American Machinists' Handbook and Dictionary of Shop Terms

AMERICAN MACHINISTS' HANDBOOK

McGraw-Hill Book Co. Inc

PUBLISHERS OF BOOKS FOR

Coal Age ▽ Electric Railway Journal
Electrical World ▽ Engineering News-Record
American Machinist ▽ The Contractor
Engineering & Mining Journal ▽ Power
Metallurgical & Chemical Engineering
Electrical Merchandising

American Machinists' Handbook

AND

DICTIONARY OF SHOP TERMS

A REFERENCE BOOK OF MACHINE SHOP AND
DRAWING ROOM DATA, METHODS AND
DEFINITIONS

BY

FRED H. COLVIN

Member American Society of Mechanical Engineers and Franklin Institute
Associate editor of the *American Machinist*, Author of " *Machine
Shop Arithmetic*," " *Machine Shop Calculations*,"
" *American Machinists' Grinding Book*,"
" *The Hill Kink Books*," etc., etc.

AND

FRANK A. STANLEY

Member American Society of Mechanical Engineers and Franklin Institute
Associate editor of the *American Machinist*, Author of " *Accurate
Tool Work*," " *Automatic Screw Machines*," " *American
Machinists' Grinding Book*," " *The Hill
Kink Books*," etc.

SECOND EDITION
THOROUGHLY REVISED AND ENLARGED
FOURTEENTH IMPRESSION
TOTAL ISSUE, 147,000

McGRAW-HILL BOOK COMPANY, Inc.

239 WEST 39TH STREET. NEW YORK

LONDON: HILL PUBLISHING CO., Ltd.
6 & 8 BOUVERIE ST., E. C.

1914

PREFACE TO SECOND EDITION

EVER since the first printing of this book, the authors have been studying ways and means of making it better, and the addition of one hundred and sixty pages by no means gives an adequate idea of the extent to which it has been revised.

Each section has been carefully studied to make it cover the changed and changing conditions of shop and drawing-room work in the hope of making it even more valuable than before.

Many of the changes have been due to suggestions made by users of the Handbook, and we shall appreciate a continuance of their interest and assistance in pointing out possibilities of improvement.

. THE AUTHORS.

PREFACE TO THE FIRST EDITION

EVERY man engaged in mechanical work of any kind, regardless of his position in the shop or drawing room, frequently requires information that is seldom remembered and is not usually available when wanted.

With this in mind it has been our endeavor to present in convenient form such data as will be of value to practical men in the various branches of machine work. While some of the matter included may seem elementary, it was considered necessary in order to make the work complete. Much of the information has never before been available to the mechanic without tiresome search and consultation.

We believe that the Dictionary section will be found of service to the younger mechanics and in helping to establish standard names for various parts which are now more or less confused in different sections of the country.

Our indebtedness to various manufacturers and individuals is hereby acknowledged, and in the back of the book will be found a list of such authorities with page references to the information furnished by them.

We dare not hope that no errors will be found and we shall be glad to have them pointed out and to receive any suggestions as to additions or other changes which may add to the value of the book.

THE AUTHORS.

CONTENTS

SCREW THREADS

Cutting Screw Threads

viii CONTENTS

viii CONTENTS

viii   CONTENTS

TWIST DRILLS AND TAPS

TÁPS

FILES

• WORK BENCHES

SOLDERING

GEARING

MILLING AND MILLING CUTTERS

Cam Milling

Indexing

Milling Cutter Reamer and Tap Flutes

Lapping

BROACHES AND BROACHING

BOLTS, NUTS AND SCREWS

Tables of Cap and Machine Screw Dimensions

Tables of A. S. M. E. Standard Machine Screw Dimensions

TAPERS AND DOVETAILS

Measuring Tapers

Diagrams and Tables of Standard Tapers

SHOP AND DRAWING ROOM STANDARDS

Standard Jig Parts

Tables of Dimensions of Standard Machine Parts

Miscellaneous Tables

MISCELLANEOUS INFORMATION

WIRE GAGES AND STOCK WEIGHTS

HORSE-POWER, BELTS AND SHAFTING

STEEL AND OTHER METALS

CONTENTS

SHOP TRIGONOMETRY

DICTIONARY OF SHOP TERMS

THE AMERICAN MACHINISTS' HANDBOOK

SCREW THREADS

CUTTING SCREW THREADS

NEARLY all lathes are geared so that if gears having the same number of teeth are placed on both stud and lead screw, it will cut a thread the same pitch as the lead screw. This is called being geared "even." If the lathe will not do this, then find what thread will be cut with even gears on both stud and lead screw and consider that as the pitch of lead screw. In speaking of the pitch of lead screw it will mean the thread that will be cut with even gears.

In cutting the same thread with even gears, both the work and the lead screw are turning at the same rate. To cut a faster thread, the lead screw must turn faster than the work, so the larger gear goes on the stud and the smaller on the lead screw. To cut a slower thread (finer-pitch or less lead), the larger gear goes on the screw and the smaller on the stud.

Calling the lead screw 6 to the inch, what gears shall we use to cut an 8 thread?

Multiply both the lead screw and the thread to be cut by some number (the same number for both) that will give two gears you have in the set. If the gears vary by 4 teeth, try 4 and get 24 and 32 as the gears. If by 5, you get 30 and 40 as the gears. Then as 8 is slower than 6, the large gear goes on the lead screw and the small one on the stud.

Cut an 18 thread with a 5-pitch lead screw and gears varying by 5 teeth. $5 \times 5 = 25$ and $5 \times 18 = 90$. There may not be a 90 gear, but you can use a 2 to 1 compound gear and use a 45 gear instead. That is, put the 25 gear on the stud, use any 2 to 1 combination between this and the 45 gear on the screw.

The 25 gear must drive the large gear of the 2 to 1 combination and the small gear drive the 45-tooth gear, either directly or through an intermediate.

In cutting fractional threads the same rule holds good. To cut $11\frac{1}{2}$ threads with gears that change by 4 teeth, use $4 \times 6 = 24$ and $4 \times 11\frac{1}{2} = 46$, with the 24 gear on the stud and the 46 on the screw. With gears changing by 5 this is not so easy, as $5 \times 11\frac{1}{2} = 57\frac{1}{2}$, an impossible gear. Multiplying by 10 would give 60 and 115, not much better. Multiply by 6 and get $6 \times 6 = 36$ and $6 \times 11\frac{1}{2} = 69$, neither of which is in the set. It seems as though 35 and 70 would come pretty near it, but they will cut a 12 thread instead.

To find what thread any two gears will cut, multiply the pitch of lead screw and the gear which goes on it and divide this by the gear on the stud. Suppose we try 40 on the stud and 75 on the lead

FIG. 1.— Lathe Gears for Screw-Cutting

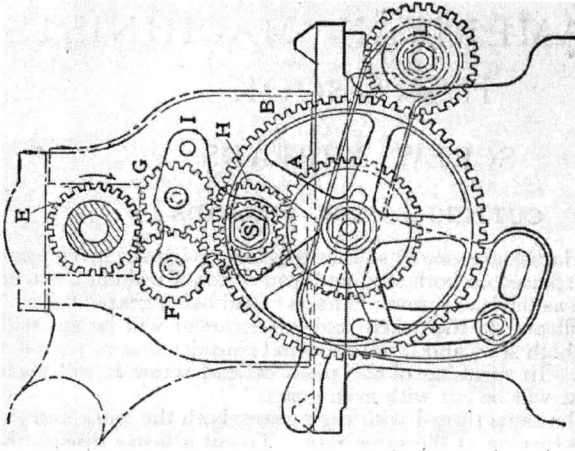

Compound Gearing

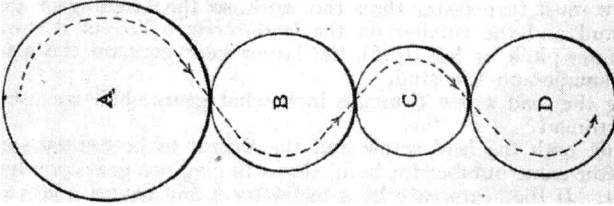

Following Motion of
a Gear Train

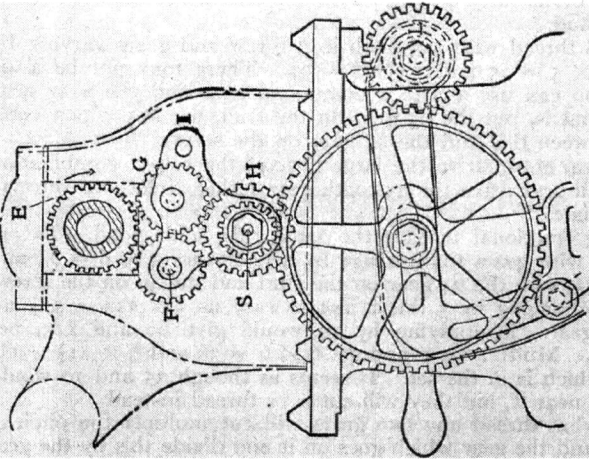

Simple Gearing

screw. Multiply 75 by 6 = 450 and divide by 40 which gives 11¼ as the thread that will be cut. Try 45 and 80. 6 × 80 = 480; divided by 45 = 10⅔, showing that the 40 and 75 are nearest and that to cut it exactly a special gear will have to be added to the set. In reality the gears would not change by 5 teeth with a 6-pitch lead screw.

Rules for screw cutting may be summed up as follows, always remembering that the lead screw is the thread that will be cut when gears having the same number of teeth are placed on both screw and stud.

Having	To Find	Rule
A = True lead of screw and B = Thread to be cut	C = Gear for stud and D = Gear for screw	Multiply both A and B by any one number that will give gears in the set. Put gear A on stud and gear B on lead screw.
A = True lead of screw B = Thread to be cut C = Gear for stud	D = Gear for screw	Multiply B by C and divide by A.
A = True lead of screw B = Thread to be cut D = Gear for screw	C = Gear for stud	Multiply A by D and divide by B
A = True lead of screw C = Gear for stud D = Gear for screw	B = Thread that will be cut	Multiply A by D and divide by C

GEARS FOR SCREW-CUTTING

GEAR trains for screw-cutting are usually arranged similarly to the illustration, Fig. 1. If the gear E on the lathe spindle has the same number of teeth as the gear H on the stud S, the lathe is geared even, i.e., gears having the same teeth placed on both stud and lead screw will cut a thread like the lead screw. As shown, the gears are out of mesh because the tumbler gears F and G do not mesh with E; but moving the handle I down throws F into mesh with E so the drive is through E, F, G, H, S and intermediate to L, driving it so as to cut a right-hand screw if it is a right-hand thread, as is usually the case. Raising handle I cuts out F entirely and reverses the direction of the lead screw.

To follow the motion of a train of gears, take a stick (or your finger if they are *not* running) and trace the motion from the driver to the end as shown by the dotted lines in *A*, *B*, *C* and *D*.

When a lathe is compound geared the stud gear drives an auxiliary gear as *A*, which multiplies or reduces the motion as the case may be. It will readily be seen, if the stud drives *A* and *B* drives *L*, the motion will be exactly doubled because *A* has one-half the number of teeth in *B*.

A SCREW-THREAD ANGLE TABLE

The accompanying table gives the angle of helix of various pitches and diameters with respect to a line perpendicular to the axis. These angles were worked out with the idea of using them for grinding thread tools for threads of various pitches upon different diameters of work. This table will enable one to set the protractor at the proper angle of side clearance for the work in hand and grind the thread tool correctly without guesswork. This is based on the outside diameter. For coarse and multiple threads it is better to figure on the pitch diameter.

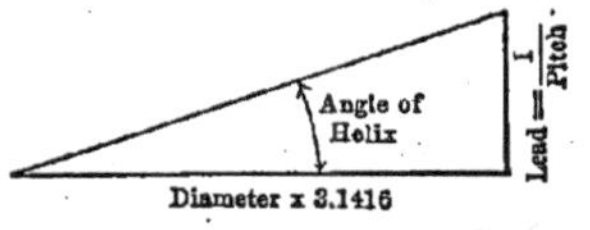

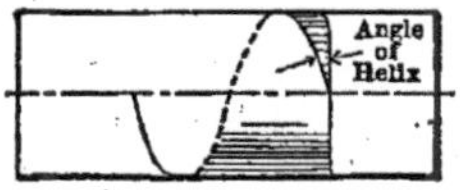

Thread Angle Table

THREADS PER INCH = *P*

Diam. of Work	1	2	3	4	5	6	7	8	9	10	11	12
1/4"	50°-54	32°-31	22°-59	17°-39	14°-18	11°-59	10°-19	9°- 2	8°- 3	7°-58	7°-11	6°- 3
3/8"	40°-23	23°- 1	15°-48	12°-16	9°-39	8°- 8	7°-13	6°-37	5°-23	5°-20	4°-49	4°-24
1/2"	32°-30	17°-41	11°-58	9°- 3	7°-16	6°-37	5°-40	4°-33	4°- 3	4°- 1	3°-37	3°- 3
5/8"	27°- 2	14°-18	9°-38	7°-15	5°-49	5°- 8	4°-10	3°-52	3°-15	3°-13	2°-54	2°-26
3/4"	23°- 5	12°- 1	8°- 8	6°- 4	4°-52	4°- 3	3°-52	3°- 3	2°-43	2°-41	2°-19	2°- 2
7/8"	20°- 4	10°-20	7°- 1	5°-12	4°-10	3°-28	2°-59	2°-37	2°-19	2°-18	2°- 4	1°-50
1 "	17°-39	9°- 2	6°- 2	4°-33	3°-39	3°- 2	2°-36	2°-17	2°- 2	2°-	1°-48	1°-31
1 1/8"	15°-49	8°- 4	5°-23	4°- 4	3°-15	2°-42	2°-19	2°- 2	1°-48	1°-47	1°-37	1°-21
1 1/4"	14°-10	7°-12	4°-48	3°-39	2°-55	2°-26	2°- 2	1°-50	1°-44	1°-37	1°-27	1°-13
1 3/8"	13°- 4	6°-37	4°-25	3°-19	2°-40	2°-13	1°-54	1°-36	1°-29	1°-28	1°-19	1°- 6
1 1/2"	11°-59	6°- 4	4°- 3	3°- 3	2°-26	2°- 2	1°-44	1°-31	1°-21	1°-20	1°-13	1°- 1
1 5/8"	11°- 6	5°-36	3°-44	2°-49	2°-15	1°-52	1°-36	1°-21	1°-15	1°-14	1°- 7	56′
1 3/4"	10°-26	5°-16	3°-29	2°-37	2°- 5	1°-44	1°-29	1°-18	1°-10	1°- 8	1°- 2	53′
1 7/8"	9°-39	4°-52	3°-15	2°-26	1°-57	1°-37	1°-23	1°-13	1°- 5	1°- 4	58′	49′
2 "	9°- 4	4°-34	3°- 3	2°-18	1°-50	1°-31	1°-18	1°- 8	1°- 1	1°- 0	54′	47′
2 1/4"	8°- 8	4°- 9	2°-42	2°- 2	1°-37	1°-21	1°- 8	1°- 1	54′	53′	49′	41′
2 1/2"	7°-15	3°-39	2°-26	1°-49	1°-28	1°-16	1°- 3	55′	49′	48′	43′	37′
2 3/4"	6°-37	3°-19	2°-13	1°-40	1°-22	1°- 7	57′	50′	45′	44′	40′	33′
3 "	6°- 4	3°- 3	2°- 2	1°-31	1°-13	1°- 1	52′	46′	41′	40′	36′	30′

While the table is worked out for single threads, it can be used for double or triple threads by considering the lead equal to the advance of the work in one revolution instead of $\frac{1}{p}$, as given in the table.

It is customary in many shops to have several thread tools in stock to cut these various thread angles, each cutting within a certain range of angles. This table will be useful in determining the best range for each thread tool.

$$P = \text{Pitch} = \text{Threads per inch.} \quad \frac{1}{P} = \text{Lead} = L$$

$$D = \text{Diameter of work in inches.} \quad \pi = 3.1416 = \frac{C}{D}$$

$$C = \text{Circumference of Work in inches} = \pi D$$

$$\frac{L}{C} = \frac{\text{Lead}}{\text{Circumference of Work}} = \frac{\frac{1}{P}}{\pi D} = \text{Tangent of Angle}$$

Find Angle in Table of Tangents

THREAD ANGLE TABLE

THREADS PER INCH = P

Diam. of Work	13	14	15	16	18	20	22	24	26	28	30	32
¼"	5°-36	5°-12	4°-51	4°-33	4°-3	3°-39	3°-19	3°-1	2°-45	2°-36	2°-25	2°-17
⅜"	3°-45	3°-28	3°-14	3°-3	2°-43	2°-26	2°-13	2°-1	1°-53	1°-44	1°-37	1°-31
½"	2°-49	2°-36	2°-26	2°-17	2°-2	1°-49	1°-40	1°-31	1°-24	1°-18	1°-13	1°-8
⅝"	2°-12	2°-5	1°-57	1°-48	1°-37	1°-28	1°-20	1°-13	1°-8	1°-3	59'	54'
¾"	1°-53	1°-44	1°-37	1°-31	1°-21	1°-13	1°-7	1°-1	57'	53'	49'	46'
⅞"	1°-37	1°-30	1°-24	1°-18	1°-10	1°-3	57'	53'	49'	45'	42'	39'
1"	1°-24	1°-18	1°-13	1°-8	1°-1	55'	50'	45'	42'	39'	36'	34'
1⅛"	1°-15	1°-11	1°-5	1°-1	54'	49'	45'	40'	38'	35'	32'	30'
1¼"	1°-7	1°-3	50'	54'	49'	44'	40'	37'	34'	31'	29'	27'
1⅜"	1°-1	57'	57'	50'	44'	40'	36'	33'	31'	28'	27'	25'
1½"	56'	52'	49'	46'	40'	36'	33'	30'	28'	26'	24'	23'
1⅝"	52'	48'	45'	42'	37'	34'	31'	28'	26'	24'	23'	21'
1¾"	48'	45'	42'	40'	35'	31'	28'	26'	24'	22'	21'	19'
1⅞"	45'	42'	39'	37'	33'	29'	27'	24'	23'	21'	19'	18'
2"	42'	40'	36'	34'	31'	27'	25'	22'	21'	19'	18'	17'
2¼"	37'	35'	32'	30'	27'	24'	22'	20'	19'	18'	16'	15'
2½"	34'	31'	29'	27'	24'	22'	20'	18'	17'	15'	14'	14'
2¾"	31'	28'	26'	25'	22'	20'	18'	17'	16'	14'	13'	13'
3"	28'	26'	24'	23'	20'	18'	17'	15'	14'	13'	12'	11'

Figs. 2 and 3 show side and front elevations of the thread tool and of the protractor as applied to obtain the proper angle of side clearance to cut a right-hand screw thread. The front edge of the thread tool is used to determine the angle of side clearance. Fig. 4 shows a section taken along the line *a b*, Fig. 2. It will be noticed that line *e f* is shorter than *G H* to give clearance to the cutting edges of the thread tool, and also that *G R* is equal to *H R* and *e S* is equal to *f S*. The angle of the helix at half the depth of the thread, Fig. 5, can be used, if desired, and can be approximated to from the table, or figured exactly by the method given at the top of the table.

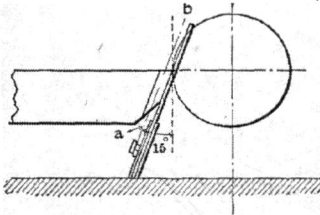

FIG. 2

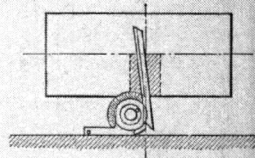

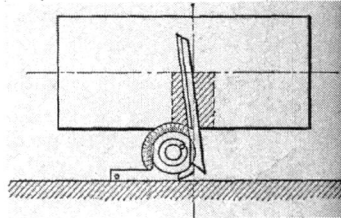

FIG. 3

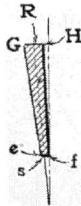

FIG. 4

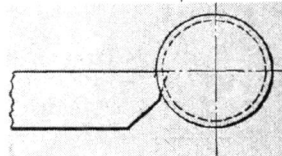

FIG. 5

The Use of the Protractor

METRIC THREADS

Metric threads are measured in millimeter but are calculated by the threads per centimeter. Any lathe with a pair of compound or "translating gears" with 50 and 127 teeth, can cut metric threads, the large gear being driven from the stud. Then the gears for the number of threads per centimeter are figured the same as threads per inch as on page 3.

MULTIPLE THREAD CUTTING

THE accompanying table will be found useful when cutting multiple threads. When one thread is cut, the feed nut may be opened (the spindle of course being stopped) and the carriage moved along by hand the distance given in the table; the nut is then closed on the screw and the next thread cut. This is a quick and sure method of starting the second, third or fourth thread where the lead screw of the lathe is of the pitch given in the table.

TABLE FOR MULTIPLE THREAD CUTTING

Cut	Thread on Lead Screw	Move Carriage
DOUBLE		
1	Even	$\frac{1}{2}$ inch
$1\frac{1}{4}$	Any	2 inch
$1\frac{1}{2}$	Any	1 inch
2	4	$\frac{1}{4}$ inch
$2\frac{1}{4}$	Any	2 inch
$2\frac{1}{2}$	Any	1 inch
3	Even	$\frac{1}{2}$ inch
$3\frac{1}{4}$	Any	2 inch
$3\frac{1}{2}$	Any	1 inch
4	8	$\frac{1}{8}$ inch
$4\frac{1}{4}$	Any	2 inch
$4\frac{1}{2}$	Any	1 inch
5	Even	$\frac{1}{2}$ inch
$5\frac{1}{2}$	Any	1 inch
TRIPLE		
1	6	$\frac{1}{3}$" or 2 threads on lead screw
$1\frac{1}{4}$	6	$1\frac{1}{3}$" or 8 threads on lead screw
$1\frac{1}{2}$	6	$\frac{2}{3}$" or 4 threads on lead screw
2	6	$\frac{1}{6}$" or 1 thread on lead screw
$2\frac{1}{4}$	6	$1\frac{1}{3}$" or 8 threads on lead screw
$2\frac{1}{2}$	6	$\frac{2}{3}$" or 4 threads on lead screw
JADRUPLE		
1	4	$\frac{1}{4}$ inch
$1\frac{1}{4}$	Any	1 inch
$1\frac{1}{2}$	Even	$\frac{1}{2}$ inch
2	8	$\frac{1}{8}$ inch
$2\frac{1}{4}$	Any	1 inch
$2\frac{1}{2}$	Even	$\frac{1}{2}$ inch

To cut a double thread screw $3\frac{1}{2}$ to the inch: the lathe must be ared the same as for a single, triple or quadruple thread. The ol will of course have to be the same width and the depth of cut e same as for a 7 per inch screw. After the first thread is cut it ill appear very shallow and wide. With the lathe spindle idle, e nut is opened and the carriage moved (in either direction) 1 ch; the nut is then closed on the lead screw and the tool is in the oper position to make the second cut.

If the carriage were moved 2 inches, the tool could follow exactly e first groove cut. In the case of a triple-thread screw, if the carage were moved 3 inches, the tool would follow its original path, d it would do the same in the case of a quadruple thread if moved inches.

The carriage can, of course, be moved 1 inch and the nut closed no matter what the pitch of the lead screw may be (unless it is fractional), but in order to close the nut after moving ½ inch, the screw must have some even number of threads per inch.

As will be seen by referring to the table, a lead screw with any even number of threads per inch is used in a number of cases, while in several other instances the screw may be of any pitch — either odd or even. In certain cases 4 and 8 per inch lead screws are specified; and in cutting triple threads a 6 per inch screw is required.

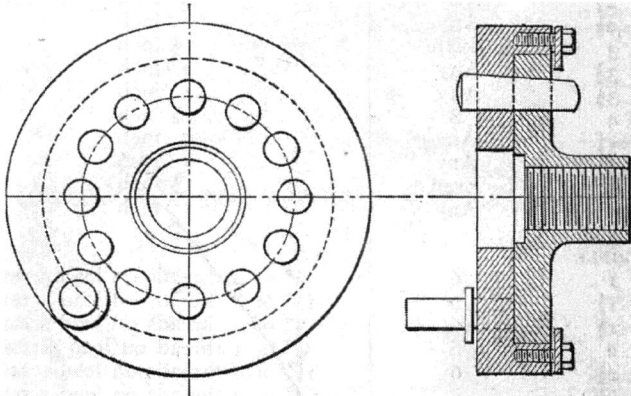

FIG. 6. — Face-Plate for Multiple Thread Cutting

FACE-PLATE FOR MULTIPLE THREAD CUTTING

FIG. 6 shows a face-plate fixture used on various numbers of threads. On an ordinary driving plate is fitted a plate having, as shown, twelve holes enabling one to get two, three, four or six leads if required. This ring carries the driving stud, and is clamped at the back of the plate by two bolts as an extra safeguard. All that is necessary in operation is to slack off the bolts, withdraw the index pin, move the plate the number of holes required, and re-tighten the bolts. It is used on different lathes, as occasion requires, by making the driving plates alike and drilling a hole for the index pin. It is found that the index pin works best when made taper, and a light tap is sufficient to loosen or fix it.

CUTTING DIAMETRAL PITCH WORMS IN THE LATHE

THE accompanying table is to be used in cases where fractional worm-thread cutting is necessary for diametrical pitch worm threads to mesh into diametral-pitch worm gears.

TABLE OF CHANGE GEARS FOR DIAMETRAL PITCH WORMS

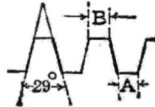

Diametral Pitch	Single Depth	Width of Tool Point A	Width of Top of Thread B	Pitch of Lead Screw							
				2	3	4	5	6	7	8	10
2	1.078"	.487"	.526"	22/7	33/7	44/7	55/7	66/7	77/7	88/7	110/7
2½	.862"	.390"	.421"	88/35	132/35	176/35	44/7	264/35	44/5	352/35	440/35
3	.719"	.325"	.350"	44/21	22/7	88/21	110/21	44/7	22/3	176/21	220/21
3½	.616"	.278"	.300"	88/49	132/49	176/49	220/49	264/49	44/7	352/49	440/49
4	.540"	.243"	.263"	11/7	33/14	22/7	55/14	33/7	11/2	44/7	55/7
5	.431"	.195"	.210"	44/35	66/35	88/35	22/7	132/35	22/5	176/35	44/7
6	.360"	.162"	.175"	22/21	11/7	44/21	55/21	22/7	11/3	88/21	110/21
7	.308"	.139"	.150"	44/49	66/49	88/49	110/49	132/49	22/7	176/49	220/49
8	.270"	.122"	.131"	11/14	33/28	11/7	55/28	33/14	11/4	22/7	55/14
9	.240"	.108"	.117"	44/63	22/21	88/63	110/63	44/21	22/9	176/63	220/63
10	.216"	.097"	.105"	22/35	33/35	44/35	11/7	66/35	11/5	88/35	22/7
11	.196"	.088"	.096"	4/7	6/7	8/7	10/7	12/7	2	16/7	20/7
12	.180"	.081"	.088"	11/21	11/14	22/21	55/42	11/7	11/6	44/21	55/21
14	.154"	.069"	.075"	22/49	33/49	44/49	55/49	66/49	11/7	88/49	110/49
16	.135"	.061"	.066"	11/28	33/56	11/14	55/56	33/28	11/8	11/7	55/28
18	.120"	.054"	.058"	22/63	11/21	44/63	55/63	22/21	11/9	88/63	110/63
20	.108"	.048"	.053"	11/35	33/70	22/35	11/14	33/35	11/10	44/35	11/7
24	.090"	.040"	.044"	11/42	11/28	11/21	55/84	11/14	11/12	22/21	55/42
28	.077"	.034"	.038"	11/49	33/98	22/49	55/98	33/49	11/14	44/49	55/49
32	.067"	.030"	.033"	11/56	33/112	11/28	55/112	33/56	11/16	11/14	55/56
40	.054"	.024"	.026"	11/70	33/140	11/35	11/28	33/70	11/20	22/35	11/14
48	.045"	.020"	.022"	11/84	11/56	11/42	55/168	11/28	11/24	11/21	55/84

Formula: $\dfrac{22 \times \text{Lead Screw}}{7 \times \text{Diametral Pitch}}$ } = Ratio of Wheels.

355 to 113 is more accurate but requires odd gears; a 71 tooth gear and a 5 to 1 compound gives 355.

In the first column is found the diametral pitch to be cut. In the second column is found the corresponding single depth of the worm thread. Under the third column is found the width of the tool at the point, the tool being the regular 29-degree included angle. In the fourth column is found the width at the top of the worm thread. The next heading in the chart is "Pitch of lead screw," and here are found different pitches of lead screws from 2 to 10.

Example: Suppose it is desired to cut a worm thread of 4 diametral pitch on a single-geared lathe having a 6-pitch lead screw. Now, opposite 4 in the first column find the single depth of worm thread, or 0.540 inch; and continuing in the same direction from left to right, under the next column find the width of the worm-thread tool at the point or end, which is 0.243 inch, and so on to the next column where is found the width of the worm thread at the top, which is 0.263 inch. Say there is a 6-pitch lead screw on the lathe. Then follow right on in the same direction until coming to the square under 6, and the gear, will be in the ratio of $\frac{3}{7}$. Of course there is no 7 gear on the lathe, so simply bring the fraction $\frac{3}{7}$ to higher denominations, say, $\frac{3}{7} \times \frac{3}{3} = \frac{9}{21}$: that is, put the 99 gear on the spindle or stud, and the 21 gear on the screw. Then use a gear of any convenient size to act as an intermediate gear, and thus connect the gear on the spindle with the gear on the screw. Taking the fraction $\frac{3}{7}$ and multiplying the numerator and denominator by 4, would give $\frac{12}{28}$ as the two gears to be used. It will be seen that this last fraction simply changes the number of teeth in the gears, but does not change the value of the fraction; thus there is the same ratio of gears.

Take another case: Suppose it is desired to cut a 20-diametral pitch worm thread in a lathe having a 4-pitch lead screw. What would be the necessary gears to cut the desired thread? Next to 20 in the first column is found the single depth of the worm thread, which is 0.108 inch. Continuing on, reading from left to right as in the first case, and 0.048 inch is found as the width of the tool at the point. In the next column is found the width at the top of the worm thread, which in this case is 0.053 inch. Under column 4, and opposite 20, are found the gears necessary for cutting a 20-diametral pitch worm thread in a lathe with a 4-pitch lead screw. The gears thus found, namely, $\frac{22 \text{ stud}}{35 \text{ screw}}$ may not be in the regular set of gears furnished with the lathe. In that case double up on both and make it $\frac{44 \text{ stud}}{70 \text{ screw}}$, which is the same in value. The two examples thus worked out could have been cut on lathes with lead screws having any number of threads per inch, with the same result. One point in cutting these threads is that the tool must be of exact dimensions all over, for if it is not exactly 29 degrees included angle, or the point is not as it should be for width, then there will be an error in the worm thread all around.

THE BROWN & SHARPE 29-DEGREE WORM THREAD AND THE ACME 29-DEGREE STANDARD SCREW THREAD

THERE seems to be some confusion among mechanics regarding the 29-degree Acme standard screw thread and the Brown & Sharpe 29-degree worm thread.

The sketches, Figs. 7 and 8, show plainly the difference between threads of the same pitch in the two systems. The sectional views are of threads of one-inch linear pitch drawn to scale to the proportions given by the thread formulas in connection with the complete tables of the two systems of threads as given on pages following. The clearance for bottom of thread is the same, 0.010 inch, for all pitches. See formula on page 24 for correct dimensions.

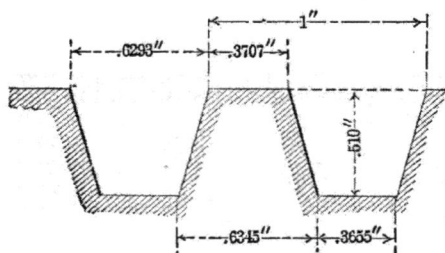

Fig. 7 — Acme 29-Degree Screw Thread

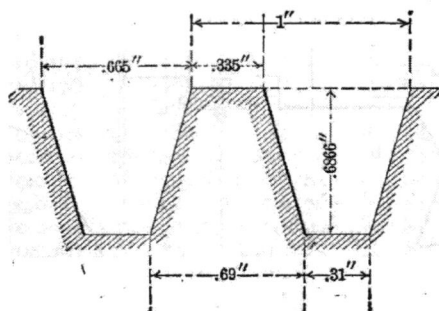

Fig. 8. — Brown & Sharpe 29-Degree Worm Thread

The worm thread is based on the linear pitch of the worm and proportions figured same as rack tooth with varying clearances in bottom. B. & S. 29-deg. screw thread has a uniform clearance of 0.005 inch for all pitches. Do not confuse the two threads.

MEASUREMENT OF V-TOOLS

THE accompanying table of angle measurements should prove of convenience to all who make tools for cutting angles or make the gages for these tools.

The principle here adopted is that, on account of the difficulty and in some cases the impossibility of measuring the tool at its point, the measurement is taken on the angle of the tool at a given distance from the point. In this case the true measurement will be less than the actual measurement by an amount equal to twice the tangent of half of the angle multiplied by the distance of the line of measurement from the point.

For making the measurement the Brown & Sharpe gear-tooth caliper may be used. Fig. 9 shows this tool in position for measuring. The depth vernier A is set to a given depth h, and the measurement is taken by means of the vernier B. The width of the tool point x is equal to the measurement on the line $a\,b$ less $2h\left(tan.\dfrac{C}{2}\right)$. To use the table, h is always taken to be $\frac{1}{16}$ inch, which is found to be a convenient depth for most work. If a greater depth is required, all that is necessary is to multiply the figures given by the ratio of the required depth to $\frac{1}{16}$ inch. For instance, if the depth is required

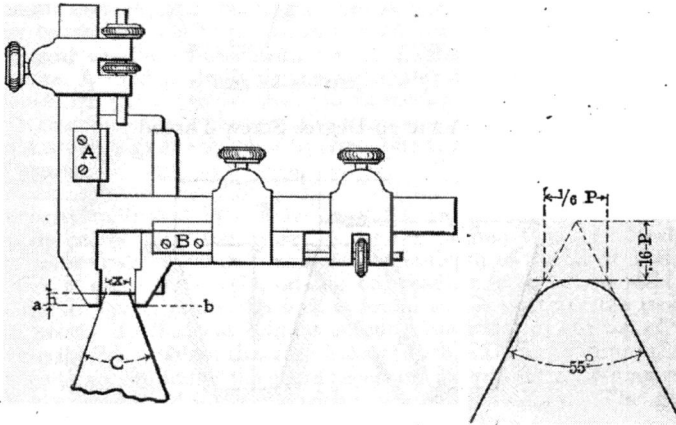

FIG. 9. —Measuring Thread Tools

to be $\frac{1}{8}$ inch, the figures given are multiplied by 2. In the great majority of cases, $\frac{1}{16}$ will be found a suitable value for h, when to find the width of the point x it is merely necessary to deduct the value of $\dfrac{tan.\dfrac{C}{2}}{8}$ for the angle required, which can be obtained at a glance from the table.

In the case of the Sellers or United States standard thread, the point of the tool should be one-eighth of the pitch of the screw, while in the Whitworth standard, as shown, the point of the tool would be one-sixth of the pitch if it were not rounded. By using these figures in combination with the table, it can be determined when sufficient has been ground from the point of the tool.

The table is called "Table for Angle Measurements," because if a sharp angle, that is, one without the point ground away, is measured as above, this measurement, by reference to the table, will give the angle direct.

TABLE FOR V-TOOL ANGLE MEASUREMENTS

Degrees	$tan.\dfrac{C}{2}$ $\dfrac{}{8}$	Degrees	$tan.\dfrac{C}{2}$ $\dfrac{}{8}$	Degrees	$tan.\dfrac{C}{2}$ $\dfrac{}{8}$
1	0.0011	31	0.0346	61	0.0736
2	0.0022	32	0.0358	62	0.0751
3	0.0033	33	0.0370	63	0.0766
4	0.0044	34	0.0382	64	0.0781
5	0.0055	35	0.0394	65	0.0796
6	0.0066	36	0.0406	66	0.0811
7	0.0077	37	0.0418	67	0.0827
8	0.0088	38	0.0430	68	0.0843
9	0.0099	39	0.0442	69	0.0859
10	0.0110	40	0.0454	70	0.0875
11	0.0121	41	0.0466	71	0.0891
12	0.0132	42	0.0489	72	0.0908
13	0.0143	43	0.0492	73	0.0925
14	0.0154	44	0.0505	74	0.0942
15	0.0165	45	0.0518	75	0.0959
16	0.0176	46	0.0531	76	0.0976
17	0.0187	47	0.0544	77	0.0994
18	0.0198	48	0.0557	78	0.1012
19	0.0209	49	0.0570	79	0.1030
20	0.0220	50	0.0583	80	0.1048
21	0.0231	51	0.0596	81	0.1067
22	0.0242	52	0.0609	82	0.1086
23	0.0253	53	0.0623	83	0.1105
24	0.0264	54	0.0637	84	0.1125
25	0.0275	55	0.0651	85	0.1145
26	0.0286	56	0.0665	86	0.1165
27	0.0298	57	0.0679	87	0.1186
28	0.0310	58	0.0693	88	0.1207
29	0.0322	59	0.0707	89	0.1228
30	0.0334	60	0.0721	90	0.1250

GRINDING THE FLAT ON THREAD TOOLS

To facilitate grinding the correct width of flat for the single-point inserted tool to cut United States standard form of threads the accompanying table on pages 14 and 15 has been prepared. The distance from the point of the tool to the back is first measured with the micrometer, then the point of the tool may be ground off until the micrometer measurement from the back is equal to the whole depth minus dimension A, when we may be sure, without undertaking the difficult job of measuring it directly, that the flat B has the proper width. The dimensions A and B for pitches from 1 to 64 threads per inch are included in the table.

TABLE FOR GRINDING FLAT END OF TOOL FOR CUTTING U. S. FORM OF THREAD

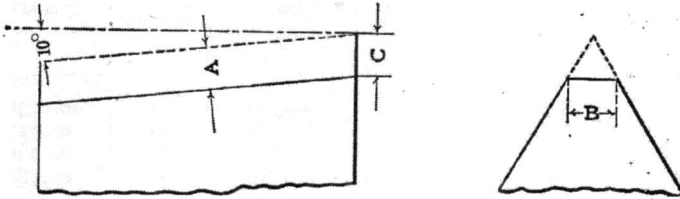

Threads per Inch	Pitch	A	B	C	Double Depth	Depth
1	1.000	.1064	.125	.1082	1.299	.6495
2	.5000	.0532	.0625	.0541	.6495	.3247
3	.3333	.0355	.0416	.0360	.433	.2165
4	.2500	.0266	.0312	.0270	.3247	.1623
5	.2000	.0213	.0250	.0216	.2598	.1299
6	.1666	.0177	.0208	.0180	.2165	.1082
7	.1428	.0152	.0178	.0154	.1855	.0927
8	.1250	.0133	.0156	.0135	.1623	.0812
9	.1111	.0118	.0138	.0120	.1443	.0721
10	.1000	.0106	.0125	.0108	.1299	.0649
11	.0909	.00963	.0113	.0098	.1180	.0592
12	.0833	.00886	.0104	.0090	.1082	.0541
13	.0769	.00818	.0096	.0083	.0999	.0499
14	.0714	.00758	.0089	.0077	.0920	.0460
15	.0666	.00707	.0083	.0071	.0866	.0433
16	.0625	.00673	.0079	.0068	.0812	.0406
17	.0588	.00620	.0073	.0063	.0764	.0382
18	.0555	.00588	.0069	.0059	.0721	.0360
19	.0526	.00554	.0065	.0056	.0683	.0341
20	.0500	.00530	.0062	.0054	.0649	.0324
21	.0476	.00503	.0059	.0051	.0618	.0309
22	.0454	.0048	.0056	.0049	.0590	.0295
23	.0431	.00451	.0053	.0046	.0564	.0282
24	.0416	.00433	.0052	.0045	.0541	.0270
25	.0400	.00426	.0050	.0043	.0519	.0259
26	.0384	.00409	.0048	.0041	.0491	.0245
27	.0370	.00393	.0046	.0040	.0481	.0240
28	.0357	.00375	.0044	.0038	.0463	.0231
29	.0344	.00366	.0043	.0037	.0447	.0223
30	.0333	.00354	.0041	.0036	.0433	.0216
31	.0322	.00341	.0040	.0035	.0419	.0209
32	.0312	.00332	.0039	.0034	.0405	.0202

TABLE FOR GRINDING FLAT END OF TOOL FOR CUTTING U. S. FORM OF THREAD

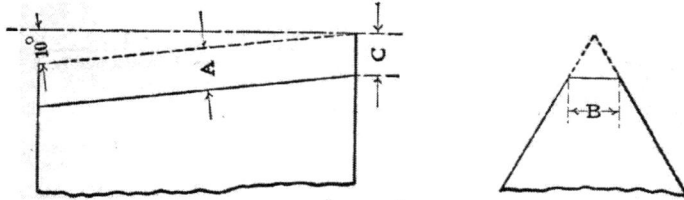

Threads per Inch	Pitch	A	B	C	Double Depth	Depth
33	.0303	.00315	.0037	.0032	.0393	.0196
34	.0294	.00307	.0036	.0031	.0382	.0191
35	.0285	.00295	.0035	.0030	.0370	.0185
36	.0277	.00289	.0034	.00295	.0360	.0180
37	.0270	.00281	.0033	.00286	.0350	.0175
38	.0263	.00272	.00325	.00282	.0341	.0170
39	.0256	.00268	.00320	.00277	.0333	.0166
40	.0250	.00264	.00312	.00270	.0324	.0162
41	.0243	.00255	.00303	.00262	.0319	.0159
42	.0238	.00251	.00295	.00257	.0309	.01545
43	.0232	.00247	.00290	.00251	.0302	.01520
44	.0227	.00238	.00283	.00245	.0295	.0147
45	.0222	.00233	.00277	.00240	.0290	.0145
46	.0217	.00230	.00271	.00235	.0282	.0141
47	.0212	.00225	.00265	.00230	.0274	.0137
48	.0208	.00221	.00260	.00225	.0270	.0135
49	.0204	.00217	.00255	.00220	.0263	.0131
50	.0200	.00213	.00250	.00216	.0258	.0129
51	.0196	.00208	.00245	.00212	.0254	.0127
52	.0192	.00204	.00240	.00208	.0249	.01245
53	.0188	.00200	.00235	.00203	.0245	.01225
54	.0185	.00196	.00231	.00200	.02405	.01202
55	.0181	.00192	.00226	.00196	.0236	.0118
56	.0178	.00189	.00222	.00192	.0232	.0116
57	.0175	.00185	.00218	.00189	.0228	.0114
58	.0172	.00184	.00215	.00186	.0223	.01115
59	.0169	.00180	.00211	.00183	.02201	.0110
60	.0166	.00177	.00208	.00180	.02165	.01082
61	.0163	.00173	.00203	.00177	.02119	.01059
62	.0161	.00172	.00202	.00175	.02095	.01047
63	.0158	.00169	.00198	.00171	.02061	.01030
64	.0156	.00167	.00196	.00169	.02029	.01014

TABLE OF U. S. STANDARD SCREW THREADS

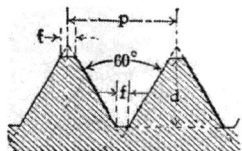

$$\text{Formula} \begin{cases} p = \text{Pitch} = \dfrac{1}{\text{No. Threads per Inch}} \\ d = \text{Depth} = p \times .64952 \\ f = \text{Flat} = \dfrac{p}{8} \end{cases}$$

Diam. of Screw	Threads to Inch	Pitch	Depth of Thread	Diam. at Root of Thread	Width of Flat
¼	20	.0500	.0325	.185	.0063
5/16	18	.0556	.0361	.2403	.0069
3/8	16	.0625	.0405	.2936	.0078
7/16	14	.0714	.0464	.3447	.0089
½	13	.0769	.0499	.4001	.0096
9/16	12	.0833	.0541	.4542	.0104
5/8	11	.0909	.0591	.5069	.0114
¾	10	.1000	.0649	.6201	.0125
7/8	9	.1111	.0721	.7307	.0139
1	8	.1250	.0812	.8376	.0156
1⅛	7	.1429	.0928	.9394	.0179
1¼	7	.1429	.0928	1.0644	.0179
1⅜	6	.1667	.1082	1.1585	.0208
1½	6	.1667	.1082	1.2835	.0208
1⅝	5½	.1818	.1181	1.3888	.0227
1¾	5	.2000	.1299	1.4902	.0250
1⅞	5	.2000	.1299	1.6152	.0250
2	4½	.2222	.1444	1.7113	.0278
2¼	4½	.2222	.1444	1.9613	.0278
2½	4	.2500	.1624	2.1752	.0313
2¾	4	.2500	.1624	2.4252	.0313
3	3½	.2857	.1856	2.6288	.0357
3¼	3½	.2857	.1856	2.8788	.0357
3½	3¼	.3077	.1998	3.1003	.0385
3¾	3	.3333	.2165	3.3170	.0417
4	3	.3333	.2165	3.5670	.0417
4¼	2⅞	.3478	.2259	3.7982	.0435
4½	2¾	.3636	.2362	4.0276	.0455
4¾	2⅝	.3810	.2474	4.2551	.0476
5	2½	.4000	.2598	4.4804	.0500
5¼	2½	.4000	.2598	4.7304	.0500
5½	2⅜	.4210	.2735	4.9530	.0526
5¾	2⅜	.4210	.2735	5.2030	.0526
6	2¼	.4444	.2882	5.4226	.0556

TABLE OF SHARP "V" SCREW THREADS

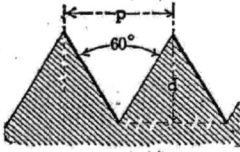

Formula $\begin{cases} p = \text{Pitch} = \dfrac{1}{\text{No. Threads per Inch}} \\ d = \text{Depth} = p \times .86603 \end{cases}$

Diam. of Screw	No. Threads per Inch	Pitch	Depth of Thread	Diam. at Root of Thread
1/4	20	.0500	.0433	.1634
5/16	18	.0556	.0481	.2163
3/8	16	.0625	.0541	.2667
7/16	14	.0714	.0618	.3140
1/2	12	.0833	.0722	.3557
9/16	12	.0833	.0722	.4182
5/8	11	.0909	.0787	.4676
11/16	11	.0909	.0787	.5301
3/4	10	.1000	.0866	.5768
13/16	10	.1000	.0866	.6393
7/8	9	.1111	.0962	.6826
15/16	9	.1111	.0962	.7451
1	8	.1250	.1083	.7835
1 1/8	7	.1429	.1237	.8776
1 1/4	7	.1429	.1237	1.0026
1 3/8	6	.1667	.1443	1.0864
1 1/2	6	.1667	.1443	1.2114
1 5/8	5	.2000	.1733	1.2784
1 3/4	5	.2000	.1733	1.4034
1 7/8	4 1/2	.2222	.1924	1.4902
2	4 1/2	.2222	.1924	1.6152
2 1/8	4 1/2	.2222	.1924	1.7402
2 1/4	4 1/2	.2222	.1924	1.8652
2 3/8	4 1/2	.2222	.1924	1.9902
2 1/2	4	.2500	.2165	2.0670
2 5/8	4	.2500	.2165	2.1920
2 3/4	4	.2500	.2165	2.3170
2 7/8	4	.2500	.2165	2.4420
3	3 1/2	.2857	.2474	2.5052
3 1/8	3 1/2	.2857	.2474	2.6301
3 1/4	3 1/2	.2857	.2474	2.7551
3 3/8	3 1/4	.3077	.2666	2.8418
3 1/2	3 1/4	.3077	.2666	2.9668
3 5/8	3 1/4	.3077	.2666	3.0918
3 3/4	3	.3333	.2886	3.1727
3 7/8	3	.3333	.2886	3.2977
4	3	.3333	.2886	3.4227

SCREW THREADS

TABLE OF WHITWORTH STANDARD SCREW THREADS

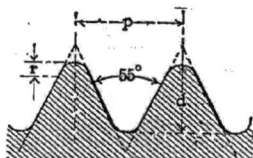

$$\text{Formula} \begin{cases} p = \text{Pitch} = \dfrac{1}{\text{No. Threads per Inch}} \\ d = \text{Depth} = p \times .64033 \\ r = \text{Radius} = p \times .1373 \end{cases}$$

Diam. of Screw	No. of Threads per inch	Pitch	Depth of Thread	Diam. at Root of Thread
$\frac{1}{4}$	20	.0500	.0320	.1860
$\frac{5}{16}$	18	.0556	.0356	.2414
$\frac{3}{8}$	16	.0625	.0400	.2950
$\frac{7}{16}$	14	.0714	.0457	.3460
$\frac{1}{2}$	12	.0833	.0534	.3933
$\frac{9}{16}$	12	.0833	.0534	.4558
$\frac{5}{8}$	11	.0909	.0582	.5086
$\frac{11}{16}$	11	.0909	.0582	.5711
$\frac{3}{4}$	10	.1000	.0640	.6219
$\frac{13}{16}$	10	.1000	.0640	.6844
$\frac{7}{8}$	9	.1111	.0711	.7327
1	8	.1250	.0800	.8399
$1\frac{1}{8}$	7	.1429	.0915	.9420
$1\frac{1}{4}$	7	.1429	.0915	1.0670
$1\frac{3}{8}$	6	.1667	.1067	1.1616
$1\frac{1}{2}$	6	.1667	.1067	1.2866
$1\frac{5}{8}$	5	.2000	.1281	1.3689
$1\frac{3}{4}$	5	.2000	.1281	1.4939
2	$4\frac{1}{2}$	.2222	.1423	1.7154
$2\frac{1}{4}$	4	.2500	.1601	1.9298
$2\frac{1}{2}$	4	.2500	.1601	2.1798
$2\frac{3}{4}$	$3\frac{1}{2}$	.2857	.1830	2.3841
3	$3\frac{1}{2}$	.2857	.1830	2.6341
$3\frac{1}{4}$	$3\frac{1}{4}$	.3077	.1970	2.8560
$3\frac{1}{2}$	$3\frac{1}{4}$	.3077	.1970	3.1060
$3\frac{3}{4}$	3	.3333	.2134	3.3231
4	3	.3333	.2134	3.5731
$4\frac{1}{2}$	$2\frac{7}{8}$	.3478	.2227	4.0546
5	$2\frac{3}{4}$	.3636	.2328	4.5343
$5\frac{1}{2}$	$2\frac{5}{8}$	.3810	.2439	5.0121
6	$2\frac{1}{2}$	.4000	.2561	5.4877

TABLE OF BRITISH ASSOCIATION SCREW THREADS

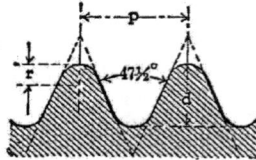

Formula $\begin{cases} p = \text{Pitch} \\ d = \text{Depth} = p \times .6 \\ r = \text{Radius} = \dfrac{2 \times p}{11} \end{cases}$

Number	Diam. of Screw mm.	Approximate Diam. Inches	Pitch mm.	Approximate Pitch Inches	Depth of Thread mm.	Diam. at Root of Thread mm.
0	6.0	.236	1.0	.0394	.6	4.8
1	5.3	.209	.9	.0354	.54	4.22
2	4.7	.185	.81	.0319	.485	3.73
3	4.1	.161	.73	.0287	.44	3.22
4	3.6	.142	.66	.0260	.395	2.81
5	3.2	.126	.59	.0232	.355	2.49
6	2.8	.110	.53	.0209	.32	2.16
7	2.5	.098	.48	.0189	.29	1.92
8	2.2	.087	.43	.0169	.26	1.68
9	1.9	.075	.39	.0154	.235	1.43
10	1.7	.067	.35	.0138	.21	1.28
11	1.5	.059	.31	.0122	.185	1.13
12	1.3	.051	.28	.0110	.17	.96
13	1.2	.047	.25	.0098	.15	.9
14	1.0	.039	.23	.0091	.14	.72
15	.9	.035	.21	.0083	.125	.65
16	.79	.031	.19	.0075	.115	.56
17	.70	.028	.17	.0067	.10	.50
18	.62	.024	.15	.0059	.09	.44
19	.54	.021	.14	.0055	.085	.37
20	.48	.019	.12	.0047	.07	.34
21	.42	.017	.11	.0043	.065	.29
22	.37	.015	.10	.0039	.06	.25
23	.33	.013	.09	.0035	.055	.22
24	.29	.011	.08	.0031	.05	.19
25	.25	.010	.07	.0028	.04	.17

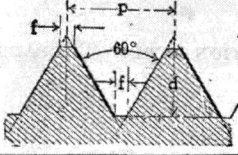

$$\text{Formula} \begin{cases} p = \text{Pitch} \\ d = \text{Depth} = p \times .6495 \\ f = \text{Flat} = \dfrac{p}{8} \end{cases}$$

Diameter of Screw mm.	Pitch mm.	Diameter at Root of Thread mm.	Width of Flat mm.
3	0.5	2.35	.06
4	0.75	3.03	.09
5	0.75	4.03	.09
6	1.0	4.70	.13
7	1.0	5.70	.13
8	1.0	6.70	.13
8	1.25	6.38	.16
9	1.0	7.70	.13
9	1.25	7.38	.16
10	1.5	8.05	.19
11	1.5	9.05	.19
12	1.5	10.05	.19
12	1.75	9.73	.22
14	2.0	11.40	.25
16	2.0	13.40	.25
18	2.5	14.75	.31
20	2.5	16.75	.31
22	2.5	18.75	.31
22	3.0	18.10	.38
24	3.0	20.10	.38
26	3.0	22.10	.38
27	3.0	23.10	.38
28	3.0	24.10	.38
30	3.5	25.45	.44
32	3.5	27.45	.44
33	3.5	28.45	.44
34	3.5	29.45	.44
36	4.0	30.80	.5
38	4.0	32.80	.5
39	4.0	33.80	.5
40	4.0	34.80	.5
42	4.5	36.15	.56
44	4.5	38.15	.56
45	4.5	39.15	.56
46	4.5	40.15	.56
48	5.0	41.51	.63
50	5.0	43.51	.63
52	5.0	45.51	.63
56	5.5	48.86	.69
60	5.5	52.86	.69
64	6.0	56.21	.75
68	6.0	60.21	.75
72	6.5	63.56	.81
76	6.5	67.56	.81
80	7.0	70.91	.88

TABLE OF INTERNATIONAL STANDARD SCREW THREADS

DIMENSIONS IN MILLIMETERS

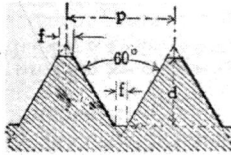

$$\text{Formula} \begin{cases} p = \text{Pitch} \\ d = \text{Depth} = p \times .64952 \\ f = \text{Flat} = \dfrac{p}{8} \end{cases}$$

Diam. of Screw	Pitch	Diam. of Screw	Pitch	Diam. of Screw	Pitch	Diam. of Screw	Pitch
6	1.00	18	2.50	39	4.00	68	6.00
7	1.00	20	2.50	42	4.50	72	6.50
8	1.25	22	2.50	45	4.50	76	6.50
9	1.25	24	3.00	48	5.00	80	7.00
10	1.50	27	3.00	52	5.00	88	7.50
11	1.50	30	3.50	56	5.50	96	8.00
12	1.75	33	3.50	60	5.50	116	9.00
14	2.00	36	4.00	64	6.00	136	10.00
16	2.00						

The "International Standard" is the same, with modifications noted, as that now in general use in France.

INTERNATIONAL STANDARD THREADS

At the "Congress International pour L'Unification des Filetages," held in Zurich, October 24, 1898, the following resolutions were adopted:

The Congress has undertaken the task of unifying the threads of machine screws. It recommends to all those who wish to adopt the metric system of threads to make use of the proposed system. This system is the one which has been established by the "Society for the Encouragement of National Industries," with the following modification adopted by this Congress.

1. The clearance at the bottom of thread shall not exceed $\frac{1}{18}$ part of the hight of the original triangle. The shape of the bottom of the thread resulting from said clearance is left to the judgment of the manufacturers. However, the Congress recommends rounded profile for said bottom.

3. The table for Standard Diameters accepted is the one which has been proposed by the Swiss Committee of Action. (This table is given above.) It is to be noticed especially that 1.25 mm. pitch is adopted for 8 mm. diameter, and 1.75 mm. pitch for 12 mm. diameter. The pitches of sizes between standard diameters indicated in the table are to be the same as for the next smaller standard diameter.

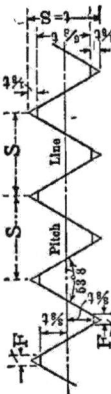

Table of German Löwenherz Thread Commonly Used on the Continent in Fine Work

The table gives sizes for the German Löwenherz thread, which is used very extensively for fine threads on measuring instruments and similar work in Germany. It was designed by Doctor Löwenherz, Berlin, in 1894.

| Diameter | | Pitch | | Approx. No. of Thds. per Inch | Root Diameter | | Pitch Diameter | | Width of Flat | Tap Drills | |
Mm.	Inches	Mm.	Inches		Mm.	Inches	Mm.	Inches	Inches (F)	Mm.	Approx. Inch Size
1.0	0.03937	0.25	0.0098	101.6	0.625	0.0246	0.812	0.0320	0.0012	0.64	0.025
1.2	0.04724	0.25	0.0098	101.6	0.825	0.0325	1.012	0.0398	0.0012	0.84	0.033
1.4	0.05512	0.30	0.0118	84.7	0.950	0.0374	1.175	0.0463	0.0015	0.97	0.038
1.7	0.06693	0.35	0.0138	72.6	1.175	0.0463	1.437	0.0566	0.0017	1.20	0.047
2.0	0.07874	0.40	0.0157	63.5	1.400	0.0551	1.700	0.0669	0.002	1.44	0.058
2.3	0.09055	0.40	0.0157	63.5	1.700	0.0669	2.000	0.07874	0.002	1.74	0.069
2.6	0.10236	0.45	0.0177	56.4	1.925	0.0758	2.260	0.0890	0.0022	1.97	0.077
3.0	0.11811	0.50	0.0197	50.8	2.250	0.0886	2.620	0.1031	0.0025	2.30	0.091
3.5	0.13780	0.60	0.0236	42.3	2.600	0.1024	3.050	0.1201	0.0029	2.65	0.104
4.0	0.15748	0.70	0.0276	36.3	2.950	0.1161	3.470	0.1367	0.0034	3.00	0.118
4.5	0.17717	0.75	0.0295	33.9	3.375	0.1329	3.930	0.1547	0.0037	3.43	0.134
5	0.19685	0.80	0.0315	31.7	3.800	0.1496	4.400	0.1732	0.0039	3.87	0.152
5.5	0.21654	0.90	0.0354	28.2	4.150	0.1634	4.825	0.1900	0.0044	4.23	0.166
6.0	0.23622	1.00	0.0394	25.4	4.500	0.1772	5.250	0.2067	0.0049	4.60	0.181
7.0	0.27560	1.10	0.0433	23.1	5.350	0.2106	6.175	0.2431	0.0054	5.45	0.215
8.0	0.31496	1.20	0.0472	21.1	6.200	0.2441	7.100	0.2795	0.0059	6.30	0.248
9.0	0.35433	1.30	0.0512	19.5	7.050	0.2776	8.025	0.3159	0.0064	7.15	0.280
10	0.39370	1.40	0.0551	18.1	7.900	0.3110	8.954	0.3525	0.0069	8.00	0.315
12	0.47244	1.60	0.0630	15.9	9.600	0.3780	10.800	0.4252	0.0079	9.70	0.382
14	0.55118	1.80	0.0709	14.1	11.300	0.4449	12.650	0.4984	0.0089	11.40	0.449
16	0.62992	2.00	0.0787	12.7	13.000	0.5118	14.500	0.5709	0.0098	13.10	0.516
18	0.70866	2.20	0.0866	11.5	14.700	0.5787	16.350	0.6442	0.0108	14.82	0.591
20	0.78740	2.40	0.0945	10.6	16.400	0.6457	18.200	0.7165	0.0118	16.52	0.656
22	0.86614	2.80	0.1102	9.1	17.800	0.7008	19.900	0.7835	0.0138	17.93	0.706
24	0.94498	2.80	0.1102	9.1	19.800	0.7795	21.900	0.8622	0.0138	19.93	0.783
26	1.02362	3.20	0.126	7.9	21.200	0.8346	23.600	0.9291	0.0157	21.35	0.840
28	1.10236	3.20	0.126	7.9	23.200	0.9134	25.600	1.0079	0.0157	23.35	0.919
30	1.18110	3.60	0.1417	7.1	24.600	0.9685	27.300	1.0748	0.0177	24.75	0.970

ROLLED THREADS

The rolled thread process dates back more than 50 years and was first patented in England. It was first used on comparatively rough work such as track bolts but has come to be used on such fine work as the sizing of taps and screws for micrometers.

The thread is forced up into the dies so that the finished screw is larger than the original wire by about the depth of one thread. In this way the size of the wire to use for any screw may be found by subtracting the depth of one thread from the outside diameter of the screw. This is $\dfrac{.866}{\text{threads per inch}}$. Exact allowance depends on material being rolled and other conditions.

The dies are usually flat plates of steel, having grooves of the same pitch and shape as the thread to be rolled. The dies can be easily laid out as follows:

Draw a horizontal line equal in length to the circumference of the *wire* or *blank*, and at its end draw a vertical line equal to the lead of the screw. The diagonal line made by joining these two points shows the angle of incline of the grooves. This can be done more easily if both the circumference and the pitch are laid out to *ten times* their actual dimensions.

DIMENSIONS OF BLANKS FOR U. S. S. ROLLED THREAD SCREWS
(REED & PRINCE MFG. CO.)

Size	T. P. I.	A	Size	T. P. I.	A
$\frac{1}{8}$	40	.1074 .1054	$\frac{9}{16}$	12	.5063 .5031
$\frac{3}{16}$	24	.1586 .1566	$\frac{5}{8}$	11	.5638 .5605
$\frac{1}{4}$	20	.2157 .2137	$\frac{3}{4}$	10	.6828 .6794
$\frac{5}{16}$	18	2745 .2715	$\frac{7}{8}$	9	.8006 .7972
$\frac{3}{8}$	16	.3325 .3295	1	8	.9165 .9131
$\frac{7}{16}$	14	.3890 .3860	$1\frac{1}{8}$	7	1.0298 1.0262
$\frac{1}{2}$	13	.4480 .4450	$1\frac{1}{4}$	7	1.1548 1.1512

ACME 29° SCREW THREADS

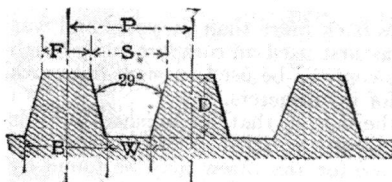

N = No. of Threads per Inch.

$P = \frac{1}{N}$ = Linear Pitch

$D = .5 P + .01$

$F = .3707 P$

W = .3707 P − .0052

S = .0293 P

B = .6293 P + .0052

The Acme standard thread is an adaptation of the most commonly used style of Worm Thread and is intended to take the place of the square thread.

It is a little shallower than the worm thread, but the same depth as the square thread and much stronger than the latter.

The various parts of the Acme standard thread are obtained as follows:

Width of Point of Tool for Screw Thread =

$$\frac{.3707}{\text{No. of Threads per inch}} - .0052.$$

Width of Screw or Nut Thread = $\dfrac{.3707}{\text{No. of Threads per inch}}$.

Diameter of Screw at Root =

$$\text{Diameter of Screw} - \left(\frac{1}{\text{No. of Threads per inch}} + .020 \right).$$

Depth of Thread = $\dfrac{1}{2 \times \text{No. of Threads per inch}} + .010.$

TABLE OF ACME 29° SCREW THREAD PARTS

N	P	D	F	W	S	B
Number of Threads per Inch	Pitch of Single Thread	Depth of Thread	Width of Top of Thread	Width of Space at Bottom of Thread	Width of Space at Top of Thread	Thickness at Root of Thread
1	1.0	.5100	.3707	.3655	.6293	.6345
1¼	.750	.3850	.2780	.2728	.4720	.4772
2	.500	.2600	.1853	.1801	.3147	.3199
3	.3333	.1767	.1235	.1183	.2098	.2150
4	.250	.1350	.0927	.0875	.1573	.1625
5	.200	.1100	.0741	.0689	.1259	.1311
6	.1666	.0933	.0618	.0566	.1049	.1101
7	.1428	.0814	.0529	.0478	.0899	.0951
8	.125	.0725	.0463	.0411	.0787	.0839
9	.1111	.0655	.0413	.0361	.0699	.0751
10	.10	.0600	.0371	.0319	.0629	.0681

ACME 29° TAP THREADS

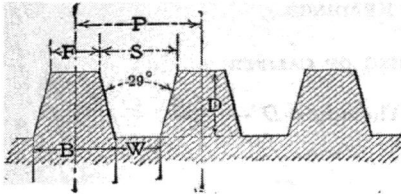

N = No. of Threads per Inch

$P = \frac{1}{N} = $ Linear Pitch

$D = .5\,P + .02$

$F = .3707\,P - .0052$

$W = .3707\,P - .0052$

$S = .6293\,P + .0052$

$B = .6293\,P + .0052$

THE Acme standard tap-thread is cut with the same width of tool as the screw-thread and the diameter at the root is the same for tap and screw. Clearance at bottom of thread between screw and nut is obtained by boring the nut blank .020 oversize.

The outside diameter of the tap is made .020 larger than the screw to give clearance between top of screw-thread and bottom of nut.

Width of Point of Tool for Tap-Thread =
$$\frac{.3707}{\text{No. of Threads per Inch}} - .0052.$$

$$\text{Width of Thread} = \frac{.3707}{\text{No. of Threads per Inch}} - .0052$$

Diameter of Tap = Diameter of Screw + .020.

Diameter of Tap at Root =
$$\text{Diameter of Tap} - \left(\frac{1}{\text{No. of Threads per Inch}} + .040. \right)$$

$$\text{Depth of Thread} = \frac{1}{2 \times \text{No. of Threads per Inch}} + .020.$$

TABLE OF ACME STANDARD 29° TAP-THREAD PARTS

N.	P	D	F	W	S	B
Number of Threads per Inch	Pitch of Single Thread	Depth of Thread	Width of Top of Thread	Width of Space at Bottom of Thread	Width of Space at Top of Thread	Thickness at Root of Thread
1	1.0	.5200	.3655	.3655	.6345	.6345
1½	.750	.3950	.2728	.2728	.4772	.4772
2	.500	.2700	.1801	.1801	.3199	.3199
3	.3333	.1867	.1183	.1183	.2150	.2150
4	.250	.1450	.0875	.0875	.1625	.1625
5	.200	.1200	.0689	.0689	.1311	.1311
6	.1666	.1033	.0566	.0566	.1101	.1101
7	.1428	.0914	.0478	.0478	.0951	.0951
8	.125	.0825	.0411	.0411	.0839	.0839
9	.1111	.0755	.0361	.0361	.0751	.0751
10	.10	.0700	.0319	.0319	.0681	.0681

Brown & Sharpe Screw Thread Micrometer Caliper
Readings

READING OF CALIPER

$$\text{For U. S. Threads} = D - \frac{.6495}{P}$$

U. S. Standard Threads

Diam.	Pitch	Caliper Reading		Diam.	Pitch	Caliper Reading	
D	P	$D - \dfrac{.6495}{P}$	$\dfrac{.6495}{P}$	D	P	$D - \dfrac{.6495}{P}$	$\dfrac{.6495}{P}$
64			.0101	$\frac{1}{4}$	20	.2176	.0324
62			.0105	$\frac{5}{16}$	18	.2765	.0360
60			.0108	$\frac{3}{8}$	16	.3344	.0406
58			.0112	$\frac{7}{16}$	14	.3911	.0464
56			.0116	$\frac{1}{2}$	13	.4501	.0499
54			.0120	$\frac{9}{16}$	12	.5084	.0541
52			.0125	$\frac{5}{8}$	11	.566	.0590
50			.0130	$\frac{3}{4}$	10	.6851	.0649
48			.0135	$\frac{7}{8}$	9	.8029	.0721
46			.0141	1	8	.9188	.0812
44			.0148	$1\frac{1}{8}$	7	1.0322	.0928
42			.0155	$1\frac{1}{4}$	7	1.1572	.0928
40			.0162	$1\frac{3}{8}$	6	1.2668	.1082
38			.0171	$1\frac{1}{2}$	6	1.3918	.1082
36			.0180	$1\frac{5}{8}$	$5\frac{1}{2}$	1.507	.1180
34			.0191	$1\frac{3}{4}$	5	1.6201	.1299
32			.0203	$1\frac{7}{8}$	5	1.7451	.1299
30			.0217	2	$4\frac{1}{2}$	1.8557	.1443
28			.0232	$2\frac{1}{2}$	4	2.3376	.1624
26			.0250	3	$3\frac{1}{2}$	2.8145	.1855
24			.0271	$3\frac{1}{2}$	$3\frac{1}{4}$	3.3002	.1998
22			.0295	4	3	3.7835	.2165

As there is no standard of diameter for the finer pitches, the columns for diameter and caliper reading are left blank. The column on the right gives the number to be subtracted from the diameter to obtain the caliper reading.

For explanation of screw thread micrometer caliper, refer to page 28.

BROWN & SHARPE SCREW THREAD MICROMETER CALIPER READINGS

READING OF CALIPER

$$\text{For "V" Threads} = D - \frac{.866}{P}$$

"V." THREADS

Diam.	Pitch	Caliper Reading		Diam.	Pitch	Caliper Reading	
D	P	$D - \frac{.866}{P}$	$\frac{.866}{P}$	D	P	$D - \frac{.866}{P}$	$\frac{.866}{P}$
	64		.0135	$\frac{1}{4}$	24	.2139	.0361
	62		.0140	$\frac{1}{4}$	20	.2067	.0433
	60		.0144	$\frac{5}{16}$	20	.2692	.0433
	58		.0149	$\frac{5}{16}$	18	.2644	.0481
	56		.0155	$\frac{3}{8}$	18	.3269	.0481
	54		.0160	$\frac{3}{8}$	16	.3209	.0541
	52		.0167	$\frac{7}{16}$	16	.3834	.0541
	50		.0173	$\frac{7}{16}$	14	.3756	.0619
	48		.0180	$\frac{1}{2}$	14	.4381	.0619
	46		.0188	$\frac{1}{2}$	13	.4334	.0666
	44		.0197	$\frac{9}{16}$	12	.4278	.0722
	42		.0206	$\frac{9}{16}$	14	.5006	.0619
	40		.0217	$\frac{9}{16}$	12	.4903	.0722
	38		.0228	$\frac{5}{8}$	11	.5463	.0787
	36		.0241	$\frac{5}{8}$	10	.5384	.0866
	34		.0255	$\frac{11}{16}$	10	.6009	.0866
	32		.0271	$\frac{3}{4}$	10	.6634	.0866
	30		.0289	$\frac{7}{8}$	9	.7788	.0962
	28		.0309	1	8	.8918	.1082
	26		.0333	$1\frac{1}{8}$	8	1.0168	.1082
				$1\frac{1}{4}$	7	1.1263	.1237
				$1\frac{1}{2}$	6	1.3557	.1443

As there is no standard of diameter for the finer pitches, the columns for diameter and caliper reading are left blank. The column on the right gives the number to be subtracted from the diameter to obtain the caliper reading.

For explanation of screw thread micrometer caliper, refer to page 28.

BROWN & SHARPE SCREW THREAD MICROMETER CALIPER
READINGS

READING OF CALIPER

For Whitworth Threads $= D - \dfrac{.640}{P}$

WHITWORTH STANDARD THREADS

Diam.	Pitch	Caliper Reading	
D	P	$D - \dfrac{.640}{P}$	$\dfrac{.640}{P}$
$\frac{1}{4}$	20	.2180	.0320
$\frac{5}{16}$	18	.2769	.0355
$\frac{3}{8}$	16	.3350	.0400
$1\frac{7}{16}$	14	.3918	.0457
$\frac{1}{2}$	12	.4467	.0533
$\frac{9}{16}$	12	.5092	.0533
$\frac{5}{8}$	11	.5668	.0582
$\frac{11}{16}$	11	.6293	.0582
$\frac{3}{4}$	10	.6860	.0640
$\frac{13}{16}$	10	.7485	.0640
$\frac{7}{8}$	9	.8039	.0711
$\frac{15}{16}$	9	.8664	.0711
1	8	.9200	.0800
$1\frac{1}{8}$	7	1.0336	.0914
$1\frac{1}{4}$	7	1.1586	.0914
$1\frac{3}{8}$	6	1.2684	.1066
$1\frac{1}{2}$	6	1.3934	.1066
$1\frac{5}{8}$	5	1.4970	.1280
$1\frac{3}{4}$	5	1.6220	.1280
$1\frac{7}{8}$	$4\frac{1}{2}$	1.7328	.1422
2	$4\frac{1}{2}$	1.8578	.1442
$2\frac{1}{8}$	$4\frac{1}{2}$	1.9828	.1422

SCREW-THREAD MICROMETER CALIPER

THE Brown & Sharpe thread micrometer is fitted with pointed spindle and "V" anvil as in Fig. 10, to measure the actual thread on the cut surface. Enough of the point is removed and the bottom of the "V" is carried low enough so that the anvil and spindle clear the top and bottom of the thread and rest directly on the sides of the thread.

As it measures one-half of the depth of the thread from the top, on each side, the diameter of the thread as indicated by the caliper, or the pitch diameter, is the full size of the thread less the depth of one thread.

This depth may be found as follows;

Depth of   V   threads = .866 ÷ number of threads to 1″
  "   " U. S. Std.   "   = .6495 ÷   "   "   "   " "
  "   " Whitworth   "   = .64 ÷   "   "   "   " "

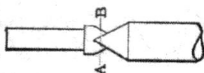

FIG. 10. — Spindle and Anvil of Thread Micrometer

As the U. S. thread is flatted ⅛ of its own depth on top, it follows that the pitch diameter of the thread is increased ⅛ on each side, equaling ¼ of the whole depth and instead of the constant .866 we use the constant .6495, which is ¾ of .866.

When the point and anvil are in contact the o represents a line drawn through the plane $A\ B$, Fig. 10, and if the caliper is opened, say to .500, it represents the distance of the two planes .500″ apart. The preceding tables are used in connection with the micrometer.

MEASURING EXTERNAL SCREW-THREAD DIAMETERS WITH MICROMETERS AND WIRES

It is frequently necessary, especially in making a tap or thread-plug gage, to measure the thread diameter on the thread angle in addition to measuring on top of the thread and at the bottom of the thread groove, and unless calipers made expressly for such work are at hand, the measurement on the thread angle is not made with any degree of accuracy or is omitted entirely. The accompanying sketches, Figs. 11, 12 and 13, formulas, and tables, are worked out for convenience in screw-thread inspection, so that by using ordinary micrometer calipers and wire of the diameter called for in the table the standard threads can be compared with the figures given.

Threads of Special Diameter

For threads of special diameter the values of x, x_1 or x_2 can be readily computed from the formula corresponding to the method of measuring to be used. The method shown in Fig. 11 at x is liable to lead to an error unless care be taken that the diameter on top of the thread is correct, and also that the flatted surface on the top of the threads is concentric with the rest of the thread. The concentricity of the flatted surface can be tested by measuring, as at x, Fig. 11, at several points on a plane through the axis and at right angles to it. The wire used must be round and of uniform diameter.

BROWN & SHARPE SCREW THREAD MICROMETER CALIPER READINGS

READING OF CALIPER

For Whitworth Threads $= D - \dfrac{.640}{P}$

WHITWORTH STANDARD THREADS

Diam.	Pitch	Caliper Reading	
D	P	$D - \dfrac{.640}{P}$	$\dfrac{.640}{P}$
$\frac{1}{4}$	20	.2180	.0320
$\frac{5}{16}$	18	.2769	.0355
$\frac{3}{8}$	16	.3350	.0400
$\frac{7}{16}$	14	.3918	.0457
$\frac{1}{2}$	12	.4467	.0533
$\frac{9}{16}$	12	.5092	.0533
$\frac{5}{8}$	11	.5668	.0582
$\frac{11}{16}$	11	.6293	.0582
$\frac{3}{4}$	10	.6860	.0640
$\frac{13}{16}$	10	.7485	.0640
$\frac{7}{8}$	9	.8039	.0711
$\frac{15}{16}$	9	.8664	.0711
1	8	.9200	.0800
$1\frac{1}{8}$	7	1.0336	.0914
$1\frac{1}{4}$	7	1.1586	.0914
$1\frac{3}{8}$	6	1.2684	.1066
$1\frac{1}{2}$	6	1.3934	.1066
$1\frac{5}{8}$	5	1.4970	.1280
$1\frac{3}{4}$	5	1.6220	.1280
$1\frac{7}{8}$	$4\frac{1}{2}$	1.7328	.1422
2	$4\frac{1}{2}$	1.8578	.1442
$2\frac{1}{8}$	$4\frac{1}{2}$	1.9828	.1422

SCREW-THREAD MICROMETER CALIPER

THE Brown & Sharpe thread micrometer is fitted with pointed spindle and "V." anvil as in Fig. 10, to measure the actual thread on the cut surface. Enough of the point is removed and the bottom of the "V" is carried low enough so that the anvil and spindle clear the top and bottom of the thread and rest directly on the sides of the thread.

As it measures one-half of the depth of the thread from the top, on each side, the diameter of the thread as indicated by the caliper, or the pitch diameter, is the full size of the thread less the depth of one thread.

This depth may be found as follows;

Depth of   V   threads = .866 ÷ number of threads to 1"
  "   " U. S. Std.   "   = .6495 ÷   "   "   "   "   " "
  "   " Whitworth   "   = .64 ÷   "   "   "   "   " "

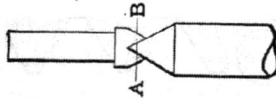

FIG. 10. — Spindle and Anvil of Thread Micrometer

As the U. S. thread is flatted $\frac{1}{8}$ of its own depth on top, it follows that the pitch diameter of the thread is increased $\frac{1}{8}$ on each side, equaling $\frac{1}{4}$ of the whole depth and instead of the constant .866 we use the constant .6495, which is $\frac{3}{4}$ of .866.

When the point and anvil are in contact the o represents a line drawn through the plane A B, Fig. 10, and if the caliper is opened, say to .500, it represents the distance of the two planes .500" apart. The preceding tables are used in connection with the micrometer.

MEASURING EXTERNAL SCREW-THREAD DIAMETERS WITH MICROMETERS AND WIRES

It is frequently necessary, especially in making a tap or thread-plug gage, to measure the thread diameter on the thread angle in addition to measuring on top of the thread and at the bottom of the thread groove, and unless calipers made expressly for such work are at hand, the measurement on the thread angle is not made with any degree of accuracy or is omitted entirely. The accompanying sketches, Figs. 11, 12 and 13, formulas, and tables, are worked out for convenience in screw-thread inspection, so that by using ordinary micrometer calipers and wire of the diameter called for in the table the standard threads can be compared with the figures given.

Threads of Special Diameter

For threads of special diameter the values of x, x_1 or x_2 can be readily computed from the formula corresponding to the method of measuring to be used. The method shown in Fig. 11 at x is liable to lead to an error unless care be taken that the diameter on top of the thread is correct, and also that the flatted surface on the top of the threads is concentric with the rest of the thread. The concentricity of the flatted surface can be tested by measuring, as at x, Fig. 11, at several points on a plane through the axis and at right angles to it. The wire used must be round and of uniform diameter.

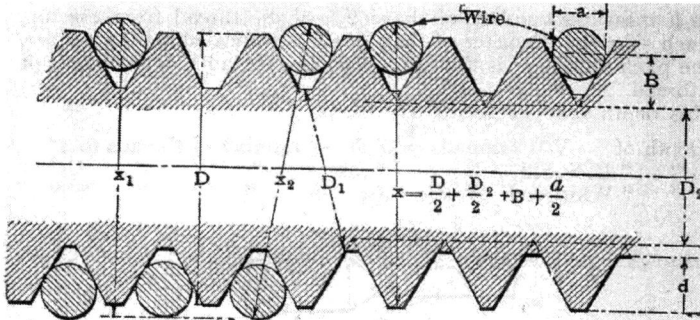

FIG. 11. — Measuring U. S. Standard Threads

D = outside diameter of thread.
D_1 = root diameter measured in thread groove.
n = number of threads per inch of length.
d = depth of thread.
p = distance from center to center of adjacent threads.
f = width of flat on U. S. Standard thread.
a = diameter of wire used.
B = distance from apex of thread angle at root, to center of wire.
D_2 = diameter of cylinder touched by apexes of thread angles.
x = diameter from top of threads on one side of tap or bolt, to top of wire laid in thread groove on opposite side.

U. S. Standard Thread

$$p = \text{lead} = \frac{1}{n}, \text{ for single threads.}$$

$$d = p \times .6495 = \frac{.6495}{n}.$$

$$D_1 = \sqrt{(D - 2d)^2 + \left(\frac{\text{lead}}{2}\right)^2}.$$

$$f = \frac{p}{8}.$$

$$a = \text{from } p, \text{ max; to } p \times .505, \text{ min.}$$

$$B = \frac{a}{2} \div \sin 30° = a.$$

$$D_2 = D - \frac{1.5155}{n}.$$

$$x = \frac{D}{2} + \frac{D_2}{2} + B + \frac{a}{2}.$$

$$x_1 = D_2 + 2B + a.$$

$$x_2 = \sqrt{(D_2 + 2B)^2 + \left(\frac{\text{lead}}{2}\right)^2} + a.$$

Table for Measuring U. S. Standard Threads with Micrometers and Wires

D	n	D_1	D_2	a	B	$\left(\frac{\text{lead}}{2}\right)^2$	x	x_1	x_2
$\frac{1}{4}''$	20	.1867	.1742	.04	.04	.000625	.2721	.2942	.2955
$\frac{5}{16}''$	18	.2419	.2283	.04	.04	.000771	.3304	.3483	.3495
$\frac{3}{8}''$	16	.2954	.2803	.04	.04	.000976	.3876	.4003	.4016
$\frac{7}{16}''$	14	.3465	.3292	.04	.04	.001274	.4433	.4492	.4507
$\frac{1}{2}''$	13	.4019	.3834	.06	.06	.001479	.5317	.5634	.5647
$\frac{9}{16}''$	12	.4561	.4362	.06	.06	.001735	.5893	.6162	.6177
$\frac{5}{8}''$	11	.5089	.4872	.06	.06	.002065	.6461	.6672	.6681
$\frac{11}{16}''$	11	.5712	.5497	.06	.06	.002065	.7086	.7297	.7312
$\frac{3}{4}''$	10	.6221	.5984	.06	.06	.0025	.7643	.7784	.7801
$\frac{13}{16}''$	10	.6844	.6609	.06	.06	.0025	.8267	.8409	.8425
$\frac{7}{8}''$	9	.7327	.7066	0.10	0.10	.003086	.9408	1.0066	1.0083
$\frac{15}{16}''$	9	.7950	.7691	0.10	0.10	.003086	1.0033	1.0691	1.0706
$1''$	8	.8399	.8105	0.10	0.10	.003906	1.0553	1.1105	1.1124
$1\frac{1}{8}''$	7	.9421	.9085	0.10	0.10	.005102	1.1667	1.2085	1.2107
$1\frac{1}{4}''$	7	1.0668	1.0335	0.10	0.10	.005102	1.2917	1.3335	1.3355
$1\frac{3}{8}''$	6	1.1614	1.1224	0.10	0.10	.006944	1.3987	1.4224	1.4250
$1\frac{1}{2}''$	6	1.2862	1.2474	0.10	0.10	.006944	1.5237	1.5474	1.5497
$1\frac{5}{8}''$	$5\frac{1}{2}$	1.3917	1.3494	0.15	0.15	.008263	1.7122	1.7994	1.8019
$1\frac{3}{4}''$	5	1.4935	1.4469	0.15	0.15	.010	1.8234	1.8969	1.8997
$1\frac{7}{8}''$	5	1.6182	1.5719	0.15	0.15	.010	1.9484	2.0219	2.0245
$2''$	$4\frac{1}{2}$	1.7149	1.6632	0.15	0.15	.012343	2.0566	2.1132	2.1163
$2\frac{1}{8}''$	$4\frac{1}{2}$	1.8393	1.7882	0.15	0.15	.012343	2.1816	2.2382	2.2411
$2\frac{1}{4}''$	$4\frac{1}{2}$	1.9641	1.9132	0.15	0.15	.012343	2.3066	2.3632	2.3667
$2\frac{3}{8}''$	4	2.0540	1.9961	0.15	0.15	.015625	2.4105	2.4461	2.4495
$2\frac{1}{2}''$	4	2.1787	2.1211	0.15	0.15	.015625	2.5355	2.5711	2.5742
$2\frac{3}{4}''$	4	2.4284	2.3711	0.15	0.15	.015625	2.7855	2.8211	2.8240
$3''$	$3\frac{1}{2}$	2.6326	2.5670	0.20	0.20	.020392	3.0835	3.1670	3.1704
$3\frac{1}{4}''$	$3\frac{1}{2}$	2.8823	2.8170	0.20	0.20	.020392	3.3335	3.4170	3.4200
$3\frac{1}{2}''$	$3\frac{1}{4}$	3.1041	3.0337	0.20	0.20	.023654	3.5668	3.6337	3.6368
$3\frac{3}{4}''$	3	3.3211	3.2448	0.20	0.20	.02775	3.7974	3.8448	3.8486
$4''$	3	3.5708	3.4948	0.20	0.20	.02775	4.0474	4.0948	4.0983
$4\frac{1}{4}''$	$2\frac{7}{8}''$	3.8019	3.7228	0.20	0.20	.03024	4.2864	4.3228	4.3264
$4\frac{1}{2}''$	$2\frac{3}{4}''$	4.0318	3.9489	0.20	0.20	.03305	4.5244	4.5500	4.5530
$4\frac{3}{4}''$	$2\frac{5}{8}''$	4.2592	4.1728	0.20	0.20	.03625	4.7614	4.7728	4.7767
$5''$	$2\frac{1}{2}''$	4.4848	4.3938	0.20	0.20	.040	4.9970	4.9938	4.9980
$5\frac{1}{4}''$	$2\frac{1}{2}''$	4.7346	4.6438	0.20	0.20	.040	5.2470	5.2438	5.2477
$5\frac{1}{2}''$	$2\frac{3}{8}''$	4.9574	4.8619	0.20	0.20	.04431	5.4810	5.4619	5.4661
$5\frac{3}{4}''$	$2\frac{3}{8}''$	5.2072	5.1119	0.20	0.20	.04431	5.7310	5.7119	5.7160
$6''$	$2\frac{1}{4}''$	5.4271	5.3264	0.20	0.20	.049373	5.9632	5.9264	5.9307

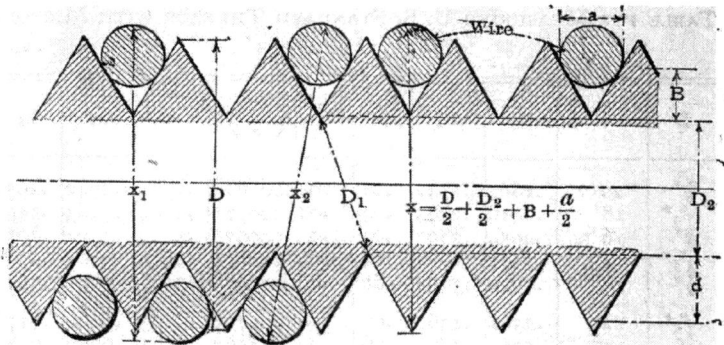

FIG. 12. — Measuring 60-Degree V-Threads

D = outside diameter of thread.
D_1 = root diameter measured in thread groove.
n = number of threads per inch of length.
d = depth of thread.
p = distance from center to center of adjacent threads.
a = diameter of wire used.
B = distance from apex of thread angle at root, to center of wire.
D_2 = diameter of cylinder touched by apexes of thread angles.
x = diameter from top of threads on one side of tap or bolt, to top of wire laid in thread groove on opposite side.

60° V Thread

$$p = \text{lead} = \frac{1}{n}, \text{ for single threads.}$$

$$d = p \times .866, = \frac{.866}{n}.$$

$$D_1 = \sqrt{(D - 2d)^2 + \left(\frac{\text{lead}}{2}\right)^2}.$$

$$a = \frac{p}{.866}, \text{max; to } p \times .577, \text{ min.}$$

$$B = \frac{a}{2} \div \sin 30° = a.$$

$$D_2 = D - \frac{1.732}{n}.$$

$$x = \frac{D}{2} + \frac{D_2}{2} + B + \frac{a}{2}.$$

$$x_1 = D_2 + 2B + a.$$

$$x_2 = \sqrt{(D_2 + 2B)^2 + \left(\frac{\text{lead}}{2}\right)^2} + a.$$

TABLE FOR MEASURING 60-DEGREE V-THREADS WITH MICROMETERS AND WIRES

D	n	D_1	D_2	a	B	$\left(\dfrac{\text{lead}}{2}\right)^2$	x	x_1	x_2
1/4″	20	.1653	.1634	0.04	0.04	.000625	.2667	.2834	.2846
5/16″	18	.2180	.2163	0.04	0.04	.000771	.3244	.3363	.3375
3/8″	16	.2685	.2667	0.04	0.04	.0009765	.3808	.3867	.3881
7/16″	14	.3158	.3138	0.06	0.06	.0001274	.4656	.4938	.4957
1/2″	12	.3580	.3557	0.06	0.06	.001735	.5178	.5357	.5375
9/16″	12	.4202	.4182	0.06	0.06	.001735	.5803	.5982	.5998
5/8″	11	.4697	.4676	0.06	0.06	.0020657	.6363	.6476	.6492
11/16″	11	.5319	.530	0.06	0.06	.0020657	.6987	.7100	.7115
3/4″	10	.5789	.5768	0.10	0.10	.0025	.8134	.8768	.8784
13/16″	10	.6412	.6393	0.10	0.10	.0025	.8759	.9393	.9413
7/8″	9	.6847	.6826	0.10	0.10	.003086	.9288	.9826	.9843
15/16″	9	.7470	.7450	0.10	0.10	.003086	.9912	1.045	1.0466
1″	8	.7859	.7835	0.10	0.10	.003906	1.0417	1.0835	1.0854
1 1/8″	7	.8803	.8776	0.10	0.10	.005102	1.1513	1.1776	1.1800
1 1/4″	7	1.0050	1.0026	0.10	0.10	.005102	1.2763	1.3026	1.3047
1 3/8″	6	1.0895	1.0863	0.15	0.15	.006944	1.4556	1.5363	1.5388
1 1/2″	6	1.2141	1.2113	0.15	0.15	.006944	1.5806	1.6613	1.6635
1 5/8″	5	1.2825	1.2786	0.15	0.15	.010	1.6768	1.7286	1.7317
1 3/4″	5	1.4071	1.4036	0.15	0.15	.010	1.8018	1.8536	1.8565
1 7/8″	4½	1.4941	1.490	0.15	0.15	.012343	1.9075	1.9400	1.9434
2″	4½	1.6188	1.615	0.15	0.15	.012343	2.0325	2.0650	2.0682
2 1/8″	4½	1.7435	1.740	0.15	0.15	.012343	2.1575	2.1900	2.1930
2 1/4″	4½	1.8683	1.8651	0.15	0.15	.012343	2.2825	2.3150	2.3178
2 3/8″	4½	1.9930	1.990	0.15	0.15	.012343	2.4075	2.440	2.4426
2 1/2″	4	2.0707	2.067	0.20	0.20	.015625	2.5835	2.670	2.6670
2 3/4″	4	2.3203	2.317	0.20	0.20	.015625	2.8335	2.917	2.9196
3″	3½	2.5089	2.505	0.20	0.20	.020392	3.0525	3.105	3.1085
3 1/4″	3½	2.7587	2.755	0.20	0.20	.020392	3.3025	3.355	3.3582
3 1/2″	3¼	2.9711	2.967	0.20	0.20	.023654	3.5335	3.567	3.5705
3 3/4″	3	3.1770	3.1727	0.20	0.20	.02775	3.7613	3.7727	3.7765
4″	3	3.4266	3.4227	0.20	0.20	.02775	4.0113	4.0227	4.0263

WATCH SCREW THREADS

WATCH screw threads are of sharp V-form and generally 45-degree angle for screws used in nickel and brass; though 60 degrees for use in steel. The Waltham Watch Company and others use the centimeter as the unit for all measurements with the exception of the pitch, which is based on the inch; the Waltham threads being 110, 120, 140, 160, 170, 180, 200, 220, 240, 254, per inch and the diameters ranging from 0.120 to 0.035 cm.

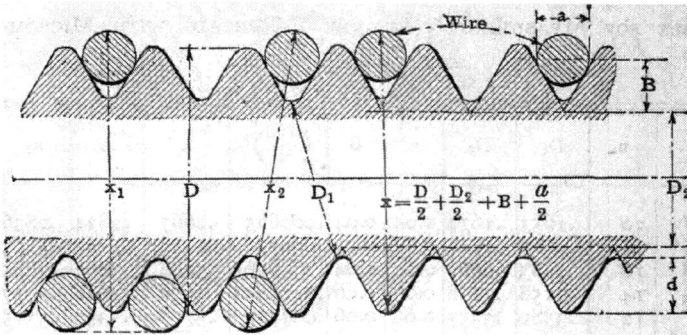

FIG. 13. — Measuring Whitworth Threads.

D = outside diameter of thread.
D_1 = root diameter measured in thread groove.
n = number of threads per inch of length.
d = depth of thread.
p = distance from center to center of adjacent threads.
r = radius on Whitworth thread.
a = diameter of wire used.
B = distance from apex of thread angle at root, to center of wire.
D_2 = diameter of cylinder touched by apexes of thread angles.
x = diameter from top of threads on one side of tap or bolt, to top of wire laid in thread groove on opposite side.

WHITWORTH THREAD

p = lead = $\frac{1}{n}$, for single threads.

$d = p \times .64033 = \frac{.64033}{n}$.

$D_1 = \sqrt{(D - 2d)^2 + \left(\frac{lead}{2}\right)^2}$.

$r = p \times .1373$.
$a = p \times .84$, max; to $p \times .454$, min.

$B = \frac{a}{2} \div \sin 27° 30' = \frac{a}{.9235}$.

$D_2 = D - \frac{1.600825}{n}$.

$x = \frac{D}{2} + \frac{D_2}{2} + B + \frac{a}{2}$.

$x_1 = D_2 + 2B + a$.

$x_2 = \sqrt{(D_2 + 2B)^2 + \left(\frac{lead}{2}\right)^2} + a$.

TABLE FOR MEASURING WHITWORTH THREADS WITH MICROMETERS AND WIRES

D	n	D_1	D_2	a	B	$\left(\frac{\text{lead}}{2}\right)^2$	x	x_1	x_2
1/4″	20	.1875	.1699	0.04	.04331	.000625	.2733	.2965	.2977
5/16″	18	.2428	.2235	0.04	.04331	.000771	.3313	.3501	.3514
3/8″	16	.2965	.2749	0.04	.04331	.000976	.3883	.4015	.4029
7/16″	14	.344	.3231	0.04	.04331	.001274	.4436	.4497	.4512
1/2″	12	.3953	.3666	0.06	.06496	.001735	.5232	.5563	.5582
9/16″	12	.4576	.4291	0.06	.06496	.001735	.5907	.6190	.6204
5/8″	11	.5105	.4794	0.06	.06496	.002065	.6372	.6693	.6710
11/16″	11	.5728	.5420	0.06	.06496	.002065	.7097	.7319	.7334
3/4″	10	.6239	.5899	0.06	.06496	.0025	.7649	.7798	.7815
13/16″	10	.6862	.6524	0.06	.06496	.0025	.8274	.8423	.8438
7/8″	9	.7348	.6971	0.06	.06496	.003086	.8810	.8870	.8882
15/16″	9	.797	.7596	0.06	.06496	.003086	.9435	.9495	.9512
1″	8	.8422	.7999	0.10	.10839	.003906	1.0583	1.1167	1.1185
1 1/8″	7	.9447	.8963	0.10	.10839	.005102	1.169	1.2131	1.2153
1 1/4″	7	1.0693	1.0213	0.10	.10839	.005102	1.294	1.3381	1.340
1 3/8″	6	1.1644	1.1082	0.10	.10839	.006944	1.400	1.4250	1.4276
1 1/2″	6	1.2892	1.2332	0.10	.10839	.006944	1.525	1.5500	1.5523
1 5/8″	5	1.3726	1.3048	0.15	.16242	.010	1.7023	1.7796	1.7826
1 3/4″	5	1.497	1.4298	0.15	.16242	.010	1.8273	1.9046	1.9074
1 7/8″	4½	1.5942	1.5193	0.15	.16242	.012343	1.9345	1.9941	1.9973
2″	4½	1.7185	1.6443	0.15	.16242	.012343	2.0595	2.1191	2.1221
2 1/8″	4½	1.8437	1.7693	0.15	.16242	.012343	2.1845	2.2441	2.2470
2 1/4″	4	1.9338	1.8498	0.15	.16242	.015625	2.2873	2.3246	2.328
2 3/8″	4	2.0585	1.9750	0.15	.16242	.015625	2.4123	2.4498	2.453
2 1/2″	4	2.1833	2.100	0.15	.16242	.015625	2.5373	2.5748	2.5778
2 3/4″	3½	2.3882	2.2926	0.20	.21567	.020392	2.837	2.9240	2.9276
3″	3½	2.6397	2.5426	0.20	.21567	.020392	3.087	3.1740	3.1773
3 1/4″	3½	2.860	2.7574	0.20	.21567	.023654	3.3194	3.3887	3.3924
3 1/2″	3½	3.1098	3.0074	0.20	.21567	.023654	3.5694	3.6387	3.642
3 3/4″	3	3.327	3.2164	0.20	.21567	.027755	3.799	3.8477	3.8515
4″	3	3.5768	3.4664	0.20	.21567	.027755	4.049	4.0977	4.1012
4 1/4″	2 7/8	3.808	3.693	0.20	.21567	.030241	4.287	4.3243	4.328
4 1/2″	2 7/8	4.0582	3.943	0.20	.21567	.030241	4.537	4.5743	4.578
4 3/4″	2 3/4	4.2878	4.168	0.20	.21567	.033051	4.7746	4.7993	4.8025
5″	2 3/4	4.5376	4.418	0.20	.21567	.033051	5.0245	5.0493	5.0524
5 1/4″	2 5/8	4.7658	4.640	0.20	.21567	.036252	5.2607	5.2713	5.275
5 1/2″	2 5/8	5.0156	4.890	0.20	.21567	.036252	5.5107	5.5213	5.5248
5 3/4″	2 1/2	5.2415	5.110	0.20	.21567	.040	5.7455	5.7413	5.7446
6″	2 1/2	5.4913	5.360	0.20	.21567	.040	5.9955	5.9913	5.9944

MEASURING FINE PITCH SCREW-THREAD DIAMETERS

THE accompanying table should be of service to those using the three-wire system of measurement as the constants cover the finer pitches and may be easily applied to screw threads of any diameter. The diagrams, Fig. 14, make the method of application so plain that no description appears necessary.

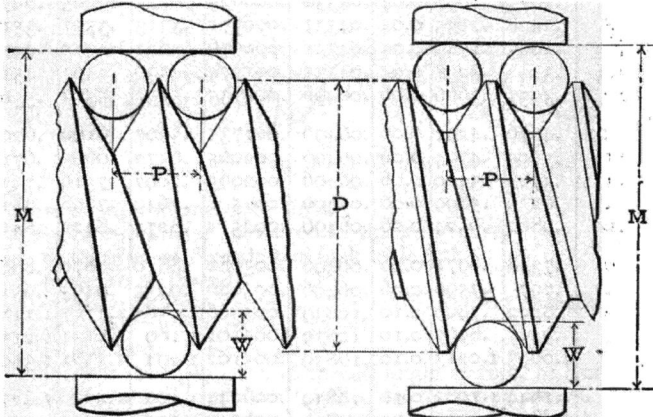

Formulas:

For V Thread

$$D = (M - 3 W) + 1.732\ P.$$
$$M = (D - 1.732\ P) + 3 W.$$

For Sellers Thread

$$D = (M - 3 W) + 1.5155\ P.$$
$$M = (D - 1.5155\ P) + 3 W.$$

FIG. 14. — Measuring Fine Pitch Threads

CONSTANTS FOR USE WITH THE 3-WIRE SYSTEM OF MEASURING SCREW THREADS

Threads per Inch	For V Thread 1.732 P =	For Sellers Thread 1.5155 P=	Threads per Inch	For V Thread 1.732 P =	For Sellers Thread 1.5155 P =
8	.21650	.18943	25	.06928	.06062
9	.19244	.16839	28	.06185	.05412
10	.17320	.15155	32	.05412	.04736
11	.15745	.13777	36	.04811	.04210
12	.14433	.12629	40	.04330	.03789
13	.13323	.11658	48	.03608	.03157
14	.12371	.10825	50	.03464	.03031
16	.10825	.09472	56	.03093	.02706
18	.09622	.08419	64	.02706	.02368
20	.08660	.07578	80	.02165	.01894
22	.07872	.06889	100	.01732	.01516
24	.07216	.06314			

MEASURING METRIC SCREW THREAD DIAMETERS

The tables and formulas given herewith in connection with Fig. 15 should be of value to those engaged in work requiring the frequent production of thread gages or special taps in the metric sizes. The three wire system is used as in the preceding tables, the wires being applied as indicated.

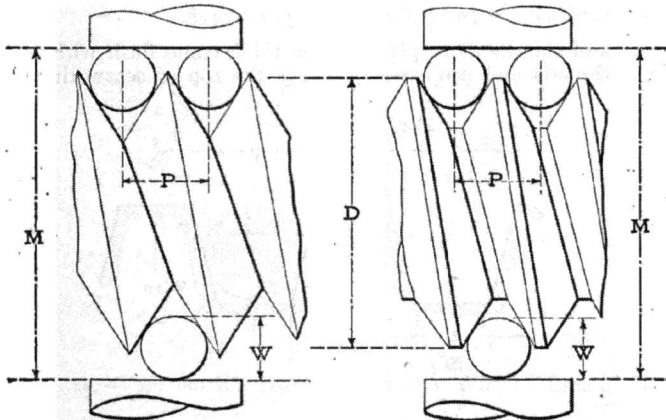

Formulas:

For V Threads

For Threads with Flat Top and Bottom equal to $\frac{1}{8}$ of the Pitch

$$D = (M - 3 W) + 1.732 P.$$
$$M = (D - 1.732 P.) + 3 W.$$

$$D = (M - 3 W) + 1.5155 P.$$
$$M = (D - 1.5155 P.) + 3 W.$$

FIG. 15. — Measuring Metric Threads

CONSTANTS FOR USE IN MEASURING METRIC SCREW THREADS BY THE 3-WIRE SYSTEM

Pitch m-m	Pitch Inches	1.732P	1.5155P	Pitch m-m	Pitch Inches	1.732P	1.5155P
0.5	.01969	.03410	.02984	4.5	.17717	.30686	.26850
0.75	.02953	.05109	.04475	5.0	.19685	.34094	.29833
1.0	.03937	.06819	.05966	5.5	.21654	.37500	.32816
1.25	.04921	.08523	.07458	6.0	.23622	.40913	.35799
1.5	.05900	.09719	.08941	6.5	.25591	.43773	.38783
1.75	.06890	.11933	.10442	7.0	.27559	.47677	.41766
2.0	.07874	.13638	.11933	7.5	.29528	.51092	.44749
2.5	.09843	.16948	.14917	8.0	.31496	.54551	.47732
3.0	.11811	.20456	.17899	9.0	.35433	.60870	.53699
3.5	.13780	.23867	.20784	10.00	.39370	.68189	.59665
4.0	.15748	.26775	.23866				

MEASURING ACME 29-DEGREE THREADS

THE diameter of a wire which will be flush with tops of thread on tap when laid in the Acme thread groove, Fig. 16, will be found as follows:

Rad. of wire section = side opp. = side adj. × tan. 37° 45′ =

$$\frac{p \times .6293 + .0052}{2} \times .77428.$$

Diam. of wire = $(p \times .6293 + .0052) .77428.$

Wires of the diameter given in the table come flush with the tops of tap threads and project .010 above the top of screw threads.

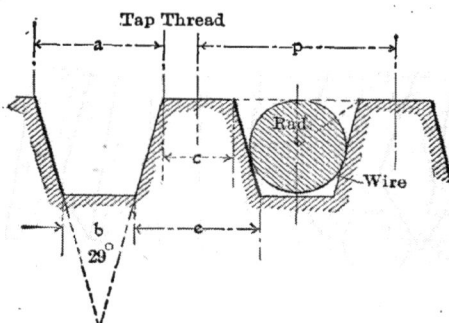

FIG. 16. — Measuring Acme Threads

TABLE OF WIRE SIZES FOR MEASURING ACME STANDARD 29° SCREW AND TAP THREADS

Threads per Inch	Pitch	Diam. of Wire
1	1.	0.4913
$1\frac{1}{3}$	.750	0.3694
$1\frac{1}{2}$	.6666	0.3288
$1\frac{3}{4}$	.5774	0.2824
2	.500	0.2476
$2\frac{1}{2}$	.400	0.1989
3	.3333	0.1664
4	.250	0.1258
5	.200	0.1014
6	.1666	0.0852
7	.1428	0.0736
8	.125	0.0649
9	.1111	0.0581
10	.100	0.0527

MEASURING BROWN & SHARPE 29-DEGREE WORM THREADS

THE diameter of wire for Brown & Sharpe worm thread, Fig. 17, for each pitch, that will rest in the thread groove on the thread angle and be flush with the tops of the finished threads, is found as follows;

Rad. of wire section (see table) = side opp. = side adj. × tan.

$37° 46' = \dfrac{0.665\,P}{2} \times 0.77428 = 0.257448\,P$ and diam. of wire = $0.5149\,P$.

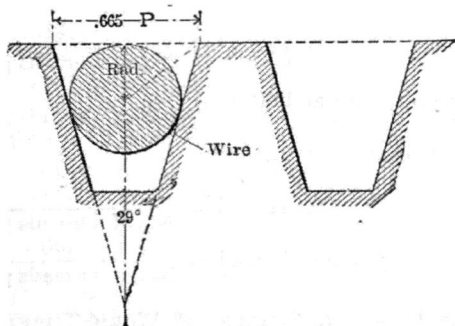

FIG. 17. — Measuring Brown & Sharpe Worm Threads.

TABLE OF WIRE SIZES FOR MEASURING B. & S. 29° WORM THREADS

Threads per Inch	Pitch	Diam. of Wire
$\frac{1}{2}$	2.	1.0298
$\frac{4}{7}$	1.750	0.9010
$\frac{2}{3}$	1.500	0.7723
$\frac{4}{5}$	1.250	0.6436
1	1.0	0.5149
$1\frac{1}{2}$	.6666	0.3432
2	.5	0.2574
$2\frac{1}{2}$	.4	0.2060
3	.3333	0.1716
$3\frac{1}{2}$	.2857	0.1471
4	.250	0.1287
$4\frac{1}{2}$	.2222	0.1144
5	.2	0.1030
6	.1666	0.0858
7	.1428	0.0735
8	.125	0.0643
9	.1111	0.0572
10	.10	0.0515
12	.0833	0.0429
16	.0625	0.0322
20	.050	0.0257

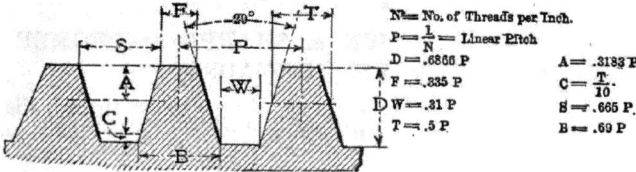

N = No. of Threads per Inch.

$P = \frac{1}{N} =$ Linear Pitch

$D = .6866\ P$ $A = .3183\ P$

$F = .335\ P$ $C = \frac{T}{10}$

$W = .31\ P$ $S = .665\ P$

$T = .5\ P$ $B = .69\ P$

$$\text{Pitch} = \frac{1}{\text{No. of Threads per inch}}$$

$$\text{Depth of Thread} = \frac{.6866}{\text{No. of Threads per inch}}$$

$$\text{Width of Top of Thread} = \frac{.335}{\text{No. of Threads per inch}}$$

$$\text{Width of Space at Bottom} = \frac{.310}{\text{No. of Threads per inch}}$$

$$\text{Clearance at Bottom of Thread} = \frac{\text{Thickness at Pitch Line}}{10}$$

$$\text{Width of Space at Top of Thread} = \frac{.665}{\text{No. of Threads per inch}}$$

$$\text{Thickness at Root of Thread} = \frac{.69}{\text{No. of Threads per inch}}$$

TABLE OF BROWN & SHARPE 29° WORM THREAD PARTS

	P	D	F	W	T	A	C	S	B
Number of Threads Per Inch	Pitch of Single Thread	Depth of Thread	Width of Top of Thread	Width of Space at Bottom	Thickness of Thread at Pitch Line	Thread Above Pitch Line	Clearance at Bottom of Thread	Width of Space at Top	Thickness at Root of Thread
1	1.0	.6866	.3350	.3100	.5000	.3183	.05	.665	.69
1¼	.8	.5492	.2680	.2480	.4000	.2546	.04	.532	.552
1½	.6666	.4577	.2233	.2066	.3333	.2122	.0333	.4433	.4599
2	.5	.3433	.1675	.1550	.2500	.1592	.0250	.3325	.345
2½	.4	.2746	.1340	.1240	.2000	.1273	.0200	.2660	.276
3	.3333	.2289	.1117	.1033	.1666	.1061	.0166	.2216	.2299
3½	.2857	.1962	.0957	.0886	.1429	.0909	.0143	.1901	.2011
4	.250	.1716	.0838	.0775	.1250	.0796	.0125	.1637	.1725
4½	.2222	.1526	.0744	.0689	.1111	.0707	.0111	.1478	.1533
5	.2	.1373	.0670	.0620	.1000	.0637	.0100	.1330	.138
6	.1666	.1144	.0558	.0517	.0833	.0531	.0083	.1108	.115
7	.1428	.0981	.0479	.0443	.0714	.0455	.0071	.095	.0985
8	.125	.0858	.0419	.0388	.0625	.0398	.0062	.0818	.0862
9	.1111	.0763	.0372	.0344	.0555	.0354	.0055	.0739	.0766
10	.10	.0687	.0335	.0310	.0500	.0318	.005	.0665	.069
12	.0833	.0572	.0279	.0258	.0416	.0265	.0042	.0551	.0575
16	.0625	.0429	.0209	.0194	.0312	.0199	.0031	.0409	.0431
20	.050	.0343	.0167	.0155	.0250	.0159	.0025	.0332	.0345

WORM WHEEL HOBS

Hobs are made larger in diameter than the worm they are used with by the amount of two clearances. The Brown & Sharpe method is to make the clearance one-tenth of the thickness of the tooth on the pitch line or .05 inch for a worm of one pitch. If the worm was 3 inches outside diameter, which would be a fair proportion for this pitch, the outside diameter of the hob would be $3 + (2 \times .05) = 3.1$ inches. The thread tool would be .31 inch wide at the point and would cut $.6366 + .1 = .7366$ deep, leaving the top of the thread the same thickness as the bottom, which is different from the worm.

The land L should be made as near the proportions given as possible.

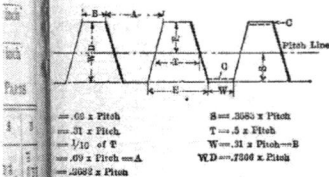

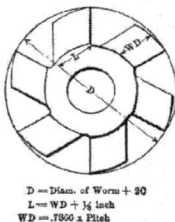

A = .69 x Pitch
B = .31 x Pitch
F = 1/10 of T
L = .69 x Pitch = A
E = .3682 x Pitch

S = .3683 x Pitch
T = .5 x Pitch
W = .31 x Pitch = B
WD = .7366 x Pitch

D = Diam. of Worm + 2C
L = WD + ¼ inch
WD = .7366 x Pitch

FIG. 18. — Section of Hob Thread   FIG. 19. — End View of Hob

The diagram Fig. 18 shows the shape and proportions of the thread of a worm hob, and Fig. 19 shows the proportions for the depth of tooth, the lead and the outside diameter. In these diagrams:

A = Width of space at top of tooth.
B = Width of thread at top.
C = Clearance or difference between the hob and worm.
D = Diameter of hob.
E = Width of tooth at bottom.
F = Hight above pitch line.
L = Width of land or tooth at bottom.
S = Depth below pitch line.
T = Width at pitch line.
W = Width of space at bottom.
WD = Whole depth of tooth.

Brown & Sharpe allow clearance at the point of the tooth only for worm wheels, but at both point and bottom when hobbing spur gears.

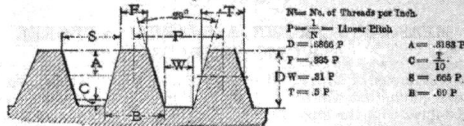

N = No. of Threads per Inch.
P = $\frac{1}{N}$ = Linear Pitch
D = .6866 P   A = .3183 P
F = .335 P   C = $\frac{P}{10}$
W = .31 P   S = .665 P
T = .5 P   B = .69 P

$$\text{Pitch} = \frac{1}{\text{No. of Threads per inch}}$$

$$\text{Depth of Thread} = \frac{.6866}{\text{No. of Threads per inch}}$$

$$\text{Width of Top of Thread} = \frac{.335}{\text{No. of Threads per inch}}$$

$$\text{Width of Space at Bottom} = \frac{.310}{\text{No. of Threads per inch}}$$

$$\text{Clearance at Bottom of Thread} = \frac{\text{Thickness at Pitch Line}}{10}$$

$$\text{Width of Space at Top of Thread} = \frac{.665}{\text{No. of Threads per inch}}$$

$$\text{Thickness at Root of Thread} = \frac{.69}{\text{No. of Threads per inch}}$$

TABLE OF BROWN & SHARPE 29° WORM THREAD PARTS

	P	D	F	W	T	A	C	S	
Number of Threads Per Inch	Pitch of Single Thread	Depth of Thread	Width of Top of Thread	Width of Space at Bottom	Thickness of Thread at Pitch Line	Thread Above Pitch Line	Clearance at Bottom of Thread	Width of Space at Top	Thickness at
1	1.0	.6866	.3350	.3100	.5000	.3183	.05	.665	.6
1¼	.8	.5492	.2680	.2480	.4000	.2546	.04	.532	.5
1½	.6666	.4577	.2233	.2066	.3333	.2122	.0333	.4433	.4
2	.5	.3433	.1675	.1550	.2500	.1592	.0250	.3325	.3
2½	.4	.2746	.1340	.1240	.2000	.1273	.0200	.2660	.2
3	.3333	.2289	.1117	.1033	.1666	.1061	.0166	.2216	.2
3½	.2857	.1962	.0957	.0886	.1429	.0909	.0143	.1901	.1
4	.250	.1716	.0838	.0775	.1250	.0796	.0125	.1637	.1
4½	.2222	.1526	.0744	.0689	.1111	.0707	.0111	.1478	.1
5	.2	.1373	.0670	.0620	.1000	.0637	.0100	.1330	.1
6	.1666	.1144	.0558	.0517	.0833	.0531	.0083	.1108	.1
7	.1428	.0981	.0479	.0443	.0714	.0455	.0071	.095	.0
8	.125	.0858	.0419	.0388	.0625	.0398	.0062	.0818	.0
9	.1111	.0763	.0372	.0344	.0555	.0354	.0055	.0739	.0
10	.10	.0687	.0335	.0310	.0500	.0318	.005	.0665	.0
12	.0833	.0572	.0279	.0258	.0416	.0265	.0042	.0551	.0
16	.0625	.0429	.0209	.0194	.0312	.0199	.0031	.0409	.0
20	.050	.0343	.0167	.0155	.0250	.0159	.0025	.0332	.0

WORM WHEEL HOBS

Hobs are made larger in diameter than the worm they are used with by the amount of two clearances. The Brown & Sharpe method is to make the clearance one-tenth of the thickness of the tooth on the pitch line or .05 inch for a worm of one pitch. If the worm was 3 inches outside diameter, which would be a fair proportion for this pitch, the outside diameter of the hob would be $3 + (2 \times .05) = 3.1$ inches. The thread tool would be .31 inch wide at the point and would cut $.6366 + .1 = .7366$ deep, leaving the top of the thread the same thickness as the bottom, which is different from the worm.

The land L should be made as near the proportions given as possible.

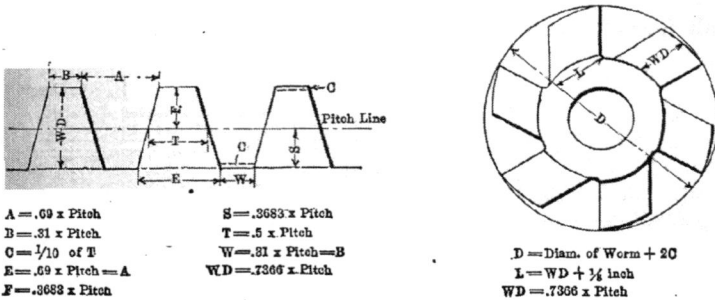

A = .69 x Pitch
B = .31 x Pitch
C = 1/10 of T
E = .69 x Pitch = A
F = .3683 x Pitch

S = .3683 x Pitch
T = .5 x Pitch
W = .81 x Pitch = B
WD = .7366 x Pitch

D = Diam. of Worm + 2C
L = WD + 1/4 inch
WD = .7366 x Pitch

FIG. 18. — Section of Hob Thread   FIG. 19. — End View of Hob

The diagram Fig. 18 shows the shape and proportions of the thread of a worm hob, and Fig. 19 shows the proportions for the depth of tooth, the lead and the outside diameter. In these diagrams:

A = Width of space at top of tooth.
B = Width of thread at top.
C = Clearance or difference between the hob and worm.
D = Diameter of hob.
E = Width of tooth at bottom.
F = Hight above pitch line.
L = Width of land or tooth at bottom.
S = Depth below pitch line.
T = Width at pitch line.
W = Width of space at bottom.
WD = Whole depth of tooth.

Brown & Sharpe allow clearance at the point of the tooth only for worm wheels, but at both point and bottom when hobbing spur gears.

PIPE AND PIPE THREADS

BRIGGS STANDARD PIPE THREADS

The particulars in the following paragraph regarding this system of pipe standards are from a paper by the late Robert Briggs, C.E., read in 1882, before the Institution of Civil Engineers of Great Britain.

The taper employed has an inclination to 1 in 32 to the axis. The thread employed has an angle of 60 degrees; it is slightly rounded off, both at the top and at the bottom, so that the hight or depth of the thread, instead of being exactly equal to the pitch $\times$ .866 is only four-fifths of the pitch, or equal to $0.8\frac{1}{n}$, if n be the number of

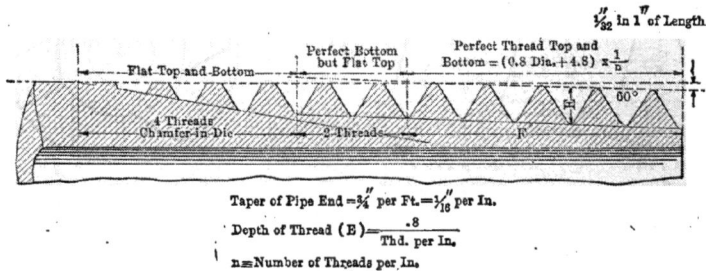

FIG. 1. — Longitudinal Section of Briggs Pipe Thread

threads per inch. For the length of tube-end throughout which the screw-thread continues perfect, the formula used is $(0.8 D + 4.8)$ $\times \frac{1}{n}$, where D is the actual external diameter of the tube throughout its parallel length, and is expressed in inches. Further back, beyond the perfect threads, come two having the same taper at the bottom, but imperfect at the top. The remaining imperfect portion of the screw-thread, furthest back from the extremity of the tube, is not essential in any way to this system of joint; and its imperfection is simply incidental to the process of cutting the thread at a single operation.

Thread Section

The threads as produced at the pipe-end in the Briggs system are represented clearly in the longitudinal section, Fig. 1.

Here the threads that are perfect at top and bottom are shown at F, the depth being indicated at E. Back of the perfect threads

ire represented the two threads with perfect bottom and flat tops
ind behind these are the imperfect threads produced by the chamfer
)r bell mouth of the threading die. A table giving the general
limensions of wrought iron tubes in the Briggs system will be found
)n page 40, while complete data pertaining to the thread depths,
engths of perfect and imperfect portions, allowances for making the
oint in screwing the pipe into the fitting, gaging allowances, etc.,
ire contained in the tables on pages 47 and 48.

In cutting pipe threads with a lathe tool as in threading taper
work in general, the tool should be set at right angles to the axis
)f the piece and not square with the conical surface.

STANDARD DIMENSIONS OF WROUGHT-IRON WELDED TUBES
BRIGGS STANDARD

Diameter of Tubes			Thickness of Metal Inches	Screwed Ends	
Nominal Inside Inches	Actual Inside Inches	Actual Outside Inches		Number of Threads per Inch	Length of Perfect Thread Inches
$\frac{1}{8}$	0.270	0.405	0.068	27	0.19
$\frac{1}{4}$	0.364	0.540	0.088	18	0.29
$\frac{3}{8}$	0.494	0.675	0.091	18	0.30
$\frac{1}{2}$	0.623	0.840	0.109	14	0.39
$\frac{3}{4}$	0.824	1.050	0.113	14	0.40
1	1.048	1.315	0.134	$11\frac{1}{2}$	0.51
$1\frac{1}{4}$	1.380	1.660	0.140	$11\frac{1}{2}$	0.54
$1\frac{1}{2}$	1.610	1.900	0.145	$11\frac{1}{2}$	0.55
2	2.067	2.375	0.154	$11\frac{1}{2}$	0.58
$2\frac{1}{2}$	2.468	2.875	0.204	8	0.89
3	3.067	3.500	0.217	8	0.95
$3\frac{1}{2}$	3.548	4.000	0.226	8	1.00
4	4.026	4.500	0.237	8	1.05
$4\frac{1}{2}$	4.508	5.000	0.246	8	1.10
5	5.045	5.563	0.259	8	1.16
6	6.065	6.625	0.280	8	1.26
7	7.023	7.625	0.301	8	1.36
8	7.982	8.625	0.322	8	1.46
*9	9.000	9.688	0.344	8	1.57
10	10.019	10.750	0.366	8	1.68

* By the action of the manufacturers of wrought-iron pipe and
)oiler tubes, at a meeting held in New York, May 9, 1889, a change
n size of actual outside diameter of 9-inch pipe was adopted, mak-
ng the latter 9.625 instead of 9.688 inches, as given in the table of
3riggs standard pipe diameters.

The table below shows the British pipe and pipe threads, sizes recommended by the Engineering Standards Committee.

BRITISH STANDARD PIPE THREADS

Nominal Diameter of Pipe	Approximate Outside Diameter of Pipe	Gage Diameter, Top of Thread	Double Depth of Thread	Bottom Diameter of Thread at Gage Point	Number of Thread per Inch	Distance of Gage Diameter from End of Pipe			Outside Diameter of Threads at End of Pipe	Inside Diameter of Thread at End of Pipe
						Standard	Maximum	Minimum		
1/8	13/32	0.383	0.046	0.337	28	5/32	0.18	0.13	0.373	0.327
1/4	17/32	0.518	0.067	0.451	19	3/16	0.22	0.16	0.506	0.439
3/8	11/16	0.656	0.067	0.589	19	1/4	0.29	0.21	0.640	0.573
1/2	27/32	0.825	0.091	0.734	14	1/4	0.29	0.21	0.809	0.718
5/8	15/16	0.902	0.091	0.811	14	1/4	0.29	0.21	0.886	0.795
3/4	1 1/16	1.041	0.091	0.950	14	3/8	0.44	0.31	1.018	0.927
7/8	1 7/32	1.189	0.091	1.098	14	3/8	0.44	0.31	1.166	1.075
1	1 11/32	1.309	0.116	1.193	11	3/8	0.44	0.31	1.286	1.170
1 1/4	1 11/16	1.650	0.116	1.534	11	1/2	0.58	0.42	1.619	1.503
1 1/2	1 29/32	1.882	0.116	1.766	11	1/2	0.58	0.42	1.851	1.735
1 3/4	2 5/32	2.116	0.116	2.000	11	5/8	0.73	0.52	2.077	1.961
2	2 3/8	2.347	0.116	2.231	11	5/8	0.73	0.52	2.308	2.192
2 1/4	2 5/8	2.587	0.116	2.471	11	11/16	0.80	0.57	2.544	2.801
2 1/2	3	2.960	0.116	2.844	11	11/16	0.80	0.57	2.917	3.043
2 3/4	3 1/4	3.210	0.116	3.094	11	13/16	0.95	0.68	3.159	3.293
3	3 1/2	3.460	0.116	3.344	11	13/16	0.95	0.68	3.409	3.293
3 1/4	3 3/4	3.700	0.116	3.584	11	7/8	1.02	0.73	3.645	3.529
3 1/2	4	3.950	0.116	3.834	11	7/8	1.02	0.73	3.895	3.779
3 3/4	4 1/4	4.200	0.116	4.084	11	7/8	1.02	0.73	4.145	4.029
4	4 1/2	4.450	0.116	4.334	11	1	1.17	0.83	4.387	4.271
4 1/2	5	4.950	0.116	4.834	11	1	1.17	0.83	4.887	4.771
5	5 1/2	5.450	0.116	5.334	11	1 1/8	1.31	0.94	5.380	5.264
5 1/2	6	5.950	0.116	5.834	11	1 1/4	1.46	1.04	5.872	5.756
6	6 1/2	6.450	0.116	6.334	11	1 3/8	1.60	1.15	6.364	6.248
7	7 1/2	7.450	0.128	7.322	10	1 3/8	1.60	1.15	7.364	7.236
8	8 1/2	8.450	0.128	8.322	10	1 1/2	1.75	1.25	8.356	8.228
9	9 1/2	9.450	0.128	9.322	10	1 1/2	1.75	1.25	9.356	9.228
10	10 1/2	10.450	0.128	10.322	10	1 5/8	1.90	1.35	10.348	10.220
11	11 1/2	11.450	0.160	11.290	8	1 5/8	1.90	1.35	11.348	11.188
12	12 1/2	12.450	0.160	12.290	8	1 5/8	1.90	1.35	12.348	12.188
13	13 3/4	13.680	0.160	13.520	8	1 5/8	1.90	1.35	13.578	13.418
14	14 3/4	14.680	0.160	14.520	8	1 3/4	2.04	1.46	14.571	14.411
15	15 3/4	15.680	0.160	15.520	8	1 3/4	2.04	1.46	15.571	15.411
16	16 3/4	16.680	0.160	16.520	8	1 7/8	2.19	1.56	16.563	16.403
17	17 3/4	17.680	0.160	17.520	8	2	2.33	1.67	17.555	17.395
18	18 3/4	18.680	0.160	18.520	8	2	2.33	1.67	18.555	18.395

Taper of pipe ends = 1/16″ to 1″. Whitworth standard threads.

Tap Drills for Pipe Taps

The sizes of Twist Drills to be used in boring holes, to be reamed with Pipe Reamers, and Threaded with Pipe Taps, are as follows:

Size Pipe Tap	BRIGGS Thread	Drill	WHITWORTH Thread	Drill	Size Pipe Tap	BRIGGS Thread	Drill	WHITWORTH Thread	Drill
1/8	27	21/64	28	5/16	1 3/4			11	1 15/16
1/4	18	27/64	19	27/64	2	11 1/2	2 3/16	11	2 5/32
3/8	18	9/16	19	9/16	2 1/4			11	2 3/8
1/2	14	11/16	14	11/16	2 1/2	8	2 9/16	11	2 5/8
5/8			14	33/32	2 3/4			11	3
3/4	14	29/32	14	29/32	3	8	3 1/8	11	3 1/4
7/8			14	1 1/16	3 1/4			11	3 1/2
1	11 1/2	1 1/8	11	1 1/8	3 1/2	8	3 11/16	11	3 3/4
1 1/4	11 1/2	1 15/32	11	1 15/32	3 3/4			11	4
1 1/2	11 1/2	1 25/32	11	1 23/32	4	8	4 3/16	11	4 1/4

Metric Pipe Threads

Nominal Inside Pipe Diameter in Inches	Inside Pipe Diameter in Millimeters	External Thread Diameter in Millimeters	Internal Thread Diameter in Millimeters	Number of Threads per Inch
1/8		10	8.3	19
1/4	6.35	13	11.3	19
3/8	9.52	16.5	14.8	19
1/2	12.70	20.5	18.2	14
5/8	15.87	23	20.7	14
3/4	19.05	26.5	24.2	14
1	25.40	33	30	11
1 1/4	31.75	42	39	11
1 1/2	38.10	48	45	11
1 3/4	44.45	52	49	11
2	50.30	59.7	56.7	11
2 1/2	63.50	76	73	11
3	76.20	89	86	11
3 1/2	88.90	101.5	98.5	11
4	101.60	114	111	11

THE table below shows the British pipe and pipe threads, siz… recommended by the Engineering Standards Committee.

BRITISH STANDARD PIPE THREADS

Nominal Diameter of Pipe	Approximate Outside Diameter of Pipe	Gage Diameter, Top of Thread	Double Depth of Thread	Bottom Diameter of Thread at Gage Point	Number of Thread per Inch	Distance of Gage Diameter from End of Pipe			Outside Diameter of Threads at End of Pipe	Inside Diameter of Thread at …
						Standard	Maximum	Minimum		
1/8	13/32	0.383	0.046	0.337	28	5/32	0.18	0.13	0.373	0.3…
1/4	17/32	0.518	0.067	0.451	19	3/16	0.22	0.16	0.506	0.4…
3/8	21/32	0.656	0.067	0.589	19	1/4	0.29	0.21	0.640	0.…
1/2	27/32	0.825	0.091	0.734	14	1/4	0.29	0.21	0.809	0.…
5/8	29/32	0.902	0.091	0.811	14	1/4	0.29	0.21	0.886	0.…
3/4	1 1/16	1.041	0.091	0.950	14	3/8	0.44	0.31	1.018	0.…
7/8	1 7/32	1.189	0.091	1.098	14	3/8	0.44	0.31	1.166	1.…
1	1 11/32	1.309	0.116	1.193	11	3/8	0.44	0.31	1.286	1.…
1 1/4	1 11/16	1.650	0.116	1.534	11	1/2	0.58	0.42	1.619	1.…
1 1/2	1 29/32	1.882	0.116	1.766	11	1/2	0.58	0.42	1.851	1.…
1 3/4	2 5/32	2.116	0.116	2.000	11	5/8	0.73	0.52	2.077	1.…
2	2 3/8	2.347	0.116	2.231	11	5/8	0.73	0.52	2.308	2.…
2 1/4	2 5/8	2.587	0.116	2.471	11	11/16	0.80	0.57	2.544	2.…
2 1/2	3	2.960	0.116	2.844	11	11/16	0.80	0.57	2.917	3.…
2 3/4	3 1/4	3.210	0.116	3.094	11	13/16	0.95	0.68	3.159	3.…
3	3 1/2	3.460	0.116	3.344	11	13/16	0.95	0.68	3.409	3…
3 1/4	3 3/4	3.700	0.116	3.584	11	7/8	1.02	0.73	3.645	3…
3 1/2	4	3.950	0.116	3.834	11	7/8	1.02	0.73	3.895	3…
3 3/4	4 1/4	4.200	0.116	4.084	11	7/8	1.02	0.73	4.145	4…
4	4 1/2	4.450	0.116	4.334	11	1	1.17	0.83	4.387	4…
4 1/2	5	4.950	0.116	4.834	11	1	1.17	0.83	4.887	4…
5	5 1/2	5.450	0.116	5.334	11	1 1/8	1.31	0.94	5.380	5…
5 1/2	6	5.950	0.116	5.834	11	1 1/4	1.46	1.04	5.872	5…
6	6 1/2	6.450	0.116	6.334	11	1 3/8	1.60	1.15	6.364	6…
7	7 1/2	7.450	0.128	7.322	10	1 3/8	1.60	1.15	7.364	7…
8	8 1/2	8.450	0.128	8.322	10	1 1/2	1.75	1.25	8.356	8…
9	9 1/2	9.450	0.128	9.322	10	1 1/2	1.75	1.25	9.356	9…
10	10 1/2	10.450	0.128	10.322	10	1 5/8	1.90	1.35	10.348	10…
11	11 1/2	11.450	0.160	11.290	8	1 5/8	1.90	1.35	11.348	11…
12	12 1/2	12.450	0.160	12.290	8	1 5/8	1.90	1.35	12.348	12…
13	13 3/4	13.680	0.160	13.520	8	1 5/8	1.90	1.35	13.578	13…
14	14 3/4	14.680	0.160	14.520	8	1 3/4	2.04	1.46	14.571	14…
15	15 3/4	15.680	0.160	15.520	8	1 3/4	2.04	1.46	15.571	15…
16	16 3/4	16.680	0.160	16.520	8	1 7/8	2.19	1.56	16.563	16…
17	17 3/4	17.680	0.160	17.520	8	2	2.33	1.67	17.555	17…
18	18 3/4	18.680	0.160	18.520	8	2	2.33	1.67	18.555	18…

Taper of pipe ends = 1/16″ to 1″. Whitworth standard threads.

Tap Drills for Pipe Taps

The sizes of Twist Drills to be used in boring holes, to be reamed with Pipe Reamers, and Threaded with Pipe Taps, are as follows:

Size Pipe Tap	BRIGGS Thread	BRIGGS Drill	WHITWORTH Thread	WHITWORTH Drill	Size Pipe Tap	BRIGGS Thread	BRIGGS Drill	WHITWORTH Thread	WHITWORTH Drill
$\frac{1}{8}$	27	$\frac{21}{64}$	28	$\frac{5}{16}$	$1\frac{3}{4}$			11	$1\frac{15}{16}$
$\frac{1}{4}$	18	$\frac{27}{64}$	19	$\frac{27}{64}$	2	$11\frac{1}{2}$	$2\frac{3}{16}$	11	$2\frac{5}{32}$
$\frac{3}{8}$	18	$\frac{9}{16}$	19	$\frac{9}{16}$	$2\frac{1}{4}$			11	$2\frac{13}{32}$
$\frac{1}{2}$	14	$1\frac{1}{16}$	14	$1\frac{1}{16}$	$2\frac{1}{2}$	8	$2\frac{9}{16}$	11	$2\frac{25}{32}$
$\frac{5}{8}$			14	$\frac{25}{32}$	$2\frac{3}{4}$			11	3
$\frac{3}{4}$	14	$\frac{29}{32}$	14	$\frac{29}{32}$	3	8	$3\frac{3}{16}$	11	$3\frac{1}{4}$
$\frac{7}{8}$			14	$1\frac{1}{16}$	$3\frac{1}{4}$			11	$3\frac{1}{2}$
1	$11\frac{1}{2}$	$1\frac{1}{8}$	11	$1\frac{1}{8}$	$3\frac{1}{2}$	8	$3\frac{11}{16}$	11	$3\frac{3}{4}$
$1\frac{1}{4}$	$11\frac{1}{2}$	$1\frac{15}{32}$	11	$1\frac{15}{32}$	$3\frac{3}{4}$			11	4
$1\frac{1}{2}$	$11\frac{1}{2}$	$1\frac{23}{32}$	11	$1\frac{23}{32}$	4	8	$4\frac{3}{16}$	11	$4\frac{1}{4}$

Metric Pipe Threads

Nominal Inside Pipe Diameter in Inches	Inside Pipe Diameter in Millimeters	External Thread Diameter in Millimeters	Internal Thread Diameter in Millimeters	Number of Threads per Inch
$\frac{1}{8}$		10	8.3	19
$\frac{1}{4}$	6.35	13	11.3	19
$\frac{3}{8}$	9.52	16.5	14.8	19
$\frac{1}{2}$	12.70	20.5	18.2	14
$\frac{5}{8}$	15.87	23	20.7	14
$\frac{3}{4}$	19.05	26.5	24.2	14
1	25.40	33	30	11
$1\frac{1}{4}$	31.75	42	39	11
$1\frac{1}{2}$	38.10	48	45	11
$1\frac{3}{4}$	44.45	52	49	11
2	50.30	59.7	56.7	11
$2\frac{1}{2}$	63.50	76	73	11
3	76.20	89	86	11
$3\frac{1}{2}$	88.90	101.5	98.5	11
4	101.60	114	111	11

THE PIPE JOINT IN THE BRIGGS SYSTEM

THE illustrations below and the tables on pages 43 and 44, represent the relation of the reamer, tap, die and testing gages in the preparation of the Briggs pipe end and fitting preliminary to making up the joint.

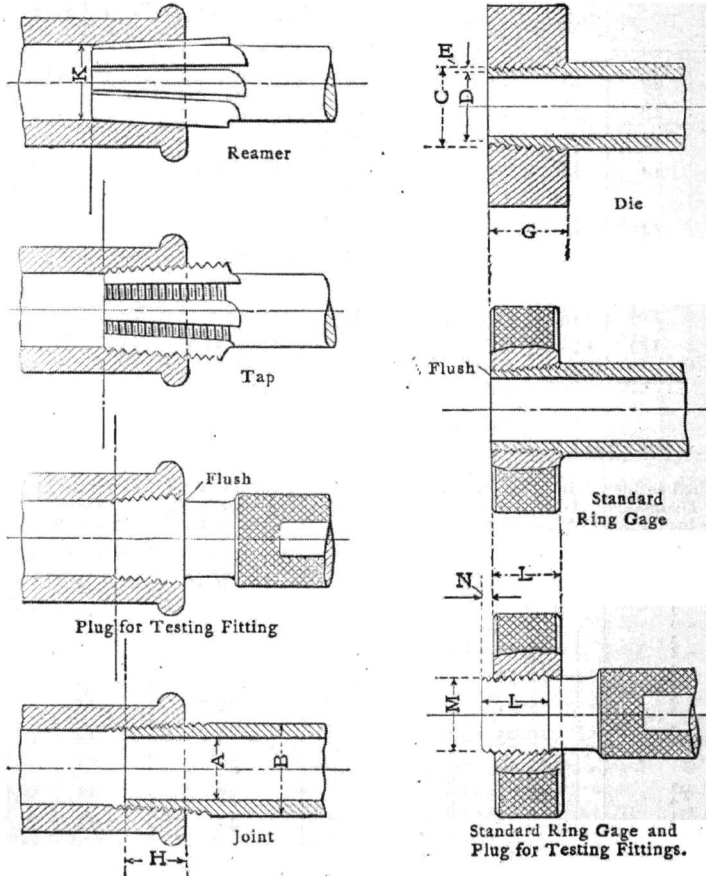

FIG. 2. — Reamer, Tap, Die and Gages for Briggs Pipe Standard

The illustrations to the left in Fig. 2 show the relative distances that the pipe reamer, tap, testing plug and pipe end are run into the fitting in making the joint; while at the right are shown the die and ring gage on the pipe end, and the relative diameters of the standard ring gage and the testing plug for the fittings.

In pipe fitting the end of the pipe should always be cut to fit the Briggs standard pipe gage. The fitting should be tapped small in order to insure a tight joint. Theoretically the joint should be tight when the pipe end has been screwed into the fitting a distance represented at H in the diagrams, Fig. 2 and following tables. However, to allow for errors the thread on the pipe is actually cut two threads beyond H. Similarly the fitting should be tapped two threads deeper than distance H.

The following table used in conjunction with the illustrations in Fig. 2, contains information as to length and number of perfect and imperfect threads; distance and number of turns the pipe screws into fitting by hand and with wrench, or the total length and number of threads of joint; ring and plug gage data for testing tools; besides general pipe dimensions, drill and reamer sizes, etc.

BRIGGS PIPE THREAD TABLE (See page 46)

Dia. of Pipe		Actual Outside	No. of Threads per Inch	Dia. at End of Pipe	Dia. at Bottom of Th'd	Depth of Thread	Length of Perfect Threads	No. of Perfect Threads
Nominal Inside	Actual Inside							
	A	B		C	D	E	H	
$\frac{1}{8}''$	.270″	.405″	27	.393″	.334″	.029″	.19″	5.13
$\frac{1}{4}''$	.364″	.540″	18	.522″	.433″	.044″	.29″	5.22
$\frac{3}{8}''$	.494″	.675″	18	.656″	.568″	.044″	.30″	5.4
$\frac{1}{2}''$	.623″	.840″	14	.815″	.701″	.057″	.39″	5.46
$\frac{3}{4}''$	.824″	1.050″	14	1.025″	.911″	.057″	.40″	5.6
1 ″	1.048″	1.315″	11½	1.283″	1.144″	.069″	.51″	5.87
1¼″	1.380″	1.660″	11½	1.626″	1.488″	.069″	.54″	6.21
1½″	1.610″	1.900″	11½	1.866″	1.728″	.069″	.55″	6.33
2 ″	2.067″	2.375″	11½	2.339″	2.201″	.069″	.58″	6.67
2½″	2.468″	2.875″	8	2.819″	2.619″	.100″	.89″	7.12
3 ″	3.067″	3.500″	8	3.441″	3.241″	.100″	.95″	7.6
3½″	3.548″	4.000″	8	3.938″	3.738″	.100″	1.00″	8.0
4 ″	4.026″	4.500″	8	4.434″	4.234″	.100″	1.05″	8.4
4½″	4.508″	5. ″	8	4.931″	4.731″	.100″	1.10″	8.8
5 ″	5.045″	5.563″	8	5.490″	5.290″	.100″	1.16″	9.28
6 ″	6.065″	6.625″	8	6.546″	6.346″	.100″	1.26″	10.08
7 ″	7.023″	7.625″	8	7.540″	7.340″	.100″	1.36″	10.88
8 ″	7.982″	8.625″	8	8.534″	8.334″	.100″	1.46″	11.68
9 ″	9.000″	9.625″	8	9.527″	9.327″	.100″	1.57″	12.56
10 ″	10.019″	10.750″	8	10.645″	10.445″	.100″	1.68″	13.44

(Table Continued on Page 48)

BRIGGS PIPE THREAD TABLE — Continued. (See page 46)

Nominal Dia. of Pipe	Total Length of Th'd and Thickness of Die	No. of Turns Pipe Screws into Fitting by Hand	Distance Pipe Screws into Fitting by Hand	No. of Turns "Take Up" with Wrench	Amount of "Take Up" with Wrench	No. of Th'ds on Plug and Ring Gage	Length of Thread on Plug and Ring Gage	Dia. of End of Plug for Testing Fittings	No. of Th'ds Inspection Plug Projects through Ring	Distance Inspection Plug Projects through Ring	Dia. of Drill to be used with Pipe Reamer	Dia. of End of Pipe Reamer Before Chamfering
	G						L	M		N		K
$\frac{1}{8}$"	.4120"	4.1256	.1528"	3	.1110"	7.1256	.2638"	.3861"	3	.1110"	$\frac{21}{64}$"	.320"
$\frac{1}{4}$"	.6240"	3.9834	.2213"	$3\frac{1}{4}$	.1805"	7.2324	.4018"	.5107"	$3\frac{1}{4}$	.1805"	$\frac{27}{64}$"	.414"
$\frac{3}{8}$"	.6300"	4.0914	.2273"	$3\frac{1}{4}$	.1805"	7.3404	.4078"	.6447"	$3\frac{1}{4}$	.1805"	$\frac{9}{16}$"	.539"
$\frac{1}{2}$"	.8194"	3.9718	.2837"	$3\frac{1}{2}$	.250"	7.4718	.5337"	.7994"	$3\frac{1}{2}$	.250"	$\frac{11}{16}$"	.648"
$\frac{3}{4}$"	.8315"	4.1398	.2957"	$3\frac{1}{2}$	.250"	7.6398	.5457"	1.0094"	$3\frac{1}{2}$	.250"	$\frac{29}{32}$"	.867"
1"	1.0305"	4.3562	.3788"	$3\frac{1}{2}$	.304"	7.8522	.6828"	1.2640"	$3\frac{1}{2}$	.304"	$1\frac{1}{8}$"	1.101"
$1\frac{1}{4}$"	1.0545"	4.6322	.4028"	$3\frac{1}{2}$	.304"	8.1282	.7068"	1.607"	$3\frac{1}{2}$	.304"	$1\frac{15}{32}$"	1.449"
$1\frac{1}{2}$"	1.0713"	4.8243	.4195"	$3\frac{1}{2}$	.304"	8.3203	.7235"	1.847"	$3\frac{1}{2}$	.304"	$1\frac{23}{32}$"	1.695"
2"	1.1043"	4.6978	.4085"	4	.348"	8.6998	.7565"	2.3173"	4	.348"	$2\frac{3}{16}$"	2.164"
$2\frac{1}{2}$"	1.6375"	5.1000	.6375"	4	.500"	9.1	1.1375"	2.787"	4	.500"	$2\frac{9}{16}$"	2.554"
3"	1.7000"	5.1000	.6375"	$4\frac{1}{2}$	.5625"	9.6	1.2000"	3.4058"	$4\frac{1}{2}$	.5625"	$3\frac{3}{16}$"	3.180"
$3\frac{1}{2}$"	1.7500"	5.5000	.6875"	$4\frac{1}{2}$	.5625"	10.0	1.2500"	3.9028"	$4\frac{1}{2}$	.5625"	$3\frac{11}{16}$"	3.680"
4"	1.8000"	5.9000	.7375"	$4\frac{1}{2}$	.5625"	10.4	1.3000"	4.3988"	$4\frac{1}{2}$	.5625"	$4\frac{3}{16}$"	4.180"
$4\frac{1}{2}$"	1.8500"	6.3000	.7875"	$4\frac{1}{2}$	.5625"	10.8	1.3500"	4.8958"	$4\frac{1}{2}$	.5625"		
5"	1.9063"	6.2504	.7813"	5	.625"	11.2504	1.4063"	5.4509"	5	.625"		
6"	2.0125"	7.1000	.8875"	5	.625"	12.1	1.5125"	6.5069"	5	.625"		
7"	2.1125"	8.0000	1.0000"	4.9	.6125"	12.9	1.6125"	7.5017"	4.9	.6125"		
8"	2.2125"	8.5040	1.0630"	5.196	.6495"	13.7	1.7125"	8.4934"	5.196	.6495"		
9"	2.3125"	9.0400	1.1300"	5.46	.6825"	14.5	1.8125"	9.4843"	5.46	.6825"		
10"	2.4250"	9.6800	1.2100"	5.72	.7150"	15.4	1.9250"	10.6003"	5.72	.7150"		

GAGE SETS FOR BRIGGS PIPE AND FITTINGS

THE gages manufactured by the Pratt & Whitney Company for makers and users of pipe and fittings include three distinct sets for each size of pipe, and these are illustrated in Fig. 3. Set No. 1 consists of a ring and plug conforming in all dimensions to the Briggs standard, and is known as the standard reference set. The plug screws into the ring with faces flush — as indicated by the position of the two gages. The flat milled on the plug shows the depth to which the latter should enter the fitting to allow for screwing up with tongs to make a steam-tight joint; the ring, of course, screws on to the pipe flush with the end.

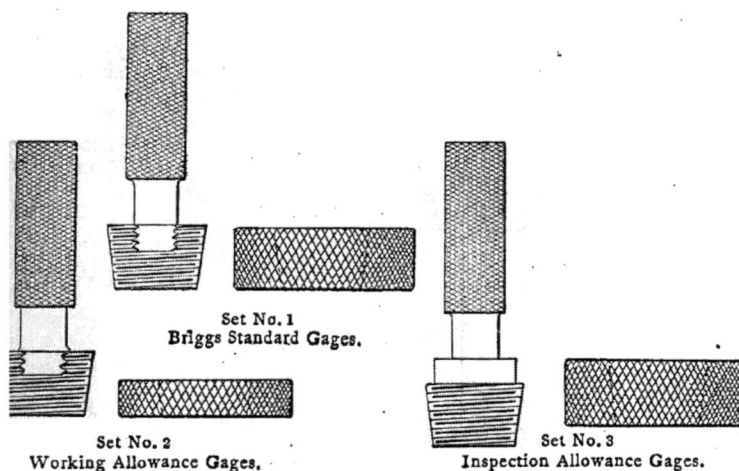

Set No. 1
Briggs Standard Gages.

Set No. 2
Working Allowance Gages.

Set No. 3
Inspection Allowance Gages.

FIG. 3. — Briggs Pipe Thread Gages

Set No. 2 — the working allowance set — consists of the plug already described and a ring whose thickness is equal to the standard ring less the allowance for screwing up the joint. As the plug and ring threads are of the same diameter at the small end, the bottom surfaces come flush when the two members are screwed together. It will be noted that, as the plug enters the fitting only to the bottom of the flat at the side, and the ring screws on to the pipe only far enough to bring the outer face flush with the pipe end, there are a few threads on, or in, the work beyond the reach of the gages; hence with this type of gage a reasonable amount of wear may be permitted at the end of the tap or the mouth of the die without causing the rejection of the work.

The plug and ring in set No. 3 are inspection allowance gages, the ring being the same in all particulars as the standard gage in set No. 1, while the plug is longer than Nos. 1 and 2 by an amount equal to the allowance for screwing up for a tight joint, this extra length being represented by the cylindrical portion at the rear of the thread cone. When the gages are screwed together the back of the cylindrical section comes flush with the ring face and the threaded end of the plug projects through the ring, as indicated, a distance equal to the length of the cylinder, or the screwing-up allowance. This plug will enter a perfect fitting until the back of the threaded section is flush with the end of the fitting, thus testing the full depth of the tapped thread in the same way that the standard ring gage covers the thread on the pipe end, and at the same time showing that the fitting is tapped to right diameter to allow the joint to screw up properly.

NATIONAL STANDARD HOSE COUPLING

This standard for fire hose couplings was adopted by the National Fire Protection Association May 26, 1905 and has since been approved and adopted by various other organizations.

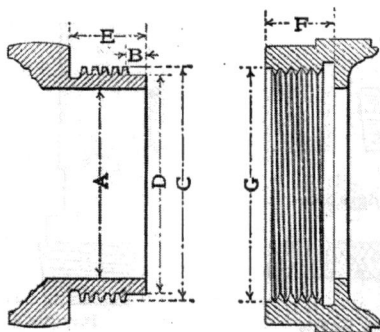

FIG. 4.—National Standard Hose Coupling

DIMENSIONS OF NATIONAL STANDARD HOSE COUPLINGS

A	Inside Diameter of Hose Couplings...	$2\frac{1}{2}$	3	$3\frac{1}{2}$	$4\frac{1}{2}$
B	Length of Blank End on Male Part...	$\frac{1}{4}$	$\frac{1}{4}$	$\frac{1}{4}$	$\frac{1}{4}$
C	Outside Diameter of Thread, Finished	$3\frac{1}{16}$	$3\frac{5}{8}$	$4\frac{1}{4}$	$5\frac{3}{4}$
D	Diameter at Root of Thread.........	2.8715	3.3763	4.0013	5.3970
E	Total Length of Male End	1	$1\frac{1}{8}$	$1\frac{1}{8}$	$1\frac{7}{8}$
	Number of Threads per inch	$7\frac{1}{2}$	6	6	4
F	Length of Female Thread..........	$\frac{7}{8}$	1	1	$1\frac{1}{4}$
G	Diameter of Top of Female Thread ..	3.0925	3.6550	4.28	5.80

NOTE:—The above to be of the 60-deg. V-thread pattern with one-hundredth inch cut off the top of thread and one-hundredth inch left in the bottom of the $2\frac{1}{2}$-inch, 3-inch, and $3\frac{1}{2}$-inch couplings, and two hundredths inch in like manner for the $4\frac{1}{2}$-inch couplings, and with one-quarter inch blank end on male part of coupling in each case; female ends to be cut $\frac{1}{8}$-inch shorter for endwise clearance. They should also be bored out .03 inch larger in the $2\frac{1}{2}$-inch, 3 and $3\frac{1}{2}$-inch sizes, and .05 inch larger on the $4\frac{1}{2}$-inch size in order to make up easily and without jamming or sticking.

TWIST DRILLS

THE twist-drill is perhaps one of the most efficient tools in use as, although one half is cut away in the flutes, it has a very large cutting surface in proportion to its cross-sectional area. This is made possible by the fact that the work helps to support the drill and the feed pressure on the drill tends to force the point into a cone-shaped hole which centers it.

In addition to the radial relief or backing-off behind the cutting edge, twist-drills have longitudinal clearance by decreasing the diameter from the point toward the shank, varying from .00025 to .0015 per inch of length. This prevents binding and is essential in accurate drilling.

To increase the strength the web is increased gradually in thickness from the point toward the shank by drawing the cutters apart. This decreases chip room and to avoid this defect the spiral is increased in pitch and the flute widened to make up the chip room.

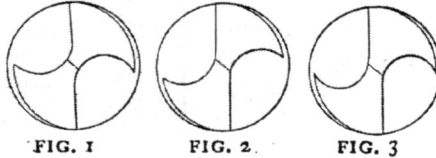

FIG. 1   FIG. 2   FIG. 3

Grooves of Twist Drills

The shape of the groove affects the power and the shape of the chip and experiments by the Cleveland Twist-Drill Company are interesting. The groove in Fig. 1 does not give a good cutting edge, especially near the center, as it does not allow a full curl to the chip. Fig. 2 is a very free cutting-groove, the chips curl up to the full size of the groove and this reduces the power required to bend the chips. Fig. 3 is an even better form as it rolls a chip with each turn conical so that one lays inside the other and makes a much shorter chip from the same depth of hole.

The angle of spirals varies from 18 to 35 degrees according to the ideas of the maker. In theory the finer the pitch or the greater the angle, the easier it should be to cut and curl the chip. But this gives a weak cutting edge and reduces the ability to carry off the heat, and it does not clear itself of chips so well. After a long series of tests the same firm adopted $27\frac{1}{2}$ degrees for the spiral. This angle makes the spiral groove of all drills start at the point with a pitch equal to six diameters of the blank, the increase in twist being a constant function of the angular movement of rotation of the drill blank. This angle is based on holes from one to three diameters deep. For deeper holes a smaller angle might be advisable and greater angle for holes of less depth. There is practically no difference in torsional stress with the angle between 25 and 30 degrees.

51

SHARPENING DRILLS

Drills should be sharpened so as to cut the right size and with as little power as possible. To cut the right size both lips must be the same length and the same angle. A gage as shown in Fig. 4 will help both to get the angle and to grind them central. This gives the usual lip edge of 59 degrees. Fig. 5 shows how you can see if both lips are ground alike, but does not give the angle. Fig. 6 is a suggestion by Professor Sweet of relieving the drill back of the cutting edge, making it similar to a flat drill in this respect.

For drilling brass or for any thin stock where the drill goes clear through, it is best to grind the cutting edge parallel with the axis of

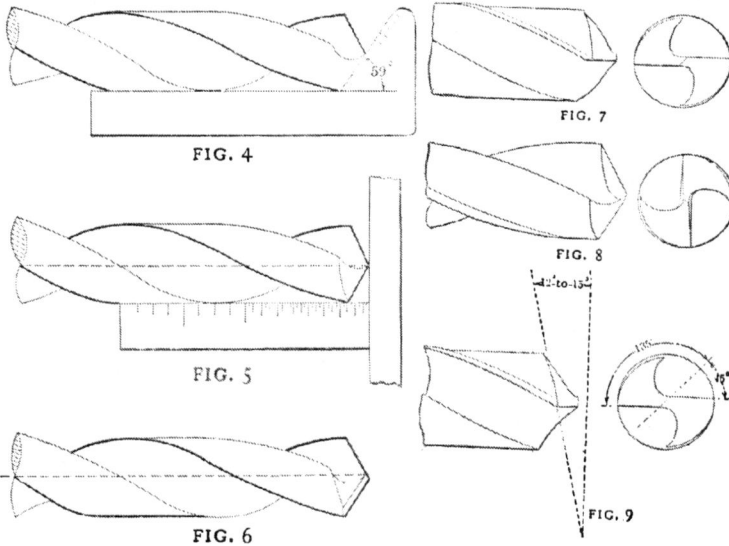

FIG. 4

FIG. 7

FIG. 5

FIG. 8

FIG. 6

FIG. 9

Grinding Twist Drills

the drill. This does away with the tendency to draw into the work. Fig. 7 shows how this is done.

It is sometimes necessary to thin the point of the drill to get best results. This requires care in grinding but can be done as shown in Fig. 8.

The best all-around clearance angle is 12 degrees, though for softer metals 15 degrees can be used. The 12 degrees is the angle at the cutting edge, but this should increase back of the cutting edge so that the line across the web should be 45 degrees, with the cutting edges. This is important, as it not only saves power but prevents splitting in hard service. The point of the drill should look like Fig. 7 or Fig. 8. Fig. 9 shows the clearance angle and the right angles for the drill point.

SPEED OF DRILLS

Learn to run drills at their proper speed to secure the most work with fewest grindings and breakages. The best practise is to use a speed that will give 30 feet a minute cutting speed for steel, 35 feet or cast iron and 60 feet for brass. This means that the cutting edge must run fast enough to make these speeds. For drilling steel with $\frac{1}{16}$-inch drill this means 1834 revolutions a minute, while for brass it would be 3668 revolutions. The table gives the speeds without any figuring for all drills up to 3 inches. These speeds require plenty of lubricant. This is for carbon steel drills.

These speeds can be exceeded in many cases even with carbon drills, and can be doubled with high speed drills, in fact from 75 to 150 feet is not uncommon with 200 feet a possibility under good conditions. The feeds in the table below can also be doubled in many cases.

TABLE OF DRILL FEEDS

Diam. of Drill	Inches of Feed per Minute at Cutting Speed of							
	30 Feet–Steel		35 Feet–Iron			60 Feet–Brass		
	Rev. per Minute	Feed .004-.007		Rev. per Minute	.004-.007		Rev. per Minute	.004-.007 per Revolution	
$\frac{1}{16}$	1834	7.33	12.83	2140	8.56	14.97	3668	14.66	25.76
$\frac{1}{8}$	917	3.66	6.41	1070	4.28	7.49	1834	7.33	12.83
$\frac{3}{16}$	611	2.44	4.27	713	2.85	4.99	1222	4.88	8.58
$\frac{1}{4}$	458	1.83	3.20	535	2.14	3.74	917	3.66	6.44
		Feed .007	.015		.007	.015		.007	.015
$\frac{5}{16}$	367	2.57	5.5	428	3	6.42	733	5.14	11
$\frac{3}{8}$	306	2.14	4.6	357	2.5	5.35	611	4.28	9.2
$\frac{7}{16}$	262	1.83	3.9	306	2.14	4.58	524	3.66	7.8
$\frac{1}{2}$	229	1.60	3.43	268	1.87	4.	459	3.20	6.86
$\frac{5}{8}$	184	1.28	2.75	214	1.50	3.21	367	2.57	5.5
$\frac{3}{4}$	153	1.07	2.3	178	1.25	2.67	306	2.14	4.6
$\frac{7}{8}$	131	.91	1.95	153	1.07	2.29	262	1.88	3.93
1	115	.80	1.71	134	.93	2	229	1.60	3.43
$1\frac{1}{8}$	102	.71	1.53	119	.83	1.79	204	1.43	3.06
$1\frac{1}{4}$	91.8	.64	1.37	107	.75	1.61	183	1.28	2.75
$1\frac{3}{8}$	83.3	.58	1.25	97.2	.68	1.45	167	1.17	2.51
$1\frac{1}{2}$	76.3	.53	1.15	89.2	.62	1.38	153	1.07	2.3
$1\frac{5}{8}$	70.5	.49	1.05	82.2	.57	1.23	141	.99	2.11
$1\frac{3}{4}$	65.5	.45	.97	76.4	.53	1.15	131	.94	1.96
$1\frac{7}{8}$	61.1	.42	.92	71.3	.50	1.07	122	.85	1.81
2	57.3	.40	.85	66.9	.46	1.	115	.80	1.73
$2\frac{1}{4}$	51	.36	.71	59.4	.41	.89	102	.71	1.53
$2\frac{1}{2}$	45.8	.32	.68	53.5	.37	.80	91.7	.64	1.37
$2\frac{3}{4}$	41.7	.29	.62	48.6	.34	.73	83.4	.58	1.21
3	38.2	.27	.57	44.6	.31	.67	76.4	.53	1.15

Feed of Drills

The feed of drills is usually given in parts of an inch per revolution, 0.004 to 0.007 inch for drills of ¼ inch and smaller and 0.007 to 0.015 inch for larger drills being recommended. This has been worked out into the table for the standard speeds to show inches of feed per minute for the three speeds given, which is more convenient. This is not an iron-clad rule but should be used with judgment. For high-speed steel these figures can be just about doubled.

Data for Drilling Cast Iron at Feed of 1″ per Min.

Size of Drill	Feed per Rev.	Thrust in Lbs.	H.P. for 1 Inch Feed per Min.	Size of Drill	Feed per Rev.	Thrust in Lbs.	H.P. for 1 Inch Feed per Min.
1	.02	1300	.0035		.06	8000	.02
	.04	2600	.0063	2½	.02	3200	.008
	.06	3900	.010		.04	6500	.016
1½	.02	2000	.005		.06	9700	.024
	.04	3900	.010	3	.02	3750	.009
	.06	5800	.015		.04	7700	.019
2	.02	2500	.006		.06	11500	.029
	.04	5300	.013				

For carbon steel the values run from 1½ to 3 times these for cast iron, increasing with the feed per revolution.

One inch flat twisted drills have been run from 313 to 575 r. p. m., with feeds of 11.27 and 28.1 inches per minute and required from 5.22 to 11.60 actual horse power.

Torque Required to Drill Cast Iron

Diam. of Drill	Feed in Inch per Rev.	Pounds Torque at 1 foot Radius	H.P. per Rev.	Diam of Drill	Feed in Inch per Rev.	Pounds Torque at 1 foot Radius	H.P. per Rev.
1	.02	50	.009		.06	390	.072
	.04	80	.014	2½	.02	200	.038
	.06	120	.023		.04	400	.076
1½	.02	75	.014		.06	600	.114
	.04	150	.028	3	.02	280	.053
	.06	225	.042		.04	575	.109
2	.02	125	.023		.06	870	.167
	.04	255	.048				

DRILL TROUBLES

Twist-drills will stand more strain in proportion to their size and weight than almost any other tool, and when a good drill gives trouble it is pretty safe to say some of the conditions are wrong.

If it chips on the edge, the lip clearance is too great and fails to support the cutting edge or the feed is too heavy. Ease off on the feed first and then watch the grinding.

If it splits in the web it is either ground wrong, *i e.*, does not have the center lip at the angle of 45 degrees or the feed is altogether too heavy.

If the outer corner wears, it shows that the speed is too great. This is particularly noticeable on cast iron.

DRILL POINTERS

In most cases it is better to use high speeds almost to the point where the drill corners commence to wear with a light feed than to use slower speed and heavy feed.

This is specially true of drilling in automatic machines where the holes are not more than twice as deep as the diameter where drills are flooded with lard oil. With deeper holes the chips are harder to get rid of and it is better to use slower speeds and heavier feeds as the drilled hole gets deeper. Speeds of 10,000 r. p. m. for drills $\frac{1}{16}$ in. and smaller are not uncommon.

Watch the drill chip and try to grind so that it will come out in a small compact roll. It is better to have this continuous clear to bottom of hole if possible.

In drilling brass use a heavier feed especially on automatic machines, as it helps to work out the chips. If you lubricate at all, flood the work. Twist-drills ground as for steel often catch and "hog in" on brass, especially at the bottom of the hole, where it breaks through. To avoid this, grind the lead or rake from the cutting edge.

In drilling hard material use turpentine as a lubricant.

Drills feed easier by thinning the extreme point if this is carefully done. This is important in hand feeding.

High-speed drills work best when warm. Lubricant should be heated to 150 degrees F. when starting drills to work; they will soon maintain the proper temperature.

SPECIAL DRILLS AND THEIR USES

Ratchet-drills have a square taper shank, are used in hand-ratchet braces and in air-driven drills. Used in bridge building, structural and repair work.

The shell drill, Fig. 10, is used after a two-groove drill in chucking out cored holes or for enlarging holes that have been made with a two-groove drill. It has a taper hole and a number of sizes can be used on the same arbor.

Wire drills and jobbers or machinists drills both have round shanks and only differ in size. Wire drills are made to a twist-drill gage and the others to a jobbers or fractional gage.

Blacksmith drills all have a $\frac{1}{2}$-inch shank $2\frac{1}{2}$ inches long, so as to all fit the same holder. There is a flat on the shank for set-screw.

The straightway or Farmers drill has the same clearance as a twist-drill but the flutes are straight. It is used mostly in drilling brass and soft metals or in drilling cross holes or castings where blow holes may be found, as it is less likely to run than the twist-drill.

Oil drills have the advantage of the cutting edge being kept cool and of the chips being forced back through the grooves which reduces friction to a minimum. They are used for all kinds of drilling, mostly deep hole work. In cast-iron drilling air is sometimes used to blow out the chips and keep the drill cool. They are generally used in a screw or chucking machine or a lathe fitted for this work. Where the drill is held stationary and the work revolves, the oil is pumped to the connection and flows through the holes in the drill as in Fig. 11.

Where the drill revolves as in a drill press, the oil is pumped into a collar which remains stationary while the drill socket revolves, as in Fig. 12. An oil groove around the socket and holes through to the drill connects with the holes in the drill itself. Other types are shown in Figs. 13 and 14. The latter is used mostly

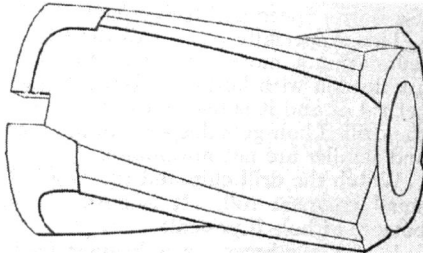

FIG. 10. — Shell Drill

in screw or chucking machine turrets where the oil is pumped into the center of the turret and into the large hole in the shank of the drill.

The hollow drill shown in Fig. 15 is used for deep drilling or long holes and is used in a lathe or some similar machine fitted for the purpose. It has a hole lengthwise through the shank connecting with the grooves of the drill. The shank can be threaded and fitted to a metal tube of such length as desired. The outside of the drill has a groove the whole length of the body. The lubricant is conveyed to the point of the drill on the outside through these grooves, while the hollow tube admits of the passage of oil and chips from the point. In using this drill the hole is first started with a short drill the size of the hole desired and drilled to a depth equal to the length of the body of the hollow drill to be used. The body of the hollow drill acts as a packing, compelling the oil to follow the grooves and the chips to flow out through the hollow shank.

Three and four groove drills are used for chucking out cored holes or enlarged holes that are first drilled with a two-groove drill. They are much better than a two-groove drill for use in cored holes or to follow another drill. The ends of the drills, Fig. 16 and 17, indicate that they are not made to drill from solid stock but for enlarging a hole already made.

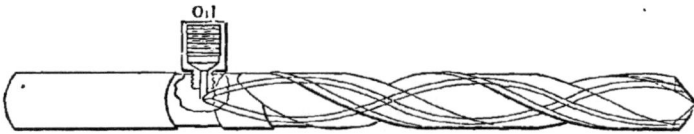

FIG. 11

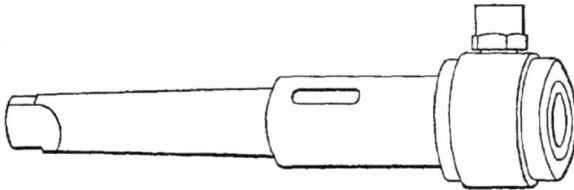

FIG. 12

FIG. 13

FIG. 14

FIG. 15

FIG. 16

FIG. 17

The following tables give standard drill sizes in various ways, each being very convenient for certain classes of work:

DECIMAL EQUIVALENTS OF NOMINAL SIZES OF DRILLS

Inch	M.M.	Wire Gage	Decimals of an Inch	Inch	M.M.	Wire Gage	Decimals of an Inch	Inch	M.M.	Wire Gage	Decimals of an Inch
$\frac{1}{64}$		80	.0135		1.2		.047244			37	.104
		79	.0145		1.3		.051181		2.7		.1063
			.015625			55	.052			36	.1065
	.4		.01574			54	.055	$\frac{7}{64}$			.109375
		78	.016		1.4		.055118			35	.11
		77	.018		1.5		.05905		2.8		.11024
	.5		.01968			53	.0595			34	.111
		76	.020	$\frac{1}{16}$			.0625			33	.113
		75	.021		1.6		.06299		2.9		.11417
		74	.0225			52	.0635			32	.116
	.6		.02362		1.7		.066929		3		.11811
		73	.024			51	.067			31	.12
		72	.025			50	.07	$\frac{1}{8}$	3.1		.12205
		71	.026		1.8		.070866				.125
	.7		.02756			49	.073		3.2		.12598
		70	.028		1.9		.0748			30	.1285
		69	.02925			48	.076		3.3		.12992
		68	.031	$\frac{5}{64}$			.078125		3.4		.13386
$\frac{1}{32}$			.03125			47	.0785			29	.136
	.8		.031496		2		.07874		3.5		.1378
		67	.032			46	.081			28	.1405
		66	.033			45	.082	$\frac{9}{64}$			.140625
		65	.035		2.1		.082677		3.6		.14173
	.9		.03543			44	.086			27	.144
		64	.036		2.2		.086614		3.7		.14567
		63	.037			43	.089			26	.147
		62	.038		2.3		.09055			25	.1495
		61	.039			42	.0935		3.8		.14961
	1		.03937	$\frac{3}{32}$			.09375			24	.152
		60	.04		2.4		.09448		3.9		.15354
		59	.041			41	.096			23	.154
		58	.042			40	.098	$\frac{5}{32}$			.15625
		57	.043		2.5		.098425			22	.157
	1.1		.043307			39	.0995		4		.15748
		56	.0465			38	.1015			21	.159
$\frac{8}{64}$			.046875		2.6		.102362			20	.161

DECIMAL EQUIVALENTS OF NOMINAL SIZES OF DRILLS, *Continued*

Inch	M.M.	Wire Gage	Decimals of an Inch	Inch	M.M.	Letter Sizes	Decimals of an Inch	Inch	M.M.	Letter Sizes	Decimals of an Inch
	4.1		.16142			A	.234			P	.323
	4.2		.16536	15/64			.234375	21/64			.328125
		19	.166		6		.23622			Q	.332
	4.3		.16929			B	.238		8.5		.33465
		18	.1695		6.1		.24015		8.6		.33859
11/64			.171875			C	.242			R	.339
		17	.173		6.2		.2441	11/32			.34375
	4.4		.17323			D	.246		8.8		.34646
		16	.177		6.3		.24803			S	.348
	4.5		.17717	1/4		E	.25		9		.35433
		15	.18		6.4		.25197			T	.358
	4.6		.1811		6.5		.25591	23/64			.359375
		14	.182			F	.257		9.2		.36221
		13	.185		6.6		.25984			U	.368
	4.7		.18504			G	.261		9.5		.37402
3/16			.1875		6.7		.26377	3/8			.375
	4.8		.18898	17/64			.265625			V	.377
		12	.189			H	.266		9.6		.37796
		11	.191		6.8		.26772		9.8		.38583
	4.9		.19291		6.9		.27165			W	.386
		10	.1935			I	.272	25/64			.390625
		9	.196		7		.27559		10		.3937
	5		.19685			J	.277			X	.397
		8	.199		7.1		.27952			Y	.404
	5.1		.20079			K	.281	13/32			.40625
		7	.201	9/32			.28125			Z	.413
13/64			.203125		7.2		.28347		10.5		.4134
		6	.204		7.3		.2874	27/64			.421875
	5.2		.20473			L	.29		11		.43307
		5	.2055		7.4		.29133	7/16			.4375
	5.3		.20866			M	.295		11.5		.45276
		4	.209		7.5		.29528	29/64			.453125
	5.4		.2126	19/64			.296875	15/32			.46875
		3	.213		7.6		.29922		12		.47244
	5.5		.21654			N	.302	31/64			.484375
7/32			.21875		7.7		.30314		12.5		.4921
	5.6		.22047		7.8		.30709	1/2			.5
		2	.221		7.9		.31102				
	5.7		.22441	5/16			.3125				
		1	.228		8.		.31496				
	5.8		.22835			O	.316				
	5.9		.23228		8.2		.32284				

Decimal Equivalents of Nominal Sizes of Drills, *Continued*

Inch	M.M.	Decimals of an Inch	Inch	M.M.	Decimals of an Inch	Inch	M.M.	Decimals of an Inch
	13	.51181	43/64		.671875	27/32		.84375
33/64		.515625	11/16		.6875		21.5	.84646
17/32		.53125		17.5	.689	55/64		.859375
	13.5	.5315	45/64		.703125		22	.86614
35/64		.546875		18	.70866	7/8		.875
	14	.55118	23/32		.71875		22.5	.88583
9/16		.5625		18.5	.72835	57/64		.890625
	14.5	.57087	47/64		.734375		23	.90551
37/64		.578125		19	.74803	29/32		.90625
	15	.59055	3/4		.75	59/64		.921875
19/32		.59375	49/64		.765625		23.5	.9252
39/64		.609375		19.5	.76772	15/16		.9375
	15.5	.61024	25/32		.78125		24	.94488
5/8		.625		20	.7874	61/64		.953125
	16	.62992	51/64		.796875		24.5	.9646
41/64		.640625		20.5	.8071	31/32		.96875
	16.5	.6496	13/16		.8125		25	.98425
21/32		.65625		21	.82677	63/64		.984375
	17	.66929	53/64		.828125	1		1.

Letter Sizes of Drills

Diameter Inches	Decimals of 1 Inch	Diameter Inches	Decimals of 1 Inch
A 15/64	.234	N	.302
B	.238	O 5/16	.316
C	.242	P 21/64	.323
D	.246	Q	.332
E 1/4	.250	R 11/32	.339
F	.257	S	.348
G	.261	T 23/64	.358
H 17/64	.266	U	.368
I	.272	V 3/8	.377
J	.277	W 25/64	.386
K 9/32	.281	X	.397
L	.290	Y 13/32	.404
M 19/64	.295	Z	.413

DECIMAL EQUIVALENTS OF DRILL SIZES FROM $\frac{1}{2}''$ TO NO. 80

Size	Decimal Equivalent	Size	Decimal Equivalent	Size	Decimal Equivalent
$\frac{1}{2}$	0.500	3	0.213	$\frac{3}{32}$	0.0937
$\frac{31}{64}$	0.4843	4	0.209	42	0.0935
$\frac{15}{32}$	0.4687	5	0.2055	43	0.089
$\frac{29}{64}$	0.4531	6	0.204	44	0.086
$\frac{7}{16}$	0.4375	$\frac{13}{64}$	0.2031	45	0.082
$\frac{27}{64}$	0.4218	7	0.201	46	0.081
Z	0.413	8	0.199	47	0.0785
$\frac{13}{32}$	0.4062	9	0.196	$\frac{5}{64}$	0.0781
Y	0.404	10	0.1935	48	0.076
X	0.397	11	0.191	49	0.073
$\frac{25}{64}$	0.3906	12	0.189	50	0.070
W	0.386	$\frac{3}{16}$	0.1875	51	0.067
V	0.377	13	0.185	52	0.0635
$\frac{3}{8}$	0.375	14	0.182	$\frac{1}{16}$	0.0625
U	0.368	15	0.180	53	0.0595
$\frac{23}{64}$	0.3593	16	0.177	54	0.055
T	0.358	17	0.173	55	0.052
S	0.348	$\frac{11}{64}$	0.1718	$\frac{3}{64}$	0.0468
$\frac{11}{32}$	0.3437	18	0.1695	56	0.0465
R	0.339	19	0.166	57	0.043
Q	0.332	20	0.161	58	0.042
$\frac{21}{64}$	0.3281	21	0.159	59	0.041
P	0.323	22	0.157	60	0.040
O	0.316	$\frac{5}{32}$	0.1562	61	0.039
$\frac{5}{16}$	0.3125	23	0.154	62	0.038
N	0.302	24	0.152	63	0.037
$\frac{19}{64}$	0.2968	25	0.1495	64	0.036
M	0.295	26	0.147	65	0.035
L	0.290	27	0.144	66	0.033
$\frac{9}{32}$	0.2812	$\frac{9}{64}$	0.1406	$\frac{1}{32}$	0.0312
K	0.281	28	0.1405	67	0.032
J	0.277	29	0.136	68	0.031
I	0.272	30	0.1285	69	0.029
H	0.266	$\frac{1}{8}$	0.125	70	0.028
$\frac{17}{64}$	0.2656	31	0.120	71	0.026
G	0.261	32	0.116	72	0.025
F	0.257	33	0.113	73	0.024
E-$\frac{1}{4}$	0.250	34	0.111	74	0.0225
D	0.246	35	0.110	75	0.021
C	0.242	$\frac{7}{64}$	0.1093	76	0.020
B	0.238	36	0.1065	77	0.018
$\frac{15}{64}$	0.2343	37	0.104	$\frac{1}{64}$	0.0156
A	0.234	38	0.1015	78	0.016
1	0.228	39	0.0995	79	0.0145
2	0.221	40	0.098	80	0.0135
$\frac{7}{32}$	0.2187	41	0.096		

TAP DRILL SIZES FOR REGULAR THREADS

THESE sizes give an allowance above the bottom of thread on sizes $\frac{3}{16}$ to 2; varying respectively as follows: for "V" threads, .010 to .055 inch; for U. S. S. and Whitworth threads, .005 to .027 inch. These are found by adding to the size at bottom of thread, $\frac{1}{4}$ of the pitch for "V" threads, and $\frac{1}{8}$ of the pitch for U. S. S. and Whitworth, the pitch being equal to 1 inch divided by the number of threads per inch. In practice it is better to use a larger drill if the exact size called for cannot be had.

Size Tap	No. of Threads	Size of Drill			Size Tap	No. of Threads	Size of Drills		
		U. S. S.	V	W			U. S. S.	V	W
$1\frac{3}{16}$	24	.138	.111	.129	$1\frac{13}{16}$	9	.808	.790	.810
$\frac{1}{4}$	20	.191	.184	.192	1	8	.854	.832	.856
$1\frac{5}{16}$	18	.248	.239	.249	$1\frac{1}{16}$	8	.917	.894	.919
$\frac{3}{8}$	16	.302	.293	.303	$1\frac{1}{8}$	7	.957	.932	.960
$1\frac{7}{16}$	14	.354	.345	.355	$1\frac{1}{4}$	7	1.082	1.057	1.085
$\frac{1}{2}$	13	.409	.399	.410	$1\frac{5}{16}$	6	1.179	1.144	1.182
$\frac{9}{16}$	12	.402	.391	.403	$1\frac{3}{8}$	6	1.304	1.269	1.307
$1\frac{9}{16}$	12	.465	.453	.466	$1\frac{3}{8}$	$5\frac{1}{2}$	1.412	1.372	1.416
$\frac{5}{8}$	11	.518	.506	.520	$1\frac{1}{2}$	5	1.390	1.347	1.394
$1\frac{11}{16}$	11	.581	.568	.583	$1\frac{1}{2}$	5	1.515	1.472	1.519
$\frac{3}{4}$	10	.632	.618	.634	$1\frac{3}{4}$	5	1.640	1.597	1.644
$1\frac{13}{16}$	10	.695	.680	.697	$1\frac{7}{8}$	$4\frac{1}{2}$	1.614	1.566	1.619
$\frac{7}{8}$	9	.745	.728	.747	2"	$4\frac{1}{2}$	1.739	1.691	1.744

A very simple rule, which is good enough in many cases, is: Subtract the pitch of one thread from the diameter of the tap. A $\frac{3}{8}$-inch tap 16-thread would be $\frac{3}{8}$ minus $\frac{1}{16} = \frac{5}{16}$ drill; a $\frac{3}{4}$-inch tap, ten-thread, would be $\frac{3}{4}$ minus $\frac{1}{10} = \frac{75}{100} - \frac{10}{100}$ or $0.75 - 0.10 = \frac{65}{100}$ or 0.65, or a little over $\frac{5}{8}$ of an inch, so a $\frac{5}{8}$-inch drill will do nicely. With a 1-inch tap we have $1 - \frac{1}{8} = \frac{7}{8}$-inch drill, which is a little large but leaves enough thread for most cases.

TAP DRILLS FOR S. A. E. (A. L. A. M.) THREADS

Size of Tap	Threads per Inch	Size of Drill, Inches	Size of Tap	Threads per Inch	Size of Drill, Inches
$\frac{1}{4}$	28	$\frac{7}{32}$	$\frac{3}{4}$	16	$\frac{43}{64}$
$\frac{5}{16}$	24	$\frac{17}{64}$	$\frac{7}{8}$	14	$\frac{51}{64}$
$\frac{3}{8}$	24	$\frac{21}{64}$	1	14	$\frac{59}{64}$
$\frac{7}{16}$	20	$\frac{3}{8}$	$1\frac{1}{8}$	12	$1\frac{1}{32}$
$\frac{1}{2}$	20	$\frac{29}{64}$	$1\frac{1}{4}$	12	$1\frac{9}{64}$
$\frac{9}{16}$	18	$\frac{33}{64}$	$1\frac{3}{8}$	12	$1\frac{17}{64}$
$\frac{5}{8}$	18	$\frac{37}{64}$	$1\frac{1}{2}$	12	$1\frac{25}{64}$
$\frac{11}{16}$	16	$\frac{39}{64}$			

The tap should be between 0.002 and 0.003 inch large for clearance between top and bottom of threads.

TAP DRILLS

For Machine Screw Taps

THESE drills will give a thread full enough for all practical purposes, but not a *full* thread as this is very seldom required in practical work. Further data along this line will be found in the tables which follow.

TAP DRILLS

Sizes of Taps	No. of Threads	Sizes of Drills	Sizes of Taps	No. of Threads	Sizes of Drills
2	48	48	12	24	19
2	56	46	13	20	17
2	64	45	13	24	15
3	40	48	14	20	14
3	48	47	14	22	13
3	56	45	14	24	11
4	32	45	15	18	12
4	36	43	15	20	10
4	40	42	15	24	7
5	30	41	16	16	10
5	32	40	16	18	7
5	36	38	16	20	5
5	40	36	16	24	1
6	30	39	17	16	7
6	32	37	17	18	4
6	36	35	17	20	2
6	40	33	18	16	2
7	28	32	18	18	1
7	30	31	18	20	B
7	32	30	19	16	C
8	24	31	19	18	D
8	30	30	19	20	E
8	32	29	20	16	E
9	24	29	20	18	E
9	28	27	20	20	F
9	30	26	22	16	H
9	32	24	22	18	I
10	24	26	24	14	K
10	28	24	24	16	L
10	30	23	24	18	M
10	32	21	26	14	O
11	24	20	26	16	P
11	28	19	28	14	R
11	30	18	28	16	S
12	20	21	30	14	T
12	22	19	30	16	U

DIMENSIONS FOR TWIST DRILLS

FOR BORING HOLES TO BE THREADED WITH U. S. FORM OF THREAD TAPS $\frac{1}{16}$ to $\frac{17}{64}$ INCH DIAMETER

Diameter Inches	No. of Threads to the Inch	Exact Diameter Bottom of Thread Inches	Gage No. of Drill	Diameter Inches	No. of Threads to the Inch	Exact Diameter Bottom of Thread Inches	Gage No. of Drill
$\frac{1}{16}$	60	.041	57	$\frac{1}{4}$	26	.200	6
$\frac{1}{16}$	64	.042	56	$\frac{5}{64}$	56	.055	53
$\frac{3}{32}$	48	.067	50	$\frac{5}{64}$	60	.056	53
$\frac{3}{32}$	50	.068	50	$\frac{7}{64}$	40	.077	46
$\frac{3}{32}$	56	.071	49	$\frac{7}{64}$	44	.080	45
$\frac{3}{32}$	60	.072	48	$\frac{7}{64}$	48	.082	44
$\frac{1}{8}$	40	.093	41	$\frac{9}{64}$	32	.100	38
$\frac{1}{8}$	44	.096	40	$\frac{9}{64}$	36	.105	36
$\frac{1}{8}$	48	.098	39	$\frac{7}{64}$	40	.108	34
$\frac{5}{32}$	32	.116	31	$\frac{11}{64}$	32	.131	29
$\frac{5}{32}$	36	.120	31	$\frac{1}{4}$	36	.136	28
$\frac{5}{32}$	40	.124	30	$\frac{1}{4}$	40	.139	28
$\frac{3}{16}$	24	.133	29	$\frac{13}{64}$	24	.149	24
$\frac{3}{16}$	28	.141	27	$\frac{13}{64}$	28	.157	21
$\frac{3}{16}$	30	.144	26	$\frac{13}{64}$	32	.162	19
$\frac{3}{16}$	32	.147	25	$\frac{13}{64}$	36	.167	18
$\frac{3}{16}$	36	.152	23	$\frac{15}{64}$	24	.180	13
$\frac{7}{32}$	24	.164	19	$\frac{15}{64}$	28	.188	10
$\frac{7}{32}$	28	.172	16	$\frac{15}{64}$	32	.194	8
$\frac{7}{32}$	32	.178	14	$\frac{15}{64}$	36	.198	7
$\frac{7}{32}$	36	.183	12	$\frac{17}{64}$	18	.193	9
$\frac{1}{4}$	18	.178	14	$\frac{17}{64}$	20	.201	5
$\frac{1}{4}$	20	.185	12	$\frac{17}{64}$	24	.211	3
$\frac{1}{4}$	22	.190	10	$\frac{17}{64}$	26	.216	2
$\frac{1}{4}$	24	.196	8	$\frac{17}{64}$	32	.225	1

DRILLS AND REAMERS FOR DOWEL PINS

SIZES OF ROD		DRILLS AND REAMERS FOR DRIVE FITS			DRILLS FOR CLEARANCE	
No. of Gage (Stubbs Steel Wire)	Dia.	Size of Drill	Dia. of Drill	Dia. of Reamer	Size of Drill	Dia. of Drill
54	.055	No. 55	.052		No. 54	.055
45	.081	" 47	.0785		" 46	.081
33	.112	" 36	.1065	.110	" 33	.113
30	.127	" 31	.120	.125	" 30	.1285
21	.157	" 24	.152	.155	" 22	.157
10	.191	" 13	.185	.189	" 11	.191
	.252	C	.242	.250 --.2505	F	.257
	.315	$\frac{1}{8}$ Reamer Drill	.307	.3125--.313	O	.316
V	.377	$\frac{3}{8}$ "	.366	.375 --.3755	V	.377
	.439	$\frac{16}{}$ "	.427	.4375--.438		
	.503	$\frac{1}{2}$ "	.489	.500 --.5005		
	.628	$\frac{5}{8}$ "	.616	.625 --.6255		
	.753	$\frac{3}{4}$ "	.734 ($\frac{47}{64}$)	.750 --.7505		

DOUBLE DEPTH OF THREADS

Threads per in.	V Threads D D	U. S. St'd D D	Whit. St'd D D	Threads per in.	V Threads D D	U. S. St'd D D	Whit. St'd D D
2	.86650	.64950	.64000	28	.06185	.04639	.04571
2¼	.77022	.57733	.56888	30	.05773	.04330	.04266
2⅜	.72960	.54694	.53894	32	.05412	.04059	.04000
2½	.69320	.51960	.51200	34	.05097	.03820	.03764
2⅝	.66015	.49485	.48761	36	.04811	.03608	.03555
2¾	.63019	.47236	.46545	38	.04560	.03418	.03368
2⅞	.60278	.45182	.44521	40	.04330	.03247	.03200
3	.57733	.43300	.42666	42	.04126	.03093	.03047
3¼	.53323	.39966	.39384	44	.03936	.02952	.03136
3½	.49485	.37114	.36571	46	.03767	.02823	.02782
4	.43300	.32475	.32000	48	.03608	.02706	.02666
4½	.38488	.28869	.28444	50	.03464	.02598	.02560
5	.34660	.25980	.25600	52	.03332	.02498	.02461
5½	.31490	.23618	.23272	54	.03209	.02405	.02370
6	.28866	.21650	.21333	56	.03093	.02319	.02285
7	.24742	.18557	.18285	58	.02987	.02239	.02206
8	.21650	.16237	.16000	60	.02887	.02165	.02133
9	.19244	.14433	.14222	62	.02795	.02095	.02064
10	.17320	.12990	.12800	64	.02706	.02029	.02000
11	.15745	.11809	.11636	66	.02625	.01968	.01939
11½	.15069	.11295	.11121	68	.02548	.01910	.01882
12	.14433	.10825	.10666	70	.02475	.01855	.01828
13	.13323	.09992	.09846	72	.02407	.01804	.01782
14	.12357	.09278	.09142	74	.02341	.01752	.01729
15	.11555	.08660	.08533	76	.02280	.01714	.01673
16	.10825	.08118	.08000	78	.02221	.01665	.01641
18	.09622	.07216	.07111	80	.02166	.01623	.01600
20	.08660	.06495	.06400	82	.02113	.01584	.01560
22	.07872	.05904	.05818	84	.02063	.01546	.01523
24	.07216	.05412	.05333	86	.02015	.01510	.01476
26	.0661	.04996	.04923	88	.01957	.01476	.01454
27	.06418	.04811	.04740	90	.01925	.01443	.01422

This gives the depth to allow for a full thread in a nut or similar iece of work for threads for 2 to 90 per inch, regardless of the diam-ter. A special nut for a 2-inch bolt, 20 threads per inch, U. S. tandard would have a hole 2. — .06495 = 1.93505 inches in diam-ter bored in it.

SIZES OF TAP DRILLS FOR TAPS WITH "V" THREAD

Diam. Tap, in Inches	Threads per Inch	Size of Drill, Number	Diam. Tap, in Inches	Threads per Inch	Size of Drill	Diam. Tap, in Inches	Threads per Inch	Size of Drill, Inches	Diam. Tap, in Inches	Threads per Inch	Size of Drill, Inches
$\frac{3}{32}$	48	50	$\frac{7}{32}$	24	No. 20	$\frac{19}{32}$	12	$\frac{31}{64}$	$1\frac{7}{32}$	7	$1\frac{1}{64}$
$\frac{3}{32}$	52	50	$\frac{7}{32}$	28	No. 17	$\frac{19}{32}$	14	$\frac{1}{2}$	$1\frac{7}{32}$	8	$1\frac{3}{64}$
$\frac{3}{32}$	54	49	$\frac{7}{32}$	30	No. 16		10	$\frac{31}{64}$	$1\frac{1}{4}$	7	$1\frac{5}{64}$
$\frac{3}{32}$	56	49	$\frac{7}{32}$	32	No. 15		11	$\frac{1}{2}$	$1\frac{9}{32}$	7	$1\frac{5}{64}$
$\frac{3}{32}$	60	48	$\frac{1}{4}$	24	No. 16		12	$\frac{5}{16}$	$1\frac{5}{16}$	7	$1\frac{7}{64}$
$\frac{7}{64}$	32	50	$\frac{1}{4}$	28	No. 12		10	$\frac{1}{2}$	$1\frac{5}{16}$	7	$1\frac{9}{64}$
$\frac{7}{64}$	36	49	$\frac{1}{4}$	32	No. 10		11		$1\frac{3}{8}$	6	$1\frac{1}{8}$
$\frac{7}{64}$	40	47	$\frac{1}{4}$	18	No. 17		12	$\frac{33}{64}$	$1\frac{3}{8}$	6	$1\frac{9}{32}$
$\frac{7}{64}$	48	44	$\frac{1}{4}$	20	No. 14		11	$\frac{9}{16}$	$1\frac{7}{16}$	6	$1\frac{11}{64}$
$\frac{7}{64}$	56	43	$\frac{1}{4}$	24	No. 9		12		$1\frac{15}{32}$	6	$1\frac{7}{32}$
$\frac{1}{8}$	32	44	$\frac{9}{32}$	16	$\frac{13}{64}$ in.		11		$1\frac{1}{2}$	6	$1\frac{11}{44}$
$\frac{1}{8}$	36	43	$\frac{9}{32}$	18	No. 3		12		$1\frac{17}{32}$	6	$1\frac{21}{64}$
$\frac{1}{8}$	40	42	$\frac{9}{32}$	20	No. 1		10		$1\frac{9}{16}$	6	$1\frac{23}{64}$
$\frac{1}{8}$	42	41	$\frac{5}{16}$	16	$\frac{15}{64}$ in.		11	$\frac{5}{8}$	$1\frac{5}{8}$	6	$1\frac{25}{64}$
$\frac{1}{8}$	48	39	$\frac{5}{16}$	18	F		12	$\frac{41}{64}$	$1\frac{5}{8}$	5	$1\frac{23}{64}$
$\frac{9}{64}$	30	41	$\frac{5}{16}$	16	$\frac{17}{64}$ in.		10		$1\frac{11}{16}$	$5\frac{1}{2}$	$1\frac{25}{64}$
$\frac{9}{64}$	32	40	$\frac{5}{16}$	18	J		11		$1\frac{11}{16}$	5	$1\frac{27}{64}$
$\frac{9}{64}$	36	37	$\frac{5}{16}$	14	L		12		$1\frac{11}{16}$	$5\frac{1}{2}$	$1\frac{29}{64}$
$\frac{9}{64}$	40	34	$\frac{5}{16}$	16	$\frac{19}{64}$ in.		10	$\frac{43}{64}$	$1\frac{11}{16}$	5	$1\frac{29}{64}$
$\frac{5}{32}$	30	33	$\frac{11}{32}$	18	N		10		$1\frac{3}{4}$	$5\frac{1}{2}$	$1\frac{31}{64}$
$\frac{5}{32}$	32	32	$\frac{11}{32}$	14	P		9		$1\frac{3}{4}$	5	$1\frac{29}{32}$
$\frac{5}{32}$	36	31	$\frac{11}{32}$	16	$\frac{21}{64}$ in.		10	$\frac{3}{4}$	$1\frac{3}{4}$	5	$1\frac{29}{64}$
$\frac{5}{32}$	40	30	$\frac{3}{8}$	18	R		9		$1\frac{25}{32}$	5	$1\frac{31}{64}$
$\frac{11}{64}$	32	30	$\frac{3}{8}$	14	S		9		$1\frac{13}{16}$	5	$1\frac{33}{64}$
$\frac{11}{64}$	36	29	$\frac{3}{8}$	16	$\frac{3}{8}$ in.	I	8		$1\frac{27}{32}$	5	$1\frac{35}{64}$
$\frac{3}{16}$	24	29	$\frac{7}{16}$	14	W	$1\frac{1}{32}$	8		$1\frac{7}{8}$	$4\frac{1}{2}$	$1\frac{33}{64}$
$\frac{3}{16}$	28	28	$\frac{7}{16}$	16	$\frac{25}{64}$ in.	$1\frac{1}{16}$	8		$1\frac{7}{8}$	5	$1\frac{35}{64}$
$\frac{3}{16}$	30	27	$\frac{1}{2}$	13	X	$1\frac{3}{32}$	8		$1\frac{29}{32}$	$4\frac{1}{2}$	$1\frac{37}{64}$
$\frac{3}{16}$	32	26	$\frac{1}{2}$	14	$\frac{13}{32}$ in.	$1\frac{1}{8}$	7		$1\frac{29}{32}$	5	$1\frac{9}{16}$
$\frac{3}{16}$	36	24	$\frac{17}{32}$	12	$\frac{27}{64}$ in.	$1\frac{1}{8}$	8		$1\frac{15}{16}$	$4\frac{1}{2}$	$1\frac{39}{64}$
$\frac{13}{64}$	24	26	$\frac{17}{32}$	13	$\frac{27}{64}$ in.	$1\frac{5}{32}$	7		$1\frac{15}{16}$	5	$1\frac{41}{64}$
$\frac{13}{64}$	28	22	$\frac{9}{16}$	14	$\frac{7}{16}$ in.	$1\frac{5}{32}$	8		$1\frac{31}{32}$	$4\frac{1}{2}$	$1\frac{43}{64}$
$\frac{13}{64}$	32	20	$\frac{9}{16}$	12	$\frac{29}{64}$ in.	$1\frac{3}{16}$	7		$1\frac{31}{32}$	5	$1\frac{43}{64}$
$\frac{13}{64}$	36	18	$\frac{9}{16}$	14	$\frac{29}{32}$ in.	$1\frac{3}{16}$	8	$1\frac{3}{64}$	2	$4\frac{1}{2}$	$1\frac{45}{64}$

This table gives similar information but in a way that would be more convenient in some cases.

TAPPING AND THREADING SPEEDS

For tapping in cast iron, the F. E. Wells & Son Company, Greenfield, Mass., recommends the following speeds:

$\frac{1}{4}$	$\frac{3}{8}$	$\frac{1}{2}$	$\frac{5}{8}$	$\frac{3}{4}$ inch holes
382	255	191	153	127

using an oil or soda compound.

For soft steel and iron:

$\frac{1}{4}$	$\frac{3}{8}$	$\frac{1}{2}$	$\frac{5}{8}$	$\frac{3}{4}$ inch holes
229	153	115	91	76

using oil as a lubricant.

The National Machine Company, Hartford, Conn., uses 233 revolutions per minute up to $\frac{1}{4}$ inch diameter and 140 revolutions per minute for sizes between $\frac{1}{4}$ and $\frac{1}{2}$ inch, using a screw-cutting oil as a lubricant.

They tap holes as deep as four tap diameters by power.

For threading cast iron in machines of the bolt-cutter type, the Landis Machine Company, Waynesboro, Penn., gives these speeds:

$\frac{1}{4}$	$\frac{3}{8}$	$\frac{1}{2}$	$\frac{3}{4}$	1	$1\frac{1}{2}$	2 inches
200	150	125	100	85	55	45

with petroleum as a lubricant.

For soft steel and iron:

$\frac{1}{4}$	$\frac{3}{8}$	$\frac{1}{2}$	$\frac{3}{4}$	1	$1\frac{1}{2}$	2 inches
280	220	175	140	115	75	60

with compound or screw-cutting oil, using a $2\frac{1}{2}$-inch belt at 1200 feet per minute. The speeds are for high-speed steel dies. Some users run the machines at a much higher rate.

THREADING PIPE

The Bignall & Keeler Manufacturing Company, Edwardsville, Ill., aims to have its pipe-threading machines run at a cutting speed of 15 feet per minute. The machine for handling pipe from $\frac{1}{4}$ to 2 inches uses a $3\frac{1}{2}$-inch belt at about 940 feet per minute. They advise nothing but lard oil on the dies.

The Standard Engineering Company, Ellwood City, Penn., also recommends a cutting speed of 15 feet per minute, using a 3-inch belt at 730 feet per minute.

It will be understood in all the cases cited that the figures given are merely a guide as to what can be done and not record performances in any particular. Soft stock can be run very fast, and hard, gritty stock is very hard on the dies.

The only general rule, in the case of dies, is to run as fast as possible without undue heating of the dies.

DRILL END LENGTHS

It is often necessary in designing brass castings to allow for drilling to a certain depth so as to give the thickness of metal A necessary at the bottom of the hole to withstand pressure.

The table gives the dimension C for usual sizes of drills. This is deducted from B to give the actual thickness of metal at A.

DRILL END LENGTHS

Dia.	C	C in nearest 1/64	Gage No.	Dia.	C	C in nearest 1/64	Gage No.	Dia.	C	C in nearest 1/64
2	0.60086	39/64	1	0.2280	0.06850	5/64	41	0.0960	0.02884	2/64
1 15/16	0.58208	37/64	2	0.2210	0.06640	4/64	42	0.0935	0.02809	2/64
1 7/8	0.56331	36/64	3	0.2130	0.06400	4/64	43	0.0890	0.02674	2/64
1 13/16	0.54453	35/64	4	0.2090	0.06279	4/64	44	0.0860	0.02584	2/64
1 3/4	0.52576	34/64	5	0.2055	0.06174	4/64	45	0.0820	0.02464	2/64
1 11/16	0.50698	1/2	6	0.2040	0.06129	4/64	46	0.0810	0.02433	2/64
1 5/8	0.48820	31/64	7	0.2010	0.06039	4/64	47	0.0785	0.02358	2/64
1 9/16	0.46942	30/64	8	0.1990	0.05979	4/64	48	0.0760	0.02283	1/64
1 1/2	0.45065	29/64	9	0.1960	0.05888	4/64	49	0.0730	0.02193	1/64
1 7/16	0.43187	28/64	10	0.1935	0.05813	4/64	50	0.0700	0.02103	1/64
1 3/8	0.41309	26/64	11	0.1910	0.05738	4/64	51	0.0670	0.02013	1/64
1 5/16	0.39431	25/64	12	0.1890	0.05678	4/64	52	0.0635	0.01908	1/64
1 1/4	0.37554	24/64	13	0.1850	0.05558	4/64	53	0.0595	0.01788	1/64
1 3/16	0.35676	23/64	14	0.1820	0.05468	4/64	54	0.0550	0.01652	1/64
1 1/8	0.33798	22/64	15	0.1800	0.05408	3/64	55	0.0520	0.01562	1/64
1 1/16	0.31931	20/64	16	0.1770	0.05318	3/64	56	0.0465	0.01397	1/64
1	0.30046	19/64	17	0.1730	0.05197	3/64	57	0.0430	0.01292	1/64
31/32	0.29104	19/64	18	0.1695	0.05092	3/64	58	0.0420	0.01262	1/64
15/16	0.28165	18/64	19	0.1660	0.04987	3/64	59	0.0410	0.01232	1/64
29/32	0.27226	17/64	20	0.1610	0.04837	3/64	60	0.0400	0.01202	1/64
7/8	0.26288	17/64	21	0.1590	0.04777	3/64	61	0.0390	0.01172	1/64
27/32	0.25349	16/64	22	0.1570	0.04717	3/64	62	0.0380	0.01142	1/64
13/16	0.24410	16/64	23	0.1540	0.04627	3/64	63	0.0370	0.01112	1/64
25/32	0.23471	15/64	24	0.1520	0.04567	3/64	64	0.0360	0.01082	1/64
3/4	0.22532	14/64	25	0.1495	0.04491	3/64	65	0.0350	0.01052	1/64
23/32	0.21593	14/64	26	0.1470	0.04416	3/64	66	0.0330	0.00991	1/64
11/16	0.20655	13/64	27	0.1440	0.04326	3/64	67	0.0320	0.00961	1/64
21/32	0.19716	13/64	28	0.1405	0.04221	3/64	68	0.0310	0.00931	1/64
5/8	0.18777	12/64	29	0.1360	0.04086	3/64	69	0.0293	0.00879	1/64
19/32	0.17838	11/64	30	0.1285	0.03861	2/64	70	0.0280	0.00841	1/64
9/16	0.16900	11/64	31	0.1200	0.03605	2/64	71	0.0260	0.00781	1/64
17/32	0.15960	10/64	32	0.1160	0.03485	2/64	72	0.0250	0.00751	1/64
1/2	0.15022	10/64	33	0.1130	0.03395	2/64	73	0.0240	0.00721	1/64
15/32	0.14083	9/64	34	0.1110	0.03335	2/64	74	0.0225	0.00676	1/64
7/16	0.13144	8/64	35	0.1100	0.03305	2/64	75	0.0210	0.00631	1/64
13/32	0.12205	8/64	36	0.1065	0.03200	2/64	76	0.0200	0.00601	1/64
3/8	0.11266	7/64	37	0.1040	0.03124	2/64	77	0.0180	0.00541	1/64
11/32	0.10327	7/64	38	0.1015	0.03049	2/64	78	0.0160	0.00481	..
5/16	0.09388	6/64	39	0.0995	0.02989	2/64	79	0.0145	0.00436	..
9/32	0.08450	5/64	40	0.0980	0.02944	2/64	80	0.0135	0.00406	..
1/4	0.07511	5/64								
7/32	0.06572	4/64								
3/16	0.05633	4/64								
5/32	0.04942	3/64								
1/8	0.03755	2/64								
3/32	0.02817	2/64								
1/16	0.01878	1/64								
1/32	0.00939	1/64								

Formula, $C = \dfrac{0.60086 \; \text{Diam.}}{2}$

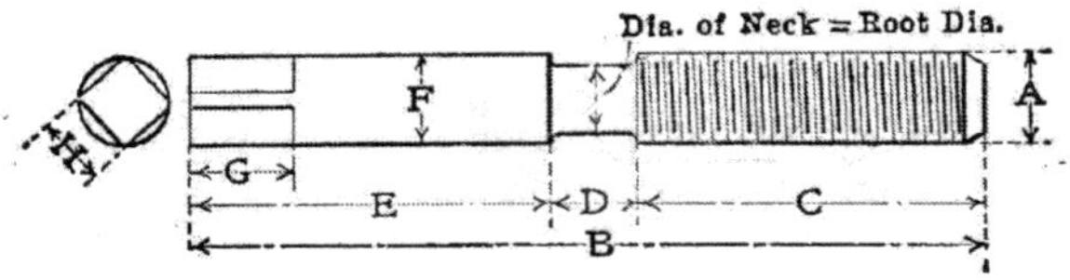

DIMENSIONS OF MACHINE SCREW TAPS

Number of Tap	Diameter of Tap	Number of Threads per Inch	Total Length	Length of Thread	Length of Neck	Length of Shank	Diameter of Shank	Length of Square	Size of Square	No. of Flutes
	A		B	C	D	E	F	G	H	
1	.071	64	1 3/4	9/16	No neck used on these.	1 3/16	.125	3/16	3/32	3
1 1/2	.081	56	1 3/4	9/16		1 3/16	.125	3/16	3/32	3
2	.089	56	1 3/4	9/16		1 3/16	.125	3/16	3/32	3
3	.101	48	1 7/8	5/8		1 1/4	.125	3/16	3/32	3
4	.113	36	2	11/16		1 5/16	.125	3/16	3/32	3
5	.125	36	2 1/8	3/4		1 3/8	.125	7/32	3/32	3
6	.141	32	2 1/8	3/4		1 3/8	.141	7/32	7/64	3
7	.154	32	2 1/8	3/4		1 3/8	.154	7/32	7/64	3
8	.166	32	2 1/4	13/16	1/8	1 5/16	.166	7/32	1/8	4
9	.180	30	2 1/4	7/8	1/8	1 1/4	.180	1/4	1/8	4
10	.194	24	2 1/4	7/8	1/8	1 1/4	.194	1/4	5/32	4
11	.206	24	2 3/8	7/8	1/8	1 1/4	.206	1/4	5/32	4
12	.221	24	2 3/8	15/16	1/8	1 5/16	.221	9/32	5/32	4
13	.234	22	2 1/2	1	3/16	1 5/16	.234	9/32	3/16	4
14	.246	20	2 5/8	1 1/16	3/16	1 3/8	.246	9/32	3/16	4
15	.261	20	2 3/4	1 1/8	3/16	1 7/16	.261	5/16	3/16	4
16	.272	18	2 3/4	1 1/8	3/16	1 7/16	.272	5/16	7/32	4
18	.298	18	2 3/4	1 1/8	3/16	1 7/16	.298	5/16	7/32	4
20	.325	16	3	1 1/4	1/4	1 1/2	.325	11/32	1/4	4
22	.350	16	3	1 1/4	1/4	1 1/2	.350	11/32	1/4	4
24	.378	16	3 1/4	1 1/4	5/16	1 11/16	.378	3/8	9/32	4
26	.404	16	3 1/4	1 1/4	5/16	1 11/16	.404	3/8	5/16	4
28	.430	14	3 1/2	1 3/8	5/16	1 13/16	.430	13/32	5/16	4
30	.456	14	3 1/2	1 3/8	5/16	1 13/16	.456	7/16	11/32	4

These are for the American Screw Company's Standard screws that have been in use for many years.

MACHINE SCREW TAPS — (WELLS BROS. CO.)

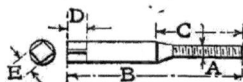

Size	Threads per Inch	Size Steel	Outside Dia. Thread		Whole Length	Length Thread	Length Square	Diam. Square
			Max.	Min.				
			A		B	C	D	E
0	80	.147	.063	.061	1 9/16	1 1/4	3/32	.112
1	72	.147	.076	.074	1 5/8	1 1/4	3/32	.112
2	64	.147	.089	.088	1 7/8	1 3/8	3/32	.112
3	56	.147	.103	.101	1 13/16	1 7/16	3/32	.112
4	48	.147	.116	.114	1 11/16	1 5/8	7/64	.112
5	44	.147	.129	.127	1 31/32	1 9/16	3/32	.112
6	40	.147	.142	.140	2 1/32	1 5/8	3/32	.112
7	36	.165	.155	.153	2 5/32	1 23/32	1/4	.124
8	36	.174	.169	.167	2 7/8	1 3/4	1/8	.131
9	32	.187	.181	.179	2 15/16	1 13/16	1/8	.140
10	30	.200	.194	.192	2 1/2	1 31/32	1/8	.150
11		.215	.206	.204	2 1/2	1	1/8	.161
12	28	.226	.220	.218	2 7/8	1 1/16	9/32	.170
13		.252	.239	.237	2 17/32	1 9/32	9/32	.189
14	24	.252	.246	.244	2 17/32	1 1/16	9/32	.189
15		.258	.258	.256	2 5/8	1 1/8	9/32	.194
16	22	.278	.273	.270	2 21/32	1 1/8	5/16	.209
18	20	.304	.299	.296	2 3/4	1 9/32	1 5/16	.228
20	20	.332 / .328	.325	.322	2 13/16	1 11/32	1 3/8	.249
22	18	.370 / .366	.351	.348	2 7/8	1 7/32	1 5/8	.278
24	16	.387 / .383	.377	.374	2 15/16	1 9/32	1 5/8	.215
26	16	.418 / .414	.403	.400	3	1 5/16	1 1/2	.236
28	14	.449 / .445	.430	.427	3 3/16	1 3/8	1 1/2	.249
30	14	.480 / .476	.456	.453	3 1/4	1 7/16	1 1/2	.268

Size	Pitch Dia.		Size	Pitch Dia.		Size	Pitch Dia.	
	Max.	Min.		Max.	Min.		Max.	Min.
0 × 80	.0538	.0528	7 × 36	.1359	.1345	16 × 22	.2421	.2403
1 × 72	.066	.065	7 × 32	.1337	.1323	16 × 20	.2394	.2374
1 × 64	.065	.064	7 × 30	.1325	.131	18 × 20	.2652	.2634
2 × 64	.078	.0769	8 × 36	.1489	.1475	18 × 18	.2618	.2598
2 × 56	.0767	.0756	8 × 32	.1467	.1453	20 × 20	.2912	.2894
3 × 56	.0897	.0886	8 × 30	.1454	.144	20 × 18	.2878	.2858
3 × 48	.0879	.0868	9 × 32	.1598	.1583	22 × 18	.3138	.3118
4 × 48	.1010	.0998	9 × 30	.1584	.1569	22 × 16	.3094	.3074
4 × 40	.0984	.0972	9 × 24	.1532	.1517	24 × 18	.3398	.3378
4 × 36	.0967	.0955	10 × 30	.1716	.170	24 × 16	.3354	.3334
5 × 44	.1129	.1116	10 × 32	.1729	.1713	26 × 16	.3614	.3594
5 × 40	.1115	.1102	10 × 24	.166	.1647	26 × 14	.3557	.3537
5 × 36	.1098	.1085	12 × 28	.1961	.1944	28 × 16	.3874	.3854
6 × 40	.1246	.1232	12 × 24	.1927	.1907	28 × 14	.3818	.3797
6 × 36	.1229	.1215	14 × 24	.2184	.2167	30 × 16	.4154	.4134
6 × 32	.1207	.1193	14 × 20	.2134	.2114	30 × 14	.4077	.4056

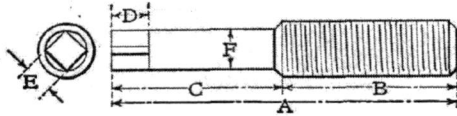

DIMENSIONS OF HAND TAPS
(WELLS BROS. CO.)

						Small Shank Taps U. S. S., Whit. and all V Taps Incl. $3\frac{1}{2}''$ over	
Size	Pitch	Total Length	Length Thread	Length Shank	Length Square	Diam. Square	Diam. Shank
		A	B	C	D	E	F
$\frac{1}{4}$	20	$2\frac{1}{4}$	$\frac{31}{32}$	$1\frac{11}{32}$	$\frac{9}{32}$	.134	.173–.175
$\frac{5}{16}$	18	$2\frac{5}{8}$	$1\frac{3}{16}$	$1\frac{7}{16}$	$1\frac{5}{16}$	.176	.228–.230
$\frac{3}{8}$	16	$2\frac{7}{8}$	$1\frac{1}{4}$	$1\frac{5}{8}$	$\frac{3}{8}$	.217	.283–.285
$\frac{7}{16}$	14	$3\frac{1}{16}$	$1\frac{3}{8}$	$1\frac{11}{16}$	$\frac{13}{32}$	.254	.330–.332
$\frac{1}{2}$	St'd	$3\frac{1}{4}$	$1\frac{3}{8}$	$1\frac{7}{8}$	$\frac{7}{16}$	.286	.373–.375
$\frac{9}{16}$	12	$3\frac{5}{8}$	$1\frac{7}{8}$	2	$\frac{15}{32}$	.321	.429
$\frac{5}{8}$	11	$3\frac{13}{16}$	$1\frac{3}{4}$	$2\frac{1}{16}$	$\frac{15}{32}$	.359	.479
$\frac{11}{16}$	11	4	$1\frac{7}{8}$	$2\frac{1}{8}$	$\frac{1}{2}$	.406	.542
$\frac{3}{4}$	10	$4\frac{1}{4}$	2	$2\frac{1}{4}$	$\frac{17}{32}$	.442	.590
$\frac{13}{16}$	10	$4\frac{7}{16}$	$2\frac{1}{8}$	$2\frac{5}{16}$	$\frac{9}{16}$	.489	.652
$\frac{7}{8}$	9	$4\frac{11}{16}$	$2\frac{1}{4}$	$2\frac{7}{16}$	$\frac{5}{8}$	.523	.697
$\frac{15}{16}$	9	$4\frac{7}{8}$	$2\frac{3}{8}$	$2\frac{1}{2}$	$\frac{11}{16}$	.569	.759
1	8	$5\frac{1}{8}$	$2\frac{7}{16}$	$2\frac{11}{16}$	$\frac{3}{4}$	.600	.800
$1\frac{1}{16}$	St'd	$5\frac{5}{16}$	$2\frac{7}{16}$	$2\frac{7}{8}$	$\frac{25}{32}$	.647	.862
$1\frac{1}{8}$	7	$5\frac{7}{16}$	$2\frac{5}{8}$	$2\frac{13}{16}$	$\frac{13}{16}$	.672	.896
$1\frac{3}{16}$	7	$5\frac{11}{16}$	$2\frac{11}{16}$	$2\frac{7}{8}$	$\frac{27}{32}$	.719	.959
$1\frac{1}{4}$	7	$5\frac{11}{16}$	$2\frac{3}{4}$	$2\frac{15}{16}$	$\frac{7}{8}$	.766	1.021
$1\frac{5}{16}$	St'd	$5\frac{13}{16}$	$2\frac{13}{16}$	3	$1\frac{1}{16}$	.813	1.084
$1\frac{3}{8}$	6	6	$2\frac{7}{8}$	$3\frac{1}{8}$	$1\frac{1}{16}$	.831	1.108
$1\frac{7}{16}$	6	$6\frac{1}{8}$	$2\frac{15}{16}$	$3\frac{3}{16}$	1	.878	1.170
$1\frac{1}{2}$	6	$6\frac{1}{4}$	3	$3\frac{1}{4}$	1	.925	1.233
$1\frac{9}{16}$	St'd	$6\frac{7}{16}$	$3\frac{1}{16}$	$3\frac{3}{8}$	$1\frac{1}{16}$	.971	1.296
$1\frac{5}{8}$	St'd	$6\frac{9}{16}$	$3\frac{1}{8}$	$3\frac{7}{16}$	$1\frac{3}{16}$	.978	1.305
$1\frac{11}{16}$	St'd	$6\frac{11}{16}$	$3\frac{3}{16}$	$3\frac{1}{2}$	$1\frac{1}{4}$	1.025	1.367
$1\frac{3}{4}$	5	$6\frac{13}{16}$	$3\frac{1}{4}$	$3\frac{9}{16}$	$1\frac{1}{4}$	1.072	1.430
$1\frac{13}{16}$	5	7	$3\frac{5}{16}$	$3\frac{11}{16}$	$1\frac{5}{16}$	1.119	1.492
$1\frac{7}{8}$	St'd	$7\frac{1}{8}$	$3\frac{3}{8}$	$3\frac{3}{4}$	$1\frac{5}{16}$	1.139	1.519
$1\frac{15}{16}$	St'd	$7\frac{1}{4}$	$3\frac{7}{16}$	$3\frac{13}{16}$	1	1.186	1.582
2	$4\frac{1}{2}$	$7\frac{3}{8}$	$3\frac{1}{2}$	$3\frac{7}{8}$	1	1.233	1.644
$2\frac{1}{8}$	$4\frac{1}{2}$	$7\frac{11}{16}$	$3\frac{5}{8}$	$4\frac{1}{16}$	1	1.327	1.769
$2\frac{1}{4}$	St'd	$7\frac{3}{4}$	$3\frac{3}{4}$	$4\frac{1}{16}$	$1\frac{1}{16}$	1.421	1.894
$2\frac{3}{8}$	St'd	$8\frac{1}{4}$	$3\frac{7}{8}$	$4\frac{3}{8}$	$1\frac{1}{16}$	1.514	2.019
$2\frac{1}{2}$	4	$8\frac{1}{2}$	4	$4\frac{1}{2}$	$1\frac{3}{16}$	1.575	2.100
$2\frac{5}{8}$	4	$8\frac{13}{16}$	$4\frac{1}{8}$	$4\frac{11}{16}$	1	1.668	2.225
$2\frac{3}{4}$	St'd	$9\frac{1}{16}$	$4\frac{1}{4}$	$4\frac{13}{16}$	$1\frac{3}{16}$	1.762	2.350
$2\frac{7}{8}$	St'd	$9\frac{3}{8}$	$4\frac{3}{8}$	5	$1\frac{9}{16}$	1.856	2.475
3	$3\frac{1}{2}$	$9\frac{5}{8}$	$4\frac{1}{2}$	$5\frac{1}{8}$	$1\frac{9}{16}$	1.906	2.542

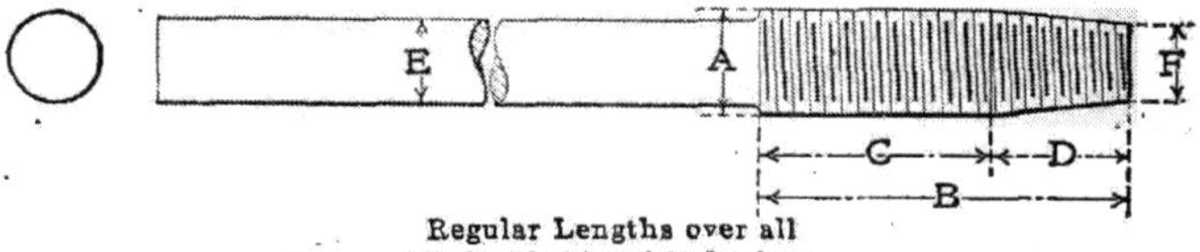

Regular Lengths over all are 11, 12, 14 and 15 Inches.

DIMENSIONS OF TAPPER TAPS

Diameter of Tap	Number of Threads per Inch		Length of Thread	Length of Straight Part	Length of Chamfered Part	Diameter of Shank E		Diameter of Point F		No. of Flutes
A	U. S. St'd	V. St'd	B	C	D	U. S. St'd	V. St'd	U. S. St'd	V. St'd	
1/4	20	20	1 3/4	1 1/8	5/8	0.170	0.150	0.179	0.158	4
5/16	18	18	2	1 1/4	3/4	0.225	0.200	0.234	0.210	4
3/8	16	16	2	1 1/4	3/4	0.280	0.250	0.287	0.261	4
7/16	14	14	2 1/4	1 3/8	7/8	0.330	0.300	0.338	0.307	4
1/2	13	12	2 1/4	1 3/8	7/8	0.385	0.340	0.393	0.348	4
9/16	12	12	2 1/2	1 1/2	1	0.440	0.400	0.446	0.411	4
5/8	11	11	2 1/2	1 1/2	1	0.490	0.455	0.499	0.462	4
11/16	11	11	2 1/2	1 1/2	1	0.555	0.515	0.561	0.523	4
3/4	10	10	2 3/4	1 5/8	1 1/8	0.605	0.560	0.611	0.570	4
13/16	10	10	2 3/4	1 5/8	1 1/8	0.670	0.625	0.673	0.631	4
7/8	9	9	3	1 3/4	1 1/4	0.720	0.675	0.722	0.675	4
15/16	9	9	3	1 3/4	1 1/4	0.780	0.730	0.783	0.736	4
1	8	8	3 1/2	2	1 1/2	0.820	0.770	0.828	0.775	4
1 1/8	7	7	3 1/2	2	1 1/2	0.925	0.860	0.928	0.869	4
1 1/4	7	7	3 1/2	2	1 1/2	1.050	0.985	1.053	0.993	4
1 3/8	6	6	4	2 3/8	1 5/8	1.145	1.070	1.147	1.075	4
1 1/2	6	6	4	2 3/8	1 5/8	1.270	1.195	1.272	1.200	4

NOTE. — Tapper taps differ from machine taps in not having a square on the end of the shank. They are used in nut tapping machines, the nuts being run over the tap on to the shank and when full the tap is removed and the nuts slid off. The tap is then replaced for another lot of nuts.

Dimensions of Briggs Standard Pipe Taps
(Wells Bros. Co.)

Size	Th'ds per Inch	Length					Diameter					Thds.	Flute	Straight	
		A	B	C	D	E	F	G	H	J	K			Outside	Pitch
$\frac{1}{8}$	27	$2\frac{1}{8}$	$\frac{3}{4}$	$1\frac{3}{8}$	$\frac{3}{8}$	$\frac{3}{32}$	.373	.309	.420	$\frac{5}{16}$	.234	27	4	.402	.374
$\frac{1}{4}$	18	$2\frac{7}{16}$	$1\frac{1}{16}$	$1\frac{3}{8}$	$\frac{7}{16}$	$\frac{3}{16}$	.493	.397	.559	$\frac{7}{16}$	.328	18	4	.536	.494
$\frac{3}{8}$	18	$2\frac{9}{16}$	$1\frac{1}{16}$	$1\frac{1}{2}$	$\frac{1}{2}$	$\frac{3}{16}$	.628	.532	.694	$\frac{9}{16}$	.421	18	4	.670	.628
$\frac{1}{2}$	14	$3\frac{1}{8}$	$1\frac{3}{8}$	$1\frac{3}{4}$	$\frac{5}{8}$	$\frac{7}{32}$	.779	.656	.865	$\frac{11}{16}$	.515	14	4	.834	.780
$\frac{3}{4}$	14	$3\frac{1}{4}$	$1\frac{3}{8}$	$1\frac{7}{8}$	$\frac{11}{16}$	$\frac{7}{32}$	.989	.866	1.075	$\frac{29}{32}$	.679	14	4	1.043	.989
1	$11\frac{1}{2}$	$3\frac{3}{4}$	$1\frac{3}{4}$	2	$\frac{13}{16}$	$\frac{1}{4}$	1.240	1.091	1.350	$1\frac{1}{8}$	.843	$11\frac{1}{2}$	5	1.305	1.240
$1\frac{1}{4}$	$11\frac{1}{2}$	4	$1\frac{3}{4}$	$2\frac{1}{4}$	$\frac{15}{16}$	$\frac{1}{4}$	1.584	1.434	1.693	$1\frac{5}{16}$	.984	$11\frac{1}{2}$	5	1.648	1.583
$1\frac{1}{2}$	$11\frac{1}{2}$	$4\frac{1}{4}$	$1\frac{3}{4}$	$2\frac{1}{2}$	1	$\frac{1}{4}$	1.822	1.672	1.932	$1\frac{1}{2}$	1.125	$11\frac{1}{2}$	6	1.888	1.823
2	$11\frac{1}{2}$	$4\frac{1}{2}$	$1\frac{3}{4}$	$2\frac{3}{4}$	$1\frac{1}{8}$	$\frac{1}{4}$	2.297	2.147	2.405	$1\frac{7}{8}$	1.406	$11\frac{1}{2}$	6	2.361	2.296
$2\frac{1}{2}$	8	$5\frac{1}{2}$	$2\frac{9}{16}$	$2\frac{15}{16}$	$1\frac{1}{4}$	$\frac{3}{8}$	2.761	2.545	2.921	$2\frac{1}{4}$	1.687	8	6	2.850	2.756
3	8	6	$2\frac{5}{8}$	$3\frac{3}{8}$	$1\frac{3}{8}$	$\frac{3}{8}$	3.383	3.167	3.547	$2\frac{5}{8}$	1.968	8	6	3.472	3.378
$3\frac{1}{2}$	8	$6\frac{1}{2}$	$2\frac{11}{16}$	$3\frac{13}{16}$	$1\frac{1}{2}$	$\frac{3}{8}$	3.879	3.663	4.047	$2\frac{13}{16}$	2.150	8	6	3.969	3.875
4	8	$6\frac{3}{4}$	$2\frac{3}{4}$	4	$1\frac{5}{8}$	$\frac{3}{8}$	4.375	4.159	4.547	3	2.250	8	6	4.465	4.371

Taper $\frac{3}{4}''$ per foot = $\frac{1}{16}''$ per inch.
"F" = Diameter at point before plugging.

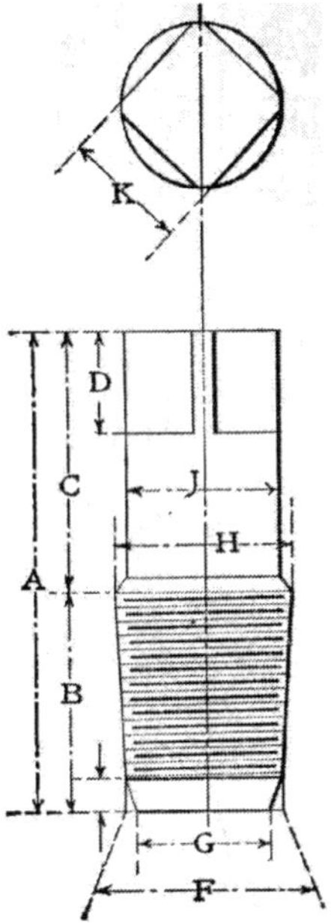

STOVE BOLT TAPS (WELLS BROS. CO.)

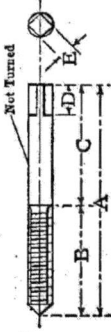

Size	No. Th'ds per Inch	Size Stock Used	Outside Diameter Max.	Min.	Pitch Diameter Max.	Min.	Root Dia.	Width of Flat at Root	A	B	C	D	E
$\frac{1}{8}$	32	.147	.127	.125	.120	.118	.097	.0063 20 U.S.S.	$1\frac{31}{32}$	$1\frac{3}{16}$	$1\frac{5}{32}$	$\frac{7}{32}$	.112
$\frac{5}{32}$	28	.174	.168	.166	.152	.150	.120	.0069 18 U.S.S.	$2\frac{7}{32}$	$2\frac{7}{32}$	$1\frac{3}{8}$	$\frac{1}{4}$	.131
$\frac{3}{16}$	24	.215	.202	.200	.182	.180	.150	.0078 16 U.S.S.	$2\frac{13}{32}$	$3\frac{1}{32}$	$1\frac{7}{16}$	$\frac{1}{4}$	.159
$\frac{7}{32}$	22	.252	.229	.227	.206	.204	.160	.0089 14 U.S.S.	$2\frac{1}{2}$	1	$1\frac{1}{2}$	$\frac{9}{32}$	.189
$\frac{1}{4}$	18	.278	.263	.260	.233	.231	.194	.0114 11 U.S.S.	$2\frac{1}{2}$	$3\frac{1}{32}$	$1\frac{17}{32}$	$\frac{9}{32}$	.207
$\frac{5}{16}$	18	.328	.320	.317	.2907	.2887	.249	.0104 12 U.S.S.	$2\frac{5}{8}$	$1\frac{1}{16}$	$1\frac{9}{16}$	$\frac{5}{16}$	.246
$\frac{3}{8}$	16	.370	.355	.352	.320	.318	.278	.0125 10 U.S.S.	$2\frac{7}{8}$	$1\frac{1}{4}$	$1\frac{5}{8}$	$\frac{3}{8}$	.278

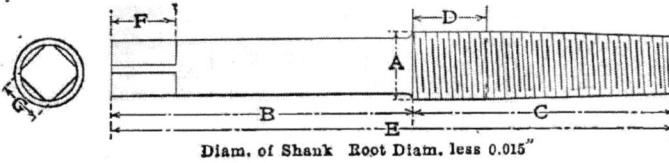

Diam. of Shank   Root Diam. less 0.015"

DIMENSIONS OF TAPER DIE TAPS

Diameter of Tap	Length of Shank	Length of Thread	Length of Straight Thread	Total Length	Length of Square	Size of Square	Number of Flutes
A	B	C	D	E	F	G	
$\frac{1}{4}$	$1\frac{1}{2}$	2	$\frac{1}{4}$	$3\frac{1}{2}$	$\frac{9}{16}$	$\frac{1}{8}$	5
$\frac{5}{16}$	$1\frac{1}{2}$	$2\frac{1}{4}$	$\frac{5}{16}$	4	$\frac{5}{8}$	$\frac{5}{32}$	5
$\frac{3}{8}$	$1\frac{1}{2}$	3	$\frac{3}{8}$	$4\frac{1}{2}$	$\frac{11}{16}$	$\frac{3}{16}$	5
$\frac{7}{16}$	$1\frac{3}{4}$	$3\frac{1}{2}$	$\frac{7}{16}$	5	$\frac{11}{16}$	$\frac{1}{4}$	5
$\frac{1}{2}$	2	$3\frac{1}{2}$	$\frac{1}{2}$	$5\frac{1}{2}$	$\frac{3}{4}$	$\frac{9}{32}$	5
$\frac{9}{16}$	$2\frac{1}{4}$	$3\frac{3}{4}$	$\frac{9}{16}$	6	$\frac{13}{16}$	$\frac{5}{16}$	5
$\frac{5}{8}$	$2\frac{1}{2}$	4	$\frac{5}{8}$	$6\frac{1}{2}$	$\frac{15}{16}$	$\frac{11}{32}$	6
$\frac{11}{16}$	$2\frac{3}{4}$	$4\frac{1}{4}$	$\frac{11}{16}$	7	$\frac{7}{8}$	$\frac{7}{16}$	6
$\frac{3}{4}$	3	$4\frac{1}{2}$	$\frac{3}{4}$	$7\frac{1}{2}$	$\frac{7}{8}$	$\frac{7}{16}$	6
$\frac{13}{16}$	$3\frac{1}{4}$	$4\frac{3}{4}$	$\frac{13}{16}$	8	$\frac{15}{16}$	$\frac{1}{2}$	6
$\frac{7}{8}$	$3\frac{1}{2}$	5	$\frac{7}{8}$	$8\frac{1}{2}$	1	$\frac{1}{2}$	6
$\frac{15}{16}$	$3\frac{1}{2}$	$5\frac{1}{4}$	$\frac{15}{16}$	$8\frac{3}{4}$	1	$\frac{9}{16}$	6
1	$3\frac{1}{2}$	$5\frac{1}{2}$	1	9	$1\frac{1}{16}$	$\frac{5}{8}$	6
$1\frac{1}{8}$	$3\frac{1}{2}$	$5\frac{3}{4}$	$1\frac{1}{8}$	$9\frac{1}{4}$	$1\frac{1}{8}$	$\frac{11}{16}$	6
$1\frac{1}{4}$	$3\frac{1}{2}$	6	$1\frac{1}{4}$	$9\frac{1}{2}$	$1\frac{3}{16}$	$\frac{3}{4}$	7
$1\frac{3}{8}$	$3\frac{3}{8}$	$6\frac{1}{4}$	$1\frac{3}{8}$	$9\frac{3}{4}$	$1\frac{5}{16}$	$\frac{13}{16}$	7
$1\frac{1}{2}$	$3\frac{3}{8}$	$6\frac{3}{8}$	$1\frac{1}{2}$	10	$1\frac{3}{8}$	$\frac{15}{16}$	7
$1\frac{5}{8}$	$3\frac{3}{8}$	$6\frac{5}{8}$	$1\frac{5}{8}$	$10\frac{1}{4}$	$1\frac{7}{16}$	1	7
$1\frac{3}{4}$	$3\frac{3}{8}$	$6\frac{3}{4}$	$1\frac{3}{4}$	$10\frac{1}{2}$	$1\frac{1}{2}$	$1\frac{1}{16}$	8
$1\frac{7}{8}$	$3\frac{3}{8}$	$7\frac{1}{8}$	$1\frac{7}{8}$	$10\frac{3}{4}$	$1\frac{5}{8}$	$1\frac{1}{8}$	8
2	$3\frac{3}{8}$	$7\frac{7}{8}$	2	11	$1\frac{11}{16}$	$1\frac{1}{4}$	8

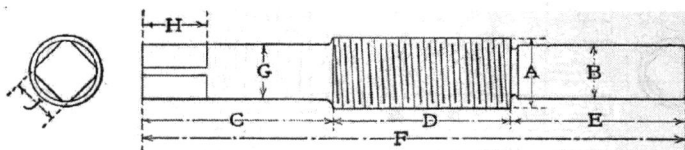

DIMENSIONS OF SELLERS HOBS

Diameter of Hob	Number of Threads per Inch		Diameter of Pilot B		Length of Shank	Length of Thread	Length of Pilot	Total Length	Diameter of Shank G		Length of Square	Size of Square	No. of Flutes
A	U.S. St'd	V. St'd	U.S. St'd	V. St'd	C	D	E	F	U.S.St'd	V. St'd	H	J	
$\frac{1}{4}$	20	20	$\frac{3}{16}$	$\frac{5}{32}$	2	$1\frac{1}{8}$	$1\frac{1}{8}$	$4\frac{1}{4}$	0.170	0.150	$\frac{3}{4}$	$\frac{1}{8}$	6
$\frac{5}{16}$	18	18	$\frac{3}{16}$	$\frac{3}{16}$	2	$1\frac{1}{4}$	$1\frac{1}{4}$	$4\frac{1}{2}$	0.225	0.200	$\frac{3}{4}$	$\frac{3}{32}$	6
$\frac{3}{8}$	16	16	$\frac{1}{4}$	$\frac{1}{4}$	$2\frac{1}{8}$	$1\frac{7}{16}$	$1\frac{7}{16}$	5	0.280	0.250	$\frac{3}{4}$	$\frac{3}{16}$	6
$\frac{7}{16}$	14	14	$\frac{5}{16}$	$\frac{1}{4}$	$2\frac{1}{8}$	$1\frac{9}{16}$	$1\frac{9}{16}$	$5\frac{1}{4}$	0.330	0.300	$\frac{13}{16}$	$\frac{1}{4}$	6
$\frac{1}{2}$	13	12	$\frac{3}{8}$	$\frac{5}{16}$	$2\frac{1}{8}$	$1\frac{11}{16}$	$1\frac{11}{16}$	$5\frac{3}{4}$	0.385	0.340	$\frac{13}{16}$	$\frac{5}{32}$	8
$\frac{9}{16}$	12	12	$\frac{3}{8}$	$\frac{3}{8}$	$2\frac{1}{4}$	$1\frac{7}{8}$	$1\frac{7}{8}$	6	0.440	0.400	$\frac{7}{8}$	$\frac{1}{4}$	8
$\frac{5}{8}$	11	11	$\frac{1}{2}$	$\frac{3}{8}$	$2\frac{1}{4}$	$2\frac{1}{8}$	$2\frac{1}{8}$	$6\frac{1}{2}$	0.490	0.455	$\frac{7}{8}$	$\frac{11}{32}$	8
$\frac{11}{16}$	11	11	$\frac{1}{2}$	$\frac{1}{2}$	$2\frac{1}{4}$	$2\frac{1}{8}$	$2\frac{1}{8}$	7	0.555	0.515	$\frac{7}{8}$	$\frac{3}{32}$	8
$\frac{3}{4}$	10	10	$\frac{1}{2}$	$\frac{1}{2}$	$2\frac{1}{2}$	$2\frac{1}{2}$	$2\frac{1}{2}$	$7\frac{1}{2}$	0.605	0.560	$\frac{7}{8}$	$\frac{7}{16}$	8
$\frac{13}{16}$	10	10	$\frac{1}{2}$	$\frac{1}{2}$	$2\frac{1}{2}$	$2\frac{3}{4}$	$2\frac{3}{4}$	8	0.670	0.625	$\frac{15}{16}$	$\frac{1}{2}$	8
$\frac{7}{8}$	9	9	$\frac{11}{16}$	$\frac{1}{2}$	$2\frac{1}{2}$	3	3	$8\frac{1}{2}$	0.715	0.675	$\frac{15}{16}$	$\frac{1}{2}$	8
$\frac{15}{16}$	9	9	$\frac{11}{16}$	$\frac{11}{16}$	$2\frac{1}{2}$	$3\frac{1}{4}$	$3\frac{1}{4}$	9	0.780	0.730	1	$\frac{9}{16}$	10
1	8	8	$\frac{11}{16}$	$\frac{11}{16}$	$2\frac{5}{8}$	$3\frac{7}{16}$	$3\frac{7}{16}$	$9\frac{1}{2}$	0.825	0.770	1	$\frac{5}{8}$	10
$1\frac{1}{8}$	7	7	$\frac{7}{8}$	$\frac{11}{16}$	$2\frac{5}{8}$	$3\frac{9}{16}$	$3\frac{9}{16}$	$9\frac{3}{4}$	0.925	0.860	$1\frac{1}{16}$	$\frac{11}{16}$	10
$1\frac{1}{4}$	7	7	$\frac{7}{8}$	$\frac{7}{8}$	$2\frac{5}{8}$	$3\frac{11}{16}$	$3\frac{11}{16}$	10	1.050	0.985	$1\frac{1}{16}$	$\frac{3}{4}$	10
$1\frac{3}{8}$	6	6	$1\frac{1}{16}$	$\frac{7}{8}$	$2\frac{5}{8}$	$3\frac{13}{16}$	$3\frac{13}{16}$	$10\frac{1}{2}$	1.145	1.070	$1\frac{1}{8}$	$\frac{13}{16}$	10
$1\frac{1}{2}$	6	6	$1\frac{1}{16}$	$1\frac{1}{16}$	$2\frac{5}{8}$	$4\frac{1}{8}$	$4\frac{1}{8}$	11	1.270	1.200	$1\frac{3}{16}$	$\frac{15}{16}$	10
$1\frac{5}{8}$	$5\frac{1}{2}$	5	$1\frac{5}{16}$	$1\frac{1}{8}$	$2\frac{3}{4}$	$4\frac{3}{8}$	$4\frac{3}{8}$	$11\frac{1}{2}$	1.375	1.265	$1\frac{1}{4}$	1	12
$1\frac{3}{4}$	5	5	$1\frac{5}{16}$	$1\frac{5}{16}$	$2\frac{3}{4}$	$4\frac{5}{8}$	$4\frac{5}{8}$	12	1.475	1.390	$1\frac{1}{4}$	$1\frac{1}{16}$	12
$1\frac{7}{8}$	5	$4\frac{1}{2}$	$1\frac{1}{2}$	$1\frac{5}{16}$	$2\frac{3}{4}$	$4\frac{7}{8}$	$4\frac{7}{8}$	$12\frac{1}{2}$	1.600	1.475	$1\frac{5}{16}$	$1\frac{1}{8}$	12
2	$4\frac{1}{2}$	$4\frac{1}{2}$	$1\frac{1}{2}$	$1\frac{1}{2}$	$2\frac{3}{4}$	$5\frac{1}{8}$	$5\frac{1}{8}$	13	1.700	1.600	$1\frac{3}{8}$	$1\frac{1}{4}$	12

NOTE. — The Sellers hob is designed to be run on centers, the work, such as hand or die chasers, being held against it and fed along by the lathe carriage.

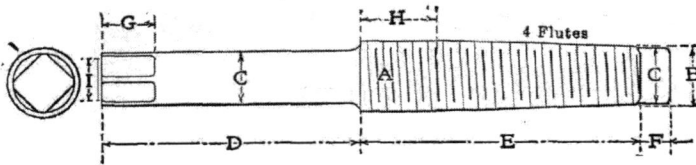

STANDARD SQUARE-THREAD TAPS

Size	A	B	C	D	E	F	G	H	I
Diameter ⅝".. (1)	35/64	1/2	1/2	3 5/8	3 1/4	1/2	9/16	5/8	7/16
(2)	19/32	17/32	1/2	3 5/8	3 1/4	1/2	9/16	5/8	7/16
Pitch 8 ...... (3)	5/8	21/64	1/2	3 5/8	3 1/4	1/2	9/16	5/8	7/16
Diameter ¾".. (1)	41/64	37/64	87/64	3 3/4	3 3/8	1/2	3/4	3/4	7/16
(2)	45/64	5/8	55/64	3 3/4	3 3/8	1/2	3/4	3/4	7/16
Pitch 6 ...... (3)	3/4	11/16	55/64	3 3/4	3 3/8	1/2	3/4	3/4	7/16
Diameter ⅞".. (1)	3/4	21/32	21/32	4	3 3/4	1/2	13/16	7/8	1/2
(2)	13/16	47/64	31/32	4	3 3/4	1/2	13/16	7/8	1/2
Pitch 4½ ..... (3)	7/8	51/64	31/32	4	3 3/4	1/2	13/16	7/8	1/2
Diameter 1".. (1)	57/64	51/64	51/64	4 1/2	4 1/4	1/2	15/16	1	5/8
(2)	61/64	7/8	51/64	4 1/2	4 1/4	1/2	15/16	1	5/8
Lead D'BL ⅔" (3)	1	15/16	51/64	4 1/2	4 1/4	1/2	15/16	1	5/8
Diameter 1⅛.. (1)	61/64	55/64	55/64	4 3/4	4 3/8	1/2	1	1 1/8	11/16
(2)	1 3/32	15/16	55/64	4 3/4	4 3/8	1/2	1	1 1/8	11/16
(3)	1 5/64	1 1/64	55/64	4 3/4	4 3/8	1/2	1	1 1/8	11/16
Pitch 3½ ...... (4)	1 1/8	1 1/16	55/64	4 3/4	4 3/8	1/2	1	1 1/8	11/16
Diameter 1⅜". (1)	1 13/64	1 1/8	1 1/8	5 1/4	4 5/8	5/8	1 1/8	1 3/8	7/8
(2)	1 9/32	1 3/16	1 1/8	5 1/4	4 5/8	5/8	1 1/8	1 3/8	7/8
(3)	1 21/64	1 11/64	1 1/8	5 1/4	4 5/8	5/8	1 1/8	1 3/8	7/8
Lead D'BL ½" (4)	1 3/8	1 5/16	1 1/8	5 1/4	4 5/8	5/8	1 1/8	1 3/8	7/8

NOTE. — While in theory the thread and the space are both one half the pitch in practice it is necessary to make the thread a little more than half in order to allow clearance for the screw that goes into the threaded hole. The amount of this clearance depends on the character of the work and varies from .001 inch up. Some also make the tap so that the screw will only bear on the top or bottom and the sides.

FILES

FILES are designated both by the spacing of their teeth and the shape or cross-section of steel on which the teeth are cut; the size always referring to their length which is measured from the point cutting to the end of the file proper but the measurement never includes the tang which fits into the handle.

TERMS USED

The back of a file is the convex or rounding side of half-round, cabinet and other files having a similar shape.

A file is Bellied when it is full or large in the center.

A Blunt file is the same size its whole length instead of being tapered.

An Equalling file is one which looks blunt but which has a slight belly or curve from joint to tang.

A Float file is a coarse single cut made for use on soft metals or wood and frequently used by plumbers.

A Safe-edge is an edge left smooth or blank so that the file will not cut if it strikes against the side of a slot or similar work.

The Tang is the small pointed end forged down for fitting into the handle.

Three square files are double cut and have teeth only on the sides, while taper saw files are usually single cut and have teeth on the edge as well as the sides. This makes the taper saw files broad on the edge or without sharp corners, while the three square files have very sharp corners.

A special angle tooth file is made for brass work. The first cut is square across the file, while the second is at quite an acute angle, about 60 degrees from the first cut.

Doctor files are very similar to these except that the first cut is about 15 degrees instead of being square across the file.

A lock file has safe edge and the teeth only go about one third the way across from each side leaving the center blank. The teeth are single cut.

HIGHT OF WORK

The work should be at a convenient hight which will usually vary from 40 to 44 inches for most men with an average of 42 inches. This means the hight of the work, not the bench.

PICKLING BATH

A good pickle to soften and loosen the scale on cast iron before filing is made of two or three parts of water to one part of sulphuric acid. Immerse castings for a short time.

For brass castings use a pickle of five parts water to one part nitric acid.

78

ROUGH

MIDDLE

HALF WAY

BASTARD

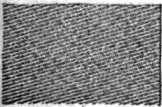

SECOND CUT

SMOOTH

Actual Tooth Spacing of Single Cut Files

ROUGH

MIDDLE

BASTARD

SECOND CUT

SMOOTH

DEAD SMOOTH

Actual Tooth Spacing of Double Cut Files

FILES

78

ROUGH

MIDDLE

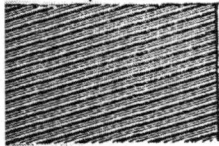

HALF WAY

BASTARD

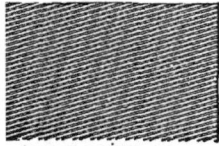

SECOND CUT

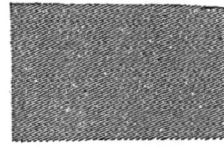

SMOOTH

Actual Tooth Spacing of Single Cut Files

ROUGH

MIDDLE

BASTARD

SECOND CUT

SMOOTH

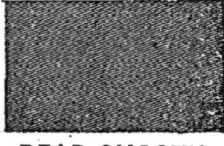

DEAD SMOOTH

Actual Tooth Spacing of Double Cut Files

The Teeth of Files

The cut of a file or the number of teeth per inch vary with the length of the file itself and the kind of a file, and is a little confusing, as a rough cut in a small file may be as fine as a second cut of a larger size. The cuts used on regular 12-inch files are shown in the illustration and represents the practice of Henry Disston & Sons. The same makers also supply the table of cuts per inch used on their machines, which are as follows. •

Regular Taper Files

Length, inches. — 2½, 3, 3½, 4, 4½, 5, 5½, 6, 6½, 7, 8, 9, 10,
Teeth per inch — 64, 56, 52, 50, 48, 46, 44, 42, 42, 40, 38, 36, 34.
Slim Tapers — 64, 64, 60, 58, 56, 52, 50, 50, 46, 46, 44, 40, 38.

Mill File, Bastard Cut

Length — 4, 5, 6, 7, 8, 9, 10, 11, 12, 13, 14, 15, 16, 17, 18, 20 in.
Teeth — 56, 50, 48, 46, 44, 42, 40, 38, 36, 34, 32, 30, 28, 26, 24, 22
per inch.

Flat File, Bastard Cut

48, 42, 38, 36, 32, 30, 26, 24, 22, 20, 20, 18, 18, 16, 16, 14.
Single cut files usually have teeth at about 25 degrees and in double cut files the other cut is usually from 45 to 50 degrees. Fine machinists files are made in ten numbers from 00 to 8.

The Shapes of Files

In the following pages the shapes of standard files are shown. The names are as follows:

1. Metal saw — blunt.
2. Three-square or triangular.
3. Barrette.
4. Slitting.
5. Square.
6. Round or rat-tail.
7. Pippin.
8 Knife.
9. Crossing.
10. Half-round.
11. Crochet.
12. Warding.
13. Extra narrow pillar.
14. Narrow pillar.
15 Pillar.
16 Hand.

Files are cut in two ways, single and double The first has but a single line of cuts across the surface, at an angle with the file body but parallel to each other. The double-cut file has two lines of cuts, at an angle with each other, and the second cut being usually finer than the first. Some prefer the single cut, for filing in the lathe. Rasps have single teeth forced up with a punch.

The old method of designating the cuts were rough, coarse, bastard, second cut, smooth and dead smooth. . Some makers are now using a series of numbers — usually eight to ten — instead of the six designations by name formerly employed. The uses of the various cuts depend on the shop in question and must be learned from observation and experience in each case.

The grades of cut used by them run from No 00 to No. 8, and while it is hard to exactly compare them with the old-style designations, it will be found that No. 00 is about the same as a bastard, No. 1 as a second cut, No. 2 or 3 with a smooth, and Nos. 6 to 8 with a dead smooth file.

1

2

3

4

5

6

7

8

9

10

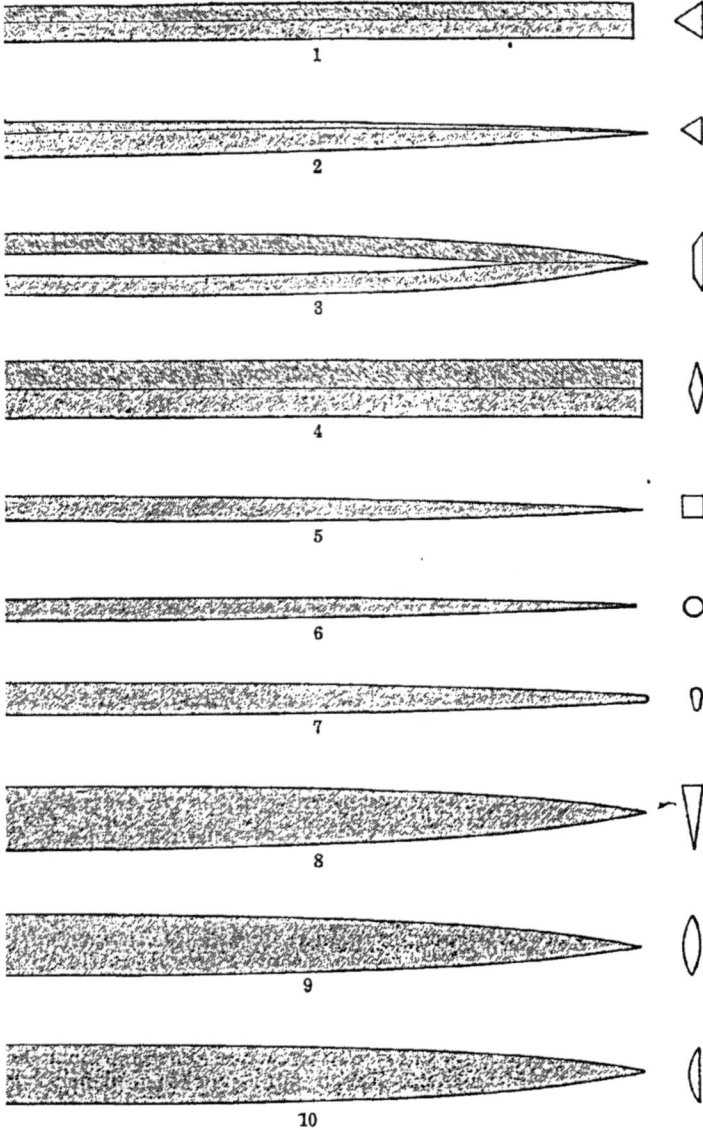

The Standard Shapes of Files

11

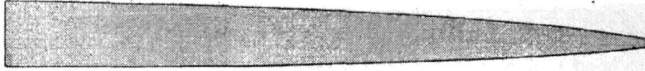

12

13

14

15

16

The Standard Shapes of Files

WHEN A FILE CUTS BEST

One who has given the matter careful attention, and has built file-testing machines, Edward G. Herbert, of Manchester, England, has come to the conclusion that a file does not cut best when it is new but after it has been used for some little time, say 2500 strokes or the filing away of one cubic inch of metal. Another curious feature is that its usefulness seems to come to a sudden instead of a gradual end.

A bastard file having 25 teeth to the inch, operating on a surface one inch square with a pressure of 30 pounds, which is about equal to heavy hand filing, gives 25 cutting edges about one inch long, which likens it somewhat to a broad cutting tool in a planer.

In cutting a file the metal is forced up in a sort of a bur, and occasionally the top of the tooth slopes over backward which is the reason that a file often cuts better after these are broken or worn off. Then, too, when a file is new all the teeth are not of the same hight and only a few points cut. As they wear down more teeth come into contact and do more work.

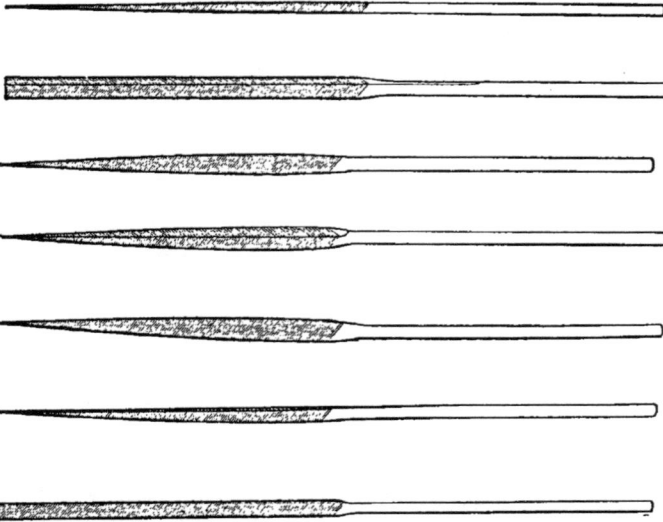

Needle Files for Fine Work

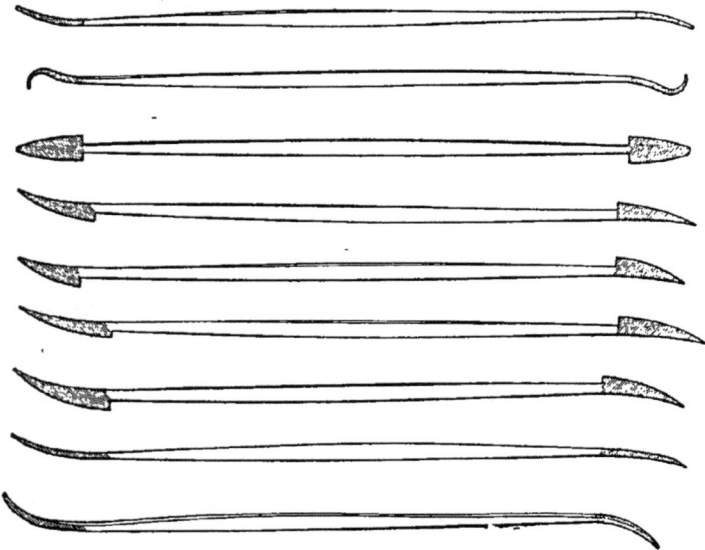

Die Sinkers Files or Riffles

WORK BENCHES

THE duties of a bench vary with the shop in which it is located according to the work that is to be done on it or at it. If it is simply a filing bench, the main requirement is that it support a vise firmly and at the proper hight. If an assembling bench, these are not the important features, and just what it does need depends on the kind of work being handled.

For the average shop work we want a bench that is rigid; that will stand chipping and filing; that can be used in testing work on a surface plate or in handling jigs and fixtures; that will not splinter badly nor yet injure a tool should it happen to drop on it. For the toolmaker the cast-iron bench top has many advantages, but both the bench and the tool are very liable to be marred by dropping the tool on it, so that for general use we rely on wood as in the days of old, except that a bench with solid 2- or 3-inch planking the whole width is now too expensive to consider. We no longer want the bench braced up against the side of the shop but set it out from

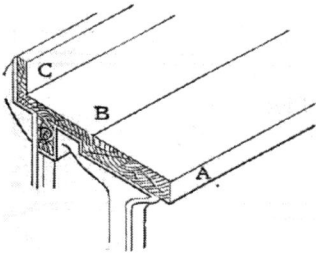

FIG. 1. Good for Ordinary Work.   FIG. 2. Another Method.

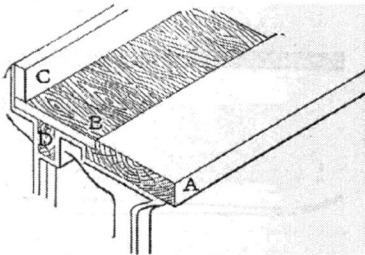

the wall to allow the heat to rise and the air to circulate, as well as giving the sprinklers a chance to get at a fire on the floor near the walls.

The use of a lighter board at the back has become so common that the New Britain Machine Company's design for a bench leg is made for this construction as shown in Fig. 1. This also shows the backboard *B* rabbeted to the plank *A*, which supports it all along the front edge, and it is also supported by the stringer *D*, which runs the whole length of the bench. These supports, in addition to the cross bearing of the legs every 6 or 8 feet, give the backboard a stiffness that was unknown where they are simply laid flush and not rabbeted and the stringer is absent.

Benches made without these supports are open to the serious objection that the backboard springs down when a heavy weight, such as a jig or surface plate, is put on the bench and throws them out of level.

All cracks are more or less of a nuisance in bench work, but in this case any shrinkage can be taken up by wedging against the iron support of the board *C* and the edge of the backboard *B*.

Another style bench with this same leg is shown in Fig. 2. Here
he front plank A and the backboard C are the same as before, but
nstead of having one backboard, this part of the bench is made up
)f narrow strips as B, fitting into rabbet in plank A and supported
)y the stringer D as before. These narrow boards can be either
ongued and grooved hardwood flooring, or can be square edges, as
)referred; in either case any shrinkage can be taken up by forcing
he boards together.

A cheaper form of bench is shown in Fig. 3, where the heavy
)lanking is entirely dispensed with and the boards B run the full
vidth of the bench as shown. Running along the front, underneath
he main boards is a soft plank A which supports the edge of the
)ench where the most work comes, and under the back is the 2 × 6-
nch stringer as before. Here, too, the boards can be either notched
)r square edge, each having its advocates; the objection raised
against the tongue and groove being that the edges are apt to split
)ff from heavy articles dropping on them. An advantage claimed
or the boards running this way is that work going on or off the

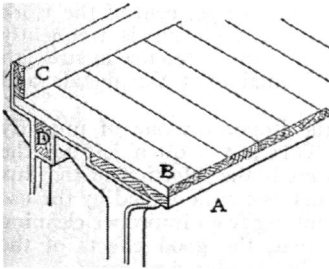

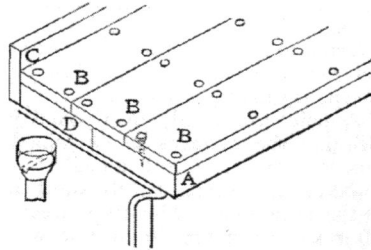

FIG. 3. A Cheaper Way.   FIG. 4. A good but
                                  expensive Construction.

)ench is always in the direction of the grain of the wood and that
'ewer splinters are formed on that account. In either Figs. 2 or 3
any local wear can be remedied by replacing the worn board with a
1ew one. Some object to the end of the grain at the front of a bench.

The material used in any of these can be varied to suit the individual requirements. Maple is generally considered the best wood
'or a bench, while others prefer ash. For the backboards hard pine
s often used and even cheaper woods will answer if necessary, al-
:hough it probably pays to use maple all through if you can afford
t.

Still another style of bench is shown in Fig. 4 and one which was
designed to be serviceable and have a long life without so much
regard to first cost as the others. The bench leg was flat on top,
the first layer of maple planks A and D and on top, narrower boards
of the same material. These were fastened with long wood screws,
holes being countered and plugged as shown.

The theory of this construction is that the boards are sure to be
more thoroughly seasoned than the planks, consequently the planks

will shrink the most and tend to draw the top boards closer together. It certainly makes a solid bench, but the first cost is rather high.

Benches are also occasionally built up from small blocks so as to present an end grain on the top, the same as butchers' blocks. One shop we know of surfaces these when worn by putting them on a Daniels' planer and substituting a circular saw for the swinging knives. This saws the top very smooth and leaves a good surface. Others glue up strips on edge and plane down to a smooth surface so as to do away with all cracks. Zinc or even heavy paper covers are often used where fine work is being assembled to prevent its finding its way into cracks and crevices.

The usual work bench is from 33 to 35 inches from the floor to the top, about 29 or 30 inches wide, and has the front plank 3 inches with backboards 1 inch thick. A cast-iron leg of this type weighs about 50 pounds.

SOLDERING

ALMOST every one thinks he can solder, yet if we examine the work carefully we will find that only about 10 per cent of the work is really done as it should be. Thorough soldering is frequently referred to as sweating, and it is remarkable the difference in strength between a well-fitted and "sweated" junction of the metals and one as ordinarily soldered.

A point frequently overlooked is the important one of properly cleaning the surfaces to be joined. This is too often left for the flux to correct. Another neglected point is the selection of the flux to be used, although nearly all of the metals can be joined by the use of the same flux. The after effects resulting from improper cleaning after soldering are frequently worse than the good effects of the soldering. This is particularly noticeable in electrical work.

For strength, fit the parts accurately. The more accurate the fitting the stronger the result. Use a solder with as high a melting point as possible. Apply the proper heat as it should be. The nearer the temperature of work to be joined is brought to the fusing point of the solder the better will be the union, since the solder will flow more readily.

Fluxes for Different Metals

There are on the market a number of fluxes or soldering salts that are giving good satisfaction. A form that is non-corrosive and very popular with electrical workers is the soldering stick in which the ingredients are molded into stick form about 1 inch diameter and 6 inches long.

The action and use of a flux in soldering are to remove and prevent the formation of an oxide during the operation of soldering, and to allow the solder to flow readily and to unite more firmly with the surfaces to be joined.

For sheet tin, on the best work rosin or colophony is used; but owing to the ease of applying and rapidity of working, zinc chloride or acid is more generally used. Beeswax can also be used, as also almost any of the pastes, fats or liquids prepared for the purpose.

For lead, a flux of oil and rosin in equal parts works very well. Tallow is also a good flux. Rosin or colophony is much used, and zinc chloride will keep the surfaces in good condition.

Lead burning is a different operation from soldering, and at the present time almost a lost art. The surfaces must be bright and free from oxide; solder is not used as a flux, but a piece of lead and rosin or oil.

For brass, zinc chloride or almost any of the soldering preparations is used. Care must be taken to remove any scale or oxide if a good joint is wanted. On new metal this is not much trouble, but on old or repair work it is sometimes exceedingly difficult. This is particularly noticeable on metal patterns that have been in use for some time. The scraper must be brought into use to remove it. Many use with considerable success an acid dip such as is commonly used by electro platers, for removing the oxide. Oily or greasy work can be cleaned by the use of potash or lye, but care must be exercised that the brass is not left too long in the solution, especially if it contains any joints previously soldered, since the action set up will dissolve the solder entirely or roughen up the joint to such an extent as to require refinishing.

For copper, the same fluxes as for brass are used. On old work it is almost always necessary to scrape the parts to be joined to get the solder to hold. A particularly difficult piece of work to solder is an old bath tub. The grease and soap form a layer that is impervious to any of the fluxes, and it must be carefully removed entirely if good work is wanted.

For zinc, use muriatic acid almost full strength or chloride of zinc solution. Zinc is the metal that has a "critical temperature" more than any other metal except the softer alloys. If the iron is overheated, the zinc is melted and a hole burned in the metal; even if this does not occur, the surface of the metal is roughened and there is formed on the soldering copper an alloy that will not flow but simply makes a pasty mass. At the correct heat the solder will flow readily and unite firmly with the metal. Especially if the work is to be painted, care should be taken to neutralize and wash off any excess of acid or soldering solution, as it is impossible to cause paint to adhere properly unless this is done.

For galvanized iron, use muriatic acid, chloride of zinc solution or rosin, and be sure to see that the acid is neutralized if the work is to be painted. Many cornices and fronts are made of this metal and are very unsightly in a short time after being painted, particularly at the joints, owing to lack of care in removing the excess flux.

An action that is not usually taken into consideration in the joining of galvanized iron or zinc with copper, as is sometimes done, is the electrical action set up by the metals if any moisture is present. This is very noticeable in cities where the acid from the atmosphere assists in the action. It will nearly always be found that the zinc or galvanized iron has been greatly injured at the places joined.

For wrought iron or steel, zinc chloride is best. The iron or steel, to make good work, should be previously freed from scale or oxide and tinned before joining. Where the oxide is not very heavy, the iron can be cleaned by brushing with muriatic acid and rubbing with a piece of zinc.

The Fluxes Themselves

The above paragraphs give the fluxes adapted to the various metals; the fluxes themselves are as follows:

Hydrochloric or muriatic acid. The ordinary commercial acid is much used in full strength or slightly diluted to solder zinc, particularly where the zinc is old or covered with an oxide. ·

Rosin or colophony, powdered, is commonly used for copper, tin and lead, and very generally by canneries and packing houses on account of its non-poisonous qualities. It is also used mixed with common olive oil. Turpentine can also be used as a flux. Beeswax is a good but expensive flux. Tallow is also used for lead pipe, but is more frequently mixed with rosin.

Palm or cocoa oil will work well, but is more generally used in the manufacture of tin plate. The common green olive oil works very well with the more fusible solders.

As expedients we can use a piece of common stearine candle or a piece of common brown rosin soap or cheap furniture varnish, which is largely composed of rosin. Paraffin, vaseline and stearine are recommended for use with some of the alloys for soldering aluminum.

Chloride of zinc, acid, or soldering liquid, is the most commonly used of all the fluxes; as usually prepared, simply dissolve as much scrap zinc in the ordinary commercial muriatic acid as it will take up. But if it is diluted with an equal quantity of water and a small quantity of sal ammoniac is added it works much better and is less likely to rust the articles soldered. If they are of iron or steel, about 2 ounces to the pint of solution is about the proper quantity of powdered sal ammoniac to add.

In preparing this solution, a glass or porcelain vessel should be used; owing to the corrosive fumes, it should be done in a well-ventilated place. Use a vessel of ample capacity, since there is considerable foaming or boiling of the mixture.

Soldering liquid, non-corrosive, is also prepared by dissolving the zinc in the acid as above and adding one fourth of the quantity of aqua ammonia to neutralize the acid, then diluting with an equal quantity of water.

Soldering liquid, neither corrosive nor poisonous. Dissolve $1\frac{1}{2}$ parts glycerin, 12 parts water, and add $1\frac{1}{2}$ parts lactic acid.

Soldering paste. When a solution of chloride is mixed with starch paste, a syrupy liquid is formed which makes a flux for soldering.

Soldering fat or paste. Melt 1 pound of tallow and add 1 pound of common olive oil. Stir in 8 ounces of powdered rosin; let this boil up and when partially cool, add with constant stirring, $\frac{1}{4}$ pint of water that has been saturated with powdered sal ammoniac. Stir constantly until cool. By adding more rosin to make it harder, this can be formed into sticks. A very good acid mixture for cleaning work to be soldered is equal parts of nitric and sulphuric acid and water. *Never pour the water into the acid.*

Cleaning and Holding Work

For copper work a dilute sulphuric acid is best. Articles of lead and zinc can be cleaned with a potash solution, but care must be exercised as the alkalies attack these metals. For zinc, a dilute solution of sulphuric or muriatic acid will clean the surface.

For cleaning or removing the oxide or other foreign material, scrapers and files are frequently used. An old file bent at the ends and with the corners flaring makes a handy tool. Grind the edge sharp and make as hard as possible.

To enable difficult points to be "filled," sometimes a small piece of moist clay pressed into shape to form the desired shape can be used to advantage as a guide for the solder. Another use of the clay is to embed the parts in, to hold them in position for soldering.

Plaster of paris is also used for this purpose, but is sometimes difficult to remove, especially in hollow pieces. A dilute solution of muriatic acid will help to get this out, however.

Castings containing aluminum are always harder to solder than other alloys. In some instances where the percentage of aluminum is high, it is necessary to copperplate the parts to be joined before a satisfactory joint can be made. In nearly every instance the work can be "stuck" together, but not actually soldered.

In metal-pattern making too little attention is given to both the fitting of the parts and the selection of the solder to joint the work. A good grade should always be used, and it must be borne in mind that the higher the melting point of the solder the stronger the joint.

A very good job of soldering can be done on work that will permit of it by carefully fitting the parts, laying a piece of tin foil, covered on both sides with a flux, between the parts to be joined and pressing them tightly together. Heat until the foil is melted. This is very good in joining broken parts of brass and bronze work. If they fit well together, they can frequently be joined in this manner so that the joint is very strong and almost imperceptible.

Soldering Cast Iron

For cast iron, the flux is usually regarded as a secret. A number of methods are in use; one of the oldest and least satisfactory is to brush the surfaces thoroughly with a brass scratch brush. Brush until the surface is coated with brass, then tin this surface and solder as usual. If plating facilities are to be had, copperplate the parts and solder together. This method has been used very successfully for a number of years.

A fair substitute for the above is to clean the surfaces thoroughly and copperplate them with a solution of sulphate of copper: about ounce sulphate of copper, ½ pint water, ½ ounce sulphuric acid. Brush this solution on or dip into the solution, rinse off and dry it well before soldering.

Another method is to tin the cast iron. To do this, first remove all scale until the surface is clean and bright. The easiest way to do this is with the emery wheel. Dip in a lye to remove any grease, and rinse the lye off; then dip into muriatic acid of the usual strength.

Then go over the surface with rosin and a half and half solder. It may be necessary to dip into the acid several times to get the piece thoroughly tinned. Rubbing the surface of the iron with a piece of zinc while the acid is still on it will facilitate the tinning.

Another method of soldering cast iron is to clean the surface as in the previous operation and then brush over with chloride of zinc solution and sprinkle powdered sal ammoniac on it; then heat until. the sal ammoniac smokes. Dip into melted tin and remove the surplus; repeat if not thoroughly tinned. Half tin and half lead works well as a solder for this.

Commutator wires and electrical connections should never be soldered by using an acid solution, owing to the corrosive action afterward. A good flux is an alcoholic solution of rosin.

Cold Soldering for Metals, Glass, Porcelain, etc.

Precipitate the copper from a solution of the sulphate by putting in strips of zinc. Place the copper powder in a porcelain or wedgewood mortar and mix it with from 20 to 30 parts of sulphuric acid of 1.85 degrees Baumé. Then add 70 parts of mercury when well mixed, wash well with water to remove the excess of acid and allow it to cool. To use it, heat it and pound it well in an iron mortar until it becomes plastic. It can then be used and adheres very firmly when cold. No flux is needed, but the surfaces must be clean. This is used where heat cannot be used, or to join metal parts to glass or porcelain.

A solution of copper for copperplating steel or cast iron before soldering will work by simply immersing the work in it. This is also useful to copper the surface of dies and tools to enable the mechanic to "lay out" or scribe the work so that the lines can be readily seen. Take copper sulphate $3\frac{1}{2}$ ounces, sulphuric acid $3\frac{1}{2}$ ounces, water 1 to 2 gallons. Dissolve the copper in the water and add the acid.

Solders and Fusible Alloys

Solders act under constant stress considerably like plastic or semi-fluid material. Their fluidity resembles that of tar or gum, and their distortion with time is greater than would be thought. In a series of tests a notable point brought out was the varying degrees of strength with age. Tensile strength increases with the percentage of tin present, but when the solder's age is considered as a factor, the product possesses its maximum value at 60 per cent. tin, showing this property as similar to that of the melting point and depending upon chemical composition.

For general work, the solder requiring resistance to stress is 60 per cent. tin, but for work requiring little mechanical strength, such as sealing, a lower per cent. of tin may be used.

Generally speaking, all solders are alloys of lead and tin. The more lead the alloy contains, above 40 per cent., the higher is its melting point, as also the less lead it contains, below 40 per cent., the lower is its melting point.

The melting point of alloys which fuse at a low temperature may be found by tying a small wire around a fragment of alloy and hanging it in a bath of water. A thermometer should be kept in the bath and the temperature increased slowly until the alloy melts. The melting point of the alloy can then be noted by the temperature of the bath. For higher temperature a bath of paraffin or oil is used. If bismuth is added to these alloys the melting point is lower, as bismuth possesses the quality of expanding on cooling, a property which is very unusual in metals. Bismuth is used not only to make the alloy or solder more easily worked, by diminishing its melting point, but if sufficient quantity be present its expansive tendency counterbalances the effects of the contraction of the other metals, and the total result is the prevention or reduction of shrinkage in the mold. The addition of cadmium still farther lowers the melting point of such alloys as those of bismuth, lead and tin, which in themselves have very low melting points.

COMPOSITION AND MELTING POINT OF SOLDERS AND FUSIBLE ALLOYS

Alloy	Lead	Tin	Bismuth	Other Constituents	Melting Point	
					Cent.	Fahr.
Solder 1	96.15	3.85			292	558
Solder 2	90.9	9.1			283	541
Solder 3	83.3	16.7			266	511
Solder 4	75.0	25.0			250	482
Solder 5	66.7	33.3			227	441
Solder 6	50.0	50.0			188	370
Solder 7	40.0	60.0			168	334
Solder 8	33.3	66.7			171	340
Solder 9	33.3	33.3	33.3	Zinc	140	284
1. Steam boiler plug	48.4		12.8	38.8	171	340
2. Steam boiler plug .	44.5		22.2	33.3	141	285
3. Steam boiler plug .	42.1		42.1	15.8	123	253
4. Steam boiler plug .	10.0	40.0	50.0		116	240
Sir Isaac Newton's.	30.0	20.0	50.0		100	212
Suitable for casts .	31.25	18.75	50.0		98	208
Rose's alloy	28.1	21.9	50.0		95	203
D'Arcet's alloy ...	25.0	25.0	50.0	Cadmium	93	200
Wood's alloy	25.0	12.5	50.0	12.5	60	140
Lipowitz's alloy ..	26.9	12.7	50.0	10.4	66	150
Expanding alloy ..	66.7		8.3	25.0	66	150

Hard solders sometimes contain more or less copper. A substantial solder contains 60 per cent. copper, 20 per cent. tin and 20 per cent. zinc. An easily melted yellow, hard solder contains about 45 per cent. copper and 55 per cent. zinc. This solder is really a brass, but at times is used for soldering, binding and filling purposes.

Nearly all aluminum solders are alloys of tin and aluminum that contain from 15 to 25 per cent. aluminum. A small per cent. of copper or nickel, never exceeding 2 or 3 per cent., is sometimes used. The exact point of separation between a fusible metal and a non-fusible one is very uncertain, thus several additional alloys are given in the table. In filling up imperfections in ornamental castings for plugs in electrical wiring and on boilers in engineering work, fusible alloys are used. Sometimes defects in structural steel have been filled in with expanding alloy, after being dressed in a coat of point. The United States Government rules call for pure Banca tin for boiler plugs, but this is not essential and any good tin will serve the purpose.

Experiments have been made in an engineering college quite recently for the purpose of finding the way of making solder joints, as well as measuring their tensile strength. Any pressure upon the solder at the moment of setting diminishes the strength of the joint. Thus, in making a solder joint, the upper piece should be held above the lower one, the solder fused by means of two blow torches, and the pieces brought together by very slow and easy pressure. By employing this method, which differs from that commonly called "sweating," the joint is less liable to be broken, as the crystalline composition of the resulting mass contains less resistance at this time.

In addition it is found that there is remarkable variation with time of the tensile strength of such joints, which is also in accord with what would be considered proper by engineering science in this field. Under any circumstances the average strength attained does not exceed 27,000 pounds per square inch, and was obtained from solder made with three-fifths of its composition tin.

ARSENAL "HOT DIP" PROCESS FOR TINNING

Use a metal composed of 80 parts of lead to 20 parts of tin by weight. The steel plate to be tinned is first pickled in a bath of 40 parts of water to one part of sulphuric acid by volume. After pickling, the metal is washed in clean water to remove all traces of the pickling acid. The work is then dipped in a flux which is made by dissolving zinc in hydrochloric acid until it is saturated. After dipping in the flux, the pieces are dipped in the melted metal (80% lead — 20% tin) until thoroughly coated and are then shaken off and thrown in a pile to cool.

A Method of Tinning Brass Parts

Brass parts are placed in layers in a screened basket with tin plates between each layer. They are then placed in a copper tank filled with water supplied with steam coil and brought to a boiling point. Sufficient amount of Cream of Tartar is added until the parts are properly plated. Four hours are required to properly tin these parts.

Small parts are placed in a cheese cloth bag in a solution of one pint of phosphoric acid (U.S.P. 50%) to four gallons of water. Heat to a boiling point until pins begin to turn white, requiring about two hours. Remove and place in linseed oil. They are then rolled on staw boards to remove the surplus oil.

GEARING

GEAR TEETH — SHAPES OF

Cycloidal or Epicycloidal. — A curved tooth generated by the point of a circle rolling away from the gear wheel or rack.

Involute. — A curved tooth generated by unwinding a tape or string from a cylinder. The rack tooth has straight sides.

Involute Standard. — The standard gear tooth has a 14½ degree pressure angle which means that the teeth of a standard rack have straight sides 14½ degrees from the vertical.

Involute — Stubbed. — A tooth shorter than the standard and usually with a 20-degree pressure angle.

GEARS — TEETH AND PARTS

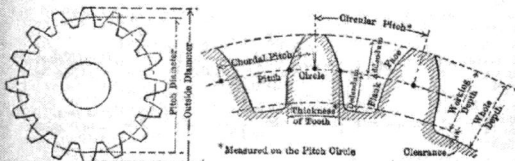

FIG. 1. — Part of Gear Teeth

Addendum. — Length from pitch line to outside.

Chordal Pitch. — Distance from center to center of teeth in a straight line.

Circular Pitch. — Distance from center to center of teeth measured on the pitch circle.

Clearance. — Extra depth of space between teeth.

Dedendum. — Length from pitch line to base of tooth.

Diametral Pitch. — Number of teeth divided by the pitch diameter or the teeth to each inch of diameter.

Face. — Working surface of tooth outside of pitch line.

Flank. — Working surface of tooth below pitch line.

Outside Diameter. — Total diameter over teeth.

Pitch Diameter. — Diameter at the pitch line.

Pitch Line. — Line of contact of two cylinders which would have the same speed ratios as the gears.

Linear Pitch. — Sometimes used in rack measurement. Same as circular pitch of a gear.

Nearly all aluminum solders are alloys of tin and aluminum that contain from 15 to 25 per cent. aluminum. A small per cent. of copper or nickel, never exceeding 2 or 3 per cent., is sometimes used. The exact point of separation between a fusible metal and a nonfusible one is very uncertain, thus several additional alloys are given in the table. In filling up imperfections in ornamental castings for plugs in electrical wiring and on boilers in engineering work, fusible alloys are used. Sometimes defects in structural steel have been filled in with expanding alloy, after being dressed in a coat of point. The United States Government rules call for pure Banca tin for boiler plugs, but this is not essential and any good tin will serve the purpose.

Experiments have been made in an engineering college quite recently for the purpose of finding the way of making solder joints, as well as measuring their tensile strength. Any pressure upon the solder at the moment of setting diminishes the strength of the joint. Thus, in making a solder joint, the upper piece should be held above the lower one, the solder fused by means of two blow torches, and the pieces brought together by very slow and easy pressure. By employing this method, which differs from that commonly called "sweating," the joint is less liable to be broken, as the crystalline composition of the resulting mass contains less resistance at this time.

In addition it is found that there is remarkable variation with time of the tensile strength of such joints, which is also in accord with what would be considered proper by engineering science in this field. Under any circumstances the average strength attained does not exceed 27,000 pounds per square inch, and was obtained from solder made with three-fifths of its composition tin.

ARSENAL "HOT DIP" PROCESS FOR TINNING

Use a metal composed of 80 parts of lead to 20 parts of tin by weight. The steel plate to be tinned is first pickled in a bath of 40 parts of water to one part of sulphuric acid by volume. After pickling, the metal is washed in clean water to remove all traces of the pickling acid. The work is then dipped in a flux which is made by dissolving zinc in hydrochloric acid until it is saturated. After dipping in the flux, the pieces are dipped in the melted metal (80% lead — 20% tin) until thoroughly coated and are then shaken off and thrown in a pile to cool.

A Method of Tinning Brass Parts

Brass parts are placed in layers in a screened basket with tin plates between each layer. They are then placed in a copper tank filled with water supplied with steam coil and brought to a boiling point. Sufficient amount of Cream of Tartar is added until the parts are properly plated. Four hours are required to properly tin these parts.

Small parts are placed in a cheese cloth bag in a solution of one pint of phosphoric acid (U.S.P. 50%) to four gallons of water. Heat to a boiling point until pins begin to turn white, requiring about two hours. Remove and place in linseed oil. They are then rolled on staw boards to remove the surplus oil.

GEARING

GEAR TEETH — SHAPES OF

Cycloidal or Epicycloidal. — A curved tooth generated by the point of a circle rolling away from the gear wheel or rack.

Involute. — A curved tooth generated by unwinding a tape or string from a cylinder. The rack tooth has straight sides.

Involute Standard. — The standard gear tooth has a $14\frac{1}{2}$ degree pressure angle which means that the teeth of a standard rack have straight sides $14\frac{1}{2}$ degrees from the vertical.

Involute — Stubbed. — A tooth shorter than the standard and usually with a 20-degree pressure angle.

GEARS — TEETH AND PARTS

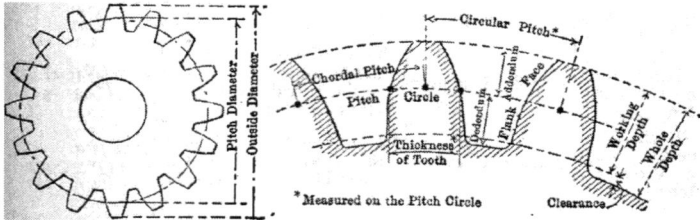

FIG. 1. — Part of Gear Teeth

Addendum. — Length from pitch line to outside.

Chordal Pitch. — Distance from center to center of teeth in a straight line.

Circular Pitch. — Distance from center to center of teeth measured on the pitch circle.

Clearance. — Extra depth of space between teeth.

Dedendum. — Length from pitch line to base of tooth.

Diametral Pitch. — Number of teeth divided by the pitch diameter or the teeth to each inch of diameter.

Face. — Working surface of tooth outside of pitch line.

Flank. — Working surface of tooth below pitch line.

Outside Diameter. — Total diameter over teeth.

Pitch Diameter. — Diameter at the pitch line.

Pitch Line. — Line of contact of two cylinders which would have the same speed ratios as the gears.

Linear Pitch. — Sometimes used in rack measurement. Same as circular pitch of a gear.

23

Having	To Get	Rule	Formula
The Diametral Pitch	The Circular Pitch	Divide 3.1416 by the Diametral Pitch	$P' = \dfrac{3.1416}{P}$
The Pitch Diameter and the Number of Teeth ...	The Circular Pitch	Divide Pitch Diameter by the product of .3183 and Number of Teeth	$P' = \dfrac{D'}{.3183\,N}$
The Outside Diameter and the Number of Teeth ...	The Circular Pitch	Divide Outside Diameter by the product of .3183 and Number of Teeth plus 2	$P' = \dfrac{D}{.3183\,N + 2}$
The Number of Teeth and the Circular Pitch	Pitch Diameter	The continued product of the Number of Teeth, the Circular Pitch and .3183	$D' = N P' \,.3183$
The Number of Teeth and the Outside Diameter ...	Pitch Diameter	Divide the product of Number of Teeth and Outside Diameter by Number of Teeth plus 2	$D' = \dfrac{N D}{N + 2}$
The Outside Diameter and the Circular Pitch	Pitch Diameter	Subtract from the Outside Diameter the product of the Circular Pitch and .6366	$D' = D - (P'.6366)$
Addendum and the Number of Teeth ...	Pitch Diameter	Multiply the Number of Teeth by the Addendum	$D' = N s$
The Number of Teeth and the Circular Pitch	Outside Diameter	The continued product of the Number of Teeth plus 2, the Circular Pitch and .3183	$D = (N + 2)\, P'\,.3183$
The Pitch Diameter and the Circular Pitch	Outside Diameter	Add to the Pitch Diameter the product of the Circular Pitch and .6366....	$D = D' + (P'.6366)$
The Number of Teeth and the Addendum........	Outside Diameter	Multiply Addendum by Number of Teeth plus 2	$D = s\,(N + 2)$
The Pitch Diameter and the Circular Pitch	Number of Teeth	Divide the product of Pitch Diameter and 3.1416 by the Circular Pitch	$N = \dfrac{D'\,3.1416}{P'}$
The Circular Pitch	Thickness of Tooth	One half the Circular Pitch	$t = \dfrac{P'}{2}$
The Circular Pitch	Addendum	Multiply the Circular Pitch by .3183 or $s = \dfrac{D'}{N}$	$s = P'\,.3183$
The Circular Pitch	Root	Multiply the Circular Pitch by .3683	$s + f = P'\,.3683$
The Circular Pitch	Working Depth	Multiply the Circular Pitch by .6366	$D'' = P'\,.6366$
The Circular Pitch	Whole Depth	Multiply the Circular Pitch by .6866	$D'' = P'\,.6866$
The Circular Pitch	Clearance	Multiply the Circular Pitch by .05	$f = P'\,.05$
Thickness of Tooth	Clearance	One tenth the Thickness of Tooth at Pitch Line	$f = \dfrac{t}{10}$

Having	To Get	Rule	Formula
The Circular Pitch	The Diametral Pitch	Divide 3.1416 by the Circular Pitch	$P = \dfrac{3.1416}{P'}$
The Pitch Diameter and the Number of Teeth ...	The Diametral Pitch	Divide Number of Teeth by Pitch Diameter	$P = \dfrac{N}{D'}$
The Outside Diameter and the Number of Teeth	The Diametral Pitch	Divide Number of Teeth plus 2 by Outside Diameter	$P = \dfrac{N+2}{D}$
The Number of Teeth and the Diametral Pitch	Pitch Diameter	Divide Number of Teeth by the Diametral Pitch	$D' = \dfrac{N}{P}$
The Number of Teeth and the Outside Diameter......	Pitch Diameter	Divide the Product of Outside Diameter and Number of Teeth by Number of Teeth plus 2	$D' = \dfrac{DN}{N+2}$
The Outside Diameter and the Diametral Pitch ...	Pitch Diameter	Subtract from the Outside Diameter the quotient of 2 divided by the Diametral Pitch...............	$D' = D - \dfrac{2}{P}$
Addendum and the Number of Teeth ...	Pitch Diameter	Multiply Addendum by the Number of Teeth	$D' = sN$
The Number of Teeth and the Diametral Pitch	Outside Diameter	Divide Number of Teeth plus 2 by the Diametral Pitch.................	$D = \dfrac{N+2}{P}$
The Pitch Diameter and the Diametral Pitch	Outside Diameter	Add to the Pitch Diameter the quotient of 2 divided by the Diametral Pitch	$D = D' + \dfrac{2}{P}$
The Pitch Diameter and the Number of Teeth ...	Outside Diameter	Divide the Number of Teeth plus 2, by the quotient of number of Teeth divided by Pitch Diameter	$D = \dfrac{N+2}{\frac{N}{D'}}$
The Number of Teeth and Addendum ..	Outside Diameter	Multiply the Number of Teeth plus 2 by Addendum	$D = (N+2)s$
The Pitch Diameter and the Diametral Pitch	Number of Teeth	Multiply Pitch Diameter by the Diametral Pitch	$N = D'P$
The Outside Diameter and the Diametral Pitch	Number of Teeth	Multiply Outside Diameter by the Diametral Pitch and subtract 2	$N = DP - 2$
The Diametral Pitch	Thickness of Tooth	Divide 1.5708 by the Diametral Pitch	$t = \dfrac{1.5708}{P}$
The Diametral Pitch	Addendum	Divide 1 by the Diametral Pitch or $s = \dfrac{D'}{N}$	$s = \dfrac{1}{P}$
The Diametral Pitch	Root	Divide 1.157 by the Diametral Pitch	$s + f = \dfrac{1.157}{P}$
The Diametral Pitch	Working Depth	Divide 2 by the Diametral Pitch.................	$D'' = \dfrac{2}{P}$
The Diametral Pitch	Whole Depth	Divide 2.157 by the Diametral Pitch	$D'' + f = \dfrac{2.157}{P}$
The Diametral Pitch	Clearance	Divide .157 by the Diametral Pitch.................	$f = \dfrac{.157}{P}$
Thickness of Tooth	Clearance	Divide Thickness of Tooth at pitch line by 10	$f = \dfrac{t}{10}$

TABLE OF CORRESPONDING DIAMETRAL AND CIRCULAR PITCHES

TABLE No. 1		TABLE No. 2	
Diametral Pitch	Circular Pitch	Circular Pitch	Diametral Pitch
1¼	2.5133	2	1.571
1½	2.0944	1⅞	1.676
1¾	1.7952	1¾	1.795
2	1.571	1⅝	1.933
2¼	1.396	1½	2.094
2½	1.257	1 7/16	2.185
2¾	1.142	1⅜	2.285
3	1.047	1 5/16	2.394
3½	.898	1¼	2.513
4	.785	1 3/16	2.646
5	.628	1⅛	2.793
6	.524	1 1/16	2.957
7	.449	1	3.142
8	.393	15/16	3.351
9	.349	7/8	3.590
10	.314	13/16	3.867
11	.286	3/4	4.189
12	.262	11/16	4.570
14	.224	5/8	5.027
16	.196	9/16	5.585
18	.175	1/2	6.283
20	.157	7/16	7.181
22	.143	3/8	8.378
24	.131	5/16	10.053
26	.121	1/4	12.566
28	.112	3/16	16.755
30	.105	1/8	25.133
32	.098	1/16	50.266
36	.087		
40	.079		
48	.065		

No. 1 table shows the diametral pitches with the corresponding circular pitches.

No. 2 table shows the circular pitches with the corresponding diametral pitches.

It is most natural to think of gears in circular or linear pitch and we soon get to know the size of any pitch, as 12, as being a little over ¼ inch from center to center. But the diametral system has many advantages in figuring gear blanks, center distances, etc.

The Center Distance of any pair of spur gears is found by adding one-half the pitch diameter of both gears.

CONSTANTS FOR DETERMINING CHORDAL PITCH AND RADIUS OF SPUR GEARS

P = Chordal Pitch of Teeth.
R = Radius of Pitch Circle.
N = Number of Teeth.
C = Constant. (See table below.)

$$\text{Chordal pitch} = \frac{\text{Radius of pitch circle}}{\text{Constant for number of teeth}}.$$

Radius of pitch circle = Constant × chordal pitch.

$$\text{Constant for any number of teeth} = \frac{\text{Radius of pitch circle}}{\text{Chordal pitch of teeth}}.$$

EXAMPLES: 1. What is radius of pitch circle of a gear having 45 teeth, 1¾ inch pitch? Follow 40 in table to column 5 (making 45 teeth), and find 7.168. Multiply by pitch, 1¾ inch, and get 12.54 inches radius or 25.08 pitch diameter.

2. What is the chordal pitch of a gear 32 inches pitch diameter, 67 teeth? Follow 60 in table to column 7 and find 10.668. Divide radius (½ of 32 = 16 inches) by constant. 16 ÷ 10.668 = 1.5 inch pitch.

3. What number of teeth has a gear of 1.5 inch chordal pitch and pitch diameter 32 inches? Divide by 2 to get radius. Divide this by chordal pitch which will give constant. 16 ÷ 1.5 = 10.666. Look in table for this constant which will be found to represent 67 teeth.

TABLE OF CONSTANTS

N	O	1	2	3	4	5	6	7	8	9
0	0.000	0.000	0.500	0.577	0.707	0.851	1.000	1.152	1.307	1.462
10	1.618	1.774	1.932	2.089	2.247	2.405	2.563	2.721	2.879	3.038
20	3.196	3.355	3.513	3.672	3.831	3.989	4.148	4.307	4.465	4.624
30	4.783	4.942	5.101	5.260	5.419	5.578	5.737	5.896	6.055	6.214
40	6.373	6.532	6.691	6.850	7.009	7.168	7.327	7.486	7.645	7.804
50	7.963	8.122	8.281	8.440	8.599	8.758	8.918	9.077	9.236	9.395
60	9.554	9.713	9.872	10.031	10.190	10.349	10.508	10.668	10.827	10.986
70	11.145	11.304	11.463	11.622	11.781	11.940	12.099	12.258	12.418	12.577
80	12.736	12.895	13.054	13.213	13.372	13.531	13.690	13.849	14.008	14.168
90	14.327	14.486	14.645	14.804	14.963	15.123	15.282	15.441	15.600	15.759
100	15.918	16.077	16.236	16.395	16.554	16.713	16.873	17.032	17.191	17.350
110	17.509	17.668	17.828	17.987	18.146	18.305	18.464	18.624	18.783	18.942
120	19.101	19.260	19.419	19.579	19.738	19.897	20.056	20.215	20.375	20.534
130	20.693	20.852	21.011	21.170	21.330	21.489	21.648	21.807	21.966	22.126
140	22.285	22.444	22.603	22.762	22.921	23.081	23.240	23.399	23.558	23.717
150	23.877	24.036	24.195	24.354	24.513	24.672	24.832	24.991	25.150	25.309
160	25.468	25.627	25.787	25.946	26.105	26.264	26.423	26.583	26.742	26.901
170	27.060	27.219	27.378	27.538	27.697	27.856	28.015	28.174	28.334	28.493
180	28.652	28.811	28.970	29.129	29.289	29.448	29.607	29.766	29.925	30.085
190	30.242	30.403	30.562	30.721	30.880	31.040	31.199	31.358	31.517	31.676
200	31.830	31.989	32.148	32.307	32.446	32.625	32.785	32.944	33.103	33.262
210	33.427	33.586	33.746	33.905	34.064	34.223	34.382	34.542	34.701	34.860
220	35.019	35.178	35.337	35.497	35.656	35.815	35.974	36.133	36.293	36.452
230	36.611	36.770	36.929	37.088	37.248	37.407	37.566	37.725	37.884	38.044
240	38.203	38.362	38.521	38.680	38.839	38.999	39.158	39.317	39.476	39.635
250	39.795									

GEARING

Gear Wheels

TABLE OF TOOTH PARTS — DIAMETRAL PITCH IN FIRST COLUMN

Diametral Pitch	Circular Pitch	Thickness of Tooth on Pitch Line	Addendum and $\frac{1"}{P}$	Working Depth of Tooth	Depth of Space below Pitch Line	Whole Depth of Tooth
P	P'	t	s	D''	$s+f$	$D''+f$
½	6.2832	3.1416	2.0000	4.0000	2.3142	4.3142
¾	4.1888	2.0944	1.3333	2.6666	1.5428	2.8761
1	3.1416	1.5708	1.0000	2.0000	1.1571	2.1571
1¼	2.5133	1.2566	.8000	1.6000	.9257	1.7257
1½	2.0944	1.0472	.6666	1.3333	.7714	1.4381
1¾	1.7952	.8976	.5714	1.1429	.6612	1.2326
2	1.5708	.7854	.5000	1.0000	.5785	1.0785
2¼	1.3963	.6981	.4444	.8888	.5143	.9587
2½	1.2566	.6283	.4000	.8000	.4628	.8628
2¾	1.1424	.5712	.3636	.7273	.4208	.7844
3	1.0472	.5236	.3333	.6666	.3857	.7190
3½	.8976	.4488	.2857	.5714	.3306	.6163
4	.7854	.3927	.2500	.5000	.2893	.5393
5	.6283	.3142	.2000	.4000	.2314	.4314
6	.5236	.2618	.1666	.3333	.1928	.3595
7	.4488	.2244	.1429	.2857	.1653	.3081
8	.3927	.1963	.1250	.2500	.1446	.2696
9	.3491	.1745	.1111	.2222	.1286	.2397
10	.3142	.1571	.1000	.2000	.1157	.2157
11	.2856	.1428	.0909	.1818	.1052	.1961
12	.2618	.1309	.0833	.1666	.0964	.1798
13	.2417	.1208	.0769	.1538	.0890	.1659
14	.2244	.1122	.0714	.1429	.0826	.1541

To obtain the size of any part of a diametral pitch not given in the table, divide the corresponding part of 1 diametral pitch by the pitch required.

As it is natural to think of gear pitches as the distance between teeth the same as threads, it is well to fix in the mind the approximate center distances of the pitches most in use. Or it is easy to remember that if the diametral pitch be divided by 3⅐ we have the teeth per inch on the pitch line. By this method we easily see that in a 10 diametral pitch gear there are approximately 3 teeth per inch while in a 22 diametral pitch there will be just 7 teeth to the inch.

TABLE OF TOOTH PARTS — *Continued*

DIAMETRAL PITCH IN FIRST COLUMN

Diametral Pitch	Circular Pitch	Thickness of Tooth on Pitch Line	Addendum and $\frac{1''}{P}$	Working Depth of Tooth	Depth of Space below Pitch Line	Whole Depth of Tooth
P	P'	t	s	D''	$s+f$	$D''+f$
15	.2094	.1047	.0666	.1333	.0771	.1438
16	.1963	.0982	.0625	.1250	.0723	.1348
17	.1848	.0924	.0588	.1176	.0681	.1269
18	.1745	.0873	.0555	.1111	.0643	.1198
19	.1653	.0827	.0526	.1053	.0609	.1135
20	.1571	.0785	.0500	.1000	.0579	.1079
22	.1428	.0714	.0455	.0909	.0526	.0980
24	.1309	.0654	.0417	.0833	.0482	.0898
26	.1208	.0604	.0385	.0769	.0445	.0829
28	.1122	.0561	.0357	.0714	.0413	.0770
30	.1047	.0524	.0333	.0666	.0386	.0719
32	.0982	.0491	.0312	.0625	.0362	.0674
34	.0924	.0462	.0294	.0588	.0340	.0634
36	.0873	.0436	.0278	.0555	.0321	.0599
38	.0827	.0413	.0263	.0526	.0304	.0568
40	.0785	.0393	.0250	.0500	.0289	.0539
42	.0748	.0374	.0238	.0476	.0275	.0514
44	.0714	.0357	.0227	.0455	.0263	.0490
46	.0683	.0341	.0217	.0435	.0252	.0469
48	.0654	.0327	.0208	.0417	.0241	.0449
50	.0628	.0314	.0200	.0400	.0231	.0431
56	.0561	.0280	.0178	.0357	.0207	.0385
60	.0524	.0262	.0166	.0333	.0193	.0360

To obtain the size of any part of a diametral pitch not given in the table, divide the corresponding part of 1 diametral pitch by the pitch required.

As it is natural to think of gear pitches as the distance between teeth the same as threads, it is well to fix in the mind the approximate center distances of the pitches most in use. Or it is easy to remember that if the diametral pitch be divided by $3\frac{1}{7}$ we have the teeth per inch on the pitch line. By this method we easily see that in a 10 diametral pitch gear there are approximately 3 teeth per inch while in a 22 diametral pitch there will be just 7 teeth to the inch.

Gear Wheels

TABLE OF TOOTH PARTS — CIRCULAR PITCH IN FIRST COLUMN

Circular Pitch	Threads or Teeth per Inch Linear	Diametral Pitch	Thickness of Tooth on Pitch Line	Addendum and Module	Working Depth of Tooth	Depth of Space below Pitch Line	Whole Depth of Tooth	Width of Thread-Tool at End	Width of Thread at Top
P'	$\frac{1''}{P'}$	P	t	s	D''	$s+f$	$D''+f$	$P'\times.31$	$P'\times.335$
2	1/2	1.5708	1.0000	.6366	1.2732	.7366	1.3732	.6200	.6700
1 7/8	8/15	1.6755	.9375	.5968	1.1937	.6906	1.2874	.5813	.6281
1 3/4	4/7	1.7952	.8750	.5570	1.1141	.6445	1.2016	.5425	.5863
1 5/8	8/13	1.9333	.8125	.5173	1.0345	.5985	1.1158	.5038	.5444
1 1/2	2/3	2.0944	.7500	.4775	.9549	.5525	1.0299	.4650	.5025
1 7/16	16/23	2.1855	.7187	.4576	.9151	.5294	.9870	.4456	.4816
1 3/8	8/11	2.2848	.6875	.4377	.8754	.5064	.9441	.4262	.4606
1 1/3	3/4	2.3562	.6666	.4244	.8488	.4910	.9154	.4133	.4466
1 5/16	16/21	2.3936	.6562	.4178	.8356	.4834	.9012	.4069	.4397
1 1/4	4/5	2.5133	.6250	.3979	.7958	.4604	.8583	.3875	.4188
1 3/16	16/19	2.6456	.5937	.3780	.7560	.4374	.8156	.3681	.3978
1 1/8	8/9	2.7925	.5625	.3581	.7162	.4143	.7724	.3488	.3769
1 1/16	16/17	2.9568	.5312	.3382	.6764	.3913	.7295	.3294	.3559
1	1	3.1416	.5000	.3183	.6366	.3683	.6866	.3100	.3350
15/16	1 1/15	3.3510	.4687	.2984	.5968	.3453	.6437	.2906	.3141
7/8	1 1/7	3.5904	.4375	.2785	.5570	.3223	.6007	.2713	.2931
13/16	1 3/13	3.8666	.4062	.2586	.5173	.2993	.5579	.2519	.2722
4/5	1 1/4	3.9270	.4000	.2546	.5092	.2946	.5492	.2480	.2680
3/4	1 1/3	4.1888	.3750	.2387	.4775	.2762	.5150	.2325	.2513
11/16	1 5/11	4.5696	.3437	.2189	.4377	.2532	.4720	.2131	.2303
2/3	1 1/2	4.7124	.3333	.2122	.4244	.2455	.4577	.2066	.2233
5/8	1 3/5	5.0265	.3125	.1989	.3979	.2301	.4291	.1938	.2094
3/5	1 2/3	5.2360	.3000	.1910	.3820	.2210	.4120	.1860	.2010
4/7	1 3/4	5.4978	.2857	.1819	.3638	.2105	.3923	.1771	.1914
9/16	1 7/9	5.5851	.2812	.1790	.3581	.2071	.3862	.1744	.1884

To obtain the size of any part of a circular pitch not given in the table, multiply the corresponding part of 1″ pitch by the pitch required.

As an example take a gear having 21 diametral pitch to find the various tooth parts. Take 1 diametral pitch and divide 3.1416 by 21 to find the corresponding circular pitch, which is .14951. The tooth thickness is 1.5708 ÷ 21 = .748; the addendum is 1.÷ 21 = .04761; the working depth is 2.÷ 21. = .09522; the depth below

Table of Tooth Parts

CIRCULAR PITCH IN FIRST COLUMN

Circular Pitch	Threads or Teeth per Inch Linear	Diametral Pitch	Thickness of Tooth on Pitch Line	Addendum and Module	Working Depth of Tooth	Depth of Space below Pitch Line	Whole Depth of Tooth	Width of Thread-Tool at End	Width of Thread at Top
P'	$\frac{1''}{P'}$	P	t	s	D''	$s+f$	$D''+f$	$P' \times .31$	$P' \times .335$
$\frac{1}{2}$	2	6.2832	.2500	.1592	.3183	.1842	.3433	.1550	.1675
$\frac{4}{9}$	$2\frac{1}{4}$	7.0685	.2222	.1415	.2830	.1637	.3052	.1378	.1489
$\frac{7}{16}$	$2\frac{2}{7}$	7.1808	.2187	.1393	.2785	.1611	.3003	.1356	.1466
$\frac{3}{7}$	$2\frac{1}{3}$	7.3304	.2143	.1364	.2728	.1578	.2942	.1328	.1436
$\frac{2}{5}$	$2\frac{1}{2}$	7.8540	.2000	.1273	.2546	.1473	.2746	.1240	.1340
$\frac{3}{8}$	$2\frac{2}{3}$	8.3776	.1875	.1194	.2387	.1381	.2575	.1163	.1256
$\frac{4}{11}$	$2\frac{3}{4}$	8.6394	.1818	.1158	.2316	.1340	.2498	.1127	.1218
$\frac{1}{3}$	3	9.4248	.1666	.1061	.2122	.1228	.2289	.1033	.1117
$\frac{5}{16}$	$3\frac{1}{5}$	10.0531	.1562	.0995	.1989	.1151	.2146	.0969	.1047
$\frac{3}{10}$	$3\frac{1}{3}$	10.4719	.1500	.0955	.1910	.1105	.2060	.0930	.1005
$\frac{2}{7}$	$3\frac{1}{2}$	10.9956	.1429	.0909	.1819	.1052	.1962	.0886	.0957
$\frac{1}{4}$	4	12.5664	.1250	.0796	.1591	.0921	.1716	.0775	.0838
$\frac{2}{9}$	$4\frac{1}{2}$	14.1372	.1111	.0707	.1415	.0818	.1526	.0689	.0744
$\frac{1}{5}$	5	15.7080	.1000	.0637	.1273	.0737	.1373	.0620	.0670
$\frac{3}{16}$	$5\frac{1}{3}$	16.7552	.0937	.0597	.1194	.0690	.1287	.0581	.0628
$\frac{2}{11}$	$5\frac{1}{2}$	17.2788	.0909	.0579	.1158	.0670	.1249	.0564	.0609
$\frac{1}{6}$	6	18.8496	.0833	.0531	.1061	.0614	.1144	.0517	.0558
$\frac{2}{13}$	$6\frac{1}{2}$	20.4203	.0769	.0489	.0978	.0566	.1055	.0477	.0515
$\frac{1}{7}$	7	21.9911	.0714	.0455	.0910	.0526	.0981	.0443	.0479
$\frac{2}{15}$	$7\frac{1}{2}$	23.5619	.0666	.0425	.0850	.0492	.0917	.0414	.0446
$\frac{1}{8}$	8	25.1327	.0625	.0398	.0796	.0460	.0858	.0388	.0419
$\frac{1}{9}$	9	28.2743	.0555	.0354	.0707	.0409	.0763	.0344	.0372
$\frac{1}{10}$	10	31.4159	.0500	.0318	.0637	.0368	.0687	.0310	.0335
$\frac{1}{16}$	16	50.2655	.0312	.0199	.0398	.0230	.0429	.0194	.0209
$\frac{1}{20}$	20	62.8318	.0250	.0159	.0318	.0184	.0343	.0155	.0167

To obtain the size of any part of a circular pitch not given in the table, multiply the corresponding part of 1″ pitch by the pitch required.

pitch line is $1.1571 \div 21 = .0551$ and the whole depth is $2.1571 \div 21 = .1027$ inches. These could also have been obtained by splitting the difference between the figures for 20 and 22 pitch. The same can be done for circular pitch except that we multiply instead of divide.

DIAGRAM FOR CAST-GEAR TEETH

THE accompanying diagram (Fig. 2) for laying out teeth for cast gears will be found useful by the machinist, patternmaker and draftsman. The diagram for circular pitch gears is similar to the one given by Professor Willis, while the one for diametral pitch was obtained by using the relation of diametral to circular pitch.

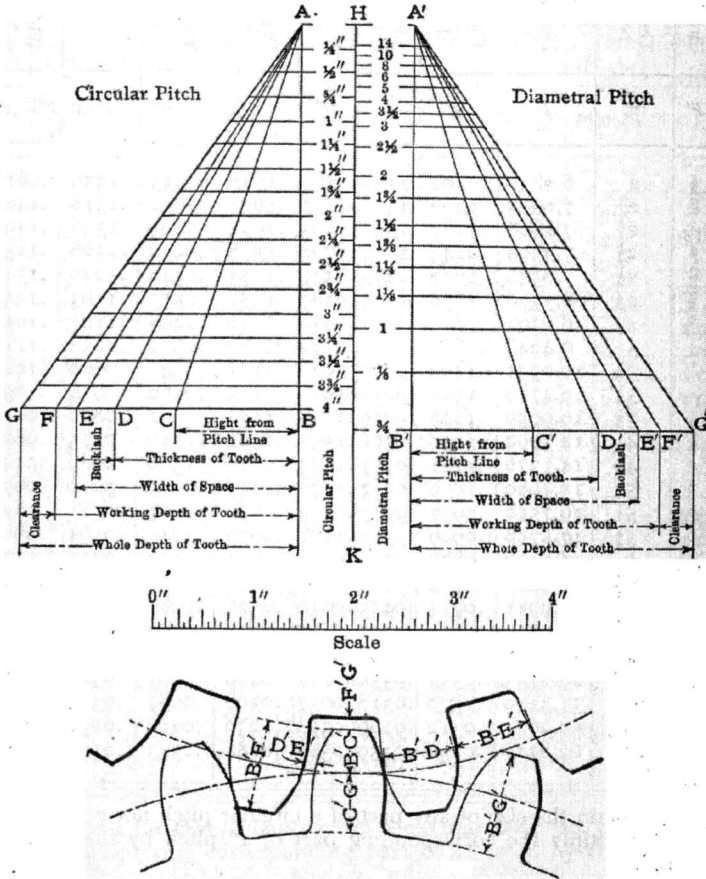

FIGS. 2 and 3.

By the diagram the relative size of a tooth may be easily determined. For example, if we contemplate using a gear of 2 diametral pitch, by referring to line $H K$, which shows the comparative distance between centers of teeth, on the pitch line, it will be observed that ı diametral pitch is but little greater than $1\frac{1}{2}$ inches circular pitch, or exactly 1.57 inches circular pitch. This result is obtained by dividing 3.1416 by the diametral pitch (3.1416 divided by 2 equals .57). In similar manner, if the circular pitch is known, the diametral pitch which corresponds to it is found by dividing 3.1416 by the circular pitch; for example, the diametral pitch which corresponds to 3 inches circular pitch is by the line $H\ K$ a little greater than 1 diametral pitch, or exactly 1.047 (3 1416 divided by 3 equals 1.047).

The proportions of a tooth may be determined for either diametral or circular pitch by using the corresponding diagram.

Continue, for illustration, the 2 diametral pitch. We have found, above, the distance between centers of teeth on the pitch line to be a little more than $1\frac{1}{2}$ inches (1.57 inches). The hight of tooth above pitch line $B'\ C'$ will be found on the horizontal line corresponding to 2 pitch. The distance between the lines $A'\ B'$ and $A'\ C'$ on this line may be taken in the dividers and transferred to the scale below. Thus we find the hight of the tooth to be $\frac{1}{1}\frac{5}{6}$ inch. In the same manner the thickness of tooth $B'\ D'$, width of space $B'\ E'$, working depth $B'\ F'$ and whole depth of tooth $B'\ G'$ may be determined.

The backlash or space between the idle surfaces of the teeth of two gear wheels when in mesh is given by the distance $D'\ E'$. The clearance or distance between the point of one tooth and the bottom of space into which it meshes is given by the distance $F'\ G'$. The backlash and clearance will vary according to the class of work for which the gears are to be used and the accuracy of the molded product. For machine molded gears which are to run in enclosed cases, or where they may be kept well oiled and free from dirt, the backlash and clearance may be reduced to a very small amount, while for gears running where dirt is likely to get into the teeth, or where irregularities due to molding, uneven shrinkage, and like causes, enter into the construction, there must be a greater allowance. The diagram is laid out for the latter case. Those who have more favorable conditions for which to design gears should vary the diagram to suit their conditions. This can be done by increasing $B\ D$ and decreasing $B\ E$, and by increasing $B\ C$ or decreasing $B\ G$, or both. to get the clearance that will best meet the required conditions. The same kind of diagram could be laid out for cut gears, but as tables are usually at hand which give the dimensions of the parts of such gears, figured to thousandths of an inch, it would be as well to consult one of these.

LAYING OUT SPUR GEAR BLANKS

DECIDE upon the size wanted, remembering that 12-pitch teeth are $\frac{2}{12}$ deep and 8-pitch — as in the drawing — $\frac{2}{8}$ deep, etc. Should t be 8 pitch, as shown in the cut, draw a circle measuring as many eighths of an inch in diameter as there are to be teeth in the gear. This circle is called the Pitch Line. Then with a radius $\frac{1}{8}$ of an inch larger, draw another circle from the same center, which will give the outside diameter of the gear, or $\frac{2}{8}$ larger than the pitch circle. Thus we have for the diameter of an 8-pitch gear of 24 teeth, $\frac{26}{8}$. Should there be 16 teeth, as in the small spur gear in the cut, the outside diameter would be $1\frac{8}{8}$, the number of teeth being always two less than there are eighths — *when it is* 8 *pitch* — in the outside diameter.

The distance from the pitch line to the bottom of the teeth is the same as to the top, excepting the clearance, which varies from $\frac{1}{8}$ of the pitch to $\frac{1}{16}$ of the thickness of the tooth at the pitch line. This latter is used by Brown & Sharpe and many others, but the clearance being provided for in the cutters the two gears would be laid out to mesh together just $\frac{2}{8}$.

These rules apply to all pitches, so that the outside diameter of a 5-pitch gear with 24 teeth would be $2\frac{6}{5}$; if a 3-pitch gear with 40 teeth it would be $\frac{42}{3}$. Again, if a blank be $4\frac{1}{8}$ ($2\frac{5}{8}$) in diameter, and cut 6 pitch, it should contain 23 teeth.

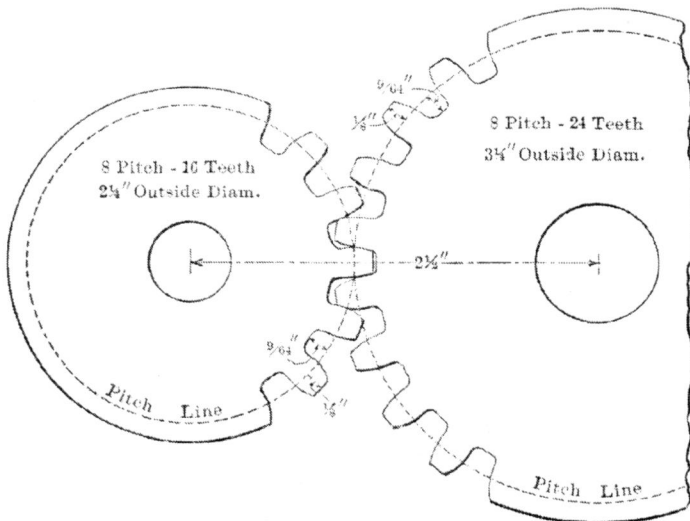

FIG. 4. — Laying out a Pair of Gears

ACTUAL SIZE OF DIAMETRAL PITCHES

It is not always easy to judge or imagine just how large a given pitch is when measured by the diametral system. To make it easy to see just what any pitch looks like the actual sizes of twelve diametral pitches are given on the following page, ranging from 20 to 4 teeth per inch of diameter on the pitch line, so that a good idea of the size of any of these teeth can be had at a glance.

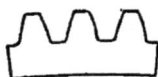

20 P.

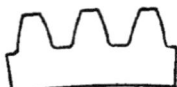

18 P.

16 P.

14 P,

12 P.   10 P.

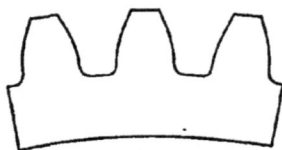

9 P.

8 P.

7 P.

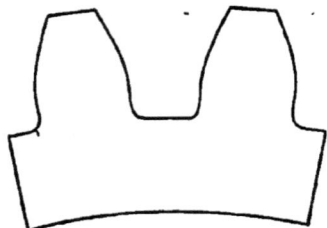

6 P.

5 P.   4 P.

LAYING OUT SINGLE CURVE TOOTH

A VERY simple method of laying out a standard tooth is shown in Fig. 5, and is known as the single curve method. Having calculated the various proportions of the tooth by rules already given, draw the pitch, outside, working depth and clearance or whole depth circles as shown. With a radius one half the pitch radius draw the semicircle from the center to the pitch circle. Take one quarter the pitch radius and with one leg at top of pitch circle strike arc cutting the semicircle. This is the center for the first tooth curve and locates the base circle for all the tooth arcs. Lay off the tooth thickness and space distances around the pitch circle and draw the tooth curves through these points with the tooth curve radius already found. The fillets in the tooth corners may be taken as one seventh of the space between the tops of the teeth.

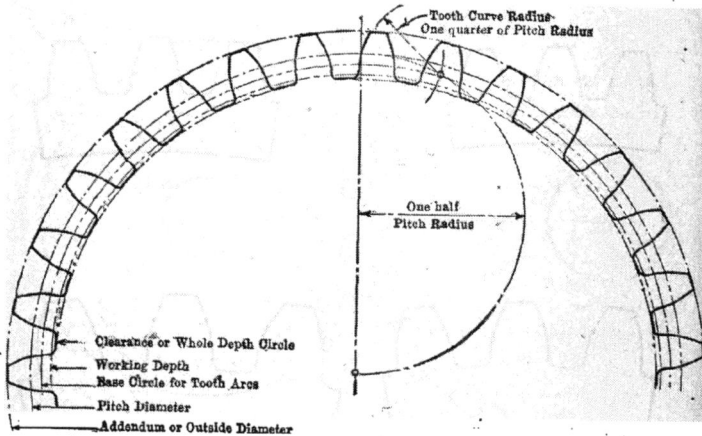

FIG. 5. — Single Curve Tooth

PRESSURE ANGLES

WE next come to pressure angles of gear teeth, which means the angle at which one tooth presses against the other and can best be shown by the pinion and rack, Figs. 6 and 7.

The standard tooth has a 14½ degree pressure angle, probably because it was so easy for the millwright to lay it out as he could obtain the angle without a protractor by using the method shown for laying out a thread tool (see Fig. 14). As the sides of an involute rack tooth are straight, and at the pressure angle from the perpendicular, draw the line of pressure at 14½ degrees from the pitch line. The base circle of the tooth arcs can be found by drawing a line from the center of the gear to the line of pressure and at right angles to it as shown, or by the first method, and working from this the tooth

:urve can be drawn by either the single-curve method or, as is more
ısual, by stopping the curve from two or more points on this same
:ircle.

The difference between the $14\frac{1}{2}$- and 20-degree pressure angles
:an be seen by comparing Figs. 6 and 7. Not only is the tooth
:horter, but the base is broader. The base circle for the tooth arcs
s found in the same way as before.

This form of tooth is largely used in automobile transmission and
;imilar work. William Sellers & Co. use a 20 degree pressure
ıngle with a tooth of standard length.

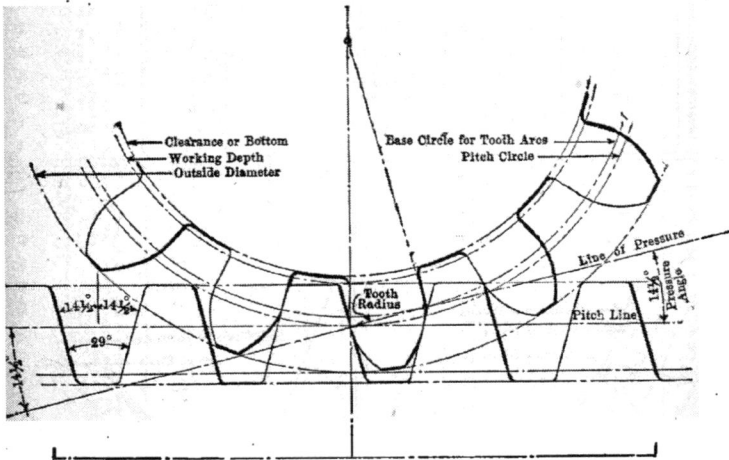

FIG. 6. — Standard Tooth

STUB-TOOTH GEARS

ANY tooth shorter than the regular standard length is called a
'stub" tooth, but like the bastard thread there have been many
:inds. In 1899 the Fellows Gear Shaper Company introduced a
;hort tooth with a 20-degree pressure angle instead of the usual $14\frac{1}{2}$-
legree. This gives a broader flank to the tooth and makes a stronger
;ear, especially for small pinions where strength is needed. While
:he Fellows tooth is shorter than the standard tooth there is no fixed
·elation between them, as, on account of the tooth depth graduations
)f the gear shaper, it was thought best to give the new tooth depth
n the same scale which is shown in the following table. This means
:hat if the pitch is 4 it has the depth of a 5-pitch standard tooth
livided as shown. The clearance is one-quarter the addendum or
ledendum.

TABLE OF TOOTH DIMENSIONS OF THE FELLOWS STUB–TOOTH GEAR

Cutters Marked Pitch	Stub Tooth Pitch	Has Depth of Standard Tooth	Thickness on Pitch Line	Addendum	Dedendum and Clearance
4/5	4	5	.3925	.200	.250
5/7	5	7	.314	.1429	.1785
6/8	6	8	.2617	.125	.1562
7/9	7	9	.2243	.111	.1389
8/10	8	10	.1962	.100	.125
9/11	9	11	.1744	.0909	.1137
10/12	10	12	.157	.0833	.1042
12/14	12	14	.1308	.0714	.0893

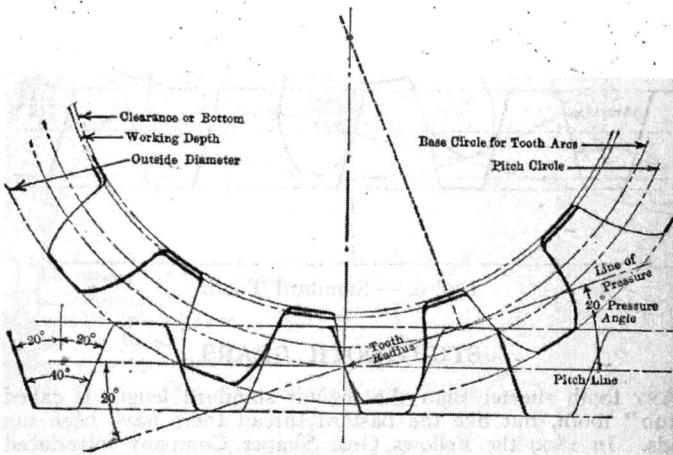

FIG. 7. — Stubbed Tooth

The Nuttall Company also use a 20-degree stub tooth, but have a
fixed length or depth in the following proportions.

Addendum   = .25 × circular pitch instead of .3683.
Dedendum   = .30 × circular pitch instead of .3683.
Working depth = .50 × circular pitch instead of .6366.
Clearance   = .05 × circular pitch same as standard.
Whole depth = .55 × circular pitch instead of .6866.

TABLE FOR TURNING AND CUTTING GEAR BLANKS

FOR STANDARD LENGTH TOOTH

Pitch	16	12	10	8	Pitch	16	12	10	8
Depth of Tooth	.135	.180	.216	.270	Depth of Tooth	.135	.180	.216	.270
No. of Teeth	Outside Diameter				No. of Teeth	Outside Diameter			
10	$\frac{3}{4}$	I	$1\frac{2}{10}$	$1\frac{1}{2}$	51	$3\frac{3}{16}$	$4\frac{5}{12}$	$5\frac{3}{10}$	$6\frac{3}{8}$
11	$1\frac{3}{16}$	$1\frac{1}{12}$	$1\frac{3}{10}$	$1\frac{5}{8}$	52	$3\frac{3}{8}$	$4\frac{1}{2}$	$5\frac{4}{10}$	$6\frac{1}{2}$
12	$\frac{7}{8}$	$1\frac{1}{12}$	$1\frac{4}{10}$	$1\frac{3}{4}$	53	$3\frac{7}{16}$	$4\frac{7}{12}$	$5\frac{5}{10}$	$6\frac{5}{8}$
13	$1\frac{1}{16}$	$1\frac{1}{8}$	$1\frac{5}{10}$	$1\frac{7}{8}$	54	$3\frac{1}{2}$	$4\frac{8}{12}$	$5\frac{5}{10}$	7
14	I	$1\frac{4}{12}$	$1\frac{6}{10}$	2	55	$3\frac{9}{16}$	$4\frac{9}{12}$	$5\frac{6}{10}$	$7\frac{1}{8}$
15	$1\frac{1}{16}$	$1\frac{5}{12}$	$1\frac{7}{10}$	$2\frac{1}{8}$	56	$3\frac{5}{8}$	$4\frac{10}{12}$	$5\frac{7}{10}$	$7\frac{1}{4}$
16	$1\frac{1}{8}$	$1\frac{6}{12}$	$1\frac{8}{10}$	$2\frac{1}{4}$	57	$3\frac{11}{16}$	$4\frac{11}{12}$	$5\frac{8}{10}$	$7\frac{3}{8}$
17	$1\frac{3}{16}$	$1\frac{7}{12}$	$1\frac{9}{10}$	$2\frac{3}{8}$	58	$3\frac{3}{4}$	5	6	$7\frac{1}{2}$
18	$1\frac{1}{4}$	$1\frac{8}{12}$	2	$2\frac{1}{2}$	59	$3\frac{13}{16}$	$5\frac{1}{12}$	$6\frac{1}{10}$	$7\frac{5}{8}$
19	$1\frac{5}{16}$	$1\frac{9}{12}$	$2\frac{1}{10}$	$2\frac{5}{8}$	60	$3\frac{7}{8}$	$5\frac{2}{12}$	$6\frac{2}{10}$	$7\frac{3}{4}$
20	$1\frac{3}{8}$	$1\frac{10}{12}$	$2\frac{2}{10}$	$2\frac{3}{4}$	61	$3\frac{15}{16}$	$5\frac{3}{12}$	$6\frac{3}{10}$	$7\frac{7}{8}$
21	$1\frac{7}{16}$	$1\frac{11}{12}$	$2\frac{3}{10}$	$2\frac{7}{8}$	62	4	$5\frac{4}{12}$	$6\frac{4}{10}$	8
22	$1\frac{1}{2}$	2	$2\frac{4}{10}$	3	63	$4\frac{1}{16}$	$5\frac{5}{12}$	$6\frac{5}{10}$	$8\frac{1}{8}$
23	$1\frac{9}{16}$	$2\frac{1}{12}$	$2\frac{5}{10}$	$3\frac{1}{8}$	64	$4\frac{1}{8}$	$5\frac{6}{12}$	$6\frac{6}{10}$	$8\frac{1}{4}$
24	$1\frac{5}{8}$	$2\frac{2}{12}$	$2\frac{6}{10}$	$3\frac{1}{4}$	65	$4\frac{3}{16}$	$5\frac{7}{12}$	$6\frac{7}{10}$	$8\frac{3}{8}$
25	$1\frac{11}{16}$	$2\frac{3}{12}$	$2\frac{7}{10}$	$3\frac{3}{8}$	66	$4\frac{1}{4}$	$5\frac{8}{12}$	$6\frac{8}{10}$	$8\frac{1}{2}$
26	$1\frac{3}{4}$	$2\frac{4}{12}$	$2\frac{8}{10}$	$3\frac{1}{2}$	67	$4\frac{5}{16}$	$5\frac{9}{12}$	$6\frac{9}{10}$	$8\frac{5}{8}$
27	$1\frac{13}{16}$	$2\frac{5}{12}$	$2\frac{9}{10}$	$3\frac{5}{8}$	68	$4\frac{3}{8}$	$5\frac{10}{12}$	7	$8\frac{3}{4}$
28	$1\frac{7}{8}$	$2\frac{6}{12}$	3	$3\frac{3}{4}$	69	$4\frac{7}{16}$	$5\frac{11}{12}$	$7\frac{1}{10}$	$8\frac{7}{8}$
29	$1\frac{15}{16}$	$2\frac{7}{12}$	$3\frac{1}{10}$	$3\frac{7}{8}$	70	$4\frac{1}{2}$	6	$7\frac{2}{10}$	9
30	2	$2\frac{8}{12}$	$3\frac{2}{10}$	4	71	$4\frac{9}{16}$	$6\frac{1}{12}$	$7\frac{3}{10}$	$9\frac{1}{8}$
31	$2\frac{1}{16}$	$2\frac{9}{12}$	$3\frac{3}{10}$	$4\frac{1}{8}$	72	$4\frac{5}{8}$	$6\frac{2}{12}$	$7\frac{4}{10}$	$9\frac{1}{4}$
32	$2\frac{1}{8}$	$2\frac{10}{12}$	$3\frac{4}{10}$	$4\frac{1}{4}$	73	$4\frac{11}{16}$	$6\frac{3}{12}$	$7\frac{5}{10}$	$9\frac{3}{8}$
33	$2\frac{3}{16}$	$2\frac{11}{12}$	$3\frac{5}{10}$	$4\frac{3}{8}$	74	$4\frac{3}{4}$	$6\frac{4}{12}$	$7\frac{6}{10}$	$9\frac{1}{2}$
34	$2\frac{1}{4}$	3	$3\frac{6}{10}$	$4\frac{1}{2}$	75	$4\frac{13}{16}$	$6\frac{5}{12}$	$7\frac{7}{10}$	$9\frac{5}{8}$
35	$2\frac{5}{16}$	$3\frac{1}{12}$	$3\frac{7}{10}$	$4\frac{5}{8}$	76	$4\frac{7}{8}$	$6\frac{6}{12}$	$7\frac{8}{10}$	$9\frac{3}{4}$
36	$2\frac{3}{8}$	$3\frac{2}{12}$	$3\frac{8}{10}$	$4\frac{3}{4}$	77	$4\frac{15}{16}$	$6\frac{7}{12}$	$7\frac{9}{10}$	$9\frac{7}{8}$
37	$2\frac{7}{16}$	$3\frac{3}{12}$	$3\frac{9}{10}$	$4\frac{7}{8}$	78	5	$6\frac{8}{12}$	8	10
38	$2\frac{1}{2}$	$3\frac{4}{12}$	4	5	79	$5\frac{1}{16}$	$6\frac{9}{12}$	$8\frac{1}{10}$	$10\frac{1}{8}$
39	$2\frac{9}{16}$	$3\frac{5}{12}$	$4\frac{1}{10}$	$5\frac{1}{8}$	80	$5\frac{1}{8}$	$6\frac{10}{12}$	$8\frac{2}{10}$	$10\frac{1}{4}$
40	$2\frac{5}{8}$	$3\frac{6}{12}$	$4\frac{2}{10}$	$5\frac{1}{4}$	81	$5\frac{3}{16}$	$6\frac{11}{12}$	$8\frac{3}{10}$	$10\frac{3}{8}$
41	$2\frac{11}{16}$	$3\frac{7}{12}$	$4\frac{3}{10}$	$5\frac{3}{8}$	82	$5\frac{1}{4}$	7	$8\frac{4}{10}$	$10\frac{1}{2}$
42	$2\frac{3}{4}$	$3\frac{8}{12}$	$4\frac{4}{10}$	$5\frac{1}{2}$	83	$5\frac{5}{16}$	$7\frac{1}{12}$	$8\frac{5}{10}$	$10\frac{5}{8}$
43	$2\frac{13}{16}$	$3\frac{9}{12}$	$4\frac{5}{10}$	$5\frac{5}{8}$	84	$5\frac{3}{8}$	$7\frac{2}{12}$	$8\frac{6}{10}$	$10\frac{3}{4}$
44	$2\frac{7}{8}$	$3\frac{10}{12}$	$4\frac{6}{10}$	$5\frac{3}{4}$	85	$5\frac{7}{16}$	$7\frac{3}{12}$	$8\frac{7}{10}$	$10\frac{7}{8}$
45	$2\frac{15}{16}$	$3\frac{11}{12}$	$4\frac{7}{10}$	$5\frac{7}{8}$	86	$5\frac{1}{2}$	$7\frac{4}{12}$	$8\frac{8}{10}$	11
46	3	4	$4\frac{8}{10}$	6	87	$5\frac{9}{16}$	$7\frac{5}{12}$	$8\frac{9}{10}$	$11\frac{1}{8}$
47	$3\frac{1}{16}$	$4\frac{1}{12}$	$4\frac{9}{10}$	$6\frac{1}{8}$	88	$5\frac{5}{8}$	$7\frac{6}{12}$	9	$11\frac{1}{4}$
48	$3\frac{1}{8}$	$4\frac{2}{12}$	5	$6\frac{1}{4}$	89	$5\frac{11}{16}$	$7\frac{7}{12}$	$9\frac{1}{10}$	$11\frac{3}{8}$
49	$3\frac{3}{16}$	$4\frac{3}{12}$	$5\frac{1}{10}$	$6\frac{3}{8}$	90	$5\frac{3}{4}$	$7\frac{8}{12}$	$9\frac{2}{10}$	$11\frac{1}{2}$
50	$3\frac{1}{4}$	$4\frac{4}{12}$	$5\frac{2}{10}$	$6\frac{1}{2}$	91	$5\frac{13}{16}$	$7\frac{9}{12}$	$9\frac{3}{10}$	$11\frac{5}{8}$

TABLE OF TOOTH DIMENSIONS OF THE FELLOWS STUB-TOOTH GEA

Cutters Marked Pitch	Stub Tooth Pitch	Has Depth of Standard Tooth	Thickness on Pitch Line	Addendum	Dedendum an Clearance
	4	5	.3925	.200	.250
	5	7	.314	.1429	.1785
	6	8	.2617	.125	.1562
	7	9	.2243	.111	.1389
	8	10	.1962	.100	.125
	9	11	.1744	.0909	.1137
	10	12	.157	.0833	.1042
	12	14	.1308	.0714	.0893

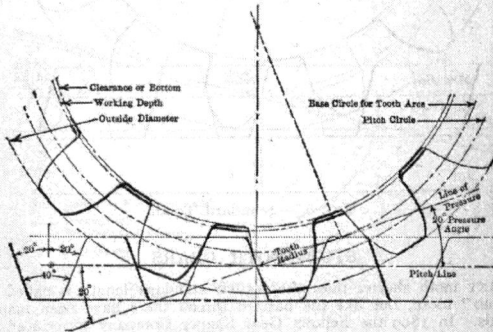

FIG. 7. — Stubbed Tooth

The Nuttall Company also use a 20-degree stub tooth, but have fixed length or depth in the following proportions.

Addendum = .25 × circular pitch instead of .3683.
Dedendum = .30 × circular pitch instead of .3683.
Working depth = .50 × circular pitch instead of .6366.
Clearance = .05 × circular pitch same as standard.
Whole depth = .55 × circular pitch instead of .6866.

TABLE FOR TURNING AND CUTTING GEAR BLANKS

FOR STANDARD LENGTH TOOTH

Pitch	16	12	10	8	Pitch	16	12	10	8
Depth of Tooth	.135	.180	.216	.270	Depth of Tooth	.135	.180	.216	.270
No. of Teeth	Outside Diameter				No. of Teeth	Outside Diameter			
10	$\frac{3}{4}$	1	$1\frac{2}{10}$	$1\frac{1}{2}$	51	$3\frac{5}{16}$	$4\frac{5}{12}$	$5\frac{8}{10}$	$6\frac{5}{8}$
11	$1\frac{13}{16}$	$1\frac{1}{12}$	$1\frac{3}{10}$	$1\frac{5}{8}$	52	$3\frac{3}{8}$	$4\frac{6}{12}$	$5\frac{4}{10}$	$6\frac{3}{4}$
12	$\frac{7}{8}$	$1\frac{5}{12}$	$1\frac{5}{10}$	$1\frac{3}{4}$	53	$3\frac{7}{16}$	$4\frac{7}{12}$	$5\frac{5}{10}$	$6\frac{7}{8}$
13	$\frac{15}{16}$	$1\frac{8}{12}$	$1\frac{6}{10}$	$1\frac{7}{8}$	54	$3\frac{1}{2}$	$4\frac{8}{12}$	$5\frac{6}{10}$	7
14	1	$1\frac{4}{12}$	$1\frac{6}{10}$	2	55	$3\frac{9}{16}$	$4\frac{9}{12}$	$5\frac{7}{10}$	$7\frac{1}{8}$
15	$1\frac{1}{16}$	$1\frac{1}{2}$	$1\frac{7}{10}$	$2\frac{1}{8}$	56	$3\frac{5}{8}$	$4\frac{10}{12}$	$5\frac{8}{10}$	$7\frac{1}{4}$
16	$1\frac{1}{8}$	$1\frac{6}{12}$	$1\frac{8}{10}$	$2\frac{1}{4}$	57	$3\frac{11}{16}$	$4\frac{11}{12}$	$5\frac{9}{10}$	$7\frac{3}{8}$
17	$1\frac{3}{16}$	$1\frac{7}{12}$	$1\frac{9}{10}$	$2\frac{3}{8}$	58	$3\frac{3}{4}$	5	6	$7\frac{1}{2}$
18	$1\frac{1}{4}$	$1\frac{8}{12}$	2	$2\frac{1}{2}$	59	$3\frac{13}{16}$	$5\frac{1}{12}$	$6\frac{1}{10}$	$7\frac{5}{8}$
19	$1\frac{5}{16}$	$1\frac{9}{12}$	$2\frac{1}{10}$	$2\frac{5}{8}$	60	$3\frac{7}{8}$	$5\frac{2}{12}$	$6\frac{2}{10}$	$7\frac{3}{4}$
20	$1\frac{3}{8}$	$1\frac{10}{12}$	$2\frac{2}{10}$	$2\frac{3}{4}$	61	$3\frac{15}{16}$	$5\frac{3}{12}$	$6\frac{3}{10}$	$7\frac{7}{8}$
21	$1\frac{7}{16}$	$1\frac{11}{12}$	$2\frac{3}{10}$	$2\frac{7}{8}$	62	4	$5\frac{1}{2}$	$6\frac{4}{10}$	8
22	$1\frac{1}{2}$	2	$2\frac{4}{10}$	3	63	$4\frac{1}{16}$	$5\frac{5}{12}$	$6\frac{5}{10}$	$8\frac{1}{8}$
23	$1\frac{9}{16}$	$2\frac{1}{12}$	$2\frac{5}{10}$	$3\frac{1}{8}$	64	$4\frac{1}{8}$	$5\frac{6}{12}$	$6\frac{6}{10}$	$8\frac{1}{4}$
24	$1\frac{5}{8}$	$2\frac{2}{12}$	$2\frac{6}{10}$	$3\frac{1}{4}$	65	$4\frac{3}{16}$	$5\frac{7}{12}$	$6\frac{7}{10}$	$8\frac{3}{8}$
25	$1\frac{11}{16}$	$2\frac{3}{12}$	$2\frac{7}{10}$	$3\frac{3}{8}$	66	$4\frac{1}{4}$	$5\frac{8}{12}$	$6\frac{8}{10}$	$8\frac{1}{2}$
26	$1\frac{3}{4}$	$2\frac{4}{12}$	$2\frac{8}{10}$	$3\frac{1}{2}$	67	$4\frac{5}{16}$	$5\frac{9}{12}$	$6\frac{10}{10}$	$8\frac{5}{8}$
27	$1\frac{13}{16}$	$2\frac{5}{12}$	$2\frac{9}{10}$	$3\frac{5}{8}$	68	$4\frac{3}{8}$	$5\frac{10}{12}$	7	$8\frac{3}{4}$
28	$1\frac{7}{8}$	$2\frac{6}{12}$	3	$3\frac{3}{4}$	69	$4\frac{7}{16}$	$5\frac{11}{12}$	$7\frac{1}{10}$	$8\frac{7}{8}$
29	$1\frac{15}{16}$	$2\frac{7}{12}$	$3\frac{1}{10}$	$3\frac{7}{8}$	70	$4\frac{1}{2}$	6	$7\frac{2}{10}$	9
30	2	$2\frac{8}{12}$	$3\frac{1}{10}$	4	71	$4\frac{9}{16}$	$6\frac{1}{12}$	$7\frac{3}{10}$	$9\frac{1}{8}$
31	$2\frac{1}{16}$	$2\frac{9}{12}$	$3\frac{1}{10}$	$4\frac{1}{8}$	72	$4\frac{5}{8}$	$6\frac{2}{12}$	$7\frac{4}{10}$	$9\frac{1}{4}$
32	$2\frac{1}{8}$	$2\frac{10}{12}$	$3\frac{1}{10}$	$4\frac{1}{4}$	73	$4\frac{11}{16}$	$6\frac{3}{12}$	$7\frac{5}{10}$	$9\frac{3}{8}$
33	$2\frac{3}{16}$	$2\frac{11}{12}$	$3\frac{5}{10}$	$4\frac{3}{8}$	74	$4\frac{3}{4}$	$6\frac{4}{12}$	$7\frac{6}{10}$	$9\frac{1}{2}$
34	$2\frac{1}{4}$	3	$3\frac{1}{10}$	$4\frac{1}{2}$	75	$4\frac{13}{16}$	$6\frac{5}{12}$	$7\frac{7}{10}$	$9\frac{5}{8}$
35	$2\frac{5}{16}$	$3\frac{1}{12}$	$3\frac{7}{10}$	$4\frac{5}{8}$	76	$4\frac{7}{8}$	$6\frac{6}{12}$	$7\frac{8}{10}$	$9\frac{3}{4}$
36	$2\frac{3}{8}$	$3\frac{2}{12}$	$3\frac{8}{10}$	$4\frac{3}{4}$	77	$4\frac{15}{16}$	$6\frac{7}{12}$	$7\frac{9}{10}$	$9\frac{7}{8}$
37	$2\frac{7}{16}$	$3\frac{3}{12}$	$3\frac{1}{10}$	$4\frac{7}{8}$	78	5	$6\frac{8}{12}$	8	10
38	$2\frac{1}{2}$	$3\frac{4}{12}$	4	5	79	$5\frac{1}{16}$	$6\frac{9}{12}$	$8\frac{1}{10}$	$10\frac{1}{8}$
39	$2\frac{9}{16}$	$3\frac{5}{12}$	$4\frac{1}{10}$	$5\frac{1}{8}$	80	$5\frac{1}{8}$	$6\frac{10}{12}$	$8\frac{2}{10}$	$10\frac{1}{4}$
40	$2\frac{5}{8}$	$3\frac{6}{12}$	$4\frac{1}{10}$	$5\frac{1}{4}$	81	$5\frac{3}{16}$	$6\frac{11}{12}$	$8\frac{3}{10}$	$10\frac{3}{8}$
41	$2\frac{11}{16}$	$3\frac{7}{12}$	$4\frac{1}{10}$	$5\frac{3}{8}$	82	$5\frac{1}{4}$	7	$8\frac{4}{10}$	$10\frac{1}{2}$
42	$2\frac{3}{4}$	$3\frac{8}{12}$	$4\frac{4}{10}$	$5\frac{1}{2}$	83	$5\frac{5}{16}$	$7\frac{1}{12}$	$8\frac{5}{10}$	$10\frac{5}{8}$
43	$2\frac{13}{16}$	$3\frac{9}{12}$	$4\frac{1}{10}$	$5\frac{5}{8}$	84	$5\frac{3}{8}$	$7\frac{2}{12}$	$8\frac{6}{10}$	$10\frac{3}{4}$
44	$2\frac{7}{8}$	$3\frac{10}{12}$	$4\frac{1}{10}$	$5\frac{3}{4}$	85	$5\frac{7}{16}$	$7\frac{3}{12}$	$8\frac{7}{10}$	$10\frac{7}{8}$
45	$2\frac{15}{16}$	$3\frac{11}{12}$	$4\frac{7}{10}$	$5\frac{7}{8}$	86	$5\frac{1}{2}$	$7\frac{4}{12}$	$8\frac{8}{10}$	11
46	3	4	$4\frac{1}{10}$	6	87	$5\frac{9}{16}$	$7\frac{5}{12}$	$8\frac{9}{10}$	$11\frac{1}{8}$
47	$3\frac{1}{16}$	$4\frac{1}{12}$	$4\frac{1}{10}$	$6\frac{1}{4}$	88	$5\frac{5}{8}$	$7\frac{6}{12}$	9	$11\frac{1}{4}$
48	$3\frac{1}{8}$	$4\frac{1}{12}$	5	$6\frac{1}{2}$	89	$5\frac{11}{16}$	$7\frac{7}{12}$	$9\frac{1}{10}$	$11\frac{3}{8}$
49	$3\frac{3}{16}$	$4\frac{3}{12}$	$5\frac{1}{10}$	$6\frac{3}{8}$	90	$5\frac{3}{4}$	$7\frac{8}{12}$	$9\frac{2}{10}$	$11\frac{1}{2}$
50	$3\frac{1}{4}$	$4\frac{4}{12}$	$5\frac{1}{10}$	$6\frac{1}{2}$	91	$5\frac{13}{16}$	$7\frac{9}{12}$	$9\frac{8}{10}$	$11\frac{5}{8}$

TABLE FOR TURNING AND CUTTING GEAR BLANKS

FOR STANDARD LENGTH TOOTH

Pitch	16	12	10	8	Pitch	16	12	10	8
Depth of Tooth	.135	.180	.216	.270	Depth of Tooth	.135	.180	.216	.270
No. of Teeth	Outside Diameter				No. of Teeth	Outside Diameter			
92	$5\frac{7}{8}$	$7\frac{10}{12}$	$9\frac{4}{10}$	$11\frac{3}{4}$	133	$8\frac{7}{16}$	$11\frac{3}{12}$	$13\frac{5}{10}$	$16\frac{7}{8}$
93	$5\frac{15}{16}$	$7\frac{11}{12}$	$9\frac{5}{10}$	$11\frac{7}{8}$	134	$8\frac{1}{2}$	$11\frac{4}{12}$	$13\frac{6}{10}$	17
94	6	8	$9\frac{6}{10}$	12	135	$8\frac{9}{16}$	$11\frac{5}{12}$	$13\frac{7}{10}$	$17\frac{1}{8}$
95	$6\frac{1}{16}$	$8\frac{1}{12}$	$9\frac{7}{10}$	$12\frac{1}{8}$	136	$8\frac{5}{8}$	$11\frac{6}{12}$	$13\frac{8}{10}$	$17\frac{1}{4}$
96	$6\frac{1}{8}$	$8\frac{2}{12}$	$9\frac{8}{10}$	$12\frac{1}{4}$	137	$8\frac{11}{16}$	$11\frac{7}{12}$	$13\frac{9}{10}$	$17\frac{3}{8}$
97	$6\frac{3}{16}$	$8\frac{3}{12}$	$9\frac{9}{10}$	$12\frac{3}{8}$	138	$8\frac{3}{4}$	$11\frac{8}{12}$	14	$17\frac{1}{2}$
98	$6\frac{1}{4}$	$8\frac{4}{12}$	10	$12\frac{1}{2}$	139	$8\frac{13}{16}$	$11\frac{9}{12}$	$14\frac{1}{10}$	$17\frac{5}{8}$
99	$6\frac{5}{16}$	$8\frac{5}{12}$	$10\frac{1}{10}$	$12\frac{5}{8}$	140	$8\frac{7}{8}$	$11\frac{10}{12}$	$14\frac{2}{10}$	$17\frac{3}{4}$
100	$6\frac{3}{8}$	$8\frac{6}{12}$	$10\frac{2}{10}$	$12\frac{3}{4}$	141	$8\frac{15}{16}$	$11\frac{11}{12}$	$14\frac{3}{10}$	$17\frac{7}{8}$
101	$6\frac{7}{16}$	$8\frac{7}{12}$	$10\frac{3}{10}$	$12\frac{7}{8}$	142	9	12	$14\frac{4}{10}$	18
102	$6\frac{1}{2}$	$8\frac{8}{12}$	$10\frac{4}{10}$	13	143	$9\frac{1}{16}$	$12\frac{1}{12}$	$14\frac{5}{10}$	$18\frac{1}{8}$
103	$6\frac{9}{16}$	$8\frac{9}{12}$	$10\frac{5}{10}$	$13\frac{1}{8}$	144	$9\frac{1}{8}$	$12\frac{2}{12}$	$14\frac{6}{10}$	$18\frac{1}{4}$
104	$6\frac{5}{8}$	$8\frac{10}{12}$	$10\frac{6}{10}$	$13\frac{1}{4}$	145	$9\frac{3}{16}$	$12\frac{3}{12}$	$14\frac{7}{10}$	$18\frac{3}{8}$
105	$6\frac{11}{16}$	$8\frac{11}{12}$	$10\frac{7}{10}$	$13\frac{3}{8}$	146	$9\frac{1}{4}$	$12\frac{4}{12}$	$14\frac{8}{10}$	$18\frac{1}{2}$
106	$6\frac{3}{4}$	9	$10\frac{8}{10}$	$13\frac{1}{2}$	147	$9\frac{5}{16}$	$12\frac{5}{12}$	$14\frac{9}{10}$	$18\frac{5}{8}$
107	$6\frac{13}{16}$	$9\frac{1}{12}$	$10\frac{9}{10}$	$13\frac{5}{8}$	148	$9\frac{3}{8}$	$12\frac{6}{12}$	15	$18\frac{3}{4}$
108	$6\frac{7}{8}$	$9\frac{2}{12}$	11	$13\frac{3}{4}$	149	$9\frac{7}{16}$	$12\frac{7}{12}$	$15\frac{1}{10}$	$18\frac{7}{8}$
109	$6\frac{15}{16}$	$9\frac{3}{12}$	$11\frac{1}{10}$	$13\frac{7}{8}$	150	$9\frac{1}{2}$	$12\frac{8}{12}$	$15\frac{2}{10}$	19
110	7	$9\frac{4}{12}$	$11\frac{2}{10}$	14	151	$9\frac{9}{16}$	$12\frac{9}{12}$	$15\frac{3}{10}$	$19\frac{1}{8}$
111	$7\frac{1}{16}$	$9\frac{5}{12}$	$11\frac{3}{10}$	$14\frac{1}{8}$	152	$9\frac{5}{8}$	$12\frac{10}{12}$	$15\frac{4}{10}$	$19\frac{1}{4}$
112	$7\frac{1}{8}$	$9\frac{6}{12}$	$11\frac{4}{10}$	$14\frac{1}{4}$	153	$9\frac{11}{16}$	$12\frac{11}{12}$	$15\frac{5}{10}$	$19\frac{3}{8}$
113	$7\frac{3}{16}$	$9\frac{7}{12}$	$11\frac{5}{10}$	$14\frac{3}{8}$	154	$9\frac{3}{4}$	13	$15\frac{6}{10}$	$19\frac{1}{2}$
114	$7\frac{1}{4}$	$9\frac{8}{12}$	$11\frac{6}{10}$	$14\frac{1}{2}$	155	$9\frac{13}{16}$	$13\frac{1}{12}$	$15\frac{7}{10}$	$19\frac{5}{8}$
115	$7\frac{5}{16}$	$9\frac{9}{12}$	$11\frac{7}{10}$	$14\frac{5}{8}$	156	$9\frac{7}{8}$	$13\frac{2}{12}$	$15\frac{8}{10}$	$19\frac{3}{4}$
116	$7\frac{3}{8}$	$9\frac{10}{12}$	$11\frac{8}{10}$	$14\frac{3}{4}$	157	$9\frac{15}{16}$	$13\frac{3}{12}$	$15\frac{9}{10}$	$19\frac{7}{8}$
117	$7\frac{7}{16}$	$9\frac{11}{12}$	$11\frac{9}{10}$	$14\frac{7}{8}$	158	10	$13\frac{4}{12}$	16	20
118	$7\frac{1}{2}$	10	12	15	159	$10\frac{1}{16}$	$13\frac{5}{12}$	$16\frac{1}{10}$	$20\frac{1}{8}$
119	$7\frac{9}{16}$	$10\frac{1}{12}$	$12\frac{1}{10}$	$15\frac{1}{8}$	160	$10\frac{1}{8}$	$13\frac{6}{12}$	$16\frac{2}{10}$	$20\frac{1}{4}$
120	$7\frac{5}{8}$	$10\frac{2}{12}$	$12\frac{2}{10}$	$15\frac{1}{4}$	161	$10\frac{3}{16}$	$13\frac{7}{12}$	$16\frac{3}{10}$	$20\frac{3}{8}$
121	$7\frac{11}{16}$	$10\frac{3}{12}$	$12\frac{3}{10}$	$15\frac{3}{8}$	162	$10\frac{1}{4}$	$13\frac{8}{12}$	$16\frac{4}{10}$	$20\frac{1}{2}$
122	$7\frac{3}{4}$	$10\frac{4}{12}$	$12\frac{4}{10}$	$15\frac{1}{2}$	163	$10\frac{5}{16}$	$13\frac{9}{12}$	$16\frac{5}{10}$	$20\frac{5}{8}$
123	$7\frac{13}{16}$	$10\frac{5}{12}$	$12\frac{5}{10}$	$15\frac{5}{8}$	164	$10\frac{3}{8}$	$13\frac{10}{12}$	$16\frac{6}{10}$	$20\frac{3}{4}$
124	$7\frac{7}{8}$	$10\frac{6}{12}$	$12\frac{6}{10}$	$15\frac{3}{4}$	165	$10\frac{7}{16}$	$13\frac{11}{12}$	$16\frac{7}{10}$	$20\frac{7}{8}$
125	$7\frac{15}{16}$	$10\frac{7}{12}$	$12\frac{7}{10}$	$15\frac{7}{8}$	166	$10\frac{1}{2}$	14	$16\frac{8}{10}$	21
126	8	$10\frac{8}{12}$	$12\frac{8}{10}$	16	167	$10\frac{9}{16}$	$14\frac{1}{12}$	$16\frac{9}{10}$	$21\frac{1}{8}$
127	$8\frac{1}{16}$	$10\frac{9}{12}$	$12\frac{9}{10}$	$16\frac{1}{8}$	168	$10\frac{5}{8}$	$14\frac{2}{12}$	17	$21\frac{1}{4}$
128	$8\frac{1}{8}$	$10\frac{10}{12}$	13	$16\frac{1}{4}$	169	$10\frac{11}{16}$	$14\frac{3}{12}$	$17\frac{1}{10}$	$21\frac{3}{8}$
129	$8\frac{3}{16}$	$10\frac{11}{12}$	$13\frac{1}{10}$	$16\frac{3}{8}$	170	$10\frac{3}{4}$	$14\frac{4}{12}$	$17\frac{2}{10}$	$21\frac{1}{2}$
130	$8\frac{1}{4}$	11	$13\frac{2}{10}$	$16\frac{1}{2}$	171	$10\frac{13}{16}$	$14\frac{5}{12}$	$17\frac{3}{10}$	$21\frac{5}{8}$
131	$8\frac{5}{16}$	$11\frac{1}{12}$	$13\frac{3}{10}$	$16\frac{5}{8}$	172	$10\frac{7}{8}$	$14\frac{6}{12}$	$17\frac{4}{10}$	$21\frac{3}{4}$
132	$8\frac{3}{8}$	$11\frac{2}{12}$	$13\frac{4}{10}$	$16\frac{3}{4}$	173	$10\frac{15}{16}$	$14\frac{7}{12}$	$17\frac{5}{10}$	$21\frac{7}{8}$

Pitch Diameters of Standard Gears

The accompanying tables require little explanation, being simply given to save time in laying out gear trains. Having the diametral pitch and the number of teeth, the pitch diameter is easily found from the tables. They also show the corresponding circular pitch, designated by C. P.

Having the pitch diameter, the outside diameter can easily be found by adding two parts of the pitch of standard gears. The outside diameter of any gear with standard teeth is the same as the pitch diameter of two more teeth.

PITCH DIAMETER OF GEARS WHEN DIAMETRAL PITCH AND THE NUMBER OF TEETH ARE KNOWN

D.P. C.P.	1.5 2.094	2 1.571	2.5 1.257	3 1.047	4 0.785	5 0.628	6 0.524	8 0.393	10 0.3142	12 0.2618	14 0.2244	16 0.1963	20 0.1571
No. T													
15	10.000	7.50	6.00	5.000	3.75	3.00	2.500	1.875	1.5	1.250	1.071	0.937	0.75
16	10.666	8.00	6.40	5.333	4.00	3.20	2.666	2.000	1.6	1.333	1.142	1.000	0.80
17	11.333	8.50	6.80	5.666	4.25	3.40	2.833	2.125	1.7	1.416	1.214	1.062	0.85
18	12.000	9.00	7.20	6.000	4.50	3.60	3.000	2.250	1.8	1.500	1.285	1.125	0.90
19	12.666	9.50	7.60	6.333	4.75	3.80	3.166	2.375	1.9	1.583	1.357	1.187	0.95
20	13.333	10.00	8.00	6.666	5.00	4.00	3.333	2.500	2.0	1.666	1.428	1.250	1.00
21	14.000	10.50	8.40	7.000	5.25	4.20	3.500	2.625	2.1	1.750	1.500	1.312	1.05
22	14.666	11.00	8.80	7.333	5.50	4.40	3.666	2.750	2.2	1.833	1.571	1.375	1.10
23	15.333	11.50	9.20	7.666	5.75	4.60	3.833	2.875	2.3	1.916	1.642	1.437	1.15
24	16.000	12.00	9.60	8.000	6.00	4.80	4.000	3.000	2.4	2.000	1.714	1.500	1.20
25	16.666	12.50	10.00	8.333	6.25	5.00	4.166	3.125	2.5	2.083	1.785	1.562	1.25
26	17.333	13.00	10.40	8.666	6.50	5.20	4.333	3.250	2.6	2.176	1.857	1.625	1.30
27	18.000	13.50	10.80	9.000	6.75	5.40	4.500	3.375	2.7	2.250	1.928	1.687	1.35
28	18.666	14.00	11.20	9.333	7.00	5.60	4.666	3.500	2.8	2.333	2.000	1.750	1.40
29	19.333	14.50	11.60	9.666	7.25	5.80	4.833	3.625	2.9	2.416	2.071	1.812	1.45
30	20.000	15.00	12.00	10.000	7.50	6.00	5.000	3.750	3.0	2.500	2.142	1.875	1.50
31	20.666	15.50	12.40	10.333	7.75	6.20	5.166	3.875	3.1	2.583	2.214	1.937	1.55
32	21.333	16.00	12.80	10.666	8.00	6.40	5.333	4.000	3.2	2.666	2.285	2.000	1.60
33	22.000	16.50	13.20	11.000	8.25	6.60	5.500	4.125	3.3	2.750	2.357	2.062	1.65
34	22.666	17.00	13.60	11.333	8.50	6.80	5.666	4.250	3.4	2.833	2.428	2.125	1.70
35	23.333	17.50	14.00	11.666	8.75	7.00	5.833	4.375	3.5	2.916	2.500	2.187	1.75

PITCH DIAMETER OF GEARS WHEN DIAMETRAL PITCH AND THE NUMBER OF TEETH ARE KNOWN. (Continued)

D.P.	1.5	2	2.5	3	4	5	6	8	10	12	14	16	20
C.P.	2.094	1.571	1.257	1.047	0.785	0.628	0.524	0.393	0.3142	0.2618	0.2244	0.1963	0.1571
No. T													
36	24.000	18.00	14.40	12.000	9.00	7.20	6.000	4.500	3.6	3.000	2.571	2.250	1.80
37	24.666	18.50	14.80	12.333	9.25	7.40	6.166	4.625	3.7	3.083	2.642	2.312	1.85
38	25.333	19.00	15.20	12.666	9.50	7.60	6.333	4.750	3.8	3.176	2.714	2.375	1.90
39	26.000	19.50	15.60	13.000	9.75	7.80	6.500	4.875	3.9	3.250	2.785	2.437	1.95
40	26.666	20.00	16.00	13.333	10.00	8.00	6.666	5.000	4.0	3.333	2.857	2.500	2.00
41	27.333	20.50	16.40	13.666	10.25	8.20	6.833	5.125	4.1	3.416	2.928	2.562	2.05
42	28.000	21.00	16.80	14.000	10.50	8.40	7.000	5.250	4.2	3.500	3.000	2.625	2.10
43	28.666	21.50	17.20	14.333	10.75	8.60	7.166	5.375	4.3	3.583	3.071	2.687	2.15
44	29.333	22.00	17.60	14.666	11.00	8.80	7.333	5.500	4.4	3.666	3.142	2.750	2.20
45	30.000	22.50	18.00	15.000	11.25	9.00	7.500	5.625	4.5	3.750	3.214	2.812	2.25
46	30.666	23.00	18.40	15.333	11.50	9.20	7.666	5.750	4.6	3.833	3.285	2.875	2.30
47	31.333	23.50	18.80	15.666	11.75	9.40	7.833	5.875	4.7	3.916	3.357	2.937	2.35
48	32.000	24.00	19.20	16.000	12.00	9.60	8.000	6.000	4.8	4.000	3.428	3.000	2.40
49	32.666	24.50	19.60	16.333	12.25	9.80	8.166	6.125	4.9	4.083	3.500	3.062	2.45
50	33.333	25.00	20.00	16.666	12.50	10.00	8.333	6.250	5.0	4.170	3.571	3.125	2.50
51	34.000	25.50	20.40	17.000	12.75	10.20	8.500	6.375	5.1	4.250	3.642	3.187	2.55
52	34.666	26.00	20.80	17.333	13.00	10.40	8.666	6.500	5.2	4.333	3.714	3.250	2.60
53	35.333	26.50	21.20	17.666	13.25	10.60	8.833	6.625	5.3	4.416	3.785	3.312	2.65
54	36.000	27.00	21.60	18.000	13.50	10.80	9.000	6.750	5.4	4.500	3.857	3.375	2.70
55	36.666	27.50	22.00	18.333	13.75	11.00	9.166	6.875	5.5	4.583	3.928	3.437	2.75
56	37.333	28.00	22.40	18.666	14.00	11.20	9.333	7.000	5.6	4.666	4.000	3.500	2.80
57	38.000	28.50	22.80	19.000	14.25	11.40	9.500	7.125	5.7	4.750	4.071	3.562	2.85
58	38.666	29.00	23.20	19.333	14.50	11.60	9.666	7.250	5.8	4.833	4.142	3.625	2.90
59	39.333	29.50	23.60	19.666	14.75	11.80	9.833	7.375	5.9	4.916	4.214	3.687	2.95
60	40.000	30.00	24.00	20.000	15.00	12.00	10.000	7.500	6.0	5.000	4.285	3.750	3.00
61	40.666	30.50	24.40	20.333	15.25	12.20	10.166	7.625	6.1	5.083	4.357	3.812	3.05
62	41.333	31.00	24.80	20.666	15.50	12.40	10.333	7.750	6.2	5.176	4.428	3.875	3.10
63	42.000	31.50	25.20	21.00	15.75	12.60	10.500	7.875	6.3	5.250	4.500	3.937	3.15
64	42.666	32.00	25.60	21.333	16.00	12.80	10.666	8.000	6.4	5.333	4.571	4.000	3.20
65	43.333	32.50	26.00	21.666	16.25	13.00	10.833	8.125	6.5	5.416	4.642	4.062	3.25
66	44.000	33.00	26.40	22.000	16.50	13.20	11.000	8.250	6.6	5.500	4.714	4.125	3.30

D.P.: — C.P.: No. T	20 / 0.1571	16 / 0.1963	14 / 0.2244	12 / 0.2618	10 / 0.3142	8 / 0.393	6 / 0.524	5 / 0.628	4 / 0.785	3 / 1.047	2.5 / 1.257	2 / 1.571	1.5 / 2.094
67	3.35	4.187	4.785	5.583	6.7	8.375	11.166	13.40	16.75	22.333	26.80	33.50	44.666
68	3.40	4.250	4.857	5.666	6.8	8.500	11.333	13.60	17.00	22.666	27.20	34.00	45.333
69	3.45	4.312	4.928	5.750	6.9	8.625	11.500	13.80	17.25	23.000	27.60	34.50	46.000
70	3.50	4.375	5.000	5.833	7.0	8.750	11.666	14.00	17.50	23.333	28.00	35.00	46.666
71	3.55	4.437	5.071	5.916	7.1	8.875	11.833	14.20	17.75	23.666	28.40	35.50	47.333
72	3.60	4.500	5.142	6.000	7.2	9.000	12.000	14.40	18.00	24.000	28.80	36.00	48.000
73	3.65	4.562	5.214	6.083	7.3	9.125	12.166	14.60	18.25	24.333	29.20	36.50	48.666
74	3.70	4.625	5.285	6.166	7.4	9.250	12.333	14.80	18.50	24.666	29.60	37.00	49.333
75	3.75	4.687	5.357	6.250	7.5	9.375	12.500	15.00	18.75	25.000	30.00	37.50	50.000
76	3.80	4.750	5.428	6.333	7.6	9.500	12.666	15.20	19.00	25.333	30.40	38.00	50.666
77	3.85	4.812	5.500	6.416	7.7	9.625	12.833	15.40	19.25	25.666	30.80	38.50	51.333
78	3.90	4.875	5.571	6.500	7.8	9.750	13.000	15.60	19.50	26.000	31.20	39.00	52.000
79	3.95	4.937	5.642	6.583	7.9	9.875	13.166	15.80	19.75	26.333	31.60	39.50	52.666
80	4.00	5.000	5.714	6.666	8.0	10.000	13.333	16.00	20.00	26.666	32.00	40.00	53.333
81	4.05	5.062	5.785	6.750	8.1	10.125	13.500	16.20	20.25	27.000	32.40	40.50	54.000
82	4.10	5.125	5.857	6.833	8.2	10.250	13.666	16.40	20.50	27.333	32.80	41.00	54.666
83	4.15	5.187	5.928	6.916	8.3	10.375	13.833	16.60	20.75	27.666	33.20	41.50	55.333
84	4.20	5.250	6.000	7.000	8.4	10.500	14.000	16.80	21.00	28.000	33.60	42.00	56.000
85	4.25	5.312	6.071	7.083	8.5	10.625	14.166	17.00	21.25	28.333	34.00	42.50	56.666
86	4.30	5.375	6.142	7.166	8.6	10.750	14.333	17.20	21.50	28.666	34.40	43.00	57.333
87	4.35	5.437	6.214	7.250	8.7	10.875	14.500	17.40	21.75	29.000	34.80	43.50	58.000
88	4.40	5.500	6.285	7.333	8.8	11.000	14.666	17.60	22.00	29.333	35.20	44.00	58.666
89	4.45	5.562	6.357	7.416	8.9	11.125	14.833	17.80	22.25	29.666	35.60	44.50	59.333
90	4.50	5.625	6.428	7.500	9.0	11.250	15.000	18.00	22.50	30.000	36.00	45.00	60.000
91	4.55	5.687	6.500	7.583	9.1	11.375	15.166	18.20	22.75	30.333	36.40	45.50	60.666
92	4.60	5.750	6.571	7.666	9.2	11.500	15.333	18.40	23.00	30.666	36.80	46.00	61.333
93	4.65	5.812	6.642	7.750	9.3	11.625	15.500	18.60	23.25	31.000	37.20	46.50	62.000
94	4.70	5.875	6.714	7.833	9.4	11.750	15.666	18.80	23.50	31.333	37.60	47.00	62.666
95	4.75	5.937	6.785	7.916	9.5	11.875	15.833	19.00	23.75	31.666	38.00	47.50	63.333
96	4.80	6.000	6.857	8.000	9.6	12.000	16.000	19.20	24.00	32.000	38.40	48.00	64.000
97	4.85	6.062	6.928	8.083	9.7	12.125	16.166	19.40	24.25	32.333	38.80	48.50	64.666
98	4.90	6.125	7.000	8.166	9.8	12.250	16.333	19.60	24.50	32.666	39.20	49.00	65.333
99	4.95	6.187	7.071	8.250	9.9	12.375	16.500	19.80	24.75	33.000	39.60	49.50	66.000

PITCH DIAMETER OF GEARS WHEN DIAMETRAL PITCH AND THE NUMBER OF TEETH ARE KNOWN. (Continued)

D.P. C.P. No. T	1.5 2.094	2 1.571	2.5 1.257	3 1.047	4 0.785	5 0.628	6 0.524	8 0.393	10 0.3142	12 0.2618	14 0.2244	16 0.1963	20 0.1571
100	66.666	50.00	40.00	33.333	25.00	20.00	16.666	12.500	10.0	8.333	7.142	6.250	5.00
101	67.333	50.50	40.40	33.666	25.25	20.20	16.835	12.625	10.1	8.416	7.214	6.312	5.05
102	68.000	51.00	40.80	34.000	25.50	20.40	17.000	12.750	10.2	8.500	7.285	6.375	5.10
103	68.666	51.50	41.20	34.333	25.75	20.60	17.166	12.875	10.3	8.583	7.357	6.437	5.15
104	69.333	52.00	41.60	34.666	26.00	20.80	17.333	13.000	10.4	8.666	7.428	6.500	5.20
105	70.000	52.50	42.00	35.000	26.25	21.00	17.500	13.125	10.5	8.750	7.500	6.562	5.25
106	70.666	53.00	42.40	35.333	26.50	21.20	17.666	13.250	10.6	8.833	7.571	6.625	5.30
107	71.333	53.50	42.80	35.666	26.75	21.40	17.833	13.375	10.7	8.916	7.642	6.687	5.35
108	72.000	54.00	43.20	36.000	27.00	21.60	18.000	13.500	10.8	9.000	7.714	6.750	5.40
109	72.666	54.50	43.60	36.333	27.25	21.80	18.166	13.625	10.9	9.083	7.785	6.812	5.45
110	73.333	55.00	44.00	36.666	27.50	22.00	18.333	13.750	11.0	9.166	7.857	6.875	5.50
111	74.000	55.50	44.40	37.000	27.75	22.20	18.500	13.875	11.1	9.250	7.928	6.937	5.55
112	74.666	56.00	44.80	37.333	28.00	22.40	18.666	14.000	11.2	9.333	8.000	7.000	5.60
113	75.333	56.50	45.20	37.666	28.25	22.60	18.833	14.125	11.3	9.416	8.071	7.062	5.65
114	76.000	57.00	45.60	38.000	28.50	22.80	19.000	14.250	11.4	9.500	8.142	7.125	5.70
115	76.666	57.50	46.00	38.333	28.75	23.00	19.166	14.375	11.5	9.583	8.214	7.187	5.75
116	77.333	58.00	46.40	38.666	29.00	23.20	19.333	14.500	11.6	9.666	9.285	7.250	5.80
117	78.000	58.50	46.80	39.000	29.25	23.40	19.500	14.625	11.7	9.750	8.357	7.312	5.85
118	78.666	59.00	47.20	39.333	29.50	23.60	19.666	14.750	11.8	9.833	8.428	7.375	5.90
119	79.333	59.50	47.60	39.666	29.75	23.80	19.833	14.875	11.9	9.916	8.500	7.437	5.95
120	80.000	60.00	48.00	40.000	30.00	24.00	20.000	15.000	12.0	10.000	8.571	7.500	6.00
121	80.666	60.50	48.40	40.333	30.25	24.20	20.166	15.125	12.1	10.083	8.642	7.562	6.05
122	81.333	61.00	48.80	40.666	30.50	24.40	20.333	15.250	12.2	10.176	8.714	7.625	6.10
123	82.000	61.50	49.20	41.000	30.75	24.60	20.666	15.375	12.3	10.250	8.785	7.687	6.15
124	82.666	62.00	49.60	41.333	31.00	24.80	20.833	15.500	12.4	10.333	8.857	7.750	6.20
125	83.333	62.50	50.00	41.666	31.25	25.00	21.000	15.625	12.5	10.416	8.928	7.812	6.25
126	84.000	63.00	50.40	42.000	31.50	25.20	21.166	15.750	12.6	10.500	9.000	7.875	6.30
127	84.666	63.50	50.80	42.333	31.75	25.40	21.333	15.875	12.7	10.583	9.071	7.937	6.35
128	85.333	64.00	51.20	42.666	32.00	25.60		16.000	12.8	10.666	9.142	8.000	6.40

B. & S. INVOLUTE GEAR TOOTH CUTTERS

No. 1 will cut wheels from 135 teeth to a rack.
No. 1½ will cut wheels from 80 teeth to 134 teeth.
No. 2 will cut wheels from 55 teeth to 134 teeth.
No. 2½ will cut wheels from 42 teeth to 54 teeth.
No. 3 will cut wheels from 35 teeth to 54 teeth.
No. 3½ will cut wheels from 30 teeth to 34 teeth.
No. 4 will cut wheels from 26 teeth to 34 teeth.
No. 4½ will cut wheels from 23 teeth to 25 teeth.
No. 5 will cut wheels from 21 teeth to 25 teeth.
No. 5½ will cut wheels from 19 teeth to 20 teeth.
No. 6 will cut wheels from 17 teeth to 20 teeth.
No. 6½ will cut wheels from 15 teeth to 16 teeth.
No. 7 will cut wheels from 14 teeth to 16 teeth.
No. 7½ will cut wheels from 13 teeth to 14 teeth.
No. 8 will cut wheels from 12 teeth to 13 teeth.

The eight cutters represented by the whole numbers constitute the regular set of cutters generally used for each pitch of tooth. The half numbers increase the set to 15 and gives teeth which are theoretically more correct. In some work special cutters are used for each gear but the 15 cutters in a set offer all that most cases require.

TABLE SHOWING DEPTH OF SPACE AND THICKNESS OF TOOTH
IN SPUR WHEELS, WHEN CUT WITH THESE CUTTERS

Pitch of Cutter	Depth to be cut in Gear Inches	Thickness of Tooth at Pitch Line. Inches	Pitch of Cutter	Depth to be cut in Gear Inches	Thickness of Tooth at Pitch Line. Inches
1¼	1.726	1.257	11	.196	.143
1½	1.438	1.047	12	.180	.131
1¾	1.233	.898	14	.154	.112
2	1.078	.785	16	.135	.098
2¼	.958	.697	18	.120	.087
2½	.863	.628	20	.108	.079
2¾	.784	.570	22	.098	.071
3	.719	.523	24	.090	.065
3½	.616	.448	26	.083	.060
4	.539	.393	28	.077	.056
5	.431	.314	30	.072	.052
6	.359	.262	32	.067	.049
7	.308	.224	36	.060	.044
8	.270	.196	40	.054	.039
9	.240	.175	48	.045	.033
10	.216	.157			

BLOCK INDEXING IN CUTTING GEAR TEETH

Block or intermittent indexing is a method to increase the output of gear cutters by allowing the feed and cutting speed to be increased without unduly heating the work. This is done by jumping from the tooth just cut to a tooth far enough away to escape the local heating and on the following rounds to cut the intermediate teeth. While the indexing takes a trifle more time, the heat is distributed so that faster cutting can be done without heating and dulling the cutter.

The following table gives the indexing of gears from 25 to 200 teeth and is worked out for the Brown & Sharpe gear cutter but can be modified to suit other machines.

INDEX TABLE FOR SPACING IN BLOCKS ON THE BROWN AND SHARPE GEAR CUTTER

Teeth to be Cut	No. Indexed at Once	First Driver	First Follower	Second Driver	Second Follower	Turns of Locking Disc
25	4	100	50	72	30	4
26	3	100	50	90	52	4
27	2	100	50	90	54	4
28	3	100	50	90	56	4
29	2	100	50	90	58	4
30	3	100	50	90	60	2
31	1	100	50	90	62	4
32	3	100	50	90	64	4
33	3	100	50	96	88	4
34	3	100	48	90	56	4
35	4	100	30	90	40	4
36	3	100	30	90	74	4
37	3	100	30	90	76	4
38	3	100	30	90	78	4
39	3	100	30	90	80	4
40	4	100	30	90	82	4
41	5	100	50	90	84	4
42	5	100	30	90	86	4
43	5	100	30	90	88	4
44	3	100	30	90	90	4
45	5	100	30	90	92	4
46	5	100	50	72	94	4
47	5	100	30	90	96	4
48	7	100	30	90	40	4
49	5	100	30	90	68	4
50	5	100	50	84	40	4
51	4	100	30	96	68	2

Teeth to be Cut	No. Indexed at Once	First Driver	First Follower	Second Driver	Second Follower	Turns of Locking Disc
52	5	100	30	90	52	2
54	4	100	30	90	54	2
55	4	100	30	90	44	2
56	4	100	30	90	56	2
57	4	100	30	84	76	2
58	7	100	30	90	58	2
60	5	100	30	90	40	2
62	5	100	30	96	62	2
63	4	100	30	90	56	2
64	5	100	30	90	64	2
65	5	100	44	90	52	2
66	4	100	30	90	40	2
67	5	100	46	90	67	2
68	3	100	50	90	68	2
69	3	100	30	84	70	2
70	5	100	30	90	72	2
72	5	100	30	96	74	2
74	7	100	70	90	50	2
75	5	100	30	84	76	2
76	4	100	30	90	44	2
77	5	100	70	90	78	2
78	5	100	30	96	80	2
80	5	100	30	84	52	2
81	4	100	30	90	82	2
82	3	100	50	90	84	2
84	4	100	30	96	68	2
85	4	100	50	84	68	2

Teeth to be Cut	No. Indexed at Once	First Driver	First Follower	Second Driver	Second Follower	Turns of Locking Disc
86	5	100	30	90	86	2
87	7	100	30	84	58	2
88	5	100	30	72	88	2
90	5	100	30	90	50	2
91	7	100	30	90	52	2
92	3	100	30	84	92	2
93	5	100	30	96	62	2
94	5	100	50	96	94	2
95	4	100	30	90	76	2
96	5	100	30	90	96	2
98	5	100	30	90	98	2
99	10	100	30	84	44	2
100	7	100	50	90	40	2
102	5	100	44	90	52	2
104	5	100	30	90	60	2
105	4	100	46	90	44	2
108	7	100	50	72	40	2
110	5	100	50	84	56	2
111	5	100	30	90	76	2
112	5	100	30	84	46	2
114	7	100	70	90	58	2
115	8	100	50	96	78	2
116	5	100	30	96	68	2
117	8	100	70	70	40	2
119	3	100	50	70	44	2
120	7	100	30	96	44	2
121	4	60	66	—	—	2

Teeth to be Cut	No. Indexed at Once	First Driver	First Follower	Second Driver	Second Follower	Turns of Locking Disc
123	7	100	30	84	86	2
124	5	100	30	84	62	2
125	5	100	30	84	50	2
126	5	100	30	90	42	2
128	7	100	30	84	64	2
129	7	100	30	84	86	2
130	5	100	30	84	52	2
132	4	100	30	96	40	2
133	5	100	30	90	76	2
134	5	100	50	90	67	2
135	7	100	30	90	54	2
136	5	100	30	90	68	2
138	5	100	92	90	40	2
140	3	100	30	90	70	2
141	5	100	94	88	52	2
143	6	100	66	90	58	2
144	5	100	60	96	40	2
145	6	100	58	96	74	2
147	5	100	60	72	59	2
148	5	100	60	84	76	2
150	7	100	68	90	60	2
152	5	100	56	72	66	2
153	5	100	60	90	62	2
154	6	100	72	70	78	2
155	5	100	50	84	68	2
156	7	100	66	96	40	2
160	7	100	50	84	44	2

Teeth to be Cut	No. Indexed at Once	First Driver	First Follower	Second Driver	Second Follower	Turns of Locking Disc
161	5	100	70	68	46	2
162	7	100	60	90	52	2
164	5	100	60	84	66	2
165	5	100	50	90	84	2
168	6	96	60	90	78	2
169	5	70	52	90	68	2
170	5	100	50	90	76	2
171	5	100	60	90	86	2
172	8	100	60	96	58	2
174	5	100	60	90	50	2
175	5	100	60	90	52	2
176	9	99	56	70	92	2
180	5	100	60	72	74	2
182	6	100	60	84	60	2
184	5	100	50	48	84	2
185	5	100	44	90	70	2
186	5	100	60	80	96	2
187	5	100	60	84	84	2
188	7	100	60	90	70	2
189	5	100	50	84	96	2
190	7	100	60	84	66	2
192	5	100	50	90	78	2
195	5	100	60	90	66	2
196	5	100	50	84	40	2
198	7	100	50	—	—	2
200	7	60	60	84	—	2

THE DIMENSIONS OF GEARS BY METRIC PITCH

Module is the pitch diameter in mm. divided by the number of teeth in the gear.

Pitch diameter in mm. is the Module multiplied by the number of teeth in the gear.

M = Module.

D' = The pitch diameter of gear.

D = The whole diameter of gear.

N = The number of teeth in gear.

D'' = The working depth of teeth.

t = Thickness of teeth on pitch line.

f = Amount added to depth for clearance.

Then

$$M = \frac{D'}{N} \text{ or } \frac{D}{N + 2}.$$

$$D' = N\,M.$$

$$D = (N + 2)\,M.$$

$$N = \frac{D'}{M} \text{ or } \frac{D}{M} - 2.$$

$$D'' = 2\,M.$$

$$t = M\,1.5708.$$

$$f = \frac{M\,1.5708}{10} = .157\,M.$$

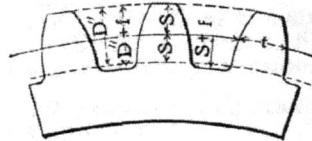

FIG. 8

The Module is equal to the part marked "S" in cut, measured in mm. and parts of mm.

Example: Module = 3.50 mm. 100 teeth.

Pitch diameter = 3.5 × 100 = 350 mm.

Whole diameter = (100 + 2) × 3.5 = 357 mm.

PITCHES COMMONLY USED — MODULE IN MILLIMETERS

Module	Corresponding English Diametral Pitch	Module	Corresponding English Diametral Pitch
½ mm.	50.800	4.5 mm.	5.644
¾	33.867	5	5.080
1	25.400	5.5	4.618
1.25	20.320	6	4.233
1.5	16.933	7	3.628
1.75	14.514	8	3.175
2	12.700	9	2.822
2.25	11.288	10	2.540
2.5	10.160	11	2.309
2.75	9.236	12	2.117
3	8.466	14	1.814
3.5	7.257	16	1.587
4	6.350		

SPROCKET WHEELS FOR BLOCK CENTER CHAINS

N = No. of Teeth. $E = \dfrac{180°}{N}$

C = Diameter of Round Part of Chain Block. $\text{Tan } D =$

$$\dfrac{\text{Sin. } E}{\dfrac{B}{A} + \text{Cos. } E}$$

B = Center to Center of holes in Chain Block.

A = Center to Center of holes in side links. Pitch Diam. $= \dfrac{A}{\text{Sin. } D}$

Outside Diam. = Pitch Diam. + C.

Bottom Diam. = Pitch Diam. − C.

In calculating the diameter of Sprocket Wheels the Bottom Diameter is the most important.

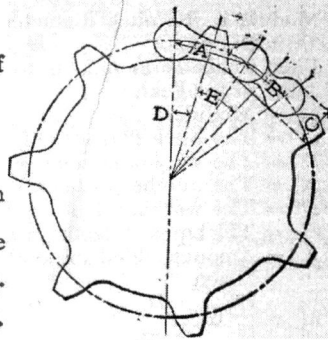

FIG. 9

DIAMETER OF SPROCKET WHEELS — FOR BLOCK CHAINS 1″ PITCH $A = .6″$. $B = .4″$. $C = .325″$.

No. of Teeth	Pitch Diameter Inches	Outside Diameter Inches	Bottom Diameter Inches
6	1.935	2.260	1.610
7	2.250	2.575	1.925
8	2.566	2.891	2.241
9	2.882	3.207	2.557
10	3.198	3.523	2.873
11	3.515	3.840	3.190
12	3.832	4.157	3.507
13	4.149	4.474	3.824
14	4.466	4.791	4.141
15	4.784	5.109	4.459
16	5.102	5.427	4.777
17	5.420	5.745	5.095
18	5.738	6.063	5.413
19	6.056	6.381	5.731
20	6.374	6.699	6.049
21	6.692	7.017	6.367
22	7.010	7.335	6.685
23	7.328	7.653	7.003
24	7.646	7.971	7.321
25	7.964	8.289	7.639
26	8.282	8.607	7.957
27	8.600	8.925	8.275
28	8.918	9.243	8.593
29	9.237	9.562	8.912
30	9.556	9.881	9.231

**Calculating Diameters of
Sprocket Wheels for Roller Chains**

N = Number of Teeth in Sprocket
P = Pitch of Chain
D = Diameter of Roller

$$A = \frac{360°}{N}$$

Pitch Diameter $= \dfrac{P}{\text{Sin. } \frac{1}{2} A}$

Outside Diameter = Pitch Diameter + D
Bottom Diameter = Pitch Diameter − D

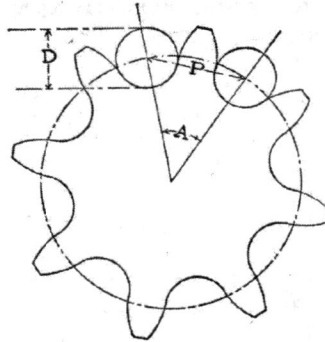

FIG. 10

Diameter of Sprocket Wheels for Roller Chains 1″ pitch where $D = .45$.

DIAMETER OF SPROCKET WHEELS FOR ROLLER CHAINS OF 1″ PITCH
WHEN $D = .45″$

No. of Teeth	Pitch Diameter in Inches	Outside Diameter in Inches	Bottom Diameter in Inches
6	2.	2.45	1.55
7	2.305	2.755	1.855
8	2.613	3.063	2.163
9	2.923	3.373	2.473
10	3.236	3.686	2.786
11	3.549	3.999	3.099
12	3.863	4.313	3.413
13	4.179	4.629	3.729
14	4.494	4.944	4.044
15	4.809	5.259	4.359
16	5.125	5.575	4.675
17	5.442	5.892	4.992
18	5.758	6.208	5.308
19	6.122	6.572	5.672
20	6.392	6.842	5.942
21	6.747	7.197	6.297
22	7.025	7.475	6.575
23	7.344	7.794	6.894
24	7.661	8.111	7.211
25	7.979	8.429	7.529
26	8.296	8.746	7.846
27	8.614	9.064	8.164
28	8.932	9.382	8.482
29	9.249	9.699	8.799
30	9.566	10.016	9.116

A TABLE FOR DIMENSIONS FOR MITER GEARS

THE accompanying table is of service in determining the principal dimensions of miter gears (center angle 45 degrees), the number of teeth and the pitch being known. The table covers most of the possible number of teeth from 12 to 60, inclusive, and pitches from 2 to 10, inclusive, omitting 9. Values for face and cut angles correspond with designations in Fig. 11.

A TABLE OF DIMENSIONS FOR MITER GEARS

MITER GEARS, CENTER ANGLE 45 DEGREES

No. of Teeth	Pitch Diameters								Outside Diameters								Face Angle	Cut Angle
	2 P.	3 P.	4 P.	5 P.	6 P.	7 P.	8 P.	10 P.	2 P.	3 P.	4 P.	5 P.	6 P.	7 P.	8 P.	10 P.		
12	6	4	3	$2\frac{2}{5}$	2	$1\frac{5}{7}$	$1\frac{1}{2}$	$1\frac{2}{10}$	6.71	4.48	3.35	2.68	2.24	1.92	1.68	1.34	51°43′	37°14′
13	$6\frac{1}{2}$	$4\frac{1}{3}$	$3\frac{1}{4}$	$2\frac{3}{5}$	$2\frac{1}{6}$	$1\frac{6}{7}$	$1\frac{5}{8}$	$1\frac{3}{10}$	7.21	4.80	3.60	2.88	2.40	2.06	1.81	1.44	51°12′	37°49′
14	7	$4\frac{2}{3}$	$3\frac{1}{2}$	$2\frac{4}{5}$	$2\frac{2}{6}$	2	$1\frac{3}{4}$	$1\frac{4}{10}$	7.71	5.14	3.85	3.08	2.57	2.20	1.93	1.54	50°47′	38°20′
15	$7\frac{1}{2}$	5	$3\frac{3}{4}$	3	$2\frac{3}{6}$	$2\frac{1}{7}$	$1\frac{7}{8}$	$1\frac{5}{10}$	8.21	5.46	4.10	3.28	2.73	2.35	2.06	1.64	50°23′	38°46′
16	8	$5\frac{1}{3}$	4	$3\frac{1}{5}$	$2\frac{4}{6}$	$2\frac{2}{7}$	2	$1\frac{6}{10}$	8.71	5.80	4.35	3.48	2.90	2.49	2.18	1.74	50°03′	39°09′
17	$8\frac{1}{2}$	$5\frac{2}{3}$	$4\frac{1}{4}$	$3\frac{2}{5}$	$2\frac{5}{6}$	$2\frac{3}{7}$	$2\frac{1}{8}$	$1\frac{7}{10}$	9.21	6.14	4.60	3.68	3.07	2.63	2.31	1.84	49°45′	39°30′
18	9	6	$4\frac{1}{2}$	$3\frac{3}{5}$	3	$2\frac{4}{7}$	$2\frac{1}{4}$	$1\frac{8}{10}$	9.71	6.48	4.85	3.88	3.24	2.77	2.43	1.94	49°29′	39°48′
19	$9\frac{1}{2}$	$6\frac{1}{3}$	$4\frac{3}{4}$	$3\frac{4}{5}$	$3\frac{1}{6}$	$2\frac{5}{7}$	$2\frac{3}{8}$	$1\frac{9}{10}$	10.21	6.80	5.10	4.08	3.40	2.92	2.56	2.04	49°15′	40°04′
20	10	$6\frac{2}{3}$	5	4	$3\frac{2}{6}$	$2\frac{6}{7}$	$2\frac{1}{2}$	2	10.71	7.14	5.35	4.28	3.57	3.06	2.68	2.14	49°03′	40°19′
21	$10\frac{1}{2}$	7	$5\frac{1}{4}$	$4\frac{1}{5}$	$3\frac{3}{6}$	3	$2\frac{5}{8}$	$2\frac{1}{10}$	11.21	7.46	5.60	4.48	3.73	3.20	2.81	2.24	48°51′	40°32′
22	11	$7\frac{1}{3}$	$5\frac{1}{2}$	$4\frac{2}{5}$	$3\frac{4}{6}$	$3\frac{1}{7}$	$2\frac{3}{4}$	$2\frac{2}{10}$	11.71	7.80	5.85	4.68	3.90	3.35	2.93	2.34	48°41′	40°45′
23	$11\frac{1}{2}$	$7\frac{2}{3}$	$5\frac{3}{4}$	$4\frac{3}{5}$	$3\frac{5}{6}$	$3\frac{2}{7}$	$2\frac{7}{8}$	$2\frac{3}{10}$	12.21	8.14	6.10	4.88	4.07	3.49	3.06	2.44	48°31′	40°56′
24	12	8	6	$4\frac{4}{5}$	4	$3\frac{3}{7}$	3	$2\frac{4}{10}$	12.71	8.48	6.35	5.08	4.24	3.63	3.18	2.54	48°22′	41°06′
25	$12\frac{1}{2}$	$8\frac{1}{3}$	$6\frac{1}{4}$	5	$4\frac{1}{6}$	$3\frac{4}{7}$	$3\frac{1}{8}$	$2\frac{5}{10}$	13.21	8.80	6.60	5.28	4.40	3.77	3.31	2.64	48°14′	41°15′
26	13	$8\frac{2}{3}$	$6\frac{1}{2}$	$5\frac{1}{5}$	$4\frac{2}{6}$	$3\frac{5}{7}$	$3\frac{1}{4}$	$2\frac{6}{10}$	13.71	9.14	6.85	5.48	4.57	3.92	3.43	2.74	48°07′	41°24′
27	$13\frac{1}{2}$	9	$6\frac{3}{4}$	$5\frac{2}{5}$	$4\frac{3}{6}$	$3\frac{6}{7}$	$3\frac{3}{8}$	$2\frac{7}{10}$	14.21	9.46	7.10	5.68	4.73	4.06	3.56	2.84	48°00′	41°32′
28	14	$9\frac{1}{3}$	7	$5\frac{3}{5}$	$4\frac{4}{6}$	4	$3\frac{1}{2}$	$2\frac{8}{10}$	14.71	9.80	7.35	5.88	4.90	4.20	3.68	2.94	47°54′	41°39′
29	$14\frac{1}{2}$	$9\frac{2}{3}$	$7\frac{1}{4}$	$5\frac{4}{5}$	$4\frac{5}{6}$	$4\frac{1}{7}$	$3\frac{5}{8}$	$2\frac{9}{10}$	15.21	10.14	7.60	6.08	5.07	4.35	3.81	3.04	47°47′	41°46′
30	15	10	$7\frac{1}{2}$	6	5	$4\frac{2}{7}$	$3\frac{3}{4}$	3	15.71	10.48	7.85	6.28	5.24	4.49	3.93	3.14	47°42′	41°53′
31	$15\frac{1}{2}$	$10\frac{1}{3}$	$7\frac{3}{4}$	$6\frac{1}{5}$	$5\frac{1}{6}$	$4\frac{3}{7}$	$3\frac{7}{8}$	$3\frac{1}{10}$	16.21	10.80	8.10	6.48	5.40	4.63	4.06	3.24	47°37′	41°59′
32	16	$10\frac{2}{3}$	8	$6\frac{2}{5}$	$5\frac{2}{6}$	$4\frac{4}{7}$	4	$3\frac{2}{10}$	16.71	11.14	8.35	6.68	5.57	4.77	4.18	3.34	47°32′	42°04′
33	$16\frac{1}{2}$	11	$8\frac{1}{4}$	$6\frac{3}{5}$	$5\frac{3}{6}$	$4\frac{5}{7}$	$4\frac{1}{8}$	$3\frac{3}{10}$	17.21	11.46	8.60	6.88	5.73	4.92	4.31	3.44	47°27′	42°10′
34	17	$11\frac{1}{3}$	$8\frac{1}{2}$	$6\frac{4}{5}$	$5\frac{4}{6}$	$4\frac{6}{7}$	$4\frac{1}{4}$	$3\frac{4}{10}$	17.71	11.80	8.85	7.08	5.90	5.06	4.43	3.54	47°23′	42°15′
35	$17\frac{1}{2}$	$11\frac{2}{3}$	$8\frac{3}{4}$	7	$5\frac{5}{6}$	5	$4\frac{3}{8}$	$3\frac{5}{10}$	18.21	12.14	9.10	7.28	6.07	5.20	4.56	3.64	47°19′	42°19′
36	18	12	9	$7\frac{1}{5}$	6	$5\frac{1}{7}$	$4\frac{1}{2}$	$3\frac{6}{10}$	18.71	12.48	9.35	7.48	6.24	5.35	4.68	3.74	47°15′	42°24′
37	$18\frac{1}{2}$	$12\frac{1}{3}$	$9\frac{1}{4}$	$7\frac{2}{5}$	$6\frac{1}{6}$	$5\frac{2}{7}$	$4\frac{5}{8}$	$3\frac{7}{10}$	19.21	12.80	9.60	7.68	6.40	5.49	4.81	3.84	47°11′	42°28′
38	19	$12\frac{2}{3}$	$9\frac{1}{2}$	$7\frac{3}{5}$	$6\frac{2}{6}$	$5\frac{3}{7}$	$4\frac{3}{4}$	$3\frac{8}{10}$	19.71	13.14	9.85	7.88	6.57	5.63	4.93	3.94	47°08′	42°32′
40	20	$13\frac{1}{3}$	10	8	$6\frac{4}{6}$	$5\frac{5}{7}$	5	4	20.71	13.80	10.35	8.28	6.90	5.92	5.18	4.14	47°01′	42°39′
42	21	14	$10\frac{1}{2}$	$8\frac{2}{5}$	7	6	$5\frac{1}{4}$	$4\frac{2}{10}$	21.71	14.48	10.85	8.68	7.24	6.20	5.43	4.34	46°56′	42°46′
44	22	$14\frac{2}{3}$	11	$8\frac{4}{5}$	$7\frac{2}{6}$	$6\frac{2}{7}$	$5\frac{1}{2}$	$4\frac{4}{10}$	22.71	15.14	11.35	9.08	7.57	6.49	5.68	4.54	46°50′	42°52′
46	23	$15\frac{1}{3}$	$11\frac{1}{2}$	$9\frac{1}{5}$	$7\frac{4}{6}$	$6\frac{4}{7}$	$5\frac{3}{4}$	$4\frac{6}{10}$	23.71	15.80	11.85	9.48	7.90	6.77	5.93	4.74	46°46′	42°58′
48	24	16	12	$9\frac{3}{5}$	8	$6\frac{6}{7}$	6	$4\frac{8}{10}$	24.71	16.48	12.35	9.88	8.24	7.06	6.18	4.94	46°42′	43°06′
50	25	$16\frac{2}{3}$	$12\frac{1}{2}$	10	$8\frac{2}{6}$	$7\frac{1}{7}$	$6\frac{1}{4}$	5	25.71	17.14	12.85	10.28	8.57	7.35	6.43	5.14	46°37′	43°12′
54	27	18	$13\frac{1}{2}$	$10\frac{4}{5}$	9	$7\frac{5}{7}$	$6\frac{3}{4}$	$5\frac{4}{10}$	27.71	18.48	13.85	11.08	9.24	7.92	6.93	5.54	46°31′	43°18′
58	29	$19\frac{1}{3}$	$14\frac{1}{2}$	$11\frac{3}{5}$	$9\frac{4}{6}$	$8\frac{2}{7}$	$7\frac{1}{4}$	$5\frac{8}{10}$	29.71	19.80	14.85	11.88	9.90	8.49	7.43	5.94	46°24′	43°24′
60	30	20	15	12	10	$8\frac{4}{7}$	$7\frac{1}{2}$	6	30.71	20.48	15.35	12.28	10.24	8.77	7.68	6.14	46°21′	43°30′

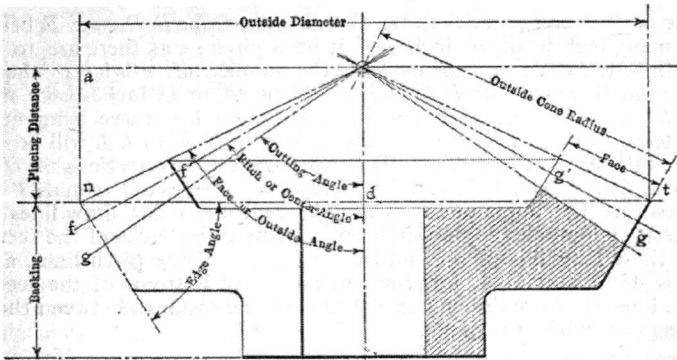

FIG. 11. — Bevel Gear Parts

BEVEL GEARS

BEVEL Gears are used to transmit power when shafts are not parallel. They can be made for any angle, but are more often at right angles than any other. Right angle bevel gears are often called miter gears. The teeth are or should be radial so that they are longer at the outer end. The names of parts are shown in Fig. 11. These should be noted carefully, particularly the face angles. The earlier editions measured *face angle* at right angles to the axis, but this is now changed as shown.

LAYING OUT BEVEL GEAR BLANKS

In laying out bevel gears, first decide upon the pitch, and draw the center lines $B B$ and $C C$, intersecting at right angles at A as shown in Fig. 12. Then draw the lines $D D$ to $E E$ the same distance each

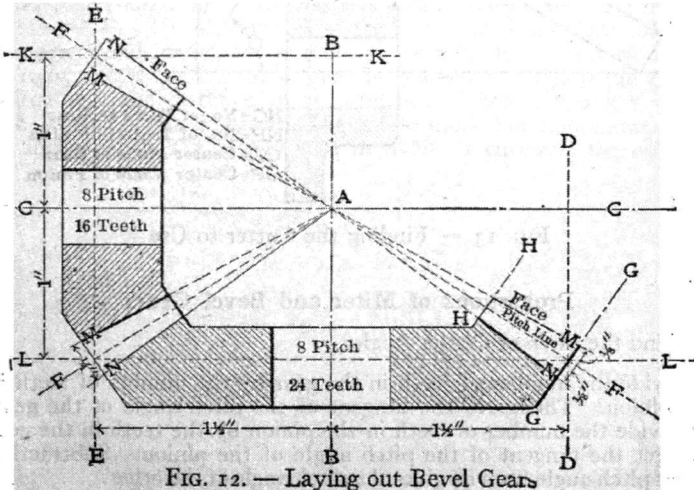

FIG. 12. — Laying out Bevel Gears

side of *B B* and parallel to it; the distance from *D D* to *E E* being
as many eighths of an inch — if it be 8 pitch — as there are to be
teeth in the gear. In the example the number of teeth is 24; there-
fore the distance from *D D* to *E E* will be $\frac{24}{8}$, or $1\frac{1}{2}$ inches each side
of *B B*. *K K* and *L L* are similarly drawn, but there being only
16 teeth in the small gear, the distance from *K K* to *L L* will be $\frac{16}{8}$,
or 1 inch each side of *C C*. Then through the intersections of *D D*
and *L L*, *E E* and *L L*, and *E E* and *K K*, draw the diagonals *F A*.
These are the pitch lines. Through the same point draw lines as
G G at right angles to the pitch lines, forming the backs of the teeth.
On these lines lay off $\frac{1}{8}$ of an inch each side of the pitch lines, and
draw *M A* and *N A*, forming the faces and bottoms of the teeth.
The lines *H H* are drawn parallel to *G G*, the distance between them
being the width of the face.

The face of the larger gear should be turned to the lines *M A*, and
the small gear to *N A*. For other pitches the same rules apply. If
4 pitch, use 4ths instead of 8ths; if 3 pitch, 3ds, and so on.

Bevel gears should always be turned to the exact diameters and
angles of the drawings and the teeth cut at the correct angle.

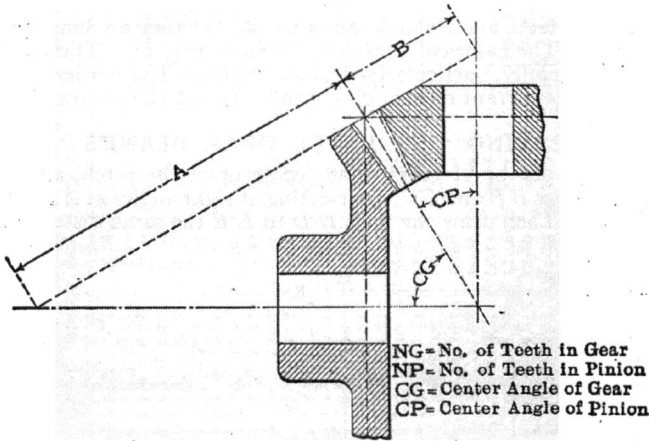

NG = No. of Teeth in Gear
NP = No. of Teeth in Pinion
CG = Center Angle of Gear
CP = Center Angle of Pinion

FIG. 13. — Finding the Cutter to Use

Proportions of Miter and Bevel Gears

To Find the Pitch or Center Angle:

Divide the number of teeth in the gear by the number of teeth in
the pinion. This gives the tangent of the pitch angle of the gear.
Or divide the number of teeth in the pinion by the teeth in the gear
and get the tangent of the pitch angle of the pinion. Subtracting
either pitch angle from 90 gives the pitch angle of the other.

To Find the Outside Diameter:

Multiply the cosine of the pitch angle by twice the addendum and add the pitch diameter.

To Find the Outside Cone Radius or Apex Distance:

Multiply the secant of the pitch angle of the pinion by ½ the pitch diameter of the gear.

To Find the Face and Cutting Angles:

Divide the addendum by the outside cone radius or apex distance. This gives the tangent of the addendum or outside angle. Subtract this angle from the pitch angle of the pinion to obtain the cutting angle of the pinion, and the face angle of the gear. Subtract the same addendum angle from the center angle of the gear to obtain the cutting angle of the gear and the face angle of the pinion. This gives a uniform clearance and is especially for use with rotary cutters.

To Find Hight of Addendum at Small End of Tooth:

Divide the addendum at the large end of the tooth by the outside cone radius. This gives the decrease in hight of the addendum for each inch of gear face. Multiply this by the length of the gear face and subtract the result from the addendum of the large end of the tooth. The difference is the hight of the addendum at the small end of the tooth.

CUTTERS FOR BEVEL GEARS

Lay out the bevel gears and draw lines A and B at right angles to the center angle line. Extend this to the center lines and measure A and B. The distance A = the radius of a spur gear of the same pitch, and finding the number of teeth in such a gear we have the right cutter for the bevel gear in question. Calling the gears 8 pitch and the distance A = 4 inches. Then $2 \times 4 \times 8 = 64$ teeth, so that a No. 2 cutter is the one to use. For the pinion, if B is 2 inches, then $2 \times 2 \times 8 = 32$ or a No. 4 cutter is the one to use.

USING THE BEVEL GEAR TABLE

TAKE a pair of bevel gears 24 and 72 teeth, 8 diametral pitch. Divide the pinion by the gear — 24 ÷ 72 = .3333. This is the tangent of the center angle of pinion. Look in the seven columns under center angles for the nearest number to this. The nearest is .3346 in the center column, as all these are decimals to four places. Follow this out to the left and find 18 in the center angle column. As the .3346 is in the column marked .50 the center angle of the pinion is 18.50 degrees. Looking to the right under center angles for gears find 71 and add the .50 making the gear angle 71.50 degrees. Thus:

Center angle of pinion 18 5 degrees.
Center angle of gear 71.5 degrees.

In the first column opposite 18 is 36. Divide this by the number of teeth in the pinion, 24, and get 1.5 degrees. This is the angle increase for this pair of gears, and is the amount to be added to the center angle to get the face angle and to be deducted to get the cut angles. This gives

Pinion center angle 18.5 + 1.5 = 20 degrees face angle.
Pinion center angle 18.5 − 1.5 = 17 degrees cut angle.
Gear center angle 71.5 + 1 5 = 73 degrees face angle.
Gear center angle 71.5 − 1 5 = 70 degrees cut angle.

For the outside diameter go to the column of diameter increase and in line with 18 find 1.90. Divide this by the pitch, 8, and get .237, which is the diameter increase for the pinion. Follow the same line to the right and find .65 for the gear increase. Divide this by the pitch, .8, and get .081 for gear increase. This gives

Pinion, 24 teeth, 8 pitch = 3 inches + .237 = 3.237 in. outside dia.
Gear, 72 teeth, 8 pitch = 9 inches + .081 = 9.081 in. outside dia.

TO SELECT THE CUTTER

Another way of selecting the cutter is to divide the number of teeth in the gear by the cosine of the center angle C and the answer is the number of teeth in a spur gear from which to select the cutter. For the pinion the process is the same except the number of teeth in the pinion is divided by the sine of the center angle. Formula

$$\text{Tangent of } CG = \frac{NG}{NP}. \qquad \text{Tangent of } CP = \frac{NP}{NG}.$$

$$\text{Number of teeth to use in selecting cutter for gear} = \frac{NG}{Cos\ CG}.$$

$$\text{Number of teeth to use in selecting cutter for pinion} = \frac{NP}{Sin\ CG}.$$

Any pair of gears can be figured out in the same way, bearing in mind that when finding the center angle for the gear, to read the parts of a degree from the decimals at the bottom, and that for the pinion they are at the top. In the example worked out the tangent came in the center column so that it made no difference. If, however, the tangent had been .3476 we read the pinion angle at the top, 19.17 degrees and the gear angle at the bottom, 70.83. By noting that the sum of the two angles is 90 degrees, we can be sure we are right.

BEVEL GEAR TABLE
SHAFT ANGLES 90°

Angle Increase; Divide by Teeth in Pinion	Diameter Increase; Divide by Pitch for Pinion	Center Angle Degrees for Pinion	Center Angle Hundredth Degrees							Center Angle Degrees for Gear	Diameter Increase; Divide by Pitch for Gear
			Left-hand Column read here								
			0	.17	.33	.50	.67	.83	1.00		
1	2.00	0	.0000	.0029	.0058	.0087	.0116	.0145	.0175	89	.03
2	2.00	1	.0175	.0204	.0233	.0262	.0291	.0320	.0349	88	.07
4	2.00	2	.0349	.0378	.0407	.0437	.0466	.0495	.0524	87	.10
6	2.00	3	.0524	.0553	.0582	.0612	.0641	.0670	.0699	86	.14
8	1.99	4	.0699	.0729	.0758	.0787	.0816	.0846	.0875	85	.17
10	1.99	5	.0875	.0904	.0934	.0963	.0992	.1022	.1051	84	.21
12	1.99	6	.1051	.1080	.1110	.1139	.1169	.1198	.1228	83	.24
14	1.98	7	.1228	.1257	.1278	.1317	.1346	.1376	.1405	82	.28
16	1.98	8	.1405	.1435	.1465	.1495	.1524	.1554	.1584	81	.31
18	1.98	9	.1584	.1614	.1644	.1673	.1703	.1733	.1763	80	.34
20	1.97	10	.1763	.1793	.1823	.1853	.1883	.1914	.1944	79	.38
22	1.96	11	.1944	.1974	.2004	.2035	.2065	.2095	.2126	78	.41
24	1.96	12	.2126	.2156	.2186	.2217	.2247	.2278	.2309	77	.45
26	1.95	13	.2309	.2339	.2370	.2401	.2432	.2462	.2493	76	.48
28	1.94	14	.2493	.2524	.2555	.2586	.2617	.2648	.2679	75	.51
30	1.93	15	.2679	.2711	.2742	.2773	.2805	.2836	.2867	74	.55
32	1.92	16	.2867	.2899	.2931	.2962	.2994	.3026	.3057	73	.58
34	1.91	17	.3057	.3089	.3121	.3153	.3185	.3217	.3249	72	.62
36	1.90	18	.3249	.3281	.3314	.3346	.3378	.3411	.3443	71	.65
37	1.89	19	.3443	.3476	.3508	.3541	.3574	.3607	.3640	70	.68
39	1.88	20	.3640	.3673	.3706	.3739	.3772	.3805	.3839	69	.71
41	1.86	21	.3839	.3872	.3906	.3939	.3973	.4006	.4040	68	.75
43	1.85	22	.4040	.4074	.4108	.4142	.4176	.4210	.4245	67	.78
45	1.84	23	.4245	.4279	.4314	.4348	.4383	.4417	.4452	66	.81
47	1.82	24	.4452	.4487	.4522	.4557	.4592	.4628	.4663	65	.84
49	1.81	25	.4663	.4699	.4734	.4770	.4806	.4841	.4877	64	.88
50	1.79	26	.4877	.4913	.4950	.4986	.5022	.5059	.5095	63	.91
52	1.78	27	.5095	.5132	.5169	.5206	.5243	.5280	.5317	62	.93
54	1.76	28	.5317	.5354	.5392	.5430	.5467	.5505	.5543	61	.97
56	1.74	29	.5543	.5581	.5619	.5658	.5696	.5735	.5774	60	1.00
57	1.73	30	.5774	.5812	.5851	.5890	.5930	.5969	.6009	59	1.03
59	1.71	31	.6009	.6048	.6088	.6128	.6168	.6208	.6249	58	1.05
61	1.69	32	.6249	.6289	.6330	.6371	.6412	.6453	.6494	57	1.08
63	1.67	33	.6494	.6536	.6577	.6619	.6661	.6703	.6745	56	1.11
64	1.65	34	.6745	.6787	.6830	.6873	.6916	.6959	.7002	55	1.14
66	1.63	35	.7002	.7046	.7089	.7133	.7177	.7221	.7265	54	1.17
68	1.61	36	.7265	.7310	.7355	.7400	.7445	.7490	.7536	53	1.20
69	1.59	37	.7536	.7581	.7627	.7673	.7720	.7766	.7813	52	1.23
71	1.57	38	.7813	.7860	.7907	.7954	.8002	.8050	.8098	51	1.25
72	1.55	39	.8098	.8146	.8195	.8243	.8292	.8342	.8391	50	1.28
73	1.53	40	.8391	.8441	.8491	.8541	.8591	.8642	.8693	49	1.31
75	1.51	41	.8693	.8744	.8796	.8847	.8899	.8952	.9004	48	1.33
77	1.48	42	.9004	.9057	.9110	.9163	.9217	.9271	.9325	47	1.36
79	1.46	43	.9325	.9380	.9435	.9490	.9545	.9601	.9657	46	1.39
80	1.43	44	.9657	.9713	.9770	.9827	.9884	.9942	1.0000	45	1.41
81	1.41	45	1.0000	1.0058	1.0117	1.0176	1.0235	1.0295	1.0355	44	1.43
			1.00	.83	.67	.50	.33	.17	0		

Right Hand Column read here

SPIRAL GEARS

THE term spiral gear is usually applied to gears having angular teeth and which do not have their shafts or axis in parallel lines, and usually at right angles. Spiral gears take the place of bevel gears and give a smoother action as well as allowing greater speed ratios in a given space. When gears with angular or skew teeth run on parallel shafts they are usually called helical gears.

THE CALCULATION OF FORTY-FIVE DEGREE SPIRAL GEARS

Pitch of Cutter	Pitch Diam.	Pitch of Spiral in Inches to One Turn	No. of Teeth in Spur in Same Curvature	Outside Diam.	Thickness of Tooth at Pitch Line (Normal)	Depth of Tooth	Clearance	Circular Pitch (Normal)
	Multiply by Number of Teeth in Spiral Gear			Add to P.D.				
2	0.70710	2.22142	2.828	1.0000	0.7854	1.0785	0.0785	1.5708
2¼	0.62855	1.97464	2.828	0.8888	0.6981	0.9587	0.0699	1.3963
2½	0.56566	1.77707	2.828	0.8000	0.6283	0.8628	0.0628	1.2566
2¾	0.51425	1.61556	2.828	0.7273	0.5712	0.7844	0.0572	1.1424
3	0.47140	1.48094	2.828	0.6666	0.5236	0.7190	0.0524	1.0472
3½	0.40406	1.26939	2.828	0.5714	0.4488	0.6163	0.0449	0.8976
4	0.35355	1.11071	2.828	0.5000	0.3927	0.5393	0.0393	0.7854
5	0.28283	0.88853	2.828	0.4000	0.3142	0.4314	0.0314	0.6283
6	0.23570	0.74047	2.828	0.3333	0.2618	0.3595	0.0262	0.5236
7	0.20203	0.63469	2.828	0.2857	0.2244	0.3081	0.0224	0.4488
8	0.17677	0.55534	2.828	0.2500	0.1963	0.2696	0.0196	0.3927
9	0.15714	0.49367	2.828	0.2222	0.1745	0.2397	0.0175	0.3491
10	0.14143	0.44431	2.828	0.2000	0.1571	0.2157	0.0157	0.3142
11	0.12856	0.40388	2.828	0.1818	0.1428	0.1961	0.0143	0.2856
12	0.11785	0.37024	2.828	0.1666	0.1309	0.1798	0.0131	0.2618
14	0.10101	0.31733	2.828	0.1429	0.1122	0.1541	0.0112	0.2244
16	0.08836	0.27759	2.828	0.1250	0.0982	0.1348	0.0098	0.1963
18	0.07855	0.24677	2.828	0.1111	0.0873	0.1198	0.0088	0.1745
20	0.07071	0.22214	2.828	0.1000	0.0785	0.1079	0.0079	0.1571
22	0.06428	0.20194	2.828	0.0909	0.0714	0.0980	0.0071	0.1428
24	0.05892	0.18510	2.828	0.0833	0.0654	0.0898	0.0065	0.1309
26	0.05437	0.17081	2.828	0.0769	0.0604	0.0829	0.0060	0.1208
28	0.05050	0.15865	2.828	0.0714	0.0561	0.0770	0.0056	0.1122
30	0.04713	0.14806	2.828	0.0666	0.0524	0.0719	0.0053	0.1047
32	0.04425	0.13901	2.828	0.0625	0.0491	0.0674	0.0050	0.0982
36	0.03929	0.12343	2.828	0.0555	0.0436	0.0599	0.0043	0.0785
40	0.03533	0.11099	2.828	0.0500	0.0393	0.0539	0.0039	0.0873
48	0.02944	0.09249	2.828	0.0417	0.0327	0.0449	0.0033	0.0654

In considering speed ratios for spiral gears the driving gear can be taken as a worm having as many threads as there are teeth and the driven as the worm wheel with its number of teeth, so that one revolution of the driver will turn a point on the pitch circle of the driven gear as many inches as the lead of the teeth of the driver.

Divide this by the circumference of the pitch circle of the driven gear to get the revolutions of the driven.

While the subject of spiral gears is rather complex if considered broadly, most of the difficulties disappear when they have a tooth angle of 45 degrees. It is perhaps for this reason that from 75 to 90 per cent. of the spiral gears used are made with this angle.

This has the added advantage of being the most durable, although there is but a trifling increase in wear down to 30 degrees and the wear at 20 degrees is not serious. In cases of necessity even 12 degrees can be used without destructive wear.

Where higher speed ratios than can be had with a 45-degree angle tooth are necessary, they can be laid out as will be shown later and can be cut on most milling machines. The usual change gears allow about two thousand different spirals to be cut.

Where the angles are not 45 degrees, the gear with the greatest angle must always be the driver.

All of the tooth parts are derived from the normal pitch while the pitch diameters are derived from the circular pitch. These are never the same in two gears of a pair except when both are 45 degrees.

As the diameter of a spiral gear does not indicate its speed ratio, the terms *driven* and *follower* are used in place of gear and pinion.

45-DEGREE SPIRAL GEAR

These gears are the simplest of all spirals to lay out and to make, the required speed ratios being obtained by varying the diameters, precisely as with spur or bevel gears, the rules for the speed ratio being the same in both cases. Moreover, the various factors required in laying out and making such gears can be reduced to the simple table shown.

Such a table has been worked out by E. J. Kearney. With it any one can quickly make the few calculations connected with any pair of 45-degree gears having teeth between 2 and 48 diametral pitch. This table will be found on preceding page:

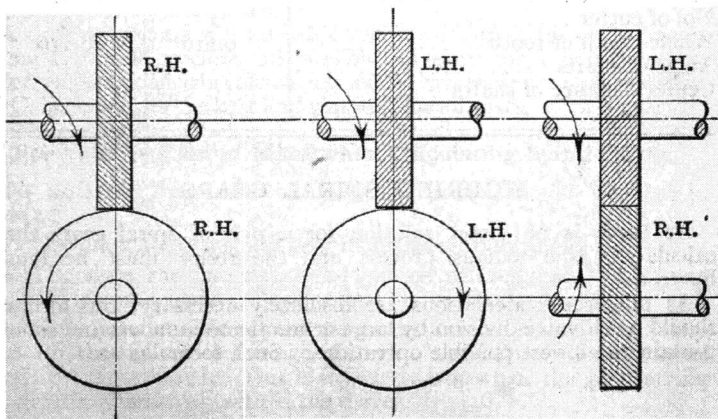

EXAMPLE

Let it be desired to construct a pair of spiral gears with 35 teeth in the gear and 16 teeth in the pinion, using a 10 pitch cutter. Using table on page 126 we have

Pitch diameter = 0.14143 × 35 = 4.950.

Outside diameter = 4.950 + 0.200 = 5.150.

Pitch in inches to one turn of spiral = 0.44431 × 35 = 15.550.

NOTE. — A slight variation in one turn makes no practical difference, hence the ordinary change gears furnished with a universal miller will usually be found sufficient.

Number of teeth in spur with same curvature = 2.828 × 35 = 98.980.

Looking at B & S spur-gear cutter list, we see that 99 is between 55 and 134, therefore we select a No. 2 cutter.

In a similar manner using 16 as a multiplier we obtain the data for the pinion. This gives 2.262 as pitch diameter so that the center distance = $\frac{4.950 + 2.262}{2}$ = 3.606.

THE VARIOUS DIMENSIONS FOLLOW

	Gear	Pinion
Number of teeth	35	16
Pitch diameter	4.950	2.262
Outside diameter	5.150	2.462
Pitch in inches to one turn	15.550	7.108
Angle of spiral	45°	45°
Pitch of cutter	10	10
No. of cutter	2	3
Whole depth of tooth	0.216	0.216
Angle of shafts	90°	
Center distance of shafts	3.606	

FIGURING SPIRAL GEARS

As there is no direct solution for a pair of spiral gears their calculation is a tedious process and the result must be found by trial.

As numerous calculations are absolutely necessary, this formula should not involve division by large or fractional numbers and should contain the fewest possible operations. Such formulas are:

Let

C = Center distance,
P = Diametral pitch,
N_1 = Number of teeth in the driver,
N_2 = Number of teeth in the follower,
S_1 = Spiral angle of driver,
S_2 = Spiral angle of follower.

Then,

$$2C = \frac{(secant\ S_1\ N_1) + (secant\ S_2\ N_2)}{P}.$$

That is, the sum of the secant of the driving angle times the number of teeth in the driver, and the secant of the follower angle times the number of teeth in it divided by the diametral pitch equals twice the center distance. This formula is derived as follows: The secant of the spiral angle times the pitch diameter of a spur gear of the same number of teeth and pitch equals the pitch diameter of a spiral gear of that angle, the pitch of the spur gear being the same as the normal pitch of the spiral gear. Now for a spur gear the number of teeth divided by the diametral pitch equals the pitch diameter. Therefore,

the secant of the spiral angle $\times \dfrac{N}{P}$ = *the pitch diameter of a spiral gear.*

The combined pitch diameters times the center distance are equal to

$$\left(Secant\ S_1 \times \frac{N_1}{P.}\right) + \left(Secant\ S_2 \times \frac{N_2}{P.}\right)$$

or $(secant\ S_1\ N_1) + (secant\ S_2\ N_2)$ for one diametral pitch.

The quantity *secant* $S_1\ N_1$ is the pitch diameter for the driver and *secant* $S_2\ N_2$ is the pitch diameter of the follower. To obtain the center distance for any other pitch, it is simply necessary to divide this last result by that pitch.

A table of secants will furnish constants covering the entire range of angles; and therefore, all possible solutions for a pair of gears. After long experience in calculating spiral gears these are recommended by C. H. Logue as the best and simplest for all cases.

Points to be Kept in Mind when Calculating Spiral Gears

To assist in their use the following points should be kept in mind:

1. The diameter of a spiral gear increases with its angle.

2. Therefore, the diameter of the follower will reduce as the driving angle is increased, although not necessarily in the same ratio.

3. It is quite possible for the center distance to remain practically constant through quite a range of angles, the follower decreasing as the driver is increased. This is especially true when the gear having the greater number of teeth is the driver.

4. If the center distance is too great when the driving angle is 45 degrees — it must not go below that in any case —a lower number of teeth must be selected for both driver and follower, while maintaining the same ratio, and another trial made using a much higher angle for the driver.

5. The center distance will increase with the angle of the driver. This increase is more rapid when reducing than when increasing the speed of the follower.

6. The number of teeth selected for each trial must be in proportion to the desired ratio.

7. Forty-five degrees is commonly accepted as the most efficient driving angle.

Selecting Secants and Trial Numbers of Teeth

To calculate a pair of spiral gears, select secants for the desired angles, assuming the normal pitch, try out the value of 2 C with trial numbers of teeth for driver and follower.

If the value 2 C is too small increase the number of teeth and try again. A very few calculations will show the number of teeth to secure the closest result.

If the center distance thus found is not as desired the angles must be shifted, keeping in mind the general laws governing the change of the center distance with the angle.

It is often found that when the desired center distance is reached the driving angle is too large to be desirable. The only alternative is to change the normal pitch and try again. A slide rule will give approximate results.

When there are limitations placed on the diameter of one or both of the gears the following formula is of value. It may also serve as a check on the above calculations. The pitch diameters are assumed.

$$Tan.\ S_1 = \frac{\left(\begin{array}{c} pitch\ diameter\ of\ driver\ \times \\ number\ of\ revolutions\ of\ driver \end{array}\right)}{\left(\begin{array}{c} pitch\ diameter\ of\ follower\ \times \\ number\ of\ revolutions\ of\ follower \end{array}\right)}.$$

This will set a limit on the driving angle S_1, to exceed which means that the gear will be too large.

REAL PITCHES FOR CIRCULAR PITCH
SPIRAL GEARS

THE accompanying table will be found convenient in figuring particulars for spiral gearing, as it eliminates much of the work by shortening the process, thus making it quite an easy and simple matter to find the dimensions for either helical gears with axes parallel to each other or for gears with right-angle drive.

Formulas for use with the table are as follows: Circumference on pitch line = real pitch multiplied by number of teeth.

Lead of Spiral = Circumference on pitch line divided by the tangent.

Pitch Diameter = Circumference divided by 3.1416.

For whole diameter add the same amount above pitch line as for spur wheels of the same pitch as the normal pitch

The following is an example of the use of the table: A pair of wheels is required to be: Ratio, 6 to 1; normal pitch, 1 in ; driver, 6 teeth; follower, 36 teeth; angle for driver, 66 degrees; angle for follower, 24 degrees.

Referring to the table we find that the real pitch for the driver is 2.4585.

2.4585 × 6 (*teeth*) = 14.751 (*circumference on pitch line*).

Cir. 14.751 ÷ 2.246 (*tangent*) = 6.567 (*lead of spiral*).

Cir. 14.751 ÷ 3.1416 = 4.695 (*pitch diameter*).

For the follower the real pitch is 1.0946.

1.0946 × 36 = 39 4056 (*circumference*).

Cir. 39.4056 ÷ 0.4452 (*tangent*) = 88.512 (*lead of spiral*).

Cir. 39.4056 ÷ 3.1416 = 12.543 (*pitch diameter*).

Another method of finding the lead of spiral is to multiply the real pitch by the number of teeth, but for this purpose take the real pitch of the mating wheel.

In the above example we should have

Real pitch of follower, 1.0946 × 6 = 6,5676 (*lead of spiral*).

Real pitch of driver, 2.4585 × 36 = 88.506.

It will be noticed that there is a slight difference in the result but this is unimportant, as it is only brought about by the dropping of a few decimal points in the tangent.

TABLE OF REAL PITCHES FOR CIRCULAR PITCH SPIRAL GEARS

Angles from Axis		1/4″		5/16″		3/8″		7/16″		1/2″		5/8″		3/4″	
Driver	Follower	Driver	Fol-lower	Driver	Fol-lower	Driver	Fol-lower	Driver	Fol-lower	Driver	Fol-lower	Driver	Fol-lower	Driver	Fol-lower
80°	10°	1.4306	0.2538	1.7996	0.3173	2.1595	0.3808	2.5194	0.4442	2.8793	0.5077	3.5992	0.6346	4.3190	0.7616
79°	11°	1.3102	0.2546	1.6377	0.3183	1.9653	0.3820	2.2928	0.4457	2.6304	0.5093	3.2755	0.6366	3.9306	0.7640
78°	12°	1.2024	0.2556	1.5030	0.3195	1.8036	0.3833	2.1042	0.4473	2.4049	0.5112	3.0060	0.6390	3.6072	0.7666
77°	13°	1.1113	0.2565	1.3892	0.3207	1.6669	0.3848	1.9440	0.4490	2.2226	0.5131	2.7784	0.6414	3.3338	0.7696
76°	14°	1.0334	0.2576	1.2917	0.3220	1.5500	0.3865	1.8084	0.4509	2.0668	0.5153	2.5834	0.6440	3.1000	0.7730
75°	15°	0.9659	0.2591	1.2074	0.3238	1.4489	0.3885	1.6903	0.4529	1.9318	0.5181	2.4148	0.6476	2.8978	0.7772
74°	16°	0.9069	0.2600	1.1337	0.3250	1.3605	0.3901	1.5872	0.4551	1.8139	0.5201	2.2674	0.6502	2.7210	0.7802
73°	17°	0.8550	0.2614	1.0688	0.3268	1.2826	0.3931	1.4964	0.4575	1.7101	0.5228	2.1377	0.6536	2.5652	0.7842
72°	18°	0.8090	0.2628	1.0112	0.3286	1.2135	0.3943	1.4157	0.4600	1.6180	0.5257	2.0225	0.6572	2.4270	0.7886
71°	19°	0.7678	0.2644	0.9598	0.3305	1.1518	0.3966	1.3438	0.4627	1.5357	0.5288	1.9196	0.6610	2.3036	0.7932
70°	20°	0.7309	0.2660	0.9137	0.3325	1.0964	0.3990	1.2791	0.4656	1.4619	0.5320	1.8274	0.6651	2.1928	0.7981
69°	21°	0.6976	0.2678	0.8720	0.3347	1.0464	0.4017	1.2208	0.4686	1.3952	0.5356	1.7440	0.6694	2.0928	0.8034
68°	22°	0.6673	0.2696	0.8342	0.3370	1.0010	0.4044	1.1679	0.4718	1.3346	0.5392	1.6684	0.6740	2.0020	0.8088
67°	23°	0.6398	0.2716	0.7993	0.3395	0.9597	0.4074	1.1120	0.4752	1.2796	0.5432	1.5996	0.6790	1.9194	0.8148
66°	24°	0.6146	0.2736	0.7683	0.3420	0.9220	0.4105	1.0756	0.4789	1.2292	0.5472	1.5366	0.6841	1.8440	0.8210
65°	25°	0.5915	0.2758	0.7394	0.3448	0.8873	0.4137	1.0352	0.4827	1.1830	0.5516	1.4788	0.6866	1.7746	0.8274
64°	26°	0.5702	0.2781	0.7129	0.3477	0.8554	0.4172	0.9980	0.4868	1.1406	0.5563	1.4258	0.6954	1.7108	0.8344
63°	27°	0.5507	0.2806	0.6885	0.3507	0.8260	0.4209	0.9636	0.4910	1.1014	0.5612	1.3766	0.7014	1.6520	0.8418
62°	28°	0.5325	0.2831	0.6656	0.3539	0.7988	0.4247	0.9319	0.4955	1.0650	0.5662	1.3312	0.7078	1.5976	0.8494
61°	29°	0.5157	0.2858	0.6446	0.3573	0.7735	0.4287	0.9024	0.5002	1.0314	0.5716	1.2892	0.7146	1.5470	0.8574
60°	30°	0.5000	0.2886	0.6250	0.3608	0.7500	0.4330	0.8750	0.5051	1.0000	0.5773	1.2500	0.7216	1.5000	0.8660
59°	31°	0.4853	0.2916	0.6067	0.3646	0.7281	0.4375	0.8494	0.5104	0.9708	0.5833	1.2134	0.7292	1.4562	0.8750
58°	32°	0.4717	0.2948	0.5897	0.3685	0.7076	0.4422	0.8256	0.5159	0.9435	0.5890	1.1794	0.7370	1.4152	0.8844
57°	33°	0.4590	0.2981	0.5738	0.3726	0.6885	0.4471	0.8033	0.5216	0.9180	0.5962	1.1476	0.7452	1.3770	0.8942
56°	34°	0.4470	0.3015	0.5588	0.3769	0.6706	0.4523	0.7824	0.5277	0.8941	0.6031	1.1176	0.7538	1.3412	0.9046
55°	35°	0.4358	0.3052	0.5448	0.3815	0.6538	0.4578	0.7627	0.5341	0.8717	0.6104	1.0896	0.7630	1.3076	0.9156
54°	36°	0.4253	0.3090	0.5316	0.3862	0.6380	0.4635	0.7443	0.5408	0.8506	0.6180	1.0632	0.7724	1.2760	0.9270
53°	37°	0.4154	0.3130	0.5192	0.3913	0.6231	0.4695	0.7269	0.5478	0.8308	0.6260	1.0384	0.7826	1.2462	0.9390
52°	38°	0.4060	0.3172	0.5076	0.3965	0.6091	0.4759	0.7161	0.5552	0.8121	0.6345	1.0152	0.7930	1.2182	0.9518
51°	39°	0.3972	0.3217	0.4965	0.4021	0.5959	0.4825	0.6952	0.5628	0.7945	0.6434	0.9930	0.8042	1.1918	0.9650
50°	40°	0.3889	0.3264	0.4861	0.4079	0.5834	0.4895	0.6806	0.5711	0.7778	0.6527	0.9722	0.8159	1.1668	0.9790
49°	41°	0.3810	0.3312	0.4763	0.4140	0.5716	0.4969	0.6668	0.5797	0.7621	0.6625	0.9526	0.8280	1.1432	0.9938
48°	42°	0.3736	0.3364	0.4670	0.4205	0.5604	0.5046	0.6538	0.5887	0.7472	0.6728	0.9340	0.8410	1.1208	1.0092
47°	43°	0.3665	0.3418	0.4582	0.4272	0.5498	0.5127	0.6415	0.5982	0.7331	0.6836	0.9164	0.8544	1.0996	1.0254
46°	44°	0.3598	0.3475	0.4498	0.4344	0.5398	0.5213	0.6298	0.6082	0.7197	0.6950	0.8996	0.8688	1.0796	1.0426
45°	45°	0.3536	0.3536	0.4419	0.4419	0.5303	0.5303	0.6187	0.6187	0.7071	0.7071	0.8839	0.8839	1.0606	1.0606

AXIS		½"		¾"		1"		1¼"		1½"		1¾"		Tangent of Angle	
Driver	Follower	Driver	Follower	Driver	Follower	Driver	Follower	Driver	Follower	Driver	Follower	Driver	Follower	Driver	Follower
80°	10°	5.0388	0.8884	5.7587	1.0154	6.4285	1.1123	7.1683	1.2602	7.8192	1.3962	8.6580	1.5230	5.6713	0.1763
79°	11°	4.5856	0.8614	5.2407	1.0187	5.8901	1.1160	6.5510	1.2732	7.2601	1.4007	7.8011	1.5280	5.1446	0.1944
78°	12°	4.2084	0.8016	4.8298	1.0203	5.4109	1.1201	6.0122	1.2780	6.6134	1.4057	7.8146	1.5335	4.7046	0.2126
77°	13°	3.8898	0.8686	4.4454	1.0203	5.0001	1.1240	5.5568	1.2828	6.1125	1.4111	6.6681	1.5394	4.3315	0.2309
76°	14°	3.6168	0.9018	4.1336	1.0300	4.6500	1.1591	5.1669	1.2882	5.6837	1.4171	6.2004	1.5459	4.0108	0.2493
75°	15°	3.3966	0.9058	3.8637	1.0353	4.3466	1.1658	4.8296	1.2952	5.3126	1.4241	5.7955	1.5513	3.7321	0.2679
74°	16°	3.1744	0.9102	3.6279	1.0403	4.0814	1.1703	4.5348	1.3004	4.9684	1.4304	5.4419	1.5504	3.4874	0.2867
73°	17°	2.9928	0.9150	3.4203	1.0457	3.8478	1.1764	4.2754	1.3071	4.7029	1.4378	5.1304	1.5585	3.2709	0.3057
72°	18°	2.8314	0.9200	3.2360	1.0515	3.6405	1.1829	4.0450	1.3143	4.4495	1.4457	4.8340	1.5771	3.0777	0.3249
71°	19°	2.6876	0.9254	3.0715	1.0576	3.4454	1.1868	3.8394	1.3220	4.2333	1.4542	4.6072	1.5864	2.9042	0.3443
70°	20°	2.5580	0.9312	2.9238	1.0641	3.2862	1.1972	3.6548	1.3302	4.0202	1.4632	4.3857	1.5962	2.7475	0.3640
69°	21°	2.4476	0.9376	2.7904	1.0711	3.1391	1.2050	3.4886	1.3389	3.8363	1.4728	4.1856	1.6097	2.6051	0.3839
68°	22°	2.3358	0.9434	2.6604	1.0785	3.0030	1.2133	3.3369	1.3480	3.6795	1.4829	4.0041	1.6178	2.4751	0.4040
67°	23°	2.2240	0.9504	2.5593	1.0865	2.8792	1.2214	3.1991	1.3580	3.4805	1.5037	3.8380	1.6295	2.3559	0.4245
66°	24°	2.1512	0.9578	2.4595	1.0946	2.7959	1.2314	3.0734	1.3682	3.3865	1.5051	3.6870	1.6418	2.2460	0.4452
65°	25°	2.0701	0.9651	2.3662	1.1033	2.6619	1.2417	2.9577	1.3779	3.2515	1.5171	3.5493	1.6550	2.1445	0.4663
64°	26°	1.9900	0.9730	2.2811	1.1127	2.5663	1.2517	2.8511	1.3908	3.1507	1.5208	3.4216	1.6639	2.0503	0.4877
63°	27°	1.9272	0.9820	2.2026	1.1223	2.4780	1.2624	2.7533	1.4029	3.0385	1.5433	3.3040	1.6833	1.9626	0.5095
62°	28°	1.8638	0.9910	2.1300	1.1326	2.3953	1.2696	2.6625	1.4157	2.9288	1.5572	3.1950	1.6988	1.8807	0.5317
61°	29°	1.8048	1.0004	2.0626	1.1433	2.3205	1.2741	2.5781	1.4292	2.8561	1.5742	3.0949	1.7150	1.8040	0.5543
60°	30°	1.7500	1.0102	2.0000	1.1548	2.2500	1.2852	2.5000	1.4433	2.7500	1.5877	3.0040	1.7320	1.7321	0.5774
59°	31°	1.6988	1.0208	1.9415	1.1667	2.1843	1.2900	2.4269	1.4583	2.6606	1.6042	2.9134	1.7499	1.6643	0.6009
58°	32°	1.6512	1.0318	1.8870	1.1790	2.1229	1.3125	2.3583	1.4740	2.5947	1.6213	2.8360	1.7687	1.6003	0.6249
57°	33°	1.6006	1.0432	1.8360	1.1920	2.0655	1.3266	2.2951	1.4904	2.5346	1.6395	2.7451	1.7785	1.5399	0.6494
56°	34°	1.5648	1.0554	1.7883	1.2055	2.0118	1.3414	2.2353	1.5077	2.4580	1.6585	2.6824	1.8003	1.4826	0.6745
55°	35°	1.5254	1.0682	1.7434	1.2202	1.9614	1.3560	2.1793	1.5260	2.3972	1.6786	2.6151	1.8311	1.4281	0.7002
54°	36°	1.4886	1.0816	1.7012	1.2356	1.9139	1.3734	2.1266	1.5449	2.3392	1.6997	2.5510	1.8541	1.3764	0.7265
53°	37°	1.4538	1.0950	1.6614	1.2511	1.8693	1.3905	2.0770	1.5652	2.2847	1.7247	2.4924	1.8781	1.3270	0.7536
52°	38°	1.4327	1.1104	1.6242	1.2690	1.8273	1.4086	2.0303	1.5862	2.2333	1.7440	2.4304	1.9035	1.2799	0.7813
51°	39°	1.3904	1.1256	1.5890	1.2807	1.7850	1.4276	1.9861	1.6084	2.1847	1.7693	2.3535	1.9381	1.2349	0.8098
50°	40°	1.3612	1.1442	1.5557	1.3054	1.7502	1.4426	1.9446	1.6317	2.1391	1.7919	2.3336	1.9581	1.1918	0.8391
49°	41°	1.3336	1.1591	1.5240	1.3250	1.7148	1.4686	1.9054	1.6820	2.0958	1.8019	2.2863	1.9875	1.1463	0.8693
48°	42°	1.3076	1.1774	1.4941	1.3456	1.6613	1.4906	1.8681	1.7089	2.0540	1.8102	2.2417	2.0184	1.1106	0.9004
47°	43°	1.2839	1.1961	1.4662	1.3673	1.6495	1.5138	1.8328	1.7317	2.0161	1.8601	2.1994	2.0510	1.0724	0.9325
46°	44°	1.2596	1.2164	1.4395	1.3901	1.6194	1.5382	1.7994	1.7317	1.9702	1.9114	2.1593	2.0852	1.0355	0.9657
45°	45°	1.2374	1.2374	1.4142	1.4142	1.5910	1.5010	1.7678	1.7058	1.9445	1.9445	2.1213	2.1213	1.0000	1.0000

TABLE OF REAL PITCHES FOR CIRCULAR PITCH SPIRAL GEARS

Angles from Axis		½" Driver	½" Fol-lower	⅝" Driver	⅝" Fol-lower	¾" Driver	¾" Fol-lower	⅞" Driver	⅞" Fol-lower	1" Driver	1" Fol-lower	1¼" Driver	1¼" Fol-lower	1½" Driver	1½" Fol-lower
Driver	Fol-lower														
80°	10°	1.4396	0.2538	1.7906	0.3173	2.1595	0.3808	2.5194	0.4442	2.8793	0.5077	3.5992	0.6346	4.4199	0.7016
79°	11°	1.3102	0.2546	1.6377	0.3183	2.1053	0.3820	2.2928	0.4457	2.6304	0.5093	3.2755	0.6366	3.9356	0.7040
78°	12°	1.2024	0.2550	1.5930	0.3195	1.8326	0.3833	2.1042	0.4473	2.4049	0.5112	3.0060	0.6390	3.6072	0.7066
77°	13°	1.1113	0.2565	1.3892	0.3207	1.6669	0.3848	1.9449	0.4490	2.2326	0.5131	2.7784	0.6414	3.3338	0.7096
76°	14°	1.0334	0.2576	1.2917	0.3220	1.5500	0.3865	1.8284	0.4509	2.0668	0.5153	2.5834	0.6440	3.1000	0.7130
75°	15°	0.9659	0.2591	1.2074	0.3230	1.4489	0.3885	1.6903	0.4529	1.9318	0.5181	2.4148	0.6476	2.8978	0.7712
74°	16°	0.9069	0.2600	1.1337	0.3250	1.3905	0.3901	1.5872	0.4551	1.8139	0.5201	2.2674	0.6502	2.7210	0.7302
73°	17°	0.8550	0.2614	1.0688	0.3268	1.2826	0.3921	1.4964	0.4575	1.7101	0.5228	2.1377	0.6536	2.5652	0.7342
72°	18°	0.8090	0.2628	1.0112	0.3286	1.2135	0.3943	1.4157	0.4600	1.6180	0.5257	2.0225	0.6572	2.4270	0.7386
71°	19°	0.7678	0.2644	0.9598	0.3305	1.1518	0.3966	1.3438	0.4627	1.5357	0.5288	1.9196	0.6610	2.3036	0.7932
70°	20°	0.7309	0.2663	0.9137	0.3325	1.0964	0.3990	1.2791	0.4656	1.4719	0.5320	1.8374	0.6651	2.1928	0.7981
69°	21°	0.6976	0.2678	0.8720	0.3347	1.0464	0.4017	1.2208	0.4686	1.3952	0.5352	1.7240	0.6694	2.0928	0.8034
68°	22°	0.6673	0.2696	0.8342	0.3370	0.9997	0.4044	1.1670	0.4718	1.3346	0.5392	1.6681	0.6740	2.0020	0.8588
67°	23°	0.6398	0.2716	0.7995	0.3395	0.9597	0.4074	1.1120	0.4752	1.2796	0.5437	1.5996	0.6790	1.9194	0.8148
66°	24°	0.6146	0.2736	0.7683	0.3420	0.8854	0.4105	1.0750	0.4789	1.2302	0.5472	1.5366	0.6841	1.8440	0.8210
65°	25°	0.5915	0.2758	0.7394	0.3448	0.8873	0.4137	1.0352	0.4827	1.1830	0.5516	1.4788	0.6896	1.7746	0.8224
64°	26°	0.5703	0.2783	0.7130	0.3477	0.8554	0.4172	0.9980	0.4868	1.1406	0.5563	1.4258	0.6956	1.7108	0.8344
63°	27°	0.5507	0.2806	0.6884	0.3507	0.8295	0.4209	0.9630	0.4910	1.1014	0.5612	1.3766	0.7014	1.6520	0.8494
62°	28°	0.5325	0.2831	0.6656	0.3539	0.7988	0.4247	0.9310	0.4955	1.0650	0.5662	1.3312	0.7054	1.5976	0.8404
61°	29°	0.5157	0.2858	0.6446	0.3573	0.7735	0.4287	0.9024	0.5002	1.0314	0.5716	1.2892	0.7146	1.5470	0.8574
60°	30°	0.5000	0.2886	0.6250	0.3608	0.7500	0.4330	0.8759	0.5051	1.0000	0.5773	1.2500	0.7216	1.5000	0.8660
59°	31°	0.4853	0.2916	0.6067	0.3646	0.7281	0.4375	0.8494	0.5104	0.9708	0.5833	1.2134	0.7292	1.4562	0.8750
58°	32°	0.4717	0.2948	0.5897	0.3685	0.7076	0.4422	0.8256	0.5159	0.9435	0.5890	1.1794	0.7370	1.4152	0.8844
57°	33°	0.4590	0.2981	0.5738	0.3726	0.6885	0.4471	0.8033	0.5216	0.9180	0.5962	1.1476	0.7452	1.3770	0.8942
56°	34°	0.4470	0.3015	0.5538	0.3769	0.6706	0.4523	0.7824	0.5277	0.8941	0.6031	1.1176	0.7538	1.3412	0.9046
55°	35°	0.4358	0.3052	0.5448	0.3815	0.6538	0.4578	0.7627	0.5341	0.8717	0.6104	1.0896	0.7630	1.3076	0.9156
54°	36°	0.4252	0.3088	0.5316	0.3862	0.6380	0.4635	0.7443	0.5408	0.8506	0.6180	1.0632	0.7724	1.2760	0.9270
53°	37°	0.4154	0.3130	0.5192	0.3913	0.6231	0.4695	0.7269	0.5478	0.8308	0.6260	1.0384	0.7826	1.2462	0.9390
52°	38°	0.4060	0.3172	0.5076	0.3965	0.6091	0.4759	0.7161	0.5552	0.8121	0.6345	1.0152	0.7930	1.2182	0.9518
51°	39°	0.3972	0.3217	0.4965	0.4021	0.5959	0.4825	0.6952	0.5628	0.7945	0.6434	0.9930	0.8042	1.1918	0.9650
50°	40°	0.3886	0.3264	0.4858	0.4079	0.5831	0.4895	0.6806	0.5711	0.7778	0.6527	0.9722	0.8159	1.1668	0.9790
49°	41°	0.3810	0.3312	0.4763	0.4140	0.5716	0.4968	0.6668	0.5795	0.7621	0.6623	0.9526	0.8286	1.1432	0.9938
48°	42°	0.3736	0.3364	0.4670	0.4205	0.5604	0.5046	0.6538	0.5887	0.7472	0.6728	0.9340	0.8410	1.1208	1.0092
47°	43°	0.3695	0.3418	0.4582	0.4272	0.5498	0.5127	0.6415	0.5982	0.7331	0.6830	0.9164	0.8544	1.0996	1.0146

Angles from Axis		Normal Pitches												Tangent of Angle	
		7/8″		1″		1 1/8″		1 1/4″		1 3/8″		1 1/2″			
Driver	Follower	Driver	Follower	Driver	Follower	Driver	Follower	Driver	Follower	Driver	Follower	Driver	Follower	Driver	Follower
80°	10°	5.0389	0.8885	5.7588	1.0154	6.4786	1.1424	7.1985	1.2693	7.9183	1.3962	8.6382	1.5231	5.6713	0.1763
79°	11°	4.5857	0.8914	5.2408	1.0187	5.8959	1.1461	6.5511	1.2734	7.2061	1.4007	7.8613	1.5281	5.1446	0.1944
78°	12°	4.2085	0.8946	4.8097	1.0223	5.4110	1.1501	6.0122	1.2779	6.6134	1.4057	7.2146	1.5335	4.7046	0.2126
77°	13°	3.8897	0.8980	4.4454	1.0263	5.0011	1.1546	5.5568	1.2829	6.1124	1.4112	6.6681	1.5395	4.3315	0.2309
76°	14°	3.6169	0.9018	4.1336	1.0306	4.6503	1.1594	5.1670	1.2883	5.6837	1.4171	6.2004	1.5459	4.0108	0.2493
75°	15°	3.3807	0.9059	3.8637	1.0353	4.3467	1.1647	4.8296	1.2941	5.3126	1.4235	5.7956	1.5529	3.7321	0.2679
74°	16°	3.1745	0.9103	3.6280	1.0403	4.0814	1.1703	4.5349	1.3004	4.9884	1.4304	5.4419	1.5604	3.4874	0.2867
73°	17°	2.9928	0.9150	3.4203	1.0457	3.8478	1.1764	4.2754	1.3071	4.7029	1.4378	5.1305	1.5685	3.2709	0.3057
72°	18°	2.8316	0.9200	3.2361	1.0515	3.6406	1.1829	4.0451	1.3143	4.4496	1.4458	4.8541	1.5772	3.0777	0.3249
71°	19°	2.6876	0.9254	3.0716	1.0576	3.4550	1.1898	3.8394	1.3220	4.2234	1.4542	4.6073	1.5864	2.9042	0.3443
70°	20°	2.5583	0.9312	2.9238	1.0642	3.2893	1.1972	3.6548	1.3302	4.0202	1.4632	4.3857	1.5963	2.7475	0.3640
69°	21°	2.4416	0.9373	2.7904	1.0711	3.1392	1.2050	3.4880	1.3389	3.8368	1.4728	4.1856	1.6067	2.6051	0.3839
68°	22°	2.3358	0.9437	2.6695	1.0785	3.0031	1.2133	3.3368	1.3482	3.6705	1.4830	4.0042	1.6178	2.4751	0.4040
67°	23°	2.2394	0.9506	2.5593	1.0864	2.8792	1.2221	3.1991	1.3580	3.5190	1.4938	3.8390	1.6295	2.3559	0.4245
66°	24°	2.1513	0.9578	2.4586	1.0946	2.7659	1.2315	3.0732	1.3683	3.3806	1.5051	3.6879	1.6420	2.2460	0.4452
65°	25°	2.0704	0.9655	2.3662	1.1034	2.6620	1.2413	2.9578	1.3792	3.2535	1.5171	3.5493	1.6551	2.1445	0.4663
64°	26°	1.9960	0.9735	2.2812	1.1126	2.5663	1.2517	2.8515	1.3908	3.1366	1.5298	3.4218	1.6689	2.0503	0.4877
63°	27°	1.9274	0.9821	2.2027	1.1223	2.4780	1.2626	2.7534	1.4029	3.0287	1.5432	3.3040	1.6835	1.9626	0.5095
62°	28°	1.8638	0.9910	2.1301	1.1326	2.3963	1.2741	2.6626	1.4157	2.9288	1.5573	3.1951	1.6989	1.8807	0.5317
61°	29°	1.8048	1.0004	2.0627	1.1434	2.3205	1.2862	2.5783	1.4292	2.8362	1.5721	3.0940	1.7150	1.8040	0.5543
60°	30°	1.7500	1.0104	2.0000	1.1547	2.2500	1.2991	2.5000	1.4434	2.7500	1.5877	3.0000	1.7321	1.7321	0.5774
59°	31°	1.6989	1.0208	1.9416	1.1666	2.1843	1.3125	2.4270	1.4583	2.6697	1.6041	2.9124	1.7499	1.6643	0.6009
58°	32°	1.6512	1.0318	1.8871	1.1792	2.1230	1.3266	2.3589	1.4740	2.5947	1.6214	2.8306	1.7688	1.6003	0.6249
57°	33°	1.6066	1.0433	1.8361	1.1924	2.0656	1.3414	2.2951	1.4905	2.5246	1.6395	2.7541	1.7885	1.5399	0.6494
56°	34°	1.5648	1.0554	1.7883	1.2062	2.0118	1.3570	2.2354	1.5078	2.4589	1.6586	2.6824	1.8093	1.4826	0.6745
55°	35°	1.5255	1.0682	1.7434	1.2208	1.9614	1.3734	2.1793	1.5260	2.3972	1.6786	2.6152	1.8312	1.4281	0.7002
54°	36°	1.4886	1.0816	1.7013	1.2361	1.9140	1.3906	2.1266	1.5451	2.3393	1.6996	2.5520	1.8541	1.3764	0.7265
53°	37°	1.4539	1.0956	1.6616	1.2521	1.8693	1.4087	2.0771	1.5652	2.2848	1.7217	2.4925	1.8782	1.3270	0.7536
52°	38°	1.4212	1.1104	1.6243	1.2690	1.8273	1.4276	2.0303	1.5863	2.2334	1.7449	2.4364	1.9035	1.2799	0.7813
51°	39°	1.3904	1.1259	1.5890	1.2868	1.7876	1.4476	1.9863	1.6084	2.1849	1.7693	2.3835	1.9301	1.2349	0.8098
50°	40°	1.3613	1.1422	1.5557	1.3054	1.7502	1.4686	1.9447	1.6318	2.1391	1.7949	2.3336	1.9581	1.1918	0.8391
49°	41°	1.3337	1.1594	1.5243	1.3250	1.7148	1.4906	1.9053	1.6563	2.0959	1.8219	2.2864	1.9875	1.1504	0.8693
48°	42°	1.3077	1.1774	1.4945	1.3456	1.6813	1.5138	1.8681	1.6820	2.0549	1.8502	2.2417	2.0184	1.1106	0.9004
47°	43°	1.2830	1.1964	1.4663	1.3673	1.6495	1.5382	1.8329	1.7092	2.0161	1.8801	2.1994	2.0510	1.0724	0.9325
46°	44°	1.2596	1.2164	1.4396	1.3902	1.6195	1.5639	1.7994	1.7377	1.9794	1.9115	2.1593	2.0853	1.0355	0.9657
45°	45°	1.2374	1.2374	1.4142	1.4142	1.5910	1.5910	1.7678	1.7678	1.9445	1.9445	2.1213	2.1213	1.0000	1.0000

SPUR-GEAR CUTTERS FOR SPIRAL GEARS

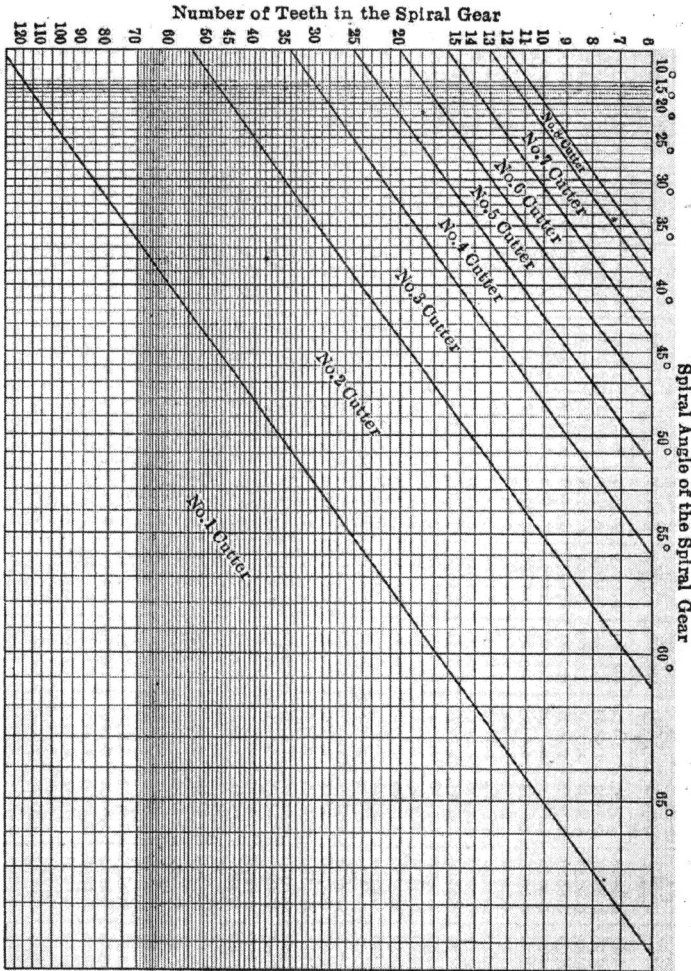

Number of Teeth in the Spiral Gear

Spiral Angle of the Spiral Gear

No. 8 Cutter
No. 7 Cutter
No. 6 Cutter
No. 5 Cutter
No. 4 Cutter
No. 3 Cutter
No. 2 Cutter
No. 1 Cutter

To find the number of a spur-gear cutter to be used in cutting a given spiral gear, locate the intersection of lines traced from the points representing the number of teeth and the spiral angle on the two scales. The number in the area on the chart within which the intersection falls is the cutter number of Brown & Sharpe's involute cutter system required.

SPIRAL GEAR TABLE

WHILE it is better in every case to understand the principles involved before using a table as this tends to prevent errors, they can be used with good results by simply following directions carefully. The subject of spiral gears is so much more complicated than other gears that many will prefer to depend entirely on the tables.

This table gives the circular pitch and addendum or the diametral pitch and lead of spirals for one diametral pitch and with teeth having angles of from 1 to 89 degrees to 45 and 45 degrees. For other pitches divide the addendum given and the spiral number by the required pitch and multiply the results by the required number of teeth. This will give the pitch diameter and lead of spiral for each wheel. For the outside diameter add two diametral pitches as in spur gearing.

Suppose we want a pair of spiral gears with 10 and 80 degree angles, 8 diametral pitch cutter, with 16 teeth in the small gear, having 10-degree angle and 10 teeth in the large gear with its 80-degree angle.

Find the 10-degree angle of spiral and in the third column find 1.0154. Divide by pitch, 8, and get .1269. Multiply this by number of teeth — .1269 × 16 = 2.030 = pitch diameter. Add 2 pitches — two ⅛ = ¼ and 2.030 + .25 = 2.28 inches outside diameter.

The lead of spiral for 10 degrees for small wheel is 18.092. Divide by pitch = 18.092 ÷ 8 = 2.2615. Multiply by number of teeth, 2.2615 × 16 = 36.18, the lead of spiral, which means that it makes one turn in 36.18 inches.

For the other gear with its 80-degree angle, find the addendum, 5.7587. Divide by pitch, 8, = .7198. Multiply by number of teeth, 10 = 7.198. Add two pitches, or .25, gives 7.448 as outside diameter.

The lead of spiral is 3.1901. Dividing by pitch, 8 = .3988. Multiplying by number of teeth = 3.988 the lead of spiral.

. When racks are to mesh with spiral gears, divide the number in the circular pitch columns for the given angle by the required diametral pitch to get the corresponding circular pitch.

If we want to make a rack to mesh with a 40-degree spiral gear of 8 pitch: Look for circular pitch opposite 40 and find 4.101. Dividing by 8 gives .512 as the circular pitch for this angle. The greater the angle the greater the circular or linear pitch, as can be seen by trying an 80-degree angle. Here the circular pitch is 2.261 inches.

SPIRAL GEAR TABLE

SHAFT ANGLES 90° FOR ONE DIAMETRAL PITCH

Angle of Spiral Degrees	To obtain the circular pitch for one tooth, divide by the required diametral pitch	To obtain the pitch diameter, divide by the required diametral pitch and multiply the quotient by the required number of teeth	To obtain the lead of spiral, divide by the required diametral pitch and multiply quotient by the required number of teeth		To obtain the pitch diameter, divide by the required diametral pitch and multiply the quotient by the required number of teeth	To obtain the circular pitch for one tooth, divide by the required diametral pitch.	Angle of Spiral in Degrees
	Circular Pitch	One Tooth or Addend.	Lead of Spirals		One Tooth or Addendum	Circular Pitch	
Small Wheel	Small Wheel	Small Wheel	Small Wheel	Large Wheel	Large Wheel	Large Wheel	Large Wheel
1	3.1419	1.0001	180.05	3.1420	57.298	180.01	89
2	3.1435	1.0006	90.020	3.1435	28.653	90.016	88
3	3.1457	1.0013	60.032	3.1458	19.107	60.026	87
4	3.1491	1.0024	45.038	3.1492	14.335	45.035	86
5	3.1535	1.0038	37.077	3.1527	11.473	36.044	85
6	3.1589	1.0055	30.056	3.1589	9.5667	30.055	84
7	3.1652	1.0075	25.728	3.1651	8.2055	25.778	83
8	3.1724	1.0098	22.573	3.1724	7.1852	22.573	82
9	3.1806	1.0124	20.082	3.1807	6.3924	20.082	81
10	3.1900	1.0154	18.092	3.1901	5.7587	18.092	80
11	3.2003	1.0187	16.464	3.2003	5.2408	16.464	79
12	3.2145	1.0232	15.076	3.2105	4.8097	15.104	78
13	3.2242	1.0263	13.966	3.2294	4.4454	13.988	77
14	3.2377	1.0306	12.986	3.2378	4.1335	12.986	76
15	3.2522	1.0352	12.138	3.2524	3.8637	12.138	75
16	3.2679	1.0402	11.393	3.2678	3.6279	11.397	74
17	3.2848	1.0456	10.417	3.2821	3.4203	10.745	73
18	3.3116	1.0514	10.192	3.3032	3.2360	10.166	72
19	3.3225	1.0576	9.6494	3.3225	3.0715	9.6494	71
20	3.3430	1.0641	9.1848	3.3433	2.9238	9.1854	70
21	3.3650	1.0711	8.7662	3.3652	2.7904	8.7663	69
22	3.3882	1.0785	8.3862	3.3833	2.6694	8.3862	68
23	3.4127	1.0863	8.0399	3.4129	2.5593	8.0403	67
24	3.4451	1.0946	7.7379	3.4391	2.4585	7.7242	66
25	3.4661	1.1033	7.4332	3.4663	2.3662	7.4336	65
26	3.4953	1.1126	7.1664	3.4952	2.2811	7.1663	64
27	3.5258	1.1223	6.9198	3.5257	2.2026	6.9197	63
28	3.5579	1.1325	6.6912	3.5575	2.1300	6.6916	62
29	3.5918	1.1433	6.4799	3.5919	2.0626	6.4799	61
30	3.6276	1.1547	6.2778	3.6277	2.0000	6.2832	60
31	3.6650	1.1666	6.0979	3.6652	1.9416	6.0997	59
32	3.7043	1.1791	5.9282	3.7044	1.8870	5.9282	58
33	3.7457	1.1923	5.7710	3.7459	1.8360	5.7680	57
34	3.7894	1.2062	5.6181	3.7826	1.7882	5.6178	56
35	3.8349	1.2207	5.4754	3.8351	1.7434	5.4770	55
36	3.8830	1.2360	5.3431	3.8834	1.7013	5.3448	54
37	3.9336	1.2521	5.2201	3.9261	1.6616	5.2200	53
38	3.9867	1.2690	5.1028	3.9921	1.6242	5.1026	52
39	4.0482	1.2867	4.9866	4.0416	1.5890	4.9920	51
40	4.1010	1.3054	4.8873	4.1012	1.5557	4.8874	50
41	4.1626	1.3250	4.7885	4.1540	1.5242	4.7884	49
42	4.2273	1.3456	4.6949	4.2272	1.4944	4.6948	48
43	4.2956	1.3673	4.6065	4.2956	1.4662	4.6062	47
44	4.3671	1.3901	4.5223	4.3675	1.4395	4.5225	46
45	4.4428	1.4142	4.4428	4.4428	1.4142	4.4428	45

THREADS OF WORMS

WORMS are cut with threads having a total angle of 29 degrees, similar to the Acme thread. Some use the same proportions as for the Acme, but most use a deeper thread such as the Brown & Sharpe, which is .6866 deep instead of .51 for a one-inch pitch as in the Acme. It is not easy to cut odd fractional pitches in most lathes, so regular pitches are cut and the circular pitch of the worm wheel is allowed to come in fractional measurements for pitch diameters and center distances. Having determined on the reduction as 40 to 1, the relative proportions can be considered as follows:

Assume a thread of 4 to the inch for the worm or a lead of ¼ inch. Then as the reduction of 40 to 1 there must be 40 teeth in the worm gear, ¼ inch from center to center of teeth or 10 inches in circumference on the pitch line or 3.18 inches. If a reduction of 20 to 1 is wanted we can use the same gear but cut a double thread of 2 per inch, which will give the same distance between teeth, but the worm gear will be moved two teeth every revolution of the worm.

Some of the commonly used proportions are:

$$\text{Pitch diam. of worm gear} = \frac{\text{No. of teeth} \times \text{pitch in inches}}{3.1416}.$$

$$\text{Diametral pitch} = \frac{3.1416}{\text{Linear pitch}}.$$

$$\text{Throat diam. of worm gear} = \text{Pitch diam.} + \frac{2}{\text{Diam. Pitch}}.$$

Outside diameter of gear for 60° sides = throat diameter + 2 (.13397 throat radius.)

Whole depth of tooth of worm or worm gear = .6866 × linear pitch.

Width at top of tooth of worm = .335 × linear pitch.
Width of bottom of tooth of worm = .31 × linear pitch.
Outside diam. of worm — single thread = 4 × linear pitch.
Outside diam. of worm — double thread = 5 × linear pitch.
Outside diam. of worm — triple thread = 6 × linear pitch.
Face of worm gear = ½ to ¾ outside diameter of worm.

Width of Face

A COMMON practice for determining the width of face or thickness of worm wheels is shown in Fig. 15. Draw the diameter of the worm and lay off 60 degrees as shown; this gives the width of working face, the sides being made straight from the bottom of the teeth. Others make the face equal to ¾ the outside diameter of worm, but ½ the diameter of the worm is more common.

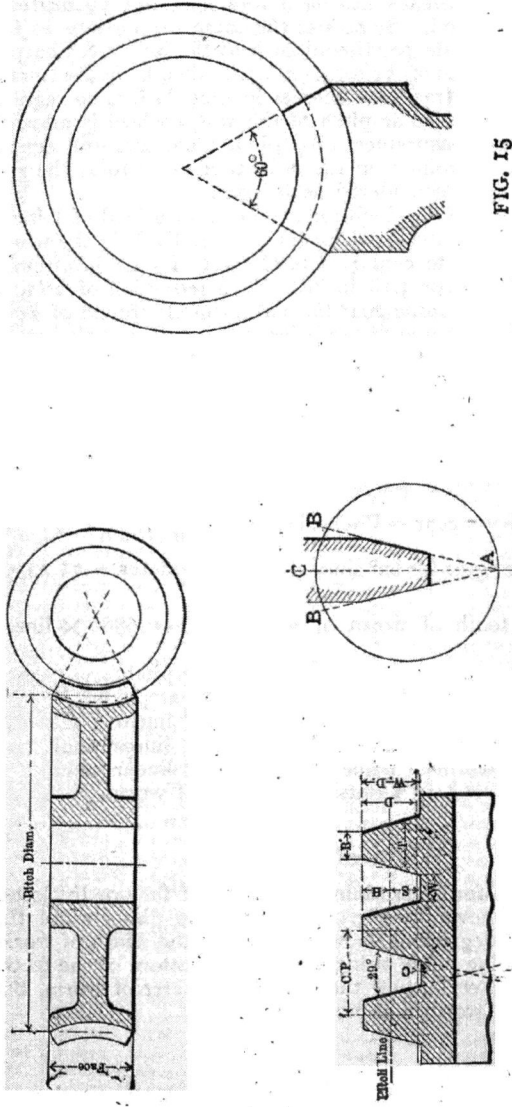

FIG. 15

FIG. 14

To Find the Pitch Diameter. (Given pitch and number of teeth.)

Rule.— Multiply the number of teeth by the circular pitch and divide by 3.1416.

Example.— Number of teeth 96; Circular pitch, $\frac{1}{4}$. Then $96 \times \frac{1}{4} = 24$. $24 \div 3.1416 = 7.639 =$ pitch diameter.

Note.— Diameter of Hob. equals diameter of Worm plus twice the clearance "C."

TABLE OF PROPORTIONS OF WORM THREADS TO RUN IN WORM WHEELS

C.P. Circular Pitch	pi. Threads per Inch	D.P. Dia-metrical Pitch	H. Tooth above Pitch-Line	D. Working Depth of Tooth	C. Clearance	S. Depth of Space below Pitch Line	W.D. Whole Depth of Tooth	T. Thickn. of Tooth on Pitch Line	W.= Width of Thread Tool at End	B. Width of Thread at Top
C.P. Inches	$pi.=\dfrac{1}{C.P.}$	$D.P.=\dfrac{\pi}{C.P.}$	$H.=\dfrac{1}{D.P.}$	$D.=2\times\dfrac{1}{D.P.}$	$C.=\dfrac{T}{10}$	$S.=H.+C.$	$W.D.=D.+C.$	$T.=\dfrac{C.P.}{2}$	$W.=.31\times C.P.$	$B.=.335\times C.P.$
2	½	1.5708	.6366	1.2732	.1000	.7366	1.3732	1.0000	.6200	.6708
1¾	4/7	1.7952	.5570	1.1141	.0875	.6445	1.2016	.8750	.5425	.5862
1½	⅔	2.0944	.4775	.9549	.0750	.5525	1.0299	.7500	.4650	.5025
1¼	⅘	2.5133	.3979	.7958	.0625	.4604	.8583	.6250	.3875	.4187
1	1	3.1416	.3183	.6366	.0500	.3683	.6866	.5000	.3100	.3350
¾	1⅓	4.1888	.2387	.4775	.0375	.2762	.5150	.3750	.2325	.2512
⅔	1½	4.7124	.2122	.4244	.0333	.2455	.4577	.3333	.2066	.2233
½	2	6.2832	.1592	.3183	.0250	.1842	.3433	.2500	.1550	.1675
⅖	2½	7.8540	.1273	.2546	.0200	.1473	.2746	.2000	.1240	.1340
⅓	3	9.4248	.1061	.2122	.0166	.1227	.2288	.1666	.1033	.1117
2/7	3½	10.9956	.0909	.1819	.0143	.1052	.1962	.1429	.0886	.0957
¼	4	12.5664	.0796	.1591	.0125	.0921	.1716	.1250	.0775	.0838
2/9	4½	14.1372	.0707	.1415	.0111	.0818	.1526	.1111	.0689	.0744
⅕	5	15.7080	.0637	.1273	.0100	.0737	.1373	.1000	.0620	.0670
⅙	6	18.8496	.0531	.1061	.0083	.0614	.1144	.0833	.0517	.0558
1/7	7	21.9911	.0455	.0910	.0071	.0526	.0981	.0714	.0443	.0479
⅛	8	25.1327	.0398	.0796	.0062	.0460	.0858	.0625	.0388	.0419
1/9	9	28.2743	.0354	.0707	.0055	.0409	.0763	.0555	.0344	.0372
1/10	10	31.4159	.0318	.0637	.0050	.0368	.0687	.0500	.0310	.0335
1/12	12	37.6992	.0265	.0530	.0042	.0307	.0572	.0416	.0258	.0279
1/14	14	43.9824	.0227	.0454	.0036	.0263	.0490	.0357	.0221	.0239
1/16	16	50.2655	.0199	.0398	.0031	.0230	.0429	.0312	.0194	.0209
1/18	18	56.5488	.0176	.0352	.0025	.0201	.0377	.0255	.0172	.0186

Note.—The above table refers to single threads only. For Multiple threads, divide the sizes given in the table for the same **lead**, by 2 for double, 3 for triple, 4 for quadruple threads, etc.

To find the Pitch Diameter (given pitch and number of teeth).

Rule.—Multiply the number of teeth by the circular pitch and divide by 3.1416.

Example.—Number of teeth, 96; Circular pitch, ¼. Then $96 \times ¼ = 24$. $24 \div 3.1416 = 7.639 =$ pitch diameter.—*Note.*—Diameter of Hob equals diameter of Worm plus twice the clearance "C."

SPEEDS AND FEEDS FOR GEAR CUTTING

(Cincinnati Gear Cutting Machine Co.)

Range of different sizes of machines as follows:

No. 3. Up to and including 4 diametral pitch.
No. 4. Up to and including 3 diametral pitch.
No. 5. Up to and including 2 diametral pitch.
No. 6. Up to and including 1¾ diametral pitch.
No. 7. Up to and including 1 diametral pitch.

For Carbon Steel Cutters Running at a Peripheral Speed of 35 Feet per Minute on Cast Iron and 30 Feet per Minute on Steel

Diametral Pitch of Gear	Feed in In. per Min. Finishing in one Cut				Feed in In. per Min. for Roughing Cut .010 to .030 in. Left for Finishing Cut				Feed in In. per Min. for Finishing Cut			
	Cast Iron	Soft Steel	High Carbon Steel	Nickel Steel	Cast Iron	Soft Steel	High Carbon Steel	Nickel Steel	Cast Iron	Soft Steel	High Carbon Steel	Nickel Steel
1					1 5/8	1 1/4	1	1	2 1/16	1 5/8	1 5/8	1 1/4
1¼					1 5/8	1 1/4	1	1	2 1/16	1 5/8	1 5/8	1 1/4
1½					2 1/16	1 5/8	1 1/4	1	2 11/16	2 1/16	2 1/16	1 5/8
1¾	2 1/16	1 11/16	1 5/16	1	3 3/8	2 11/16	2 1/16	1 11/16	4 3/8	3 3/8	2 11/16	2 1/16
2	2 1/2	2	1 11/16	1 1/4	4 1/16	3 1/8	2 1/2	2	4 1/16	3 1/8	2 1/2	2
2½	2 1/2	2	1 11/16	1 1/4	4 1/16	3 1/8	2 1/2	2	4 1/16	3 1/8	2 1/2	2
3	3 7/16	2 1/2	1 5/8	1 1/4	4 1/16	3 7/16	2 1/2	2	4 1/4	3 7/16	2 1/2	2
4	3 7/16	2 1/2	2	1 5/8	4 1/4	3 7/16	2 1/2	2	4 1/4	3 7/16	2 1/2	2
5	3 7/16	2 1/2	2	1 5/8	4 1/4	3 7/16	2 1/2	2	4 1/4	3 7/16	2 1/2	2
6	3 7/16	2 1/2	2	1 5/8	4 1/4	3 7/16	2 1/2	2	4 1/4	3 7/16	2 1/2	2
7	3 7/16	2 1/2	2	1 5/8	4 1/4	3 7/16	2 1/2	2	4 1/4	3 7/16	2 1/2	2
8	3 7/16	2 1/2	2	1 5/8	5 7/16	4 1/4	3 7/16	2 1/2	5 7/16	4 1/4	3 7/16	2 1/2
9	4 1/4	3 7/16	2 1/2	2	5 7/16	4 1/4	3 7/16	2 1/2	5 7/16	4 1/4	3 7/16	2 1/2
10	4 1/4	3 7/16	2 1/2	2	5 7/16	4 1/4	3 7/16	2 1/2	5 7/16	4 1/4	3 7/16	2 1/2

For High Speed Steel Cutters Running at a Peripheral Speed of 55 Feet per Minute on Cast Iron and 80 Feet per Minute on Steel

Diametral Pitch of Gear	Feed in In. per Min. Finishing in one Cut				Feed in In. per Min. for Roughing Cut .010 to .030 in. Left for Finishing Cut				Feed in In. per Min. for Finishing Cut			
	Cast Iron	Soft Steel	High Carbon Steel	Nickel Steel	Cast Iron	Soft Steel	High Carbon Steel	Nickel Steel	Cast Iron	Soft Steel	High Carbon Steel	Nickel Steel
1					2	1 5/8	1 5/8	1 1/4	2 11/16	2 11/16	2 11/16	2 1/16
1¼					2 1/2	2	2	1 5/8	3 5/16	3 5/16	3 5/16	2 11/16
1½					3 3/8	2 1/16	2 1/16	2 1/16	4 3/8	4 3/8	4 3/8	3 3/8
1¾	2 11/16	2 1/16	2 1/16	1 11/16	4 3/8	3 3/8	3 3/8	2 11/16	5 9/16	5 9/16	5 9/16	4 3/8
2	3 1/8	2 1/2	2 1/2	1 15/16	5 1/8	4	4	3 1/8	6 9/16	6 9/16	6 9/16	5 1/8
2½	3 1/8	2 1/2	2 1/2	1 15/16	5 1/8	4	4	3 1/8	6 9/16	6 9/16	6 9/16	5 1/8
3	3 7/16	2 1/2	2 1/2	2	5 7/16	4 1/4	4 1/4	3 7/16	6 13/16	6 13/16	6 13/16	5 7/16
4	3 7/16	2 1/2	2 1/2	2	5 7/16	4 1/4	4 1/4	3 7/16	6 13/16	6 13/16	6 13/16	6 13/16
5	3 7/16	2 1/2	2 1/2	2	5 7/16	4 1/4	4 1/4	3 7/16	6 13/16	6 13/16	6 13/16	6 13/16
6	4 1/4	3 7/16	3 7/16	2 1/2	5 7/16	4 1/4	4 1/4	3 7/16	6 13/16	6 13/16	6 13/16	6 13/16
7	4 1/4	3 7/16	3 7/16	2 1/2	5 7/16	4 1/4	4 1/4	3 7/16	6 13/16	6 13/16	6 13/16	6 13/16
8	4 1/4	3 7/16	3 7/16	2 1/2	5 7/16	4 1/4	4 1/4	3 7/16	6 13/16	6 13/16	6 13/16	6 13/16
9	5 7/16	4 1/4	4 1/4	3 7/16	6 13/16	5 7/16	5 7/16	4 1/4	8 1/2	8 1/2	8 1/2	8 1/2
10	5 7/16	4 1/4	4 1/4	3 7/16	6 13/16	5 7/16	5 7/16	4 1/4	8 1/2	8 1/2	8 1/2	8 1/2

MILLING AND MILLING CUTTERS

MILLING MACHINE FEEDS AND SPEEDS

The determining of the proper feeds of milling cutters in the past was usually a matter of guesswork, or experience, as a good many would term it, no absolute rule of any kind having ever been established.

A guide for determining the proper feed of milling cutters is found in ascertaining the thickness of the chip per tooth of the cutter.

Taking, for example, an average size milling cutter working in cast iron, say $2\frac{1}{2}$ inches diameter, 3 inches long, with eighteen teeth, which is quite commonly used, and it will be found that the thickness of the chip per tooth is quite small, resulting in .0018 inch, with a table feed of 2 inches per minute. This is entirely too slow. Now, comparing this cut of .0018 inch with a lathe tool cut, it will be seen that such a chip in a milling cutter is much smaller and is far more injurious to the cutter than a heavier feed, since the cutting edge of a tool will hold up longer in cutting into the metal instead of scraping it.

A cutter is very seldom ruined by the feed, but is generally ruined by overspeeding it. For instance, with a cutter of thirty teeth with a table feed of .300 inch per revolution, the chip per tooth will then only be $\frac{.300}{30T} = .010$ inch thick — still quite a light cut when comparing it with a lathe tool chip. Hence in many cases of milling, if the feeds are guided by the thickness of chip per tooth, a much faster feed would be used, since it is evident that the heaviest feeds, comaratively, give only a thin chip per tooth.

CUTTING SPEEDS

The Brown & Sharpe Mfg. Co. recommends a cutting speed of 65 feet per minute for carbon and 80 to 100 feet per minute for high speed milling cutters under average conditions. On soft cast iron, having a tensile strength of about 13,000 pounds — the feed recommended is 0.148 inches per revolution or about 9 inches per minute for carbon cutters. With a medium cast iron of about 23,000 pounds tensile strength, the same speed is maintained but the feed reduced about $\frac{1}{3}$ or to 6 inches per minute. For high speed cutters the feed can run up to 0.26 inch per revolution on the softer iron.

On steel of 65,000 tensile strength, with a cut 6 inches wide by $\frac{3}{16}$ inch deep, a feed of 16 inches per minute can be maintained for long periods. At 60 revolutions per minute and a feed of 0.262 per revolution 18 cubic inches per minute was removed with 21 horsepower.

It is not always advisable to maintain the highest cutter speeds as a slower speed and heavier feed will prevent vibration and chatter. These are not maximum results but can be attained under regular working conditions. The horsepower required for removing a cubic inch of metal per minute on the milling machine may be safely considered as $1\frac{1}{4}$ horsepower for steel and $\frac{3}{4}$ horsepower for cast iron.

THE ACTION OF A MILLING CUTTER

Experiments carried on with cutters at the works of the Cincinnati Milling Machine Company and extending over several years, have led to results of general interest. These tests covered milling cutters of various types.

The action of the ordinary milling cutter is not a true cutting action, as it is commonly understood. By a true cutting action is meant the driving of a wedge-shaped tool between the work and the chip and, although this definition is not based on a generally accepted meaning of the term, it is believed that it expresses fairly well what most mechanics understand by cutting. Practically all milling cutters have their teeth radial and this, of course, excludes the possibility of driving a wedge between chip and work. The tooth compresses the metal until it produces a strain great enough to cause a plane of cleavage at some angle with the direction of the cutter. It then begins to compress a new piece, push it off, and so on. This at least *seems* to be the action of the cutter, judging by the form of the chips. These chips are in the form of needles or small bars.

The chip taken by a milling cutter varies very materially from those taken by a lathe or planer tool. These latter tools make chips of uniform section, whereas the section of a milling chip increases from zero to a maximum.

Fig. 1 shows a milling chip as it would appear, if no compression or distortion took place. The proportions are very much exaggerated, so as to bring its typical shape clearer into view. The width $A\,B$ at the top is equal to the feed per tooth. The height $B\,C$ is the depth of cut. The length $B\,D$ is the width of cut. The section $M\,N\,O\,P$, shown halfway on the chip, is a normal section and a measure of the amount of work which was done at the time the cutter passed the point M.

Fig. 2 shows the action of a milling cutter, with center O, when the cutter is rotating and the work is feeding at the same time. The tooth $A\,B$ sweeps through the path $B\,C$. When the point B has reached the position B_1, a new tooth starts cutting. By this time O has advanced to position O_2, and the new tooth $A_2\,B_2$ is not yet in a vertical position, when the point B_2 touches the work. When the cutter revolves, this point B_2 must penetrate into the work and compress the metal of the work. The result will be spring in the arbor. When this spring has assumed certain proportions, the blade or tooth

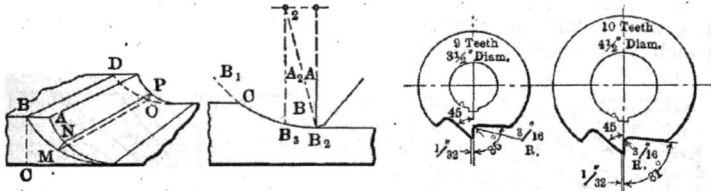

FIG. 1 — Chip Assumed to be produced by Cutter without distortion

FIG. 2. — Action of Milling Cutter

FIG. 3. — Coarse pitch Milling Cutter

begins to remove a chip. This may be assumed to take place in the position B_3, the tooth simply gliding over the work from B_2 to B_3. This action must necessarily be very harmful to the cutter, and it was believed that this, perhaps more than any other action of the cutter, caused its dulling. It would be especially severe with light cuts, as a relatively small amount of spring would allow the point B_2 to travel through a large arc. It would be quite possible that a tooth should fail entirely to take a chip, and that the succeeding tooth would take a chip of double the amount.

This peculiar action of the milling cutter is inherent in its construction and cannot be avoided. This question then is how to minimize these harmful results.

Another feature, which limits the ability of a milling cutter to remove metal, is the proportion between the chip to be removed and the amount of space between two adjoining teeth. Such a limitation does not exist with lathe or planer tools, where the chips have unlimited space in which to flow off.

FORM OF TOOTH IN THE NEW CUTTER

The foregoing considerations led to a gradual evolution of spiral milling cutters. At first, the number of teeth of spiral mills was only slightly diminished, as it was thought that some element which was not considered might affect the result. Gradually the spacing was increased and the cutters, as now used, have taken the forms shown in Fig. 3.

Two standard sizes are used, although other sizes are required for special cutters and special gangs. The standard diameters are $3\frac{1}{2}$ inches and $4\frac{1}{2}$ inches. The $3\frac{1}{2}$-inch diameter cutters are made with nine, and the $4\frac{1}{2}$-inch diameter cutters with ten teeth, which corresponds to a spacing of about $1\frac{1}{4}$ inches. The point of the tooth has a land of $\frac{1}{32}$ inch, and the back of the tooth forms an angle of 45 degrees with the radial line. The chip space is approximately four times as great as in the usual standard cutter of the present time and is formed with a $\frac{3}{16}$-inch radius at the bottom.

RESULTS OF TESTS

Very satisfactory results were obtained with these cutters. Figs. 4, 5, and 6 show the results of tests made with cutters with ⅝-inch, ¾-inch and 1⅛-inch spacing. Cuts were taken on cast-iron test

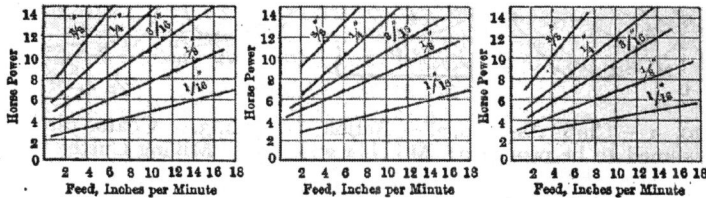

Milling Cutters and their Efficiency

blocks. It will be noticed that the same amount of power is required to take a cut ¼-inch deep and with 10.4 feed with a cutter of ⅝-inch pitch, and a cut ¼ inch deep and with 13.5 feed but with a cutter 1⅛-inch pitch.

Therefore there is a large increase in the amount of metal which can be removed with the same amount of horsepower, by using these wide-spaced cutters. It was also found that for roughing on the ordinary work in the shop a cutter with the wider-spaced teeth would remain sharp for a longer period, notwithstanding that feeds had been increased.

THE FINISH OF THE WORK

It is a common belief that better finish can be obtained with teeth closely spaced, but experience with the wide-spaced cutter shows that there is no ground for this belief. The grade of finish may be expressed by the distance between successive marks on the work. These marks are revolution marks and not tooth marks. It is practically impossible to avoid these revolution marks. They are caused by the cutter not being exactly round or quite concentric with the hole, by the hole not being of exactly the same size as the arbor, by the arbor not being round, by the straight part of the arbor not being concentric with the taper shank, by the taper shank not being round or of the same taper exactly as the taper hole in the spindle, by this taper hole being out of line with the spindle, by looseness between the spindle and its bearings, etc. Each of these items is very small in any good milling machine; yet the accumulation of these little errors is sufficient to cause a mark, and this mark needs to have a depth of only a fraction of a thousandth of an inch to be very plainly visible. As these marks are caused by conditions which return once for every revolution of the cutter, it is plain that the spacing of the teeth can have no effect on the distance between them and, therefore, on the grade of finish. This has been proven by actual tests.

THE CHIP BREAKER

It is generally believed that for finishing alone a milling cutter should be used without chip breakers, the effect of the chip breaker being to scratch the surface. To overcome this trouble, chip break-

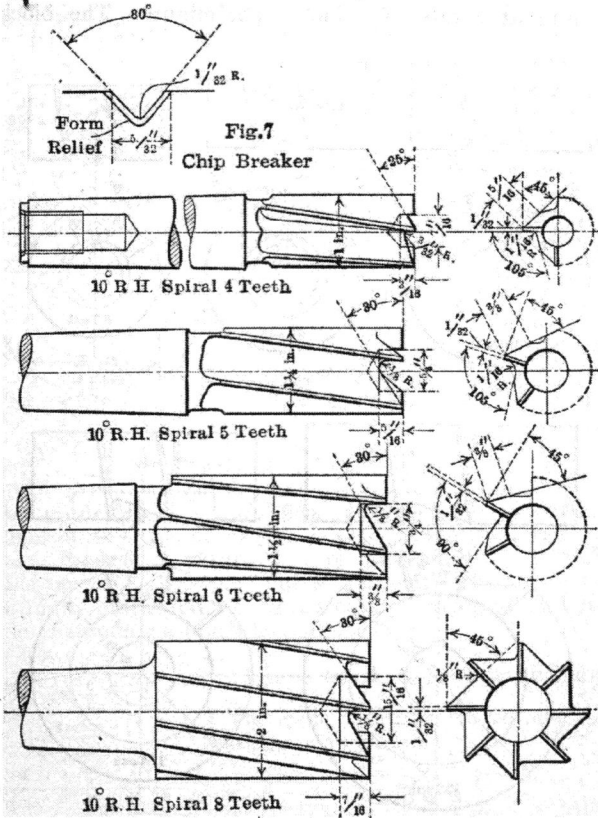

Fig. 7
Chip Breaker

10° R.H. Spiral 4 Teeth

10° R.H. Spiral 5 Teeth

10° R.H. Spiral 6 Teeth

10° R.H. Spiral 8 Teeth

FIG. 8.—Taper Shank End Mills

ers are made as shown in Fig. 7 with clearance at both corners. This prevents the tearing up of metal with the result that a cutter with these chip breakers produces as good a finish as one without chip breakers.

END MILLS

Fig. 8 shows the end mills which are now considered standard by the Cincinnati Milling Machine Company and which fill practically all requirements. They are made in sizes of 1 inch, 1¼ inches, 1½ inches and 2 inches in diameter, the smallest with four, and the largest with eight teeth. In order to preserve the strength of the teeth it is necessary to mill the back of the teeth of the three smaller sizes with two faces. Their action is remarkably free. A 2-inch taper shank end mill milled a slot $1\frac{1}{8}$ inches deep in a solid block of cast iron at a rate of 6 inches per minute. The block was

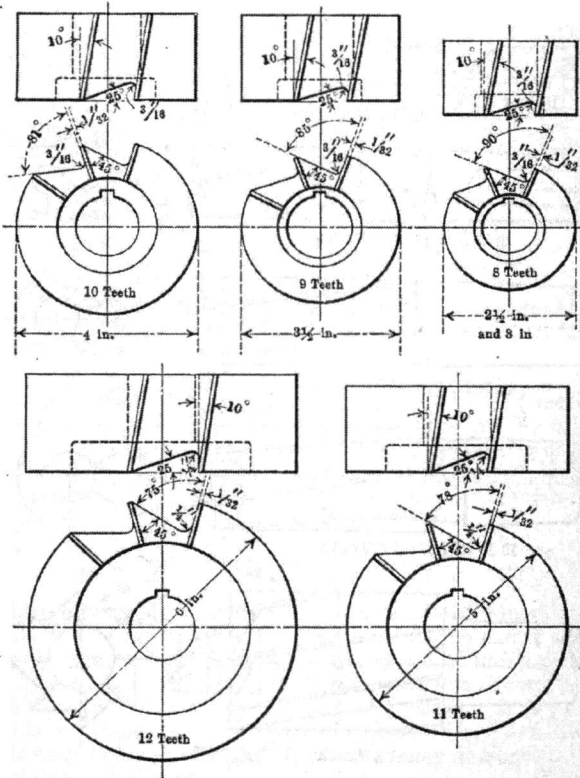

FIG. 9. — Spiral Shell Cutters

clamped to the table of the milling machine and the knee was fed upward. The same cutter would remove from the end of the casting a section $1\frac{1}{2}$ inches wide and $1\frac{1}{2}$ inches deep. Under the latter conditions, the chips would free themselves from the cutter and these chips were rolled up in pieces much like the chips obtained from a broad planer tool, when taking a finishing cut. This cut was taken with a feed of 11 inches per minute. Another similar cut, but 1 inch and $1\frac{1}{8}$ inches in section, was taken with a feed of 33 inches per minute.

Fig. 9 shows the shell end mills of the wide-spaced type, which are now considered standard for their use by the Cincinnati Milling Machine Company, and Figs. 10 and 11 show the side mills.

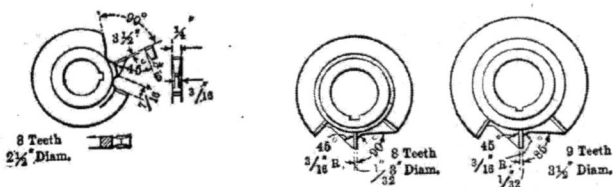

FIG. 10. — Side Mills

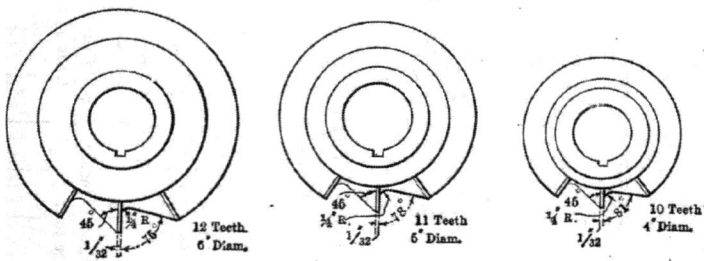

FIG. 11. — Side Mills

When milling steel, a heavy flow of oil on a milling cutter, forced by means of an oil pump, is just as essential as the great volume of oil which is used on automatic screw machine tools, which would not hold up one-half hour if not so flushed. The life of a milling cutter amply lubricated will be materially prolonged and it will be capable of standing a much heavier feed.

LEADS OF B. & S. CUTTER SPIRALS

The leads of the Brown & Sharpe Cutter Spirals are as follows:

$$\mathrm{Tan}\ \alpha = \frac{C}{L}$$

Diam. of Cutter	Lead	Diam. of Cutter	Lead
$\frac{1}{2}''$	$7.29''$	$2''$	$31.5''$
$\frac{5}{8}-\frac{3}{4}''$	$9.52''$	$2\frac{1}{4}-2\frac{1}{2}''$	$36''$
$\frac{7}{8}''$	$13.71''$	$2\frac{3}{4}-3''$	$48''$
$1 -1\frac{1}{4}''$	$17.14''$	$3\frac{1}{2}-3\frac{3}{4}''$	$60''$
$1\frac{1}{2}''$	$23.33''$	$4''$	$68.57''$
$1\frac{3}{4}''$	$28''$		

TABLE OF PITCHES AND APPROXIMATE ANGLES FOR CUTTING SPIRALS ON THE UNIVERSAL MILLING MACHINE

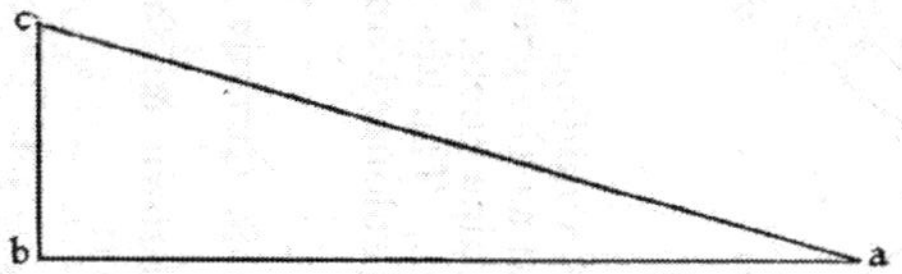

To find the angle for cutters of a larger diameter than given in the table, make a drawing as shown in the diagram; the angle b being a right angle. Let $b\,c$ equal the circumference. Let $a\,b$ equal the pitch. Connect $c\,a$ by a line, and measure the angle a with a protractor; or divide the circumference by the lead and the quotient will be the tangent of the angle. Find the angle in a table of tangents.

Diameter of Mill, Cutter, or Drill to be Cut

Inches

Values Given Under Diameters are Angles in Degrees

$$\text{The lead in inches in one turn} = \frac{10 \times \text{Gear on Worm} \times \text{2nd Gear on Stud}}{\text{Gear on Screw} \times \text{1st Gear on Stud}}$$

Pitch in Inches to one Turn	Gear on Screw	Second Gear on Stud	First Gear on Stud	Gear on Worm	⅛	¼	⅜	½	⅝	¾	⅞	1	1¼	1½	1¾	2	2¼	2½	2¾	3	3¼	3½	3¾	4
1.25	72	24	64	24	17¾	32¼																		
1.46	72	28	64	24	14¾	28	38½																	
1.56	72	30	64	24	14¼	26¾	37																	
1.67	72	32	64	24	12¾	25	34¼	43¼																

																									45	44¼	44¼
																							45	42½	42¼	42	
																				44	43	42¼	40	39¾	39½		
																43½	41¼	40¼	39½	37½	37	37¼	36½				
												44¼	43¼	43	40½	38¾	37½	36½	34½	34½	34						
										44¼	43½	41	40¼	39½	37	36½	35½	34	33½	31¾	31¼	31					
									42	41½	41¼	40¼	39½	37	36¼	36	33½	32	30½	30¼	30	28½	28	27¾			
							44¼	41¾	41¼	41	37¾	37¼	36¼	35¼	33	32½	32	29½	28	27	26½	24½	24¼	24¼			
						43½	41½	39	36½	36	33	27	26¾	25¾	25½	23¾	22½	22	21	20½	18½	18¼	17¼	17	16¾		
					44¼	44½	39	37	35	33	31¼	26¾	25½	25¼	23½	23	22½	20½	20¼	19¼	18¾	18¼	17¼	17	16¾		
				44¾	43¼	40½	39	36	35¼	33½	31¼	29½	27¾	26¾	24¼	23¾	23	22½	20½	20¼	19¾	18¼	17	16¼	16	15	14¾
			43¼	40½	39	36	32¾	31¼	29½	27¾	25½	23½	23¾	21	19½	18	17¾	17¼	15¾	14¾	13½	12½	12¼	12¼			
		45	43¼	41¼	38	35¼	34	31¼	28	26¾	25¼	23¾	22	20¾	20	17¾	17¼	16½	16¼	15	14½	14¼	13¾	13¼	12½	12¼	12
	39	37	35	32	29¾	28¼	25¼	23	20½	19½	17½	16½	16	14½	13¾	13¼	12½	12	11¼	10¾	10¼	10	9¼	8¾	8½	8½	
31	29¼	27¼	25	23	21¾	19¼	17¾	16¼	15½	14½	13¼	12¼	12	11	10¾	10¼	10	9½	9	8¾	8¼	8	7½	7¼	7	6¾	6¼
21¼	20¼	19¼	17	15¼	15	13¾	13¼	11¾	11¼	10¾	9¾	9	8½	8¼	8	7¼	7	6¾	6½	6½	6¼	6	5½	5¼	5	4¾	4¾
11¼	10¼	9¾	8¾	8	7¼	7	6	5¾	5¼	5	4½	4	4	3½	3¼	3¼	3¼	3	3	2¾	2¾	2½	2½	2¼	2	2	2
1.94	2.08	2.22	2.50	2.78	2.92	3.24	3.70	3.89	4.17	4.53	4.86	5.33	5.44	6.12	6.22	6.48	6.67	7.29	7.41	7.62	8.33	9.00	9.33	9.52	10.29	10.37	10.50
72	72	72	72	72	72	72	72	64	72	72	72	72	64	72	72	56	64	72	72	56	72	64	72	56	56	72	64
28	40	28	48	28	56	28	32	24	48	28	56	32	28	28	40	40	40	32	40	48	40	40	32	56	56		
64	64	56	64	56	64	48	48	48	72	48	56	64	40	40	40	48	48	48	48	32	32	30	40	40	48	40	
32	24	32	24	40	24	40	40	56	40	56	40	48	56	56	56	64	56	64	64	48	72	56	64	72	64	48	

TABLE OF PITCHES AND APPROXIMATE ANGLES FOR CUTTING SPIRALS ON THE UNIVERSAL MILLING MACHINE

(Continued)

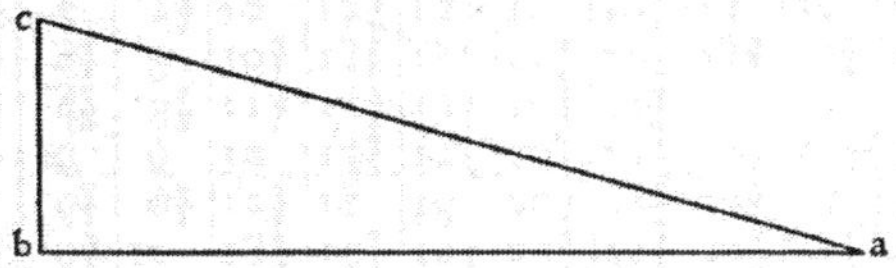

To find the angle for cutters of a larger diameter than given in the table, make a drawing as shown in the diagram; the angle b being a right angle. Let a b equal the circumference. Let b c equal the pitch. Connect c a by a line, and measure the angle a with a protractor; or divide the circumference by the lead and the quotient will be the tangent of the angle. Find the angle in a table of tangents.

Diameter of Mill, Cutter, or Drill to be Cut

Inches

Values Given Under Diameters are Angles in Degrees

Pitch in Inches to one Turn	Gear on Screw	Second Gear on Stud	First Gear on Stud	Gear on Worm	⅛	¼	⅜	½	⅝	¾	⅞	1	1¼	1½	1¾	2	2¼	2½	2¾	3	3¼	3½	3¾	4
10.67	72	48	40	64	2	4	6¼	8¼	10¼	12¼	14¼	16½	20¼	24	27¼	30½	33½	36½	39	41½	43¼			
10.94	64	40	32	56	2	4	6	8¼	10¼	12	14	16¼	20	23½	26¾	30	33	35¾	38¼	40¾	43	44¼		
11.11	72	40	32	64	2	4	6	8	10	11¾	13¾	16	19¾	23	26¼	29½	32¼	35¼	38	40¼	42½	44¼		
11.66	72	48	32	56	1¾	3¾	5¾	7½	9½	11¼	13¼	15¼	18¼	22	25¼	28½	31¼	34	36½	39	41¼	43½		

12.00	13.12	13.33	13.71	15.24	15.56	15.75	16.87	17.14	18.75	19.29	19.59	19.69	21.43	22.50	23.33	26.25	26.67	28.00	30.86	31.50	36.00	41.14	45.00	48.00	51.43	60.00	68.57
48	64	72	56	72	72	40	64	56	48	56	56	64	56	64	48	40	40	40	40	40	32	40	32	32	28
32	48	48	48	48	56	72	48	48	40	48	48	56	40	56	56	56	56	56	48	56	64	64	56	64	64
40	32	28	40	28	32	64	32	32	32	28	32	24	28	32	24	28	32	32	28	28	24	28	24	24
72	56	56	64	64	64	56	72	64	72	72	64	72	72	72	64	64	72	72	72	72	72	72	72

MILLING HEART-SHAPED CAMS

ONE method of producing heart-shaped cams is as follows:

Lay out the curve of the cam roughly, as in Fig. 1. Drill and re-move the outside stock, being sure to leave sufficient stock to over-come errors in laying out. Put the cam on the nut arbor and tighten securely. If the roll of the cam is ⅜ radius, select a milling cutter having the same radius, as the roll of the cam must come to the lowest point, which it would not be able to do if a cutter of a smaller radius than that of the roll were used. It would also make a difference to the other points on the curve of the cam, which is not quite so apparent at first glance.

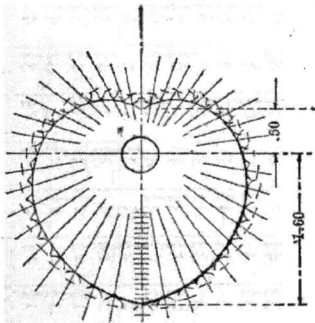

FIG. 1. — Method of Laying Out Cam

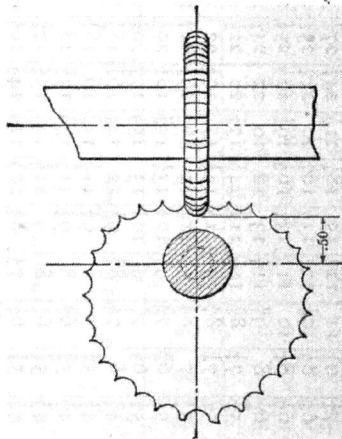

FIG. 2. — Position of Cam and Cutter when Commencing to Mill

Selecting an Index

THE next operation is to place the cam between centers on the milling machine, having the cutter in line with the vertical radius of the cam, at its lowest point. Next choose an index circle which will give a division of the cam such that the rise of each division will be in thousandths of an inch, if possible. For this cam take a circle which will give 200 divisions. As this will make 100 divisions on a side, the rise of each division will be 0.011 of an inch. Now raise the table to the required hight, starting at the lowest point of the cam, and mill across, as in Fig. 2.

Moving the Table

For the other cuts lower the table 0.011 each time, and revolve the cam one division until the highest point of the cam is reached, then raise the table 0.011 for each division of the cam.

When the cam comes from the milling machine there will be found to be small grooves left between the cuts. These may be easily removed by smoothing off with a file without impairing the accuracy of the cam.

Most screw-machine cams can be made in this manner, and they will be found to be more accurate than if laid out and filed to the line, and also much easier to make after one has become accustomed to the method.

MILLING CAMS BY GEARING UP THE DIVIDING HEAD

By the method here shown, cams of any rise may be milled with the gears regularly furnished with the milling-machine.

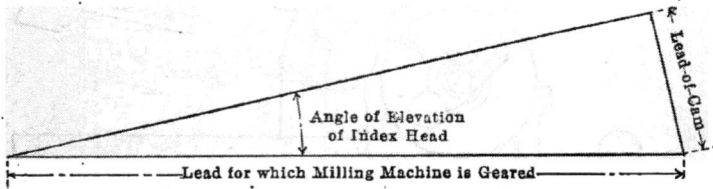

Angle of Elevation of Index Head

Lead-of-Cam

Lead for which Milling Machine is Geared

FIG. 3.—Diagram for Angle of Index Head

With the head set vertically the lead of the cam would be the same as the lead for which the machine is geared, while with the head horizontal and the milling spindle also, a concentric arc, or rest, would be milled on the cam, regardless of how the machine was geared. By inclining the head and milling spindle, we can produce any lead on the cam less than that for which the machine is geared.

The method of finding the inclination at which to set the index head is shown in Fig. 3, and is simply the solution of a plain right-angled triangle, in which the hypothenuse represents the lead of the machine, and one of the other sides represents the lead we wish to produce on the cam. By dividing the latter by the former we get the sine of the angle of inclination.

Take for illustration a plate cam having ⅛-inch rise in 300 degrees.

$$\frac{360}{300} \times \tfrac{1}{8} = 0.15,$$

which is the lead we want on the cam, while the slowest lead for which the B & S. machine can be geared is 0.67

$$\frac{0.15}{0.67} = 0.224.$$

Consulting a table of sines, we find 0.224 approximates closely the sine of 13 degrees, which is the angle at which to set the head, and if the milling spindle is also set at the same angle, the edge of the cam will be parallel with the shaft on which it is to run. Fig. 4 shows a milling-machine set for this job.

When a cam has several lobes of different leads, we gear the machine up for a lead somewhat longer than the longest one called for in that cam, and then all the different lobes can be milled with the one setting of gears, by simply altering the inclination of head and milling spindle for each different lead on the cam.

If the diameter of the cam and the inclination of the head will admit, it is better to mill on the under side of the cam, as that brings the mill and the table nearer together and thus increases rigidity, besides enabling us to easily see any lines that may be laid out on the flat face of the cam. Also the chips do not accumulate on the work.

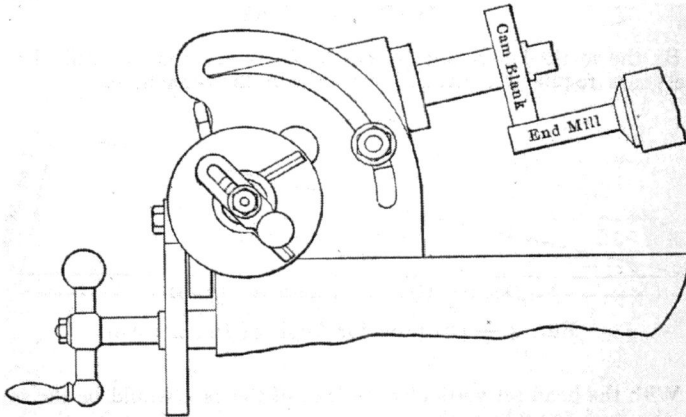

Fig. 4.—Dividing Head Set for Cam Milling

The work is fed against the cutter by turning the index crank, and on coming back for another cut we turn the handle of the milling-machine table. As a result the work will recede from the cutter before the cam blank commences to turn, owing to back lash in the gears, thus preventing the cutter from dragging over the work while running back.

In this way we use to advantage what is ordinarily considered a defect in machine construction.

The milling-machine, when used as shown in Fig. 4, will be found to be more rigid than when the head is set in the vertical position, and the cams will work more smoothly on account of the shearing action of the cutter.

One possible objection to the method here advocated is the necessity of using, in some cases, an end mill of extra length of tooth. In practise, an end mill ⅜-inch diameter and with a 3½-inch length of tooth is not unusual; but the results in both speed and quality will be found entirely satisfactory.

TABLES OF SETTINGS FOR MILLING SCREW MACHINE CAMS

COMPUTED BY THE CINCINNATI MILLING MACHINE CO.

ON the preceding pages an explanation is given of the methods of computing the angle at which to set the dividing head and milling head for cutting spiral screw machine cams or other cams of similar form to any desired lead. For leads below o.6 inch the method referred to will be of direct service, but where the lead is greater than o.6 inch the following tables can be used to great advantage as these give at once the settings of dividing head and vertical milling attachment for leads from o.6 inch to 6 inches.

These tables give all the information necessary and it only remains for the milling machine operator to select the lead of the desired cam from the tables and set up for the corresponding change gears and angles.

In setting the vertical milling attachment read the angle direct from the dial. Example: if the angle given in the table is 39½ degrees, set the spindle 39½ degrees from its vertical position.

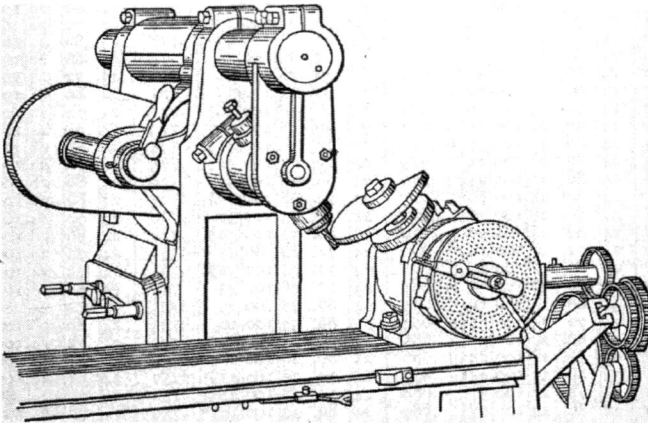

FIG. 5. — Milling Cams

In setting the dividing head, subtract the angle in the table from 90 degrees. The difference represents the angle to which the dividing head spindle must be raised from the horizontal position.

Example: The angle given in the table is 39½ degrees. 90 degrees — 39½ degrees equals 50½ degrees.

Set the dividing head spindle 50½ degrees up from the horizontal position. This angle is read direct from the dial. The set up is shown in Fig. 5.

The tables may of course be used in connection with the cutting of any other similar cams.

Lead	Gear on Worm	1st Intermediate	2nd Intermediate	Gear on Screw	Angle
.600	24	86	24	100	26½
.601	24	86	24	100	26
.602	24	86	24	100	26
.603	24	86	28	100	39½
.604	24	72	24	100	41
.605	24	86	24	100	25½
.606	24	86	28	100	39
.607	24	86	24	100	25
.608	24	72	24	100	40½
.609	24	86	24	100	24½
.610	24	86	24	100	24½
.611	24	86	28	100	38½
.612	24	86	24	100	24
.613	24	72	24	100	40
.614	24	86	24	100	23½
.615	24	86	28	100	38
.616	24	86	24	100	23
.617	24	72	24	100	39½
.618	24	72	24	100	39½
.619	24	86	24	100	22½
.620	24	86	28	100	37½
.621	24	86	24	100	22
.622	24	72	24	100	39
.623	24	86	24	100	21½
.624	24	86	28	100	37
.625	24	86	24	100	21
.626	24	86	32	100	45½
.627	24	86	24	100	20½
.628	24	86	28	100	36½
.629	24	86	24	100	20
.630	24	72	24	100	38
.631	24	86	32	100	45
.632	24	86	28	100	36
.633	24	86	24	100	19
.634	24	72	24	100	37½
.635	24	86	24	100	18½
.636	24	86	28	100	35½
.637	24	86	32	100	44½
.638	24	72	24	100	37
.639	24	86	24	100	17½
.640	24	86	28	100	35
.641	24	86	24	100	17
.642	24	86	32	100	44
.643	24	86	28	100	34½
.644	24	86	24	100	15
.645	24	86	24	100	15½
.646	24	86	24	100	15½
.647	24	86	24	100	15
.648	24	86	32	100	43½
.649	24	86	24	100	14½

Lead	Gear on Worm	1st Intermediate	2nd Intermediate	Gear on Screw	Angle
.650	24	86	24	100	14
.651	24	86	28	100	33½
.652	24	86	24	100	13½
.653	24	86	32	100	43
.654	24	86	24	100	12½
.655	24	86	24	100	12
.656	24	86	24	100	11½
.657	24	86	24	100	11
.658	24	86	32	100	42½
.659	24	72	24	100	34½
.660	24	86	24	100	10
.661	24	86	28	100	32
.662	24	86	28	100	32
.663	24	72	24	100	34
.664	24	86	32	100	42
.665	24	72	28	100	44½
.666	24	86	28	100	31½
.667	24	72	24	100	33½
.668	24	64	24	100	42
.669	24	72	24	86	44
.670	24	86	28	100	31
.671	24	72	24	100	33
.672	24	86	28	100	30½
.673	24	86	28	100	30½
.674	24	64	24	100	41½
.675	24	72	24	100	32½
.676	24	86	28	100	30
.677	24	72	28	100	43½
.678	24	72	24	100	32
.679	24	86	32	100	40½
.680	24	72	24	86	43
.681	24	72	24	100	31½
.682	24	72	28	100	43
.683	24	86	28	100	29
.684	24	86	32	100	40
.685	24	72	24	86	42½
.686	24	86	28	100	28½
.687	24	72	28	100	42½
.688	24	72	28	100	42½
.689	24	86	32	100	39½
.690	24	86	28	100	28
.691	24	72	24	86	42
.692	24	86	28	100	27½
.693	24	72	28	100	42
.694	24	86	32	100	39
.695	24	64	24	100	39½
.696	24	86	28	100	27
.697	24	72	24	86	41½
.698	24	72	28	100	41½
.699	24	86	32	100	38½

Lead	Gear on Worm	1st Intermediate	2nd Intermediate	Gear on Screw	Angle
.700	24	72	24	100	29
.701	24	72	24	86	41
.702	24	86	28	100	26
.703	24	72	24	100	28½
.704	24	86	32	100	38
.705	24	86	28	100	25½
.706	24	72	24	100	28
.707	24	72	24	86	40½
.708	24	86	28	100	25
.709	24	72	28	100	40½
.710	24	72	24	100	27½
.711	24	86	28	100	24½
.712	24	72	24	86	40
.713	24	72	24	100	27
.714	24	64	24	100	37½
.715	24	72	28	100	40
.716	24	86	28	100	23½
.717	24	72	24	86	39½
.718	24	86	32	100	36½
.719	24	86	28	100	23
.720	24	72	28	100	39½
.721	24	86	28	100	22½
.722	24	72	28	100	25½
.723	24	64	24	100	36½
.724	24	86	28	100	22
.725	24	72	24	100	25
.726	24	86	28	100	21½
.727	24	86	32	100	35½
.728	24	72	24	100	24
.729	24	86	28	100	21
.730	24	72	28	100	38½
.731	24	72	24	100	24
.732	24	86	28	100	20½
.733	24	72	24	86	38
.734	24	86	28	100	20
.735	24	72	28	100	38
.736	24	86	28	100	19½
.737	24	64	24	100	35
.738	24	72	24	86	37½
.739	24	72	28	100	37½
.740	24	72	28	100	37½
.741	24	86	28	100	18½
.742	24	72	24	100	22
.743	24	86	28	100	18
.744	24	72	28	100	21½
.745	24	72	28	100	37
.746	24	64	24	100	34
.747	24	86	28	100	17
.748	24	72	24	86	36½
.749	24	86	28	100	16½

Lead	Gear on Worm	1st Intermediate	2nd Intermediate	Gear on Screw	Angle	Lead	Gear on Worm	1st Intermediate	2nd Intermediate	Gear on Screw	Angle	Lead	Gear on Worm	1st Intermediate	2nd Intermediate	Gear on Screw	Angle
.750	24	72	28	100	36½	.800	24	72	28	100	31	.850	24	72	24	86	24
.751	24	86	28	100	16	.801	24	72	24	86	30½	.852	24	64	24	100	19
.752	24	72	24	100	20	.802	24	64	24	86	40	.851	24	72	28	100	24
.753	24	86	32	100	32½	.803	24	86	32	100	26	.853	24	72	24	86	23½
.754	24	72	24	100	19½	.804	28	86	32	100	39½	.854	24	86	32	100	17
.755	24	72	28	100	36	.805	24	72	32	100	41	.855	24	64	28	100	35½
.756	24	86	28	100	14½	.806	24	86	32	100	25½	.856	24	86	32	100	16½
.757	24	72	24	86	35½	.807	24	64	24	86	39½	.857	24	64	24	86	35
.758	24	86	28	100	14	.808	24	72	28	100	30	.858	24	64	24	100	17½
.759	24	64	24	100	32½	.809	24	64	24	100	26	.859	24	72	24	86	22½
.760	24	72	28	100	35½	.810	28	86	32	100	39	.860	24	64	28	100	35
.761	24	86	28	100	13	.811	24	72	32	100	40½	.861	24	72	28	86	37½
.762	24	72	24	86	35	.812	24	72	28	100	29½	.862	24	72	28	100	22½
.763	24	72	24	100	17½	.813	24	72	24	86	29	.863	24	64	24	100	16½
.764	24	86	28	100	12	.814	24	64	24	86	39	.864	28	86	32	100	34
.765	24	72	24	100	17	.815	28	86	32	100	38½	.865	24	64	24	100	16
.766	24	72	24	86	34½	.816	24	72	28	100	29	.866	24	86	32	100	14
.767	24	72	24	100	16½	.817	24	72	24	86	28½	.867	24	64	24	100	15½
.768	24	86	28	100	10½	.818	24	72	28	86	41	.868	24	72	28	100	21½
.769	24	86	28	100	10	.819	24	86	32	100	23½	.869	24	64	24	100	15
.770	24	86	32	100	30½	.820	24	72	28	100	28½	.870	24	86	32	100	13
.771	24	72	24	86	34	.821	24	72	24	86	28	.871	24	64	24	100	14½
.772	24	72	24	100	15	.822	24	86	32	100	23	.872	24	86	32	100	12½
.773	24	86	32	100	30	.823	24	72	32	100	39½	.873	24	64	24	100	14
.774	24	72	24	100	14½	.824	24	72	28	100	28	.874	24	72	24	86	20
.775	24	64	24	100	30½	.825	24	72	24	86	27½	.875	24	86	32	100	11½
.776	24	72	24	100	14	.826	28	86	32	100	37½	.876	24	64	28	100	33½
.777	24	86	32	100	29½	.827	24	72	28	100	27½	.877	24	64	24	100	13
.778	24	72	28	100	33½	.828	24	86	32	100	22	.878	24	86	32	100	10½
.779	24	72	24	100	13	.829	24	86	40	100	42	.879	24	64	24	100	12½
.780	24	72	24	86	33	.830	24	64	24	86	37½	.880	24	64	24	100	12
.781	24	72	24	100	12½	.831	24	72	28	86	40	.881	24	64	28	100	33
.782	24	72	28	100	33	.832	24	72	24	86	26½	.882	24	64	24	100	11½
.783	24	64	24	100	29½	.833	24	56	24	100	36	.883	24	64	24	86	32½
.784	24	72	24	100	11½	.834	24	86	32	100	21	.884	28	86	32	100	32
.785	24	86	32	100	28½	.835	24	72	32	100	38½	.885	24	64	24	100	10½
.786	28	86	32	100	41	.836	24	72	24	86	26	.886	24	64	24	100	10
.787	24	64	24	100	29	.837	24	72	28	86	30½	.887	24	72	24	86	17½
.788	24	72	24	100	10	.838	24	56	24	100	35½	.888	24	64	24	86	32
.789	24	72	24	86	32	.839	24	86	32	100	20	.889	24	72	24	86	17
.790	24	64	24	86	41	.840	24	64	24	100	21	.890	24	72	28	100	17½
.791	24	64	24	100	28½	.841	24	72	32	100	38	.891	24	56	24	100	30
.792	24	86	32	100	27½	.842	24	86	32	100	19½	.892	24	72	24	86	16½
.793	24	72	24	86	31½	.843	24	72	28	86	39	.893	28	86	32	100	31
.794	24	72	28	86	43	.844	24	86	32	100	19	.894	24	72	24	86	16
.795	24	72	28	100	31½	.845	24	72	28	100	25	.895	24	64	28	100	31½
.796	24	64	24	86	40½	.846	24	64	24	100	20	.896	24	72	24	86	15½
.797	24	72	24	86	31	.847	24	86	32	100	18½	.897	24	72	28	100	16
.708	28	86	32	100	40	.848	24	64	24	100	19½	.898	24	72	24	86	15
.799	24	72	32	100	41½	.849	24	86	32	100	18	.899	24	72	28	100	15½

Lead	Gear on Worm	1st Intermediate	2nd Intermediate	Gear on Screw	Angle	Lead	Gear on Worm	1st Intermediate	2nd Intermediate	Gear on Screw	Angle	Lead	Gear on Worm	1st Intermediate	2nd Intermediate	Gear on Screw	Angle
.900	24	56	24	100	29	.950	24	72	32	86	40	1.000	24	86	44	100	35½
.901	24	72	28	100	15	.951	24	56	24	100	22½	1.001	24	56	24	100	13½
.902	24	72	24	86	14	.952	28	86	32	100	24	1.002	28	86	32	100	16
.903	24	72	28	100	14½	.953	24	64	24	86	24½	1.003	24	56	24	100	13
.904	24	72	24	86	13½	.954	24	56	24	100	22	1.004	28	86	32	100	15½
.905	24	72	28	100	14	.955	24	72	32	100	26½	1.005	24	56	24	100	12½
.906	24	72	24	86	13	.956	24	64	28	86	38½	1.006	24	56	24	100	12
.907	24	72	28	100	13½	.957	24	56	24	100	21½	1.007	24	64	24	86	16
.908	24	72	24	86	12½	.958	24	72	28	86	28	1.008	24	56	24	100	11½
.909	24	72	28	100	13	.959	24	72	32	100	26	1.009	28	86	32	100	14½
.910	24	72	32	100	31½	.960	24	64	24	86	23½	1.010	24	56	24	100	11
.911	24	72	28	100	12½	.961	24	86	44	100	38½	1.011	28	86	32	100	14
.912	24	72	28	100	12	.962	24	72	28	86	27½	1.012	24	56	24	100	10½
.913	24	72	24	86	11	.963	28	86	32	100	22½	1.013	24	56	24	100	10
.914	24	72	28	100	11½	.964	24	56	24	100	20½	1.014	24	64	24	86	14½
.915	24	72	32	100	31	.965	24	64	32	100	36½	1.015	28	86	32	100	13
.916	24	72	24	86	10	.966	28	86	32	100	22	1.016	24	64	24	86	14
.917	24	72	28	100	10½	.967	24	56	24	100	20	1.017	28	86	32	100	12½
.918	24	64	28	100	29	.968	24	56	24	86	36	1.018	24	64	24	86	13½
.919	24	72	28	100	10	.969	24	64	28	86	37½	1.019	28	86	32	100	12
.920	28	86	32	100	28	.970	24	56	24	100	19½	1.020	24	64	24	86	13
.921	24	56	24	100	26½	.971	24	72	28	86	26½	1.021	28	86	32	100	11½
.922	24	64	28	86	41	.972	86	44	32	64	6	1.022	24	64	24	86	12½
.923	24	64	28	100	28½	.973	24	56	24	100	19	1.023	28	86	32	100	11
.924	28	86	32	100	27½	.974	24	64	24	86	21½	1.024	24	64	24	86	12
.925	24	56	24	100	26	.975	24	72	32	100	24	1.025	24	64	28	100	12½
.926	24	64	32	100	39½	.976	28	86	32	100	20½	1.026	24	64	24	86	11½
.927	24	64	28	100	28	.977	24	64	28	100	21½	1.027	24	64	28	100	12
.928	24	64	28	86	40½	.978	24	56	24	100	18	1.028	24	64	24	86	11
.929	24	56	24	100	25½	.979	28	86	32	100	20	1.029	24	64	28	100	11½
.930	24	72	28	86	31	.980	24	64	28	100	21	1.030	24	64	24	86	10½
.931	24	64	28	100	27½	.981	24	64	24	86	20½	1.031	24	64	28	100	11
.932	28	72	32	100	41½	.982	28	86	32	100	19½	1.032	24	64	28	100	10½
.933	24	64	24	86	27	.983	24	72	28	86	25	1.033	24	72	32	100	14½
.934	24	86	44	100	40½	.984	24	56	24	100	17	1.034	24	64	28	100	10
.935	24	72	28	86	30½	.985	28	86	32	100	19	1.035	24	72	32	100	14
.936	24	56	24	100	24½	.986	24	72	32	100	22½	1.036	24	56	24	86	30
.937	24	64	24	86	26½	.987	24	64	24	86	19½	1.037	24	72	32	100	13½
.938	24	72	32	100	28½	.988	28	86	32	100	18½	1.038	24	72	28	86	17
.939	24	64	32	100	38½	.989	24	56	24	100	16	1.039	24	64	32	100	30
.940	24	56	24	100	24	.990	24	64	24	86	19	1.040	24	72	32	100	13
.941	24	64	24	86	26	.991	28	86	32	100	18	1.041	24	56	24	86	29½
.942	24	72	32	100	28	.992	24	56	24	100	15½	1.042	24	72	32	100	12½
.943	24	72	32	86	40½	.993	24	64	24	86	18½	1.043	24	72	28	86	16
.944	24	56	24	100	23½	.994	24	56	24	100	15	1.044	24	72	32	100	12
.945	24	64	24	86	25½	.995	24	72	28	86	23½	1.045	24	86	40	100	20½
.946	24	72	32	100	27½	.996	24	56	24	100	14½	1.046	24	72	32	100	11½
.947	24	56	24	100	23	.997	24	56	24	86	33½	1.047	24	72	32	100	11
.948	28	86	32	100	24½	.998	24	56	24	100	14	1.048	24	72	28	86	15
.949	24	64	24	86	25	.999	28	86	32	100	16½	1.049	24	72	32	100	10½

Lead	Gear on Worm	1st Intermediate	2nd Intermediate	Gear on Screw	Angle	Lead	Gear on Worm	1st Intermediate	2nd Intermediate	Gear on Screw	Angle	Lead	Gear on Worm	1st Intermediate	2nd Intermediate	Gear on Screw	Angle
1.050	24	72	28	86	14½	1.150	24	56	24	86	16	1.250	24	64	28	72	31
1.052	24	86	40	100	19½	1.152	28	86	44	100	36½	1.252	28	86	40	100	16
1.054	24	72	28	86	14	1.154	24	64	28	86	19	1.254	24	64	32	86	26
1.056	24	56	24	86	28	1.156	24	64	32	100	15½	1.256	24	64	28	72	30½
1.058	24	86	40	100	18½	1.158	24	56	24	86	14½	1.258	28	86	40	100	15
1.060	28	86	40	100	35½	1.160	24	56	24	86	14	1.260	28	86	40	100	14½
1.062	24	72	28	86	12	1.162	24	64	32	100	14½	1.262	32	56	24	100	23
1.064	24	86	40	100	17½	1.164	24	64	32	100	14	1.264	24	72	40	100	18½
1.066	24	56	24	86	27	1.166	24	72	40	100	29	1.266	28	86	40	100	13½
1.068	24	64	28	86	29	1.168	24	56	24	86	12½	1.268	24	72	40	100	18
1.070	24	86	40	100	16½	1.170	24	56	24	86	12	1.270	24	72	44	100	30
1.072	28	72	32	100	30½	1.172	24	56	24	86	11½	1.272	28	72	32	86	28½
1.074	24	64	32	100	26½	1.174	24	56	24	86	11	1.274	28	86	40	100	12
1.076	24	64	32	86	39½	1.176	24	56	24	86	10½	1.276	28	86	40	100	11½
1.078	24	86	40	100	15	1.178	24	56	24	86	10	1.278	28	86	40	100	11
1.080	24	86	40	100	14½	1.180	24	64	32	100	10½	1.280	28	86	40	100	10½
1.082	28	86	44	100	41	1.182	24	64	32	100	10	1.282	28	86	40	100	10
1.084	24	56	24	86	25	1.184	24	64	32	100	9½	1.284	24	72	40	100	15½
1.086	28	86	40	100	33½	1.186	24	86	44	100	15	1.286	40	64	24	100	31
1.088	24	56	24	86	24½	1.188	24	72	40	100	27	1.288	24	72	40	100	15
1.090	24	72	32	86	28½	1.190	24	64	28	86	13	1.290	24	72	40	100	14½
1.092	24	86	40	100	12	1.192	24	64	28	86	12½	1.292	32	56	24	100	19½
1.094	24	86	40	100	11½	1.194	24	64	28	86	12	1.294	24	86	48	100	15
1.096	24	86	40	100	11	1.196	28	72	32	100	16	1.296	24	72	40	100	13½
1.098	28	72	32	100	28	1.198	24	72	32	86	15	1.298	24	64	32	86	21½
1.100	28	72	32	86	40½	1.200	24	72	32	86	14½	1.300	24	86	48	100	14
1.102	24	64	28	86	25½	1.202	24	64	28	86	10	1.302	24	64	32	86	21
1.104	24	86	44	100	26	1.204	28	72	32	100	14½	1.304	24	72	40	100	12
1.106	40	64	24	100	42½	1.206	24	72	32	86	13½	1.306	24	72	40	100	11½
1.108	24	86	44	100	25½	1.208	24	72	32	86	13	1.308	24	72	40	100	11
1.110	24	72	32	86	26½	1.210	28	72	32	100	13½	1.310	24	64	28	72	26
1.112	24	72	40	100	33½	1.212	28	72	32	100	13	1.312	40	64	24	100	29
1.114	24	64	32	86	37	1.214	24	86	48	100	25	1.314	28	86	44	100	23½
1.116	24	56	24	86	21	1.216	32	56	24	100	27½	1.316	28	64	32	100	20
1.118	28	72	32	100	26	1.218	24	72	40	100	24	1.318	24	86	48	100	10½
1.120	24	56	24	86	20½	1.220	28	86	40	100	20½	1.320	24	86	48	100	10
1.122	24	86	44	100	24	1.222	24	72	40	100	23½	1.322	28	72	32	86	24
1.124	24	56	24	86	20	1.224	28	86	40	100	20	1.324	32	56	24	100	15
1.126	24	86	44	100	23½	1.226	24	72	48	100	40	1.326	32	86	40	100	27
1.128	24	64	32	100	20	1.228	28	86	44	100	31	1.328	28	64	32	100	18½
1.130	24	72	40	100	32	1.230	28	64	32	100	28½	1.330	32	56	24	100	14
1.132	24	64	28	86	22	1.232	24	72	40	100	22½	1.332	28	64	32	100	18
1.134	24	56	24	86	18½	1.234	24	86	48	100	23	1.334	24	64	32	86	17
1.136	24	64	28	86	21½	1.236	24	72	40	100	22	1.336	32	56	24	100	13
1.138	24	64	32	100	18½	1.238	28	86	40	100	18	1.338	32	56	24	100	12½
1.140	24	64	28	86	21	1.240	24	72	40	100	21½	1.340	24	72	44	100	24
1.142	24	64	32	86	35	1.242	28	86	40	100	17½	1.342	28	64	32	100	16½
1.144	24	56	24	86	17	1.244	24	72	40	100	21	1.344	24	64	32	86	15½
1.146	24	86	44	100	21	1.246	32	72	40	100	45½	1.346	32	56	24	100	11
1.148	24	64	32	100	17	1.248	28	86	40	100	16½	1.348	32	56	24	100	10½

Lead	Gear on Worm	1st Intermediate	2nd Intermediate	Gear on Screw	Angle
1.350	32	56	24	100	10
1.352	28	64	32	100	15
1.354	24	64	32	86	14
1.356	24	64	32	86	13½
1.358	28	64	32	100	14
1.360	28	72	32	86	20
1.362	24	64	32	86	12½
1.364	24	64	32	86	12
1.366	24	64	28	72	20½
1.368	28	72	32	86	19
1.370	28	86	44	100	17
1.372	24	64	32	86	10½
1.374	24	64	32	86	10
1.376	28	72	32	86	18
1.378	28	86	44	100	16
1.380	28	72	32	86	17½
1.382	24	64	32	72	34
1.384	28	86	44	100	15
1.386	40	64	24	100	22½
1.388	28	64	32	86	31½
1.390	28	86	44	100	14
1.392	44	64	24	100	32½
1.394	28	72	32	86	15½
1.396	28	86	44	100	13
1.398	28	72	32	86	15
1.400	40	64	24	100	21
1.402	28	86	44	100	12
1.404	28	72	32	86	14
1.406	28	86	44	100	11
1.408	24	64	28	72	15
1.410	28	72	32	86	13
1.412	24	64	28	72	14½
1.414	24	72	44	100	15½
1.416	24	64	44	86	42½
1.418	28	72	32	86	11½
1.420	28	72	32	86	11
1.422	40	64	24	100	18½
1.424	28	64	32	86	29
1.426	24	64	28	72	12
1.428	28	86	48	100	24
1.430	32	86	40	100	16
1.432	24	72	44	100	12½
1.434	24	64	28	72	10½
1.436	24	64	28	72	10
1.438	24	72	44	100	11½
1.440	24	72	44	100	11
1.442	24	72	44	100	10½
1.444	32	86	40	100	14
1.446	24	72	44	86	32
1.448	28	72	40	100	21½
1.450	32	86	40	100	13
1.452	40	64	24	100	14½
1.454	28	86	48	100	21½
1.456	24	72	40	86	20
1.458	32	86	40	100	11½
1.460	24	44	32	86	44
1.462	40	64	24	100	13
1.464	40	64	24	100	12½
1.466	24	72	40	86	19
1.468	28	64	40	100	33
1.470	40	64	24	100	11½
1.472	40	64	24	100	11
1.474	24	72	40	86	18
1.476	28	72	40	100	18½
1.478	24	72	40	86	17½
1.480	28	72	40	100	18
1.482	24	72	40	86	17
1.484	28	72	40	100	17½
1.486	24	72	40	86	16½
1.488	28	72	40	100	17
1.490	24	72	40	86	16
1.492	28	72	40	100	16½
1.494	24	72	40	86	15
1.496	28	72	40	100	16
1.498	32	64	40	100	41½
1.500	28	64	40	100	31
1.502	28	86	48	100	16
1.504	24	72	40	86	14
1.506	28	72	40	100	14½
1.508	24	72	48	100	19½
1.510	24	72	40	86	13
1.512	24	64	44	86	38
1.514	24	72	48	86	35½
1.516	24	72	40	86	12
1.518	32	86	44	100	22
1.520	28	86	48	100	13½
1.522	24	72	40	86	11
1.524	24	72	40	86	10½
1.526	24	72	40	86	10
1.528	32	86	44	100	21
1.530	28	72	40	100	10½
1.532	28	72	40	100	10
1.534	28	86	48	100	11
1.536	32	72	40	86	42
1.538	24	72	48	100	16
1.540	28	100	56	72	45
1.542	24	72	48	100	15½
1.544	28	64	32	86	18½
1.546	24	72	48	100	15
1.548	28	64	32	86	18
1.550	44	64	24	100	20
1.552	24	72	48	100	14
1.554	24	64	40	86	27
1.556	24	64	32	72	21
1.558	24	72	44	86	24
1.560	44	64	24	100	19
1.562	24	72	48	100	12½
1.564	24	72	44	86	23½
1.566	32	86	44	100	17
1.568	24	72	48	100	11½
1.570	32	72	40	100	28
1.572	28	64	32	86	15
1.574	32	86	44	100	16
1.576	24	72	48	100	10
1.578	44	64	24	100	17
1.580	28	64	32	86	14
1.582	28	64	24	100	16½
1.584	40	56	24	100	22½
1.586	28	64	32	86	13
1.588	32	86	44	100	15½
1.590	44	64	24	100	15½
1.592	28	64	32	86	12
1.594	44	64	24	100	15
1.596	28	64	44	100	34
1.598	28	64	32	86	11
1.600	44	56	24	100	21
1.602	24	64	32	72	16
1.604	32	86	44	100	11½
1.606	24	64	32	72	15½
1.608	44	64	24	100	13
1.610	32	86	44	100	10½
1.612	32	86	44	100	10
1.614	44	64	24	100	12
1.616	24	56	24	100	19½
1.618	24	64	32	72	14
1.620	44	64	24	100	11
1.622	44	64	24	100	10½
1.624	24	64	32	72	13
1.626	24	72	44	86	17½
1.628	24	64	32	72	12½
1.630	24	64	32	72	12
1.632	28	72	44	100	10½
1.634	24	64	32	72	17½
1.636	24	64	32	72	11
1.638	32	86	48	100	23½
1.640	28	72	40	86	25
1.642	24	64	32	72	10
1.644	24	64	40	86	19½
1.646	28	72	40	86	24½
1.648	40	56	24	100	16

Lead	Gear on Worm	1st Intermediate	2nd Intermediate	Gear on Screw	Angle
1.650	28	64	40	100	19½
1.652	40	56	24	100	15½
1.654	24	72	44	86	14
1.656	28	72	44	100	14½
1.658	24	72	44	86	13½
1.660	28	72	44	100	14
1.662	32	86	48	100	21½
1.664	28	72	44	100	13½
1.666	28	64	32	72	31
1.668	24	72	44	86	12
1.670	28	72	44	100	12½
1.672	24	64	40	86	16½
1.674	24	72	44	86	11
1.676	24	72	44	86	10½
1.678	28	64	40	100	16½
1.680	28	72	44	100	11
1.682	28	72	44	100	10½
1.684	32	86	48	100	19½
1.686	28	64	40	100	15½
1.688	40	56	24	100	10
1.690	28	64	40	100	15
1.692	24	64	40	86	14
1.694	32	72	44	100	30
1.696	24	64	40	86	13½
1.698	28	64	40	100	14
1.700	32	72	40	100	17
1.702	28	64	40	100	13½
1.704	28	64	40	72	45½
1.706	24	64	40	86	12
1.708	28	64	40	100	12½
1.710	28	72	40	86	19
1.712	24	64	40	86	11
1.714	32	64	40	100	31
1.716	28	72	40	86	18½
1.718	24	64	40	86	10
1.720	28	72	40	86	18
1.722	24	44	32	86	32
1.724	28	100	56	86	19
1.726	24	56	40	86	30
1.728	32	72	40	100	13½
1.730	28	72	40	86	17
1.732	32	72	40	100	13
1.734	28	72	40	86	16½
1.736	32	72	40	100	12½
1.738	32	56	40	100	40½
1.740	32	86	48	100	13
1.742	32	72	40	100	11½
1.744	32	86	48	100	12½
1.746	24	64	44	86	24½
1.748	32	72	40	100	10½
1.750	32	86	48	100	11½
1.752	28	100	56	86	16
1.754	28	72	48	100	20
1.756	32	86	48	100	10½
1.758	32	72	44	100	26
1.760	28	72	48	100	19½
1.762	28	64	32	72	25
1.764	24	72	48	86	18½
1.766	28	72	40	86	12½
1.768	32	72	48	100	34
1.770	28	72	48	100	18½
1.772	44	56	24	100	20
1.774	24	72	48	86	17½
1.776	28	72	40	86	11
1.778	44	56	24	100	19½
1.780	28	100	56	86	12½
1.782	32	64	40	100	27
1.784	24	56	40	86	26½
1.786	28	100	56	86	11½
1.788	24	72	48	86	16
1.790	28	100	56	86	11
1.792	28	100	56	86	10½
1.794	44	56	24	100	18
1.796	28	64	32	72	22½
1.798	24	64	44	86	20½
1.800	32	72	44	100	23
1.802	28	64	32	72	22
1.804	32	72	44	86	37½
1.806	24	56	40	86	25
1.808	28	72	48	100	14½
1.810	28	72	48	86	33
1.812	24	72	48	86	13
1.814	24	64	44	86	19
1.816	24	72	48	86	12½
1.818	28	72	44	86	24
1.820	24	64	44	86	18½
1.822	44	56	24	100	15
1.824	40	86	44	100	27
1.826	24	72	48	86	11
1.828	24	56	40	86	23½
1.830	28	72	48	100	11½
1.832	24	72	48	86	10
1.834	44	56	24	100	13½
1.836	28	72	48	100	10½
1.838	44	56	40	100	38
1.840	24	64	44	86	16½
1.842	32	72	40	86	27
1.844	28	64	32	72	18½
1.846	28	64	44	100	16½
1.848	44	56	24	100	11½
1.850	28	64	44	100	16
1.852	28	72	44	86	21½
1.854	44	56	24	100	10½
1.856	24	64	40	72	27
1.858	24	64	44	86	14½
1.860	32	72	44	100	18
1.862	24	64	44	86	14
1.864	28	64	44	100	14½
1.866	24	64	44	86	13½
1.868	28	64	44	100	14
1.870	24	64	44	86	13
1.872	28	64	44	100	13½
1.874	24	64	44	86	12½
1.876	28	64	44	100	13
1.878	28	64	32	72	15
1.880	24	64	44	86	11½
1.882	28	64	32	72	14½
1.884	24	64	44	86	11
1.886	28	64	44	100	11½
1.888	28	72	44	86	18½
1.890	24	64	44	86	10
1.892	32	72	48	100	27½
1.894	28	64	32	72	13
1.896	28	64	44	100	10
1.898	28	64	32	72	12½
1.900	28	64	40	86	21
1.902	28	64	32	72	12
1.904	24	64	48	86	24½
1.906	32	72	44	100	13
1.908	28	64	32	72	11
1.910	32	72	44	100	12½
1.912	28	64	32	72	10½
1.914	28	64	32	72	10
1.916	24	56	40	86	16
1.918	28	72	44	86	15½
1.920	32	72	44	100	11
1.922	28	72	44	86	15
1.924	28	64	40	86	19
1.926	32	72	44	100	10
1.928	28	64	44	86	30½
1.930	24	56	40	86	14½
1.932	32	64	40	100	15
1.934	24	56	40	86	14
1.936	32	64	40	100	14½
1.938	24	56	40	86	14
1.940	28	64	48	100	22½
1.942	24	56	40	86	13
1.944	32	56	40	86	43
1.946	28	72	44	86	12
1.948	32	72	40	86	19½

Lead	Gear on Worm	1st Intermediate	2nd Intermediate	Gear on Screw	Angle	Lead	Gear on Worm	1st Intermediate	2nd Intermediate	Gear on Screw	Angle	Lead	Gear on Worm	1st Intermediate	2nd Intermediate	Gear on Screw	Angle
1.950	28	72	44	86	11½	2.050	28	64	48	100	12½	2.150	32	72	44	86	19
1.952	40	86	44	100	17½	2.052	28	64	44	86	23½	2.152	32	64	44	100	12
1.954	24	64	48	86	21	2.054	28	64	48	100	12	2.154	24	64	44	72	20
1.956	32	72	48	100	23½	2.056	40	86	48	100	23	2.156	32	64	44	100	11½
1.958	40	86	44	100	17	2.058	24	64	48	86	10½	2.158	24	56	40	72	25
1.960	28	72	44	86	10	2.060	32	72	48	100	15	2.160	32	64	44	100	11
1.962	48	56	24	100	17½	2.062	24	56	40	72	30	2.162	40	86	48	100	14½
1.964	24	64	40	72	19½	2.064	44	48	28	100	36½	2.164	32	64	40	86	21½
1.966	28	64	40	86	15	2.066	32	56	40	86	39	2.166	32	64	48	100	25½
1.968	40	86	44	100	16	2.068	28	64	48	100	10	2.168	32	56	48	100	18½
1.970	32	64	40	100	10	2.070	32	72	48	100	14	2.170	32	72	48	86	29
1.972	48	56	24	100	16½	2.072	32	56	40	100	25	2.172	28	64	44	86	14
1.974	28	44	32	86	13½	2.074	32	72	48	100	13½	2.174	32	56	40	100	18
1.976	28	64	44	86	28	2.076	28	72	48	86	17	2.176	56	64	32	100	39
1.978	24	44	32	86	13	2.078	32	72	48	100	13	2.178	40	72	44	100	27
1.980	28	64	48	100	19½	2.080	32	64	44	100	19	2.180	40	86	48	100	12½
1.982	24	44	32	86	12½	2.082	32	72	48	100	12½	2.182	28	72	56	86	30½
1.984	28	48	40	86	43	2.084	28	64	40	72	31	2.184	24	56	44	72	33½
1.986	24	44	32	86	12	2.086	32	72	48	100	12	2.186	32	72	44	86	16
1.988	28	56	32	72	26½	2.088	28	100	56	72	16½	2.188	28	56	32	72	10
1.990	28	64	40	86	12	2.090	32	72	48	100	11½	2.190	32	56	40	86	34½
1.992	48	56	24	100	14½	2.092	28	72	48	86	15½	2.192	40	86	48	100	11
1.994	28	64	40	86	11½	2.094	32	72	48	100	11	2.194	28	64	40	72	25½
1.996	24	44	32	86	10½	2.096	28	64	44	86	20½	2.196	40	86	48	100	10½
1.998	28	64	40	86	11	2.098	32	64	44	100	17½	2.198	44	86	48	100	26½
2.000	48	56	24	100	13½	2.100	28	44	32	86	27½	2.200	24	56	40	72	22½
2.002	40	86	44	100	12	2.102	28	72	48	86	14½	2.202	32	72	44	86	14½
2.004	28	64	40	86	10	2.104	28	100	56	72	15	2.204	28	64	44	86	10
2.006	40	86	44	100	11½	2.106	28	72	48	86	14	2.206	32	72	44	86	14
2.008	48	56	24	100	12½	2.108	40	44	24	100	15	2.208	32	56	40	100	15
2.010	32	72	40	86	13½	2.110	28	64	44	86	19½	2.210	48	100	56	86	45
2.012	48	56	24	100	12	2.112	40	44	24	100	14½	2.212	32	64	40	86	18
2.014	32	72	40	86	13	2.114	28	56	32	72	18	2.214	24	64	44	72	15
2.016	40	86	44	100	10	2.116	28	64	44	86	19	2.216	32	72	44	86	13
2.018	32	72	40	86	12½	2.118	28	100	56	72	13½	2.218	32	56	40	100	14
2.020	28	72	48	86	21½	2.120	28	72	48	86	12½	2.220	32	72	44	86	12½
2.022	32	72	40	86	12	2.122	28	100	56	72	13	2.222	28	64	48	86	24½
2.024	28	64	48	100	15½	2.124	28	72	48	86	12	2.224	32	72	44	86	12
2.026	48	56	24	100	10	2.126	28	100	56	72	12½	2.226	44	86	48	100	25
2.028	28	64	48	100	15	2.128	28	64	44	86	18	2.228	32	72	44	86	11½
2.030	24	64	40	72	13	2.130	28	100	56	72	12	2.230	32	64	40	86	16½
2.032	32	72	40	86	10½	2.132	24	64	44	72	21½	2.232	32	72	44	86	11
2.034	24	64	40	72	12½	2.134	28	100	56	72	11½	2.234	44	48	28	100	29½
2.036	32	72	40	86	10	2.136	28	56	32	72	16	2.236	32	72	44	86	10½
2.038	28	64	48	100	14	2.138	28	72	48	86	10	2.238	24	64	44	72	12½
2.040	32	72	48	100	17	2.140	24	56	40	72	26	2.240	32	56	40	100	11½
2.042	28	64	48	100	13½	2.142	28	100	56	72	10½	2.242	24	64	44	72	12
2.044	40	44	24	100	20½	2.144	40	72	48	100	36½	2.244	32	56	40	100	11
2.046	28	64	48	100	13	2.146	28	56	32	72	15	2.246	24	64	44	72	11½
2.048	24	64	40	72	10½	2.148	44	86	48	100	29	2.248	32	56	40	100	10½

Lead	Gear on Worm	1st Intermediate	2nd Intermediate	Gear on Screw	Angle
2.250	24	64	44	72	11
2.255	32	64	48	100	20
2.260	44	56	32	100	26
2.265	28	44	32	86	17
2.270	28	44	32	86	16½
2.275	32	64	40	86	12
2.280	28	64	44	72	31½
2.285	44	86	48	100	21½
2.290	24	44	40	86	25½
2.295	32	64	48	100	17
2.300	24	56	40	72	15
2.305	24	56	40	72	14½
2.310	24	56	40	72	14
2.315	24	56	40	72	13½
2.320	28	44	32	86	11½
2.325	28	44	32	86	11
2.330	40	100	56	72	41½
2.335	28	64	48	86	17
2.340	24	56	48	72	35
2.345	24	56	40	72	10
2.350	28	64	44	72	28½
2.355	44	86	48	100	16½
2.360	32	64	48	100	10½
2.365	24	56	48	86	8½
2.370	44	56	32	100	19½
2.375	28	64	48	86	13½
2.380	32	100	56	72	17
2.385	32	72	56	86	34½
2.390	28	64	40	72	10½
2.395	40	72	44	100	11½
2.400	56	64	32	100	31
2.405	28	64	48	86	10
2.410	32	100	56	72	14½
2.415	44	86	48	100	10½
2.420	32	100	56	72	13½
2.425	32	100	56	72	13
2.430	32	100	56	72	12½
2.435	32	72	48	86	11
2.440	32	72	48	86	10½
2.445	44	56	32	100	13½
2.450	24	64	48	72	11½
2.455	40	72	48	100	23
2.460	28	64	48	72	32½
2.465	32	64	44	86	15½
2.470	28	40	32	86	18½
2.475	32	64	40	72	27
2.480	44	48	28	100	15
2.485	28	72	56	86	11
2.490	28	72	56	86	10½
2.495	24	44	40	86	10½
2.500	28	64	48	72	31
2.505	24	56	44	72	17
2.510	28	40	44	86	45½
2.515	32	64	44	86	10½
2.520	44	48	28	100	11
2.525	48	56	32	100	23
2.530	24	56	44	72	15
2.535	32	56	40	86	17½
2.540	32	64	48	86	24½
2.545	32	56	44	86	29½
2.550	28	64	44	72	17½
2.555	32	56	40	86	16
2.560	32	64	48	86	23½
2.565	28	40	32	86	10
2.570	44	48	40	100	45½
2.575	24	56	44	72	10½
2.580	40	72	56	86	44½
2.585	32	56	40	86	13½
2.590	32	56	40	86	13
2.595	44	40	32	120	42½
2.600	32	56	40	86	12
2.605	32	56	40	86	11½
2.610	32	56	40	72	20
2.615	44	48	40	100	44½
2.620	28	64	44	72	11½
2.625	44	56	24	64	27
2.630	48	56	32	100	16½
2.635	40	100	56	72	34½
2.640	48	100	56	72	45
2.645	24	40	44	86	30½
2.650	40	56	44	86	30½
2.655	56	64	32	100	18½
2.660	44	48	40	100	43½
2.665	28	64	48	72	24
2.670	28	48	44	72	41½
2.675	48	64	28	56	44½
2.680	28	44	48	86	41
2.685	48	100	56	72	44
2.690	40	64	44	100	12
2.695	40	64	44	100	11½
2.700	28	44	48	86	40½
2.705	56	64	32	100	15
2.710	40	72	56	86	41½
2.715	40	56	44	86	42
2.720	48	64	28	56	43½
2.725	44	48	40	100	42
2.730	48	100	56	72	43
2.735	44	40	32	100	39
2.740	28	44	48	86	39½
2.745	40	72	44	86	15
2.750	28	64	48	72	19½
2.755	44	40	32	100	38½
2.760	28	44	48	86	39
2.765	48	64	28	56	42½
2.770	28	48	44	72	39
2.775	40	72	44	86	12½
2.780	40	72	44	86	12
2.785	24	44	48	72	40
2.790	28	48	44	72	38½
2.795	32	48	40	72	41
2.800	24	56	48	72	11½
2.805	24	56	48	72	11
2.810	44	56	24	64	17½
2.815	28	44	40	86	18
2.820	40	56	44	86	39½
2.825	32	56	44	72	36
2.830	48	64	28	56	41
2.835	28	48	40	72	29
2.840	40	56	44	86	39
2.845	28	44	40	86	16
2.850	28	56	64	86	40
2.855	28	44	48	86	36½
2.860	40	56	44	86	38½
2.865	24	44	48	72	38
2.870	44	48	48	86	38½
2.875	40	64	48	86	34½
2.880	48	100	56	72	39½
2.885	24	44	48	72	37½
2.890	44	48	40	100	38
2.895	32	56	44	72	34
2.900	28	44	40	86	11½
2.905	40	72	48	86	20½
2.910	28	44	40	86	10½
2.915	28	40	44	86	35½
2.920	28	48	44	72	35
2.925	40	64	44	86	33
2.930	32	64	44	72	16½
2.935	48	64	28	56	38½
2.940	40	64	48	86	35½
2.945	40	72	56	86	35½
2.950	40	64	48	100	10½
2.955	48	64	28	56	38
2.960	24	44	48	72	35½
2.965	32	64	44	72	14
2.970	32	64	48	72	27
2.975	40	56	44	86	35½
2.980	48	40	28	100	27½
2.985	52	100	40	100	35½
2.990	28	48	44	72	33
2.995	48	64	28	56	37

Lead	Gear on Worm	1st Intermediate	2nd Intermediate	Gear on Screw	Angle
3.000	40	100	56	64	31
3.005	40	64	48	86	30½
3.010	28	56	64	86	36
3.015	48	64	28	56	36½
3.020	48	100	56	72	36
3.025	40	100	56	72	13½
3.030	40	64	44	72	37½
3.035	24	40	48	86	25
3.040	44	48	40	100	34
3.045	32	64	48	72	24
3.050	40	56	44	100	14
3.055	56	44	28	86	42½
3.060	28	44	48	86	30½
3.065	40	56	44	86	33
3.070	28	40	44	86	31
3.075	44	48	40	100	33
3.080	40	64	48	86	28
3.085	28	56	64	86	34
3.090	48	64	28	56	34½
3.095	48	100	56	72	34
3.100	24	44	48	72	31½
3.105	40	100	56	64	27½
3.110	44	48	40	100	32
3.115	28	48	40	72	16
3.120	44	64	48	100	19
3.125	32	56	44	72	26½
3.130	32	56	48	86	11
3.135	28	44	48	86	28
3.140	32	56	48	86	10
3.145	48	64	28	56	33
3.150	28	44	48	86	27½
3.155	28	64	56	72	22
3.160	44	48	40	100	30½
3.165	24	44	48	72	29½
3.170	28	48	40	72	12
3.175	32	48	40	72	31
3.180	40	56	44	86	29½
3.185	40	100	56	64	24½
3.190	28	56	64	86	31
3.195	44	72	48	86	20½
3.200	48	100	56	72	31
3.205	28	40	44	86	26½
3.210	24	44	48	72	28
3.215	40	64	48	72	39½
3.220	56	44	28	86	39
3.225	24	44	48	72	27½
3.230	48	40	28	100	16
3.235	32	72	64	86	12
3.240	24	44	48	72	27
3.245	28	40	44	86	25
3.250	44	64	48	100	10
3.255	32	48	40	72	28½
3.260	32	56	44	72	21
3.265	48	100	56	72	29
3.270	40	56	44	86	26½
3.275	44	40	32	100	21½
3.280	48	64	28	56	29
3.285	32	48	40	72	27½
3.290	32	44	40	86	13½
3.295	24	44	48	72	25
3.300	32	48	40	72	27
3.305	40	72	56	86	24
3.310	44	48	40	100	25½
3.315	32	48	40	72	20½
3.320	28	40	44	86	22
3.325	40	56	44	86	24½
3.330	28	56	64	86	26½
3.335	28	64	56	72	11½
3.340	40	64	44	72	29
3.345	32	44	48	86	34½
3.350	44	48	40	100	24
3.355	48	100	56	72	26
3.360	40	56	48	100	11½
3.365	28	40	44	86	20
3.370	48	64	28	56	26
3.375	44	48	40	100	23
3.380	32	56	48	72	27½
3.385	48	64	28	56	25½
3.390	48	40	32	100	28
3.395	32	56	44	72	13½
3.400	40	56	44	86	21½
3.405	28	44	48	86	16½
3.410	32	48	40	72	23
3.415	28	40	44	86	17½
3.420	32	40	48	86	40
3.425	28	56	64	86	23
3.430	28	44	48	86	15
3.435	44	48	40	100	20½
3.440	48	100	56	64	35
3.445	28	44	48	86	14
3.450	28	56	64	86	22
3.455	40	56	44	86	19
3.460	40	72	56	86	17
3.465	32	64	56	72	27
3.470	28	48	56	86	24
3.475	40	56	44	86	18
3.480	28	48	44	72	12½
3.485	40	56	44	86	17½
3.490	32	40	44	86	31½
3.495	24	44	48	72	16
3.500	28	48	44	72	11
3.505	28	48	44	72	10½
3.510	40	72	56	86	14
3.515	28	40	44	86	11
3.520	24	44	48	72	14½
3.525	44	48	40	100	16
3.530	40	56	44	86	15
3.535	24	44	48	72	13½
3.540	48	100	56	72	18½
3.545	40	56	44	86	14
3.550	24	44	48	72	12½
3.555	40	56	48	100	19½
3.560	40	56	44	86	13
3.565	40	64	44	72	21
3.570	48	100	56	72	17
3.575	24	44	48	72	10½
3.580	44	48	40	100	12½
3.585	48	40	32	100	21
3.590	40	64	48	72	30½
3.595	56	40	28	100	23½
3.600	44	48	40	100	11
3.605	48	64	28	56	16
3.610	28	56	64	86	14
3.615	32	44	40	72	26½
3.620	48	40	32	100	19½
3.625	44	56	48	100	16
3.630	32	48	40	72	11½
3.635	28	40	48	86	21½
3.640	28	56	64	86	12
3.645	48	100	56	72	12½
3.650	40	72	64	86	28
3.655	32	64	56	72	20
3.660	28	48	56	86	15½
3.665	48	100	56	72	11
3.670	48	100	56	72	10½
3.675	48	64	28	56	11½
3.680	32	56	48	72	15
3.685	28	48	56	86	14
3.690	56	48	24	64	32½
3.695	44	56	48	100	11½
3.700	48	40	32	100	15½
3.705	32	56	48	72	13½
3.710	44	100	56	64	15½
3.715	28	48	56	86	12
3.720	32	56	48	72	15
3.725	56	44	28	86	26
3.730	48	64	32	56	29½
3.735	40	64	44	72	12
3.740	56	44	28	86	25½
3.745	40	64	48	72	26

Lead	Gear on Worm	1st Intermediate	2nd Intermediate	Gear on Screw	Angle	Lead	Gear on Worm	1st Intermediate	2nd Intermediate	Gear on Screw	Angle	Lead	Gear on Worm	1st Intermediate	2nd Intermediate	Gear on Screw	Angle
3.750	32	44	48	86	22½	4.000	28	40	48	72	31	4.250	28	48	56	72	20½
3.755	40	64	44	72	10½	4.005	40	64	48	72	16	4.255	56	40	28	86	21
3.760	44	64	48	86	11½	4.010	56	40	32	100	26½	4.260	44	72	64	86	20½
3.765	32	64	56	72	14½	4.015	40	64	48	72	15½	4.265	56	44	28	64	40
3.770	48	40	32	100	11	4.020	40	72	64	86	13½	4.270	44	64	56	86	17½
3.775	48	100	56	64	26	4.025	40	64	48	72	15	4.275	32	44	56	86	25½
3.780	40	56	48	86	18½	4.030	32	40	48	86	25½	4.280	28	40	48	72	23½
3.785	40	48	44	72	42	4.035	44	64	56	72	41	4.285	40	56	44	72	11
3.790	32	48	44	72	21½	4.040	48	64	32	56	19½	4.290	28	48	56	72	19
3.795	56	40	28	100	14½	4.045	56	48	44	100	38	4.295	56	48	24	64	11
3.800	56	44	28	86	23½	4.050	40	72	64	86	11½	4.300	44	72	64	86	19
3.805	44	72	56	86	17	4.055	40	48	44	86	18	4.305	44	56	48	86	11
3.810	56	40	32	86	43	4.060	40	64	48	72	13	4.310	32	44	56	86	24½
3.815	56	44	28	86	23	4.065	44	64	48	72	27½	4.315	28	48	56	72	18
3.820	56	40	28	100	13	4.070	44	72	64	86	26½	4.320	44	64	48	72	19½
3.825	44	72	56	86	16	4.075	56	44	28	86	10½	4.325	44	72	64	86	18
3.830	40	64	56	72	38	4.080	44	56	48	86	21½	4.330	28	56	64	72	13
3.835	28	40	48	86	11	4.085	56	48	24	64	21	4.335	56	40	28	86	18
3.840	32	48	44	72	19½	4.090	40	64	48	72	11	4.340	72	48	24	64	39½
3.845	28	44	48	72	25	4.095	28	48	56	72	25½	4.345	64	48	24	72	40½
3.850	40	64	48	72	22½	4.100	48	100	56	64	12½	4.350	28	48	56	72	16½
3.855	56	40	28	100	10½	4.105	44	72	64	86	25½	4.355	28	56	64	72	11½
3.860	56	40	28	100	10	4.110	48	64	32	56	16½	4.360	32	44	56	86	23
3.865	56	40	28	86	32	4.115	40	56	44	72	19½	4.365	56	40	32	100	13
3.870	32	40	44	86	19	4.120	48	64	32	56	16	4.370	56	40	28	86	16½
3.875	32	48	44	72	18	4.125	28	44	48	72	13½	4.375	32	44	56	86	22½
3.880	32	44	56	86	35	4.130	48	100	56	64	10½	4.380	48	72	64	86	28
3.885	44	72	56	86	12½	4.135	32	56	64	86	13½	4.385	40	48	64	86	45
3.890	40	64	48	72	21	4.140	28	40	48	72	27½	4.390	56	40	32	100	11½
3.895	40	48	44	86	24	4.145	28	48	56	72	24	4.395	44	64	56	86	11
3.900	56	44	28	72	38	4.150	48	64	32	56	14½	4.400	40	56	48	72	22½
3.905	28	44	48	72	23	4.155	44	72	64	86	24	4.405	44	64	48	72	16
3.910	56	48	32	64	40	4.160	56	40	32	86	37	4.410	56	44	24	64	22½
3.915	48	64	32	56	24	4.165	44	64	56	86	21½	4.415	40	56	48	72	22
3.920	32	44	40	72	14	4.170	44	64	48	72	24½	4.420	48	72	64	86	42
3.925	40	56	48	86	10	4.175	56	44	24	86	29	4.425	64	40	32	86	42
3.930	56	44	28	86	18½	4.180	56	40	28	86	23½	4.430	28	48	56	72	12½
3.935	32	48	44	72	15	4.185	40	56	44	72	16½	4.435	48	64	56	72	40½
3.940	40	64	48	72	19	4.190	64	48	32	72	45	4.440	44	72	64	86	12½
3.945	48	64	32	56	23	4.195	28	40	48	72	26	4.445	56	48	44	100	30
3.950	48	72	56	86	24½	4.200	48	64	32	56	11½	4.450	32	44	56	86	20
3.955	32	44	48	86	13	4.205	48	44	40	100	15½	4.455	86	56	24	72	29½
3.960	28	44	48	72	21	4.210	56	40	32	100	20	4.460	40	56	48	72	20½
3.965	56	48	24	64	25	4.215	48	44	40	100	15	4.465	44	64	48	72	13
3.970	32	44	48	86	12	4.220	32	44	56	86	27	4.470	44	48	56	86	41½
3.975	32	56	64	72	38½	4.225	48	44	40	100	14½	4.475	28	40	48	72	16½
3.980	32	40	44	86	13½	4.230	28	40	48	72	25	4.480	40	44	28	86	28
3.985	40	64	48	72	17	4.235	40	56	44	72	14	4.485	56	44	28	72	25
3.990	44	56	48	86	24½	4.240	32	44	48	72	29	4.490	32	48	56	72	30
3.995	40	64	48	72	16½	4.245	56	48	24	64	14	4.495	32	44	48	72	22

Lead	Gear on Worm	1st Intermediate	2nd Intermediate	Gear on Screw	Angle	Lead	Gear on Worm	1st Intermediate	2nd Intermediate	Gear on Screw	Angle	Lead	Gear on Worm	1st Intermediate	2nd Intermediate	Gear on Screw	Angle
4.500	56	44	32	64	45	4.750	32	44	48	72	11½	5.000	48	64	56	72	31
4.505	56	44	28	64	36	4.755	64	40	32	86	37	5.005	56	44	28	64	26
4.510	44	64	56	72	32½	4.760	44	56	64	86	35½	5.010	56	48	28	64	11
4.515	48	64	44	56	40	4.765	64	48	24	56	33½	5.015	40	48	44	72	10
4.520	86	56	24	72	28	4.770	86	56	24	72	37	5.020	40	44	56	86	32
4.525	40	48	56	86	33½	4.775	86	56	24	64	34	5.025	64	48	32	72	32
4.530	56	72	64	86	38½	4.780	40	64	56	72	10½	5.030	56	48	44	100	11½
4.535	40	44	56	86	40	4.785	44	56	48	72	24	5.035	44	56	48	72	16
4.540	64	48	32	72	40	4.790	44	56	64	86	35	5.040	32	44	56	72	27
4.545	72	56	24	64	19½	4.795	86	56	24	72	20½	5.045	64	48	24	56	28
4.550	48	72	64	86	23½	4.800	64	44	32	86	27½	5.050	48	64	40	56	19½
4.555	56	44	28	72	23	4.805	44	48	86	86	38½	5.055	56	48	44	100	10
4.560	48	64	56	86	21	4.810	48	64	56	86	10	5.060	86	64	28	72	14½
4.565	28	40	48	72	12	4.815	32	40	44	72	10	5.065	86	48	24	72	32
4.570	32	44	48	72	19½	4.820	40	44	56	86	35½	5.070	40	56	64	86	17½
4.575	32	44	56	86	15	4.825	64	48	32	72	35½	5.075	40	44	56	86	31
4.580	48	64	44	56	39	4.830	86	56	24	64	33	5.080	64	48	32	72	31
4.585	32	44	56	86	14½	4.835	48	64	40	56	25½	5.085	86	56	24	64	28
4.590	48	64	56	86	20	4.840	56	48	28	64	18½	5.090	32	48	56	72	11
4.595	32	44	56	86	14	4.845	32	56	64	72	17½	5.095	56	40	32	86	12
4.600	40	56	48	72	15	4.850	56	44	28	72	11½	5.100	32	40	48	72	17
4.605	32	44	86	86	13½	4.855	86	56	24	72	18½	5.105	40	44	64	86	41
4.610	40	56	48	72	14½	4.860	44	48	56	86	35½	5.110	56	72	64	86	28
4.615	32	44	56	86	13	4.865	40	44	48	86	16½	5.115	40	48	56	86	19½
4.620	40	56	48	72	14	4.870	48	72	64	86	11	5.120	44	40	48	86	33½
4.625	44	56	48	72	28	4.875	40	56	64	86	23½	5.125	56	44	28	64	23
4.630	86	56	24	64	36½	4.880	86	44	24	72	41½	5.130	64	40	32	86	30½
4.635	40	44	48	86	24	4.885	48	64	44	56	34	5.135	40	56	64	86	15
4.640	40	56	48	72	13	4.890	44	48	56	86	35	5.140	40	44	56	86	32
4.645	48	64	56	86	18	4.895	32	56	64	72	15½	5.145	40	48	56	86	18½
4.650	32	40	44	72	18	4.900	72	44	24	86	37	5.150	48	64	56	72	28
4.655	56	44	32	64	43	4.905	64	44	32	86	25	5.155	86	40	24	72	44
4.660	64	40	32	86	38½	4.910	86	56	24	64	31½	5.160	40	48	56	86	18
4.665	40	44	56	86	38	4.915	72	48	28	64	41½	5.165	44	64	56	72	15
4.670	64	48	32	72	38	4.920	48	64	56	72	32½	5.170	72	44	24	56	42½
4.675	48	64	44	56	37½	4.925	56	40	32	86	19	5.175	32	40	48	72	14
4.680	64	48	24	56	35	4.930	56	48	28	64	15	5.180	56	72	64	86	26½
4.685	56	44	24	64	11	4.935	56	72	64	86	31½	5.185	56	40	48	100	39½
4.690	32	44	56	72	34	4.940	32	56	64	72	13½	5.190	40	56	64	86	29½
4.695	40	64	56	72	15	4.945	86	56	24	72	15	5.195	44	48	56	86	29½
4.700	44	56	64	86	36½	4.950	32	56	64	72	13	5.200	64	48	24	56	24½
4.705	48	72	64	86	18½	4.955	56	40	28	64	36	5.205	64	32	28	72	48
4.710	32	56	64	72	22	4.960	32	56	64	72	12½	5.210	44	56	64	86	27
4.715	56	48	28	64	22½	4.965	64	40	32	86	33½	5.215	72	48	24	64	24
4.720	56	48	28	72	17½	4.970	64	48	32	72	33	5.220	48	64	56	72	26½
4.725	56	48	44	100	23	4.975	44	64	56	72	21½	5.225	48	56	64	86	35
4.730	44	56	64	86	36	4.980	86	48	24	72	33½	5.230	44	64	56	72	12
4.735	44	48	56	86	37½	4.985	44	56	64	86	31½	5.235	40	56	64	86	10
4.740	72	56	24	64	10½	4.990	72	48	24	64	27½	5.240	86	56	24	64	24½
4.745	56	44	28	72	16½	4.995	32	44	56	72	28	5.245	32	44	56	72	22

Lead	Gear on Worm	1st Intermediate	2nd Intermediate	Gear on Screw	Angle	Lead	Gear on Worm	1st Intermediate	2nd Intermediate	Gear on Screw	Angle	Lead	Gear on Worm	1st Intermediate	2nd Intermediate	Gear on Screw	Angle
5.250	56	40	28	64	31	5.500	64	32	28	72	45	5.750	64	48	32	72	14
5.255	44	56	64	86	26	5.505	56	72	64	86	18	5.755	86	48	24	72	15½
5.260	64	48	24	56	23	5.510	72	56	32	64	31	5.760	86	64	40	72	39½
5.265	48	64	56	72	25½	5.515	44	48	56	86	22½	5.765	44	48	56	86	15
5.270	44	48	56	86	28	5.520	64	40	32	86	22	5.770	64	44	28	56	37½
5.275	40	44	56	86	27	5.525	86	44	24	72	32	5.775	48	64	44	56	11½
5.280	64	48	32	72	27	5.530	72	48	32	64	42½	5.780	40	44	56	86	12½
5.285	64	40	32	72	42	5.535	56	72	64	86	17	5.785	64	48	32	72	12½
5.290	56	44	48	100	30	5.540	64	40	32	86	21½	5.790	64	40	32	86	13½
5.295	44	48	56	86	27½	5.545	40	44	56	86	20½	5.795	86	48	24	72	14
5.300	40	44	48	72	29	5.550	56	72	64	86	16½	5.800	64	44	24	56	21½
5.305	64	40	32	86	27	5.555	48	64	44	56	19½	5.805	44	48	56	72	35½
5.310	56	44	28	64	17½	5.560	48	44	56	86	38½	5.810	86	48	28	72	33½
5.315	56	40	28	72	12½	5.565	64	40	32	72	38½	5.815	86	44	24	64	37½
5.320	44	56	64	86	24½	5.570	86	40	24	72	39	5.820	64	44	24	56	21
5.325	56	40	28	72	12	5.575	86	48	24	72	21	5.825	64	40	32	72	35
5.330	64	44	32	86	10	5.580	40	44	56	86	19½	5.830	86	48	24	72	12½
5.335	64	48	24	56	21	5.585	86	44	24	72	31	5.835	64	40	32	86	11½
5.340	86	56	24	64	22	5.590	40	48	64	72	41	5.840	44	48	56	72	35
5.345	86	48	24	72	26½	5.595	56	40	28	64	24	5.845	64	40	32	86	11
5.350	72	48	24	64	18	5.600	86	56	24	64	13½	5.850	86	56	32	72	31
5.355	40	56	64	72	32½	5.605	48	64	44	56	18	5.855	48	44	56	86	34½
5.360	64	44	32	72	34	5.610	40	44	56	72	37½	5.860	64	40	32	72	34½
5.365	44	48	56	86	26	5.615	86	44	24	64	40	5.865	64	40	28	72	10½
5.370	64	48	24	56	20	5.620	64	48	32	72	18½	5.870	72	48	32	64	38½
5.375	86	44	28	72	24	5.625	86	56	32	72	34½	5.875	56	40	44	100	17½
5.380	32	44	56	72	18	5.630	86	48	24	72	19½	5.880	86	56	32	72	30½
5.385	56	72	64	86	21½	5.635	48	44	64	56	17	5.885	72	44	28	56	44
5.390	86	48	24	72	25½	5.640	56	72	64	86	13	5.890	44	56	64	72	12½
5.395	32	44	56	72	17½	5.645	44	40	56	86	38	5.895	44	40	48	72	36½
5.400	56	32	28	72	37½	5.650	48	44	56	72	16½	5.900	56	64	40	48	36
5.405	64	44	28	56	42	5.655	64	44	32	72	29	5.905	40	44	48	72	13
5.410	44	48	56	86	25	5.660	48	64	56	72	14	5.910	72	48	32	64	38
5.415	86	64	40	72	43½	5.665	48	64	44	56	16	5.915	40	48	64	72	37
5.420	72	48	24	64	15½	5.670	56	40	44	100	23	5.920	40	48	56	72	24
5.425	48	64	44	56	23	5.675	56	32	28	72	33½	5.925	86	64	32	56	39½
5.430	86	64	32	56	45	5.680	86	44	28	72	18	5.930	86	44	24	64	36
5.435	64	48	32	72	23½	5.685	44	56	64	86	13½	5.935	72	44	28	64	34
5.440	44	56	64	86	21½	5.690	48	44	64	86	45½	5.940	86	56	32	72	29½
5.445	48	64	44	56	22½	5.695	48	64	44	56	12½	5.945	44	40	48	86	14½
5.450	64	48	24	56	17½	5.700	56	72	64	86	10	5.950	72	48	32	64	37½
5.455	64	48	32	72	23	5.705	40	44	56	86	15½	5.955	44	56	64	72	11½
5.460	64	40	32	86	23½	5.710	64	48	32	72	15½	5.960	40	44	48	72	10½
5.465	44	56	64	72	38½	5.715	40	48	64	72	39½	5.965	40	48	56	72	23
5.470	72	48	24	64	13½	5.720	40	44	56	72	36	5.970	44	40	48	72	35½
5.475	64	48	32	72	22½	5.725	86	44	24	72	28½	5.975	56	44	48	100	12
5.480	48	56	64	72	44	5.730	48	64	44	56	13½	5.980	44	48	56	72	33
5.485	72	48	32	64	43	5.735	48	64	56	72	10½	5.985	40	48	64	72	19½
5.490	86	44	24	64	41½	5.740	44	56	64	86	11	5.990	72	48	32	64	37
5.495	44	48	56	86	23	5.745	72	48	32	64	40	5.995	44	48	64	86	28½

PLAIN AND DIFFERENTIAL INDEXING ON BROWN & SHARPE MILLING MACHINES

THE general arrangement of the universal dividing head is illustrated in Figs. 1, 2, and 3. As indicated by the diagrammatic sketch Fig. 2, the worm wheel A is secured to the main spindle of the spiral head and rotated by means of the worm shaft and single-threaded worm B. The index plate (having rows of equally spaced holes) remains stationary during the dividing operation, and is fitted with adjustable sector arms which obviate the necessity of counting the number of holes through which the index crank requires to be moved each time a division is made on the surface of the work. · The stan-

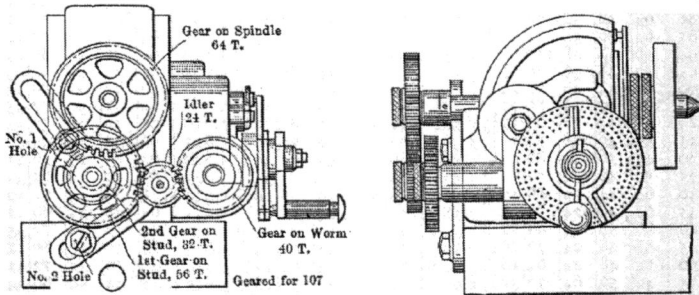

FIG. 1. — Brown & Sharpe Dividing Head Arranged for
Differential Indexing

dard ratio between the worm B and the worm wheel A is 1:40; and · to find the movement of the index crank for any required division, the following formula is employed: The movement of the index crank $= \dfrac{40}{N}$ where N is the number of equal divisions required.

Example: Let it be required to divide the circumference of a piece of work into 48 equal parts.

The movement of the index crank for each division $= \dfrac{40}{48} = \dfrac{5}{6}$ *revolutions.*

An index plate having a row of 18 holes would be chosen, and the sector arms set to limit the movement of the index crank to 15 spaces for $\dfrac{5}{6} = \dfrac{15}{18}$.

GENERAL PRINCIPLE OF DIFFERENTIAL INDEXING

The number of equal divisions which may be obtained by simple indexing (with the index plates usually provided by milling-machine makers) is strictly limited, and does not meet all the requirements called for in practice.

Differential indexing provides the most convenient way of overcoming this difficulty, this method being simpler than compound indexing. In the differential system the dividing operation is performed as in simple indexing, the only difference being that the index plate instead of remaining stationary during the process of indexing, is made to move relatively to the index crank, being connected to the main spindle of the spiral head by a set of change gears, which may be arranged to give either a *positive* or *negative* movement to the

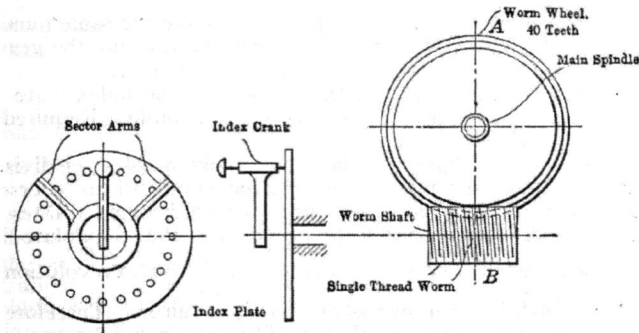

Fig. 2

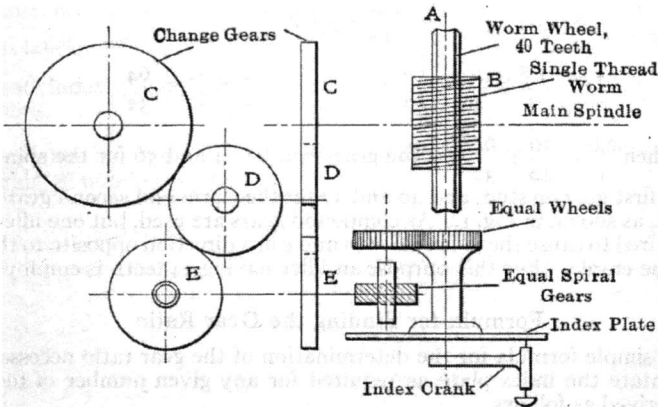

Fig. 3

index plate; whichever is found necessary to determine the *actual* motion which must be given to the index crank in order to satisfy the formula given above for simple indexing: *Actual movement of the index crank* $= \dfrac{40}{N}$.

The two views in Fig. 1 and the diagram, Fig. 3, will serve to give an idea of the arrangement of the gearing, which is adopted in differential indexing.

For any movement of the index crank the motion is transmitted to the index plate (which is free to rotate on the worm shaft) as follows: The index crank drives through the worm shaft and worm B to the worm wheel A, which in turn transmits the motion through the change gears, spiral gears and equal gears, the last of which is connected directly to the index plate. The last pair of gears being equal and driven through equal spiral gears, whatever number of revolutions are given to the gear E, the index plate will make the same number. It is therefore convenient to consider the revolutions of the gear E, as the revolutions of the index plate in all calculations.

To illustrate the influence of the gearing on the index plate and indexing operation, consider the following example: Required to index for 107 divisions:

If we use the plate having 20 holes and move 8 holes per division, as in simple indexing for 100 divisions, 100 moves will of course be required to rotate the worm 40 turns, which in turn rotates the spindle once. If now we make 107 moves with the index plate fixed as in simple indexing, we will obtain $107 \times \dfrac{8}{20} = 42.8$ revolutions of the worm, which is 2.8 in excess of what is required. Therefore the index plate must be geared so that it will move back 2.8 turns while the spindle is revolving once; that is, the ratio of the gearing must be 2.8 to 1.

$$\frac{2.8}{1} = \frac{2.8}{2} \times \frac{2}{1}$$

$$\frac{2.8}{2} \times \frac{20}{20} = \frac{56}{40} \qquad\qquad \frac{2}{1} \times \frac{32}{32} = \frac{64}{32}$$

Then $\dfrac{2.8}{1} = \dfrac{56}{40} \times \dfrac{64}{32}$ and the gears will be 64 and 56 for the spindle and first gear on stud, and 40 and 32 for the worm and second gear on stud, as shown in Fig. 1. As compound gears are used, but one idler is required to cause the index plate to move in a direction opposite to that of the crank. For this purpose an idler having 24 teeth is employed.

Formula for Finding the Gear Ratio

A simple formula for the determination of the gear ratio necessary to rotate the index plate as required for any given number of teeth is derived as follows:

Let N equal the number of divisions required to be indexed.

Let n equal some number either greater or smaller than N, which can be obtained directly by simple indexing.

Let $\dfrac{40}{n}$ equal the index setting; that is the setting of the sector arms for each movement of the index crank;

Then $n - N \times \dfrac{40}{n}$ equals the gear ratio.

If the number chosen for n is greater than the number of divisions required (N) the index plate must be geared to have a positive motion, that is to rotate in the same direction as the index crank. If the number n is less than N the index plate is geared to have a negative motion, that is, to rotate in opposite direction to the crank.

Application of the Formula

Suppose we wish to obtain 63 divisions: choose any number for n which may be obtained by simple indexing, say 60, then

$$(n - N) = (60 - 63) = -3$$

This number (-3) when multiplied by the value of the index setting will give the gear ratio. The index setting equals $\frac{40}{n}$, equals $\frac{40}{60}$, then

$$(n - N)\frac{40}{n} = -3 \times \frac{40}{60} = -\frac{60}{30} \text{ or } \frac{2}{1} \text{ as the gear ratio.}$$

We can therefore use gears of 48 and 24 teeth, the 48 gear being the driver and the 24 gear the follower; that is, the 48 gear being on the spindle and the 24 gear on the worm. As n is smaller than N the idlers are arranged to give a negative movement to the index plate.

The index setting is found above as $\frac{40}{n}$ which equals $\frac{40}{60}$ or $\frac{2}{3}$. We can thus use the 39 hole circle in the index plate and set the sector for 26 holes, this giving the setting as $\frac{26}{39}$ or $\frac{2}{3}$; that is, we set the sector and index pin exactly the same as for simple indexing of 60 divisions.

The tables on the following pages give the dividing head gears for indexing all numbers up to 730.

Number of Divisions	Index Circle	No. of Turns of Index	Gear on Worm	No. 1 Hole		Gear on Spindle	Idlers	
				First Gear on Stud	Second Gear on Stud		No. 1 Hole	No. 2 Hole
2	Any	20						
3	39	$13\frac{13}{39}$						
4	Any	10						
5	Any	8						
6	39	$6\frac{26}{39}$						
7	49	$5\frac{35}{49}$						
8	Any	5						
9	27	$4\frac{12}{27}$						
10	Any	4						
11	33	$3\frac{21}{33}$						
12	39	$3\frac{13}{39}$						
13	39	$3\frac{3}{39}$						
14	49	$2\frac{42}{49}$						
15	39	$2\frac{26}{39}$						
16	20	$2\frac{10}{20}$						
17	17	$2\frac{6}{17}$						
18	27	$2\frac{6}{27}$						
19	19	$2\frac{2}{19}$						
20	Any	2						
21	21	$1\frac{19}{21}$						
22	33	$1\frac{23}{33}$						
23	23	$1\frac{17}{23}$						
24	39	$1\frac{26}{39}$						
25	20	$1\frac{12}{20}$						
26	39	$1\frac{21}{39}$						
27	27	$1\frac{13}{27}$						
28	49	$1\frac{21}{49}$						
29	29	$1\frac{19}{29}$						
30	39	$1\frac{13}{39}$						
31	31	$1\frac{9}{31}$						
32	20	$1\frac{5}{20}$						
33	33	$1\frac{7}{33}$						
34	17	$1\frac{3}{17}$						
35	49	$1\frac{7}{49}$						
36	27	$1\frac{3}{27}$						
37	37	$1\frac{3}{37}$						
38	19	$1\frac{1}{19}$						
39	39	$1\frac{1}{39}$						
40	Any	1						
41	41	$\frac{40}{41}$						
42	21	$\frac{20}{21}$						

Number of Divisions	Index Circle	No. of Turns of Index	Gear on Worm	No. 1 Hole		Gear on Spindle	Idlers	
				First Gear on Stud	Second Gear on Stud		No. 1 Hole	No. 2 Hole
43	43							
44	33							
45	27							
46	23							
47	47							
48	18							
49	49							
50	20							
51	17		24			48	24	44
52	39							
53	49		56	40	24	72		
54	27							
55	33							
56	49							
57	21		56			40	24	44
58	29							
59	39		48			32	44	
60	39							
61	39		48			32	24	44
62	31							
63	39		24			48	24	44
64	16							
65	39							
66	33							
67	21		28			48	44	
68	17							
69	20		40			56	24	44
70	49							
71	18		72			40	24	
72	27							
73	21		28			48	24	44
74	37							
75	15							
76	19							
77	20		32			48	44	
78	39							
79	20		48			24	44	
80	20							
81	20		48			24	24	44
82	41							
83	20		32			48	24	44

Number of Divisions	Index Circle	No. of Turns of Index	Gear on Worm	No. 1 Hole First Gear on Stud	No. 1 Hole Second Gear on Stud	Gear on Spindle	Idlers No. 1 Hole	Idlers No. 2 Hole
84	21							
85	17							
86	43							
87	15		40			24	24	44
88	33							
89	18		72			32	44	
90	27							
91	39		24			48	24	44
92	23							
93	18		24			32	24	44
94	47							
95	19							
96	21		28			32	24	44
97	20		40			48	44	
98	49							
99	20		56	28	40	32		
100	20							
101	20		72	24	40	•48		24
102	20		40			32	24	44
103	20		40			48	24	44
104	39							
105	21							
106	43		86	24	24	48		
107	20		40	56	32	64		24
108	27							
109	16		32			28	24	44
110	33							
111	39		24			72	32	
112	39		24			64	44	
113	39		24			56	44	
114	39		24			48	44	
115	23							
116	29							
117	39		24			24	56	
118	39		48			32	44	
119	39		72			24	44	
120	39							
121	39		72			24	24	44
122	39		48			32	24	44
123	39		24			24	24	44
124	31							

Number of Divisions	Index Circle	No. of Turns of Index	Gear on Worm	No. 1 Hole		Gear on Spindle	Idlers	
				First Gear on Stud	Second Gear on Stud		No. 1 Hole	No. 2 Hole
125	39	$\frac{13}{39}$	24			40	24	44
126	39	$\frac{13}{39}$	24			48	24	44
127	39	$\frac{13}{39}$	24			56	24	44
128	16	$\frac{5}{16}$						
129	39	$\frac{13}{39}$	24			72	24	44
130	39	$\frac{12}{39}$						
131	20	$\frac{10}{20}$	40			28	44	
132	33	$\frac{6}{33}$						
133	21	$\frac{6}{21}$	24			48	44	
134	21	$\frac{6}{21}$	28			48	44	
135	27	$\frac{2}{27}$						
136	17	$\frac{5}{17}$						
137	21	$\frac{6}{21}$	28			24	56	
138	21	$\frac{6}{21}$	56			32	44	
139	21	$\frac{6}{21}$	56	32	48	24		
140	49	$\frac{14}{49}$						
141	18	$\frac{1}{18}$	48			40	44	
142	21	$\frac{6}{21}$	56			32	24	44
143	21	$\frac{6}{21}$	28			24	24	44
144	18	$\frac{1}{18}$						
145	29	$\frac{2}{29}$						
146	21	$\frac{6}{21}$	28			48	24	44
147	21	$\frac{6}{21}$	24			48	24	44
148	37	$\frac{6}{37}$						
149	21	$\frac{6}{21}$	28			72	24	44
150	15	$\frac{4}{15}$						
151	20	$\frac{5}{20}$	32			72	44	
152	19	$\frac{5}{19}$						
153	20	$\frac{5}{20}$	32			56	44	
154	20	$\frac{5}{20}$	32			48	44	
155	31	$\frac{8}{31}$						
156	39	$\frac{10}{39}$						
157	20	$\frac{5}{20}$	32			24	56	
158	20	$\frac{5}{20}$	48			24	44	
159	20	$\frac{5}{20}$	64	32	56	28		
160	20	$\frac{5}{20}$						
161	20	$\frac{5}{20}$	64	32	56	28		24
162	20	$\frac{5}{20}$	48			24	24	44
163	20	$\frac{5}{20}$	32			24	24	44
164	41	$\frac{4}{41}$						
165	33	$\frac{8}{33}$						

Number of Divisions	Index Circle	No. of Turns of Index	Gear on Worm	No. 1 Hole First Gear on Stud	No. 1 Hole Second Gear on Stud	Gear on Spindle	Idlers No. 1 Hole	Idlers No. 2 Hole
166	20	$\frac{5}{20}$	32			48	24	44
167	20	$\frac{5}{20}$	32			56	24	44
168	21	$\frac{5}{21}$						
169	20	$\frac{5}{20}$	32			72	24	44
170	17	$\frac{4}{17}$						
171	21	$\frac{5}{21}$	56			40	24	44
172	43	$\frac{10}{43}$						
173	18	$\frac{4}{18}$	72	56	32	64		
174	18	$\frac{4}{18}$	24			32	56	
175	18	$\frac{4}{18}$	72	40	32	64		
176	18	$\frac{4}{18}$	72	24	24	64		
177	18	$\frac{4}{18}$	72			48	24	
178	18	$\frac{4}{18}$	72			32	44	
179	18	$\frac{4}{18}$	72	24	48	32		
180	18	$\frac{4}{18}$						
181	18	$\frac{4}{18}$	72	24	48	32		24
182	18	$\frac{4}{18}$	72			32	24	44
183	18	$\frac{4}{18}$	48			32	24	44
184	23	$\frac{2}{23}$						
185	37	$\frac{8}{37}$						
186	18	$\frac{4}{18}$	48			64	24	44
187	18	$\frac{4}{18}$	72	48	24	56		24
188	47	$\frac{10}{47}$						
189	18	$\frac{4}{18}$	32			64	24	44
190	19	$\frac{4}{19}$						
191	20	$\frac{4}{20}$	40			72	24	
192	20	$\frac{4}{20}$	40			64	44	
193	20	$\frac{4}{20}$	40			56	44	
194	20	$\frac{4}{20}$	40			48	44	
195	39	$\frac{8}{39}$						
196	49	$\frac{10}{49}$						
197	20	$\frac{4}{20}$	40			24	56	
198	20	$\frac{4}{20}$	56	28	40	32		
199	20	$\frac{4}{20}$	100	40	64	32		
200	20	$\frac{4}{20}$						
201	20	$\frac{4}{20}$	72	24	40	24		24
202	20	$\frac{4}{20}$	72	24	40	48		24
203	20	$\frac{4}{20}$	40			24	24	44
204	20	$\frac{4}{20}$	40			32	24	44
205	41	$\frac{8}{41}$						
206	20	$\frac{4}{20}$	40			48	24	44

Number of Divisions	Index Circle	No. of Turns of Index	Gear on Worm	No. 1 Hole		Gear on Spindle	Idlers	
				First Gear on Stud	Second Gear on Stud		No. 1 Hole	No. 2 Hole
207	20	$\frac{4}{20}$	40			56	24	44
208	20	$\frac{4}{20}$	40			64	24	44
209	20	$\frac{4}{20}$	40			72	24	44
210	21	$\frac{4}{21}$						
211	16	$1\frac{3}{16}$	64			28	44	
212	43	$1\frac{8}{43}$	86	24	24	48		
213	27	$2\frac{5}{27}$	72			40	44	
214	20	$\frac{4}{20}$	40	56	32	64		24
215	43	$\frac{8}{43}$						
216	27	$\frac{5}{27}$						
217	21	$\frac{4}{21}$	48			64	24	44
218	16	$\frac{3}{16}$	64			56	24	44
219	21	$\frac{4}{21}$	28			48	24	44
220	33	$\frac{6}{33}$						
221	17	$1\frac{7}{17}$	24			24	56	
222	18	$\frac{8}{18}$	24			72	44	
223	43	$\frac{8}{43}$	86	48	24	64		24
224	18	$1\frac{8}{18}$	24			64	44	
225	27	$2\frac{8}{27}$	24			40	24	44
226	18	$1\frac{8}{18}$	24			56	44	
227	49	$\frac{8}{49}$	56	64	28	72		
228	18	$1\frac{8}{18}$	24			48	44	
229	18	$\frac{8}{18}$	24			44	48	
230	23	$\frac{4}{23}$						
231	18	$1\frac{8}{18}$	32			48	44	
232	29	$\frac{5}{29}$						
233	18	$\frac{8}{18}$	48			56	44	
234	18	$\frac{8}{18}$	24			24	56	
235	47	$\frac{8}{47}$						
236	18	$\frac{3}{18}$	48			32	44	
237	18	$1\frac{8}{18}$	48			24	44	
238	18	$1\frac{8}{18}$	72			24	44	
239	18	$1\frac{3}{18}$	72	24	64	32		
240	18	$1\frac{3}{18}$						
241	18	$1\frac{3}{18}$	72	24	64	32		24
242	18	$1\frac{3}{18}$	72			24	24	44
243	18	$1\frac{3}{18}$	64			32	24	44
244	18	$1\frac{3}{18}$	48			32	24	44
245	49	$\frac{8}{49}$						
246	18	$1\frac{3}{18}$	24			24	24	44
247	18	$1\frac{3}{18}$	48			56	24	44

Number of Divisions	Index Circle	No. of Turns of Index	Gear on Worm	No. 1 Hole		Gear on Spindle	Idlers	
				First Gear on Stud	Second Gear on Stud		No. 1 Hole	No. 2 Hole
248	31	3 5/31						
249	18	1 3/18	32			48	24	44
250	18	1 3/18	24			40	24	44
251	18	1 3/18	48	44	32	64		24
252	18	1 3/18	24			48	24	44
253	33	3 5/33	24			40	56	
254	18	1 3/18	24			56	24	44
255	18	1 3/18	48	40	24	72		24
256	18	1 3/18	24			64	24	44
257	49	4 3/49	56	48	28	64		24
258	43	7 3/43	32			64	24	44
259	21	2 1/21	24			72	44	
260	39	3 6/39						
261	29	2 4/29	48	64	24	72		
262	20	2 0/20	40			28	44	
263	49	4 6/49	56	64	28	72		24
264	33	3 5/33						
265	21	2 8/21	56	40	24	72		
266	21	2 1/21	32			64	44	
267	27	2 4/27	72			32	44	
268	21	2 1/21	28			48	44	
269	20	3 0/20	64	32	40	28		24
270	27	2 4/27						
271	21	2 8/21	56			72	24	
272	21	2 4/21	56			64	24	
273	21	2 2/21	24			24	56	
274	21	3 3/21	56			48	44	
275	21	2 2/21	56			40	44	
276	21	1 8/21	56			32	44	
277	21	2 2/21	56			24	44	
278	21	2 2/21	56	32	48	24		
279	27	2 7/27	24			32	24	44
280	49	4 0/49						
281	21	2 2/21	72	24	56	24		24
282	43	6 6/43	86	24	24	56		
283	21	2 2/21	56			24	24	44
284	21	2 8/21	56			32	24	44
285	21	2 2/21	56			40	24	44
286	21	2 2/21	56			48	24	44
287	21	2 2/21	24			24	24	44
288	21	2 2/21	28			32	24	44

Number of Divisions	Index Circle	No. of Turns of Index	Gear on Worm	No. 1 Hole		Gear on Spindle	Idlers	
				First Gear on Stud	Second Gear on Stud		No. 1 Hole	No. 2 Hole
289	21	$2\frac{3}{21}$	56			72	24	44
290	29	$2\frac{4}{29}$						
291	15	$1\frac{3}{15}$	40			48	44	
292	21	$2\frac{3}{21}$	28			48	24	44
293	15	$2\frac{2}{15}$	48	32	40	56		
294	21	$2\frac{3}{21}$	24			48	24	44
295	15	$1\frac{3}{15}$	48			32	44	
296	37	$3\frac{3}{37}$						
297	33	$4\frac{4}{33}$	28	48	24	56		
298	21	$2\frac{3}{21}$	28			72	24	44
299	23	$2\frac{3}{23}$	24			24	56	
300	15	$1\frac{3}{15}$						
301	43	$6\frac{3}{43}$	24			48	24	44
302	16	$1\frac{2}{16}$	32			72	24	
303	15	$1\frac{2}{15}$	72	24	40	48		24
304	16	$1\frac{2}{16}$	24			48	44	
305	15	$1\frac{2}{15}$	48			32	24	44
306	15	$1\frac{2}{15}$	40			32	24	44
307	15	$1\frac{2}{15}$	72	48	40	56		24
308	16	$1\frac{2}{16}$	32			48	44	
309	15	$1\frac{2}{15}$	40			48	24	44
310	31	$3\frac{1}{31}$						
311	16	$1\frac{2}{16}$	64	24	24	72		
312	39	$3\frac{3}{39}$						
313	16	$1\frac{2}{16}$	32			28	56	
314	16	$1\frac{2}{16}$	32			24	56	
315	16	$1\frac{2}{16}$	64			40	24	
316	16	$1\frac{2}{16}$	64			32	44	
317	16	$1\frac{2}{16}$	64			24	44	
318	16	$1\frac{2}{16}$	56	28	48	24		
319	29	$2\frac{4}{29}$	48	64	24	72		24
320	16	$1\frac{2}{16}$						
321	16	$1\frac{2}{16}$	72	24	64	24		24
322	23	$2\frac{3}{23}$	32			64	24	44
323	16	$1\frac{2}{16}$	64			24	24	44
324	16	$1\frac{2}{16}$	64			32	24	44
325	16	$1\frac{2}{16}$	64			40	24	44
326	16	$1\frac{2}{16}$	32			24	24	44
327	16	$1\frac{2}{16}$	32			28	24	44
328	41	$\frac{2}{41}$						
329	16	$1\frac{2}{16}$	64	24	24	72		24

Number of Divisions	Index Circle	No. of Turns of Index	Gear on Worm	No. 1 Hole		Gear on Spindle	Idlers	
				First Gear on Stud	Second Gear on Stud		No. 1 Hole	No. 2 Hole
330	33	4/33						
331	15	1 2/15	64	44	24	48		24
332	16	1 2/16	32		*	48	24	44
333	18	1 2/18	24			72	44	
334	16	1 2/16	32			56	24	44
335	33	4/33	72	48	44	40		24
336	16	1 2/16	32			64	24	44
337	43	4 5/43	86	40	32	56		
338	16	1 2/16	32			72	24	44
339	18	1 2/18	24			56	44	
340	17	1 7/17						
341	43	4 5/43	86	24	32	40		
342	18	1 2/18	32			64	44	
343	15	1 5/15	40	64	24	86		24
344	43	4 5/43						
345	18	1 2/18	24			40	56	
346	18	1 2/18	72	56	32	64		
347	43	4 5/43	86	24	32	40		24
348	18	1 2/18	24			32	56	
349	18	1 2/18	72	44	24	48		
350	18	1 2/18	72	40	32	64		
351	18	1 2/18	24			24	56	
352	18	1 2/18	72	24	24	64		
353	18	1 2/18	72			56	24	
354	18	1 2/18	72			48	24	
355	18	1 4/18	72			40	24	
356	18	1 2/18	72			32	24	
357	18	1 2/18	72			24	44	
358	18	1 2/18	72	32	48	24		
359	43	4 5/43	86	48	32	100		24
360	18	1 2/18						
361	19	1 2/19	32			64	44	
362	18	1 2/18	72	28	56	32		24
363	18	1 2/18	72			24	24	44
364	18	1 2/18	72			32	24	44
365	20	2 6/20	32	48	24	56		
366	18	1 2/18	48			32	24	44
367	18	1 2/18	72			56	24	24
368	18	1 2/18	72	24	24	64		24
369	41	4/41	32	56	28	64		
370	37	4/37						

Number of Divisions	Index Circle	No. of Turns of Index	Gear on Worm	No. 1 Hole		Gear on Spindle	Idlers	
				First Gear on Stud	Second Gear on Stud		No. 1 Hole	No. 2 Hole
371	21	$\frac{2}{21}$	32	56	24	64		
372	18	$\frac{2}{18}$	48			64	24	44
373	20	$\frac{2}{20}$	40	48	32	72		
374	18	$\frac{1}{18}$	72	64	32	56		24
375	18	$\frac{1}{18}$	24			40	24	44
376	47	$\frac{5}{47}$						
377	29	$\frac{2}{29}$	24			24	56	
378	18	$\frac{1}{18}$	32			64	24	44
379	20	$\frac{2}{20}$	48	56	40	72		
380	19	$\frac{1}{19}$						
381	18	$\frac{1}{18}$	24			56	24	44
382	20	$\frac{2}{20}$	40			72	24	
383	20	$\frac{2}{20}$	40			68 [1]	44	
384	20	$\frac{2}{20}$	40			64	44	
385	20	$\frac{2}{20}$	32			48	44	
386	20	$\frac{2}{20}$	40			56	44	
387	43	$\frac{4}{43}$	32	56	28	64		
388	20	$\frac{2}{20}$	40			48	44	
389	20	$\frac{2}{20}$	40			44	56	
390	39	$\frac{3}{39}$						
391	20	$\frac{2}{20}$	48	24	40	72		
392	49	$\frac{5}{49}$						
393	20	$\frac{2}{20}$	40			28	44	
394	20	$\frac{2}{20}$	40			24	56	
395	20	$\frac{2}{20}$	64			32	44	
396	20	$\frac{2}{20}$	56	28	40	32		
397	20	$\frac{2}{20}$	64	24	40	32		
398	20	$\frac{2}{20}$	100	40	64	32		
399	21	$\frac{2}{21}$	32			64	44	
400	20	$\frac{2}{20}$						
401	21	$\frac{2}{21}$	56	32	24	76 [1]		
402	21	$\frac{2}{21}$	28			48	44	
403	20	$\frac{2}{20}$	64	24	40	32		24
404	20	$\frac{2}{20}$	72	24	40	48		24
405	20	$\frac{2}{20}$	64			32	24	44
406	20	$\frac{2}{20}$	40			24	24	44
407	20	$\frac{2}{20}$	40			28	24	44
408	20	$\frac{2}{20}$	40			32	24	44
409	20	$\frac{2}{20}$	40	24	32	48		24
410	41	$\frac{4}{41}$						

NOTE. Special gears in this and following tables are 46, 47, 52, 58, 68, 70, 76, 84.   [1] Special gear.

Number of Divisions	Index Circle	No. of Turns of Index	Gear on Worm	No. 1 Hole		Gear on Spindle	Idlers	
				First Gear on Stud	Second Gear on Stud		No. 1 Hole	No. 2 Hole
411	21	2 2/1	28			24	56	
412	20	2 2/0	40			48	24	44
413	21	2 2/1	48			32	44	
414	21	2 2/1	56			32	44	
415	20	2 2/0	32			48	24	44
416	20	2 2/0	40			64	24	44
417	21	2 4/0	56	32	48	24		
418	20	2 2/0	40			72	24	44
419	33	3 4/3	44	28	24	72		
420	21	2 2/1						
421	20	2 2/0	48	56	40	72		24
422	20	2 2/0	40	44	32	64		24
423	21	2 2/1	72	24	56	48		24
424	43	4 4/3	86	24	24	48		
425	21	2 2/1	72	48	56	40		24
426	21	2 2/1	56			32	24	44
427	20	2 2/0	40	48	32	72		24
428	20	2 2/0	40	56	32	64		24
429	21	2 2/1	28			24	24	44
430	43	4 4/3						
431	21	2 2/1	72	44	28	48		24
432	20	2 2/0	40	56	28	64		24
433	20	2 2/0	40	44	24	72		24
434	21	2 2/1	48			64	24	44
435	21	2 2/1	28			40	24	44
436	20	2 2/0	40	48	24	72		24
437	23	2 2/3	32			64	44	
438	21	2 2/1	28			48	24	44
439	43	4 4/3	86	24	24	72		24
440	33	3 3/3						
441	21	2 2/1	32			64	24	44
442	20	2 2/0	40	56	24	72		24
443	20	2 2/0	40	48	24	86		24
444	21	2 2/1	56	48	24	64		24
445	33	3 3/3	64	32	44	40		24
446	33	3 3/3	44			24	24	48
447	21	2 2/1	28			72	24	44
448	20	2 2/0	40	64	24	72		24
449	33	3 8/3	64	32	44	72		24
450	33	3 3/3	44			40	24	32

Number of Divisions	Index Circle	No. of Turns of Index	Gear on Worm	No. 1 Hole		Gear on Spindle	Idlers	
				First Gear on Stud	Second Gear on Stud		No. 1 Hole	No. 2 Hole
451	33	$\frac{8}{33}$	24			24	24	44
452	33	$\frac{8}{33}$	44			48	24	40
453	33	$\frac{8}{33}$	44			52 [1]	24	40
454	49	$\frac{4}{49}$	56	64	28	72		
455	49	$\frac{4}{49}$	28	40	32	64		
456	21	$\frac{2}{21}$	56	64	24	72		24
457	33	$\frac{8}{33}$	44		.	68 [1]	24	40
458	33	$\frac{8}{33}$	44			72	24	24
459	27	$\frac{2}{27}$	24	48	24	72		
460	23	$\frac{2}{23}$						
461	33	$\frac{8}{33}$	44	28	24	72		24
462	33	$\frac{8}{33}$	32			64	24	44
463	21	$\frac{2}{21}$	56	64	24	86		24
464	33	$\frac{8}{33}$	44	48	28	56		24
465	33	$\frac{8}{33}$	44	24	24	100		24
466	49	$\frac{4}{49}$	56	48	28	64		
467	33	$\frac{8}{33}$	44	48	32	72		24
468	39	$\frac{8}{39}$	28	48	24	56		
469	49	$\frac{4}{49}$	28			48	44	
470	47	$\frac{4}{47}$						
471	49	$\frac{4}{49}$	56	32	28	76 [1]		
472	49	$\frac{4}{49}$	56	32	28	72		
473	33	$\frac{8}{33}$	48	64	32	72		24
474	49	$\frac{4}{49}$	56	32	28	64		
475	49	$\frac{4}{49}$	56	40	28	48		
476	49	$\frac{4}{49}$	56			64	24	
477	27	$\frac{2}{27}$	24	48	24	56		
478	49	$\frac{4}{49}$	56	24	28	64		
479	49	$\frac{4}{49}$	56	32	28	44		
480	49	$\frac{4}{49}$	56	32	28	40		
481	37	$\frac{8}{37}$	24			24	56	
482	33	$\frac{8}{33}$	44	56	24	72		24
483	49	$\frac{4}{49}$	56			32	44	
484	49	$\frac{4}{49}$	56	24	28	32		
485	23	$\frac{2}{23}$	46 [1]	24	24	100		24
486	27	$\frac{2}{27}$	32	56	28	64		
487	39	$\frac{8}{39}$	24	72	52 [1]	44		
488	33	$\frac{8}{33}$	44	64	24	72		24
489	23	$\frac{2}{23}$	46 [1]	58 [1]	32	64		24
490	49	$\frac{4}{49}$						

[1] Special gear.

Number of Divisions	Index Circle	No. of Turns of Index	Gear on Worm	No. 1 Hole		Gear on Spindle	Idlers	
				First Gear on Stud	Second Gear on Stud		No. 1 Hole	No. 2 Hole
491	33	$\frac{3}{33}$	44	68¹	24	72		24
492	41	$\frac{3}{41}$	28	48	24	56		
493	29	$\frac{2}{29}$	32	64	24	72		
494	39	$\frac{3}{39}$	32			64	44	
495	27	$\frac{2}{27}$	32	40	24	64		
496	49	$\frac{4}{49}$	56	24	28	32		24
497	49	$\frac{4}{49}$	56			32	24	44
498	27	$\frac{2}{27}$	48	56	24	64		
499	49	$\frac{4}{49}$	56	24	28	48		24
500	49	$\frac{4}{49}$	56	32	28	40		24
501	49	$\frac{4}{49}$	56	32	28	44		24
502	49	$\frac{4}{49}$	56	32	28	48		24
503	23	$\frac{2}{23}$	46¹	64	32	86		24
504	49	$\frac{4}{49}$	56			64	24	24
505	49	$\frac{4}{49}$	56	40	28	48		24
506	49	$\frac{4}{49}$	56	32	28	64		24
507	39	$\frac{3}{39}$	24			24	56	
508	49	$\frac{4}{49}$	56	32	28	72		24
509	49	$\frac{4}{49}$	56	32	28	76¹		24
510	49	$\frac{4}{49}$	56	40	28	64		24
511	49	$\frac{4}{49}$	28			48	24	44
512	49	$\frac{4}{49}$	56	44	28	64		24
513	27	$\frac{2}{27}$	32			64	44	
514	49	$\frac{4}{49}$	56	48	28	64		24
515	27	$\frac{2}{27}$	72	32	24	100		
516	43	$\frac{3}{43}$	32	56	28	64		
517	49	$\frac{4}{49}$	56	48	28	72		24
518	49	$\frac{4}{49}$	28			64	24	44
519	27	$\frac{2}{27}$	72	56	32	64		
520	39	$\frac{3}{39}$						
521	27	$\frac{2}{27}$	72	76¹	48	64		
522	29	$\frac{2}{29}$	48	64	24	72		
523	27	$\frac{2}{27}$	72	68¹	48	64		
524	27	$\frac{2}{27}$	72	32	24	64		
525	27	$\frac{2}{27}$	72	40	32	64		
526	49	$\frac{4}{49}$	56	64	28	72		24
527	31	$\frac{3}{31}$	32	64	24	72		
528	27	$\frac{2}{27}$	72	24	24	64		
529	27	$\frac{2}{27}$	72	44	48	64		
530	15	$\frac{1}{15}$	24	56	32	64		

¹ Special gear.

Number of Divisions	Index Circle	No. of Turns of Index	Gear on Worm	No. 1 Hole First Gear on Stud	No. 1 Hole Second Gear on Stud	Gear on Spindle	Idlers No. 1 Hole	Idlers No. 2 Hole
531	27	$2\frac{2}{7}$	72			48	24	
532	27	$2\frac{2}{7}$	72	32	48	64		
533	27	$2\frac{2}{7}$	72	32	48	56		
534	27	$2\frac{2}{7}$	72			32	44	
535	27	$2\frac{2}{7}$	72	32	48	40		
536	39	$3\frac{8}{9}$	52 [1]			64	24	44
537	27	$2\frac{2}{7}$	72	28	56	32		
538	29	$2\frac{3}{9}$	58 [1]	56	24	72		
539	49	$4\frac{2}{9}$	28	48	24	56		24
540	27	$2\frac{2}{7}$						
541	39	$3\frac{8}{9}$	52 [1]	56	32	48		24
542	39	$3\frac{8}{9}$	52 [1]	44	32	64		24
543	27	$2\frac{2}{7}$	72	24	48	32		24
544	15	$1\frac{1}{5}$	40	56	24	64		
545	15	$1\frac{1}{5}$	32	44	24	64		
546	39	$3\frac{8}{9}$	32			64	24	44
547	27	$2\frac{2}{7}$	72	32	48	56		24
548	27	$2\frac{2}{7}$	72	32	48	64		24
549	27	$2\frac{2}{7}$	72			48	24	24
550	15	$1\frac{1}{5}$	32	40	24	64		
551	29	$2\frac{2}{9}$	32			64	44	
552	27	$2\frac{2}{7}$	72	24	24	64		24
553	49	$4\frac{2}{9}$	28	48	24	72		24
554	27	$2\frac{2}{7}$	72	56	48	64		24
555	15	$1\frac{1}{5}$	24			72	44	
556	15	$1\frac{1}{5}$	24	44	40	64		
557	15	$1\frac{1}{5}$	40	32	24	86		
558	27	$2\frac{2}{7}$	48			64	24	44
559	39	$3\frac{8}{9}$	24			72	24	44
560	43	$4\frac{3}{3}$	86	40	32	64		
561	27	$2\frac{2}{7}$	72	56	32	64		24
562	27	$2\frac{2}{7}$	72	44	24	64		24
563	29	$2\frac{8}{9}$	58 [1]			68 [1]	44	
564	43	$4\frac{8}{3}$	86	24	24	56		
565	15	$1\frac{1}{5}$	24			56	44	
566	43	$3\frac{4}{3}$	86	24	24	44		
567	15	$1\frac{1}{5}$	32	44	40	64		
568	15	$1\frac{1}{5}$	40	32	24	64		
569	29	$2\frac{2}{9}$	58 [1]			44	24	
570	15	$1\frac{1}{5}$	32			64	44	

[1] Special gear.

Number of Divisions	Index Circle	No. of Turns of Index	Gear on Worm	First Gear on Stud	Second Gear Stud	Gear on Spindle	No. 1 Hole	No. 2 Hole
				No. 1 Hole			Idlers	
571	43	$\frac{8}{43}$	86	28	64	32		
572	15	$\frac{1}{15}$	40	28	24	64		
573	15	$\frac{1}{15}$	40			72	24	
574	41	$\frac{4}{41}$	32			64	24	44
575	15	$\frac{1}{15}$	24			40	44	
576	15	$\frac{1}{15}$	40			64	24	
577	43	$\frac{8}{43}$	86	32	64	44		24
578	15	$\frac{1}{15}$	48	44	40	64		
579	15	$\frac{2}{29}$	40			56	44	
580	29	$\frac{1}{15}$						
581	15	$\frac{1}{15}$	48	32	40	76 [1]		
582	15	$\frac{2}{27}$	40			48	44	
583	27	$\frac{1}{15}$	72	64	24	86		24
584	15	$\frac{1}{15}$	48	32	40	64		
585	15	$\frac{1}{15}$	24			24	56	
586	15	$\frac{2}{29}$	72	48	40	56		
587	29	$\frac{1}{15}$	58 [1]			28	24	44
588	15	$\frac{1}{15}$	40			32	44	
589	15	$\frac{1}{15}$	72	44	40	48		
590	15	$\frac{1}{15}$	48			32	44	
591	15	$\frac{1}{15}$	40			24	44	
592	16	$\frac{1}{16}$	24			72	44	
593	15	$\frac{1}{15}$	72	28	40	48		
594	33	$\frac{2}{33}$	32	56	28	64		
595	15	$\frac{1}{15}$	72			24	44	
596	15	$\frac{1}{15}$	72	24	40	32		
597	33	$\frac{2}{33}$	44	56	24	72		
598	16	$\frac{1}{16}$	64	56	24	72		
599	43	$\frac{3}{43}$	86	44	24	84		24
600	15	$\frac{1}{15}$						
601	29	$\frac{2}{29}$	58 [1]	56	48	72		24
602	43	$\frac{8}{43}$	32			64	24	44
603	15	$\frac{1}{15}$	72	24	40	24		24
604	16	$\frac{1}{16}$	32			72	24	
605	15	$\frac{1}{15}$	72			24	24	44
606	15	$\frac{1}{15}$	72	24	40	48		24
607	15	$\frac{1}{15}$	72	28	40	48		24
608	16	$\frac{1}{16}$	32			64	44	
609	15	$\frac{1}{15}$	40			24	24	44
610	15	$\frac{1}{15}$	48			32	24	44

[1] Special gear.

Number of Divisions	Index Circle	No. of Turns of Index	Gear on Worm	No. 1 Hole		Gear on Spindle	No. 2 Hole	
				First Gear on Stud	Second Gear on Stud		No. 1 Hole	No. 2 Hole
611	15	$1\frac{1}{5}$	72	44	40	48		24
612	15	$1\frac{1}{5}$	40			32	24	44
613	16	$1\frac{1}{5}$	64	48	32	72		
614	15	$1\frac{1}{5}$	72	48	40	56		24
615	15	$1\frac{1}{5}$	24			24	24	44
616	16	$1\frac{1}{5}$	32			48	44	
617	33	$2\frac{2}{3}$	44	32	24	86		
618	15	$1\frac{1}{5}$	40			48	24	44
619	16	$1\frac{1}{5}$	48	28	32	72		
620	31	$3\frac{1}{31}$						
621	15	$1\frac{1}{5}$	40			56	24	44
622	16	$1\frac{1}{6}$	64	24	24	72		
623	16	$1\frac{1}{6}$	64	24	24	68[1]		
624	16	$1\frac{1}{6}$	24			24	56	
625	15	$1\frac{1}{5}$	24			40	24	44
626	16	$1\frac{1}{6}$	32			28	56	
627	15	$1\frac{1}{5}$	40			72	24	44
628	16	$1\frac{1}{6}$	32			24	56	
629	16	$1\frac{1}{6}$	64			44	24	
630	16	$1\frac{1}{6}$	64			40	24	
631	16	$1\frac{1}{6}$	64	28	56	72		
632	16	$1\frac{1}{6}$	64			32	44	
633	16	$1\frac{1}{6}$	64			28	44	
634	16	$1\frac{1}{6}$	64			24	44	
635	15	$1\frac{1}{5}$	24			56	24	44
636	16	$1\frac{1}{6}$	56	28	48	24		
637	49	$4\frac{3}{9}$	24			24	56	
638	29	$2\frac{2}{9}$	48	64	24	72		24
639	33	$3\frac{2}{3}$	44	28	32	64		
640	16	$1\frac{1}{6}$						
641	33	$3\frac{2}{3}$	44	32	48	76[1]		
642	16	$1\frac{1}{6}$	72	24	64	24		24
643	16	$1\frac{1}{6}$	64	28	56	24		24
644	49	$4\frac{3}{9}$	56			32	44	
645	15	$1\frac{1}{5}$	24			72	24	44
646	16	$1\frac{1}{6}$	64			24	24	44
647	16	$1\frac{1}{6}$	64			28	24	44
648	16	$1\frac{1}{6}$	64			32	24	44
649	33	$3\frac{2}{3}$	72			48	24	
650	16	$1\frac{1}{6}$	64			40	24	44

[1] Special gear.

Number of Divisions	Index Circle	No. of Turns of Index	Gear on Worm	No. 1 Hole		Gear on Spindle	No. 2 Hole	
				First Gear on Stud	Second Gear on Stud		No. 1 Hole	No. 2 Hole
651	16	$1\frac{1}{16}$	64			44	24	24
652	16	$1\frac{1}{16}$	32			24	24	44
653	33	$2\frac{2}{33}$	72	28	44	48		
654	16	$1\frac{1}{16}$	64			56	24	
655	16	$1\frac{1}{16}$	64	40	32	48		24
656	16	$1\frac{1}{16}$	24			24	24	44
657	18	$1\frac{1}{18}$	32	48	24	56		
658	16	$1\frac{1}{16}$	64	24	24	72		24
659	16	$1\frac{1}{16}$	64	24	24	76[1]		24
660	33	$2\frac{2}{33}$						
661	16	$1\frac{1}{16}$	64	56	48	72		24
662	16	$1\frac{1}{16}$	64	44	24	48		24
663	17	$1\frac{1}{17}$	24			24	56	
664	16	$1\frac{1}{16}$	32			48	24	44
665	49	$4\frac{8}{49}$	56			40	24	44
666	18	$1\frac{1}{18}$	24			72	44	
667	16	$1\frac{1}{16}$	64	48	32	72		24
668	16	$1\frac{1}{16}$	32			56	24	44
669	33	$2\frac{2}{33}$	44			24	24	24
670	33	$2\frac{2}{33}$	72	48	44	40		24
671	33	$2\frac{2}{33}$	72			48	24	24
672	18	$1\frac{1}{18}$	24			64	44	
673	16	$1\frac{1}{16}$	48	44	32	72		24
674	33	$2\frac{2}{33}$	72	56	44	48		24
675	33	$2\frac{2}{33}$	44			40	24	24
676	16	$1\frac{1}{16}$	32			72	24	44
677	18	$1\frac{1}{18}$	48	32	24	86		
678	18	$1\frac{1}{18}$	24			56	44	
679	49	$4\frac{8}{49}$	28			44	24	40
680	17	$1\frac{2}{17}$						
681	33	$2\frac{2}{33}$	44			56	24	24
682	33	$2\frac{2}{33}$	48			64	24	24
683	16	$1\frac{1}{16}$	32			86	24	44
684	18	$1\frac{1}{18}$	32			64	44	
685	18	$1\frac{1}{18}$	24	56	48	40		
686	15	$1\frac{1}{15}$	40	64	24	86		24
687	18	$1\frac{1}{18}$	24			44	48	
688	16	$1\frac{1}{16}$	24			72	24	44
689	39	$3\frac{3}{39}$	24	48	24	56		
690	18	$1\frac{1}{18}$	24			40	56	

[1] Special gear.

Number of Divisions	Index Circle	No. of Turns of Index	Gear on Worm	No. 1 Hole		Gear on Spindle	Idlers	
				First Gear on Stud	Second Gear on Stud		No. 1 Hole	No. 2 Hole
691	18	$\frac{1}{18}$	48	32	24	58 ¹		
692	18	$\frac{1}{18}$	72	56	32	64		
693	18	$\frac{1}{18}$	32			48	44	
694	17	$\frac{1}{17}$	68 ¹			56	24	44
695	18	$\frac{1}{18}$	72	24	24	100		
696	18	$\frac{1}{18}$	24			32	56	
697	17	$\frac{1}{17}$	24			24	24	44
698	18	$\frac{1}{18}$	72	44	24	48		
699	18	$\frac{1}{18}$	48			56	44	
700	18	$\frac{1}{18}$	72	40	32	64		
701	17	$\frac{1}{17}$	68 ¹	48	32	56		24
702	18	$\frac{1}{18}$	24			24	56	
703	19	$\frac{1}{19}$	24			72	44	
704	18	$\frac{1}{18}$	72	24	24	64		
705	18	$\frac{1}{18}$	48			40	44	
706	18	$\frac{1}{18}$	72			56	24	
707	18	$\frac{1}{18}$	72			52 ¹	24	
708	18	$\frac{1}{18}$	72			48	24	
709	18	$\frac{1}{18}$	72			44	24	
710	18	$\frac{1}{18}$	72			40	24	
711	18	$\frac{1}{18}$	64			32	44	
712	18	$\frac{1}{18}$	72			32	24	
713	18	$\frac{1}{18}$	72			28	44	
714	18	$\frac{1}{18}$	72			24	44	
715	18	$\frac{1}{18}$	72	32	64	40		
716	18	$\frac{1}{18}$	72	28	56	32		
717	18	$\frac{1}{18}$	72	24	64	32		
718	33	$\frac{2}{33}$	44	58 ¹	24	64		24
719	17	$\frac{1}{17}$	68 ¹	52 ¹	24	72		24
720	18	$\frac{1}{18}$						
721	21	$\frac{1}{21}$	24	64	32	68 ¹		
722	19	$\frac{1}{19}$	32			64	44	
723	18	$\frac{1}{18}$	72	24	64	32		24
724	18	$\frac{1}{18}$	72	28	56	32		24
725	18	$\frac{1}{18}$	72	24	48	40		24
726	18	$\frac{1}{18}$	72			24	24	44
727	18	$\frac{1}{18}$	72			28	24	44
728	18	$\frac{1}{18}$	72			32	24	44
729	18	$\frac{1}{18}$	64			32	24	44
730	20	$\frac{1}{20}$	32	48	24	56		

¹ Special gear.

TABLE FOR INDEXING ANGLES—INDEX PLATES (See Explanation on page 191)

Holes	15	16	17	18	19	20	21	23	27	29	31	33	37	39	41	43	47	49
1	0.0666	0.0625	0.0588	0.0555	0.0526	0.0500	0.0476	0.0435	0.0370	0.0345	0.0323	0.0303	0.0270	0.0256	0.0244	0.0233	0.0213	0.0204
2	0.1333	0.1250	0.1176	0.1111	0.1053	0.1000	0.0952	0.0870	0.0741	0.0690	0.0645	0.0606	0.0541	0.0513	0.0488	0.0465	0.0426	0.0408
3	0.2000	0.1875	0.1765	0.1666	0.1579	0.1500	0.1429	0.1304	0.1111	0.1034	0.0968	0.0909	0.0811	0.0769	0.0732	0.0698	0.0638	0.0612
4	0.2667	0.2500	0.2353	0.2222	0.2105	0.2000	0.1904	0.1739	0.1481	0.1379	0.1290	0.1212	0.1081	0.1026	0.0976	0.0930	0.0851	0.0816
5	0.3333	0.3125	0.2941	0.2777	0.2632	0.2500	0.2381	0.2174	0.1852	0.1724	0.1613	0.1515	0.1351	0.1282	0.1220	0.1163	0.1064	0.1020
6	0.4000	0.3750	0.3529	0.3333	0.3158	0.3000	0.2857	0.2609	0.2222	0.2069	0.1935	0.1818	0.1622	0.1538	0.1463	0.1395	0.1277	0.1224
7	0.4667	0.4375	0.4118	0.3888	0.3684	0.3500	0.3333	0.3043	0.2593	0.2414	0.2258	0.2121	0.1892	0.1795	0.1707	0.1628	0.1489	0.1429
8	0.5333	0.5000	0.4706	0.4444	0.4211	0.4000	0.3810	0.3478	0.2963	0.2759	0.2581	0.2424	0.2162	0.2051	0.1951	0.1860	0.1702	0.1633
9	0.6000	0.5625	0.5294	0.5000	0.4737	0.4500	0.4286	0.3913	0.3333	0.3103	0.2903	0.2727	0.2432	0.2308	0.2195	0.2093	0.1915	0.1837
10	0.6666	0.6250	0.5882	0.5555	0.5263	0.5000	0.4762	0.4348	0.3703	0.3448	0.3226	0.3030	0.2703	0.2564	0.2439	0.2326	0.2128	0.2040
11	0.7333	0.6875	0.6471	0.6111	0.5789	0.5500	0.5238	0.4783	0.4074	0.3793	0.3548	0.3333	0.2973	0.2821	0.2683	0.2558	0.2340	0.2245
12	0.8000	0.7500	0.7059	0.6666	0.6316	0.6000	0.5714	0.5217	0.4444	0.4138	0.3871	0.3636	0.3243	0.3077	0.2927	0.2791	0.2553	0.2449
13	0.8666	0.8125	0.7647	0.7222	0.6842	0.6500	0.6190	0.5652	0.4815	0.4483	0.4194	0.3939	0.3514	0.3333	0.3171	0.3023	0.2766	0.2653
14	0.9333	0.8750	0.8230	0.7777	0.7368	0.7000	0.6666	0.6087	0.5185	0.4827	0.4516	0.4242	0.3784	0.3590	0.3415	0.3256	0.2979	0.2857
15		0.9375	0.8824	0.8333	0.7895	0.7500	0.7143	0.6522	0.5555	0.5172	0.4839	0.4545	0.4054	0.3846	0.3659	0.3488	0.3191	0.3061
16			0.9412	0.8888	0.8421	0.8000	0.7619	0.6957	0.5924	0.5517	0.5161	0.4848	0.4324	0.4103	0.3902	0.3721	0.3404	0.3265
17				0.9444	0.8947	0.8500	0.8095	0.7391	0.6296	0.5862	0.5484	0.5151	0.4594	0.4359	0.4146	0.3954	0.3617	0.3469
18					0.9474	0.9000	0.8571	0.7826	0.6666	0.6207	0.5806	0.5454	0.4865	0.4615	0.4390	0.4186	0.3830	0.3673
19						0.9500	0.9048	0.8261	0.7037	0.6552	0.6129	0.5757	0.5135	0.4872	0.4634	0.4419	0.4043	0.3878
20							0.9524	0.8696	0.7407	0.6897	0.6452	0.6060	0.5405	0.5128	0.4878	0.4651	0.4255	0.4082
21								0.9130	0.7777	0.7241	0.6774	0.6363	0.5676	0.5385	0.5122	0.4884	0.4468	0.4286
22								0.9565	0.8148	0.7586	0.7097	0.6666	0.5946	0.5641	0.5366	0.5116	0.4681	0.4490
23									0.8519	0.7931	0.7419	0.6969	0.6216	0.5897	0.5610	0.5349	0.4894	0.4694
24									0.8888	0.8276	0.7742	0.7272	0.6486	0.6154	0.5854	0.5581	0.5106	0.4898

Holes	INDEX PLATES									
	27	29	31	33	37	39	41	43	47	49
25	0.9259	0.8621	0.8065	0.7575	0.6757	0.6410	0.6097	0.5814	0.5319	0.5102
26	0.9630	0.8966	0.8387	0.7878	0.7027	0.6666	0.6341	0.6047	0.5532	0.5306
27		0.9310	0.8710	0.8181	0.7297	0.6923	0.6585	0.6279	0.5745	0.5510
28			0.9032	0.8484	0.7568	0.7179	0.6829	0.6512	0.5957	0.5714
29			0.9355	0.8787	0.7838	0.7436	0.7073	0.6744	0.6170	0.5918
30			0.9677	0.9090	0.8108	0.7692	0.7317	0.6977	0.6383	0.6122
31				0.9393	0.8378	0.7949	0.7561	0.7209	0.6596	0.6326
32				0.9696	0.8647	0.8205	0.7805	0.7442	0.6809	0.6531
33					0.8919	0.8462	0.8049	0.7674	0.7021	0.6735
34					0.9189	0.8718	0.8293	0.7907	0.7234	0.6939
35					0.9459	0.8974	0.8537	0.8140	0.7447	0.7143
36					0.9730	0.9231	0.8780	0.8372	0.7660	0.7347
37						0.9487	0.9024	0.8605	0.7872	0.7551
38						0.9743	0.9268	0.8837	0.8085	0.7755
39							0.9512	0.9070	0.8298	0.7959
40							0.9756	0.9302	0.8511	0.8163
41								0.9535	0.8723	0.8367
42								0.9768	0.8936	0.8571
43									0.9149	0.8775
44									0.9362	0.8980
45									0.9574	0.9184
46									0.9787	0.9388
47										0.9592
48										0.9796

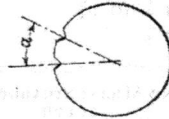

TABLE FOR INDEXING ANGLES

The table saves many calculations when obtaining proper index for angles, either in degrees, minutes or seconds, or all three collectively. An example will readily show its application.

The angle to be indexed is one of 31 deg., 17 min., 11 sec. Reducing the angle to seconds = 112,631. One turn of the crank = 9 deg, which reduced to seconds = 32,400.

$$\frac{112,631}{32,400} = 3.4762 \ turns.$$

We find in the table 0.4762 = $\frac{10}{21}$; thus, three turns and 10 holes on the 21 circle give correct results to four decimal places.

MILLING CUTTER, REAMER AND TAP FLUTES

THE following tables give the number of teeth or flutes suitable for milling in various types of cutters, reamers, taps, etc., and also show the forms of fluting cutters used.

END MILLS

STRAIGHT TEETH		SPIRAL TEETH	
Dia. Mill	No. Teeth	Dia. Mill	No. Teeth
$\frac{1}{4}$	6	$\frac{1}{4}$ to $\frac{1}{2}$	8
$\frac{5}{16}$ to $\frac{9}{16}$	8	$\frac{9}{16}$ to $\frac{15}{16}$	10
$\frac{5}{8}$ to 1	10	1 to $1\frac{1}{4}$	12
$1\frac{1}{8}$ to $1\frac{3}{8}$	12	$1\frac{3}{8}$ to $1\frac{1}{2}$	14
$1\frac{1}{2}$	14		

SHELL END MILLS; STRAIGHT OR SPIRAL TEETH		INSERTED TOOTH CUTTERS, P. & W. FORM	
Dia. Mill	No. Teeth	Dia. Cutter	No. Blades
		4	10
		5	12
		6	16
		7	18
$1\frac{1}{4}$ to $1\frac{9}{16}$	16	8	20
$1\frac{5}{8}$ to $2\frac{9}{16}$	18	10	24
$2\frac{5}{8}$ to 3	20	12	28

METAL SLITTING CUTTERS

Thickness	Pitch	Thickness	Pitch
$\frac{1}{32}$	$\frac{3}{16}$	$\frac{5}{32}$	$\frac{5}{16}$
$\frac{1}{16}$	$\frac{1}{4}$	$\frac{3}{16}$	$\frac{11}{32}$
$\frac{3}{32}$	$\frac{9}{32}$	$\frac{1}{4}$	$\frac{3}{8}$
$\frac{1}{8}$	$\frac{5}{16}$		

SCREW SLOTTING CUTTERS

Cutters thinner than $\frac{1}{32}$ cut $\frac{3}{64}$ pitch.
Cutters $\frac{1}{32}$ to $\frac{3}{64}$ thick cut $\frac{1}{16}$ pitch.
Cutters over $\frac{3}{64}$ thick cut $\frac{3}{32}$ pitch.

Plain Milling Cutters	
Dia. of Cutter	No. of Teeth
2 to $2\frac{3}{4}$	18
3 to $3\frac{3}{4}$	20
4 to 5	22
$5\frac{1}{4}$ to 6	24
$6\frac{1}{4}$ to $8\frac{3}{4}$	26
9 to $9\frac{1}{4}$	28
$9\frac{1}{2}$ to 10	30
$10\frac{1}{4}$ to 11	32

FLUTING CUTTERS

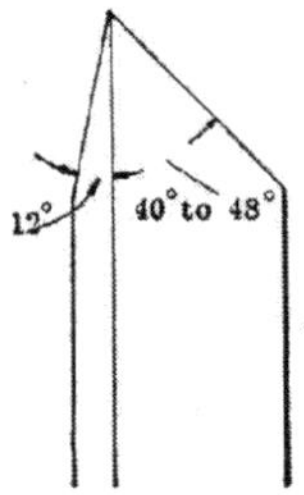

Form of Cutter for Milling Teeth in Plain Milling Cutters.

Plain cutters of $\frac{3}{4}$-inch face and over are generally made with spiral teeth. The 12-degree angle on side of fluting cutter gives ample clearance for cutting spiral grooves with the 12-degree face set on the center line of the work.

Side or Straddle Mills	
Dia. of Cutter	No. of Teeth
2	16
$2\frac{1}{2}$	20
$2\frac{3}{4}$ to $3\frac{1}{2}$	24
$3\frac{3}{4}$ to $4\frac{1}{4}$	26
5 to $5\frac{3}{4}$	28
6 to $6\frac{3}{4}$	30
7 to $7\frac{3}{4}$	32
8 to $8\frac{3}{4}$	34

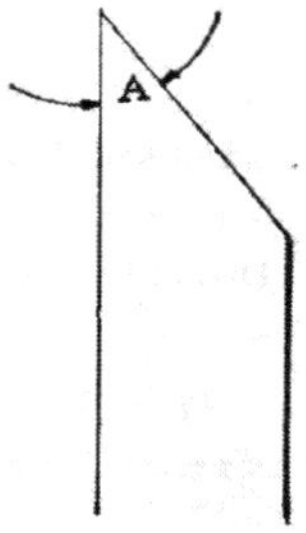

Angular Cutter for Milling Teeth in Straddle Milling Cutters.

For milling teeth on periphery of straddle mills use angular cutter with 60 degree angle at *A;* for milling teeth on sides of cutters use 70°, 75° or 80° cutter according to number of teeth in cutter to be milled.

CORNER ROUNDING CUTTERS

Dia. Cutter	Rad. Circle	No. Teeth
2	$\frac{1}{16}$ to $\frac{1}{8}$	14
$2\frac{1}{4}$	$\frac{5}{32}$ to $\frac{1}{4}$	12
$2\frac{3}{4}$ to $3\frac{1}{2}$	$\frac{5}{16}$ to $\frac{5}{8}$	10
$3\frac{3}{4}$	$\frac{11}{16}$ to $\frac{3}{4}$	8

CONCAVE AND CONVEX CUTTERS

Dia. Cutter	Dia. Circle	No. Teeth
2	$\frac{1}{8}$ to $\frac{1}{4}$	12
$2\frac{1}{4}$ to $3\frac{1}{2}$	$\frac{3}{8}$ to $1\frac{1}{8}$	10
$3\frac{1}{2}$ to 4	$1\frac{1}{4}$ to 2	8

ANGULAR CUTTERS

Dia. of Cutter	No. of Teeth
$2\frac{1}{2}$	18
$2\frac{3}{4}$	20
3	22

DOUBLE ANGLE CUTTERS

Dia. of Cutter	No. of Teeth
$2\frac{1}{2}$ to 3	22

CUTTERS FOR SPIRAL MILLS

Dia. of Cutters	No. of Teeth
$2\frac{1}{2}$	18
$2\frac{3}{4}$	20
3	22

Angular Cutter for Milling Teeth in Corner Rounding, Concave and Convex Cutters.

Cutter for Milling Teeth in Angular Cutters, Double Angle Cutters and Cutters for Spiral Mills. To cut Teeth on side A of this Cutter use 60° Cutter. To cut side B use 70°–75° Cutter.

HAND TAPS	
Dia. of Tap	No. Flutes
$1\frac{3}{2}$ to $1\frac{3}{4}$	4
$1\frac{7}{8}$ to $2\frac{3}{4}$	6
3 to 4	8
3 to 4 mm.	3
5 to 44 mm.	4
46 to 50 mm.	6

MACHINE SCREW TAPS	
Dia. of Tap	No. Flutes
No. 1 to 7	3
No. 8 to 30	4

TAPPER TAPS	
Dia. of Tap	No. Flutes
$\frac{1}{2}$ to $1\frac{5}{8}$	4
$1\frac{3}{4}$ to 2	5
$2\frac{1}{4}$	6

MACHINE OR NUT TAPS	
Dia. of Tap	No. Flutes
$\frac{3}{16}$ to $\frac{5}{16}$	4
$\frac{3}{8}$ to $2\frac{1}{4}$	5
$2\frac{3}{8}$ to 3	6
$3\frac{1}{4}$ to 4	7

SCREW MACHINE TAPS	
Dia. of Tap	No. Flutes
$\frac{1}{4}$ to $1\frac{1}{2}$	4
$1\frac{9}{16}$ to 2	6

TAP FLUTING CUTTER

With

3 Flutes in Tap, B = $\frac{3}{4}$ Dia. Tap

4 Flutes in Tap, B = $\frac{1}{2}$ Dia. Tap

5 Flutes in Tap, B = $\frac{13}{32}$ Dia. Tap

6 Flutes in Tap, B = $\frac{11}{32}$ Dia. Tap

7 Flutes in Tap, B = $\frac{9}{32}$ Dia. Tap

8 Flutes in Tap, B = $\frac{1}{4}$ Dia. Tap

With

3 Flutes in Tap, E = $\frac{9}{32}$ Dia. Tap

4 Flutes in Tap, E = $\frac{1}{4}$ Dia. Tap

5 Flutes in Tap, E = $\frac{13}{64}$ Dia. Tap

6 Flutes in Tap, E = $\frac{11}{64}$ Dia. Tap

7 Flutes in Tap, E = $\frac{5}{32}$ Dia. Tap

8 Flutes in Tap, E = $\frac{9}{64}$ Dia. Tap

In milling taps with the convex cutter the cutter must be central with the tap.

TAPER PIPE TAPS	
Dia. of Tap	No. of Flutes
$\frac{1}{8}$ to $\frac{1}{2}$	4
$\frac{3}{4}$	4 or 5
1 to $1\frac{1}{2}$	5
2	7
$2\frac{1}{2}$	8
3	9
$3\frac{1}{2}$ to 4	11

STRAIGHT PIPE TAPS	
Dia. of Tap	No. of Flutes
$\frac{1}{4}$ to $\frac{1}{2}$	4
$\frac{3}{4}$ to $1\frac{1}{4}$	5
$1\frac{1}{2}$	6
2	7
$2\frac{1}{2}$	8
3	9
$3\frac{1}{2}$	10

TAP FLUTING CUTTERS

B   A

Cutter A is a regular tap fluting cutter that may be used if preferred for fluting any kind of tap in place of convex cutter B.

PIPE HOBS

Dia. Hob	No. Flutes	Dia. Hob	No. Flutes	Dia. Hob	No. Flutes
$\frac{1}{8}$ to $\frac{1}{4}$	6	1	12	3	28
$\frac{3}{8}$	8	$1\frac{1}{4}$ to $1\frac{1}{2}$	16	$3\frac{1}{2}$	34
$\frac{1}{2}$	9	2	20	4	36
$\frac{3}{4}$	10	$2\frac{1}{2}$	24	$4\frac{1}{2}$	46

HOB FLUTING CUTTER

SELLERS HOBS

Dia. Hobs	No. Flutes	Dia. Hob	No. Flutes
$\frac{1}{4}$ to $\frac{7}{16}$	6	$1\frac{1}{2}$ to $2\frac{1}{2}$	12
$\frac{1}{2}$ to $\frac{7}{8}$	8	$2\frac{5}{8}$ to $2\frac{7}{8}$	14
$\frac{15}{16}$ to $1\frac{3}{8}$	10	3 to 4	16

HOB TAPS

Dia. Hob	No. Flutes
$\frac{1}{4}$ to $\frac{1}{2}$	6
$\frac{9}{16}$ to $\frac{13}{16}$	8
$\frac{7}{8}$ to $1\frac{1}{2}$	10
$1\frac{5}{8}$ to 2	12

In fluting hobs leave land $\frac{3}{16}$ inch wide on top.

SHELL REAMERS

Dia. of Reamer	No. of Flutes	Dia. of Reamer	No. of Flutes	Dia. of Reamer	No. of Flutes
$\frac{1}{4}$ to $\frac{3}{8}$	6	$\frac{21}{32}$ to $1\frac{1}{2}$	10	$2\frac{9}{32}$ to $2\frac{3}{4}$	14
$\frac{13}{32}$ to $\frac{5}{8}$	8	$1\frac{17}{32}$ to $2\frac{1}{4}$	12	$2\frac{25}{32}$ to 4	16

CUTTERS FOR FLUTING REAMERS

Dia. of Reamer	R = Radius of Corner	Dia. of Reamer	R = Radius of Corner
$\frac{1}{8}$ to $\frac{3}{16}$	0	$1\frac{1}{8}$ to $1\frac{1}{2}$	$\frac{1}{16}$
$\frac{1}{4}$ to $\frac{3}{8}$	$\frac{1}{64}$	$1\frac{9}{16}$ to $2\frac{1}{4}$	$\frac{5}{64}$
$\frac{1}{2}$ to $\frac{5}{8}$	$\frac{1}{32}$	$2\frac{5}{16}$ to 3	$\frac{3}{16}$
$\frac{3}{4}$ to 1	$\frac{3}{64}$		

Dia. of Reamer	A = Am't Cutting Edge is Ahead of Center	Dia. of Reamer	A = Am't Cutting Edge is Ahead of Center
$\frac{1}{4}$	.011	$1\frac{1}{2}$	.066
$\frac{3}{8}$	.016	$1\frac{3}{4}$	.076
$\frac{1}{2}$	.022	2	.087
$\frac{5}{8}$	.027	$2\frac{1}{4}$	.098
$\frac{3}{4}$	.033	$2\frac{1}{2}$	.109
$\frac{7}{8}$	.038	$2\frac{3}{4}$	.120
1	.044	3	.131
$1\frac{1}{4}$	.055		

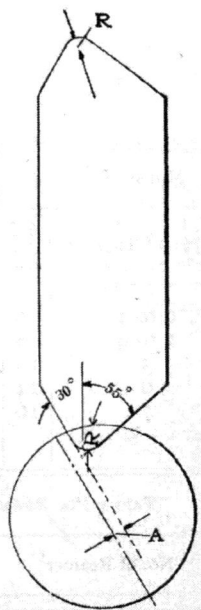

The type of cutter shown may be used for all classes of reamers except rose reamers.

Rose Chucking Reamers

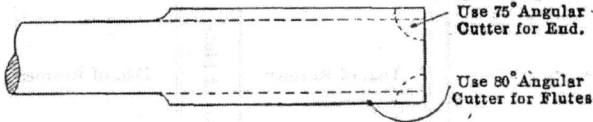

Use 75° Angular Cutter for End.

Use 80° Angular Cutter for Flutes

Depth of Groove = $\frac{1}{8}$ to $\frac{1}{6}$ Dia.

Dia. of Reamer	No. of End Cuts	No. of Flutes	Dia. of Reamer	No. of End Cuts	No. of Flutes
$\frac{1}{8}$ to $\frac{1}{2}$	6	3	$1\frac{3}{4}$ to 2	12	6
$\frac{5}{8}$ to 1	8	4	$2\frac{1}{4}$ to $2\frac{1}{2}$	14	7
$1\frac{1}{8}$ to $1\frac{1}{2}$	10	5	$2\frac{3}{4}$ to 3	16	8

Taper Reamers

Morse Taper		B. & S. Taper		Jarno Taper	
No. of Taper	No. of Flutes	No. of Taper	No. of Flutes	No. of Taper	No. of Flutes
o to 1	6	1 to 5	6	2	4
2 to 4	8	6 to 10	8	3 to 4	6
5	10	11 to 12	10	5 to 10	8
6	14	13	12	11 to 15	10
7	16	14 to 16	14	16 to 18	12
		16 to 18	16	19 to 20	14

Taper Pin Reamers		Locomotive Taper Reamers	
No. of Reamer	No. of Flutes	Dia. of Reamer	No. of Flutes
oooo to oo	4	$\frac{1}{4}$ to $\frac{1}{2}$	6
o to 7	6	$\frac{9}{16}$ to $1\frac{1}{4}$	8
8 to 10	8	$1\frac{5}{16}$ to $1\frac{3}{4}$	10
11 to 14	10	$1\frac{13}{16}$ to 2	12

CENTER REAMERS

DIAMETER OF STRADDLE MILL FOR FLUTING (3 FLUTES)

Size of Reamer	Outside Dia. of Cutter	Size of Reamer	Outside Dia. of Cutter
$\frac{1}{4}''$ cut	$2\frac{1}{2}$	$\frac{3}{4}''$ cut	$3\frac{1}{2}$
$\frac{3}{8}''$ cut	$2\frac{3}{4}$	$\frac{7}{8}''$ cut	$3\frac{3}{4}$
$\frac{1}{2}''$ cut	3	$1''$ cut	4
$\frac{5}{8}''$ cut	$3\frac{1}{4}$		

CUTTER KEYWAYS

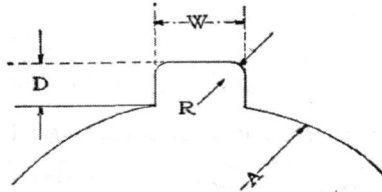

SQUARE KEYWAY

Dia. Hole, A	$\frac{3}{8}-\frac{9}{16}$	$\frac{5}{8}-\frac{7}{8}$	$\frac{15}{16}-1\frac{1}{8}$	$1\frac{3}{16}-1\frac{3}{8}$	$1\frac{7}{16}-1\frac{3}{4}$	$1\frac{13}{16}-2$	$2\frac{1}{16}-2\frac{1}{2}$	$2\frac{9}{16}-3$
Width Key, W	$\frac{3}{32}$	$\frac{1}{8}$	$\frac{3}{32}$	$\frac{1}{16}$	$\frac{1}{4}$	$\frac{5}{16}$	$\frac{3}{8}$	$\frac{7}{16}$
Depth, D....	$\frac{3}{64}$	$\frac{1}{16}$	$\frac{5}{64}$	$\frac{3}{32}$	$\frac{1}{8}$	$\frac{5}{32}$	$\frac{3}{16}$	$\frac{3}{16}$
Radius, R ...	.020	.030	.035	.040	.050	.060	.060	.060

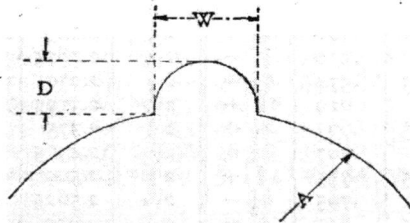

HALF-ROUND KEYWAY

Dia. Hole, A.	$\frac{3}{8}-\frac{5}{8}$	$\frac{11}{16}-\frac{13}{16}$	$\frac{7}{8}-1\frac{3}{16}$	$1\frac{1}{4}-1\frac{7}{16}$	$1\frac{1}{2}-2$	$2\frac{1}{16}-2\frac{7}{16}$	$2\frac{1}{2}-3$
Width, W....	$\frac{1}{8}$	$\frac{3}{16}$	$\frac{1}{4}$	$\frac{5}{16}$	$\frac{3}{8}$	$\frac{7}{16}$	$\frac{1}{2}$
Depth, D....	$\frac{1}{16}$	$\frac{3}{32}$	$\frac{1}{8}$	$\frac{3}{32}$	$\frac{3}{16}$	$\frac{3}{32}$	$\frac{1}{4}$

Width of Slot A Inches	Diameter of Neck of Cutter Inches	Width of Slot B Inches	Depth C Inches	Extreme Limit D Inches
$\frac{1}{4}$	$\frac{7}{32}$	$\frac{1}{2}$	$\frac{5}{32}$	$\frac{5}{16}$
$\frac{5}{16}$	$\frac{9}{32}$	$\frac{5}{8}$	$\frac{3}{32}$	$\frac{3}{8}$
$\frac{3}{8}$	$\frac{11}{32}$	$\frac{11}{16}$	$\frac{3}{32}$	$\frac{7}{16}$
$\frac{7}{16}$	$\frac{3}{8}$	$\frac{13}{16}$	$\frac{7}{32}$	$\frac{7}{16}$
$\frac{1}{2}$	$\frac{7}{16}$	$\frac{15}{16}$	$\frac{9}{32}$	$\frac{9}{16}$
$\frac{5}{8}$	$\frac{17}{32}$	$1\frac{3}{16}$	$\frac{13}{32}$	$\frac{3}{4}$
$\frac{3}{4}$	$\frac{21}{32}$	$1\frac{5}{16}$	$\frac{11}{32}$	1
$\frac{7}{8}$	$\frac{25}{32}$	$1\frac{1}{8}$	$\frac{11}{16}$	$1\frac{1}{16}$
1	$\frac{29}{32}$	$1\frac{7}{8}$	$\frac{13}{16}$	$1\frac{3}{16}$

These cutters are made $\frac{1}{32}$ inch larger in diameter and $\frac{1}{64}$ inch greater in thickness than the figures given, to allow for sharpening.

LARGEST SQUARES THAT CAN BE MILLED ON ROUND STOCK

Diam. of Stock	Decimal Equivalent	Size of Square	Nearest Fraction	Diam. of Stock	Decimal Equivalent	Size of Square	Nearest Fraction
$\frac{1}{8}$	.125	.088	$\frac{3}{32}$ −	$1\frac{9}{16}$	1.5625	1.105	$1\frac{7}{64}$ −
$\frac{3}{16}$	.1875	.133	$\frac{1}{8}$ +	$1\frac{5}{8}$	1.625	1.149	$1\frac{5}{32}$ −
$\frac{1}{4}$	.250	.177	$\frac{11}{64}$ −	$1\frac{11}{16}$	1.6875	1.193	$1\frac{3}{16}$ +
$\frac{5}{16}$	.3125	.221	$\frac{7}{32}$ +	$1\frac{3}{4}$	1.750	1.237	$1\frac{15}{64}$ −
$\frac{3}{8}$	.375	.265	$\frac{17}{64}$ −	$1\frac{13}{16}$	1.8125	1.282	$1\frac{9}{32}$ −
$\frac{7}{16}$	.4375	.309	$\frac{5}{16}$ −	$1\frac{7}{8}$	1.875	1.326	$1\frac{21}{64}$ −
$\frac{1}{2}$	.500	.354	$\frac{23}{64}$ −	$1\frac{15}{16}$	1.9375	1.370	$1\frac{3}{8}$ −
$\frac{9}{16}$	.5625	.398	$\frac{25}{64}$ +	2	2.000	1.414	$1\frac{13}{32}$ +
$\frac{5}{8}$	.625	.442	$\frac{7}{16}$ +	$2\frac{1}{16}$	2.0625	1.458	$1\frac{29}{64}$ +
$\frac{11}{16}$	.6875	.486	$\frac{31}{64}$ −	$2\frac{1}{8}$	2.125	1.502	$1\frac{1}{2}$ +
$\frac{3}{4}$	.750	.530	$\frac{17}{32}$ −	$2\frac{3}{16}$	2.1875	1.547	$1\frac{35}{64}$ −
$\frac{13}{16}$	.8125	.574	$\frac{37}{64}$ −	$2\frac{1}{4}$	2.250	1.591	$1\frac{19}{32}$ −
$\frac{7}{8}$	.875	.619	$\frac{5}{8}$ −	$2\frac{5}{16}$	2.3125	1.635	$1\frac{41}{64}$ −
$\frac{15}{16}$	.9375	.663	$\frac{21}{32}$ +	$2\frac{3}{8}$	2.375	1.679	$1\frac{43}{64}$ +
1	1.000	.707	$\frac{45}{64}$ +	$2\frac{7}{16}$	2.4375	1.723	$1\frac{23}{32}$ +
$1\frac{1}{16}$	1.0625	.755	$\frac{3}{4}$ +	$2\frac{1}{2}$	2.500	1.768	$1\frac{49}{64}$ +
$1\frac{1}{8}$	1.125	.795	$\frac{51}{64}$ −	$2\frac{9}{16}$	2.5625	1.813	$1\frac{13}{16}$ −
$1\frac{3}{16}$	1.1875	.840	$\frac{27}{32}$ −	$2\frac{5}{8}$	2.625	1.856	$1\frac{55}{64}$ −
$1\frac{1}{4}$	1.250	.884	$\frac{57}{64}$ −	$2\frac{11}{16}$	2.6875	1.900	$1\frac{29}{32}$ −
$1\frac{5}{16}$	1.3125	.928	$\frac{59}{64}$ +	$2\frac{3}{4}$	2.750	1.944	$1\frac{15}{16}$ +
$1\frac{3}{8}$	1.375	.972	$\frac{31}{32}$ +	$2\frac{13}{16}$	2.8125	1.989	$1\frac{63}{64}$ +
$1\frac{7}{16}$	1.4375	1.016	$1\frac{1}{64}$ +	$2\frac{7}{8}$	2.875	2.033	$2\frac{1}{32}$ +
$1\frac{1}{2}$	1.500	1.061	$1\frac{1}{16}$ −	$2\frac{15}{16}$	2.9375	2.077	$2\frac{5}{64}$ −
Side of Largest Square = Dia. of Stock × .707				3	3.000	2.121	$2\frac{1}{8}$ −

TABLE OF DIVISIONS CORRESPONDING TO GIVEN CIRCUMFERENTIAL DISTANCES

This table gives approximate number of divisions and distances apart on circumference, corresponding to a known diameter of work. It is useful in milling-machine work in cutting mills, saws, ratchets, etc.

Dia. of Work	$\frac{1}{32}''$	$\frac{1}{16}''$	$\frac{1}{8}''$	$\frac{3}{16}''$	$\frac{1}{4}''$	$\frac{5}{16}''$	$\frac{3}{8}''$	$\frac{7}{16}''$	$\frac{1}{2}''$	$\frac{9}{16}''$	$\frac{5}{8}''$	$\frac{11}{16}''$	$\frac{3}{4}''$	$\frac{7}{8}''$	$1''$
$\frac{1}{4}$	25	12	6												
$\frac{5}{16}$	31	16	8												
$\frac{3}{8}$	38	19	9	6											
$\frac{7}{16}$	44	22	11	7	5										
$\frac{1}{2}$	50	25	13	8	6										
$\frac{5}{8}$	63	31	16	10	8	6									
$\frac{3}{4}$	75	38	19	13	9	8	6								
$\frac{7}{8}$	88	44	22	15	11	9	7	6							
I	100	50	25	17	13	10	8	7	6						
$\frac{1}{4}$	126	63	31	21	16	13	10	9	8	7	6				
$\frac{1}{2}$	150	75	38	25	19	15	13	11	10	8	7				
$\frac{3}{4}$	176	88	44	29	22	18	15	13	11	10	9	8	7	6	
2	200	100	50	34	25	20	17	14	12	11	10	9	8	7	6
$\frac{1}{4}$	226	113	56	38	28	23	19	16	14	13	11	10	9	8	7
$\frac{1}{2}$	251	125	63	42	31	25	21	18	16	14	12	11	10	9	8
$\frac{3}{4}$	277	138	69	46	35	28	23	20	17	15	14	13	12	10	9
3	302	151	75	50	38	30	25	22	19	17	15	15	13	11	9
$\frac{1}{4}$	327	163	82	54	41	33	27	23	20	18	16	15	14	12	10
$\frac{1}{2}$	352	176	88	59	44	35	30	25	22	20	18	16	15	13	11
$\frac{3}{4}$	378	189	94	63	47	38	31	27	24	21	19	17	16	14	12
4	402	201	100	67	50	40	34	29	25	22	20	18	17	15	13
$\frac{1}{4}$	428	214	107	71	53	43	36	31	27	24	21	19	18	15	13
$\frac{1}{2}$	454	227	114	76	57	45	38	32	28	25	23	21	19	16	14
$\frac{3}{4}$	478	239	119	79	60	48	40	34	30	27	24	22	20	17	15
5	503	252	126	84	63	50	42	36	31	28	25	23	21	18	16
$\frac{1}{4}$	528	264	132	88	66	53	44	38	33	29	26	24	22	19	16
$\frac{1}{2}$	554	277	138	92	69	55	46	40	35	31	27	25	23	20	17
$\frac{3}{4}$	579	289	145	96	73	58	48	41	36	32	28	26	24	21	18
6	604	302	151	101	76	61	50	44	38	34	30	27	25	22	19

For example: A straddle mill, say, 5 inches in diameter, is to be cut with teeth $\frac{7}{16}$ apart. Without a table of this kind the workman will have to go to the trouble of multiplying the diameter by 3.1416 and then divide by $\frac{7}{16}$ to find the number of teeth to set up for. In the table, under $\frac{7}{16}$ and opposite 5, he can find at once the number of divisions, as 36. Where the table shows an odd number of teeth, one more or less can, of course, be taken if it is important to have even number of teeth.

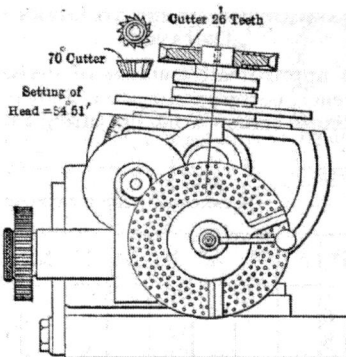

MILLING SIDE TEETH IN MILLING CUTTERS

THE table gives the angle at which to set the dividing head of a miller when milling the side teeth in milling cutters.

MILLING SIDE TEETH IN MILLING CUTTERS. ANGLE TO SET DIVIDING HEAD

No. of Teeth	ANGLE OF CUTTER USED							
	45°	50°	60°	65°	70°	75°	80°	85°
6				36° 08'	50° 55'	62° 21'	57° 08'	81° 17'
7			43° 36'	54° 13'	62° 50'	70° 22'	72° 13'	83° 42'
8		32° 57'	54° 44'	61° 30'	68° 39'	74° 04'	77° 13'	84° 52'
9	32° 58'	45° 15'	61° 01'	66° 58'	72° 13'	77° 00'	81° 29'	85° 47'
10	43° 24'	52° 26'	65° 12'	70° 12'	74° 40'	78° 46'	82° 38'	86° 14'
12	54° 44'	61° 02'	70° 32	74° 23'	77° 52'	81° 06'	84° 09'	87° 06'
14	61° 12	66° 10'	73° 51'	77° 01'	79° 54'	82° 35'	85° 08'	87° 35'
16	65° 32	69° 40'	76° 10'	78° 52'	81° 20'	83° 37'	85° 49'	87° 55'
18	68° 39'	72° 13'	77° 52'	80° 13'	82° 23'	84° 21'	86° 19'	88° 10'
20	71° 03'	74° 11'	79° 11'	81° 17'	83° 13'	85° 00'	86° 43'	88° 22'
22	72° 55'	75° 44'	80° 14'	82° 08'	83° 52'	85° 29'	87° 02'	88° 31'
24	74° 28'	77° 00'	81° 06'	82° 49'	84° 24'	85° 53°	87° 18'	88° 39'
26	75° 44'	78° 04'	81° 49'	83° 33'	84° 51'	86° 12'	87° 30'	88° 45'
28	76° 49'	78° 58'	82° 26'	83° 53'	85° 14'	86° 29'	87° 42'	88° 51'
30	77° 44'	79° 43'	82° 57'	84° 18'	85° 34'	86° 44'	87° 51'	88° 56'
32	78° 32'	80° 23'	83° 24'	84° 40'	85° 51'	86° 56'	87° 59'	89° 00'
34	79° 14'	80° 59'	83° 48'	85° 00'	86° 06'	87° 08'	88° 07'	89° 04'
36	79° 51'	81° 29'	84° 09'	85° 17'	86° 19'	87° 17'	88° 13'	89° 07'
38	80° 24'	81° 58'	84° 29'	85° 32'	86° 31'	87° 26'	88° 18'	89° 09'
40	80° 53'	82° 22'	84° 45'	85° 46'	86° 42'	87° 34'	88° 24'	89° 12'
42	81° 20'	82° 44'	85° 00'	85° 58'	86° 51'	87° 41'	88° 29'	89° 14'

The table shows the angle to the nearest minute, but as an ordinary dividing head is not graduated to read in minutes, the nearest quarter degree is taken.

CUTTING SPEEDS FOR COLD SAW CUTTING-OFF MACHINES

The table on page 204 shows the practice of the Brown & Sharpe Mfg. Co. The semi-high speed still is used for soft steel but high speed is recommended for cutting tool steel. A good lard cutting oil is preferred though it can be dark colored and more impure than for screw machines.

The experience of this company has led to the adoption of the saw tooth shown herewith. This allows a slower speed and coarser feed than finer teeth, and cuts stock more easily and quickly.

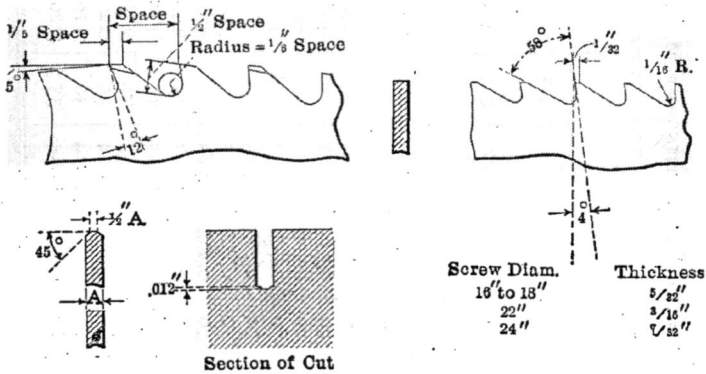

Section of Cut

Screw Diam.	Thickness
16" to 18"	5/22"
22"	3/16"
24"	7/32"

Newton Machine Tool Works recommend a high speed and light feed for steel low in carbon and manganese to keep the chip thin as possible. Up to 35-point carbon use 60 to 65 feet per minute for solid blades. From 35 to 50-point carbon, 55 to 60 feet per minute and less feed. Above 50-point carbon use inserted tooth saws. With inserted tooth saws speeds can be from 50 to 80 feet per minute on 50 to 70-point carbon, but only on heavy, rigid machines. For cutting sprues in steel foundries a solid tooth saw with a speed of 55 feet per minute and a feed of $\frac{1}{4}$ to $\frac{3}{8}$ inch per minute is recommended.

The work should be flooded at all times with any good cutting compound which does not rust. A good mixture is: whale oil, 9 quarts; pure lard oil, 2 gallons; sal soda, 15 pounds; and 40 gallons of water.

The Tindel-Morris Co. give $\frac{3}{4}$ inch per minute as a safe feed for steel bars of 45-point carbon from 2 to 10 inches in diameter. The speed of inserted tooth saws is given as 25 to 30 feet per minute, as this, with a coarse feed, gives good results. This is with $\frac{3}{4}$ inch spacing between teeth. Liberal power is needed — a 36-inch saw requiring from 10 to 15 horsepower.

TABLE OF CUTTING SPEEDS FOR COLD SAW CUTTING-OFF MACHINES

Diameter of Stock	Diameter of Saw	Machinery and Soft Steel					Tool Steel					High-speed Tool Steel				
		Number of Teeth in Saw	Cutting Speed of Saw, Ft. per Min.	Feed of Saw, Inches per Min.	Revolutions of Saw per Min.	Approx. Min. to Cut Off One Piece	Number of Teeth in Saw	Cutting Speed of Saw, Ft. per Min.	Feed of Saw, Inches per Min.	Revolutions of Saw per Min.	Approx. Min. to Cut Off One Piece	Number of Teeth in Saw	Cutting Speed of Saw, Ft. per Min.	Feed of Saw, Inches per Min.	Revolutions of Saw per Min.	Approx. Min. to Cut Off One Piece
2	16	76	50	0.88	11.93	2¼	108	70	0.666	16.71	3	108	50	0.250	11.93	8
2½	16	76	50	0.833	11.93	3	108	70	0.555	16.71	4½	108	50	0.250	11.93	10
3	16	76	50	0.750	11.93	4	108	70	0.500	16.71	6	108	50	0.250	11.93	12
3½	18	76	50	0.70	10.61	5	108	70	0.466	16.71	7½	108	50	0.225	10.61	15½
4	18	76	50	0.66	10.61	6	108	70	0.444	14.85	9	108	50	0.210	10.61	19
4½	18	76	50	0.642	10.61	7	108	70	0.409	14.85	11	108	50	0.195	10.61	23
5	18	76	50	0.588	10.61	8½	108	70	0.384	14.85	13	108	50	0.178	10.61	28
5½	22	86	50	0.55	8.68	10	108	70	0.366	14.85	15	108	50	0.166	8.68	33
6	22	86	50	0.50	8.68	12	120	70	0.333	12.15	18	120	50	0.153	8.68	39
6½	22	86	50	0.464	7.95	14	120	70	0.309	12.15	21	120	50	0.138	7.95	47
7	24	86	50	0.411	7.95	17	120	70	0.280	11.14	25	120	50	0.126	7.95	55
7½	24	86	50	0.357	7.95	21	120	70	0.250	11.14	30	120	50	0.116	7.95	64
8	24	86	50	0.397	7.95	26	120	70	0.228	11.14	35	120	50	0.108	7.95	74

TURNING AND BORING

THE accompanying table is a ready means of figuring machine time on turned, bored or faced work.

The ordinary method employed is to ascertain the number of feet in the circumference of the piece by multiplying the diameter in inches by 3.1416 and dividing by 12. The next step consists of dividing the length by the feed used, which gives the entire number of revolutions the piece must make.

CONSTANTS FOR CUTTING TIME, IN MINUTES

FEED IN INCHES	CUTTING SPEED						
Two Cuts at	15 Feet	18 Feet	20 Feet	25 Feet	30 Feet	35 Feet	40 Feet
1–64 1–32	1.676	1.396	1.257	1.005	0.8378	0.7181	0.6281
1–32 1–16	0.8378	0.6981	0.6283	0.5027	0.4189	0.3590	0.3141
1–16 1– 8	0.4189	0.3491	0.3142	0.2513	0.2094	0.1795	0.1570
1– 8 1– 4	0.2094	0.1745	0.1571	0.1257	0.1047	0.0898	0.0785
One Cut at							
1–64	1.117	0.9308	0.8378	0.6702	0.5585	0.4787	0.4189
1–32	0.5585	0.4654	0.4189	0.3351	0.2793	0.2394	0.2094
1–16	0.2792	0.2327	0.2094	0.1676	0.1396	0.1197	0.1047
1– 8	0.1396	0.1164	0.1047	0.0838	0.0698	0.0598	0.0524
1– 4	0.0698	0.0582	0.0524	0.0419	0.0349	0.0299	0.0262
Two Cuts at	45 Feet	50 Feet	60 Feet	70 Feet	80 Feet	90 Feet	100 Feet
1–64 1–32	0.5581	0.5027	0.4189	0.3590	0.3142	0.2793	0.2513
1–32 1–16	0.2793	0.2513	0.2094	0.1705	0.1571	0.1396	0.1257
1–16 1– 8	0.1396	0.1257	0.1047	0.0898	0.0785	0.0698	0.0628
1– 8 1– 4	0.0698	0.0683	0.0524	0.0449	0.0393	0.0349	0.0314
One Cut at							
1–64	0.3723	0.3351	0.2793	0.2394	0.2094	0.1852	0.1676
1–32	0.1862	0.1676	0.1396	0.1197	0.1047	0.0931	0.0838
1–16	0.0931	0.0838	0.0698	0.0598	0.0524	0.0465	0.0419
1– 8	0.0465	0.0419	0.0349	0.0299	0.0262	0.0233	0.0209
1– 4	0.0233	0.0209	0.0175	0.0150	0.0131	0.0116	0.0105

Having the circumference in feet and the number of revolutions, it is necessary to multiply them to find the entire number of feet traveled. Dividing this result by the speed of cut in feet per minute will give the actual cutting time in minutes.

The figuring is not complicated in any way, but it has the disadvantage of taking too much time. It can be resolved into the following formula:

$$\frac{Diameter \times 3.1416 \times length\ in\ inches}{12 \times speed \times feed\ in\ inches} = time\ in\ minutes.$$

The known factors in the case can be resolved into a constant which is directly dependent on the feed and speed; hence, a table covering a wide range of speeds and feeds is necessary for their proper use.

One part of the table gives constants for two cuts at $\frac{1}{64}$-inch and $\frac{1}{32}$-inch feed, up to $\frac{1}{8}$-inch and $\frac{1}{4}$-inch feed, at any speed from 15 feet to 100 feet per minute. The rest of the table gives constants for one cut at $\frac{1}{64}$-inch up to and including $\frac{1}{4}$-inch feed, also at any speed from 15 feet to 100 feet per minute.

A typical computation is as follows:

A piece 4 inches in diameter, 10 inches long, is turned with two cuts at $\frac{1}{16}$-inch and $\frac{1}{32}$-inch feed, each with a cutting speed of 20 feet per minute. Diameter $\times$ length in inches $\times$ constant = time in minutes. $4 \times 10 \times 0.6283 = 26$ minutes.

If, for the purpose of accuracy it is thought advisable, in connection with these two cuts, to run another cut over, the constant 0.6283 is added to a constant for the third feed used. If this feed is $\frac{1}{64}$-inch, then we have $0.6283 + 0.8378 = 1.4661$, the constant for three cuts, one of $\frac{1}{16}$-inch, one of $\frac{1}{32}$-inch, and one of $\frac{1}{64}$-inch feed.

TABLE HAS WIDE APPLICATION

There is hardly a combination of feeds and speeds that it is not possible to secure by inspection from the table. By interpolation an added number can be secured.

The table can be adapted, on account of its wide range, to the known individual performance of any lathe or boring mill in the shop. No slide rule or any special operations are necessary to secure the desired results, merely a knowledge of multiplication.

For flange facing it is possible to use the table with the same ease as for boring and turning by figuring on the main diameter.

ROTARY CUTTING SPEED

An easy method of calculating the cutting speed of a lathe tool or milling cutter is to divide the number of revolutions by 4 and multiply by the diameter in *inches*. This gives the cutting speed in *feet* per minute. Dividing 3.1416 by 12 gives .262 and .25 is very close after allowing for belt slip.

Let D = diam. of work, cutter or boring bar,

N = revolutions per minute.

C = cutting speed in feet per minute.

$$C = D \times \frac{N}{4}. \qquad N = \frac{4 \times C}{D}. \qquad D = \frac{4 \times C}{N}.$$

LATHE TOOL TESTS

In testing steels for lathe and similar tools it has become customary to use standard material, speeds, feeds and depth of cut. In some cases tools are run until they break down, in others they are passed if they stand up for a specified time. A 20-point carbon steel is often selected and cuts $\frac{1}{4}$ inch deep with $\frac{1}{16}$ to $\frac{1}{8}$ inch feed at cutting speeds of from 60 to 90 feet per minute.

The U. S. Navy Department specifies that a $\frac{7}{8}$-inch lathe tool shall stand up for 20 minutes with a $\frac{3}{16}$-inch cut and $\frac{1}{16}$-inch feed at 60 feet per minute without regrinding; the material must be at least 80,000-lb. tensile, and 50,000-lb. elastic limit with a 25 per cent. elongation in 2 inches. The steel is annealed before the test.

CUTTING LUBRICANTS

Cast iron is usually worked dry, but when hard cast-iron gears are to be cut, as with three cutters, the first cut through will work better with strong soda water. It makes an objectionable mess, but the work will be done faster and the cutters keep sharper longer than with the dry process of cutting.

Brass and babbitt are usually cut dry, but to hand-ream brass and babbitt is sometimes difficult if the reamer is a little dull. Kerosene and turpentine are used with good results. Cast iron can be hand-reamed easily with tallow and graphite, mixed, and the hole will be kept just the size of the reamer. Copper can be worked well with lard-oil and turpentine mixed.

In boring babbitt bushings and rod boxes in a lathe or boring mill, it is very difficult to work the material dry as the chips have a great tendency to roll around the tool and into a hard ball, tearing the metal and making a rough ragged hole. In this case kerosene and lard-oil mixed will work well.

Cheap oil is sometimes used as a lubricant for cutting, but soap water or soda water is better for iron and steel shafting and with a sharp tool and light finish cut the work will be smooth enough to polish without filing.

Rawhide is a very peculiar substance to work, and to drill it with a twist drill is a tedious job, as the flutes will clog and stick if run dry. A cake of soap held against the drill will prevent all trouble and sticking of drills. It is bad practice to use oil on rawhide as it injures the fiber and loosens the glue. Drills should be run at very high speed in rawhide to work well.

Turpentine is good in some cases where fitting is done, such as scraping lay-out plates, or face plates. Oil will form a coating so that marks cannot be seen plainly, but turpentine will prove beneficial on this kind of work if used freely. The marks can be seen plainly, and the work is a great deal easier to scrape than with an oil surface, as the oil glazes over the surface and makes it hard to start a tool.

GRINDING AND LAPPING

GRINDING WHEELS AND GRINDING

The Commercial Abrasives

EMERY, corundum, carborundum, and alundum are the ordinary commercial abrasive materials. They vary in hardness, though it does not follow that the hardest grit is the best for cutting purposes; the shape and form of fracture of the particles must also be taken into consideration. We may imagine a wheel made up from diamonds, the hardest substance in nature, and whose individual kernels were of spherical form; it is quite obvious that it would be of little service as a cutting agent; on the other hand, if these kernels were crystalline or conchoidal in form it would probably be the ideal grinding wheel.

Emery is a form of corundum found with a variable percentage of impurity; it is of a tough consistency and breaks with a conchoidal fracture.

Corundum is an oxide of aluminum of a somewhat variable purity according to the neighborhood in which it is mined; its fracture is conchoidal and generally crystalline.

Carborundum is a silicide of carbon and is a product of the electric furnace; it breaks with a sharp crystalline fracture.

Alundum is an artificial product, being a fused oxide of aluminum. It is of uniform quality with about 98 per cent. of purity. It breaks with a sharp, conchoidal crystalline fracture and has all the toughness of emery.

Grit and Bond

A GRINDING wheel is made up of the "grit" or cutting material, and the bond. The cutting efficiency of a wheel depends largely on the grit; the grade of hardness depends principally on the bonding material used. The efficiency in grinding a given metal is dependent largely upon the "temper," or resistance to fracture, and, as noted above, upon the character of fracture of the grit or cutting grains of the wheel.

The function of the bond is not only to hold the cutting particles of the wheel together and to give the wheel the proper factor of safety at the speed it is to be run, but it must also be possible to vary its tensile strength to fit the work it is called upon to do. We often hear the operator say that the wheel is too hard or too soft. He means that the bond retains the cutting teeth so long that they become dulled, and this wheel is inefficient; or, in the case of a soft wheel, the bond has not been strong enough to hold the cutting teeth and they are pulled out of the wheel before they have done the work expected.

The bond to be used for a given operation depends on the wheel
and work speeds, area of wheel in contact with the work, vibration in
wheel spindle or work, shape and weight of work, and many other
like variables.

Wheels are bonded by what are known as the vitrified, silicate,
elastic and rubber processes. No one bond makes a superior wheel
for all purposes; each one has its field.

The vitrified bond is made of fused clays, is unchanged by heat
or cold, and can be made in a greater range of hardness than any
other bond. It does not completely fill the voids between the grains,
and, therefore, a wheel bonded in this way having more clearance
than any other, is adaptable for all kinds of grinding except where
the wheel is not thick enough to withstand side pressure. This bond
has no elasticity.

The silicate bond is composed of clays fluxed by silicate of soda at
low temperatures. It is not as stable as the vitrified bond as regards
dampness, gives less clearance between grains, and has a range of
hardness below that of the vitrified in the harder grades. This bond
has no elasticity and will not make a safe wheel of extreme thinness.

The elastic bond is composed of shellac and other gums. It completely fills the voids of the wheel, has a limited range of grades, has
a high tensile strength and elasticity, and can be used for the making
of very thin wheels. The rubber or vulcanite bond has the general
characteristics of the elastic, but its grades of hardness cannot be
varied to the same extent and its uses are limited.

Grain and Grade

GRINDING wheels are made in various combinations of coarseness
and hardness to meet the variety of conditions under which they
are used. The cutting material is crushed and graded from coarse
to fine in many sizes designated by number. Thus the sizes of grain
used in the Norton wheels are numbered 10, 12, 14, 16, 20, 24, 30,
36, 46, 50, 60, 70, 80, 90, 100, 120, 150, 180, 200. Finer grades
known as flour are also used, sometimes these being designated as
F, FF, FFF, etc. By No. 20 grain is meant a size that will pass
through a grading sieve having 20 meshes to the linear inch.

The term "grade" refers to the degree of hardness of the wheel or
the resistance of the cutting particles under grinding pressure. A
wheel from which the cutting particles are easily broken, causing it
to wear rapidly, is called soft, while one which retains its particles
longer is called hard.

Minimum Thickness of Wheels

Tables 1, 2, and 3 by the Norton Company, show minimum thickness of wheels made by the different processes. A wheel of fine grit
can be made thinner than a wheel of coarse grit, and have the same
factor of safety. The minimum thickness depends upon both the
diameter and the coarseness of the grit used.

For example, a 24-inch vitrified wheel of No. 10 or No. 12 grain
should not be made thinner than 2 inches, while if a grain No. 36 or
finer is used it is considered a safe wheel at 1 inch thick.

TABLE 1. — MINIMUM THICKNESS OF ELASTIC WHEELS

Diameter in Inches	Grain				
	14 and 16	20 and 24	30 and 36	46 and 60	70 and finer
	Minimum Thickness of Wheels in Inches				
28 to 30	3/4	3/4	3/4	3/4	3/4
24 to 26	5/8	5/8	1/2	1/2	1/2
20 to 22	1/2	1/2	3/8	3/8	3/8
16 to 18	3/8	3/8	1/4	1/4	1/4
14 to 15	1/4	1/4	1/16	1/16	1/16
10 to 12	3/16	3/16	1/8	1/8	1/8
7 to 9	3/16	1/8	1/8	1/16	1/16
5 to 6	3/16	1/8	1/16	1/16	1/32
3 to 4	3/16	1/8	1/16	1/32	1/32
1 to 2	3/16	1/8	1/16	1/32	1/64

TABLE 2. — MINIMUM THICKNESS OF VITRIFIED WHEELS

Diameter in Inches	Grain							
	10 and 12	14 and 16	20 and 24	30	36	46	50 to 120	150 and finer
	Minimum Thickness of Wheel in Inches							
32 to 36	2½	2½	2	2	2	2	2	2
24 to 30	2	2	1½	1¼	1	1	1	1
20 to 22	1½	1½	1¼	1¼	1	3/4	3/4	3/4
16 to 18	1½	1½	1	1	3/4	3/4	1/2	1/2
14 to 15	1¼	1¼	3/4	3/4	1/2	1/2	3/8	3/8
10 to 12	1¼	1¼	5/8	5/8	1/2	3/8	3/8	1/4
7 to 9	1	1	3/8	3/8	5/16	1/4	1/4	3/16
5 to 6	1	1	3/8	3/8	1/4	1/4	1/4	3/16
3 to 4		1	3/4	3/8	1/4	3/16	1/8	1/8
1 to 2			3/4		1/4	1/8	1/8	1/8
Smaller than 1 In.							1/16	1/16

TABLE 3.—MINIMUM THICKNESS OF SILICATE WHEELS

	Grain											
	10, 12, 14, and 16		20 and 24		30		36		40 and 50		60 to 120	150 and finer
	Wire Web											
	With	Without	With	Without	With	Without	With	Without	With	Without	Without	
Diameter in Inches	Minimum Thickness of Wheel in Inches											
44 to 48	3		3	2	3	2	3	2	3	2	2	2
38 to 42	$2\frac{1}{2}$		$2\frac{1}{2}$	2	$2\frac{1}{2}$	2	$2\frac{1}{2}$	2	$2\frac{1}{2}$	2	2	2
32 to 36	$2\frac{1}{2}$		$2\frac{1}{2}$	2	$2\frac{1}{2}$	$1\frac{1}{2}$	$2\frac{1}{2}$	$1\frac{1}{2}$	$2\frac{1}{2}$	$1\frac{1}{2}$	$1\frac{1}{2}$	$1\frac{1}{2}$
28 to 30	2		2	2	2	2	2	1	2	1	1	1
24 to 26	2		$1\frac{1}{2}$	$1\frac{1}{2}$	2	1	2	1	2	1	1	1
20 to 22	$1\frac{3}{4}$		$1\frac{1}{2}$	$1\frac{1}{2}$	$1\frac{1}{4}$	1	$1\frac{1}{4}$	1	$1\frac{1}{4}$	1	1	1
16 to 18	$1\frac{1}{2}$		1	1	1	$\frac{3}{4}$	1	$\frac{3}{4}$	1	$\frac{3}{4}$	$\frac{3}{4}$	$\frac{3}{4}$
14 to 15	$1\frac{1}{2}$		1	1	1	$\frac{3}{4}$	1	$\frac{3}{4}$	1	$\frac{3}{4}$	$\frac{3}{4}$	$\frac{3}{4}$
10 to 12	$1\frac{1}{2}$		$\frac{3}{4}$	$\frac{3}{4}$	$\frac{3}{4}$	$\frac{1}{2}$	$\frac{3}{4}$	$\frac{1}{2}$	$\frac{3}{4}$	$\frac{3}{8}$	$\frac{3}{8}$	$\frac{3}{8}$
7 to 9			$\frac{3}{4}$	$\frac{3}{4}$	$\frac{3}{4}$	$\frac{1}{2}$	$\frac{3}{4}$	$\frac{1}{2}$	$\frac{3}{4}$	$\frac{3}{8}$	$\frac{3}{8}$	$\frac{3}{8}$
5 to 6						$\frac{1}{2}$		$\frac{1}{4}$		$\frac{1}{4}$	$\frac{1}{4}$	$\frac{1}{4}$
3 to 4						$\frac{1}{2}$		$\frac{1}{4}$		$\frac{1}{4}$	$\frac{1}{4}$	$\frac{1}{8}$
1 to 2						$\frac{1}{2}$		$\frac{1}{4}$		$\frac{3}{16}$	$\frac{1}{8}$	$\frac{1}{8}$

Grading of Wheels

OF the many firms engaged in the manufacture of grinding wheels there are probably no two which have a similar method of grading or designating the hardness of their wheeeels. The Norton Company, which is probably the oldest in the field, uses the letter method, which may be said to be the simplest. That is, they take *M* for their medium-hard wheel and the letters before M denote in regular alphabetical progression the progressively softer wheels. Moreover they use a + mark for denoting wheels which vary in temper from the standards. Thus a wheel may be harder than the standard K, and still be not so hard as the standard L; in this case it is known as K +. The Carborundum Company adopts a somewhat similar method of grading, the difference being that although M denotes its medium-hard wheel the letters before M denote the progressively harder grades. Various other American companies use the letter method of grading to some extent, but all have individual ideas as to what degree of hardness should constitute an M or medium-grade wheel. Then there are firms both in America and on the continent of Europe which discard the letter method of grading or else use it in conjunction with numbers or fractions of numbers such as 2H, $1\frac{1}{2}$M and so on.

The selection of suitable wheels for machine grinding may be said to be governed by the following points, namely, the texture of the material to be ground, the arc of wheel contact with work and the quality of finish required. The first and last of these points can for convenience' sake be taken in conjunction. The quality of surface finish is dependent on the condition of the wheel face and depth of cut rather than on the fineness of the grit in the wheel. A wheel of so fine a grit as 100 will give an indifferent finish if it is not turned true and smooth.

It may be assumed that for all general purposes the aim in view is to procure a wheel which will fulfil two conditions, that is, that it shall first remove stock rapidly and at the same time give a decent finish. Wheels made from a combination of grit of different sizes are the best for this purpose, as may be seen from the following explanation. Coarse wheels of an even number of grit will remove stock faster than will fine wheels of an even number, because their depth of cut or penetration is greater. They, however, fail in giving a high surface finish except in grinding very hard material, because they are not compact enough.

The Combination Grit Wheel

WITH the combination wheel the conditions are different and it seems better at removing stock than does the coarse, even grit wheel. It may be safe to assume from this that something of a *grindstone action* takes place, that is, that the finer particles of grit become detached from the bond and both roll and cut in their imprisoned condition between the larger particles. For finishing purposes this wheel has all the compactness and smooth face of a wheel which was made solely from its finest number of grit; and for roughing, it enables a depth of cut to be got which is within the capacity of its largest kernels.

With regard to the texture or hardness of material ground it may be taken as a general rule that the harder the material is, the softer the bond of wheel should be, and that cast iron and hardened steel bear some relation to each other as far as grinding wheels are concerned, for the same wheel is usually suitable for both materials.

Too large an assortment of wheels is likely to lead to confusion and we may take the Norton plain cylindrical grinding machine as being a case in point of a limited assortment of wheels; at the same time it will be a starting point to illustrate choice of wheels under various grinding conditions. In this machine four different grade wheels, all of 24 combination grit, are found sufficient for all classes of material that it is ordinarily required to grind. These include high- and low-carbon steels, cast iron, chilled iron, and bronze or composition metals. These wheels are graded J, K, L, and M.

Hard Wheels

ONE of the greatest advantages accruing from grinding is that it ignores the non-homogeneity of material and that it machines work with the lightest known method of tool pressure, thus avoiding all deflections and distortions of material which are a natural result of

the more severe machining processes. Yet these objects are too
often defeated by the desire for hard and long-lived wheels. A wheel
that is too hard or whose bond will not crumble sufficiently under
the pressure of cut will displace the work and give rise to many
unforeseen troubles. It is also a prolific cause of vibration which
is antagonistic to good and accurate work. The advantage claimed
for it, that it gives a better surface finish, is a deceptive one, for it
mostly obtains this finish at the expense of accuracy. Quality of
finish, that is, accurate finish, is merely a question of arranging of
work speed, condition of wheel face and depth of cut. In the machine mentioned the suitability of wheels to materials and conditions
is found to be as follows, the wheels being in each case of a combination of alundum grit:

For hard chilled iron and large diameters of cast iron and
    hardened steel .... 24 J
For medium chilled iron and medium diameters of cast iron
    and hardened steel and bronze..................... 24 K
For all grades of steel which are not hardened and for bronze 24 L
For very low carbon machine steels .... 24 M

The table given may, speaking generally, be what would be chosen
in the way of wheels for the materials given, and in actual practice
they soon give evidence as to whether they are suitable. It may be
gathered from the table that diameter of work is a factor in the choice
of a wheel. This refers to area of wheel contact and is governed
by what is shown in the table when broad differences of diameter
occur; for instance, it might be necessary to use the K wheel for a
large diameter of high carbon steel if the L wheel was evidently too
hard.

Speed and Efficient Cutting

The efficient cutting of a wheel depends very much on the speed
of the work, and an absence of knowledge in this respect may often
lead to a suitable wheel's rejection. Revolving the wheel at the
speed recommended by the maker is the first necessity, and if it is
found unsuitable after experimenting with various speeds it should
be changed for a softer or harder one as the conditions indicate.
Starting from the point that a wheel is desired that shall remove
the maximum amount of stock with the minimum amount of wear
on the wheel, the indications and method of procedure may be as
follows; only it must be understood that this refers to cases where
an ample supply of water is being delivered at the *grinding point.*

If, after trying all reasonable work speeds, a wheel should burn the
work, or refuse to cut without excessive pressure, or persistently
glaze the surface of the work, it is too hard for that particular work
and material and may be safely rejected. If, after trying all reasonably reduced work speeds, a wheel should lose its size quickly and
show all signs of rapid wear, it is too soft for that particular work and
material and may be rejected. These indications refer to all ordinary cases and it may be gathered that the most economical wheel
is that which acts in such a manner as to be a medium between the
two cases. There is still another point to bear in mind with regard
to the size of the grit in the wheel, but which refers more especially

to very hard materials such as chilled iron. Either a coarse or combination wheel may go on cutting efficiently in roughing cuts because pressure is exerted, but may begin to glaze when this pressure is much relieved as in finishing cuts. A careful microscopic scrutiny of a wheel that displays this tendency would seem to lead to the following assumption:

When a Wheel is Sharp

THE wheel face when newly trued with the diamond tool, which is necessary to obtain an accurate finish, shows a promiscuous arrangement of particles, some of which present points and others present a broader face with a rough and granular surface. When the wheel is presented to the hard surface of the work the high points of this granular face and the sharp contour of the kernels will go on cutting until they are dulled and worn down, after which their face

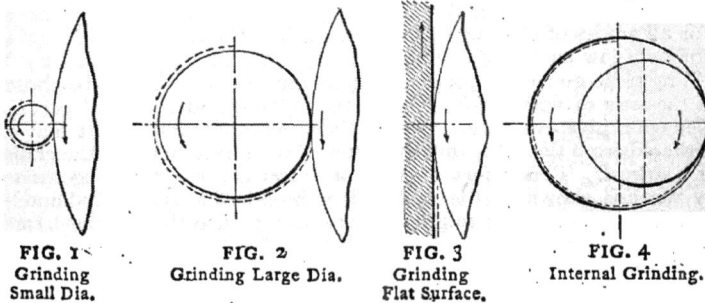

FIG. 1
Grinding
Small Dia.

FIG. 2
Grinding Large Dia.

FIG. 3
Grinding
Flat Surface.

FIG. 4
Internal Grinding.

Contact of Wheel

area is too great to enter the surface without undue pressure. When the wheel has reached this condition the microscope shows these broader-faced kernels polished to a metallic luster, which bears out the explanation tendered and also makes the remedy quite apparent. This is to use a wheel of very fine grit for finishing purposes in these cases or else keep the coarser wheel in condition by repeated dressings with the diamond tool.

Wheel Contact

REFERENCE to Figs. 1 to 4 will show what actual practice requires in the choice of a wheel so far as the question of wheel contact is concerned. A wheel is shown in contact with four different varieties of work, all of which we will suppose to be of the same material, the depth of cut, much exaggerated, being the same in each case. In the first case it is a shaft of small diameter, and the wheel contact being the smallest the harder grade of wheel would be suitable, comparatively speaking. Assuming that this wheel was found to be suitable it would probably require a softer wheel for the next case, which is a shaft of larger diameter, and the wheel contact proportionately greater. To continue the comparison still further, the third case shows the wheel engaged in grinding a flat surface, and the fourth is a wheel grinding internally. In each case practice demands that the wheel shall be progressively softer in bond or grade and is some proof of a consistency in the action of grinding wheels.

The Contact Area of a Wheel

THE most probable explanation of this may be that as the contact area increases more work is required from each individual kernel of grit and it the sooner becomes dulled; this requires that the bond must be more friable both to allow it to escape easily and to minimize the pressure required to make the wheel cut as the cutting area becomes greater. Following on this reasoning we are able to choose a list of wheels which would be suitable for almost all purposes, and which would be as follows if of Norton grade:

For plain cylindrical grinding
J K L M
For grinding plane surfaces
H I J K
For internal grinding
F H I J

This collection of wheels would be suitable for almost any type of grinding machines, though when the wheels are exceptionally narrow a grade or one-half grade higher might be possible; it would, of course, be a matter for a little trial and experiment. The wheels for external cylindrical work may preferably be combination wheels, but for plane surface and internal work they are better made of single grit, about 36 or 46. The great contact area of wheel in these two classes of work is liable to generate much heat so that an open and porous wheel is preferable.

Wheel Pressure and Wear

As the wheel is a disk built up from a numerous assortment of minute cutting tools which are held in position by a more or less friable bond, in using it we must bring it to bear on the work with a pressure that shall not be so great as to tear these minute tools from their setting until their cutting efficiency is exhausted, for if we do so we are wasting the wheel. To gage the exact amount of the pressure required is a matter of judgment and experience, though where automatic feeds are provided on a machine the right amount of pressure or feed is soon determined. It will also be readily understood that a regular automatic feed is more reliable for the purpose than a possibly erratic hand one. The automatic feed may be set to give a certain depth of cut at each pass of the wheel, and its amount of wear noted; if this wear be found excessive the depth of cut may be reduced. It must not be here forgotten that work speed also enters into this consideration and that a high work speed will tend to wear the wheel excessively; inversely a reduced work speed will reduce the amount of wear. Having these points in mind the right combination of depth of cut and work speed is soon arrived at, and an approximate judgment attained for the future.

Grinding Allowances

THE amount of stock left for removal by the grinding wheel and the method of preparing the work have both much bearing on the economic use of grinding wheels, and heavy and unnoticed losses often occur through want of a few precautionary measures. The necessary amount of stock to leave on a piece of work as a grinding allowance depends firstly on the type of machine employed, the class of labor engaged in preparing it, and whether it has to be hardened or otherwise.

In powerful machines, which will remove stock rapidly, the grinding allowance may be anything up to $\frac{1}{32}$ inch. There are many cases of an especial character when the grinding allowance stated may be exceeded to advantage so long as discretion is used. Straight shafts may often be ground direct from the black bar of raw material $\frac{1}{16}$ inch above finished size, or when shafts of this character must have large reduction on the ends they can be roughly reduced in the turret lathe while in their black state and finished outright more economically in the grinding machine. Very hard qualities of steels or chilled rolls are other cases where it is often more economical to use the grinding machine without any previous machining process, and though there may be sometimes an alarming waste of abrasive material its cost is as nothing compared with other savings that are made.

Grinding allowances for hardened work are usually larger than for soft work, to allow for possible distortion; so that individual experience alone can determine the amount to be left. It is sufficient to say that the allowances on case-hardened or carbonized work should not be excessive; otherwise the hardened surface may be ground away.

Grinding Hardened Work

As far as the actual grinding of hardened work goes, it is indispensable that the whole portion of a piece that is to be ground should be roughed over previous to the final finishing; if it is at all possible to allow some little time to elapse between the two operations so much the better, more especially if it has bent in hardening and been afterward straightened; this will allow of the development of any strain that may be present. Both for special and standard work in a factory a table of grinding allowances can be compiled as a result of experience and posted in a conspicuous position. If this be done and trouble taken to see that it is adhered to, it will save much trouble and be a means of avoiding much unnecessary expense.

It is necessary to slightly undercut the corners of shoulders so as to preserve the corner of the grinder's wheel intact. A piece of work should never be prepared in such a manner as to form a radius on the corner of the wheel, for to get the wheel face flat again means much waste of wheel and wear of diamond. Where fillets or radii are necessary they are better got out with a tool, for even if they are to be ground they must be turned good to allow the wheel to conform to their shape. The only excusable reason for grinding a round corner is when the work is hardened or in some special case where the expense incurred is warranted.

GRINDING ALLOWANCES FOR VARIOUS LENGTHS AND DIAMETERS

Table 4 shows the practice of the Landis Tool Company, in reference to grinding allowances. This table covers work up to 12 inches diameter, and lengths to 48 inches.

TABLE 4. — ALLOWANCES FOR GRINDING

(LANDIS TOOL CO.)

length / Diam.	3″	6″	9″	12″	15″	18″	24″	30″	36″	42″	48″
½	.010	.010	.010	.010	.015	.015	.015	.020	.020	.020	.020
¾	.010	.010	.010	.010	.015	015	.015	.020	.020	.020	.020
1	.010	.010	.010	.015	.015	.015	.015	.020	.020	.020	.020
1¼	.010	.010	.015	.015	.015	.015	.015	.020	.020	.020	.020
1½	.010	.015	.015	.015	.015	.015	.020	.020	.020	.020	.020
2	.015	.015	.015	.015	.015	.020	.020	.020	.020	.020	.025
2¼	.015	.015	.015	.015	.020	.020	.020	.020	.020	.025	.025
2½	.015	.015	.015	.020	.020	.020	.020	.020	.025	.025	.025
3	.015	.015	.020	.020	.020	.020	.020	.025	.025	.025	.025
3½	.015	.020	.020	.020	.020	.020	.025	.025	.025	.025	.025
4	.020	.020	.020	.020	.020	.025	.025	.025	.025	.025	.030
4½	.020	.020	.020	.020	.025	.025	.025	.025	.025	.030	.030
5	.020	.020	.020	.025	.025	.025	.025	.025	.030	.030	.030
6	.020	.020	.025	.025	.025	.025	.025	.030	.030	.030	.030
7	.020	.025	.025	.025	.025	.025	.030	.030	.030	.030	.030
8	.025	.025	.025	.025	.025	.030	.030	.030	.030	.030	.030
9	.025	.025	.025	.025	.030	.030	.030	.030	.030	.030	.030
10	.025	.025	.025	.030	.030	.030	.030	.030	.030	.030	.030
11	.025	.025	.030	.030	.030	.030	.030	.030	.030	.030	.030
12	.030	.030	.030	.030	.030	.030	.030	.030	.030	.030	.030

OTHER GRINDING ALLOWANCES

TABLE 5 gives the allowances of the Brown & Sharpe Mfg. Co. in rough turning work for the grinding department. Limit gages of the form shown are used, the dimensions in the table covering work up to 2 inches diameter.

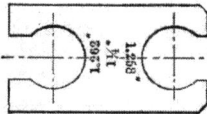

TABLE 5.— LIMIT GAGE SIZES FOR LATHE WORK WHICH IS TO BE FINISHED BY GRINDING

(BROWN & SHARPE MFG. CO.)

Size	Not go on	Go on	Size	Not go on	Go on	Size	Not go on	Go on
	Inches			Inches			Inches	
3/8	0.383	0.387	15/16	0.9455	0.9495	1 1/2	1.508	1.512
7/16	0.4455	0.4495	1	1.008	1.012	1 9/16	1.5705	1.5745
1/2	0.508	0.512	1 1/16	1.0705	1.0745	1 5/8	1.633	1.637
9/16	0.5705	0.5745	1 1/8	1.133	1.137	1 11/16	1.6955	1.6995
5/8	0.633	0.637	1 3/16	1.1955	1.1995	1 3/4	1.758	1.762
11/16	0.6955	0.6995	1 1/4	1.258	1.262	1 13/16	1.8205	1.8245
3/4	0.758	0.762	1 5/16	1.3205	1.3245	1 7/8	1.883	1.8875
13/16	0.8205	0.8245	1 3/8	1.383	1.387	1 15/16	1.9455	1.949
7/8	0.883	0.887	1 7/16	1.4455	1.4495	2	2.008	2.012

Use of Water

WATER should be applied at the right spot. This spot must be right at the *grinding point*, whether it be internal, external, or plane-surface work, and must be delivered with sufficient force to keep the wheel face clean. If this is not done there is a kind of mud accumulated at the grinding point, which causes glazing. Water is, or should be, used in grinding process not as a means of quenching heat but rather to prevent its creation and radiation, and so the actual grinding point is the best place to apply it.

It is a necessary means of keeping the work at an equable temperature so as to obviate distortion and to make the matter of taking dimensions an actuality rather than a guessing matter. This applies equally to all kinds of grinding.

The Use of Diamonds

HERE it is perhaps well to give the question of diamonds some little consideration as they are sometimes a very expensive item. A diamond is a very essential part of a grinding machine's equipment, for in its absence a good and highly finished grade of work is an impossibility. It is perhaps unnecessary to state that they should be the hardest rough stones procurable, and that the larger they are the cheaper they are in the end. With regard to their size: This is a known proportionate element in their price per carat, but a large stone allows of a more secure hold in its setting and so the danger of losing it is reduced. As a further precaution against this danger the diamond tool should always be held by mechanical means when using it except in cases which are unavoidable; this may be in cases where profile shapes have to be turned on the wheel face. An attempt to turn by hand a perfectly flat face on a wheel, which is necessary for finishing, must of a necessity end in failure.

As a means of preservation of the diamond a full stream of water should be run on it when in use and many light chips are preferable to a few heavy ones. The main thing is to watch that it does not get unduly heated, for this is disastrous to it. Where large quantities of material have to be removed from a wheel the ordinary wheel dresser may be employed to reduce the bulk of the stock, and the diamond only used for finishing to shape.

Setting the Diamonds

DIAMONDS may be obtained ready fixed in suitable holders or the rough stones may be bought and set by any competent toolmaker. The illustrations show various methods by which they may be held securely and require but little explanation. First, Fig. 5 is the method most commonly used, the diamond being either peened or brazed in position. One disadvantage of this method is that the diamond is apt to break with a chance blow of the peening chisel, or the heat from brazing will sometimes cause fractures; neither is it so easily reset when its point becomes dulled as are the other methods shown. Fig. 6 requires no explanation except that it is advisable to pack the diamond with shredded asbestos fiber to act as a cushion; this method allows of quick resetting. Fig. 7 consists

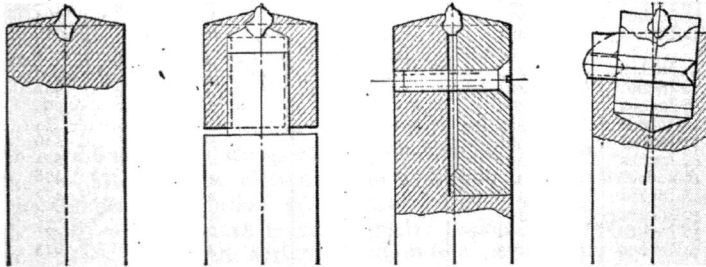

FIG. 5   FIG. 6   FIG. 7   FIG. 8

Methods of Setting Diamonds

of a small steel cap tapped out to fit the stock as shown. Enough shredded asbestos fiber is inserted between the diamond and stock to hold it firmly in position. This method also allows of quick and safe resetting. The fourth method, Fig. 8, is covered by patent rights and its advantage can be seen at a glance; as the diamond wears, the small peg containing it can be revolved in the stock to present a new cutting edge and be so clamped in position.

Speed Tables, Rules for Surface Speeds, etc.

THE table below gives the number of revolutions per minute at which grinding wheels of diameters ranging from 1 to 60 inches must be operated to secure peripheral velocities of 4000, 5000, 5500 and 6000 feet per minute. Ordinarily a speed of 5000 feet per minute is employed, though sometimes the speed is somewhat lower or higher for certain cases.

GRINDING WHEEL SPEEDS

Diameter Wheel	Rev. per Minute for Surface Speed of 4000 ft.	Rev. per Minute for Surface Speed of 5000 ft.	Rev. per Minute for Surface Speed of 5500 ft.	Rev. per Minute for Surface Speed of 6000 ft.
1 Inch	15,279	19,099	21,000	22,918
2 Inches	7,639	9,549	10,500	11,459
3 Inches	5,093	6,366	7,350	7,639
4 Inches	3,820	4,775	5,250	5,730
5 Inches	3,056	3,820	4,200	4,584
6 Inches	2,546	3,183	3,500	3,820
7 Inches	2,183	2,728	3,000	3,274
8 Inches	1,910	2,387	2,600	2,865
10 Inches	1,528	1,910	2,100	2,292
12 Inches	1,273	1,592	1,750	1,910
14 Inches	1,091	1,364	1,500	1,637
16 Inches	955	1,194	1,300	1,432
18 Inches	849	1,061	1,150	1,273
20 Inches	764	955	1,050	1,146
22 Inches	694	868	950	1,042
24 Inches	637	976	875	955
26 Inches	586	733	800	879
28 Inches	546	683	750	819
30 Inches	509	637	700	764
32 Inches	477	596	650	716
34 Inches	449	561	620	674
36 Inches	424	531	580	637
38 Inches	402	503	550	603
40 Inches	382	478	525	573
42 Inches	364	455	500	546
44 Inches	347	434	475	521
46 Inches	332	415	455	498
48 Inches	318	397	440	477
50 Inches	306	383	420	459
52 Inches	294	369	405	441
54 Inches	283	354	390	425
56 Inches	273	341	375	410
58 Inches	264	330	360	396
60 Inches	255	319	350	383

The exact speed at which any specified wheel should be run depends upon several conditions, such as the type of machine, character of work and wheel, quality of finish desired and various other factors referred to at other places in this book. Wheels are ordinarily run in practice from about 4000 to 6000 feet per minute, though in some cases a speed as high as 7500 feet has been employed. An average speed recommended by most wheel makers is 5000 feet. To allow an ample margin of safety it is recommended that wheel speeds should not exceed 6000 feet per minute.

The table of circumferences below will be of service in connection with the finding of surface speeds and spindle revolutions per minute.

CIRCUMFERENCES OF GRINDING WHEELS

Diameter of Wheel in Inches	Circumference of Wheel in Feet	Diameter of Wheel in Inches	Circumference of Wheel in Feet	Diameter of Wheel in Inches	Circumference of Wheel in Feet
1	.262	25	6.546	49	12.838
2	.524	26	6.807	50	13.090
3	.785	27	7.069	51	13.352
4	1.047	28	7.330	52	13.613
5	1.309	29	7.592	53	13.875
6	1.571	30	7.854	54	14.137
7	1.833	31	8.116	55	14.499
8	2.094	32	8.377	56	14.661
9	2.356	33	8.639	57	14.923
10	2.618	34	8.901	58	15.184
11	2.880	35	9.163	59	15.446
12	3.142	36	9.425	60	15.708
13	3.403	37	9.687	61	15.970
14	3.665	38	9.948	62	16.232
15	3.927	39	10.210	63	16.493
16	4.189	40	10.472	64	16.755
17	4.451	41	10.734	65	17.017
18	4.712	42	10.996	66	17.279
19	4.974	43	11.257	67	17.541
20	5.236	44	11.519	68	17.802
21	5.498	45	11.781	69	18.064
22	5.760	46	12.043	70	18.326
23	6.021	47	12.305	71	18.588
24	6.283	48	12.566	72	18.850

Thus, to find the surface speed of a wheel in feet per minute:

Rule. — Multiply the circumference as obtained from the table, by the number of revolutions per minute.

Example. — A wheel 18 inches diameter makes 1060 revolutions per minute. What is the surface speed, in feet, per minute?

$$4.712 \times 1060 = 5000 \text{ feet surface speed.}$$

When the surface speed and wheel diameter are given, to find the number of revolutions of the wheel spindle:

Rule. — Divide the surface speed in feet per minute by the circumference.

Example. — A wheel 24 inches diameter is to be run at 6000 feet surface speed per minute. How many revolutions should the wheel make?

$6000 \div 6.283 = 962$, number of revolutions per minute the wheel should make.

GRADING ABRASIVE WHEELS

THE Norton Company uses 26 grade marks, the Carborundum Company 19, while the Safety Emery Wheel Company uses 40. The following table is a comparison between the grade designations of the Norton Company and the Carborundum Company. Intermediate letters between the grade designations indicate relative degrees of hardness between them; the Norton Company manufacturing four degrees of each designation, while the Carborundum Company manufactures three.

Norton Co.	Grade Designation	Carborundum Co.
A.........................	Extremely or Very Soft	 V
B...................		.... U
C.............		.... T
D.........		
E.....	Soft	.... S
F........		.... R
G.............		.... Q
H..................		
I......................	Medium Soft	.... P
J...............		.... O
K.............		
L..........		.... N
M ...	Medium	.... M
N		 L
O		
P		.... K
Q	Medium Hard	.... J
R		 I
S		.... H
T		
U	Hard	.... G
V.........		.... F
W		.... E
X		
Y	Extremely or Very Hard	.... D
Z		

The Safety Emery Wheel Company's grade list is an arbitrary one with the following designations:

C. Extra Soft   H. Very Soft
A. Soft   M. Medium Soft

P. Medium   I. Medium Hard
O. Hard   N. Very Hard
E. Extra Hard   D. Special Extra Hard

Intermediate figures between those designated as soft, medium soft, etc., indicate so many degrees harder or softer, *e.g.*, A¼ is one degree harder than soft. A¾ is three degrees harder than soft or one degree softer than medium soft.

NUMBERS AND GRADES OF ABRASIVE WHEELS

In the following table for the selection of grades will be found a comparison of the grading used by the Norton Company, and that of the Carborundum Company:

Class of Work	Norton Co.		Carborundum Co.	
	Number Usually Furnished	Grade Usually Furnished	Number Usually Furnished	Grade Usually Furnished
Large Cast Iron and Steel Castings	16 to 20	Q to R	16 to 24	G to H
Small Cast Iron and Steel Castings	20 to 30	P to Q	20 to 30	G to H
Large Malleable Iron Castings ..	16 to 20	Q to R	16 to 24	G to H
Small Malleable Iron Castings ..	20 to 30	P to Q	20 to 30	H to I
Chilled Iron Castings	16 to 20	Q to R	16 to 24	H
Wrought Iron	16 to 30	P to Q	16 to 24	F to H
Brass Castings...............	16 to 30	O to P	20 to 36	H to I
Bronze Castings	16 to 30	P to Q	20 to 30	I
Rough Work in General........	16 to 30	P to Q	20 to 30	H
General Machine Shop Use	30 to 46	O to P	24 to 36	G to J
Lathe and Planer Tools	30 to 46	N to O	30 to 36	I to J
Small Tools	36 to 100	N to P	50 to 80	I to J
Wood-working Tools	36 to 60	M to N	40 to 60	L to M
Twist Drills (Hand Grinding)...	36 to 60	M to N	60	I to J
Twist Drills (Special Machines).	46 to 60	K to M	50	L to O
Reamers, Taps, Milling Cutters, etc. (Hand Grind)...........	46 to 100	N to P	50 to 80	K to N
Reamers, Taps, Milling Cutters, etc. (Spec. Mach.)...........	46 to 60	H to K	50 to 60	L to M
Edging and Jointing Agricultural Implements	16 to 30	Q to R	141 to 24	G to I
Grinding Plow Points..........	16 to 30	P to Q	20 to 24	H
Surfacing Plow Bodies	20 to 30	N to O	16 to 20	G
Stove Mounting...............	20 to 36	P to Q	24 to 30	G
Finishing Edges of Stoves	30 to 46	O to P	24 to 30	G
Drop Forgings	20 to 30	P to Q	24 to 36	G to I
Gumming and Sharpening Saws.	36 to 60	M to N	403–603	J to L
Planing Mill and Paper Cutting Knives	30 to 46	J to K	202—60 to 80	M to R
Car Wheel Grinding..........	20 to 30	O to P	16 to 24	H

THE SHAPES OF WHEELS

ALTHOUGH grinding wheels are manufactured in a great variety of shapes and sizes, there are a few general forms into which they may be grouped. Practically all of the hundreds of commonly used shapes made for the various types of grinding machines and for the different kinds of work come under some one of these classifications, the most common of which may be designated as "disk," "cup," "cylin-.

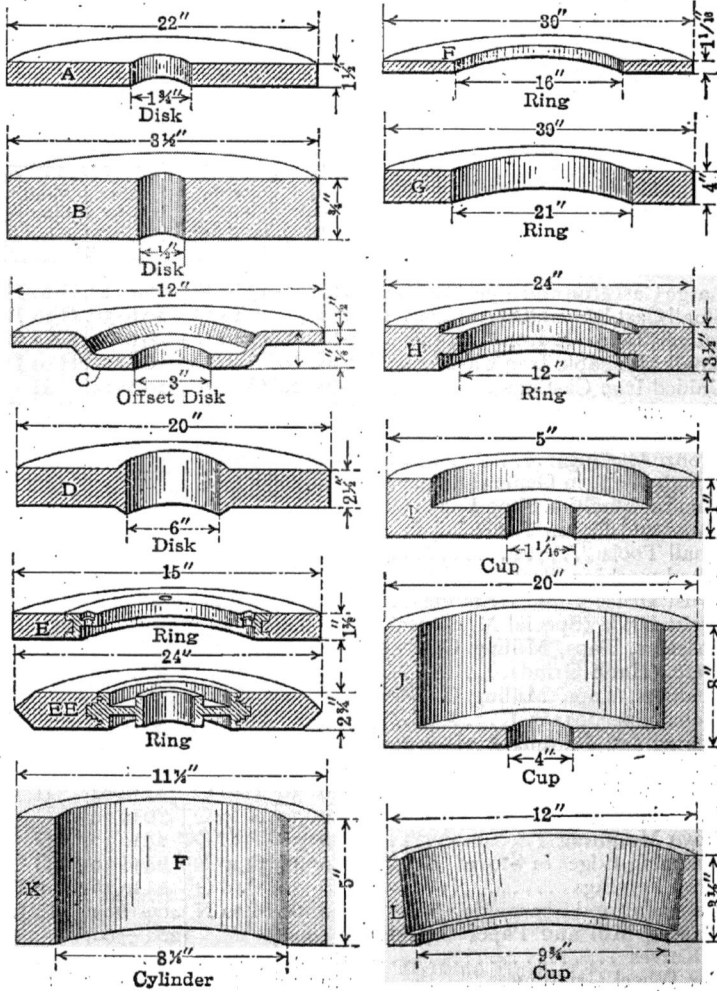

FIG. 9. — Shapes of Wheels

der" and "saucer" wheels. These shapes and some of their modifications are included in the groups of wheels illustrated in Figs. 9-10. These wheels are in most cases made in numerous widths and diameters, and the dimensions given in any such instances merely

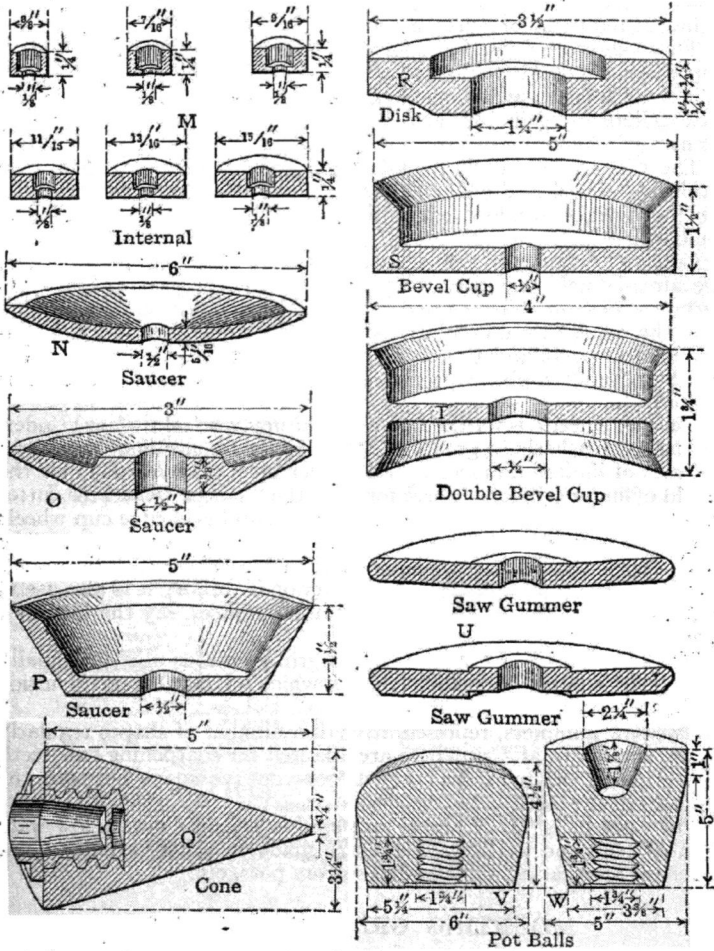

FIG. 10 — Shapes of Wheels

show the proportions of one size of wheel selected as typical from the comprehensive lists of wheel manufacturers' products.

Of the wheels shown, *A* and *B* are plain disks; *C* is an offset disk used on cylindrical grinders for grinding close up to a gear, collar, or piston head of large radius; *D* is a disk wheel for different makes of tool and roll grinders, E, EE, F, G and H are "ring" wheels which are modifications of the disk type. The two wheels E and EE are made on large iron centers and are for use on the Sellers tool grinders. The other ring wheels referred to are adapted for mounting on large iron centers, and all such wheels are for service on machines where only a limited reduction of wheel diameter is permissible.

The shallow cup wheel I is for drill grinders and the larger, deeper cup wheel J is of a type used extensively on knife-grinding machinery. Wheels of this shape and of suitable dimensions, are also used on roll and cylindrical grinders, and in the smaller sizes on cutters and reamer grinders.

The wheel K is a plain cylinder for grinding on the end the same as the cup wheels. Such cylinders are used in various proportions on vertical surface grinders, edge grinders, etc. They are held in ring chucks.

Cup and cylinder wheels are coming more and more into use and are already made in a great variety of diameters and widths. On certain classes of grinding operations they have marked advantages over the regular form of wheel as the same diameter is always maintained, thus avoiding the necessity of a change in speed, and the grinding is accomplished on a flat surface instead of one that is curved.

The cup wheel L is for the Pratt & Whitney vertical surface grinder.

The small wheels in group M are for internal grinding operations in holes of limited diameter. The larger internal wheel R is for the Heald cylinder grinder. Three forms of the "saucer" wheel for cutter grinders are illustrated at N, O and P, and two bevel-edge cup wheels are shown at S, and T, both being made for cutter grinder use. The double-edge cup wheel can be used for sharpening both sides of a straddle mill without reversing the latter on its arbor; it is also useful in such operations as grinding out parallel surfaces, say the jaws of a snap gage.

The conical wheel at Q is for a tool grinder and is used principally for sharpening pattern makers' gouges which are beveled on the inside of the curve.

Two saw gummers, representative of a number of shapes regularly made, are shown at U. These are adapted for sharpening saw teeth and grinding down in the "gullet" or concave space between the bottoms of the teeth.

The "pot balls" at N and W are used in grinding out hollow ware such as pots and kettles. These are made in great variety to suit spherical receptacles, skillets, flat bottom pots, etc.

MOUNTING GRINDING WHEELS

One of the most important considerations in connection with the use of grinding wheels is that they shall be properly mounted upon suitably proportioned spindles and between properly designed flanges. A wheel which is crowded upon a spindle of weak design, or which is cramped between two imperfect flanges that are either too small or take a bearing upon the wheel at the wrong point, is subjected to conditions as likely to cause an accident as is an excessive rate of speed.

The vast number of abrasive wheels in use upon the class of machines commonly known as bench and floor grinders, grinding wheel stands, emery grinders, etc., and which are so generally in service at various points about the machine shop, blacksmith shop and foundry, makes it desirable that something should be said here in reference to the best methods of mounting wheels on such apparatus.

In the first place, the machine itself should be of rigid construction, with spindle of ample proportions; the bearings should be well fitted; and kept well oiled so that the arbor will not become overheated and by expanding, break the wheel; and the machine should be securely fastened on substantial foundations not only to insure safety but in order to secure better results with the wheel.

The following sizes of spindles are recommended by the Norton Company and by some other wheelmakers, except where the grinding wheels are extra thick:

Wheel	Spindle
6 in. diameter and less	$\frac{1}{2}$ in.
8 in. diameter and less	$\frac{5}{8}$ in.
10 in. diameter and less	$\frac{3}{4}$ in.
12 in. diameter and less	1 in.
14 in. diameter and less	$1\frac{1}{4}$ in.
16 in. diameter and less	$1\frac{1}{2}$ in.
18 to 20 in. diameter	$1\frac{3}{4}$ in.
22 to 24 in. diameter	2 in.
Larger than 24 in.	$2\frac{1}{4}$ to 3 in.

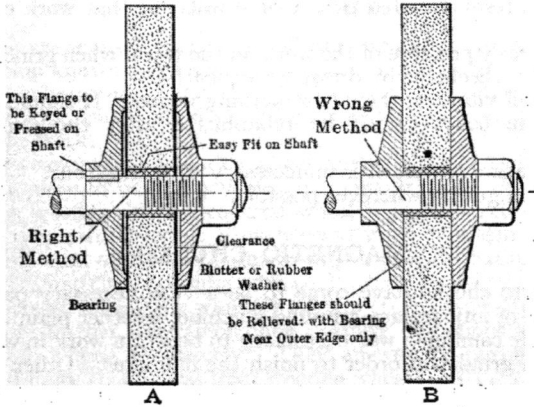

FIG. 11 — Right and wrong way to mount wheels

The flanges should be relieved as at A in Fig. 11, and they should be at least one-half the diameter of the wheel and have a true bearing at the outer edge. The inner flange should never be loose but in all cases should be fixed on the spindle. Under no circumstances should the flanges be allowed to be less than one-third the diameter of the wheel. Wheels must not be allowed to run when held only by a nut in place of a flange, as the nut is liable to crawl and cause accident.

Compressible washers of pulp or rubber, slightly larger than the flanges, should be used between the flanges and the wheel as shown at A, Fig. 11. These distribute the pressure evenly when the flanges are tightened, by taking up any imperfections in the wheel or flanges.

The hole in the wheel bushing should be 0.005 inch larger than standard size spindles. This permits the wheel to slide on the spindle without cramping and insures a good fit not only on the spindle but against the inside flange, which is essential.

The flanges should be tightened only enough to hold the wheel firmly, thus avoiding unnecessary strain.

General Suggestions

HANDLE all wheels with the greatest care in unpacking, storing, delivering, etc. Wheels are frequently cracked by rough usage before they are ever placed on the grinding machine. The man in charge of the storeroom should inspect each wheel before giving it out to the workman.

Wheels should be stored in a dry place.

A wheel used in wet grinding should not be left overnight partly immersed in water.

When mounting wheels do not screw up the nut too tight; it should be set up only enough so that the flanges hold the wheel firmly.

Keep all rests adjusted close to the wheel so that work cannot be caught.

Avoid heavy pressure of the work on the wheel when grinding.

Keep the wheel true by dressing frequently.

If a wheel vibrates, there is something wrong. It should be trued up and the boxes should be rebabbitted after the journals are trued up.

Never hack a wheel; it is unnecessary and dangerous.

Use wheel guards wherever possible.

MAGNETIC CHUCKS

MAGNETIC chucks have come to be a very necessary part of the equipment of any surface grinding machine, whether plain or rotary. Before their coming it was customary to bed thin work in wax on the platen of a grinder in order to finish the flat sides. Other flat work had to be held in "fingers" on special fixtures, and on account of their being very thin and easily sprung, it was difficult to secure really accurate work.

The magnetic chuck holds the thinnest pieces of iron or steel firmly, draws down any slight spring in the work and prevents springing when strains are released during the grinding operations.

The chuck face is divided into magnet poles, separated by babbit or other non-magnetic metals, and coils of insulated wire from these into electromagnets when current is applied. For rotary work, the electric current is supplied by brushes running against insulated contract rings on the outside. Current can be supplied from any incandescent lamp socket on a direct current circuit.

Alternating current cannot be used.

A No. o chuck having a face 10 × 14 inches uses about one-half as much power as a 16 candle-power lamp.

Hints for Using Magnetic Chucks

The chucks should not be taken apart.

Nothing but iron or steel can be held on the chucks.

The holding power depends on the amount of work surface in contact with the chuck.

Work can be held on edge by using adjustable back rest.

Very thin work can be held for grinding on the edges by laying it against the back rest and backing it up with a parallel strip.

Thin work will not hold as well as thick work.

In packing a number of small pieces on a chuck at one setting, it is better to separate them a little with strips of non-magnetic material.

Do not plug up the vent holes in the chuck.

Keep water away from the switch, the brushes and the interior of the chuck.

Magnetic chucks do not take the place of all other chucks.

Do not use water on chucks except where they are made for it.

Chucks are usually wound for 110 or 220 volts *for direct current only.*

POLISHING WHEELS

THERE are many varieties of polishing wheels in use, the principal kinds being known as wooden wheels, compressed wheels, canvas and muslin, seahorse and felt wheels. For good work, and economy in abrasive, glue and labor cost, wheels and methods must be selected to suit the work.

A few years ago, the wooden wheel covered with leather and turned to fit the piece to be polished, was universally used. At the present time, the wooden, leather-covered wheel is used largely on flat surfaces and on work where it is necessary to maintain good edges. When this kind of a wheel is made with a double coating of leather, it makes a first-class finishing wheel.

Compressed wheels, or wheels having a steel center are made with surfaces of leather, canvas or linen. Many tool shops are equipped with these wheels exclusively. They answer all purposes and are safer and more economical than wooden wheels.

They are also used largely on cutlery and for polishing chilled plows. The compressed wheel is of strong construction, is very durable and easily kept in balance.

Canvas and muslin wheels are used extensively for polishing stoves, shovels, plows, brass, cast iron and steel. For roughing out and dry lining on irregular pieces, they have proved very satisfactory. They hold the abrasive well and require no washing off as they can be cleaned with a buff stick or an abrasive brick.

Many concerns, such as plow-, shovel- and hoemakers, buy the canvas and muslin and make their own wheels.

Sea-horse wheels are very expensive, most concerns buying the hides and making their own wheels.

Where a high-grade polish is required, there is probably no wheel which can compare with the wheel made of sea horse. They are largely used on guns, pistols and cutlery.

Felt wheels are largely used by stovemakers for finishing surfaces. Bull neck wheels are also used for this purpose.

The felt wheels are made from white Spanish and Mexican felt and are extensively used for finishing on certain classes of work.

Care of Polishing Wheels

POLISHING wheels should be kept in perfect balance and running true at all times. A wheel out of balance wastes time; glue and abrasive, and will not do as good work.

The most efficient glue and the best abrasive are the cheapest in the long run.

The glue pots should be kept clean and the glue properly cooked before using.

It is also important to heat the abrasive before applying.

The wheels should be kept properly cleaned and thoroughly covered with the abrasive.

The wheels should be selected for the particular work the same as in grinding and only the wheel best adapted should be used at all times.

Polishing operations are usually divided into three classes: roughing, dry fining, and finishing or oiling.

The abrasives used for roughing usually run from numbers 20 to 80. For dry fining, from numbers 90 to 120. The numbers used for finishing run from 150 to XF.

For both roughing out and dry fining, the polishing wheels should be used dry. For finishing, the wheels are first worn down a little and then oil, beeswax, tallow and similar substances are used on the wheel. This, together with the abrasive, brings up a fine finish.

Speed of Buffing Wheels

Wood, leather covered	7,000 ft. per minute
Walrus	8,000 ft. per minute
Rag wheels	7,000 ft. per minute
Hair-brush wheels	12,000 ft. per minute
Ohio grindstone	2,500 ft. per minute
Huron grindstone	3,500 ft. per minute

LAPPING

LAPPING may be defined as the process of finishing the surface of a piece of work by means of another piece of material, called a lap, the surface of which is charged with an abrasive.

Laps are roughly divided into three general classes. First, those where the form of the lap makes a line contact with the work, and the work is, if cylindrical, revolved to develop the cylindrical form, or, if straight, in one direction, is moved back and forth under the lap. Second, those which are used for straight surfaces with a full contact on the lap, and third, those which are used for male and female cylindrical surfaces with a full contact on the lap. In all cases the material from which the lap is made must be softer than the work. If this is not so, the abrasive will charge the work and cut the lap, instead of the lap cutting the work.

The first class is used in the place of emery wheels, either where the work is too small to use an ordinary wheel or where a form is to be ground on the work and an emery wheel will not keep its shape. They are usually made of machinery steel and the abrasive used is crushed diamond rolled into the surface. In rolling in the diamond

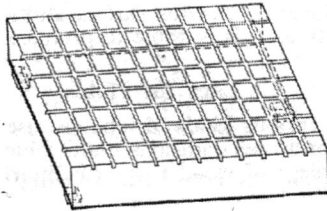

FIG. 1. — A Lapping Plate for Flat Work

dust the sharp corners of the particles cause them to bed securely into the surface of the lap, and if a good quality of diamond is used, a lap will grind all day without recharging. Oil is used to lubricate the work and carry away the dust from the grinding. If a diamond lap is run dry the particles of diamond tear and raise "burs" in the work, which strip the lap very quickly. The speed should be about two-thirds that for an emery wheel of the same size; for if it is excessive, the lap will wear smooth and glaze instead of cutting. This kind of lap is used mainly in watch and clock shops, and shops making watch tools, sub-press dies, and similar work.

Lapping Flat Surfaces

In lapping flat surfaces, which are usually on hardened steel, a cast-iron plate is used as a lap and emery as an abrasive. In order that the plate may stay reasonably straight, it should either be quite thick, or else ribbed sufficiently to make it rigid, and in any case it should be supported on three feet, the same as a surface place. For

rough work or "blocking down," as it is called, the lap works better
if scored with narrow grooves, about $\frac{1}{2}$ inch apart, both lengthways
and crossways, thus dividing the plate into small squares, as in Fig. 1.
The emery is sprinkled loosely on the block, wet with lard oil
and the work rubbed on it; care is taken to press hardest on the highest spots. The emery and oil get in the grooves, and are continually
rolling in and out, getting between the plate and the work and are
crushed into the cast iron, thus charging it thoroughly in a short
time. About No. 100 or No. 120 emery is best for this purpose.

After blocking down, or if the work has first been ground on a
surface grinder, the process is different. A plain plate is used
with the best quality of flour of emery as an abrasive, as the least
lump or coarseness will scratch the work so that it will be very hard
to get the scratches out. Instead of oil benzine is used as a lubricant and the lap should be cleaned off and fresh benzine and emery
applied as often as it becomes sticky. The work should be tried
from time to time with a straight-edge and care taken not to let the
emery run in and out from under the work, as this will cause the edges
to abrade more than the center, and will especially mar the corners.
After getting a good surface, the plate and work should be cleaned
perfectly dry, and then rubbed. The charging in the plate will
cut just enough to remove whatever emery may have become charged
in the work, will take away the dull surface and leave it as smooth as
glass and as accurate as it is possible to produce.

Laps for Holes

In lapping holes various kinds of laps are used, according to the
accuracy required, and the conditions under which the work is done.
The simplest is a piece of wood turned cylindrical with a longitu-

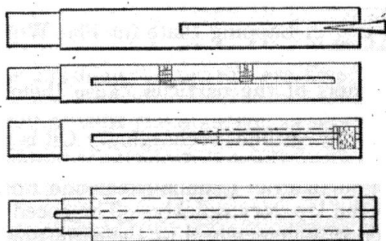

FIG. 2. — Laps for Holes

dinal groove or split in which the edge of a piece of emery cloth is
inserted. This cloth is wound around the wood until it fills the hole
in the work. This is only fit for smoothing or enlarging rough holes
and usually leaves them more out of round and bell-mouthed than
they were at first. Another lap used for the same purpose — and
which produces better results — is made by turning a piece of copper, brass, or cast iron to fit the hole and splitting it longitudinally
for some distance from the end. Loose emery is sprinkled over it,

with lard oil for a lubricant, and a taper wedge is driven into the end for adjustment as the lap wears.

For lapping common drill bushings, cam rolls, etc., in large quantities, where a little bell-mouthing can be allowed, and yet a reasonably good hole is required, a great many shops use adjustable copper laps made with more care than the above. One way of making them is to split the lap nearly the whole length, but leaving both ends solid. One side is drilled and tapped for spreading screws for adjustment. Either one screw half-way down the split may be used or two screws dividing the split into thirds. Another and better means of adjustment is to drill a small longitudinal hole a little over half the length of the lap, enlarge it for half its length, and tap the large end for some distance. This is done before splitting. Into this hole a long screw with a taper point is fitted so that when tightened it tries to force itself into a small hole, thus spreading the lap.

For nice work there is nothing better than a lead lap. Lead charges easily, holds the emery firmly and does not scratch or score the work. It is easy to fit to the work and holds its shape well for light cuts. Under hard usage, however, it wears easily. For this reason, while laps for a single hole or a special job are sometimes cast on straight arbors, where much lapping is done it is customary to mold the laps to taper arbors with means for a slight adjustment. After any extensive adjustment the lap will be out of true and must be turned off. All of these laps, as shown in Fig. 2, are to be held by one end in a lathe chuck, and the work run back and forth on them by hand, or by means of a clamp held in the hand. If a clamp is used care should be taken not to spring the work.

How to Do Good Lapping

THERE are several points which must be taken into consideration in order to get good results in lapping holes. The most important is that the lap shall always fill the hole. If this condition is not complied with the weight of the work and the impossibility of holding it exactly right will cause it to lap out of round, or if it is out of round at the start the lap will be free to follow the original surface. If the lap fits, it will bear hardest on the high spots and lap them off. Next in importance to getting a round hole is to have it straight. To attain this end the lap should be a little longer than the work, so that it will lap the whole length of the hole at once, and not have a tendency to follow any curvature there may be in it. What is known as bell-mouthing, or lapping large on the ends, is hard to prevent, especially if the emery is sprinkled on the lap and the work shoved on it while it is running. The best way to avoid this condition when using cast-iron or copper laps, which do not charge easily, is to put the emery in the slot, near the center of the lap, and after the work is shoved on squirt oil in the slot to float the emery. Then, when the lathe is started the emery will carry around and gradually work out to the ends, lapping as it goes. Where lead is used the emery can be put on where it is desired to have the lap cut and rolled in with a flat strip of iron. It will not come out easily, so will not spread to any extent, and it is possible with a lap charged in this manner to avoid cutting the ends of the hole at all. The work should always be kept in motion back and forth to avoid lumping of the emery and cuttings which will score grooves in the work.

Ring Gage and Other Work

RING gages are lapped with a lead lap. They are first ground straight and smooth to within .0005 inch of size, and then, when lapped, are cooled as well as cleaned, before trying the plug, by

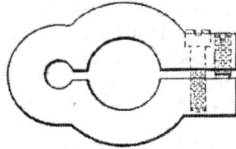

FIG. 3.—A Lap for Plugs

placing them in a pail of benzine for a long enough time to bring them down to the temperature of the room. Some shops leave a thin collar projection from each side around the hole, so that, if there is any bell-mouthing, it will be in these collars, which are ground off after the lapping is done.

Other metals are lapped in this same manner, except that the abrasive is different. Cast iron is lapped with emery, but charges to some extent. This charging can be taken out without changing the work materially by rubbing it by hand with flour of emery cloth. In lapping bronze or brass, crocus and Vienna lime are used. Crocus is used with a cast-iron or lead lap, and the charging is removed by running the work for a few seconds on a hardwood stick which fits the hole. Unslaked Vienna lime, freshly crushed, is used with a lead or hardwood lap, and does not charge. It does a nice job, but is very slow, and is only used in watch factories.

For lapping plug gages, pistons, and other cylindrical articles, a cast-iron lap is usually used, split and fitted with a closing and a spreading screw, as shown in Fig. 3. Sometimes, where a very fine finish is required, or where the work is not hardened, the hole is made larger than the work, and a lead ring cast into it.

DIAMOND POWDER IN THE MACHINE SHOP

THE diamond used for this purpose, costing 85 cents per carat, is an inferior grade of diamond, not so hard as the black diamond used for drills and truing emery wheels, and not of a clear and perfect structure to permit it to enter the gem class. Many are a mixed black and white, others yellow and some pink; many are clear but flaky. Then there is the small débris from diamond cutting, which is reduced to powder and sells somewhat cheaper; but some find it more economical to use the above and powder it themselves, as the débris from diamond cutting is of a flaky nature, and does not charge into the lap so well.

Assuming there is 25 carats to reduce to powder, proceed as follows:

Into a mortar, as shown at Fig. 4, place about 5 carats, using an 8-ounce hammer to crush it. It takes from 3 to 4 minutes' steady pounding to reduce it to a good average. Scrape the powder free from the bottom and the sides and empty into one half pint of oil. The oil used is the best olive oil obtainable, and is held in a cup-shaped receptacle that will hold a pint and one half. The 25 carats being reduced to powder, and in the oil, stir it until thoroughly mixed, and allow to stand 5 minutes; then pour off to another dish. The diamond that remains in the dish· is coarse and should be washed in benzine and allowed to dry, and should be repounded, unless extremely coarse diamond is desired. In that case label it No. o. Now stir that which has been poured from No. o, and allow to stand 10 minutes. Then pour off into another dish. The residue will be No. 1. Repeat the operation, following the table below.

.The settlings can be put into small dishes for convenient use, enough oil staying with the diamond to give it the consistency of paste. The dishes can be obtained from a jewelers' supply house.

TABLE FOR SETTLING DIAMOND POWDER

To obtain No. o — 5 minutes.   To obtain No. 3 — 1 hour.
To obtain No. 1 — 10 minutes.   To obtain No. 4 — 2 hours.
To obtain No. 2 — 30 minutes.   To obtain No. 5 — 10 hours.
To obtain No. 6 — until oil is clear.

Diamond is seldom hammered; it is generally rolled into the metal. For instance, several pieces of wire of various diameters charged with diamond may be desired for use in die work. Place the wire and a small portion of the diamond between two hardened surfaces, and under pressure roll back and forth until thoroughly charged. No. 2 diamond in this case is generally used. Or one can form the metal any desired shape and apply diamond and use a roll, as Fig. 6, to force the diamond into the metal. This is then a file which will work hard steel, but the moment this diamond file, or lap, is crowded it is stripped of the diamond, and is consequently of no use. It is to be used with comparatively light pressure.

Diamond Laps

COPPER is the best metal. It takes the diamond readily, and retains it longer than other metals; brass next, then bessemer steel. The latter is used when it is wished to preserve a form that is often used.

For sharpening small, flat drills, say 0.008 to 0.100, a copper lap mounted on a taper shank, as in Fig. 5 and charged on the face with No. 2 diamond, using pressure on the roll, makes a most satisfactory method of sharpening drills. The diamond lasts for a long time if properly used, and there is no danger of drawing the temper on the drill. It is much quicker than any other method of sharpening.

To charge the lap use the roll, Fig. 7, supported on a T rest pressing firmly against the lap, being careful to have the roll on the center; otherwise instead of charging the lap it will be grinding the roll. The diamond may be spread either on the lap or the roll, and the first charging usually takes twice the amount of diamond that subsequent charging takes. To avoid loss of diamond, wash the

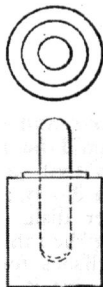

FIG. 5

FIG. 6

FIG. 7

FIG. 4

Diamond Lap Tools

lap in a dish of benzine kept exclusively for that purpose. This can be reclaimed by burning the metal with acids, and the diamond can be resettled.

For the grinding of taper holes in hard spindles or for position work in hard plates, where holes are too small to allow the use of emery wheels, No. 1 diamond does the work beautifully. Or if it is wished to grind sapphire centers or plugs as stops, etc., a bessemer lap made in the form of a wheel and charged with diamond on the diameter does the work nicely.

Nos. 5 and 6 diamond are used on boxwood laps, mounted on taper plugs or chucks, and the diamond smeared on with the finger. The lap is run at high speed and used for fine and slow cutting which also gives a high polish.

REAMER AND CUTTER GRINDING

Reamer Clearances

AFTER constant experimenting for a period of more than a year, the Cincinnati Milling Machine Company succeeded in establishing tables for four styles of reamers for obtaining what they consider to be the best clearances, the object being to grind clearances on reamers which would ream the greatest number of smooth holes with a minimum amount of wear. The four styles of reamers are as follows: Hand reamers for steel, hand reamers for gray iron and bronze, chucking reamers for gray iron and bronze, chucking reamers for steel. The company uses adjustable blade reamers almost exclusively, all of which are ground in the toolroom on their universal cutter and tool grinder. High speed steel reamers cling to nickel steel and do not cut it as well as carbon steel.

Fig. 1 is a cross-section of a hand reamer. Two clearance lines, *A* and *B*, are ground on the blades, *a* being the cutting clearance and *b* the second clearance called for in the table. The object of giving the adjustment for the second clearance so minutely is to provide a proper width of land, which equals .025 inch on all hand reamers for gray iron or bronze, and 0.005 inch on hand reamers for steel.

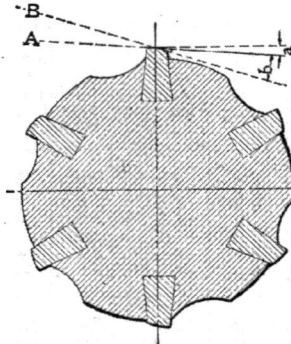

FIG. 1. — Cross-section of Hand Reamer

Chucking reamers for gray iron and bronze have, in this system, 23-degree beveled ends as shown in Fig. 2, and are provided with two clearances along the blades, for which the settings are given in Table 3. The beveled ends have only one clearance which is equal to the second clearance given in Table 3. Fig. 3 shows a chucking reamer for reaming steel. In these reamers the blades are circular ground to the exact size of hole to be reamed and without clearance, the 45-

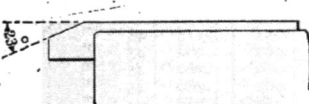

FIG. 2. — Chucking Reamer   FIG. 3. — Chucking Reamer
Blade for Gray Iron and Bronze   Blade for Steel

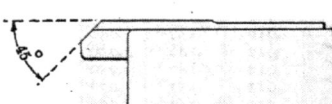

degree beveled ends only having clearance as given in Table 4. On all reamers of this style the blades are ground from .015 to .020 inch below size half of their length toward the shank end.

In grinding the clearances for the various kinds of reamers as given in Table 1, 2, and 3, the tooth rest is held stationary on the emery wheel head of the grinder, while in grinding the 45-degree beveled ends on the chucking reamers for steel, the tooth rest is supported from the grinder table and travels with the work. The front end of the hand reamer blades are tapered about 0.004 per inch. The back ends of the blades are also slightly tapered to prevent injuring the holes when backing the reamer out.

	REAMER CLEARANCE — Ground with Cup Wheel 3″ dia.—Tooth Rest to be Set Central with Emery Wheel Spindle. Set Work holding Centers above Emery Wheel Center by Amount given below in Tables No. 1-2 and 3						Set Tooth Rest Below Work Holding Centers. Amount given Below in Table No. 4	
	TABLE 1 — Hand Reamer for Steel Cut'g Clearance Land .006 Wide		TABLE 2 — Hand Reamer for Cast Iron and Bronze Cut'g Clearance Land .025 Wide		TABLE 3 — Chucking Reamer for Cast Iron and Bronze Cut'g Clearance Land .025 Wide		TABLE 4 — Chucking Reamers for Steel Circular Ground	
Size of Reamer	For Cutting Clearance	For Second Clearance	For Cutting Clearance	For Second Clearance	For Cutting Clearance	For Second Clearance	Angle on End of Blade	For Cutting Clearance on Angle
1/2″	.012	.052	.032	.072	.040	.080	45 Degrees	.080
9/16″	.012	.057	.032	.072	.040	.080	45 "	.080
5/8″	.012	.062	.032	.072	.040	.090	45 "	.090
11/16″	.012	.067	.035	.095	.040	.100	45 "	.100
3/4″	.012	.072	.035	.095	.040	.100	45 "	.100
13/16″	.012	.077	.037	.095	.045	.125	45 "	.125
7/8″	.012	.082	.040	.120	.045	.125	45 "	.125
15/16″	.012	.087	.040	.120	.045	.125	45 "	.125
1″	.012	.092	.040	.120	.045	.125	45 "	.125
1 1/16″	.012	.097	.040	.120	.045	.125	45 "	.125
1 1/8″	.012	.102	.040	.120	.045	.125	45 "	.125
1 3/16″	.012	.106	.042	.122	.045	.125	45 "	.125
1 1/4″	.012	.112	.045	.145	.050	.160	45 "	.160
1 5/16″	.012	.118	.045	.145	.050	.160	45 "	.160
1 3/8″	.012	.122	.045	.145	.050	.160	45 "	.175
1 7/16″	.012	.127	.045	.145	.055	.175	45 "	.175
1 1/2″	.012	.132	.048	.168	.055	.175	45 "	.175
1 9/16″	.012	.137	.050	.170	.055	.175	45 "	.175
1 5/8″	.012	.142	.050	.170	.060	.200	45 "	.200
1 11/16″	.012	.147	.050	.170	.060	.200	45 "	.200
1 3/4″	.012	.152	.052	.192	.060	.200	45 "	.200
1 13/16″	.012	.157	.052	.192	.060	.200	45 "	.200
1 7/8″	.012	.162	.056	.196	.060	.200	45 "	.200
1 15/16″	.012	.167	.056	.196	.064	.200	45 "	.200
2″	.012	.172	.056	.216	.064	.224	45 "	.225
2 1/8″	.012	.172	.056	.216	.064	.224	45 "	.225
2 1/4″	.012	.172	.059	.219	.064	.224	45 "	.225
2 3/8″	.012	.172	.059	.219	.064	.224	45 "	.225
2 1/2″	.012	.172	.063	.223	.064	.224	45 "	.225
2 5/8″	.012	.172	.063	.223	.064	.224	45 "	.225
2 3/4″	.012	.172	.063	.223	.068	.228	45 "	.230
2 7/8″	.012	.172	.063	.223	.068	.228	45 "	.230
3″	.012	.172	.065	.225	.072	.232	45 "	.230
3 1/8″	.012	.172	.065	.225	.072	.232	45 "	.230
3 1/4″	.012	.172	.065	.225	.075	.235	45 "	.235
3 3/8″	.012	.172	.065	.225	.075	.235	45 "	.235
3 1/2″	.012	.172	.065	.225	.077	.237	45 "	.240
	Mount Tooth Rest on Emery Wheel Head						Mount Tooth Rest on Table of Machine	

REAMER CLEARANCE Ground with Cup Wheel 3″ dia.—Tooth Rest to be Set Central with Emery Wheel Spindle. Set Work holding Centers above Emery Wheel Center by Amount given below in Tables No. 1-2 and 3							Set Tooth Rest Below Work Holding Centers Amount given Below in Table No. 4	
TABLE 1 Hand Reamer for Steel Cut'g Clearance Land .006 Wide			TABLE 2 Hand Reamer for Cast Iron and Bronze Cut'g Clearance Land .025 Wide		TABLE 3 Chucking Reamer for Cast Iron and Bronze Cut'g Clearance Land .025 Wide		TABLE 4 Chucking Reamers for Steel Circular Ground	
Size of Reamer	For Cutting Clearance	For Second Clearance	For Cutting Clearance	For Second Clearance	For Cutting Clearance	For Second Clearance	Angle on End of Blade	For Cutting Clearance on Angle
2 13/16″	.012	.172	.065	.225	.077	.237	45 Degrees	.240
2 7/8 ″	.012	.172	.070	.230	.080	.240	45 "	.240
2 15/16″	.012	.172	.070	.230	.080	.240	45 "	.240
3″	.012	.172	.072	.232	.080	.240	45 "	.240
3 1/16″	.012	.172	.072	.232	.080	.240	45 "	.240
3 1/8 ″	.012	.172	.075	.235	.083	.240	45 "	.240
3 3/16″	.012	.172	.075	.235	.083	.243	45 "	.240
3 1/4 ″	.012	.172	.078	.238	.083	.243	45 "	.245
3 5/16″	.012	.172	.078	.238	.087	.243	45 "	.245
3 3/8 ″	.012	.172	.081	.241	.087	.247	45 "	.245
3 7/16″	.012	.172	.081	.241	.090	.247	45 "	.245
3 1/2 ″	.012	.172	.084	.244	.090	.250	45 "	.250
3 9/16″	.012	.172	.084	.244	.090	.250	45 "	.250
3 5/8 ″	.012	.172	.087	.247	.093	.253	45 "	.250
3 11/16″	.012	.172	.087	.247	.093	.253	45 "	.250
3 3/4 ″	.012	.172	.090	.250	.097	.257	45 "	.255
3 13/16″	.012	.172	.090	.250	.097	.257	45 "	.255
3 7/8 ″	.012	.172	.093	.253	.100	.260	45 "	.255
3 15/16″	.012	.172	.093	.253	.100	.260	45 "	.255
4 ″	.012	.172	.096	.256	.104	.264	45 "	.260
4 1/16″	.012	.172	.096	.256	.104	.264	45 "	.260
4 1/8 ″	.012	.172	.096	.256	.104	.264	45 "	.260
4 3/16″	.012	.172	.096	.256	.106	.266	45 "	.260
4 1/4 ″	.012	.172	.096	.256	.106	.266	45 "	.265
4 5/16″	.012	.172	.096	.256	.106	.266	45 "	.265
4 3/8 ″	.012	.172	.096	.256	.108	.268	45 "	.265
4 7/16″	.012	.172	.096	.256	.108	.268	45 "	.265
4 1/2 ″	.012	.172	.100	.260	.108	.268	45 "	.265
4 9/16″	.012	.172	.100	.260	.108	.268	45 "	.265
4 5/8 ″	.012	.172	.100	.260	.110	.270	45 "	.270
4 11/16″	.012	.172	.100	.260	.110	.270	45 "	.270
4 3/4 ″	.012	.172	.104	.264	.114	.274	45 "	.275
4 13/16″	.012	.172	.104	.264	.114	.274	45 "	.275
4 7/8 ″	.012	.172	.106	.266	.116	.276	45 "	.275
4 15/16″	.012	.172	.106	.266	.116	.276	45 "	.275
5 ″	.012	.172	.110	.270	.118	.278	45 "	.275
5 3/8 ″	.012	.172	.118	.278				
Mount Tooth Rest on Emery Wheel Head							Mount Tooth Rest on Table of Machine	

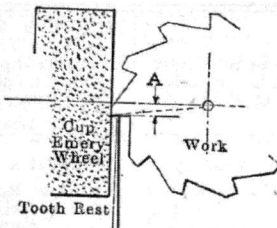

CUP WHEEL CLEARANCE TABLE

For setting tooth rest to obtain 5° or 7° clearance when grinding peripheral teeth of milling cutters with cup-shaped wheel. Tooth rest is set below work centers as at *A*, the distance being found in the table below.

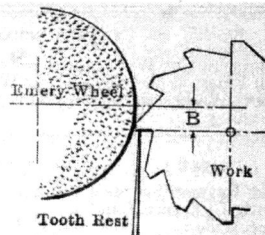

DISK WHEEL CLEARANCE TABLE

Giving distance *B* for setting work centers and tooth rest below center of wheel spindle to obtain 5° or 7° clearance with wheels of different diameters when grinding with periphery of disk wheel.

Dia. Cutter Inches	For 5° Clearance A =	For 7° Clearance A =	Dia. of Emery Wheel Inches	For 5° Clearance B =	For 7° Clearance B =
$\frac{1}{4}$	.011	.015	2	.0937	.125
$\frac{3}{8}$	.015	.022	$2\frac{1}{4}$	.099	.141
$\frac{1}{2}$	.022	.030	$2\frac{1}{2}$	.110	.156
$\frac{5}{8}$	.028	.037	$2\frac{3}{4}$	.125	.172
$\frac{3}{4}$	.033	.045	3	.132	.187
$\frac{7}{8}$	.037	.052	$3\frac{1}{4}$	.143	.203
I	.044	.060	$3\frac{1}{2}$	.154	.219
$1\frac{1}{4}$	.055	.075	$3\frac{3}{4}$	.165	.234
$1\frac{1}{2}$	.066	.090	4	.176	.250
$1\frac{3}{4}$	.077	.105	$4\frac{1}{4}$	.187	.265
2	.088	.120	$4\frac{1}{2}$	.198	.281
$2\frac{1}{4}$	.099	.135	$4\frac{3}{4}$	.209	.297
$2\frac{1}{2}$	.110	.150	5	.220	.312
$2\frac{3}{4}$	.121	.165	$5\frac{1}{4}$	.231	.328
3	.132	.180	$5\frac{1}{2}$	.242	.344
$3\frac{1}{2}$	.154	.210	$5\frac{3}{4}$	.253	.359
4	.176	.240	6	.264	.375
$4\frac{1}{2}$	.198	.270	$6\frac{1}{4}$	.275	.390
5	.220	.300	$6\frac{1}{2}$	.286	.406
$5\frac{1}{2}$	.242	.330	$6\frac{3}{4}$	.297	.421
6	.264	.360	7	.308	.437

OILSTONES AND THEIR USES

Natural Stones

THE following particulars regarding the well-known Arkansas and Washita stones are given by the Pike Manufacturing Company:

Arkansas stones are made from rock quarried in the Ozark mountains of Arkansas, and are prepared for commercial purposes in two grades, hard and soft.

Hard Arkansas is composed of pure silica and its sharpening qualities are due to small, sharp-pointed grains, or crystals, of hexagonal shape, which are much harder than steel and will, therefore, cut away and sharpen steel tools. The extreme fineness of texture makes this stone, of necessity, a slow cutter, but in the very density of the crystals of which it is composed lies its virtue as a sharpener.

Soft Arkansas stone is not quite so fine-grained and hard as the hard Arkansas, but it cuts faster and is better for some kinds of mechanical work. It is especially adapted for sharpening the tools used by wood carvers, file makers, pattern makers, and all workers in hard wood.

Washita stone is also found in the Ozark mountains in Arkansas and is similar to the Arkansas stone, being composed of nearly pure silica, but is much more porous. It is known as the best natural stone for sharpening carpenters' and general wood workers' tools. This stone is found in various grades, from perfectly crystallized and porous grit to vitreous flint and hard sandstone. The sharpness of the grit depends entirely upon its crystallization, the best oilstones being made from very porous crystals.

In addition to the regular rectangular sections, natural stones are made in such shapes as square, triangular, round, flat, bevel, diamond, oval, pointed, knife edge.

Artificial Oilstones

ARTIFICIAL oilstones are manufactured in a multitude of shapes and sizes and are adapted for sharpening all kinds of tools. Such stones are made by the Norton Company of alundum and crystolon, the former being known as India oilstones, the latter as crystolon sharpening stones. Similar shapes are manufactured by the American Emery Wheel Works, and the Carborundum Company also makes such stones in great variety.

The stones are made in three grades or grits, coarse, medium and fine. The coarse stones are used in machine shops for sharpening very dull or nicked tools, machine knives, and for general use where fast cutting is desired.

Medium stones are sharpening mechanics' tools in general, more particularly those used by carpenters and in wood-working shops.

Fine stones are adapted for engravers, die workers, cabinet makers and other users of tools requiring a very fine, keen-cutting edge.

Of the great variety of shapes and sizes a number adapted especially for machine shop purposes are illustrated half size in Fig. 1. Of these, Nos. 0, 1, 1½, 2, 24 and 29 are for sharpening lathe and planer tools, and for use after grinding; Nos. 23, 25, 56 and 56½ for reamers; Nos. 13, 14 and 15 for taps; Nos. 4, 5, 6, 7, 8, 9, 10, 11, 12 and 26 for dies.

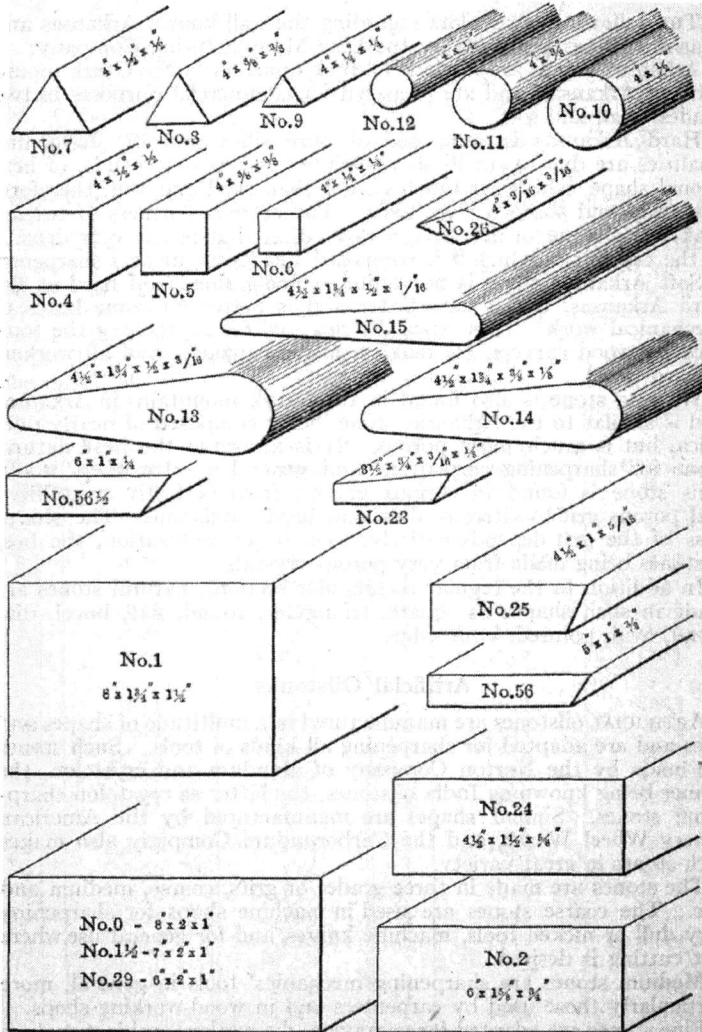

Fig. 1.—Shapes of Oilstones

A few shapes and sizes for curved-edge wood-working tools are Nos. 10, 11, 12, 13, 14, 15, in Fig. 1. Rectangular shapes for straightedge tools like chisels, plane bits, planer knives, scrapers, paper-cutting knives and other tools with broad flat edges are Nos. 0, 1, 1½, 2, 24, 29, in Fig. 1.

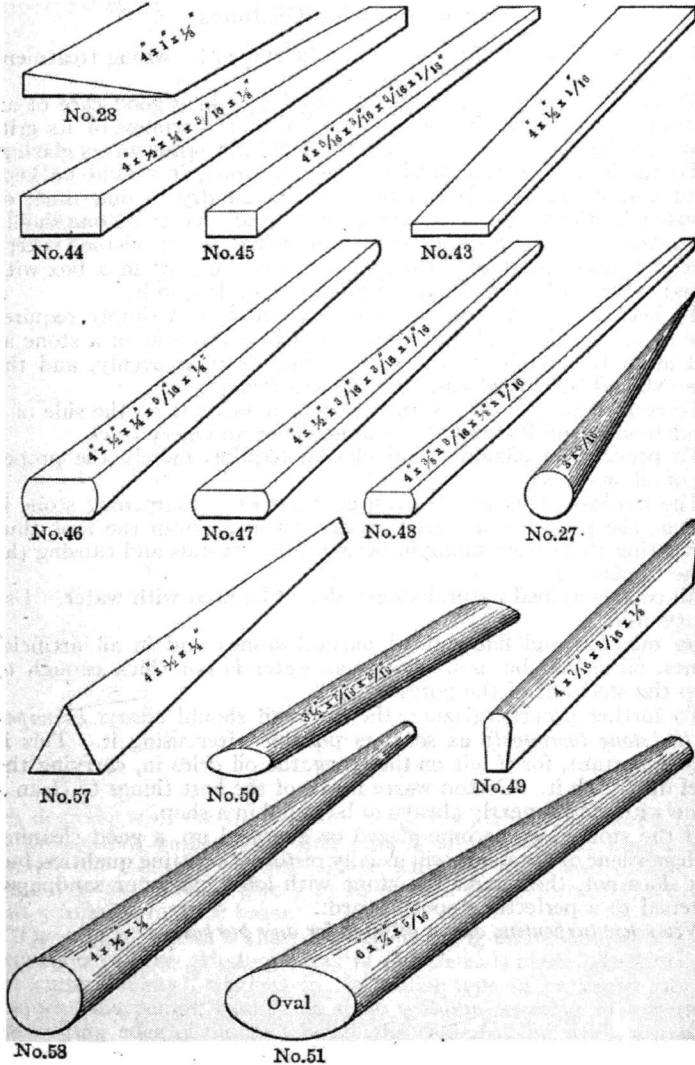

FIG. 2. — Shapes of Oilstones

Fig. 2 shows some of the sizes and shapes particularly adapted for mold and die work, watch and clock makers' tools, etc. Other shapes suitable for such purposes are shown by Nos. 4, 5, 6, 7, 8, 9 and 26 in Fig. 1 and No. 51 in Fig. 2.

How to Care for Oilstones

LIKE anything else, an oilstone can be ruined by wrong treatment and lack of care.

There are three objects to be attained in taking good care of an oilstone: first, to retain the original life and sharpness of its grit; second, to keep its surface flat and even; third, to prevent its glazing.

To retain the original freshness of the stone, it should be kept clean and moist. To let an oilstone remain dry a long time, or expose it to the air, tends to harden it. A new natural stone should be soaked in oil for several days before using. If an oilstone is kept in a dry place (most of them are) it should be kept in a box with closed cover, and a few drops of fresh, clean oil left on it.

To keep the surface of an oilstone flat and even simply requires care in using. Tools should be sharpened on the edge of a stone as well as in the middle to prevent wearing down unevenly, and the stone should be turned end for end occasionally.

To restore an even, flat surface grind the oilstone on the side of a grindstone or rub it down with sandstone or an emery brick.

To prevent an oilstone from glazing requires merely the proper use of oil or water.

The purpose of using either oil or water on a sharpening stone is to float the particles of steel that are cut away from the tool, thus preventing them from filling in between the crystals and causing the stone to glaze.

All coarse-grained natural stones should be used with water. Use plenty of it.

On medium and fine-grained natural stones and in all artificial stones, oil should be used always, as water is not thick enough to keep the steel out of the pores.

To further prevent glazing, the dirty oil should *always be wiped off the stone thoroughly* as soon as possible after using it. This is very important, for if left on the stone, the oil dries in, carrying the steel dust with it. Cotton waste is one of the best things to clean a stone with, and is nearly always to be found in a shop.

If the stone does become glazed or gummed up, a good cleaning with gasolene or ammonia will usually restore its cutting qualities, but if it does not, then scour the stone with loose emery or sandpaper fastened to a perfectly smooth board.

Never use turpentine on an oilstone for any purpose.

SCREW MACHINE TOOLS, SPEEDS AND FEEDS

BOX TOOLS AND CUTTERS

THE general principles of two types of box tools using respectively tangent and radial cutters are represented in Figs. 1 and 2. The former type is generally used for roughing and the latter for finishing. The tangent cutter in the type of box tool shown in Fig. 1 lies in a slot formed parallel to the bottom of the box but at an angle, usually

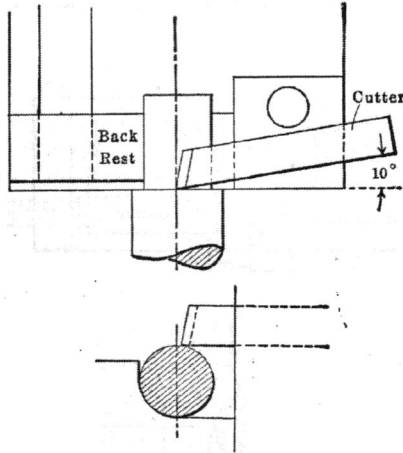

FIG. 1. — Roughing Box Tool with Tangent Cutter

ten degrees, with the front of the box, thus giving the desired rake at the cutting point. Finishing cutters of the type in Fig. 2 are straight on the end, located square with the work and ordinarily ground as indicated to give 7 to 10 degrees front clearance for steel and 5 to 8 degrees for brass.

The tangent cutter is sharpened by grinding on the end, and compensation for the grinding away of the metal is made by adjusting the cutter forward, whereas in the radial type of cutter in Fig. 2, frequent sharpening cannot be done without resulting in lowering the cutting edge of the tool below the center of the work, unless a substantial part of the tool be sacrificed. The radial tool, however, is easily ground accurately on face a, which is the edge governing the finish; while the corresponding face on the tangent tool is rather difficult to grind so as to produce as smooth work.

245

The sizes of steel recommended for box-tool cutters are as follows: For box tools used for stock diameters up to $\frac{5}{16}$ inch, $\frac{3}{16}$ inch square; up to $\frac{3}{8}$ inch diameter, $\frac{7}{32}$ inch square; up to $\frac{1}{2}$ inch diameter, $\frac{1}{4}$ inch square; up to $\frac{3}{4}$ inch diameter, $\frac{5}{16}$ inch square; up to 1 inch diameter, $\frac{3}{8}$ inch square; up to $1\frac{1}{2}$ inches diameter, $\frac{1}{2}$ inch square.

HOLLOW MILLS

THE teeth of hollow mills should be radial or ahead of the center. With the cutting edge ahead of the center, as in Fig. 3, the chips as produced are caused to move outward away from the work and prevented from disfiguring it. With the cutting edge below the center, rough turning will result. With the cutting edge greatly above the center, chattering occurs. About one tenth of the cutting diameter is a good average amount to cut the teeth ahead of the center.

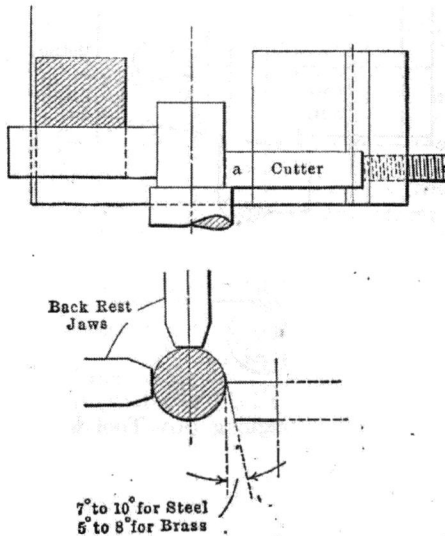

a Cutter

Back Rest
Jaws

7° to 10° for Steel
5° to 8° for Brass

FIG. 2. — Finishing Box Tool with
Radial Cutter

When the chips produced from any turning or boring cut curl nicely, it is indicative of a free cutting action; but these chips are very troublesome on the automatic screw machine. In making hollow mills for the automatic, part or all of the rake to the cutting edge is generally sacrificed.

The table under the hollow mill in Fig. 3 gives proportions of mills from $\frac{1}{16}$ to $\frac{3}{4}$ diameter, showing the amount to cut the teeth ahead of the center, the taper of the hole, etc.

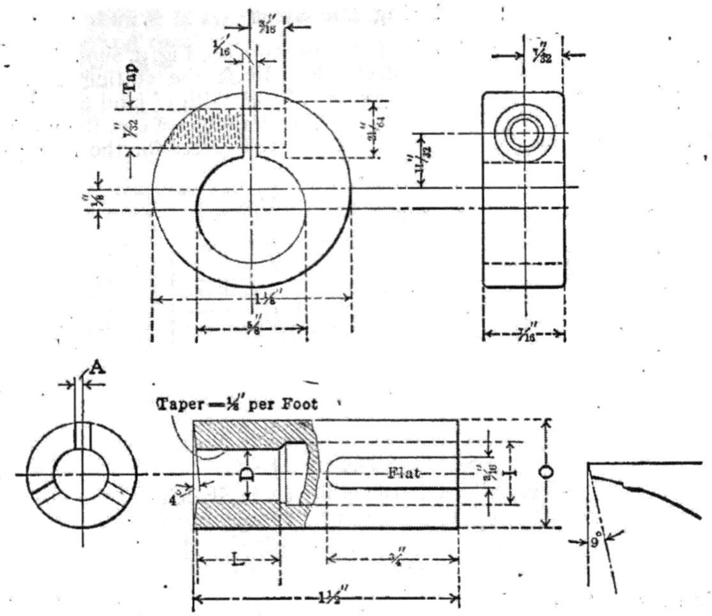

D = Finishing..	$\frac{1}{16}$	$\frac{3}{32}$	$\frac{1}{8}$	$\frac{5}{32}$	$\frac{3}{16}$	$\frac{7}{32}$	$\frac{1}{4}$	$\frac{9}{32}$	$\frac{5}{16}$	$\frac{3}{8}$	$\frac{1}{2}$	$\frac{5}{8}$	$\frac{3}{4}$
D = Roughing .	.072	.104	.135	.166	.197	.229	.26	.291	.322	.385	.510	.635	.760
L =	$\frac{1}{8}$	$\frac{1}{4}$	$\frac{5}{16}$	$\frac{5}{16}$	$\frac{3}{8}$	$\frac{3}{8}$	$\frac{7}{16}$	$\frac{7}{16}$	$\frac{1}{2}$	$\frac{5}{8}$	$\frac{3}{4}$	$\frac{7}{8}$	1
$A = \frac{D}{10} =$	.006	.009	.012	.015	.019	.022	.025	.028	.031	.038	.050	.063	.075
I =	$\frac{3}{16}$	$\frac{3}{16}$	$\frac{3}{16}$	$\frac{3}{16}$	$\frac{3}{16}$	$\frac{3}{8}$	$\frac{3}{8}$	$\frac{3}{8}$	$\frac{3}{8}$	$\frac{7}{16}$	$\frac{7}{16}$	$1\frac{1}{8}$	$1\frac{3}{8}$
O =	$\frac{3}{8}$	$\frac{3}{8}$	$\frac{3}{8}$	$\frac{3}{8}$	$\frac{3}{8}$	$\frac{3}{8}$	$\frac{3}{8}$	$\frac{3}{8}$	$\frac{3}{8}$	1	$1\frac{1}{4}$	$1\frac{3}{8}$	$1\frac{5}{8}$

FIG. 3.—Hollow Mill Dimensions

DIES AND TAPS

IT is good practice in making spring screw dies to either hob out the thread with a hob tap 0.005 to 0.015 inch over-size, according to size, and in use to spring the prongs to proper cutting size by a clamping ring, or to tap the die out from the rear with a hob tap tapering from $\frac{3}{16}$ inch to $\frac{1}{4}$ inch per foot, leaving the front end about 0.002 inch over cutting size, and in this case also to use a clamping ring. Both of these schemes are for the purpose of obtaining back clearance and are effective. Of the two the use of the taper hob is to be preferred.

Spring Die Sizes

The table of dimensions for spring screw dies, Fig. 4, should prove of service, particularly for steel. For brass the cutting edge is radial, thus eliminating dimension A. The width of land at bottom of thread is usually made about $\frac{1}{4}$ outside diameter of cut, the milling between flutes being 70 degrees, leaving 50 degrees for the prong in the case of three-flute dies.

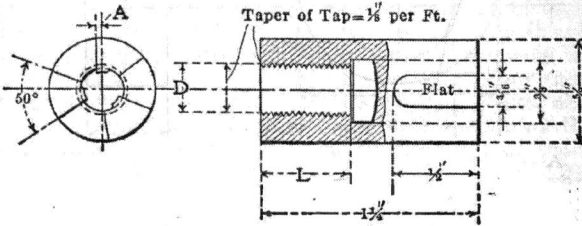

SMALL SIZES OF DIES
(Over all Dimensions Given in Sketch)

$D =$	$\frac{1}{16}$	$\frac{3}{8}$	$\frac{3}{16}$	$\frac{1}{4}$	$\frac{5}{16}$	No. 3	4	6	8	10	12
Threads P. I. =	64	40	32	20	18	56	40	32	24-32	24-32	24-32
$A = \dfrac{D}{10}$	.003	.012	.019	.025	.031	.010	.011	.014	.016	0.19	.021
$L =$	$\frac{3}{16}$	$\frac{9}{32}$	$\frac{3}{8}$	$\frac{1}{2}$	$\frac{1}{2}$	$\frac{7}{32}$	$\frac{1}{4}$	$\frac{9}{32}$	$\frac{5}{16}$	$\frac{11}{32}$	$\frac{3}{8}$

SIZES $\frac{3}{8}$ TO 1 INCH

	$\frac{3}{8}$ to $\frac{1}{2}$	$\frac{1}{2}$ to $\frac{3}{4}$	$\frac{3}{4}$ to 1
$D =$	$\frac{3}{8}$ to $\frac{1}{2}$	$\frac{1}{2}$ to $\frac{3}{4}$	$\frac{3}{4}$ to 1
Th's P.I. =	Std.	Std.	Std.
$A =$	$D \div 10$	$D \div 10$	$D \div 10$
$L =$	$\frac{3}{4}$	$1''$	$1\frac{1}{2}$
O.S. Dia.	$1''$	$1\frac{1}{8}$	$1\frac{5}{8}$
Length	$2''$	$2\frac{1}{4}''$	$2\frac{1}{2}''$

FIG. 4. — Spring Die Dimensions

Sizing Work for Threading

In boring holes previously to tapping they should be somewhat larger than the theoretical diameter at bottom of thread, as the crowding action of the tap will cause the metal to flow some and compensate for this. Where no allowance is made, frequent tap breakage is liable to occur and torn threads in the work also. On external work it is for the same reasons advisable to turn the work undersize and the following table gives good average allowances for both internal and external work.

ALLOWANCES FOR THREADING IN THE SCREW MACHINE

Threads per Inch	External Work Turn Undersize	Internal Work Increase Over Theoretical Bottom of Thread
28	0.002	0.004
24	0.002	0.0045
22	0.0025	0.005
20	0.0025	0.0055
16	0.003	0.006
14	0.003	0.0065
13	0.0035	0.007
12	0.0035	0.007
11	0.0035	0.0075
10	0.004	0.008
9	0.004	0.0085
8	0.0045	0.009
7	0.0045	0.0095
6	0.005	0.010

Tap Length and Number of Lands

The number of teeth in taps and the width of land should be regulated by the diameter and pitch of work as well as the nature of the material being cut. On fine threads, where a drunken thread is to be insured against, more teeth are required than on a coarser pitch of the same diameter. A good average number of teeth on taps for United States standard threads is given in the following table. With

Outside Dia.	No. of Flutes	Width of Land
$\frac{3}{16}$	4	$\frac{3}{64}$
$\frac{1}{4}$	4	$\frac{1}{16}$
$\frac{5}{16}$	4	$\frac{5}{64}$
$\frac{3}{8}$	4	$\frac{3}{32}$
$\frac{7}{16}$	4	$\frac{7}{64}$
$\frac{1}{2}$	4	$\frac{1}{8}$
$\frac{5}{8}$	4	$\frac{5}{32}$
$\frac{3}{4}$	4	$\frac{3}{16}$
$\frac{7}{8}$	4	$\frac{7}{32}$
1	4	$\frac{1}{4}$
$1\frac{1}{4}$	4	$\frac{5}{16}$

too few teeth and too short land very little support is afforded and this may cause chattering; too much land in contact causes heat due to excessive friction, welding of chips and torn threads.

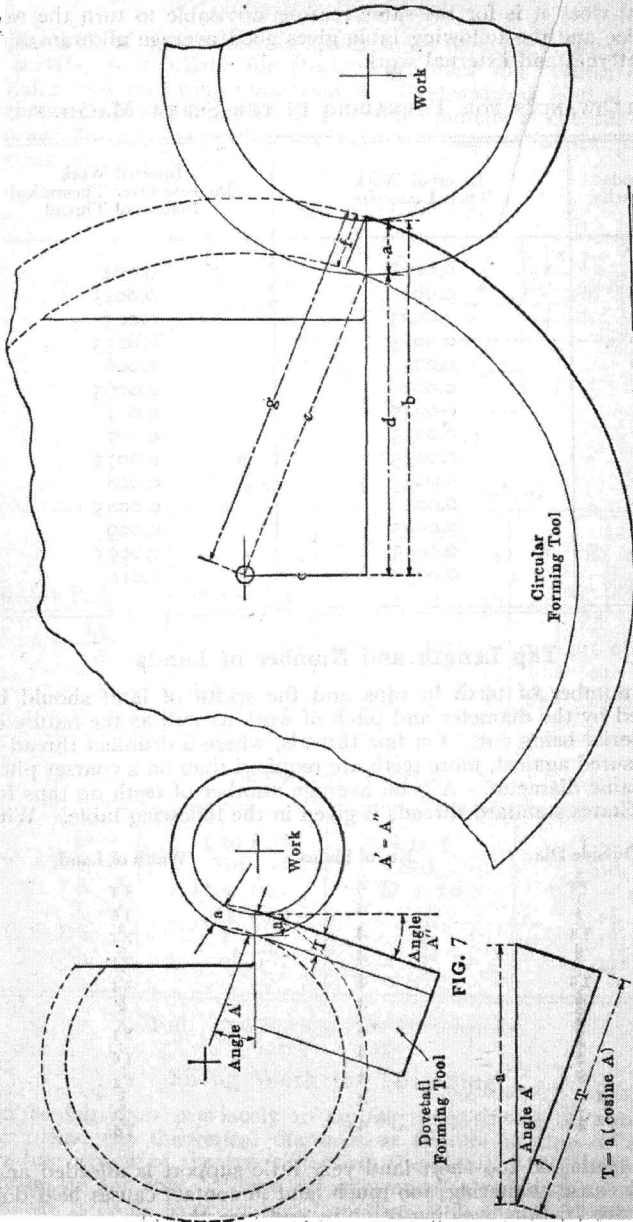

Forming Tool Diameters and Depths

FIG. 7

FIG. 8

FIG. 9

Work

Circular
Forming Tool

Dovetail
Forming Tool

Angle A'

Angle A'

Angle A'

A' - A"

Work

$$l = g - \sqrt{g^2 + a^2 - (2\ a)\sqrt{g^2 - c^2}}$$

$$T = a\ (\text{cosine } A)$$

FORMING TOOLS

THE two types of forming cutters commonly used in the screw machine are shown in Figs. 5 and 6. The circular forming cutter in Fig. 5 is usually cut away from $\frac{1}{8}$ to $\frac{3}{16}$ inch below center to give suitable cutting clearance and the center of the tool post on which it is mounted is a corresponding amount above the center of the machine, so that the cutting edge of the circular tool is brought on

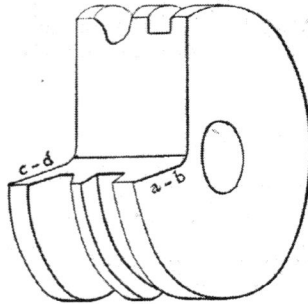

FIG. 5. — Circular Forming Tool

the center line of the work. The relative clearance ordinarily obtained by circular cutters and dovetail tools of the type shown in Fig. 6, is indicated in Fig. 7. It is obvious that with a given material the larger the diameter of the work the greater the angle of clearance required. Clearance angles are seldom less than 7 degrees or over 12 degrees.

The diameter of circular forming tools is an important matter for consideration. A small diameter has a more pronounced change of

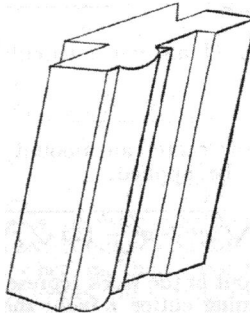

FIG. 6. — Dovetail Forming Tool

clearance angle than a large diameter. In fact, when of an exceedingly large diameter the circular tool approaches in cutting action the dovetail type of tool which is usually provided with about 10 degrees clearance. Circular tools usually range from about $1\frac{1}{4}$ to 3 inches diameter, depending upon the size of machine in which they are used.

Getting the Tool Diameters at Different Points

In order to make a circular or a dovetail type of tool so that the contour of its cutting edge is such as to produce correct work, the amount a circular tool is cut below center, as at c in Fig. 8, and the clearance angle of a dovetail tool as at A', Fig. 7 must be known. Thus, referring to Fig. 8, the forming tool shown cuts two different diameters on the work, the step between being represented by dimension a. To find-depth f to which the forming tool must be finished on the center line to give the correct depth of cut a in the work (the

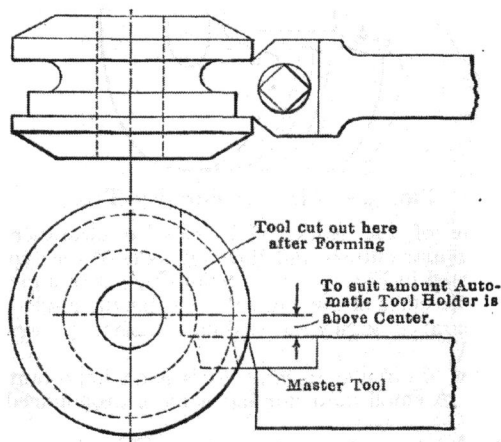

Tool cut out here
after Forming

To suit amount Auto-
matic Tool Holder is
above Center.

Master Tool

Fig. 10. — Finishing a Circular Tool

cutter being milled below center an amount represented by c) the following formula may be applied:

$$f = g - \sqrt{g^2 + a^2 - (2a\sqrt{g^2 - c^2})}.$$

Suppose the depth of cut in the work represented by a to be 0.152″; the radius g of the forming cutter 1 inch; the distance c which the forming tool is milled below center, $\frac{3}{16}$ inch. Applying the above formula to find f and substituting the values just given for the letters in the formula we have $f = 1 - \sqrt{1 + .0231 - (.304\sqrt{1 - .03516)}}$

$= 1 - \sqrt{1 + .0231 - (.304 \times .9823)}$

$= 1 - \sqrt{.724485} = 1 - .8512 = .1488$

Then $f = .1488$

Dovetail Tool Depths

If a similar piece of work is to be formed with a dovetail type of cutter, the distance T, Figs. 7 and 9, to which it is necessary to plane the tool shoulder in order that it may cut depth a correctly in the work, is found by the formula: $T = a$ (cosine A'). As 10 degrees is the customary clearance on this form of tool, the cosine of this angle, which is .98481, may be considered a constant, making reference to a table of cosines unnecessary as a rule. Assuming the same depth for a as in the previous case, that is .152 inch, and multiplying by .98481, gives .1496 inch as the depth of T to which the tool must be planed.

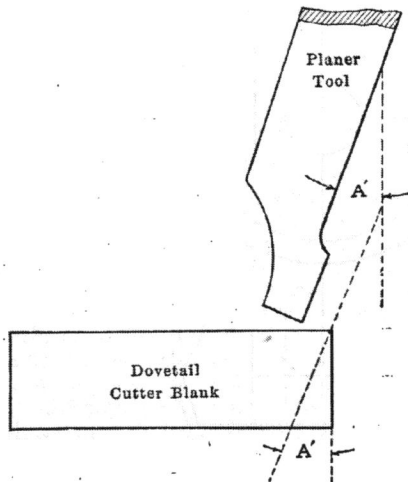

FIG. 11. — Finishing a Dovetail Forming Tool

While it frequently is necessary or advisable to determine by calculation the dimension computed in the preceding examples, in the majority of cases when making a cutter with a master tool of the same outline as the model, the correct form in the circular cutter is obtained automatically by dropping the master tool to the same distance below the lathe center as the circular cutter is to be milled off center and then feeding it in to finish the cutter. This procedure, shown in Fig. 10, assures the correct shape at all points being produced on the exact working plane of the cutter. Similarly, in finishing a dovetail cutter in the planer or shaper, the master tool may be set as in Fig. 11 at the same angle with the cutter (usually 10 degrees) as the latter will afterward be applied to the work.

CIRCULAR TOOL FOR CONICAL POINTS

WHEN a circular cutter is to be made for forming a conical surface on a piece as in Fig. 12, a master tool of the exact angle required on the work may be used for finishing the cutter in the same way as the tool in Fig. 9 is applied; that is, the master is to be dropped below center the amount the cutter center is to be above the work center when in operation. The distance is represented by A in Fig. 12. Another method, which avoids the necessity of making a master tool, is to set the compound rest of the lathe to the exact angle required (in this case 30 degrees with the center line) and with a horizontal

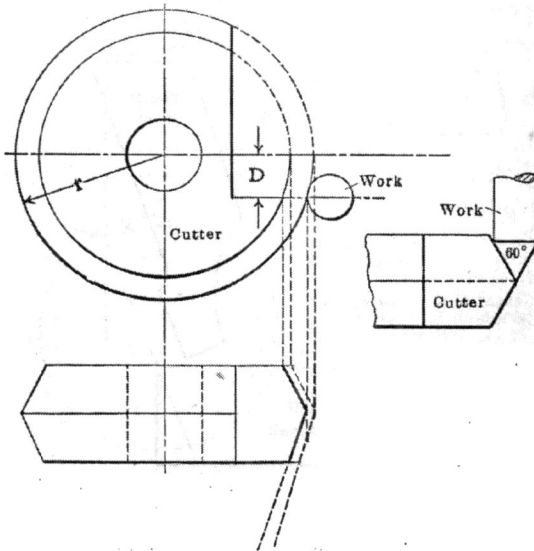

FIG. 12.— Circular Forming Tool for Conical Points

cutting tool set at distance D below center, turn off one side of the cutter blank and then set the compound rest around the other way and face off the other side. If desired a similar method may be followed for grinding the forming cutter after hardening. The arbor carrying the cutter should be located either above or below the grinding wheel a distance equal to $D\dfrac{(R + r)}{r}$ where D equals the depth the cutter is milled below center, r the radius of the cutter, and R the radius of the emery wheel. Assuming D to be .187 ($\frac{3}{16}$) inch; R, 2.5 inches; and r, 1 inch, the vertical distance between centers of forming tool and grinding wheel centers would equal .187 $\dfrac{(1 + 2.5)}{1}$ = .187 (3.5) = .6562 ($\frac{21}{32}$) inch.

FINDING DIAMETERS OF CIRCULAR
FORMING TOOLS

IN making circular forming tools it is oftentimes desirable to check the finished tool or finish a tool by grinding. It may also be advantageous to know the exact diameter a tool should be turned while making it, in order that calipering may be more convenient and certain. Methods of computing the diameter at different points are given on page 252, but in many cases of this kind the following tables will greatly facilitate matters, particularly when making circular forming tools for Brown & Sharpe automatic screw machines:

Suppose, for example, we have a piece to make like Fig. 13, on the No. 2 Brown & Sharpe automatic screw machine. The largest diameter of the circular forming tool would produce the smallest

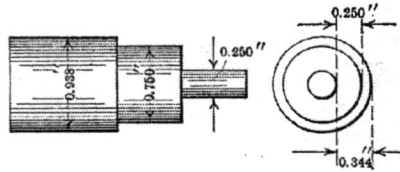

FIG. 13. — The piece to be made

diameter of the piece, which is 0.250 inch. The difference between this 0.250-inch diameter and the step of the 0.750-inch diameter is (0.750 — 0.250 inch) ÷ 2 = 0.250 inch.

The largest diameter of the circular forming tool for the No. 2 machine is 3 inches, which corresponds to a radius of 1.49998 inches with a base line of 1.479 inch for the triangle completed by the perpendicular joining the cutting line of the tool with the parallel line passing through the center of the tool.

The hypothenuse of the triangle is formed by the radius joining the intersection of the base line and the circumference of the tool as in Fig. 14. Subtracting 0.250 inch from 1.479 inches we have 1.229 inches, which, in Table 4, corresponds to a radius of 1.25417 inches, and multiplying by 2 gives a diameter of 2.50834 inches, to which to turn the cutter to correctly form the 0.750-inch diameter on the piece, Fig. 13.

Considering the largest diameter of the piece and taking the height of the second step above the first diameter, we have $\dfrac{0.938 - 0.25}{2} =$ 0.344 inch, and subtracting from 1.479 = 1.135 for the base line, which, in Table 4, corresponds to a radius of 1.16221. Multiplying by 2 gives a diameter of 2.3244 to turn the cutter to in order to produce the 0.938-inch diameter on the work. Tables 2, 3 and 4 are for cutters of the dimensions given in Table 1.

These tables are figured in steps of 0.001 inch for the capacity of the machines. A difference of a fractional part of a thousandth can be added to the radius if the step is a part of a thousandth over the base-line figures, which are given in even thousandths. For illustration: Say the base-line figure is 1.4765 inches. In the table 1.476 inches corresponds to a radius of 1.49702; add 0.0005 inch to 1.49702 and the radius will be as near correct as it is practicable to make a cutter.

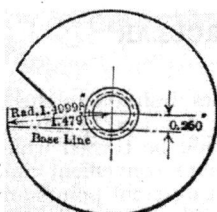

.FIG. 14

TABLE 1.—DIMENSIONS OF CUTTERS FOR B. & S. AUTOMATIC SCREW MACHINES

Mach. No.	Approx. Diam.	Max. Radius	Max. Base Line	Distance Above or Below Center
2	3″	1.49998″	1.479″	0.250″
o	2¼″	1.12474″	1.109″	0.1875″
oo	1¾″	0.87497″	0.866″	0.125″

TABLE 2.—FOR FINDING DIAMETERS OF CIRCULAR FORMING TOOLS FOR BROWN & SHARPE NO. oo AUTOMATIC SCREW MACHINE

No. oo		No. oo		No. oo		No. oo		No. oo	
Base Line	Radius	Base Line	Radius	Base Line	Radius	Base Line	Radius	Base Line	Radius
.866	.87497	.841	.85024	.815	.82453	.789	.79884	.763	.77317
.865	.87398	.840	.84925	.814	.82354	.788	.79785	.762	.77218
.864	.87300	.839	.84826	.813	.82255	.787	.79686	.761	.77120
.863	.87201	.838	.84727	.812	.82156	.786	.79588	.760	.77021
.862	.87102	.837	.84628	.811	.82058	.785	.79489	.759	.76922
.861	.87003	.836	.84529	.810	.81959	.784	.79390	.758	.76823
.860	.86904	.835	.84430	.809	.81860	.783	.79291	.757	.76725
.859	.86805	.834	.84332	.808	.81761	.782	.79193	.756	.76626
.858	.86706	.833	.84233	.807	.81662	.781	.79094	.755	.76528
.857	.86607	.832	.84134	.806	.81564	.780	.78995	.754	.76429
.856	.86508	.831	.84035	.805	.81465	.779	.77896	.753	.76330
.855	.86409	.830	.83936	.804	.81366	.778	.78798	.752	.76232
.854	.86310	.829	.83837	.803	.81267	.777	.78699	.751	.76133
.853	.86211	.828	.83738	.802	.81168	.776	.78600	.750	.76035
.852	.86112	.827	.83639	.801	.81069	.775	.78502	.749	.75936
.851	.86013	.826	.83540	.800	.80971	.774	.78403	.748	.75837
.850	.85914	.825	.83442	.799	.80872	.773	.78304	.747	.75739
.849	.85815	.824	.83343	.798	.80773	.772	.78205	.746	.75640
.848	.85716	.823	.83244	.797	.80674	.771	.78107	.745	.75541
.847	.85617	.822	.83145	.796	.80576	.770	.78008	.744	.75443
.846	.85518	.821	.83046	.795	.80477	.769	.77909	.743	.75344
.845	.85420	.820	.82947	.794	.80378	.768	.77811	.742	.75246
.844	.85321	.819	.82848	.793	.80279	.767	.77712	.741	.75147
.843	.85222	.818	.82750	.792	.80180	.766	.77613	.740	.75048
.842	.85123	.817	.82651	.791	.80082	.765	.77515		
		.816	.82552	.790	.79983	.764	.77416		

NOTE.—In the above Table 2 and Tables 3 and 4, it should be noted, as explained on page 255, that the Base Line dimensions in the columns under that heading and in the diagram, Fig. 14, are actually the distance of the cutting edge of the tool from the center of the cutter, the latter being used in the machine a certain distance either above or below the spindle center corresponding to Table 1. The distance from the cutting edge to center is therefore shorter than the true cutter radius by the amount indicated in the tables.

TABLE 3.—FOR FINDING DIAMETERS OF CIRCULAR FORMING TOOLS FOR BROWN & SHARPE NO. 0 AUTOMATIC SCREW MACHINE

No. 0		No. 0		No. 0		No. 0		No. 0	
Base Line	Radius	Base Line	Radius	Base Line	Radius	Base Line	Radius	Base Line	Radius
1.109	1.12474	1.060	1.07646	1.010	1.02726	.960	.97813	.910	.92911
1.108	1.12375	1.059	1.07547	1.009	1.02627	.959	.97715	.909	.92813
1.107	1.12277	1.058	1.07448	1.008	1.02529	.958	.97617	.908	.92715
1.106	1.12178	1.057	1.07350	1.007	1.02431	.957	.97519	.907	.92617
1.105	1.12079	1.056	1.07252	1.006	1.02332	.956	.97421	.906	.92519
1.104	1.11981	1.055	1.07153	1.005	1.02234	.955	.97323	.905	.92421
1.103	1.11882	1.054	1.07055	1.004	1.02136	.954	.97225	.904	.92324
1.102	1.11784	1.053	1.06956	1.003	1.02038	.953	.97127	.903	.92226
1.101	1.11685	1.052	1.06857	1.002	1.01939	.952	.97028	.902	.92128
1.100	1.11586	1.051	1.06759	1.001	1.01841	.951	.96930	.901	.92030
1.099	1.11488	1.050	1.06661	1.000	1.01743	.950	.96832	.900	.91932
1.098	1.11389	1.049	1.06563	.999	1.01644	.949	.96734	.899	.91834
1.097	1.11291	1.048	1.06464	.998	1.01546	.948	.96636	.898	.91732
1.096	1.11192	1.047	1.06366	.997	1.01448	.947	.96538	.897	.91638
1.095	1.11094	1.046	1.06267	.996	1.01349	.946	.96440	.896	.91540
1.094	1.10995	1.045	1.06169	.995	1.01251	.945	.96342	.895	.91442
1.093	1.10896	1.044	1.06070	.994	1.01153	.944	.96244	.894	.91345
1.092	1.10798	1.043	1.05972	.993	1.01055	.943	.96146	.893	.91247
1.091	1.10699	1.042	1.05874	.992	1.00957	.942	.96047	.892	.91149
1.090	1.10601	1.041	1.05775	.991	1.00858	.941	.95949	.891	.91051
1.089	1.10502	1.040	1.05677	.990	1.00760	.940	.95851	.890	.90953
1.088	1.10404	1.039	1.05578	.989	1.00662	.939	.95753	.889	.90855
1.087	1.10305	1.038	1.05480	.988	1.00563	.938	.95655	.888	.90757
1.086	1.10207	1.037	1.05381	.987	1.00465	.937	.95557	.887	.90660
1.085	1.10108	1.036	1.05283	.986	1.00367	.936	.95459	.886	.90562
1.084	1.10009	1.035	1.05185	.985	1.00269	.935	.95361	.885	.90464
1.083	1.09911	1.034	1.05086	.984	1.00170	.934	.95263	.884	.90366
1.082	1.09813	1.033	1.04988	.983	1.00072	.933	.95165	.883	.90268
1.081	1.09714	1.032	1.04889	.982	.99974	.932	.95067	.882	.90170
1.080	1.09616	1.031	1.04791	.981	.99875	.931	.94969	.881	.90073
1.079	1.09517	1.030	1.04693	.980	.99777	.930	.94871	.880	.89975
1.078	1.09418	1.029	1.04594	.979	.99679	.929	.94773	.879	.89877
1.077	1.09319	1.028	1.04496	.978	.99581	.928	.94675	.878	.89779
1.076	1.09221	1.027	1.04398	.977	.99483	.927	.94577	.877	.89681
1.075	1.09123	1.026	1.04299	.976	.99384	.926	.94479	.876	.89584
1.074	1.09024	1.025	1.04200	.975	.99286	.925	.94381	.875	.89486
1.073	1.08926	1.024	1.04102	.974	.99188	.924	.94283	.874	.89388
1.072	1.08828	1.023	1.04004	.973	.99090	.923	.94185	.873	.89290
1.071	1.08729	1.022	1.03906	.972	.98991	.922	.94087	.872	.89193
1.070	1.08630	1.021	1.03807	.971	.98893	.921	.93989	.871	.89095
1.069	1.08532	1.020	1.03709	.970	.98795	.920	.93891	.870	.88997
1.068	1.08433	1.019	1.03611	.969	.98697	.919	.93793	.869	.88899
1.067	1.08335	1.018	1.03512	.968	.98559	.918	.93695	.868	.88802
1.066	1.08236	1.017	1.03414	.967	.98501	.917	.93597	.867	.88704
1.065	1.08138	1.016	1.03316	.966	.98402	.916	.93499	.866	.88607
1.064	1.08039	1.015	1.03217	.965	.98304	.915	.93401	.865	.88508
1.063	1.07941	1.014	1.03119	.964	.98206	.914	.93303	.864	.88411
1.062	1.07842	1.013	1.03021	.963	.98108	.913	.93205	.863	.88313
1.061	1.07744	1.012	1.02922	.962	.98010	.912	.93107	.862	.88216
		1.011	1.02824	.961	.97912	.911	.93009	.861	.88118
								.860	.88020
								.859	.87922

TABLE 4. — FOR FINDING DIAMETERS OF CIRCULAR FORMING
TOOLS FOR BROWN & SHARPE NO. 2 AUTOMATIC
SCREW MACHINE

No. 2		No. 2		No. 2		No. 2		No. 2	
Base Line	Radius	Base Line	Radius	Base Line	Radius	Base Line	Radius	Base Line	Radius
1.479	1.49998	1.430	1.45168	1.380	1.40246	1.330	1.35329	1.280	1.30419
1.478	1.49899	1.429	1.45070	1.379	1.40148	1.329	1.35231	1.279	1.30320
1.477	1.49801	1.428	1.44982	1.378	1.40050	1.328	1.35133	1.278	1.30222
1.476	1.49702	1.427	1.44873	1.377	1.39952	1.327	1.35035	1.277	1.30124
1.475	1.49604	1.426	1.44775	1.376	1.39853	1.326	1.34936	1.276	1.30026
1.474	1.49505	1.425	1.44676	1.375	1.39754	1.325	1.34838	1.275	1.29928
1.473	1.49406	1.424	1.44578	1.374	1.39656	1.324	1.34740	1.274	1.29830
1.472	1.49308	1.423	1.44479	1.373	1.39558	1.323	1.34641	1.273	1.29732
1.471	1.49209	1.422	1.44381	1.372	1.39459	1.322	1.34543	1.272	1.29633
1.470	1.49110	1.421	1.44282	1.371	1.39360	1.321	1.34445	1.271	1.29535
1.469	1.49012	1.420	1.44184	1.370	1.39262	1.320	1.34347	1.270	1.29437
1.468	1.48913	1.419	1.44085	1.369	1.39164	1.319	1.34248	1.269	1.29339
1.467	1.48815	1.418	1.43987	1.368	1.39066	1.318	1.34150	1.268	1.29241
1.466	1.48716	1.417	1.43874	1.367	1.38967	1.317	1.34052	1.267	1.29143
1.465	1.48618	1.416	1.43790	1.366	1.38869	1.316	1.33954	1.266	1.29045
1.464	1.48519	1.415	1.43090	1.365	1.38770	1.315	1.33855	1.265	1.28947
1.463	1.48421	1.414	1.43593	1.364	1.38672	1.314	1.33757	1.264	1.28848
1.462	1.48322	1.413	1.43495	1.363	1.38574	1.313	1.33659	1.263	1.28750
1.461	1.48223	1.412	1.43396	1.362	1.38475	1.312	1.33560	1.262	1.28652
1.460	1.48125	1.411	1.43298	1.361	1.38377	1.311	1.33462	1.261	1.28554
1.459	1.48026	1.410	1.43199	1.360	1.38279	1.310	1.33364	1.260	1.28456
1.458	1.47928	1.409	1.43100	1.359	1.38181	1.309	1.33266	1.259	1.28358
1.457	1.47829	1.408	1.43002	1.358	1.38082	1.308	1.33168	1.258	1.28260
1.456	1.47731	1.407	1.42905	1.357	1.37984	1.307	1.33069	1.257	1.28162
1.455	1.47632	1.406	1.42805	1.356	1.37885	1.306	1.32971	1.256	1.28064
1.454	1.47534	1.405	1.42707	1.355	1.37786	1.305	1.32873	1.255	1.27966
1.453	1.47435	1.404	1.42608	1.354	1.37689	1.304	1.32775	1.254	1.27868
1.452	1.47337	1.403	1.42510	1.353	1.37590	1.303	1.32677	1.253	1.27770
1.451	1.47238	1.402	1.42411	1.352	1.37492	1.302	1.32578	1.252	1.27672
1.450	1.47139	1.401	1.42313	1.351	1.37393	1.301	1.32480	1.251	1.27574
1.449	1.47041	1.400	1.42215	1.350	1.37295	1.300	1.32382	1.250	1.27476
1.448	1.46944	1.399	1.42116	1.349	1.37197	1.299	1.32284	1.249	1.27377
1.447	1.46846	1.398	1.42118	1.348	1.37098	1.298	1.32186	1.248	1.27279
1.446	1.46745	1.397	1.41919	1.347	1.37000	1.297	1.32087	1.247	1.27181
1.445	1.46647	1.396	1.41821	1.346	1.36902	1.296	1.31989	1.246	1.27083
1.444	1.46548	1.395	1.41723	1.345	1.36804	1.295	1.31891	1.245	1.26985
1.443	1.46459	1.394	1.41624	1.344	1.36705	1.294	1.31793	1.244	1.26887
1.442	1.46351	1.393	1.41526	1.343	1.36607	1.293	1.31695	1.243	1.26789
1.441	1.46253	1.392	1.41427	1.342	1.36509	1.292	1.31596	1.242	1.26691
1.440	1.46154	1.391	1.41329	1.341	1.36410	1.291	1.31498	1.241	1.26593
1.439	1.46056	1.390	1.41230	1.340	1.36312	1.290	1.31400	1.240	1.26495
1.438	1.45957	1.389	1.41132	1.339	1.36214	1.289	1.31301	1.239	1.26397
1.437	1.45853	1.388	1.41033	1.338	1.36116	1.288	1.31203	1.238	1.26299
1.436	1.45759	1.387	1.40935	1.337	1.36017	1.287	1.31106	1.237	1.26201
1.435	1.45661	1.386	1.40837	1.336	1.35919	1.286	1.31008	1.236	1.26103
1.434	1.45563	1.385	1.40738	1.335	1.35820	1.285	1.30909	1.235	1.26005
1.433	1.45464	1.384	1.40640	1.334	1.35722	1.284	1.30811	1.234	1.25907
1.432	1.45366	1.383	1.40541	1.333	1.35624	1.283	1.30713	1.233	1.25809
1.431	1.45267	1.382	1.40443	1.332	1.35526	1.282	1.30615	1.232	1.25711
		1.381	1.40345	1.331	1.35428	1.281	1.30517	1.231	1.25613

TABLE 4. — FOR FINDING DIAMETERS OF CIRCULAR FORMING TOOLS FOR BROWN & SHARPE NO. 2 AUTOMATIC SCREW MACHINE

No. 2		No. 2		No. 2		No. 2		No. 2	
Base Line	Radius	Base Line	Radius	Base Line	Radius	Base Line	Radius	Base Line	Radius
1.230	1.25515	1.178	1.20424	1.126	1.15342	1.074	1.10271	1.022	1.05213
1.229	1.25417	1.177	1.20326	1.125	1.15244	1.073	1.10174	1.021	1.05116
1.228	1.25319	1.176	1.20228	1.124	1.15147	1.072	1.10076	1.020	1.05019
1.227	1.25221	1.175	1.20130	1.123	1.15049	1.071	1.09979	1.019	1.04920
1.226	1.25123	1.174	1.20032	1.122	1.14951	1.070	1.09882	1.018	1.04825
1.225	1.25025	1.173	1.19934	1.121	1.14854	1.069	1.09784	1.017	1.04728
1.224	1.24927	1.172	1.19837	1.120	1.14756	1.068	1.09687	1.016	1.04631
1.223	1.24829	1.171	1.19739	1.119	1.14659	1.067	1.09590	1.015	1.04533
1.222	1.24731	1.170	1.19641	1.118	1.14561	1.066	1.09492	1.014	1.04436
1.221	1.24633	1.169	1.19543	1.117	1.14463	1.065	1.09395	1.013	1.04339
1.220	1.24535	1.168	1.19446	1.116	1.14366	1.064	1.09298	1.012	1.04242
1.219	1.24437	1.167	1.19348	1.115	1.14268	1.063	1.09200	1.011	1.04145
1.218	1.24339	1.166	1.19250	1.114	1.14171	1.062	1.09103	1.010	1.04048
1.217	1.24241	1.165	1.19152	1.113	1.14073	1.061	1.09006	1.009	1.03951
1.216	1.24143	1.164	1.19054	1.112	1.13976	1.060	1.08908	1.008	1.03854
1.215	1.24045	1.163	1.18957	1.111	1.13878	1.059	1.08811	1.007	1.03757
1.214	1.23947	1.162	1.18859	1.110	1.13780	1.058	1.08714	1.006	1.03660
1.213	1.23849	1.161	1.18761	1.109	1.13683	1.057	1.08616	1.005	1.03563
1.212	1.23752	1.160	1.18663	1.108	1.13586	1.056	1.08519	1.004	1.03466
1.211	1.23654	1.159	1.18566	1.107	1.13488	1.055	1.08422	1.003	1.03369
1.210	1.23556	1.158	1.18468	1.106	1.13390	1.054	1.08324	1.002	1.03273
1.209	1.23458	1.157	1.18370	1.105	1.13293	1.053	1.08227	1.001	1.03175
1.208	1.23360	1.156	1.18272	1.104	1.13195	1.052	1.08130	1.000	1.03078
1.207	1.23262	1.155	1.18175	1.103	1.13098	1.051	1.08032	.999	1.02981
1.206	1.23164	1.154	1.18077	1.102	1.13000	1.050	1.07935	.998	1.02884
1.205	1.23066	1.153	1.17979	1.101	1.12903	1.049	1.07838	.997	1.02787
1.204	1.22968	1.152	1.17881	1.100	1.12805	1.048	1.07741	.996	1.02690
1.203	1.22870	1.151	1.17784	1.099	1.12708	1.047	1.07643	.995	1.02593
1.202	1.22772	1.150	1.17686	1.098	1.12610	1.046	1.07546	.994	1.02496
1.201	1.22675	1.149	1.17588	1.097	1.12513	1.045	1.07449	.993	1.02399
1.200	1.22577	1.148	1.17491	1.096	1.12415	1.044	1.07352	.992	1.02302
1.199	1.22479	1.147	1.17393	1.095	1.12318	1.043	1.07254	.991	1.02205
1.198	1.22381	1.146	1.17295	1.094	1.12220	1.042	1.07157	.990	1.02108
1.197	1.22283	1.145	1.17197	1.093	1.12123	1.041	1.07060	.989	1.02011
1.196	1.22185	1.144	1.17100	1.092	1.12025	1.040	1.06963	.988	1.01914
1.195	1.22087	1.143	1.17002	1.091	1.11928	1.039	1.06865	.987	1.01817
1.194	1.21989	1.142	1.16904	1.090	1.11830	1.038	1.06768	.986	1.01720
1.193	1.21891	1.141	1.16807	1.089	1.11733	1.037	1.06671	.985	1.01623
1.192	1.21793	1.140	1.16709	1.088	1.11635	1.036	1.06574	.984	1.01526
1.191	1.21696	1.139	1.16612	1.087	1.11538	1.035	1.06477	.983	1.01429
1.190	1.21598	1.138	1.16514	1.086	1.11440	1.034	1.06379	.982	1.01332
1.189	1.21500	1.137	1.16416	1.085	1.11343	1.033	1.06282	.981	1.01235
1.188	1.21402	1.136	1.16318	1.084	1.11246	1.032	1.06185	.980	1.01139
1.187	1.21304	1.135	1.16221	1.083	1.11148	1.031	1.06088	.979	1.01042
1.186	1.21206	1.134	1.16123	1.082	1.11051	1.030	1.05991	.978	1.00945
1.185	1.21108	1.133	1.16025	1.081	1.10953	1.029	1.05893	.977	1.00848
1.184	1.21011	1.132	1.15928	1.080	1.10856	1.028	1.05796	.976	1.00751
1.183	1.20913	1.131	1.15830	1.079	1.10758	1.027	1.05699	.975	1.00654
1.182	1.20815	1.130	1.15732	1.078	1.10661	1.026	1.05602	.974	1.00557
1.181	1.20717	1.129	1.15635	1.077	1.10563	1.025	1.05505	.973	1.00460
1.180	1.20619	1.128	1.15537	1.076	1.10466	1.024	1.05408	.972	1.00363
1.179	1.20521	1.127	1.15440	1.075	1.10369	1.023	1.05310	.971	1.00267
								.970	1.00170

HARDENING SPRING COLLETS AND FEED CHUCKS

Before hardening collets it is common practice to open them somewhat to insure their having a given tension after hardening and tempering so that they will open and release the stock the instant they are themselves freed by the chucking mechanism. This opening of the chuck must be carefully attended to or an eccentric and unsatisfactory job will result. Sometimes a simple fixture having a cone pointed spindle is used for this purpose, the collet being held centrally while the cone plunger is forced between the chuck jaws to open them evenly the necessary amount. No matter how much care is taken in this operation, the effect is lost unless the hardening is properly attended to and only grinding will produce a perfectly true collet.

Preventing Distortion. — Some toolmakers take the precaution of leaving a thin fin of metal at the front end of the collet in each saw slot as at A, Fig. 15, in order that when hardened there shall be no chance of distortion due to unequal springing of the jaws. This metal tie or bridge at the ends of the jaws is removed by grinding out with a thin slitting wheel or lap. Another method, shown at B, also leaves a narrow ring at the front end to run on grinder center while collet is ground outside. The ring at the end of the nose may be ground off leaving the collet ready for use.

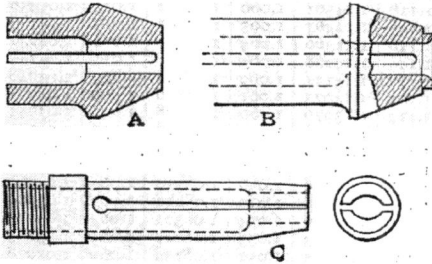

FIG. 15

Another method of preventing trouble in hardening is to insert a piece of metal, say $\frac{1}{32}$ inch thicker than the width of the saw slot, in the front end of the slots and then wire the nose of the chuck tightly so as to retain the steel pieces during the hardening process. The collet must be heated uniformly and dipped so as to insure all three prongs being cooled simultaneously. With the best of care a collet that is hardened but not ground afterward will generally require touching up on the conical portion of one or two of the prongs to insure its running true. It is not difficult, however, to make the collet run true within 0.002 inch by polishing one or two prongs.

In order that the collet may close parallel it must be fairly long and the outside of each prong or jaw may be relieved by filing so as to insure its bearing along the center line on the conical surface. It must be carefully tempered at the ends of slots to prevent breaking.

Feed Chucks. — Feed chucks need no such refinement in their production. They are usually closed after slitting on opposite sides so that after hardening they will maintain a constant grip on the stock sufficient to feed it forward when it is released by the chuck. The idea is indicated at C, Fig. 15. Ordinarily the hole for the stock should be bored a little over size otherwise the corners of the feed chuck jaws when drawn back over the stock will mar the surface.

TABLE 1. CUTTING SPEEDS AND FEEDS FOR SCREW STOCK

Dia. of Stock	1/32 Inch Chip			Dia. of Stock	1/16 Inch Chip			Dia. of Stock	1/8 Inch Chip			Dia. of Stock	1/4 Inch Chip		
	Feet Surface Speed	Rev. per Min.	Feed per Rev.		Feet Surface Speed	Rev. per Min.	Feed per Rev.		Feet Surface Speed	Rev. per Min.	Feed per Rev.		Feet Surface Speed	Rev. per Min.	Feed per Rev.
1/8	80	2445	.002	1/4	60	916	.0035	3/8	55	560	.004	3/4	50	254	.004
3/16	70	1426	.003	3/8	60	611	.004	1/2	55	420	.005	1	50	191	.005
1/4	70	1069	.004	1/2	60	458	.005	3/4	55	280	.006	1 1/4	45	137	.005
3/8	70	713	.005	3/4	55	280	.006	1	50	191	.007	1 1/2	45	114	.006
1/2	60	458	.006	1	55	210	.007	1 1/4	50	152	.007	1 3/4	45	98	.006
3/4	60	305	.007	1 1/4	55	168	.007	1 1/2	45	114	.007	2	40	76	.006
1	60	229	.008	1 1/2	50	127	.007	1 3/4	45	98	.007	2 1/4	40	68	.007
1 1/4	60	183	.008	1 3/4	50	109	.008	2	40	76	.008	2 1/2	40	61	.007

With high speed steel tools the speeds in these tables may be increased about 30 per cent and feeds 10 to 20 per cent.

TABLE 2. CUTTING SPEEDS AND FEEDS FOR BRASS

Dia. of Stock	1/32 Inch Chip			Dia. of Stock	1/16 Inch Chip			Dia. of Stock	1/8 Inch Chip			Dia. of Stock	1/4 Inch Chip		
	Feet Surface Speed	Rev. per Min.	Feed per Rev.		Feet Surface Speed	Rev. per Min.	Feed per Rev.		Feet Surface Speed	Rev. per Min.	Feed per Rev.		Feet Surface Speed	Rev. per Min.	Feed per Rev.
1/8	180	5500	.003	1/4	180	2748	.004	3/8	165	1680	.004	3/4	150	762	.005
3/16	180	3668	.004	3/8	180	1833	.005	1/2	165	1260	.006	1	150	573	.006
1/4	180	2748	.005	1/2	180	1374	.0065	3/4	165	840	.007	1 1/4	135	411	.007
3/8	180	1833	.006	3/4	165	840	.0075	1	150	573	.008	1 1/2	135	342	.008
1/2	180	1374	.008	1	165	630	.0085	1 1/4	150	456	.009	1 3/4	135	294	.008
3/4	180	915	.010	1 1/4	165	504	.010	1 1/2	135	342	.010	2	120	228	.009
1	180	687	.011	1 1/2	150	381	.012	1 3/4	135	294	.010	2 1/4	120	204	.009
1 1/4	180	549	.012	1 3/4	150	327	.012	2	120	228	.011	2 1/2	120	183	.010

SPEEDS AND FEEDS FOR SCREW MACHINE WORK

THE accompanying tables of speeds and feeds for different types of tools used on materials commonly worked in the automatic screw machine have been compiled from data accumulated and thoroughly tested during extended experience in this class of work.

It is, of course, impossible, where a series of tools is used on an automatic machine, to select speeds theoretically correct for every tool carried by the turret and cross slide. A compromise is necessary and therefore speeds are selected which will fall within the range suitable for the different tools.

Speeds and Feeds for Turning

Tables 1 and 2, page 261, cover turning speeds and feeds for bright-drawn stock (screw stock) and brass, with various depths of chip (that is, stock removed on a side) from $\frac{1}{32}$ up to $\frac{1}{4}$ inch. These feeds and speeds and depths of cut are figured more especially for such tools

TABLE 3. SPEEDS AND FEEDS FOR FINISH BOX TOOL

Finished Diameter of Work	SCREW STOCK			BRASS ROD			Amount advisable to remove on a side
	Feet Surface Speed	Rev. per Min.	Feed per Rev.	Feet Surface Speed	Rev. per Min.	Feed per Rev.	
$\frac{1}{8}$	80	2445	.0045	180	5500	.0045	.0025
$1\frac{3}{16}$	70	1426	.0055	180	3668	.0055	.0025
$\frac{1}{4}$	65	993	.0075	180	2750	.0075	.0045
$\frac{1}{2}$	60	458	.011	180	1375	.011	.006
$\frac{3}{4}$	60	305	.012	180	917	.012	.006
1	60	229	.012	175	668	.012	.0065
$1\frac{1}{2}$	55	140	.014	170	433	.014	.007
2	50	95	.014	170	325	.014	.008

With high speed steel tools the above speeds may be increased about 30 per cent and feeds 10 to 20 per cent.

as roughing boxes where the cut, though frequently heavy, is taken by a single cutting tool. For a $\frac{3}{16}$-inch chip the feeds for various diameters of stock are practically midway between those tabulated for $\frac{1}{8}$-and $\frac{1}{4}$-inch chips. The feed per revolution for $\frac{3}{8}$ chip taken on diameters $1\frac{1}{4}$ inch and larger is the same as given for $\frac{1}{4}$ inch chip, the speed also being the same for corresponding diameters. Where hollow mills are used on steel and the work is divided among three or more cutting edges the feed per revolution for a given depth of chip is about 25 per cent coarser than given for box tools; with both classes of tools the feeds are, of course increased as the diameter of the stock increases, the peripheral speeds being reduced as the feeds grow coarser. The speeds and feeds for finishing box tools as used on screw stock and brass are given in Table 3, the last column indicating the amount of stock which, generally speaking, it is advisable to remove in order to produce a good surface.

Forming-tool Speeds and Feeds

Speeds and feeds for forming tools are given in Tables 4 and 5. It will be seen that after a work diameter of about $\frac{1}{4}$ inch has been reached, a tool about $\frac{1}{8}$-inch wide is adapted to take the coarsest feed, tools from this width up to approximately $\frac{3}{16}$ (such as commonly employed for cutting-off purposes) admitting of heavier crowding as a rule than either the narrower or wider tools.

TABLE 4. SPEEDS FOR FORMING

Dia. of Work	Screw Stock		Brass Rod		Dia. of Work	Screw Stock		Brass Rod	
	Feet Surface Speed	Rev. per Min.	Feet Surface Speed	Rev. per Min.		Feet Surface Speed	Rev. per Min.	Feet Surface Speed	Rev. per Min.
$\frac{1}{8}$	75	2292	200	6112	$\frac{5}{8}$	60	360	175	1050
$\frac{3}{16}$	75	1528	200	4074	$\frac{3}{4}$	60	305	175	882
$\frac{1}{4}$	70	1069	185	2827	1	60	229	175	667
$\frac{3}{8}$	65	662	185	1885	$1\frac{1}{2}$	60	153	170	432
$\frac{1}{2}$	65	497	185	1414	2	50	96	170	324

With high speed steel tools the above speeds may be increased about 30 per cent.

TABLE 5. FEEDS FOR FORMING TOOLS

Width of Form	Smallest Diameter of Form							
	$\frac{1}{16}$	$\frac{1}{8}$	$\frac{3}{16}$	$\frac{1}{4}$	$\frac{3}{8}$	$\frac{1}{2}$	$\frac{3}{4}$	$1\frac{1}{2}$
$\frac{1}{16}$	.0007	.0008	.001	.0012	.0012	.0012	.0012	.0012
$\frac{1}{8}$	.0005	.0008	.001	.0012	.0015	.0020	.0025	.0025
$\frac{1}{4}$		.0007	.001	.001	.0015	.0015	.0018	.0018
$\frac{3}{8}$			.0009	.001	.001	.0012	.0015	.0015
$\frac{1}{2}$			.0008	.0009	.001	.001	.0015	.0015
$\frac{3}{4}$				.0008	.0009	.001	.0011	.0012
1					.0008	.0009	.001	.0012
$1\frac{1}{2}$					.0007	.0007	.0009	.0011
2							.0007	.001

With cutting-off tools of high speed steel the above feeds may be increased 10 to 10 per cent.

Drilling Speeds and Feeds

Drilling speeds and feeds are given in Table 6. While these speeds are based on much higher peripheral velocities than drill-makers as a rule recommend for general purposes, it should be noted that conditions for drilling in the automatic, on the ordinary run of work, are usually ideal so far as lubrication, steadiness of feed, etc., are concerned, and it is possible where the holes drilled are comparatively shallow and the drill has ample opportunity for cooling during operation of the other tools, to maintain speeds that would be considered too high to be attempted in general shop practice.

TABLE 6. DRILLING FEEDS AND SPEEDS

Dia. of Drill	SCREW STOCK Feed per Rev. of Drill	SCREW STOCK R.P.M. at 60 Ft. Peripheral Speed	BRASS ROD Feed per Rev.	BRASS ROD R.P.M. at 175 Ft. Peripheral Speed	Dia. of Drill	SCREW STOCK Feed per Rev.	SCREW STOCK R.P.M. at 55 Ft. Peripheral Speed	BRASS ROD Feed per Rev.	BRASS ROD R.P.M. at 165 Ft. Peripheral Speed
1/16	.0013	3667	.0017	10696	1/2	.005	420	.0065	1260
5/64	.0016	2933	.002	8555	9/16	.0057	373	.0074	1120
3/32	.0018	2445	.0023	7130	5/8	.0059	336	.0077	1008
1/8	.0025	1833	.0033	5348	11/16	.006	305	.0078	917
5/32	.003	1421	.0039	4144	3/4	.0065	280	.0084	841
3/16	.004	1222	.0052	3565	7/8	.0075	240	.0097	702
7/32	.004	1048	.0052	3050			50 Ft.		150 Ft.
1/4	.0045	916	.0058	2674	1	.0085	191	.0110	573
9/32	.0045	815	.0058	2377	1 1/4	.0095	152	.0123	458
5/16	.0045	733	.0058	2139	1 1/2	.011	127	.0143	382
3/8	.0045	611	.0061	1783	1 3/4	.013	109	.0169	327
7/16	.005	524	.0065	1528	2	.014	96	.0182	294

With high speed drills the above speeds may be increased about 30 per cent.

Speeds and Feeds for Reaming

Table 7 is made up of speed and feed data for reamers. In this table the feed for different classes of material has been considered as constant for any given diameter of reamer, although it is probable that with certain materials, especially on brass alloys, etc., the feed per revolution might be increased somewhat, to advantage, over the rates given. These feeds have been tabulated, however, as representing highly satisfactory practice in reaming the materials listed.

TABLE 7. REAMING FEEDS AND SPEEDS

Feed per Rev.	Amount to Remove on Dia.	REV. PER MIN.		Dia. of Reamer	Feed per Rev.	Amount to Remove on Dia.	REV. PER MIN.	
		Screw Stock at 40 Ft.	Brass Rod at 130 Ft.				Screw Stock at 40 Ft.	Brass Rod at 130 Ft.
.005	.0045	1222	3972	1¼	.018	.010	122	397
.006	.0045	815	2648	1½	.020	.010	102	331
.007	.006	611	1986	1¾	.022	.010	87	284
.0085	.006	407	1324	2	.024	.013	76	248
.0105	.008	306	993	2¼	.026	.013	68	220
.012	.008	245	795	2½	.028	.013	61	199
.014	.008	204	662	2¾	.030	.013	56	181
.016	.010	153	497	3	.032	.013	51	165

With high speed reamers the above speeds may be increased about 20 per cent.

Threading, Counterboring, Etc.

Table 8 explains itself and, while giving speeds for threading work th dies, should be of equal value in establishing speeds for tapping.

TABLE 8. SPEEDS FOR DIES. STANDARD THREADS
WITH HIGH-SPEED STEEL DIES

SCREW STOCK		BRASS ROD		Dia. of Thread	SCREW STOCK		BRASS ROD	
Feet Surface Speed	Rev. per Min.	Feet Surface Speed	Rev. per Min.		Feet Surface Speed	Rev. per Min.	Feet Surface Speed	Rev. per Min.
40	1222	135	4126	¼	35	178	115	586
40	611	125	1909	1	30	115	110	420
35	356	120	1222	1¼	30	92	100	306
35	267	120	917	1½	30	76	90	229
35	210	120	715	2	25	48	85	162

For carbon steel dies run at 50 to 75 % of above speeds.

For feeds for counterbores from ¾ inch to 2 inches diameter, bles 1 and 2 for turning may be followed where the counterbores to a depth from one half to three quarters their diameter. Where ting deeper than about one diameter, the feeds should be decreased; such depths it is well to withdraw the counterbore during the ting operation to free it from chips.

Drilling Speeds and Feeds

Drilling speeds and feeds are given in Table 6. While the speeds are based on much higher peripheral velocities than drill makers as a rule recommend for general purposes, it should be noted that conditions for drilling in the automatic, on the ordinary run of work, are usually ideal so far as lubrication, steadiness of feed, etc., are concerned, and it is possible where the holes drilled are comparatively shallow and the drill has ample opportunity for cooling during operation of the other tools, to maintain speeds that would be considered too high to be attempted in general shop practice.

TABLE 6. DRILLING FEEDS AND SPEEDS

Dia. of Drill	SCREW STOCK		BRASS ROD		Dia. of Drill	SCREW STOCK		BRASS R.	
	Feed per Rev. of Drill	R.P.M. at 60 Ft. Peripheral Speed	Feed per Rev.	R.P.M. at 175 Ft. Peripheral Speed		Feed per Rev.	R.P.M. at 55 Ft. Peripheral Speed	Feed per Rev.	R. 16 Pe. S
1/16	.0013	3667	.0017	10696	1/2	.005	420	.0065	1
3/64	.0016	2933	.002	8555	17/32	.0057	373	.0074	1
3/32	.0018	2445	.0023	7130	9/16	.0059	336	.0077	1
1/8	.0025	1833	.0033	5348	11/16	.006	305	.0078	
5/32	.003	1421	.0039	4144	3/4	.0065	280	.0084	
3/16	.004	1222	.0052	3565	7/8	.0075	240	.0097	
7/32	.004	1048	.0052	3050			50 Ft.		15 ft.
1/4	.0045	916	.0058	2674	1	.0085	191	.0110	
9/32	.0045	815	.0058	2377	1 1/4	.0095	152	.0123	
5/16	.0045	733	.0058	2139	1 1/2	.011	127	.0143	
3/8	.0045	611	.0061	1783	1 3/4	.013	109	.0169	
7/16	.005	524	.0065	1528	2	.014	96	.0182	

With high speed drills the above speeds may be increased about 30 per cen

Speeds and Feeds for Reaming

Table 7 is made up of speed and feed data for reamers. In this table the feed for different classes of material has been considered as constant for any given diameter of reamer, although is probable that with certain materials, especially on brass alloys, the feed per revolution might be increased somewhat, to advantage, over the rates given. These feeds have been tabulated, however as representing highly satisfactory practice in reaming the materials listed.

TABLE 7. REAMING FEEDS AND SPEEDS

Dia. of Reamer	Feed per Rev.	Amount to Remove on Dia.	Rev. per Min. Screw Stock at 40 Ft.	Brass Rod at 130 Ft.	Dia. of Reamer	Feed per Rev.	Amount to Remove on Dia.	Rev. per Min. Screw Stock at 40 Ft.	Brass Rod at 130 Ft.
	.005	.0045	1222	3972	1¼	.018	.010	122	397
	.006	.0045	815	2648	1½	.020	.010	102	331
	.007	.006	611	1986	1¾	.022	.010	87	284
	.0085	.006	407	1324	2	.024	.013	76	248
	.0105	.008	306	993	2¼	.026	.013	68	220
	.012	.008	245	795	2½	.028	.013	61	199
	.014	.008	204	662	2¾	.030	.013	56	181
1	.016	.010	153	497	3	.032	.013	51	165

With high speed reamers the above speeds may be increased about 20 per cent.

Threading, Counterboring, Etc.

Table 8 explains itself and, while giving speeds for threading work with dies, should be of equal value in establishing speeds for tapping.

TABLE 8. SPEEDS FOR DIES. STANDARD THREADS
WITH HIGH-SPEED STEEL DIES

Dia. of Thread	Screw Stock Feet Surface Speed	Rev. per Min.	Brass Rod Feet Surface Speed	Rev. per Min.	Dia. of Thread	Screw Stock Feet Surface Speed	Rev. per Min.	Brass Rod Feet Surface Speed	Rev. per Min.
	40	1222	135	4126	¾	35	178	115	586
	40	611	125	1909	1	30	115	110	420
	35	356	120	1222	1¼	30	92	100	306
	35	267	120	917	1½	30	76	90	229
	35	210	120	715	2	25	48	85	162

For carbon steel dies run at 50 to 75 % of above speeds.

For feeds for counterbores from ¾ inch to 2 inches diameter, Tables 1 and 2 for turning may be followed where the counterbores cut to a depth from one half to three quarters their diameter. Where cutting deeper than about one diameter, the feeds should be decreased; in such depths it is well to withdraw the counterbore during the cutting operation to free it from chips.

PUNCH PRESS TOOLS

METHOD OF FINDING THE DIAMETERS OF SHELL BLANKS

THIS method for the finding of diameters of shell blanks, applies also to some other shapes which frequently occur in practice.

The method is based upon the surface of the shell in comparison with the area of the blank and should therefore be used only when light material is to be considered. In case of the flanged shapes the width of the flange should be small in proportion to the diameter.

CYLINDRICAL SHELL

Fig. 1 shows a cylindrical shell of the diameter d and the depth h. To find the diameter of the blank, lay down the diameter d of the shell twice on a horizontal line, Fig. 2, add to this a distance equal to four times the depth h of the shell and describe a semicircle of which the total distance is the diameter. The vertical line D from the intersecting point with the circle to the horizontal line gives the desired blank diameter. Line D is to be drawn at a distance d from the end of the horizontal.

FLANGED SHELLS

If the shell has a flange as in Fig. 3, add four times the width of this flange to the horizontal line and proceed as above; see Fig. 4.

In the case of a hemisphere, Fig. 5, lay down the diameter three times on the horizontal line and draw the vertical line at the distance d from the end, as in Fig. 6.

If the hemisphere has a flange as in Fig. 7, add a distance equal to twice the width of the flange to the horizontal line, as in Fig. 8. In any case, the length of the vertical line D gives the desired diameter of blank.

TAPER SHELLS

If a shell with tapering sides, Fig. 9, has to be drawn, multiply first the bottom diameter by itself and divide the product by the sum of the two diameters d_1 and d in order to obtain the length x. Otherwise proceed as shown in Fig. 10.

FLANGED TAPER SHELLS

If the taper shell has a flange of the width a, Fig. 11, add to the base line of the diagram twice this width, as shown in Fig. 12.

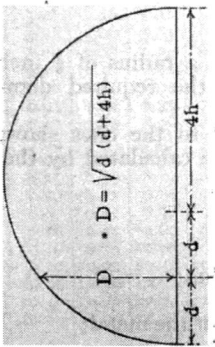

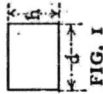

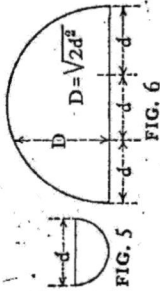

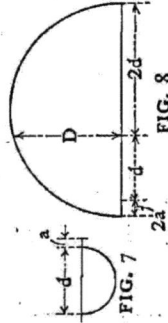

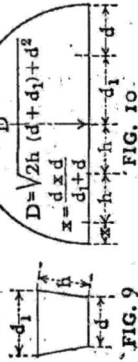

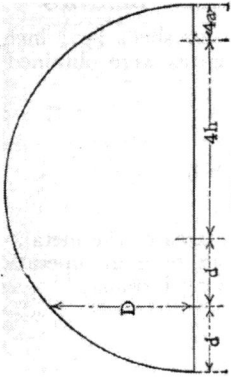

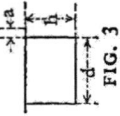

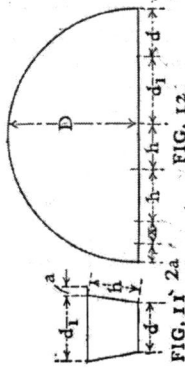

Finding the Diameters of Shell Blanks

FIG. 1
FIG. 2 $D=\sqrt{d\,(d+4h)}$

FIG. 3
FIG. 4

FIG. 5
FIG. 6 $D=\sqrt{2d^2}$

FIG. 7
FIG. 8

FIG. 9
FIG. 10 $D=\sqrt{2h\,(d+d_1)+d^2}$ $x=\dfrac{d\times d}{d_1+d}$

FIG. 11
FIG. 12

TABLE OF DIAMETERS OF SHELL BLANKS

THE table shows the diameters of blanks for shells $\frac{1}{4}$ x $\frac{1}{4}$ inch to 6 x 6 inches inclusive, by $\frac{1}{4}$ inches. The figures were obtained by the formula given on page 267:

$$D = \sqrt{d(d + 4h)}$$

where,

d = Diameter of finished shell.
h = Hight of finished shell.

They were also checked by figuring on the area of the metal.

If it is desired to punch the metal in one or more operations, get the mean hight of the shell by the following formula;

$$m = \frac{h\,t}{T}$$

where

m = Mean hight of finished shell.
h = Hight of finished shell.
t = Thickness of finished shell.
T = Thickness of metal before drawing.

Suppose for example, a shell 2 inches diameter by 6 inches high; thickness of metal before drawing, 0.040 inch; finish thickness of shell, 0.020 inch. Then

$$m = \frac{h\,t}{T} = \frac{6 \times 0.020}{0.040} = 3 \text{ inches.}$$

By using this hight, from the table we find a shell 2 inches diameter by 3 inches high requires a blank 5.29 inches diameter.

When the shell has rounded corners at the bottom, subtract the radius of the corner from the figures given in the table. Thus, in

FIG. 13

the last example, suppose the shell to have a radius of $\frac{1}{8}$ inch on the corner; 5.29 − 0.125 = 5.165 inches, the required diameter of the blanks.

When a shell has a cross-section similar to the ones shown in Fig. 13, the required blank diameter may be calculated by the following formula:

$$d = 1.1284 \sqrt{\frac{W}{w\,t}},$$

where

d = Diameter of blank in inches;
W = Weight of shell;
w = Weight of one cubic inch of the metal;
t = Thickness of shell.

DIAMETER OF BLANKS FOR SHELLS, ¼ x ¼ INCH TO 6 x 6 INCHES

Shell Diameter	Hight of Shell											
	¼″	½″	¾″	1″	1¼″	1½″	1¾″	2″	2¼″	2½″	2¾″	3″
¼″	0.56	0.75	0.90	1.03 (E)	1.14	1.25	1.35	1.44	1.52	1.60	1.68	1.75
½″	0.87	1.12	1.32	1.50	1.66	1.80	1.94	2.06	2.18	2.29	2.40	2.50
¾″	1.14	1.44	1.68	1.89	2.08	2.25	2.41	2.56	2.70	2.84	2.97	3.09
1″	1.41	1.73	2.00	2.24	2.45	2.65	2.83	3.00	3.16	3.32	3.46	3.61
1¼″	1.68	2.01	2.30	2.56	2.79	3.01	3.21	3.40	3.58	3.75	3.91	4.07
1½″	1.94	2.29	2.60	2.87	3.12	3.36	3.57	3.78	3.97	4.15	4.33	4.50
1¾″	2.19	2.56	2.88	3.17	3.44	3.68	3.91	4.13	4.34	4.53	4.72	4.91
2″	2.45	2.83	3.16	3.46	3.74	4.00	4.24	4.47	4.69	4.90	5.10	5.29
2¼″	2.70	3.09	3.44	3.75	4.04	4.31	4.56	4.80	5.03	5.25	5.46	5.66
2½″	2.96	3.36	3.71	4.03	4.33	4.61	4.87	5.12	5.36	5.59	5.81	6.02
2¾″	3.21	3.61	3.98	4.31	4.62	4.91	5.18	5.44	5.68	5.92	6.15	6.37
3″	3.46	3.87	4.24	4.58	4.90	5.20	5.48	5.74	6.00	6.25	6.48	6.71
3¼″	3.71	4.13	4.51	4.85	5.18	5.48	5.77	6.04	6.31	6.56	6.80	7.04
3½″	3.97	4.39	4.77	5.12	5.45	5.77	6.06	6.34	6.61	6.87	7.12	7.36
3¾″	4.22	4.64	5.03	5.39	5.73	6.05	6.35	6.64	6.91	7.18	7.44	7.69
4″	4.47	4.90	5.29	5.66	6.00	6.32	6.63	6.93	7.21	7.48	7.75	8.00
4¼″	4.72	5.15	5.55	5.92	6.27	6.60	6.91	7.22	7.50	7.78	8.05	8.31
4½″	4.98	5.41	5.81	6.19	6.54	6.87	7.19	7.50	7.79	8.08	8.35	8.62
4¾″	5.22	5.66	6.07	6.45	6.80	7.15	7.47	7.78	8.08	8.37	8.65	8.92
5″	5.48	5.92	6.32	6.71	7.07	7.42	7.75	8.06	8.37	8.66	8.94	9.22
5¼″	5.73	6.17	6.58	6.97	7.33	7.68	8.02	8.34	8.65	8.95	9.24	9.52
5½″	5.98	6.42	6.84	7.23	7.60	7.95	8.29	8.62	8.93	9.23	9.53	9.81
5¾″	6.23	6.68	7.09	7.49	7.86	8.22	8.56	8.89	9.21	9.52	9.81	10.10
6″	6.48	6.93	7.35	7.75	8.12	8.49	8.83	9.17	9.49	9.80	10.10	10.39

Shell Diameter	Hight of Shell											
	3¼″	3½″	3¾″	4″	4¼″	4½″	4¾″	5″	5¼″	5½″	5¾″	6″
¼″	1.82	1.89	1.95	2.01	2.08	2.14	2.19	2.25	2.30	2.36	2.41	2.46
½″	2.60	2.69	2.78	2.87	2.96	3.04	3.12	3.21	3.29	3.36	3.44	3.50
¾″	3.21	3.33	3.44	3.54	3.65	3.75	3.85	3.95	4.04	4.13	4.22	4.31
1″	3.74	3.87	4.00	4.12	4.24	4.36	4.47	4.58	4.69	4.80	4.90	5.00
1¼″	4.22	4.37	4.51	4.64	4.77	4.91	5.03	5.15	5.27	5.39	5.50	5.62
1½″	4.66	4.82	4.98	5.12	5.27	5.41	5.55	5.68	5.81	5.94	6.06	6.18
1¾″	5.08	5.26	5.41	5.58	5.73	5.88	6.03	6.17	6.31	6.45	6.58	6.71
2″	5.48	5.66	5.83	6.00	6.16	6.32	6.48	6.63	6.78	6.93	7.07	7.21
2¼″	5.86	6.05	6.23	6.41	6.58	6.75	6.91	7.07	7.23	7.39	7.54	7.69
2½″	6.22	6.42	6.61	6.80	6.98	7.16	7.33	7.50	7.66	7.82	7.98	8.14
2¾″	6.58	6.79	6.99	7.18	7.37	7.55	7.73	7.91	8.08	8.25	8.41	8.58
3″	6.93	7.14	7.35	7.55	7.75	7.94	8.12	8.31	8.49	8.66	8.83	9.00
3¼″	7.27	7.49	7.70	7.91	8.11	8.31	8.50	8.69	8.88	9.06	9.24	9.41
3½″	7.60	7.83	8.05	8.26	8.47	8.67	8.87	9.07	9.26	9.45	9.63	9.81
3¾″	7.92	8.16	8.38	8.61	8.82	9.03	9.24	9.44	9.63	9.83	10.02	10.20
4″	8.25	8.49	8.72	8.94	9.17	9.38	9.59	9.80	10.00	10.20	10.39	10.58
4¼″	8.56	8.81	9.04	9.28	9.50	9.72	9.94	10.15	10.36	10.56	10.76	10.96
4½″	8.87	9.12	9.37	9.60	9.84	10.06	10.28	10.50	10.71	10.92	11.12	11.32
4¾″	9.18	9.44	9.69	9.93	10.16	10.40	10.62	10.84	11.06	11.27	11.48	11.69
5″	9.49	9.75	10.00	10.25	10.49	10.72	10.95	11.18	11.40	11.62	11.83	12.04
5¼″	9.79	10.05	10.31	10.56	10.81	11.05	11.28	11.51	11.74	11.96	12.18	12.39
5½″	10.08	10.36	10.62	10.87	11.12	11.37	11.61	11.84	12.07	12.30	12.52	12.74
5¾″	10.38	10.66	10.92	11.18	11.44	11.69	11.93	12.17	12.40	12.63	12.85	13.08
6″	10.68	10.95	11.23	11.49	11.75	12.00	12.25	12.49	12.73	12.96	13.19	13.42

PUNCH AND DIE ALLOWANCE FOR ACCURATE WORK

In the blanking, perforating and forming of flat stock in the power press for parts of adding machines, typewriters, etc., it is generally desired to make two different kinds of cuts with the dies used. First, to leave the outside of the blank of a semi-smooth finish, with sharp corners, free from burrs, and with the least amount of rounding on the cutting side. Second, to leave the holes and slots that are per-

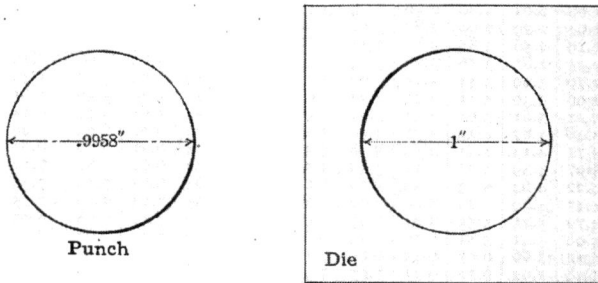

FIG. 14. — Blanking Tools

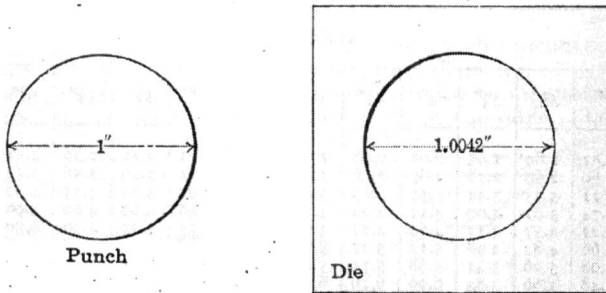

FIG. 15. — Perforating Tools

forated in the parts as smooth and straight as possible, and true to size. The table given is the result of considerable experimenting on this class of work, and has stood the test of years of use since it was compiled.

The die always governs the size of the work passing through it. The punch governs the size of the work that it passes through. In blanking work the die is made to the size of the work wanted and the punch smaller. In perforating work the punch is made to the size of the work wanted and the die larger than the punch. The clearance between the die and punch governs the results obtained.

Figs. 14 and 15 show the application of the table in determining the clearance for blanking or perforating hard rolled steel .060 inch thick. The clearance given in the table for this thickness of metal is .0042, and Fig. 14 shows that for blanking to exactly 1 inch diameter this amount is deducted from the diameter of the punch, while for perforating the same amount is added, as in Fig. 15, to the diameter of the die. For a sliding fit make punch and die .00025 to .0005 inch larger; and for a driving fit make punch and die .0005 to .0015 inch smaller.

TABLE OF ALLOWANCES FOR PUNCH AND DIE FOR DIFFERENT THICKNESS AND MATERIALS

Thickness of Stock Inch	Clearance for Brass and Soft Steel Inch	Clearance for Medium Rolled Steel Inch	Clearance for Hard Rolled Steel Inch
.010	.0005	.0006	.0007
.020	.001	.0012	.0014
.030	.0015	.0018	.0021
.040	.002	.0024	.0028
.050	.0025	.003	.0035
.060	.003	.0036	.0042
.070	.0035	.0042	.0049
.080	.004	.0048	.0056
.090	.0045	.0054	.0063
.100	.005	.006	.007
.110	.0055	.0066	.0077
.120	.006	.0072	.0084
.130	.0065	.0078	.0091
.140	.007	.0084	.0098
.150	.0075	.009	.0105
.160	.008	.0096	.0112
.170	.0085	.0102	.0119
.180	.009	.0108	.0126
.190	.0095	.0114	.0133
.200	.010	.012	.014

CLEARANCE FOR PUNCHES AND DIES FOR BOILER WORK

THE practice of the Baldwin Locomotive Works on sizes up to $1\frac{1}{4}$ inches is to make the punch $\frac{1}{64}$ inch below nominal size and the die $\frac{1}{64}$ inch above size, which gives $\frac{1}{32}$ inch clearance. Above $1\frac{1}{4}$ inches the punches are made to nominal size and the dies $\frac{1}{32}$ inch large, which allows the same clearance as before. The taper on dies below $1\frac{1}{4}$ inches is 1 inch in 12; on sizes above $1\frac{1}{4}$ inches it is half this or $\frac{1}{2}$ inch in 12 inches.

LUBRICANT FOR PRESS TOOLS

ALTHOUGH there are some shops in which no lubricant is used when working sheet metal, and where good results are obtained, still it is best to use a lubricant on all classes of sheet-metal work.

For all cutting dies on brass and steel a heavy animal oil is best. Pure lard oil is very satisfactory, although expensive.

When punching copper, or German silver, a thin coating of lard oil or sperm oil should be spread over the sheets or strips before punching. A good way to do this evenly is to coat one sheet thickly and then feed it through a pair of rolls, after which a number of other sheets may be run through the rolls and thus coated evenly. For drawn work this method of coating the sheets from which the shells are to be drawn will be found to be the best, as the coating of oil on the stock will be very thin and it will not be found necessary to clean the shells afterward, the oil having disappeared during the blanking and drawing process. When oil is applied with a pad or brush the coating will be so thick that it will be necessary to clean the article produced.

DRAWING STEEL SHELLS

In drawing steel shells a mixture of equal parts of oil and black lead is very useful, and while it may be used warm it does not affect the work as much as the speed of the drawing press does; the thicker the stock the slower must be the speed of the punch. A heavy grease with a small proportion of white lead mixed in with it is also recommended for this purpose.

If the drawing die is very smooth and hard at the corner of the "draw," or edge of the die, the liability of clogging will be reduced to a minimum. Often it will help to give to the die a lateral polish by taking a strip of emery cloth and changing the grain of the polish from circular to the same direction as the drawing.

LUBRICANTS FOR BRASS

For drawing brass or copper a clean soap water is considered most satisfactory. One of the largest brass firms in this country uses a preparation made by putting 15 pounds of Fuller's soap in a barrel of hot water, and boiling until all the lumps are dissolved. This is used as hot as possible. If the work is allowed to lie in the water until a slime has formed on the shell it will draw all the better. A soap that is strong in resin or potash will not give good results.

In drawing zinc the water should be hot, or the percentage of broken shells will be large.

Aluminum is an easy metal to draw, but it hardens up very quickly. For lubricants lard oil, melted Russian tallow and vaseline are all good. The lubricant should be applied to both sides of the metal.

BROACHES AND BROACHING

BROACHING is being used more and more to finish holes and even for slots and the outside of pieces of work. In most cases it is used to change a round hole to a square or other shape, such as the four or ten key ways used in automobile transmission.

The chip cut by each tooth varies from 0.001 to 0.007 inch, according to the material being cut and the accuracy required. The teeth are usually undercut from 6 to 10 degrees to give a curl to the chip, while the top clearance is about 30 degrees. Some English practice

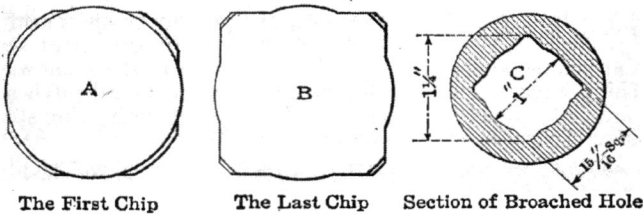

| The First Chip | The Last Chip | Section of Broached Hole |

FIG. 1

undercuts 25 degrees, having top nearly flat. The distance between teeth varies according to the length of the hole being broached, the spacing being larger for long holes so as not to have too many teeth engaged at once, three being a good number. Spacing varies with length of hole.

In broaching square holes from the round, or in other cases where there is a decided change of shape, the first teeth take the widest cut as at A, Fig. 1. This evens up the work of the different teeth

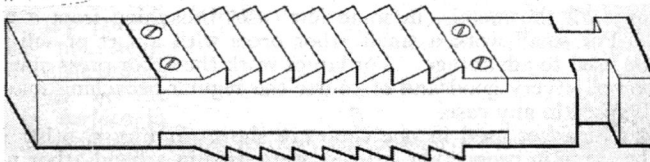

FIG. 2

as to the length of surface cut as the hole approaches a square as seen at B.

The blank for the cutting part of each broach is first turned taper by an amount equal to the total cut of the teeth. The tooth spaces are then turned $\frac{1}{2}$ inch apart and about $\frac{3}{32}$ inch deep, this depending on the diameter of the broach, as it must not be unduly weakened; it is then milled $1\frac{3}{8}$ inch square as shown. The longer the hole the more chip room must be provided.

Where the hole or other surface to be broached is short, the teeth are often cut on an angle to give a shearing cut. This is also done to prevent chatter at times, another remedy being to space the teeth unevenly as with reamers.

The solid broach is used more than any other. But as tool steel is apt to spring in hardening, and to break out teeth at times, some use built-up or sectional broaches, especially on large work where the solid broach costs heavily. Some use low carbon steel, case hardened. These sectional broaches are made in a variety of ways, Figs. 2 to 4 showing a few examples. In Fig. 2 sections are set in on the side, while in Figs. 3 and 4 the sections are practically disks held on a central arbor. In some cases several teeth are made on one section. Fig. 4 is made in the same way for broaching internal gears having 66 teeth, 20 diametral pitch and ½ inch face. Each tooth cuts 0.006, the last three teeth being straight to insure the size being accurate.

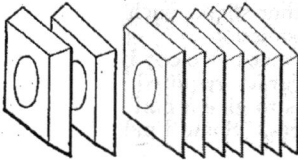

FIG. 3

FIG. 4

BROACHING ROUND HOLES

Round holes have been broached instead of reamed in some places for many years and the practice is growing. It was formerly confined to soft metal, such as shaft bearings, but is now being made to cover all the metals, in some few cases broaching from a cored hole. For small work a small arbor press with a sort of sub-press can be used to advantage. For larger work the arbor press operated by power is very good and of course the regular broaching machine can be used in any case.

Two broaches used in one shop are shown in Fig. 5, other sizes can be made in proportion. These were used in a hand arbor press. The first 5 or 6 teeth do most of the cutting as these broaches only finish the holes instead of reaming. In some cases with broaches for soft metal bearings and even in cast iron, the large end is left plain and a trifling amount larger than the last tooth. It then acts as a burnisher and compresses the metal. This requires a large amount of power.

In broaching round holes in cast iron, the broach was made from 0.0002 to 0.0003 inch larger than the nominal size and the land was 0.012 as shown. The holes were drilled close to size so as to leave very little work for the broach. In this case about 0.002 inch was left for broaching.

The comparison between broaching and reaming in this case is interesting. The reamers would wear appreciably below size in 25 holes while one broach finished 5000 holes to size.

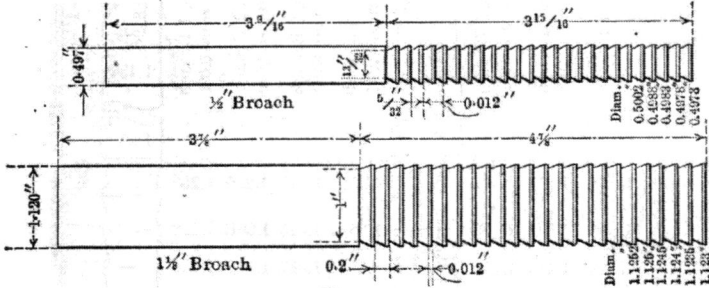

FIG. 5

TO SAVE TIME IN BROACHING OUT SQUARE HOLES

The fit of the gears on a square shaft depends almost entirely on the flat surfaces at or near the corners. With this in mind, it is an economy to bore or drill the round hole in the gear slightly larger than the diameter across the flats of the squared shaft, as shown in Fig. 6.

Taking a $1\frac{1}{4}$-inch square shaft and boring the hole $\frac{1}{16}$ inch larger or $1\frac{5}{16}$ inches in diameter, we see in the illustration exactly what this would mean. The amount of metal to be cut out would be materially reduced, the portion A to B not being touched by the broach in any way. Yet the remaining surface in the corners would be ample to carry all the load of the gears at work, and the clearance A to B would allow the best of lubrication.

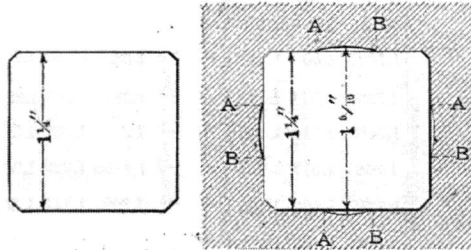

FIG. 6

The center relief, as shown, gives considerable added chip space as well as reduces the amount of chip, thus allowing a heavier chip per tooth. This may either reduce the length of the broach or allow a longer hole (such as two gears at once) to be broached with the same length of broach.

The set of 7 broaches shown in Fig. 7 show the practice of the Brown & Sharpe Mfg. Co. in making automobile transmission gears. The gears are of a tough alloy steel making the 7 necessary to secure an accurate hole of $1\frac{1}{4}$ inches across the flats. Each broach is $30\frac{1}{2}$ inches long, the cutting portion being only $17\frac{1}{2}$ inches. The method of holding the shank can be readily seen.

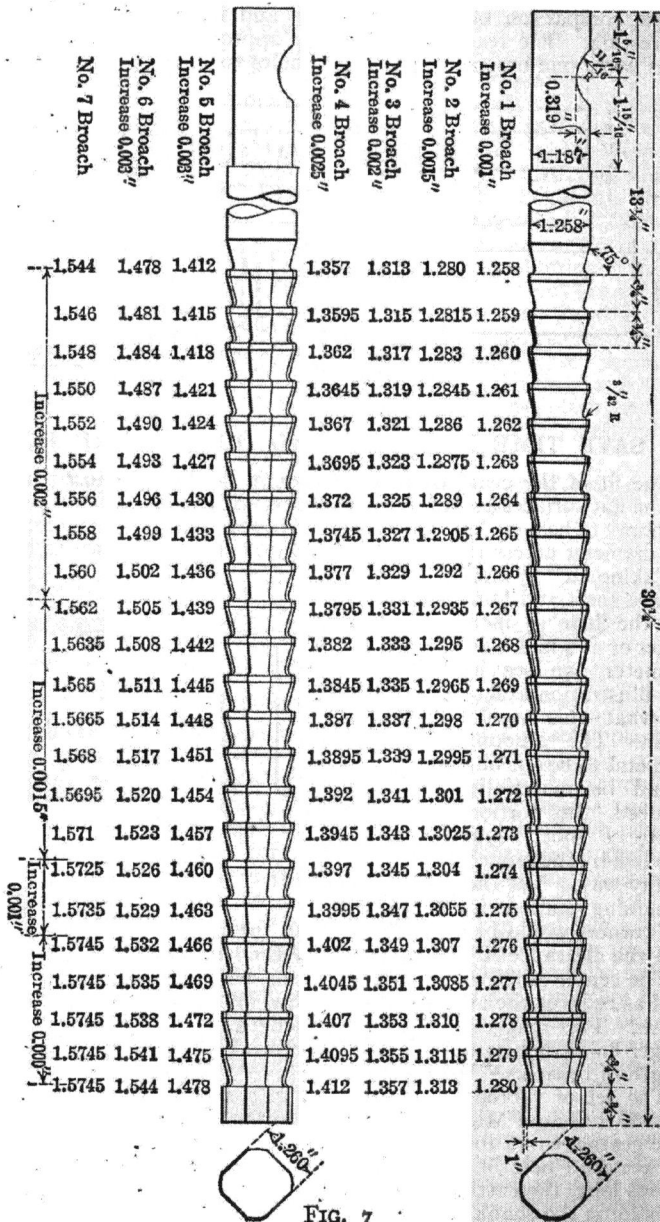

No. 7 Broach	No. 6 Broach Increase 0.003"	No. 5 Broach Increase 0.003"	No. 4 Broach Increase 0.0025"	No. 3 Broach Increase 0.002"	No. 2 Broach Increase 0.0005"	No. 1 Broach Increase 0.001"
1.544	1.478	1.412	1.357	1.313	1.280	1.258
1.546	1.481	1.415	1.3595	1.315	1.2815	1.259
1.548	1.484	1.418	1.362	1.317	1.283	1.260
1.550	1.487	1.421	1.3645	1.319	1.2845	1.261
1.552	1.490	1.424	1.367	1.321	1.286	1.262
1.554	1.493	1.427	1.3695	1.323	1.2875	1.263
1.556	1.496	1.430	1.372	1.325	1.289	1.264
1.558	1.499	1.433	1.3745	1.327	1.2905	1.265
1.560	1.502	1.436	1.377	1.329	1.292	1.266
1.562	1.505	1.439	1.3795	1.331	1.2935	1.267
1.5635	1.508	1.442	1.382	1.333	1.295	1.268
1.565	1.511	1.445	1.3845	1.335	1.2965	1.269
1.5665	1.514	1.448	1.387	1.337	1.298	1.270
1.568	1.517	1.451	1.3895	1.339	1.2995	1.271
1.5695	1.520	1.454	1.392	1.341	1.301	1.272
1.571	1.523	1.457	1.3945	1.343	1.3025	1.273
1.5725	1.526	1.460	1.397	1.345	1.304	1.274
1.5735	1.529	1.463	1.3995	1.347	1.3055	1.275
1.5745	1.532	1.466	1.402	1.349	1.307	1.276
1.5745	1.535	1.469	1.4045	1.351	1.3085	1.277
1.5745	1.538	1.472	1.407	1.353	1.310	1.278
1.5745	1.541	1.475	1.4095	1.355	1.3115	1.279
1.5745	1.544	1.478	1.412	1.357	1.313	1.280

FIG. 7

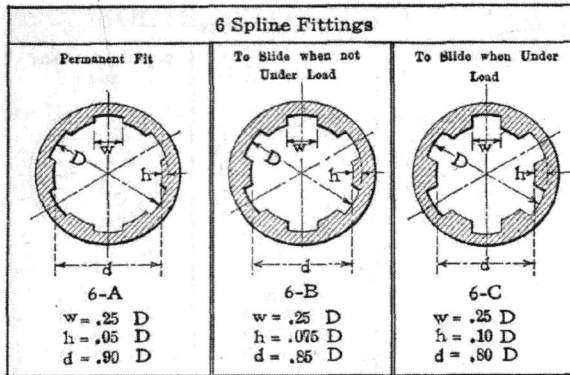

6-SPLINE FITTINGS FOR AUTOMOBILES

From sixth Report of Broaches Division S.A.E. Accepted at
Meeting of Society, January, 1914

Nominal Diam.	D	d	w	T	D	d	w	T	D	d	w	T
3/4	.750	.675	.188	80	.750	.638	.188	117	.750	.600	.188	152
	.749	.674	.187		.749	.637	.187		.749	.599	.187	
7/8	.875	.788	.219	109	.875	.744	.219	159	.875	.700	.219	207
	.874	.787	.218		.874	.743	.218		.874	.699	.218	
1	1.000	.900	.250	143	1.000	.850	.250	208	1.000	.800	.250	270
	.999	.899	.249		.999	.849	.249		.999	.799	.249	
1 1/8	1.125	1.013	.281	180	1.125	.956	.281	263	1.125	.900	.281	342
	1.124	1.012	.280		1.124	1.955	.280		1.124	.899	.280	
1 1/4	1.250	1.125	.313	223	1.250	1.063	.313	325	1.250	1.000	.313	421
	1.249	1.124	.312		1.249	1.062	.312		1.249	.999	.312	
1 3/8	1.375	1.238	.344	269	1.375	1.169	.344	393	1.375	1.100	.344	510
	1.374	1.237	.343		1.374	1.168	.343		1.374	1.099	.343	
1 1/2	1.500	1.350	.375	321	1.500	1.275	.375	468	1.500	1.200	.375	608
	1.499	1.349	.374		1.499	1.274	.374		1.499	1.199	.374	
1 5/8	1.625	1.463	.406	376	1.625	1.381	.406	550	1.625	1.300	.406	713
	1.624	1.462	.405		1.624	1.380	.405		1.624	1.299	.405	
1 3/4	1.750	1.575	.438	436	1.750	1.488	.438	637	1.750	1.400	.438	827
	1.749	1.574	.437		1.749	1.487	.437		1.749	1.399	.437	
2	2.000	1.800	.500	570	2.000	1.700	.500	833	2.000	1.600	.500	1080
	1.998	1.798	.498		1.998	1.608	.498		1.998	1.598	.498	
2 1/4	2.250	2.025	.563	721	2.250	1.913	.563	1052	2.250	1.800	.563	1367
	2.248	2.023	.561		2.248	1.912	.561		2.248	1.798	.561	
2 1/2	2.500	2.250	.625	891	2.500	2.125	.625	1300	2.500	2.000	.625	1688
	2.498	2.248	.623		2.498	2.123	.623		2.498	1.998	.623	
3	3.000	2.700	.750	1283	3.000	2.550	.750	1873	3.000	2.400	.750	2430
	2.998	2.698	.748		2.998	2.548	.748		2.998	2.398	.748	

$T = 1000 \times 6$ (No. of Splines) $\times$ Mean Radius $\times h \times 1 =$ inch-pounds torque capacity per inch bearing length at 1000 lbs. pressure per square inch on sides of splines. No allowance is made for radii on corners nor for clearances.

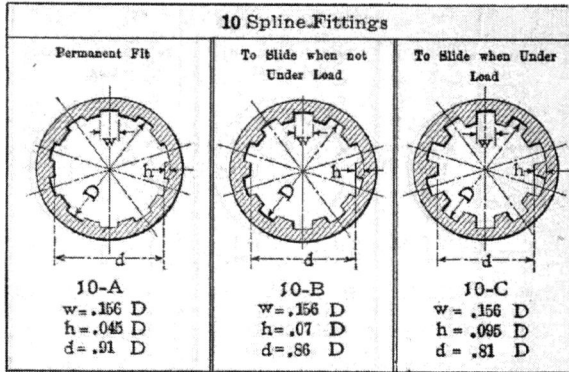

10 Spline Fittings		
Permanent Fit	To Slide when not Under Load	To Slide when Under Load
10-A	10-B	10-C
w = .156 D	w = .156 D	w = .156 D
h = .045 D	h = .07 D	h = .095 D
d = .91 D	d = .86 D	d = .81 D

10-SPLINE FITTINGS FOR AUTOMOBILES

From Sixth Report of Broaches Division S.A.E.   Accepted at Meeting of Society, January, 1914

Nominal Diam.	D	d	w	T	D	d	w	T	D	d	w	T
$\frac{3}{4}$	.750 .749	.683 .682	.117 .116	120	.750 .749	.645 .644	.117 .116	183	.750 .749	.608 .607	.117 .116	241
$\frac{7}{8}$	.875 .874	.796 .795	.137 .136	165	.875 .874	.753 .752	.137 .136	248	.875 .874	.709 .708	.137 .136	329
1	1.000 .999	.910 .909	.156 .155	215	1.000 .999	.860 .859	.156 .155	326	1.000 .999	.810 .809	.156 .155	430
$1\frac{1}{8}$	1.125 1.124	1.024 1.023	.176 .175	271	1.125 1.124	.968 .967	.176 .175	412	1.125 1.124	.911 .910	.176 .175	545
$1\frac{1}{4}$	1.250 1.249	1.138 1.137	.195 .194	336	1.250 1.249	1.075 1.074	.195 .194	508	1.250 1.249	1.013 1.012	.195 .194	672
$1\frac{3}{8}$	1.375 1.374	1.251 1.250	.215 .214	406	1.375 1.374	1.183 1.182	.215 .214	614	1.375 1.374	1.114 1.113	.215 .214	813
$1\frac{1}{2}$	1.500 1.499	1.365 1.364	.234 .233	483	1.500 1.499	1.290 1.289	.234 .233	732	1.500 1.499	1.215 1.214	.234 .233	967
$1\frac{5}{8}$	1.625 1.624	1.479 1.478	.254 .253	566	1.625 1.624	1.398 1.397	.254 .253	860	1.625 1.624	1.316 1.315	.254 .253	1135
$1\frac{3}{4}$	1.750 1.749	1.593 1.592	.273 .272	658	1.750 1.749	1.505 1.504	.273 .272	997	1.750 1.749	1.418 1.417	.273 .272	1316
2	2.000 1.998	1.820 1.818	.312 .310	860	2.000 1.998	1.720 1.718	.312 .310	1302	2.000 1.998	1.620 1.618	.312 .310	1720
$2\frac{1}{4}$	2.250 2.248	2.048 2.046	.351 .349	1088	2.250 2.248	1.935 1.933	.351 .349	1647	2.250 2.248	1.823 1.821	.351 .349	2176
$2\frac{1}{2}$	2.500 2.498	2.275 2.273	.390 .388	1343	2.500 2.498	2.150 2.148	.390 .388	2034	2.500 2.498	2.025 2.023	.390 .388	2688
3	3.000 2.998	2.730 2.728	.468 .466	1934	3.000 2.998	2.580 2.578	.468 .466	2929	3.000 2.998	2.430 2.428	.468 .466	3869

T = 1000 $\times$ 10 (No. of Splines) $\times$ Mean Radius $\times$ h $\times$ 1 = inch-pounds torque capacity per inch bearing length at 1000 lbs. pressure per square inch on sides of Splines. No allowance is made for radii on corners nor for clearances.

BOLTS, NUTS AND SCREWS

U. S. STANDARD BOLTS AND NUTS

THE U. S. Standard for bolts, nuts, etc., called also Sellers' Standard, Franklin Institute Standard, and American Standard, was recommended in 1864 by the Franklin Institute for general adoption by engineers. (*See Note*).

STRENGTH OF U. S. STANDARD BOLTS FROM ¼ TO 3″ DIAMETER

Bolt		Areas		Tensile Strength			Shearing Strength			
							Full Bolt		Bottom of Thread	
Diameter of Bolt	No. of Threads per Inch	Full Bolt	Bottom of Thread	At 10,000 lbs. per Sq. In.	At 12,500 lbs. per Sq. In.	At 17,500 lbs. per Sq. In.	At 7,500 lbs. per Sq. In.	At 10,000 lbs. per Sq. In.	At 7,500 lbs. per Sq. In.	At 10,000 lbs. per Sq. In.
¼	20	.049	.027	270	340	470	380	490	200	270
5⁄16	18	.077	.045	450	570	790	580	770	340	450
⅜	16	.110	.068	680	850	1,190	830	1,100	510	680
7⁄16	14	.150	.093	930	1,170	1,630	1,130	1,500	700	930
½	13	.196	.126	1,260	1,570	2,200	1,470	1,960	940	1,260
9⁄16	12	.248	.162	1,620	2,030	2,840	1,860	2,480	1,220	1,620
⅝	11	.307	.202	2,020	2,520	3,530	2,300	3,070	1,510	2,020
¾	10	.442	.302	3,020	3,770	5,290	3,310	4,420	2,270	3,020
⅞	9	.601	.419	4,190	5,240	7,340	4,510	6,010	3,150	4,190
1	8	.785	.551	5,510	6,890	9,640	5,890	7,850	4,130	5,510
1⅛	7	.994	.693	6,930	8,660	12,130	7,450	9,940	5,200	6,930
1¼	7	1.227	.890	8,890	11,120	15,570	9,200	12,270	6,670	8,900
1⅜	6	1.485	1.054	10,540	13,180	18,450	11,140	14,850	7,910	10,540
1½	6	1.767	1.294	12,940	16,170	22,640	13,250	17,670	9,700	12,940
1⅝	5½	2.074	1.515	15,150	18,940	26,510	15,550	20,740	11,360	15,150
1¾	5	2.405	1.745	17,450	21,800	30,520	18,040	24,050	13,080	17,440
1⅞	5	2.761	2.049	20,490	25,610	35,860	20,710	27,610	15,370	20,490
2	4½	3.142	2.300	23,000	28,750	40,250	23,560	31,420	17,250	23,000
2¼	4½	3.976	3.021	30,210	37,770	52,870	29,820	39,760	22,660	30,210
2½	4	4.909	3.716	37,160	46,450	65,040	36,820	49,090	27,870	37,160
2¾	4	5.940	4.620	46,200	57,750	80,840	44,580	59,400	34,650	46,200
3	3½	7.069	5.428	54,280	67,850	94,990	53,020	70,690	40,710	54,280

NOTE.—The distance between parallel sides of the bolt head and nut for a rough bolt is one and one-half diameters of the bolt plus one-eighth of an inch. The thickness of the head in this system for a rough bolt is equal to one-half the distance between its parallel sides. The thickness of the nut is equal to the diameter of the bolt. It was originally recommended in this system that the thickness of the head for a finished bolt be equal to the thickness of the nut, and that the distance between the parallel sides of a bolt head and nut and the thickness of the nut be one-sixteenth inch less for finished parts than for rough. However, it is the practice of bolt and nut manufacturers to make finished U. S. nuts to the same dimensions as established for rough ones, and where finished heads are required to the U. S. Standard they are customarily made to the same dimensions as rough heads unless otherwise specified.

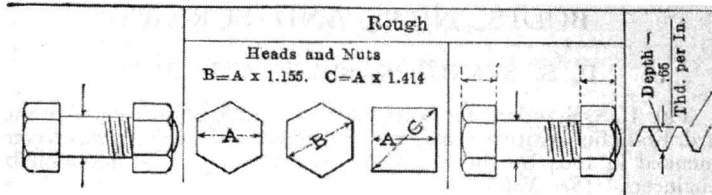

Rough

Heads and Nuts
B=A x 1.155. C=A x 1.414

Depth = .65 Thd. per In.

U. S. STANDARD BOLTS AND NUTS
ROUGH

Dia. of Bolt	Threads per Inch	Across Flats	Across Corners		Thickness		Depth of Thread
			B	C	Head	Nut	
$\frac{1}{4}$	20	$\frac{1}{2}$	$\frac{37}{64}$	$\frac{23}{32}$	$\frac{1}{4}$	$\frac{1}{4}$	.0325
$\frac{5}{16}$	18	$\frac{19}{32}$	$\frac{11}{16}$	$\frac{27}{32}$	$\frac{19}{64}$	$\frac{5}{16}$	.0361
$\frac{3}{8}$	16	$\frac{11}{16}$	$\frac{51}{64}$	$\frac{31}{32}$	$\frac{11}{32}$	$\frac{3}{8}$	.0406
$\frac{7}{16}$	14	$\frac{25}{32}$	$\frac{29}{32}$	$1\frac{7}{64}$	$\frac{25}{64}$	$\frac{7}{16}$	.0464
$\frac{1}{2}$	13	$\frac{7}{8}$	$1\frac{1}{64}$	$1\frac{1}{4}$	$\frac{7}{16}$	$\frac{1}{2}$	.0500
$\frac{9}{16}$	12	$\frac{31}{32}$	$1\frac{1}{8}$	$1\frac{3}{8}$	$\frac{31}{64}$	$\frac{9}{16}$	.0542
$\frac{5}{8}$	11	$1\frac{1}{16}$	$1\frac{15}{64}$	$1\frac{1}{2}$	$\frac{17}{32}$	$\frac{5}{8}$	.0590
$\frac{3}{4}$	10	$1\frac{1}{4}$	$1\frac{29}{64}$	$1\frac{25}{32}$	$\frac{5}{8}$	$\frac{3}{4}$	.0650
$\frac{7}{8}$	9	$1\frac{7}{16}$	$1\frac{43}{64}$	$2\frac{1}{16}$	$\frac{23}{32}$	$\frac{7}{8}$	.0722
I	8	$1\frac{5}{8}$	$1\frac{7}{8}$	$2\frac{19}{64}$	$\frac{13}{16}$	I	.0812
$1\frac{1}{8}$	7	$1\frac{13}{16}$	$2\frac{3}{32}$	$2\frac{9}{16}$	$\frac{29}{32}$	$1\frac{1}{8}$	.0928
$1\frac{1}{4}$	7	2	$2\frac{5}{16}$	$2\frac{53}{64}$	I	$1\frac{1}{4}$	.0928
$1\frac{3}{8}$	6	$2\frac{3}{16}$	$2\frac{17}{32}$	$3\frac{3}{32}$	$1\frac{3}{32}$	$1\frac{3}{8}$	.1083
$1\frac{1}{2}$	6	$2\frac{3}{8}$	$2\frac{3}{4}$	$3\frac{23}{64}$	$1\frac{3}{16}$	$1\frac{1}{2}$	.1083
$1\frac{3}{4}$	5	$2\frac{3}{4}$	$3\frac{3}{16}$	$3\frac{57}{64}$	$1\frac{3}{8}$	$1\frac{3}{4}$	.1300
2	$4\frac{1}{2}$	$3\frac{1}{8}$	$3\frac{39}{64}$	$4\frac{27}{64}$	$1\frac{9}{16}$	2	.1444
$2\frac{1}{4}$	$4\frac{1}{2}$	$3\frac{1}{2}$	$4\frac{3}{64}$	$4\frac{61}{64}$	$1\frac{3}{4}$	$2\frac{1}{4}$	.1444
$2\frac{1}{2}$	4	$3\frac{7}{8}$	$4\frac{31}{64}$	$5\frac{31}{64}$	$1\frac{15}{16}$	$2\frac{1}{2}$	.1625
$2\frac{3}{4}$	4	$4\frac{1}{4}$	$4\frac{29}{32}$	$6\frac{1}{64}$	$2\frac{1}{8}$	$2\frac{3}{4}$	.1625
3	$3\frac{1}{2}$	$4\frac{5}{8}$	$5\frac{11}{32}$	$6\frac{17}{32}$	$2\frac{5}{16}$	3	.1857

NOTE. — U. S. Government Standard Bolts and Nuts are made to above U. S. or Sellers' Standard Rough Dimensions. The sizes of finished bolt heads and nuts are the same as the sizes of the rough ones, that is for finished work the forgings must be larger than for rough, thus the same wrench may be used on both black and finished heads and nuts.

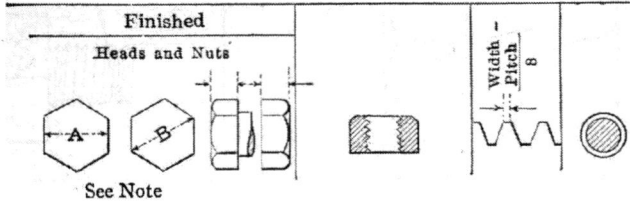

Finished
Heads and Nuts

A B

$\dfrac{\text{Width}}{\text{Pitch}} = 8$

See Note

U. S. STANDARD BOLTS AND NUTS. — FINISHED HEADS AND NUTS

FINISHED HEADS AND NUTS

Dia. of Bolt	Across Flats (See Note)	Across Corners (See Note)	Thickness	Exact Size of Hole	Tap Drill Used	Width of Flat	Area at Root of Thread	Safe Strain in lbs. Iron at 50,000 lbs. per Sq. In. Factor of Safety = 5
$\frac{1}{4}$	$\frac{7}{16}$	$\frac{1}{2}$	$\frac{3}{16}$	.185	.191	.0063	.0260	260
$\frac{5}{16}$	$\frac{17}{32}$	$\frac{39}{64}$	$\frac{1}{4}$	.2408	.246	.0069	.0452	452
$\frac{3}{8}$	$\frac{5}{8}$	$\frac{23}{32}$	$\frac{5}{16}$	.2938	$\frac{19}{64}$	.0078	.0677	677
$\frac{7}{16}$	$\frac{23}{32}$	$\frac{53}{64}$	$\frac{3}{8}$	.3447	$\frac{23}{64}$	.0089	.0932	932
$\frac{1}{2}$	$\frac{13}{16}$	$\frac{15}{16}$	$\frac{7}{16}$	.4001	$\frac{13}{32}$	.0096	.1257	1257
$\frac{9}{16}$	$\frac{29}{32}$	$1\frac{1}{64}$	$\frac{1}{2}$	.4542	$\frac{15}{32}$	.0104	.1620	1620
$\frac{5}{8}$	1	$1\frac{5}{32}$	$\frac{9}{16}$	.5069	$\frac{33}{64}$	.0114	.2018	2018
$\frac{3}{4}$	$1\frac{3}{16}$	$1\frac{21}{64}$	$\frac{11}{16}$	.6201	$\frac{5}{8}$	.0124	.3020	3020
$\frac{7}{8}$	$1\frac{3}{8}$	$1\frac{19}{32}$	$\frac{13}{16}$	.7307	$\frac{47}{64}$	.0139	.4194	4194
1	$1\frac{9}{16}$	$1\frac{13}{16}$	$\frac{15}{16}$	.8376	$\frac{27}{32}$	.0156	.5509	5509
$1\frac{1}{8}$	$1\frac{3}{4}$	$2\frac{1}{64}$	$1\frac{1}{16}$	.9394	$\frac{61}{64}$	.0179	.6930	6930
$1\frac{1}{4}$	$1\frac{15}{16}$	$2\frac{15}{64}$	$1\frac{3}{16}$	1.0644	$1\frac{5}{64}$	.0179	.8890	8890
$1\frac{3}{8}$	$2\frac{1}{8}$	$2\frac{29}{64}$	$1\frac{5}{16}$	1.1585	$1\frac{11}{64}$	.0208	1.054	10540
$1\frac{1}{2}$	$2\frac{5}{16}$	$2\frac{43}{64}$	$1\frac{7}{16}$	1.2835	$1\frac{19}{64}$	.0208	1.293	12930
$1\frac{3}{4}$	$2\frac{11}{16}$	$3\frac{5}{64}$	$1\frac{11}{16}$	1.4902	$1\frac{33}{64}$	.0250	1.744	17440
2	$3\frac{1}{16}$	$3\frac{17}{32}$	$1\frac{13}{16}$	1.7113	$1\frac{23}{32}$	.0278	2.3	23000
$2\frac{1}{4}$	$3\frac{7}{16}$	$3\frac{31}{32}$	$2\frac{3}{16}$	1.9613	$1\frac{31}{32}$	.0278	3.021	30210
$2\frac{1}{2}$	$3\frac{13}{16}$	$4\frac{13}{32}$	$2\frac{7}{16}$	2.1752	$2\frac{3}{16}$	.0313	3.714	37140
$2\frac{3}{4}$	$4\frac{3}{16}$	$4\frac{27}{32}$	$2\frac{11}{16}$	2.4252	$2\frac{7}{16}$	.0313	4.618	46180
3	$4\frac{9}{16}$	$5\frac{3}{32}$	$2\frac{15}{16}$	2.6288	$2\frac{41}{64}$	.0357	5.427	54270

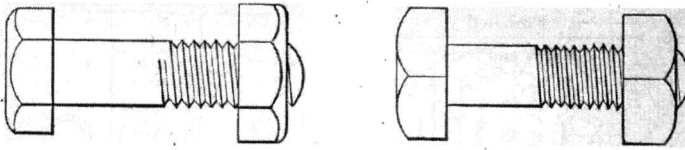

MACHINE BOLTS WITH MANUFACTURERS STD. HEADS

Dia. of Bolt	No. of Threads per Inch	HEX. AND SQUARE HEADS (National Machinery Co.)			HEX. AND SQUARE NUTS			
		Across Flats Square Heads	Across Flats Hex. Heads	Thickness Sq. and Hex. Heads	Across Flats Hex. and Sq.	Across Corners Hex. Nut	Across Corners Square Nut	Thickness Hex. and Sq.
$\frac{1}{4}$	20	$\frac{3}{8}$	$\frac{7}{16}$	$\frac{3}{16}$	$\frac{7}{16}$	$\frac{1}{2}$	$\frac{5}{8}$	$\frac{3}{16}$
$1\frac{5}{16}$	18	$\frac{15}{32}$	$\frac{17}{32}$	$\frac{1}{4}$	$\frac{17}{32}$	$\frac{39}{64}$	$\frac{3}{4}$	$\frac{1}{4}$
$\frac{3}{8}$	16	$\frac{9}{16}$	$\frac{5}{8}$	$\frac{9}{32}$	$\frac{5}{8}$	$\frac{23}{32}$	$\frac{57}{64}$	$\frac{5}{16}$
$\frac{7}{16}$	14	$\frac{21}{32}$	$\frac{23}{32}$	$\frac{21}{64}$	$\frac{23}{32}$	$\frac{53}{64}$	1	$\frac{3}{8}$
$\frac{1}{2}$	13	$\frac{3}{4}$	$\frac{13}{16}$	$\frac{3}{8}$	$\frac{13}{16}$	$\frac{15}{16}$	$1\frac{5}{32}$	$\frac{7}{16}$
$\frac{9}{16}$	12	$\frac{27}{32}$	$\frac{29}{32}$	$\frac{27}{64}$	$\frac{29}{32}$	$1\frac{1}{64}$	$1\frac{9}{32}$	$\frac{1}{2}$
$\frac{5}{8}$	11	$\frac{15}{16}$	1	$\frac{17}{32}$	1	$1\frac{5}{32}$	$1\frac{27}{64}$	$\frac{9}{16}$
$\frac{3}{4}$	10	$1\frac{1}{8}$	$1\frac{3}{16}$	$\frac{9}{16}$	$1\frac{3}{16}$	$1\frac{21}{64}$	$1\frac{21}{32}$	$\frac{11}{16}$
$\frac{7}{8}$	9	$1\frac{5}{16}$	$1\frac{3}{8}$	$\frac{21}{32}$	$1\frac{3}{8}$	$1\frac{19}{32}$	$1\frac{15}{16}$	$\frac{13}{16}$
1	8	$1\frac{1}{2}$	$1\frac{9}{16}$	$\frac{3}{4}$	$1\frac{9}{16}$	$1\frac{13}{16}$	$2\frac{13}{64}$	$\frac{15}{16}$
$1\frac{1}{8}$	7	$1\frac{11}{16}$	$1\frac{3}{4}$	$\frac{27}{32}$	$1\frac{13}{16}$	$2\frac{3}{32}$	$2\frac{9}{16}$	$1\frac{1}{8}$
$1\frac{1}{4}$	7	$1\frac{7}{8}$	$1\frac{15}{16}$	$\frac{15}{16}$	2	$2\frac{5}{16}$	$2\frac{53}{64}$	$1\frac{1}{4}$
$1\frac{3}{8}$	6	$2\frac{1}{16}$	$2\frac{1}{8}$	$1\frac{1}{16}$	$2\frac{3}{16}$	$2\frac{17}{32}$	$3\frac{3}{32}$	$1\frac{3}{8}$
$1\frac{1}{2}$	6	$2\frac{1}{4}$	$2\frac{5}{16}$	$1\frac{1}{8}$	$2\frac{3}{8}$	$2\frac{3}{4}$	$3\frac{23}{64}$	$1\frac{1}{2}$
$1\frac{5}{8}$	$5\frac{1}{2}$	$2\frac{7}{16}$	$2\frac{1}{2}$	$1\frac{7}{32}$	$2\frac{9}{16}$	$2\frac{31}{32}$	$3\frac{5}{8}$	$1\frac{5}{8}$
$1\frac{3}{4}$	5	$2\frac{5}{8}$	$2\frac{11}{16}$	$1\frac{5}{16}$	$2\frac{3}{4}$	$3\frac{3}{16}$	$3\frac{57}{64}$	$1\frac{3}{4}$
$1\frac{7}{8}$	5	$2\frac{13}{16}$	$2\frac{7}{8}$	$1\frac{13}{32}$	$2\frac{15}{16}$	$3\frac{13}{32}$	$4\frac{5}{32}$	$1\frac{7}{8}$
2	$4\frac{1}{2}$	3	$3\frac{1}{16}$	$1\frac{1}{2}$	$3\frac{1}{8}$	$3\frac{39}{64}$	$4\frac{27}{64}$	2

NOTE. — Nuts supplied by different makers for manufacturers standard bolts vary somewhat as regards thickness. The above nut sizes are Hoopes and Townsend Standard.

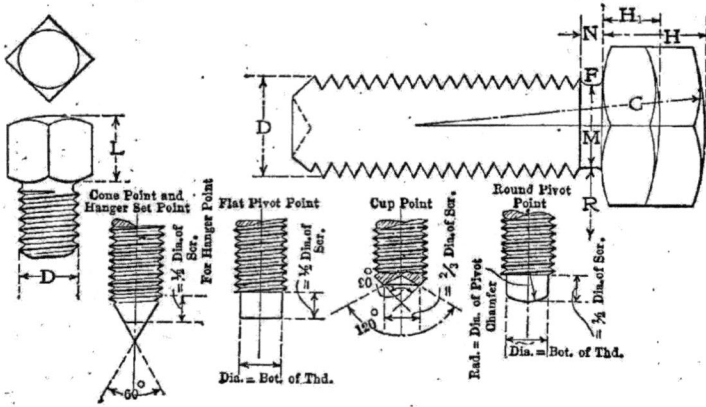

SET SCREWS

				HARTFORD MACHINE SCREW CO. STANDARD					
Dia. of Screw	No. of Threads per Inch	Length of Head	Length of Head	Length of Low Head	Radius of Crown	Dia. of Neck	Radius of Neck	Fillet — Neck	Length of Neck
D		L	H	H_1	C	M	R	F	N
$\frac{1}{4}$	20	$\frac{1}{4}$	$\frac{7}{32}$	$\frac{1}{8}$	$\frac{5}{8}$	$\frac{7}{32}$	$\frac{1}{4}$	.019	.075
$\frac{5}{16}$	18	$\frac{5}{16}$	$\frac{35}{128}$	$\frac{5}{32}$	$\frac{25}{32}$	$\frac{35}{128}$	$\frac{5}{16}$	.021	.083
$\frac{3}{8}$	16	$\frac{3}{8}$	$\frac{21}{64}$	$\frac{3}{16}$	$\frac{15}{16}$	$\frac{21}{64}$	$\frac{3}{8}$	.023	.094
$\frac{7}{16}$	14	$\frac{7}{16}$	$\frac{49}{128}$	$\frac{7}{32}$	$1\frac{3}{32}$	$\frac{49}{128}$	$\frac{7}{16}$	.027	.107
$\frac{1}{2}$	13	$\frac{1}{2}$	$\frac{7}{16}$	$\frac{1}{4}$	$1\frac{1}{4}$	$\frac{7}{16}$	$\frac{1}{2}$	.031	.125
$\frac{9}{16}$	12	$\frac{9}{16}$	$\frac{63}{128}$	$\frac{9}{32}$	$1\frac{13}{32}$	$\frac{63}{128}$	$\frac{9}{16}$	.032	.125
$\frac{5}{8}$	11	$\frac{5}{8}$	$\frac{35}{64}$	$\frac{5}{16}$	$1\frac{9}{16}$	$\frac{35}{64}$	$\frac{5}{8}$	.034	.130
$\frac{3}{4}$	10	$\frac{3}{4}$	$\frac{21}{32}$	$\frac{3}{8}$	$1\frac{7}{8}$	$\frac{21}{32}$	$\frac{3}{4}$	.037	.150
$\frac{7}{8}$	9	$\frac{7}{8}$	$\frac{49}{64}$	$\frac{7}{16}$	$2\frac{3}{16}$	$\frac{49}{64}$	$\frac{7}{8}$	.041	.166
I	8	I	$\frac{7}{8}$	$\frac{1}{2}$	$2\frac{1}{2}$	$\frac{7}{8}$	I	.047	.187

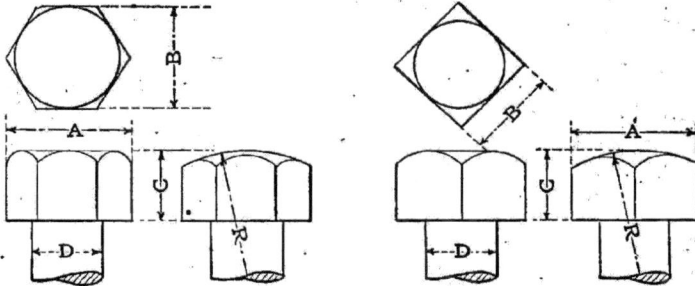

HARTFORD MACHINE SCREW CO., STANDARD

		HEXAGON HEAD CAP SCREWS				SQUARE HEAD CAP SCREWS			
Dia. of Screw	No. of Threads per In.	Distance Across Corners	Distance Across Flats	Thickness of Head	Radius of Head	Distance Across Corners	Distance Across Flats	Thickness of Head	Radius of Head
D		A	B	C	R	A	B	C	R
$\frac{1}{4}$	20	$\frac{1}{2}$	$\frac{7}{16}$	$\frac{1}{4}$	$\frac{3}{4}$	$\frac{17}{32}$	$\frac{3}{8}$	$\frac{1}{4}$	$\frac{25}{32}$
$\frac{5}{16}$	18	$\frac{37}{64}$	$\frac{1}{2}$	$\frac{5}{16}$	$\frac{55}{64}$	$\frac{5}{8}$	$\frac{7}{16}$	$\frac{5}{16}$	$\frac{15}{16}$
$\frac{3}{8}$	16	$\frac{21}{32}$	$\frac{9}{16}$	$\frac{3}{8}$	$\frac{31}{32}$	$\frac{45}{64}$	$\frac{1}{2}$	$\frac{3}{8}$	$1\frac{1}{16}$
$\frac{7}{16}$	14	$\frac{23}{32}$	$\frac{5}{8}$	$\frac{7}{16}$	$1\frac{5}{64}$	$\frac{51}{64}$	$\frac{9}{16}$	$\frac{7}{16}$	$1\frac{3}{16}$
$\frac{1}{2}$	13	$\frac{7}{8}$	$\frac{3}{4}$	$\frac{1}{2}$	$1\frac{9}{32}$	$\frac{57}{64}$	$\frac{5}{8}$	$\frac{1}{2}$	$1\frac{5}{16}$
$\frac{9}{16}$	12	$\frac{15}{16}$	$\frac{13}{16}$	$\frac{9}{16}$	$1\frac{13}{32}$	$\frac{31}{32}$	$\frac{11}{16}$	$\frac{9}{16}$	$1\frac{15}{32}$
$\frac{5}{8}$	11	$1\frac{1}{64}$	$\frac{7}{8}$	$\frac{5}{8}$	$1\frac{1}{2}$	$1\frac{1}{16}$	$\frac{3}{4}$	$\frac{5}{8}$	$1\frac{19}{32}$
$\frac{3}{4}$	10	$1\frac{5}{32}$	1	$\frac{3}{4}$	$1\frac{23}{32}$	$1\frac{15}{64}$	$\frac{7}{8}$	$\frac{3}{4}$	$1\frac{27}{32}$
$\frac{7}{8}$	9	$1\frac{19}{64}$	$1\frac{1}{8}$	$\frac{7}{8}$	$1\frac{15}{16}$	$1\frac{19}{32}$	$1\frac{1}{8}$	$\frac{7}{8}$	$2\frac{3}{8}$
1	8	$1\frac{7}{16}$	$1\frac{1}{4}$	1	$2\frac{5}{32}$	$1\frac{49}{64}$	$1\frac{1}{4}$	1	$2\frac{21}{32}$
$1\frac{1}{8}$	7	$1\frac{19}{32}$	$1\frac{3}{8}$	$1\frac{1}{8}$	$2\frac{3}{8}$	$1\frac{15}{16}$	$1\frac{3}{8}$	$1\frac{1}{8}$	3
$1\frac{1}{4}$	7	$1\frac{47}{64}$	$1\frac{1}{2}$	$1\frac{1}{4}$	$2\frac{19}{32}$	$2\frac{1}{8}$	$1\frac{1}{2}$	$1\frac{1}{4}$	$3\frac{3}{16}$

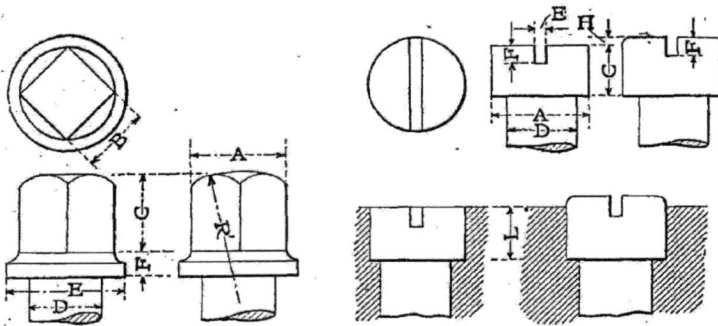

Dia. of Screw	No. of Threads per Inch	COLLAR HEAD SCREWS						FILLISTER HEAD CAP SCREWS (P. & .W. St'd)						
		Distance Across Corners	Distance Across Flats	Length of Head	Dia. of Collar	Thickness of Collar	Radius of Head	Dia. of Head	Length of Flat Head	Hight of Round Corner	Length of Round Head	Width of Slot	Depth of Slot	Depth of Counterbore
D		A	B	C	E	F	R	A	C	H	C+H	E	F	L
$\frac{1}{8}$	40	$\frac{11}{64}$	$\frac{1}{8}$	$\frac{9}{64}$	$\frac{1}{4}$	$\frac{1}{16}$	$\frac{1}{4}$	$\frac{11}{64}$	$\frac{3}{32}$	$\frac{1}{32}$	$\frac{1}{8}$	.025	$\frac{1}{32}$	$\frac{3}{32}$
$\frac{3}{16}$	32	$\frac{17}{64}$	$\frac{3}{16}$	$\frac{7}{32}$	$\frac{11}{32}$	$\frac{5}{64}$	$\frac{3}{8}$	$\frac{1}{4}$	$\frac{1}{8}$	$\frac{3}{32}$	$\frac{5}{32}$	.039	$\frac{3}{64}$	$\frac{1}{8}$
$\frac{1}{4}$	20	$\frac{11}{32}$	$\frac{1}{4}$	$\frac{9}{32}$	$\frac{7}{16}$	$\frac{3}{32}$	$\frac{1}{2}$	$\frac{11}{32}$	$\frac{5}{32}$	$\frac{1}{32}$	$\frac{3}{16}$	.058	$\frac{5}{64}$	$\frac{5}{32}$
$\frac{5}{16}$	18	$\frac{7}{16}$	$\frac{5}{16}$	$\frac{11}{32}$	$\frac{1}{2}$	$\frac{1}{8}$	$\frac{11}{16}$	$\frac{7}{16}$	$\frac{3}{16}$	$\frac{3}{64}$	$\frac{15}{64}$	.071	$\frac{5}{64}$	$\frac{3}{16}$
$\frac{3}{8}$	16	$\frac{17}{32}$	$\frac{3}{8}$	$\frac{13}{32}$	$\frac{5}{8}$	$\frac{5}{32}$	$\frac{13}{16}$	$\frac{1}{2}$	$\frac{1}{4}$	$\frac{5}{64}$	$\frac{19}{64}$	.086	$\frac{7}{64}$	$\frac{1}{4}$
$\frac{7}{16}$	14	$\frac{5}{8}$	$\frac{7}{16}$	$\frac{15}{32}$	$\frac{11}{16}$	$\frac{5}{32}$	$\frac{15}{16}$	$\frac{9}{16}$	$\frac{1}{4}$	$\frac{3}{64}$	$\frac{19}{64}$	.099	$\frac{7}{64}$	$\frac{1}{4}$
$\frac{1}{2}$	13	$\frac{45}{64}$	$\frac{1}{2}$	$\frac{9}{16}$	$\frac{13}{16}$	$\frac{13}{64}$	$1\frac{7}{16}$	$\frac{11}{16}$	$\frac{5}{16}$	$\frac{3}{64}$	$\frac{23}{64}$	.112	$\frac{1}{8}$	$\frac{5}{16}$
$\frac{9}{16}$	12	$\frac{51}{64}$	$\frac{9}{16}$	$\frac{5}{8}$	$\frac{15}{16}$	$\frac{7}{32}$	$1\frac{3}{16}$	$\frac{3}{4}$	$\frac{3}{8}$	$\frac{3}{64}$	$\frac{23}{64}$	.133	$\frac{9}{64}$	$\frac{3}{8}$
$\frac{5}{8}$	11	$\frac{57}{64}$	$\frac{5}{8}$	$\frac{11}{16}$	1	$\frac{1}{4}$	$1\frac{5}{16}$	$\frac{7}{8}$	$\frac{7}{16}$	$\frac{1}{16}$	$\frac{1}{2}$	.133	$\frac{5}{32}$	$\frac{7}{16}$
$\frac{3}{4}$	10	$1\frac{1}{16}$	$\frac{3}{4}$	$\frac{13}{16}$	$1\frac{1}{4}$	$\frac{5}{16}$	$1\frac{9}{16}$	$1\frac{1}{16}$	$\frac{1}{2}$	$\frac{1}{16}$	$\frac{9}{16}$	.133	$\frac{3}{16}$	$\frac{1}{2}$
$\frac{7}{8}$	9							$1\frac{3}{16}$	$\frac{9}{16}$	$\frac{1}{16}$	$\frac{5}{8}$	.133	$\frac{7}{32}$	$\frac{9}{16}$
1	8							$1\frac{3}{8}$	$\frac{5}{8}$	$\frac{1}{16}$	$\frac{11}{16}$	.165	$\frac{1}{4}$	$\frac{5}{8}$

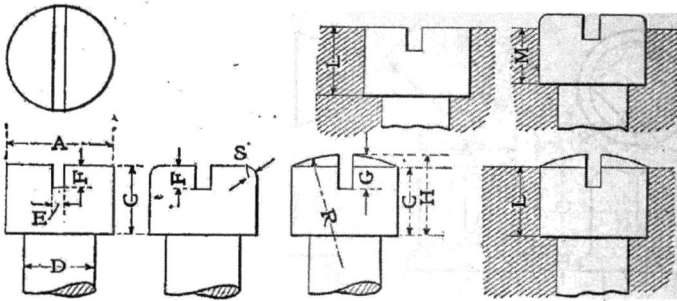

FLAT, ROUND AND OVAL FILLISTER HEAD CAP SCREWS

Dia. of Screw	No. of Threads per Inch	Dia. of Head	Length of Flat and Round Head	Radius of Corner	Length of Oval Head	Radius of Crown	Width of Slot	Depth of Slot	Depth of Slot Oval Head	Depth of Counter Bore, Flat and Oval Head	Depth of Counterbore Round Head
D		A	C	S	H	R	E	F	G	L	M
$\frac{1}{8}$	40	$\frac{3}{16}$	$\frac{1}{8}$	$\frac{1}{32}$	$\frac{9}{64}$	$\frac{1}{4}$	.032	$\frac{1}{16}$	$\frac{5}{64}$	$\frac{1}{8}$	$\frac{3}{32}$
$\frac{3}{16}$	32	$\frac{1}{4}$	$\frac{3}{16}$	$\frac{1}{32}$	$\frac{7}{32}$	$\frac{5}{16}$	.040	$\frac{1}{16}$	$\frac{3}{32}$	$\frac{3}{16}$	$\frac{3}{32}$
$\frac{1}{4}$	20	$\frac{3}{8}$	$\frac{1}{4}$	$\frac{1}{32}$	$\frac{9}{32}$	$\frac{1}{2}$	.064	$\frac{1}{16}$	$\frac{3}{32}$	$\frac{1}{4}$	$\frac{7}{32}$
$\frac{5}{16}$	18	$\frac{7}{16}$	$\frac{5}{16}$	$\frac{1}{16}$	$\frac{23}{64}$	$\frac{5}{8}$	.072	$\frac{5}{64}$	$\frac{1}{8}$	$\frac{5}{16}$	$\frac{1}{4}$
$\frac{3}{8}$	16	$\frac{9}{16}$	$\frac{3}{8}$	$\frac{1}{16}$	$\frac{15}{32}$	$\frac{3}{4}$	.091	$\frac{3}{32}$	$\frac{9}{64}$	$\frac{3}{8}$	$\frac{5}{16}$
$\frac{7}{16}$	14	$\frac{5}{8}$	$\frac{7}{16}$	$\frac{1}{16}$	$\frac{1}{2}$	$\frac{7}{8}$	.102	$\frac{7}{64}$	$\frac{11}{64}$	$\frac{7}{16}$	$\frac{3}{8}$
$\frac{1}{2}$	13	$\frac{3}{4}$	$\frac{1}{2}$	$\frac{1}{16}$	$\frac{9}{16}$	$1\frac{1}{16}$	.114	$\frac{1}{8}$	$\frac{3}{16}$	$\frac{1}{2}$	$\frac{7}{16}$
$\frac{9}{16}$	12	$\frac{13}{16}$	$\frac{9}{16}$	$\frac{1}{16}$	$\frac{41}{64}$	$1\frac{1}{8}$	.114	$\frac{9}{64}$	$\frac{7}{32}$	$\frac{9}{16}$	$\frac{1}{2}$
$\frac{5}{8}$	11	$\frac{7}{8}$	$\frac{5}{8}$	$\frac{1}{16}$	$\frac{45}{64}$	$1\frac{1}{4}$	.128	$\frac{5}{32}$	$\frac{15}{64}$	$\frac{5}{8}$	$\frac{9}{16}$
$\frac{3}{4}$	10	1	$\frac{3}{4}$	$\frac{1}{16}$	$\frac{27}{32}$	$1\frac{1}{2}$	.133	$\frac{3}{16}$	$\frac{9}{32}$	$\frac{3}{4}$	$\frac{11}{16}$
$\frac{7}{8}$	9	$1\frac{1}{8}$	$\frac{7}{8}$	$\frac{1}{16}$	$\frac{63}{64}$	$1\frac{5}{8}$	.133	$\frac{7}{32}$	$\frac{21}{64}$	$\frac{7}{8}$	$\frac{13}{16}$
1	8	$1\frac{1}{4}$	1	$\frac{3}{32}$	$1\frac{1}{8}$	$1\frac{3}{4}$	.165	$\frac{1}{4}$	$\frac{3}{8}$	1	$\frac{29}{32}$

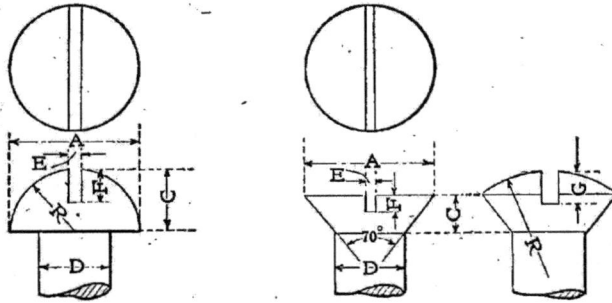

Dia. of Screw	No. of Threads per Inch	Button Head Cap Screws					Flat and Oval Countersunk Head Cap Screws					
		Dia. of Head	Length of Head	Radius of Head	Width of Slot	Depth of Slot	Dia. of Head	Length of Flat Head	Radius of Crown	Width of Slot	Depth of Slot Flat Head	Depth of Slot Oval Head
D		A	C	R	E	F	A	C	R	E	F	G
$\frac{1}{8}$	40	$\frac{7}{32}$	$\frac{7}{64}$	$\frac{7}{64}$	.035	$\frac{3}{64}$	$\frac{1}{4}$	$\frac{3}{32}$	$\frac{3}{8}$	.040	$\frac{3}{64}$	$\frac{3}{64}$
$\frac{3}{16}$	32	$\frac{5}{16}$	$\frac{5}{32}$	$\frac{5}{32}$	.051	$\frac{1}{16}$	$\frac{3}{8}$	$\frac{9}{64}$	$\frac{9}{16}$	.064	$\frac{1}{16}$	$\frac{1}{16}$
$\frac{1}{4}$	20	$\frac{7}{16}$	$\frac{7}{32}$	$\frac{7}{32}$	.072	$\frac{5}{64}$	$\frac{15}{32}$	$\frac{5}{32}$	$\frac{29}{32}$	.072	$\frac{5}{64}$	$\frac{5}{64}$
$\frac{5}{16}$	18	$\frac{9}{16}$	$\frac{9}{32}$	$\frac{9}{32}$	.091	$\frac{3}{32}$	$\frac{5}{8}$	$\frac{7}{32}$	$\frac{15}{16}$	.102	$\frac{3}{32}$	$\frac{3}{32}$
$\frac{3}{8}$	16	$\frac{5}{8}$	$\frac{5}{16}$	$\frac{5}{16}$	.102	$\frac{7}{64}$	$\frac{3}{4}$	$\frac{17}{64}$	$1\frac{1}{8}$	.114	$\frac{7}{64}$	$\frac{7}{64}$
$\frac{7}{16}$	14	$\frac{3}{4}$	$\frac{3}{8}$	$\frac{3}{8}$	.114	$\frac{1}{8}$	$\frac{13}{16}$	$\frac{17}{64}$	$1\frac{7}{32}$	.114	$\frac{1}{8}$	$\frac{1}{8}$
$\frac{1}{2}$	13	$\frac{13}{16}$	$\frac{13}{32}$	$\frac{13}{32}$	.114	$\frac{5}{32}$	$\frac{7}{8}$	$\frac{17}{64}$	$1\frac{5}{16}$	.128	$\frac{5}{32}$	$\frac{5}{32}$
$\frac{9}{16}$	12	$\frac{15}{16}$	$\frac{15}{32}$	$\frac{15}{32}$	.114	$\frac{11}{64}$	1	$\frac{5}{16}$	$1\frac{1}{2}$	.133	$\frac{11}{64}$	$\frac{11}{64}$
$\frac{5}{8}$	11	1	$\frac{1}{2}$	$\frac{1}{2}$	.133	$\frac{3}{16}$	$1\frac{1}{8}$	$\frac{23}{64}$	$1\frac{11}{16}$	.133	$\frac{3}{16}$	$\frac{3}{16}$
$\frac{3}{4}$	10	$1\frac{1}{4}$	$\frac{5}{8}$	$\frac{5}{8}$	.133	$\frac{7}{32}$	$1\frac{3}{8}$	$\frac{7}{16}$	$2\frac{1}{16}$	.133	$\frac{7}{32}$	$\frac{7}{32}$

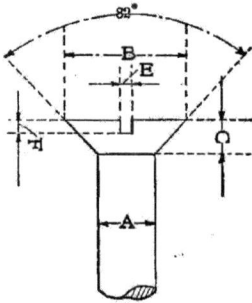

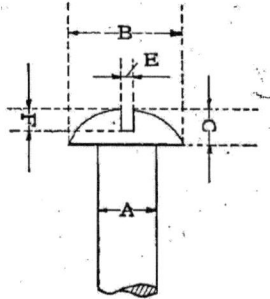

MACHINE SCREWS. AMERICAN SCREW COMPANY

No.	A	FLAT HEAD				ROUND HEAD			
		B	C	E	F	B	C	E	F
2	.0842	.1631	.0454	.030	.0151	.1544	.0672	.030	.0403
3	.0973	.1894	.0530	.032	.0177	.1786	.0746	.032	.0448
4	.1105	.2158	.0605	.034	.0202	.2028	.0820	.034	.0492
5	.1236	.2421	.0681	.036	.0227	.2270	.0894	.036	.0536
6	.1368	.2684	.0757	.039	.0252	.2512	.0968	.039	.0580
7	.1500	.2947	.0832	.041	.0277	.2754	.1042	.041	.0625
8	.1631	.3210	.0908	.043	.0303	.2996	.1116	.043	.0670
9	.1763	.3474	.0984	.045	.0328	.3238	.1190	.045	.0714
10	.1894	.3737	.1059	.048	.0353	.3480	.1264	.048	.0758
12	.2158	.4263	.1210	.052	.0403	.3922	.1412	.052	.0847
14	.2421	.4790	.1362	.057	.0454	.4364	.1560	.057	.0936
16	.2684	.5316	.1513	.061	.0504	.4806	.1708	.061	.1024
18	.2947	.5842	.1665	.066	.0555	.5248	.1856	.066	.1114
20	.3210	.6368	.1816	.070	.0605	.5690	.2004	.070	.1202
22	.3474	.6895	.1967	.075	.0656	.6106	.2152	.075	.1291
24	.3737	.7421	.2118	.079	.0706	.6522	.2300	.079	.1380
26	.4000	.7421	.1967	.084	.0656	.6938	2448	.084	.1469
28	.4263	.7948	.2118	.088	.0706	.7354	.2596	.088	.1558
30	.4526	.8474	.2270	.093	.0757	.7770	.2744	.093	.1646

Dimensions given are maximum, the necessary working variations being below them.

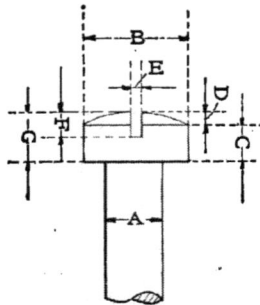

MACHINE SCREWS. AMERICAN SCREW COMPANY

| No. | A | FILLISTER HEAD | | | | | G |
		B	C	D	E	F	
2	.0842	.1350	.0549	.0126	.030	.0338	.0675
3	.0973	.1561	.0634	.0146	.032	.0390	.0780
4	.1105	.1772	.0720	.0166	.034	.0443	.0886
5	.1236	.1984	.0806	.0186	.036	.0496	.0992
6	.1368	.2195	.0892	.0205	.039	.0549	.1097
7	.1500	.2406	.0978	.0225	.041	.0602	.1203
8	.1631	.2617	.1063	.0245	.043	.0654	.1308
9	.1763	.2828	.1149	.0265	.045	.0707	.1414
10	.1894	.3040	.1235	.0285	.048	.0760	.1520
12	.2158	.3462	.1407	.0324	.052	.0866	.1731
14	.2421	.3884	.1578	.0364	.057	.0971	.1942
16	.2684	.4307	.1750	.0403	.061	.1077	.2153
18	.2947	.4729	.1921	.0443	.066	.1182	.2364
20	.3210	.5152	.2093	.0483	.070	.1288	.2576
22	.3474	.5574	.2267	.0520	.075	.1384	.2787
24	.3737	.5996	.2436	.0562	.079	.1499	.2998
26	.4000	.6419	.2608	.0601	.084	.1605	.3209
28	.4263	.6841	.2779	.0641	.088	.1710	.3420
30	.4526	.7264	.2951	.0681	.093	.1816	.3632

AMERICAN SCREW COMPANY. STANDARD THREADS PER INCH

No.	2	3	4	5	6	7	8	9	10	12
Threads per Inch	48 56 64	48 56	32, 36 40		30 32 36	30 32	30 32 36	24, 30, 32		20 24

No.	14	16	18	20	22	24	26	28	30
Threads per Inch	18 20. 24	16, 18, 20 .		16, 18		14 16 18		14, 16	

A.S.M.E. STANDARD PROPORTIONS OF MACHINE SCREWS

THE diagram and tables herewith show the proportions of machine screws as recommended by the committee of the American Society of Mechanical Engineers on Standard Proportions for Machine Screws, the report of this committee being adopted by the Society at its spring meeting, 1907.

The included angle is 60 degrees, and the flat at top and bottom of thread is one eighth of the pitch for the basic or standard diameter. There is a uniform increment of 0.013 inch, between all sizes from 0.06 to 0.19 (numbers 0 to 10 in the tables which follow) and of 0.026 inch in the remaining sizes. This change has been made in the interest of simplicity and because the resulting pitch diameters are more nearly in accord with the pitch diameters of screws in present use.

The pitches are a function of the diameter as expressed by the formula

$$\text{Threads per inch} = \frac{6.5}{D + 0.02},$$

with the results given approximately, so as to avoid the use of fractional threads.

The diagram shows the various sizes for both 16 and 72 threads per inch, and shows, among other things, the allowable difference in the flat surface, between the maximum tap and the minimum screw, this variation being from one-eighth to one sixteenth.

The minimum tap conforms to the basic standard in all respects, except diameter. The difference between the minimum tap and the maximum screw provides an allowance for error in pitch and for wear of tap in service.

The form of tap thread shown is recommended as being stronger and more serviceable than the so-called V-thread, but as some believe a strict adherence to the form shown might add to the cost of small taps, they have decided that taps having the correct angle and pitch diameter are permissible even with the V-thread. This will allow a large proportion of the taps now in stock to be utilized.

The tables given by the committee were combined into the present compact form by the Corbin Screw Corporation.

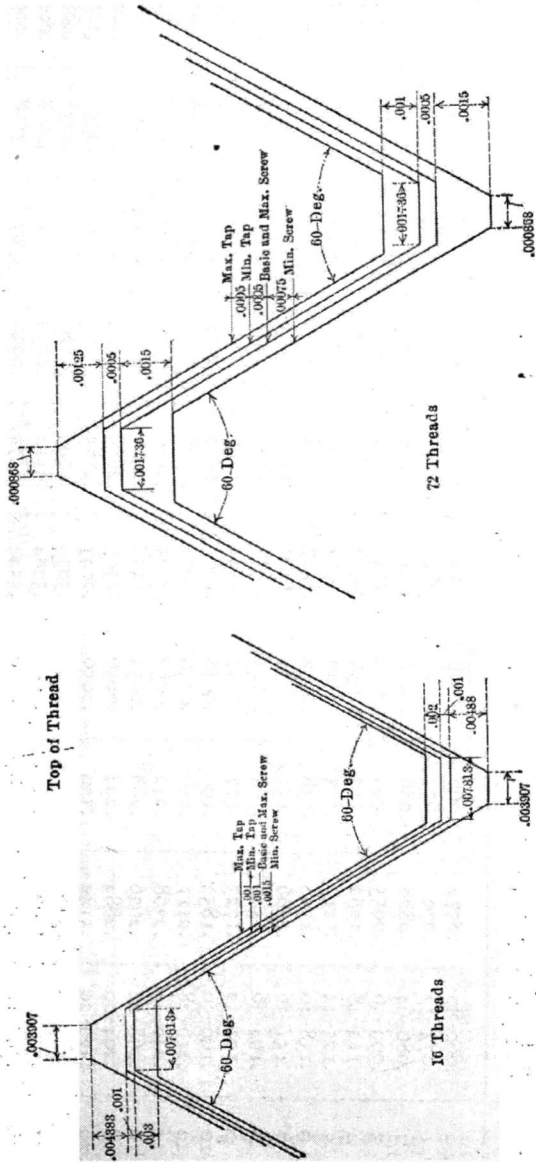

Diagram Showing Form of Basic Maximum and Minimum Screw and Tap Threads
A. S. M. E. Machine Screw Standard

A. S. M. E. Standard Machine Screws

No.	Size, Out. Dia. and Thds. P. I.	Outside Diameters			Pitch Diameters			Root Diameters		
		Minimum	Maximum	Difference	Minimum	Maximum	Difference	Minimum	Maximum	Difference
0	.060-80	.0572	.060	.0028	.0505	.0519	.0014	.0410	.0438	.0028
1	.073-72	.070	.073	.003	.0625	.064	.0015	.052	.055	.0030
2	.086-64	.0828	.086	.0032	.0743	.0759	.0016	.0624	.0657	.0033
3	.099-56	.0955	.099	.0035	.0857	.0874	.0017	.0721	.0758	.0037
4	.112-48	.1082	.112	.0038	.0966	.0985	.0019	.0807	.0849	.0042
5	.125-44	.1210	.125	.0040	.1082	.1102	.0020	.0910	.0955	.0045
6	.138-40	.1338	.138	.0042	.1197	.1218	.0021	.1007	.1055	.0048
7	.151-36	.1466	.151	.0044	.1308	.1330	.0022	.1097	.1149	.0052
8	.164-36	.1596	.164	.0044	.1438	.146	.0022	.1227	.1279	.0052
9	.177-32	.1723	.177	.0047	.1544	.1567	.0023	.1307	.1364	.0057
10	.190-30	.1852	.190	.0048	.166	.1684	.0024	.1407	.1467	.0060
12	.216-28	.2111	.216	.0049	.1904	.1928	.0024	.1633	.1696	.0063
14	.242-24	.2368	.242	.0052	.2123	.2149	.0026	.1808	.1879	.0071
16	.268-22	.2626	.268	.0054	.2358	.2385	.0027	.2014	.209	.0076
18	.294-20	.2884	.294	.0056	.2587	.2615	.0028	.2208	.229	.0082
20	.320-20	.3144	.320	.0056	.2847	.2875	.0028	.2468	.255	.0082
22	.346-18	.3402	.346	.0058	.3070	.3099	.0029	.2649	.2738	.0089
24	.372-16	.366	.372	.0060	.3284	.3314	.0030	.281	.2908	.0098
26	.398-16	.392	.398	.0060	.3544	.3574	.0030	.307	.3168	.0098
28	.424-14	.4178	.424	.0062	.3745	.3776	.0031	.3204	.3312	.0108
30	.450-14	.4438	.450	.0062	.4005	.4036	.0031	.3464	.3572	.0108

Taps for A. S. M. E. Standard Machine Screws

No.	Size — Out. Dia. and Thds. P. In.	Outside Diameters			Pitch Diameters			Root Diameters			Tap Drill Diameters
		Minimum	Maximum	Difference	Minimum	Maximum	Difference	Minimum	Maximum	Difference	
0	.060–80	.0609	.0632	.0023	.0528	.0538	.001	.0447	.0466	.0019	.0465
1	.073–72	.074	.0765	.0025	.065	.066	.001	.056	.058	.0020	.0595
2	.086–64	.0871	.0898	.0027	.0770	.0781	.0011	.0668	.0689	.0021	.070
3	.099–56	.1002	.1033	.0031	.0886	.0897	.0011	.077	.0793	.0023	.0785
4	.112–48	.1133	.1168	.0035	.0998	.101	.0012	.0862	.0887	.0025	.089
5	.125–44	.1263	.1301	.0038	.1116	.1129	.0013	.0968	.0995	.0027	.0995
6	.138–40	.1394	.1435	.0041	.1232	.1246	.0014	.1069	.1097	.0028	.110
7	.151–36	.1525	.1569	.0044	.1345	.1359	.0014	.1164	.1193	.0029	.120
8	.164–36	.1655	.1699	.0044	.1475	.1489	.0014	.1294	.1323	.0029	.136
9	.177–32	.1786	.1835	.0049	.1583	.1598	.0015	.138	.1411	.0031	.1405
10	.190–30	.1916	.1968	.0052	.170	.1716	.0016	.1483	.1515	.0032	.152
12	.216–28	.2176	.2232	.0056	.1944	.1961	.0017	.1712	.1745	.0033	.173
14	.242–24	.2438	.250	.0062	.2167	.2184	.0017	.1897	.1932	.0035	.1935
16	.268–22	.2698	.2765	.0067	.2403	.2421	.0018	.2108	.2144	.0036	.213
18	.294–20	.2959	.3031	.0072	.2634	.2652	.0018	.2309	.2346	.0037	.234
20	.320–20	.3219	.3291	.0072	.2894	.2912	.0018	.2569	.2606	.0037	.261
22	.346–18	.3479	.3559	.0080	.3118	.3138	.0020	.2757	.2796	.0039	.281
24	.372–16	.374	.3828	.0088	.3334	.3354	.0020	.2928	.2968	.0040	.2968
26	.398–16	.400	.4088	.0088	.3594	.3614	.0020	.3188	.3228	.0040	.323
28	.424–14	.4261	.4359	.0098	.3797	.3818	.0021	.3333	.3374	.0041	.339
30	.450–14	.4521	.4619	.0098	.4057	.4078	.0021	.3593	.3634	.0041	.368

A. S. M. E. Special Machine Screws

No.	Size Out. Dia. and Thds. P.I.	Outside Diameters			Pitch Diameters			Root Diameters		
		Minimum	Maximum	Difference	Minimum	Maximum	Difference	Minimum	Maximum	Difference
1	.073–64	.0698	.073	.0032	.0613	.0629	.0016	.0494	.0527	.0033
2	.086–56	.0825	.086	.0035	.0727	.0744	.0017	.0591	.0628	.0037
3	.099–48	.0952	.099	.0038	.0836	.0855	.0019	.0677	.0719	.0042
4	.112–40	.1078	.112	.0042	.0937	.0958	.0021	.0747	.0795	.0048
	36	.1076	.112	.0044	.0918	.094	.0022	.0707	.0759	.0052
5	.125–40	.1208	.125	.0042	.1067	.1088	.0021	.0877	.0925	.0048
	36	.1206	.125	.0044	.1048	.107	.0022	.0837	.0889	.0052
6	.138–36	.1336	.138	.0044	.1178	.120	.0022	.0967	.1019	.0052
	32	.1333	.138	.0047	.1154	.1177	.0023	.0917	.0974	.0057
7	.151–32	.1463	.151	.0047	.1284	.1307	.0023	.1047	.1104	.0057
	30	.1462	.151	.0048	.1270	.1294	.0024	.1017	.1077	.0060
8	.164–32	.1593	.164	.0047	.1414	.1437	.0023	.1177	.1234	.0057
	30	.1592	.164	.0048	.1400	.1424	.0024	.1147	.1207	.0060
9	.177–30	.1722	.177	.0048	.1529	.1553	.0024	.1277	.1337	.0060
	24	.1718	.177	.0052	.1473	.1499	.0026	.1158	.1229	.0071
10	.190–32	.1853	.190	.0047	.1674	.1697	.0023	.1437	.1494	.0057
	24	.1848	.190	.0052	.1603	.1629	.0026	.1288	.1359	.0071
12	.216–24	.2108	.216	.0052	.1863	.1889	.0026	.1548	.1619	.0071
14	.242–20	.2364	.242	.0056	.2067	.2095	.0028	.1688	.1770	.0082
16	.268–20	.2624	.268	.0056	.2327	.2355	.0028	.1948	.203	.0082
18	.294–18	.2882	.294	.0058	.255	.2579	.0029	.2129	.2218	.0089
20	.320–18	.3142	.320	.0058	.281	.2839	.0029	.2389	.2478	.0089
22	.346–16	.340	.346	.0060	.3024	.3054	.0030	.255	.2648	.0098
24	.372–18	.3662	.372	.0058	.333	.3359	.0029	.2909	.2998	.0089
26	.398–14	.3918	.398	.0062	.3485	.3516	.0031	.2944	.3052	.0108
28	.424–16	.418	.424	.0060	.3804	.3834	.0030	.333	.3428	.0098
30	.450–16	.444	.450	.0060	.4064	.4094	.0030	.359	.3688	.0098

No.	Size Out. Dia. and Thds. P. In.	Outside Diameters			Pitch Diameters			Root Diameters			Tap Drill Diameters
		Minimum	Maximum	Difference	Minimum	Maximum	Difference	Minimum	Maximum	Difference	
1	.073–64	.0741	.0768	.0027	.064	.0651	.0011	.0538	.0559	.0021	.055
2	.086–56	.0872	.0903	.0031	.0756	.0767	.0011	.064	.0663	.0023	.067
3	.099–48	.1003	.1038	.0035	.0868	.088	.0012	.0732	.0757	.0025	.076
4	.112–40	.1134	.1175	.0041	.0972	.0986	.0014	.0809	.0837	.0028	.082
	36	.1135	.1179	.0044	.0955	.0969	.0014	.0774	.0803	.0029	.081
5	.125–40	.1264	.1305	.0041	.1102	.1116	.0014	.0939	.0967	.0028	.098
	36	.1265	.1309	.0044	.1085	.1099	.0014	.0904	.0933	.0029	.0935
6	.138–36	.1395	.1439	.0044	.1215	.1229	.0014	.1034	.1063	.0029	.1065
	32	.1396	.1445	.0049	.1193	.1208	.0015	.099	.1021	.0031	.1015
7	.151–32	.1526	.1575	.0049	.1323	.1338	.0015	.112	.1151	.0031	.116
	30	.1526	.1578	.0052	.131	.1326	.0016	.1093	.1125	.0032	.113
8	.164–32	.1656	.1705	.0049	.1453	.1468	.0015	.125	.1281	.0031	.1285
	30	.1656	.1708	.0052	.144	.1456	.0016	.1223	.1255	.0032	.1285
9	.177–30	.1786	.1838	.0052	.1569	.1585	.0016	.1353	.1385	.0032	.1405
	24	.1788	.185	.0062	.1517	.1534	.0017	.1247	.1282	.0035	.1285
10	.190–32	.1916	.1965	.0049	.1713	.1728	.0015	.151	.1541	.0031	.154
	24	.1918	.198	.0062	.1647	.1664	.0017	.1377	.1412	.0035	.1405
12	.216–24	.2178	.224	.0062	.1907	.1924	.0017	.1637	.1672	.0035	.166
14	.242–20	.2439	.2511	.0072	.2114	.2132	.0018	.1789	.1826	.0037	.182
16	.268–20	.2699	.2771	.0072	.2374	.2392	.0018	.2049	.2086	.0037	.209
18	.294–18	.2959	.3039	.008	.2598	.2618	.002	.2237	.2276	.0039	.228
20	.320–18	.3219	.3299	.008	.2858	.2878	.002	.2497	.2536	.0039	.257
22	.346–16	.348	.3568	.0088	.3074	.3094	.002	.2668	.2708	.004	.272
24	.372–18	.3739	.3819	.008	.3378	.3398	.002	.3017	.3056	.0039	.3125
26	.398–14	.4001	.4099	.0098	.3537	.3558	.0021	.3073	.3114	.0041	.316
28	.424–16	.426	.4348	.0088	.3854	.3874	.002	.3448	.3488	.004	.348
30	.450–16	.452	.4608	.0088	.4114	.4134	.002	.3708	.3748	.004	.377

PROPORTIONS OF MACHINE SCREW HEADS
A. S. M. E. Standard

THE four standard heads are given herewith. These proportions are based on and include the diameter of the screw, diameter of the head, thickness of head, width and depth of slot, radius for round and fillister heads, and included angle of the flat-head screw.

OVAL FILLISTER HEAD MACHINE SCREWS. A. S. M. E. STANDARD

OVAL FILLISTER HEAD SCREWS

A = Diameter of Body.

$B = 1.64A - .009$ = Diam. of Head and Rad. for Oval

$C = 0.66A - .002$ = Hight of Side

$D = .173A + .015$

$E = \frac{1}{2}F$ = Depth of Slot

$F = .134B + C$ = Hight of Head.

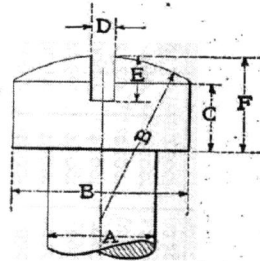

A	B	C	D	E	F
.060	.0894	.0376	.025	.025	.0496
.073	.1107	.0461	.028	.030	.0609
.086	.132	.0548	.030	.036	.0725
.099	.153	.0633	.032	.042	.0838
.112	.1747	.0719	.034	.048	.0953
.125	.196	.0805	.037	.053	.1068
.138	.217	.089	.039	.059	.1180
.151	.2386	.0976	.041	.065	.1296
.164	.2599	.1062	.043	.071	.1410
.177	.2813	.1148	.046	.076	.1524
.190	.3026	.1234	.048	.082	.1639
.216	.3452	.1405	.052	.093	.1868
.242	.3879	.1577	.057	.105	.2097
.268	.4305	.1748	.061	.116	.2325
.294	.4731	.192	.066	.128	.2554
.320	.5158	.2092	.070	.140	.2783
.346	.5584	.2263	.075	.150	.3011
.372	.6011	.2435	.079	.162	.3240
.398	.6437	.2606	.084	.173	.3469
.424	.6863	.2778	.088	.185	.3698
.450	.727	.295	.093	.201	.4024

FLAT FILLISTER HEAD MACHINE SCREWS. A. S. M. E. STANDARD

FLAT FILLISTER HEAD SCREWS

A = Diameter of Body
B = $1.64A - .009$ = Diam. of Head.
C = $0.66A - .002$ = Hight of Head
D = $0.173A + .015$ = Width of Slot
E = $\frac{1}{2}C$ = Depth of Slot

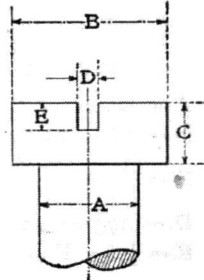

A	B	C	D	E
.060	.0894	.0376	.025	.019
.073	.1107	.0461	.028	.023
.086	.132	.0548	.030	.027
.099	.153	.0633	.032	.032
.112	.1747	.0719	.034	.036
.125	.196	.0805	.037	.040
.138	.217	.0890	.039	.044
.151	.2386	.0976	.041	.049
.164	.2599	.1062	.043	.053
.177	.2813	.1148	.046	.057
.190	.3026	.1234	.048	.062
.216	.3452	.1405	.052	.070
.242	.3879	.1577	.057	.079
.268	.4305	.1748	.061	.087
.294	.4731	.1920	.066	.096
.320	.5158	.2092	.070	.104
.346	.5584	.2263	.075	.113
.372	.601	.2435	.079	.122
.398	.6437	.2606	.084	.130
.424	.6863	.2778	.088	.139
.450	.727	.295	.093	.147

FLAT HEAD MACHINE SCREWS. A. S. M. E. STANDARD

FLAT HEAD SCREWS

A = Diameter of Body

$B = 2A - .008$ = Diam. of Head

$G = \dfrac{A - .008}{1.739}$ = Depth of Head

$D = .173A + .015$ = Width of Slot

$E = \frac{1}{3}C$ = Depth of Slot

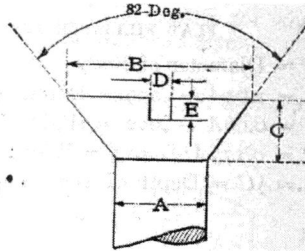

A	B	C	D	E
.060	.112	.029	.025	.010
.073	.138	.037	.028	.012
.086	.164	.045	.030	.015
.099	.190	.052	.032	.017
.112	.216	.060	.034	.020
.125	.242	.067	.037	.022
.138	.262	.075	.039	.025
.151	.294	.082	.041	.027
.164	.320	.090	.043	.030
.177	.346	.097	.046	.032
.190	.372	.105	.048	.035
.216	.424	.120	.052	.040
.242	.472	.135	.057	.045
.268	.528	.150	.061	.050
.294	.580	.164	.066	.055
.320	.632	.179	.070	.060
.346	.682	.194	.075	.065
.372	.732	.209	.079	.070
.398	.788	.224	.084	.075
.424	.840	.239	.088	.080
.450	.892	.254	.093	.085

ROUND HEAD MACHINE SCREWS. A. S. M. E. STANDARD

ROUND HEAD SCREWS

A = Diameter of Body.

B = $1.85A - .005$ = Diam. of Head

C = $.7A$ = Hight of Head

D = $.173A + .015$ = Width of Slot

E = $\frac{1}{2}C + .01$ = Depth of Slot

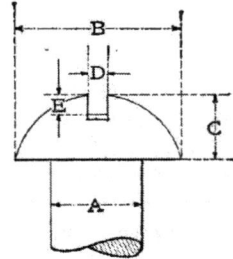

A	B	C	D	E
.060	.106	.042	.025	.031
.073	.130	.051	.028	.035
.086	.154	.060	.030	.040
.099	.178	.069	.032	.044
.112	.202	.078	.034	.049
.125	.226	.087	.037	.053
.138	.250	.096	.039	.058
.151	.274	.105	.041	.062
.164	.298	.114	.043	.067
.177	.322	.123	.046	.071
.190	.346	.133	.048	.076
.216	.394	.151	.052	.085
.242	.443	.169	.057	.094
.268	.491	.187	.061	.103
.294	.539	.205	.066	.112
.320	.587	.224	.070	.122
.346	.635	.242	.075	.131
.372	.683	.260	.079	.140
.398	.731	.278	.084	.149
.424	.779	.296	.088	.158
.450	.827	.315	.093	.167

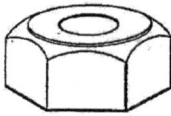

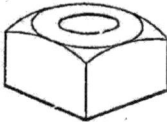

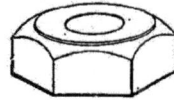

HOT PRESSED AND COLD PUNCHED NUTS

U. S. STANDARD HOT PRESSED AND COLD PUNCHED NUTS				COLD PUNCHED CHECK AND JAM NUTS			
HEXAGON AND SQUARE				HEXAGON			
Dia. Bolt	Across Flats	Thickness	Dia. Hole	Dia. Bolt	Across Flats	Thickness	Dia. Hole
$\frac{1}{4}$	$\frac{1}{2}$	$\frac{1}{4}$	$\frac{5}{16}$	$\frac{1}{4}$	$\frac{1}{2}$	$\frac{3}{16}$	$\frac{13}{64}$
$\frac{5}{16}$	$\frac{19}{32}$	$\frac{5}{16}$	$\frac{1}{4}$	$\frac{5}{16}$	$\frac{19}{32}$	$\frac{7}{32}$	$\frac{1}{4}$
$\frac{3}{8}$	$\frac{11}{16}$	$\frac{3}{8}$	$\frac{9}{64}$	$\frac{3}{8}$	$\frac{11}{16}$	$\frac{1}{4}$	$\frac{19}{64}$
$\frac{7}{16}$	$\frac{25}{32}$	$\frac{7}{16}$	$\frac{13}{32}$	$\frac{7}{16}$	$\frac{25}{32}$	$\frac{5}{16}$	$\frac{23}{64}$
$\frac{1}{2}$	$\frac{7}{8}$	$\frac{1}{2}$	$\frac{13}{32}$	$\frac{1}{2}$	$\frac{7}{8}$	$\frac{5}{16}$	$\frac{13}{32}$
$\frac{9}{16}$	$\frac{31}{32}$	$\frac{9}{16}$	$\frac{29}{64}$	$\frac{9}{16}$	$\frac{31}{32}$	$\frac{11}{32}$	$\frac{29}{64}$
$\frac{5}{8}$	$1\frac{1}{16}$	$\frac{5}{8}$	$\frac{33}{64}$	$\frac{5}{8}$	$1\frac{1}{16}$	$\frac{3}{8}$	$\frac{33}{64}$
$\frac{3}{4}$	$1\frac{1}{4}$	$\frac{3}{4}$	$\frac{5}{8}$	$\frac{3}{4}$	$1\frac{1}{4}$	$\frac{7}{16}$	$\frac{5}{8}$
$\frac{7}{8}$	$1\frac{7}{16}$	$\frac{7}{8}$	$\frac{47}{64}$	$\frac{7}{8}$	$1\frac{7}{16}$	$\frac{1}{2}$	$\frac{47}{64}$
1	$1\frac{5}{8}$	1	$\frac{27}{32}$	1	$1\frac{5}{8}$	$\frac{9}{16}$	$\frac{27}{32}$
$1\frac{1}{8}$	$1\frac{13}{16}$	$1\frac{1}{8}$	$\frac{15}{16}$	$1\frac{1}{8}$	$1\frac{13}{16}$	$\frac{5}{8}$	$\frac{15}{16}$
$1\frac{1}{4}$	2	$1\frac{1}{4}$	$1\frac{1}{16}$	$1\frac{1}{4}$	2	$\frac{3}{4}$	$1\frac{1}{16}$
$1\frac{3}{8}$	$2\frac{3}{16}$	$1\frac{3}{8}$	$1\frac{5}{32}$	$1\frac{3}{8}$	$2\frac{3}{16}$	$\frac{13}{16}$	$1\frac{5}{32}$
$1\frac{1}{2}$	$2\frac{3}{8}$	$1\frac{1}{2}$	$1\frac{9}{32}$	$1\frac{1}{2}$	$2\frac{3}{8}$	$\frac{7}{8}$	$1\frac{9}{32}$
$1\frac{5}{8}$	$2\frac{9}{16}$	$1\frac{5}{8}$	$1\frac{25}{64}$	$1\frac{5}{8}$	$2\frac{9}{16}$	$\frac{15}{16}$	$1\frac{25}{64}$
$1\frac{3}{4}$	$2\frac{3}{4}$	$1\frac{3}{4}$	$1\frac{1}{2}$	$1\frac{3}{4}$	$2\frac{3}{4}$	1	$1\frac{1}{2}$
$1\frac{7}{8}$	$2\frac{15}{16}$	$1\frac{7}{8}$	$1\frac{5}{8}$	$1\frac{7}{8}$	$2\frac{15}{16}$	$1\frac{1}{16}$	$1\frac{5}{8}$
2	$3\frac{1}{8}$	2	$1\frac{23}{32}$	2	$3\frac{1}{8}$	$1\frac{1}{8}$	$1\frac{23}{32}$
$2\frac{1}{8}$	$3\frac{5}{16}$	$2\frac{1}{8}$	$1\frac{13}{16}$				
$2\frac{1}{4}$	$3\frac{1}{2}$	$2\frac{1}{4}$	$1\frac{15}{16}$				
$2\frac{3}{8}$	$3\frac{11}{16}$	$2\frac{3}{8}$	$2\frac{1}{16}$				
$2\frac{1}{2}$	$3\frac{7}{8}$	$2\frac{1}{2}$	$2\frac{1}{4}$				
$2\frac{3}{4}$	$4\frac{1}{4}$	$2\frac{3}{4}$	$2\frac{27}{64}$				
3	$4\frac{5}{8}$	3	$2\frac{5}{8}$				

Finished case-hardened and semi-finished nuts are made to the above dimensions. Semi-finished nuts are tapped and faced true on the bottom.

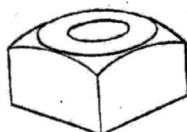

HOT PRESSED NUTS

HOT PRESSED NUTS, MANUFACTURERS STANDARD				HOT PRESSED AND FORGED NUTS, MANUFACTURERS STANDARD			
HEXAGON				SQUARE			
Dia. Bolt	Across Flats	Thickness	Dia. Hole	Dia. Bolt	Across Flats	Thickness	Dia. Hole
$\frac{1}{4}$	$\frac{1}{2}$	$\frac{1}{4}$	$\frac{7}{32}$	$\frac{1}{4}$	$\frac{1}{2}$	$\frac{1}{4}$	$\frac{7}{32}$
$\frac{5}{16}$	$\frac{9}{16}$	$\frac{5}{16}$	$\frac{9}{32}$	$\frac{5}{16}$	$\frac{9}{16}$	$\frac{5}{16}$	$\frac{9}{32}$
$\frac{3}{8}$	$\frac{5}{8}$	$\frac{3}{8}$	$\frac{11}{32}$	$\frac{3}{8}$	$\frac{5}{8}$	$\frac{3}{8}$	$\frac{11}{32}$
$\frac{7}{16}$	$\frac{7}{8}$	$\frac{7}{16}$	$\frac{25}{64}$	$\frac{7}{16}$	$\frac{7}{8}$	$\frac{7}{16}$	$\frac{25}{64}$
$\frac{1}{2}$	I	$\frac{1}{2}$	$\frac{7}{16}$	$\frac{1}{2}$	I	$\frac{1}{2}$	$\frac{7}{16}$
$\frac{9}{16}$	$1\frac{1}{8}$	$\frac{9}{16}$	$\frac{1}{2}$	$\frac{9}{16}$	$1\frac{1}{8}$	$\frac{9}{16}$	$\frac{1}{2}$
$\frac{5}{8}$	$1\frac{1}{4}$	$\frac{5}{8}$	$\frac{9}{16}$	$\frac{5}{8}$	$1\frac{1}{4}$	$\frac{5}{8}$	$\frac{9}{16}$
$\frac{3}{4}$	$1\frac{3}{8}$	$\frac{3}{4}$	$\frac{21}{32}$	$\frac{3}{4}$	$1\frac{1}{2}$	$\frac{3}{4}$	$\frac{21}{32}$
$\frac{7}{8}$	$1\frac{5}{8}$	$\frac{7}{8}$	$\frac{25}{32}$	$\frac{7}{8}$	$1\frac{3}{4}$	$\frac{7}{8}$	$\frac{25}{32}$
I	$1\frac{3}{4}$	I	$\frac{7}{8}$	I	2	I	$\frac{7}{8}$
$1\frac{1}{8}$	2	$1\frac{1}{4}$	$1\frac{1}{32}$	$1\frac{1}{8}$	$2\frac{1}{4}$	$1\frac{1}{8}$	$1\frac{1}{32}$
$1\frac{1}{4}$	$2\frac{1}{4}$	$1\frac{3}{8}$	$1\frac{3}{32}$	$1\frac{1}{4}$	$2\frac{1}{2}$	$1\frac{1}{4}$	$1\frac{3}{32}$
$1\frac{3}{8}$	$2\frac{1}{2}$	$1\frac{1}{2}$	$1\frac{3}{16}$	$1\frac{3}{8}$	$2\frac{3}{4}$	$1\frac{3}{8}$	$1\frac{3}{16}$
$1\frac{1}{2}$	$2\frac{3}{4}$	$1\frac{5}{8}$	$1\frac{5}{16}$	$1\frac{1}{2}$	3	$1\frac{1}{2}$	$1\frac{5}{16}$
$1\frac{5}{8}$	3	$1\frac{3}{4}$	$1\frac{7}{16}$	$1\frac{5}{8}$	$3\frac{1}{4}$	$1\frac{5}{8}$	$1\frac{7}{16}$
$1\frac{3}{4}$	$3\frac{1}{4}$	$1\frac{7}{8}$	$1\frac{9}{16}$	$1\frac{3}{4}$	$3\frac{1}{2}$	$1\frac{3}{4}$	$1\frac{9}{16}$
$1\frac{7}{8}$	$3\frac{1}{2}$	2	$1\frac{11}{16}$	$1\frac{7}{8}$	$3\frac{3}{4}$	$1\frac{7}{8}$	$1\frac{11}{16}$
2	$3\frac{1}{2}$	2	$1\frac{13}{16}$	2	4	2	$1\frac{13}{16}$
$2\frac{1}{8}$	$3\frac{3}{4}$	$2\frac{1}{8}$	$1\frac{7}{8}$	$2\frac{1}{8}$	4	$2\frac{1}{8}$	$1\frac{7}{8}$
$2\frac{1}{4}$	$3\frac{3}{4}$	$2\frac{1}{4}$	2	$2\frac{1}{4}$	$4\frac{1}{4}$	$2\frac{1}{4}$	2
$2\frac{3}{8}$	4	$2\frac{3}{8}$	$2\frac{1}{8}$	$2\frac{3}{8}$	$4\frac{1}{4}$	$2\frac{3}{8}$	$2\frac{1}{8}$
$2\frac{1}{2}$	$4\frac{1}{4}$	$2\frac{1}{2}$	$2\frac{1}{4}$	$2\frac{1}{2}$	$4\frac{1}{2}$	$2\frac{1}{2}$	$2\frac{1}{4}$
$2\frac{3}{4}$	$4\frac{1}{2}$	$2\frac{3}{4}$	$2\frac{7}{16}$	$2\frac{3}{4}$	$4\frac{3}{4}$	$2\frac{3}{4}$	$2\frac{7}{16}$
3	$4\frac{3}{4}$	3	$2\frac{11}{16}$	3	5	3	$2\frac{11}{16}$
$3\frac{1}{4}$	5	$3\frac{1}{4}$	$2\frac{15}{16}$	$3\frac{1}{4}$	$5\frac{1}{2}$	$3\frac{1}{4}$	$2\frac{15}{16}$
$3\frac{1}{2}$	$5\frac{1}{4}$	$3\frac{1}{2}$	$3\frac{1}{8}$	$3\frac{1}{2}$	6	$3\frac{1}{2}$	$3\frac{1}{8}$

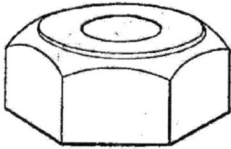

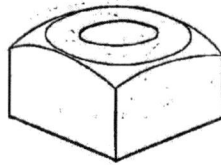

COLD PUNCHED NUTS, MANUFACTURERS STANDARD

HEXAGON				SQUARE			
Dia. Bolt	Across Flats	Thickness	Dia. Hole	Dia. Bolt	Across Flats	Thickness	Dia. Hole
$\frac{1}{4}$	$\frac{1}{2}$	$\frac{1}{4}$	$\frac{7}{32}$	$\frac{1}{4}$	$\frac{1}{2}$	$\frac{1}{4}$	$\frac{7}{32}$
$\frac{5}{16}$	$\frac{5}{8}$	$\frac{5}{16}$	$\frac{9}{32}$	$\frac{5}{16}$	$\frac{5}{8}$	$\frac{5}{16}$	$\frac{9}{32}$
$\frac{3}{8}$	$\frac{3}{4}$	$\frac{3}{8}$	$\frac{11}{32}$	$\frac{3}{8}$	$\frac{3}{4}$	$\frac{3}{8}$	$\frac{11}{32}$
$\frac{7}{16}$	$\frac{7}{8}$	$\frac{7}{16}$	$\frac{13}{32}$	$\frac{7}{16}$	$\frac{7}{8}$	$\frac{7}{16}$	$\frac{13}{32}$
$\frac{1}{2}$	$\frac{7}{8}$	$\frac{1}{2}$	$\frac{7}{16}$	$\frac{1}{2}$	$\frac{7}{8}$	$\frac{1}{2}$	$\frac{7}{16}$
$\frac{1}{2}$	1	$\frac{1}{2}$	$\frac{7}{16}$	$\frac{1}{2}$	1	$\frac{1}{2}$	$\frac{7}{16}$
$\frac{9}{16}$	1	$\frac{9}{16}$	$\frac{1}{2}$	$\frac{9}{16}$	$1\frac{1}{8}$	$\frac{9}{16}$	$\frac{9}{16}$
$\frac{5}{8}$	$1\frac{1}{8}$	$\frac{9}{16}$	$\frac{9}{16}$	$\frac{5}{8}$	$1\frac{1}{8}$	$\frac{5}{8}$	$\frac{9}{16}$
$\frac{5}{8}$	$1\frac{3}{16}$	$\frac{5}{8}$	$\frac{9}{16}$	$\frac{5}{8}$	$1\frac{1}{4}$	$\frac{5}{8}$	$\frac{19}{32}$
$\frac{3}{4}$	$1\frac{1}{4}$	$\frac{3}{4}$	$\frac{9}{16}$	$\frac{3}{4}$	$1\frac{1}{2}$	$\frac{3}{4}$	$\frac{21}{32}$
$\frac{3}{4}$	$1\frac{5}{16}$	$\frac{3}{4}$	$\frac{21}{32}$	$\frac{7}{8}$	$1\frac{1}{2}$	$\frac{7}{8}$	$\frac{25}{32}$
$\frac{7}{8}$	$1\frac{7}{16}$	$\frac{7}{8}$	$\frac{23}{32}$	$\frac{7}{8}$	$1\frac{5}{8}$	$\frac{7}{8}$	$\frac{25}{32}$
$\frac{7}{8}$	$1\frac{1}{2}$	$\frac{3}{4}$	$\frac{23}{32}$	$\frac{7}{8}$	$1\frac{3}{4}$	$\frac{7}{8}$	$\frac{25}{32}$
$\frac{7}{8}$	$1\frac{1}{2}$	$\frac{7}{8}$	$\frac{23}{32}$	1	$1\frac{5}{8}$	1	$\frac{7}{8}$
$\frac{7}{8}$	$1\frac{11}{16}$	1	$\frac{25}{32}$	1	2	1	$\frac{7}{8}$
$\frac{7}{8}$	$1\frac{5}{8}$	$\frac{7}{8}$	$\frac{31}{32}$	$1\frac{1}{8}$	2	$1\frac{1}{8}$	$1\frac{5}{16}$
$\frac{7}{8}$	$1\frac{13}{16}$	1	$\frac{31}{32}$	$1\frac{1}{8}$	$2\frac{1}{4}$	$1\frac{1}{8}$	$1\frac{5}{16}$
1	$1\frac{3}{4}$	1	$\frac{7}{8}$	$1\frac{1}{4}$	$2\frac{1}{4}$	$1\frac{1}{4}$	$1\frac{1}{16}$
1	$1\frac{3}{4}$	$1\frac{1}{8}$	$\frac{7}{8}$	$1\frac{1}{4}$	$2\frac{1}{2}$	$1\frac{1}{4}$	$1\frac{1}{16}$
$1\frac{1}{8}$	2	$1\frac{1}{4}$	$\frac{15}{16}$	$1\frac{3}{8}$	$2\frac{3}{4}$	$1\frac{3}{8}$	$1\frac{1}{16}$
$1\frac{1}{4}$	$2\frac{1}{4}$	$1\frac{3}{8}$	$1\frac{1}{16}$	$1\frac{1}{2}$	3	$1\frac{1}{2}$	$1\frac{3}{16}$
$1\frac{3}{8}$	$2\frac{1}{2}$	$1\frac{1}{2}$	$1\frac{5}{16}$	$1\frac{3}{4}$	$3\frac{1}{4}$	$1\frac{3}{4}$	$1\frac{9}{16}$
$1\frac{1}{2}$	$2\frac{3}{4}$	$1\frac{5}{8}$	$1\frac{5}{16}$	$1\frac{7}{8}$	$3\frac{1}{2}$	$1\frac{7}{8}$	$1\frac{11}{16}$
$1\frac{5}{8}$	3	$1\frac{3}{4}$	$1\frac{7}{16}$	2	4	2	$1\frac{13}{16}$
$1\frac{3}{4}$	$3\frac{1}{4}$	$1\frac{7}{8}$	$1\frac{9}{16}$				
$1\frac{7}{8}$	$3\frac{1}{2}$	2	$1\frac{11}{16}$				
2	$3\frac{1}{2}$	2	$1\frac{13}{16}$				
2	$3\frac{3}{4}$	$2\frac{1}{8}$	$1\frac{13}{16}$				

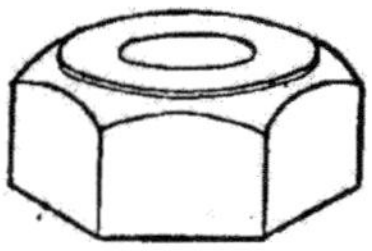

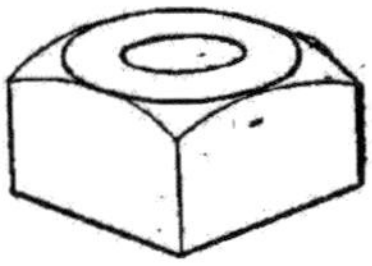

HOT PRESSED NUTS. MANUFACTURERS STANDARD NARROW GAGE SIZES

Hexagon				Square			
Dia. Bolt	Across Flats	Thick-ness	Dia. Hole	Dia. Bolt	Across Flats	Thick-ness	Dia. Hole
				$\frac{1}{8}$	$\frac{11}{32}$	$\frac{5}{32}$	$\frac{3}{32}$
				$\frac{3}{16}$	$\frac{13}{32}$	$\frac{3}{16}$	$\frac{5}{32}$
				$\frac{1}{4}$	$\frac{15}{32}$	$\frac{7}{32}$	$\frac{7}{32}$
				$\frac{5}{16}$	$\frac{9}{16}$	$\frac{9}{32}$	$\frac{9}{32}$
$\frac{3}{8}$	$\frac{11}{16}$	$\frac{3}{8}$	$\frac{21}{64}$	$\frac{3}{8}$	$\frac{11}{16}$	$\frac{3}{8}$	$\frac{21}{64}$
$\frac{7}{16}$	$\frac{25}{32}$	$\frac{7}{16}$	$\frac{25}{64}$	$\frac{7}{16}$	$\frac{25}{32}$	$\frac{7}{16}$	$\frac{25}{64}$
$\frac{1}{2}$	$\frac{7}{8}$	$\frac{1}{2}$	$\frac{7}{16}$	$\frac{1}{2}$	$\frac{7}{8}$	$\frac{1}{2}$	$\frac{7}{16}$
$\frac{9}{16}$	1	$\frac{9}{16}$	$\frac{1}{2}$	$\frac{9}{16}$	1	$\frac{9}{16}$	$\frac{1}{2}$
$\frac{5}{8}$	$1\frac{1}{8}$	$\frac{5}{8}$	$\frac{9}{16}$	$\frac{5}{8}$	$1\frac{1}{8}$	$\frac{5}{8}$	$\frac{9}{16}$
$\frac{3}{4}$	$1\frac{1}{4}$	$\frac{3}{4}$	$\frac{21}{32}$	$\frac{3}{4}$	$1\frac{3}{8}$	$\frac{3}{4}$	$\frac{21}{32}$
$\frac{7}{8}$	$1\frac{1}{2}$	$\frac{7}{8}$	$\frac{49}{64}$	$\frac{7}{8}$	$1\frac{5}{8}$	$\frac{7}{8}$	$\frac{49}{64}$
1	$1\frac{5}{8}$	1	$\frac{7}{8}$	1	$1\frac{3}{4}$	1	$\frac{7}{8}$
$1\frac{1}{8}$	2	$1\frac{1}{8}$	$\frac{31}{32}$	$1\frac{1}{8}$	2	$1\frac{1}{8}$	$\frac{31}{32}$
$1\frac{1}{4}$	$2\frac{1}{4}$	$1\frac{1}{4}$	$1\frac{3}{32}$	$1\frac{1}{4}$	$2\frac{1}{4}$	$1\frac{1}{4}$	$1\frac{3}{32}$
$1\frac{3}{8}$	$2\frac{1}{2}$	$1\frac{1}{2}$	$1\frac{3}{16}$	$1\frac{3}{8}$	$2\frac{1}{2}$	$1\frac{1}{2}$	$1\frac{3}{16}$
$1\frac{1}{2}$	$2\frac{1}{2}$	$1\frac{1}{2}$	$1\frac{5}{16}$	$1\frac{1}{2}$	$2\frac{1}{2}$	$1\frac{1}{2}$	$1\frac{5}{16}$

DIMENSIONS OF WHITWORTH STANDARD HEXAGONAL NUTS AND BOLT-HEADS

Dia. of Bolt	Width of Nut or Bolt Head across Flats	Hight of Bolt Head	Dia. of Bolt	Width of Nut or Bolt Head across Flats	Hight of Bolt Head
$\frac{1}{8}$	.338	.109	$1\frac{1}{4}$	2.048	1.094
$\frac{3}{16}$	.448	.164	$1\frac{3}{8}$	2.215	1.203
$\frac{1}{4}$	.525	.219	$1\frac{1}{2}$	2.413	1.312
$\frac{5}{16}$	.601	.273	$1\frac{5}{8}$	2.576	1.422
$\frac{3}{8}$	.709	.328	$1\frac{3}{4}$	2.758	1.531
$\frac{7}{16}$	.820	.383	$1\frac{7}{8}$	3.018	1.641
$\frac{1}{2}$	.919	.437	2	3.149	1.750
$\frac{9}{16}$	1.011	.492	$2\frac{1}{8}$	3.337	1.859
$\frac{5}{8}$	1.101	.547	$2\frac{1}{4}$	3.546	1.969
$\frac{11}{16}$	1.201	.601	$2\frac{3}{8}$	3.750	2.078
$\frac{3}{4}$	1.301	.656	$2\frac{1}{2}$	3.894	2.187
$\frac{13}{16}$	1.390	.711	$2\frac{5}{8}$	4.049	2.297
$\frac{7}{8}$	1.479	.766	$2\frac{3}{4}$	4.181	2.406
$\frac{15}{16}$	1.574	.820	$2\frac{7}{8}$	4.346	2.516
1	1.670	.875	3	4.531	2.625
$1\frac{1}{8}$	1.860	.984			

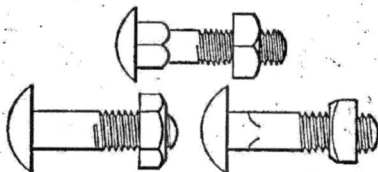

BUTTON HEAD MACHINE AND LOOM BOLTS
HOOPES & TOWNSEND CO.

Diameter Bolt..	3/16	1/4	5/16	3/8	7/16	1/2	9/16	5/8	3/4	7/8	1
Diameter Head.	1/2	5/8	13/16	15/16	1 1/16	1 1/8	1 5/16	1 3/8	1 5/8	1 7/8	2 1/8
Thickness of Head........	5/32	1/8	5/32	3/16	1/4	1/4	5/16	3/8	1/2	5/8	3/4

CARRIAGE BOLTS
UPSON NUT CO.

Diameter Bolt..	3/16	1/4	5/16	3/8	7/16	1/2	9/16	5/8	3/4	7/8	1
Diameter Head.	7/16	9/16	11/16	13/16	15/16	1 1/16	1 3/16	1 5/16	1 9/16	1 13/16	2 1/16
Thickness of Head........	3/32	1/8	5/32	3/16	7/32	1/4	9/32	5/16	3/8	7/16	1/2

LENGTHS OF BOLTS

SQUARE HEAD, Hexagon Head, Button Head, Round Head and Cone Head bolts are measured under the head. Countersunk Head bolts, bolt ends and rods are measured over all.

LENGTHS OF THREADS CUT ON BOLTS

Length of Bolts	1/4 & 5/16	3/8 & 7/16	1/2 & 9/16	5/8	3/4	7/8	1	1 1/8	1 1/4
1 to 1 1/2" ...	3/4	7/8	1	1 1/4	..	..	..	..	..
1 5/8 to 2" ...	7/8	1	1	1 1/4	1 1/2	1 3/4	..	..	..
2 1/8 to 2 1/2" ...	1	1	1	1 1/4	1 1/2	1 3/4	1 1/4	..	..
2 5/8 to 3" ...	1	1	1	1 1/4	1 1/2	1 3/4	2	2 1/4	..
3 1/8 to 4" ...	1	1	1 1/4	1 1/4	1 1/2	1 3/4	2	2 1/4	2 1/2
4 1/8 to 8" ...	1	1 1/4	1 1/4	1 1/2	1 1/2	1 3/4	2	2 3/4	3
8 1/8 to 12" ...	1	1 1/4	1 1/2	1 3/4	2	2 1/4	2 1/2	3	3 1/4
12 1/8 to 20" ...	1	1 1/2	2	2	2	2 1/2	3	3 1/4	3 1/2

Bolts longer than 20 inches and larger than 1 1/4 inch in diameter are usually threaded about 3 times the diameter of the rod.

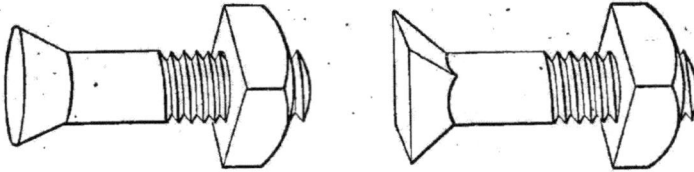

ROUND AND SQUARE COUNTERSUNK HEAD BOLTS

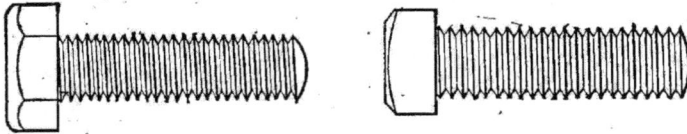

Diameter Bolt	$\frac{1}{4}$	$\frac{5}{16}$	$\frac{3}{8}$	$\frac{7}{16}$	$\frac{1}{2}$	$\frac{9}{16}$	$\frac{5}{8}$	$\frac{3}{4}$	$\frac{7}{8}$	1
Diameter Round Head	$\frac{1}{2}$	$\frac{19}{32}$	$\frac{11}{16}$	$\frac{25}{32}$	$\frac{7}{8}$	$\frac{31}{32}$	$1\frac{1}{16}$	$1\frac{1}{4}$	$1\frac{7}{16}$	$1\frac{5}{8}$
Distance across Flats Square Head	$\frac{1}{2}$	$\frac{19}{32}$	$\frac{11}{16}$	$\frac{25}{32}$	$\frac{7}{8}$	$\frac{31}{32}$	$1\frac{1}{16}$	$1\frac{1}{4}$	$1\frac{7}{16}$	$1\frac{5}{8}$
Thickness Square and Round Heads	$\frac{3}{16}$	$\frac{3}{16}$	$\frac{7}{32}$	$\frac{1}{4}$	$\frac{1}{4}$	$\frac{9}{32}$	$\frac{5}{16}$	$\frac{11}{32}$	$\frac{13}{32}$	$\frac{7}{16}$

TAP BOLTS

Diameter Bolt	$\frac{1}{4}$	$\frac{5}{16}$	$\frac{3}{8}$	$\frac{7}{16}$	$\frac{1}{2}$	$\frac{9}{16}$	$\frac{5}{8}$	$\frac{3}{4}$	$\frac{7}{8}$	1
No. of Threads per Inch	20	18	16	14	13	12	11	10	9	8
Across Flats Hex. and Square Heads	$\frac{3}{8}$	$\frac{15}{32}$	$\frac{9}{16}$	$\frac{21}{32}$	$\frac{3}{4}$	$\frac{27}{32}$	$\frac{15}{16}$	$1\frac{1}{8}$	$1\frac{5}{16}$	$1\frac{1}{2}$
Across Corners Hex. Head	$\frac{7}{16}$	$\frac{9}{16}$	$\frac{21}{32}$	$\frac{3}{4}$	$\frac{55}{64}$	$\frac{31}{32}$	$1\frac{5}{64}$	$1\frac{9}{64}$	$1\frac{33}{64}$	$1\frac{23}{32}$
Across Corners Square Head	$\frac{17}{32}$	$\frac{21}{32}$	$\frac{51}{64}$	$\frac{15}{16}$	$1\frac{1}{16}$	$1\frac{3}{16}$	$1\frac{21}{64}$	$1\frac{21}{32}$	$1\frac{55}{64}$	$2\frac{1}{8}$
Thickness Hex. and Square Heads	$\frac{3}{16}$	$\frac{1}{4}$	$\frac{5}{16}$	$\frac{3}{8}$	$\frac{7}{16}$	$\frac{1}{2}$	$\frac{17}{32}$	$\frac{5}{8}$	$\frac{3}{4}$	$\frac{7}{8}$

STOVE BOLT DIAMETERS AND THREADS

Dia. of Bolt	$\frac{1}{8}$	$\frac{5}{32}$	$\frac{3}{16}$	$\frac{7}{32}$	$\frac{1}{4}$	$\frac{5}{16}$	$\frac{3}{8}$
No. of Threads per Inch	32	28	24	22	18	18	16

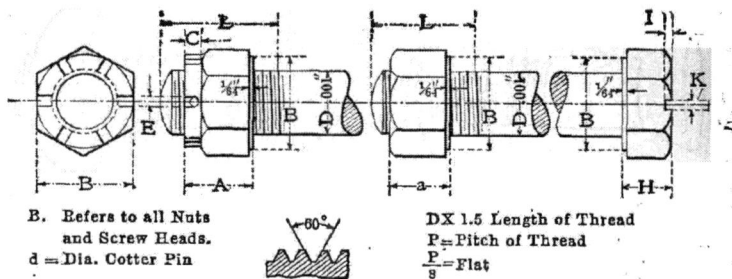

B. Refers to all Nuts and Screw Heads.
d = Dia. Cotter Pin

DX1.5 Length of Thread
P = Pitch of Thread
$\frac{P}{9}$ = Flat

All heads and nuts to be semi-finished. All screws to be of steel not less than 100,000 pounds tensile strength and 60,000 pounds elastic limit per square inch. Screws, screw heads and plain nuts to be left soft. Castle nuts to be case-hardened. Where screws are to be used in soft material such as cast iron, brass, bronze or aluminum, the U. S. S. pitches are to be used. Body diameter to be 0.001 inch less than nominal diameter with a plus tolerance of zero and a minus tolerance of 0.002 inch. Nuts shall fit without perceptible shake. This was originally known as the A. L. A. M. Standard, but is now the S. A. E. (Society Automobile Engineers).

Automobile Screw and Nut Standards Adopted by the S. A. E.

D	$\frac{1}{4}$	$\frac{5}{16}$	$\frac{3}{8}$	$\frac{7}{16}$	$\frac{1}{2}$	$\frac{9}{16}$	$\frac{5}{8}$	$\frac{11}{16}$	$\frac{3}{4}$	$\frac{7}{8}$	I
P	28	24	24	20	20	18	18	16	16	14	14
A	$\frac{9}{32}$	$\frac{21}{64}$	$\frac{13}{32}$	$\frac{29}{64}$	$\frac{9}{16}$	$\frac{39}{64}$	$\frac{23}{32}$	$\frac{49}{64}$	$\frac{13}{16}$	$\frac{29}{32}$	I
a	$\frac{7}{32}$	$\frac{17}{64}$	$\frac{21}{64}$	$\frac{3}{8}$	$\frac{7}{16}$	$\frac{31}{64}$	$\frac{35}{64}$	$\frac{19}{32}$	$\frac{21}{32}$	$\frac{49}{64}$	$\frac{7}{8}$
B	$\frac{7}{16}$	$\frac{1}{2}$	$\frac{9}{16}$	$\frac{5}{8}$	$\frac{3}{4}$	$\frac{7}{8}$	$\frac{15}{16}$	I	$1\frac{1}{16}$	$1\frac{1}{4}$	$1\frac{7}{16}$
C	$\frac{3}{32}$	$\frac{3}{32}$	$\frac{1}{8}$	$\frac{1}{8}$	$\frac{3}{16}$	$\frac{3}{16}$	$\frac{1}{4}$	$\frac{1}{4}$	$\frac{1}{4}$	$\frac{1}{4}$	$\frac{1}{4}$
E	$\frac{5}{64}$	$\frac{5}{64}$	$\frac{1}{8}$	$\frac{1}{8}$	$\frac{1}{8}$	$\frac{5}{32}$	$\frac{5}{32}$	$\frac{5}{32}$	$\frac{5}{32}$	$\frac{5}{32}$	$\frac{5}{32}$
H	$\frac{3}{16}$	$\frac{15}{64}$	$\frac{9}{32}$	$\frac{21}{64}$	$\frac{3}{8}$	$\frac{27}{64}$	$\frac{15}{32}$	$\frac{33}{64}$	$\frac{9}{16}$	$\frac{21}{32}$	$\frac{3}{4}$
I	$\frac{3}{32}$	$\frac{7}{64}$	$\frac{1}{8}$	$\frac{1}{8}$	$\frac{1}{8}$	$\frac{1}{8}$	$\frac{1}{8}$	$\frac{1}{8}$	$\frac{1}{8}$	$\frac{1}{8}$	$\frac{1}{8}$
K	$\frac{1}{16}$	$\frac{1}{16}$	$\frac{3}{32}$	$\frac{3}{32}$	$\frac{3}{32}$	$\frac{3}{32}$	$\frac{3}{32}$	$\frac{3}{32}$	$\frac{3}{32}$	$\frac{3}{32}$	$\frac{3}{32}$
d	$\frac{1}{16}$	$\frac{1}{16}$	$\frac{3}{32}$	$\frac{3}{32}$	$\frac{3}{32}$	$\frac{1}{8}$	$\frac{1}{8}$	$\frac{1}{8}$	$\frac{1}{8}$	$\frac{1}{8}$	$\frac{1}{8}$
L	$\frac{3}{8}$	$\frac{15}{32}$	$\frac{9}{16}$	$\frac{21}{32}$	$\frac{3}{4}$	$\frac{27}{32}$	$\frac{15}{16}$	$1\frac{1}{32}$	$1\frac{1}{8}$	$1\frac{5}{16}$	$1\frac{1}{2}$

PLANER NUTS

Diameter of Bolt	$\frac{1}{2}$	$\frac{5}{8}$	$\frac{3}{4}$	$\frac{7}{8}$	1	$1\frac{1}{8}$	$1\frac{1}{4}$
No. of Threads per Inch	13	11	10	9	8	7	7
Across Flats	$\frac{7}{8}$	$1\frac{1}{16}$	$1\frac{1}{4}$	$1\frac{7}{16}$	$1\frac{5}{8}$	$1\frac{13}{16}$	2
Thickness	$\frac{13}{16}$	1	$1\frac{1}{8}$	$1\frac{5}{16}$	$1\frac{7}{16}$	$1\frac{3}{4}$	$2\frac{1}{16}$

COUPLING BOLTS

Diameter of Bolt	$\frac{1}{2}$	$\frac{5}{8}$	$\frac{3}{4}$	$\frac{7}{8}$	1	$1\frac{1}{8}$	$1\frac{1}{4}$
No. of Threads per Inch	13	11	10	9	8	7	7
Short Diameter of Head	$\frac{7}{8}$	$1\frac{1}{16}$	$1\frac{1}{4}$	$1\frac{7}{16}$	$1\frac{5}{8}$	$1\frac{13}{16}$	2
Length of Head	$\frac{1}{2}$	$\frac{5}{8}$	$\frac{3}{4}$	$\frac{7}{8}$	1	$1\frac{1}{8}$	$1\frac{1}{4}$
Thickness of Nut	$\frac{1}{2}$	$\frac{5}{8}$	$\frac{3}{4}$	$\frac{7}{8}$	1	$1\frac{1}{8}$	$1\frac{1}{4}$
Short Diameter of Nut	$\frac{7}{8}$	$1\frac{1}{16}$	$1\frac{1}{4}$	$1\frac{7}{16}$	$1\frac{5}{8}$	$1\frac{13}{16}$	2

PLANER HEAD BOLTS AND NUTS

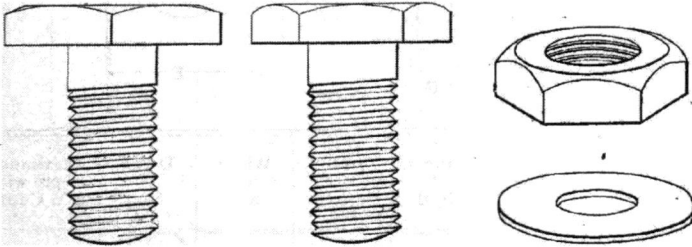

Diameter of Bolt	$\frac{1}{2}$	$\frac{9}{16}$	$\frac{5}{8}$	$\frac{11}{16}$	$\frac{3}{4}$
No. of Threads per Inch	12	12	12	12	12
Short Diameter of Head	$\frac{7}{8}$	1	$1\frac{1}{8}$	$1\frac{1}{8}$	$1\frac{1}{4}$
Length of Head	$\frac{5}{16}$	$\frac{5}{16}$	$\frac{3}{8}$	$\frac{3}{8}$	$\frac{7}{16}$
Short Diameter of Nuts	$1\frac{1}{8}$	$1\frac{1}{8}$	$1\frac{1}{4}$	$1\frac{1}{4}$	$1\frac{1}{16}$
Thickness of Nuts	$\frac{3}{8}$	$\frac{3}{8}$	$\frac{3}{8}$	$\frac{3}{8}$	$\frac{1}{2}$
Washers for Planer Head Bolts	$\frac{1}{2}$	$\frac{9}{16}$	$\frac{5}{8}$	$\frac{11}{16}$	$\frac{3}{4}$
Diameter of Washers	$1\frac{7}{16}$	$1\frac{7}{16}$	$1\frac{1}{2}$	$1\frac{9}{16}$	$1\frac{13}{16}$
Thickness of Washers	$\frac{1}{16}$	$\frac{1}{16}$	$\frac{1}{16}$	$\frac{1}{16}$	$\frac{3}{32}$

DEPTHS TO DRILL AND TAP FOR STUDS

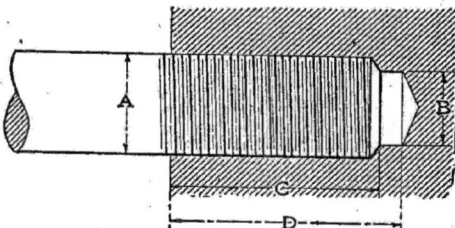

Dia. of Stud	A	$\frac{1}{4}$	$\frac{5}{16}$	$\frac{3}{8}$	$\frac{7}{16}$	$\frac{1}{2}$	$\frac{9}{16}$	$\frac{5}{8}$	$\frac{3}{4}$	$\frac{7}{8}$	1
Dia. of Drill C. I.	B	$\frac{13}{64}$	$\frac{17}{64}$	$\frac{5}{16}$	$\frac{3}{8}$	$\frac{21}{64}$	$\frac{15}{32}$	$\frac{17}{32}$	$\frac{41}{64}$	$\frac{3}{4}$	$\frac{55}{64}$
Depth of Thread	C	$\frac{3}{8}$	$\frac{15}{32}$	$\frac{9}{16}$	$\frac{21}{32}$	$\frac{3}{4}$	$\frac{27}{32}$	$\frac{15}{16}$	$1\frac{1}{8}$	$1\frac{1}{16}$	$1\frac{1}{2}$
Depth to Drill	D	$\frac{7}{16}$	$\frac{17}{32}$	$\frac{5}{8}$	$\frac{23}{32}$	$\frac{27}{32}$	$\frac{15}{16}$	$1\frac{1}{32}$	$1\frac{1}{4}$	$1\frac{7}{16}$	$1\frac{5}{8}$

BOLT HEADS FOR STANDARD T-SLOTS

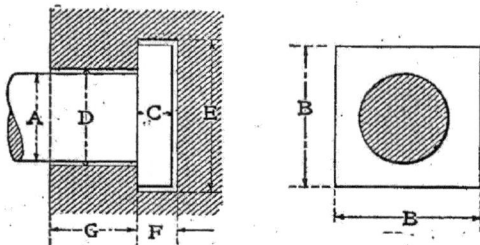

Dia. of Bolt	Width of Head	Thickness of Head	Width of Slot	Width of Slot	Depth of Slot	Maximum Depth with St'd Cutter
A	B	C	D	E	F	G
$\frac{1}{4}$	$\frac{9}{16}$	$\frac{1}{8}$	$\frac{5}{16}$	$\frac{5}{8}$	$\frac{5}{32}$	$\frac{3}{8}$
$\frac{5}{16}$	$\frac{5}{8}$	$\frac{3}{16}$	$\frac{3}{8}$	$\frac{11}{16}$	$\frac{7}{32}$	$\frac{7}{16}$
$\frac{3}{8}$	$\frac{3}{4}$	$\frac{3}{16}$	$\frac{7}{16}$	$\frac{13}{16}$	$\frac{7}{32}$	$\frac{7}{16}$
$\frac{7}{16}$	$\frac{7}{8}$	$\frac{1}{4}$	$\frac{1}{2}$	$\frac{15}{16}$	$\frac{9}{32}$	$\frac{9}{16}$
$\frac{1}{2}$	$1\frac{1}{8}$	$\frac{5}{16}$	$\frac{5}{8}$	$1\frac{1}{16}$	$\frac{9}{32}$	$\frac{3}{4}$
$\frac{5}{8}$	$1\frac{1}{4}$	$\frac{1}{2}$	$\frac{3}{4}$	$1\frac{5}{16}$	$\frac{17}{32}$	1
$\frac{3}{4}$	$1\frac{9}{16}$	$\frac{5}{8}$	$\frac{7}{8}$	$1\frac{5}{8}$	$\frac{1}{1}$	$1\frac{1}{16}$
$\frac{7}{8}$	$1\frac{13}{16}$	$\frac{3}{4}$	1	$1\frac{7}{8}$	$\frac{13}{16}$	$1\frac{3}{16}$

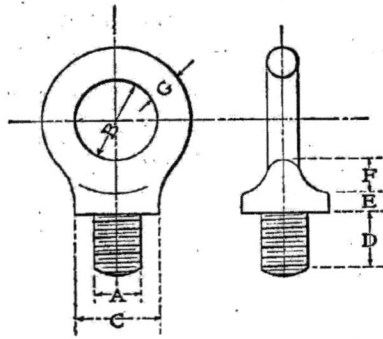

EYE BOLTS

A	B	C	D	E	F	G
$\frac{3}{8}$	2	$\frac{3}{4}$	$\frac{7}{8}$	$\frac{3}{16}$	$\frac{3}{8}$	$\frac{5}{16}$
$\frac{1}{2}$	$2\frac{1}{8}$	1	1	$\frac{1}{4}$	$\frac{1}{2}$	$\frac{3}{8}$
$\frac{5}{8}$	$2\frac{1}{4}$	$1\frac{1}{4}$	$1\frac{1}{8}$	$\frac{5}{16}$	$\frac{5}{8}$	$\frac{1}{2}$
$\frac{3}{4}$	$2\frac{3}{8}$	$1\frac{1}{16}$	$1\frac{1}{4}$	$\frac{5}{16}$	$\frac{11}{16}$	$\frac{9}{16}$
$\frac{7}{8}$	$2\frac{1}{2}$	$1\frac{11}{16}$	$1\frac{3}{8}$	$\frac{3}{8}$	$\frac{3}{4}$	$\frac{5}{8}$
1	$2\frac{7}{8}$	$1\frac{7}{8}$	$1\frac{1}{2}$	$\frac{7}{16}$	$\frac{7}{8}$	$\frac{3}{4}$
$1\frac{1}{8}$	$2\frac{7}{8}$	$2\frac{3}{8}$	$1\frac{5}{8}$	$\frac{1}{2}$	1	$\frac{13}{16}$
$1\frac{1}{4}$	3	$2\frac{3}{8}$	$1\frac{3}{4}$	$\frac{1}{2}$	$1\frac{1}{8}$	$\frac{7}{8}$
$1\frac{3}{8}$	$3\frac{1}{8}$	$2\frac{5}{8}$	$1\frac{7}{8}$	$\frac{9}{16}$	$1\frac{3}{16}$	1
$1\frac{1}{2}$	$3\frac{1}{4}$	$2\frac{3}{4}$	2	$\frac{5}{8}$	$1\frac{1}{4}$	$1\frac{1}{16}$
$1\frac{5}{8}$	$3\frac{3}{8}$	3	$2\frac{1}{8}$	$\frac{11}{16}$	$1\frac{3}{8}$	$1\frac{1}{8}$
$1\frac{3}{4}$	$3\frac{1}{2}$	$3\frac{1}{4}$	$2\frac{1}{4}$	$\frac{3}{4}$	$1\frac{1}{2}$	$1\frac{1}{4}$
$1\frac{7}{8}$	$3\frac{5}{8}$	$3\frac{1}{2}$	$2\frac{3}{8}$	$\frac{13}{16}$	$1\frac{5}{8}$	$1\frac{5}{16}$
2	$3\frac{3}{4}$	$3\frac{3}{4}$	$2\frac{1}{2}$	$\frac{7}{8}$	$1\frac{3}{4}$	$1\frac{3}{8}$

SPRING COTTERS

No. of Wire Gage	13	12	11	10	9	8	7	6
Dia. Inches	$\frac{3}{32}$	$\frac{7}{64}$	$\frac{1}{8}$	$\frac{9}{64}$	$\frac{5}{32}$	$\frac{11}{64}$	$\frac{3}{16}$	$\frac{13}{64}$
Lengths. Inches	$\frac{1}{2}$ to 2	$\frac{1}{2}$ to 2	$\frac{1}{2}$ to $2\frac{1}{2}$	$\frac{1}{2}$ to $2\frac{1}{2}$	$\frac{1}{2}$ to $2\frac{1}{2}$	$\frac{1}{2}$ to $2\frac{1}{2}$	$\frac{3}{4}$ to 3	$\frac{3}{4}$ to 3

No. of Wire Gage	5	4	1				
Dia. Inches	$\frac{7}{32}$	$\frac{1}{4}$	$\frac{5}{16}$	$\frac{3}{8}$	$\frac{7}{16}$	$\frac{1}{2}$	$\frac{5}{8}$
Lengths. Inches	1 to 3	1 to 4	1 to 4	$1\frac{1}{2}$ to 4	$1\frac{1}{4}$ to 5	2 to 6	3 to 6

Regular Lengths vary by $\frac{1}{4}$ inch up to 4 inches and by 1 inch from 4 to 6 inches. Lengths are measured under the eye.

ROUND AND SQUARE WASHERS

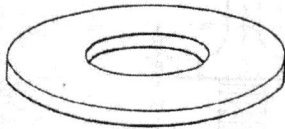

U. S. STANDARD WASHERS

Size of Bolt	Size of Hole	Outside Diameter	Thickness Wire Gage No.
$\frac{3}{16}$	$\frac{1}{4}$	$\frac{9}{16}$	18 $(\frac{3}{64})$
$\frac{1}{4}$	$\frac{5}{16}$	$\frac{3}{4}$	16 $(\frac{1}{16})$
$\frac{5}{16}$	$\frac{3}{8}$	$\frac{7}{8}$	16 $(\frac{1}{16})$
$\frac{3}{8}$	$\frac{7}{16}$	1	14 $(\frac{5}{64})$
$\frac{7}{16}$	$\frac{1}{2}$	$1\frac{1}{4}$	14 $(\frac{5}{64})$
$\frac{1}{2}$	$\frac{9}{16}$	$1\frac{3}{8}$	12 $(\frac{3}{32})$
$\frac{9}{16}$	$\frac{5}{8}$	$1\frac{1}{2}$	12 $(\frac{3}{32})$
$\frac{5}{8}$	$\frac{11}{16}$	$1\frac{3}{4}$	10 $(\frac{1}{8})$
$\frac{3}{4}$	$\frac{13}{16}$	2	10 $(\frac{1}{8})$
$\frac{7}{8}$	$\frac{15}{16}$	$2\frac{1}{4}$	9 $(\frac{5}{32})$
1	$1\frac{1}{16}$	$2\frac{1}{2}$	9 $(\frac{5}{32})$
$1\frac{1}{8}$	$1\frac{1}{4}$	$2\frac{3}{4}$	9 $(\frac{5}{32})$
$1\frac{1}{4}$	$1\frac{3}{8}$	3	9 $(\frac{5}{32})$
$1\frac{3}{8}$	$1\frac{1}{2}$	$3\frac{1}{4}$	8 $(\frac{11}{64})$
$1\frac{1}{2}$	$1\frac{5}{8}$	$3\frac{1}{2}$	8 $(\frac{11}{64})$
$1\frac{5}{8}$	$1\frac{3}{4}$	$3\frac{3}{4}$	8 $(\frac{11}{64})$
$1\frac{3}{4}$	$1\frac{7}{8}$	4	8 $(\frac{11}{64})$
$1\frac{7}{8}$	2	$4\frac{1}{4}$	8 $(\frac{11}{64})$
2	$2\frac{1}{8}$	$4\frac{1}{2}$	8 $(\frac{11}{64})$
$2\frac{1}{4}$	$2\frac{3}{8}$	$4\frac{3}{4}$	6 $(\frac{3}{16})$
$2\frac{1}{2}$	$2\frac{5}{8}$	5	5 $(\frac{7}{32})$

NARROW GAGE WASHERS

Size of Bolt	Size of Hole	Outside Diameter	Thickness Wire Gage No.
$\frac{1}{4}$	$\frac{5}{16}$	$\frac{5}{8}$	16 $(\frac{1}{16})$
$\frac{5}{16}$	$\frac{3}{8}$	$\frac{3}{4}$	16 $(\frac{1}{16})$
$\frac{3}{8}$	$\frac{7}{16}$	$\frac{7}{8}$	16 $(\frac{1}{16})$
$\frac{7}{16}$	$\frac{1}{2}$	$1\frac{1}{8}$	14 $(\frac{5}{64})$
$\frac{1}{2}$	$\frac{9}{16}$	$1\frac{1}{4}$	12 $(\frac{8}{32})$
$\frac{9}{16}$	$\frac{5}{8}$	$1\frac{3}{8}$	12 $(\frac{8}{32})$
$\frac{5}{8}$	$\frac{11}{16}$	$1\frac{1}{2}$	10 $(\frac{1}{8})$
$\frac{3}{4}$	$\frac{13}{16}$	$1\frac{3}{4}$	10 $(\frac{1}{8})$
$\frac{7}{8}$	$\frac{15}{16}$	2	9 $(\frac{5}{32})$
1	$1\frac{1}{16}$	$2\frac{1}{4}$	9 $(\frac{5}{32})$
$1\frac{1}{8}$	$1\frac{1}{4}$	$2\frac{1}{2}$	9 $(\frac{5}{32})$
$1\frac{1}{4}$	$1\frac{3}{8}$	$2\frac{3}{4}$	9 $(\frac{5}{32})$
$1\frac{3}{8}$	$1\frac{1}{2}$	3	8 $(\frac{11}{64})$
$1\frac{1}{2}$	$1\frac{5}{8}$	$3\frac{1}{4}$	8 $(\frac{11}{64})$

SQUARE WASHERS
STANDARD SIZES

Size of Bolt	Size of Hole	Width	Thickness
$\frac{3}{8}$	$\frac{7}{16}$	$1\frac{1}{2}$	$\frac{1}{8}$
$\frac{7}{16}$	$\frac{1}{2}$	$1\frac{3}{4}$	$\frac{1}{8}$
$\frac{1}{2}$	$\frac{9}{16}$	2	$\frac{8}{16}$
$\frac{5}{8}$	$\frac{11}{16}$	$2\frac{1}{4}$	$\frac{1}{4}$
$\frac{3}{4}$	$\frac{13}{16}$	$2\frac{1}{2}$	$\frac{1}{4}$
$\frac{7}{8}$	$\frac{15}{16}$	3	$\frac{1}{4}$
1	$1\frac{1}{32}$	$3\frac{1}{2}$	$\frac{3}{8}$
$1\frac{1}{8}$	$1\frac{3}{16}$	4	$\frac{3}{8}$
$1\frac{1}{4}$	$1\frac{5}{16}$	$4\frac{1}{2}$	$\frac{3}{8}$
$1\frac{3}{8}$	$1\frac{1}{2}$	5	$\frac{3}{8}$
$1\frac{1}{2}$	$1\frac{5}{8}$	6	$\frac{3}{8}$
$1\frac{3}{4}$	$1\frac{7}{8}$	6	$\frac{3}{8}$
2	$2\frac{1}{8}$	6	$\frac{3}{8}$

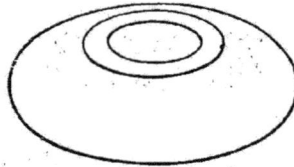

CAST-IRON WASHERS

Size of Bolt	Outside Diameter	Thickness	Size of Bolt	Outside Diameter	Thickness
$\frac{3}{8}$	$1\frac{1}{2}$	$\frac{5}{16}$	$1\frac{1}{8}$	$4\frac{1}{2}$	1
$\frac{1}{2}$	2	$\frac{3}{8}$	$1\frac{1}{4}$	5	$1\frac{1}{8}$
$\frac{5}{8}$	$2\frac{1}{2}$	$\frac{1}{2}$	$1\frac{3}{8}$	$5\frac{1}{2}$	$1\frac{1}{4}$
$\frac{3}{4}$	3	$\frac{5}{8}$	$1\frac{1}{2}$	6	$1\frac{3}{8}$
$\frac{7}{8}$	$3\frac{1}{2}$	$\frac{3}{4}$	$1\frac{3}{4}$	7	$1\frac{1}{2}$
1	4	$\frac{7}{8}$	2	$7\frac{1}{2}$	$1\frac{5}{8}$

RIVETING WASHERS

Size of Rivet	Size of Hole	Outside Diameter	Thickness Wire Gage	Size of Rivet	Size of Hole	Outside Diameter	Thickness Wire Gag
7 (.180)	$\frac{3}{16}$	$\frac{1}{2}$	18	$\frac{3}{8}$	$\frac{13}{32}$	$1\frac{1}{4}$	12
6 (.203)	$\frac{7}{32}$	$\frac{9}{16}$	18	$\frac{7}{16}$	$\frac{15}{32}$	1	14
.5 (.220)	$\frac{15}{64}$	$\frac{5}{8}$	18	$\frac{7}{16}$	$\frac{15}{32}$	$1\frac{1}{4}$	12
$\frac{1}{4}$	$\frac{17}{64}$	$\frac{5}{8}$	16	$\frac{1}{2}$	$\frac{17}{32}$	$1\frac{1}{8}$	12
$\frac{1}{4}$	$\frac{17}{64}$	$\frac{3}{4}$	16	$\frac{1}{2}$	$\frac{17}{32}$	$1\frac{1}{4}$	12
$\frac{5}{16}$	$\frac{11}{32}$	$\frac{3}{4}$	14	$\frac{1}{2}$	$\frac{21}{32}$	$1\frac{1}{2}$	11
$\frac{5}{16}$	$\frac{11}{32}$	$\frac{7}{8}$	14	$\frac{5}{8}$	$\frac{21}{32}$	$1\frac{1}{2}$	11
$\frac{3}{8}$	$\frac{13}{32}$	$\frac{7}{8}$	14	$\frac{5}{8}$	$\frac{21}{32}$	$1\frac{3}{4}$	10
$\frac{3}{8}$	$\frac{13}{32}$	1	14				

MACHINE AND WOOD SCREW GAGE

No. of Screw Gage	Size of Number in Decimals	No. of Screw Gage	Size of Number in Decimals	No. of Screw Gage	Size of Number in Decimals	No. of Screw Gage	Size of Number in Decimals
000	.03152	12	.21576	25	.38684	38	.55792
00	.04468	13	.22892	26	.40000	39	.57108
0	.05784	14	.24208	27	.41316	40	.58424
1	.07100	15	.25524	28	.42632	41	.59740
2	.08416	16	.26840	29	.43948	42	.61056
3	.09732	17	.28156	30	.45264	43	.62372
4	.11048	18	.29472	31	.46580	44	.63688
5	.12364	19	.30788	32	.47896	45	.65004
6	.13680	20	.32104	33	.49212	46	.66320
7	.14996	21	.33420	34	.50528	47	.67636
8	.16312	22	.34736	35	.51844	48	.68952
9	.17628	23	.36052	36	.53160	49	.70268
10	.18944	24	.37368	37	.54476	50	.71584
11	.20260						

The difference between consecutive sizes is .01316"

Cone Point

Gimlet Point

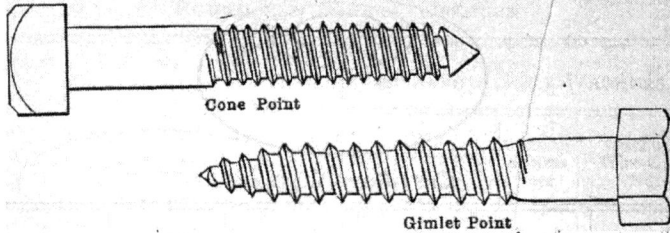

COACH AND LAG SCREWS

Diameter Screw	$\frac{1}{4}$	$\frac{5}{16}$	$\frac{3}{8}$	$\frac{7}{16}$	$\frac{1}{2}$	$\frac{9}{16}$	$\frac{5}{8}$	$\frac{3}{4}$	$\frac{7}{8}$	1
No. of Threads per Inch	10	$9\frac{1}{2}$	7	7	6	5	5	$4\frac{1}{2}$	$4\frac{1}{2}$	3
Across Flats Hex. and Square Heads	$\frac{3}{8}$	$\frac{15}{32}$	$\frac{9}{16}$	$\frac{21}{32}$	$\frac{3}{4}$	$\frac{27}{32}$	$\frac{15}{16}$	$1\frac{1}{8}$	$1\frac{5}{16}$	$1\frac{1}{2}$
Thickness Hex. and Square Heads	$\frac{3}{16}$	$\frac{1}{4}$	$\frac{5}{16}$	$\frac{3}{8}$	$\frac{7}{16}$	$\frac{1}{2}$	$\frac{17}{32}$	$\frac{5}{8}$	$\frac{3}{4}$	$\frac{7}{8}$

LENGTHS OF THREADS ON COACH AND LAG SCREWS

OF ALL DIAMETERS

Length of Screw	Length of Thread	Length of Screw	Length of Thread
$1\frac{1}{2}''$	To Head	$5''$	$4''$
$2''$	$1\frac{1}{2}''$	$5\frac{1}{2}''$	$4''$
$2\frac{1}{2}''$	$2''$	$6''$	$4\frac{1}{2}''$
$3''$	$2\frac{1}{4}''$	$7''$	$5''$
$3\frac{1}{2}''$	$2\frac{1}{2}''$	$8''$	$6''$
$4''$	$3''$	$9''$	$6''$
$4\frac{1}{2}''$	$3\frac{1}{2}''$	10 to 12''	$7''$

LAG-SCREW TEST

(SCREWS DRAWN OUT OF YELLOW PINE)

Test by Hoopes and Townsend

Diameter Screw	$\frac{1}{2}$ in.	$\frac{5}{8}$ in.	$\frac{3}{4}$ in.	$\frac{7}{8}$ in.	1 in.
Depth in Wood	$3\frac{1}{2}$ in.	4 in.	4 in.	5 in.	6 in.
Force in Pounds	4,960	6,000	7,685	11,500	12,620

WOOD SCREWS

Wood screws range in size from No. 0 to No. 30, by the American Screw Company's gage and in lengths from ¼ inch to 6 inches. The increase in length is by eights of an inch up to 1 inch, then by quarters of an inch up to 3 inches and by half inches up to 5 inches. As a rule the threaded portion is about seven tenths of the total length. The included angle of the flat head is 82 degrees. The table below gives the body and head diameters, and the threads per inch as generally cut, although there is no fixed standard as to number of threads which is universally adhered to by all wood-screw manufacturers.

Flat headed wood-screws include the head in the length given. With round headed screws, one half the head is generally included in the length although the practice is not uniform.

WOOD-SCREW DIMENSIONS

(ANGLE OF FLAT HEAD = 82 DEGREES)

Screw Gage	Diameter of Screw	Diameter of Head	Threads per Inch	No. of Screw Gage	Diameter of Screw	Diameter of Head	Threads per Inch
0	.05784 1/16 −	.110 7/64 +	32	16	.26840 17/64 +	.526 17/32 −	9
1	.07100 5/64 −	.136 9/64 +	28	17	.28156 9/32	.552 35/64 +	9
2	.08416 5/64 +	.162 5/32 +	26	18	.29472 19/64 −	.578 37/64 −	8
3	.09732 3/32 +	.188 3/16	24	19	.30788 5/16 −	.604 39/64 −	8
4	.11048 7/64 +	.214 7/32 −	22	20	.32104 21/64 −	.630 5/8 +	8
5	.12364 1/8 −	.240 15/64 +	20	21	.33420 21/64 +	.656 21/32 −	8
6	.13680 9/64 −	.266 17/64 +	18	22	.34736 11/32 +	.682 11/16 −	7
7	.14996 5/32 −	.292 19/64	16	23	.36052 23/64 −	.708 45/64 +	7
8	.16312 5/32 +	.318 5/16 +	15	24	.37368 3/8 −	.734 47/64 −	7
9	.17628 11/64 +	.344 11/32 +	14	25	.38684 25/64 −	.760 49/64 −	7
10	.18944 3/16 +	.370 3/8 −	13	26	.40000 25/64 −	.786 25/32 +	6
11	.20260 13/64 −	.396 25/64 +	12	27	.41316 53/128 +	.812 13/16	6
12	.21576 7/32 −	.422 27/64	11	28	.42632 27/64 +	.838 27/32 −	6
13	.22892 15/64 −	.448 29/64 −	11	29	.43948 7/16 +	.864 55/64 +	6
14	.24208 1/4 −	.474 15/32 +	10	30	.45264 29/64	.890 57/64	6
15	.25524 1/4 +	.500 1/2	10				

U. S. Navy Boiler Rivets

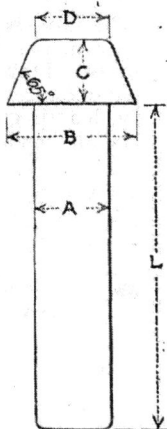

A	B	C	D	Weight of 10 heads	Weight per inch of shank L
$\frac{1}{2}$	$\frac{15}{16}$	$\frac{7}{16}$	$\frac{1}{2}$	.531	.0556
$\frac{9}{16}$	1	$\frac{1}{2}$	$\frac{9}{16}$	.713	.0704
$\frac{5}{8}$	$1\frac{1}{8}$	$\frac{9}{16}$	$\frac{5}{8}$	1.007	.0869
$\frac{11}{16}$	$1\frac{1}{4}$	$\frac{5}{8}$	$\frac{11}{16}$	1.372	.1052
$\frac{3}{4}$	$1\frac{5}{16}$	$\frac{5}{8}$	$\frac{3}{4}$	1.551	.1251
$\frac{13}{16}$	$1\frac{7}{16}$	$\frac{11}{16}$	$\frac{13}{16}$	2.033	.1470
$\frac{7}{8}$	$1\frac{1}{2}$	$\frac{11}{16}$	$\frac{7}{8}$	2.258	.1703
$\frac{15}{16}$	$1\frac{5}{8}$	$\frac{3}{4}$	$\frac{15}{16}$	2.871	.1956
1	$1\frac{3}{4}$	$\frac{13}{16}$	1	3.584	.2225
$1\frac{1}{16}$	$1\frac{11}{16}$	$\frac{13}{16}$	$1\frac{1}{16}$	3.910	.2512
$1\frac{1}{8}$	$1\frac{11}{16}$	$\frac{7}{8}$	$1\frac{1}{8}$	4.761	.2816
$1\frac{3}{16}$	2	$\frac{7}{8}$	$1\frac{3}{16}$	5.170	.3137
$1\frac{1}{4}$	$2\frac{1}{8}$	$\frac{15}{16}$	$1\frac{1}{4}$	6.215	.3477
$1\frac{5}{16}$	$2\frac{1}{4}$	1	$1\frac{5}{16}$	7.391	.3833
$1\frac{3}{8}$	$2\frac{3}{8}$	$1\frac{1}{16}$	$1\frac{3}{8}$	8.490	.4207
$1\frac{7}{16}$	$2\frac{1}{2}$	$1\frac{1}{8}$	$1\frac{7}{16}$	9.941	.4599
$1\frac{1}{2}$	$2\frac{5}{8}$	$1\frac{3}{16}$	$1\frac{1}{2}$	11.507	.5006
$1\frac{9}{16}$	$2\frac{3}{4}$	$1\frac{1}{4}$	$1\frac{9}{16}$	13.242	.5433
$1\frac{5}{8}$	$2\frac{7}{8}$	$1\frac{5}{16}$	$1\frac{5}{8}$	15.146	.5876
$1\frac{11}{16}$	3	$1\frac{3}{8}$	$1\frac{11}{16}$	17.300	.6336
$1\frac{3}{4}$	$3\frac{1}{8}$	$1\frac{7}{16}$	$1\frac{3}{4}$	19.485	.6815

U. S. Navy Hull and Tank Rivet Heads

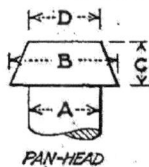

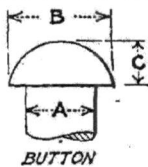

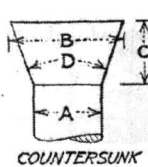

PAN-HEAD   BUTTON   COUNTERSUNK

Pan-head				Button			Countersunk			
A	B	C	D	A	B	C	A	B	C	D
$\frac{1}{4}$	$\frac{7}{16}$	$\frac{5}{16}$	$\frac{1}{4}$	$\frac{1}{4}$	$\frac{7}{16}$	$\frac{13}{32}$	$\frac{1}{4}$	$\frac{3}{8}$	$\frac{3}{32}$	60
$\frac{3}{8}$	$\frac{5}{8}$	$\frac{5}{16}$	$\frac{3}{8}$	$\frac{3}{8}$	$\frac{5}{8}$	$\frac{5}{16}$	$\frac{3}{8}$	$\frac{5}{8}$	$\frac{3}{32}$	60
$\frac{1}{2}$	$\frac{13}{16}$	$\frac{3}{8}$	$\frac{1}{2}$	$\frac{1}{2}$	$\frac{13}{16}$	$\frac{3}{8}$	$\frac{1}{2}$	$\frac{13}{16}$	$\frac{1}{4}$	60
$\frac{5}{8}$	1	$\frac{7}{16}$	$\frac{5}{8}$	$\frac{5}{8}$	1	$\frac{7}{16}$	$\frac{5}{8}$	$1\frac{1}{16}$	$\frac{3}{8}$	60
$\frac{3}{4}$	$1\frac{3}{16}$	$\frac{1}{2}$	$\frac{3}{4}$	$\frac{3}{4}$	$1\frac{3}{16}$	$\frac{1}{2}$	$\frac{3}{4}$	$1\frac{5}{32}$	$\frac{1}{2}$	45
$\frac{7}{8}$	$1\frac{5}{16}$	$\frac{9}{16}$	$\frac{7}{8}$	$\frac{7}{8}$	$1\frac{5}{16}$	$\frac{9}{16}$	$\frac{7}{8}$	$1\frac{1}{4}$	$\frac{11}{16}$	45
1	$1\frac{1}{2}$	$\frac{5}{8}$	1	1	$1\frac{1}{2}$	$\frac{5}{8}$	1	$1\frac{5}{16}$	$\frac{11}{16}$	37
$1\frac{1}{8}$	$1\frac{5}{8}$	$\frac{11}{16}$	$1\frac{1}{8}$	$1\frac{1}{8}$	$1\frac{5}{8}$	$\frac{11}{16}$	$1\frac{1}{8}$	$1\frac{3}{8}$	$\frac{11}{16}$	37
$1\frac{1}{4}$	$1\frac{13}{16}$	$\frac{3}{4}$	$1\frac{1}{4}$	$1\frac{1}{4}$	$1\frac{13}{16}$	$\frac{3}{4}$	$1\frac{1}{4}$	$1\frac{29}{32}$	1	37

LENGTH OF ROUND HEAD RIVETS FOR DIFFERENT THICKNESSES OF METAL

To find the required length of a rivet when thickness of metal between rivet heads is given, assuming the rivet hole to be $\frac{1}{16}$ inch larger than the rivet before it is heated, refer to the table below. Grip in inches means thickness of metal between rivet heads.

Grip in Inches.	Diameter in Inches				
	$\frac{1}{2}$	$\frac{5}{8}$	$\frac{3}{4}$	$\frac{7}{8}$	1
	Length in Inches.				
$\frac{1}{2}$	$1\frac{1}{2}$	$1\frac{3}{4}$	$1\frac{7}{8}$	2	$2\frac{1}{8}$
$\frac{5}{8}$	$1\frac{5}{8}$	$1\frac{7}{8}$	2	$2\frac{1}{8}$	$2\frac{1}{4}$
$\frac{3}{4}$	$1\frac{3}{4}$	2	$2\frac{1}{8}$	$2\frac{1}{4}$	$2\frac{3}{8}$
$\frac{7}{8}$	$1\frac{7}{8}$	$2\frac{1}{8}$	$2\frac{1}{4}$	$2\frac{3}{8}$	$2\frac{1}{2}$
1	2	$2\frac{1}{4}$	$2\frac{3}{8}$	$2\frac{1}{2}$	$2\frac{5}{8}$
$1\frac{1}{8}$	$2\frac{1}{8}$	$2\frac{3}{8}$	$2\frac{1}{2}$	$2\frac{5}{8}$	$2\frac{3}{4}$
$1\frac{1}{4}$	$2\frac{1}{4}$	$2\frac{1}{2}$	$2\frac{5}{8}$	$2\frac{3}{4}$	$2\frac{7}{8}$
$1\frac{3}{8}$	$2\frac{3}{8}$	$2\frac{5}{8}$	$2\frac{3}{4}$	$2\frac{7}{8}$	3
$1\frac{1}{2}$	$2\frac{1}{2}$	$2\frac{3}{4}$	3	$3\frac{1}{8}$	$3\frac{1}{4}$
$1\frac{5}{8}$	$2\frac{5}{8}$	$2\frac{7}{8}$	$3\frac{1}{8}$	$3\frac{1}{4}$	$3\frac{3}{8}$
$1\frac{3}{4}$	$2\frac{3}{4}$	3	$3\frac{1}{4}$	$3\frac{3}{8}$	$3\frac{1}{2}$
$1\frac{7}{8}$	$2\frac{7}{8}$	$3\frac{1}{8}$	$3\frac{3}{8}$	$3\frac{1}{2}$	$3\frac{5}{8}$
2	3	$3\frac{1}{4}$	$3\frac{1}{2}$	$3\frac{5}{8}$	$3\frac{3}{4}$
$2\frac{1}{8}$	$3\frac{1}{8}$	$3\frac{3}{8}$	$3\frac{5}{8}$	$3\frac{3}{4}$	$3\frac{7}{8}$
$2\frac{1}{4}$	$3\frac{1}{4}$	$3\frac{1}{2}$	$3\frac{3}{4}$	$3\frac{7}{8}$	4
$2\frac{3}{8}$	$3\frac{3}{8}$	$3\frac{5}{8}$	$3\frac{7}{8}$	4	$4\frac{1}{8}$
$2\frac{1}{2}$	$3\frac{1}{2}$	$3\frac{3}{4}$	4	$4\frac{1}{8}$	$4\frac{1}{4}$
$2\frac{5}{8}$	$3\frac{5}{8}$	$3\frac{7}{8}$	$4\frac{1}{8}$	$4\frac{1}{4}$	$4\frac{3}{8}$
$2\frac{3}{4}$	$3\frac{3}{4}$	4	$4\frac{1}{4}$	$4\frac{3}{8}$	$4\frac{1}{2}$
$2\frac{7}{8}$	$3\frac{7}{8}$	$4\frac{1}{8}$	$4\frac{3}{8}$	$4\frac{1}{2}$	$4\frac{5}{8}$
3	4	$4\frac{1}{4}$	$4\frac{1}{2}$	$4\frac{5}{8}$	$4\frac{3}{4}$
$3\frac{1}{8}$	$4\frac{1}{8}$	$4\frac{3}{8}$	$4\frac{5}{8}$	$4\frac{3}{4}$	$4\frac{7}{8}$
$3\frac{1}{4}$	$4\frac{1}{4}$	$4\frac{1}{2}$	$4\frac{3}{4}$	$4\frac{7}{8}$	5
$3\frac{3}{8}$	$4\frac{3}{8}$	$4\frac{5}{8}$	$4\frac{7}{8}$	5	$5\frac{1}{8}$
$3\frac{1}{2}$	$4\frac{1}{2}$	$4\frac{3}{4}$	5	$5\frac{1}{8}$	$5\frac{1}{4}$
$3\frac{5}{8}$	$4\frac{5}{8}$	$4\frac{7}{8}$	$5\frac{1}{8}$	$5\frac{1}{4}$	$5\frac{3}{8}$
$3\frac{3}{4}$	$4\frac{3}{4}$	5	$5\frac{1}{4}$	$5\frac{3}{8}$	$5\frac{1}{2}$
$3\frac{7}{8}$	$4\frac{7}{8}$	$5\frac{1}{8}$	$5\frac{3}{8}$	$5\frac{1}{2}$	$5\frac{5}{8}$
4	5	$5\frac{1}{4}$	$5\frac{1}{2}$	$5\frac{3}{4}$	$5\frac{3}{4}$
$4\frac{1}{4}$	$5\frac{1}{8}$	$5\frac{1}{2}$	$5\frac{3}{4}$	6	$6\frac{1}{8}$
$4\frac{1}{2}$	$5\frac{1}{2}$	$5\frac{3}{4}$	$6\frac{1}{4}$	$6\frac{1}{4}$	$6\frac{1}{2}$
$4\frac{3}{4}$	$5\frac{3}{4}$	$6\frac{1}{8}$	$6\frac{1}{2}$	$6\frac{1}{2}$	$6\frac{3}{4}$
5	$6\frac{1}{8}$	$6\frac{3}{8}$	$6\frac{3}{4}$	$6\frac{7}{8}$	7

CALIPERING AND FITTING

THE VERNIER AND HOW TO READ IT

THIS method of measuring or of dividing known distances into very small parts is credited to the invention of Pierre Vernier in 1631. The principle is shown in Figs. 1 to 3 and its application in Figs. 4 and 5. In Figs. 1 and 2 both distances 0–1 are the same but they are divided into different divisions. Calling 0 — 1 = 1 inch then in Fig. 1 it is clear that moving the lower seal one division will divide

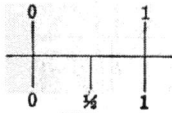

FIG. 1

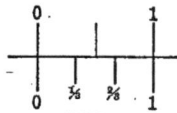

FIG. 2

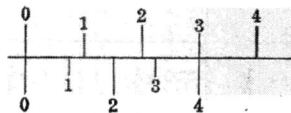

FIG. 3

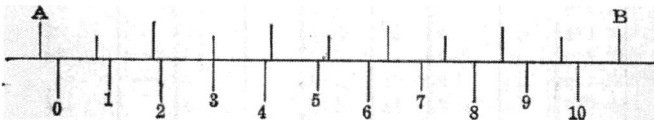

FIG. 4

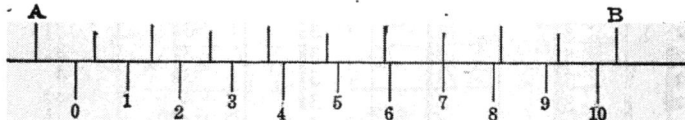

FIG. 5

Vernier Reading

the upper one in half. In Fig. 2 the upper scale is divided in half and the lower one in thirds. If the lower scale is moved either way until ⅓ or ⅔ comes under the end line, it has moved ⅓ of an inch but if either of these are moved to the center line then it is only moved ½ of this amount or ⅙

Figure 3 shows the usual application of the principle except that it is divided in four parts instead of ten. Here both the scales have four parts but on the lower scale the four parts just equal three parts of the upper scale. It is evident that if we move the lower scale so that 0 goes to 1 and 4 goes to 4 that it will be moved ¼ the length of the distance 0 — 4 on the upper scale. If this distance was 1 inch, each division on the upper scale equals ¼ inch and moving the lower scale so that the line 1 just matches the line next to 0 on the upper scale gives ¼ of one of these divisions or $\frac{1}{16}$ of an inch.

Figures 4 and 5 show the usual application in which the lower or vernier scale is divided into 10 parts which equals 9 parts of the upper scale. The same division holds good, however, and when the lower scale is moved so that the first division of the vernier just matches the first line of the scale, it has been moved just one tenth of a division. In Fig. 4 the third lines match so that it has moved $\frac{2}{10}$ and in Fig. 5, $\frac{7}{10}$ of a division. So if A B is one inch then each division is $\frac{1}{10}$ of an inch and each line of the vernier is $\frac{1}{10}$ of that or $\frac{1}{100}$ of an inch.

To find the reading of any vernier, divide one division of the upper or large scale by the number of divisions in the small scale. So if we had a vernier with 16 divisions in each, the large scale being 1 inch long, then the movement of one division is $\frac{1}{16}$ of $\frac{1}{16}$ or $\frac{1}{256}$ of an inch.

READING THE MICROMETER

THE commercial micrometer consists of a frame, the anvil or fixed measuring point, the spindle which has a thread cut 40 to the inch on the portion inside the sleeve or barrel and the thimble which goes outside the sleeve and turns the spindle. One turn of the

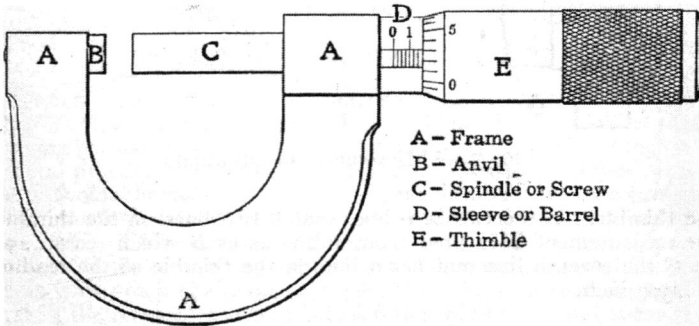

A – Frame
B – Anvil
C – Spindle or Screw
D – Sleeve or Barrel
E – Thimble

FIG. 6. — Micrometer

screw moves the spindle $\frac{1}{40}$ or .025 of an inch and the marks on the sleeve show the number of turns the screw is moved. Every fourth graduation is marked 1, 2, 3, etc., representing tenths of an inch or as each mark is .025 the first four means .025 × 4 = .100, the third means .025 × 4 × 3 = .300.

The thimble has a beveled edge divided into 25 parts and numbered 0, 5, 10, 15, 20 and to 0 again. Each of these mean $\frac{1}{25}$ of a turn or $\frac{1}{25}$ of $\frac{1}{40}$ = $\frac{1}{1000}$ of an inch. To read, multiply the marks on the barrel by 25 and add the graduations on the edge of the thimble. In the cut there are 7 marks on the sleeve and 3 on the thimble so we say 7 × 25 = 175, plus 3 = 178 or .178.

In shop practice it is common to read them without any multiplying by using mental addition. Beginning at the largest number shown on the sleeve and calling it hundreds and add 25 for each mark, we say in the case show 100 and 25, 50, 75 and then add the numbers shown on the thimble 3, making .178 in all. If it showed 4 and one mark, with the thimble showing 8 marks, the reading would be 400 + 25 + 8 = 433 thousandths or .433.

THE TEN-THOUSANDTH MICROMETER

THIS adds a vernier to the micrometer sleeve or barrel as shown in Fig. 7, which is read the same as any vernier as has been explained. First note the thousandths as in the ordinary micrometer and then look at the line on the sleeve which just matches a line on

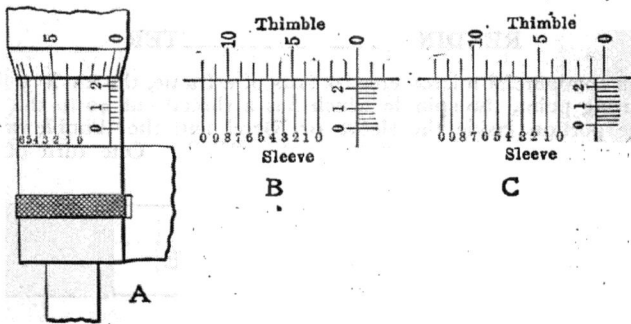

FIG. 7. — Micrometer Graduations

the thimble. If the two zero lines match two lines on the thimble, the measurement is in even thousandths as at B which reads .250. At C the seventh line matches a line on the thimble so the reading is .2507 inch.

MEASURING THREE-FLUTED TOOLS WITH THE MICROMETER

THE sketch, Fig. 8 on page 319, shows a V-block or gage for measuring three-fluted drills, counterbores, etc.

The angle being 60 degrees, the distances A, B, and C are equal. Consequently to determine the correct diameter of the piece to be measured, apply the gage as indicated in the sketch and deduct one third of the total measurement.

The use of this gage has a decided advantage over the old way of soldering on a piece of metal opposite a tooth or boring out a ring to fit to.

Using a standard 60-degree triangle for setting and a few different sizes of standard cylindrical plug gages for testing, the V-block may be easily and very accurately made.

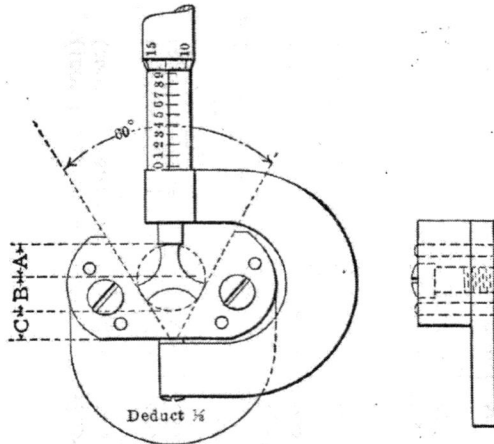

FIG. 8. — Measuring Three-Fluted Tools

PRESS AND RUNNING FITS

Parallel Press, Drive and Close Fits

TABLE 1, page 320, gives the practice of the C. W. Hunt Company, New York, for press, drive and close or hand fits for parallel shafts ranging between one and ten inches in diameter. In accordance with general practice, the holes for all parallel fits are made standard, except for unavoidable variation due to the wear of the reamer, the variation from standard diameter for the various kinds of fits being made in the shaft. This variation is, however, not positive, but is made between limits of accuracy or tolerance. Taking the case of a press fit on a two-inch shaft, for example, it will be seen that the hole — that is, the reamer — is kept between the correct size and 0.002 inch below size, while the shaft must be between 0.002 and 0.003 inch over size. For a drive or hand fit the limits for the hole are the same as for a press fit, while the shaft in the former case must be between 0.001 and 0.002 large and in the latter between 0.001 and 0.002 small.

Parallel Running Fits

Table 2, page 321, gives in the same way the allowances made by the same concern for parallel running fits of three grades of closeness. The variations allowed in the holes are not materially different from those of the preceding table, but the shafts are, of course, below instead of above the nominal size.

In all cases the tables apply to steel shafts and cast-iron wheels or other members. In the right-hand columns of the tables the formulas from which the allowances are calculated are given, and from which the range of tables may be extended.

TABLE 1. LIMITS TO DIAMETERS OF PARALLEL SHAFTS AND BUSHINGS (SHAFTS CHANGING)

Diameters		1 in.	2 in.	3 in.	4 in.	5 in.	Formula:
Press Fit	Shaft	+.001	+.002	+.003	+.004	+.005	+(.001 d +.000)
		+.002	+.003	+.004	+.005	+.006	+(.001 d +.001)
Drive Fit	Shaft	+.0005	+.001	+.0015	+.002	+.0025	+(.0005 d +.000)
		+.0015	+.002	+.0025	+.003	+.0035	+(.0005 d +.001)
Hand Fit	Shaft	−.001	−.001	−.001	−.002	−.002	....
		−.002	−.002	−.002	−.003	−.003	....
All Fits	Hole	+.000	+.000	+.000	+.000	+.000	....
		−.002	−.002	−.002	−.003	−.003	....

Diameters		6 in.	7 in.	8 in.	9 in.	10 in.	Formula:
Press Fit	Shaft	+.006	+.007	+.008	+.009	+.010	+(.001 d +.000)
		+.007	+.008	+.009	+.010	+.011	+(.001 d +.001)
Drive Fit	Shaft	+.003	+.0035	+.004	+.0045	+.005	+(.0005 d +.000)
		+.004	+.0045	+.005	+.0055	+.006	+(.0005 d +.001)
Hand Fit	Shaft	−.002	−.003	−.003	−.003	−.003	....
		−.003	−.004	−.004	−.004	−.004	....
All Fits	Hole	+.000	+.000	+.000	+.000	+.000	....
		−.003	−.004	−.004	−.004	−.004	....

TABLE 2. LIMITS TO DIAMETERS OF PARALLEL JOURNALS AND BEARINGS (JOURNALS CHANGING)

Diameters		1 in.	2 in.	3 in.	4 in.	5 in.	Formula:
Close Fit	Shaft {	−.003 / −.005	−.004 / −.006	−.005 / −.007	−.006 / −.008	−.007 / −.009	−(.001 d + .002) / −(.001 d + .004)
Free Fit	Shaft {	−.008 / −.011	−.009 / −.012	−.010 / −.013	−.011 / −.014	−.012 / −.015	−(.001 d + .007) / −(.001 d + .010)
Loose Fit	Shaft {	−.023 / −.028	−.026 / −.031	−.029 / −.034	−.032 / −.037	−.035 / −.040	−(.003 d + .020) / −(.003 d + .025)
All Fits	Hole {	+.000 / −.002	+.000 / −.002	+.000 / −.002	+.000 / −.002	+.000 / −.003	....

Diameters		6 in.	7 in.	8 in.	9 in.	10 in.	Formula:
Close Fit	Shaft {	−.008 / −.010	−.009 / −.011	−.010 / −.012	−.011 / −.013	−.012 / −.014	−(.001 d + .002) / −(.001 d + .004)
Free Fit	Shaft {	−.013 / −.016	−.014 / −.017	−.015 / −.018	−.016 / −.019	−.017 / −.020	−(.001 d + .007) / −(.001 d + .010)
Loose Fit	Shaft {	−.038 / −.043	−.041 / −.044	−.044 / −.049	−.047 / −.052	−.050 / −.055	−(.003 d + .020) / −(.003 d + .025)
All Fits	Hole {	+.000 / −.003	+.000 / −.003	+.000 / −.004	+.000 / −.004	+.000 / −.004	....

Shrink Fits

Table 3 gives the practice of the General Electric Company, Schenectady, New York, in regard to shrink fits, the same allowances also being made for press fits on heavy work such as couplings, etc.

TABLE 3. ALLOWANCES FOR SHRINK FITS

Dia. In.	Allowance	Dia. In.	Allowance	Dia. In.	Allowance
1	.001	20	.008	42	.0143
2	.0015	22	.0088	44	.015
3	.0020	24	.0093	46	.0155
4	.0028	26	.0098	48	.016
6	.0035	28	.0105	60	.020
8	.0045	30	.011	72	.024
10	.0053	32	.0115	84	.027
12	.0058	34	.012	96	.030
14	.0065	36	.0128	108	.033
16	.007	38	.0133	120	.0355
18	.0075	40	.0138	132	.038
				144	.040

LIMITS FOR GAGES

THE Newall Engineering Company, when developing their system of limit gages, investigated the practice of the leading English, Continental and American engineering concerns relative to allowances for different kinds of fits and prepared a table which is the average of all the data received, every point included being covered by the practice of some prominent establishment. The limits and allowances thus arrived at for shop gages are given in Table 4, which is self-explanatory.

TABLE 4. LIMITS AND ALLOWANCES IN SHOP GAGES FOR DIFFERENT KINDS OF FITS

Nominal Diameters	$\frac{1}{2}''$	$1''$	$2''$	$3''$	$4''$	$5''$	$6''$
Over size	.00025	.00050	.00075	.00100	.00100	.00100	.00150
Under size	.00025	.00025	.00025	.00050	.00050	.00050	.00050
Margin	.00050	.00075	.00100	.00150	.00150	.00200	.00200

Limits in Plug Gages for Standard Holes

(*Table Continued on Page 323*)

TABLE 4 *Continued.* — LIMITS IN SHOP GAGES

Allowances — over Standard — for Force Fits

Nominal Diameters	½	1″	2″	3″	4″	5″	6″
Mean............	.00075	.00175	.00350	.00525	.00700	.00900	.01100
High	.00100	.00200	.00400	.00600	.00800	.01000	.01200
Low............	.00050	.00150	.00300	.00450	.00600	.00800	.01000
Margin	.00050	.00050	.00100	.00150	.00200	.00200	.00200

Allowances — over Standard — for Driving Fits

Nominal Diameters	½″	1″	2″	3″	4″	5″	6″
Mean..........	.000375	.000875	.00125	.00200	.00250	.00300	.00350
High	.00050	.00100	.00150	.00250	.00300	.00350	.00400
Low	.00025	.00075	.00100	.00150	.00200	.00250	.00300
Margin	.00025	.00025	.00050	.00100	.00100	.00100	.00100

Allowances — Below Standard — for Push or Keying Fits

Nominal Diameters	½″	1″	2″	3″	4″	5″	6″
High	.00025	.00050	.00100	.00150	.00200	.00200	.00200
Low...........	.00075	.00100	.00150	.00200	.00250	.00250	.00250
Margin	.00050	.00050	.00050	.00050	.00050	.00050	.00050

Clearances for Running Fits

Class of Gage	Diameters	½″	1	2″	3″	4″	5″	6″
X.	Mean	.00150	.00200	.00260	.00320	.00380	.00440	.00500
	High	.00100	.00125	.00175	.00200	.00250	.00300	.00350
	Low	.00200	.00275	.00350	.00425	.00500	.00575	.00650
	Margin	.00100	.00150	.00175	.00225	.00250	.00275	.00300
Y.	Mean	.00100	.00150	.00190	.00230	.00270	.00310	.00350
	High	.00075	.00100	.00125	.00150	.00200	.00225	.00250
	Low	.00125	.00200	.00250	.00300	.00350	.00400	.00450
	Margin	.00050	.00100	.00125	.00150	.00150	.00175	.00200
Z.	Mean	.000625	.00100	.00120	.00140	.00160	.00180	.00200
	High	.00050	.00075	.00075	.00100	.00100	.00125	.00125
	Low	.00075	.00125	.00150	.00200	.00225	.00250	.00275
	Margin	.00025	.00050	.00075	.00100	.00125	.00125	.00150

Class X is suitable for engine and other work requiring easy fits.
Class Y is suitable for high speeds and good average machine work.
Class Z is suitable for fine tool work.

Limits For Work Ground to Various Classes of Fits

Table 5 gives the limits used by the Brown and Sharpe Manufacturing Company in grinding work to various classes of fits required in machine manufacture.

TABLE 5 — GRINDING LIMITS FOR CYLINDRICAL PIECES
As Adopted by Brown and Sharpe Mfg. Co.

RUNNING FITS — ORDINARY SPEED

To ½-inch diameter, inc.	0.00025 to 0 00075	Small
To 1-inch diameter, inc.	0.00075 to 0.0015	Small
To 2-inch diameter, inc.	0.0015 to 0 0025	Small
To 3½-inch diameter, inc.	0.0025 to 0.0035	Small
To 6-inch diameter, inc.	0.0035 to 0 005	Small

RUNNING FITS — HIGH SPEED, HEAVY PRESSURE AND ROCKER SHAFTS

To ½-inch diameter, inc.	0 0005 to 0.001	Small
To 1-inch diameter, inc.	0.001 to 0 002	Small
To 2-inch diameter, inc.	0.002 to 0 003	Small
To 3½-inch diameter, inc.	0.003 to 0.0045	Small
To 6-inch diameter, inc.	0.0045 to 0.0065	Small

SLIDING FITS

To ½-inch diameter, inc.	0 00025 to 0.0005	Small
To 1-inch diameter, inc.	0.0005 to 0.001	Small
To 2-inch diameter, inc.	0 001 to 0.002	Small
To 3½-inch diameter, inc.	0.002 to 0.0035	Small
To 6-inch diameter, inc.	0.003 to 0.005	Small

STANDARD FITS

To ½-inch diameter, inc.	Standard to 0 00025	Small
To 1-inch diameter, inc.	Standard to 0.0005	Small
To 2-inch diameter, inc.	Standard to 0.001	Small
To 3½-inch diameter, inc.	Standard to 0.0015	Small
To 6-inch diameter, inc.	Standard to 0.002	Small

DRIVING FITS — FOR SUCH PIECES AS ARE REQUIRED TO BE READILY TAKEN APART

To ½-inch diameter, inc.	Standard to 0.00025	Large
To 1-inch diameter, inc.	0.00025 to 0.0005	Large
To 2-inch diameter, inc.	0.0005 to 0.00075	Large
To 3½-inch diameter, inc.	0.00075 to 0.001	Large
To 6-inch diameter, inc.	0.001 to 0.0015	Large

DRIVING FITS

To ½-inch diameter, inc.	0.0005 to 0.001	Large
To 1-inch diameter, inc.	0.001 to 0.002	Large
To 2-inch diameter, inc.	0.002 to 0.003	Large
To 3½-inch diameter, inc.	0.003 to 0.004	Large
To 6-inch diameter, inc.	0.004 to 0.005	Large

TABLE 5 *Continued*

FORCING FITS

To ½-inch diameter, inc. . . .	0 00075 to 0.0015	Large
To 1-inch diameter, inc. . .	0.0015 to 0.0025	Large
To 2-inch diameter, inc. .. .	0.0025 to 0.004	Large
To 3½-inch diameter, inc. . . .	0.004 to 0.006	Large
To 6-inch diameter, inc. . .	0.006 to 0.009	Large

SHRINKING FITS — FOR PIECES TO TAKE HARDENED SHELLS ⅜ INCH THICK AND LESS

To ½-inch diameter, inc.	0.00025 to 0 0005	Large
To 1-inch diameter, inc.	0.0005 to 0.001	Large
To 2-inch diameter, inc.	0.001 to 0 0015	Large
To 3½-inch diameter, inc.	0.0015 to 0.002	Large
To 6-inch diameter, inc.	0.002 to 0.003	Large

SHRINKING FITS — FOR PIECES TO TAKE SHELLS, ETC., HAVING A THICKNESS OF MORE THAN ⅜ INCH

To ½-inch diameter, inc.	0.0005 to 0.001	Large
To 1-inch diameter, inc.	0.001 to 0.0025	Large
To 2-inch diameter, inc. .	0.0025 to 0.0035	Large
To 3½-inch diameter, inc. . . .	0 0035 to 0.005	Large
To 6-inch diameter, inc.	0.005 to 0 007	Large

GRINDING LIMITS FOR HOLES

To ½-inch diameter, inc.	Standard to 0 0005	Large
To 1-inch diameter, inc.	Standard to 0 00075	Large
To 2-inch diameter, inc.	Standard to 0.001	Large
To 3½-inch diameter, inc.	Standard to 0.0015	Large
To 6-inch diameter, inc.	Standard to 0.002	Large
To 12-inch diameter, inc.	Standard to 0.0025	Large

Metric Allowances For Fits of All Classes

Table 6 covers allowances worked out by the Newall Engineering Company for use in connection with metric measurements; the allowances being given in decimals of a millimeter.

The Newall system is based on a hole "basis," which means that all holes are produced as near the standard size as commercially possible and the allowances are made in the shaft or other fitting. The first part of the table shows the tolerances allowable in a standard hole for two grades of work which are designated by classes A and B. The remainder of the table covers fits of various classes.

TABLE 6 — THE NEWALL STANDARD
Tables of Allowances for Various Classes of Fits in Millimeters
Tolerances in Standard Holes for Two Grades of Work

Nominal Dia.	Up to 15	16–25	26–50	51–75	76–100	101–125	126–150
High limit	+ 0.007	+ 0.013	+ 0.019	+ 0.026	+ 0.026	+ 0.026	+ 0.039
Low limit.....	− 0.007	− 0.007	− 0.007	− 0.013	− 0.013	− 0.013	− 0.013
Tolerance.....	0.014	0.020	0.026	0.039	0.039	0.039	0.052
High limit	+ 0.013	+ 0.019	+ 0.026	+ 0.032	+ 0.039	+ 0.045	+0.051
Low limit.....	− 0.013	−0.013	− 0.013	− 0.019	− 0.019	− 0.019	− 0.026
Tolerance.....	0.026	0.032	0.039	0.052	0.058	0.064	0.077

Force and Shrink Fits

Nominal Dia.	Up to 15	16–25	26–50	51–75	76–100	101–125	126–150
High limit	+ 0.026	+ 0.051	+ 0.102	+ 0.153	+ 0.204	+ 0.255	+ 0.306
Low limit.....	+ 0.013	+ 0.038	+ 0.077	+ 0.115	+ 0.152	+ 0.203	+ 0.254
Tolerance.....	0.013	0.013	0.025	0.038	0.052	0.052	0.052

Driving Fits

Nominal Dia.	Up to 15	16–25	26–50	51–75	76–100	101–125	126–150
High limit	+ 0.013	+ 0.026	+ 0.039	+ 0.064	+ 0.077	+ 0.089	+ 0.102
Low limit.....	+ 0.007	+ 0.019	+ 0.026	+ 0.039	+ 0.051	+ 0.063	+ 0.076
Tolerance.....	0.006	0.007	0.013	0.025	0.026	0.026	0.026

Push Fits — Go in Easy but will not Turn

Nominal Dia.	Up to 15	16–25	26–50	51–75	76–100	101–125	126–150
High limit	− 0.006	− 0.006	− 0.006	− 0.012	− 0.012	− 0.012	− 0.012
Low limit.....	− 0.019	− 0.019	− 0.019	− 0.026	− 0.026	− 0.026	− 0.026
Tolerance.....	0.013	0.013	0.013	0.014	0.014	0.014	0.014

Running Fits for Engine and Similar Work

Nominal Dia.	Up to 15	16–25	26–50	51–75	76–100	101–125	126–150
High limit	− 0.025	− 0.032	− 0.045	− 0.051	− 0.063	− 0.076	− 0.089
Low limit.....	− 0.051	− 0.070	− 0.090	− 0.108	− 0.127	− 0.146	− 0.165
Tolerance.....	0.026	0.038	0.045	0.057	0.064	0.070	0.076

Running Fits for Good Average Machine Work

Nominal Dia.	Up to 15	16–25	26–50	51–75	76–100	101–125	126–150
High limit	− 0.019	− 0.025	− 0.032	− 0.038	− 0.051	− 0.057	− 0.063
Low limit:....	− 0.032	− 0.051	− 0.064	− 0.076	− 0.089	− 0.101	− 0.114
Tolerance.....	0.013	0.026	0.032	0.038	0.038	0.044	0.051

Running Fits for Fine Tool Work

Nominal Dia.	Up to 15	16–25	26–50	51–75	76–100	101–125	126–150
High limit	− 0.012	− 0.019	− 0.019	− 0.025	− 0.025	− 0.032	− 0.032
Low limit.....	− 0.019	− 0.032	− 0.039	− 0.051	− 0.057	− 0.064	− 0.070
Tolerance.....	0.007	0.013	0.020	0.026	0.032	0.032	0.038

Press Fits For Wheel Hubs

THE practice of the Boston Elevated Railroad is to allow 8 tons per inch of diameter. An excess of 2 tons total pressure is allowed for cast iron, while the minimum pressure may be from 8 to 13 tons below the normal according to diameter, as shown by the following table. These are for cast iron hubs with the cone 5 inches in diameter — $7\frac{1}{2}$ inches long. For cast steel or wrought iron 20 per cent greater pressure is allowed.

Diameter of Fit	Minimum Pressure	Maximum Pressure	Variation Allowed in Tons
$2\frac{1}{2}$ to $2\frac{15}{16}$	12	22	
3 to $3\frac{7}{16}$	16	26	
$3\frac{1}{2}$ to $3\frac{15}{16}$	20	30	10
4 to $4\frac{7}{16}$	24	34	
$4\frac{1}{2}$ to $4\frac{15}{16}$	28	38	
5 to $5\frac{7}{16}$	31	42	11
$5\frac{1}{2}$ to $5\frac{15}{16}$	35	46	
6 to $6\frac{7}{16}$	38	50	12
$6\frac{1}{2}$ to $6\frac{15}{16}$	42	54	
7 to $7\frac{7}{16}$	45	58	13
$7\frac{1}{2}$ to $7\frac{15}{16}$	49	62	
8 to $8\frac{7}{16}$	52	66	14
$8\frac{1}{2}$ to $8\frac{15}{16}$	56	70	
9 to $9\frac{7}{16}$	59	74	15
$9\frac{1}{2}$ to $9\frac{15}{16}$	63	78	
10 to $10\frac{7}{16}$	67	82	

RUNNING FITS FOR POWER TRANSMISSION MACHINERY

The Dodge Manufacturing Company has different standards for different classes of work for running fits. Their ordinary bearings vary from $\frac{1}{64}$ inch for 1 inch to a little over $\frac{1}{32}$ for 6 inches. Their clutch sleeves, which are babbitted, run very much closer, varying from 0.008 to about 0.0015 inch. Loose pulleys are sometimes made as close as 0.003 inch on the smaller sizes. The company has found that a good standard on loose pulleys is about $\frac{1}{64}$ on a $2\frac{1}{2}$ inch hole and varying proportionately for diameters above and below that. This is very much freer than most people recommend, but it has been found that in the general trade there is more difficulty in having a little too tight a fit than there is in having the fit a little too loose.

MAKING ALLOWANCES WITH THE CALIPERS FOR RUNNING, SHRINK, AND PRESS FITS

ONE of the familiar devices of the machinist consists in giving the inside calipers a certain amount of side play, when it is desirable to obtain a measure minutely less than the full diameter of the hole, as in making a loose or running fit, or a sliding fit as of a plunger in a cylinder. Thus in Fig, 9, A is the diameter of the bore, B the caliper setting and C the side play permitted the caliper in the hole.

In the table below is given a list of the reduced dimensions for different amounts of side play of the calipers in a 12-inch hole. From this, the dimensions may be obtained for holes of other diameters by division. Where in the table the side play is 2 inches, if we divide the items by 4 we have the side play and the reduced dimension for a 3-inch hole, or 0.5 inch and 2.9894 inches respectively.

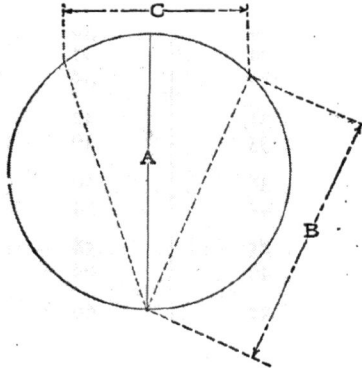

FIG. 9. — Side Play of the Calipers

TABLE OF REDUCED DIAMETERS INDICATED BY INSIDE CALIPERS FOR DIFFERENT AMOUNTS OF SIDE PLAY IN A 12-INCH HOLE

Side play

0.1	11.9999
0.2	11.9991
0.4	11.9983
0.6	11.9962
0.8	11.9933
1.0	11.9895
1.2	11.9849
1.4	11.9795
1.6	11.9730
1.8	11.9660
2.0	11.9579
2.2	11.9490
2.4	11.9391
2.5	11.9339
3.0	11.9044

Axial Inclination of the Calipers in Measuring for Shrink or Press Fits

In the case worked out on page 328, it was desired to produce a hole slightly larger than the piece to go into it, or a piece slightly smaller than the hole. In operations where a hole is wanted somewhat smaller than the piece to be shrunk or pressed into it, a similar plan of measuring can be employed, and a table giving the tightness can be computed. The sketch, Fig. 10, will serve to make the meaning clear. The distance A is the diameter of a hole and line a is the length of a gage the exact size of the piece to be pressed or shrunk into the hole. The distance b is the amount the gage lacks of assuming a position square or at a right angle to the axis of the hole.

It is an easy matter to make a table as suggested. It is only necessary to find the different lengths for the hypotenuse a for the right-angle triangle of which A is the constant base and b the perpendicular, taking b at different lengths from $\frac{1}{8}$ inch to 2 inches. Assuming the diameter to be 12 inches, then the lengths indicated for different inclinations in the direction of the axis will be as given in the following table.

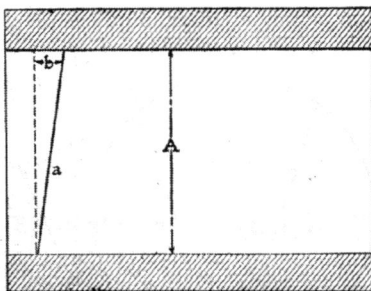

FIG. 10. — Inclination of the Calipers for Press Fits

TABLE FOR AXIAL INCLINATION OF CALIPERS IN ALLOWING FOR SHRINK OR FORCE FITS IN A 12-INCH HOLE

Inclination of calipers	
$\frac{1}{8}$ inch	12.00065
$\frac{1}{4}$ inch	12.00260
$\frac{3}{8}$ inch	12.00580
$\frac{1}{2}$ inch	12.01040
$\frac{5}{8}$ inch	12.01626
$\frac{3}{4}$ inch	12.02340
$\frac{7}{8}$ inch	12.03180
1 inch	12.04159
$1\frac{1}{4}$ inches	12.06490
$1\frac{1}{2}$ inches	12.09338
$1\frac{3}{4}$ inches	12.12689
2 inches	12.16550

Side Play of Calipers in Boring Holes Larger than a Piece of Known Diameter

The following is an approximate rule for obtaining the variation in the size of a hole corresponding to a given amount of side play in the calipers. The rule has the merit of extreme simplicity and can be applied equally well to all diameters except the very smallest. In most cases the calculation is so simple that it can be done mentally without having recourse to pencil or paper.

The Calculation

Let A in Fig. 11 = side play of calipers or end measuring rod *in sixteenths of an inch.*

B = dimensions to which calipers are set, or length of measuring rod *in inches.*

C = difference between diameter of hole and length of B *in thousandths of an inch.*

Then $C = \dfrac{A^2}{2B}$, within a very small limit.

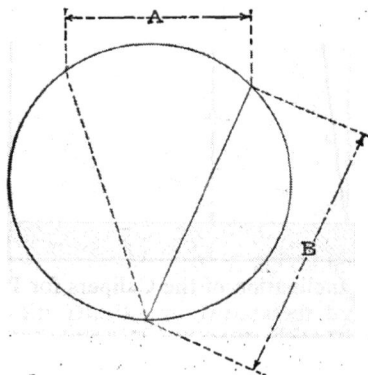

FIG. 11. — Caliper Side Play

Example: A standard end measuring rod, $5\frac{1}{2}$ inches long, has $\frac{3}{8}$ inch of side play in a hole. What is the size of the hole? In this case $A = 6$ and $B = 5\frac{1}{2}$. Apply the above formula:

$$C = \frac{6 \times 6}{11} = \frac{36}{11} = 3.27 \text{ thousandths of an inch, or } 0.00327 \text{ inch.}$$

The diameter of the hole, therefore, is $5\frac{1}{2} + 0.00327$ or 5.50327.

The method will be found to be correct within a limit of about 0.0002 inch if the amount of side play is not more than one eighth of the diameter of the hole for holes up to 6 inches diameter; within 0.0005 inch for holes from 6 inches up to 12 inches; and within 0.001 for holes from 12 inches up to 24 inches.

Allowing for Running and Driving Fits

This rule has been found to be useful for boring holes of large diameters in which allowances have to be made for running or driving fits, as only a single measuring rod for each nominal size is required. The rods should be of standard length, or a known amount less than standard, the allowances being obtained by varying the amount of side play when boring. The rule is also capable of determining limits, as the maximum and minimum amount of side play allowable can be specified. The measuring rods should be tapered at each end and the points slightly rounded. For accurate work, the body of the rod should be encased in some non-conducting material to nullify the effect of the heat of the hand.

In comparing this method with that described on page 330, it should be remembered that the conditions are reversed — that is to say, the first method is for setting calipers to a given dimension *smaller* than a hole of known diameter, whereas the method now described is for boring a hole a given amount *larger* than a gage of known length.

In measuring the side play it is sufficient to take it to the nearest sixteenth of an inch, and if anything like accuracy is required it should be measured not guessed at.

DIMENSIONS OF KEYS AND KEY-SEATS

THE following rules and table on page 332, as prepared by Baker Bros., Toledo, Ohio, give dimension of keys and key-seats.

The width of the key should equal one fourth the diameter of the shaft.

The thickness of the key should equal one sixth the diameter of the shaft.

The depth in the hub for a straight key-seat should be one half the thickness of the key.

The depth in the hub at the large end, for a taper key-seat, should be three fifths the thickness of the key.

The taper for all key-seats should be $\frac{3}{16}$ inch in 1 foot of length.

The depth to be cut in the hub for taper key-seats, at the large end, is greater than those cut straight, for the reason that unless this is done the depth in the hub at the small end will not be sufficient, especially in long key-seats.

The depths of key-seats in the table are given in thousandths of an inch and measured from the edge of the key-seat, and not from the center. In this manner the exact depth of key-seat can be measured at any time after it is cut.

For extra long key-seats the depth cut in the hub may be slightly increased, but for the average work the table will be found correct.

DIMENSIONS OF KEYS AND KEY-SEATS. (BAKER BROS.)

Size of Hole	Decimal Equivalent	Preferred Width of Key-Seat	Nearest Size of Cutter	Preferred Thickness of Key	Nearest Fractional Thickness	Depth to be Cut in Hub for Straight Key	Depth at Large End for Taper Key
1	1.	.25	1/4	.166	3/16	.093	.112
1 1/16	1.062	.265	1/4	.177	3/16	.093	.112
1 1/8	1.125	.281	1/4	.187	3/16	.093	.112
1 3/16	1.187	.296	5/16	.198	7/32	.109	.131
1 1/4	1.25	.312	5/16	.208	7/32	.109	.131
1 5/16	1.312	.328	5/16	.219	7/32	.109	.131
1 3/8	1.375	.343	3/8	.229	1/4	.125	.15
1 7/16	1.437	.359	3/8	.239	1/4	.125	.15
1 1/2	1.5	.375	3/8	.25	1/4	.125	.15
1 9/16	1.562	.39	3/8	.26	1/4	.125	.15
1 5/8	1.625	.406	7/16	.271	9/32	.141	.168
1 11/16	1.687	.421	7/16	.281	9/32	.141	.168
1 3/4	1.75	.437	7/16	.292	9/32	.141	.168
1 13/16	1.812	.453	7/16	.302	9/32	.141	.168
1 7/8	1.875	.468	1/2	.312	11/32	.171	.206
1 15/16	1.937	.484	1/2	.323	11/32	.171	.206
2	2.	.5	1/2	.333	11/32	.171	.206
2 1/16	2.062	.515	1/2	.344	11/32	.171	.206
2 1/8	2.125	.531	1/2	.354	11/32	.171	.206
2 3/16	2.187	.547	1/2	.364	11/32	.171	.206
2 1/4	2.25	.563	1/2	.375	11/32	.171	.206
2 5/16	2.312	.578	1/2	.385	11/32	.171	.206
2 3/8	2.375	.593	5/8	.396	7/16	.218	.262
2 7/16	2.437	.609	5/8	.406	7/16	.218	.262
2 1/2	2.5	.625	5/8	.416	7/16	.218	.262
2 9/16	2.562	.641	5/8	.427	7/16	.218	.262
2 5/8	2.625	.656	5/8	.437	7/16	.218	.262
2 11/16	2.687	.672	5/8	.448	7/16	.218	.262
2 3/4	2.75	.687	5/8	.458	7/16	.218	.262
2 13/16	2.812	.703	5/8	.469	7/16	.218	.262
2 7/8	2.875	.719	3/4	.479	1/2	.25	.3
2 15/16	2.937	.734	3/4	.49	1/2	.25	.3
3	3.	.75	3/4	.5	1/2	.25	.3
3 1/8	3.125	.781	3/4	.521	1/2	.25	.3
3 3/16	3.187	.797	3/4	.531	1/2	.25	.3
3 1/4	3.25	.812	3/4	.542	1/2	.25	.3
3 3/8	3.375	.844	7/8	.562	5/8	.312	.375
3 7/16	3.437	.859	7/8	.573	5/8	.312	.375
3 1/2	3.5	.875	7/8	.583	5/8	.312	.375
3 5/8	3.625	.906	7/8	.604	5/8	.312	.375
3 11/16	3.687	.923	7/8	.614	5/8	.312	.375
3 3/4	3.75	.937	7/8	.625	5/8	.312	.375
3 7/8	3.875	.969	1	.646	11/16	.343	.412
3 15/16	3.937	.984	1	.656	11/16	.343	.412
4	4.	1.	1	.666	11/16	.343	.412

DIMENSIONS OF STRAIGHT KEYS

ANOTHER system of keys used by a good many manufacturers is given in the table following, the sizes of shafts ranging by sixteenths from $\frac{5}{16}$ inch to 4 inches and by eighths from 4 to 6 inches. The keys are square until the $1\frac{1}{4}$ inch shaft is reached, when the thickness of the key becomes $\frac{1}{16}$ less than the width. With the $4\frac{1}{4}$ size the thickness of the key becomes $\frac{1}{8}$ inch less than the width and this difference is constant up to the $5\frac{1}{8}$ shaft when the width exceeds the thickness by $\frac{3}{16}$ inch, this difference in the two dimensions continuing throughout the remainder of the table.

DIMENSIONS OF STRAIGHT KEYS

Dia. of Shaft	Width of Key	Thickness of Key	Dia. of Shaft	Width of Key	Thickness of Key	Dia. of Shaft	Width of Key	Thickness of Key	Dia. of Shaft	Width of Key	Thickness of Key
0			1 1/4	1/4	3/16	2 1/2	1/2	7/16	3 3/4	3/4	11/16
1/16			1 5/16	1/4	3/16	2 9/16	1/2	7/16	3 13/16	3/4	11/16
1/8			1 3/8	1/4	3/16	2 5/8	1/2	7/16	3 7/8	13/16	3/4
3/16			1 7/16	1/4	3/16	2 11/16	1/2	7/16	3 15/16	13/16	3/4
1/4	3/32	3/32	1 1/2	5/16	1/4	2 3/4	9/16	1/2	4	13/16	3/4
5/16	3/32	3/32	1 9/16	5/16	1/4	2 13/16	9/16	1/2	4 1/8	13/16	3/4
3/8	1/8	1/8	1 5/8	5/16	1/4	2 7/8	9/16	1/2	4 1/4	7/8	3/4
7/16	1/8	1/8	1 11/16	5/16	1/4	2 15/16	9/16	1/2	4 3/8	7/8	3/4
1/2	1/8	1/8	1 3/4	3/8	5/16	3	5/8	9/16	4 1/2	15/16	13/16
9/16	1/8	1/8	1 13/16	3/8	5/16	3 1/16	5/8	9/16	4 5/8	15/16	13/16
5/8	3/16	3/16	1 7/8	3/8	5/16	3 1/8	5/8	9/16	4 3/4	15/16	13/16
11/16	3/16	3/16	1 15/16	3/8	5/16	3 3/16	5/8	9/16	4 7/8	1	7/8
3/4	3/16	3/16	2	7/16	3/8	3 1/4	11/16	5/8	5	1	7/8
13/16	3/16	3/16	2 1/16	7/16	3/8	3 5/16	11/16	5/8	5 1/8	1 1/16	7/8
7/8	3/16	3/16	2 1/8	7/16	3/8	3 3/8	11/16	5/8	5 1/4	1 1/16	7/8
15/16	1/4	1/4	2 3/16	7/16	3/8	3 7/16	11/16	5/8	5 3/8	1 1/8	15/16
1	1/4	1/4	2 1/4	1/2	7/16	3 1/2	3/4	11/16	5 1/2	1 1/8	15/16
1 1/16	1/4	1/4	2 5/16	1/2	7/16	3 9/16	3/4	11/16	5 5/8	1 1/8	15/16
1 1/8	1/4	1/4	2 3/8	1/2	7/16	3 5/8	3/4	11/16	5 3/4	1 3/16	1
1 3/16	1/4	1/4	2 7/16	1/2	7/16	3 11/16	3/4	11/16	5 7/8	1 3/16	1
									6	1 3/16	1

SQUARE FEATHER KEYS AND STRAIGHT KEY SIZES

THE tables on page 334 give the sizes of square feather keys and regular straight keys in accordance with the practice of Jones & Laughlin, Pittsburg. For taper keys, this concern and many others use a $\frac{1}{8}$-inch per foot taper.

Square Feather Key Sizes. (Jones & Laughlin)

Dia. of Shaft	Size of Key	Dia. of Shaft	Size of Key
1 to 1 $\frac{1}{5}$	$\frac{1}{4} \times \frac{1}{4}$	3 $\frac{3}{16}$ to 3 $\frac{3}{8}$	$\frac{13}{16} \times \frac{13}{16}$
1 $\frac{3}{16}$ to 1 $\frac{3}{8}$	$\frac{5}{16} \times \frac{5}{16}$	3 $\frac{7}{16}$ to 3 $\frac{5}{8}$	$\frac{7}{8} \times \frac{7}{8}$
1 $\frac{7}{16}$ to 1 $\frac{5}{8}$	$\frac{3}{8} \times \frac{3}{8}$	3 $\frac{11}{16}$ to 3 $\frac{7}{8}$	$\frac{15}{16} \times \frac{15}{16}$
1 $\frac{11}{16}$ to 1 $\frac{7}{8}$	$\frac{7}{16} \times \frac{7}{16}$	3 $\frac{15}{16}$ to 4 $\frac{1}{8}$	1×1
1 $\frac{15}{16}$ to 2 $\frac{1}{4}$	$\frac{1}{2} \times \frac{1}{2}$	4 $\frac{3}{16}$ to 4 $\frac{3}{8}$	$1\frac{1}{16} \times 1\frac{1}{16}$
2 $\frac{3}{16}$ to 2 $\frac{3}{8}$	$\frac{9}{16} \times \frac{9}{16}$	4 $\frac{7}{16}$ to 4 $\frac{3}{4}$	$1\frac{1}{8} \times 1\frac{1}{8}$
2 $\frac{7}{16}$ to 2 $\frac{5}{8}$	$\frac{5}{8} \times \frac{5}{8}$	4 $\frac{13}{16}$ to 5 $\frac{1}{4}$	$1\frac{1}{4} \times 1\frac{1}{4}$
2 $\frac{11}{16}$ to 2 $\frac{7}{8}$	$\frac{11}{16} \times \frac{11}{16}$	5 $\frac{5}{16}$ to 5 $\frac{3}{4}$	$1\frac{3}{8} \times 1\frac{3}{8}$
2 $\frac{15}{16}$ to 3 $\frac{1}{8}$	$\frac{3}{4} \times \frac{3}{4}$	5 $\frac{13}{16}$ to 6 $\frac{1}{4}$	$1\frac{1}{2} \times 1\frac{1}{2}$

Straight Key Sizes. (Jones & Laughlin)

Dia. of Shaft	Size of Key	Dia. of Shaft	Size of Key
1 to 1 $\frac{1}{8}$	$\frac{1}{4} \times \frac{3}{16}$	3 $\frac{3}{16}$ to 3 $\frac{3}{8}$	$\frac{13}{16} \times \frac{17}{32}$
1 $\frac{3}{16}$ to 1 $\frac{3}{8}$	$\frac{5}{16} \times \frac{7}{32}$	3 $\frac{7}{16}$ to 3 $\frac{5}{8}$	$\frac{7}{8} \times \frac{19}{32}$
1 $\frac{7}{16}$ to 1 $\frac{5}{8}$	$\frac{3}{8} \times \frac{1}{4}$	3 $\frac{11}{16}$ to 3 $\frac{7}{8}$	$\frac{15}{16} \times \frac{5}{8}$
1 $\frac{11}{16}$ to 1 $\frac{7}{8}$	$\frac{7}{16} \times \frac{9}{32}$	3 $\frac{15}{16}$ to 4 $\frac{1}{8}$	$1 \times \frac{11}{16}$
1 $\frac{15}{16}$ to 2 $\frac{1}{8}$	$\frac{1}{2} \times \frac{5}{16}$	4 $\frac{3}{16}$ to 4 $\frac{3}{8}$	$1\frac{1}{16} \times \frac{11}{16}$
2 $\frac{3}{16}$ to 2 $\frac{3}{8}$	$\frac{9}{16} \times \frac{3}{8}$	4 $\frac{7}{16}$ to 4 $\frac{1}{4}$	$1\frac{1}{8} \times \frac{3}{4}$
2 $\frac{7}{16}$ to 2 $\frac{5}{8}$	$\frac{5}{8} \times \frac{13}{32}$	4 $\frac{13}{16}$ to 5 $\frac{1}{4}$	$1\frac{1}{4} \times \frac{27}{32}$
2 $\frac{11}{16}$ to 2 $\frac{7}{8}$	$\frac{11}{16} \times \frac{15}{32}$	5 $\frac{5}{16}$ to 5 $\frac{3}{4}$	$1\frac{3}{8} \times \frac{29}{32}$
2 $\frac{15}{16}$ to 3 $\frac{1}{8}$	$\frac{3}{4} \times \frac{1}{2}$	5 $\frac{13}{16}$ to 6 $\frac{1}{4}$	$1\frac{1}{2} \times 1$

The Barth Key

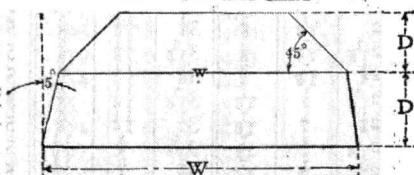

No. of Key	w	W	D
1	$\frac{1}{8}$	.132	$1\frac{5}{28}$
2	$\frac{5}{32}$	.165	$\frac{3}{64}$
3	$\frac{3}{16}$	.199	$\frac{1}{16}$
4	$\frac{1}{4}$	.264	$\frac{5}{64}$
5	$\frac{5}{16}$	.329	$\frac{3}{32}$

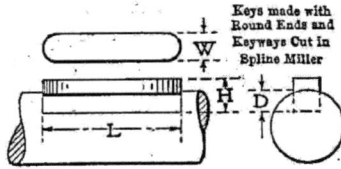

Keys made with Round Ends and Keyways Cut in Spline Miller

The Length "L" may vary from the table given, but must at least be equal to (2 × W). The maximum length of slot which can be cut in the Spline Milling machine in one cut; is (4″ + W). Note that the Width (W) is in all cases equal to the depth (D).

PRATT & WHITNEY KEY SYSTEM

Key No.	L	W	H	D	Key No.	L	W	H	D
1	$\frac{1}{2}$	$\frac{1}{16}$	$\frac{3}{32}$	$\frac{1}{16}$	22	$1\frac{3}{8}$	$\frac{1}{4}$	$\frac{3}{8}$	$\frac{1}{4}$
2		$\frac{3}{32}$	$\frac{9}{64}$	$\frac{3}{32}$	23		$\frac{5}{16}$	$\frac{15}{32}$	$\frac{5}{16}$
3		$\frac{1}{8}$	$\frac{3}{16}$	$\frac{1}{8}$	F		$\frac{3}{8}$	$\frac{9}{16}$	$\frac{3}{8}$
4	$\frac{5}{8}$	$\frac{3}{32}$	$\frac{9}{64}$	$\frac{3}{32}$	24	$1\frac{1}{2}$	$\frac{1}{4}$	$\frac{3}{8}$	$\frac{1}{4}$
5		$\frac{1}{8}$	$\frac{3}{16}$	$\frac{1}{8}$	25		$\frac{5}{16}$	$\frac{15}{32}$	$\frac{5}{16}$
6		$\frac{5}{32}$	$\frac{15}{64}$	$\frac{5}{32}$	G		$\frac{3}{8}$	$\frac{9}{16}$	$\frac{3}{8}$
7	$\frac{3}{4}$	$\frac{1}{8}$	$\frac{3}{16}$	$\frac{1}{8}$	51	$1\frac{3}{4}$	$\frac{1}{4}$	$\frac{3}{8}$	$\frac{1}{4}$
8		$\frac{5}{32}$	$\frac{15}{64}$	$\frac{5}{32}$	52		$\frac{5}{16}$	$\frac{15}{32}$	$\frac{5}{16}$
9		$\frac{3}{16}$	$\frac{9}{32}$	$\frac{3}{16}$	53		$\frac{3}{8}$	$\frac{9}{16}$	$\frac{3}{8}$
10	$\frac{7}{8}$	$\frac{5}{32}$	$\frac{15}{64}$	$\frac{5}{32}$	26	2	$\frac{3}{16}$	$\frac{9}{32}$	$\frac{3}{16}$
11		$\frac{3}{16}$	$\frac{9}{32}$	$\frac{3}{16}$	27		$\frac{1}{4}$	$\frac{3}{8}$	$\frac{1}{4}$
12		$\frac{7}{32}$	$\frac{21}{64}$	$\frac{7}{32}$	28		$\frac{5}{16}$	$\frac{15}{32}$	$\frac{5}{16}$
A		$\frac{1}{4}$	$\frac{3}{8}$	$\frac{1}{4}$	29		$\frac{3}{8}$	$\frac{9}{16}$	$\frac{3}{8}$
13	1	$\frac{3}{16}$	$\frac{9}{32}$	$\frac{3}{16}$	54	$2\frac{1}{4}$	$\frac{1}{4}$	$\frac{3}{8}$	$\frac{1}{4}$
14		$\frac{7}{32}$	$\frac{21}{64}$	$\frac{7}{32}$	55		$\frac{5}{16}$	$\frac{15}{32}$	$\frac{5}{16}$
15		$\frac{1}{4}$	$\frac{3}{8}$	$\frac{1}{4}$	56		$\frac{3}{8}$	$\frac{9}{16}$	$\frac{3}{8}$
B		$\frac{5}{16}$	$\frac{15}{32}$	$\frac{5}{16}$	57		$\frac{7}{16}$	$\frac{21}{32}$	$\frac{7}{16}$
16	$1\frac{1}{8}$	$\frac{3}{16}$	$\frac{9}{32}$	$\frac{3}{16}$	58	$2\frac{1}{2}$	$\frac{5}{16}$	$\frac{15}{32}$	$\frac{5}{16}$
17		$\frac{7}{32}$	$\frac{21}{64}$	$\frac{7}{32}$	59		$\frac{3}{8}$	$\frac{9}{16}$	$\frac{3}{8}$
18		$\frac{1}{4}$	$\frac{3}{8}$	$\frac{1}{4}$	60		$\frac{7}{16}$	$\frac{21}{32}$	$\frac{7}{16}$
C		$\frac{5}{16}$	$\frac{15}{32}$	$\frac{5}{16}$	61		$\frac{1}{2}$	$\frac{3}{4}$	$\frac{1}{2}$
19	$1\frac{1}{4}$	$\frac{3}{16}$	$\frac{9}{32}$	$\frac{3}{16}$	30	3	$\frac{3}{8}$	$\frac{9}{16}$	$\frac{3}{8}$
20		$\frac{7}{32}$	$\frac{21}{64}$	$\frac{7}{32}$	31		$\frac{7}{16}$	$\frac{21}{32}$	$\frac{7}{16}$
21		$\frac{1}{4}$	$\frac{3}{8}$	$\frac{1}{4}$	32		$\frac{1}{2}$	$\frac{3}{4}$	$\frac{1}{2}$
D		$\frac{5}{16}$	$\frac{15}{32}$	$\frac{5}{16}$	33		$\frac{9}{16}$	$\frac{27}{32}$	$\frac{9}{16}$
E		$\frac{3}{8}$	$\frac{9}{16}$	$\frac{3}{8}$	34		$\frac{5}{8}$	$\frac{15}{16}$	$\frac{5}{8}$

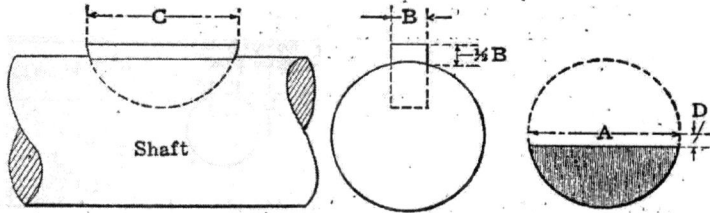

Shaft

WHITNEY KEYS AND CUTTERS. NOS. 1 TO 26
(Woodruff's Patent)

No. of Key and Cutter	Dia. of Cutter	Thickness of Key and Cutter	Length of Key	Key Cut Below Center	No. of Key and Cutter	Dia. of Cutter	Thickness of Key and Cutter	Length of Key	Key Cut Below Center
	A	B	C	D		A	B	C	D
1	$\frac{1}{2}$	$\frac{1}{16}$	$\frac{1}{2}$	$\frac{3}{64}$	16	$1\frac{1}{8}$	$\frac{3}{16}$	$1\frac{1}{8}$	$\frac{5}{64}$
2	$\frac{1}{2}$	$\frac{3}{32}$	$\frac{1}{2}$	$\frac{3}{64}$	17	$1\frac{1}{8}$	$\frac{7}{32}$	$1\frac{1}{8}$	$\frac{5}{64}$
3	$\frac{1}{2}$	$\frac{1}{8}$	$\frac{1}{2}$	$\frac{3}{64}$	18	$1\frac{1}{8}$	$\frac{1}{4}$	$1\frac{1}{8}$	$\frac{5}{64}$
4	$\frac{5}{8}$	$\frac{3}{32}$	$\frac{5}{8}$	$\frac{1}{16}$	C	$1\frac{1}{8}$	$\frac{5}{16}$	$1\frac{1}{8}$	$\frac{5}{64}$
5	$\frac{5}{8}$	$\frac{1}{8}$	$\frac{5}{8}$	$\frac{1}{16}$	19	$1\frac{1}{4}$	$\frac{3}{16}$	$1\frac{1}{4}$	$\frac{5}{64}$
6	$\frac{5}{8}$	$\frac{5}{32}$	$\frac{5}{8}$	$\frac{1}{16}$	20	$1\frac{1}{4}$	$\frac{7}{32}$	$1\frac{1}{4}$	$\frac{5}{64}$
7	$\frac{3}{4}$	$\frac{1}{8}$	$\frac{3}{4}$	$\frac{1}{16}$	21	$1\frac{1}{4}$	$\frac{1}{4}$	$1\frac{1}{4}$	$\frac{5}{64}$
8	$\frac{3}{4}$	$\frac{5}{32}$	$\frac{3}{4}$	$\frac{1}{16}$	D	$1\frac{1}{4}$	$\frac{5}{16}$	$1\frac{1}{4}$	$\frac{5}{64}$
9	$\frac{3}{4}$	$\frac{3}{16}$	$\frac{3}{4}$	$\frac{1}{16}$	E	$1\frac{1}{4}$	$\frac{3}{8}$	$1\frac{1}{4}$	$\frac{5}{64}$
10	$\frac{7}{8}$	$\frac{5}{32}$	$\frac{7}{8}$	$\frac{1}{16}$	22	$1\frac{3}{8}$	$\frac{1}{4}$	$1\frac{3}{8}$	$\frac{3}{32}$
11	$\frac{7}{8}$	$\frac{3}{16}$	$\frac{7}{8}$	$\frac{1}{16}$	23	$1\frac{3}{8}$	$\frac{5}{16}$	$1\frac{3}{8}$	$\frac{3}{32}$
12	$\frac{7}{8}$	$\frac{7}{32}$	$\frac{7}{8}$	$\frac{1}{16}$	F	$1\frac{3}{8}$	$\frac{3}{8}$	$1\frac{3}{8}$	$\frac{3}{32}$
A	$\frac{7}{8}$	$\frac{1}{4}$		$\frac{1}{16}$	24	$1\frac{1}{2}$	$\frac{1}{4}$	$1\frac{1}{2}$	$\frac{7}{64}$
13	1	$\frac{3}{16}$	1	$\frac{1}{16}$	25	$1\frac{1}{2}$	$\frac{5}{16}$	$1\frac{1}{2}$	$\frac{7}{64}$
14	1	$\frac{7}{32}$	1	$\frac{1}{16}$	G	$1\frac{1}{2}$	$\frac{3}{8}$	$1\frac{1}{2}$	$\frac{7}{64}$
15	1	$\frac{1}{4}$	1	$\frac{1}{16}$					
B	1	$\frac{5}{16}$	1	$\frac{1}{16}$					

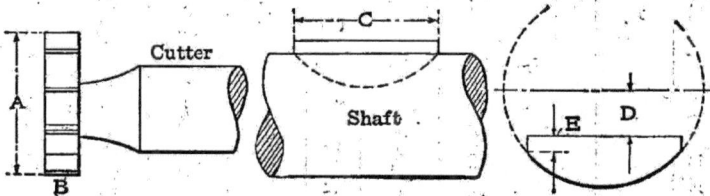

Cutter

Shaft

NOTE: Refer to table at top of page 337 for values of dimension E.

WHITNEY KEYS AND CUTTERS. NOS. 26 TO 36

No. of Key and Cutter	Dia. of Cutter	Thickness of Key and Cutter	Length of Key	Key Cut Below Center	Flat at End of Key	No. of Key and Cutter	Dia. of Cutter	Thickness of Key and Cutter	Length of Key	Key Cut Below Center	Flat at End of Key
	A	B	C	D	E		A	B	C	D	E
26	$2\frac{1}{8}$	$\frac{3}{16}$	$1\frac{23}{32}$	$\frac{17}{32}$	$\frac{3}{32}$	30	$3\frac{1}{2}$	$\frac{3}{8}$	$2\frac{7}{8}$	$\frac{13}{16}$	$\frac{3}{16}$
27	$2\frac{1}{8}$	$\frac{1}{4}$	$1\frac{25}{32}$	$\frac{9}{32}$	$\frac{3}{32}$	31	$3\frac{1}{2}$	$\frac{7}{16}$	$2\frac{7}{8}$	$\frac{13}{16}$	$\frac{3}{16}$
28	$2\frac{1}{8}$	$\frac{5}{16}$	$1\frac{29}{32}$	$\frac{21}{32}$	$\frac{3}{32}$	32	$3\frac{1}{2}$	$\frac{1}{2}$	$2\frac{7}{8}$	$\frac{13}{16}$	$\frac{3}{16}$
29	$2\frac{1}{8}$	$\frac{3}{8}$	$1\frac{31}{32}$	$\frac{17}{32}$	$\frac{3}{32}$	33	$3\frac{1}{2}$	$\frac{9}{16}$	$2\frac{7}{8}$	$\frac{13}{16}$	$\frac{3}{16}$
R	$2\frac{3}{4}$	$\frac{1}{4}$	$2\frac{1}{16}$	$\frac{5}{8}$	$\frac{1}{8}$	34	$3\frac{1}{2}$	$\frac{5}{8}$	$2\frac{7}{8}$	$\frac{13}{16}$	$\frac{3}{16}$
S	$2\frac{3}{4}$	$\frac{5}{16}$	$2\frac{5}{16}$	$\frac{5}{8}$	$\frac{1}{8}$	35	$3\frac{1}{2}$	$\frac{11}{16}$	$2\frac{7}{8}$	$\frac{13}{16}$	$\frac{3}{16}$
T	$2\frac{3}{4}$	$\frac{3}{8}$	$2\frac{5}{16}$	$\frac{5}{8}$	$\frac{1}{8}$	36	$3\frac{1}{2}$	$\frac{3}{4}$	$2\frac{7}{8}$	$\frac{13}{16}$	$\frac{3}{16}$
U	$2\frac{3}{4}$	$\frac{7}{16}$	$2\frac{5}{16}$	$\frac{5}{8}$	$\frac{1}{8}$						
V	$2\frac{3}{4}$	$\frac{1}{2}$	$2\frac{5}{16}$	$\frac{5}{8}$	$\frac{1}{8}$						

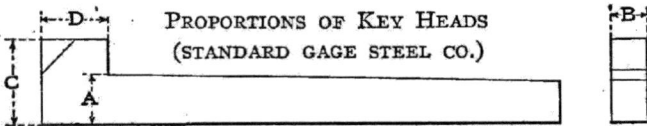

PROPORTIONS OF KEY HEADS
(STANDARD GAGE STEEL CO.)

A	B	C	D	A	B	C	D
$\frac{1}{8}$	$\frac{1}{8}$	$\frac{1}{4}$	$\frac{7}{32}$	$1\frac{5}{8}$	$1\frac{5}{8}$	$2\frac{3}{4}$	$1\frac{7}{8}$
$\frac{3}{16}$	$\frac{3}{16}$	$\frac{5}{16}$	$\frac{9}{32}$	$1\frac{11}{16}$	$1\frac{11}{16}$	$2\frac{7}{8}$	$1\frac{15}{16}$
$\frac{1}{4}$	$\frac{1}{4}$	$\frac{3}{8}$	$\frac{11}{32}$	$1\frac{3}{4}$	$1\frac{3}{4}$	3	2
$\frac{5}{16}$	$\frac{5}{16}$	$\frac{9}{16}$	$\frac{13}{32}$	$1\frac{13}{16}$	$1\frac{13}{16}$	$3\frac{1}{8}$	$2\frac{1}{16}$
$\frac{3}{8}$	$\frac{3}{8}$	$\frac{11}{16}$	$\frac{15}{32}$	$1\frac{7}{8}$	$1\frac{7}{8}$	$3\frac{3}{8}$	$2\frac{1}{8}$
$\frac{7}{16}$	$\frac{7}{16}$	$\frac{3}{4}$	$\frac{17}{32}$	$1\frac{15}{16}$	$1\frac{15}{16}$	$3\frac{5}{8}$	$2\frac{3}{16}$
$\frac{1}{2}$	$\frac{1}{2}$	$\frac{7}{8}$	$\frac{7}{8}$	2	2	$3\frac{3}{4}$	$2\frac{1}{4}$
$\frac{9}{16}$	$\frac{9}{16}$	1	$\frac{21}{32}$	$2\frac{1}{16}$	$2\frac{1}{16}$	$3\frac{7}{8}$	$2\frac{7}{16}$
$\frac{5}{8}$	$\frac{5}{8}$	$1\frac{1}{8}$	$\frac{23}{32}$	$2\frac{1}{8}$	$2\frac{1}{8}$	4	$2\frac{1}{2}$
$\frac{11}{16}$	$\frac{11}{16}$	$1\frac{3}{16}$	$\frac{25}{32}$	$2\frac{3}{16}$	$2\frac{3}{16}$	$4\frac{1}{8}$	$2\frac{9}{16}$
$\frac{3}{4}$	$\frac{3}{4}$	$1\frac{1}{4}$	$\frac{7}{8}$	$2\frac{1}{4}$	$2\frac{1}{4}$	$4\frac{1}{4}$	$2\frac{5}{8}$
$\frac{13}{16}$	$\frac{13}{16}$	$1\frac{5}{16}$	$\frac{15}{16}$	$2\frac{5}{16}$	$2\frac{5}{16}$	$4\frac{3}{8}$	$2\frac{11}{16}$
$\frac{7}{8}$	$\frac{7}{8}$	$1\frac{1}{2}$	1	$2\frac{3}{8}$	$2\frac{3}{8}$	$4\frac{1}{2}$	$2\frac{3}{4}$
$\frac{15}{16}$	$\frac{15}{16}$	$1\frac{5}{8}$	$1\frac{1}{8}$	$2\frac{7}{16}$	$2\frac{7}{16}$	$4\frac{5}{8}$	$2\frac{13}{16}$
1	1	$1\frac{3}{4}$	$1\frac{1}{8}$	$2\frac{1}{2}$	$2\frac{1}{2}$	$4\frac{3}{4}$	$2\frac{7}{8}$
$1\frac{1}{16}$	$1\frac{1}{16}$	$1\frac{3}{4}$	$1\frac{3}{16}$	$2\frac{9}{16}$	$2\frac{9}{16}$	$4\frac{7}{8}$	$2\frac{15}{16}$
$1\frac{1}{8}$	$1\frac{1}{8}$	$1\frac{7}{8}$	$1\frac{5}{16}$	$2\frac{5}{8}$	$2\frac{5}{8}$	5	3
$1\frac{3}{16}$	$1\frac{3}{16}$	$1\frac{15}{16}$	$1\frac{3}{8}$	$2\frac{11}{16}$	$2\frac{11}{16}$	$5\frac{1}{8}$	$3\frac{1}{16}$
$1\frac{1}{4}$	$1\frac{1}{4}$	2	$1\frac{7}{16}$	$2\frac{3}{4}$	$2\frac{3}{4}$	$5\frac{1}{4}$	$3\frac{1}{8}$
$1\frac{5}{16}$	$1\frac{5}{16}$	$2\frac{1}{8}$	$1\frac{1}{2}$	$2\frac{13}{16}$	$2\frac{13}{16}$	$5\frac{3}{8}$	$3\frac{3}{16}$
$1\frac{3}{8}$	$1\frac{3}{8}$	$2\frac{1}{4}$	$1\frac{9}{16}$	$2\frac{7}{8}$	$2\frac{7}{8}$	$5\frac{1}{4}$	$3\frac{1}{4}$
$1\frac{7}{16}$	$1\frac{7}{16}$	$2\frac{3}{8}$	$1\frac{5}{8}$	$2\frac{15}{16}$	$2\frac{15}{16}$	$5\frac{1}{4}$	$3\frac{5}{16}$
$1\frac{1}{2}$	$1\frac{1}{2}$	$2\frac{1}{2}$	$1\frac{3}{4}$	3	3	$5\frac{3}{8}$	$3\frac{1}{2}$
$1\frac{9}{16}$	$1\frac{9}{16}$	$2\frac{5}{8}$	$1\frac{13}{16}$				

TABLE FOR FINDING TOTAL KEYWAY DEPTH

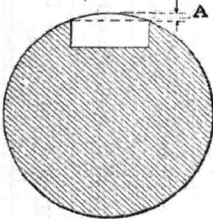

In the column marked "Size of Shaft" find the number representing the size; then to the right find the column representing the keyway to be cut and the decimal there is the distance *A*, which added to the depth of the keyway will give the total depth from the point where the cutter first begins to cut.

Size of Shaft	$\frac{1}{4}$ Keyway	$\frac{5}{16}$ Keyway	$\frac{3}{8}$ Keyway	$\frac{7}{16}$ Keyway	$\frac{1}{2}$ Keyway
$\frac{1}{2}$	0.0325	. . . .	. . . .	. . . .	. . . .
$\frac{9}{16}$	0.0289	. . . .	. . . .	. . . .	. . . .
$\frac{5}{8}$	0.0254	0.0413	. . . .	. . . .	. . . .
$\frac{11}{16}$	0.0236	0.0379	. . . .	. . . .	. . . .
$\frac{3}{4}$	0.022	0.0346	0.0511	. . . .	. . . .
$\frac{13}{16}$	0.0198	0.0314	0.0465	. . . .	. . . .
$\frac{7}{8}$	0.0177	0.0283	0.042	0.0583	. . . .
$\frac{15}{16}$	0.0164	0.0264	0.0392	0.0544	. . . .
I	0.0152	0.0246	0.0365	0.0506	0.067
$1\frac{1}{16}$	0.0143	0.0228	0.0342	0.0476	0.0625
$1\frac{1}{8}$	0.0136	0.021	0.0319	0.0446	0.0581
$1\frac{3}{16}$	0.0131	0.0204	0.0304	0.0421	0.0551
$1\frac{1}{4}$	0.0127	0.0198	0.029	0.0397	0.0522
$1\frac{5}{16}$	0.0123	0.0191	0.0279	0.038	0.0499
$1\frac{3}{8}$	0.012	0.0185	0.0268	0.0364	0.0477
$1\frac{7}{16}$	0.0114	0.0174	0.0254	0.0346	0.0453
$1\frac{1}{2}$	0.011	0.0164	0.024	0.0328	0.0429
$1\frac{9}{16}$	0.0107	0.0158	0.0231	0.0309	0.0412
$1\frac{5}{8}$	0.0105	0.0153	0.0221	0.0291	0.0395
$1\frac{11}{16}$	0.0102	0.0147	0.0214	0.0282	0.0383
$1\frac{3}{4}$	0.0099	0.0142	0.0207	0.0274	0.0371
$1\frac{13}{16}$	0.0095	0.0136	0.0198	0.0265	0.0355
$1\frac{7}{8}$	0.0093	0.013	0.019	0.0257	0.0339
$1\frac{15}{16}$	0.009	0.0127	0.0184	0.025	0.0328
2	0.0088	0.0124	0.0179	0.0243	0.0317
$2\frac{1}{16}$	0.0083	0.0117	0.0173	0.0236	0.0308
$2\frac{1}{8}$	0.0078	0.0111	0.0168	0.0229	0.0299
$2\frac{3}{16}$	0.0073	0.0109	0.0163	0.0222	0.0291
$2\frac{1}{4}$	0.007	0.0107	0.0159	0.0216	0.0282

TABLE FOR FINDING TOTAL KEYWAY DEPTH

In the column marked "Size of Shaft" find the number representing the size; then to the right find the column representing the keyway to be cut and the decimal there is the distance A, which added to the depth of the keyway will give the total depth from the point where the cutter first begins to cut.

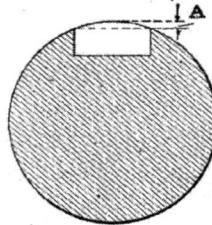

Size of Shaft	$\frac{1}{4}$ Keyway	$\frac{5}{16}$ Keyway	$\frac{3}{8}$ Keyway	$\frac{7}{16}$ Keyway	$\frac{1}{2}$ Keyway
$2\frac{5}{16}$	0.0068	0.0104	0.0155	0.0209	0.0274
$2\frac{3}{8}$	0.0066	0.0102	0.0152	0.0202	0.0267
$2\frac{7}{16}$	0.0064	0.01	0.0149	0.0198	0.026
$2\frac{1}{2}$	0.0063	0.0098	0.0146	0.0194	0.0253
$2\frac{9}{16}$	0.0061	0.0094	0.0142	0.0189	0.0247
$2\frac{5}{8}$	0.006	0.009	0.0139	0.0185	0.0242
$2\frac{11}{16}$	0.0059	0.0089	0.0136	0.018	0.0236
$2\frac{3}{4}$	0.0058	0.0088	0.0133	0.0176	0.023
$2\frac{13}{16}$	0.0057	0.0086	0.0129	0.0172	0.0226
$2\frac{7}{8}$	0.0056	0.0084	0.0126	0.0168	0.022
$2\frac{15}{16}$	0.0054	0.0083	0.0122	0.0164	0.0216
3	0.0053	0.0081	0.0119	0.0161	0.0211
$3\frac{1}{16}$	0.0052	0.008	0.0116	0.0158	0.0207
$3\frac{1}{8}$	0.0051	0.0078	0.0114	0.0155	0.0202
$3\frac{3}{16}$	0.005	0.0076	0.0112	0.0152	0.0198
$3\frac{1}{4}$	0.0049	0.0075	0.011	0.0149	0.0194
$3\frac{5}{16}$	0.0048	0.0074	0.0108	0.0146	0.0191
$3\frac{3}{8}$	0.0047	0.0072	0.0106	0.0143	0.0187
$3\frac{7}{16}$	0.0046	0.0071	0.0104	0.014	0.0184
$3\frac{1}{2}$	0.0045	0.007	0.0102	0.0138	0.018
$3\frac{9}{16}$	0.0044	0.0069	0.0101	0.0135	0.0188
$3\frac{5}{8}$	0.0043	0.0067	0.01	0.0133	0.0174
$3\frac{11}{16}$	0.0042	0.0066	0.0099	0.0131	0.0171
$3\frac{3}{4}$	0.0042	0.0065	0.0098	0.0128	0.0168
$3\frac{13}{16}$	0.0041	0.0064	0.0097	0.0126	0.0166
$3\frac{7}{8}$	0.0041	0.0063	0.0096	0.0124	0.0163
$3\frac{15}{16}$	0.0041	0.0062	0.0095	0.0123	0.0161
4	0.004	0.0061	0.0094	0.0121	0.016

TAPERS FOR KEYS, ETC., FROM $\frac{1}{16}$ TO 1 INCH PER FOOT. AMOUNT OF TAPER FOR LENGTHS VARYING BY $\frac{1}{2}$ INCH

Taper per Foot	LENGTH										
	1	1½	2	2½	3	3½	4	4½	5	5½	6
$\frac{1}{16}$	.0052	.0078	.0104	.0130	.0156	.0182	.0208	.0234	.0260	.0286	.0312
$\frac{1}{8}$	.0104	.0156	.0208	.0260	.0312	.0364	.0416	.0468	.0520	.0572	.0625
$\frac{3}{16}$	.0156	.0234	.0312	.0390	.0468	.0546	.0625	.0703	.0781	.0859	.0937
$\frac{1}{4}$	.0208	.0312	.0416	.0520	.0625	.0729	.0833	.0937	.1041	.1145	.1250
$\frac{5}{16}$	.0260	.0390	.0520	.0650	.0781	.0911	.1041	.1171	.1302	.1432	.1562
$\frac{3}{8}$	.0312	.0468	.0625	.0780	.0937	.1092	.1250	.1406	.1562	.1718	.1875
$\frac{7}{16}$	.0364	.0546	.0729	.0911	.1093	.1275	.1458	.1640	.1822	.2004	.2187
$\frac{1}{2}$	.0416	.0624	.0833	.1041	.1250	.1457	.1666	.1874	.2083	.2291	.2500
$\frac{9}{16}$	.0468	.0702	.0937	.1171	.1406	.1641	.1875	.2109	.2343	.2577	.2812
$\frac{5}{8}$	.0520	.0780	.1041	.1301	.1562	.1823	.2083	.2343	.2604	.2864	.3125
$\frac{11}{16}$	.0572	.0858	.1145	.1431	.1718	.2004	.2291	.2577	.2864	.3150	.3437
$\frac{3}{4}$	.0625	.0938	.1250	.1563	.1875	.2188	.2500	.2813	.3125	.3438	.3750
$\frac{13}{16}$	.0677	.1016	.1354	.1693	.2031	.2370	.2708	.3047	.3385	.3724	.4062
$\frac{7}{8}$	.0729	.1094	.1458	.1823	.2187	.2552	.2916	.3281	.3645	.4010	.4375
$\frac{15}{16}$	.0781	.1172	.1562	.1953	.2343	.2734	.3125	.3515	.3906	.4296	.4687
1	.0833	.1250	.1666	.2083	.2500	.2916	.3333	.3749	.4166	.4582	.5000

Taper per Foot	LENGTH										
	6½	7	7½	8	8½	9	9½	10	10½	11	11½
$\frac{1}{16}$	.0338	.0364	.0390	.0416	.0442	.0468	.0494	.0520	.0546	.0572	.0598
$\frac{1}{8}$	.0677	.0729	.0781	.0833	.0885	.0937	.0989	.1041	.1093	.1145	.1197
$\frac{3}{16}$	.1015	.1093	.1171	.1250	.1328	.1406	.1484	.1562	.1640	.1718	.1796
$\frac{1}{4}$	.1354	.1458	.1562	.1666	.1770	.1875	.1979	.2083	.2187	.2291	.2395
$\frac{5}{16}$	.1692	.1822	.1952	.2083	.2213	.2343	.2473	.2604	.2734	.2864	.2994
$\frac{3}{8}$	.2031	.2187	.2343	.2500	.2656	.2812	.2968	.3125	.3281	.3437	.3593
$\frac{7}{16}$	.2369	.2552	.2734	.2916	.3098	.3281	.3463	.3645	.3827	.4010	.4192
$\frac{1}{2}$	.2708	.2916	.3124	.3333	.3541	.3750	.3958	.4166	.4374	.4583	.4791
$\frac{9}{16}$	.3046	.3281	.3515	.3750	.3984	.4218	.4452	.4687	.4921	.5156	.5390
$\frac{5}{8}$	.3385	.3645	.3905	.4166	.4426	.4687	.4947	.5208	.5468	.5729	.5989
$\frac{11}{16}$	.3723	.4010	.4296	.4583	.4869	.5156	.5442	.5729	.6015	.6302	.6588
$\frac{3}{4}$	.4063	.4375	.4688	.5000	.5313	.5625	.5938	.6250	.6563	.6875	.7188
$\frac{13}{16}$	.4401	.4739	.5078	.5416	.5755	.6093	.6432	.6770	.7109	.7447	.7786
$\frac{7}{8}$	.4739	.5104	.5468	.5833	.6197	.6562	.6926	.7291	.7655	.8020	.8384
$\frac{15}{16}$	.5078	.5468	.5859	.6250	.6640	.7031	.7422	.7812	.8203	.8593	.8984
1	.5416	.5833	.6249	.6666	.7082	.7500	.7917	.8333	.8750	.9166	.9583

TAPERS AND DOVETAILS

MEASURING TAPERS

An Accurate Taper Gage

THE gage illustrated in Fig. 1 is an exceedingly accurate device for the gaging of tapers.

It is evident that if two round disks of unequal diameter are placed on a surface plate a certain distance apart, two straight-edges touching these two disks will represent a certain taper. It is also evident

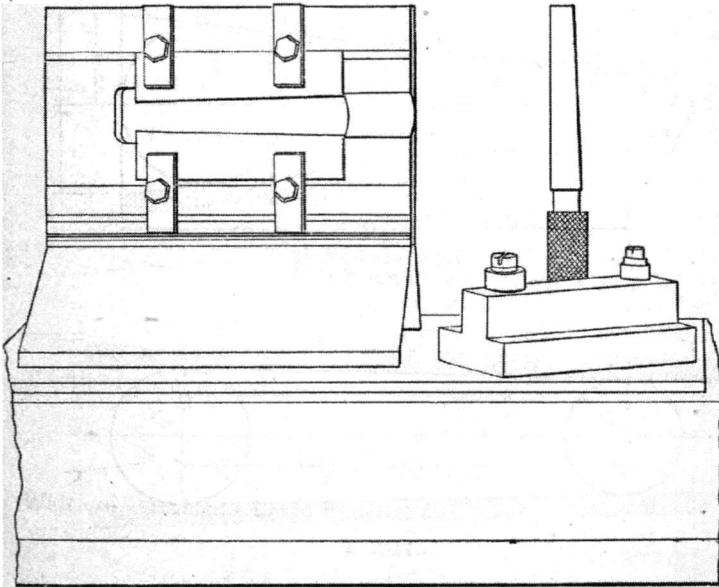

FIG. 1. — Accurate Taper Gage

that with the measuring instruments now in use it is a simple matter to measure accurately the diameters of the two disks, and the distance these disks are apart. These three dimensions accurately and positively determine the taper represented by the straight-edges touching the rolls. If a record is made of these three dimensions these conditions can be reproduced at any time, thus making it possible to duplicate a taper piece even though the part may not at the time be accessible.

The formulas on the following pages may be of service in connection with a gage of this character:

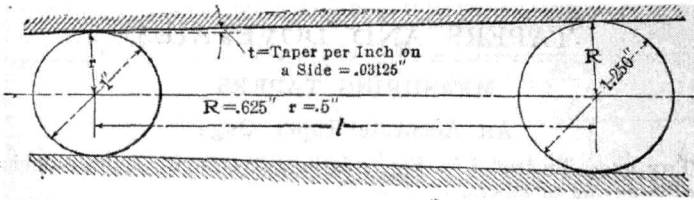

t=Taper per Inch on
a Side = .03125″

R = .625″   r = .5″

Taper per Foot = ¾″
FIG. 2

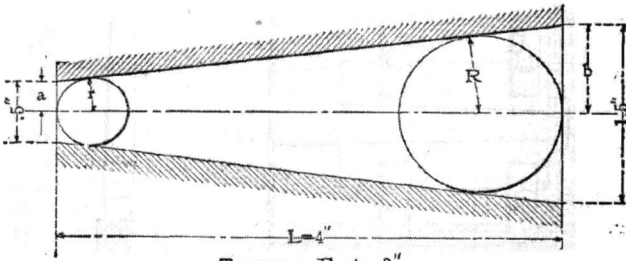

L = 4″

Taper per Foot = 3″
FIG. 3

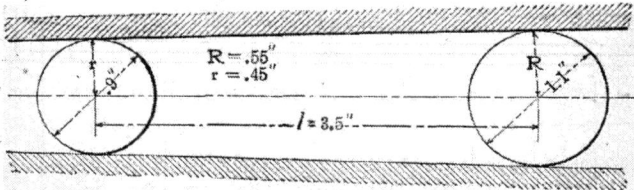

R = .55″
r = .45″

l = 3.5″

FIG. 4

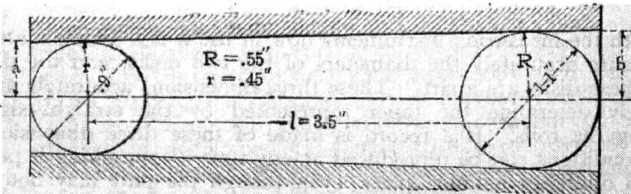

R = .55″
r = .45″

l = 3.5″

FIG. 5
Applications of Taper Gage

Formulas for Use in Connection with Taper Gage

To find Center Distance (l), refer to Fig. 2.

$$l = \frac{R - r}{t} \sqrt{1 + t^2}$$

To find Disk Diameters, refer to Fig. 3.

$$r = \frac{a}{L}\left[\sqrt{L^2 + (b - a)^2} + (b + a) \right]$$

Dia. Small Disk $= 2\, r$

$$R = \frac{b}{L}\left[\sqrt{L^2 + (b - a)^2} - (b - a) \right]$$

Dia. Large Disk $= 2\, R$

To find Taper Per Foot (T), refer to Fig. 4.

$$T = 24 \left(\frac{R - r}{\sqrt{l^2 - (R - r)^2}} \right)$$

To find Width of Opening at Ends, refer to Fig. 5.

$$a = r \sqrt{\frac{l - (R - r)}{l + (R - r)}}$$

Width of opening at Small End $= 2\, a$.

$$b = R \sqrt{\frac{l + (R - r)}{l - (R - r)}}$$

Width of Opening at Large End $= 2\, b$.

Applications of Formulas

To Find Center Distance Between Disks

Suppose there are two disks as shown in Fig. 2, whose diameters are respectively $1\frac{1}{4}$ and 1 inch. It is desired to construct a taper of $\frac{3}{4}$ to the foot and the center distance l between disks must be determined in order that the gage jaws when touching both disks shall give that taper.

Let $R =$ radius of large disk, or 0.625 inch.
$r =$ radius of small disk, or 0.500 inch.
$t =$ taper per inch on side, or
$$\frac{0.750}{24} = 0.03125 \text{ inch.}$$

Then

$$l = \frac{R - r}{t} \sqrt{1 + t^2} =$$

$$\frac{0.125}{0.03125} \sqrt{1.000976} = 4 \times 1.0005 = 4.002 \text{ inches.}$$

To Find Disk Diameters

Suppose the gage jaws are to be set as in Fig. 3 for a three-inch per foot taper whose length is to be four inches. The small end is to be exactly $\frac{1}{2}$ inch and the large end for this taper will, therefore, be $1\frac{1}{2}$ inches. What diameter must the disks be made so that when the jaws are in contact with them and the distance L over the disks measures 4 inches, the taper will be exactly three inches per foot? Here a represents $\frac{1}{2}$ the width of opening at the small end, and b one half the width of opening at the large end. The radius of the small disk may be found by the formula:

$$r = \frac{a}{L} \left\{ \sqrt{L^2 + (b - a)^2} + (b - a) \right\}.$$

Then

$$r = \frac{0.250}{4} \left(\sqrt{16 + 0.25} + 0.5 \right)$$

$$= 0.0625 (4.0311 + 0.5) = 0.2832.$$

Diameter small disk $= 0.2832$ inch $\times 2 = 0.5664$ inch. For the large disk:

$$R = \frac{b}{L} \left\{ \sqrt{L^2 + (b - a)^2} - (b - a) \right\}.$$

Then

$$R = \frac{0.75}{4} \left(\sqrt{16 + 0.25} - 0.5 \right)$$

$$= 0.1875 (4.0311 - 0.5) = 0.6621.$$

Diameter large disk $= 0.6621$ inch $\times 2 = 1.3242$ inches.

To Find Taper Per Foot

In duplicating a taper the gage jaws may be set to the model and by placing between the jaws a pair of disks whose diameters are known the taper per foot may be readily found. For example, the jaws in Fig. 4 are set to a certain model, two disks 0.9 and 1.1 inch diameter are placed between them and the distance over the disks measured, from which dimension l (which is 3.5 inches) is readily found by subtracting half the diameters of the disks. Here l represents the center distance as in Fig. 2. To determine the taper per foot which may be represented by T, the formula is:

$$T = 24 \left(\frac{R - r}{\sqrt{l^2 - (R - r)^2}} \right).$$

Then

$$T = 24 \left(\frac{0.1}{\sqrt{12.25 - 0.01}} \right) = 24 \left(\frac{0.1}{3.4985} \right) = 0.684$$

Taper per foot = 0.684 inch.

To Find Width of Opening at Ends

If, with the ends of the gage jaws flush with a line tangent to the disk peripheries as in Fig. 5, it is required to find the width of the opening at the small end where a represents one half that width, the following formula may be applied, the disks being as in the last example 0.9 and 1.1 inch diameter respectively, and the center distance 3.5 inches:

$$a = r \sqrt{\frac{l - (R - r)}{l + (R - r)}}$$

Then

$$a = 0.45 \sqrt{\frac{3.5 - (.55 - .45)}{3.5 + (.55 - .45)}}$$

$$= 0.45 \sqrt{\frac{3.4}{3.6}} = 0.45 \sqrt{.94444} = .4373$$

0.4373 inch × 2 = 0.8746 inch width of opening at small end of gage.

Similarly the width of opening at the large end of the gage may be found as follows, where b = half the width of the large end:

$$b = R \sqrt{\frac{l + (R - r)}{l - (R - r)}}$$

Then

$$b = 0.55 \sqrt{\frac{3.5 + (.55 - .45)}{3.5 - (.55 - 45)}}$$

$$= 0.55 \sqrt{\frac{3.6}{3.4}} = 0.55 - 1.05882 = .56595$$

0.56595 inch × 2 = 1.1319 inch = width of opening at large end.

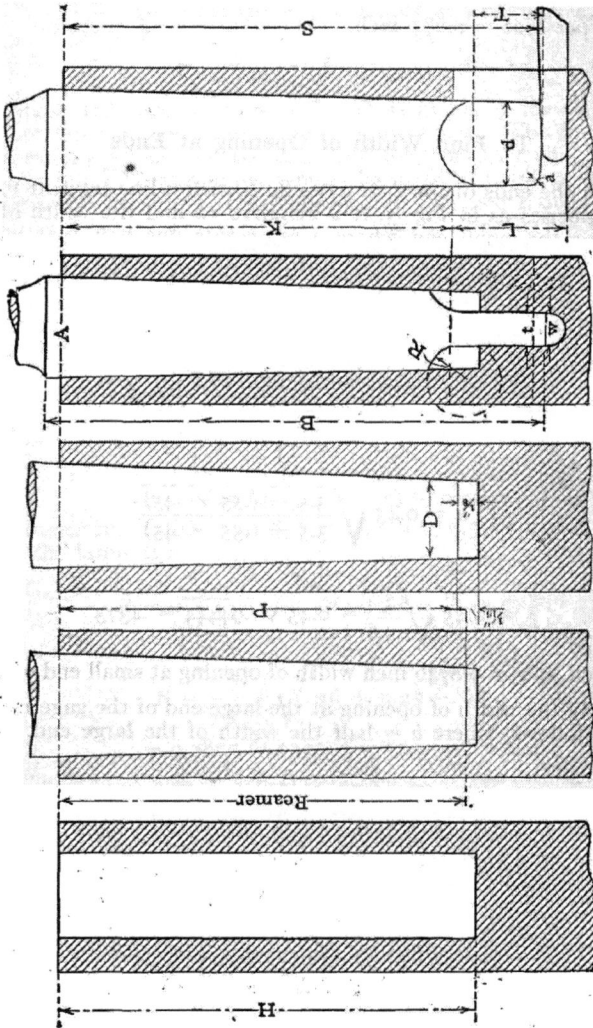

Brown & Sharpe Standard Tapers

Taper of Key = $1\frac{3}{4}''$ per Ft.

BROWN & SHARPE TAPERS

Number of Taper	D Dia. of Plug at Small End	A Dia. at End of Socket for length P.	P Standard Plug Depth	B Whole Length of Shank	H Depth of Hole	K End of Socket to Keyway	L Length of Keyway	W Width of Key-way	T Length of Tongue	d Dia. of Tongue	t Thickness of Tongue	R Radius of Mill for Tongue	a Radius of Tongue	S Shank Depth	Taper per Foot	Taper per Inch
1	.20	.2391	15/16	1-1/4	1-1/16	1-5/16	3/8	.135		.170	1/8	9/16	.030	1-3/16	.500	.0416
2	.25	.2995	1-3/16	1-9/16	1-5/16	1-5/8	3/8	.166		.220	5/32	3/16	.030	1-7/16	.500	.0416
3	.312	.3952	2	2	1-11/16	1-3/4	1/2	.197		.280	3/16	3/16	.040	1-11/16	.500	.0416
4	.35	.4020	1-1/4	2	1-11/16	1-3/4	1/2	.228		.320	7/32	3/16	.050	1-7/8	.500	.0416
5	.45	.5229	1-3/8	2-1/2	2-1/16	2-1/8	1/2	.260		.420	1/4	5/16	.060	2-1/8	.500	.0416
6	.50	.5989	1-3/4	2-7/8	2-1/2	2-5/8	5/8	.291		.460	9/32	5/16	.060	2-7/16	.500	.0416
7	.60	.7250	3/16	3-1/2	3	3-1/8	3/4	.322		.560	11/32	3/8	.070	3-3/16	.500	.0416
8	.75	.8985	4	4-1/4	3-5/8	3-3/4	1	.353		.710	7/16	7/16	.080	3-15/16	.500	.0416
9	.90	1.0770	4-1/4	4-5/8	4	4-1/8	1	.385		.860	1/2	1/2	.100	4-11/16	.500	.0416
10	.90	1.0667	5	5-1/2	5	5-1/8	1-1/4	.385		.860	1/2	1/2	.100	5-5/16	.500	.0416
10	1.0446	1.2596	5-1/16	6-1/4	5-1/2	5-5/8	1-3/8	.447		1.010	19/32	5/8	.110	6-1/8	.5016	.043
11	1.0446	1.2891	6-3/4	7-3/4	7	7-1/8	1-3/8	.447		1.010	19/32	5/8	.110	7-11/16	.5016	.043
12	1.25	1.5312	7-1/4	8-3/8	7-1/2	7-5/8	1-1/2	.510		1.210	23/32	3/4	.130	8-1/16	.500	.0416
13	1.50	1.7968	8-1/4	8-3/4	8	8-1/8	1-5/8	.510		1.460	7/8	7/8	.150	9-3/16	.500	.0416
14	1.75	2.0729	8-1/2	9-1/2	9	9-1/8	1-5/8	.572		1.710	1	1	.170	9-9/16	.500	.0416
15	2.	2.3437	9-1/4	10	9-1/2	9-5/8	1-3/4	.635		1.960	1-5/32	1-1/8	.190	10-1/4	.500	.0416
16	2.25	2.6145	9-3/4	10-1/2	10		1-7/8			2.210			.210		.500	.0416
17	2.50	2.8855	10-1/4							2.450			.230		.500	.0416
18	2.75														.500	.0416
	3.00															

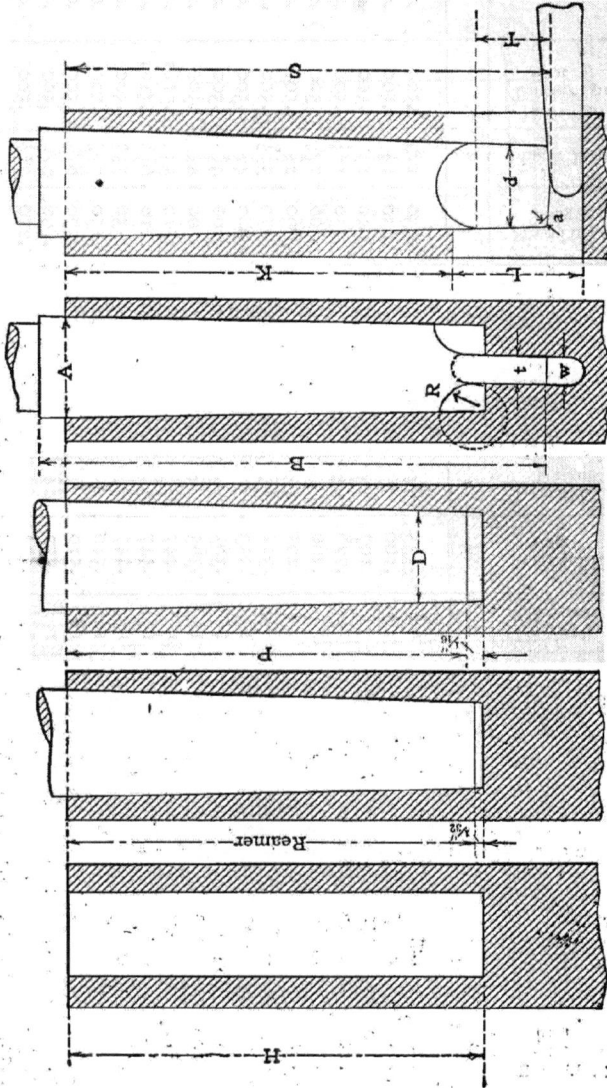

MORSE TAPERS

	Sym.	0	1	2	3	4	5	6	7
No. of Taper		0	1	2	3	4	5	6	7
Dia. of Plug at Small End	D	.252	.369	.572	.778	1.02	1.475	2.116	2.75
Dia. at End of Socket	A	.356	.475	.7	.938	1.231	1.748	2.494	3.27
Standard Plug Depth	P	2	2⅛	2 9/16	3 3/16	4 1/16	5 3/16	7¼	10
Whole Length of Shank	B	2 11/32	2 7/16	3⅛	3⅞	4⅞	6⅛	8 9/16	11⅝
Depth of Hole	H	2 1/32	2 3/16	2⅝	3¼	4⅛	5¼	7⅜	10⅝
End of Socket to Keyway	K	1 15/16	2 1/16	2¼	3 1/16	3⅞	4 7/16	7	9½
Length of Key-way	L	9/16	¾	⅞	1 3/16	1¼	1½	1¾	2⅝
Width of Key-way	W	.160	.213	.26	.322	.478	.635	.76	1.135
Length of Tongue	T	¼	⅜	7/16	9/16	⅝	¾	1⅛	1⅜
Dia. of Tongue	d	.235	.343	17/32	23/32	31/32	1 13/32	2	2⅝
Thickness of Tongue	t	5/32	13/64	¼	5/16	15/32	⅝	¾	1⅛
Radius of Mill for Tongue	R	5/32	3/16	¼	9/32	5/16	⅜	½	¾
Radius of Tongue	a	.04	.05	.06	.08	.10	.12	.15	.18
Shank Depth	S	2 7/32	2 7/16	2 15/16	3 11/16	4⅝	5⅞	8¼	11¼
Taper per Foot		.625	.600	.602	.602	.623	.630	.626	.625
Taper per Inch		.05208	.05	.05016	.05016	.05191	.0525	.05216	.05208
No. of Key		0	1	2	3	4	5	6	7

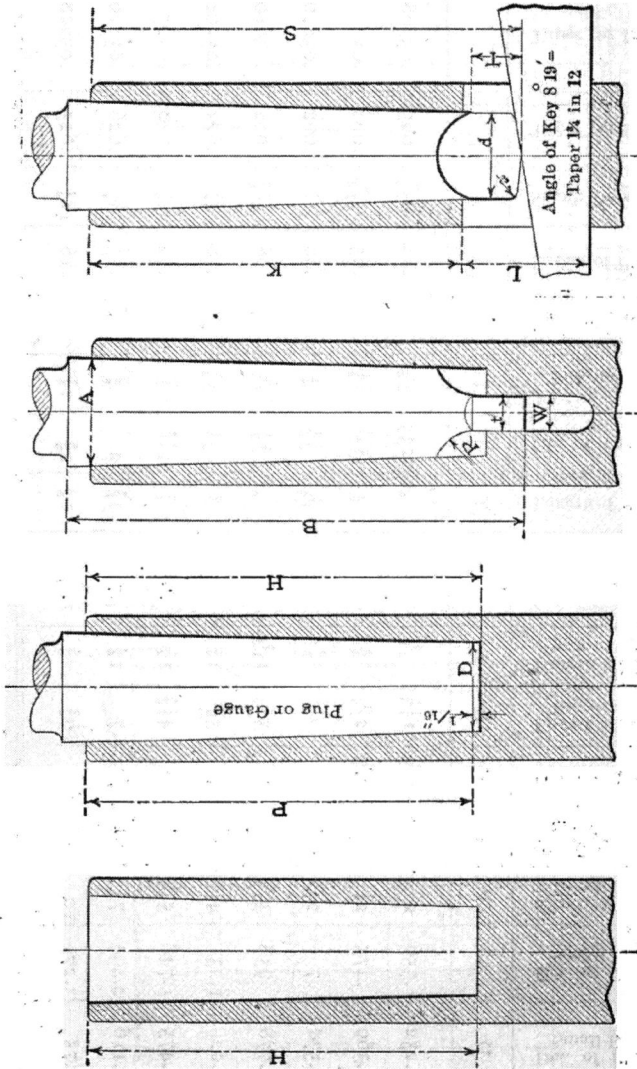

Morse Short Shanks. Where the original tangs on drills have been broken, the shanks can be reduced in length and provided with thicker and wider tangs for insuring a stronger drive, the shanks being fitted to a tang gage for short shank sockets. The short shank drills are then used in sleeves and sockets which are made externally to fit the regular Morse socket and spindle holes.

MORSE TAPERS — SHORT SHANKS

No. of Taper	Diam. of Plug at Small End (D)	Diam. at End of Socket (A)	Whole Length of Shank (B)	Shank Depth (S)	Depth of Hole (H)	Standard Plug Depth (P)	Thickness of Tongue (t)	Length of Tongue (T)	Rad. of Mill for Tongue (R)	Diameter of Tongue (d)	Radius of Tongue (a)	Width of Keyway (W)	Length of Keyway (L)	End of Socket to Keyway (K)	Taper per Foot	Taper per Inch	No. of Key
0	.271	.356	$1\frac{31}{32}$	$1\frac{27}{32}$	$1\frac{23}{32}$	$1\frac{5}{8}$	.186 .188	$\frac{1}{4}$	$\frac{3}{16}$	.258	$\frac{3}{64}$	.193 .196	$\frac{5}{8}$	$1\frac{17}{32}$	.625	.05208	0
1	.388	.475	$2\frac{1}{8}$	2	$1\frac{15}{16}$	$1\frac{3}{4}$	.249 .251	$\frac{3}{8}$	$\frac{1}{4}$	.371	$\frac{1}{16}$	.260 .263	$1\frac{3}{16}$	$1\frac{21}{32}$	.600	.050	1
2	.600	.700	$2\frac{9}{16}$	$2\frac{3}{8}$	$2\frac{1}{16}$	2	.374 .376	$\frac{7}{16}$	$\frac{9}{32}$	.575	$\frac{1}{8}$	.385 .388	$1\frac{5}{16}$	$1\frac{15}{16}$	.602	.05016	2
3	.816	.938	$3\frac{1}{8}$	$3\frac{1}{8}$	$2\frac{7}{8}$	$2\frac{1}{16}$	.499 .501	$\frac{9}{16}$	$\frac{5}{16}$	.783	$\frac{3}{16}$	.512 .516	$1\frac{5}{16}$	$2\frac{5}{16}$	.602	.05016	3
4	1.062	1.231	$4\frac{1}{16}$	$4\frac{1}{8}$	$3\frac{5}{16}$	$3\frac{1}{4}$	.624 .626	$\frac{5}{8}$	$\frac{3}{8}$	1.023	$\frac{3}{16}$	.637 .641	$1\frac{1}{2}$	$2\frac{11}{32}$	.623	.05191	4
5	1.532	1.748	$5\frac{1}{8}$	$6\frac{1}{4}$	$4\frac{3}{16}$	$4\frac{1}{8}$	.999 1.001	$\frac{3}{4}$	$\frac{1}{2}$	1.483	$\frac{1}{8}$	1.012 1.016	2	$3\frac{11}{32}$	.630	.0525	5
6	2.201	2.494	$7\frac{1}{16}$	$6\frac{1}{4}$	$5\frac{3}{16}$	$5\frac{5}{8}$	1.248 1.251	$1\frac{1}{8}$	$\frac{5}{8}$	2.128	$\frac{1}{4}$	1.263 1.268	$2\frac{1}{4}$	$5\frac{1}{16}$	.626	.05216	6
7	2.857	3.270	$9\frac{1}{16}$	$9\frac{1}{16}$	$8\frac{1}{16}$	$7\frac{7}{16}$	1.623 1.627	$1\frac{3}{8}$	$\frac{3}{4}$	2.769	$\frac{1}{8}$	1.639 1.644	$3\frac{5}{8}$	$7\frac{1}{8}$	.625	.05208	7

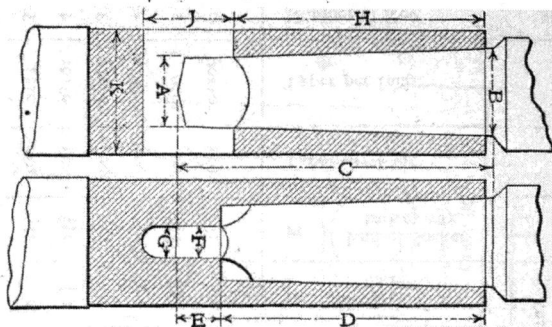

The Standard Tool Company's Standard Taper Shanks

No. of Taper	Diameter Small End of Shank	Diameter Large End of Shank	Total Length of Shank	Depth Hole in Socket	Length Tongue to End Socket Hole	Thickness of Tongue
	A	B	C	D	E	F
0	.2406	.3626	$2\frac{11}{32}$	$2\frac{1}{32}$	$\frac{3}{16}$	$\frac{5}{32}$
1	.3533	.4814	$2\frac{9}{16}$	$2\frac{3}{16}$	$\frac{5}{16}$	$\frac{3}{16}$
2	.5531	.7099	$3\frac{1}{8}$	$2\frac{5}{8}$	$\frac{5}{16}$	$\frac{1}{4}$
3	.7529	.9472	$3\frac{7}{8}$	$3\frac{1}{4}$	$\frac{7}{16}$	$\frac{5}{16}$
4	.9908	1.2438	$4\frac{7}{8}$	$4\frac{1}{8}$	$\frac{1}{2}$	$\frac{15}{32}$
5	1.4390	1.7605	$6\frac{1}{8}$	$5\frac{1}{4}$	$\frac{5}{8}$	$\frac{5}{8}$
6	2.0638	2.5104	$8\frac{9}{16}$	$7\frac{3}{8}$	$\frac{7}{8}$	$\frac{3}{4}$
7	2.6849	3.2903	$11\frac{5}{8}$	$10\frac{1}{8}$	$1\frac{1}{8}$	$1\frac{1}{8}$

No. of Taper	Width of Keyway	End of Socket of Keyway	Length of Keyway	Diameter of Socket	Taper per Foot	Taper per Inch
	G	H	J	K		
0	$\frac{11}{64}$	$1\frac{15}{16}$	$\frac{9}{16}$	$\frac{9}{16}$	.625	.05208
1	$\frac{7}{32}$	$2\frac{1}{16}$	$\frac{3}{4}$	$\frac{25}{32}$	.600	.05000
2	$\frac{17}{64}$	$2\frac{1}{2}$	$\frac{15}{16}$	$1\frac{1}{16}$	.602	.05016
3	$\frac{21}{64}$	$3\frac{1}{16}$	$1\frac{1}{8}$	$1\frac{5}{16}$	.602	.05016
4	$\frac{31}{64}$	$3\frac{5}{8}$	$1\frac{7}{16}$	$1\frac{11}{16}$	.623	.05191
5	$\frac{41}{64}$	$4\frac{15}{16}$	$1\frac{3}{4}$	$2\frac{7}{16}$	.630	.05250
6	$\frac{43}{64}$	7	$2\frac{1}{4}$	$2\frac{3}{8}$	.626	.05216
7	$1\frac{9}{64}$	$9\frac{1}{2}$	$2\frac{5}{8}$	...	.625	.05208

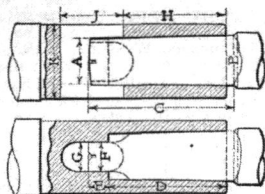

THE STANDARD TOOL COMPANY'S SHORT TAPER

No. of Taper	Diameter Small End of Shank	Diameter Large End of Shank	Total Length of Shank	Depth Hole in Socket	Length Tongue to End Socket Hole	Thickness of Tongue
	A	B	C	D	E	F
1	.378	.484	2¼	1¾	¼	3/16
2	.587	.706	2⅜	1¹⁵⁄₁₆	⁵⁄₁₆	½
3	.800	.941	2⅝	2¼		⅝
4	1.050	1.244	3⅛	3	⁹⁄₁₆	⅝
5	1.515	1.757	4⅝	3¾		1
6	2.169	2.501	6⅜	5		1¼
7	2.815	3.283	9	7¼	1	1½

No. of Taper	Width of Keyway	End of Socket to Keyway	Length of Keyway	Diameter of Socket	Taper per Foot	Taper per Inch
	G	H	J	K		
1	.263	1¾	¾	⅝	.600	.0500
2	.388	1¾	1	1¹⁄₁₆	.602	.05016
3	.520	2	1¼	1⅝	.602	.05016
4	.645	2¹¹⁄₁₆	1½	1⁷⁄₁₆	.623	.05191
5	1.020	3½	2	2¹⁄₁₆	.630	.0525
6	1.270	4⅝	2½	2⅜	.626	.05216
7	1.520	7	3		.625	.05208

THE STANDARD TOOL CO'S. SHORT TAPER SHANKS

THE table shows the short taper shanks of the Standard Tool Company for giving a tang of increased strength.

Sockets and sleeves are furnished, made with the outside taper to fit the regular taper of spindles of drill presses; the inner taper being suitable for the short shanks and also made with both outside and inside taper, conforming to the new standard, and these latter interchange or nest into each other.

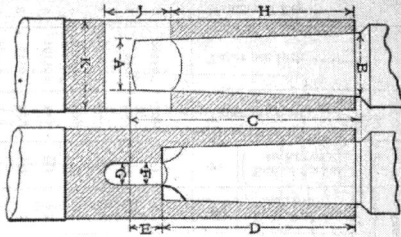

The Standard Tool Company's Standard Taper Shanks

No. of Taper	Diameter Small End of Shank	Diameter Large End of Shank	Total Length of Shank	Depth Hole in Socket	Length Tongue to End Socket Hole	Thickness of Tongue
	A	B	C	D	E	F
0	.2406	.3626	2 11/32	2 7/32	1/8	
1	.3533	.4814	2 9/16	2 3/16	1/8	
2	.5531	.7099	3 1/8	2 5/8	7/16	
3	.7529	.9472	3 7/8	3 1/4	1/16	
4	.9908	1.2438	4 7/8	4 1/8		
5	1.4390	1.7605	6 1/8	5 1/4		
6	2.0638	2.5104	8 9/16	7 3/8		
7	2.6849	3.2903	11 5/8	10 1/2	1 1/8	1 3/8

No. of Taper	Width of Keyway	End of Socket of Keyway	Length of Keyway	Diameter of Socket	Taper per Foot	Taper per Inch
	G	H	J	K		
0	1 1/4	1 15/16	7/8	9/16	.625	.0520
1	7/16	2 1/16	1/4	25/32	.600	.0500
2	7/16	2 1/2	1/8	1 1/3	.602	.0501
3	9/16	3 1/8	1 1/4	1 11/16	.602	.0501
4	5/8	3 5/8	1 7/16	1 11/16	.623	.0519
5	3/4	4 1/16	1 1/4	2 1/8	.630	.0525
6	1 1/4	7	2 1/4	2 5/8	.626	.0521
7	1 5/16	9 1/2	2 3/8	...	.625	.0520

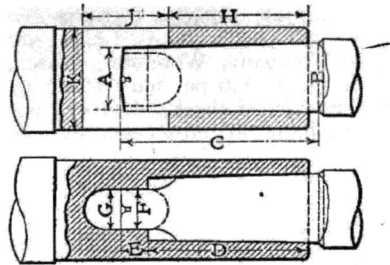

THE STANDARD TOOL COMPANY'S SHORT TAPER

No. of Taper	Diameter Small End of Shank	Diameter Large End of Shank	Total Length of Shank	Depth Hole in Socket	Length Tongue to End Socket Hole	Thickness of Tongue
	A	B	C	D	E	F
1	.378	.484	$2\frac{1}{8}$	$1\frac{3}{4}$	$\frac{1}{4}$	$\frac{1}{4}$
2	.587	.706	$2\frac{3}{8}$	$1\frac{15}{16}$	$\frac{5}{16}$	$\frac{3}{8}$
3	.800	.941	$2\frac{8}{16}$	$2\frac{1}{4}$	$\frac{3}{8}$	$\frac{1}{2}$
4	1.050	1.244	$3\frac{1}{4}$	3	$\frac{9}{16}$	$\frac{5}{8}$
5	1.515	1.757	$4\frac{5}{8}$	$3\frac{3}{4}$	$\frac{5}{8}$	1
6	2.169	2.501.	$6\frac{3}{8}$	5	$\frac{3}{4}$	$1\frac{1}{4}$
7	2.815	3.283	9	$7\frac{3}{4}$	1	$1\frac{1}{2}$

No. of Taper	Width of Keyway	End of Socket to Keyway	Length of Keyway	Diameter of Socket	Taper per Foot	Taper per Inch
	G	H	J	K		
1	.263	$1\frac{5}{8}$	$\frac{3}{4}$	$\frac{25}{32}$	.600	.0500
2	.388	$1\frac{3}{4}$	1	$1\frac{1}{8}$	.602	.05016
3	.520	2	$1\frac{1}{4}$	$1\frac{5}{16}$	.602	.05016
4	.645	$2\frac{11}{16}$	$1\frac{1}{2}$	$1\frac{11}{16}$	.623	.05191
5	1.020	$3\frac{1}{4}$	2	$2\frac{1}{16}$	.630	.0525
6	1.270	$4\frac{3}{8}$	$2\frac{1}{2}$	$2\frac{7}{8}$	.626	.05216
7	1.520	7	3		.625	.05208

THE STANDARD TOOL CO'S. SHORT TAPER SHANKS

THE table shows the short taper shanks of the Standard Tool Company for giving a tang of increased strength.

Sockets and sleeves are furnished, made with the outside taper to fit the regular taper of spindles of drill presses; the inner taper being suitable for the short shanks and also made with both outside and inside taper, conforming to the new standard, and these latter interchange or nest into each other.

THE REED TAPER

THE F. E. Reed Company, Worcester, Mass., uses in its lathe spindles the 1 in 20 taper (0.6 per foot) which the Jarno system is based on. The diameters of the Reed tapers, however, differ from the Jarno, and the lengths in most cases are somewhat less. The dimensions are given in the table below.

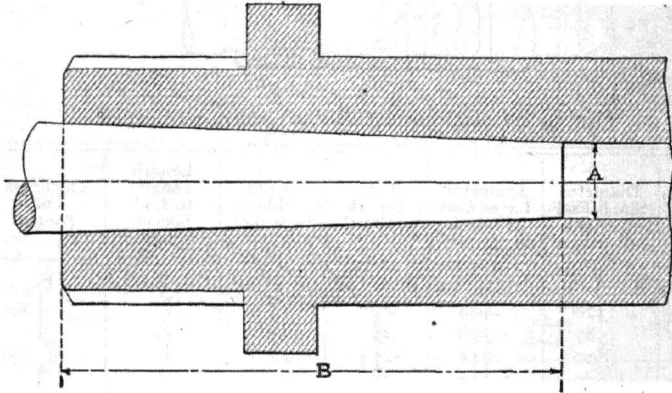

F. E. REED LATHE CENTER TAPERS

TAPER PER FOOT = 0.6 INCH.   TAPER PER INCH = 0.05 INCH

Size of Lathe	Dia. of Small End of Taper	Length of Taper	Size of Lathe	Dia. of Small End of Taper	Length of Taper
	A	B		A	B
12"	$\frac{9}{16}$	$3\frac{5}{8}$	20"	$1\frac{1}{2}$	$5\frac{5}{16}$
14"	$\frac{15}{16}$	$4\frac{1}{8}$	22"	$1\frac{1}{2}$	$5\frac{5}{16}$
16"	$1\frac{1}{4}$	$4\frac{5}{8}$	24"	$1\frac{3}{4}$	$5\frac{1}{2}$
Special 16"	$1\frac{3}{4}$	$4\frac{3}{8}$	27"	$1\frac{3}{4}$	$5\frac{1}{2}$
18"	$1\frac{1}{4}$	$5\frac{1}{16}$	30"	2	$5\frac{3}{4}$

THE JARNO TAPER

WHILE the majority of American tool builders use the Brown & Sharpe taper in their milling-machine spindles and the Morse taper in their lathes, a number of firms, among them the Pratt & Whitney Company, Hartford, Conn., and the Norton Grinding Company, Worcester, Mass., have adopted the "Jarno" taper, the proportions of which are given in the accompanying table. In this system the taper of which is 0.6 inch per foot or 1 in 20, the number of the taper is the key by which all the dimensions are immediately determined without the necessity even of referring to the table. That is, the number of the taper is the number of tenths of an inch in diameter at the small end, the number of eighths of an inch at the large end, and the number of halves of an inch in length or depth. For example: the No. 6 taper is six eighths ($\frac{3}{4}$) inch diameter at large end, six tenths ($\frac{6}{10}$) diameter at the small end and six halves (3 inches) in length. Similarly, the No. 16 taper is $\frac{16}{8}$, or 2 inches diameter at the large end; $\frac{16}{10}$ or 1.6 inches at the small end; $\frac{16}{2}$ or 8 inches in length.

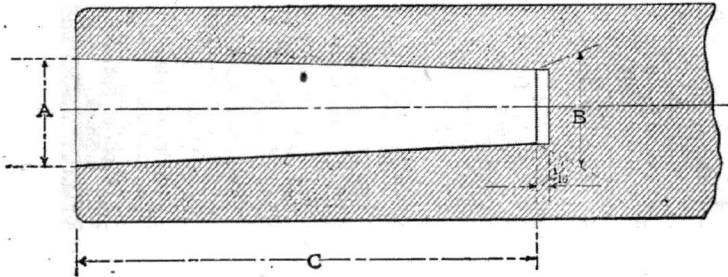

JARNO TAPERS

TAPER PER FOOT = 0.6 INCH.　　TAPER PER INCH = 0.05 INCH.

$$\text{Dia. Large End} = \frac{\text{No. of Taper}}{8}$$

$$\text{Dia. Small End} = \frac{\text{No. of Taper}}{10}$$

$$\text{Length of Taper} = \frac{\text{No. of Taper}}{2}$$

No. of Taper	Dia. Large End	Dia. Small End	Length of Taper	No. of Taper	Dia. Large End	Dia. Small End	Length of Taper
	A	B	C		A	B	C
1	.125	.10	.5	11	1.375	1.10	5.5
2	.250	.20	1.	12	1.500	1.20	6.0
3	.375	.30	1.5	13	1.625	1.30	6.5
4	.500	.40	2.0	14	1.750	1.40	7.0
5	.625	.50	2.5	15	1.875	1.50	7.5
6	.750	.60	3.0	16	2.000	1.60	8.0
7	.875	.70	3.5	17	2.125	1.70	8.5
8	1.000	.80	4.0	18	2.250	1.80	9.0
9	1.125	.90	4.5	19	2.375	1.90	9.5
10	1.250	1.00	5.0	20	2.500	2.00	10.0

SELLERS TAPERS

Dia. of Drill	Dia. of Shank at Gage Point B	Length of Shank from Point B	Length of Drill Body from Point B	Total Length of Drill	Length of Shank Over All	Dia. at Reduced Portion of Shank	Length of Reduced Portion of Shank	Approximate Pitch of Spiral Grooves	Width of Spline in Shank	Depth of Spline in Shank	Width of Key	Hight of Key
A	B	C			D	E	F		G	H	I	K
$\frac{1}{4}$	$\frac{1}{2}$	$2\frac{1}{4}$	$4\frac{1}{4}$	$6\frac{1}{2}$	$2\frac{5}{16}$	$\frac{11}{32}$	$1\frac{3}{16}$	3.70	$\frac{3}{32}$	$\frac{5}{64}$	$\frac{5}{64}$	$\frac{9}{64}$
$\frac{5}{16}$	"	"	$4\frac{1}{4}$	$6\frac{1}{2}$	"	"	"	3.70	"	"	"	"
$\frac{3}{8}$	"	"	$4\frac{3}{4}$	7	"	"	"	3.70	"	"	"	"
$\frac{7}{16}$	"	"	$5\frac{1}{4}$	$7\frac{1}{2}$	"	"	"	3.70	"	"	"	"
$\frac{1}{2}$	"	"	$5\frac{3}{4}$	8	"	"	"	5.32	"	"	"	"
$\frac{9}{16}$	$1\frac{1}{16}$	$2\frac{3}{4}$	$6\frac{1}{4}$	8	$2\frac{7}{8}$	$\frac{1}{2}$	$1\frac{1}{4}$	5.32	$\frac{1}{8}$	$\frac{3}{32}$	$\frac{7}{64}$	$\frac{11}{64}$
$\frac{5}{8}$	"	"	$6\frac{3}{4}$	$9\frac{1}{2}$	"	"	"	5.32	"	"	"	"
$\frac{11}{16}$	"	"	$6\frac{1}{2}$	$9\frac{1}{2}$	"	"	"	6.24	"	"	"	"
$\frac{3}{4}$	"	"	$7\frac{1}{4}$	10	"	"	"	6.24	"	"	"	"
$\frac{13}{16}$	"	"	$7\frac{1}{4}$	10	"	"	"	6.24	"	"	"	"
$\frac{7}{8}$	$\frac{7}{8}$	$3\frac{1}{2}$	8	$11\frac{1}{2}$	$3\frac{11}{16}$	$\frac{5}{8}$	$\frac{5}{8}$	7.28	"	"	"	"
$\frac{15}{16}$	"	"	8	$11\frac{1}{2}$	"	"	"	7.28	"	"	"	"
1	"	"	$8\frac{1}{2}$	12	"	"	"	9.50	"	"	"	"
$1\frac{1}{16}$	"	"	$8\frac{1}{2}$	12	"	"	"	"	"	"	"	"
$1\frac{1}{8}$	$1\frac{1}{8}$	$4\frac{1}{2}$	9	$13\frac{1}{2}$	$4\frac{3}{4}$	$\frac{25}{32}$	$\frac{3}{8}$	"	$\frac{3}{16}$	$\frac{1}{8}$	$\frac{11}{64}$	$\frac{15}{64}$
$1\frac{3}{16}$	"	"	9	$13\frac{1}{2}$	"	"	"	"	"	"	"	"
$1\frac{1}{4}$	"	"	9	$13\frac{1}{2}$	"	"	"	"	"	"	"	"
$1\frac{5}{16}$	"	"	9	$13\frac{1}{2}$	"	"	"	"	"	"	"	"
$1\frac{3}{8}$	"	"	$9\frac{1}{2}$	14	"	"	"	"	"	"	"	"
$1\frac{7}{16}$	"	"	$9\frac{1}{2}$	14	"	"	"	"	"	"	"	"
$1\frac{1}{2}$	"	"	10	$14\frac{1}{2}$	"	"	"	"	"	"	"	"
$1\frac{9}{16}$	"	"	10	$14\frac{1}{2}$	"	"	"	"	"	"	"	"
$1\frac{5}{8}$	$1\frac{5}{8}$	$6\frac{1}{2}$	10	$16\frac{1}{2}$	$6\frac{3}{4}$	$1\frac{1}{8}$	$1\frac{7}{16}$	13.72	$\frac{1}{4}$	$\frac{3}{32}$	$\frac{15}{64}$	$\frac{21}{64}$
$1\frac{11}{16}$	"	"	10	$16\frac{1}{2}$	"	"	"	"	"	"	"	"
$1\frac{3}{4}$	"	"	$10\frac{1}{2}$	17	"	"	"	"	"	"	"	"
$1\frac{13}{16}$	"	"	$10\frac{1}{2}$	17	"	"	"	"	"	"	"	"
$1\frac{7}{8}$	"	"	11	$17\frac{1}{2}$	"	"	"	"	"	"	"	"
$1\frac{15}{16}$	"	"	11	$17\frac{1}{2}$	"	"	"	"	"	"	"	"
2	"	"	$11\frac{1}{2}$	18	"	"	"	"	"	"	"	"

THE SELLERS' TAPER

THE system of tapers used by William Sellers & Company, Inc., of Philadelphia, Pa., in lathes, drilling and boring machines, is given in the preceding table. The taper is $\frac{3}{4}$ inch per foot and each size of taper is splined as shown for a key the dimensions of which are included in the table. The pitch of the spiral for the drills used by the company is also included.

TAPER PINS AND REAMERS

TAPER REAMERS AND PINS

(PRATT & WHITNEY CO.)

Taper = $\frac{1}{4}$ inch per foot or .0208 inch per inch

Size. No.	Dia. of Small End of Reamer	Dia. of Large End of Reamer	Length of Flute	Total Length of Reamer	Size Drill for Reamer	Longest Limit Length of Pin	Dia. of Large End of Pin	Approx. Fractional Size at Large End of Pin
0	0.135"	.162"	$1\frac{5}{16}$"	2"	28	1"	.156"	$\frac{5}{32}$"
1	.146"	.179"	$1\frac{9}{16}$"	$2\frac{3}{8}$"	25	$1\frac{1}{4}$"	.172"	$\frac{11}{64}$"
2	.162"	.200"	$1\frac{13}{16}$"	$2\frac{11}{16}$"	19	$1\frac{1}{2}$"	.193"	$\frac{3}{16}$"
3	.183"	.226"	$2\frac{1}{16}$"	3"	12	$1\frac{3}{4}$"	.219"	$\frac{7}{32}$"
4	.208"	.257"	$2\frac{3}{8}$"	$3\frac{7}{16}$"	3	2"	.250"	$\frac{1}{4}$"
5	.240"	.300"	$2\frac{7}{8}$"	$4\frac{3}{8}$"	$\frac{1}{4}$	$2\frac{1}{2}$"	.289"	$\frac{9}{32}$"
6	.279"	.354"	$3\frac{5}{8}$"	5"	$\frac{9}{32}$	$3\frac{1}{4}$"	.341"	$\frac{11}{32}$"
7	.331"	.423"	$4\frac{7}{16}$"	$6\frac{1}{16}$"	$\frac{11}{32}$	$3\frac{3}{4}$"	.409"	$\frac{13}{32}$"
8	.398"	.507"	$5\frac{1}{4}$"	$7\frac{1}{16}$"	$\frac{13}{32}$	$4\frac{1}{2}$"	.492"	$\frac{31}{64}$"
9	.482"	.609"	$6\frac{1}{8}$"	$8\frac{1}{8}$"	$\frac{31}{64}$	$5\frac{1}{4}$"	.591"	$\frac{19}{32}$"
10	.581"	.727"	7"	$9\frac{1}{2}$"	$\frac{19}{32}$	6"	.706"	$\frac{23}{32}$"
11	.706"	.878"	$8\frac{1}{4}$"	$11\frac{1}{4}$"	$\frac{23}{32}$	$7\frac{1}{4}$"	.857"	$\frac{55}{64}$"
12	.842"	1.050"	10"	$13\frac{3}{8}$"	$\frac{55}{64}$	$8\frac{1}{4}$"	1.013"	$1\frac{1}{64}$"
13	1.009"	1.259"	12"	16"	$1\frac{1}{64}$	$10\frac{3}{4}$"	1.233"	$1\frac{15}{64}$"

These reamer sizes are so proportioned that each overlaps the size smaller about $\frac{1}{2}$ inch.

Table of Drill Sizes for Taper Pins

Drill Sizes for Taper Pins

The table gives the drill sizes for taper pins ranging in lengths by ¼ inch from No. 0, ¾ inch long, to No. 10, 6 inches long. The diameter of the small end of the pin for each length is given in the fourth column with the drill size in the fifth column.

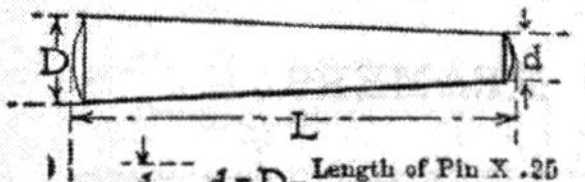

$$d = D - \frac{\text{Length of Pin} \times .25}{12}$$

No. Pin	L	D	d	No. of Drill
0	¾″	0.156″	0.1404″	28
0	1″	0.156″	0.1352″	29
1	¾″	0.172″	0.1564″	22
1	1″	0.172″	0.1512″	24
1	1¼″	0.172″	0.146″	26
2	¾″	0.193″	0.1774″	16
2	1″	0.193″	0.1722″	17
2	1¼″	0.193″	0.167″	18
2	1½″	0.193″	0.1618″	20
3	¾″	0.219″	0.2034″	6
3	1″	0.219″	0.1982″	8
3	1¼″	0.219″	0.193″	10
3	1½″	0.219″	0.1878″	12
3	1¾″	0.219″	0.1825″	14
4	¾″	0.250″	0.2344″	15/64″
4	1″	0.250″	0.2292″	15/64″
4	1¼″	0.250″	0.224″	1
4	1½″	0.250″	0.2187″	2
4	1¾″	0.250″	0.2135″	3
4	2″	0.250″	0.2083″	4
5	¾″	0.289″	0.2734″	17/64″
5	1″	0.289″	0.2682″	17/64″
5	1¼″	0.289″	0.263″	17/64″
5	1½″	0.289″	0.2577″	1/4″
5	1¾″	0.289″	0.2525″	1/4″
5	2″	0.289″	0.2473″	1/4″
5	2¼″	0.289″	0.2421″	15/64″
6	¾″	0.341″	0.3254″	21/64″
6	1″	0.341″	0.3201″	21/64″
6	1¼″	0.341″	0.315″	5/16″
6	1½″	0.341″	0.310″	5/16″
6	1¾″	0.341″	0.3045″	19/64″
6	2″	0.341″	0.2994″	19/64″
6	2¼″	0.341″	0.2941″	19/64″
6	2½″	0.341″	0.2889″	9/32″
6	2¾″	0.341″	0.2837″	9/32″
6	3″	0.341″	0.2785″	9/32″
6	3¼″	0.341″	0.2733″	17/64″
7	1″	0.409″	0.3881″	25/64″

No. of Pin	L	D	d	No. of Drill
7	1¼″	0.409″	0.3829″	25/64″
7	1½″	0.409″	0.3777″	3/8″
7	1¾″	0.409″	0.3725″	3/8″
7	2″	0.409″	0.3673″	3/8″
7	2¼″	0.409″	0.3621″	23/64″
7	2½″	0.409″	0.3569″	23/64″
7	2¾″	0.409″	0.3517″	23/64″
7	3″	0.409″	0.3465″	11/32″
7	3¼″	0.409″	0.3413″	11/32″
7	3½″	0.409″	0.3361″	11/32″
7	3¾″	0.409″	0.3309″	21/64″
8	1¼″	0.492″	0.466″	15/32″
8	1½″	0.492″	0.4608″	15/32″
8	1¾″	0.492″	0.4555″	29/64″
8	2″	0.492″	0.4503″	29/64″
8	2¼″	0.492″	0.4451″	29/64″
8	2½″	0.492″	0.4399″	7/16″
8	2¾″	0.492″	0.4347″	7/16″
8	3″	0.492″	0.4295″	7/16″
8	3¼″	0.492″	0.4243″	27/64″
8	3½″	0.492″	0.4191″	27/64″
8	3¾″	0.492″	0.4139″	27/64″
8	4″	0.492″	0.4087″	13/32″
8	4¼″	0.492″	0.4035″	13/32″
8	4½″	0.492″	0.3982″	13/32″
9	1½″	0.591″	0.5597″	9/16″
9	1¾″	0.591″	0.5545″	35/64″
9	2″	0.591″	0.5493″	35/64″
9	2¼″	0.591″	0.5441″	35/64″
9	2½″	0.591″	0.5389″	35/64″
9	2¾″	0.591″	0.5337″	17/32″
9	3″	0.591″	0.5285″	17/32″
9	3¼″	0.591″	0.5233″	17/32″
9	3½″	0.591″	0.5181″	33/64″
9	3¾″	0.591″	0.5129″	33/64″
9	4″	0.591″	0.5077″	33/64″
9	4¼″	0.591″	0.5025″	1/2″
9	4½″	0.591″	0.4972″	1/2″
9	4¾″	0.591″	0.4929″	1/2″
9	5″	0.591″	0.4868″	31/64″
9	5¼″	0.591″	0.4816″	31/64″
9	5½″	0.591″	0.4764″	31/64″
10	1½″	0.706″	0.6747″	43/64″
10	1¾″	0.706″	0.6695″	43/64″
10	2″	0.706″	0.6643″	43/64″
10	2¼″	0.706″	0.6591″	21/32″
10	2½″	0.706″	0.6539″	21/32″
10	2¾″	0.706″	0.6487″	21/32″
10	3″	0.706″	0.6435″	41/64″
10	3¼″	0.706″	0.6383″	41/64″
10	3½″	0.706″	0.6331″	41/64″
10	3¾″	0.706″	0.6278″	5/8″
10	4″	0.706″	0.6226″	5/8″
10	4¼″	0.706″	0.6174″	5/8″
10	4½″	0.706″	0.6122″	39/64″
10	4¾″	0.706″	0.6078″	39/64″
10	5″	0.706″	0.6018″	39/64″
10	5¼″	0.706″	0.5966″	19/32″
10	5½″	0.706″	0.5914″	19/32″
10	5¾″	0.706″	0.5862″	19/32″
10	6″	0.706″	0.581″	37/64″

STANDARD TAPER PINS USED BY THE U. S. ORDNANCE DEPARTMENT

The accompanying tables show the standard taper and split pin used by the Ordnance Department of the U. S. Army as revised up to July 20, 1912. The first table shows the standard taper pins and the retaining split pins used in the end. The pins are ¼-inch taper per foot. They have tapered head and point to allow for upsetting, either in driving or removing pins from the work.

The first table gives the number of the pin and the diameter at the small end in the first two columns. The next three columns show the sizes of the shaft and collars in which these pins are used, while the last two columns show the split pins which are used in some cases on the small end of the taper pin to prevent accidental withdrawal from the hole.

The second table shows the dimensions of the standard split pin used in connection with the taper pins, and gives the diameter and the length manufactured. The tapered points are shown by the drawing to be the length of the diameter of the split pin, with the small end of the taper 0.75 of the diameter.

STANDARD TAPER PINS and Retaining Split Pins

TAPER PINS 0.25 per Ft. Taper		WORK USED IN SHAFTS		COLLARS	Retaining SPLIT PINS	
Number	DIA. AT SMALL END D	Min. Diam.	Max. Diam.	Max. Diam.	DIAM.	LENGTH
	0.0625		0.3	0.75		
0	0.09375	0.3	0.5	1		
0	0.135	0.5	0.75	1.125	0.0468	0.3125
2	0.162	0.75	1	1.625	0.0625	0.375
2	0.208	1	1.5	2.125	0.0781	0.4375
4	0.279	1.5	2	3.25	0.09375	0.5
6	0.388	2	3	4.875	0.125	0.75
8	0.581	3	4.5	8.625	0.156	1
12	0.842	4.5	6.5	9.625	0.203	1.25

STANDARD SPLIT PINS

ALL PINS BELOW THIS LINE ARE COMMERCIAL SIZES

DIAM.	LENGTHS MANUFACTURED														
0.0468	0.3125	0.5	0.75												
0.0625	0.375	0.5625	0.8125												
0.0781	0.4375	0.625	0.75	1											
0.09375	0.5	0.625	0.75	1	1.25	1.5	1.75	2							
0.125	0.5	0.75	1	1.25	1.5	1.75	2	2.25	2.5						
0.156	0.5	0.75	1	1.25	1.5	1.75	2	2.25	2.5						
0.203	0.5	0.75	1	1.25	1.5	1.75	2	2.25	2.5	2.75	3				
0.25		0.75	1	1.25	1.5	1.75	2	2.25	2.5	2.75	3	3.25	3.5	3.75	4
0.375			1	1.25	1.5	1.75	2	2.25	2.5	2.75	3	3.25	3.5	3.75	4
0.5					1.5	1.75	2	2.25	2.5	2.75	3	3.25	3.5	3.75	4 — Also 5 and 6 inch
0.625							2	2.25	2.5	2.75	3	3.25	3.5	3.75	4 — Also 5 and 6 inch

Split Pin through

Lengths — 0.75 D

D = Nominal Diam. or Diam. of Hole to Receive Pin

0.75 D

TAPERS FROM $\frac{1}{16}$ TO $1\frac{1}{4}$ INCH PER FOOT
AMOUNT OF TAPER FOR LENGTHS UP TO 24 INCHES

Length of Tapered Portion	Taper per Foot									
	$\frac{1}{16}$	$\frac{3}{32}$	$\frac{1}{8}$	$\frac{1}{4}$	$\frac{3}{8}$	$\frac{1}{2}$	$\frac{5}{8}$	$\frac{3}{4}$	1	$1\frac{1}{4}$
$\frac{1}{32}$	.0002	.0002	.0003	.0007	.0010	.0013	.0016	.0020	.0026	.0033
$\frac{1}{16}$	.0003	.0005	.0007	.0013	.0020	.0026	.0033	.0039	.0052	.0065
$\frac{3}{32}$	.0007	.0010	.0013	.0026	.0039	.0052	.0065	.0078	.0104	.0130
$\frac{1}{8}$	.0010	.0015	.0020	.0039	.0059	.0078	.0098	.0117	.0156	.0195
$\frac{5}{32}$	.0013	.0020	.0026	.0052	.0078	.0104	.0130	.0136	.0208	.0260
$\frac{3}{16}$	.0016	.0024	.0033	.0065	.0098	.0130	.0163	.0195	.0260	.0326
$\frac{7}{32}$	.0020	.0029	.0039	.0078	.0117	.0156	.0195	.0234	.0312	.0391
$\frac{1}{4}$	.0023	.0034	.0046	.0091	.0137	.0182	.0228	.0273	.0365	.0456
$\frac{9}{32}$	.0026	.0039	.0052	.0104	.0156	.0208	.0260	.0312	.0417	.0521
$\frac{5}{16}$	.0029	.0044	.0059	.0117	.0176	.0234	.0293	.0352	.0469	.0586
$\frac{11}{32}$	.0033	.0049	.0065	.0130	.0195	.0260	.0326	.0391	.0521	.0651
$\frac{3}{8}$	.0036	.0054	.0072	.0143	.0215	.0286	.0358	.0430	.0573	.0716
$\frac{13}{32}$	.0039	.0059	.0078	.0156	.0234	.0312	.0391	.0469	.0625	.0781
$\frac{7}{16}$	.0042	.0063	.0085	.0169	.0254	.0339	.0423	.0508	.0677	.0846
$\frac{15}{32}$	.0046	.0068	.0091	.0182	.0273	.0365	.0456	.0547	.0729	.0911
$\frac{1}{2}$	.0049	.0073	.0098	.0195	.0293	.0391	.0488	.0586	.0781	.0977
1	.0052	.0078	.0104	.0208	.0312	.0417	.0521	.0625	.0833	.1042
2	.0104	.0156	.0208	.0417	.0625	.0833	.1042	.125	.1667	.2083
3	.0156	.0234	.0312	.0625	.0937	.1250	.1562	.1875	.250	.3125
4	.0208	.0312	.0417	.0833	.125	.1667	.2083	.250	.3333	.4167
5	.0260	.0391	.0521	.1042	.1562	.2083	.2604	.3125	.4167	.5208
6	.0312	.0469	.0625	.125	.1875	.250	.3125	.375	.500	.625
7	.0365	.0547	.0729	.1458	.2187	.2917	.3646	.4375	.5833	.7292
8	.0417	.0625	.0833	.1667	.250	.3333	.4167	.500	.6667	.8333
9	.0469	.0703	.0937	.1875	.2812	.375	.4687	.5625	.750	.9375
10	.0521	.0781	.1042	.2083	.3125	.4167	.5208	.625	.8333	1.0417
11	.0573	.0859	.1146	.2292	.3437	.4583	.5729	.6875	.9167	1.1458
12	.0625	.0937	.125	.250	.375	.500	.625	.750	1.000	1.250
13	.0677	.1016	.1354	.2708	.4062	.5417	.6771	.8125	1.0833	1.3542
14	.0729	.1094	.1458	.2917	.4375	.5833	.7292	.875	1.1667	1.4583
15	.0781	.1172	.1562	.3125	.4687	.625	.7812	.9375	1.250	1.5625
16	.0833	.125	.1667	.3333	.500	.6667	.8333	1.000	1.3333	1.6667
17	.0885	.1328	.1771	.3542	.5312	.7083	.8854	1.0625	1.4167	1.7708
18	.0937	.1406	.1875	.3750	.5625	.750	.9375	1.125	1.500	1.875
19	.0990	.1484	.1979	.3958	.5937	.7917	.9896	1.1875	1.5833	1.9792
20	.1042	.1562	.2083	.4167	.625	.8333	1.0417	1.250	1.6667	2.0833
21	.1094	.1641	.2187	.4375	.6562	.875	1.0937	1.3125	1.750	2.1875
22	.1146	.1719	.2292	.4583	.6875	.9167	1.1458	1.375	1.8333	2.2917
23	.1198	.1797	.2396	.4792	.7187	.9583	1.1970	1.4375	1.9167	2.3958
24	.125	.1875	.250	.500	.750	1.000	1.250	1.500	2.000	2.500

TAPERS PER FOOT IN INCHES AND CORRESPONDING ANGLES

Taper per Foot	Included Angle			Angle with Center Line			Taper per Foot	Included Angle			Angle with Center Line		
	Deg.	Min.	Sec.	Deg.	Min.	Sec.		Deg.	Min.	Sec.	Deg.	Min.	Sec.
1/64	0	4	28	0	2	14	1	4	46	18	2	23	9
1/32	0	8	58	0	4	29	1 1/8	5	21	44	2	40	52
1/16	0	17	54	0	8	57	1 1/4	5	57	48	2	58	54
3/32	0	26	52	0	13	26	1 3/8	6	33	26	3	16	43
1/8	0	35	48	0	17	54	1 1/2	7	9	10	3	34	35
5/32	0	44	44	0	22	22	1 5/8	7	44	48	3	52	24
3/16	0	53	44	0	26	52	1 3/4	8	20	26	4	10	13
7/32	1	2	34	0	31	17	1 7/8	8	56	2	4	28	1
1/4	1	11	36	0	35	48	2	9	31	36	4	45	48
9/32	1	20	30	0	40	15	2 1/4	10	42	42	5	21	21
5/16	1	29	30	0	44	45	2 1/2	11	53	36	5	56	48
11/32	1	38	22	0	49	11	2 3/4	13	4	24	6	32	12
3/8	1	47	24	0	53	42	3	14	15	0	7	7	30
13/32	1	56	24	0	58	12	3 1/4	15	25	24	7	42	42
7/16	2	5	18	1	2	39	3 1/2	16	35	40	8	17	50
15/32	2	14	16	1	7	8	3 3/4	17	45	40	8	52	50
1/2	2	23	10	1	11	35	4	18	55	28	9	27	44
17/32	2	32	4	1	16	2	4 1/4	20	5	2	10	2	31
9/16	2	41	4	1	20	32	4 1/2	21	14	2	10	37	1
19/32	2	50	2	1	25	1	4 3/4	22	23	22	11	11	41
5/8	2	59	42	1	29	51	5	23	32	12	11	46	6
21/32	3	7	56	1	33	58	5 1/4	24	40	42	12	20	21
11/16	3	16	54	1	38	27	5 1/2	25	48	48	12	54	24
23/32	3	25	50	1	42	55	5 3/4	26	56	46	13	28	23
3/4	3	34	44	1	47	22	6	28	4	2	14	2	1
25/32	3	43	44	1	51	52	6 1/4	29	11	34	14	35	47
13/16	3	52	38	1	56	19	6 1/2	30	18	26	15	9	13
27/32	4	1	36	2	0	48	6 3/4	31	25	2	15	42	31
7/8	4	10	32	2	5	16	7	32	31	12	16	15	36
29/32	4	19	34	2	9	47	7 1/4	33	36	40	16	48	20
15/16	4	28	24	2	14	12	7 1/2	34	42	30	17	21	15
31/32	4	37	20	2	18	40	7 3/4	35	47	32	17	53	46
							8	36	52	12	18	26	6

Table for Computing Tapers
The Tabulated Quantities = Twice the Tangent of Half the Angle.

Deg.	0′	10′	20′	30′	40′	50′	60′
0	.00000	.00290	.00582	.00872	.01164	.01454	.01746
1	.01746	.02036	.02326	.02618	.02910	.03200	.03492
2	.03492	.03782	.04072	.04364	.04656	.04946	.05238
3	.05238	.05528	.05820	.06110	.06402	.06692	.06984
4	.06984	.07276	.07566	.07858	.08150	.08440	.08732
5	.08732	.09024	.09316	.09606	.09898	.10190	.10482
6	.10482	.10774	.11066	.11356	.11648	.11940	.12232
7	.12232	.12524	.12816	.13108	.13400	.13694	.13986
8	.13986	.14278	.14570	.14862	.15156	.15448	.15740
9	.15740	.16034	.16326	.16618	.16912	.17204	.17498
10	.17498	.17790	.18084	.18378	.18670	.18964	.19258
11	.19258	.19552	.19846	.20138	.20432	.20726	.21020
12	.21020	.21314	.21610	.21904	.22198	.22492	.22788
13	.22788	.23082	.23376	.23672	.23966	.24262	.24556
14	.24556	.24852	.25148	.25444	.25738	.26034	.26330
15	.26330	.26626	.26922	.27218	.27516	.27812	.28108
16	.28108	.28404	.28702	.28998	.29296	.29592	.29890
17	.29890	.30188	.30486	.30782	.31080	.31378	.31676
18	.31676	.31976	.32274	.32572	.32870	.33170	.33468
19	.33468	.33768	.34066	.34366	.34666	.34966	.35266
20	.35266	.35566	.35866	.36166	.36466	.36768	.37068
21	.37068	.37368	.37670	.37972	.38272	.38574	.38876
22	.38876	.39178	.39480	.39782	.40084	.40388	.40690
23	.40690	.40994	.41296	.41600	.41904	.42208	.42512
24	.42512	.42816	.43120	.43424	.43728	.44034	.44338
25	.44338	.44644	.44950	.45256	.45562	.45868	.46174
26	.46174	.46480	.46786	.47094	.47400	.47708	.48016
27	.48016	.48324	.48632	.48940	.49248	.49556	.49866
28	.49866	.50174	.50484	.50794	.51004	.51414	.51724
29	.51724	.52034	.52344	.52656	.52966	.53278	.53590
30	.53590	.53902	.54214	.54526	.54838	.55152	.55464
31	.55464	.55778	.56092	.56406	.56720	.57034	.57350
32	.57350	.57664	.57980	.58294	.58610	.58926	.59242
33	.59242	.59560	.59876	.60194	.60510	.60828	.61146
34	.61146	.61464	.61782	.62102	.62420	.62740	.63060
35	.63060	.63380	.63700	.64020	.64342	.64662	.64984
36	.64984	.65306	.65628	.65950	.66272	.66596	.66920
37	.66920	.67242	.67566	.67890	.68216	.68540	.68866
38	.68866	.69192	.69516	.69844	.70170	.70496	.70824
39	.70824	.71152	.71480	.71808	.72136	.72464	.72794
40	.72794	.73124	.73454	.73784	.74114	.74446	.74776
41	.74776	.75108	.75440	.75774	.76106	.76440	.76772
42	.76772	.77106	.77442	.77776	.78110	.78446	.78782
43	.78782	.79118	.79454	.79792	.80130	.80468	.80806
44	.80806	.81144	.81482	.81822	.82162	.82502	.82842
45	.82842	.83184	.83526	.83866	.84210	.84552	.84894

TABLE FOR COMPUTING TAPERS

The Tabulated Quantities = Twice the Tangent of Half the Angle.

Deg.	0′	10′	20′	30′	40′	50′	60′
46	.84894	.85238	.85582	.85926	.86272	.86616	.86962
47	.86962	.87308	.87656	.88002	.88350	.88698	.89046
48	.89046	.89394	.89744	.90094	.90444	.90794	.91146
49	.91146	.91496	.91848	.92202	.92554	.92908	.93262
50	.93262	.93616	.93970	.94326	.94682	.95038	.95396
51	.95396	.95752	.96110	.96468	.96828	.97186	.97546
52	.97546	.97906	.98268	.98630	.98990	.99354	.99716
53	.99716	1.00080	1.00444	1.00808	1.01174	1.01538	1.01906
54	1.01906	1.02272	1.02638	1.03006	1.03376	1.03744	1.04114
55	1.04114	1.04484	1.04854	1.05226	1.05596	1.05970	1.06342
56	1.06342	1.06716	1.07090	1.07464	1.07840	1.08214	1.08592
57	1.08592	1.08968	1.09346	1.09724	1.10102	1.10482	1.10862
58	1.10862	1.11242	1.11624	1.12006	1.12388	1.12770	1.13154
59	1.13154	1.13538	1.13924	1.14310	1.14696	1.15082	1.15470
60	1.15470	1.15858	1.16248	1.16636	1.17026	1.17418	1.17810
61	1.17810	1.18202	1.18594	1.18988	1.19382	1.19776	1.20172
62	1.20172	1.20568	1.20966	1.21362	1.21762	1.22160	1.22560
63	1.22560	1.22960	1.23362	1.23764	1.24166	1.24570	1.24974
64	1.24974	1.25378	1.25784	1.26190	1.26598	1.27006	1.27414
65	1.27414	1.27824	1.28234	1.28644	1.29056	1.29468	1.29882
66	1.29882	1.30296	1.30710	1.31126	1.31542	1.31960	1.32378
67	1.32378	1.32796	1.33216	1.33636	1.34056	1.34478	1.34902
68	1.34902	1.35326	1.35750	1.36176	1.36602	1.37028	1.37456
69	1.37456	1.37984	1.38314	1.38744	1.39176	1.39608	1.40042
70	1.40042	1.40476	1.40910	1.41346	1.41782	1.42220	1.42658
71	1.42658	1.43098	1.43538	1.43980	1.44422	1.44864	1.45308
72	1.45308	1.45754	1.46200	1.46646	1.47094	1.47542	1.47992
73	1.47992	1.48442	1.48894	1.49348	1.49800	1.50256	1.50710
74	1.50710	1.51168	1.51624	1.52084	1.52544	1.53004	1.53466
75	1.53466	1.53928	1.54392	1.54856	1.55322	1.55790	1.56258
76	1.56258	1.56726	1.57196	1.57668	1.58140	1.58612	1.59088
77	1.59088	1.59562	1.60040	1.60516	1.60996	1.61476	1.61966
78	1.61956	1.62440	1.62922	1.63406	1.63892	1.64380	1.64868
79	1.64868	1.65356	1.65846	1.66338	1.66830	1.67324	1.67820
80	1.67820	1.68316	1.68814	1.69312	1.69812	1.70314	1.70816
81	1.70816	1.71320	1.71824	1.72332	1.72836	1.73348	1.73858
82	1.73858	1.74368	1.74882	1.75396	1.75910	1.76428	1.76946
83	1.76946	1.77464	1.77984	1.78506	1.79030	1.79554	1.80080
84	1.80080	1.80608	1.81138	1.81668	1.82198	1.82732	1.83266
85	1.83266	1.83802	1.84340	1.84878	1.85418	1.85960	1.86504
86	1.86504	1.87048	1.87594	1.88142	1.88690	1.89240	1.89792
87	1.89792	1.90346	1.90902	1.91458	1.92016	1.92576	1.93138
88	1.93138	1.93700	1.94266	1.94832	1.95400	1.95968	1.96540
89	1.96540	1.97112	1.97686	1.98262	1.98840	1.99420	2.00000
90	2.						

Refer to page 364 for explanation of table.

TABLE FOR USE IN COMPUTING TAPERS

In the table on pages 362 and 363 the quantities when expressed in inches represent the taper per inch corresponding to various angles advancing by 10 minutes from 10 minutes to 90 degrees. If an angle is given as, say, $27\frac{1}{2}$ degrees and it is desired to find the corresponding taper in inches, the amount, 0.4894 may be taken directly from the table. This is the taper per inch of length measured as in Fig. 6, along the axis. The taper in inches per foot of length is found by multiplying

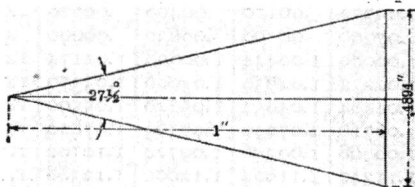

Fig. 6. — Taper per Inch and Corresponding Angle

the tabulated quantity by 12, and in this particular case would be 0.4894″ × 12 = 5.8728″. Where the included angle is not found directly in the table, the taper per inch is found as follows: Assume that the angle in question is $12\frac{1}{4}$ degrees, then the nearest angles in the table are 12° 10′ and 12° 20′, the respective quantities tabulated under these angles being 0.21314 and 0.21610. The difference between the two is 0.00296, and as $12\frac{1}{4}°$ is half way between 12° 10′ and 12° 20′ one half of 0.00296, or 0.00148 is added to 0.21314, giving 0.21462″ as the taper of a piece 1 inch in length and of an included angle of $12\frac{1}{4}$ degree. The taper per foot equals 0.21362″ × 12 = 2.5634″.

TABLE FOR DIMENSIONING DOVETAIL SLIDES AND GIBS

The table on page 365 is figured for machine-tool work, so as to enable one to tell at a glance the amount to be added or subtracted in dimensioning dovetail slides and their gibs, for the usual angles up to 60 degrees. The column for 45-degree dovetails is omitted, as A and B would, of course, be alike for this angle.

In the application of the table, assuming a base with even dimensions, as in the sketch Fig. 7, to obtain the dimensions x and y of the slide Fig. 8, allowing for the gib which may be assumed to be $\frac{1}{4}$ inch thick, the perpendicular depth of the dovetail being $\frac{5}{8}$ inch, and the angle 60 degrees, look under column A for $\frac{5}{8}$ inch and it will be found opposite this that B is 0.360 inch, which subtracted from 2 inches gives 1.640 inches, the dimension x. To find y first get the dimension 1.640 inches, then under the column for 60-degree gibs (where C is $\frac{1}{4}$ inch), D is found to be 0.289 inch, which is added to 1.640, giving 1.929 inches.

In practice this dimension is usually made a little larger, say to the nearest 64th, to allow for fitting the gib.

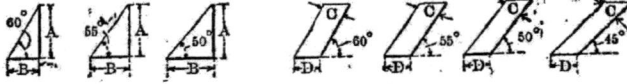

TABLE FOR DIMENSIONING DOVETAIL SLIDES AND GIBS

A	B	B	B	C	D	D	D	D
$\frac{1}{32}$″	.018″	.022″	.027″	$\frac{1}{8}$″	.144″	.152″	.163″	.176″
$\frac{1}{16}$″	.036″	.044″	.053″	$\frac{3}{16}$″	.216″	.228″	.244″	.264″
$\frac{1}{8}$″	.072″	.087″	.105″	$\frac{1}{4}$″	.289″	.305″	.326″	.353″
$\frac{1}{4}$″	.144″	.175″	.210″	$\frac{5}{16}$″	.361″	.381″	.407″	.442″
$\frac{3}{8}$″	.216″	.262″	.314″	$\frac{3}{8}$″	.433″	.457″	.489″	.530″
$\frac{1}{2}$″	.288″	.350″	.420″	$\frac{1}{2}$″	.577″	.610″	.652″	.707″
$\frac{5}{8}$″	.360″	.437″	.525″	$\frac{5}{8}$″	.721″	.762″	.815″	.883″
$\frac{3}{4}$″	.433″	.525″	.629″	$\frac{3}{4}$″	.866″	.915″	.979″	1.060″
$\frac{7}{8}$″	.505″	.612″	.734″	$\frac{7}{8}$″	1.010″	1.067″	1.142″	1.237″
1″	.577″	.700″	.839″	1″	1.154″	1.220″	1.305″	1.414″
$1\frac{1}{8}$″	.649″	.787″	.944″					
$1\frac{1}{4}$″	.721″	.875″	1.049″					
$1\frac{3}{8}$″	.794″	.962″	1.153″					
$1\frac{1}{2}$″	.866″	1.050″	1.259″					
$1\frac{3}{4}$″	1.010″	1.225″	1.469″					
2″	1.154″	1.400″	1.677″					
$2\frac{1}{4}$″	1.298″	1.575″	1.888″					
$2\frac{1}{2}$″	1.442″	1.750″	2.097″					
$2\frac{3}{4}$″	1.588″	1.925″	2.307″					
3″	1.732″	2.100″	2.517″					
$3\frac{1}{2}$″	2.020″	2.450″	2.937″					
4″	2.308″	2.800″	3.356″					
$4\frac{1}{2}$″	2.598″	3.150″	3.776″					
5″	2.885″	3.501″	4.195″					

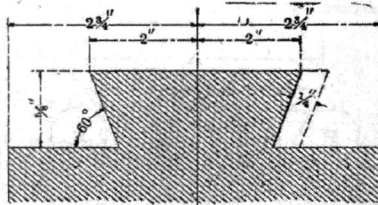

FIG. 7

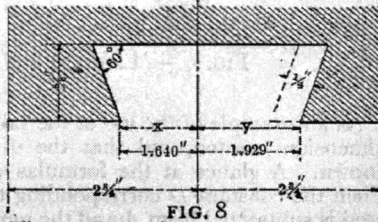

FIG. 8

MEASURING EXTERNAL AND INTERNAL DOVETAILS

THE accompanying table of constants is for use with the plug method of sizing dovetail gages, etc. The constants are calculated for the plugs and angles most in use; and to use them a knowledge of arithmetic is all that is required. The formulas by which they were obtained are added for the convenience of those who may have an unusual angle to make.

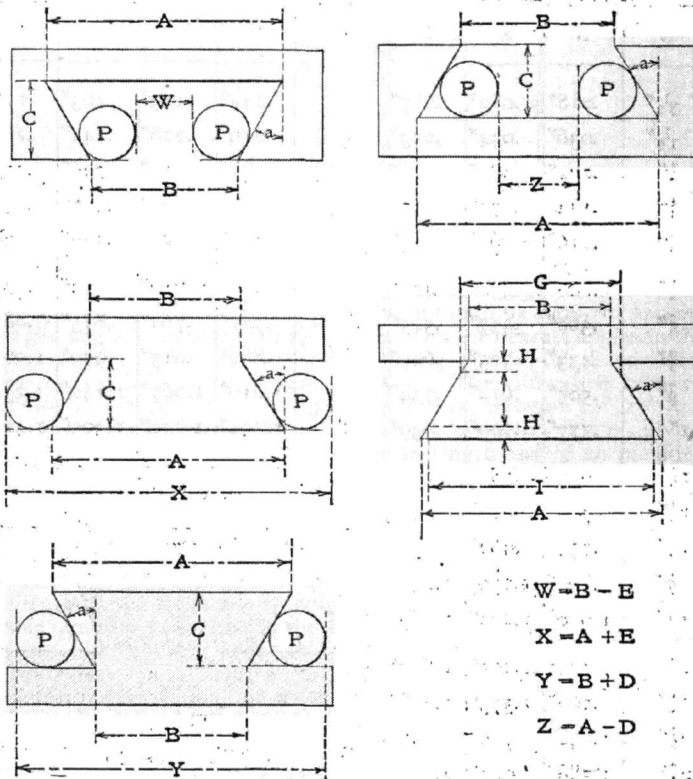

$$W = B - E$$
$$X = A + E$$
$$Y = B + D$$
$$Z = A - D$$

FIG. 9. — External and Internal Dovetails

As an example of the use of the table, suppose that Z, Fig. 9, is the dimension wanted, and that the dimension A and the angle a are known. A glance at the formulas above shows that $Z = A - D$. Then the constant D corresponding to the size of plug and the angle used is subtracted from A and the remainder equals Z. For instance, if $A = 4"$, the plug used $= \frac{3}{8}"$, and the angle $= 30$ degrees, then $Z = A - D = 4" - 1.0245" = 2.9755"$.

If A is not known but B and C are given, according to the formula below the table $A = B + C F$. Then if $B = 3.134''$, $C = \frac{3}{4}''$, and the angle is 30 degrees, as before, $A = B + C F = 3.134'' + (.75'' \times 1.1547) = 4''$, whence Z can be found, as already shown.

If the corners of the dovetail are flat, as shown in Fig. 9 at I and G, and the dimensions I and H and the angles are known, it will be found from the formulas below the table that A also $= I + H F$; so that if $I = 3.8557''$, $H = \frac{1}{8}''$, and the angle = 30 degrees, then $A = I + H F = 3.8557'' + (.125'' \times 1.1547) = 4''$, from which Z is found as before.

CONSTANTS FOR DOVETAILS

Plug		60°	55°	50°	45°	40°	35°	30°
$\frac{1}{4}''$	D	1.1830	1.0429	.9368	.8535	.7861	.7302	.6830
	E	.3170	.3233	.3410	.3536	.3666	.3802	.3943
$\frac{3}{8}''$	D	1.7745	1.5643	1.4053	1.2803	1.1792	1.0954	1.0245
	E	.4755	.4932	.5115	.5303	.5499	.5702	.5915
$\frac{1}{2}''$	D	2.3660	2.0858	1.8730	1.7070	1.5722	1.4604	1.3660
	E	.6340	.6576	.6820	.7072	.7332	.7603	.7886
$\frac{3}{4}''$	D	3.5490	3.1286	2.8106	2.5606	2.3584	2.1903	2.0490
	E	.9510	.9864	1.0230	1.0606	1.0998	1.1404	1.1830
	F	3.4641	2.8563	2.3836	2	1.6782	1.4004	1.1547

$$A = B + CF = I + HF$$

$$B = A - CF = G - HF$$

$$E = P\left(\cot. \frac{90 + a}{2}\right) + P$$

$$D = P\left(\cot. \frac{90 - a}{2}\right) + P$$

$$F = 2 \tan a$$

TOOL FOR LAYING OUT ANGLES ACCURATELY

THE bevel gage here shown is for laying out angles accurately. In using this gage set a vernier caliper or large "micrometer" to twice the sine of half the angle desired, multiplied by ten, add one

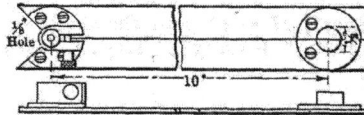

half inch and open the gage till it fits the vernier; this gives the angle within the limits of the measuring tool and the radius of the gage. The eighth-inch hole in the center is for a setting plug when it is desirable to lay out an angle from a given center.

The table gives the measurements over the half disks required for setting the arms of the gage to give any angle from 1 to 45 degrees, and also the setting for any number of holes in a circle from 3 to 22.

TABLE FOR SETTING TOOL FOR LAYING OUT ANGLES

GAGE SETTING FOR EVEN DEGREES

Angle Degrees	Measurement Over Disks	Angle Degrees	Measurement Over Disks	Angle Degrees	Measurement Over Disks	Angle Degrees	Measurement Over Disks
1	0.6746	12	2.5906	23	4.4874	34	6.3474
2	0.8490	13	2.764	24	4.6582	35	6.5142
3	1.0236	14	2.9374	25	4.8288	36	6.6804
4	1.1980	15	3.1106	26	4.9980	37	6.846
5	1.3724	16	3.2834	27	5.1690	38	7.0114
6	1.5468	17	3.4562	28	5.3384	39	7.1762
7	1.7210	18	3.6286	29	5.5176	40	7.3404
8	1.8952	19	3.8010	30	5.6764	41	7.5042
9	2.0692	20	3.9730	31	5.8448	42	7.6674
10	2.2432	21	4.1448	32	6.0128	43	7.830
11	2.4170	22	4.3162	33	6.1804	44	7.9922
						45	8.1536

GAGE SETTINGS FOR HOLES IN A CIRCLE

No. of Holes in Circle	Measurement Over Disks	No. of Holes in Circle	Measurement Over Disks	No. of Holes in Circle	Measurement Over Disks	No. of Holes in Circle	Measurement Over Disks
3	17.8206	8	8.1536	13	5.2864	18	3.9730
4	14.6422	9	7.3404	14	4.9504	19	3.7918
5	12.2558	10	6.6802	15	4.6582	20	3.6286
6	10.5	11	6.1346	16	4.4018	21	3.4808
7	9.1776	12	5.6762	17	4.1750	22	3.3462

SHOP AND DRAWING ROOM STANDARDS

STANDARD JIG PARTS

Drill Bushings

WHEN drilling and reaming operations are to be performed in the same jig, two slip bushings, one for the drill and the other for the reamer, should be used; if the jig is to be used for a large number of parts, the hole for the bushings should in turn be bushed with a steel lining to prevent wearing. The soft cast-iron will wear rapidly if this is not done, and the jig will soon have to be rebored and rebushed.

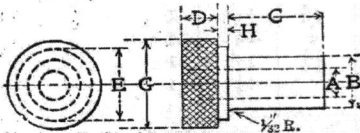

FIG. 1
Loose Bushings

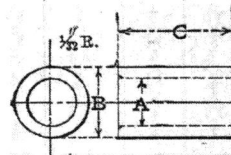

FIG. 2
Fixed Bushings

LOOSE BUSHINGS							FIXED BUSHINGS		
A	B	C	D	E	G	H	A	B	C
No. 52	$\frac{1}{4}$	$\frac{9}{16}$	$\frac{1}{4}$	$\frac{7}{16}$	$\frac{9}{16}$	$\frac{1}{16}$	52	$\frac{1}{4}$	$\frac{9}{16}$
No. 30	$\frac{5}{16}$	$\frac{5}{8}$	$\frac{5}{16}$	$\frac{1}{2}$	$\frac{5}{8}$	$\frac{1}{16}$	30	$\frac{5}{16}$	$\frac{9}{16}$
No. 12	$\frac{3}{8}$	$\frac{5}{8}$	$\frac{5}{16}$	$\frac{9}{16}$	$\frac{11}{16}$	$\frac{1}{16}$	12	$\frac{3}{8}$	$\frac{9}{16}$
$\frac{1}{4}$	$\frac{1}{2}$	$\frac{11}{16}$	$\frac{3}{8}$	$\frac{11}{16}$	$\frac{13}{16}$	$\frac{1}{16}$	$\frac{1}{4}$	$\frac{1}{2}$	$\frac{11}{16}$
$\frac{5}{16}$	$\frac{9}{16}$	$\frac{3}{4}$	$\frac{7}{16}$	$\frac{5}{16}$	$\frac{15}{16}$	$\frac{1}{16}$	$\frac{5}{16}$	$\frac{9}{16}$	$\frac{3}{4}$
$\frac{3}{8}$	$\frac{5}{8}$	$\frac{13}{16}$	$\frac{3}{8}$	$\frac{13}{16}$	$\frac{15}{16}$	$\frac{1}{16}$	$\frac{3}{8}$	$\frac{5}{8}$	$\frac{13}{16}$
$\frac{7}{16}$	$\frac{11}{16}$	$\frac{13}{16}$	$\frac{7}{8}$	$\frac{7}{8}$	1	$\frac{1}{16}$	$\frac{7}{16}$	$\frac{11}{16}$	$\frac{11}{16}$
$\frac{3}{4}$	$\frac{3}{4}$	$\frac{7}{8}$	$\frac{7}{16}$	$\frac{15}{16}$	$1\frac{1}{16}$	$\frac{1}{16}$	$\frac{3}{4}$	$\frac{3}{4}$	$\frac{11}{16}$
$\frac{9}{16}$	$\frac{13}{16}$	$\frac{7}{8}$	$\frac{7}{16}$	1	$1\frac{1}{8}$	$\frac{1}{16}$	$\frac{9}{16}$	$\frac{13}{16}$	$\frac{3}{4}$
$\frac{5}{8}$	$\frac{7}{8}$	$\frac{15}{16}$	$\frac{1}{2}$	$1\frac{1}{16}$	$1\frac{3}{16}$	$\frac{1}{16}$	$\frac{5}{8}$	$\frac{7}{8}$	$\frac{3}{4}$
$\frac{11}{16}$	$\frac{15}{16}$	1	$\frac{9}{16}$	$1\frac{1}{8}$	$1\frac{1}{4}$	$\frac{1}{16}$	$\frac{11}{16}$	$\frac{15}{16}$	$1\frac{13}{16}$
$\frac{3}{4}$	$1\frac{1}{16}$	1	$\frac{9}{16}$	$1\frac{1}{4}$	$1\frac{1}{16}$	$\frac{1}{16}$	$\frac{3}{4}$	1	$\frac{7}{8}$
$\frac{13}{16}$	$1\frac{1}{8}$	$1\frac{1}{16}$	$\frac{9}{16}$	$1\frac{5}{16}$	$1\frac{1}{2}$	$\frac{1}{16}$	$\frac{13}{16}$	$1\frac{1}{16}$	$\frac{7}{8}$
$\frac{7}{8}$	$1\frac{1}{4}$	$1\frac{1}{8}$	$\frac{5}{8}$	$1\frac{7}{16}$	$1\frac{3}{8}$	$\frac{1}{16}$	$\frac{7}{8}$	$1\frac{1}{8}$	$1\frac{15}{16}$
$\frac{15}{16}$	$1\frac{5}{16}$	$1\frac{3}{16}$	$\frac{5}{8}$	$1\frac{1}{2}$	$1\frac{11}{16}$	$\frac{1}{16}$	$\frac{15}{16}$	$1\frac{1}{16}$	1
1	$1\frac{3}{8}$	$1\frac{1}{4}$	$\frac{11}{16}$	$1\frac{9}{16}$	$1\frac{3}{4}$	$\frac{1}{16}$	1	$1\frac{1}{4}$	1

Three different styles of bushings with their dimensions are shown in Figs. 1, 2 and 3. These can be blanked out in quantities and finished to required sizes as needed, and should be made of tool steel. Allowances should be made in the blanks for grinding and

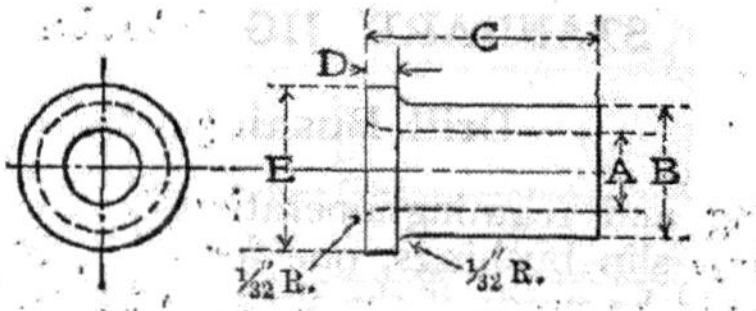

A	B	C	D	E	A	B	C	D	E
$\frac{1}{4}$	$\frac{7}{16}$	$\frac{9}{16}$	$\frac{3}{32}$	$\frac{15}{16}$	$\frac{11}{16}$	$1\frac{1}{16}$	$1\frac{1}{16}$	$\frac{1}{8}$	$1\frac{1}{8}$
$\frac{5}{16}$	$\frac{1}{2}$	$\frac{3}{4}$	$\frac{3}{32}$	$\frac{5}{8}$	1	$1\frac{1}{16}$	$1\frac{1}{8}$	$\frac{1}{8}$	$1\frac{3}{16}$
$\frac{3}{8}$	$\frac{9}{16}$	$\frac{13}{16}$	$\frac{3}{32}$	$\frac{11}{16}$	$1\frac{1}{8}$	$1\frac{1}{16}$	$1\frac{3}{16}$	$\frac{1}{8}$	$1\frac{1}{4}$
$\frac{7}{16}$	$\frac{5}{8}$	$\frac{7}{8}$	$\frac{3}{32}$	$\frac{3}{4}$	$1\frac{1}{4}$	$1\frac{1}{8}$	$1\frac{1}{4}$	$\frac{3}{32}$	$1\frac{5}{16}$
$\frac{1}{2}$	$\frac{11}{16}$	$\frac{7}{8}$	$\frac{3}{32}$	$\frac{13}{16}$	$1\frac{1}{4}$	$1\frac{3}{16}$	$1\frac{5}{16}$	$\frac{3}{32}$	$1\frac{3}{8}$
$\frac{9}{16}$	$\frac{3}{4}$	$\frac{15}{16}$	$\frac{1}{8}$	$\frac{15}{16}$	1	$1\frac{1}{4}$	$1\frac{5}{16}$	$\frac{3}{32}$	$1\frac{7}{16}$
$\frac{5}{8}$	$\frac{7}{8}$	1	$\frac{1}{8}$	$1\frac{1}{16}$					

FIG. 3. — Fixed Bushings

lapping after hardening. Fig. 1 shows a slip bushing; Fig. 2 a stationary bushing, and Fig. 3 a stationary bushing where tools with stop collars are to be used. Such bushings as shown in Figs. 2 and 3 are also used for linings for slip bushings.

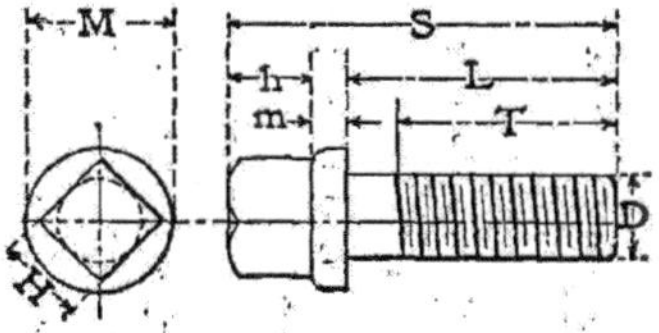

FIG. 4
Collar-Head Jig Screws.

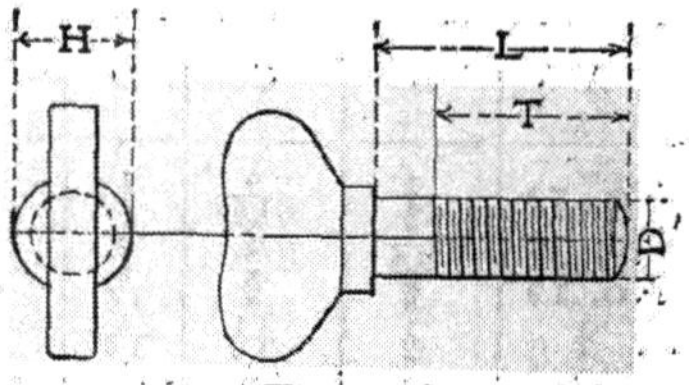

FIG. 5
Winged Jig Screws

D	Thrd.	L	T	h	m	H	M	S	D	Thrd.	H	L	T
$\frac{1}{4}$	20	1	$\frac{3}{4}$	$\frac{1}{4}$	$\frac{3}{32}$	$\frac{1}{4}$	$\frac{7}{16}$	$1\frac{1}{2}$	$\frac{1}{4}$	20	$\frac{3}{8}$	1	$\frac{3}{4}$
$\frac{5}{16}$	18	1	$\frac{3}{4}$	$\frac{5}{16}$	$\frac{1}{8}$	$\frac{5}{16}$	$\frac{1}{2}$	$1\frac{7}{16}$	$\frac{5}{16}$	18	$\frac{7}{16}$	1	$\frac{3}{4}$
$\frac{3}{8}$	16	$1\frac{1}{2}$	1	$\frac{3}{8}$	$\frac{1}{8}$	$\frac{3}{8}$	$\frac{3}{8}$	2	$\frac{3}{8}$	16	$\frac{1}{2}$	$1\frac{1}{2}$	1
$\frac{7}{16}$	14	2	$1\frac{1}{2}$	$\frac{7}{16}$	$\frac{5}{16}$	$\frac{7}{16}$	$1\frac{1}{2}$	$2\frac{5}{8}$					
$\frac{1}{2}$	13	2	$1\frac{1}{2}$	$\frac{1}{2}$	$\frac{3}{16}$	$\frac{1}{2}$	$\frac{9}{16}$	$2\frac{11}{16}$					

Binding Screws

Binding-screws should be made in various sizes and with threads to conform to the standard taps with which the shop is provided. When drills of a very large size are used, a screw with a square or hexagon head is best, as the work requires firm clamping. If the drills used are small, a winged screw will be sufficient and more convenient, as it will require less time to manipulate. Some good screws for clamping straps are shown in Figs. 4 and 5. Of course the screws can be made of any length desired.

When the work is to be held against the seat or a stop by means of a set-screw, such screws as shown in Figs. 6 and 7 will be found very useful. If, however, the work is very light, a wing screw can be used.

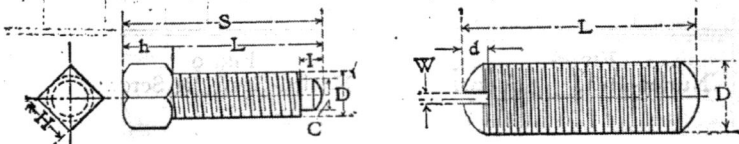

D	Thrd.	L	h	I	C	H	S	D	Thrd.	L	W	d
$\frac{1}{4}$	20	1	$\frac{1}{4}$	$\frac{1}{4}$	$\frac{5}{32}$	$\frac{1}{4}$	$1\frac{1}{4}$	$\frac{1}{4}$	20	$\frac{3}{4}$	.040	$\frac{3}{32}$
$\frac{5}{16}$	18	1	$\frac{5}{16}$	$\frac{5}{16}$	$\frac{13}{64}$	$\frac{5}{16}$	$1\frac{5}{16}$	$\frac{5}{16}$	18	1	.057	$\frac{3}{32}$
$\frac{3}{8}$	16	$1\frac{1}{2}$	$\frac{3}{8}$	$\frac{3}{8}$	$\frac{5}{64}$	$\frac{3}{8}$	$1\frac{3}{8}$	$\frac{3}{8}$	16	1	$\frac{1}{16}$	$\frac{1}{8}$
$\frac{7}{16}$	14	$1\frac{1}{2}$	$\frac{7}{16}$	$\frac{7}{16}$	$\frac{11}{16}$	$\frac{7}{16}$	$1\frac{15}{16}$	$\frac{7}{16}$	14	$1\frac{1}{2}$	$\frac{5}{64}$	$\frac{1}{8}$
$\frac{1}{2}$	13	$1\frac{1}{2}$	$\frac{1}{2}$	$\frac{3}{16}$	$\frac{11}{32}$	$\frac{1}{2}$	2	$\frac{1}{2}$	13	$1\frac{1}{2}$	$\frac{5}{64}$	$\frac{1}{8}$

Fig. 6	Fig. 7
Square-Head Jig Screws	Headless Jig Screws

Supporting Screws

Figs. 8 and 9 show screws that are useful in supporting work against the thrust of drills when the work is of such a nature that it cannot be supported otherwise.

Locking Screws

A convenient hinge-cover locking screw is shown in Fig. 10. This screw, when used, should be adjusted so that only a quarter turn will be needed to clamp or release the cover, which should be slotted to admit the head of the screw.

The different sizes of the styles of screws shown are not only used with drilling jigs, but are equally useful with other jigs and fixtures. These screws should be made of screw stock and case-hardened.

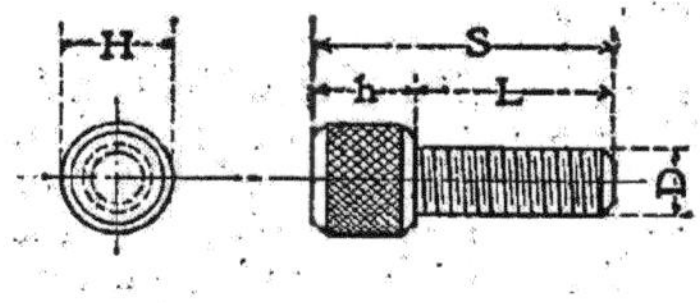

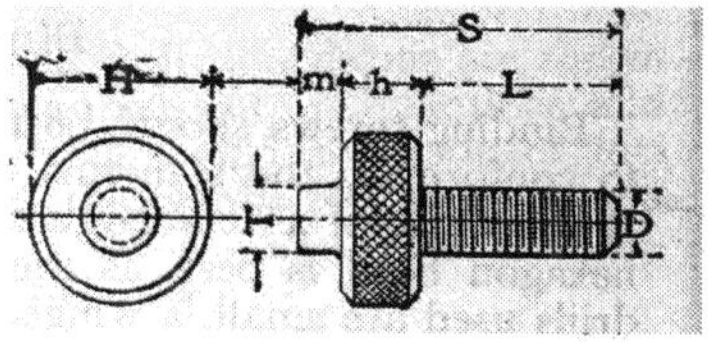

D	Thrd.	L	h	S	H	D	Thrd.	L	h	m	S	H	T
$\frac{1}{4}$	20	$\frac{3}{4}$	$\frac{3}{8}$	$1\frac{1}{8}$	$\frac{1}{2}$	$\frac{1}{4}$	20	$\frac{3}{4}$	$\frac{5}{16}$	$\frac{3}{16}$	$1\frac{1}{4}$	$\frac{3}{8}$	$\frac{1}{4}$
$\frac{5}{16}$	18	1	$\frac{1}{2}$	$1\frac{1}{2}$	$\frac{9}{16}$	$\frac{5}{16}$	18	1	$\frac{3}{8}$	$\frac{7}{32}$	$1\frac{19}{32}$	$\frac{7}{16}$	$\frac{5}{16}$
$\frac{3}{8}$	16	1	$\frac{9}{16}$	$1\frac{9}{16}$	$\frac{5}{8}$	$\frac{3}{8}$	16	1	$\frac{7}{16}$	$\frac{1}{4}$	$1\frac{11}{16}$	1	$\frac{3}{8}$

Fig. 8
Nurled-Head Jig Screws

Fig. 9
Nurled-Head Jig Screws

Strap Dimensions

A convenient strap to use with these jigs is shown in Fig. 11. The straps should be made of bessemer steel and case-hardened after finishing. The slot G can be located in the proper position and made of such dimensions as to allow the strap to be slipped back out of the way when work is being placed in and taken from the jig.

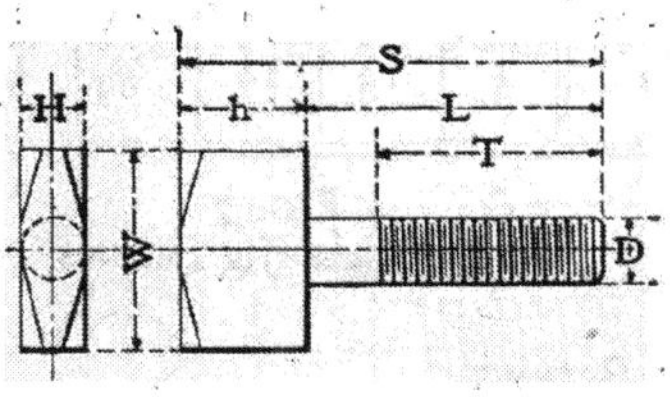

Fig. 10. — Locking Jig Screws

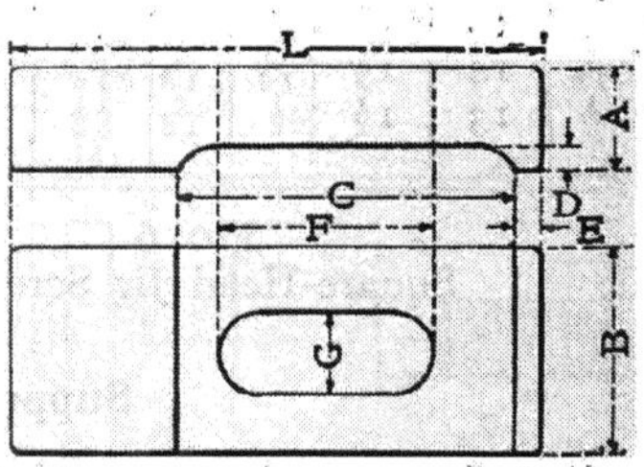

Fig. 11. — Jig Straps

D	Thrd.	H	h	L	S	T	W	A	B	C	D	E	L
$\frac{3}{16}$	18	$\frac{5}{16}$	$\frac{5}{8}$	$1\frac{1}{2}$	$2\frac{1}{8}$	$1\frac{1}{8}$	$1\frac{1}{16}$	$\frac{1}{2}$	1	$1\frac{5}{8}$	$\frac{1}{8}$	$\frac{1}{8}$	$2\frac{1}{2}$
$\frac{1}{4}$	16	$\frac{3}{8}$	$1\frac{1}{16}$	$1\frac{5}{8}$	$2\frac{5}{16}$	$1\frac{1}{8}$	$1\frac{3}{16}$	$\frac{1}{2}$	1	$1\frac{5}{8}$	$\frac{1}{4}$	$\frac{3}{16}$	3
$\frac{5}{16}$	14	$\frac{7}{16}$	$\frac{3}{4}$	$1\frac{3}{4}$	$2\frac{5}{8}$	$1\frac{1}{4}$	$1\frac{5}{16}$		$1\frac{1}{4}$	2	$\frac{3}{8}$	$\frac{5}{16}$	$3\frac{1}{2}$
$\frac{1}{2}$	13	$\frac{1}{2}$	$\frac{7}{8}$	$1\frac{7}{8}$	$2\frac{7}{8}$	$1\frac{1}{4}$	$1\frac{5}{16}$		$1\frac{1}{4}$	2	$\frac{1}{4}$	$\frac{3}{16}$	$3\frac{1}{2}$
									$1\frac{1}{4}$	2		$\frac{5}{16}$	4

HAND WHEELS. (Pratt & Whitney Co.)

Section x-x

Section y-y

A	B	C	D	E	F	G	H	J	K	L	M	O	P	Tap	Spline	Handle No.	No. of Arms
3 in.														5/16 — 28	3/32 × 3/32	00	3
4														5/16 — 28	3/32 × 3/32	0	3
4½														3/8 — 24	3/64 × 3/32	1	3
5														3/8 — 24		1	3
6														3/8 — 24		2	3
7														3/8 — 24		3	3
8														3/8 — 24		4	3
9														3/8 — 24		4	3
10														7/16 — 20		5	3
11														7/16 — 20		5	3
12														1/2 — 16		6	3

HANDLES FOR HAND-WHEELS

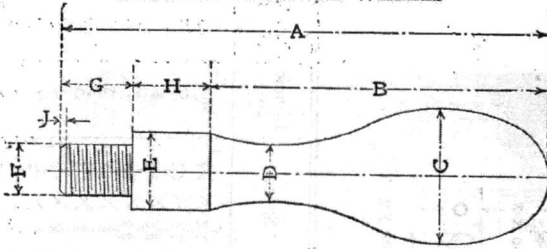

No.	A	B	C	D	E	F	G	H	J	P. I.
∞	$1\frac{15}{16}$	$1\frac{5}{16}$	$\frac{17}{32}$	$\frac{1}{4}$	$\frac{3}{8}$	$\frac{5}{16}$	$\frac{3}{8}$	$\frac{1}{4}$	$\frac{1}{32}$	28
0	$2\frac{11}{16}$	$1\frac{15}{16}$	$\frac{11}{16}$	$\frac{11}{32}$	$\frac{15}{16}$	$\frac{5}{16}$	$\frac{3}{8}$	$\frac{3}{8}$	$\frac{1}{32}$	28
1	$2\frac{15}{16}$	2	$\frac{15}{16}$	$\frac{13}{32}$	$\frac{15}{32}$	$\frac{9}{32}$	$\frac{3}{8}$	$\frac{9}{16}$	$\frac{1}{32}$	24
2	$3\frac{7}{16}$	$2\frac{3}{8}$	1	$\frac{7}{16}$	$\frac{1}{2}$	$\frac{3}{8}$	$\frac{1}{2}$	$\frac{9}{16}$	$\frac{1}{32}$	24
3	$3\frac{15}{16}$	$2\frac{15}{16}$	$1\frac{1}{8}$	$\frac{15}{32}$	$\frac{19}{32}$	$\frac{3}{8}$	$\frac{1}{2}$	$\frac{5}{8}$	$\frac{3}{32}$	24
4	$4\frac{1}{4}$	$3\frac{3}{8}$	$1\frac{1}{4}$	$\frac{1}{2}$	$\frac{19}{32}$	$\frac{3}{8}$	$\frac{1}{2}$	$\frac{5}{8}$	$\frac{1}{32}$	24
5	$4\frac{3}{4}$	$3\frac{7}{16}$	$1\frac{5}{16}$	$\frac{15}{16}$	$\frac{23}{32}$	$\frac{7}{16}$	$\frac{1}{2}$	$\frac{13}{16}$	$\frac{1}{32}$	20
6	$5\frac{3}{16}$	$3\frac{5}{8}$	$1\frac{7}{16}$	$\frac{5}{8}$			$\frac{11}{16}$	$\frac{7}{8}$	$\frac{1}{32}$	16

KNOBS

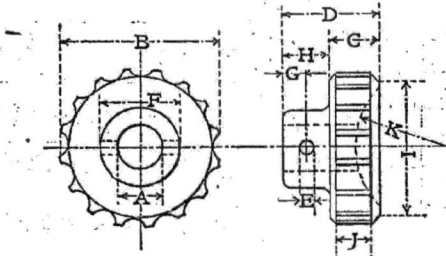

A	B	C	D	E	F	G	H	I	J	K
$\frac{3}{16}$	1	$\frac{3}{16}$	$\frac{15}{32}$	$\frac{3}{32}$	$\frac{7}{16}$	$\frac{1}{8}$	$\frac{1}{4}$	$1\frac{5}{16}$	$\frac{5}{32}$	
$\frac{1}{4}$	$1\frac{1}{16}$	$\frac{5}{16}$	$\frac{11}{16}$	$\frac{5}{32}$	$\frac{9}{16}$	$\frac{3}{8}$	$\frac{3}{8}$	$1\frac{1}{16}$	$\frac{1}{4}$	
$\frac{5}{16}$	$1\frac{1}{16}$	$\frac{3}{8}$	$\frac{13}{16}$	$\frac{3}{16}$	$\frac{5}{8}$	$\frac{3}{8}$	$\frac{3}{8}$	$1\frac{1}{16}$	$\frac{1}{4}$	
$1\frac{5}{16}$	$1\frac{1}{16}$	$\frac{1}{2}$	$\frac{15}{16}$	$\frac{1}{4}$	$\frac{11}{16}$	$\frac{7}{16}$	$\frac{7}{16}$	$1\frac{3}{8}$	$\frac{3}{8}$	
$\frac{3}{8}$	$1\frac{1}{2}$	$\frac{7}{16}$	$\frac{7}{8}$	$\frac{1}{4}$	$\frac{11}{16}$	$\frac{7}{32}$	$\frac{7}{16}$	$1\frac{3}{8}$	$\frac{3}{8}$	
$\frac{7}{16}$	$1\frac{1}{2}$	$\frac{7}{16}$	$\frac{7}{8}$	$\frac{1}{4}$	$\frac{11}{16}$	$\frac{7}{32}$	$\frac{7}{16}$	$1\frac{3}{8}$	$\frac{3}{8}$	
$\frac{1}{2}$	$1\frac{3}{4}$	$\frac{9}{16}$	$1\frac{1}{16}$	$\frac{5}{16}$	$\frac{3}{4}$	$\frac{1}{2}$	$\frac{1}{2}$	$1\frac{5}{8}$	$\frac{7}{16}$	
$\frac{9}{16}$	$1\frac{3}{4}$	$\frac{9}{16}$	$1\frac{1}{16}$	$\frac{5}{16}$	$\frac{3}{4}$	$\frac{1}{2}$	$\frac{1}{2}$	$1\frac{5}{8}$	$\frac{7}{16}$	
$\frac{5}{8}$	$2\frac{1}{4}$	$\frac{11}{16}$	$1\frac{1}{4}$	$\frac{3}{16}$	$1\frac{1}{16}$	$\frac{9}{32}$	$\frac{9}{16}$	$2\frac{1}{16}$	$\frac{5}{8}$	
$1\frac{1}{16}$	$2\frac{1}{4}$	$\frac{11}{16}$	$1\frac{1}{4}$	$\frac{3}{16}$	$1\frac{1}{16}$	$\frac{9}{32}$	$\frac{9}{16}$	$2\frac{1}{16}$	$\frac{5}{8}$	
$\frac{3}{4}$	$2\frac{1}{4}$	$\frac{11}{16}$	$1\frac{1}{4}$	$\frac{3}{16}$	$1\frac{1}{16}$	$\frac{9}{32}$	$\frac{9}{16}$	$2\frac{1}{16}$	$\frac{5}{8}$	Cup Out to Suit

BALL HANDLES
(Pratt & Whitney Co.)

Center Ball

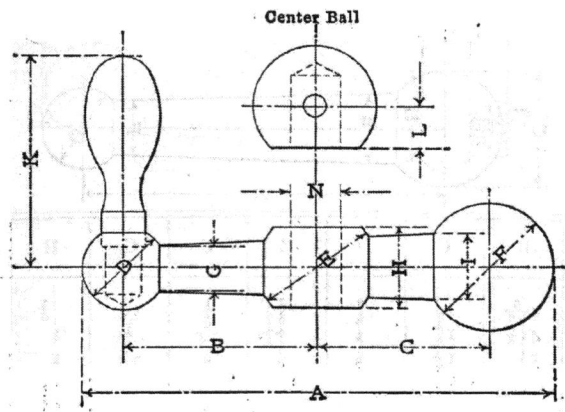

A	B	C	D	E	F	G	H	I	K	L	N
3	$1\frac{3}{16}$	1	$\frac{5}{8}$	$\frac{7}{8}$	1	$\frac{9}{16}$	$\frac{1}{2}$	$1\frac{7}{8}$	$1\frac{7}{8}$	$\frac{9}{32}$	$\frac{5}{8}$
4	$1\frac{9}{32}$	$1\frac{1}{16}$	$1\frac{1}{16}$	1	$1\frac{1}{8}$	$\frac{5}{8}$	$\frac{11}{16}$	$\frac{9}{16}$	$1\frac{15}{16}$	$\frac{5}{32}$	$\frac{7}{16}$
$4\frac{1}{2}$	$1\frac{1}{4}$	$1\frac{1}{8}$	$\frac{3}{4}$	$1\frac{1}{16}$	$1\frac{1}{4}$	$\frac{7}{16}$	$\frac{3}{4}$	$\frac{5}{8}$	$2\frac{1}{2}$	$\frac{3}{8}$	$\frac{1}{2}$
5	$2\frac{1}{16}$	$1\frac{13}{16}$	$\frac{7}{8}$	$1\frac{3}{16}$	$1\frac{3}{8}$	$\frac{1}{2}$	$\frac{13}{16}$	$\frac{11}{16}$	$2\frac{11}{16}$	$\frac{13}{32}$	$\frac{9}{16}$
$5\frac{1}{2}$	$2\frac{9}{32}$	$2\frac{1}{32}$	$1\frac{15}{16}$	$1\frac{1}{4}$	$1\frac{7}{16}$	$\frac{1}{2}$	$\frac{7}{8}$	$\frac{3}{4}$	$2\frac{1}{4}$	$\frac{7}{16}$	$\frac{9}{16}$
6	$2\frac{1}{2}$	$2\frac{7}{32}$	1	$1\frac{5}{16}$	$1\frac{9}{16}$	$\frac{1}{2}$	$\frac{15}{16}$	$\frac{3}{4}$	$3\frac{1}{8}$	$\frac{15}{32}$	$\frac{9}{16}$
7	$2\frac{21}{32}$	$2\frac{21}{32}$	$1\frac{1}{16}$	$1\frac{7}{16}$	$1\frac{11}{16}$	$\frac{9}{16}$	1	$\frac{13}{16}$	$3\frac{11}{16}$	$\frac{1}{2}$	$\frac{5}{8}$
8	$3\frac{1}{16}$	$3\frac{3}{32}$	$1\frac{1}{8}$	$1\frac{1}{2}$	$1\frac{13}{16}$	$\frac{9}{16}$	$1\frac{1}{16}$	$\frac{7}{8}$	$3\frac{3}{8}$	$\frac{17}{32}$	$\frac{5}{8}$

BINDER HANDLES

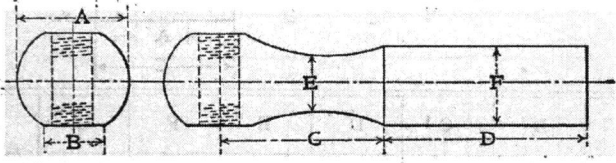

A	B		C		D		E		F		Dia. of Tap	
1	$\frac{3}{4}$		$1\frac{5}{8}$		$1\frac{5}{8}$		$\frac{7}{16}$		$\frac{3}{4}$		$\frac{7}{16}$	
$1\frac{1}{16}$	$1\frac{13}{16}$		$1\frac{3}{4}$		2		$\frac{1}{2}$		$1\frac{13}{16}$		$\frac{9}{16} - \frac{1}{2}$	
$1\frac{1}{2}$	$\frac{7}{8}$	$1\frac{1}{8}$	$2\frac{1}{8}$	$2\frac{3}{8}$	$2\frac{3}{8}$		$\frac{9}{16}$		$1\frac{1}{16}$		$\frac{1}{2} - \frac{1}{2}$	
	$1\frac{1}{2}$		$2\frac{5}{8}$		$2\frac{3}{4}$		$\frac{5}{8}$		$1\frac{1}{16}$		$\frac{5}{8} - \frac{11}{16}$	

SINGLE END BALL HANDLES. (Walcott & Wood)

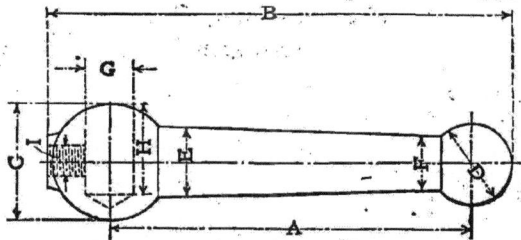

A	B	C	D	E	F	G	H	I
$3\frac{5}{16}$	$4\frac{5}{16}$	$1\frac{1}{8}$	$\frac{3}{4}$	$\frac{11}{16}$	$\frac{7}{8}$	$1\frac{5}{16}$	$\frac{7}{8}$	$\frac{5}{16}$
$3\frac{5}{8}$	$4\frac{11}{16}$	$1\frac{1}{8}$	$\frac{7}{8}$	$\frac{13}{16}$	$\frac{15}{16}$	$1\frac{9}{16}$	1	$\frac{15}{16}$
$4\frac{1}{8}$	$5\frac{1}{4}$	$1\frac{3}{8}$	1	$\frac{7}{8}$	$\frac{5}{8}$	$1\frac{9}{16}$	1	$\frac{3}{8}$
$4\frac{11}{16}$	$6\frac{1}{16}$	$1\frac{5}{8}$	1	1	$\frac{11}{16}$	$1\frac{5}{8}$	$1\frac{1}{8}$	$\frac{3}{8}$
$5\frac{5}{8}$	$6\frac{13}{16}$	$1\frac{3}{4}$	$1\frac{1}{8}$	1	$\frac{11}{16}$	$1\frac{11}{16}$	$1\frac{1}{8}$	$\frac{3}{8}$
$6\frac{1}{8}$	$7\frac{1}{16}$	2	$1\frac{7}{16}$	$1\frac{1}{8}$	$\frac{3}{4}$	$1\frac{3}{4}$	$1\frac{1}{2}$	$\frac{5}{16}$
$6\frac{5}{8}$	$7\frac{5}{16}$	2	$1\frac{1}{2}$	$1\frac{13}{16}$	$\frac{3}{4}$	$1\frac{3}{4}$	$1\frac{1}{2}$	$\frac{5}{16}$
8	$9\frac{1}{16}$	$2\frac{1}{4}$	$1\frac{5}{8}$	$1\frac{5}{8}$	$\frac{7}{8}$	$1\frac{3}{4}$	$1\frac{1}{4}$	$\frac{7}{16}$

BALL LEVER HANDLES

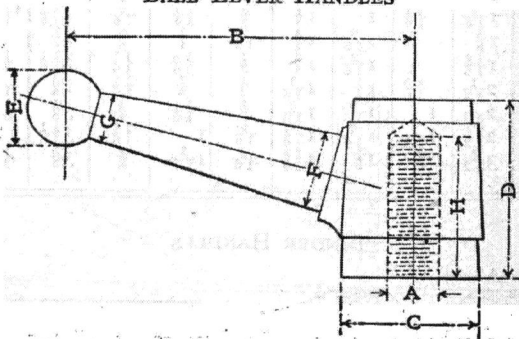

A	B	C	D	E	F	G	H
$\frac{1}{2}$	$2\frac{7}{8}$	1	$1\frac{5}{8}$	$\frac{5}{8}$	$\frac{11}{16}$	$\frac{1}{2}$	$1\frac{5}{8}$
$\frac{1}{2}$	$3\frac{15}{16}$	$1\frac{1}{8}$	$1\frac{5}{8}$	$\frac{11}{16}$	$\frac{3}{4}$	$\frac{9}{16}$	$1\frac{5}{8}$
$\frac{5}{8}$	$4\frac{3}{8}$	$1\frac{3}{16}$	$1\frac{13}{16}$	$\frac{3}{4}$	$\frac{7}{8}$	$\frac{5}{8}$	$1\frac{3}{4}$
$\frac{5}{8}$	$5\frac{7}{16}$	$1\frac{5}{16}$	$2\frac{1}{8}$	$\frac{7}{8}$	$\frac{15}{16}$	$\frac{5}{8}$	$1\frac{3}{4}$
$\frac{3}{4}$	$6\frac{1}{2}$	$1\frac{3}{8}$	$2\frac{1}{2}$	1	1	$\frac{5}{8}$	2
$\frac{3}{4}$	$7\frac{15}{16}$	$1\frac{3}{4}$	$2\frac{11}{16}$	1	1	$\frac{5}{8}$	$2\frac{1}{16}$
$\frac{3}{4}$	$8\frac{15}{16}$	$1\frac{1}{4}$	$2\frac{7}{8}$	1	$1\frac{1}{16}$	$\frac{5}{8}$	$2\frac{7}{8}$

WING NUTS

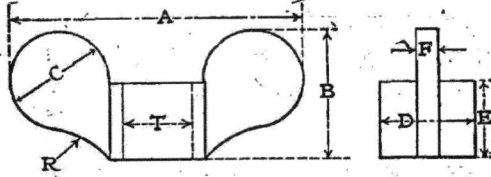

A	B	C	D	E	F	R	T
$\frac{19}{32}$	$1\frac{1}{32}$	$\frac{7}{32}$	$\frac{7}{32}$	$\frac{5}{32}$	$\frac{3}{32}$	$\frac{9}{32}$	$\frac{1}{8}$
$\frac{13}{16}$	$1\frac{5}{32}$	$\frac{5}{16}$	$\frac{1}{4}$	$\frac{1}{4}$	$\frac{1}{8}$	$\frac{3}{32}$	$\frac{5}{32}$
$1\frac{3}{16}$	$\frac{5}{8}$	$\frac{3}{8}$	$\frac{7}{16}$	$\frac{3}{8}$	$\frac{1}{8}$	$\frac{5}{16}$	$\frac{1}{4}$
$1\frac{1}{2}$	$\frac{3}{4}$	$\frac{1}{2}$	$\frac{1}{2}$	$\frac{7}{16}$	$\frac{5}{32}$	$\frac{7}{16}$	$\frac{5}{16}$
$1\frac{5}{8}$	$\frac{13}{16}$	$\frac{9}{16}$	$\frac{1}{2}$	$\frac{1}{2}$	$\frac{5}{32}$	$\frac{7}{16}$	$\frac{3}{8}$
$1\frac{15}{16}$	$\frac{7}{8}$	$\frac{5}{8}$	$\frac{5}{8}$	$\frac{9}{16}$	$\frac{5}{32}$	$\frac{1}{2}$	$\frac{7}{16}$
$2\frac{5}{16}$	$1\frac{1}{16}$	$\frac{3}{4}$	$\frac{3}{4}$	$\frac{11}{16}$	$\frac{5}{32}$	$\frac{3}{4}$	$\frac{1}{2}$

MACHINE HANDLES

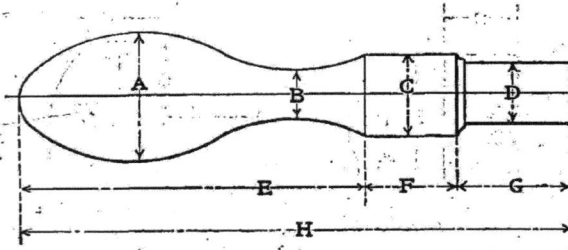

A	B	C	D	E	F	G	H
$\frac{13}{16}$	$\frac{11}{32}$	$\frac{15}{32}$	$\frac{5}{16}$	$1\frac{15}{16}$	$\frac{7}{16}$	$\frac{1}{2}$	$2\frac{7}{8}$
$\frac{15}{16}$	$\frac{13}{32}$	$\frac{15}{32}$	$\frac{5}{16}$	2	$\frac{5}{8}$	$\frac{11}{16}$	$3\frac{5}{8}$
1	$\frac{7}{16}$	$\frac{1}{2}$	$\frac{5}{16}$	$2\frac{3}{8}$	$\frac{5}{8}$	$\frac{3}{4}$	$3\frac{3}{4}$
$1\frac{3}{16}$	$\frac{15}{32}$	$\frac{19}{32}$	$\frac{5}{16}$	$2\frac{13}{16}$	$\frac{11}{16}$	$\frac{13}{16}$	$4\frac{5}{16}$
$1\frac{1}{4}$	$\frac{1}{2}$	$\frac{19}{32}$	$\frac{5}{16}$	$3\frac{3}{8}$	$\frac{3}{4}$	$\frac{13}{16}$	$4\frac{11}{16}$
$1\frac{5}{16}$	$\frac{9}{16}$	$\frac{21}{32}$	$\frac{3}{8}$	$3\frac{1}{16}$	$\frac{7}{8}$	$1\frac{1}{16}$	$5\frac{1}{8}$
$1\frac{7}{16}$	$\frac{5}{8}$	$\frac{3}{4}$	$\frac{7}{16}$	$3\frac{3}{8}$	$\frac{15}{16}$	$1\frac{1}{8}$	$5\frac{11}{16}$

THUMB NUTS

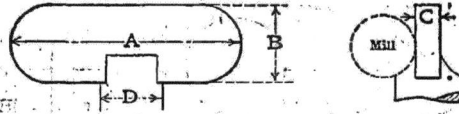

D	A	B	C	Mill
$\frac{3}{16}$	$\frac{7}{8}$	$\frac{1}{4}$	$\frac{3}{32}$	$\frac{5}{16}$
$\frac{1}{4}$	1	$\frac{5}{16}$	$\frac{1}{8}$	$\frac{5}{16}$
$\frac{5}{16}$	$1\frac{1}{4}$	$\frac{3}{8}$	$\frac{5}{32}$	$\frac{7}{16}$
$\frac{3}{8}$	$1\frac{1}{2}$	$\frac{7}{16}$	$\frac{5}{32}$	$\frac{7}{16}$
$\frac{7}{16}$	$1\frac{3}{4}$	$\frac{1}{2}$	$\frac{8}{16}$	$\frac{1}{2}$
$\frac{1}{2}$	2	$\frac{9}{16}$	$\frac{3}{16}$	$\frac{1}{2}$
$\frac{9}{16}$	$2\frac{1}{4}$	$\frac{5}{8}$	$\frac{3}{16}$	$\frac{5}{8}$
$\frac{5}{8}$	$2\frac{1}{2}$	$\frac{11}{16}$	$\frac{7}{32}$	$\frac{5}{8}$

HOOK BOLTS

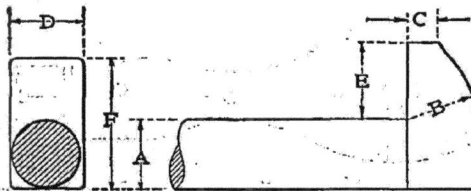

Dia. of Bolt	Thickness of Head	Thickness at End	Width of Head	Off Set of Head	Length of Head
A	B	C	D	E	F
$\frac{3}{8}$	$\frac{7}{16}$	$\frac{3}{16}$	$\frac{3}{8}$	$\frac{7}{16}$	$\frac{13}{16}$
$\frac{1}{2}$	$\frac{9}{16}$	$\frac{1}{4}$	$\frac{1}{2}$	$\frac{9}{16}$	$1\frac{1}{16}$
$\frac{5}{8}$	$\frac{11}{16}$	$\frac{5}{16}$	$\frac{5}{8}$	$\frac{11}{16}$	$1\frac{5}{16}$
$\frac{3}{4}$	$\frac{13}{16}$	$\frac{3}{8}$	$\frac{3}{4}$	$\frac{13}{16}$	$1\frac{9}{16}$
$\frac{7}{8}$	$\frac{15}{16}$	$\frac{7}{16}$	$\frac{7}{8}$	$\frac{15}{16}$	$1\frac{13}{16}$
1	$1\frac{1}{16}$	$\frac{1}{2}$	1	$1\frac{1}{16}$	$2\frac{1}{16}$

COUNTERBORES WITH INSERTED PILOTS

¾ to 1" Counterbores to have 4 Flutes
1" to 1½"   "   "   "   6   "

Diam. A	K	L	M	N	O
3/8	1 7/32	1/4	1 15/32	3/16	From 3/16" to 15/32" in 32nds.
7/16	"	"	"	"	
1/2	1 27/32	3/8	2 7/32	5/16	
9/16	"	"	"	"	From 1/2" to 31/32" in 32nds.
5/8	"	"	"	"	
11/16	"	"	"	"	
3/4	"	"	"	"	
13/16	"	"	"	"	
7/8	"	"	"	"	
15/16	"	"	"	"	
1	"	"	"	"	
1 1/16	2 11/32	1/2	2 27/32	1/2	
1 1/8	"	"	"	"	
1 3/16	"	"	"	"	From 1" to 1 15/32" in 32nds.
1 1/4	"	"	"	"	
1 5/16	"	"	"	"	
1 3/8	"	"	"	"	
1 7/16	"	"	"	"	
1 1/2	"	"	"	"	

Diam. A	B	C	D	E	F	G	H	I	J
3/8	3/16	11/32	5/16	1	1 1/2	3 1/2	3/16	1 1/16	1 1/4
7/16	"	13/32	"	1 1/32	1 9/16	3 11/16	"	1 3/32	"
1/2	"	15/32	"	1 1/16	1 5/8	3 7/8	"	1 1/8	"
9/16	5/16	17/32	1/2	1 1/8	1 11/16	4 1/8	1/4	1 5/32	1 7/8
5/8	"	19/32	"	1 3/16	1 3/4	4 5/16	"	1 3/16	"
11/16	"	21/32	"	1 1/4	1 13/16	4 1/2	"	1 7/32	"
3/4	"	23/32	"	1 5/16	1 7/8	4 11/16	"	1 1/4	"
13/16	"	25/32	"	1 3/8	1 15/16	4 15/16	"	1 9/32	"
7/8	"	27/32	"	1 7/16	2	5 1/8	"	1 5/16	"
15/16	"	29/32	"	1 1/2	2 1/16	5 3/8	"	1 11/32	"
1	"	1 1/32	"	1 9/16	2 1/8	5 5/8	"	1 3/8	"
1 1/16	1/2	1	3/4	1 5/8	2 3/16	5 15/16	5/16	1 13/32	2 3/8
1 1/8	"	1 1/16	"	1 11/16	2 1/4	6	"	1 15/32	"
1 3/16	"	1 1/16	"	1 3/4	2 5/16	6 1/4	"	1 15/32	"
1 1/4	"	1 1/8	"	1 13/16	2 3/8	6 7/16	"	1 1/2	"
1 5/16	"	1 1/8	"	1 7/8	2 7/16	6 5/8	"	1 17/32	"
1 3/8	"	1 1/4	"	1 15/16	2 1/2	6 7/8	"	1 19/32	"
1 7/16	"	1 1/4	"	2	2 9/16	7 1/16	"	1 19/32	"
1 1/2	"	1 3/8	"	2 1/16	2 5/8	7 1/16	"	1 5/8	"

DIMENSIONS OF STANDARD PLUG AND RING GAGES

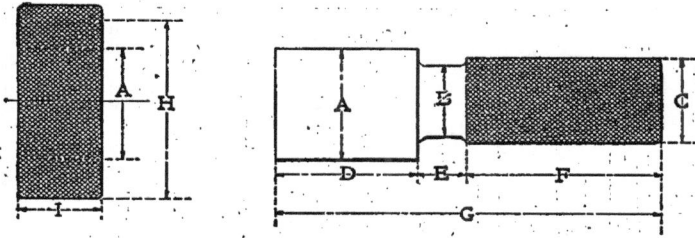

PLUG							RING	
Dia. of Plug	Dia. of Neck	Dia. of Handle	Length of Std. Plug	Length of Neck	Length of Handle	Total Length of Gage	O. S. Dia. of Ring	Thickness of Ring
A	B	C	D	E	F	G	H	I
$\frac{1}{4}$	$\frac{7}{32}$	$\frac{7}{16}$	$\frac{7}{8}$	$\frac{5}{16}$	2	$3\frac{9}{16}$	1	$\frac{1}{2}$
$\frac{5}{16}$	$\frac{9}{32}$	$\frac{7}{16}$	$\frac{15}{16}$	$\frac{5}{16}$	$2\frac{1}{8}$	$3\frac{3}{8}$	$1\frac{1}{16}$	$\frac{9}{16}$
$\frac{3}{8}$	$\frac{5}{16}$	$\frac{1}{2}$	1	$\frac{5}{16}$	$2\frac{1}{4}$	$3\frac{9}{16}$	$1\frac{1}{8}$	$\frac{5}{8}$
$\frac{7}{16}$	$\frac{3}{8}$	$\frac{1}{2}$	$1\frac{1}{16}$	$\frac{5}{16}$	$2\frac{3}{8}$	$3\frac{3}{4}$	$1\frac{3}{16}$	$\frac{5}{8}$
$\frac{1}{2}$	$\frac{7}{16}$	$\frac{9}{16}$	$1\frac{1}{8}$	$\frac{3}{8}$	$2\frac{1}{2}$	4	$1\frac{1}{4}$	$\frac{11}{16}$
$\frac{9}{16}$	$\frac{7}{16}$	$\frac{9}{16}$	$1\frac{3}{16}$	$\frac{3}{8}$	$2\frac{5}{8}$	$4\frac{3}{16}$	$1\frac{5}{16}$	$\frac{11}{16}$
$\frac{5}{8}$	$\frac{1}{2}$	$\frac{9}{16}$	$1\frac{1}{4}$	$\frac{3}{8}$	$2\frac{3}{4}$	$4\frac{3}{8}$	$1\frac{3}{8}$	$\frac{11}{16}$
$\frac{11}{16}$	$\frac{9}{16}$	$\frac{5}{8}$	$1\frac{5}{16}$	$\frac{3}{8}$	$2\frac{7}{8}$	$4\frac{9}{16}$	$1\frac{1}{2}$	$\frac{3}{4}$
$\frac{3}{4}$	$\frac{5}{8}$	$\frac{5}{8}$	$1\frac{3}{8}$	$\frac{7}{16}$	3	$4\frac{3}{4}$	$1\frac{5}{8}$	$\frac{3}{4}$
$\frac{13}{16}$	$\frac{5}{8}$	$\frac{11}{16}$	$1\frac{7}{16}$	$\frac{7}{16}$	$3\frac{1}{8}$	5	$1\frac{3}{4}$	$\frac{13}{16}$
$\frac{7}{8}$	$\frac{11}{16}$	$\frac{3}{4}$	$1\frac{1}{2}$	$\frac{7}{16}$	$3\frac{1}{8}$	$5\frac{1}{16}$	2	$\frac{7}{8}$
$\frac{15}{16}$	$\frac{11}{16}$	$\frac{3}{4}$	$1\frac{9}{16}$	$\frac{7}{16}$	$3\frac{1}{4}$	$5\frac{1}{4}$	2	$\frac{15}{16}$
1	$\frac{3}{4}$	$\frac{7}{8}$	$1\frac{5}{8}$	$\frac{1}{2}$	$3\frac{1}{4}$	$5\frac{3}{8}$	$2\frac{1}{8}$	1
$1\frac{1}{8}$	$\frac{3}{4}$	$\frac{7}{8}$	$1\frac{3}{4}$	$\frac{1}{2}$	$3\frac{1}{4}$	$5\frac{1}{2}$	$2\frac{1}{4}$	1
$1\frac{1}{4}$	$\frac{7}{8}$	1	$1\frac{3}{4}$	$\frac{1}{2}$	$3\frac{3}{8}$	$5\frac{5}{8}$	$2\frac{3}{8}$	$1\frac{1}{8}$
$1\frac{3}{8}$	1	$1\frac{1}{8}$	$1\frac{3}{4}$	$\frac{5}{8}$	$3\frac{1}{2}$	$5\frac{3}{4}$	$2\frac{1}{2}$	$1\frac{1}{8}$
$1\frac{1}{2}$	1	$1\frac{1}{8}$	$1\frac{7}{8}$	$\frac{5}{8}$	$3\frac{1}{2}$	$5\frac{7}{8}$	$2\frac{5}{8}$	$1\frac{1}{4}$
$1\frac{5}{8}$	$1\frac{1}{8}$	$1\frac{1}{4}$	2	$\frac{5}{8}$	$3\frac{1}{2}$	$6\frac{1}{8}$	$2\frac{3}{4}$	$1\frac{1}{4}$
$1\frac{3}{4}$	$1\frac{1}{8}$	$1\frac{1}{4}$	$2\frac{1}{8}$	$\frac{5}{8}$	$3\frac{1}{2}$	$6\frac{1}{8}$	3	$1\frac{1}{2}$
$1\frac{7}{8}$	$1\frac{3}{8}$	$1\frac{3}{8}$	$2\frac{1}{8}$	$\frac{5}{8}$	$3\frac{1}{2}$	$6\frac{1}{8}$	$3\frac{1}{4}$	$1\frac{1}{2}$
2	$1\frac{1}{2}$	$1\frac{3}{8}$	$2\frac{1}{4}$	$\frac{3}{4}$	$3\frac{1}{2}$	$6\frac{3}{8}$	$3\frac{1}{4}$	$1\frac{1}{2}$
$2\frac{1}{4}$	$1\frac{1}{2}$	$1\frac{3}{8}$	$2\frac{1}{4}$	$\frac{3}{4}$	$3\frac{3}{8}$	$6\frac{5}{8}$	$3\frac{3}{8}$	$1\frac{5}{8}$
$2\frac{1}{2}$	$1\frac{5}{8}$	$1\frac{1}{2}$	$2\frac{1}{4}$	$\frac{3}{4}$	$3\frac{3}{8}$	$6\frac{5}{8}$	$3\frac{3}{8}$	$1\frac{5}{8}$
$2\frac{3}{4}$	$1\frac{5}{8}$	$1\frac{1}{2}$	$2\frac{1}{2}$	$\frac{3}{4}$	$3\frac{3}{8}$	$6\frac{3}{4}$	4	$1\frac{5}{8}$
3	$1\frac{7}{8}$	$1\frac{1}{4}$	$2\frac{1}{2}$	$\frac{3}{4}$	$3\frac{3}{8}$	$6\frac{3}{4}$	$4\frac{1}{2}$	$1\frac{3}{4}$

"HB"—"DWF" Radial Bearings—Medium 300 Series
(Hess-Bright Mfg. Co.)

Medium Series

No. of Bearing	Bore A		Diameter B		Width C		Load in Lbs. and Rev. per Minute					Ball Dia.
	mm.	inches	mm.	inches	mm.	inches	200	500	800	1200	1500	
300	10	0.3937	35	1.3780	11	0.4331	220	185	160	140	125	¼
301	12	0.4724	37	1.4567	12	0.4724	265	210	175	155	130	¼
302	15	0.5906	42	1.6536	13	0.5118	285	240	210	175	155	¼
303	17	0.6693	47	1.8504	14	0.5512	395	330	285	240	220	5⁄16
304	20	0.7874	52	2.0473	15	0.5906	440	375	330	285	240	5⁄16
305	25	0.9843	62	2.4410	17	0.6693	660	550	485	395	350	3⁄8
306	30	1.1811	72	2.8347	19	0.7480	880	725	625	530	485	7⁄16
307	35	1.3780	80	3.1496	21	0.8268	1100	925	770	660	615	7⁄16
308	40	1.5748	90	3.5433	23	0.9055	1430	1165	990	835	770	1⁄2
309	45	1.7717	100	3.9370	25	0.9843	1760	1430	1265	1045	970	9⁄16
310	50	1.9685	110	4.3307	27	1.0630	2090	1715	1485	1210	1110	5⁄8
311	55	2.1654	120	4.7244	29	1.1417	2530	2070	1760	1485	1320	11⁄16
312	60	2.3622	130	5.1181	31	1.2205	2970	2420	2090	1705	1540	3⁄4
313	65	2.5591	140	5.5118	33	1.2992	3410	2795	2420	1980	1760	7⁄8
314	70	2.7559	150	5.9055	35	1.3780	3895	3190	2750	2255	2080	15⁄16
315	75	2.9528	160	6.2992	37	1.4567	4400	3630	3080	2530	2245	1
316	80	3.1496	170	6.6929	39	1.5354	4995	4070	3520	2860	2530	1 1⁄16
317	85	3.3465	180	7.0866	41	1.6142	5500	4510	3850	3190	2750	1 1⁄8
318	90	3.5433	190	7.4804	43	1.6929	6160	5015	4290	3520	3025	1 3⁄16
319	95	3.7402	200	7.8741	45	1.7717	6820	5610	4730	3850	3300	1 1⁄4
320	100	3.9370	215	8.4646	47	1.8504	7435	6050	5170	4180	3520	1 5⁄16
321	105	4.1339	225	8.8583	49	1.9291	8140	6600	5610	4510	3850	1 3⁄8
322	110	4.3307	240	9.4489	50	1.9685	9080	7875	6710	5390	4620	1 1⁄2

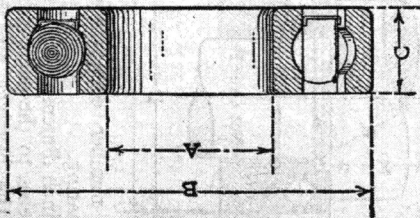

"HB"-"DWF" Thrust Collar Bearings — Medium Weight Series No. 1100
(HESS-BRIGHT MFG. CO.)

Brg. No.	1500	1000	500	300	150	100	50	25	10	Crane Hook Ld.	Weight of Brg. in Lbs.
1102	145	190	245	285	330	395	540	660	1100	1100	.09
1103	185	245	310	365	430	505	660	825	1320	1320	.13
1104	240	320	395	485	550	650	870	1089	1760	1760	.20
1105	295	395	495	585	680	770	1045	1355	2200	2420	.24
1106	330	440	550	660	770	880	1175	1520	2420	3520	.33
1107	440	550	660	880	1085	1285	1725	2245	3300	4400	.51
1108	550	660	770	990	1210	1395	1905	2400	3520	5500	.53
1109	660	770	880	1210	1540	1890	2585	3255	4620	7708	.81
1110	770	880	1100	1430	1760	2110	2880	3650	5060	8800	.88
1111	880	1100	1320	1650	2200	2465	3255	4355	6380	9900	1.25
1112	990	1210	1540	1870	2420	2605	3430	4620	6820	11000	1.28
1113	1210	1430	1760	2200	2640	3235	4235	5720	8360	13200	1.78
1114	1320	1540	1980	2420	3080	3300	4335	6070	8800	15400	1.80
1115	1430	1650	2090	2530	3300	3485	4555	6380	9240	16280	2.00
1116	1540	1760	2420	2640	3740	4180	5455	8790	11000	17600	2.35
1117	1870	2090	2860	3300	4400	4950	6600	9295	13200	22000	3.19
1118	1980	2200	2970	3520	4620	5225	6950	9790	13860	23100	3.74
1119	2200	2530	3520	4180	5280	5995	7905	11255	15400	26400	4.25
1120	2420	2640	3740	4400	5500	6510	8745	11440	16280	29040	4.95
1121	2640	3080	3960	4840	5940	7370	9845	12640	17600	33000	5.50
1123	2860	3520	4840	5500	7040	8635	11605	14830	22000	39600	6.42
1125	3080	4180	5280	6380	8140	10340	13970	17600	24400	46200	7.63
1128	3740	4840	6600	8140	10560	13510	18215	23010	28600	61600	11.46

Load in Lbs. and Rev. per Minute

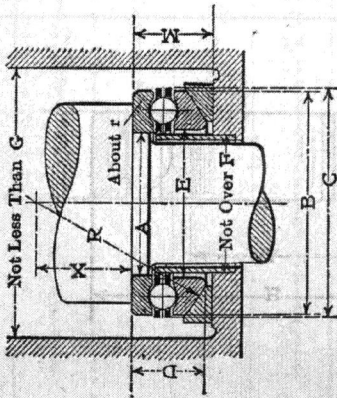

THE number completely identifies each bearing.

The inch dimensions are the nearest equivalents to the even millimeters in which the bearings are made. The metric sizes are retained to insure interchangeability of the American-made "Hess-Bright" bearings with German and French DWF. The loads cited are safe for steady speeds and constant loads.

"HB"–"DWF" Thrust Collar Bearings—Medium Weight Series No. 1100—*Continued*
(HESS-BRIGHT MFG. CO.)

With Ball Cage

Brg. No.	A mm	A in.	B mm	B in.	C mm	C in.	D mm	D in.	E mm	E in.	F in.	G in.	R mm	R in.	r mm	r in.	X mm	X in.	Balls No.	Balls Dia.
1102	10	0.3937	30	1.18	32	1.26	14	0.55	12	0.47	9/16	1 1/4	25	0.98	1	.04	9.9	0.39	8	1/4
1103	15	0.5906	35	1.38	35	1.38	15	0.59	17	0.67	3/4	1 1/2	30	1.18	1	.04	13.4	0.53	10	1/4
1104	20	0.7874	42	1.65	42	1.65	16	0.63	22	0.87	1 1/16	2 3/16	35	1.38	1	.04	16.6	0.65	13	1/4
1105	25	0.9843	47	1.85	47	1.85	17	0.67	27	1.06	1 1/4	2 1/4	35	1.38	1	.04	14.4	0.57	16	1/4
1106	30	1.1811	53	2.09	55	2.17	18	0.71	32	1.26	1 1/4	2 1/8	40	1.57	1	.04	17.8	0.70	18	5/16
1107	35	1.3780	62	2.44	64	2.52	21	0.83	37	1.46	1 1/2	2 15/16	50	1.97	1.5	.06	23.8	0.94	17	5/16
1108	40	1.5748	64	2.52	66	2.60	21	0.83	42	1.65	1 9/16	3 1/16	50	1.97	1.5	.06	22.4	0.88	18	5/16
1109	45	1.7717	73	2.87	75	2.95	25	0.98	47	1.85	1 13/16	3 1/2	60	2.36	1.5	.06	28.5	1.12	17	3/8
1110	50	1.9685	78	3.07	80	3.15	25	0.98	52	2.05	1 13/16	3 9/16	65	2.56	1.5	.06	33	1.30	19	3/8
1111	55	2.1654	88	3.46	90	3.54	28	1.10	57	2.24	2 1/16	4 1/8	70	2.76	1.5	.06	33.8	1.33	18	3/8
1112	60	2.3622	90	3.54	92	3.62	28	1.10	62	2.44	2 1/16	4 1/16	75	2.95	1.5	.06	38.1	1.50	19	7/16
1113	65	2.5951	100	3.94	102	4.02	32	1.26	67	2.64	2 5/16	4 9/16	80	3.15	2	.08	38.5	1.52	18	7/16
1114	70	2.7559	103	4.06	105	4.13	32	1.26	72	2.83	2 5/8	4 11/16	85	3.35	2	.08	42.8	1.69	19	7/16
1115	75	2.9528	110	4.33	110	4.33	32	1.26	77	3.03	2 13/16	4 15/16	90	3.54	2	.08	47.1	1.85	20	7/16
1116	80	3.1406	118	4.53	118	4.65	35	1.38	82	3.23	3	5 5/16	95	3.74	2	.08	48.5	1.91	19	1/2
1117	85	3.3465	125	4.92	132	5.20	38	1.50	88	3.46	3 1/8	5 1/16	105	4.13	2	.08	54.8	2.16	18	1/2
1118	90	3.5433	135	5.32	135	5.32	38	1.50	93	3.66	3 3/8	6	110	4.33	2.5	.10	50.2	2.33	20	1/2
1119	95	3.7402	140	5.51	145	5.71	41	1.61	98	3.86	3 3/8	6 1/4	115	4.53	2.5	.10	60.2	2.37	19	9/16
1120	100	3.9370	150	5.91	150	5.91	41	1.61	103	4.06	3 13/16	6 1/4	125	4.92	2.5	.10	70.2	2.76	20	9/16
1121	105	4.1339	155	6.10	157	6.18	46	1.81	108	4.25	4	7	130	5.12	2.5	.10	69.2	2.72	19	9/16
1123	115	4.5276	165	6.50	167	6.57	49	1.93	118	4.65	4 3/8	7 1/2	140	5.51	3	.12	74.8	2.94	19	1 1/16
1125	125	4.9213	175	6.89	180	7.09	52	2.05	128	5.04	4 3/8	8	150	5.91	3	.12	80.2	3.16	19	1 1/8
1128	140	5.5118	200	7.87	206	8.11	58	2.28	143	5.63	5 3/8	9	170	6.69	3	.12	92.5	3.64	19	1

New Departure Combined Radial and Thrust Bearings. — Cup and Cone

Bearing No.	Bore m/m	Bore in.	Diameter m/m	Diameter in.	Width m/m	Width in.	Ball Diam.	Ball No.	Chamfer C	Inside Shoulder A	Radius R	Offset D	Outside Shoulder B	Load 600 R.P.M.
0204	20	.78740	47	1.85040	14	.55118	1/4	11	.05	1.0274	1 1/16	.0788	1.4704	200
0304			52	2.04725	15	.59055	5/16	10			1/16	.0394	1.5947	250
0404														
0205	25	.98425	52	2.04725	15	.59055	9/32	11			1/16	.0394	1.6672	215
0305			62	2.44095	17	.66929	3/8	9	.05	1.2243	5/64	.0787	1.9884	360
0405			80	3.14962	21	.82677	5/16	8			3/32	.0788	2.5409	730
0206	30	1.18110	62	2.44095	16	.62992	5/16	12			5/64	.0393	2.0809	260
0306			72	2.83465	19	.74803	7/16	10	.065	1.4711	5/64	.0787	2.3621	530
0406			90	3.54332	23	.90551	1/2	8			3/32	.0787	2.9148	925
0207	35	1.37795	72	2.83465	17	.66929	3/8	12			5/64	.0394	2.3621	405
0307			80	3.14962	21	.82677	1/2	10	.065	1.6680	3/32	.0788	2.5209	735
0407			100	3.93702	25	.98425	3/4	8			3/32	.0788	3.3085	1150

No.													
0208	40	1.57481	80	3.14962	18	.70866		14	.08	1.9148	.0394	2.6571	480
0308			90	3.54332	23	.90551		10			.0787	2.8946	860
0408			110	4.33072	27	1.06299		8			.0787	3.5257	1375
0209	45	1.77166	85	3.34647	19	.74803		14	.08	2.1117	.0393	2.8539	625
0309			100	3.93702	25	.98425		10			.0788	3.2883	1040
0409			120	4.72443	29	1.14173		8			.0788	3.9194	1620
0210	50	1.96851	90	3.54332	20	.78740		16	0.85	2.3385	.0394	3.0308	710
0310			110	4.33072	27	1.06299		10			.0787	3.6620	1280
0410			130	5.11813	31	1.22047		10			.0787	4.2931	1900
0211	55	2.16536	100	3.93702	21	.82677		16	.085	2.5354	.0394	3.4245	810
0311			120	4.72443	29	1.14173		10			.0788	3.8994	1500
0411			140	5.51183	33	1.29921	1	10			.0787	4.6868	2100
0212	60	2.36221	110	4.33072	22	.86614		16	.09	2.7622	.0394	3.6422	1025
0312			130	5.11813	31	1.22047		12			.0787	4.2731	1925
0412			150	5.90554	35	1.37795		10			.0788	5.0605	2400
0213	65	2.55906	120	4.72443	23	.90551		16	.09	2.9591	.0393	4.0357	1200
0313			140	5.51183	33	1.29921		10			.0787	4.6668	2275
0413			160	6.29924	37	1.45669		10			.0787	5.4542	2750
0214	70	2.75591	125	4.92128	24	.94488		18	.095	3.1816	.0394	4.2125	1325
0314			150	5.90554	35	1.37795	1	10			.0788	5.0405	2650
0215	75	2.95277	130	5.11813	25	.98425		16	.095	3.3828	.0394	4.4094	1425
0315			160	6.29924	37	1.45669	1	10			.0787	5.4342	3000
0216	80	3.14962	140	5.51183	26	1.02362		16	.10	3.6097	.0393	4.7831	1675
0316			170	6.69296	39	1.53544		12			.0788	5.8079	3600

"SKF" Self-Aligning Radial Bearings — Medium Type — 13000

Type No.	Bore d (m/m)	Bore d (in.)	Diameter D (m/m)	Diameter D (in.)	Width B (m/m)	Width B (in.)	Width B_1 (m/m)	Width B_1 (in.)	Rad. r (m/m)	Rad. r (in.)	150	300	500	1000	1500
											Revolutions per minute — Maximum Load in Pounds				
1300	10	.3937	35	1.3780	11	.4331	....	....	1	.04	310	265	230	165	145
1301	12	.4724	37	1.4567	12	.4724	....	....	1	.04	410	350	300	230	200
1302	15	.5906	42	1.6535	13	.5118	....	....	1	.04	465	385	330	240	220
1303	17	.6693	47	1.8504	14	.5512	....	....	1	.04	665	550	465	355	310
1304	20	.7874	52	2.0472	15	.5906	....	....	1	.04	685	575	485	375	330
1305	25	.9843	62	2.4409	17	.6693	....	....	1	.04	1050	885	750	550	485
1306	30	1.1811	72	2.8346	19	.7480	....	....	2	.08	1320	1100	935	715	660
1307	35	1.3780	80	3.1496	21	.8268	....	....	2	.08	1710	1430	1210	905	770
1308	40	1.5748	90	3.5433	23	.9055	....	....	2	.08	2120	1760	1510	1150	1040
1309	45	1.7717	100	3.9370	25	.9843	....	....	2	.08	2760	2200	1990	1425	1320
1310	50	1.9685	110	4.3307	27	1.0630	....	....	2	.08	2980	2540	2200	1630	1430
1311	55	2.1654	120	4.7244	29	1.1417	....	....	2	.08	3860	3310	2810	2040	1820
1312	60	2.3622	130	5.1181	31	1.2205	....	....	2	.08	4410	3860	3250	2430	2150
1313	65	2.5591	140	5.5118	33	1.2992	....	....	3	.12	5290	4410	3860	2870	2430
1314	70	2.7559	150	5.9055	35	1.3780	....	....	3	.12	6070	5070	4410	3310	2920
1315	75	2.9528	160	6.2992	37	1.4567	....	....	3	.12	7050	5860	4960	3750	3200
1316	80	3.1496	170	6.6929	39	1.5354	....	....	3	.12	7280	6070	5300	4000	3530
1317	85	3.3465	180	7.0866	41	1.6142	49	1.929	3	.12	10300	8720	7280	5520	4850
1318	90	3.5433	190	7.4803	43	1.6929	52	2.047	3	.12	11000	9100	7830	5960	5180
1319	95	3.7402	200	7.8740	45	1.7717	54.5	2.146	3	.12	13100	10000	9500	7000	6200
1320	100	3.9370	215	8.4646	47	1.8504	58	2.283	3	.12	13600	11400	9710	7280	6620
1321	105	4.1339	225	8.8583	49	1.9291	60	2.362	3	.12	16000	13200	11200	8720	7720
1322	110	4.3307	240	9.4488	50	1.9685	64	2.520	3	.12	17400	14300	12100	9050	7950

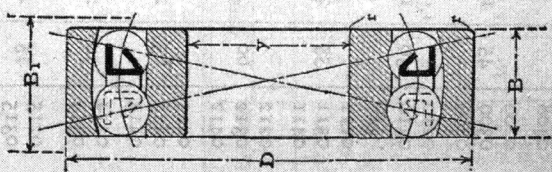

THE erection of a perpendicular by the construction of a triangle whose sides are respectively 3, 4 and 5 units in length is a familiar and handy device. The following table gives a greater range of choice in the shape or proportions of the triangle employed. The table is a list of all integral, or whole-number, right-angled triangles the units of whose least sides do not exceed 20.

Hight	Base	Hypotenuse	Hight	Base	Hypotenuse	Hight	Base	Hypotenuse
3	4	5	12	16	20	17	144	195
5	12	13	12	35	37	18	24	30
6	8	10	13	84	85	18	80	82
7	24	25	14	48	50	19	180	181
8	15	17	15	20	25	20	21	29
9	12	15	15	36	39	20	48	52
9	40	41	15	112	113	20	99	101
10	24	26	16	30	34			
11	60	61	16	63	65			

TABLE OF CHORDS

To construct any angle from the table of chords, page 388: Let the required angle be 36° 38′; the nearest angles in the table are 36° 30′ and 36° 40′, and the chords are respectively 0.6263 and 0.6291, the difference 0.0028 corresponding to an angular difference of 10′. To find the amount which must be added to 0.6263 (the chord corresponding to 36° 30′) in order to obtain the chord for a 36° 38′ arc, multiply 0.0028 by $\frac{8}{10}$ = 0.00224. 0.6263 + 0.00224 = 0.62854. Then, if the radius is 1″ and the angle 36° 38′ the chord will be 0.62854″.

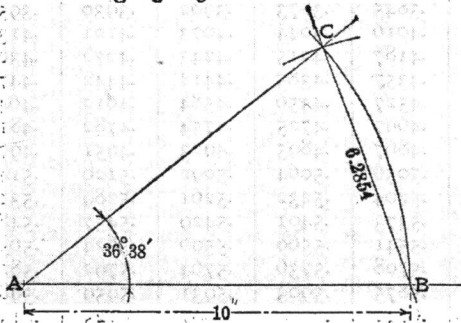

In laying out an angle as in the accompanying illustration a base line A B can be drawn, say 10 inches long, then with a radius A B and center A, arc B C can be struck. Multiply chord 0.62854 inch by 10 giving 6.2854 inches, as the radius of an arc to be struck from center B and cutting arc B C at C. Through point C draw a line A C and the angle B A C will equal 36° 38′.

Where the angle required is in even degrees or sixths of degrees (as 10′, 20′, etc.) the corresponding chord may be taken directly from the table. A 10 to 1 layout is particularly convenient as the multiplication of the tabulated chords by 10 is readily performed mentally.

TABLE OF CHORDS
THE TABULATED QUANTITIES = TWICE THE SINE OF HALF THE ARC

Deg.	0′	10′	20′	30′	40′	50′	60′
0	.0000	.0029	.0058	.0087	.0116	.0145	.0174
1	.0174	.0204	.0233	.0262	.0291	.0320	.0349
2	.0349	.0378	.0407	.0436	.0465	.0494	.0523
3	.0523	.0553	.0582	.0611	.0640	.0669	.0698
4	.0698	.0727	.0756	.0785	.0814	.0843	.0872
5	.0872	.0901	.0930	.0959	.0988	.1017	.1047
6	.1047	.1076	.1105	.1134	.1163	.1192	.1221
7	.1221	.1250	.1279	.1308	.1337	.1366	.1395
8	.1395	.1424	.1453	.1482	.1511	.1540	.1569
9	.1569	.1598	.1627	.1656	.1685	.1714	.1743
10	.1743	.1772	.1801	.1830	.1859	.1888	.1917
11	.1917	.1946	.1975	.2004	.2033	.2062	.2090
12	.2090	.2119	.2148	.2177	.2206	.2235	.2264
13	.2264	.2293	.2322	.2351	.2380	.2409	.2437
14	.2437	.2466	.2495	.2524	.2553	.2582	.2610
15	.2610	.2639	.2668	.2697	.2726	.2755	.2783
16	.2783	.2812	.2841	.2870	.2899	.2927	.2956
17	.2956	.2985	.3014	.3042	.3071	.3100	.3129
18	.3129	.3157	.3186	.3215	.3243	.3272	.3301
19	.3301	.3330	.3358	.3387	.3416	.3444	.3473
20	.3473	.3502	.3530	.3559	.3587	.3616	.3645
21	.3645	.3673	.3702	.3730	.3759	.3788	.3816
22	.3816	.3845	.3873	.3902	.3930	.3959	.3987
23	.3987	.4016	.4044	.4073	.4101	.4130	.4158
24	.4158	.4187	.4215	.4243	.4272	.4300	.4329
25	.4329	.4357	.4385	.4414	.4442	.4471	.4499
26	.4499	.4527	.4556	.4584	.4612	.4641	.4669
27	.4669	.4697	.4725	.4754	.4782	.4810	.4838
28	.4838	.4867	.4895	.4923	.4951	.4979	.5008
29	.5008	.5036	.5064	.5092	.5120	.5148	.5176
30	.5176	.5204	.5232	.5261	.5289	.5317	.5345
31	.5345	.5373	.5401	.5429	.5457	.5485	.5513
32	.5513	.5541	.5569	.5596	.5624	.5652	.5680
33	.5680	.5708	.5736	.5764	.5792	.5820	.5847
34	.5847	.5875	.5903	.5931	.5959	.5986	.6014
35	.6014	.6042	.6069	.6097	.6125	.6153	.6180
36	.6180	.6208	.6236	.6263	.6291	.6318	.6346
37	.6346	.6374	.6401	.6429	.6456	.6484	.6511
38	.6511	.6539	.6566	.6594	.6621	.6649	.6676
39	.6676	.6703	.6731	.6758	.6786	.6813	.6840
40	.6840	.6868	.6895	.6922	.6950	.6977	.7004
41	.7004	.7031	.7059	.7086	.7113	.7140	.7167
42	.7167	.7194	.7222	.7249	.7276	.7303	.7330
43	.7330	.7357	.7384	.7411	.7438	.7465	.7492
44	.7492	.7519	.7546	.7573	.7600	.7627	.7654
45	.7654	.7680	.7707	.7734	.7761	.7788	.7815

TABLE OF CHORDS

THE TABULATED QUANTITIES = TWICE THE SINE OF HALF THE ARC

Deg.	0′	10′	20′	30′	40′	50′	60′
46	.7815	.7841	.7868	.7895	.7921	.7948	.7975
47	.7975	.8001	.8028	.8055	.8081	.8108	.8135
48	.8135	.8161	.8188	.8214	.8241	.8267	.8294
49	.8294	.8320	.8347	.8373	.8400	.8426	.8452
50	.8452	.8479	.8505	.8531	.8558	.8584	.8610
51	.8610	.8636	.8663	.8689	.8715	.8741	.8767
52	.8767	.8793	.8820	.8846	.8872	.8898	.8924
53	.8924	.8950	.8976	.9002	.9028	.9054	.9080
54	.9080	.9106	.9132	.9157	.9183	.9209	.9235
55	.9235	.9261	.9286	.9312	.9338	.9364	.9389
56	.9389	.9415	.9441	.9466	.9492	.9518	.9543
57	.9543	.9569	.9594	.9620	.9645	.9671	.9696
58	.9696	.9722	.9747	.9772	.9798	.9823	.9848
59	.9848	.9874	.9899	.9924	.9949	.9975	1.0000
60	1.0000	1.0025	1.0050	1.0075	1.0100	1.0126	1.0151
61	1.0151	1.0176	1.0201	1.0226	1.0251	1.0276	1.0301
62	1.0301	1.0326	1.0350	1.0375	1.0400	1.0425	1.0450
63	1.0450	1.0475	1.0500	1.0524	1.0550	1.0574	1.0598
64	1.0598	1.0623	1.0648	1.0672	1.0697	1.0721	1.0746
65	1.0746	1.0770	1.0795	1.0819	1.0844	1.0868	1.0893
66	1.0893	1.0917	1.0941	1.0966	1.0990	1.1014	1.1039
67	1.1039	1.1063	1.1087	1.1111	1.1135	1.1159	1.1184
68	1.1184	1.1208	1.1232	1.1256	1.1280	1.1304	1.1328
69	1.1328	1.1352	1.1376	1.1400	1.1424	1.1448	1.1471
70	1.1471	1.1495	1.1519	1.1543	1.1567	1.1590	1.1614
71	1.1614	1.1638	1.1661	1.1685	1.1708	1.1732	1.1756
72	1.1756	1.1780	1.1803	1.1826	1.1850	1.1873	1.1896
73	1.1896	1.1920	1.1943	1.1966	1.1990	1.2013	1.2036
74	1.2036	1.2059	1.2083	1.2106	1.2129	1.2152	1.2175
75	1.2175	1.2198	1.2221	1.2244	1.2267	1.2290	1.2313
76	1.2313	1.2336	1.2360	1.2382	1.2405	1.2427	1.2450
77	1.2450	1.2473	1.2496	1.2518	1.2541	1.2564	1.2586
78	1.2586	1.2609	1.2631	1.2654	1.2677	1.2699	1.2721
79	1.2721	1.2744	1.2766	1.2789	1.2811	1.2833	1.2856
80	1.2856	1.2878	1.2900	1.2922	1.2945	1.2967	1.2989
81	1.2989	1.3011	1.3033	1.3055	1.3077	1.3099	1.3121
82	1.3121	1.3143	1.3165	1.3187	1.3209	1.3231	1.3252
83	1.3252	1.3274	1.3296	1.3318	1.3340	1.3361	1.3383
84	1.3383	1.3404	1.3426	1.3447	1.3469	1.3490	1.3512
85	1.3512	1.3533	1.3555	1.3576	1.3597	1.3619	1.3640
86	1.3640	1.3661	1.3682	1.3704	1.3725	1.3746	1.3767
87	1.3767	1.3788	1.3809	1.3030	1.3851	1.3872	1.3893
88	1.3893	1.3914	1.3935	1.3956	1.3977	1.3997	1.4018
89	1.4018	1.4039	1.4060	1.4080	1.4101	1.4121	1.4142
90	1.4142						

TABLE FOR SPACING HOLES IN CIRCLES

No. of Divisions in Circle	Deg. of Arc	Length of Chord Dia. 1	Length of Chord Dia. 2	Length of Chord Dia. 3	Length of Chord Dia. 4	Length of Chord Dia. 5	Length of Chord Dia. 6
3	120	.866	1.732	2.598	3.464	4.330	5.196
4	90	.707	1.414	2.121	2.828	3.536	4.243
5	72	.588	1.176	1.763	2.351	2.938	3.527
6	60	.500	1.000	1.500	2.000	2.500	3.000
7	51°–25′	.434	.868	1.302	1.736	2.170	2.604
8	45	.383	.765	1.148	1.531	1.913	2.296
9	40	.342	.684	1.026	1.368	1.710	2.052
10	36	.309	.618	.927	1.236	1.545	1.854
11	32°–43′	.282	.564	.845	1.127	1.409	1.691
12	30	.259	.518	.776	1.035	1.294	1.553
13	27°–41′	.239	.479	.718	.958	1.197	1.436
14	25°–42′	.222	.445	.667	.890	1.112	1.334
15	24	.208	.416	.624	.832	1.040	1.247
16	22°–30′	.195	.390	.585	.780	.975	1.171
17	21°–11′	.184	.367	.551	.735	.918	1.102
18	20	.174	.347	.521	.695	.868	1.041
19	18°–57′	.164	.329	.493	.658	.822	.987
20	18	.156	.318	.469	.626	.782	.937
21	17°– 8′	.149	.298	.447	.596	.745	.894
22	16°–22′	.142	.286	.427	.569	.712	.855
23	15°–39′	.136	.273	.409	.545	.681	.818
24	15	.130	.261	.392	.522	.653	.783
25	14°–24′	.125	.251	.375	.501	.627	.752
26	13°–51′	.120	.241	.361	.482	.602	.723
27	13°–20′	.116	.232	.348	.464	.580	.697
28	12°–51′	.112	.224	.336	.448	.560	.672
29	12°–25′	.108	.216	.324	.432	.540	.648
30	12	.104	.209	.314	.418	.522	.627
31	11°–37′	.101	.202	.303	.404	.505	.606
32	11°–15′	.098	.196	.294	.393	.491	.589

TABLE FOR SPACING HOLES IN CIRCLES

No. of Divisions in Circle	Deg. of Arc	Length of Chord Dia. 7	Length of Chord Dia. 8	Length of Chord Dia. 9	Length of Chord Dia. 10	Length of Chord Dia. 11	Length of Chord Dia. 12
3	120	6.062	6.928	7.794	8.660	9.526	10.392
4	90	4.950	5.657	6.364	7.071	7.778	8.485
5	72	4.115	4.702	5.290	5.878	6.465	7.053
6	60	3.500	4.000	4.500	5.000	5.500	6.000
7	51°–25′	3.037	3.471	3.905	4.339	4.773	5.207
8	45	2.679	3.061	3.444	3.827	4.210	4.592
9	40	2.394	2.736	3.078	3.420	3.762	4.104
10	36	2.163	2.472	2.781	3.090	3.399	3.708
11	32°–43′	1.973	2.254	2.536	2.818	3.100	3.381
12	30	1.812	2.069	2.329	2.588	2.847	3.106
13	27°–41′	1.676	1.915	2.154	2.394	2.633	2.873
14	25°–42′	1.557	1.779	2.000	2.224	2.446	2.669
15	24	1.455	1.663	1.871	2.079	2.287	2.495
16	22°–30′	1.366	1.561	1.756	1.951	2.146	2.341
17	21°–11′	1.286	1.469	1.653	1.837	2.020	2.204
18	20	1.216	1.389	1.563	1.737	1.910	2.084
19	18°–57′	1.151	1.316	1.480	1.645	1.809	1.974
20	18	1.095	1.251	1.408	1.564	1.721	1.877
21	17°– 8′	1.043	1.192	1.341	1.489	1.639	1.788
22	16°–22′	.996	1.139	1.281	1.423	1.566	1.708
23	15°–39′	.954	1.092	1.227	1.363	1.499	1.635
24	15	.914	1.044	1.175	1.305	1.436	1.566
25	14°–24′	.877	1.003	1.128	1.253	1.379	1.504
26	13°–51′	.843	.963	1.084	1.204	1.325	1.445
27	13°–20′	.813	.929	1.045	1.161	1.277	1.393
28	12°–51′	.784	.896	1.008	1.121	1.233	1.345
29	12°–25′	.756	.864	.972	1.080	1.188	1.296
30	12	.732	.836	.941	1.045	1.150	1.254
31	11°–37′	.707	.808	.910	1.011	1.112	1.213
32	11°–15′	.687	.785	.883	.982	1.080	1.178

TABLE FOR SPACING HOLES IN CIRCLES

THE table on pages 390 and 391 will be found of service when it is desired to space any number of holes up to and including 32, in a circle. The number of divisions or holes desired will be found in the first column, the corresponding angle included at the center being given as a convenience in the second column. The remaining column heads cover various diameters of circles from 1 to 12 inches, and under these different heads and opposite the required number of holes will be found the lengths of chords or distances between hole centers for the given circle diameter.

Thus, if it is required to space off 18 holes in an 8-inch circle, by following down the first column until 18 is reached and then reading directly to the right, in the column headed "Length of Chord-Dia 8," will be found the distance 1 389 as the chord length for that number of divisions and diameter of circle. Or, suppose a circle of 12 inches diameter is to be spaced off for a series of 27 holes to be drilled at equal distances apart. Opposite 27 found in the first column, and under the heading, "Dia. 12," will be found the chord 1 393 as the length to which the dividers may be set directly for laying off the series of holes.

If it is desired to lay off a series of holes in a circle of some diameter not given in the table, say 10 holes in an 11½-inch circle, subtract the chord for 10 holes in an 11-inch circle, or, 3 399 from the chord in the "Dia. 12" column, or 3.708, and add half the difference (.154) to 3.399, giving 3.553 as the chord or center distance between holes. Or, if 24 holes are to be equally spaced in a 20-inch circle, all that is necessary in order to find the chord, or center distance, is to find opposite 24, and in the column headed, "Dia. 10," the quantity 1.305 and multiply this by 2, giving a length of 2.610 inches as the center distance.

TABLE OF SIDES, ANGLES AND SINES

THE table on pages 393 to 397 is carried out for a much higher number of sides or spaces than are included in the preceding table and will be found useful in many cases not covered by that table. It was originally computed for finding the thicknesses of commutator bars and also for calculating the chord for spacing slots in armature punchings. In using this table the diameter of the circle is, of course, multiplied by the sine opposite the desired number of holes or sides.

Assuming for illustration that a series of 51 holes are to be equally spaced about a circle having a diameter of 17 inches, opposite 51 in the column headed "No. of Sides," find the quantity .06156 in the column headed "Sine," and multiply this quantity by 17. The product 1 0456 is the length of the chord or the required distance between centers of the holes for this circle. Or, if 40 equidistant points are to be spaced about a circle 16 inches diameter, opposite the number of sides, 40, will be found the quantity .078459 which multiplied by 16 gives 1.255 inch as the distance between centers.

MULTIPLY DIAMETER BY SINE TO GET LENGTH OF SIDE
(Angle given is half of angle subtended at center)

No. Sides	Angle Deg. Min. Sec.	Sine	No. Sides	Angle Deg. Min. Sec.	Sine
3	60	.8660254	52	3–27–41.53	.0603784
4	45	.7071067	53	3–23–46.41	.0592405
5	36	.5877852	54	3–20	.0581448
6	30	.5000000	55	3–16–21.81	.0570887
7	25–42–51.42	.4338828	56	3–12–51.42	.0560704
8	22–30	.3826834	57	3– 9–28.42	.0550877
9	20–	.3420201	58	3– 6–12.41	.0541388
10	18–	.3090170	59	3– 3– 3.05	.0532221
11	16–21–49.09	.2817325	60	3–	.0523360
12	15–	.2588190	61	2–57– 2.95	.0514787
13	13–50–46.15	.2393157	62	2–54–11.61	.0506491
14	12–51–25.71	.2225208	63	2–51–25.71	.0498458
15	12	.2079116	64	2–48– 45	.0490676
16	11–15	.1950903	65	2–46– 9.23	.0483133
17	10–35–17.64	.1837495	66	2–43–38.18	.0475819
18	10–	.1736481	67	2–41–11.64	.0468722
19	9–28–25.26	.1645945	68	2–38–49.41	.0461834
20	9–	.1564344	69	2–36–31.30	.0455145
21	8–34–17.14	.1490422	70	2–34–17.14	.0448648
22	8–10–54.54	.1423148	71	2–32– 6.76	.0442333
23	7–49–33.91	.1361666	72	2–30	.0436194
24	7–30–	.1305262	73	2–27–56.71	.0430222
25	7–12–	.1253332	74	2–25–56.75	.0424411
26	6–55–23.07	.1205366	75	2–24–	.0418757
27	6–40	.1160929	76	2–22– 6.31	.0413249
28	6–25–42.85	.1119644	77	2–20–15.58	.0407885
29	6–12–24.82	.1081189	78	2–18–27.69	.0402659
30	6–	.1045284	79	2–16–42.53	.0397565
31	5–48–23.22	.1011683	80	2–15–	.0392598
32	5–37–30	.0980171	81	2–13–20	.0387753
33	5–27–16.36	.0950560	82	2–11–42.45	.0383027
34	5–17–38.82	.0922683	83	2–10– 7.22	.0378414
35	5– 8–34.28	.0896392	84	2– 8–34.28	.0373911
36	5–	.0871557	85	2– 7– 3.54	.0369515
37	4–51–53.51	.0848058	86	2– 5–34.88	.0365220
38	4–44–12.63	.0825793	87	2– 4– 8.27	.0361023
39	4–36–55.38	.0804665	88	2– 2–43.63	.0356923
40	4–30–	.0784591	89	2– 1–20.89	.0352914
41	4–23–24.87	.0765492	90	2–	.0348995
42	4–17– 8.57	.0747301	91	1–58–40.87	.0345160
43	4–11– 9.76	.0729952	92	1–57–23.47	.0341410
44	4– 5–27.27	.0713391	93	1–56– 7.74	.0337741
45	4	.0697565	94	1–54–53.61	.0334149
46	3–54–46.95	.0682423	95	1–53–41.05	.0330633
47	3–49–47.23	.0667926	96	1–52–30.	.0327190
48	3–45–	.0654031	97	1–51–20.41	.0323818
49	3–40–24.49	.0640702	98	1–50–12.24	.0320515
50	3–36–	.0627905	99	1–49– 5.45	.0317279
51	3–31–45.88	.0615609	100	1–48–	.0314107

MULTIPLY DIAMETER BY SINE TO GET LENGTH OF SIDE
(Angle given is half of angle subtended at center)

No. Sides	Angle Deg. Min. Sec.	Sine	No. Sides	Angle Deg. Min. Sec.	Sine
101	1-46-55.84	.0310998	151	1-11-31.39	.0208037
102	1-45-52.94	.0307950	152	1-11- 3.15	.0206668
103	1-44-51.26	.0304961	153	1-10-35.29	.0205318
104	1-43-50.76	.0302029	154	1-10- 7.79	.0203985
105	1-42-51.42	.0299154	155	1- 9-40.64	.0202669
106	1-41-53.20	.0296332	156	1- 9-13.84	.0201370
107	1-40-56.07	.0293564	157	1- 8-47.38	.0200087
108	1-40-	.0290847	158	1- 8-21.26	.0198821
109	1-39- 4.95	.0288179	159	1- 7-55.47	.0197571
110	1-38-10.90	.0285560	160	1- 7-30	.0196336
111	1-37-17.83	.0282488	161	1- 7- 4.84	.0195117
112	1-36-25.71	.0280462	162	1- 6-40	.0193913
113	1-35-34.51	.0277981	163	1- 6-15.46	.0192723
114	1-34-44.21	.0275543	164	1- 5-51.21	.0191548
115	1-33-54.78	.0273147	165	1- 5-27.27	.0190387
116	1-33- 6.20	.0270793	166	1- 5- 3.61	.0189241
117	1-32-18.46	.0268479	167	1- 4-40.23	.0188107
118	1-31-31.52	.0266204	168	1- 4-17.14	.0186988
119	1-30-45.38	.0263968	169	1- 3-54.31	.0185881
120	1-30-	.0261769	170	1- 3-31.76	.0184788
121	1-29-15.37	.0259606	171	1- 3- 9.47	.0183708
122	1-28-31.47	.0257478	172	1- 2-47.44	.0182640
123	1-27-48.29	.0255386	173	1- 2-25.66	.0181584
124	1-27- 5.80	.0253326	174	1- 2- 4.13	.0180541
125	1-26-24	.0251300	175	1- 1-42.85	.0179509
126	1-25-42.85	.0249306	176	1- 1-21.81	.0178489
127	1-25- 2.36	.0247344	177	1- 1- 1.01	.0177481
128	1-24-22.50	.0245412	178	1- 0-40.44	.0176484
129	1-23-43.25	.0243509	179	1- 0-20.11	.0175498
130	1-23- 4.61	.0241637	180	1- -	.0174524
131	1-22-26.56	.0239793	181	-59-40.11	.0173559
132	1-21-49.09	.0237976	182	-59-20.43	.0172605
133	1-21-12.18	.0236188	183	-59- 0.98	.0171663
134	1-20-35.82	.0234425	184	-58-41.73	.0170730
135	1-20-	.0232689	185	-58-22.70	.0169807
136	1-19-24.70	.0230978	186	-58- 3.87	.0168894
137	1-18-49.92	.0229292	187	-57-45.24	.0167991
138	1-18-15.65	.0227631	188	-57-26.30	.0167097
139	1-17-41.87	.0225994	189	-57- 8.57	.0166214
140	1-17- 8.57	.0224380	190	-56-50.52	.0165339
141	1-16-35.74	.0222789	191	-56-32.67	.0164473
142	1-16- 3.38	.0221220	192	-56-15	.0163617
143	1-15-31.46	.0219673	193	-55-57.51	.0162769
144	1-15-	.0218148	194	-55-40.20	.0161930
145	1-14-28.96	.0216644	195	-55-23.07	.0161100
146	1-13-58.35	.0215160	196	-55- 6.12	.0160278
147	1-13-28.16	.0213697	197	-54-49.34	.0159464
148	1-12-58.37	.0212253	198	-54-32.72	.0158659
149	1-12-28.99	.0210829	199	-54-16.28	.0157862
150	1-12-	.0209424	200	-54-	.0157073

MULTIPLY DIAMETER BY SINE TO GET LENGTH OF SIDE
(Angle given is half of angle subtended at center)

No. Sides	Angle Min. Sec.	Sine	No. Sides	Angle Min. Sec.	Sine
201	53–43.88	.0156244	251	43– 1.67	.0125160
202	53–27.92	.0155518	252	42–51.43	.0124663
203	53–12.12	.0154752	253	42–41.26	.0124171
204	52–56.47	.0153993	254	42–31.18	.0123682
205	52–40.97	.0153242	255	42–21.18	.0123197
206	52–25.63	.0152498	256	42–11.25	.0122715
207	52–10.44	.0151764	257	42– 1.40	.0122238
208	51–55.38	.0151033	258	41–51.63	.0121764
209	51–40.48	.0150310	259	41–41.93	.0121294
210	51–25.71	.0149595	260	41–32.31	.0120827
211	51–11.09	.0148886	261	41–22.76	.0120364
212	50–56.60	.0148183	262	41–13.28	.0119905
213	50–42.25	.0147487	263	41– 3.88	.0119449
214	50–28.04	.0146798	264	40–54.54	.0118997
215	50–13.96	.0146115	265	40–45.28	.0118548
216	50–	.0145439	266	40–36.09	.0118102
217	49–46.17	.0144769	267	40–26.96	.0117660
218	49–32.48	.0144104	268	40–17.91	.0117221
219	49–18.91	.0143446	269	40– 8.93	.0116786
220	49– 5.46	.0142794	270	40–	.0116353
221	48–52.13	.0142148	271	39–51.14	.0115923
222	48–38.92	.0141508	272	39–42.35	.0115497
223	48–25.83	.0140874	273	39–33.63	.0115074
224	48–12.86	.0140245	274	39–24.96	.0114654
225	48–	.0139622	275	39–16.36	.0114237
226	47–47.26	.0139004	276	39– 7.83	.0113823
227	47–34.63	.0138392	277	38–59.35	.0113412
228	47–22.11	.0137785	278	38–50.94	.0113004
229	47– 9.69	.0137183	279	38–42.58	.0112599
230	46–57.39	.0136587	280	38–34.28	.0112197
231	46–45.19	.0135995	281	38–26.05	.0111798
232	46–33.10	.0135409	282	38–17.87	.0111401
233	46–21.11	.0134828	283	38– 9.75	.0111008
234	46– 9.23	.0134252	284	38– 1.69	.0110617
235	45–57.45	.0133681	285	37–53.68	.0110229
236	45–45.76	.0133115	286	17–45.73	.0109844
237	45–34.18	.0132553	287	37–37.84	.0109461
238	45–22.69	.0131996	288	37–30	.0109081
239	45–11.29	.0131444	289	37–22.21	.0108704
240	45–	.0130896	290	37–14.48	.0108329
241	44–48.80	.0130353	291	37– 6.80	.0107957
242	44–37.68	.0129814	292	36–59.18	.0107587
243	44–26.67	.0129280	293	36–51.60	.0107220
244	44–15.74	.0128750	294	36–44.08	.0106855
245	44– 4.90	.0128225	295	36–36.61	.0106493
246	43–54.15	.0127704	296	36–29.19	.0106133
247	43–43.48	.0127187	297	36–21.82	.0105776
248	43–32.40	.0126674	298	36–14.50	.0105421
249	43–22.41	.0126165	299	36– 7.22	.0105068
250	43–12	.0125661	300	36–	.0104718

MULTIPLY DIAMETER BY SINE TO GET LENGTH OF SIDE
(Angle given is half of angle subtended at center)

No. Sides	Angle Min. Sec.	Sine	No. Sides	Angle Min. Sec.	Sine
301	35–52.82	.0104370	351	30–46.15	.0089502
302	35–45.69	.0104024	352	30–40.91	.0089248
303	35–38.61	.0103681	353	30–35.69	.0088996
304	35–31.58	.0103340	354	30–30.51	.0088744
305	35–24.59	.0103001	355	30–25.35	.0088494
306	35–17.65	.0102665	356	30–20.22	.0088245
307	35–10.75	.0102330	357	30–15.12	.0087998
308	35– 3.90	.0101998	358	30–10.05	.0087753
309	34–57.09	.0101668	359	30– 5.01	.0087508
310	34–50.32	.0101340	360	30–	.0087265
311	34–43.60	.0101014	361	29–55.01	.0087023
312	34–36.92	.0100690	362	29–50.05	.0086783
313	34–30.29	.0100368	363	29–45.12	.0086544
314	34–23.69	.0100049	364	29–40.22	.0086306
315	34–17.14	.0099731	365	29–35.34	.0086070
316	34–10.63	.0099415	366	29–30.49	.0085835
317	34– 4.16	.0099102	367	29–25.67	.0085601
318	33–57.74	.0098791	368	29–20.87	.0085368
319	33–51.35	.0098482	369	29–16.10	.0085137
320	33–45	.0098174	370	29–11.35	.0084907
321	33–38.69	.0097868	371	29– 6.63	.0084678
322	33–32.42	.0097564	372	29– 1.94	.0084451
323	33–26.19	.0097261	373	28–57.27	.0084224
324	33–20	.0096961	374	28–52.62	.0083999
325	33–13.85	.0096663	375	28–48	.0083775
326	33– 7.73	.0096367	376	28–43.40	.0083552
327	33– 1.65	.0096072	377	28–38.83	.0083331
328	32–55.61	.0095779	378	28–34.28	.0083110
329	32–49.60	.0095488	379	28–29.76	.0082891
330	32–43.64	.0095198	380	28–25.26	.0082673
331	32–37.70	.0094911	381	28–20.78	.0082456
332	32–31.81	.0094625	382	28–16.33	.0082240
333	32–25.95	.0094341	383	28–11.91	.0082025
334	32–20.12	.0094059	384	28– 7.50	.0081812
335	32–14.33	.0093778	385	28– 3.12	.0081599
336	32– 8.57	.0093499	386	27–58.76	.0081387
337	32– 2.85	.0093221	387	27–54.42	.0081177
338	31–57.16	.0092945	388	27–50.10	.0080968
339	31–51.50	.0092671	389	27–45.81	.0080760
340	31–45.88	.0092398	390	27–41.54	.0080553
341	31–40.29	.0092127	391	27–37.29	.0080347
342	31–34.74	.0091858	392	27–33.06	.0080142
343	31–29.21	.0091590	393	27–28.85	.0079938
344	31–23.72	.0091324	394	27–24.67	.0079735
345	31–18.26	.0091059	395	27–20.51	.0079533
346	31–12.83	.0090796	396	27–16.36	.0079332
347	31– 7.44	.0090534	397	27–12.24	.0079132
348	31– 2.07	.0090274	398	27– 8.14	.0078934
349	30–56.73	.0090016	399	27– 4.06	.0078736
350	30–51.43	.0089758	400	27–	.0078534

MULTIPLY DIAMETER BY SINE TO GET LENGTH OF SIDE
(Angle given is half of angle subtended at center)

No. Sides	Angle Min. Sec.	Sine	No. Sides	Angle Min. Sec.	Sine
401	26–55.96	.0078343	451	23–56.81	.0069658
402	26–51.94	.0078148	452	23–53.63	.0069504
403	26–47.94	.0077954	453	23–50.46	.0069351
404	26–43.96	.0077761	454	23–47.31	.0069198
405	26–40	.0077569	455	23–44.17	.0069046
406	26–36.06	.0077378	456	23–41.05	.0068894
407	26–32.14	.0077188	457	23–37.94	.0068744
408	26–28.23	.0076999	458	23–34.84	.0068594
409	26–24.35	.0076811	459	23–31.76	.0068444
410	26–20.49	.0076623	460	23–28.69	.0068295
411	26–16.64	.0076437	461	23–25.64	.0068147
412	26–12.82	.0076251	462	23–22.60	.0067999
413	26– 9.01	.0076067	463	23–19.57	.0067852
414	26– 5.22	.0075883	464	23–16.55	.0067706
415	26– 1.45	.0075700	465	23–13.55	.0067561
416	25–57.70	.0075518	466	23–10.56	.0067416
417	25–53.96	.0075337	467	23– 7.58	.0067272
418	25–50.24	.0075157	468	23– 4.61	.0067128
419	25–46.54	.0074977	469	23– 1.66	.0066985
420	25–42.86	.0074799	470	22–58.72	.0066842
421	25–39.19	.0074621	471	22–55.79	.0066700
422	25–35.54	.0074444	472	22–52.88	.0066559
423	25–31.91	.0074268	473	22–49.98	.0066418
424	25–28.30	.0074093	474	22–47.09	.0066278
425	25–24.70	.0073919	475	22–44.21	.0066138
426	25–21.12	.0073745	476	22–41.34	.0065999
427	25–17.56	.0073573	477	22–38.49	.0065861
428	25–14.02	.0073401	478	22–35.65	.0065723
429	25–10.49	.0073230	479	22–32.82	.0065585
430	25– 6.98	.0073059	480	22–30	.0065449
431	25– 3.48	.0072890	481	22–27.20	.0065313
432	25–	.0072721	482	22–24.40	.0065178
433	24–56.54	.0072553	483	22–21.61	.0065043
434	24–53.09	.0072386	484	22–18.84	.0064909
435	24–49.66	.0072220	485	22–16.08	.0064775
436	24–46.24	.0072054	486	22–13.33	.0064641
437	24–42.84	.0071889	487	22–10.59	.0064509
438	24–39.45	.0071725	488	22– 7.87	.0064377
439	24–36.08	.0071562	489	22– 5.16	.0064245
440	24–32.73	.0071399	490	22– 2.45	.0064114
441	24–29.39	.0071237	491	21–59.75	.0063983
442	24–26.06	.0071076	492	21–57.07	.0063853
443	24–22.75	.0070916	493	21–54.40	.0063723
444	24–19.46	.0070756	494	21–51.74	.0063594
445	24–16.18	.0070597	495	21–49.09	.0063466
446	24–12.91	.0070439	496	21–46.45	.0063338
447	24– 9.66	.0070281	497	21–43.82	.0063211
448	24– 6.43	.0070124	498	21–41.20	.0063084
449	24– 3.21	.0069968	499	21–38.59	.0062957
450	24–	.0069813	500	21–36	.0062831

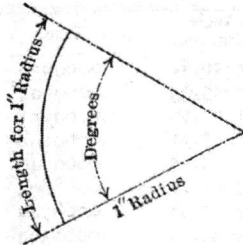

LENGTHS OF CIRCULAR ARCS

THE table gives the lengths of circular arcs to the radius of one, for angles from 1 to 180 degrees. The lengths for minutes of arcs are given at the right.

To find the length of a circular arc with radius of 1 inch and angle of 45 degrees 20 minutes. Opposite 45 degrees find 0.7854, and opposite 20 minutes 0.0058. Adding these gives 0.7912 inch as the length of arc. If the radius is 2 inches, multiply the lengths in the table by 2.

LENGTHS OF CIRCULAR ARCS TO RADIUS OF 1

Degree	Length	Degree	Length	Degree	Length	Degree	Length	Min.	Length	Min.	Length
0	0.0000	45	0.7854	90	1.5708	135	2.3562	0	0.0000	45	0.0131
1	0.0175	46	0.8029	91	1.5882	136	2.3736	1	0.0003	46	0.0134
2	0.0349	47	0.8203	92	1.6057	137	2.3911	2	0.0006	47	0.0137
3	0.0524	48	0.8378	93	1.6232	138	2.4086	3	0.0009	48	0.0140
4	0.0698	49	0.8552	94	1.6406	139	2.4260	4	0.0012	49	0.0143
5	0.0873	50	0.8728	95	1.6581	140	2.4435	5	0.0015	50	0.0145
6	0.1047	51	0.8901	96	1.6755	141	2.4609	6	0.0017	51	0.0148
7	0.1222	52	0.9076	97	1.6930	142	2.4784	7	0.0020	52	0.0151
8	0.1396	53	0.9250	98	1.7104	143	2.4958	8	0.0023	53	0.0154
9	0.1571	54	0.9425	99	1.7279	144	2.5133	9	0.0026	54	0.0157
10	0.1745	55	0.9599	100	1.7453	145	2.5307	10	0.0029	55	0.0160
11	0.1920	56	0.9774	101	1.7628	146	2.5482	11	0.0032	56	0.0163
12	0.2094	57	0.9948	102	1.7802	147	2.5656	12	0.0035	57	0.0166
13	0.2269	58	1.0123	103	1.7977	148	2.5831	13	0.0038	58	0.0169
14	0.2443	59	1.0297	104	1.8151	149	2.6005	14	0.0041	59	0.0172
15	0.2618	60	1.0472	105	1.8326	150	2.6180	15	0.0044	60	0.0175
16	0.2793	61	1.0647	106	1.8500	151	2.6354	16	0.0047		
17	0.2967	62	1.0821	107	1.8675	152	2.6529	17	0.0050		
18	0.3142	63	1.0996	108	1.8850	153	2.6704	18	0.0052		
19	0.3316	64	1.1170	109	1.9024	154	2.6878	19	0.0055		
20	0.3491	65	1.1345	110	1.9199	155	2.7052	20	0.0058		
21	0.3665	66	1.1519	111	1.9373	156	2.7227	21	0.0061		
22	0.3840	67	1.1694	112	1.9548	157	2.7402	22	0.0064		
23	0.4014	68	1.1868	113	1.9722	158	2.7576	23	0.0067		
24	0.4189	69	1.2043	114	1.9897	159	2.7751	24	0.0070		
25	0.4363	70	1.2217	115	2.0071	160	2.7925	25	0.0073		
26	0.4538	71	1.2392	116	2.0246	161	2.8100	26	0.0076		
27	0.4712	72	1.2566	117	2.0420	162	2.8274	27	0.0079		
28	0.4887	73	1.2741	118	2.0595	163	2.8449	28	0.0081		
29	0.5061	74	1.2915	119	2.0769	164	2.8623	29	0.0084		
30	0.5236	75	1.3090	120	2.0944	165	2.8798	30	0.0087		
31	0.5411	76	1.3265	121	2.1118	166	2.8972	31	0.0090		
32	0.5585	77	1.3439	122	2.1293	167	2.9147	32	0.0093		
33	0.5760	78	1.3614	123	2.1468	168	2.9322	33	0.0096		
34	0.5934	79	1.3788	124	2.1642	169	2.9496	34	0.0099		
35	0.6109	80	1.3963	125	2.1817	170	2.9671	35	0.0102		
36	0.6283	81	1.4137	126	2.1991	171	2.9845	36	0.0105		
37	0.6458	82	1.4312	127	2.2166	172	3.0020	37	0.0108		
38	0.6632	83	1.4486	128	2.2340	173	3.0194	38	0.0111		
39	0.6807	84	1.4661	129	2.2515	174	3.0369	39	0.0113		
40	0.6981	85	1.4835	130	2.2690	175	3.0543	40	0.0116		
41	0.7156	86	1.5010	131	2.2864	176	3.0718	41	0.0119		
42	0.7330	87	1.5184	132	2.3038	177	3.0892	42	0.0122		
43	0.7505	88	1.5359	133	2.3132	178	3.1067	43	0.0125		
44	0.7679	89	1.5533	134	2.3387	179	3.1241	44	0.0128		

ACTUAL CUTTING SPEED OF PLANERS IN FEET PER MINUTE

Forward Cutting Speed in Feet per Minute	Return Speed						
	2 to 1	3 to 1	4 to 1	5 to 1	6 to 1	7 to 1	8 to 1
20	13.3	15.	16	16.66	17.14	17.5	17.76
25	16.6	18.75	20	20.83	21.42	21.87	22.16
30	20.	22.5	24	25.	25.71	26.25	26.56
35	23.3	26.25	28	29.16	30.	30.62	31.04
40	26.6	30.	32	33.33	34.28	35.	35.52
45	30.	33.75	36	37.5	38.56	39.37	40.
50	33.3	37.5	40	41.66	42.84	43.75	44.48
55	36.6	41.25	44	45.83	47.12	48.12	48.95
60	40.	45.	48	50.	51.42	52.50	53.43
65	43.3	48.75	52	54.16	55.70	56.87	57.91
70	46.6	52.5	56	58.33	60.	61.25	62.3
75	50.	56.25	60	62.5	64.28	66.62	66.71

The table shows clearly that a slight increase in cutting speed is better than high return speed. A 25-foot forward speed at 4 to 1 return is much better than 8 to 1 return with 20-feet forward speed.

Economical planer speeds are given below (Cincinnati Planer Co.).

Cast Iron roughing......40 to 50 ft.; finishing......20 to 25 ft.
Steel casting and wrought iron roughing 30 to 35 ft.; finishing 20 ft.
Bronze and brass...50 to 60 ft.; Machinery steel...30 to 35 ft.

ALLOWANCES FOR BOLT HEADS AND UPSETS

STOCK ALLOWED FOR STANDARD UPSETS BY ACME MACHINERY CO.

$\frac{1}{2}$	in.	Upset to	$\frac{5}{8}$	in.	Length of	Upset,	3	in.	Stock	required,	$1\frac{3}{4}$ in.
$\frac{5}{8}$	"	"	$\frac{3}{4}$	"	"	"	$3\frac{1}{2}$	"	"	"	$1\frac{5}{8}$ "
$\frac{3}{4}$	"	"	$\frac{7}{8}$	"	"	"	$3\frac{1}{2}$	"	"	"	$1\frac{1}{2}$ "
$\frac{7}{8}$	"	"	$1\frac{1}{8}$	"	"	"	4	"	"	"	$2\frac{3}{4}$ "
1	"	"	$1\frac{1}{4}$	"	"	"	4	"	"	"	$2\frac{3}{8}$ "
$1\frac{1}{8}$	"	"	$1\frac{3}{8}$	"	"	"	$4\frac{1}{2}$	"	"	"	$2\frac{1}{4}$ "
$1\frac{1}{4}$	"	"	$1\frac{1}{2}$	"	"	"	$4\frac{1}{2}$	"	"	"	$2\frac{1}{2}$ "
$1\frac{3}{8}$	"	"	$1\frac{5}{8}$	"	"	"	5	"	"	"	$2\frac{1}{8}$ "
$1\frac{1}{2}$	"	"	$1\frac{3}{4}$	"	"	"	5	"	"	"	2 "
$1\frac{1}{2}$	"	"	$1\frac{7}{8}$	"	"	"	5	"	"	"	$2\frac{7}{8}$ "
$1\frac{5}{8}$	"	"	$1\frac{7}{8}$	"	"	"	$5\frac{1}{2}$	"	"	"	$1\frac{7}{8}$ "
$1\frac{3}{4}$	"	"	2	"	"	"	$5\frac{1}{2}$	"	"	"	$1\frac{3}{4}$ "
$1\frac{7}{8}$	"	"	$2\frac{1}{8}$	"	"	"	6	"	"	"	2 "
2	"	"	$2\frac{3}{8}$	"	"	"	6	"	"	"	$2\frac{1}{2}$ "
2	"	"	$2\frac{1}{2}$	"	"	"	6	"	"	"	$3\frac{1}{2}$ "
$2\frac{1}{4}$	"	"	$2\frac{5}{8}$	"	"	"	$6\frac{1}{2}$	"	"	"	$2\frac{1}{2}$ "
$2\frac{1}{2}$	"	"	$2\frac{7}{8}$	"	"	"	$6\frac{1}{2}$	"	"	"	$2\frac{1}{4}$ "
$2\frac{3}{4}$	"	"	$3\frac{1}{8}$	"	"	"	7	"	"	"	2 "
3	"	"	$3\frac{1}{2}$	"	"	"	7	"	"	"	$2\frac{5}{8}$ "

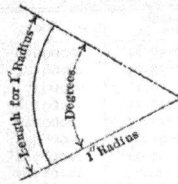

LENGTHS OF CIRCULAR ARCS

THE table gives the lengths of circu[lar]
arcs to the radius of one, for angles fr[om]
1 to 180 degrees. The lengths for minute[s of]
arcs are given at the right.

To find the length of a circular arc w[ith]
radius of 1 inch and angle of 45 degrees [20]
minutes. Opposite 45 degrees find 0.78[54]
and opposite 20 minutes 0.0058. Add[ing]
these gives 0.7912 inch as the length of [arc.]
If the radius is 2 inches, multiply the lengths in the table by 2.

LENGTHS OF CIRCULAR ARCS TO RADIUS OF 1

De-gree	Length	De-gree	Length	De-gree	Length	De-gree	Length	Min.	Length	Min.	Le[ngth]
0	0.0000	45	0.7854	90	1.5708	135	2.3562	0	0.0000	45	
1	0.0175	46	0.8029	91	1.5882	136	2.3736	1	0.0003	46	
2	0.0349	47	0.8203	92	1.6057	137	2.3911	2	0.0006	47	
3	0.0524	48	0.8378	93	1.6232	138	2.4086	3	0.0009	48	
4	0.0698	49	0.8552	94	1.6406	139	2.4260	4	0.0012	49	
5	0.0873	50	0.8727	95	1.6581	140	2.4435	5	0.0015	50	
6	0.1047	51	0.8901	96	1.6755	141	2.4609	6	0.0017	51	
7	0.1222	52	0.9076	97	1.6930	142	2.4784	7	0.0020	52	
8	0.1396	53	0.9250	98	1.7104	143	2.4958	8	0.0023	53	
9	0.1571	54	0.9425	99	1.7279	144	2.5133	9	0.0026	54	
10	0.1745	55	0.9599	100	1.7453	145	2.5307	10	0.0029	55	
11	0.1920	56	0.9774	101	1.7628	146	2.5482	11	0.0032	56	
12	0.2094	57	0.9948	102	1.7802	147	2.5656	12	0.0035	57	
13	0.2269	58	1.0123	103	1.7977	148	2.5831	13	0.0038	58	
14	0.2443	59	1.0297	104	1.8151	149	2.6005	14	0.0041	59	
15	0.2618	60	1.0472	105	1.8326	150	2.6180	15	0.0044	60	
16	0.2793	61	1.0647	106	1.8500	151	2.6354	16	0.0047		
17	0.2967	62	1.0821	107	1.8675	152	2.6529	17	0.0050		
18	0.3142	63	1.0996	108	1.8850	153	2.6704	18	0.0052		
19	0.3316	64	1.1170	109	1.9024	154	2.6878	19	0.0055		
20	0.3491	65	1.1345	110	1.9199	155	2.7052	20	0.0058		
21	0.3665	66	1.1519	111	1.9373	156	2.7227	21	0.0061		
22	0.3840	67	1.1694	112	1.9548	157	2.7402	22	0.0064		
23	0.4014	68	1.1868	113	1.9722	158	2.7576	23	0.0067		
24	0.4189	69	1.2043	114	1.9897	159	2.7751	24	0.0070		
25	0.4363	70	1.2217	115	2.0071	160	2.7925	25	0.0073		
26	0.4538	71	1.2392	116	2.0246	161	2.8100	26	0.0076		
27	0.4712	72	1.2566	117	2.0420	162	2.8274	27	0.0079		
28	0.4887	73	1.2741	118	2.0595	163	2.8449	28	0.0081		
29	0.5061	74	1.2915	119	2.0769	164	2.8623	29	0.0084		
30	0.5236	75	1.3090	120	2.0944	165	2.8798	30	0.0087		
31	0.5411	76	1.3265	121	2.1118	166	2.8972	31	0.0090		
32	0.5585	77	1.3439	122	2.1293	167	2.9147	32	0.0093		
33	0.5760	78	1.3614	123	2.1468	168	2.9322	33	0.0096		
34	0.5934	79	1.3788	124	2.1642	169	2.9496	34	0.0099		
35	0.6109	80	1.3963	125	2.1817	170	2.9671	35	0.0102		
36	0.6283	81	1.4137	126	2.1991	171	2.9845	36	0.0105		
37	0.6458	82	1.4312	127	2.2166	172	3.0020	37	0.0108		
38	0.6632	83	1.4486	128	2.2340	173	3.0194	38	0.0111		
39	0.6807	84	1.4661	129	2.2515	174	3.0369	39	0.0113		
40	0.6981	85	1.4835	130	2.2690	175	3.0543	40	0.0116		
41	0.7156	86	1.5010	131	2.2864	176	3.0718	41	0.0119		
42	0.7330	87	1.5184	132	2.3038	177	3.0892	42	0.0122		
43	0.7505	88	1.5359	133	2.3213	178	3.1067	43	0.0125		
44	0.7679	89	1.5533	134	2.3387	179	3.1241	44	0.0128		

ACTUAL CUTTING SPEED OF PLANERS IN FEET PER MINUTE

Forward Cutting Speed in Feet per Minute	Return Speed						
	2 to 1	3 to 1	4 to 1	5 to 1	6 to 1	7 to 1	8 to 1
20	13.3	15.	16	16.66	17.14	17.5	17.76
25	16.6	18.75	20	20.83	21.42	21.87	22.16
30	20.	22.5	24	25.	25.71	26.25	26.56
35	23.3	26.25	28	29.16	30.	30.62	31.04
40	26.6	30.	32	33.33	34.28	35.	35.52
45	30.	33.75	36	37.5	38.56	39.37	40.
50	33.3	37.5	40	41.66	42.84	43.75	44.48
55	36.6	41.25	44	45.83	47.12	48.12	48.95
60	40.	45.	48	50.	51.42	52.50	53.43
65	43.3	48.75	52	54.16	55.70	56.87	57.91
70	46.6	52.5	56	58.33	60.	61.25	62.3
75	50.	56.25	60	62.5	64.28	66.62	66.71

The table shows clearly that a slight increase in cutting speed is better than high return speed. A 25-foot forward speed at 4 to 1 return is much better than 8 to 1 return with 20-feet forward speed.

Economical planer speeds are given below (Cincinnati Planer Co.).

Cast Iron roughing......40 to 50 ft.; finishing......20 to 25 ft.
Steel casting and wrought iron roughing 30 to 35 ft.; finishing 20 ft.
Bronze and brass...50 to 60 ft.; Machinery steel...30 to 35 ft.

ALLOWANCES FOR BOLT HEADS AND UPSETS

STOCK ALLOWED FOR STANDARD UPSETS BY ACME MACHINERY CO.

$\frac{1}{2}$	in.	Upset to	$\frac{5}{8}$	in.	Length of Upset,	3	in.	Stock required,	$1\frac{3}{4}$	in.
$\frac{5}{8}$	"	"	$\frac{3}{4}$	"	"	$3\frac{1}{2}$	"	"	$1\frac{5}{8}$	"
$\frac{3}{4}$	"	"	$\frac{7}{8}$	"	"	$3\frac{1}{2}$	"	"	$1\frac{1}{2}$	"
$\frac{7}{8}$	"	"	$1\frac{1}{8}$	"	"	4	"	"	$2\frac{3}{4}$	"
1	"	"	$1\frac{1}{4}$	"	"	4	"	"	$2\frac{3}{8}$	"
$1\frac{1}{8}$	"	"	$1\frac{3}{8}$	"	"	$4\frac{1}{2}$	"	"	$2\frac{1}{4}$	"
$1\frac{1}{4}$	"	"	$1\frac{1}{2}$	"	"	$4\frac{1}{2}$	"	"	$2\frac{1}{2}$	"
$1\frac{3}{8}$	"	"	$1\frac{5}{8}$	"	"	5	"	"	$2\frac{1}{8}$	"
$1\frac{1}{2}$	"	"	$1\frac{3}{4}$	"	"	5	"	"	2	"
$1\frac{1}{2}$	"	"	$1\frac{7}{8}$	"	"	5	"	"	$2\frac{7}{8}$	"
$1\frac{5}{8}$	"	"	$1\frac{7}{8}$	"	"	$5\frac{1}{2}$	"	"	$1\frac{7}{8}$	"
$1\frac{3}{4}$	"	"	2	"	"	$5\frac{1}{2}$	"	"	$1\frac{3}{4}$	"
$1\frac{7}{8}$	"	"	$2\frac{1}{8}$	"	"	6	"	"	2	"
2	"	"	$2\frac{3}{8}$	"	"	6	"	"	$2\frac{1}{2}$	"
2	"	"	$2\frac{1}{2}$	"	"	6	"	"	$3\frac{1}{2}$	"
$2\frac{1}{4}$	"	"	$2\frac{5}{8}$	"	"	$6\frac{1}{2}$	"	"	$2\frac{1}{2}$	"
$2\frac{1}{2}$	"	"	$2\frac{7}{8}$	"	"	$6\frac{1}{2}$	"	"	$2\frac{1}{4}$	"
$2\frac{3}{4}$	"	"	$3\frac{1}{8}$	"	"	7	"	"	2	"
3	"	"	$3\frac{1}{2}$	"	"	7	"	"	$2\frac{5}{8}$	"

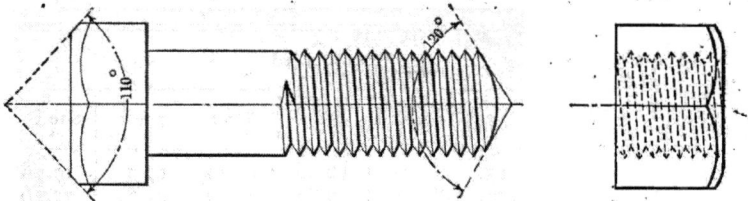

STOCK REQUIRED TO MAKE MANUFACTURER'S STANDARD BOLT
HEADS AND NUTS — ROUGH

NATIONAL MACHINERY CO.

Size of Bolt	BOLT HEADS SQUARE OR HEXAGON					NUTS SQUARE OR HEXAGON						
	Short Diameter		Thickness	Stock Required for Upset		Short Diameter		Diameter Hole	Thickness	Size Stock Required		
										Width		Thickness
	Sq.	Hexagon		Sq.	Hexagon	Sq.	Hexagon			Sq.	Hexagon	Square or Hexagon
in.	in.	in.	in.	in.	in.	in.	in.	in.	in.	in.	in.	in.
$\frac{1}{4}$	$\frac{3}{8}$	$\frac{7}{16}$	$\frac{3}{16}$	$\frac{17}{32}$	$\frac{23}{32}$	$\frac{1}{2}$	$\frac{1}{2}$	$\frac{9}{32}$	$\frac{1}{4}$	$\frac{15}{32}$	$\frac{19}{32}$	$\frac{11}{64}$
$\frac{5}{16}$	$\frac{15}{32}$	$\frac{17}{32}$	$\frac{1}{4}$	$\frac{11}{16}$	$\frac{3}{4}$	$\frac{5}{8}$	$\frac{5}{8}$	$\frac{9}{32}$	$\frac{5}{16}$	$\frac{19}{32}$	$\frac{19}{32}$	$\frac{11}{32}$
$\frac{3}{8}$	$\frac{9}{16}$	$\frac{5}{8}$	$\frac{9}{32}$	$\frac{13}{16}$	$\frac{15}{16}$	$\frac{3}{4}$	$\frac{3}{4}$	$\frac{11}{32}$	$\frac{3}{8}$	$\frac{23}{32}$	$\frac{23}{32}$	$\frac{13}{32}$
$\frac{7}{16}$	$\frac{21}{32}$	$\frac{23}{32}$	$\frac{21}{64}$	$\frac{31}{32}$	1	$\frac{7}{8}$	$\frac{7}{8}$	$\frac{13}{32}$	$\frac{7}{16}$	$1\frac{1}{8}$	$1\frac{1}{8}$	$\frac{13}{32}$
$\frac{1}{2}$	$\frac{3}{4}$	$\frac{13}{16}$	$\frac{3}{8}$	$1\frac{1}{16}$	$1\frac{3}{32}$	1	1	$\frac{7}{16}$	$\frac{1}{2}$	$1\frac{5}{16}$	$1\frac{5}{16}$	$\frac{17}{32}$
$\frac{9}{16}$	$\frac{27}{32}$	$\frac{29}{32}$	$\frac{27}{64}$	$1\frac{7}{32}$	$1\frac{1}{4}$	$1\frac{1}{8}$	$1\frac{1}{8}$	$\frac{1}{2}$	$\frac{9}{16}$	$1\frac{1}{16}$	$1\frac{1}{16}$	$\frac{19}{32}$
$\frac{5}{8}$	$1\frac{3}{16}$	1	$\frac{15}{32}$	$1\frac{5}{16}$	$1\frac{13}{32}$	$1\frac{1}{4}$	$1\frac{1}{4}$	$\frac{9}{16}$	$\frac{5}{8}$	$1\frac{3}{16}$	$1\frac{3}{16}$	$\frac{21}{32}$
$\frac{3}{4}$	$1\frac{1}{8}$	$1\frac{3}{16}$	$\frac{9}{16}$	$1\frac{5}{8}$	$1\frac{9}{16}$	$1\frac{1}{2}$	$1\frac{3}{8}$	$\frac{21}{32}$	$\frac{3}{4}$	$1\frac{7}{16}$	$1\frac{5}{16}$	$1\frac{1}{16}$
$\frac{7}{8}$	$1\frac{5}{16}$	$1\frac{3}{8}$	$\frac{21}{32}$	$1\frac{7}{8}$	$1\frac{7}{8}$	$1\frac{3}{4}$	$1\frac{5}{8}$	$\frac{25}{32}$	$\frac{7}{8}$	$1\frac{11}{16}$	$1\frac{9}{16}$	$\frac{15}{16}$
1	$1\frac{1}{2}$	$1\frac{9}{16}$	$\frac{3}{4}$	$2\frac{9}{32}$	$2\frac{3}{32}$	2	$1\frac{7}{8}$	$\frac{7}{8}$	1	$1\frac{15}{16}$	$1\frac{13}{16}$	$1\frac{1}{16}$
$1\frac{1}{8}$	$1\frac{11}{16}$	$1\frac{3}{4}$	$\frac{27}{32}$	$2\frac{13}{32}$	$2\frac{7}{32}$	$2\frac{1}{4}$	2	$\frac{15}{16}$	$1\frac{1}{8}$	$2\frac{3}{16}$	$1\frac{13}{16}$	$1\frac{5}{16}$
$1\frac{1}{4}$	$1\frac{7}{8}$	$1\frac{15}{16}$	$\frac{15}{16}$	$2\frac{11}{16}$	$2\frac{7}{16}$	$2\frac{1}{2}$	$2\frac{1}{4}$	$1\frac{9}{32}$	$1\frac{1}{4}$	$2\frac{3}{8}$	$2\frac{3}{16}$	$1\frac{1}{2}$
$1\frac{3}{8}$	$2\frac{1}{16}$	$2\frac{1}{8}$	$1\frac{1}{16}$	$3\frac{3}{32}$	$2\frac{27}{32}$	$2\frac{3}{4}$	$2\frac{1}{2}$	$1\frac{7}{16}$	$1\frac{3}{8}$	$2\frac{5}{8}$	$2\frac{3}{8}$	$1\frac{5}{8}$
$1\frac{1}{2}$	$2\frac{1}{4}$	$2\frac{5}{16}$	$1\frac{1}{8}$	$3\frac{7}{32}$	3	3	$2\frac{3}{4}$	$1\frac{15}{16}$	$1\frac{1}{2}$	$2\frac{7}{8}$	$2\frac{5}{8}$	$1\frac{3}{4}$
$1\frac{5}{8}$	$2\frac{7}{16}$	$2\frac{1}{2}$	$1\frac{7}{32}$	$3\frac{13}{32}$	$3\frac{1}{4}$	$3\frac{1}{4}$	3	$1\frac{7}{16}$	$1\frac{5}{8}$	$3\frac{1}{8}$	$2\frac{7}{8}$	$1\frac{7}{8}$
$1\frac{3}{4}$	$2\frac{5}{8}$	$2\frac{11}{16}$	$1\frac{1}{16}$	$3\frac{3}{4}$	$3\frac{13}{32}$	$3\frac{1}{2}$	$3\frac{1}{4}$	$1\frac{9}{16}$	$1\frac{3}{4}$	$3\frac{3}{8}$	$3\frac{1}{8}$	2
$1\frac{7}{8}$	$2\frac{13}{16}$	$2\frac{7}{8}$	$1\frac{13}{32}$	$4\frac{13}{32}$	$3\frac{13}{32}$	$3\frac{3}{4}$	$3\frac{1}{2}$	$1\frac{11}{16}$	$1\frac{7}{8}$	$3\frac{5}{8}$	$3\frac{3}{8}$	$2\frac{1}{8}$
2	3	$3\frac{1}{16}$	$1\frac{1}{2}$	$4\frac{1}{16}$	4	4	$3\frac{1}{2}$	$1\frac{13}{16}$	2	$3\frac{7}{8}$	$3\frac{3}{8}$	$2\frac{1}{4}$
$2\frac{1}{4}$	$3\frac{3}{8}$	$3\frac{7}{16}$	$1\frac{11}{16}$	5	$4\frac{1}{16}$	$4\frac{1}{4}$	$3\frac{3}{4}$	2	$2\frac{1}{4}$	$4\frac{1}{8}$	$3\frac{5}{8}$	$2\frac{3}{8}$
$2\frac{1}{2}$	$3\frac{3}{4}$	$3\frac{13}{16}$	$1\frac{7}{8}$	$5\frac{5}{8}$	$4\frac{13}{32}$	$4\frac{1}{2}$	$4\frac{1}{4}$	$2\frac{1}{4}$	$2\frac{1}{2}$	$4\frac{3}{8}$	$4\frac{1}{8}$	$2\frac{5}{8}$
$2\frac{3}{4}$	$4\frac{1}{8}$	$4\frac{3}{16}$	$2\frac{1}{16}$	$5\frac{29}{32}$	$5\frac{5}{8}$	$4\frac{3}{4}$	$4\frac{1}{2}$	$2\frac{7}{16}$	$2\frac{3}{4}$	$4\frac{5}{8}$	$4\frac{1}{8}$	$2\frac{7}{8}$
3	$4\frac{1}{2}$	$4\frac{7}{16}$	$2\frac{1}{4}$	$6\frac{7}{16}$	$5\frac{11}{16}$	5	$4\frac{3}{4}$	$2\frac{11}{16}$	3	$4\frac{7}{8}$	$4\frac{3}{8}$	$3\frac{1}{8}$

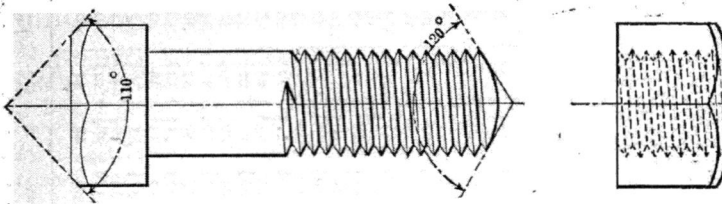

STOCK REQUIRED TO MAKE UNITED STATES STANDARD BOLT
HEADS AND NUTS — ROUGH

NATIONAL MACHINERY CO.

	BOLT HEADS SQUARE OR HEXAGON				NUTS SQUARE OR HEXAGON				
Size of Bolt	Short Diameter	Thickness	Stock Required for Upset		Short Diameter	Diameter Hole	Thickness	Size Stock Required Square or Hexagon	
			Square	Hexagon				Width	Thickness
in.	in.	in.	in.	in.	in.	in.	in.	in.	in.
$\frac{1}{4}$	$\frac{1}{2}$	$\frac{1}{4}$	$1\frac{9}{32}$	$1\frac{3}{32}$	$\frac{1}{2}$	$\frac{7}{16}$ scant	$\frac{1}{4}$	$\frac{17}{64}$	$\frac{13}{32}$
$\frac{5}{16}$	$\frac{19}{32}$	$\frac{19}{64}$	$1\frac{1}{8}$	$1\frac{1}{16}$	$\frac{19}{32}$	$\frac{1}{4}$ scant	$\frac{5}{16}$	$\frac{11}{32}$	$\frac{1}{8}$
$\frac{3}{8}$	$\frac{11}{16}$	$\frac{11}{32}$	$1\frac{1}{4}$	$1\frac{1}{4}$	$\frac{11}{16}$	$\frac{11}{32}$ scant	$\frac{3}{8}$	$\frac{3}{4}$	$1\frac{3}{8}$
$\frac{7}{16}$	$\frac{25}{32}$	$\frac{25}{64}$	$1\frac{5}{8}$	$1\frac{3}{8}$	$\frac{25}{32}$	$\frac{11}{32}$	$\frac{7}{16}$	$\frac{23}{32}$	$\frac{15}{32}$
$\frac{1}{2}$	$\frac{7}{8}$	$\frac{7}{16}$	$1\frac{23}{32}$	$1\frac{1}{2}$	$\frac{7}{8}$	$\frac{13}{32}$ scant	$\frac{1}{2}$	$1\frac{3}{8}$	$\frac{17}{32}$
$\frac{9}{16}$	$\frac{31}{32}$	$\frac{31}{64}$	$1\frac{13}{16}$	$1\frac{5}{8}$	$\frac{31}{32}$	$\frac{23}{64}$	$\frac{9}{16}$	$\frac{31}{32}$	$\frac{19}{32}$
$\frac{5}{8}$	$1\frac{1}{16}$	$\frac{17}{32}$	2	$1\frac{11}{16}$	$1\frac{1}{16}$	$\frac{1}{2}$ full	$\frac{5}{8}$	1	$\frac{21}{32}$
$\frac{3}{4}$	$1\frac{1}{4}$	$\frac{5}{8}$	$2\frac{9}{32}$	$1\frac{15}{16}$	$1\frac{1}{4}$	$\frac{5}{8}$ scant	$\frac{3}{4}$	$1\frac{3}{16}$	$1\frac{3}{8}$
$\frac{7}{8}$	$1\frac{7}{16}$	$\frac{23}{32}$	$2\frac{1}{2}$	$2\frac{3}{32}$	$1\frac{7}{16}$	$\frac{3}{4}$ scant	$\frac{7}{8}$	$1\frac{3}{8}$	$1\frac{5}{8}$
1	$1\frac{5}{8}$	$\frac{13}{16}$	$2\frac{3}{4}$	$2\frac{3}{8}$	$1\frac{5}{8}$	$\frac{7}{8}$ scant	1	$1\frac{9}{16}$	$1\frac{7}{16}$
$1\frac{1}{8}$	$1\frac{13}{16}$	$\frac{29}{32}$	3	$2\frac{19}{32}$	$1\frac{13}{16}$	$\frac{15}{16}$ full	$1\frac{1}{8}$	$1\frac{3}{4}$	$1\frac{9}{16}$
$1\frac{1}{4}$	2	1	$3\frac{1}{4}$	$2\frac{27}{32}$	2	$1\frac{1}{16}$ full	$1\frac{1}{4}$	$1\frac{7}{8}$	$1\frac{3}{4}$
$1\frac{3}{8}$	$2\frac{3}{16}$	$1\frac{3}{32}$	$3\frac{1}{8}$	3	$2\frac{3}{16}$	$1\frac{5}{32}$ full	$1\frac{3}{8}$	$2\frac{1}{16}$	$1\frac{1}{2}$
$1\frac{1}{2}$	$2\frac{3}{8}$	$1\frac{3}{16}$	$3\frac{5}{16}$	$3\frac{5}{16}$	$2\frac{3}{8}$	$1\frac{9}{32}$ full	$1\frac{1}{2}$	$2\frac{1}{4}$	$1\frac{5}{8}$
$1\frac{5}{8}$	$2\frac{9}{16}$	$1\frac{9}{32}$	$4\frac{1}{16}$	$3\frac{1}{2}$	$2\frac{9}{16}$	$1\frac{13}{32}$ scant	$1\frac{5}{8}$	$2\frac{7}{16}$	$1\frac{3}{4}$
$1\frac{3}{4}$	$2\frac{3}{4}$	$1\frac{3}{8}$	$4\frac{1}{8}$	$3\frac{3}{4}$	$2\frac{3}{4}$	$1\frac{1}{2}$ scant	$1\frac{3}{4}$	$2\frac{5}{8}$	$1\frac{7}{8}$
$1\frac{7}{8}$	$2\frac{15}{16}$	$1\frac{15}{32}$	$4\frac{5}{8}$	4	$2\frac{15}{16}$	$1\frac{5}{8}$ scant	$1\frac{7}{8}$	$2\frac{13}{16}$	2
2	$3\frac{1}{8}$	$1\frac{9}{16}$	$4\frac{7}{8}$	$4\frac{1}{4}$	$3\frac{1}{8}$	$1\frac{23}{32}$ scant	2	3	$2\frac{1}{8}$
$2\frac{1}{4}$	$3\frac{1}{2}$	$1\frac{3}{4}$	$5\frac{1}{16}$	$4\frac{11}{16}$	$3\frac{1}{2}$	$1\frac{31}{32}$ scant	$2\frac{1}{4}$	$3\frac{3}{8}$	$2\frac{3}{8}$
$2\frac{1}{2}$	$3\frac{7}{8}$	$1\frac{15}{16}$	$5\frac{13}{16}$	$5\frac{3}{16}$	$3\frac{7}{8}$	$2\frac{1}{8}$	$2\frac{1}{2}$	$3\frac{3}{4}$	$2\frac{5}{8}$
$2\frac{3}{4}$	$4\frac{1}{4}$	$2\frac{1}{8}$	$6\frac{7}{16}$	$5\frac{1}{2}$	$4\frac{1}{4}$	$2\frac{7}{16}$	$2\frac{3}{4}$	$4\frac{1}{8}$	$2\frac{7}{8}$
3	$4\frac{5}{8}$	$2\frac{5}{16}$	7	$6\frac{1}{8}$	$4\frac{5}{8}$	$2\frac{11}{16}$	3	$4\frac{1}{2}$	$3\frac{1}{8}$

TABLE OF BOARD FEET IN PIECES 1 TO 24 INCHES WIDE UP TO 24 FEET LONG

THE table herewith shows the board feet contained in planks of a given width and length. This table is of use especially to the patternmaker but may be of value to any one having to make calculations in board measure.

Length of Board in Feet

Width of Board in Inches	1'	2'	3'	4'	5'	6'	7'	8'	9'	10'	11'	12'	13'	14'	15'	16'	18'	20'	22'	24'
1"	1/12	1/6	1/4	1/3	5/12	1/2	7/12	2/3	3/4	5/6	11/12	1	1 1/12	1 1/6	1 1/4	1 1/3	1 1/2	1 2/3	1 5/6	2
2"	1/6	1/3	1/2	2/3	5/6	1	1 1/6	1 1/3	1 1/2	1 2/3	1 5/6	2	2 1/6	2 1/3	2 1/2	2 2/3	3	3 1/3	3 2/3	4
3"	1/4	1/2	3/4	1	1 1/4	1 1/2	1 3/4	2	2 1/4	2 1/2	2 3/4	3	3 1/4	3 1/2	3 3/4	4	4 1/2	5	5 1/2	6
4"	1/3	2/3	1	1 1/3	1 2/3	2	2 1/3	2 2/3	3	3 1/3	3 2/3	4	4 1/3	4 2/3	5	5 1/3	6	6 2/3	7 1/3	8
5"	5/12	5/6	1 1/4	1 2/3	2 1/12	2 1/2	2 11/12	3 1/3	3 3/4	4 1/6	4 7/12	5	5 5/12	5 5/6	6 1/4	6 2/3	7 1/2	8 1/3	9 1/6	10
6"	1/2	1	1 1/2	2	2 1/2	3	3 1/2	4	4 1/2	5	5 1/2	6	6 1/2	7	7 1/2	8	9	10	11	12
7"	7/12	1 1/6	1 3/4	2 1/3	2 11/12	3 1/2	4 1/12	4 2/3	5 1/4	5 5/6	6 5/12	7	7 7/12	8 1/6	8 3/4	9 1/3	10 1/2	11 2/3	12 5/6	14
8"	2/3	1 1/3	2	2 2/3	3 1/3	4	4 2/3	5 1/3	6	6 2/3	7 1/3	8	8 2/3	9 1/3	10	10 2/3	12	13 1/3	14 2/3	16
9"	3/4	1 1/2	2 1/4	3	3 3/4	4 1/2	5 1/4	6	6 3/4	7 1/2	8 1/4	9	9 3/4	10 1/2	11 1/4	12	13 1/2	15	16 1/2	18
10"	5/6	1 2/3	2 1/2	3 1/3	4 1/6	5	5 5/6	6 2/3	7 1/2	8 1/3	9 1/6	10	10 5/6	11 2/3	12 1/2	13 1/3	15	16 2/3	18 1/3	20
11"	11/12	1 5/6	2 3/4	3 2/3	4 7/12	5 1/2	6 5/12	7 1/3	8 1/4	9 1/6	10 1/12	11	11 11/12	12 5/6	13 3/4	14 2/3	16 1/2	18 1/3	20 1/6	22
12"	1	2	3	4	5	6	7	8	9	10	11	12	13	14	15	16	18	20	22	24
13"	1 1/12	2 1/6	3 1/4	4 1/3	5 5/12	6 1/2	7 7/12	8 2/3	9 3/4	10 5/6	11 11/12	13	14 1/12	15 1/6	16 1/4	17 1/3	19 1/2	21 2/3	23 5/6	26
14"	1 1/6	2 1/3	3 1/2	4 2/3	5 5/6	7	8 1/6	9 1/3	10 1/2	11 2/3	12 5/6	14	15 1/6	16 1/3	17 1/2	18 2/3	21	23 1/3	25 2/3	28
15"	1 1/4	2 1/2	3 3/4	5	6 1/4	7 1/2	8 3/4	10	11 1/4	12 1/2	13 3/4	15	16 1/4	17 1/2	18 3/4	20	22 1/2	25	27 1/2	30
16"	1 1/3	2 2/3	4	5 1/3	6 2/3	8	9 1/3	10 2/3	12	13 1/3	14 2/3	16	17 1/3	18 2/3	20	21 1/3	24	26 2/3	29 1/3	32
17"	1 5/12	2 5/6	4 1/4	5 2/3	7 1/12	8 1/2	9 11/12	11 1/3	12 3/4	14 1/6	15 7/12	17	18 5/12	19 5/6	21 1/4	22 2/3	25 1/2	28 1/3	31 1/6	34
18"	1 1/2	3	4 1/2	6	7 1/2	9	10 1/2	12	13 1/2	15	16 1/2	18	19 1/2	21	22 1/2	24	27	30	33	36
19"	1 7/12	3 1/6	4 3/4	6 1/3	7 11/12	9 1/2	11 1/12	12 2/3	14 1/4	15 5/6	17 5/12	19	20 7/12	22 1/6	23 3/4	25 1/3	28 1/2	31 2/3	34 5/6	38
20"	1 2/3	3 1/3	5	6 2/3	8 1/3	10	11 2/3	13 1/3	15	16 2/3	18 1/3	20	21 2/3	23 1/3	25	26 2/3	30	33 1/3	36 2/3	40
21"	1 3/4	3 1/2	5 1/4	7	8 3/4	10 1/2	12 1/4	14	15 3/4	17 1/2	19 1/4	21	22 3/4	24 1/2	26 1/4	28	31 1/2	35	38 1/2	42
22"	1 5/6	3 2/3	5 1/2	7 1/3	9 1/6	11	12 5/6	14 2/3	16 1/2	18 1/3	20 1/6	22	23 5/6	25 2/3	27 1/2	29 1/3	33	36 2/3	40 1/3	44
23"	1 11/12	3 5/6	5 3/4	7 2/3	9 7/12	11 1/2	13 5/12	15 1/3	17 1/4	19 1/6	21 1/12	23	24 11/12	26 5/6	28 3/4	30 2/3	34 1/2	38 1/3	42 1/6	46
24"	2	4	6	8	10	12	14	16	18	20	22	24	26	28	30	32	36	40	44	48

Width of Board in Inches

Table gives board feet in an inch thick plank. For other thicknesses multiply by thickness in inches.

QUICK WAY OF ESTIMATING LUMBER FOR A PATTERN

MULTIPLY length, breadth, and thickness in inches together and this by 7, pointing off three places.

Board 8 inches wide, 18 inches long, 1 inch thick. $8 \times 18 \times 1 \times 7 = 1.008$ square feet. This is .008 too much, but near enough for most work. Board $1\frac{1}{2} \times 10 \times 36 = 540 \times 7 = 3.780$. The correct answer is 3.75.

TABLE GIVING PROPORTIONATE WEIGHT OF CASTINGS TO WEIGHT OF WOOD PATTERNS

A Pattern Weighing One Pound Made of (Less weight of Core Prints)	Cast Iron	Brass	Copper	Bronze	Bell Metal	Zinc
Pine or Fir..	16	18.8	19.7	19.3	17	15.5
Oak........	9	10.1	10.4	10.3	10.9	8.6
Beech	9.7	10.9	11.4	11.3	11.9	9.1
Linden	13.4	15.1	16.7	15.5	16.3	12.9
Pear........	10.2	11.5	11.9	11.8	12.4	9.8
Birch.......	10.6	11.9	12.3	12.2	12.9	10.2
Alder.......	12.8	14.3	14.9	14.7	15.5	12.2
Mahogany ..	11.7	13.2	13.7	13.5	14.2	11.2
Brass.......	0.85	0.95	0.99	0.98	1.0	0.81

DEGREES OBTAINED BY OPENING A TWO-FOOT RULE

Degrees	Inches	Degrees	Inches	Degrees	Inches
1	.21	15	3.12	55	11.08
2	.422	20	4.17	60	12
3	.633	25	5.21	65	12.89
4	.837	30	6.21	70	13.76
5	1.04	35	7.20	75	14.61
7.5	1.57	40	8.21	80	15.43
10	2.09	45	9.20	85	16.21
14.5	3.015	50	10.12	90	16.97

Open a two-foot rule until open ends are distance apart given in table when degrees given in table can be scribed. Same results can be had with two 12-inch steel scales placed together at one end.

WEIGHT OF FILLETS

To facilitate the calculations of the weights of the different parts of a machine from the drawings, the accompanying table of areas or volumes of fillets having radii from $\frac{1}{16}$ to 3 inches can be used. It has been calculated for fillets connecting sides that are at right angles to each other.

TABLE OF AREAS OR VOLUMES OF FILLETS

Radius of Fillet in Inches	Area or Volume of Fillet in Sq. or Cubic Inches	Radius of Fillet in Inches	Area or Volume of Fillet in Sq. or Cubic Inches
$\frac{1}{16}$	.0008	$1\frac{9}{16}$	.5240
$\frac{1}{8}$	.0033	$1\frac{5}{8}$	.5667
$\frac{3}{16}$	.0075	$1\frac{11}{16}$	.6119
$\frac{1}{4}$	.0134	$1\frac{3}{4}$	.6572
$\frac{5}{16}$	.0209	$1\frac{13}{16}$	.7050
$\frac{3}{8}$	.0302	$1\frac{7}{8}$	.7543
$\frac{7}{16}$	.0410	$1\frac{15}{16}$	.8056
$\frac{1}{2}$	.0537	2	.8584
$\frac{9}{16}$	.0678	$2\frac{1}{16}$	.9129
$\frac{5}{8}$	.0838	$2\frac{1}{8}$	.9690
$\frac{11}{16}$	.1013	$2\frac{3}{16}$	1.0269
$\frac{3}{4}$	.1207	$2\frac{1}{4}$	1.0864
$\frac{13}{16}$	.1417	$2\frac{5}{16}$	1.1475
$\frac{7}{8}$	.1643	$2\frac{3}{8}$	1.2105
$\frac{15}{16}$	.1886	$2\frac{7}{16}$	1.2749
1	.2146	$2\frac{1}{2}$	1.3413
$1\frac{1}{16}$	.2423	$2\frac{9}{16}$	1.4086
$1\frac{1}{8}$	.2716	$2\frac{5}{8}$	1.4787
$1\frac{3}{16}$	.3026	$2\frac{11}{16}$	1.5500
$1\frac{1}{4}$	.3353	$2\frac{3}{4}$	1.6229
$1\frac{5}{16}$	.3697	$2\frac{13}{16}$	1.6869
$1\frac{3}{8}$	.4057	$2\frac{7}{8}$	1.7739
$1\frac{7}{16}$	.4434	$2\frac{15}{16}$	1.8518
$1\frac{1}{2}$	.4829	3	1.9314

To find the volume of a fillet by this table when the radius and length are given, multiply the value in the table opposite the given radius by the length of the fillet in inches, and this result multiplied by the weight of a cubic inch of the material will give the weight of the fillet.

LAYING OUT A SQUARE CORNER

It sometimes happens that we wish to lay out a perfectly square corner and have no square of any kind handy. Here is a way that requires nothing but a scale or rule, or even a straight stick without any graduations whatever will do. Using this stick, draw a line as *A C* (Fig. 1) and at one end of this draw the line *B D* at any angle. This line must be straight, twice as long as *A C* and

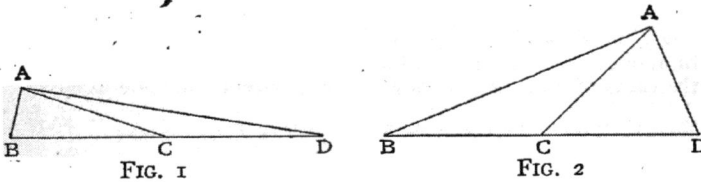

FIG. 1   FIG. 2

of equal length each side of the point *C*. Then if you join points *D A B*, you have an exact right-angle or square corner. Fig. 2 is simply another example of this, in which the line *A C* has been drawn at a very different angle to show that it works in any position. Joining the ends *D A B* as before also gives an exact right angle.

ANOTHER METHOD

Another method is by what is known as the 6, 8 and 10 rule This means that if a triangle has sides in the ratio of 6, 8 and 10, the angle is 90 degrees. Lay down a line 6 units long, either inches, feet or yards. Lay off another line 8 units long as nearly right angles as possible. Measure across the ends of the two lines and adjust until this distance is 10 units, which makes it a right angle. These distances may be 3, 4 and 5; 12, 16 and 20 or any combination in this ratio. It is largely used in laying out large corners.

SPEED FOR WOOD TURNING

A good average speed for a wood turning lathe is a surface or cutting speed of from 1,000 to 1,500 ft. per minute. Where work does not exceed 1-in. diameter the lathe may be run 3,000 r.p.m.; for 2-in. stock 2,500; for 3-in., 2,000, or a little less, and for larger stock, the speed is reduced in proportion.

COOLING HOT BEARINGS

A hot box can be cooled by pouring sulphur on the bearing. It melts at 220 degrees and puts a smooth surface on both journals and bearings. It fills oil groove but can be dissolved with benzine if machine cannot be stopped. Either stick or flowers of sulphur will do. Graphite is also good but cannot be used where the color is objectionable as in flour mills or other white stock.

WIRE GAGES AND STOCK WEIGHTS

TWIST DRILL AND STEEL WIRE GAGE SIZES

THE Twist Drill and Steel Wire Gage is used for measuring the sizes of twist drills and steel drill rods. Rod sizes by this gage should not be confused with Stubs' Steel Wire Gage sizes. The difference between the sizes of corresponding numbers in the two gages ranges from about .0005 to .004 inch, the Stubs sizes being the smaller except in the cases of a few numbers where the systems coincide exactly.

TWIST DRILL AND STEEL WIRE GAGE SIZES

No. of Gage	Dia. in Inches	No. of Gage	Dia. in Inches	No. of Gage	Dia. in Inches	No. of Gage	Dia. in Inches
1	.2280	21	.1590	41	.0960	61	.0390
2	.2210	22	.1570	42	.0935	62	.0380
3	.2130	23	.1540	43	.0890	63	.0370
4	.2090	24	.1520	44	.0860	64	.0360
5	.2055	25	.1495	45	.0820	65	.0350
6	.2040	26	.1470	46	.0810	66	.0330
7	.2010	27	.1440	47	.0785	67	.0320
8	.1990	28	.1405	48	.0760	68	.0310
9	.1960	29	.1360	49	.0730	69	.02925
10	.1935	30	.1285	50	.0700	70	.0280
11	.1910	31	.1200	51	.0670	71	.0260
12	.1890	32	.1160	52	.0635	72	.0250
13	.1850	33	.1130	53	.0595	73	.0240
14	.1820	34	.1110	54	.0550	74	.0225
15	.1800	35	.1100	55	.0520	75	.0210
16	.1770	36	.1065	56	.0465	76	.0200
17	.1730	37	.1040	57	.0430	77	.0180
18	.1695	38	.1015	58	.0420	78	.0160
19	.1660	39	.0995	59	.0410	79	.0145
20	.1610	40	.0980	60	.0400	80	.0135

STUBS' GAGES

IN using Stubs' Gages, the difference between the Stubs Iron Wire Gage and the Stubs Steel Wire Gage should be kept in mind. The Stubs Iron Wire Gage is the one commonly known as the English Standard Wire, or Birmingham Gage, and designates the Stubs soft wire sizes. The Stubs Steel Wire Gage is used in measuring drawn steel wire or drill rods of Stubs' make and is also used by many American makers of drill rods.

DIMENSIONS IN DECIMAL PARTS OF AN INCH

Number of Gage	American or Brown & Sharpe	Birmingham or Stubs' Iron Wire	Washburn & Moen Mfg. Co.	Trenton Iron Co.	Stubs' Steel Wire	Imperial Wire Gage	U. S. Standard for Plate
000000	....	......	......	......	......	.464	.46875
00000	....	......	......	.450	......	.432	.4375
0000	.46	.454	.3938	.400	......	.400	.40625
000	.40964	.425	.3625	.360	......	.372	.375
00	.3648	.380	.3310	.330	......	.348	.34375
0	.32486	.340	.3065	.305	......	.324	.3125
1	.2893	.300	.2830	.285	.227	.300	.28125
2	.25763	.284	.2625	.265	.219	.276	.265625
3	.22942	.259	.2437	.245	.212	.252	.25
4	.20431	.238	.2253	.225	.207	.232	.234375
5	.18194	.220	.2070	.205	.204	.212	.21875
6	.16202	.203	.1920	.190	.201	.192	.203125
7	.14428	.180	.1770	.175	.199	.176	.1875
8	.12849	.165	.1620	.160	.197	.160	.171875
9	.11443	.148	.1483	.145	.194	.144	.15625
10	.10189	.134	.1350	.130	.191	.128	.140625
11	.090742	.120	.1205	.1175	.188	.116	.125
12	.080808	.109	.1055	.105	.185	.104	.109375
13	.071961	.095	.0915	.0925	.182	.092	.09375
14	.064084	.083	.0800	.080	.180	.080	.078125
15	.057068	.072	.0720	.070	.178	.072	.0703125
16	.05082	.065	.0625	.061	.175	.064	.0625
17	.045257	.058	.0540	.0525	.172	.056	.05625
18	.040303	.049	.0475	.045	.168	.048	.05
19	.03589	.042	.0410	.040	.164	.040	.04375
20	.031961	.035	.0348	.035	.161	.036	.0375
21	.028462	.032	.03175	.031	.157	.032	.034375
22	.025347	.028	.0286	.028	.155	.028	.03125
23	.022571	.025	.0258	.025	.153	.024	.028125
24	.0201	.022	.0230	.0225	.151	.022	.025
25	.0179	.020	.0204	.020	.148	.020	.021875
26	.01594	.018	.0181	.018	.146	.018	.01875
27	.014195	.016	.0173	.017	.143	.0164	.0171875
28	.012641	.014	.0162	.016	.139	.0149	.015625
29	.011257	.013	.0150	.015	.134	.0136	.0140625
30	.010025	.012	.0140	.014	.127	.0124	.0125
31	.008928	.010	.0132	.013	.120	.0116	.0109375
32	.00795	.009	.0128	.012	.115	.0108	.01015625
33	.00708	.008	.0118	.011	.112	.0100	.009375
34	.006304	.007	.0104	.010	.110	.0092	.00859375
35	.005614	.005	.0095	.0095	.108	.0084	.0078125
36	.005	.004	.0090	.009	.106	.0076	.00703125
37	.004453			.0085	.103	.0068	.006640625
38	.003965			.008	.101	.0060	.00625
39	.003531			.0075	.099	.0052	
40	.003144			.007	.097	.0048	

WIRE AND DRILL SIZES ARRANGED CONSECUTIVELY

Dia. of Wire	American or B. & S.	B'ham or Stubs' Wire	Stubs' Steel Wire	Twist Drill and Steel Wire
			Gage Number	
.00314	40			
.00353	39			
.00397	38			
.004		36		
.0045	37			
.005	36	35		
.0056	35			
.0063	34			
.007		34		
.0071	33			
.008	32	33		
.0089	31			
.009		32		
.010	30	31		
.0113	29			
.012		30		
.0126	28			
.013		29	80	
.0135				80
.014		28	79	
.0142	27			
.0145				79
.015			78	
.0159	26			
.016		27	77	78
.0179	25			
.018		26	76	77
.020		25	75	76
.0201	24			
.021				75
.022		24	74	
.0225				74
.0226	23			
.023			73	
.024			72	73
.025		23		72
.0253	22			
.026			71	71
.027			70	
.028		22		70
.0285	21			
.029			69	
.0293				69
.030			68	
.031			67	68
.032	20	21	66	67
.033			65	66
.035		20	64	65
.0359	19			
.036			63	64
.037			62	63
.038			61	62
.039			60	61
.040			59	60
.0403	18			
.041			58	59
.042		19	57	58
.043				57
.045			56	
.0453	17			
.0465				56
.049		18		
.050			55	
.0508	16			
.052				55
.055			54	54
.0571	15			
.058		17	53	
.0595				53
.063			52	
.0635				52
.0641	14			
.065		16		
.066			51	
.067				51
.069			50	
.070				50
.072	13	15	49	
.073				49
.075			48	
.076				48
.077			47	
.0785				47
.079			46	
.0808	12			
.081			45	46
.082				45
.083		14		
.085			44	
.086				44
.088			43	
.089				43
.0907	11			
.092			42	
.0935				42
.095		13	41	
.096				41
.097			40	
.098				40
.099			39	
.0995				39
.101			38	
.1015				38
.1019	10			
.103			37	
.104				37
.106			36	
.1065				36
.108			35	

WIRE AND DRILL SIZES ARRANGED CONSECUTIVELY

Dia. of Wire	American or B.&S.	B'ham or Stubs' Wire	Stubs' Steel Wire	Twist Drill and Steel Wire	Dia. of Wire	American or B.&S.	B'ham or Stubs' Wire	Stubs' Steel Wire	Twist Drill and Steel Wire
	Gage Number					Gage Number			
.109		12			.203		6		
.110			34	35	.204			5	6
.111				34	.2043	4			
.112			33		.2055				5
.113				33	.207			4	
.1144	9				.209				4
.115			32		.212			3	
.116				32	.213				3
.120		11	31	31	.219			2	
.127			30		.220		5		
.1285	8			30	.221				2
.134		10	29		.227			1	
.136				29	.228				1
.139			28		.2294	3			
.1405				28	.234				A
.143			27		.238		4		B
.144				27	.242				C
.1443	7				.246				D
.146			26		.250				E
.147				26	.257				F
.148		9	25		.2576	2			
.1495				25	.259		3		
.151			24		.261				G
.152				24	.266				H
.153			23		.272				I
.154				23	.277				J
.155			22		.281				K
.157			21	22	.284		2		
.159				21	.2893	1			
.161			20	20	.290				L
.162	6				.295				M
.164			19		.300		1		
.165		8			.302				N
.166				19	.316				O
.168			18		.323				P
.1695				18	.3249	0			
.172			17		.332				Q
.173				17	.339				R
.175			16		.340		0		
.177				16	.348				S
.178			15		.358				T
.180		7	14	15	.3648	00			
.1819	5				.368				U
.182			13	14	.377				V
.185			12	13	.380		00		
.188			11		.386				W
.189				12	.397				X
.191			10	11	.404				Y
.1935				10	.4096	000			
.194			9		.413				Z
.196				9	.425		000		
.197			8		.454		0000		
.199			7	8	.460	0000			
.201			6	7					

STUBS' STEEL WIRE SIZES AND WEIGHTS

As stated in the explanatory note regarding Stubs' Gages at the bottom of page 406 the Stubs steel wire gage is used for measuring drawn steel wire and drill rods of Stubs' make and is also used by various drill rod makers in America.

STUBS' STEEL WIRE SIZES, AND WEIGHT IN POUNDS PER LINEAR FOOT

Letter and No. of Gage	Dia. in Inches	Weight per Foot	No. of Wire Gage	Dia. in Inches	Weight per Foot	No. of Wire Gage	Dia. in Inches	Weight per Foot
Z	.413	.456	10	.191	.098	46	.079	.017
Y	.404	.437	11	.188	.095	47	.077	.016
X	.397	.422	12	.185	.092	48	.075	.015
W	.386	.399	13	.182	.089	49	.072	.014
V	.377	.380	14	.180	.087	50	.069	.013
U	.368	.362	15	.178	.085	51	.066	.012
T	.358	.335	16	.175	.082	52	.063	.011
S	.348	.324	17	.172	.079	53	.058	.009
R	.339	.307	18	.168	.075	54	.055	.008
Q	.332	.295	19	.164	.072	55	.050	.007
P	.323	.280	20	.161	.069	56	.045	.006
O	.316	.267	21	.157	.066	57	.042	.0047
N	.302	.244	22	.155	.064	58	.041	.0045
M	.295	233	23	.153	.063	59	.040	.0042
L	.290	.225	24	.151	.061	60	.039	.0040
K	.281	.211	25	.148	.059	61	.038	.0039
J	.277	.205	26	.146	.057	62	.037	.0037
I	.272	.192	27	.143	.055	63	.036	.0035
H	.266	.189	28	.139	.052	64	.035	.0033
G	.261	.182	29	.134	.048	65	.033	.0029
F	.257	.177	30	.127	.043	66	.032	.0027
E	.250	.167	31	.120	.039	67	.031	.0026
D	.246	.162	32	.115	.035	68	.030	.0024
C	.242	.159	33	.112	.034	69	.029	.0022
B	.238	.152	34	.110	.032	70	.027	.0020
A	.234	.146	35	.108	.031	71	.026	.0018
1	.227	.138	36	.106	.030	72	.024	.0015
2	.219	.128	37	.103	.028	73	.023	.0014
3	.212	.120	38	.101	.027	74	.022	.0013
4	.207	.115	39	.099	.026	75	.020	.0011
5	.204	.111	40	.097	.025	76	.018	.0009
6	.201	.108	41	.095	.024	77	.016	.0007
7	.199	.106	42	.092	.023	78	.015	.0006
8	.197	.104	43	.088	.020	79	.014	.0005
9	.194	.101	44	.085	.019	80	.013	.0004
			45	.081	.018			

MUSIC WIRE SIZES

No. of Gage	Washburn & Moen	Webster & Horsefall	No. of Gage	Washburn & Moen	Webster & Horsefall	No. of Gage	Washburn & Moen	Webster & Horsefall
8–0	.0083		6	.0215	.016	19	.0414	.043
7–0	.0087		7	.023	.018	20	.0434	.045
6–0	.0095		8	.0243	.020	21	.046	.047
5–0	.010		9	.0256	.022	22	.0483	.052
4–0	.011	.006	10	.027	.024	23	.051	.055
3–0	.012	.007	11	.0284	.026	24	.055	.059
2–0	.0133	.008	12	.0296	.029	25	.0586	.061
1–0	.0144	.009	13	.0314	.031	26	.0626	.065
1	.0156	.010	14	.0326	.033	27	.0658	.070
2	.0166	.011	15	.0345	.035	28	.072	.072
3	.0178	.012	16	.036	.037	29	.076	.077
4	.0188	.013	17	.0377	.039	30	.080	.083
5	.0202	.014	18	.0395	.041			

WEIGHTS OF SHEET STEEL AND IRON
UNITED STATES STANDARD GAGE
(Adopted by U. S. Government, July 1, 1893)

Number of Gage	App. Thickness	Weight per Sq. Foot		No. of Gage	App. Thickness	Weight per Sq. Foot	
		Steel	Iron			Steel	Iron
0000000	.5	20.320	20.00	17	.05625	2.286	2.25
000000	.46875	19.050	18.75	18	.05	2.032	2.
00000	.4375	17.780	17.50	19	.04375	1.778	1.75
0000	.40625	16.510	16.25	20	.0375	1.524	1.50
000	.375	15.240	15.00	21	.03437	1.397	1.375
00	.34375	13.970	13.75	22	.03125	1.270	1.25
0	.3125	12.700	12.50	23	.02812	1.143	1.125
1	.28125	11.430	11.25	24	.025	1.016	1.
2	.26562	10.795	10.625	25	.02187	.903	.875
3	.25	10.160	10.00	26	.01875	.762	.75
4	.23437	9.525	9.375	27	.01718	.698	.687
5	.21875	8.890	8.75	28	.01562	.635	.623
6	.20312	8.255	8.125	29	.01406	.571	.562
7	.1875	7.620	7.5	30	.0125	.508	.5
8	.17187	6.985	6.875	31	.01093	.440	.437
9	.15625	6.350	6.25	32	.01015	.413	.406
10	.14062	5.715	5.625	33	.00937	.381	.375
11	.125	5.080	5.00	34	.00859	.349	.343
12	.10937	4.445	4.375	35	.00781	.317	.312
13	.09375	3.810	3.75	36	.00703	.285	.281
14	.07812	3.175	3.125	37	.00664	.271	.265
15	.07031	2.857	2.812	38	.00625	.254	.25
16	.0625	2.540	2.50				

Weight of 1 cubic foot is assumed to be 487.7 lbs. for steel plates and 480 lbs. for iron plates.

WEIGHTS OF STEEL, WROUGHT IRON, BRASS AND COPPER PLATES
AMERICAN OR BROWN & SHARPE GAGE

No. of Gage	Thickness in Inches	WEIGHT IN LBS. PER SQUARE FOOT			
		Steel	Iron	Brass	Copper
0000	.46	18.77	18.40	19.688	20.838
000	.4096	16.71	16.38	17.533	18.557
00	.3648	14.88	14.59	15.613	16.525
0	.3249	13.26	13.00	13.904	14.716
1	.2893	11.80	11.57	12.382	13.105
2	.2576	10.51	10.30	11.027	11.670
3	.2294	9.39	9.18	9.819	10.392
4	.2043	8.34	8.17	8.745	9.255
5	.1819	7.42	7.28	7.788	8.242
6	.1620	6.61	6.48	6.935	7.340
7	.1443	5.89	5.77	6.175	6.536
8	.1285	5.24	5.14	5.499	5.821
9	.1144	4.67	4.58	4.898	5.183
10	.1019	4.16	4.08	4.361	4.616
11	.0908	3.70	3.63	3.884	4.110
12	.0808	3.30	3.23	3.458	3.660
13	.0720	2.94	2.88	3.080	3.260
14	.0641	2.62	2.56	2.743	2.903
15	.0571	2.33	2.28	2.442	2.585
16	.0508	2.07	2.03	2.175	2.302
17	.0453	1.85	1.81	1.937	2.050
18	.0403	1.64	1.61	1.725	1.825
19	.0359	1.46	1.44	1.536	1.626
20	.0320	1.31	1.28	1.367	1.448
21	.0285	1.16	1.14	1.218	1.289
22	.0253	1.03	1.01	1.085	1.148
23	.0226	.922	.904	.966	1.023
24	.0201	.820	.804	.860	.910
25	.0179	.730	.716	.766	.811
26	.0159	.649	.636	.682	.722
27	.0142	.579	.568	.608	.643
28	.0126	.514	.504	.541	.573
29	.0113	.461	.452	.482	.510
30	.0100	.408	.400	.429	.454
31	.0089	.363	.356	.382	.404
32	.0080	.326	.320	.340	.360
33	.0071	.290	.284	.303	.321
34	.0063	.257	.252	.269	.286
35	.0056	.228	.224	.240	.254
36	.0050	.190	.188	.214	.226
37	.0045	.169	.167	.191	.202
38	.0040	.151	.149	.170	.180
39	.0035	.134	.132	.151	.160
40	.0031	.119	.118	.135	.142

WEIGHTS OF STEEL, WROUGHT IRON, BRASS AND COPPER PLATES
BIRMINGHAM OR STUBS' GAGE

No. of Gage	Thickness in Inches	WEIGHT IN LBS. PER SQUARE FOOT			
		Steel	Iron	Brass	Copper
0000	.454	18.52	18.16	19.431	20.556
000	.425	17.34	17.00	18.190	19.253
00	.380	15.30	15.20	16.264	17.214
0	.340	13.87	13.60	14.552	15.402
1	.300	12.24	12.00	12.840	13.590
2	.284	11.59	11.36	12.155	12.865
3	.259	10.57	10.36	11.085	11.733
4	.238	9.71	9.52	10.186	10.781
5	.220	8.98	8.80	9.416	9.966
6	.203	8.28	8.12	8.689	9.196
7	.180	7.34	7.20	7.704	8.154
8	.165	6.73	6.60	7.062	7.475
9	.148	6.04	5.92	6.334	6.704
10	.134	5.47	5.36	5.735	6.070
11	.120	4.90	4.80	5.137	5.436
12	.109	4.45	4.36	4.667	4.938
13	.095	3.88	3.80	4.066	4.303
14	.083	3.39	3.32	3.552	3.769
15	.072	2.94	2.88	3.081	3.262
16	.065	2.65	2.60	2.782	2.945
17	.058	2.37	2.32	2.482	2.627
18	.049	2.00	1.96	2.097	2.220
19	.042	1.71	1.68	1.797	1.902
20	.035	1.43	1.40	1.498	1.585
21	.032	1.31	1.28	1.369	1.450
22	.028	1.14	1.12	1.198	1.270
23	.025	1.02	1.00	1.070	1.132
24	.022	.898	.88	.941	.997
25	.020	.816	.80	.856	.906
26	.018	.734	.72	.770	.815
27	.016	.653	.64	.685	.725
28	.014	.571	.56	.599	.634
29	.013	.530	.52	.556	.589
30	.012	.490	.48	.514	.544
31	.010	.408	.40	.428	.453
32	.009	.367	.36	.385	.408
33	.008	.326	.32	.342	.362
34	.007	.286	.28	.2996	.317
35	.005	.204	.20	.214	.227
36	.004	.163	.16	.171	.181

WEIGHTS OF STEEL, IRON, BRASS AND COPPER WIRE

AMERICAN OR BROWN & SHARPE GAGE

No. of Gage	Dia. in Inches	WEIGHT IN LBS. PER 1000 LINEAR FEET			
		Steel	Iron	Brass	Copper
0000	.4600	566.03	560.74	605.18	640.51
000	.4096	448.88	444.68	479.91	507.95
00	.3648	355.99	352.66	380.67	402.83
0	.3247	282.30	279.67	301.82	319.45
1	.2893	223.89	221.79	239.35	253.34
2	.2576	177.55	175.89	189.82	200.91
3	.2294	140.80	139.48	150.52	159.32
4	.2043	111.66	110.62	119.38	126.35
5	.1819	88.548	87.720	94.666	100.20
6	.1620	70.221	69.565	75.075	79.462
7	.1447	55.685	55.165	59.545	63.013
8	.1285	44.164	43.751	47.219	49.976
9	.1144	35.026	34.699	37.437	39.636
10	.1019	27.772	27.512	29.687	31.426
11	.0907	22.026	21.820	23.549	24.924
12	.0808	17.468	17.304	18.676	19.766
13	.0720	13.851	13.722	14.809	15.674
14	.0641	10.989	10.886	11.746	12.435
15	.0571	8.712	8.631	9.315	9.859
16	.0508	6.909	6.845	7.587	7.819
17	.0453	5.478	5.427	5.857	6.199
18	.0403	4.344	4.304	4.645	4.916
19	.0359	3.445	3.413	3.684	3.899
20	.0320	2.734	2.708	2.920	3.094
21	.0285	2.167	2.147	2.317	2.452
22	.0253	1.719	1.703	1.838	1.945
23	.0226	1.363	1.350	1.457	1.542
24	.0201	1.081	1.071	1.155	1.223
25	.0179	.8571	.8491	.9163	.9699
26	.0159	.6797	.6734	.7267	.7692
27	.0142	.5391	.5340	.5763	.6099
28	.0126	.4275	.4235	.4570	.4837
29	.0113	.3389	.3358	.3624	.3835
30	.0100	.2688	.2663	.2874	.3042
31	.0089	.2132	.2113	.2280	.2413
32	.0080	.1691	.1675	.1808	.1913
33	.0071	.1341	.1328	.1434	.1517
34	.0063	.1063	.1053	.1137	.1204
35	.0056	.0844	.0836	.0901	.0956
36	.0050	.0668	.0662	.0715	.0757
37	.0045	.0530	.0525	.0567	.0600
38	.0040	.0420	.0416	.0449	.0475
39	.0035	.0333	.0330	.0356	.0375
40	.0031	.0264	.0262	.0282	.0299

WEIGHTS OF IRON, BRASS, AND COPPER WIRE
BIRMINGHAM OR STUBS' GAGE

No. of Gage	Dia. in Inches	WEIGHT IN LBS. PER 1000 LINEAR FEET		
		Iron	Brass	Copper
0000	.454	546.21	589.29	623.2
000	.425	478.65	516.41	546.1
00	.380	382.66	412.84	436.6
0	.340	306.34	330.50	349.5
1	.300	238.50	257.31	272.1
2	.284	213.74	230.60	243.9
3	.259	177.77	191.79	202.8
4	.238	150.11	161.95	171.3
5	.220	128.26	138.37	146.3
6	.203	109.20	117.82	124.6
7	.180	85.86	92.63	97.96
8	.165	72.14	77.83	82.31
9	.148	58.05	62.62	66.23
10	.134	47.58	51.34	54.29
11	.120	38.16	41.17	43.54
12	.109	31.49	33.97	35.92
13	.095	23.92	25.80	27.29
14	.083	18.26	19.70	20.83
15	.072	13.73	14.82	15.67
16	.065	11.19	12.08	12.77
17	.058	8.92	9.62	10.17
18	.049	6.36	6.86	7.259
19	.042	4.67	5.04	5.333
20	.035	3.25	3.52	3.704
21	.032	2.71	2.93	3.096
22	.028	2.08	2.24	2.370
23	.025	1.66	1.79	1.890
24	.022	1.28	1.39	1.463
25	.020	1.06	1.14	1.209
26	.018	.863	.926	.979
27	.016	.680	.732	.774
28	.014	.529	.560	.592
29	.013	.438	.483	.511
30	.012	.382	.412	.435
31	.010	.266	.286	.302
32	.009	.212	.232	.244
33	.008	.167	.183	.193
34	.007	.133	.140	.148
35	.005	.066	.071	.075
36	.004	.046	.048	.052

WEIGHTS OF STEEL AND IRON BARS PER LINEAR FOOT

| Dia. or Distance Across Flats | STEEL | | | | IRON | |
| | Weight per Foot | | | | Weight per Foot | |
	Round	Square	Hexagon	Octagon	Round	Square
$\frac{1}{16}$	.010	.013	.012	.011	.010	.013
$\frac{1}{8}$	.042	.053	.046	.044	.041	.052
$\frac{3}{16}$	.094	.119	.103	.099	.092	.117
$\frac{1}{4}$	.167	.212	.185	.177	.164	.208
$\frac{5}{16}$	.261	.333	.288	.277	.256	.326
$\frac{3}{8}$	.375	.478	.414	.398	.368	.469
$\frac{7}{16}$	.511	.651	.564	.542	.501	.638
$\frac{1}{2}$	.667	.850	.737	.708	.654	.833
$\frac{9}{16}$	.845	1.076	.932	.896	.828	1.055
$\frac{5}{8}$	1.043	1.328	1.151	1.107	1.023	1.302
$\frac{11}{16}$	1.262	1.608	1.393	1.331	1.237	1.576
$\frac{3}{4}$	1.502	1.913	1.658	1.584	1.473	1.875
$\frac{13}{16}$	1.763	2.245	1.944	1.860	1.728	2.201
$\frac{7}{8}$	2.044	2.603	2.256	2.156	2.004	2.552
$\frac{15}{16}$	2.347	2.989	2.591	2.482	2.301	2.930
1	2.670	3.400	2.947	2.817	2.618	3.333
$1\frac{1}{16}$	3.014	3.838	3.327	3.182	2.955	3.763
$1\frac{1}{8}$	3.379	4.303	3.730	3.568	3.313	4.219
$1\frac{3}{16}$	3.766	4.795	4.156	3.977	3.692	4.701
$1\frac{1}{4}$	4.173	5.312	4.605	4.407	4.091	5.208
$1\frac{5}{16}$	4.600	5.857	5.077	4.858	4.510	5.742
$1\frac{3}{8}$	5.049	6.428	5.571	5.331	4.950	6.302
$1\frac{7}{16}$	5.518	7.026	6.091	5.827	5.410	6.888
$1\frac{1}{2}$	6.008	7.650	6.631	6.344	5.890	7.500
$1\frac{9}{16}$	6.520	8.301	7.195	6.905	6.392	8.138
$1\frac{5}{8}$	7.051	8.978	7.776	7.446	6.913	8.802
$1\frac{11}{16}$	7.604	9.682	8.392	8.027	7.455	9.492
$1\frac{3}{4}$	8.178	10.41	9.025	8.635	8.018	10.21
$1\frac{13}{16}$	8.773	11.17	9.682	9.264	8.601	10.95
$1\frac{7}{8}$	9.388	11.95	10.36	9.918	9.204	11.72
$1\frac{15}{16}$	10.02	12.76	11.06	10.58	9.828	12.51
2	10.68	13.60	11.79	11.28	10.47	13.33
$2\frac{1}{8}$	12.06	15.35	13.31	12.71	11.82	15.05
$2\frac{1}{4}$	13.52	17.22	14.92	14.24	13.25	16.88
$2\frac{3}{8}$	15.07	19.18	16.62	15.88	14.77	18.80
$2\frac{1}{2}$	16.69	21.25	18.42	17.65	16.36	20.83
$2\frac{5}{8}$	18.40	23.43	20.31	19.45	18.04	22.97
$2\frac{3}{4}$	20.20	25.71	22.29	21.28	19.80	25.21
$2\frac{7}{8}$	22.07	28.10	24.36	23.28	21.64	27.55
3	24.03	30.60	26.53	25.36	23.56	30.00
$3\frac{1}{8}$	26.08	33.20	28.78	27.50	25.57	32.55
$3\frac{1}{4}$	28.20	35.92	31.10	29.28	27.65	35.21
$3\frac{3}{8}$	30.42	38.78	33.57	32.10	29.82	37.97
$3\frac{1}{2}$	32.71	41.65	36.10	34.56	32.07	40.83
$3\frac{5}{8}$	35.09	44.68	38.73	37.05	34.40	43.80
$3\frac{3}{4}$	37.56	47.82	41.45	39.68	36.82	46.88
$3\frac{7}{8}$	40.10	51.05	44.26	42.35	39.31	50.05
4	42.73	54.40	47.16	45.12	41.89	53.33

WEIGHTS OF BRASS, COPPER AND ALUMINUM BARS PER LINEAR FOOT

Dia. or Distance Across Flats	BRASS Weight per Foot			COPPER Weight per Foot		ALUMINUM Weight per Foot	
	Round	Square	Hexagon	Round	Square	Round	Square
1/16	.011	.014	.013	.012	.015	.003	.004
1/8	.045	.055	.048	.047	.060	.014	.018
3/16	.100	.125	.108	.106	.135	.032	.041
1/4	.175	.225	.194	.189	.241	.057	.072
5/16	.275	.350	.301	.296	.377	.089	.114
3/8	.395	.510	.436	.426	.542	.128	.163
7/16	.540	.690	.592	.579	.737	.174	.222
1/2	.710	.905	.773	.757	.964	.227	.290
9/16	.900	1.15	.978	.958	1.22	.288	.367
5/8	1.10	1.40	1.24	1.18	1.51	.356	.453
11/16	1.35	1.72	1.45	1.43	1.82	.430	.548
3/4	1.66	2.05	1.73	1.70	2.17	.516	.652
13/16	1.85	2.40	2.03	2.00	2.54	.601	.766
7/8	2.15	2.75	2.36	2.32	2.95	.697	.888
15/16	2.48	3.15	2.71	2.66	3.39	.800	1.02
1	2.85	3.65	3.10	3.03	3.86	.911	1.16
1 1/16	3.20	4.08	3.49	3.42	4.35	1.03	1.31
1 1/8	3.57	4.55	3.91	3.81	4.88	1.15	1.47
1 3/16	3.97	5.08	4.38	4.27	5.44	1.28	1.64
1 1/4	4.41	5.65	4.82	4.72	6.01	1.42	1.81
1 5/16	4.86	6.22	5.33	5.21	6.63	1.57	2.00
1 3/8	5.35	6.81	5.76	5.72	7.24	1.72	2.19
1 7/16	5.86	7.45	6.38	6.26	7.97	1.88	2.40
1 1/2	6.37	8.13	6.92	6.81	8.67	2.05	2.61
1 9/16	6.92	8.83	7.54	7.39	9.41	2.22	2.83
1 5/8	7.48	9.55	8.15	7.99	10.18	2.41	3.06
1 11/16	8.05	10.27	8.80	8.45	10.73	2.59	3.30
1 3/4	8.65	11.00	9.47	9.27	11.80	2.79	3.55
1 13/16	9.29	11.82	10.15	9.76	12.43	2.99	3.81
1 7/8	9.95	12.68	10.86	10.64	13.55	3.20	4.08
1 15/16	10.58	13.50	11.68	11.11	14.15	3.41	4.35
2	11.25	14.35	12.36	12.11	15.42	3.64	4.64
2 1/8	12.78	16.27	13.92	13.67	17.42	4.11	5.24
2 1/4	14.32	18.24	15.72	15.33	19.51	4.61	5.87
2 3/8	15.96	20.32	17.52	17.08	21.74	5.14	6.54
2 1/2	17.68	22.53	19.44	18.92	24.09	5.69	7.25
2 5/8	19.50	24.83	21.24	20.86	26.56	6.27	7.99
2 3/4	21.40	27.25	23.40	22.89	29.05	6.89	8.53
2 7/8	23.39	29.78	25.82	25.02	31.86	7.52	9.58
3	25.47	32.43	27.84	27.24	34.69	8.20	10.44
3 1/4	30.45	38.77	32.76	31.97	40.71	9.62	12.25
3 1/2	35.31	44.96	37.80	37.08	47.22	11.16	14.21
3 3/4	40.07	51.01	43.56	42.11	53.61	12.81	16.31
4	46.12	58.73	49.44	48.43	61.67	14.56	18.56

Weights of Flat Sizes of Steel in Pounds per Linear Foot

	½	⅝	¾	⅞	1	1⅛	1¼	1⅜	1½	1¾	2	2¼	2½	2¾	3	3½	4	5	6
⅛	.213	.266	.320	.372	.426	.479	.530	.585	.640	.745	.850	.955	1.07	1.18	1.28	1.49	1.70	2.13	2.56
3⁄16	.319	.399	.480	.558	.639	.718	.790	.878	.960	1.12	1.28	1.43	1.60	1.76	1.92	2.24	2.55	3.20	3.83
¼	.425	.533	.640	.743	.852	.958	1.06	1.17	1.28	1.49	1.70	1.91	2.13	2.34	2.56	2.98	3.40	4.26	5.11
5⁄16	.531	.665	.800	.929	1.06	1.20	1.33	1.46	1.60	1.86	2.13	2.39	2.66	2.92	3.19	3.72	4.25	5.32	6.38
⅜	.638	.798	.960	1.12	1.28	1.43	1.59	1.75	1.91	2.23	2.55	2.87	3.20	3.51	3.83	4.46	5.10	6.40	7.66
7⁄16	.744	.931	1.12	1.30	1.49	1.67	1.86	2.05	2.23	2.60	2.98	3.35	3.72	4.09	4.46	5.21	5.95	7.44	8.92
½		1.07	1.28	1.49	1.70	1.91	2.13	2.34	2.55	2.98	3.40	3.83	4.26	4.68	5.10	5.96	6.80	8.52	10.20
9⁄16		1.20	1.44	1.67	1.91	2.15	2.39	2.63	2.87	3.35	3.83	4.30	4.78	5.26	5.74	6.69	7.65	9.56	11.50
⅝			1.60	1.86	2.12	2.39	2.66	2.92	3.19	3.72	4.26	4.79	5.32	5.86	6.39	7.44	8.52	10.64	12.78
11⁄16			1.76	2.04	2.34	2.63	2.92	3.22	3.51	4.09	4.68	5.26	5.84	6.43	7.01	8.18	9.35	11.70	14.00
¾				2.23	2.55	2.86	3.19	3.50	3.83	4.46	5.10	5.74	6.40	7.02	7.65	8.92	10.20	12.80	15.30
13⁄16				2.41	2.76	3.11	3.45	3.80	4.14	4.83	5.53	6.22	6.91	7.60	8.29	9.67	11.10	13.80	16.60
⅞					2.98	3.34	3.72	4.09	4.46	5.21	5.96	6.70	7.46	8.19	8.94	10.42	11.92	14.92	17.88
15⁄16					3.19	3.59	3.98	4.38	4.78	5.58	6.38	7.17	7.97	8.77	9.56	11.20	12.80	15.90	19.10
1						3.82	4.25	4.68	5.10	5.96	6.80	7.66	8.52	9.36	10.20	11.92	13.60	17.04	20.40
1⅛							4.78	5.27	5.74	6.71	7.65	8.61	9.59	10.54	11.48	13.41	15.30	19.17	22.95
1¼								5.85	6.38	7.45	8.50	9.57	10.65	11.71	12.76	14.90	17.00	21.30	25.61
1½									7.67	8.94	10.20	11.49	12.78	14.04	15.30	17.88	20.40	25.56	30.

WEIGHTS OF SEAMLESS BRASS TUBING PER LINEAR FOOT. (1/8 TO 2 1/2 OUTSIDE DIAMETER. NOS. 1 TO 25 STUBS' GAGE)

No. of Gage	Thickness in Inches	1/8	3/16	1/4	5/16	3/8	7/16	1/2	9/16	5/8	3/4	7/8	1	1 1/4	1 1/2	1 3/4	2	2 1/4	2 1/2
1	.300	..	..	..	..	..	..	..	..	..	..	..	2.42	3.28	4.10	5.03	5.88	6.75	7.62
2	.284	..	..	..	..	..	..	..	..	..	..	..	2.35	3.16	4.03	4.80	5.57	6.45	7.26
3	.259	..	..	..	..	..	..	..	..	..	..	1.85	2.22	2.98	3.72	4.48	5.23	5.96	6.72
4	.238	..	..	..	..	..	..	..	..	..	..	1.76	2.10	2.79	3.49	4.18	4.82	5.51	6.25
5	.220	..	..	..	..	..	..	..	..	..	..	1.68	1.99	2.60	3.26	3.89	4.53	5.14	5.80
6	.203	..	..	..	..	..	..	..	..	1.00	1.29	1.58	1.88	2.46	3.04	3.60	4.20	4.80	5.39
7	.180	..	..	..	..	..	..	..	..	.90	1.19	1.44	1.71	2.23	2.77	3.28	3.78	4.33	4.83
8	.165	..	..	..	..	.40	.52	.64	.77	.87	1.11	1.35	1.59	2.07	2.54	3.02	3.50	3.98	4.46
9	.148	..	..	..	..	.39	.49	.61	.71	.82	1.04	1.25	1.46	1.89	2.32	2.75	3.17	3.60	4.03
10	.134	..	..	..	..	.38	.46	.58	.65	.77	.96	1.16	1.35	1.74	2.12	2.51	2.90	3.28	3.67
11	.120	..	..	.18	.26	.36	.43	.53	.61	.70	.87	1.05	1.22	1.57	1.91	2.27	2.16	2.96	3.31
12	.109	..	..	.177	.256	.334	.413	.491	.570	.650	.808	.965	1.12	1.43	1.76	2.07	2.39	2.70	3.01
13	.095	..	..	.170	.237	.306	.377	.445	.514	.580	.717	.855	1.00	1.27	1.55	1.82	2.09	2.37	2.65
14	.083	..	..	.160	.220	.280	.340	.400	.460	.520	.640	.760	.88	1.12	1.36	1.61	1.84	2.08	2.32
15	.072	..	.096	.144	.201	.251	.303	.355	.409	.461	.564	.667	.77	.99	1.19	1.40	1.61	1.81	2.02
16	.065	.045	.092	.138	.186	.232	.279	.326	.372	.420	.515	.609	.70	.89	1.07	1.26	1.45	1.64	1.82
17	.058	.044	.087	.128	.169	.212	.255	.295	.338	.380	.463	.548	.64	.80	.97	1.14	1.30	1.48	1.64
18	.049	.043	.078	.113	.150	.183	.220	.255	.291	.325	.397	.467	.54	.67	.82	.96	1.10	1.24	1.39
19	.042	.040	.070	.101	.130	.161	.193	.221	.252	.282	.343	.404	.46	.58	.71	.83	.95	1.07	1.19
20	.035	.036	.062	.086	.113	.136	.163	.188	.214	.238	.289	.339	.39	.49	.59	.69	.80	.893	1.00
21	.032	.034	.057	.081	.104	.128	.151	.173	.196	.219	.266	.312	.357	.450	.542	.635	.727	.820	.913
22	.028	.031	.051	.072	.093	.112	.133	.152	.174	.192	.233	.275	.315	.396	.477	.556	.638	.718	.799
23	.025	.029	.047	.066	.082	.102	.119	.136	.155	.173	.209	.245	.281	.354	.426	.497	.571	.641	.714
24	.022	.026	.042	.058	.074	.090	.107	.121	.137	.154	.186	.218	.249	.312	.376	.438	.502	.566	.629
25	.020	.024	.039	.052	.068	.081	.096	.110	.126	.140	.169	.197	.226	.285	.342	.399	.457	.516	.573

For Weights of Seamless Copper Tubing, add 5 per cent. to the weights above.

Weights of Flat Sizes of Steel in Pounds per Linear Foot

Thick.	¼	⅜	½	⅝	¾	⅞	1	1⅛	1¼	1⅜	1½	1¾	2	2¼	2½	2¾	3	3½	4	5	6
⅛			.213	.266	.320	.372	.426	.479	.530	.585	.640	.745	.850	.955	1.07	1.18	1.28	1.49	1.70	2.13	2.56
3/16		.240	.319	.399	.480	.558	.639	.718	.798	.878	.960	1.12	1.28	1.43	1.60	1.76	1.92	2.24	2.55	3.20	3.83
¼	.213	.319	.425	.531	.638	.744	.852	.958	1.06	1.17	1.28	1.49	1.70	1.91	2.13	2.34	2.56	2.98	3.40	4.26	5.11
5/16		.399	.533	.666	.799	.932	1.07	1.20	1.33	1.46	1.60	1.86	2.13	2.40	2.66	2.93	3.20	3.73	4.26	5.32	6.39
⅜		.479	.639	.799	.958	1.12	1.28	1.44	1.60	1.76	1.92	2.24	2.56	2.87	3.20	3.51	3.83	4.46	5.11	6.40	7.66
7/16			.745	.932	1.12	1.30	1.49	1.68	1.86	2.05	2.23	2.60	2.98	3.35	3.72	4.09	4.46	5.21	5.96	7.44	8.92
½			.852	1.07	1.28	1.49	1.70	1.92	2.13	2.34	2.56	2.98	3.41	3.83	4.26	4.68	5.11	5.96	6.82	8.52	10.22
9/16				1.20	1.44	1.68	1.92	2.16	2.40	2.64	2.88	3.35	3.83	4.31	4.79	5.27	5.75	6.71	7.67	9.59	11.50
⅝				1.33	1.60	1.86	2.13	2.40	2.66	2.93	3.20	3.73	4.26	4.79	5.33	5.86	6.39	7.46	8.52	10.65	12.78
11/16					1.76	2.05	2.34	2.64	2.93	3.22	3.51	4.10	4.69	5.27	5.86	6.44	7.03	8.20	9.37	11.72	14.06
¾					1.92	2.24	2.56	2.88	3.20	3.51	3.83	4.47	5.11	5.75	6.39	7.03	7.67	8.95	10.22	12.78	15.34
13/16						2.42	2.77	3.12	3.46	3.81	4.15	4.85	5.54	6.23	6.92	7.61	8.31	9.69	11.08	13.85	16.61
⅞						2.61	2.98	3.35	3.73	4.10	4.47	5.22	5.96	6.71	7.46	8.20	8.95	10.44	11.93	14.91	17.89
15/16							3.20	3.59	3.99	4.39	4.79	5.59	6.39	7.19	7.99	8.79	9.59	11.18	12.78	15.98	19.17
1							3.41	3.83	4.26	4.69	5.11	5.96	6.82	7.67	8.52	9.37	10.22	11.93	13.63	17.04	20.45
1⅛								4.31	4.79	5.27	5.75	6.71	7.67	8.63	9.59	10.54	11.50	13.42	15.34	19.17	23.01
1¼									5.33	5.86	6.39	7.46	8.52	9.59	10.65	11.72	12.78	14.91	17.04	21.30	25.56
1⅜										6.44	7.03	8.20	9.37	10.54	11.72	12.89	14.06	16.40	18.75	23.43	28.12
1½											7.67	8.95	10.22	11.50	12.78	14.06	15.34	17.89	20.45	25.56	30.67

WEIGHTS OF SEAMLESS BRASS TUBING PER LINEAR FOOT. (⅛ TO 2½ OUTSIDE DIAMETER. NOS. 1 TO 25 STUBS' GAGE)

No. of Gage	Thickness in Inches	⅛	3/16	¼	5/16	⅜	7/16	½	9/16	⅝	¾	⅞	1	1¼	1½	1¾	2	2¼	2½
1	.300												2.42	3.28	4.10	5.03	5.88	6.75	7.62
2	.284											1.85	2.35	3.16	4.03	4.80	5.57	6.45	7.26
3	.259											1.76	2.22	2.98	3.72	4.48	5.23	5.96	6.72
4	.238											1.68	2.10	2.79	3.49	4.18	4.82	5.51	6.25
5	.220										1.29	1.58	1.99	2.60	3.26	3.89	4.53	5.14	5.80
6	.203									1.00	1.19	1.44	1.88	2.46	3.04	3.60	4.20	4.80	5.39
7	.180								.795	.90	1.11	1.35	1.71	2.23	2.77	3.28	3.78	4.33	4.83
8	.165							.638	.757	.87	1.04	1.25	1.59	2.07	2.54	3.02	3.50	3.98	4.46
9	.148						.494	.601	.708	.82	.96	1.16	1.46	1.89	2.32	2.75	3.17	3.60	4.03
10	.134					.373	.469	.566	.663	.77	.87	1.05	1.35	1.74	2.12	2.51	2.90	3.28	3.67
11	.120				.267	.353	.440	.526	.613	.70	.808	.965	1.22	1.57	1.91	2.27	2.66	2.96	3.31
12	.109			.177	.256	.334	.413	.492	.570	.650	.717	.855	1.12	1.43	1.76	2.07	2.39	2.70	3.01
13	.095			.170	.237	.306	.375	.444	.513	.580	.640	.760	1.00	1.27	1.55	1.82	2.09	2.37	2.65
14	.083		.100	.160	.220	.280	.340	.399	.459	.520	.564	.667	.88	1.12	1.36	1.61	1.84	2.08	2.32
15	.072		.096	.144	.201	.251	.304	.356	.407	.461	.515	.609	.77	.99	1.19	1.40	1.61	1.81	2.02
16	.065		.092	.138	.186	.232	.279	.326	.373	.420	.463	.548	.70	.89	1.07	1.26	1.45	1.64	1.82
17	.058	.045	.087	.128	.169	.212	.254	.296	.338	.380	.463	.547	.64	.80	.97	1.14	1.30	1.48	1.64
18	.049	.043	.078	.113	.150	.183	.220	.255	.290	.325	.397	.463	.54	.67	.82	.96	1.10	1.24	1.39
19	.042	.040	.070	.101	.130	.161	.192	.222	.252	.282	.343	.404	.46	.58	.71	.83	.95	1.07	1.19
20	.035	.036	.062	.086	.113	.136	.163	.188	.213	.238	.289	.339	.39	.49	.59	.69	.80	.893	1.00
21	.032	.034	.057	.081	.104	.128	.150	.173	.196	.219	.265	.311	.357	.450	.542	.635	.727	.820	.913
22	.028	.031	.051	.072	.093	.112	.133	.151	.173	.192	.233	.274	.315	.396	.477	.556	.638	.718	.799
23	.025	.029	.047	.066	.082	.102	.119	.137	.155	.173	.209	.245	.281	.354	.426	.497	.571	.641	.714
24	.022	.026	.042	.058	.074	.090	.107	.121	.137	.154	.186	.218	.249	.312	.376	.438	.502	.566	.629
25	.020	.024	.039	.052	.068	.081	.096	.110	.126	.140	.169	.197	.226	.285	.342	.399	.457	.516	.573

For Weights of Seamless Copper Tubing, add 5 per cent. to the weights above.

HORSE-POWER, BELTS AND SHAFTING

Horse-Power

HORSE-POWER is an arbitrary unit of measurement which has been adopted for measuring the work of engines or machines. It is given as 33,000 foot pounds per minute which means 1 pound lifted 33,000 feet per minute or 33,000 pounds lifted 1 foot per minute or 330 pounds lifted 100 feet per minute, or any combination which gives 33,000 foot pounds per minute.

Steam Engine Horse-Power

In a steam engine it means the effective steam pressure per square inch, times the length of piston movement per revolution in feet, times the piston area in square inches, times the number of revolutions per minute, and all divided by 33,000. This is easily remembered by the formula

$$\frac{PLAN}{33000}$$

where

P = mean effective pressure per square inch.
L = length of a double stroke in feet.
A = area of piston in square inches.
N = number of revolutions per minute.

Electrical Power

As compared with electrical units the mechanical horse-power equals 746 watts or nearly ¾ of a kilowatt. So that a kilowatt (1000 watts) equals 1.34 horse power.

Gas Engine Horse-Power

The A. L. A. M. rating for gasoline engines, which means the rating adopted by the American Licensed Automobile Manufacturers, is based on the assumption that the piston speed is 1000 feet per minute in all cases. This gives 1500 revolutions per minute for a 4-inch stroke motor, which is about average practice. Since the defeat of the Selden patent the A. L. A. M. has ceased to exist and this is now known as the S. A. E. standard (Society of Automobile Engineers).

S. A. E. (A. L. A. M.) HORSE-POWER RATING

THE formula adopted is $\dfrac{D^2 \times N}{2\cdot5}$ and based on 1000 feet per minute piston speed. D is the cylinder bore, N the number of cylinders, and 2.5 a constant, based on the average view of the Mechanical Branch as to a fair conservative rating.

TABLE OF HORSE-POWER FOR USUAL SIZES OF MOTORS, BASED ON
S. A. E. (A. L. A. M.) FORMULA

BORE		HORSE-POWER			
Ins.	M/M	1 Cyl.	2 Cyls.	4 Cyls.	6 Cyls.
$2\frac{1}{2}$	64	$2\frac{1}{2}$	5	10	15
$2\frac{5}{8}$	68	$2\frac{3}{4}$	$5\frac{1}{2}$	11	$16\frac{1}{2}$
$2\frac{3}{4}$	70	3	6	$12\frac{1}{10}$	$18\frac{1}{5}$
$2\frac{7}{8}$	73	$3\frac{5}{16}$	$6\frac{5}{8}$	$13\frac{1}{4}$	$19\frac{7}{8}$
3	76	$3\frac{3}{5}$	$7\frac{1}{5}$	$14\frac{2}{5}$	$21\frac{3}{5}$
$3\frac{1}{8}$	79	$3\frac{15}{16}$	$7\frac{7}{8}$	$15\frac{5}{8}$	$23\frac{7}{16}$
$3\frac{1}{4}$	83	$4\frac{1}{4}$	$8\frac{1}{2}$	$16\frac{9}{10}$	$25\frac{2}{5}$
$3\frac{3}{8}$	85	$4\frac{1}{16}$	$9\frac{1}{8}$	$18\frac{1}{4}$	$27\frac{2}{5}$
$3\frac{1}{2}$	89	$4\frac{9}{10}$	$9\frac{4}{5}$	$19\frac{3}{5}$	$29\frac{2}{5}$
$3\frac{5}{8}$	92	$5\frac{1}{4}$	$10\frac{1}{2}$	$20\frac{1}{4}$	$31\frac{3}{8}$
$3\frac{3}{4}$	95	$5\frac{5}{8}$	$11\frac{1}{4}$	$22\frac{1}{2}$	$33\frac{3}{4}$
$3\frac{7}{8}$	99	6	12	24	$36\frac{1}{16}$
4	102	$6\frac{2}{5}$	$12\frac{4}{5}$	$25\frac{3}{5}$	$38\frac{2}{5}$
$4\frac{1}{8}$	105	$6\frac{13}{16}$	$13\frac{5}{8}$	$27\frac{1}{4}$	$40\frac{9}{10}$
$4\frac{1}{4}$	108	$7\frac{1}{4}$	$14\frac{1}{2}$	$28\frac{9}{10}$	$43\frac{3}{5}$
$4\frac{3}{8}$	111	$7\frac{7}{8}$	$15\frac{5}{16}$	$30\frac{5}{8}$	$45\frac{15}{16}$
$4\frac{1}{2}$	114	$8\frac{1}{10}$	$16\frac{1}{5}$	$32\frac{2}{5}$	$48\frac{3}{5}$
$4\frac{5}{8}$	118	$8\frac{9}{16}$	$17\frac{1}{5}$	$34\frac{1}{4}$	$51\frac{2}{5}$
$4\frac{3}{4}$	121	9	18	$36\frac{1}{10}$	$54\frac{1}{10}$
$4\frac{7}{8}$	124	$9\frac{1}{2}$	19	38	57
5	127	10	20	40	60
$5\frac{1}{8}$	130	$10\frac{1}{2}$	21	42	63
$5\frac{1}{4}$	133	11	22	$44\frac{1}{10}$	$66\frac{1}{5}$
$5\frac{3}{8}$	137	$11\frac{9}{16}$	23	46	$69\frac{1}{10}$
$5\frac{1}{2}$	140	$12\frac{1}{10}$	$24\frac{1}{5}$	$48\frac{2}{5}$	$72\frac{3}{5}$
$5\frac{5}{8}$	143	$12\frac{5}{8}$	$25\frac{5}{16}$	$50\frac{5}{8}$	$75\frac{15}{16}$
$5\frac{3}{4}$	146	$13\frac{1}{4}$	$26\frac{1}{2}$	53	$79\frac{1}{2}$
$5\frac{7}{8}$	149	$13\frac{13}{16}$	$27\frac{7}{8}$	$55\frac{1}{4}$	$82\frac{9}{10}$
6	152	$14\frac{2}{5}$	$28\frac{4}{5}$	$57\frac{3}{5}$	$86\frac{2}{5}$

To simplify reading of the above, the horse-power figures are approximate, but correct within one-sixteenth.

DRIVING POWER OF LEATHER BELTS

THE question of the proper size of a leather belt for a given power transmission resolves itself into a question of selecting various factors. These factors have been worked out by experiments, by analytical methods, and in practice.

The horse-power that a belt will transmit depends upon the effective tension and the belt speed. The effective tension depends upon the difference in the tensions of the two sides of the belt and on the surface friction, which depends upon the ratio of the tensions and the angle of belt contact with pulley.

Experiments and practice have shown that a belt of single thickness will stand a stress of 60 pounds per inch of width and give good results, that is, it will only require an occasional taking up and will have a fairly long life. The corresponding values for double and triple belts are 105 and 150 pounds per inch of width provided the pulleys are not too small.

Experiments have shown that on small pulleys the ratio of the tensions should not exceed 2, on medium pulleys 2.5, and on large pulleys 3. The larger the pulley, the better the contact; also the thinner the belt, the better the contact for the same size of pulley. When the pulley diameter in *feet* is three times the thickness of the belt in *inches*, or in this proportion, we get equivalent results for different thicknesses of belts. This gives us a method of classifying our pulleys. The belt has to adjust itself in passing over a pulley due to its own thickness. Some adjustment is also necessary on account of the crowning of the pulley. These adjustments account for the different ratios for the various pulley diameters. The effects of the crown and pulley diameters are not usually considered in belt rules, although they should be. The ratios given are for 180 degrees wrap and decrease with less contact.

The creep of the belt depends upon its elasticity and the load, and experiments have shown that this should not exceed 1 per cent. in good practice. In order to keep this creep below 1 per cent. it is necessary to limit the difference of tension per inch of width of single belt to 40 pounds. The corresponding values for double and triple belts are 70 and 100 pounds per inch of width. These figures are based on an average value of 20,000 for the running modulus of elasticity of leather belting.

Table 1 has been prepared on the basis of these limitations and gives a value for the factor or constant F in the equation

$$H.P. = \frac{V \times W}{F} \text{ or } W = \frac{H.P. \times F}{V}$$

in which $H P$ is the horse-power, V the belt velocity in feet per minute, and W the width in inches.

Table 2 gives corrected values for F, when the arc of contact or wrap is greater or less than 180 degrees. On large pulleys the creep may exceed 1 per cent. if the wrap is over 180 degrees, as the increased friction gives a greater difference of tensions.

To illustrate the use of the tables, we will take the following examples:

TABLE I. — FACTORS FOR 180 DEGREES OF BELT CONTACT

Diameter of pulley	Under 8"	8"–36"	Over 3 feet	Under 14"	14"–60"	Over 5 feet	Under 21"	21"–84"	Over 7 feet
Thickness of belt	Single	Single	Single	Double	Double	Double	Triple	Triple	Triple
Factor	1100	920	830	630	520	470	440	370	330
Difference of tensions	30	36	40	52.5	63	70	75	90	100
Per cent of creep	0.74	0.89	0.99	0.74	0.89	0.99	0.74	0.89	0.99
Ratio of tensions	2.00	2.50	3.00	2.00	2.50	3.00	2.00	2.50	3.00
Tension on tight side	60	60	60	105	105	105	150	150	150

TABLE II. — FACTORS FOR VARYING DEGREES OF BELT CONTACT

120°	130°	140°	150°	160°	170°	180°	190°	200°	210°	220°
1400	1330	1270	1220	1180	1140	1100	1070	1040	1010	980
1240	1170	1100	1040	990	950	920	890	860	830	810
1100	1030	980	930	890	860	830	800	770	750	730
800	760	730	700	670	650	630	610	590	570	560
700	660	630	600	570	540	520	500	480	470	460
630	590	560	530	510	490	470	450	440	430	420
560	540	520	500	480	460	440	420	410	400	390
490	470	450	430	410	390	370	350	340	330	320
440	420	400	380	360	340	330	320	310	300	290

How much horse-power will a 4-inch single belt transmit at a speed of 4600 feet per minute passing over a 12-inch pulley? The factor is 920, therefore,

$$\frac{4600 \times 4}{920} = 20 \ H.P.$$

How wide should a belt be in order to transmit 50 horse-power at 2000 feet per minute on a 36-inch pulley?

$$W = \frac{50 \times 830}{2000} = 20.7\text{-}inch \ single \ belt.$$

This gives a width of single belt beyond the usual limit, 8 inches being considered good practice for the maximum width of a single belt.

$$W = \frac{50 \times 520}{2000} = 13\text{-}inch \ double \ belt.$$

How wide should a single belt be in order to transmit 2 horse-power at 600 feet per minute over a 4-in. pulley with 140 deg. wrap? In this case we take the factor 1100 from Table 1 and in Table 2 find a corrected value for 1100 under 140 degrees of 1270.

$$W = \frac{2 \times 1270}{600} = 4.23\text{-}inch \ single \ belt.$$

How wide a belt is required for 300 horse-power at 2000 feet per minute over a 10-foot pulley?

$$W = \frac{300 \times 470}{2000} = 70.5\text{-}inch \ double \ belt.$$

This is too wide. Good practice calls for a change to triple at 48 inches unless for some special reason a narrower belt is necessary.

$$W = \frac{300 \times 330}{2000} = 49.5\text{-}inch \ triple \ belt.$$

The results given by these factors are well within working values and the belts will probably transmit 50 per cent. more power than these factors, but at the expense of the life of the belt. A liberal allowance at the beginning means less annoyance, fewer delays in taking up the belts, longer life and less cost for renewals and repairs. Belt speeds of 4000 to 4800 ft. should rarely be exceeded.

Transmission of power in mill work is by gearing, by shafting, by electric motors, and by leather and rope belting, and which of these should be used in a particular case is a problem for the engineer in charge to determine.

For successful work the pulleys must be large in diameter and must have a smooth surface where the rope bears upon them. The speed and the load on the rope must also be such as experience has shown to be economical. When these conditions are fulfilled, a rope drive is a very satisfactory method of transmitting power.

The table shows the horse-power of driving ropes and the diameter of pulleys that should be used for this purpose. This table takes into consideration the effects of the centrifugal force, so that the strain on the rope is constant on the driving side in transmitting the tabular power, no matter what the speed may be. While many engineers recommend a much larger horse-power, we believe the estimates here given are advisable except in temporary installations.

HORSE-POWER OF MANILA ROPE

Dia. of Rope	Velocity, Feet per Minute										
	1,000	1,500	2,000	2,500	3,000	3,500	4,000	4,500	5,000	5,500	6,000
3/4	2.3	3.3	4.3	5.2	6.0	6.6	7.2	7.3	7.4	7.3	6.9
7/8	3.0	4.5	5.9	7.0	8.2	9.0	9.6	9.8	10.0	9.6	9.0
1	4.0	5.9	7.7	9.2	10.6	11.8	12.7	12.9	13.0	12.7	12.0
1 1/8	5.0	7.5	9.7	11.6	13.5	14.9	16.0	16.3	16.7	16.5	15.3
1 1/4	6.3	9.1	12.0	14.3	16.7	18.5	20.0	20.2	20.7	20.1	18.9
1 3/8	7.5	10.8	14.4	17.4	20.0	22.1	23.7	24.5	24.6	24.0	22.3
1 1/2	9.0	13.5	17.4	20.7	23.0	26.3	28.7	29.0	29.5	28.6	26.7
1 5/8	10.5	15.5	20.1	24.3	27.9	30.8	32.9	34.1	34.3	33.3	31.0
1 3/4	12.3	18.0	23.6	28.2	32.7	36.4	38.5	39.4	40.5	38.7	36.0
2	16.0	23.2	30.6	46.8	42.5	46.7	50.0	51.7	52.8	50.6	47.3
2 1/4	20.0	29.6	38.6	46.6	53.6	59.2	63.6	65.8	66.3	64.4	60.3
2 1/2	25.0	36.6	47.7	57.5	66.0	71.2	78.0	80.0	81.0	79.0	73.8

DATA OF MANILA TRANSMISSION ROPE

Diameter of Rope	Square of Diameter	Approx. Wgt. per ft.	Breaking Strength	Maximum Allowable Tension	Length of Splice, Feet			Smallest Diam. of Sheaves, Inches	Maximum Number of Revolutions per Minute
					3 Strands	4 Strands	6 Strands		
3/4	.5625	.20	3,950	112	6	8	..	28	760
7/8	.7656	.26	5,400	153	6	8	..	32	650
1	1.	.34	7,000	200	7	10	14	36	570
1 1/8	1.2656	.43	8,900	253	7	10	16	40	510
1 1/4	1.5625	.53	10,900	312	7	10	16	46	460
1 3/8	1.8906	.65	13,200	378	8	12	16	50	415
1 1/2	2.25	.77	15,700	450	8	12	18	54	380
1 5/8	2.6406	.90	18,500	528	8	12	18	60	344
1 3/4	3.0625	1.04	21,400	612	8	12	18	64	330
2	4.	1.36	28,000	800	9	14	20	72	290
2 1/4	5.0625	1.73	35,400	1,012	9	14	20	82	255
2 1/2	6.25	2.13	43,700	1,250	10	16	22	90	230

Weight of transmission rope .... $= .34 \times$ diameter.^{2}
Breaking strength .... $= 7,000 \times$ diameter.^{2}
Maximum allowable tension .:....... $= 200 \times$ diameter.^{2}
Diameter smallest practicable sheave.. $= 36 \times$ diameter.
Velocity of rope (assumed).......... $= 5,400$ feet per minute.

BELT FASTENINGS

The best fastening for a belt is the cement splice. It is far beyond any form of lacing, belt hooks, riveting, or any other method of joining together the ends of a belt. The cement joint is easily applied to leather and to rubber belts, but to make a good cement splice in a canvas belt requires more time and apparatus than is usually at hand. Good glue makes a fine cement for leather belts, and fish glue is less affected by moisture than the other. Many of the liquid glues are fish glue treated with acid so as not to gelatinize when cold. A little bichromate of potash added to ordinary hot glue just before it is used will render it insoluble in water. Both lap and wedge joints are used.

Belt Hooks

There are many styles of belt hooks in use, some of the more common kind being shown in Figs. 1, 2, 3 and 4. Fig. 2 is practically a double rivet, Fig. 3 a malleable iron fastening, although similar hooks have been made of pressed steel, and Fig. 4 is the Blake stud, which has the advantage of not weakening the belt but makes a hump on the outside where the ends turn up. Fig. 5 is the Bristol hook of stamped steel which is driven in the points turned over on the other side. Fig. 6 is the Jackson belt lacing and is applied by a hand machine which screws a spiral wire across the ends of a belt. These are then flattened and a rawhide pin or a heavy soft cord used as a hinge joint between them. These joints are probably equal to 90 per cent. of the belt strength.

Lacing Belts

Belts fastened by lacing are weakened according to the amount of material punched out in making the holes to receive the lacing. It is preferable to lace with a small lacing put many times, through small holes. Such a joint is stronger than a few pieces of wide lacing through a number of large holes. Figs. 7 and 9 illustrate two forms of belt lacing, the latter being far preferable to the other. The lacing shown by Fig. 7 is in a double leather belt 5 inches wide. The width makes no difference as the strength is figured in percentage of the total width. There are four holes in this piece of belt, each hole $\frac{3}{8}$ inch in diameter. The aggregate width thus cut out of the belt is $4 \times \frac{3}{8}$ inch $= \frac{12}{8} = 1\frac{1}{2}$ inches. Then $1.5 \div 5 = 0.30$, or 30 per cent. of the belt has been cut away—nearly one-third of the total strength.

Another Method of Lacing

In Fig. 9 a different method is followed. Instead of there being a few large holes, there are more smaller ones—one fourth more, in fact. There are five holes, each $\frac{3}{16}$ inch in diameter, making a total of $\frac{15}{16}$ inch or $0.9375 \div 5 = 18\frac{3}{4}$ per cent., leaving $81\frac{1}{4}$ per cent. of the total belt strength against 70 per cent. in the belt with large holes. A first-class double leather belt will tear in two under a strain of about 500 pounds to each lace hole, the strain being applied in the holes by means of lacings.

The belt shown by Fig. 9 has 81¼ per cent. of 1.875 square inches of section, = 1.525 square inches left after cutting out the five holes. This amount is good for 3000 × 1.875 = 5625 pounds breaking strain, and as the lacing will tear out under 2500 pounds, it will be seen that we cannot afford to use lacings if the full power of the leather is to be utilized. This, under a factor of safety of 5, would be 1125 pounds to the square inch, or 1125 × 1.525 = 1715 pounds

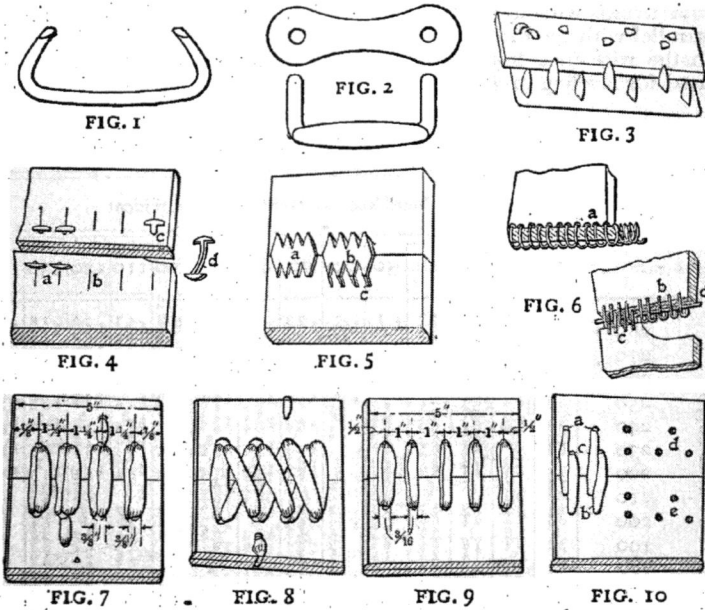

FIG. 1

FIG. 2

FIG. 3

FIG. 4

FIG. 5

FIG. 6

FIG. 7 FIG. 8 FIG. 9 FIG. 10

Belt Hooks and Lacings

working strain for the belt, or 1715 ÷ 5 = 343.5 pounds to each lace. This, too, is too much, as it is less than a factor of safety of 2.

The belt to carry 40 pounds working tension to the inch of width must also carry about 40 pounds standing tension, making a strain of 80 pounds to the inch, or 80 × 5 = 400 pounds. This is a better showing, and gives a factor of safety of 2500 ÷ 400 = 6¼. Still, we are wasting a belt of 5625 pounds ultimate strength in order to get from it 400 pounds working strain. This means a factor of safety of over 14 in the body of the belt but of only 6¼ at the lacing, which shows the advantage of a cement splice.

Fig. 10 shows a method sometimes used to relieve the lace-holes of some of the strain. Double rows of holes are punched as at *a b*, and the lacing distributed among them. As far as helping the strength of the belt is concerned, this does nothing, for all the stress put upon the belt by the lacing at *c* must be carried by the belt section at *a*; therefore this way of punching holes does not increase the section strength. Neither does staggering the holes as shown at *d* and *e*. The form of hole-punching shown at *a b c* is desirable for another reason. It distributes the lacing very nicely and does not make such a lump to thump when it passes over the pulleys.

ALINING SHAFTING BY A STEEL WIRE

A STEEL wire is often used for alining shafting by stretching it parallel with the direction of the shaft and measuring from the shaft to the wire in a horizontal direction. This steel wire can also be used for leveling or alining in a direction at right angles to the other,

SAGS OF A STEEL ALINING WIRE FOR SHAFTING

Distance in Feet, from Reel to Point of Measurement

	10	20	30	40	50	60	70	80	90	100	110	120	130	140

Distance in Feet, from Reel to Point of Support: 280, 270, 260, 250, 240, 230, 220, 210, 200, 190, 180, 170, 160, 150, 140, 130, 120, 110, 100, 90, 80, 70, 60, 50, 40, 30

Sag of the Wire in Inches

by making vertical measurements, if it is stretched under established conditions and if the sags at the points of measurement are known. The accompanying table gives the sags in inches from a truly level line passing through the points of support of the wire, at successive points beginning 10 feet from the reel and spaced 10 feet apart for a No. 17 Birmingham gage high grade piano wire, stretched with a weight of 60 pounds, wound on a reel of a minimum diameter of three and one-half inches and for total distances between the reel and point of support of the wire varying by increments of 10 feet from 40 to 280 feet. Thus a wire of any convenient length, of the kind indicated, can be selected, so long as this length is a multiple of 10 feet and between the limits specified, and the table gives the sags from a truly level line at points 10 feet apart for its entire length when it is stretched under the conditions designated. These sags

SAGS OF A STEEL ALINING WIRE FOR SHAFTING

Distance in Feet, from Reel to Point of Support	Distance in Feet, from Reel to Point of Measurement												
	150	160	170	180	190	200	210	220	230	240	250	260	270
280	$1\frac{13}{16}$	$1\frac{25}{32}$	$1\frac{47}{64}$	$1\frac{43}{64}$	$1\frac{37}{64}$	$1\frac{31}{64}$	$1\frac{23}{64}$	$1\frac{7}{32}$	$1\frac{1}{16}$	$\frac{57}{64}$	$\frac{11}{16}$	$\frac{31}{64}$	$\frac{1}{4}$
270	$1\frac{43}{64}$	$1\frac{41}{64}$	$1\frac{37}{64}$	$1\frac{1}{2}$	$1\frac{13}{32}$	$1\frac{19}{64}$	$1\frac{11}{64}$	$1\frac{1}{64}$	$\frac{55}{64}$	$\frac{43}{64}$	$\frac{29}{64}$	$\frac{15}{64}$	
260	$1\frac{17}{32}$	$1\frac{31}{64}$	$1\frac{27}{64}$	$1\frac{11}{32}$	$1\frac{15}{64}$	$1\frac{7}{64}$	$\frac{31}{32}$	$\frac{13}{16}$	$\frac{39}{64}$	$\frac{7}{16}$			
250	$1\frac{13}{32}$	$1\frac{23}{64}$	$1\frac{9}{32}$	$1\frac{3}{16}$	$1\frac{7}{64}$	$\frac{59}{64}$	$\frac{25}{32}$	$\frac{39}{64}$	$\frac{7}{16}$				
240	$1\frac{15}{64}$	$1\frac{11}{64}$	$1\frac{5}{64}$	$\frac{63}{64}$	$\frac{55}{64}$	$\frac{47}{64}$	$\frac{37}{64}$	$\frac{13}{32}$					
230	$1\frac{3}{32}$	$1\frac{1}{64}$	$\frac{59}{64}$	$\frac{13}{16}$	$\frac{45}{64}$	$\frac{35}{64}$	$\frac{3}{8}$	$\frac{13}{64}$					
220	$\frac{61}{64}$	$\frac{7}{8}$	$\frac{49}{64}$	$\frac{21}{32}$	$\frac{35}{64}$	$\frac{29}{64}$	$\frac{1}{4}$						
210	$\frac{51}{64}$	$\frac{23}{32}$	$\frac{5}{8}$	$\frac{1}{2}$	$\frac{3}{8}$	$\frac{11}{64}$							
200	$\frac{11}{16}$	$\frac{37}{64}$	$\frac{29}{64}$	$\frac{21}{64}$	$\frac{11}{64}$								
190	$\frac{35}{64}$	$\frac{7}{16}$	$\frac{5}{16}$	$\frac{5}{32}$									
180	$\frac{13}{32}$	$\frac{9}{32}$	$\frac{5}{32}$										
170	$\frac{17}{64}$	$\frac{9}{64}$											
160	$\frac{9}{64}$												

Sag of the Wire in Inches

being known, direct measurements can be made to level or aline a shaft by vertical measurements.

The method was originally developed for alining the propeller shafts of vessels, but it is equally serviceable for semi-flexible shafting, as factory line shafts.

SPEED OF SHAFTING

Line shaft speed varies with machinery it drives. Probably 250 r.p.m. is an average today, with cases of 400 r.p.m. even on 4-in. shafts and 600 to 700 r.p.m. on 2-in. shafts for high speed machinery.

HORSE POWER OF STEEL SHAFTING

For Line Shaft Service

Shaft Sizes Inches	Revolutions per Minute										Max. Dist. Between Bearings
	100	125	150	175	200	225	250	300	350	400	
1 3/16	2.4	3.1	3.7	4.3	4.9	5.5	6.1	7.3	8.5	9.7	....
1 7/16	4.3	5.3	6.4	7.4	8.5	9.5	10.5	12.7	14.8	16.9	6.8″
1 11/16	6.7	8.4	10.1	11.7	13.4	15.1	16.7	20.1	23.4	26.8	7.2″
1 15/16	10.0	12.5	15.0	17.5	20.0	22.5	25.0	30.0	35.0	40.0	8.2″
2 3/16	14.3	17.8	21.4	24.9	28.5	32.1	35.6	42.7	49.8	57.0	8.9″
2 7/16	19.5	24.4	29.3	34.1	39.0	44.1	48.7	58.5	68.2	78.0	9.6″
2 11/16	26.0	32.5	39.0	43.5	52.0	58.5	65.0	78.0	87.0	104.0	10.2″
2 15/16	33.8	42.2	50.6	59.1	67.5	75.9	84.4	101.3	118.2	135.0	10.8″
3 3/16	43.0	53.6	64.4	75.1	85.8	96.6	107.3	128.7	150.3	171.6	11.4″
3 7/16	53.6	67.0	79.4	93.8	107.2	120.1	134.0	158.8	187.6	214.4	12.0″
3 11/16	65.9	82.4	97.9	115.4	121.8	148.3	164.8	195.7	230.7	243.6	12.5″
3 15/16	80.0	100.0	120.0	140.0	160.0	180.0	200.0	240.0	280.0	320.0	....
4 7/16	113.9	142.4	170.8	199.3	227.8	256.2	284.7	341.7	398.6	455.6	....
4 15/16	156.3	195.3	234.4	273.4	312.5	351.5	390.6	468.7	546.8	625.0	....
5 1/2	207.9	260.0	311.9	363.9	415.9	459.9	520.0	623.9	727.9	830.0	....
6	270.0	337.5	495.0	472.5	540.0	607.5	675.0	810.0	945.0	1080.0	....
6 1/2	343.3	429.0	514.9	600.7	686.5	772.4	858.0	1029.0	1201.0	1372.0	....
7	428.8	535.9	643.1	750.3	847.5	964.7	1071.9	1286.0	1500.0	1695.0	....
8	640.0	800.0	960.0	1126.0	1280.0	1440.0	1600.9	1920.0	2240.0	2560.0	....

This table is based on the formula

$$M = \frac{D^3 \times R}{80}.$$ For heavier work use $M = \frac{D^3 \times R}{100}$

For head and jack shafts, supported by bearings close to main sheave or pulley so as to prevent transverse strain, the following formula may be used with safety:

$$M = \frac{D^3 \times R}{125}$$

D = Diameter of shaft in inches.
R = Number of revolutions per minute.
M = Horse-power.

Deflection of shafting from weight of pulleys and draw of belting should not be allowed in excess of .001 per foot, as this action adds very rapidly to the power cost. If this deflection is at a clutch, sleeve or roller bearing, any of them may be ruined easily and quickly. It can be reduced by using more hangers.

SPEEDS OF PULLEYS AND GEARS

The fact that the circumference of a pulley or gear is always 3.1416 or 3 1/7 times the diameter makes it easy to figure speeds by considering only the diameter of both driver and driven pulleys. Belting from one 6-inch pulley to another gives the same speed to both; but if the driving pulley is 16 inches and the driven pulley only four inches it is clear that the small pulley will turn 4 times for every turn of the large pulley. If this is reversed and the small pulley is the driver, the large pulley will only make one turn for every four of the small pulley. The same rule applies to gears if the *pitch diameter* and not the outside diameter is taken. The following rules have been arranged for convenience in finding any desired information about pulley or gear speeds.

HAVING	TO FIND	RULE
Diameter of Driving Pulley Diameter of Driven Pulley Speed of Driving Pulley	Speed of Driven Pulley	Multiply Diameter of Driving Pulley by its Speed and divide by Diameter of Driven Pulley.
Diameter of Driving Pulley Speed of Driving Pulley Speed of Driven Pulley	Diameter of Driven Pulley	Multiply Diameter of Driving Pulley by its Speed and Divide by Speed of Driven Pulley.
Diameter of Driving Pulley Diameter of Driven Pulley Speed of Driven Pulley	Speed of Driving Pulley	Multiply Diameter of Driven Pulley by its Speed and Divide by Diameter of Driving Pulley.
Diameter of Driven Pulley Speed of Driven Pulley Speed of Driving Pulley	Diameter of Driving Pulley	Multiply Diameter of Driven Pulley by its Speed and Divide by Speed of Driving Pulley.

These rules apply equally well to a number of pulley belts together or to a train of gears if *all* the driving and *all* the driven pulley diameters and speeds are grouped together.

TABLES OF CIRCUMFERENTIAL SPEEDS

THE tables on pages 432-435 which give circumferential speeds, can be used for obtaining gear and belt speeds and the speed of revolving parts of high-speed motors.

For diameters greater than those given in the tables, the speeds can be obtained by adding together the speeds for two diameters whose sum equals that of the diameter for which we require the speed. For example, to find the speed at a 120-inch diameter and 200 revolutions per minute, the following calculation is readily made:

Speed for 100-inch diameter — 5236 feet.
Speed for 20-inch diameter — 1047 feet.
Speed for 120-inch diameter — 6283 feet.

To interpolate, we can use the values given for speed for 1- to 10-inch diameters, dividing them by 10, 100, 1000, etc., to obtain speeds for tenths, hundredths, thousandths, etc.. For instance, if the speed for 550 revolutions per minute and 46.186-inch diameter is required, we proceed as follows:

For 46   in. diameter . . . .   speed = 6623 ft.
For 0.1   in. diameter = $\frac{1}{10}$ of 1-in. diameter speed =   14.4 ft.
For 0.08 in. diameter = $\frac{1}{100}$ of 8-in. diameter speed =   11.5 ft.
For 0.006 in. diameter = $\frac{1}{1000}$ of 6-in. diameter speed = . 0.9 ft.
For 46.186 in. diameter . . . . speed = 6650 ft.

CIRCUMFERENTIAL SPEEDS IN FEET PER MINUTE

(See page 431)

Diameter in Inches	Revolutions per Minute										
	50	100	150	200	250	300	350	400	450	500	550
1	13	26	39	52	65	79	92	105	118	131	144
2	26	52	79	105	131	157	183	209	236	262	288
3	39	79	118	157	196	236	275	314	353	393	432
4	52	105	157	209	262	314	367	419	471	523	576
5	65	131	196	262	328	393	458	524	589	654	720
6	79	157	236	314	393	471	550	628	707	785	863
7	92	183	275	367	458	550	641	733	825	916	1,008
8	105	209	314	419	524	628	733	838	942	1,047	1,152
9	118	236	353	471	589	707	825	942	1,060	1,178	1,296
10	131	262	393	524	655	785	916	1,047	1,178	1,309	1,440
11	144	288	432	576	720	864	1008	1,152	1,296	1,440	1,584
12	157	314	471	628	785	943	1100	1,257	1,414	1,571	1,728
13	170	340	511	681	851	1021	1191	1,361	1,532	1,701	1,872
14	183	367	550	733	916	1100	1283	1,466	1,649	1,832	2,016
15	196	393	589	785	982	1178	1375	1,571	1,767	1,963	2,160
16	209	419	628	838	1047	1257	1466	1,675	1,885	2,094	2,304
17	223	445	668	890	1113	1335	1558	1,780	2,003	2,225	2,442
18	236	471	707	943	1178	1414	1649	1,885	2,121	2,356	2,592
19	249	497	746	995	1244	1492	1741	1,990	2,238	2,487	2,736
20	262	524	785	1047	1309	1571	1833	2,094	2,356	2,618	2,880
21	275	550	825	1100	1374	1649	1924	2,199	2,474	2,749	3,024
22	288	576	864	1152	1440	1728	2016	2,304	2,592	2,880	3,168
23	301	602	903	1204	1505	1806	2107	2,409	2,710	3,011	3,312
24	314	628	943	1257	1571	1885	2199	2,513	2,827	3,142	3,456
25	327	655	982	1309	1636	1963	2291	2,618	2,945	3,273	3,600
26	340	681	1021	1361	1702	2042	2382	2,723	3,063	3,403	3,744
27	353	707	1060	1414	1767	2121	2474	2,827	3,181	3,534	3,888
28	367	733	1100	1466	1837	2199	2566	2,932	3,299	3,665	4,032
29	380	759	1139	1518	1898	2278	2657	3,037	3,417	3,796	4,176
30	393	785	1178	1571	1964	2356	2749	3,142	3,534	3,927	4,320
31	406	812	1217	1623	2029	2435	2840	3,246	3,652	4,058	4,464
32	419	838	1257	1676	2094	2513	2932	3,351	3,770	4,189	4,608
33	432	864	1296	1728	2160	2592	3024	3,456	3,888	4,320	4,752
34	445	890	1335	1780	2225	2670	3115	3,560	4,006	4,451	4,896
35	458	916	1375	1833	2291	2749	3206	3,665	4,123	4,581	5,040
36	471	943	1414	1885	2356	2827	3299	3,770	4,241	4,712	5,184
37	484	969	1453	1937	2422	2906	3390	3,875	4,359	4,843	5,328
38	497	995	1492	1990	2487	2985	3482	3,979	4,477	4,974	5,472
39	511	1021	1532	2042	2553	3063	3573	4,084	4,595	5,105	5,616
40	524	1047	1571	2094	2618	3142	3665	4,189	4,712	5,236	5,760
41	537	1073	1610	2147	2683	3220	3757	4,294	4,831	5,367	5,904
42	550	1100	1649	2199	2749	3299	3848	4,398	4,948	5,498	6,048
43	563	1126	1689	2251	2814	3377	3940	4,503	5,066	5,629	6,192
44	576	1152	1728	2304	2880	3456	4032	4,608	5,184	5,760	6,336
45	589	1178	1767	2356	2945	3534	4123	4,712	5,301	5,891	6,480
46	602	1204	1806	2408	3011	3613	4215	4,817	5,419	6,021	6,623
47	615	1231	1846	2461	3076	3692	4307	4,922	5,537	6,152	6,768
48	628	1257	1885	2513	3142	3770	4398	5,027	5,655	6,283	6,912
49	641	1283	1924	2566	3207	3849	4490	5,131	5,773	6,414	7,056
50	655	1309	1963	2618	3273	3927	4581	5,236	5,891	6,545	7,200

CIRCUMFERENTIAL SPEEDS IN FEET PER MINUTE

(See page 431)

Diameter in Inches	Revolutions per Minute										
	50	100	150	200	250	300	350	400	450	500	550
51	668	1335	2003	2670	3338	4006	4673	5,341	6,008	6,676	7,343
52	681	1361	2042	2723	3403	4084	4764	5,445	6,126	6,807	7,487
53	694	1388	2081	2775	3469	4163	4856	5,550	6,244	6,938	7,631
54	707	1414	2121	2827	3534	4241	4948	5,655	6,362	7,069	7,775
55	720	1440	2160	2880	3600	4320	5040	5,760	6,480	7,199	7,919
56	733	1466	2199	2932	3665	4398	5131	5,864	6,597	7,330	8,063
57	746	1492	2238	2985	3731	·4477	5223	5,969	6,715	7,461	8,207
58	759	1518	2278	3037	3796	4555	5314	6,074	6,833	7,592	8,351
59	772	1545	2317	3089	3862	4634	5406	6,178	6,951	7,723	8,495
60	785	1571	2356	3142	3927	4712	5498	6,283	7,069	7,854	8,639
61	799	1597	2395	3194	3992	4791	5589	6,388	7,186	7,985	8,783
62	812	1623	2435	3246	4058	4870	5681	6,493	7,304	8,116	8,927
63	825	1649	2474	3299	4123	4948	5773	6,597	7,422	8,247	9,071
64	838	1676	2513	3351	4189	5027	5864	6,702	7,540	8,378	9,215
65	851	1702	2552	3403	4254	5105	5956	6,807	7,658	8,508	9,359
66	864	1728	2592	3456	4320	5184	6048	6,912	7,775	8,640	9,503
67	877	1754	2631	3508	4385	5262	6139	7,016	7,893	8,770	9,647
68	890	1780	2670	3560	4451	5341	6231	7,121	8,011	8,901	9,791
69	903	1806	2710	3613	4516	5419	6322	7,226	8,129	9,032	9,935
70	·916	1833	2749	3665	4581	5498	6414	7,330	8,247	9,163	10,079
71	929	1859	2788	3718	4647	5576	6506	7,435	8,365	9,294	10,223
72	943	1885	2827	3770	4712	5655	6597	7,540	8,482	9,425	10,367
73	956	1911	2867	3822	4778	5733	6689	7,644	8,600	9,556	10,511
74	969	1937	2906	3875	4843	5812	6781	7,749	8,718	9,687	10,655
75	982	1964	2945	3927	4909	5890	6872	7,854	8,836	9,818	10,796
76	995	1990	2985	3979	4974	5969	6964	7,959	8,954	9,948	10,943
77	1008	2016	3024	4032	5040	6048	7056	8,063	9,072	10,079	11,087
78	1021	2042	3063	4084	5105	6126	7147	8,168	9,189	10,210	11,231
79	1034	2068	3102	4136	5171	6205	7239	8,273	9,307	10,341	11,375
80	1047	2094	3142	4189	5236	6283	7330	8,378	9,425	10,472	11,519
81	1060	2121	3181	4241	5301	6362	7422	8,482	9,543	10,603	11,663
82	1073	2147	3220	4294	5367	6440	7514	8,587	9,660	10,734	11,807
83	1087	2173	3259	4346	5432	6519	7605	8,692	9,778	10,865	11,951
84	1100	2199	3299	4398	5498	6597	7697	8,797	9,896	10,996	12,099
85	1113	2225	3338	4451	5563	6676	7789	8,901	10,014	11,127	12,235
86	1126	2251	3377	4503	5629	6754	7880	9,006	10,132	11,257	12,383
87	1139	2278	3417	4555	5694	6833	7972	9,111	10,249	11,388	12,527
88	1152	2304	3456	4607	5760	6912	8063	9,215	10,367	11,519	
89	1161	2330	3495	4660	5825	6990	8155	9,320	10,485	11,650	
90	1178	2356	3534	4712	5891	7069	8247	9,425	10,603	11,780	
91	1191	2382	3574	4765	5956	7147	8338	9,530	10,721	11,912	
92	1204	2408	3617	4817	6021	7226	8430	9,634	10,839	12,043	
93	1217	2435	3652	4870	6087	7304	8522	9,739	10,956	12,174	
94	1231	2461	3692	4922	6152	7383	8613	9,844	11,074	12,305	
95	1244	2487	3731	4974	6217	7461	8704	9,948	11,192	12,436	
96	1257	2513	3770	5027	6283	7540	8796	10,053	11,310	12,566	
97	1270	2539	3809	5079	6349	7618	8888	10,158	11,428		
98	1283	2566	3849	5131	6414	7697	8980	10,263	11,545		
99	1296	2592	3888	5183	6480	7775	9071	10,367	11,663		
100	1309	2618	3927	5236	6545	7854	9163	10,472	11,781		

CIRCUMFERENTIAL SPEEDS IN FEET PER MINUTE

Revolutions per Minute

Diameter in Inches			2,400 / 1,200 / 600	2,600 / 1,300 / 650	2,800 / 1,400 / 700	3,000 / 1,500 / 750	3,200 / 1,600 / 800	3,400 / 1,700 / 850	3,600 / 1,800 / 900	3,800 / 1,900 / 950	4,000 / 2,000 / 1,000	4,400 / 2,200 / 1,100
1			157	170	183	196	209	223	236	249	262	288
2			314	340	367	393	419	445	471	497	524	576
3			471	510	550	589	628	668	707	746	785	863
4			628	681	733	785	838	890	942	995	1,047	1,152
5			785	851	916	982	1,047	1,113	1,178	1,244	1,309	1,440
6			942	1,021	1,100	1,178	1,257	1,335	1,414	1,492	1,571	1,728
7			1,100	1,191	1,283	1,375	1,466	1,558	1,649	1,741	1,832	2,016
8			1,257	1,361	1,466	1,571	1,675	1,780	1,885	1,990	2,094	2,304
9			1,414	1,531	1,649	1,767	1,885	2,003	2,121	2,238	2,356	2,592
10			1,571	1,702	1,833	1,964	2,094	2,225	2,356	2,487	2,618	2,880
11			1,728	1,872	2,016	2,160	2,304	2,448	2,592	2,736	2,880	3,168
12			1,885	2,042	2,199	2,356	2,513	2,670	2,827	2,984	3,143	3,456
13			2,042	2,212	2,382	2,552	2,723	2,893	3,063	3,233	3,403	3,744
14			2,199	2,382	2,566	2,749	2,932	3,115	3,299	3,482	3,665	4,032
15			2,356	2,552	2,749	2,945	3,142	3,338	3,534	3,731	3,927	4,320
16			2,513	2,723	2,932	3,142	3,351	3,560	3,770	3,979	4,189	4,608
17			2,670	2,893	3,115	3,338	3,560	3,783	4,006	4,228	4,451	4,896
18			2,827	3,063	3,299	3,534	3,770	4,006	4,241	4,477	4,712	5,184
19			2,985	3,233	3,482	3,731	3,979	4,228	4,477	4,725	4,974	5,472
20			3,142	3,403	3,665	3,927	4,189	4,451	4,712	4,974	5,236	5,760
21			3,299	3,573	3,848	4,123	4,398	4,673	4,948	5,223	5,498	6,048
22			3,456	3,744	4,032	4,320	4,608	4,896	5,184	5,472	5,760	6,336
23			3,613	3,914	4,215	4,516	4,817	5,118	5,419	5,720	6,021	6,623

Diameter in Inches												
6	12	24	3,770	4,084	4,398	4,712	5,027	5,341	5,655	5,969	6,283	6,912
6¼	12½	25	3,927	4,254	4,581	4,909	5,236	5,563	5,891	6,218	6,545	7,200
6½	13	26	4,084	4,424	4,764	5,105	5,445	5,786	6,126	6,466	6,807	7,487
6¾	13½	27	4,241	4,594	4,948	5,301	5,655	6,008	6,362	6,715	7,069	7,775
7	14	28	4,398	4,764	5,131	5,498	5,864	6,231	6,597	6,963	7,330	8,063
7¼	14½	29	4,555	4,935	5,314	5,694	6,074	6,453	6,833	7,213	7,592	8,351
7½	15	30	4,712	5,105	5,498	5,890	6,283	6,676	7,069	7,461	7,854	8,639
7¾	15½	31	4,870	5,275	5,681	6,086	6,493	6,898	7,304	7,710	8,116	8,927
8	16	32	5,027	5,445	5,864	6,283	6,702	7,121	7,540	7,959	8,378	9,215
8¼	16½	33	5,184	5,615	6,048	6,479	6,912	7,343	7,775	8,207	8,640	9,503
8½	17	34	5,341	5,785	6,231	6,676	7,121	7,566	8,011	8,456	8,901	9,791
8¾	17½	35	5,498	5,956	6,414	6,872	7,330	7,789	8,247	8,705	9,163	10,079
9	18	36	5,655	6,126	6,597	7,069	7,540	8,011	8,482	8,954	9,425	10,367
9¼	18½	37	5,812	6,296	6,781	7,265	7,749	8,234	8,718	9,202	9,687	10,655
9½	19	38	5,969	6,466	6,964	7,461	7,959	8,456	8,954	9,451	9,948	10,943
9¾	19½	39	6,126	6,637	7,147	7,658	8,168	8,679	9,189	9,700	10,210	
10	20	40	6,283	6,807	7,330	7,854	8,378	8,901	9,425	9,948	10,472	
10¼	20½	41	6,440	6,977	7,514	8,050	8,587	9,124	9,660	10,197	10,734	
10½	21	42	6,597	7,147	7,697	8,247	8,797	9,346	9,896	10,446	10,990	
10¾	21½	43	6,754	7,317	7,880	8,443	9,006	9,569	10,131	10,695		
11	22	44	6,912	7,487	8,063	8,639	9,215	9,791	10,367	10,943		
11¼	22½	45	7,069	7,658	8,247	8,836	9,425	10,014	10,603			
11½	23	46	7,226	7,828	8,430	9,032	9,634	10,236	10,839			
11¾	23½	47	7,383	7,998	8,613	9,228	9,844	10,459				
12	24	48	7,540	8,168	8,797	9,425	10,053	10,681				
12¼	24½	49	7,697	8,338	8,980	9,621	10,263	10,903				
12½	25	50	7,854	8,508	9,163	9,818	10,472					
12¾	25½	51	8,011	8,679	9,346	10,014	10,681					
13	26	52	8,168	8,849	9,529	10,210	10,891					
13¼	26½	53	8,325	9,019	9,712	10,407						
13½	27	54	8,482	9,189	9,896	10,603						
13¾	27½	55	8,639	9,359	10,079	10,799						
14	28	56	8,797	9,530	10,263	10,996						
14¼	28½	57	8,954	9,700	10,446							
14½	29	58	9,111	9,870	10,629							
14¾	29½	59	9,268	10,040	10,812							
15	30	60	9,425	10,210	10,996							

Revolutions per Minute

Diameter			2,400	2,600	1,200	1,300	600	650
15¼	30½	61					9,582	10,380
15½	31	62					9,739	10,551
15¾	31½	63					9,896	10,721
16	32	64					10,053	10,891
16¼	32½	65					10,210	
16½	33	66					10,367	
16¾	33½	67					10,524	
17	34	68					10,681	
17¼	34½	69					10,839	

POWER REQUIRED BY MACHINE TOOLS

ENGINE LATHES

	Horse-power	
Swing Inches	Average work	Heavy work
12	$\frac{1}{2}$	2
14	$\frac{3}{4}$– 1	2 – 3
16	1 – 2	2 – 3
18	2 – 3	3 – 5
20–22	3	$7\frac{1}{2}$–10
24–27	5	$7\frac{1}{2}$–10
30	5 – $7\frac{1}{2}$	$7\frac{1}{2}$–10
32–36	$7\frac{1}{2}$–10	10 –15
38–42	10 –15	15 –20
48–54	15 –20	20 –25
60–84	20 –25	25 –30

AXLE LATHES

	H.P.
Single	5– $7\frac{1}{2}$–10
Double	10–15 –20
Locomotive axle ..	25

WHEEL LATHES

	H P.	Tailstock Motor H P.
48-in. car wheel ..	15–20	5
51–60 driv. wheel .	15–20	5
79–84	25–30	5
90	30–40	5–$7\frac{1}{2}$
100	40–50	5–$7\frac{1}{2}$
Quartering attach-ment	3– 5	

CYLINDER LATHES

	H.P.
40 in.	15
40-in. heavy	20
48 in.	15

VERTICAL BORING MILLS

Size	Average H P.	Heavy H.P.
36–42 in.	5 – $7\frac{1}{2}$	$7\frac{1}{2}$–10
50 in.	$7\frac{1}{2}$	$7\frac{1}{2}$–10
60–84 in.	$7\frac{1}{2}$–10	10 –15
7–12 ft.	10 –15	30 –40
14–25 ft.	15 –25	30 –40

HORIZONTAL BORING, DRILLING AND MILLING MACHINE

Dia. Spindle	Horse-power for Single Spindle
$3\frac{1}{2}$–$4\frac{1}{2}$	5 – $7\frac{1}{2}$
$4\frac{1}{2}$–$5\frac{1}{2}$	$7\frac{1}{2}$–10
$5\frac{1}{2}$–$6\frac{1}{2}$	10 –15

For double spindle, use double the horse-power.

CYLINDER BORING MACH.

Dia. Spindle	Max. Boring Diameter	Horse-power
4	20	$7\frac{1}{2}$
6	30	10
8	40	15

MISCELLANEOUS

Loco. rod boring mach.	$7\frac{1}{2}$–10
Car-box boring mach.	
6 x 12 and $5\frac{1}{2}$ x 10″ boxes	5 – $7\frac{1}{2}$
Car-wheel borer..	10 –15

PLANERS

Size	Horse-power
24 x 24 in.	3 – 5
30 x 30 in.	5 – $7\frac{1}{2}$
36 x 36 in.	10–15
48 x 48 in.	15–20
60 x 60 in.	20–25
72 x 72 in.	20–30
84 x 84 in.	30
100 x 100 in.	40

NOTE. — Normal length of bed in feet is about $\frac{1}{4}$ the width in inches.

FROG AND SWITCH PLANERS

36 x 12 in.	30
48 x 36 in.	30

PLATE PLANERS

Niles Nos. 2 and 3	10
Niles No. 5	15
Niles Nos. 6 and 7	20
Niles No. 8	20–25

ROTARY PLANERS

Dia. Cutter	Horse-power
24– 30 in.	5– 7½
36– 42 in.	10
48– 54 in.	15
60– 72 in.	20–25
84–100 in.	30–40

SHAPERS

	H.P.
12–16-in. stroke	2
18-in. stroke	2 – 3
20–24-in. stroke	3 – 5
30-in. stroke.........	5 – 7½
20-in. Traverse-head..	7½
24-in. Traverse-head..	10

CRANK SLOTTERS

Stroke	Horse-power
6– 8	3 – 5
10–12	5
14	5 – 7½
16–18	7½–10
20–30	10 –15

PLAIN MILLERS

Table Feed	Cross Feed	H.P.
34	10	7½
42	12	10
50	12	15

UNIVERSAL MILLERS

Nos. 1–1½	1 – 2
No. 2	3 – 5
No. 3	5 – 7½
No. 4	7½–10
No. 5	10 –15

VERTICAL MILLERS

Height Under Work

12–14 in.	5– 7½
18 in.	10
20 in.	15
24 in.	20

VERTICAL SLAB MILLERS

24-in. width of work	7½
32–36-in. width of work ...	10
42-in. width of work	15

HORIZONTAL SLAB MILLERS

Width Between Housings	Horse-power Average	Heavy
24–30 in.	7½–10	10–15
36 in.	10 –15	20–25
60–72 in.	25	75

CYLINDRICAL GRINDERS

Dia. Wheel	Horse-power Average	Heavy
10 in.	5	7½
14 in.	10	15
18 in.	10	15

EMERY GRINDERS

No. Wheels	Dia.	H.P.
2	6 in.	½– 1
2	10 in.	2
2	12 in.	3
2	18 in.	5 – 7½
2	24–26 in.	7½–10

MISC. GRINDERS

Type	Horse-power
Wet tool............	2–3
Flexible swing.......	3
Angle cock	3
Piston rod	3
Twist drill	2
Automatic tool	3–5
Car wheel...........	30

BUFFING HEADS

No. Wheels	Dia.	H.P.
2	6	¼– ½
2	10	1 –2
2	14	3 –5

VERTICAL DRILLS

Size	H.P.
12–20 in.	1
24–28 in.	2
30–32 in.	3
36–40 in.	5
50–60 in.	5 –7½
Sensitive drills up to ½-in.	¼– ⅜

RADIAL DRILLS

Size	Horse-power Average	Heavy
3-ft. arm	1–2	3
4-ft. arm	2–3	5 – 7½
5-6-7ft. arm	3–5	5 – 7½
8-9-10 ft. arm	5–7½	7½–10

MULTI.-SPINDLE DRILLS

Size of Drills	Up to	H P
$\frac{1}{32}-\frac{1}{4}$	6–10 spindle	3
$\frac{1}{16}-\frac{3}{8}$	6–10 spindle	5
$\frac{3}{16}-\frac{1}{2}$	6–10 spindle	7½
$\frac{1}{4}-\frac{3}{4}$	6–10 spindle	10
$\frac{3}{4}-1$	6–10 spindle	10–15
2	4 spindle	7½

GEAR CUTTERS

Size	Horse-power
36 x 9 in.	2 – 3
48 x 10 in.	3 – 5
30–60 x 12 in.	5 – 7½
72 x 14 in.	7½–10
64 x 20 in.	10–15

COLD SAWS

Dia. Saw	Horse-power
20 in.	3
26 in.	5
32 in.	7½
36 in.	10–15
42 in.	20
48 in.	25
Hacksaws	½

BOLT CUTTERS

Single	Horse-power
1, 1¼, 1½ in.	1–2
1¾, 2 in.	2–3
2½, 3½ in.	3–5
4, 6 in.	5–7½
1, 1½ in. double	2–3
2, 2½ in. double	3–5
1, 1½, 2 in. triple	3–7½

BOLT POINTERS

1½, 2½ in.	1–2

NUT TAPPERS

1, 2 in. 4-spindle	3
2 in. 6-spindle	3–5
2 in. 10-spindle	5
2 in. nut facer	3

PIPE THREADING AND CUTTING OFF MACHINES

Size of Pipe	Horse-power
¼– 2 in.	2
½– 3 in.	3
1¼– 6 in.	3–5
2 – 8 in.	3–5
3 –10 in.	5
4 –12 in.	5
8 –18 in.	7½
24 in.	10

HAMMERS

Size	Horse-power
15– 75 lb.	½–5
100–200 lb.	5 –7½

Drop hammers require approximately 1 horse-power for every 100-pound weight of hammer head.

100 lb. Bradley hammer	3
200 lb. Bradley hammer	5
350 lb. Beaudry hammer	5

BULLDOZERS, FORMING OR BENDING MACHINES

Width	Head Movement	Horse-power
29 in.	14 in.	5
34 in.	16 in.	7½
39 in.	16 in.	10
45 in.	18 in.	15
63 in.	20 in.	20

BULLDOZERS (AJAX)

No. 3	5
No. 4	7½
No. 5	10
No. 6	15
No. 7	30
No. 9	40
No. 12	50

BOLT HEADERS (HOT)

Size	Horse-power
¾–1½ in.	5– 7½
1½–2 in.	10–15

UPSETTING MACHINES

2 in.	7½–10
3 in.	10 –15
5 in.	15 –20
6 in.	20 –30

Hot Nut Machines

Size	Horse-power
$\frac{1}{2}$– $\frac{5}{8}$ in.	5
$\frac{7}{8}$–1 in.	$7\frac{1}{2}$–10
$1\frac{1}{2}$–2 in.	10 –15

Hyd. Wheel Press

Size	Horse-power
100 tons	5
200–300 tons	$7\frac{1}{2}$
400 tons	10
600 tons	15

Bending and Straightening Rolls

Width	Thickness	H P.
4– 6 in.	$\frac{5}{16}$– $\frac{3}{8}$	5
6 in.	$\frac{7}{16}$– $\frac{3}{4}$	5–15
8 in.	$\frac{7}{8}$	25
10 in.	$1\frac{1}{8}$–$1\frac{1}{2}$	35–50
24 in.	1	50

Flue Machines

	No of Flues Capacity	Horse-power
Flue Rattler	250–300	20–30
Flue Cutter		2– 3
Flue Welder		2– 3

Notching Press (Sheet-Iron)

Dia. Punch	Thickness	Horse-power
$\frac{3}{8}$ in.	$\frac{1}{4}$	1
$\frac{1}{2}$– $\frac{5}{8}$ in.	$\frac{1}{2}$– $\frac{5}{8}$	2– 3
$\frac{3}{4}$ in.	$\frac{3}{4}$	3– 5
$\frac{7}{8}$–1 in.	$\frac{1}{2}$– $\frac{3}{4}$	5
1 in.	1	$7\frac{1}{2}$
$1\frac{1}{8}$ in.	1	$7\frac{1}{2}$–10
$1\frac{3}{4}$ in.	1	10 –15
2 in.	1	10 –15
$2\frac{1}{2}$ in.	$1\frac{1}{2}$	15 –25

Multiple Punch

4 holes $\frac{5}{8}$ dia. $\frac{3}{8}$ plate $7\frac{1}{2}$–10

Shears

Gap Width	Cut $\frac{1}{2}$ Iron	Cut $\frac{3}{4}$ Iron
30–42 in.	3	5
56–60 in.	4	$7\frac{1}{2}$
72–96 in.	5	10
Bolt shears		$7\frac{1}{2}$
Double angle shears		10
Rotary bevel shears		$7\frac{1}{2}$

Plate Shears

Metal	Cut per Min.	Stroke	H.P
$\frac{3}{4}$ x 24 in.	35	3 in.	10
1 x 24 in.	20	3 in.	15
2 x 14 in.	15	$4\frac{1}{4}$ in.	30
1 x 42 in.	20	4 in.	20
$1\frac{1}{2}$ x 42 in.	15	$4\frac{1}{2}$ in.	60
$1\frac{1}{4}$ x 54 in.	18	6 in.	75
$1\frac{1}{2}$ x 72 in.	20	$5\frac{1}{2}$ in.	10
$1\frac{1}{4}$ x 100 in.	10–12	$7\frac{1}{2}$ in.	75

Lever Shears

Metal Cut	Horse-power
1 x 1 in.	5
$1\frac{1}{2}$ x $1\frac{1}{2}$ in.	$7\frac{1}{2}$
2 x 2 in.	10
6 x 1 in.	10
$2\frac{1}{2}$ x $2\frac{1}{2}$ in.	10
1 x 7 in.	15
$2\frac{3}{4}$ x $2\frac{3}{4}$ in.	15
$1\frac{1}{2}$ x 8 in.	20
$3\frac{1}{2}$ x $3\frac{1}{2}$ in.	20
$4\frac{1}{2}$ round	30

Motors Usually Employed for Cranes and Hoists

Hoist

Capacity tons	Speed ft. per min.	H.P.
5	25	15
	50	25
10	30	25
	40	40
15	20	25
20	15	25
25	10	25
	15	33
30	14	33
5 aux.	50	25
10 aux.	25	25
50	10	40
5 aux.	50	25
10 aux.	25	25

Capacity tons	Bridge Span ft.	H.P.	Trolley H P.
5	60	20	3
10	80	25	3
15	80	25	5
20	80	25	5
25	80	25	5
30	80	33	$7\frac{1}{2}$
35	80	40	$7\frac{1}{2}$–10

POWER REQUIRED FOR PLANING-MILL EQUIPMENT

BAND SAWS

Dia. Wheel	Max. width of Saw	H.P.
30 in.	$\frac{1}{2}$	2
34 in.	$\frac{1}{2}$	3
36–38 in.	$\frac{1}{2}$–$1\frac{1}{2}$	3–5
40–42 in.	$\frac{1}{2}$–$1\frac{1}{2}$	3–$7\frac{1}{2}$
40–42 in.	$2\frac{1}{2}$	10
40–42 in.	$3\frac{1}{2}$	15

CUT OFF SAWS

Dia. Saw	No. of Saws	H.P.
12–14	1	3
16	1	5
16	2	$7\frac{1}{2}$–10
30	1	$7\frac{1}{2}$

CIRCULAR RIP SAWS

14	1	5
16	1	$7\frac{1}{2}$
24	1	10
36	1	15

TIMBER SIZERS

Capacity	No. Heads	H.P.
30 x 20 in.	4	50
20 x 20 in.	4	50
30 x 10 in.	4	40
20 x 16 in.	4	40

SURFACERS

Size	No. Heads	H.P.	
30 x 6 in.	1–2	15–20	Heavy work
24 x 6 in.	1–2	15–20	
30 x 8 in.	2	30	
26 x 8 in.	2	30	
24 x 6 in.	1	5–$7\frac{1}{2}$	Light work
16 x 6 in.	1	5–$7\frac{1}{2}$	
24 x 8 in.	1	10	
30 x 8 in.	1	10	

	Horse-power
Shapers, 1–2 spin....	3–5
Borers	5–$7\frac{1}{2}$

PLANERS, MATCHERS AND FLOORING MACHINES

Size	Heads	Horse-power
9 x 8 in.	4–5	30
19 x 8 in.	4–5	30
24 x 8 in.	4–5	40

Size	Heads	Horse-power
30 x 8 in.	4–5	40
24 x 12 in.	4–5	40
30 x 12 in.	4–5	40

OUTSIDE MOULDERS

Capacity	No Heads	Horse-power
4 x 4 in.	1–2	5
4 x 4 in.	3–4	$7\frac{1}{2}$
6 x 4 in.	1–2	5
6 x 4 in.	3–4	$7\frac{1}{2}$
8 x 4 in.	4	10
10 x 4 in.	4	15
12 x 5 in.	4	20
14 x 6 in.	4	20

INSIDE MOULDERS

8 x 4 in.	4	15
10 x 4 in.	4	15
10 x 6 in	4–5	20–30
15 x 4 in.	4–5	20–30

JOINTERS

8–12 in.	2
16–24 in.	3
30–36 in.	5

TENONING MACHINES

	No. Heads	
$5\frac{1}{2}$ x 14 in.	1	3–5
$5\frac{1}{2}$ x 15 in.	2	5
23 x 9 in.	2	$7\frac{1}{2}$
54 x $4\frac{1}{2}$ in.	4–8	10–15
78 x $4\frac{1}{2}$ in.	4–8	10–15
Gainers		$7\frac{1}{2}$–10–15

BELT SANDERS

Width of Belt	Horse-power
6–14 in.	2–3
18 in.	5

COLUMN ARM

Length of Arm	Dia. of Disks	Horse-power
4–10 ft.	8 in.	3

DRUM SANDERS

Length of Drum	Horse-power
30 in.	$7\frac{1}{2}$
36 in.	10
42–48 in.	15
54–60 in.	20
72–84 in.	30

GROUP DRIVING OF MACHINES

There are many shops where group driving will be found more desirable than the use of individual motors, both as to first cost and maintenance.   This is particularly true where the machines are comparatively small and run intermittently, as the cost of motors will be much less.

Friction load of $2\frac{1}{2}$ to 3-inch shafting, with bearings 8 to 10 feet and running at 150 to 200 revolutions per minute, is about 1 horse-power for every 30 feet of shafting.   This includes the friction of countershafts of the machines driven by it.

In group driving it is usually perfectly safe to select a motor having a rated capacity of from 25 to 30 per cent. of the total power required for the machines in the group.

POWER REQUIRED FOR PUNCHING AND SHEARING

Experiments tend to show that with steel plates of 60,000 pounds tensile strength, the metal is all sheared when the punch has passed $\frac{1}{4}$ through the plate.   The following formula by L. R. Pomeroy takes this into account and also allows the motor and efficiency of 80 per cent. and the punching machine 75 per cent.

When $T =$ Full thickness of plate.
              $D =$ Diameter of hole punched.
              $N =$ Number of holes punched per minute.
              $P =$ Horse-power required to drive machine.

$$P = \frac{T^2 \times D \times N}{3.78}.$$

Taking a $\frac{1}{2}$-inch hole in a $\frac{1}{4}$-inch plate, the power required to punch 30 per minute would be

$$\frac{\frac{1}{4} \times \frac{1}{2} \times 30}{3.78} = \frac{3.75}{3.78} \text{ or about 1 horse-power.}$$

Pressure required for shearing = Length of cut $\times$ thickness in inches $\times$ shearing strength of material.   Dies with "shear" reduce this $\frac{1}{4}$ to $\frac{1}{2}$.

POWER REQUIRED TO REMOVE METAL

The power required to remove metal depends on the amount of metal removed per minute and the nature of the cutting tool.   With a cutting angle of 75 to 80 degrees, tests show that for mild steel of 40-point carbon one horse-power will remove 1.5 cubic inches of metal per minute.

For average conditions and with tools as ordinarily used, tests show that to remove one cubic inch of metal per min. requires the amount of power shown in the table.

Brass and similar alloys .... 0.2 to 0.3 H.P.
Cast iron .... 0.3 to 0.5 "
Wrought iron .... }
Mild steel (0.30% to 0.40% carbon) ...... } 0.6 "
Hard steel (0.50% carbon) .... 1.00 to 1.25 "
Very hard tire steel .... 1.50 "

Two important factors enter into the problem of power for driving machines. These are the Time Factor and the Load Factor.

$$\text{Time Factor} = \frac{\text{Actual Cutting Time}}{\text{Total Time to Complete Operation}}.$$

$$\text{Load Factor} = \frac{\text{Average Daily Load}}{\text{Full Load Rating of Motor}}.$$

Many tests give the following load factors:

The average load factor for motors driving lathes is from 10 to 25 per cent. On some special machines, as driving wheel and car wheel lathes, the cuts are all heavy, which increases the average load factor to from 30 to 40 per cent.

For extension boring mills, 5 horse-power motors are used to move the housings on from 10 feet to 16 feet mills, 7½ horse-power for from 14 feet to 20 feet mills and 10 horse-power for from 16 feet to 24 feet mills. The load factor of the driving motor on boring mill averages from 10 to 25 per cent.

The load factor of motor-driven drills is about 40 per cent. when the larger drills applicable thereto are used. If the smaller drill are used the load factor averages 25 per cent. and lower.

For the average milling operations the load factor averages from 10 to 25 per cent. On slab milling machines where large quantitie of metal are removed it will average from 30 to 40 per cent.

The work on this class of machinery is usually light and much time is required in making adjustments. Hence the load factor i rarely higher than 20 per cent.

On planers the load factor averages between 15 and 20 per cent. The motor must be large enough to reverse the table quickly, ye this peak load occurs for such short intervals that it does not in crease the average load per cycle very much.

The work done on shapers is of a varying character. With ligh work the load factor will not exceed from 15 to 20 per cent.; with heavy work, the load factor will be as high as 40 per cent.

The conditions with slotters are similar to those on shapers.

HORSE-POWER TO DRIVE MACHINES

Extensive experiments by L. R. Pomeroy show that the horse power required equals the Feed per rev. or stroke × Depth o

ut in inches $\times$ Cutting speed in feet per minute $\times$ 12 $\times$ Number
if tools cutting $\times$ a Constant which depends on the material.   This
hecks up fairly well with actual motor tests.   The constants given
re:

Cast iron	0.35 to 0.5
Wrought iron or soft steel	0.45 to 0.7
Locomotive driving wheel tires	0.70 to 1.00
Very hard steel.	1.00 to 1.10

Handling this in another way, Charles Robbins of the Westing-
.ouse Electric & Manufacturing Co. gives: The horse-power =
:ubic inches removed per minute $\times$ a Constant.   These constants
re:

Brass and similar alloys	0.2 to 0.3
Cast iron	0.3 to 0.5
Wrought iron	0.6
Mild steel (0.30 to 0.40 carbon)	0.6
Hard steel (0.50 carbon).	1.00 to 1.25
Very hard tire steel	1.50

These represent average conditions with the cutting tools ordinarily
sed.
A brief summary of the studies by Mr. Robbins gives interesting
ata on various machines.   These give factors as follows:

	Time Factor	Load Factor
ertical boring machine . . . . /	44%	27%
.adial drilling machine	41	10
ortable milling machine	54	55
ortable slotting machine	50	12
laners	55	

L. R. Pomeroy also gives a method of determining the horse-power
:quired by the belt used to drive the machine.   The formula is:

[p. = Thickness of belt in inches $\times$ Width of belt in inches $\times$
    Diameter of pulley in inches $\times$ Revolutions per minute $\times$
    Constant for kind of belt.

These constants are:

Leather belt	0.0062 to 0.0098
Cotton belt	0.0036 to 0.0068
Rubber belt	0.0050 to 0.0082

STEEL AND OTHER METALS

HEAT TREATMENT OF STEEL

THE theory of the heat treatment of steel rests upon the influence of the rate of cooling on certain molecular changes in structure occurring at different temperatures in the solid state. These changes are of two classes, critical and progressive; the former occur periodically between certain narrow temperature limits, while the latter proceed gradually with the rise in temperature, each change producing alterations in the physical characteristics. By controlling the rate of cooling, these changes can be given a permanent set, and the physical characteristics can thus be made different from those in the metal in its normal state.

The highest temperature that it is safe to submit a steel to for heat-treating is governed by the chemical composition of the steel. Pure carbon steel should be raised to about 1650 degrees Fahr., while some of the high-grade alloy steels may safely be raised to 1750 degrees Fahr., and the high-speed steels may be raised to just below the melting point, usually from 2000 to 2150 degrees Fahr. It is necessary to raise the metal to these points so that the active cooling process will have the desired effect of checking the crystallization of the structure.

Methods of Heating

Furnaces using solid fuel such as coal, coke, charcoal, etc., are the most numerous and have been used the longest. These furnaces consist of a grate to place the fuel on, an arch to reflect the heat and a plate to put the pieces on. The plate should be so arranged that the flames will not strike the pieces to be heated, and for that reason some use cast-iron or clay retorts which are open on the side toward the doors of the furnace.

Liquid fuel furnaces, which have open fires and which use liquid fuels, are not very numerous at present, but their use is increasing, owing to the ease with which the fire is handled and the cleanliness as compared with a coal, coke or charcoal fire.

Crude oil and kerosene are the fuels generally used in these furnaces, owing to their cheapness and the fact that they can be easily obtained. These fuels are usually stored in a tank near the furnaces and are pumped to them or flow by force of gravity.

Heating in Liquids

Furnaces using liquid for heating have a receptacle to hold the liquid, which is heated by coal, oil, gas or any other economical means; the liquid is kept at the highest temperature to which the piece should be heated. The piece should be heated slowly in an ordinary furnace to about 800 degrees, after which it should be immersed in the liquid bath and kept there long enough to attain the temperature of the bath and then removed to be annealed or hardened.

The bath usually consists of lead, although antimony, cyanate of potassium, chloride of barium, a mixture of chloride of barium and chloride of potassium in the proportion of 3 to 2, mercury, common salt and metallic salts have been successfully used.

This method gives good results, as no portion of the piece to be treated can reach a temperature above that of the liquid bath; a pyrometer attachment will indicate exactly when the piece has arrived at that temperature, and its surface cannot be acted upon chemically. The bath can be maintained easily at the proper temperature and the entire process is under perfect control.

When lead is used it is liable to stick to the steel unless it is pure and retard the cooling of the spots where it adheres. Impurities, such as sulphur, are liable to be absorbed by the steel and thus affect its chemical composition. With high temperatures lead and cyanate of potassium throw off poisonous vapors which make them prohibitive, and even at comparatively low temperatures these vapors are detrimental to the health of the workmen in the hardening room. The metallic salts, however, do not give off these poisonous vapors, and are much better to use for this purpose, but many times the fumes are unbearable.

Gas as Fuel

Furnaces using gaseous fuel are very numerous and are so constructed that they can use either natural gas, artificial gas, or producer gas. They are very easy to regulate and if well built are capable of maintaining a constant temperature within a wide range.

In first cost this style of furnace is greater than that of the solid fuel furnaces, but where natural or producer gas is used the cost of operating is so much less that the saving soon pays for the cost of installation. Illuminating gas, however, is more expensive than the solid fuels and is only used where high-grade work demands the best results from heat treatment.

COOLING THE STEEL

COOLING apparatus is divided into two classes — baths for hardening and the different appliances for annealing.

The baths for quenching are composed of a large variety of materials. Some of the more commonly used are as follows, being arranged according to their intensity on 0.85 per cent. carbon steel: Mercury; water with sulphuric acid added; nitrate of potassium; sal ammoniac; common salt; carbonate of lime; carbonate of magnesia; pure water; water containing soap, sugar, dextrine or alcohol; sweet milk; various oils; beef suet; tallow; wax. These baths, however, do not act under all conditions with the same relative intensity, as their conductivity and viscosity vary greatly with the temperature.

With the exception of the oils and some of the greases, the quenching effect increases as the temperature of the bath lowers. Sperm and linseed oils, however, at all temperatures between 32 and 250 degrees Fahr., act about the same as distilled water at 160 degrees.

The baths for hardening which give the best results are those in which some means are provided for keeping the liquid at an even temperature. Where but few pieces are to be quenched, or a considerable time elapses between the quenching of pieces, the bath will retain an atmospheric temperature from its own natural radiation. Where a bath is in continuous use, for quenching a large number of pieces throughout the day, some means must be provided to keep the temperature of the bath at a low even temperature. The hot pieces from the heating furnace will raise the temperature of the bath many degrees, and the last piece quenched will not be nearly as hard as the first.

Annealing

The appliances for annealing are as numerous as the baths for quenching, and where a few years ago the ashes from the forge were all that were considered necessary for properly annealing a piece of steel, to-day many special preparations are being manufactured and sold for this purpose.

The more common materials used for annealing are powdered charcoal, charred bone, charred leather, slacked lime, sawdust, sand, fire clay, magnesia or refractory earth. The piece to be annealed is usually packed in a cast-iron box, using some of these materials or combinations of them for the packing, the whole is then heated in a furnace to the proper temperature and set aside, with the cover left on, to cool gradually to the atmospheric temperature.

For certain grades of steel these materials give good results; but for all kinds of steels and for all grades of annealing the slow-cooling furnace no doubt gives the best satisfaction, as the temperature can be easily raised to the right point, kept there as long as necessary, and then regulated to cool down as slowly as is desired. The gas, oil or electric furnaces are the easiest to handle and regulate.

The Hardening Bath

In hardening steels the influence of the bath depends upon its temperature, its mass and its nature; or to express this in another way, upon its specific heat, its conductivity, its volatility and its viscosity. With other things equal, the lower the temperature of the bath, the quicker will the metal cool and the more pronounced will be the hardening effect. Thus water at 60 degrees will make steel harder than water at 150 degrees, and when the bath is in constant use the first piece quenched will be harder than the tenth or twentieth, owing to the rise in temperature of the bath. Therefore if uniform results are to be obtained in using a water bath, it must either be of a very large volume or kept cool by some mechanical means. In other words, the bath must be maintained at a constant temperature.

The mass of the bath can be made large so no great rise in temperature is made by the continuous cooling of pieces, or it can be made small and its rise in temperature used for hardening tools that are to remain fairly soft, as, if this temperature is properly regulated, the tool will not have to be re-heated and tempered later, and cracks and fissures are not as liable to occur.

Another way of arriving at the same results would be to use the double bath for quenching, that is, to have one bath of some product similar to salt which fuses at 575 degrees Fahr. Quench the piece in that until it has reached its temperature, after which it can be quenched in a cold bath or cooled in the air.

BATH FOR DRAWING TEMPER

A VERY good table from which to make up baths for drawing the temper is as follows:

Composition of Bath Lead and Tin	Melting Point in degree F.	Color of Steel at Temperature Given
14 8	420	very faint yellow
15 8	430	faint yellow
16 8	440	light straw
17 8	450	straw
18.5.......8	460	full straw
20 8	470	dark straw
24 8	480	old gold
28 8	490	brown
38 8	510	brown with purple spots
60 8	530	purple
96 8	550	deep purple
200 8	560	blue
Boiling linseed oil	600	dark blue
Melted lead	610	gray blue

These are used in a similar manner to the hardening baths, selecting the bath which gives the proper drawing temperature.

HIGH-SPEED STEELS

THESE steels are made by alloying tungsten and chromium or molybdenum and chromium with steel. These compositions completely revolutionize the points of transformation. Chromium, which has a tendency to raise the critical temperature, when added to a tungsten steel, in the proportions of 1 or 2 per cent., reduces the critical temperature to below that of the atmosphere. Tungsten and molybdenum prolong the critical range of temperatures of the steel on slow cooling so that it begins at about 1300 degrees Fahr. and spreads out all the way down to 600 degrees.

These steels are heated to 1850 degrees for the molybdenum and 2200 degrees for the tungsten, and cooled moderately fast, usually in and air blast, to give them the property known as "red-hardness." This treatment prevents the critical changes altogether and preserves the steel in what is known as the austenitic condition. The austenitic condition is one of hardness and toughness.

One rule which has given good results in heat-treating these high-speed steels is to heat slowly to 1500 degrees Fahr., then heat fast to 2200 degrees; after which cool rapidly in an air blast to 1550 degrees; then cool either rapidly or slowly to the temperature of the air. Others advocate cooling in crude oil.

CASE-HARDENING

CASE-HARDENING, carbonizing, or, as it is called in Europe, "cementation," is largely used so that the outer shell can be made hard enough to resist wear and the core of the piece can be left soft enough to withstand the shock strains to which it is subjected.

Several methods different from the old established one of packing the metal in a box filled with some carbonizing material, and then subjecting it to heat, have been devised in the last few years. Among them might be mentioned the Harveyizing process which is especially applicable to armor plate. The Harveyizing process uses a bed of charcoal over the work, the plates being pressed up against it in a pit or furnace and gas turned on so that the steel will be heated through the charcoal, thus allowing the carbon to soak in from the top.

The result of the carbonizing operation is determined by five factors, which are as follows: First, the nature of the steel; second, the nature of the carbonizing material; third, the temperature of the carbonizing furnace; fourth, the time the piece is submitted to the carbonizing process; fifth, the heat treatment which follows carbonizing.

The nature of the steel has no influence on the speed of penetration of the carbon, but has an influence on the final result of the operation.

If steel is used that has a carbon content up to 0.56 per cent., the rate of penetration in carbonizing is constant; but the higher the carbon content is, in the core, the more brittle it becomes by prolonged annealing after carbonizing. Therefore it is necessary that the carbon content should be low in the core, and for this reason a preference is given to steels containing from 0.12 to 0.15 per cent. of carbon for carbonizing or case-hardening purposes.

TABLE I. — PENETRATION OF CARBON PER HOUR WITH
DIFFERENT ALLOYS

Component of Alloys	Speed of Penetration per Hr. in Inches
0.5 per cent. manganese	0.043
1.0 per cent. manganese	0.047
1.0 per cent. chromium	0.039
2.0 per cent. chromium	0.043
2.0 per cent. nickel	0.028
5.0 per cent. nickel	0.020
0.5 per cent. tungsten	0.035
1.0 per cent. tungsten	0.036
2.0 per cent. tungsten	0.047
0.5 per cent. silicon	0.024
1.0 per cent. silicon	0.020
2.0 per cent. silicon	0.016
5.0 per cent. silicon	0.000
1.0 per cent. titanium	0.032
2.0 per cent. titanium	0.028
1.0 per cent. molybdenum	0.036
2.0 per cent. molybdenum	0.043
1.0 per cent. aluminum	0.016
3.0 per cent. aluminum	0.008

The rate of penetration for ordinary carbonizing steel under the same conditions would have been 0.035 inch. Thus it will be seen that manganese, chromium, tungsten and molybdenum increase the rate of penetration. These seem to exist in the state of a double carbide and release a part of the cementite iron.

Nickel, silicon, titanium and aluminum retard the rate of penetration — 5 per cent. of silicon reducing it to zero — and these exist in the state of solution in the iron.

The Carbonizing Materials

The nature of the carbonizing materials has an influence on the speed of penetration and it is very essential that the materials be of known chemical composition as this is the only way to obtain like results on the same steel at all times.

These materials or cements are manufactured in many special and patented preparations. The following materials are used and compounded in these preparations, but many of them give as good results when used alone as when compounded with others in varying percentages: Powdered bone; wood charcoal; charred sugar; charred leather; cyanide of potassium; ferro-cyanide of potassium; bichromate of potassium; animal black, acid cleaned. Prussiate of potash, anthracite, mixture of barium carbonate, graphite, petroleum gas, acetylene, horn, etc.

Wood charcoal is very largely used in carbonizing steels, but the value of this material varies with the wood used, the method employed in making the charcoal, and other factors. Used alone it gives the normal rate of penetration for the first hour, but after that the rate gradually decreases until at eight hours it gives the lowest rate of penetration of any of the carbonizing materials. The best wood charcoal is that made from hickory.

Powdered charcoal and bone give good results as a carbonizing material and are successfully used in carbonizing nickel-chrome steel by packing in a cast-iron pot and keeping at a temperature of about 2000 degrees Fahr. for four hours, and then cooling slowly before taking out of the pot or uncovering.

TABLE 2

Temperature Degrees Fahrenheit	Materials Used and Rate of Penetration in Inches			
	Charcoal 60 per cent. + 40 per cent. of Carbonate of Borium	Ferro-cyanide 66 per cent. + 34 per cent. of Bichromate	Ferro-cyanide Alone	Powdered Wood Charcoal Alone
1300	....	....	....	....
1475	0.020	0.033	0.020	0.020
1650	0.088	0.069	0.079	0.048
1825	0.128	0.128	0.128	0.098
2000	0.177	0.177	0.198	0.138

The speed of penetration caused by the action of different cements at different temperatures for the same time, i.e., eight hours, is best shown by Table 2.

CASE-HARDENING

Case-hardening, carbonizing, or, as it is called in Europe, "cementation," is largely used so that the outer shell can be made hard enough to resist wear and the core of the piece can be left soft enough to withstand the shock strains to which it is subjected.

Several methods different from the old established one of packing the metal in a box filled with some carbonizing material, and then subjecting it to heat, have been devised in the last few years. Among them might be mentioned the Harveyizing process which is especially applicable to armor plate. The Harveyizing process uses a bed of charcoal over the work, the plates being pressed up against it in a pit or furnace and gas turned on so that the steel will be heated through the charcoal, thus allowing the carbon to soak in from the top.

The result of the carbonizing operation is determined by the factors, which are as follows: First, the nature of the steel; second, the nature of the carbonizing material; third, the temperature of the carbonizing furnace; fourth, the time the piece is submitted to the carbonizing process; fifth, the heat treatment which follows carbonizing.

The nature of the steel has no influence on the speed of penetration of the carbon, but has an influence on the final result of the operation.

If steel is used that has a carbon content up to 0.56 per cent., the rate of penetration in carbonizing is constant; but the higher the carbon content is, in the core, the more brittle it becomes by prolonged annealing after carbonizing. Therefore it is necessary that the carbon content should be low in the core, and for this reason preference is given to steels containing from 0.12 to 0.15 per cent. of carbon for carbonizing or case-hardening purposes.

Table I. — Penetration of Carbon per Hour with Different Alloys

Component of Alloys	Speed of Penetration Hr. in In.
0.5 per cent. manganese	0.8
1.0 per cent. manganese	0.7
1.0 per cent. chromium	0.6
2.0 per cent. chromium	0.8
2.0 per cent. nickel	0.8
5.0 per cent. nickel	0.9
0.5 per cent. tungsten	0.5
1.0 per cent. tungsten	0.6
2.0 per cent. tungsten	0.7
0.5 per cent. silicon	0.4
1.0 per cent. silicon	0.9
2.0 per cent. silicon	0.6
5.0 per cent. silicon	0.9
1.0 per cent. titanium	0.2
2.0 per cent. titanium	0.8
1.0 per cent. molybdenum	0.6
2.0 per cent. molybdenum	0.8
1.0 per cent. aluminum	0.6
3.0 per cent. aluminum	0.8

The rate of penetration for ordinary carbonizing steel under the same conditions would have been 0.035 inch. Thus-it will be seen that manganese, chromium, tungsten and molybdenum increase the rate of penetration. These seem to exist in the state of a double carbide and release a part of the cementite iron.

Nickel, silicon, titanium and aluminum retard the rate of penetration — 5 per cent. of silicon reducing it to zero — and these exist in the state of solution in the iron.

The Carbonizing Materials

The nature of the carbonizing materials has an influence on the speed of penetration and it is very essential that the materials be of a known chemical composition as this is the only way to obtain like results on the same steel at all times.

These materials or cements are manufactured in many special and patented preparations. The following materials are used and compounded in these preparations, but many of them give as good results when used alone as when compounded with others in varying percentages: Powdered bone; wood charcoal; charred sugar; charred leather; cyanide of potassium; ferro-cyanide of potassium; bichromate of potassium; animal black, acid cleaned. Prussiate of potash, anthracite, mixture of barium carbonate, graphite, petroleum gas, acetylene, horn, etc.

Wood charcoal is very largely used in carbonizing steels, but the value of this material varies with the wood used, the method employed in making the charcoal, and other factors. Used alone it gives the normal rate of penetration for the first hour, but after that the rate gradually decreases until at eight hours it gives the lowest rate of penetration of any of the carbonizing materials. The best wood charcoal is that made from hickory.

Powdered charcoal and bone give good results as a carbonizing material and are successfully used in carbonizing nickel-chrome steel by packing in a cast-iron pot and keeping at a temperature of about 1000 degrees Fahr. for four hours, and then cooling slowly before taking out of the pot or uncovering.

TABLE 2

Temperature in Degrees Fahrenheit	MATERIALS USED AND RATE OF PENETRATION IN INCHES			
	Charcoal 60 per cent. + 40 per cent. of Carbonate of Borium	Ferro-cyanide 66 per cent. + 34 per cent. of Bichromate	Ferro-cyanide Alone	Powdered Wood Charcoal Alone
1300	....	....	....	....
1475	0.020	0.033	0.020	0.020
1650	0.088	0.069	0.079	0.048
1825	0.128	0.128	0.128	0.098
2000	0.177	0.177	0.198	0.138

The speed of penetration caused by the action of different cements at different temperatures for the same time, i.e., eight hours, is best shown by Table 2.

The nature of the carbonizing material has a very pronounced effect on the rate of carbonization, or the percentage of the carbon content in the surface layer of the piece, or both.

Another Test of Penetration

At the same temperature, *i.e.*, 1825 degrees Fahr., for different lengths of time and with different cements, the rate of penetration obtained was according to Table 3.

Eighty per cent. charcoal + 20 per cent. carbonate of barium, 40 per cent. charcoal + 60 per cent. carbonate of barium, ferro-cyanide alone and 66 per cent. ferro-cyanide + 34 per cent. bichromate were used with practically the same results for eight hours' time.

TABLE 3

Length of Time in Hours	MATERIALS USED AND RATE OF PENETRATION IN INCHES				
	Carbon 60 per cent. + 40 per cent. of Carbonate	Ferro-cyanide 66 per cent. + 34 per cent. of Bichromate	Powdered Wood Charcoal Alone	Charcoal and Carbonate of Potassium	Unwashed Animal Black
1	0.031	0.033	0.028	0.059	0.035
2	0.039	0.037	0.053	0.078	0.059
4	0.047	0.049	0.063	0.094	0.088
6	0.078	0.074	0.072	0.011	0.106
8	0.118	0.128	0.098	0.138	0.128

Another set of tests was carried out for a longer period of time, with other materials and at a uniform temperature of 1650 degrees Fahr., with the results given in Table 4.

TABLE 4

Length of Time in Hours	MATERIALS USED AND RATE OF PENETRATION IN INCHES		
	Charred Leather	Ground Wood Charcoal	Barium Carbonate and Wood Charcoal
2	0.045	0.028	0.055
4	0.062	0.042	0.087
8	0.080	0.062	0.111
12	0.110	0.070	0.125

In the use of hydrocarbons, or gases, a fresh supply can be kept lowing into the carbonizing receptacle and the time greatly reduced or deep penetration with an appreciable reduction of time for the hallow penetrations.

The constitution of a given steel is not the same in the hardened s in the normal state, owing to the carbon not being in the same tate. In the annealed or normal steel it is in a free state, while in a hardened steel it is in a state of solution which we may call martenite; and this contains more or less carbon according to the original arbon content of the steel. The composition, and therefore the mechanical properties, depend principally upon the carbon content, he mechanical properties being changed slowly and gradually by an ncrease in carbon.

This is best shown by Table 5 in which it will be seen that the ensile strength and elastic limit gradually increased with the increase n the percentage of carbon, both in the annealed and hardened state

TABLE 5. — EFFECT OF COMPOSITION AND HARDENING ON THE STRENGTH

	Case Harden- ing Steel	Very Low Carbon	Low Carbon	Medium Carbon	High Carbon	Very Carbon
Carbon	0.10	0.14	0.23	0.52	0.60	0.72
Silicon	0.09	0.05	0.15	0.18	0.10	0.17
Manganese	0.19	0.33	0.45	0.35	0.40	0.38
Phosphorus	0.016	0.023	0.091	0.021	0.035	0.03
Sulphur	0.025	0.052	0.062	0.043	0.025	0.06

MECHANICAL PROPERTIES WHEN ANNEALED

	Case Harden- ing Steel	Very Low Carbon	Low Carbon	Medium Carbon	High Carbon	Very Carbon
Tensile Strength (in pounds per square inch)	60,300	61,500	66,500	97,800	116,400	130,700
Elastic Limit (in pounds per square inch)	36,300	35,200	41,200	52,600	66,500	75,800
Elongation (percentage in 4 inches)...	29	27	26	20	14	9

MECHANICAL PROPERTIES WHEN HARDENED

	Case Harden- ing Steel	Very Low Carbon	Low Carbon	Medium Carbon	High Carbon	Very Carbon
Tensile Strength (in pounds per square inch)	66,400	73,100	99,400	132,100	153,400	180,100
Elastic Limit (in pounds per square inch)	40,300	39,600	54,000	81,400	102,100	105,500
Elongation (percentage in 4 inches)...	24	22	14	9	4	0

while the elongation gradually decreased. These tests were made with bar ½ inch in diameter and 4 inches in length. It will also be seen that there was considerable change in the steels which were too low in carbon to be made so hard that they could not be filed. The reduction in elongation when the test bars were heated and quenched show that the metal was harder than when in the annealed state.

Selecting the Proper Temperature for Quenching

A hardening process that will produce a steel that is as homogeneous as possible is always sought for in practice. This is easily obtained in a high-carbon steel and especially if it contains 0.85 per cent. carbon, by passing the recalescent point before quenching. The desired homogeneity is not so easily obtained, however, in the low-carbon steels as they have several points of transformation. If these are quenched at a point a little above the lowest point of transformation the carbon will pass into solution, but the solution is not homogeneous. To obtain this result it is necessary that the quenching be done from a little above the highest point of transformation. This is higher in the low- than in the high-carbon steels. In practice this calls for a quenching of the low-carbon steels as about 1650 degrees Fahr., while a high-carbon steel should be quenched at about 1450 degrees.

Testing Pyrometers

Pyrometers can be tested by placing some common salt in an iron box and heating until it melts. Put the pyrometer in the molten salt and, if correct, it will register 1441 degrees Fahr.

A Table of Fahrenheit and Centigrade thermometer scales is given on page 455.

Test of Hardness

The hardness of metals, particularly of steels which are heat treated, is now tested with either the Shore Scleroscope or the Brinnell Ball method.

THE BRINNELL TEST

The Brinnell method of testing consists of forcing a hardened steel ball of given dimension into the metal to be tested under a given pressure. The diameter of the impression made is read with a graduated microscope and the hardness found by consulting the table below. In this the ball is 10 millimeters in diameter. If, with a pressure of 3000 kilograms as indicated by the testing machine, the diameter of the depression is 3 millimeters, the hardness number is 418. Dividing this by 6 gives practically 70, as shown under the second column. According to this table, a pressure of only 500 kilograms will give a direct reading which is about the same as that of the Scleroscope. The standard pressure however is 3000 kilograms.

TABLE OF BRINNELL HARDNESS NUMERALS—STEEL BALL OF 10 MILLIMETERS DIAMETER

Diameter of Impression, Millimeters	Hardness Numeral Pressure, Kilograms		Diameter of Impression, Millimeters	Hardness Numeral Pressure, Kilograms		Diameter of Impression, Millimeters	Hardness Numeral Pressure, Kilograms		Diameter of Impression, Millimeters	Hardness Numeral Pressure, Kilograms		Diameter of Impression, Millimeters	Hardness Numeral Pressure, Kilograms	
	3000	500		3000	500		3000	500		3000	500		3000	500
2.0	946	158	3.0	418	70	4.0	228	38.0	5.0	143	23.8	6.0	95.0	15.9
2.05	898	150	3.05	402	67	4.05	223	37.0	5.05	140	23.3	6.05	94.0	15.6
2.10	857	143	3.10	387	65	4.10	217	36.0	5.10	137	22.8	6.10	92.0	15.3
2.15	817	136	3.15	375	63	4.15	212	35.0	5.15	134	22.3	6.15	90.0	15.1
2.20	782	130	3.20	364	61	4.20	207	34.5	5.20	131	21.8	6.20	89.0	14.8
2.25	744	124	3.25	351	59	4.25	202	33.6	5.25	128	21.5	6.25	87.0	14.5
2.30	713	119	3.30	340	57	4.30	196	32.6	5.30	126	21.0	6.30	86.0	14.3
2.35	683	114	3.35	332	55	4.35	192	32.0	5.35	124	20.6	6.35	84.0	14.0
2.40	652	109	3.40	321	54	4.40	187	31.2	5.40	121	20.1	6.40	82.0	13.8
2.45	627	105	3.45	311	52	4.45	183	30.4	5.45	118	19.7	6.45	81.0	13.5
2.50	600	100	3.50	302	50	4.50	179	29.7	5.50	116	19.3	6.50	80.0	13.3
2.55	578	96	3.55	293	49	4.55	174	29.1	5.55	114	19.0	6.55	79.0	13.1
2.60	555	93	3.60	286	48	4.60	170	28.4	5.60	112	18.6	6.60	77.0	12.8
2.65	532	89	3.65	277	46	4.65	166	27.8	5.65	109	18.2	6.65	76.0	12.6
2.70	512	86	3.70	269	45	4.70	163	27.2	5.70	107	17.8	6.70	74.0	12.4
2.75	495	83	3.75	262	44	4.75	159	26.5	5.75	105	17.5	6.75	73.0	12.2
2.80	477	80	3.80	255	43	4.80	156	25.9	5.80	103	17.2	6.80	71.5	11.9
2.85	460	77	3.85	248	41	4.85	153	25.4	5.85	101	16.9	6.85	70.0	11.7
2.90	444	74	3.90	241	40	4.90	149	24.9	5.90	99	16.6	6.90	69.0	11.5
2.95	430	72	3.95	235	39	4.95	146	24.4	5.95	97	16.2	6.95	68.0	11.3

SCLEROSCOPE READING

In the Shore Scleroscope, a miniature drop hammer tup falls from a fixed height to the surface of the metal being tested. The height of the rebound indicates the hardness on an arbitrary scale which has 115 divisions, these meeting all usual requirements. This method can be applied to any material which will take a permanent set under impact. For, no matter how hard the material, the falling weight, weighing about 40 grains, makes a dent which can be seen with a glass.

The following table shows the readings which will be obtained on the Scleroscope for the materials indicated, this giving the comparative hardness of the materials.

SCLEROSCOPE HARDNESS SCALE

Metal	Annealed	Hammered
Lead — cast	2– 5	3– 7
Babbitt	4– 9	
Gold	5	$8\frac{1}{2}$
Silver	$6\frac{1}{2}$	20– 30
Brass — cast	7–35	
Pure Tin — cast	8	12
Brass — drawn	10–15	20– 45
Bismuth — cast	9	
Platinum	10	17
Copper — cast	6	14– 20
Zinc — cast	8	20
Iron — pure	18	25– 30
Mild steel, 0.15 carbon	22	30– 45
Nickel Anode — cast	31	55
Iron, gray — cast	30–45	
Iron, gray — chilled		50– 90
Steel, tool, 1% carbon	30–35	40– 50
Steel, tool, 1.65% carbon	35–40	
Vanadium steel	35–45	
Chrome — Nickel	47	
Chrome — Nickel, hardened		60– 95
Steel, high speed, hardened		70–105
Steel, carbon, tool, hardened		90–110

NOTE. — These figures vary with the composition and density of the metals. They are about $\frac{1}{8}$ those of the Brinnell test for equal hardness, varying somewhat with the kind of metal.

FAHRENHEIT AND CENTIGRADE THERMOMETER SCALES

F	C	F	C	F	C	F	C	F	C
− 40	− 40.	70	21.1	185	85.	950	510.	2100	1149.
− 35	− 37.2	75	23.9	190	87.8	1000	537.8	2150	1176.5
− 30	− 34.4	80	26.7	195	90.6	1050	565.5	2200	1204.
− 25	− 31.7	85	29.4	200	93.3	1100	593.	2250	1232.
− 20	− 28.9	90	32.2	205	96.1	1150	621.	2300	1260.
− 15	− 26.1	95	35.	210	98.9	1200	648.5	2350	1287.5
− 10	− 23.3	100	37.8	212	100.	1250	676.5	2400	1315.5
− 5	− 20.6	105	40.6	215	101.7	1300	704.	2450	1343.
0	− 17.8	110	43.3	225	107.2	1350	732.	2500	1371.
+ 5	− 15.	115	46.1	250	121.2	1400	760.	2550	1399.
10	− 12.2	120	48.9	300	148.9	1450	788.	2600	1426.5
15	− 9.4	125	51.7	350	176.7	1500	816.	2650	1455.
20	− 6.7	130	54.4	400	204.4	1550	844.	2700	1483.
25	− 3.9	135	57.2	450	232.2	1600	872.	2750	1510.
30	− 1.1	140	60.	500	260.	1650	899.	2800	1537.5
32	0	145	62.8	550	287.8	1700	926.	2850	1565.
35	+ 1.7	150	65.6	600	315.6	1750	954.	2900	1593.
40	4.4	155	68.3	650	343.3	1800	982.	2950	1621.
45	7.2	160	71.1	700	371.1	1850	1010.	3000	1648.5
50	10.	165	73.9	750	398.9	1900	1038.	3050	1676.
55	12.8	170	76.7	800	426.7	1950	1065.5	3100	1705.
60	15.6	175	79.4	850	454.4	2000	1093.	3150	1732.
65	18.3	180	82.2	900	482.2	2050	1121.	3200	1760.

To convert Fahrenheit into Centigrade: Subtract 32 from Fahrenheit, divide remainder by 9 and multiply by 5.

Example: 212 Fahr.

$$\frac{32}{180} \qquad 180 \div 9 = 20. \quad 20 \times 5 = 100.$$

Ans. 212 Fahr. = 100 Cent.

Centigrade to Fahrenheit: Divide by 5, multiply by 9 and add 32.
Example: 260 Cent. ÷ 5 = 52. 52 × 9 = 468 + 32 = 500 Fahr.
Ans. 260 Cent. = 500 Fahr.

ALLOYS FOR COINAGE

	Gold	Copper	Silver	Other Constituents	Remarks
Gold coin	91.66	8.33	—	—	British standard.
" "	90.0	10.0	—	—	"Latin Union" and American.
" "	1.33	82.73	15.93	—	Roman, Septimus Severus, 265 A.D.
" "	40.35	19.63	40.02	—	Early British B.C. 50.
Silver coin	0.1	7.1	92.05	Lead 0.2	Roman B.C. 31, almost same as British silver coin.
" "	—	7.5	92.5	—	British standard.

Composition of Bronzes (Navy Department)

White Metal: PARTS
Tin 7.6
Copper 2.3
Zinc 83.3
Antimony 3.8
Lead 3.0

Hard Bronze for Piston Rings:
Tin 22.0
Copper 78.0

Bearings — Wearing Surfaces, etc.:
Copper 6
Tin 1
Zinc .... ¼

Naval Brass:
Copper 62.0
Tin 1.0
Zinc 37.0

Brazing Metal:
Copper 85.0
Zinc 15.0

Antifriction Metal:
Copper — (best refined) 3.7
Banca tin 88.8
Regulus of antimony 7.5
Well fluxed with borax and rosin in mixing.

Bearing Metal — (Pennsylvania Railroad):
Copper 77.0
Tin 8.0
Lead 15.0

Bearing Metal

In the Journal of the Franklin Institute G. H. Clamer states that 13 parts antimony and 87 parts lead make an excellent bearing metal, these being exactly the proportions which give a homogeneous structure. For heavier duty tin should be added.

Bismuth Alloys (Fusible Metals)

	Bismuth	Lead	Tin	Cadmium	Melting Point
					C°
Newton's alloys ...	50.0	31.25	18.75	—	95
Rose's " ...	50.0	28.10	24.64	—	100
Darcet's " ...	50.0	25.00	25.00	—	93
Wood's " ...	50.0	24.00	14.00	12.00	66–71
Lipowitz's " ...	50.0	27.00	13.00	10.00	60

ALLOYS

	Copper	Tin	Lead	Zinc	Nickel	Antimony	
Babbitt	8.	92.				4.	Very hard.
Bell metal	76.5	23.5					"Big Ben,"
	74.8	25.2					Westminster.
Brass	63–72			27–34			Typical brass.
" wire	70.29	0.17		29.26			
Britannia	1.46	90.62				7.81	Birmingham sheet.
Bronze........	95	4.		1.			British coinage.
	80–90	12–18		7.			Heavy bearings.
German silver ..	60			20.	20		Nickel varies.
Gun metal	91	9.					Cannons.
Mannheim gold	80–88			20–12			
Muntz metal ..	60–62			38–40			Ship sheathing.
Packfong......	43.8			40.6			Chinese alloy.
Shot metal			99.6		15.6		Trace of arsenic.
Speculum	70.24	29.11		trace			Telescope mirror.
Type metal....	2.0	10.	70			18.	
		3.2	82			14.	Stereotyping.
White metal ..	6.	82.				12.	For bearings.

Brass Alloys

Strictly, a brass is a copper-zinc alloy containing one-third zinc and two-thirds copper; whereas a bronze is a copper-tin alloy containing approximately 10 per cent. tin and 90 per cent. copper. The old-style gun metal contained from 90 to 92 per cent. copper and from 8 to 10 per cent. tin. Lead is frequently added to both these classes of alloy to make them machine more easily, and both tin and zinc are commonly used in the same alloy, so that today we have a series of copper-tin-zinc alloys of almost infinite variety. In all cases of the useful alloys of this class, however, there is present more than per cent. copper.

In most of the modern alloys tin is depended upon to give strength and zinc to cheapen the mixture. Some of the old-style gun metals contained as much as 16 per cent. tin and 84 per cent. copper, but such metals were brittle and hard. The common yellow brass employed by plumbers in making ordinary valves and fittings may considered as composed of approximately 16 pounds copper, 8 pounds zinc, and ½ pound lead. It will be noticed that this consists approximately one-third zinc and two-thirds copper, with a little lead added to improve the machining qualities. For the making of high-grade casting ingots or new metal should be used in all cases.

In making a brass the copper should be melted first and the zinc added, care being taken not to let the temperature rise too high, for if it does the zinc will ignite and burn. The lead is added last and the metal thoroughly stirred.

COMPOSITION OF BRONZES (NAVY DEPARTMENT)

White Metal: P..ts
    Tin 6
    Copper 3
    Zinc 3
    Antimony 8
    Lead 0
Hard Bronze for Piston Rings:
    Tin 0
    Copper 0
Bearings — Wearing Surfaces, etc.:
    Copper ....
    Tin ....
    Zinc ....
Naval Brass:
    Copper 0
    Tin 0
    Zinc 0
Brazing Metal:
    Copper 0
    Zinc 0
Antifriction Metal:
    Copper — (best refined) 7
    Banca tin 8
    Regulus of antimony 5
        Well fluxed with borax and rosin in mixing.
Bearing Metal — (Pennsylvania Railroad):
    Copper 0
    Tin 0
    Lead 0

BEARING METAL

In the Journal of the Franklin Institute G. H. Clamer states ..t 13 parts antimony and 87 parts lead make an excellent bea..g metal, these being exactly the proportions which give a homogen..s structure. For heavier duty tin should be added.

BISMUTH ALLOYS (FUSIBLE METALS)

	Bismuth	Lead	Tin	Cadmium	Mel.. Po..
					C
Newton's alloys ...	50.0	31.25	18.75	—	9
Rose's " ...	50.0	28.10	24.64	—	1C
Darcet's " ...	50.0	25.00	25.00	—	9
Wood's " ...	50.0	24.00	14.00	12.00	66
Lipowitz's " ...	50.0	27.00	13.00	10.00	6

Alloys

	Copper	Tin	Lead	Zinc	Nickel	Antimony	
Babbitt	8.	92.				4.	Very hard.
Bell metal	76.5	23.5					"Big Ben,"
	74.8	25.2					Westminster.
Brass	63–72			27–34			Typical brass.
" wire	70.29	0.17		29.26			
Britannia	1.46	90.62				7.81	Birmingham sheet.
Bronze........	95	4.		1.			British coinage.
	80–90	12–18		7.			Heavy bearings.
German silver..	60			20.	20		Nickel varies.
Gun metal	91	9.					Cannons.
Mannheim gold	80–88			20–12			
Muntz metal ..	60–62			38–40			Ship sheathing.
Packfong......	43.8			40.6			Chinese alloy.
Shot metal			99.6		15.6		Trace of arsenic.
Speculum	70.24	29.11		trace			Telescope mirror.
Type metal....	2.0	10.	70			18.	
		3.2	82			14.	Stereotyping.
White metal ..	6.	82.				12.	For bearings.

Brass Alloys

Strictly, a brass is a copper-zinc alloy containing one-third zinc and two-thirds copper; whereas a bronze is a copper-tin alloy containing approximately 10 per cent. tin and 90 per cent. copper. The old-style gun metal contained from 90 to 92 per cent. copper and from 8 to 10 per cent. tin. Lead is frequently added to both these classes of alloy to make them machine more easily, and both tin and zinc are commonly used in the same alloy, so that today we have a series of copper-tin-zinc alloys of almost infinite variety. In all cases in the useful alloys of this class, however, there is present more than 50 per cent. copper.

In most of the modern alloys tin is depended upon to give strength and zinc to cheapen the mixture. Some of the old-style gun metals contained as much as 16 per cent. tin and 84 per cent. copper, but such metals were brittle and hard. The common yellow brass employed by plumbers in making ordinary valves and fittings may be considered as composed of approximately 16 pounds copper, 8 pounds zinc, and ½ pound lead. It will be noticed that this consists of approximately one-third zinc and two-thirds copper, with a little lead added to improve the machining qualities. For the making of high-grade casting ingots or new metal should be used in all cases. In making a brass the copper should be melted first and the zinc added, care being taken not to let the temperature rise too high, for if it does the zinc will ignite and burn. The lead is added last and the metal thoroughly stirred.

PROPERTIES OF METALS

Metal	Melting Point	Wt. per Cu. In.	Wt. per Cu. Ft.	Tensile Strength	Specific Gravity	Chemical Symbol
Aluminum	1217	.0924	159.63	20,000	2.56	Al.
Antimony	1166	.2424	418.86		6.71	Sb.
Bismuth	518	.354	611.76		9.83	Bi.
Brass, cast	1692	.3029	523.2	24,000	8.393	
Bronze	1692	.319	550.	36,000	8.83	
Chromium	2750	.2457	429.49		6.8	Cr.
Cobalt	2714	.307	530.6		8.5	Co.
Copper	1981	.322	556.	36,000	8.9	Cu.
Gold	1945	.6979	1206.05	20,000	19.32	Au.
Iridium	4172	.8099	1400.		22.42	Ir.
Iron, cast	2700	.26	450.	16,500	7.21	Fe.
Iron, wrought	2920	.278	480.13	50,000	7.7	Fe.
Lead	621	.41	710.	3,000	11.37	Pb.
Manganese	2237	.289	499.4		8.	Mn.
Mercury	−36	.4909	848.35		13.59	Hg.
Nickel	2646	.3179	549.34		8.8	Ni.
Platinum	3191	.7769	1342.13		21.5	Pt.
Silver	1761	.3805	657.33	40,000	10.53	Ag.
Steel — cast	2450	.28	481.2	50,000	7.81	
Steel — rolled	2600	.2833	489.6	65,000	7.854	
Tin	449	.2634	455.08	4,600	7.29	Sn.
Tungsten	5430	.69	1192.31		19.10	W.
Vanadium	3146	.1987	343.34		5.50	V.
Zinc	786	.245	430.	7,500	6.86	Zn.

SHRINKAGE OF CASTINGS

Aluminum — pure .... .2031 inch per foot
    "   Nickel Alloy .... .1875 "   "   "
    "   Special Alloy .... .1718 "   "   "
Iron, Small Cylinders .... .0625 "   "   "
    " Pipes .... .125 "   "   "
    " Girders and Beams .... .100 "   "   "
    " Large Cylinders, Contraction of Diameter
        at Top .... .0625 "   "   "
    " Large Cylinders, Contraction of Diameter
        at Bottom .... .083 "   "   "
    " Large Cylinders, Contraction of Length .... .094 "   "   "
Brass — Thin .... .167 "   "   "
    " Thick .... .150 "   "   "
Copper .... .1875 "   "   "
Bismuth .... .1563 "   "   "
Lead .... .3125 "   "   "
Zinc .... .3125 "   "   "

Aluminum

Can be melted in ordinary plumbago crucibles the same as brass and will not absorb silicon or carbon to injure it unless overheated. Melts at 1217 degrees Fahr. or 625 Cent. Becomes granular and easily broken at about 1000 Fahr.

Shrinkage of pure aluminum .. ... .2031" per foot
Nickel Aluminum Casting Alloy .. .. .1875" " "
Special Casting Alloy .. .. .1718" " "

The most used alloys have a strength of about 20,000 pounds to square inch at a weight of one third that of brass.

Iron or sand molds can be used and should be poured as cool as it will run to avoid blowholes.

Burnishing. — Use a bloodstone or steel burnisher, with mixture of melted vaseline and kerosene oil or two tablespoonfuls of ground borax, dissolved in a quart of hot water and a few drops of ammonia added.

Frosting. — Clean with benzine. Dip in strong solution of caustic soda or potash, then in solution of undiluted nitric acid. Wash thoroughly in water and dry in hot sawdust.

Polishing. — Any good metal polish that will not scratch will clean aluminum. One that is recommended is made of

Stearic Acid — One part ⎫
Fuller's Earth — One part ⎬ Grind fine and mix very well.
Rotten Stone — Six parts ⎭

Castings are cleaned with a brass scratch brush, run at a high speed. Sand blasting is also used both alone and before scratch brushing.

Spinning. — A high speed, about 4000 feet per minute, is best for spinning. This means that for work 5 to 8 inches in diameter, 2800 to 2600 revolutions per minute is good, while for smaller work of 4 inches this would go up to 3200 r.p.m.

Turning. — Use a tool with shearing edge similar to a wood-cutting tool as they clear themselves better. Use kerosene or water as a lubricant, or if a bright cut is wanted use benzine. For drawing on a press use vaseline.

Soldering. — See page 92.

U. S. Armory Method of Bluing Steel. — Have work clean and free from grease. Take 10 parts of nitre and 1 part of manganese. Heat in this mixture to from 700 to 800 degrees F. and quench in oil.

STEAM HAMMERS AND DROP FORGING

WHILE it is impossible to accurately rate the capacity of steam hammers with respect to the size of work they should handle, on account of the greatly varying conditions, a few notes from the experience of the Bement works of the Niles-Bement-Pond Company will be of service.

For making an occasional forging of a given size, a smaller hammer may be used than if we are manufacturing this same piece in large quantities. If we have a 6-inch piece to forge, such as a pinion or a short shaft, a hammer of about 1100 pounds capacity would answer very nicely. But should the general work be as large as this, it would be very much better to use a 1500-pound hammer. If, on the other hand, we wish to forge 6-inch axles economically, it would be necessary to use a 7000- or 8000-pound hammer. The following table will be found convenient for reference for the proper size of hammer to be used on different classes of general blacksmith work, although it will be understood that it is necessary to modify these to suit conditions, as has already been indicated.

Diameter of Stock	Size of Hammer
3½ Inches	250 to 350 pounds
4 Inches	350 to 600 pounds
4½ Inches	600 to 800 pounds
5 Inches	800 to 1000 pounds
5 Inches	1100 to 1500 pounds

Steam hammers are always rated by the weight of the ram, and the attached parts, which include the piston and rod, nothing being added on account of the steam pressure behind the piston. This makes it a little difficult to compare them with plain drop or tilting hammers, which are also rated in the same way.

Steam hammers are usually operated at pressures varying from 75 to 100 pounds of steam per square inch, and may also be operated by compressed air at about the same pressures. It is cheaper, however, in the case of compressed air to use pressures from 60 to 80 pounds instead of going higher.

In figuring on the boiler capacity for steam hammers, there are several things to be considered, and it depends upon the number of hammers in use and the service required. It will vary from one boiler horse-power for each 100 pounds of falling weight up to three horse-power for the same weight, according to the service expected. In a shop where a number of steam hammers are being used, it is usually safe to count on the lower boiler capacity given, as it is practically safe to say that all of the hammers are never in use at the same time. In a shop with a single hammer, on the other hand, and especially where hard service is expected, it is necessary to allow the larger boiler capacity as there is no reserve to be drawn on, due to part of the hammers being idle, as in the other case.

DRAFT IN DROP FORGING DIES

In sinking dies for drop forging, it is important that the draft at the sides of the impression should be made as little as possible to avoid heavy cuts in the machining operations. It is equally important that the draft be sufficient to allow the forging to be easily withdrawn from the die, else production under the hammer will be hampered. The standard draft (or draw) for most dies is 7 degrees from the perpendicular, but other angles are used in special cases and sometimes two or three different angles of draft are used in the same die at different parts of the impression.

Figure 1 shows the plan and side elevation of a lower die where three angles of draft are advisable. The shoulders A and B are

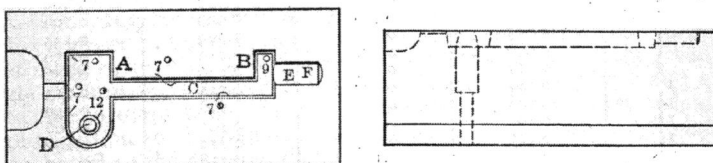

Fig. 1. — Example of Draft in Drop Forging Dies

places where the metal is likely to hug on account of the contraction of the hot metal along the part marked C, which is of comparatively small cross-section and will cool rapidly. These shoulders are given an angle of 9 degrees. The inserted tool-steel plug D, is another place where metal is likely to hug badly. It is usual to give such plugs 12 and even 15 degrees of draft on each side. Moreover, the tendency of plugs to get "jumped up," hammered over and badly heat checked is much reduced if they are given a big draft. The part marked E is semicircular and will draw easily. The end of E at F is a part of a sphere. All other sides of the impression are given 7 degrees draft. If the die is smooth and regular the forging will draw easily.

All impressions are laid out to one-eighth inch to the foot shrink rule. This allows for a shrinkage of about 0.010 inch to the inch. The same shrinkage is allowed in the thickness of forgings. For example: A forging is to be 2 inches thick with half the thickness in each die. The depth of impressions will be 1.010 inch in each die. In laying out the impression on the face of the die, allowance has been made for shrinkage in length, thickness and breadth of forging, and, in addition, for the draft on the sides. In complex dies where there are many different depths and offsets on the face of the die, the die sinker has to keep all these points constantly in mind while laying out or run the risk of spoiling the whole job.

A Table of Draft Dimensions

The allowance for 7-degree draft is easy to remember, being almost exactly $\frac{1}{32}$ inch at the face of the die for each $\frac{1}{4}$ inch of depth. Table 1 has been calculated to give the allowances in thousandths of an inch on actual depth, as measured with an ordinary depth gage. It is not usual in marking out to work closer than $\frac{1}{64}$ inch, but the

TABLE 1. — ALLOWANCE IN THOUSANDTHS OF AN INCH AT FACE OF DIE FOR STANDARD ANGLES OF DRAFT AND VARIOUS DEPTHS OF IMPRESSION

Depths in Inches	STANDARD DRAFT ANGLES IN DEGREES			
	5 Degrees	7 Degrees	9 Degrees	12 Degrees
	Inch	Inch	Inch	Inch
$\frac{1}{8}$	0.011	0.015	0.020	0.027
$\frac{1}{4}$	0.022	0.031	0.040	0.053
$\frac{3}{8}$	0.033	0.046	0.059	0.080
$\frac{1}{2}$	0.044	0.061	0.079	0.106
$\frac{5}{8}$	0.055	0.077	0.099	0.133
$\frac{3}{4}$	0.066	0.092	0.119	0.159
$\frac{7}{8}$	0.077	0.107	0.139	0.186
1	0.087	0.123	0.158	0.213
$1\frac{1}{8}$	0.098	0.138	0.178	0.239
$1\frac{1}{4}$	0.109	0.153	0.198	0.266
$1\frac{3}{8}$	0.120	0.169	0.218	0.292
$1\frac{1}{2}$	0.131	0.184	0.238	0.319
$1\frac{5}{8}$	0.142	0.200	0.257	0.345
$1\frac{3}{4}$	0.153	0.215	0.277	0.372
$1\frac{7}{8}$	0.164	0.230	0.297	0.399
2	0.175	0.246	0.317	0.425

arrangement of table in thousandths allows the nearest $\frac{1}{64}$ inch to be taken. The best plan is to take the allowance for the angle at 1 inch depth as a constant and figure out the allowance for the particular depth wanted from the expression

$$Draft\ allowance = \frac{C\,D}{1}.$$

Where C = a constant and D = the depth in inches.

MAKING TYPES

A type, shown in Fig. 2, is generally used as a guide for chipping and scraping out the spherical end of the semicircular part E. It is

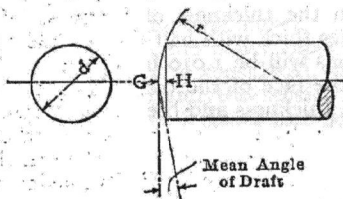

FIG. 2

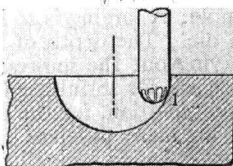

FIG. 3

not usual to make the curve on the end conform to any particular mean angle of draft. Most diesinkers merely turn the end of the type to a curve that looks right to the eye. However, uniformity is desirable in these curves and Table 2 is given as a help in that

TABLE 2. — MEAN DRAFT OF SPHERICAL END OF CYLINDRICAL TYPE

When Radius of End of Type is	Mean Angle of Draft in Degrees is
$2\frac{1}{2}$ × Diameter of Type	$5\frac{3}{4}$
$2\frac{1}{4}$ × " " "	$6\frac{1}{2}$
2 × " " "	$7\frac{1}{4}$
$1\frac{3}{4}$ × " " "	$8\frac{1}{4}$
$1\frac{1}{2}$ × " " "	$9\frac{1}{2}$

direction. It gives the values of the mean angle of draft with various radii expressed in terms of the diameter of the type. It will be noted that if the radius r is made twice the diameter of the type the mean angle of draft is $7\frac{1}{4}$ degrees. This rule is easy to remember and a good one to adopt as standard. A good and easy way to get a close approximation to the required curve is as follows: Turn a cylinder of tool steel to the required diameter. Face the end square, scratch off the distance $G H$ equal to the allowance for draft obtained from Table 1, remembering that the depth is half the diameter of the type. Turn the end to a curve which is uniform to the eye from the center to the scratched line H. After the type is hardened it is ready for use.

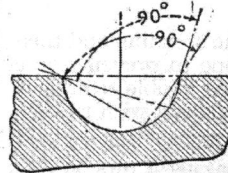

FIG. 4

Semicircular impressions are finished with ball cutters of the correct diameter. When a ball cutter of the correct diameter is not at hand and the job will not warrant making one, the following method may be used. The center line of the impression is projected to the end of the die. A semicircle is scribed on the vertical surface of the end. After the impression is roughed out, a smaller ball cutter is placed in the chuck of a diesinking machine and the knee and slides manipulated until the cutter is in proper relation to the semicircle as shown in Fig. 3. A square is used to indicate when the curves of cutter and semicircle are coincident, as at I. The micrometer dials are now set, the lateral slide locked, the knee lowered, the longitudinal slide operated until the cutter is in position over the impression and the ball tool sunk into the die until the micrometer comes to the position set at the semicircle on the end. A longitudinal cut is taken with this setting. The cutter is then placed in another lateral position and the operation of setting and cutting repeated. It may be necessary to perform this operation several times, and even then the result will be a series of gutters and ridges instead of a uniform, semicircular depression. This can be readily corrected with the scraper and riffler.

An aid in testing the accuracy of semicircular impressions is shown in Fig. 4. If the semicircle is true, the corners of the square will touch in all positions when the sides are resting on the edges of the impression. If the square rocks on the corner in any position, that spot is high and must be scraped down. This test must be made before the "flash" is milled in the die.

KNOTS AND SLINGS FOR HANDLING WORK

THE knots described have been useful in work in out-of-the-way places. No. 1 indicates the meaning of the terms employed.

No. 2, Simple or Overhand Knot. — The simplest of all knots to tie, and may be used as a stop on a rope. A free end is necessary to make it. If strained, it injures the fiber of the rope more than a figure-8 knot, and it is difficult to unmake and liable to jam.

No. 3, Double Overhand Knot. — Used for the end of a rope when it is required to prevent its going through an eye, as in a pulley block or for the end of a halter rope. Also useful for shortening a rope and may be made with any number of turns: *A* in the illustration shows the first position; *B*, the knot finished with two turns; and *C*, one with four full turns of rope.

No. 4, Figure-8 Knot (Flemish). — May be employed as a stop on a rope; is less injurious to the fiber of the rope, and more easily undone than either the single or double overhand knot. If made with the rope doubled and the bight left long, it becomes a figure-8 hoop knot.

No. 5, Stevedore Knot. — End of the rope is wrapped twice around the standing and then passed through the eye. Useful as a stop on a rope to prevent the end going through an eye, as in a pulley block (see double overhand knot). Also employed instead of sewing the rope end with twine.

No. 6, Boat Knot (Marline-spike Hitch). — Suitable for quickly making a rope ladder, or getting a temporary pull on a rope with a marline-spike. No free ends required to form this knot. Point marked *A* must always be at the back of the spike or rung of the ladder, away from the direction of the weight or pull.

No. 7, Slip Knot (Simple Running Knot). — The simplest kind of slip knot. It may be used similarly to the packer's knot, but is not so good, as it is liable to pull through and does not bind on the rope.

No. 8, Tomfool Knot (Double Running Knot). — When the loops are drawn taut and the ends tied, this makes a pair of handcuffs which it is almost impossible for the person so secured to undo. It may be used as a barrel sling, half-hitches being put on the ends, and the hook put under the knot itself. The bight marked 3 is passed through the overhand loop as shown by the dotted line.

No. 9, Flemish Loop. — This knot makes a simple loop for light work and may be used in the same way as a bowline, but is not so quickly made; neither is it so secure nor so easily undone. The security depends almost entirely upon the check knot.

No. 10, Bowline. — A generally useful knot when a loop of any sort that will not slip is required, as in a sling for lowering a man, or fastening a bucket to a rope.

No. 11, Bowline II. — A method of attaching the end of one rope to the standing of another. A half turn is put in the standing and the end of the other rope taken through as if tying an ordinary bowline. This knot is practically a sheet bend.

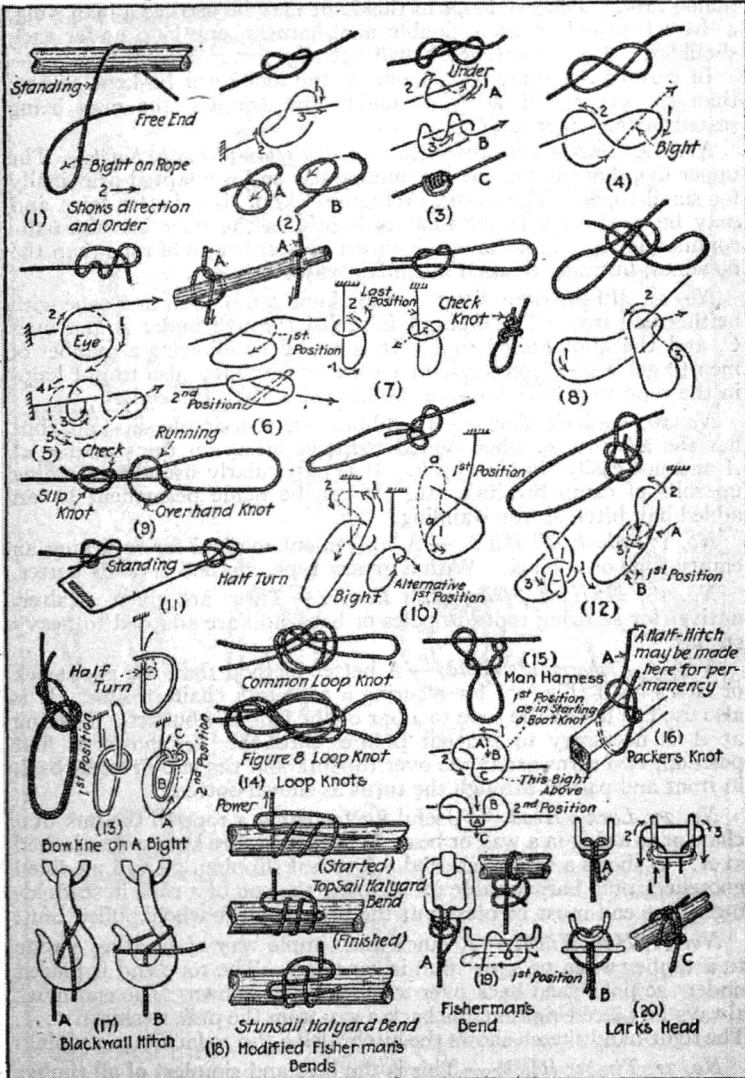

No. 12, Running Bowline. — As shown in the first position a half turn is made at A (shown dotted) and the end is passed through and to the back of the part marked B. This is a good slip knot and does not tighten on the standing, always remaining open.

No. 13, *Bowline on a Bight.* — The part marked *A* is passed behind *B* and then in the direction of the arrow to *C*. The bight *B* is then pulled taut. The two loops of this knot may be used as a man sling, a barrel sling, or as a double man-harness, one loop under each shoulder. When tightened it will not slip.

In case of an injured man, one of the loops can be kept shorter than the other and adjusted under the armpits, the man being seated in the larger loop.

No. 14, *Open-hand Loop Knot and Figure-8 Loop Knot.* — The upper loop knot is the one in common use and is adapted principally for small ropes. The lower, or Figure-8 knot, is a better form and may be used on a larger rope as it injures the fiber less than the common form. These knots require a greater length of rope than the bowlines, but may be used in similar ways.

No. 15, *Man-harness Knot.* — This knot can be tied in a rope with neither end free. The bight *A* is pulled through under *B* and over *C*, and the knot pulled taut. It is useful as allowing a number of men to get a good purchase on a rope for hauling; also to put loops in the rope to receive hooks at points other than the ends.

No. 16, *Packer's Knot.* — A modification of a simple slip knot, but has the advantage, when pulled tight, of biting on the standing at *A* and not easily slipping back. It is particularly useful for cording up rolls of camp bedding, etc. It can be made permanent by an added half hitch on the standing.

No. 17, *Blackwall Hitch.* — A convenient method for returning an empty rope on a hook. With a greasy rope, method *B* holds better.

No. 18, *Modified Fisherman's Bends.* — These are given as alternatives for securing ropes to poles or bars, and are adapted to heavy strains.

No. 19, *Fisherman's Bend.* — A better method than the gooseneck or lark's head (Fig. 20) for securing a rope to a chain or link. It is also used to fasten the rope to a bar or the bail of a bucket. Lashing at *A* is necessary to prevent pulling through. As shown in first position, two turns are taken over the link and the end brought back in front and passed through the turns as shown dotted.

No. 20, *Lark's Head.* — Useful for fastening a rope to the link of a chain or to a ring in a wall or box. It is not a secure knot unless lashed at *A*. *B* shows a toggle inserted to prevent slipping. *C* is a modified gooseneck on a bar, suitable for securing the end of a rope in scaffolding. The end must be placed at the back and the whole pulled taut.

No. 21, *Half Hitch.* — A quick and simple way of securing a rope to a timber when no great pull is expected. The rope end is placed under the pole, then back over to the right as shown. The end must always be placed right at the back away from the pull, as shown at *A*. The right-hand sketch shows the hitch with a slip to facilitate undoing.

No. 22, *Timber Hitch.* — This is the best and simplest of all timber hitches and may be used for towing or otherwise handling timber, rods, pipes, etc.; also for starting lashings on scaffolding or any kind of pole work. For raising or lowering timber, the half hitch should be placed high above the center of gravity to avoid slanting.

No. 23, Clove Hitch. — This is one of the most useful of all hitches, as it will take a strain in either direction without slackening. It is used for mooring ships heads of derricks for guy lines and all kinds of rigging work. It may be easily undone, or a bight may be put in

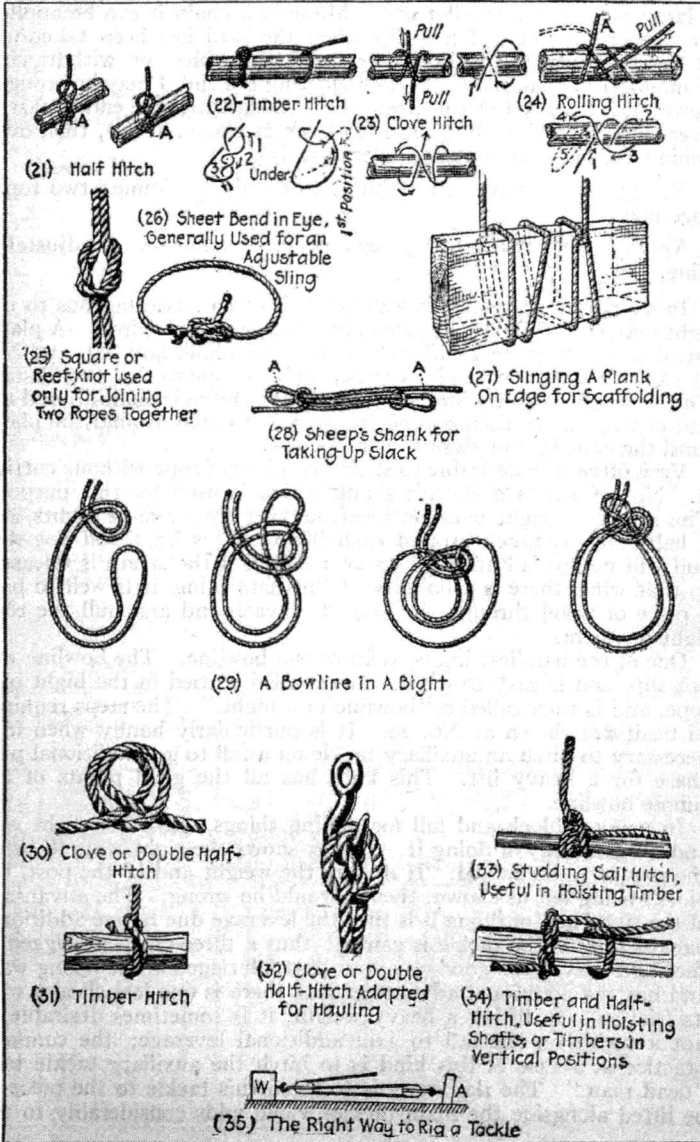

(21) Half Hitch

(22) Timber Hitch

Pull Pull

(23) Clove Hitch

T₁ Under

Pull

A

(24) Rolling Hitch

1st Position

(26) Sheet Bend in Eye, Generally Used for an Adjustable Sling

(25) Square or Reef-Knot used only for Joining Two Ropes Together

(27) Slinging A Plank On Edge for Scaffolding

(28) Sheep's Shank for Taking-Up Slack

(29) A Bowline in A Bight

(30) Clove or Double Half-Hitch

(31) Timber Hitch

(32) Clove or Double Half-Hitch Adapted for Hauling

(33) Studding Sail Hitch, Useful in Hoisting Timber

(34) Timber and Half-Hitch, Useful in Hoisting Shafts, or Timbers in Vertical Positions

W A

(35) The Right Way to Rig a Tackle

instead of one end to use as a slip. When commencing to tie the hitch on a horizontal bar, the rule is over and back below, or the reverse of the procedure in tying a half hitch.

No. 24, Rolling Hitch. — This lashing is used for getting a grip on a large rope with a smaller one. Made in a chain it can be applied to wire ropes and will not slip when the load has been taken up. It is also suitable for hauling on electric cables, or withdrawing diamond drill or other rods. For securing the end *A* may be brought down and be lashed to the large rope. In making, the end is passed over the spar twice, then returned back as shown at (3), then over behind as at (4), and up and under as at (5).

No. 25. — A square or reef knot, used only for joining two ropes together.

No. 26. — Sheet bend in an eye, generally used for an adjustable sling.

In supporting a swinging scaffold, it is often advantageous to use light material, while, at the same time, strength is required. A plank on edge is a great deal stiffer than the same plank laid flat, and No. 27 shows how to sling a plank edgewise by a rope so that it will stay. The knot used is a very simple one. A clove hitch is made around the end of the plank; then one of the parts is twisted around the plank until the ends lead as shown in the sketch.

Very often it is desirable to shorten a piece of rope without cutting it. No. 28 shows a sheep's shank which is used for this purpose. The rope is brought back on itself, making two or more bights, and a half hitch is taken around each bight. This knot will not slip, and will nearly fall apart of its own accord if the strain is released, so that when there is a liability of this happening, it is well to pass a piece of wood through the loop *A* at each end and pull the rope tight on them.

One of the handiest knots to know is a bowline. The bowline will not slip, and is easy to untie. It can also be tied in the bight of a rope, and is then called a "bowline in a bight." The steps required to tie it are shown at No. 29. It is particularly handy when it is necessary to hitch an auxiliary tackle on a fall to get additional purchase for a heavy lift. This knot has all the good points of the simple bowline.

In using a block and fall for pulling things, there is a right way and a wrong way of doing it. No. 35 shows the right way, *W* being the weight to be moved. If *A* were the weight and *W* the post, the blocks being left as shown, then it would be wrong. The advantage of the right way of doing it is that the leverage due to one additional part of rope in the tackle is gained! thus a three-part fall, rigged in the right way, is as good as a four-part fall rigged in the wrong way, and has the additional advantage that there is one less sheave with its friction. In lifting a heavy weight, it is sometimes desirable to put a tackle on the fall to gain additional leverage; the common practice in a case of this kind is to hitch the auxiliary tackle to a "dead man." The right way is to hitch this tackle to the piece to be lifted alongside the main tackle, which adds considerably to the leverage, being equivalent to one more part to the main fall besides the gain by the use of the auxiliary fall.

No. 30. — Clove or double half hitch.

No. 31. — Timber hitch.

No. 32. — Clove or double half hitch as used for hauling.

No. 33. — Studding sail hitch as used in hoisting timber.

No. 34. — Timber and half hitch. Useful in hoisting shafting or timber in a vertical position.

SAFE LOADS FOR EYE-BOLTS AND FOR ROPES AND CHAINS

TABLE 1. — SAFE LOADS FOR EYE-BOLTS

	A	Inches B	C	Safe Load, Lb.
Drop-forged steel	$\frac{1}{2}$	$1\frac{3}{8}$	$\frac{7}{8}$	1,100
	$\frac{9}{16}$	$1\frac{7}{8}$	$1\frac{3}{32}$	1,500
	$\frac{5}{8}$	$1\frac{1}{8}$	$1\frac{1}{8}$	1,800
	$\frac{3}{4}$	$1\frac{1}{8}$	$1\frac{1}{8}$	2,800
	$\frac{7}{8}$	$1\frac{3}{8}$	$1\frac{3}{8}$	3,900
	1	$2\frac{1}{16}$	$1\frac{1}{8}$	5,100
	$1\frac{1}{4}$	$2\frac{5}{8}$	$1\frac{1}{16}$	8,400
	$1\frac{1}{2}$	$2\frac{9}{16}$	1	12,200
	$1\frac{3}{4}$	$3\frac{1}{8}$	$1\frac{1}{2}$	16,500
	2	$3\frac{1}{16}$	$1\frac{5}{8}$	21,800
D.B G. iron E.L., 28,000 lb. per sq. in., welded	$1\frac{3}{4}$	3	$1\frac{1}{4}$	10,000
	$1\frac{1}{4}$	4	$1\frac{1}{2}$	11,000
	2	5	$1\frac{3}{4}$	14,000
	$2\frac{1}{2}$	6	2	16,000

TABLE 2. — SAFE LOADS ON ROPES AND CHAINS

Manila Rope, Safe Load in Tons				Wire Cable, Safe Load in Tons				Chains, Safe Load in Tons			
Diam. of Rope, In.	Single Rope	Two Part	Four Part	Diam. of Cable, In.	Single Rope	Two Part	Four Part	Diam. of Chain, In.	Single Chain	Two Part	Four Part
$\frac{1}{2}$	$\frac{1}{2}$	$\frac{3}{4}$	$\frac{3}{4}$	$\frac{1}{2}$	1	2	$3\frac{1}{2}$	$\frac{1}{4}$	$\frac{1}{2}$	$\frac{3}{4}$	$1\frac{1}{2}$
$\frac{5}{8}$	$\frac{3}{4}$	$\frac{3}{4}$	$1\frac{1}{4}$	$\frac{5}{8}$	$1\frac{1}{4}$	$3\frac{1}{2}$	$6\frac{1}{2}$	$\frac{3}{8}$	1	$1\frac{1}{4}$	3
$\frac{3}{4}$	$\frac{3}{4}$	1	2	$\frac{3}{4}$	$2\frac{1}{4}$	$4\frac{1}{2}$	9	$\frac{1}{2}$	2	$3\frac{1}{2}$	6
$\frac{7}{8}$	$\frac{7}{8}$	$1\frac{1}{2}$	$2\frac{1}{2}$	$\frac{7}{8}$	$3\frac{1}{4}$	6	12	$\frac{5}{8}$	3	5	9
1	1	2	3	1	4	8	16	$\frac{3}{4}$	5	9	15
$1\frac{1}{4}$	$1\frac{1}{4}$	$2\frac{1}{2}$	4	$1\frac{1}{4}$	6	12	24	$\frac{7}{8}$	6	$10\frac{1}{2}$	18
$1\frac{1}{2}$	2	4	6	$1\frac{1}{2}$	10	19	36	1	8	14	24
$1\frac{3}{4}$	$2\frac{1}{2}$	5	8	$1\frac{3}{4}$	13	25	48	$1\frac{1}{4}$	11	19	33
2	$3\frac{1}{2}$	$6\frac{1}{2}$	11	2	16	32	60	$1\frac{1}{4}$	13	23	39
$2\frac{1}{2}$	$4\frac{1}{2}$	8	13					$1\frac{1}{2}$	18	32	54

GENERAL REFERENCE TABLES

COMMON WEIGHTS AND MEASURES

LINEAR OR MEASURE OF LENGTH

12 inches = 1 foot.   3 feet = 1 yard.
5½ yards = 1 rod.   40 rods = furlong.
8 furlongs = 1 mile.

EQUIVALENT MEASURES

Inches	Feet	Yards	Rods	Furlongs	Mile
36 =	3 =	1			
198 =	16.5 =	5.5 =	1		
7920 =	660 =	220 =	40 =	1	
63,360 =	5280 =	1760 =	320 =	8 =	1

SQUARE MEASURE

144 square inches = 1 sq. foot.   30¼ square yards = 1 sq. rod.
9 square feet = 1 sq. yd.   160 square rods = 1 acre.
640 acres = 1 sq. mile.

EQUIVALENT MEASURE

Sq. Mi.	A.	Sq. Rd.	Sq. Yd.	Sq. Ft.	Sq. In.
1 =	640 =	102,400 =	3,097,600 =	27,878,400 =	4,014,489,600

CUBIC MEASURE

1728 cubic inches = 1 cubic foot.   128 cubic feet = 1 cord.
27 cubic feet = 1 cubic yard.   24¾ cubic feet = 1 perch.
1 cu. yd. = 27 cu. ft. = 46,656 cu. in.

WEIGHT — AVOIRDUPOIS

437.5 grains = 1 ounce.   100 pounds = 1 hundred weight.
16 ounces = 1 pound.   2000 pounds = 1 ton.
2240 pounds = 1 long ton.
1 ton = 20 cwt. = 2000 lbs. = 32,000 oz. = 14,000,000 gr.

WEIGHT = TROY

24 grains = 1 pennyweight.   20 pwt. = 1 ounce.
12 ounces = 1 pound.
1 lb. = 12 oz. = 240 pwt. = 5760 gr.

470

Dry Measure

2 pints = 1 quart. 8 quarts = 1 peck.
4 pecks = 1 bushel
1 bu. = 4 pk. = 32 qt. = 64 pt.
U. S. bushel = 2150.42 cu. in.   British = 2218.19 cu. in.

Liquid Measure

4 gills = 1 pint.   4 quarts = 1 gallon.
2 pints = 1 quart.   31½ gallons = 1 barrel.
2 barrels or 63 gals. = 1 hogshead.
1 hhd. = 2 bbl. = 63 gals. = 252 qt. = 504 pt. = 2016 gi.

The U. S. gallon contains 231 cu. in. = .134 cu. ft.
One cubic foot = 7 481 gallons.
One cubic foot weighs 62.425 lbs. at 39.2 deg. Fahr.
One gallon weighs 8.345 lbs.
For rough calculations 1 cu. ft. is called 7¼ gallons and 1 gallon
is 8⅓ lbs.

Angles or Arcs

60 seconds = 1 minute.   90 degrees = 1 rt. angle or quadrant.
60 minutes = 1 degree.   360 degrees = 1 circle.
1 circle = 360° = 21,600′ = 1,296,000″.
1 minute of arc on the earth's surface is 1 nautical mile = 1.15
imes a land mile or 6080 feet.

Weight of a Cubic Foot of Substances

Names of Substances	Average Weight Lbs.
Anthracite, solid, of Pennsylvania	93
" broken, loose	54
" " moderately shaken	58
" heaped bushel, loose	(80)
Ash, American white, dry	38
Asphaltum	87
Brass (Copper and Zinc), cast	504
" rolled	524
Brick, best pressed	150
" common hard	125
" soft, inferior	100
Brickwork, pressed brick	140
" ordinary	112
Cement, hydraulic, ground, loose, American, Rosendale	56
" " " " " Louisville	50
" " " " English, Portland	90
Cherry, dry	42
Chestnut, dry	41
Coal, bituminous, solid	84
" " broken, loose	49
" " heaped bushel, loose	(74)

WEIGHT OF A CUBIC FOOT OF SUBSTANCES — *Continued*

NAMES OF SUBSTANCES	Average Weight Lbs.
Coke, loose, of good coal	27
" " heaped bushel	38
Copper, cast	542
" rolled	548
Earth, common loam, dry, loose	76
" " " " moderately rammed	95
Ebony, dry	76
Elm, dry	35
Flint	162
Glass, common window	157
Gneiss, common	168
Gold, cast, pure, or 24 carat	1204
" pure, hammered	1217
Granite	170
Gravel, about the same as sand, which see.	
Hemlock, dry	25
Hickory, dry	53
Hornblende, black	203
Ice	58.7
Iron, cast	450
" wrought, pure	485
" " average	480
Ivory	114
Lead	711
Lignum Vitæ, dry	83
Lime, quick, ground, loose, or in small lumps	53
" " " " thoroughly shaken	75
Limestones and Marbles	168
" " " loose, in irregular fragments	96
Mahogany, Spanish, dry	53
" Honduras, dry	35
Maple, dry	49
Marbles, see Limestones.	
Masonry, of granite or limestone, well dressed	165
" " sandstone, well dressed	144
Mercury, at 32° Fahrenheit	849
Mica	183
Mortar, hardened	103
Mud, dry, close 80 to	110
" wet, fluid, maximum	120
Oak, live, dry	59
" white, dry	52
" other kinds 32 to	45
Petroleum	55
Pine, white, dry	25
" yellow, Northern	34
" " Southern	45

WEIGHT OF A CUBIC FOOT OF SUBSTANCES — *Continued*

NAMES OF SUBSTANCES	Average Weight Lbs.
Platinum	1342
Quartz, common, pure	165
Rosin	69
Salt, coarse, Syracuse, N. Y.	45
" Liverpool, fine, for table use	49
Sand, of pure quartz, dry, loose	90 to 106
" well shaken	99 to 117
" perfectly wet	120 to 140
Sandstones, fit for building	151
Shales, red or black	162
Silver	655
Slate	175
Snow, freshly fallen	5 to 12
" moistened and compacted by rain	15 to 50
Spruce, dry	25
Steel	490
Sulphur	125
Sycamore, dry	37
Tar	62
Tin, cast	459
Turf or Peat, dry, unpressed	20 to 30
Walnut, black, dry	38
Water, pure rain or distilled, at 60° Fahrenheit	62⅓
" sea	64
Wax, bees	60.5
Zinc or Spelter	437

Green timbers usually weigh from one-fifth to one-half more than dry.

WATER CONVERSION FACTORS

U. S. gallons	× 8.33	= pounds
U. S. gallons	× 0 13368	= cubic feet.
U. S. gallons	× 231	= cubic inches.
U. S gallons	× 0 83	= English gallons
U. S. gallons	× 3.78	= liters
English gallons (Imperial)	× 10	= pounds
English gallons (Imperial)	× 0.16	= cubic feet.
English gallons (Imperial)	× 277 274	= cubic inches.
English gallons (Imperial)	× 1.2	= U. S. gallons.
English gallons (Imperial)	× 4 537	= liters.
Cubic inches of water (39 1°)	× 0 036024	= pounds
Cubic inches of water (39 1°)	× 0.004329	= U. S. gallons.
Cubic inches of water (39.1°)	× 0 003607	= English gallons.
Cubic inches of water (39 1°)	× 0 576384	= ounces.
Cubic feet (of water) (39 1°)	× 62.425	= pounds.
Cubic feet (of water) (39 1°)	× 7.48	= U. S gallons.
Cubic feet (of water) (39.1°)	× 6 232	= English gallons.
Cubic feet (of water) (39.1°)	× 0.028	= tons
Pounds of water	× 27.72	= cubic inches.
Pounds of water	× 0 01602	= cubic feet.
Pounds of water	× 0 12	= U. S. gallons.
Pounds of water	× 0.10	= English gallons.

CONVENIENT MULTIPLIERS

Inches	× 0.08333	= feet.	Sq. inches	× 0.00695	= Sq. feet.
Inches	× 0.02778	= yards.	Sq. inches	× 0.0007716	= Sq. yards.
Inches	× 0.00001578	= miles.	Cu. inches	× 0.00058	= Cu. feet.
			Cu. inches	× 0.0000214	= Cu. yards.
Feet	× 0.3334	= yards.	Sq. feet	× 144	= Sq. inches.
Feet	× 0.00019	= miles.	Sq. feet	× 0.1112	= Sq. yards.
Yards	× 36	= inches.	Cu. feet	× 1728	= Cu. inches.
Yards	× 3	= feet.	Cu. feet	× 0.03704	= Cu. yards.
Yards	× 0.0005681	= miles.	Sq. yards	× 1296	= Sq. inches.
Miles	× 63360	= inches.	Sq. yards	× 9	= Sq. feet.
Miles	× 5280	= feet.	Cu. yards	× 46656	= Cu. inches.
Miles	× 1760	= yards.	Cu. yards	× 27	= Cu. feet.
Avoir. oz.	× 0.0625	= pounds.	Avoir. lbs.	× 0.0005	= tons.
Avoir. oz.	× 0.00003125	= tons.	Avoir. tons	× 32000	= ounces.
Avoir. lbs.	× 16	= ounces.	Avoir. tons	× 2000	= pounds.

THE METRIC SYSTEM

The Metric System is based on the Meter which was designed to be one ten-millionth ($\frac{1}{10000000}$) part of the earth's meridian quadrant, through Dunkirk and Formentera. Later investigations, however, have shown that the Meter exceeds one ten-millionth part by almost one part in 6400. The value of the Meter, as authorized by the U. S. Government, is 39.37 inches. The Metric system was legalized by the U. S. Government in 1866.

The three principal units are the Meter, the unit of length, the liter, the unit of capacity, and the gram, the unit of weight. Multiples of these are obtained by prefixing the Greek words: deka (10), hekto (100), and kilo (1000). Divisions are obtained by prefixing the Latin words: deci ($\frac{1}{10}$), centi ($\frac{1}{100}$), and milli ($\frac{1}{1000}$). Abbreviations of the multiples begin with a capital letter, and of the divisions with a small letter, as in the following tables:

MEASURES OF LENGTH

10 millimeters (mm)	= 1 centimeter	cm.
10 centimeters	= 1 decimeter	dm.
10 decimeters	= 1 meter	m.
10 meters	= 1 dekameter	Dm.
10 dekameters	= 1 hektometer	Hm.
10 hektometers	= 1 kilometer	Km.

MEASURES OF SURFACE (NOT LAND)

100 square millimeters (mm²)	= 1 square centimeter	cm².
100 square centimeters	= 1 square decimeter	dm².
100 square decimeters	= 1 square meter	m².

MEASURES OF VOLUME

1000 cubic millimeters (mm³)	= 1 cubic centimeter	cm³.
1000 cubic centimeters	= 1 cubic decimeter	dm³.
1000 cubic decimeters	= 1 cubic meter	m³.

MEASURES OF CAPACITY

10 milliliters (ml)	....	= 1 centiliter	....................cl.
10 centiliters ..	....	= 1 deciliter	.................dl.
10 deciliters	.. ..	= 1 liter	....l.
10 liters	.. ..	= 1 dekaliter	. ...Dl.
10 dekaliters	. .. ...	= 1 hektoliter	.. ..Hl.
10 hektoliters ...	.. ..	= 1 kiloliter	....Kl.

NOTE. — The liter is equal to the volume occupied by 1 cubic decimeter.

MEASURES OF WEIGHT

10 milligrams (mg)	. ...	= 1 centigram	....................cg.
10 centigrams	.. ..	= 1 decigram	....dg.
10 decigrams	... .	= 1 gram	... .g.
10 grams	. . ..	= 1 dekagram	....Dg.
10 dekagrams	..	= 1 hektogram	....Hg.
10 hektograms	. . .	= 1 kilogram	....Kg.
1000 kilograms	. . ..	= 1 ton	.. ..T.

NOTE. — The gram is the weight of one cubic centimeter of pure distilled water
at a temperature of 39 2° F., the kilogram is the weight of 1 liter of water; the ton is
the weight of 1 cubic meter of water.

METRIC AND ENGLISH CONVERSION TABLE

MEASURES OF LENGTH

meter = { 39 37 inches.
          3 28083 feet.
          1 0936 yds.

centimeter = .3037 inch.

millimeter = { 03937 inch, or
              1
              — inch nearly.
              25

kilometer = 0.62137 mile.

1 foot = .3048 meter.

1 inch = { 2 54 centimeters.
          25 4 millimeters.

MEASURES OF SURFACE

square meter = { 10.764 square feet.
                1.196 square yds.

square centimeter = .155 sq. in.

square millimeter = .00155 sq. in.

1 square yard = .836 square meter.

1 square foot = .0929 square meter.

1 square in. = { 6 452 sq centimeters:
                645.2 sq. millimeters.

MEASURES OF VOLUME AND CAPACITY

cubic meter = { 35 314 cubic feet.
               1.308 cubic yards.
               264 2 gallons (231 cubic inch).

cubic decimeter = { 61 023 cubic in
                   .0353 cubic ft.

cubic centimeter = .061 cubic inch.

liter = { 1 cubic decimeter.
         61.023 cubic inches.
         .0353 cubic foot.
         1.0567 quarts (U. S.)
         .2642 gallons (U. S)
         2 202 lbs. of water at 62° F.

1 cubic yard = .7645 cubic meter.

1 cubic ft. = { 02832 cubic meter.
               28 317 cubic decimeters.
               28 317 liters.

1 cubic inch = 16 387 cubic centimeters.

1 gallon (British) = 4 543 liters.

1 gallon (U. S.) = 3.785 liters.

MEASURES OF WEIGHT

gram = 15 432 grains.

kilogram = 2 2046 pounds.

metric ton = { .9842 ton of 2240 lbs.
              19 68 cwts.
              2204.6 lbs.

1 grain = 0648 grams.

1 ounce avoirdupois = 28.35 grams.

1 pound = .4536 kilograms.

1 ton of 2240 lbs. = { 1 016 metric tons.
                      1016 kilograms.

MISCELLANEOUS CONVERSION FACTORS

1 kilogram per meter = .6720 pounds per foot.
1 gram per square millimeter = 1.422 pounds per square inch.
1 kilogram per square meter = 0.2084 pounds per square foot.
1 kilogram per cubic meter = .0624 pounds per cubic foot.
1 degree centigrade = 1.8 degrees Fahrenheit.
1 pound per foot = 1.488 kilograms per meter.
1 pound per square foot = 4.882 kilograms per square meter.
1 pound per cubic foot = 16.02 kilograms per cubic meter.
1 degree Fahrenheit = .5556 degrees centigrade.
1 Calorie (French Thermal Unit) = 3.968 B. T. U. (British Thermal Unit).

$$1 \text{ Horse Power} = \begin{cases} 33,000 \text{ foot pounds per minute.} \\ 746 \text{ Watts.} \end{cases}$$

$$1 \text{ Watt (Unit of Electrical Power)} = \begin{cases} .00134 \text{ Horse Power.} \\ 44.24 \text{ foot pounds per minute} \end{cases}$$

$$1 \text{ Kilowatt} = \begin{cases} 1000 \text{ Watts.} \\ 1.34 \text{ Horse Power.} \\ 44240 \text{ foot pounds per minute.} \end{cases}$$

DECIMAL EQUIVALENTS OF FRACTIONS OF MILLIMETERS. (ADVANCING BY $\frac{1}{100}$ MM.)

mm.	Inches	mm.	Inches	mm.	Inches	mm.	Inches
$\frac{1}{100}$ =	.00039	$\frac{26}{100}$ =	.01024	$\frac{51}{100}$ =	.02008	$\frac{76}{100}$ =	.02992
$\frac{2}{100}$ =	.00079	$\frac{27}{100}$ =	.01063	$\frac{52}{100}$ =	.02047	$\frac{77}{100}$ =	.03032
$\frac{3}{100}$ =	.00118	$\frac{28}{100}$ =	.01102	$\frac{53}{100}$ =	.02087	$\frac{78}{100}$ =	.03071
$\frac{4}{100}$ =	.00157	$\frac{29}{100}$ =	.01142	$\frac{54}{100}$ =	.02126	$\frac{79}{100}$ =	.03110
$\frac{5}{100}$ =	.00197	$\frac{30}{100}$ =	.01181	$\frac{55}{100}$ =	.02165	$\frac{80}{100}$ =	.03150
$\frac{6}{100}$ =	.00236	$\frac{31}{100}$ =	.01220	$\frac{56}{100}$ =	.02205	$\frac{81}{100}$ =	.03189
$\frac{7}{100}$ =	.00276	$\frac{32}{100}$ =	.01260	$\frac{57}{100}$ =	.02244	$\frac{82}{100}$ =	.03228
$\frac{8}{100}$ =	.00315	$\frac{33}{100}$ =	.01299	$\frac{58}{100}$ =	.02283	$\frac{83}{100}$ =	.03268
$\frac{9}{100}$ =	.00354	$\frac{34}{100}$ =	.01339	$\frac{59}{100}$ =	.02323	$\frac{84}{100}$ =	.03307
$\frac{10}{100}$ =	.00394	$\frac{35}{100}$ =	.01378	$\frac{60}{100}$ =	.02362	$\frac{85}{100}$ =	.03346
$\frac{11}{100}$ =	.00433	$\frac{36}{100}$ =	.01417	$\frac{61}{100}$ =	.02402	$\frac{86}{100}$ =	.03386
$\frac{12}{100}$ =	.00472	$\frac{37}{100}$ =	.01457	$\frac{62}{100}$ =	.02441	$\frac{87}{100}$ =	.03425
$\frac{13}{100}$ =	.00512	$\frac{38}{100}$ =	.01496	$\frac{63}{100}$ =	.02480	$\frac{88}{100}$ =	.03465
$\frac{14}{100}$ =	.00551	$\frac{39}{100}$ =	.01535	$\frac{64}{100}$ =	.02520	$\frac{89}{100}$ =	.03504
$\frac{15}{100}$ =	.00591	$\frac{40}{100}$ =	.01575	$\frac{65}{100}$ =	.02559	$\frac{90}{100}$ =	.03543
$\frac{16}{100}$ =	.00630	$\frac{41}{100}$ =	.01614	$\frac{66}{100}$ =	.02598	$\frac{91}{100}$ =	.03583
$\frac{17}{100}$ =	.00669	$\frac{42}{100}$ =	.01654	$\frac{67}{100}$ =	.02638	$\frac{92}{100}$ =	.03622
$\frac{18}{100}$ =	.00709	$\frac{43}{100}$ =	.01693	$\frac{68}{100}$ =	.02677	$\frac{93}{100}$ =	.03661
$\frac{19}{100}$ =	.00748	$\frac{44}{100}$ =	.01732	$\frac{69}{100}$ =	.02717	$\frac{94}{100}$ =	.03701
$\frac{20}{100}$ =	.00787	$\frac{45}{100}$ =	.01772	$\frac{70}{100}$ =	.02756	$\frac{95}{100}$ =	.03740
$\frac{21}{100}$ =	.00827	$\frac{46}{100}$ =	.01811	$\frac{71}{100}$ =	.02795	$\frac{96}{100}$ =	.03780
$\frac{22}{100}$ =	.00866	$\frac{47}{100}$ =	.01850	$\frac{72}{100}$ =	.02835	$\frac{97}{100}$ =	.03819
$\frac{23}{100}$ =	.00906	$\frac{48}{100}$ =	.01890	$\frac{73}{100}$ =	.02874	$\frac{98}{100}$ =	.03858
$\frac{24}{100}$ =	.00945	$\frac{49}{100}$ =	.01929	$\frac{74}{100}$ =	.02913	$\frac{99}{100}$ =	.03898
$\frac{25}{100}$ =	.00984	$\frac{50}{100}$ =	.01969	$\frac{75}{100}$ =	.02953	1 =	.03937

DECIMAL EQUIVALENTS OF MILLIMETERS AND FRACTIONS OF MILLIMETERS. (ADVANCING BY $\frac{1}{50}$ MM. AND 1 MM.)

mm.	Inches	mm.	Inches	mm.	Inches	mm.	Inches
		$\frac{40}{50}$ =	.03150	31 =	1.22047	71 =	2.79527
$\frac{1}{50}$ =	.00079	$\frac{41}{50}$ =	.03228	32 =	1.25984	72 =	2.83464
$\frac{2}{50}$ =	.00157	$\frac{42}{50}$ =	.03307	33 =	1.29921	73 =	2.87401
$\frac{3}{50}$ =	.00236	$\frac{43}{50}$ =	.03386	34 =	1.33858	74 =	2.91338
$\frac{4}{50}$ =	.00315	$\frac{44}{50}$ =	.03465	35 =	1.37795	75 =	2.95275
$\frac{5}{50}$ =	.00394	$\frac{45}{50}$ =	.03543	36 =	1.41732	76 =	2.99212
$\frac{6}{50}$ =	.00472	$\frac{46}{50}$ =	.03622	37 =	1.45669	77 =	3.03149
$\frac{7}{50}$ =	.00551	$\frac{47}{50}$ =	.03701	38 =	1.49606	78 =	3.07086
$\frac{8}{50}$ =	.00630	$\frac{48}{50}$ =	.03780	39 =	1.53543	79 =	3.11023
$\frac{9}{50}$ =	.00709	$\frac{49}{50}$ =	.03858	40 =	1.57480	80 =	3.14960
$\frac{10}{50}$ =	.00787	1 =	.03937	41 =	1.61417	81 =	3.18897
$\frac{11}{50}$ =	.00866	2 =	.07874	42 =	1.65354	82 =	3.22834
$\frac{12}{50}$ =	.00945	3 =	.11811	43 =	1.69291	83 =	3.26771
$\frac{13}{50}$ =	.01024	4 =	.15748	44 =	1.73228	84 =	3.30708
$\frac{14}{50}$ =	.01102	5 =	.19685	45 =	1.77165	85 =	3.34645
$\frac{15}{50}$ =	.01181	6 =	.23622	46 =	1.81102	86 =	3.38582
$\frac{16}{50}$ =	.01260	7 =	.27559	47 =	1.85039	87 =	3.42519
$\frac{17}{50}$ =	.01339	8 =	.31496	48 =	1.88976	88 =	3.46456
$\frac{18}{50}$ =	.01417	9 =	.35433	49 =	1.92913	89 =	3.50393
$\frac{19}{50}$ =	.01496	10 =	.39370	50 =	1.96850	90 =	3.54330
$\frac{20}{50}$ =	.01575	11 =	.43307	51 =	2.00787	91 =	3.58267
$\frac{21}{50}$ =	.01654	12 =	.47244	52 =	2.04724	92 =	3.62204
$\frac{22}{50}$ =	.01732	13 =	.51181	53 =	2.08661	93 =	3.66141
$\frac{23}{50}$ =	.01811	14 =	.55118	54 =	2.12598	94 =	3.70078
$\frac{24}{50}$ =	.01890	15 =	.59055	55 =	2.16535	95 =	3.74015
$\frac{25}{50}$ =	.01969	16 =	.62992	56 =	2.20472	96 =	3.77952
$\frac{26}{50}$ =	.02047	17 =	.66929	57 =	2.24409	97 =	3.81889
$\frac{27}{50}$ =	.02126	18 =	.70866	58 =	2.28346	98 =	3.85826
$\frac{28}{50}$ =	.02205	19 =	.74803	59 =	2.32283	99 =	3.89763
$\frac{29}{50}$ =	.02283	20 =	.78740	60 =	2.36220	100 =	3.93700
$\frac{30}{50}$ =	.02362	21 =	.82677	61 =	2.40157		
$\frac{31}{50}$ =	.02441	22 =	.86614	62 =	2.44094		
$\frac{32}{50}$ =	.02520	23 =	.90551	63 =	2.48031		
$\frac{33}{50}$ =	.02598	24 =	.94488	64 =	2.51968		
$\frac{34}{50}$ =	.02677	25 =	.98425	65 =	2.55905		
$\frac{35}{50}$ =	.02756	26 =	1.02362	66 =	2.59842		
$\frac{36}{50}$ =	.02835	27 =	1.06299	67 =	2.63779		
$\frac{37}{50}$ =	.02913	28 =	1.10236	68 =	2.67716		
$\frac{38}{50}$ =	.02992	29 =	1.14173	69 =	2.71653		
$\frac{39}{50}$ =	.03071	30 =	1.18110	70 =	2.75590		

1 mm. = 0.03937 in.
1 cm. = 0.3937 "
1 dm. = 3.937 "
1 m. = 39.37 "

EQUIVALENTS OF ENGLISH INCHES IN MILLIMETERS (39.37 inches = 1 meter)

Inch	15/16	7/8	13/16	3/4	11/16	5/8	9/16	1/2	7/16	3/8	5/16	1/4	3/16	1/8	1/16	0	Inch
0	23.8	22.2	20.6	19.1	17.5	15.9	14.3	12.7	11.1	9.5	7.9	6.4	4.8	3.2	1.6	0.0	0
1	49.2	47.6	46.0	44.4	42.9	41.3	39.7	38.1	36.5	34.9	33.3	31.7	30.2	28.6	27.0	25.4	1
2	74.6	73.0	71.4	69.8	68.3	66.7	65.1	63.5	61.9	60.3	58.7	57.1	55.6	54.0	52.4	50.8	2
3	100.0	98.4	96.8	95.2	93.7	92.1	90.5	88.9	87.3	85.7	84.1	82.5	81.0	79.4	77.8	76.2	3
4	125.4	123.8	122.2	120.7	119.1	117.5	115.9	114.3	112.7	111.1	109.5	108.0	106.4	104.8	103.2	101.6	4
5	150.8	149.2	147.6	146.1	144.5	142.9	141.3	139.7	138.1	136.5	134.9	133.4	131.8	130.2	128.6	127.0	5
6	176.2	174.6	173.0	171.5	169.9	168.3	166.7	165.1	163.5	161.9	160.3	158.8	157.2	155.6	154.0	152.4	6
7	201.6	200.0	198.4	196.9	195.3	193.7	192.1	190.5	188.9	187.3	185.7	184.2	182.6	181.0	179.4	177.8	7
8	227.0	225.4	223.8	222.3	220.7	219.1	217.5	215.9	214.3	212.7	211.1	209.6	208.0	206.4	204.8	203.2	8
9	252.4	250.8	249.2	247.7	246.1	244.5	242.9	241.3	239.7	238.1	236.5	235.0	233.4	231.8	230.2	228.6	9
10	277.8	276.2	274.6	273.1	271.5	269.9	268.3	266.7	265.1	263.5	261.9	260.4	258.8	257.2	255.6	254.0	10
11	303.2	301.6	300.0	298.4	296.9	295.3	293.7	292.1	290.5	288.9	287.3	285.7	284.2	282.6	281.0	279.4	11
12	328.6	327.0	325.4	323.8	322.3	320.7	319.1	317.5	315.9	314.3	312.7	311.1	309.6	308.0	306.4	304.8	12
13	354.0	352.4	350.8	349.2	347.7	346.1	344.5	342.9	341.3	339.7	338.1	336.5	335.0	333.4	331.8	330.2	13
14	379.4	377.8	376.2	374.6	373.1	371.5	369.9	368.3	366.7	365.1	363.5	361.9	360.4	358.8	357.2	355.6	14
15	404.8	403.2	401.6	400.0	398.5	396.9	395.3	393.7	392.1	390.5	388.9	387.3	385.8	384.2	382.6	381.0	15
16	430.2	428.6	427.0	425.4	423.9	422.3	420.7	419.1	417.5	415.9	414.3	412.7	411.2	409.6	408.0	406.4	16
17	455.6	454.0	452.4	450.8	449.3	447.7	446.1	444.5	442.9	441.3	439.7	438.1	436.6	435.0	433.4	431.8	17
18	481.0	479.4	477.8	476.2	474.7	473.1	471.5	469.9	468.3	466.7	465.1	463.5	462.0	460.4	458.8	457.2	18
19	506.4	504.8	503.2	501.6	500.1	498.5	496.9	495.3	493.7	492.1	490.5	488.9	487.4	485.8	484.2	482.6	19
20	531.8	530.2	528.6	527.0	525.5	523.9	522.3	520.7	519.1	517.5	515.9	514.3	512.8	511.2	509.6	508.0	20
21	557.2	555.6	554.0	552.4	550.9	549.3	547.7	546.1	544.5	542.9	541.3	539.7	538.2	536.6	535.0	533.4	21
22	582.6	581.0	579.4	577.8	576.3	574.7	573.1	571.5	569.9	568.3	566.7	565.1	563.6	562.0	560.4	558.8	22
23	608.0	606.4	604.8	603.2	601.7	600.1	598.5	596.9	595.3	593.7	592.1	590.5	589.0	587.4	585.8	584.2	23

DECIMAL EQUIVALENTS OF FRACTIONS OF AN INCH. (ADVANCING BY 8THS, 16THS, 32NDS AND 64THS.)

8ths	32nds	64ths	64ths
$\frac{1}{8}$ = .125	$\frac{1}{32}$ = .03125	$\frac{1}{64}$ = .015625	$\frac{33}{64}$ = .515625
$\frac{1}{4}$ = .250	$\frac{3}{32}$ = .09375	$\frac{3}{64}$ = .046875	$\frac{35}{64}$ = .546875
$\frac{3}{8}$ = .375	$\frac{5}{32}$ = .15625	$\frac{5}{64}$ = .078125	$\frac{37}{64}$ = .578125
$\frac{1}{2}$ = .500	$\frac{7}{32}$ = .21875	$\frac{7}{64}$ = .109375	$\frac{39}{64}$ = .609375
$\frac{5}{8}$ = .625	$\frac{9}{32}$ = .28125	$\frac{9}{64}$ = .140625	$\frac{41}{64}$ = .640625
$\frac{3}{4}$ = .750	$\frac{11}{32}$ = .34375	$\frac{11}{64}$ = .171875	$\frac{43}{64}$ = .671875
$\frac{7}{8}$ = .875	$\frac{13}{32}$ = .40625	$\frac{13}{64}$ = .203125	$\frac{45}{64}$ = .703125
	$\frac{15}{32}$ = .46875	$\frac{15}{64}$ = .234375	$\frac{47}{64}$ = .734375
16ths.			
$\frac{1}{16}$ = .0625	$\frac{17}{32}$ = .53125	$\frac{17}{64}$ = .265625	$\frac{49}{64}$ = .765625
$\frac{3}{16}$ = .1875	$\frac{19}{32}$ = .59375	$\frac{19}{64}$ = .296875	$\frac{51}{64}$ = .796875
$\frac{5}{16}$ = .3125	$\frac{21}{32}$ = .65625	$\frac{21}{64}$ = .328125	$\frac{53}{64}$ = .828125
$\frac{7}{16}$ = .4375	$\frac{23}{32}$ = .71875	$\frac{23}{64}$ = .359375	$\frac{55}{64}$ = .859375
$\frac{9}{16}$ = .5625	$\frac{25}{32}$ = .78125	$\frac{25}{64}$ = .390625	$\frac{57}{64}$ = .890625
$\frac{11}{16}$ = .6875	$\frac{27}{32}$ = .84375	$\frac{27}{64}$ = .421875	$\frac{59}{64}$ = .921875
$\frac{13}{16}$ = .8125	$\frac{29}{32}$ = .90625	$\frac{29}{64}$ = .453125	$\frac{61}{64}$ = .953125
$\frac{15}{16}$ = .9375	$\frac{31}{32}$ = .96875	$\frac{31}{64}$ = .484375	$\frac{63}{64}$ = .984375

DECIMAL EQUIVALENTS OF FRACTIONS OF AN INCH. (ADVANCING BY 64THS.)

$\frac{1}{64}$ = .015625	$\frac{17}{64}$ = .265625	$\frac{33}{64}$ = .515625	$\frac{49}{64}$ = .765625
$\frac{1}{32}$ = .03125	$\frac{9}{32}$ = .28125	$\frac{17}{32}$ = .53125	$\frac{25}{32}$ = .78125
$\frac{3}{64}$ = .046875	$\frac{19}{64}$ = .296875	$\frac{35}{64}$ = .546875	$\frac{51}{64}$ = .796875
$\frac{1}{16}$ = .0625	$\frac{5}{16}$ = .3125	$\frac{9}{16}$ = .5625	$\frac{13}{16}$ = .8125
$\frac{5}{64}$ = .078125	$\frac{21}{64}$ = .328125	$\frac{37}{64}$ = .578125	$\frac{53}{64}$ = .828125
$\frac{3}{32}$ = .09375	$\frac{11}{32}$ = .34375	$\frac{19}{32}$ = .59375	$\frac{27}{32}$ = .84375
$\frac{7}{64}$ = .109375	$\frac{23}{64}$ = .359375	$\frac{39}{64}$ = .609375	$\frac{55}{64}$ = .859375
$\frac{1}{8}$ = .125	$\frac{3}{8}$ = .375	$\frac{5}{8}$ = .625	$\frac{7}{8}$ = .875
$\frac{9}{64}$ = .140625	$\frac{25}{64}$ = .390625	$\frac{41}{64}$ = .640625	$\frac{57}{64}$ = .890625
$\frac{5}{32}$ = .15625	$\frac{13}{32}$ = .40625	$\frac{21}{32}$ = .65625	$\frac{29}{32}$ = .90625
$\frac{11}{64}$ = .171875	$\frac{27}{64}$ = .421875	$\frac{43}{64}$ = .671875	$\frac{59}{64}$ = .921875
$\frac{3}{16}$ = .1875	$\frac{7}{16}$ = .4375	$\frac{11}{16}$ = .6875	$\frac{15}{16}$ = .9375
$\frac{13}{64}$ = .203125	$\frac{29}{64}$ = .453125	$\frac{45}{64}$ = .703125	$\frac{61}{64}$ = .953125
$\frac{7}{32}$ = .21875	$\frac{15}{32}$ = .46875	$\frac{23}{32}$ = .71875	$\frac{31}{32}$ = .96875
$\frac{15}{64}$ = .234375	$\frac{31}{64}$ = .484375	$\frac{47}{64}$ = .734375	$\frac{63}{64}$ = .984375
$\frac{1}{4}$ = .25	$\frac{1}{2}$ = .50	$\frac{3}{4}$ = .75	

DECIMAL EQUIVALENTS OF FRACTIONS BELOW ½"

Decimal Equivalents	Fractional Parts of an Inch										Decimal Equivalents
	6	7	8	12	14	16	24	28	32	64	
.015625										1	.015625
.03125									1	2	.03125
.035714								1			.035714
.041667							1				.041667
.046875										3	.046875
.0625						1			2	4	.0625
.071429					1			2			.071429
.078125										5	.078125
.083333				1			2				.083333
.09375									3	6	.09375
.107143								3			.107143
.109375										7	.109375
.125			1			2	3		4	8	.125
.140625										9	.140625
.142857		1			2			4			.142857
.15625									5	10	.15625
.166666	1			2			4				.166666
.171875										11	.171875
.178571								5			.178571
.1875						3			6	12	.1875
.203125										13	.203125
.208333							5				.208333
.214286					3			6			.214286
.21875									7	14	.21875
.234375										15	.234375
.25			2	3		4	6	7	8	16	.25
.265625										17	.265625
.28125									9	18	.28125
.285714		2			4			8			.285714
.291666							7				.291666
.296875										19	.296875
.3125						5			10	20	.3125
.321429								9			.321429
.328125										21	.328125
.333333	2			4			8				.333333
.34375									11	22	.34375
.357143					5			10			.357143
.359375										23	.359375
.375			3			6	9		12	24	.375
.390625										25	.390625
.392857								11			.392857
.40625									13	26	.40625
.41666				5			10				.41666
.421875										27	.421875
.428571		3			6			12			.428571
.4375					7				14	28	.4375
.453125										29	.453125
.458333							11				.458333
.464286								13			.464286
.46875									15	30	.46875
.484375										31	.484375
.5	3		4	6	7	8	12	14	16	32	.5

DECIMAL EQUIVALENTS OF FRACTIONS BETWEEN ½″ AND 1″

Decimal Equivalents	Fractional Parts of an Inch										Decimal Equivalents
---	6	7	8	12	14	16	24	28	32	64	---
.515625										33	.515625
.53125									17	34	.53125
.535714								15			.535714
.541666							13				.541666
.546875										35	.546875
.5625						9			18	36	.5625
.571429		4			8			16			.571429
.578125										37	.578125
.583333				7			14				.583333
.59375									19	38	.59375
.607143								17			.607143
.609375										39	.609375
.625			5			10	15		20	40	.625
.640625										41	.640625
.642867					9			18			.642867
.65625									21	42	.65625
.666666	4			8			16				.666666
.671875										43	.671875
.678571								19			.678571
.6875						11			22	44	.6875
.703125										45	.703125
.708333							17				.708333
.714286		5			10			20			.714286
.71875									23	46	.71875
.734375										47	.734375
.75			6	9		12	18	21	24	48	.75
.765625										49	.765625
.78125									25	50	.78125
.785714					11			22			.785714
.791666							19				.791666
.796875										51	.796875
.8125						13			26	52	.8125
.821429								23			.821429
.828125										53	.828125
.833333	5			10			20				.833333
.84375									27	54	.84375
.857143		6			12			24			.857143
.859375										55	.859375
.875			7			14	21		28	56	.875
.890625										57	.890625
.892857								25			.892857
.90625									29	58	.90625
.916666				11			22				.916666
.921875										59	.921875
.928571					13			26			.928571
.9375						15			30	60	.9375
.953125										61	.953125
.958333							23				.958333
.964286								27			.964286
.96875									31	62	.96875
.984375										63	.984375

DECIMAL EQUIVALENTS OF FRACTIONS AND NEAREST EQUIVALENT 64THS

Fr.	Decimal	Nearest 64th	Fr.	Decimal	Nearest 64th	Fr.	Decimal	Nearest 64th
1/32	0.0313		2/15	0.1333	1/8	7/27	0.2593	
1/31	0.0323		3/22	0.1364		6/23	0.2609	
1/30	0.0333		4/29	0.1379		5/19	0.2632	
1/29	0.0345	1/32	1/7	0.1429	9/64	4/15	0.2667	17/64
1/28	0.0357		4/27	0.1481		7/26	0.2692	
1/27	0.0370		3/20	0.1500		3/11	0.2727	
1/26	0.0385		2/13	0.1538		8/29	0.2759	
1/25	0.0400		5/32	0.1563	5/32	5/18	0.2778	
1/24	0.0417		3/19	0.1579		7/25	0.2800	
1/23	0.0435		4/25	0.1600		9/32	0.2813	9/32
1/22	0.0455		5/31	0.1613		2/7	0.2857	
1/21	0.0476	3/64	1/6	0.1667		9/31	0.2903	
1/20	0.0500		5/29	0.1724	11/64	7/24	0.2917	
1/19	0.0526		4/23	0.1739		5/17	0.2941	
1/18	0.0556		3/17	0.1765		8/27	0.2963	19/64
1/17	0.0589		5/28	0.1785		3/10	0.3000	
1/16	0.0625	1/16	2/11	0.1818		7/23	0.3043	
2/31	0.0645		5/27	0.1852		4/13	0.3077	
1/15	0.0667		3/16	0.1875	3/16	9/29	0.3103	
2/29	0.0690		4/21	0.1905		5/16	0.3125	5/16
1/14	0.0714		5/26	0.1923		6/19	0.3158	
2/27	0.0740		6/31	0.1935		7/22	0.3182	
1/13	0.0769	5/64	1/5	0.2000	13/64	8/25	0.3200	
2/25	0.0800		6/29	0.2069		9/28	0.3214	
1/12	0.0833		5/24	0.2083		10/31	0.3226	21/64
2/23	0.0870		4/19	0.2105		1/3	0.3333	
1/11	0.0909		3/14	0.2143		11/32	0.3438	11/32
3/32	0.0938	3/32	5/23	0.2174		10/29	0.3448	
2/21	0.0952		7/32	0.2188	7/32	9/26	0.3462	
3/31	0.0968		2/9	0.2222		8/23	0.3478	
1/10	0.1000		7/31	0.2258		7/20	0.3500	
3/29	0.1034		5/22	0.2273		6/17	0.3529	
2/19	0.1053		3/13	0.2308		11/31	0.3548	
3/28	0.1071		7/30	0.2333		5/14	0.3571	
1/9	0.1111	7/64	4/17	0.2353	15/64	9/25	0.3600	23/64
3/26	0.1154		5/21	0.2381		4/11	0.3636	
2/17	0.1176		6/25	0.2400		11/30	0.3667	
3/25	0.1200		7/29	0.2414		7/19	0.3684	
1/8	0.1250	1/8	1/4	0.2500	1/4	10/27	0.3704	
4/31	0.1290		8/31	0.2580		3/8	0.3750	3/8
3/23	0.1304							

DECIMAL EQUIVALENTS OF FRACTIONS AND NEAREST EQUIVALENT 64THS

Fr.	Decimal	Nearest 64th	Fr.	Decimal	Nearest 64th	Fr.	Decimal	Nearest 64th
$\frac{11}{29}$	0.3793	$\frac{3}{8}$	$\frac{16}{31}$	0.5161	$\frac{33}{64}$	$\frac{17}{27}$	0.6296	$\frac{5}{8}$
$\frac{8}{21}$	0.3810		$\frac{15}{29}$	0.5172		$\frac{12}{19}$	0.6316	
$\frac{5}{13}$	0.3846		$\frac{14}{27}$	0.5185		$\frac{19}{30}$	0.6333	
$\frac{12}{31}$	0.3871		$\frac{13}{25}$	0.5200		$\frac{7}{11}$	0.6364	
$\frac{7}{18}$	0.3889		$\frac{12}{23}$	0.5217		$\frac{16}{25}$	0.6400	$\frac{41}{64}$
$\frac{9}{23}$	0.3913	$\frac{25}{64}$	$\frac{11}{21}$	0.5238		$\frac{9}{14}$	0.6429	
$\frac{11}{28}$	0.3929		$\frac{10}{19}$	0.5263		$\frac{20}{31}$	0.6452	
$\frac{2}{5}$	0.4000		$\frac{9}{17}$	0.5294		$\frac{11}{17}$	0.6471	
$\frac{13}{32}$	0.4063	$\frac{13}{32}$	$\frac{17}{32}$	0.5313	$\frac{17}{32}$	$\frac{13}{20}$	0.6500	
$\frac{11}{27}$	0.4074		$\frac{8}{15}$	0.5333		$\frac{15}{23}$	0.6522	
$\frac{9}{22}$	0.4091		$\frac{15}{28}$	0.5357		$\frac{17}{26}$	0.6538	
$\frac{7}{17}$	0.4118		$\frac{7}{13}$	0.5385		$\frac{19}{29}$	0.6552	
$\frac{12}{29}$	0.4138		$\frac{13}{24}$	0.5417		$\frac{21}{32}$	0.6563	$\frac{21}{32}$
$\frac{5}{12}$	0.4167		$\frac{6}{11}$	0.5455	$\frac{35}{64}$	$\frac{2}{3}$	0.6667	$\frac{43}{64}$
$\frac{13}{31}$	0.4194		$\frac{17}{31}$	0.5484		$\frac{21}{31}$	0.6774	
$\frac{8}{19}$	0.4211	$\frac{27}{64}$	$\frac{11}{20}$	0.5500		$\frac{19}{28}$	0.6786	
$\frac{11}{26}$	0.4231		$\frac{16}{29}$	0.5517		$\frac{17}{25}$	0.6800	
$\frac{3}{7}$	0.4286		$\frac{5}{9}$	0.5556		$\frac{15}{22}$	0.6818	
$\frac{13}{30}$	0.4333		$\frac{14}{25}$	0.5600		$\frac{13}{19}$	0.6842	
$\frac{10}{23}$	0.4348		$\frac{9}{16}$	0.5625	$\frac{9}{16}$	$\frac{11}{16}$	0.6875	$\frac{11}{16}$
$\frac{7}{16}$	0.4375	$\frac{7}{16}$	$\frac{13}{23}$	0.5652		$\frac{20}{29}$	0.6897	
$\frac{11}{25}$	0.4400		$\frac{17}{30}$	0.5667		$\frac{9}{13}$	0.6923	
$\frac{4}{9}$	0.4444		$\frac{4}{7}$	0.5714		$\frac{16}{23}$	0.6957	
$\frac{13}{29}$	0.4483		$\frac{15}{26}$	0.5769		$\frac{7}{10}$	0.7000	
$\frac{9}{20}$	0.4500		$\frac{11}{19}$	0.5789	$\frac{37}{64}$	$\frac{19}{27}$	0.7037	$\frac{45}{64}$
$\frac{14}{31}$	0.4516	$\frac{29}{64}$	$\frac{18}{31}$	0.5806		$\frac{12}{17}$	0.7059	
$\frac{5}{11}$	0.4545		$\frac{7}{12}$	0.5833		$\frac{17}{24}$	0.7083	
$\frac{11}{24}$	0.4583		$\frac{17}{29}$	0.5862		$\frac{22}{31}$	0.7097	
$\frac{6}{13}$	0.4615		$\frac{10}{17}$	0.5882		$\frac{5}{7}$	0.7143	
$\frac{13}{28}$	0.4642		$\frac{13}{22}$	0.5909		$\frac{23}{32}$	0.7188	$\frac{23}{32}$
$\frac{7}{15}$	0.4667		$\frac{16}{27}$	0.5926		$\frac{18}{25}$	0.7200	
$\frac{15}{32}$	0.4688	$\frac{15}{32}$	$\frac{19}{32}$	0.5938	$\frac{19}{32}$	$\frac{13}{18}$	0.7222	
$\frac{8}{17}$	0.4706		$\frac{3}{5}$	0.6000		$\frac{21}{29}$	0.7241	
$\frac{9}{19}$	0.4737		$\frac{17}{28}$	0.6071		$\frac{8}{11}$	0.7273	
$\frac{10}{21}$	0.4762		$\frac{14}{23}$	0.6087	$\frac{39}{64}$	$\frac{19}{26}$	0.7308	
$\frac{11}{23}$	0.4783		$\frac{11}{18}$	0.6111		$\frac{11}{15}$	0.7333	$\frac{47}{64}$
$\frac{12}{25}$	0.4800		$\frac{19}{31}$	0.6129		$\frac{14}{19}$	0.7368	
$\frac{13}{27}$	0.4815		$\frac{8}{13}$	0.6154		$\frac{17}{23}$	0.7391	
$\frac{14}{29}$	0.4828	$\frac{31}{64}$	$\frac{13}{21}$	0.6190		$\frac{20}{27}$	0.7407	
$\frac{15}{31}$	0.4839		$\frac{18}{29}$	0.6207		$\frac{23}{31}$	0.7419	
$\frac{1}{2}$	0.5000	$\frac{1}{2}$	$\frac{5}{8}$	0.6250	$\frac{5}{8}$	$\frac{3}{4}$	0.7500	$\frac{3}{4}$

DECIMAL EQUIVALENTS OF FRACTIONS AND NEAREST EQUIVALENT 64THS

Fr.	Decimal	Nearest 64th	Fr.	Decimal	Nearest 64th	Fr.	Decimal	Nearest 64th
	0.7586			0.8387			0.9167	
	0.7600			0.8400			0.9200	
	0.7619			0.8421			0.9231	$\frac{59}{64}$
	0.7647	$\frac{49}{64}$		0.8438	$\frac{27}{32}$		0.9259	
	0.7667			0.8462			0.9286	
	0.7692			0.8500			0.9310	
	0.7727			0.8519			0.9333	
	0.7742			0.8571	$\frac{55}{64}$		0.9355	
	0.7778			0.8621			0.9375	$\frac{15}{16}$
	0.7813	$\frac{25}{32}$		0.8636			0.9412	
	0.7826			0.8667			0.9444	
	0.7857			0.8696			0.9474	
	0.7895			0.8710			0.9500	
	0.7917			0.8750	$\frac{7}{8}$		0.9524	$\frac{61}{64}$
	0.7931	$\frac{51}{64}$		0.8800			0.9545	
	0.8000			0.8824			0.9565	
	0.8065			0.8846			0.9583	
	0.8077			0.8889			0.9600	
	0.8095			0.8929	$\frac{57}{64}$		0.9615	
	0.8125	$\frac{13}{16}$		0.8947			0.9630	
	0.8148			0.8966			0.9643	
	0.8182			0.9000			0.9655	
	0.8214			0.9032			0.9667	
	0.8235			0.9048			0.9678	
	0.8261			0.9063			0.9688	$\frac{31}{32}$
	0.8276	$\frac{53}{64}$		0.9091	$\frac{29}{32}$		1.0000	
	0.8334			0.9130				

TABLE OF PRIME-NUMBER FRACTIONS

THE table shows decimal equivalents of common fractions having prime numbers for both numerator and denominator. As an example, suppose it is required to find the thread angle of a worm.

$$\text{Tangent thread angle} = \frac{\text{number threads}}{\text{diametral pitch} \times \text{pitch diameter}}.$$

Find the angle of a worm 7 diametral pitch, 5 threads, 2-inch P. diameter: $\text{Tangent angle} = \frac{5}{7} \times \frac{1}{2}$

Then from table

$$\tfrac{5}{7} = 0.7143 \quad \text{and} \quad \frac{0.7143}{2} = 0.35715$$

which is the tangent for 19 degrees 21 minutes, nearly.

PRIME NUMBER FRACTIONS AND THEIR DECIMAL EQUIVALENTS

Denominators (Prime Numbers Only)

	97	89	83	79	73	71	67	61	59	53	47	43
1	.0103	.0112	.0120	.0126	.0137	.0141	.0149	.0164	.0169	.0189	.0213	.0233
3	.0309	.0337	.0361	.0380	.0411	.0423	.0448	.0492	.0508	.0566	.0638	.0698
5	.0515	.0562	.0602	.0633	.0685	.0704	.0746	.0820	.0847	.0943	.1064	.1163
7	.0722	.0787	.0843	.0886	.0959	.0986	.1045	.1148	.1186	.1321	.1489	.1628
11	.1134	.1236	.1325	.1392	.1507	.1549	.1642	.1803	.1864	.2075	.2340	.2558
13	.1340	.1461	.1566	.1646	.1781	.1831	.1940	.2131	.2203	.2453	.2766	.3023
17	.1753	.1910	.2048	.2152	.2329	.2394	.2537	.2787	.2881	.3208	.3617	.3953
19	.1959	.2135	.2289	.2405	.2603	.2676	.2836	.3115	.3220	.3585	.4043	.4419
23	.2371	.2584	.2771	.2911	.3151	.3299	.3433	.3770	.3898	.4340	.4894	.5349
29	.2990	.3258	.3494	.3671	.3973	.4085	.4328	.4754	.4915	.5472	.6170	.6744
31	.3196	.3483	.3735	.3924	.4247	.4366	.4627	.5082	.5254	.5849	.6596	.7209
37	.3814	.4157	.4458	.4684	.5068	.5211	.5522	.6066	.6271	.6981	.7872	.8605
41	.4227	.4607	.4940	.5190	.5616	.5775	.6119	.6721	.6949	.7736	.8723	.9535
43	.4433	.4831	.5181	.5443	.5890	.6056	.6418	.7049	.7288	.8113	.9149	
47	.4845	.5281	.5663	.5949	.6438	.6620	.7015	.7705	.7966	.8868		
53	.5464	.5955	.6386	.6709	.7260	.7465	.7910	.8689	.8983			
59	.6082	.6629	.7108	.7468	.8082	.8310	.8806	.9672				
61	.6289	.6854	.7349	.7722	.8356	.8592	.9104					
67	.6907	.7528	.8072	.8481	.9178	.9437						
71	.7320	.7978	.8554	.8987	.9726							
73	.7526	.8202	.8795	.9241								
79	.8144	.8876	.9518									
83	.8557	.9326										
89	.9175											

Denominators (Prime Numbers Only)

	41	37	31	29	23	19	17	13	11	7	5	3
1	.0244	.0270	.0323	.0345	.0435	.0526	.0588	.0769	.0909	.1429	.2000	.3333
3	.0732	.0811	.0968	.1034	.1304	.1579	.1765	.2308	.2727	.4286	.6000	
5	.1220	.1351	.1613	.1724	.2174	.2632	.2941	.3846	.4545	.7143		
7	.1707	.1892	.2258	.2414	.3043	.3684	.4118	.5385	.6364			
11	.2683	.2973	.3558	.3793	.4783	.5789	.6471	.8462				
13	.3171	.3514	.4194	.4483	.5652	.6842	.7647					
17	.4146	.4595	.5484	.5862	.7391	.8947						
19	.4634	.5135	.6129	.6552	.8261							
23	.5610	.6212	.7419	.7931								
29	.7073	.7838	.9355									
31	.7561	.8778										
37	.9024											

Only those common fractions having prime numbers for both the numerator and denominator are given in table. Others can be found by simple multiplication or division.

EQUIVALENTS OF INCHES AND FRACTIONS OF INCHES IN DECIMALS OF A FOOT

In.	0 In.	1 In.	2 In.	3 In.	4 In.	5 In.
		.0833	.1667	.2500	.3333	.4167
1/32	.0026	.0859	.1693	.2526	.3359	.4193
1/16	.0052	.0885	.1719	.2552	.3385	.4219
3/32	.0078	.0911	.1745	.2578	.3411	.4245
1/8	.0104	.0938	.1771	.2604	.3438	.4271
5/32	.0130	.0964	.1797	.2630	.3464	.4297
3/16	.0156	.0990	.1823	.2656	.3490	.4323
7/32	.0182	.1016	.1849	.2682	.3516	.4349
1/4	.0208	.1042	.1875	.2708	.3542	.4375
9/32	.0234	.1068	.1901	.2734	.3568	.4401
5/16	.0260	.1094	.1927	.2760	.3594	.4427
11/32	.0286	.1120	.1953	.2786	.3620	.4453
3/8	.0313	.1146	.1979	.2813	.3646	.4479
13/32	.0339	.1172	.2005	.2839	.3672	.4505
7/16	.0365	.1198	.2031	.2865	.3698	.4531
15/32	.0391	.1224	.2057	.2891	.3724	.4557
1/2	.0417	.1253	.2083	.2917	.3750	.4583
17/32	.0443	.1276	.2091	.2943	.3776	.4609
9/16	.0469	.1302	.2135	.2969	.3802	.4635
19/32	.0495	.1328	.2161	.2995	.3828	.4661
5/8	.0521	.1354	.2188	.3021	.3854	.4688
21/32	.0547	.1380	.2214	.3047	.3880	.4714
11/16	.0573	.1406	.2240	.3073	.3906	.4740
23/32	.0599	.1432	.2266	.3099	.3932	.4766
3/4	.0625	.1458	.2292	.3125	.3958	.4792
25/32	.0651	.1484	.2318	.3151	.3984	.4818
13/16	.0677	.1510	.2344	.3177	.4010	.4844
27/32	.0703	.1536	.2370	.3203	.4036	.4870
7/8	.0729	.1563	.2396	.3229	.4063	.4896
29/32	.0755	.1589	.2422	.3255	.4089	.4922
15/16	.0781	.1615	.2448	.3281	.4115	.4948
31/32	.0807	.1641	.2474	.3307	.4141	.4974

EQUIVALENTS OF INCHES AND FRACTIONS OF INCHES IN DECIMALS OF A FOOT

In.	6 In.	7 In.	8 In.	9 In.	10 In.	11 In.
	.5000	.5833	.6667	.7500	.8333	.9167
1/32	.5026	.5859	.6693	.7526	.8359	.9193
1/16	.5052	.5885	.6719	.7552	.8385	.9219
3/32	.5078	.5911	.6745	.7578	.8411	.9245
1/8	.5104	.5938	.6771	.7604	.8438	.9271
5/32	.5130	.5964	.6797	.7630	.8464	.9297
3/16	.5156	.5990	.6823	.7656	.8490	.9323
7/32	.5182	.6016	.6849	.7682	.8516	.9349
1/4	.5208	.6042	.6875	.7708	.8542	.9375
9/32	.5234	.6068	.6901	.7734	.8568	.9401
5/16	.5260	.6094	.6927	.7760	.8594	.9427
11/32	.5286	.6120	.6953	.7786	.8620	.9453
3/8	.5313	.6146	.6979	.7813	.8646	.9479
13/32	.5339	.6172	.7005	.7839	.8672	.9505
7/16	.5365	.6198	.7031	.7865	.8698	.9531
15/32	.5391	.6224	.7057	.7891	.8724	.9557
1/2	.5417	.6250	.7083	.7917	.8750	.9583
17/32	.5443	.6276	.7109	.7943	.8776	.9609
9/16	.5469	.6302	.7135	.7969	.8802	.9635
19/32	.5495	.6328	.7161	.7995	.8828	.9661
5/8	.5521	.6354	.7188	.8021	.8854	.9688
21/32	.5547	.6380	.7214	.8047	.8880	.9714
11/16	.5573	.6406	.7240	.8073	.8906	.9740
23/32	.5599	.6432	.7266	.8099	.8932	.9766
3/4	.5625	.6458	.7292	.8125	.8958	.9792
25/32	.5651	.6484	.7318	.8151	.8984	.9818
13/16	.5677	.6510	.7344	.8177	.9010	.9844
27/32	.5703	.6536	.7370	.8203	.9036	.9870
7/8	.5729	.6563	.7396	.8229	.9063	.9896
29/32	.5755	.6589	.7422	.8255	.9089	.9922
15/16	.5781	.6615	.7448	.8281	.9115	.9948
31/32	.5807	.6641	.7474	.8307	.9141	.9974

TABLE I.—SQUARES OF NUMBERS FROM "0" to "7 28/64" BY 64THS—NUMBER

Added Fractions to Sixty-fourths	0	1	2	3	4	5	6	7
0	.000000	1.00000	4.00000	9.00000	16.00000	25.00000	36.00000	49.00000
1/64	.000244	1.03149	4.06274	9.09399	16.12524	25.15649	36.18774	49.21899
1/32	.000977	1.06348	4.12598	9.18848	16.25098	25.31348	36.37598	49.43848
3/64	.002197	1.09595	4.18970	9.28345	16.37720	25.47095	36.56470	49.65845
1/16	.003906	1.12891	4.25391	9.37891	16.50391	25.62891	36.75391	49.87891
5/64	.006104	1.16235	4.31860	9.47485	16.63110	25.78735	36.94360	50.09985
3/32	.008789	1.19629	4.38379	9.57129	16.75879	25.94629	37.13379	50.32129
7/64	.011963	1.23071	4.44946	9.66821	16.88696	26.10571	37.32446	50.54321
1/8	.015625	1.26563	4.51563	9.76563	17.01563	26.26563	37.51563	50.76563
9/64	.019775	1.30103	4.58228	9.86353	17.14478	26.42603	37.70728	50.98853
5/32	.024414	1.33691	4.64941	9.96191	17.27441	26.58691	37.89941	51.21191
11/64	.029541	1.37329	4.71704	10.06079	17.40454	26.74829	38.09204	51.43579
3/16	.035156	1.41016	4.78516	10.16016	17.53516	26.91016	38.28516	51.66016
13/64	.041260	1.44751	4.85376	10.26001	17.66626	27.07251	38.47876	51.88501
7/32	.047852	1.48535	4.92285	10.36035	17.79785	27.23535	38.67285	52.11035
15/64	.054932	1.52368	4.99243	10.46118	17.92993	27.39868	38.86743	52.33618
1/4	.062500	1.56250	5.06250	10.56250	18.06250	27.56250	39.06250	52.56250
17/64	.070557	1.60181	5.13306	10.66431	18.19556	27.72681	39.25806	52.78931
9/32	.079102	1.64160	5.20410	10.76660	18.32910	27.89160	39.45410	53.01660
19/64	.088135	1.68188	5.27563	10.86938	18.46313	28.05688	39.65063	53.24438
5/16	.097656	1.72266	5.34766	10.97266	18.59766	28.22266	39.84766	53.47266
21/64	.107666	1.76392	5.42017	11.07642	18.73267	28.38892	40.04517	53.70142
11/32	.118164	1.80566	5.49316	11.18066	18.86816	28.55566	40.24316	53.93066
23/64	.129151	1.84790	5.56665	11.28540	19.00415	28.72290	40.44165	54.16040
3/8	.140625	1.89063	5.64063	11.39063	19.14063	28.89063	40.64063	54.39063
25/64	.152588	1.93384	5.71509	11.49034	19.27759	29.05884	40.84009	54.62134
13/32	.165039	1.97754	5.79004	11.60254	19.41504	29.22754	41.04004	54.85254
27/64	.177979	2.02173	5.86548	11.70923	19.55298	29.39673	41.24048	55.08423
7/16	.191406	2.06641	5.94141	11.81641	19.69141	29.56641	41.44141	55.31641

Fraction	0	1	2	3	4	5	6	7
29/64	.205322	2.11157	6.01782	11.92407	19.83032	29.73657	41.64282	55.54907
15/32	.219726	2.15723	6.09473	12.03223	19.96073	29.90723	41.84473	55.78223
31/64	.234619	2.20337	6.17212	12.14081	20.10902	30.07837	42.04712	56.01587
1/2	.250000	2.25000	6.25000	12.25000	20.25000	30.25000	42.25000	56.25000
33/64	.265869	2.29712	6.32837	12.35962	20.39087	30.42212	42.45337	56.48462
17/32	.282227	2.34473	6.40723	12.46973	20.53223	30.59473	42.65723	56.71973
35/64	.299072	2.39282	6.48657	12.58032	20.67407	30.76782	42.86157	56.95532
9/16	.316406	2.44141	6.56641	12.69141	20.81641	30.94141	43.06641	57.19141
37/64	.334229	2.49048	6.64673	12.80298	20.95923	31.11548	43.27173	57.42798
19/32	.352539	2.54004	6.72754	12.91504	21.10254	31.29004	43.47754	57.66504
39/64	.371338	2.59009	6.80884	13.02759	21.24634	31.46509	43.68384	57.90259
5/8	.390625	2.64063	6.89063	13.14063	21.39063	31.64063	43.89063	58.14063
41/64	.410400	2.69165	6.97290	13.25415	21.53540	31.81665	44.09790	58.37915
21/32	.430664	2.74316	7.05566	13.36810	21.68066	31.99316	44.30566	58.61816
43/64	.451416	2.79517	7.13892	13.48267	21.82642	32.17017	44.51392	58.85767
11/16	.472656	2.84766	7.22266	13.59766	21.97266	32.34766	44.72266	59.09766
45/64	.494385	2.90063	7.30688	13.71313	22.11938	32.52563	44.93188	59.33813
23/32	.516602	2.95410	7.39160	13.82910	22.26660	32.70410	45.14160	59.57910
47/64	.539307	3.00806	7.47681	13.94556	22.41431	32.88306	45.35181	59.82056
3/4	.562500	3.06250	7.56250	14.06250	22.56250	33.06250	45.56250	60.06250
49/64	.586182	3.11743	7.64868	14.17993	22.71118	33.24243	45.77368	60.30493
25/32	.610352	3.17285	7.73535	14.29785	22.86035	33.42285	45.98535	60.54785
51/64	.635010	3.22876	7.82251	14.41626	23.01001	33.60376	46.19751	60.79126
13/16	.660156	3.28516	7.91016	14.53516	23.16016	33.78516	46.41016	61.03516
53/64	.685791	3.34204	7.99829	14.65454	23.31079	33.96704	46.62329	61.27954
27/32	.711914	3.39941	8.08691	14.77441	23.46191	34.14941	46.83691	61.52441
55/64	.738526	3.45728	8.17603	14.89478	23.61353	34.33228	47.05103	61.76978
7/8	.765625	3.51563	8.26563	15.01563	23.76563	34.51563	47.26563	62.01563
57/64	.793213	3.57446	8.35571	15.13696	23.91821	34.69940	47.48071	62.26196
29/32	.821289	3.63379	8.44629	15.25879	24.07129	34.88379	47.69629	62.50879
59/64	.849854	3.69360	8.53735	15.38110	24.22485	35.06860	47.91235	62.75610
15/16	.878906	3.75391	8.62891	15.50391	24.37891	35.25391	48.12891	63.00391
61/64	.908447	3.81470	8.72095	15.62720	24.53345	35.43970	48.34595	63.25220
31/32	.938477	3.87598	8.81348	15.75098	24.68848	35.62508	48.56348	63.50098
63/64	.968994	3.93774	8.90649	15.87524	24.84399	35.81274	48.78149	63.75024

Added Fractions to Sixty-fourths

Decimal Equivalents, Squares, Square Roots, Cubes and Cube Roots of Fractions; Circumferences and Areas of Circles from $\frac{1}{64}$ to 1 inch

Fraction	Dec. Equiv.	Square	Sq. Root	Cube	Cube Root	Circum. Circle	Area Circle
$\frac{1}{64}$	.015625	.000244	.1250	.000003815	.2500	.04909	.000192
$\frac{1}{32}$	.03125	.0009765	.1768	.00003052	.3150	.09818	.000767
$\frac{3}{64}$	.046875	.002197	.2165	.000103	.3606	.1473	.001726
$\frac{1}{16}$	.0625	.003906	.2500	.0002442	.3968	.1963	.003068
$\frac{5}{64}$	.078125	.006104	.2795	.0004768	.4275	.2455	.004794
$\frac{3}{32}$	.09375	.008789	.3062	.0008240	.4543	.2945	.006903
$\frac{7}{64}$	.109375	.01196	.3307	.001308	.4782	.3436	.009396
$\frac{1}{8}$	.1250	.01563	.3535	.001953	.5000	.3927	.01228
$\frac{9}{64}$	.140625	.01978	.3750	.002781	.5200	.4438	.01553
$\frac{5}{32}$	.15625	.02441	.3953	.003815	.5386	.4909	.01916
$\frac{11}{64}$	.171875	.02954	.4161	.005078	.5560	.5400	.02321
$\frac{3}{16}$	.1875	.03516	.4330	.006592	.5724	.5890	.02761
$\frac{13}{64}$	.203125	.04126	.4507	.008381	.5878	.6381	.03241
$\frac{7}{32}$	.21875	.04786	.4677	.01047	.6025	.6872	.03758
$\frac{15}{64}$	.234375	.05493	.4841	.01287	.6166	.7363	.04314
$\frac{1}{4}$	.2500	.0625	.5000	.01562	.6300	.7854	.04909
$\frac{17}{64}$	.265625	.07056	.5154	.01874	.6428	.8345	.05541
$\frac{9}{32}$	.28125	.07910	.5303	.02225	.6552	.8836	.06213
$\frac{19}{64}$	.296875	.08813	.5449	.02616	.6671	.9327	.06922
$\frac{5}{16}$	.3125	.09766	.5590	.03052	.6786	.9817	.07670
$\frac{21}{64}$	.328125	.1077	.5728	.03533	.6897	1.031	.08456
$\frac{11}{32}$	.34375	.1182	.5863	.04062	.7005	1.080	.09281
$\frac{23}{64}$	.359375	.12913	.5995	.04641	.7110	1.129	.1014
$\frac{3}{8}$	.3750	.1406	.6124	.05273	.7211	1.178	.1104
$\frac{25}{64}$	.390625	.1526	.6250	.05960	.7310	1.227	.1226
$\frac{13}{32}$	.40625	.1650	.6374	.06705	.7406	1.276	.1296
$\frac{27}{64}$	.421875	.17800	.6495	.07508	.7500	1.325	.1398
$\frac{7}{16}$	.4375	.1914	.6614	.08374	.7592	1.374	.1503
$\frac{29}{64}$	.453125	.2053	.6732	.09304	.7681	1.424	.1613
$\frac{15}{32}$	.46875	.2197	.6847	.1030	.7768	1.473	.1726
$\frac{31}{64}$	.484375	.2346	.6960	.1136	.7853	1.522	.1843
$\frac{1}{2}$	.5000	.2500	.7071	.1250	.7937	1.571	.1963

DECIMAL EQUIVALENTS, SQUARES, SQUARE ROOTS, CUBES, CUBE
ROOTS OF FRACTIONS; CIRCUMFERENCES AND AREAS OF CIR-
CLES FROM $\frac{1}{64}$ TO 1 INCH.

Frac-tion	Dec. Equiv.	Square	Sq. Root	Cube	Cube Root	Circum. Circle	Area Circle
33/64	.515625	.2659	.7181	.1371	.8019	1.620	.2088
17/32	.53125	.2822	.7289	.1499	.8099	1.669	.2217
35/64	.546875	.2991	.7395	.1636	.8178	1.718	.2349
9/16	.5625	.3164	.7500	.1780	.8255	1.767	.2485
37/64	.578125	.3342	.7603	.1932	.8331	1.816	.2625
19/32	.59375	.3525	.7706	.2093	.8405	1.865	.2769
39/64	.609375	.3713	.7806	.2263	.8478	1.914	.2916
5/8	.6250	.3906	.7906	.2441	.8550	1.963	.3068
41/64	.640625	.4104	.8004	.2629	.8621	2.013	.3223
21/32	.65625	.4307	.8101	.2826	.8690	2.062	.3382
43/64	.671875	.4514	.8197	.3033	.8758	2.111	.3545
11/16	.6875	.4727	.8292	.3250	.8826	2.160	.3712
45/64	.703125	.4944	.8385	.3476	.8892	2.209	.3883
23/32	.71875	.5166	.8478	.3713	.8958	2.258	.4057
47/64	.734375	.5393	.8569	.3961	.9022	2.307	.4236
3/4	.7500	.5625	.8660	.4219	.9086	2.356	.4418
49/64	.765625	.5862	.8750	.4488	.9148	2.405	.4604
25/32	.78125	.6104	.8839	.4768	.9210	2.454	.4794
51/64	.796875	.6350	.8927	.5060	.9271	2.503	.4987
13/16	.8125	.6602	.9014	.5364	.9331	2.553	.5185
53/64	.828125	.6858	.9100	.5679	.9391	2.602	.5386
27/32	.84375	.7119	.9186	.6007	.9449	2.651	.5592
55/64	.859375	.7385	.9270	.6347	.9507	2.700	.5801
7/8	.8750	.7656	.9354	.6699	.9565	2.749	.6013
57/64	.890625	.7932	.9437	.7064	.9621	2.798	.6230
29/32	.90625	.8213	.9520	.7443	.9677	2.847	.6450
59/64	.921875	.8499	.9601	.7835	.9732	2.896	.6675
15/16	.9375	.8789	.9682	.8240	.9787	2.945	.6903
61/64	.953125	.9084	.9763	.8659	.9841	2.994	.7135
31/32	.96875	.9385	.9843	.9091	.9895	3.043	.7371
63/64	.984375	.9690	.9922	.9539	.9948	3.093	.7610
1	1	1	1	1	1	3.1416	.7854

SQUARES, CUBES, SQUARE AND CUBE ROOTS OF NUMBERS FROM 1 TO 1000

No.	Square	Cube	Sq. Root	Cube Root	No.	Square	Cube	Sq. Root	Cube Root
1	1	1	1.0000	1.0000	51	2601	132651	7.1414	3.7084
2	4	8	1.4142	1.2599	52	2704	140608	7.2111	3.7325
3	9	27	1.7321	1.4422	53	2809	148877	7.2801	3.7563
4	16	64	2.0000	1.5874	54	2916	157464	7.3485	3.7798
5	25	125	2.2361	1.7100	55	3025	166375	7.4162	3.8030
6	36	216	2.4495	1.8171	56	3136	175616	7.4833	3.8259
7	49	343	2.6458	1.9129	57	3249	185193	7.5498	3.8485
8	64	512	2.8284	2.0000	58	3364	195112	7.6158	3.8709
9	81	729	3.0000	2.0801	59	3481	205379	7.6811	3.8930
10	100	1000	3.1623	2.1544	60	3600	216000	7.7460	3.9149
11	121	1331	3.3166	2.2240	61	3721	226981	7.8102	3.9365
12	144	1728	3.4611	2.2894	62	3844	238328	7.8740	3.9579
13	169	2197	3.6056	2.3513	63	3969	250047	7.9373	3.9791
14	196	2744	3.7417	2.4101	64	4096	262144	8.0000	4.0000
15	225	3375	3.8730	2.4662	65	4225	274625	8.0623	4.0207
16	256	4096	4.0000	2.5198	66	4356	287496	8.1240	4.0412
17	289	4913	4.1231	2.5713	67	4489	300763	8.1854	4.0615
18	324	5832	4.2426	2.6207	68	4624	314432	8.2462	4.0817
19	361	6859	4.3589	2.6684	69	4761	328509	8.3066	4.1016
20	400	8000	4.4721	2.7144	70	4900	343000	8.3666	4.1213
21	441	9261	4.5826	2.7589	71	5041	357911	8.4261	4.1408
22	484	10648	4.6904	2.8020	72	5184	373248	8.4853	4.1602
23	529	12167	4.7958	2.8439	73	5329	389017	8.5440	4.1793
24	576	13824	4.8990	2.8845	74	5476	405224	8.6023	4.1983
25	625	15625	5.0000	2.9240	75	5625	421875	8.6603	4.2172
26	676	17576	5.0990	2.9625	76	5776	438976	8.7178	4.2358
27	729	19683	5.1962	3.0000	77	5929	456533	8.7750	4.2543
28	784	21952	5.2915	3.0366	78	6084	474552	8.8318	4.2727
29	841	24389	5.3852	3.0723	79	6241	493039	8.8882	4.2908
30	900	27000	5.4772	3.1072	80	6400	512000	8.9443	4.3089
31	961	29791	5.5678	3.1414	81	6561	531441	9.0000	4.3267
32	1024	32768	5.6569	3.1748	82	6724	551368	9.0554	4.3445
33	1089	35937	5.7446	3.2075	83	6889	571787	9.1104	4.3621
34	1156	39304	5.8310	3.2396	84	7056	592704	9.1652	4.3795
35	1225	42875	5.9161	3.2711	85	7225	614125	9.2195	4.3968
36	1296	46656	6.0000	3.3019	86	7396	636056	9.2736	4.4140
37	1369	50653	6.0828	3.3322	87	7569	658503	9.3276	4.4310
38	1444	54872	6.1644	3.3620	88	7744	681472	9.3808	4.4480
39	1521	59319	6.2450	3.3912	89	7921	704969	9.4340	4.4647
40	1600	64000	6.3246	3.4200	90	8100	729000	9.4868	4.4814
41	1681	68921	6.4031	3.4482	91	8281	753571	9.5394	4.4979
42	1764	74088	6.4807	3.4760	92	8464	778688	9.5917	4.5144
43	1849	79507	6.5574	3.5034	93	8649	804357	9.6437	4.5307
44	1936	85184	6.6332	3.5303	94	8836	830584	9.6954	4.5468
45	2025	91125	6.7082	3.5569	95	9025	857375	9.7468	4.5629
46	2116	97336	6.7823	3.5830	96	9216	884736	9.7980	4.5789
47	2209	103823	6.8557	3.6088	97	9409	912673	9.8489	4.5947
48	2304	110592	6.9282	3.6342	98	9604	941192	9.8995	4.6104
49	2401	117649	7.0000	3.6593	99	9801	970299	9.9499	4.6261
50	2500	125000	7.0711	3.6840	100	10000	1000000	10.0000	4.6416

Squares, Cubes, Square and Cube Roots of Numbers from 1 to 1000

No.	Square	Cube	Sq. Root	Cube Root	No.	Square	Cube	Sq. Root	Cube Root
101	10201	1030301	10.0499	4.6570	151	22801	3442951	12.2882	5.3251
102	10404	1061208	10.0995	4.6723	152	23104	3511808	12.3288	5.3368
103	10609	1092727	10.1489	4.6875	153	23409	3581577	12.3693	5.3485
104	10816	1124864	10.1980	4.7027	154	23716	3652264	12.4097	5.3601
105	11025	1157625	10.2470	4.7177	155	24025	3723875	12.4499	5.3717
106	11236	1191016	10.2956	4.7326	156	24336	3796416	12.4900	5.3832
107	11449	1225043	10.3441	4.7475	157	24649	3869893	12.5300	5.3947
108	11664	1259712	10.3923	4.7622	158	24964	3944312	12.5698	5.4061
109	11881	1295029	10.4403	4.7769	159	25281	4019679	12.6095	5.4175
110	12100	1331000	10.4881	4.7914	160	25600	4096000	12.6491	5.4288
111	12321	1367631	10.5357	4.8059	161	25921	4173281	12.6886	5.4401
112	12544	1404928	10.5830	4.8203	162	26244	4251528	12.7279	5.4514
113	12769	1442897	10.6301	4.8346	163	26569	4330747	12.7671	5.4626
114	12996	1481544	10.6771	4.8488	164	26896	4410944	12.8062	5.4737
115	13225	1520875	10.7238	4.8629	165	27225	4492125	12.8452	5.4848
116	13456	1560896	10.7703	4.8770	166	27556	4574296	12.8841	5.4959
117	13689	1601613	10.8167	4.8910	167	27889	4657463	12.9228	5.5069
118	13924	1643032	10.8628	4.9049	168	28224	4741632	12.9615	5.5178
119	14161	1685159	10.9087	4.9187	169	28561	4826809	13.0000	5.5288
120	14400	1728000	10.9545	4.9324	170	28900	4913000	13.0384	5.5397
121	14641	1771561	11.0000	4.9461	171	29241	5000211	13.0767	5.5505
122	14884	1815848	11.0454	4.9597	172	29584	5088448	13.1149	5.5613
123	15129	1860867	11.0905	4.9732	173	29929	5177717	13.1529	5.5721
124	15376	1906624	11.1355	4.9866	174	30276	5268024	13.1909	5.5828
125	15625	1953125	11.1803	5.0000	175	30625	5359375	13.2288	5.5934
126	15876	2000376	11.2250	5.0133	176	30976	5451776	13.2665	5.6041
127	16129	2048383	11.2694	5.0265	177	31329	5545233	13.3041	5.6147
128	16384	2097152	11.3137	5.0397	178	31684	5639752	13.3417	5.6252
129	16641	2146689	11.3578	5.0528	179	32041	5735339	13.3791	5.6357
130	16900	2197000	11.4018	5.0658	180	32400	5832000	13.4164	5.6462
131	17161	2248091	11.4455	5.0788	181	32761	5929741	13.4536	5.6567
132	17424	2299968	11.4891	5.0916	182	33124	6028568	13.4907	5.6671
133	17689	2352637	11.5326	5.1045	183	33489	6128487	13.5277	5.6774
134	17956	2406104	11.5758	5.1172	184	33856	6229504	13.5647	5.6877
135	18225	2460375	11.6190	5.1299	185	34225	6331625	13.6015	5.6980
136	18496	2515456	11.6619	5.1426	186	34596	6434856	13.6382	5.7083
137	18769	2571353	11.7047	5.1551	187	34969	6539203	13.6748	5.7185
138	19044	2628072	11.7473	5.1676	188	35344	6644672	13.7113	5.7287
139	19321	2685619	11.7898	5.1801	189	35721	6751269	13.7477	5.7388
140	19600	2744000	11.8322	5.1925	190	36100	6859000	13.7840	5.7489
141	19881	2803221	11.8743	5.2048	191	36481	6967871	13.8203	5.7590
142	20164	2863288	11.9164	5.2171	192	36864	7077888	13.8564	5.7690
143	20449	2924207	11.9583	5.2293	193	37249	7189057	13.8924	5.7790
144	20736	2985984	12.0000	5.2415	194	37636	7301384	13.9284	5.7890
145	21025	3048625	12.0416	5.2536	195	38025	7414875	13.9642	5.7989
146	21316	3112136	12.0830	5.2656	196	38416	7520536	14.0000	5.8088
147	21609	3176523	12.1244	5.2776	197	38809	7645373	14.0357	5.8186
148	21904	3241792	12.1655	5.2896	198	39204	7762392	14.0712	5.8285
149	22201	3307949	12.2066	5.3015	199	39601	7880599	14.1067	5.8383
150	22500	3375000	12.2474	5.3133	200	40000	8000000	14.1421	5.8480

SQUARES, CUBES, SQUARE AND CUBE ROOTS OF NUMBERS FROM
1 TO 1000

No.	Square	Cube	Sq. Root	Cube Root	No.	Square	Cube	Sq. Root	Cube Root
201	40401	8120601	14.1774	5.8578	251	63001	15813251	15.8430	6.3080
202	40804	8242408	14.2127	5.8675	252	63504	16003008	15.8745	6.3164
203	41209	8365427	14.2478	5.8771	253	64009	16194277	15.9060	6.3247
204	41616	8489664	14.2829	5.8868	254	64516	16387064	15.9374	6.3330
205	42025	8615125	14.3178	5.8964	255	65025	16581375	15.9687	6.3413
206	42436	8741816	14.3527	5.9059	256	65536	16777216	16.0000	6.3496
207	42849	8869743	14.3875	5.9155	257	66049	16974593	16.0312	6.3579
208	43264	8998912	14.4222	5.9250	258	66564	17173512	16.0624	6.3661
209	43681	9129329	14.4568	5.9345	259	67081	17373979	16.0935	6.3743
210	44100	9261000	14.4914	5.9439	260	67600	17576000	16.1245	6.3825
211	44521	9393931	14.5258	5.9533	261	68121	17779581	16.1555	6.3907
212	44944	9528128	14.5602	5.9627	262	68644	17984728	16.1864	6.3988
213	45369	9663597	14.5945	5.9721	263	69169	18191447	16.2173	6.4070
214	45796	9800344	14.6287	5.9814	264	69696	18399744	16.2481	6.4151
215	46225	9938375	14.6629	5.9907	265	70225	18609625	16.2788	6.4232
216	46656	10077696	14.6969	6.0000	266	70756	18821096	16.3095	6.4312
217	47089	10218313	14.7309	6.0092	267	71289	19034163	16.3401	6.4393
218	47524	10360232	14.7648	6.0185	268	71824	19248832	16.3707	6.4473
219	47961	10503459	14.7986	6.0277	269	72361	19465109	16.4012	6.4553
220	48400	10648000	14.8324	6.0368	270	72900	19683000	16.4317	6.4633
221	48841	10793861	14.8661	6.0459	271	73441	19902511	16.4621	6.4713
222	49284	10941048	14.8997	6.0550	272	73984	20123648	16.4924	6.4792
223	49729	11089567	14.9332	6.0641	273	74529	20346417	16.5227	6.4872
224	50176	11239424	14.9666	6.0732	274	75076	20570824	16.5529	6.4951
225	50625	11390625	15.0000	6.0822	275	75625	20796875	16.5831	6.5030
226	51076	11543176	15.0333	6.0912	276	76176	21024576	16.6132	6.5108
227	51529	11697083	15.0665	6.1002	277	76729	21253933	16.6433	6.5187
228	51984	11852352	15.0997	6.1091	278	77284	21484952	16.6733	6.5265
229	52441	12008989	15.1327	6.1180	279	77841	21717639	16.7033	6.5343
230	52900	12167000	15.1658	6.1269	280	78400	21952000	16.7332	6.5421
231	53361	12326391	15.1987	6.1358	281	78961	22188041	16.7631	6.5499
232	53824	12487168	15.2315	6.1446	282	79524	22425768	16.7929	6.5577
233	54289	12649337	15.2643	6.1534	283	80089	22665187	16.8226	6.5654
234	54756	12812904	15.2971	6.1622	284	80656	22906304	16.8523	6.5731
235	55225	12977875	15.3297	6.1710	285	81225	23149125	16.8819	6.5808
236	55696	13144256	15.3623	6.1797	286	81796	23393656	16.9115	6.5885
237	56169	13312053	15.3948	6.1885	287	82369	23639903	16.9411	6.5962
238	56644	13481272	15.4272	6.1972	288	82944	23887872	16.9706	6.6039
239	57121	13651919	15.4596	6.2058	289	83521	24137569	17.0000	6.6115
240	57600	13824000	15.4919	6.2145	290	84100	24389000	17.0294	6.6191
241	58081	13997521	15.5242	6.2231	291	84681	24642171	17.0587	6.6267
242	58564	14172488	15.5563	6.2317	292	85264	24897088	17.0880	6.6343
243	59049	14348907	15.5885	6.2403	293	85849	25153757	17.1172	6.6419
244	59536	14526784	15.6205	6.2488	294	86436	25412184	17.1464	6.6494
245	60025	14706125	15.6525	6.2573	295	87025	25672375	17.1756	6.6569
246	60516	14886936	15.6844	6.2658	296	87616	25934336	17.2047	6.6644
247	61009	15069223	15.7162	6.2743	297	88209	26198073	17.2337	6.6719
248	61504	15252992	15.7480	6.2828	298	88804	26463592	17.2627	6.6794
249	62001	15438249	15.7797	6.2912	299	89401	26730899	17.2916	6.6869
250	62500	15625000	15.8114	6.2996	300	90000	27000000	17.3205	6.6943

SQUARES, CUBES, SQUARE AND CUBE ROOTS OF NUMBERS FROM
1 TO 1000

No.	Square	Cube	Sq. Root	Cube Root	No.	Square	Cube	Sq. Root	Cube Root
301	90601	27270901	17.3494	6.7018	351	123201	43243551	18.7350	7.0540
302	91204	27543608	17.3781	6.7092	352	123904	43614208	18.7617	7.0607
303	91809	27818127	17.4069	6.7166	353	124609	43986977	18.7883	7.0674
304	92416	28094464	17.4356	6.7240	354	125316	44361864	18.8149	7.0740
305	93025	28372625	17.4642	6.7313	355	126025	44738875	18.8414	7.0807
306	93636	28652616	17.4929	6.7387	356	126736	45118016	18.8680	7.0873
307	94249	28934443	17.5214	6.7460	357	127449	45499293	18.8944	7.0940
308	94864	29218112	17.5499	6.7533	358	128164	45882712	18.9209	7.1006
309	95481	29503629	17.5784	6.7606	359	128881	46268279	18.9473	7.1072
310	96100	29791000	17.6068	6.7679	360	129600	46656000	18.9737	7.1138
311	96721	30080231	17.6352	6.7752	361	130321	47045881	19.0000	7.1204
312	97344	30371328	17.6635	6.7824	362	131044	47437928	19.0263	7.1269
313	97969	30664297	17.6918	6.7897	363	131769	47832147	19.0526	7.1335
314	98596	30959144	17.7200	6.7969	364	132496	48228544	19.0788	7.1400
315	99225	31255875	17.7482	6.8041	365	133225	48627125	19.1050	7.1466
316	99856	31554496	17.7764	6.8113	366	133956	49027896	19.1311	7.1531
317	100489	31855013	17.8045	6.8185	367	134689	49430863	19.1572	7.1596
318	101124	32157432	17.8326	6.8256	368	135424	49836032	19.1833	7.1661
319	101761	32461759	17.8606	6.8328	369	136161	50243409	19.2094	7.1726
320	102400	32768000	17.8885	6.8399	370	136900	50653000	19.2354	7.1791
321	103041	33076161	17.9165	6.8470	371	137641	51064811	19.2614	7.1855
322	103684	33386248	17.9444	6.8541	372	138384	51478848	19.2873	7.1920
323	104329	33698267	17.9722	6.8612	373	139129	51895117	19.3132	7.1984
324	104976	34012224	18.0000	6.8683	374	139876	52313624	19.3391	7.2048
325	105625	34328125	18.0278	6.8753	375	140625	52734375	19.3649	7.2112
326	106276	34645976	18.0555	6.8824	376	141376	53157376	19.3907	7.2177
327	106929	34965783	18.0831	6.8894	377	142129	53582633	19.4165	7.2240
328	107584	35287552	18.1108	6.8964	378	142884	54010152	19.4422	7.2304
329	108241	35611289	18.1384	6.9034	379	143641	54439939	19.4679	7.2368
330	108900	35937000	18.1659	6.9104	380	144400	54872000	19.4936	7.2432
331	109561	36264691	18.1934	6.9174	381	145161	55306341	19.5192	7.2495
332	110224	36594368	18.2209	6.9244	382	145924	55742968	19.5448	7.2558
333	110889	36926037	18.2483	6.9313	383	146689	56181887	19.5704	7.2622
334	111556	37259704	18.2757	6.9382	384	147456	56623104	19.5959	7.2685
335	112225	37595375	18.3030	6.9451	385	148225	57066625	19.6214	7.2748
336	112896	37933056	18.3303	6.9521	386	148996	57512456	19.6469	7.2811
337	113569	38272753	18.3576	6.9589	387	149769	57960603	19.6723	7.2874
338	114244	38614472	18.3848	6.9658	388	150544	58411072	19.6977	7.2936
339	114921	38958219	18.4120	6.9727	389	151321	58863869	19.7231	7.2999
340	115600	39304000	18.4391	6.9795	390	152100	59319000	19.7484	7.3061
341	116281	39651821	18.4662	6.9864	391	152881	59776471	19.7737	7.3124
342	116964	40001688	18.4932	6.9932	392	153664	60236288	19.7990	7.3186
343	117649	40353607	18.5203	7.0000	393	154449	60698457	19.8242	7.3248
344	118336	40707584	18.5472	7.0068	394	155236	61162984	19.8494	7.3310
345	119025	41063625	18.5742	7.0136	395	156025	61629875	19.8746	7.3372
346	119716	41421736	18.6011	7.0203	396	156816	62099136	19.8997	7.3434
347	120409	41781923	18.6279	7.0271	397	157609	62570773	19.9249	7.3496
348	121104	42144192	18.6548	7.0338	398	158404	63044792	19.9499	7.3558
349	121801	42508549	18.6815	7.0406	399	159201	63521199	19.9750	7.3619
350	122500	42875000	18.7083	7.0473	400	160000	64000000	20.0000	7.3681

SQUARES, CUBES, SQUARE AND CUBE ROOTS OF NUMBERS FROM
1 TO 1000

No.	Square	Cube	Sq. Root	Cube Root	No.	Square	Cube	Sq. Root	Cube Root
401	160801	64481201	20.0250	7.3742	451	203401	91733851	21.2368	7.6688
402	161604	64964808	20.0499	7.3803	452	204304	92345408	21.2603	7.6744
403	162409	65450827	20.0749	7.3864	453	205209	92959677	21.2838	7.6800
404	163216	65939264	20.0998	7.3925	454	206116	93576664	21.3073	7.6857
405	164025	66430125	20.1246	7.3986	455	207025	94196375	21.3307	7.6914
406	164836	66923416	20.1494	7.4047	456	207936	94818816	21.3542	7.6970
407	165649	67419143	20.1742	7.4108	457	208849	95443993	21.3776	7.7026
408	166464	67917312	20.1990	7.4169	458	209764	96071912	21.4009	7.7082
409	167281	68417929	20.2237	7.4229	459	210681	96702579	21.4243	7.7138
410	168100	68921000	20.2485	7.4290	460	211600	97336000	21.4476	7.7194
411	168921	69426531	20.2731	7.4350	461	212521	97972181	21.4709	7.7250
412	169744	69934528	20.2978	7.4410	462	213444	98611128	21.4942	7.7306
413	170569	70444997	20.3224	7.4470	463	214369	99252847	21.5174	7.7362
414	171396	70957944	20.3470	7.4530	464	215296	99897344	21.5407	7.7418
415	172225	71473375	20.3715	7.4590	465	216225	100544625	21.5639	7.7473
416	173056	71991296	20.3961	7.4650	466	217156	101194696	21.5870	7.7529
417	173889	72511713	20.4206	7.4710	467	218089	101847563	21.6102	7.7584
418	174724	73034632	20.4450	7.4770	468	219024	102503232	21.6333	7.7639
419	175561	73560059	20.4695	7.4829	469	219961	103161709	21.6564	7.7695
420	176400	74088000	20.4939	7.4889	470	220900	103823000	21.6795	7.7750
421	177241	74618461	20.5183	7.4948	471	221841	104487111	21.7025	7.7805
422	178084	75151448	20.5426	7.5007	472	222784	105154048	21.7256	7.7860
423	178929	75686967	20.5670	7.5067	473	223729	105823817	21.7486	7.7915
424	179776	76225024	20.5913	7.5126	474	224676	106496424	21.7715	7.7970
425	180625	76765625	20.6155	7.5185	475	225625	107171875	21.7945	7.8025
426	181476	77308776	20.6398	7.5244	476	226576	107850176	21.8174	7.8079
427	182329	77854483	20.6640	7.5302	477	227529	108531333	21.8403	7.8134
428	183184	78402752	20.6882	7.5361	478	228484	109215352	21.8632	7.8188
429	184041	78953589	20.7123	7.5420	479	229441	109902239	21.8861	7.8243
430	184900	79507000	20.7364	7.5478	480	230400	110592000	21.9089	7.8297
431	185761	80062991	20.7605	7.5537	481	231361	111284641	21.9317	7.8352
432	186624	80621568	20.7846	7.5595	482	232324	111980168	21.9545	7.8406
433	187489	81182737	20.8087	7.5654	483	233289	112678587	21.9773	7.8460
434	188356	81746504	20.8327	7.5712	484	234256	113379904	22.0000	7.8514
435	189225	82312875	20.8567	7.5770	485	235225	114084125	22.0227	7.8568
436	190096	82881856	20.8806	7.5828	486	236196	114791256	22.0454	7.8622
437	190969	83453453	20.9045	7.5886	487	237169	115501303	22.0681	7.8676
438	191844	84027672	20.9284	7.5944	488	238144	116214272	22.0907	7.8730
439	192721	84604519	20.9523	7.6001	489	239121	116930169	22.1133	7.8784
440	193600	85184000	20.9762	7.6059	490	240100	117649000	22.1359	7.8837
441	194481	85766121	21.0000	7.6117	491	241081	118370771	22.1585	7.8891
442	195364	86350888	21.0238	7.6174	492	242064	119095488	22.1811	7.8944
443	196249	86938307	21.0476	7.6232	493	243049	119823157	22.2036	7.8998
444	197136	87528384	21.0713	7.6289	494	244036	120553784	22.2261	7.9051
445	198025	88121125	21.0950	7.6346	495	245025	121287375	22.2486	7.9105
446	198916	88716536	21.1187	7.6403	496	246016	122023936	22.2711	7.9158
447	199809	89314623	21.1424	7.6460	497	247009	122763473	22.2935	7.9211
448	200704	89915392	21.1660	7.6517	498	248004	123505992	22.3159	7.9264
449	201601	90518849	21.1896	7.6574	499	249001	124251499	22.3383	7.9317
450	202500	91125000	21.2132	7.6631	500	250000	125000000	22.3607	7.9370

SQUARES, CUBES, SQUARE AND CUBE ROOTS OF NUMBERS FROM
1 TO 1000

No.	Square	Cube	Sq. Root	Cube Root	No.	Square	Cube	Sq. Root	Cube Root
501	251001	125751501	22.3830	7.9423	551	303601	167284151	23.4734	8.1982
502	252004	126506008	22.4054	7.9476	552	304704	168196608	23.4947	8.2031
503	253009	127263527	22.4277	7.9528	553	305809	169112377	23.5160	8.2081
504	254016	128024064	22.4499	7.9581	554	306916	170031464	23.5372	8.2130
505	255025	128787625	22.4722	7.9634	555	308025	170953875	23.5584	8.2180
506	256036	129554216	22.4944	7.9686	556	309136	171879616	23.5797	8.2229
507	257049	130323843	22.5167	7.9739	557	310249	172808693	23.6008	8.2278
508	258064	131096512	22.5389	7.9791	558	311364	173741112	23.6220	8.2327
509	259081	131872229	22.5610	7.9843	559	312481	174676879	23.6432	8.2377
510	260100	132651000	22.5832	7.9896	560	313600	175616000	23.6643	8.2426
511	261121	133432831	22.6053	7.9948	561	314721	176558481	23.6854	8.2475
512	262144	134217728	22.6274	8.0000	562	315844	177504328	23.7065	8.2524
513	263169	135005697	22.6495	8.0052	563	316969	178453547	23.7276	8.2573
514	264196	135796744	22.6716	8.0104	564	318096	179406144	23.7487	8.2621
515	265225	136590875	22.6936	8.0156	565	319225	180362125	23.7697	8.2670
516	266256	137388096	22.7156	8.0208	566	320356	181321496	23.7908	8.2719
517	267289	138188413	22.7376	8.0260	567	321489	182284263	23.8118	8.2768
518	268324	138991832	22.7596	8.0311	568	322624	183250432	23.8328	8.2816
519	269361	139798359	22.7816	8.0363	569	323761	184220009	23.8537	8.2865
520	270400	140608000	22.8035	8.0415	570	324900	185192000	23.8747	8.2913
521	271441	141420761	22.8254	8.0466	571	326041	186169411	23.8956	8.2962
522	272484	142236648	22.8473	8.0517	572	327184	187149248	23.9165	8.3010
523	273529	143055667	22.8692	8.0569	573	328329	188132517	23.9374	8.3059
524	274576	143877824	22.8910	8.0620	574	329476	189119224	23.9583	8.3107
525	275625	144703125	22.9129	8.0671	575	330625	190109375	23.9792	8.3155
526	276676	145531576	22.9347	8.0723	576	331776	191102976	24.0000	8.3203
527	277729	146363183	22.9565	8.0774	577	332929	192100033	24.0208	8.3251
528	278784	147197952	22.9783	8.0825	578	334084	193100552	24.0416	8.3300
529	279841	148035889	23.0000	8.0876	579	335241	194104539	24.0624	8.3348
530	280900	148877000	23.0217	8.0927	580	336400	195112000	24.0832	8.3396
531	281961	149721291	23.0434	8.0978	581	337561	196122941	24.1039	8.3443
532	283024	150568768	23.0651	8.1028	582	338724	197137368	24.1247	8.3491
533	284089	151419437	23.0868	8.1079	583	339889	198155287	24.1454	8.3539
534	285156	152273304	23.1084	8.1130	584	341056	199176704	24.1661	8.3587
535	286225	153130375	23.1301	8.1180	585	342225	200201625	24.1868	8.3634
536	287296	153990656	23.1517	8.1231	586	343396	201230056	24.2074	8.3682
537	288369	154854153	23.1733	8.1281	587	344569	202262003	24.2281	8.3730
538	289444	155720872	23.1948	8.1332	588	345744	203297472	24.2487	8.3777
539	290521	156590819	23.2164	8.1382	589	346921	204336469	24.2693	8.3825
540	291600	157464000	23.2379	8.1433	590	348100	205379000	24.2899	8.3872
541	292681	158340421	23.2594	8.1483	591	349281	206425071	24.3105	8.3919
542	293764	159220088	23.2809	8.1533	592	350464	207474688	24.3311	8.3967
543	294849	160103007	23.3024	8.1583	593	351649	208527857	24.3516	8.4014
544	295936	160989184	23.3238	8.1633	594	352836	209584584	24.3721	8.4061
545	297025	161878625	23.3452	8.1683	595	354025	210644875	24.3926	8.4108
546	298116	162771336	23.3666	8.1733	596	355216	211708736	24.4131	8.4155
547	299209	163667323	23.3880	8.1783	597	356409	212776173	24.4336	8.4202
548	300304	164566592	23.4094	8.1833	598	357604	213847192	24.4540	8.4249
549	301401	165469149	23.4307	8.1882	599	358801	214921799	24.4715	8.4296
550	302500	166375000	23.4521	8.1932	600	360000	216000000	24.4949	8.4343

SQUARES, CUBES, SQUARE AND CUBE ROOTS OF NUMBERS FROM 1 TO 1000

No.	Square	Cube	Sq. Root	Cube Root	No.	Square	Cube	Sq. Root	Cube Root
601	361201	217081801	24.5153	8.4390	651	423801	275894451	25.5147	8.6668
602	362404	218167208	24.5357	8.4437	652	425104	277167808	25.5343	8.6713
603	363609	219256227	24.5561	8.4484	653	426409	278445077	25.5539	8.6757
604	364816	220348864	24.5764	8.4530	654	427716	279726264	25.5734	8.6801
605	366025	221445125	24.5967	8.4577	655	429025	281011375	25.5930	8.6845
606	367236	222545016	24.6171	8.4623	656	430336	282300416	25.6125	8.6890
607	368449	223648543	24.6374	8.4670	657	431649	283593393	25.6320	8.6934
608	369664	224755712	24.6577	8.4716	658	432964	284890312	25.6515	8.6978
609	370881	225866529	24.6779	8.4763	659	434281	286191179	25.6710	8.7022
610	372100	226981000	24.6982	8.4809	660	435600	287496000	25.6905	8.7066
611	373321	228099131	24.7184	8.4856	661	436921	288804781	25.7099	8.7110
612	374544	229220928	24.7386	8.4902	662	438244	290117528	25.7294	8.7154
613	375769	230346397	24.7588	8.4948	663	439569	291434247	25.7488	8.7198
614	376996	231475544	24.7790	8.4994	664	440896	292754944	25.7682	8.7241
615	378225	232608375	24.7992	8.5040	665	442225	294079625	25.7876	8.7285
616	379456	233744896	24.8193	8.5086	666	443556	295408296	25.8070	8.7329
617	380689	234885113	24.8395	8.5132	667	444889	296740963	25.8263	8.7373
618	381924	236029032	24.8596	8.5178	668	446224	298077632	25.8457	8.7416
619	383161	237176659	24.8797	8.5224	669	447561	299418309	25.8650	8.7460
620	384400	238328000	24.8998	8.5270	670	448900	300763000	25.8844	8.7503
621	385641	239483061	24.9199	8.5316	671	450241	302111711	25.9037	8.7547
622	386884	240641848	24.9399	8.5362	672	451584	303464448	25.9230	8.7590
623	388129	241804367	24.9600	8.5408	673	452929	304821217	25.9422	8.7634
624	389376	242970624	24.9800	8.5453	674	454276	306182024	25.9615	8.7677
625	390625	244140625	25.0000	8.5499	675	455625	307546875	25.9808	8.7721
626	391876	245314376	25.0200	8.5544	676	456976	308915776	26.0000	8.7764
627	393129	246491883	25.0400	8.5590	677	458329	310288733	26.0192	8.7807
628	394384	247673152	25.0599	8.5635	678	459684	311665752	26.0384	8.7850
629	395641	248858189	25.0799	8.5681	679	461041	313046839	26.0576	8.7893
630	396900	250047000	25.0998	8.5726	680	462400	314432000	26.0768	8.7937
631	398161	251239591	25.1197	8.5772	681	463761	315821241	26.0960	8.7980
632	399424	252435968	25.1396	8.5817	682	465124	317214568	26.1151	8.8023
633	400689	253636137	25.1595	8.5862	683	466489	318611987	26.1343	8.8066
634	401956	254840104	25.1794	8.5907	684	467856	320013504	26.1534	8.8109
635	403225	256047875	25.1992	8.5952	685	469225	321419125	26.1725	8.8152
636	404496	257259456	25.2190	8.5997	686	470596	322828856	26.1916	8.8194
637	405769	258474853	25.2389	8.6043	687	471969	324242703	26.2107	8.8237
638	407044	259694072	25.2587	8.6088	688	473344	325660672	26.2298	8.8280
639	408321	260917119	25.2784	8.6132	689	474721	327082769	26.2488	8.8323
640	409600	262144000	25.2982	8.6177	690	476100	328509000	26.2679	8.8366
641	410881	263374721	25.3180	8.6222	691	477481	329939371	26.2869	8.8408
642	412164	264609288	25.3377	8.6267	692	478864	331373888	26.3059	8.8451
643	413449	265847707	25.3574	8.6312	693	480249	332812557	26.3240	8.8493
644	414736	267089984	25.3772	8.6357	694	481636	334255384	26.3439	8.8536
645	416025	268336125	25.3969	8.6401	695	483025	335702375	26.3629	8.8578
646	417316	269586136	25.4165	8.6446	696	484416	337153536	26.3818	8.8621
647	418609	270840023	25.4362	8.6490	697	485809	338608873	26.4008	8.8663
648	419904	272097792	25.4558	8.6535	698	487204	340068392	26.4197	8.8706
649	421201	273359449	25.4755	8.6579	699	488601	341532099	26.4386	8.8748
650	422500	274625000	25.4951	8.6624	700	490000	343000000	26.4575	8.8790

SQUARES, CUBES, SQUARE AND CUBE ROOTS OF NUMBERS FROM
1 TO 1000

No.	Square	Cube	Sq. Root	Cube Root	No.	Square	Cube	Sq. Root	Cube Root
701	491401	344472101	26.4764	8.8833	751	564001	423564751	27.4044	9.0896
702	492804	345948408	26.4953	8.8875	752	565504	425259008	27.4226	9.0937
703	494209	347428927	26.5141	8.8917	753	567009	426957777	27.4408	9.0977
704	495616	348913664	26.5330	8.8959	754	568516	428661064	27.4591	9.1017
705	497025	350402625	26.5518	8.9001	755	570025	430368875	27.4773	9.1057
706	498436	351895816	26.5707	8.9043	756	571536	432081216	27.4955	9.1098
707	499849	353393243	26.5895	8.9085	757	573049	433798093	27.5136	9.1138
708	501264	354894912	26.6083	8.9127	758	574564	435519512	27.5318	9.1178
709	502681	356400829	26.6271	8.9169	759	576081	437245479	27.5500	9.1218
710	504100	357911000	26.6458	8.9211	760	577600	438976000	27.5681	9.1258
711	505521	359425431	26.6646	8.9253	761	579121	440711081	27.5862	9.1298
712	506944	360944128	26.6833	8.9295	762	580644	442450728	27.6043	9.1338
713	508369	362467097	26.7021	8.9337	763	582169	444194947	27.6225	9.1378
714	509796	363994344	26.7208	8.9378	764	583696	445943744	27.6405	9.1418
715	511225	365525875	26.7395	8.9420	765	585225	447697125	27.6586	9.1458
716	512656	367061696	26.7582	8.9462	766	586756	449455096	27.6767	9.1498
717	514089	368601813	26.7769	8.9503	767	588289	451217663	27.6948	9.1537
718	515524	370146232	26.7955	8.9545	768	589824	452984832	27.7128	9.1577
719	516961	371694959	26.8142	8.9587	769	591361	454756609	27.7308	9.1617
720	518400	373248000	26.8328	8.9628	770	592900	456533000	27.7489	9.1657
721	519841	374805361	26.8514	8.9670	771	594441	458314011	27.7669	9.1696
722	521284	376367048	26.8701	8.9711	772	595984	460099648	27.7849	9.1736
723	522729	377933067	26.8887	8.9752	773	597529	461889917	27.8029	9.1775
724	524176	379503424	26.9072	8.9794	774	599076	463684824	27.8209	9.1815
725	525625	381078125	26.9258	8.9835	775	600625	465484375	27.8388	9.1855
726	527076	382657176	26.9444	8.9876	776	602176	467288576	27.8568	9.1894
727	528529	384240583	26.9629	8.9918	777	603729	469097433	27.8747	9.1933
728	529984	385828352	26.9815	8.9959	778	605284	470910952	27.8927	9.1973
729	531441	387420489	27.0000	9.0000	779	606841	472729139	27.9106	9.2012
730	532900	389017000	27.0185	9.0041	780	608400	474552000	27.9285	9.2052
731	534361	390617891	27.0370	9.0082	781	609961	476379541	27.9464	9.2091
732	535824	392223168	27.0555	9.0123	782	611524	478211768	27.9643	9.2130
733	537289	393832837	27.0740	9.0164	783	613089	480048687	27.9821	9.2170
734	538756	395446904	27.0924	9.0205	784	614656	481890304	28.0000	9.2209
735	540225	397065375	27.1109	9.0246	785	616225	483736625	28.0179	9.2248
736	541696	398688256	27.1293	9.0287	786	617796	485587656	28.0357	9.2287
737	543169	400315553	27.1477	9.0328	787	619369	487443403	28.0535	9.2326
738	544644	401947272	27.1662	9.0369	788	620944	489303872	28.0713	9.2365
739	546121	403583419	27.1846	9.0410	789	622521	491169069	28.0891	9.2404
740	547600	405224000	27.2029	9.0450	790	624100	493039000	28.1069	9.2443
741	549801	406869021	27.2213	9.0491	791	625681	494913671	28.1247	9.2482
742	550564	408518488	27.2397	9.0532	792	627264	496793088	28.1425	9.2521
743	552049	410172407	27.2580	9.0572	793	628849	498677257	28.1603	9.2560
744	553536	411830784	27.2764	9.0613	794	630436	500566184	28.1780	9.2599
745	555025	413493625	27.2947	9.0654	795	632025	502459875	28.1957	9.2638
746	556516	415160936	27.3130	9.0694	796	633616	504358336	28.2135	9.2677
747	558009	416832723	27.3313	9.0735	797	635209	506261573	28.2312	9.2716
748	559504	418508992	27.3496	9.0775	798	636804	508169592	28.2489	9.2754
749	561001	420189749	27.3679	9.0816	799	638401	510082399	28.2666	9.2793
750	562500	421875000	27.3861	9.0856	800	640000	512000000	28.2843	9.2832

SQUARES, CUBES, SQUARE AND CUBE ROOTS OF NUMBERS FROM
1 TO 1000

No.	Square	Cube	Sq. Root	Cube Root	No.	Square	Cube	Sq. Root	Cube Root
801	641601	513922401	28.3019	9.2870	851	724201	616295051	29.1719	9.4764
802	643204	515849608	28.3196	9.2909	852	725904	618470208	29.1890	9.4801
803	644809	517781627	28.3373	9.2948	853	727609	620650477	29.2062	9.4838
804	646416	519718464	28.3549	9.2986	854	729316	622835864	29.2233	9.4875
805	648025	521660125	28.3725	9.3025	855	731025	625026375	29.2404	9.4912
806	649636	523606616	28.3901	9.3063	856	732736	627222016	29.2575	9.4949
807	651249	525557943	28.4077	9.3102	857	734449	629422793	29.2746	9.4986
808	652864	527514112	28.4253	9.3140	858	736164	631628712	29.2916	9.5023
809	654481	529475129	28.4429	9.3179	859	737881	633839779	29.3087	9.5060
810	656100	531441000	28.4605	9.3217	860	739600	636056000	29.3258	9.5097
811	657721	533411731	28.4781	9.3255	861	741321	638277381	29.3428	9.5134
812	659344	535387328	28.4956	9.3294	862	743044	640503928	29.3598	9.5171
813	660969	537367797	28.5132	9.3332	863	744769	642735647	29.3769	9.5207
814	662596	539353144	28.5307	9.3370	864	746496	644972544	29.3939	9.5244
815	664225	541343375	28.5482	9.3408	865	748225	647214625	29.4109	9.5281
816	665856	543338496	28.5657	9.3447	866	749956	649461896	29.4279	9.5317
817	667489	545338513	28.5832	9.3485	867	751689	651714363	29.4449	9.5354
818	669124	547343432	28.6007	9.3523	868	753424	653972032	29.4618	9.5391
819	670761	549353259	28.6182	9.3561	869	755161	656234909	29.4788	9.5427
820	672400	551368000	28.6356	9.3599	870	756900	658503000	29.4958	9.5464
821	674041	553387661	28.6531	9.3637	871	758641	660776311	29.5127	9.5501
822	675684	555412248	28.6705	9.3675	872	760384	663054848	29.5296	9.5537
823	677329	557441767	28.6880	9.3713	873	762129	665338617	29.5466	9.5574
824	678976	559476224	28.7054	9.3751	874	763876	667627624	29.5635	9.5610
825	680625	561515625	28.7228	9.3789	875	765625	669921875	29.5804	9.5647
826	682276	563559976	28.7402	9.3827	876	767376	672221376	29.5973	9.5683
827	683929	565609283	28.7576	9.3865	877	769129	674526133	29.6142	9.5719
828	685584	567663552	28.7750	9.3902	878	770884	676836152	29.6311	9.5756
829	687241	569722789	28.7924	9.3940	879	772641	679151439	29.6479	9.5792
830	688900	571787000	28.8097	9.3978	880	774400	681472000	29.6648	9.5828
831	690561	573856191	28.8271	9.4016	881	776161	683797841	29.6816	9.5865
832	692224	575930368	28.8444	9.4053	882	777924	686128968	29.6985	9.5901
833	693889	578009537	28.8617	9.4091	883	779689	688465387	29.7153	9.5937
834	695556	580093704	28.8791	9.4129	884	781456	690807104	29.7321	9.5973
835	697225	582182875	28.8964	9.4166	885	783225	693154125	29.7489	9.6010
836	698896	584277056	28.9137	9.4204	886	784996	695506456	29.7658	9.6046
837	700569	586376253	28.9310	9.4241	887	786769	697864103	29.7825	9.6082
838	702244	588480472	28.9482	9.4279	888	788544	700227072	29.7993	9.6118
839	703921	590589719	28.9655	9.4316	889	790321	702595369	29.8161	9.6154
840	705600	592704000	28.9828	9.4354	890	792100	704969000	29.8329	9.6190
841	707281	594823321	29.0000	9.4391	891	793881	707347971	29.8496	9.6226
842	708964	596947688	29.0172	9.4429	892	795664	709732288	29.8664	9.6262
843	710649	599077107	29.0345	9.4466	893	797449	712121957	29.8831	9.6298
844	712336	601211584	29.0517	9.4503	894	799236	714516984	29.8998	9.6334
845	714025	603351125	29.0689	9.4541	895	801025	716917375	29.9166	9.6370
846	715716	605495736	29.0861	9.4578	896	802816	719323136	29.9333	9.6406
847	717409	607645423	29.1033	9.4615	897	804609	721734273	29.9500	9.6442
848	719104	609800192	29.1204	9.4652	898	806404	724150792	29.9666	9.6477
849	720801	611960049	29.1376	9.4690	899	808201	726572699	29.9833	9.6513
850	722500	614125000	29.1548	9.4727	900	810000	729000000	30.0000	9.6549

SQUARES, CUBES, SQUARE AND CUBE ROOTS OF NUMBERS FROM
1 TO 1000

No.	Square	Cube	Sq. Root	Cube Root	No.	Square	Cube	Sq. Root	Cube Root
901	811801	731432701	30.0167	9.6585	951	904401	860085351	30.8383	9.8339
902	813604	733870808	30.0333	9.6620	952	906304	862801408	30.8545	9.8374
903	815409	736314327	30.0500	9.6656	953	908209	865523177	30.8707	9.8408
904	817216	738763264	30.0666	9.6692	954	910116	868250664	30.8869	9.8443
905	819025	741217625	30.0832	9.6727	955	912025	870983875	30.9031	9.8477
906	820836	743677416	30.0998	9.6763	956	913936	873722816	30.9192	9.8511
907	822649	746142643	30.1164	9.6799	957	915849	876467493	30.9354	9.8546
908	824464	748613312	30.1330	9.6834	958	917764	879217912	30.9516	9.8580
909	826281	751089429	30.1496	9.6870	959	919681	881974079	30.9677	9.8614
910	828100	753571000	30.1662	9.6905	960	921600	884736000	30.9839	9.8648
911	829921	756058031	30.1828	9.6941	961	923521	887503681	31.0000	9.8683
912	831744	758550528	30.1993	9.6976	962	925444	890277128	31.0161	9.8717
913	833569	761048497	30.2159	9.7012	963	927369	893056347	31.0322	9.8751
914	835396	763551944	30.2324	9.7047	964	929296	895841344	31.0483	9.8785
915	837225	766060875	30.2490	9.7082	965	931225	898632125	31.0644	9.8819
916	839056	768575296	30.2655	9.7118	966	933156	901428696	31.0805	9.8854
917	840889	771095213	30.2820	9.7153	967	935089	904231063	31.0966	9.8888
918	842724	773620632	30.2985	9.7188	968	937024	907039232	31.1127	9.8922
919	844561	776151559	30.3150	9.7224	969	938961	909853209	31.1288	9.8956
920	846400	778688000	30.3315	9.7259	970	940900	912673000	31.1448	9.8990
921	848241	781229961	30.3480	9.7294	971	942841	915498611	31.1609	9.9024
922	850084	783777448	30.3645	9.7329	972	944784	918330048	31.1769	9.9058
923	851929	786330467	30.3809	9.7364	973	946729	921167317	31.1929	9.9092
924	853776	788889024	30.3974	9.7400	974	948676	924010424	31.2090	9.9126
925	855625	791453125	30.4138	9.7435	975	950625	926859375	31.2250	9.9160
926	857476	794022776	30.4302	9.7470	976	952576	929714176	31.2410	9.9194
927	859329	796597983	30.4467	9.7505	977	954529	932574833	31.2570	9.9227
928	861184	799178752	30.4631	9.7540	978	956484	935441352	31.2730	9.9261
929	863041	801765089	30.4795	9.7575	979	958441	938313739	31.2890	9.9295
930	864900	804357000	30.4959	9.7610	980	960400	941192000	31.3050	9.9329
931	866761	806954491	30.5123	9.7645	981	962361	944076141	31.3209	9.9363
932	868624	809557568	30.5287	9.7680	982	964324	946966168	31.3369	9.9396
933	870489	812166237	30.5450	9.7715	983	966289	949862087	31.3528	9.9430
934	872356	814780504	30.5614	9.7750	984	968256	952763904	31.3688	9.9464
935	874225	817400375	30.5778	9.7785	985	970225	955671625	31.3847	9.9497
936	876096	820025856	30.5941	9.7819	986	972196	958585256	31.4006	9.9531
937	877969	822656953	30.6105	9.7854	987	974169	961504803	31.4166	9.9565
938	879844	825293672	30.6268	9.7889	988	976144	964430272	31.4325	9.9598
939	881721	827936019	30.6431	9.7924	989	978121	967361669	31.4484	9.9632
940	883600	830584000	30.6594	9.7959	990	980100	970299000	31.4643	9.9666
941	885481	833237621	30.6757	9.7993	991	982081	973242271	31.4802	9.9699
942	887364	835896888	30.6920	9.8028	992	984064	976191488	31.4960	9.9733
943	889249	838561807	30.7083	9.8063	993	986049	979146657	31.5119	9.9766
944	891136	841232384	30.7246	9.8097	994	988036	982107784	31.5278	9.9800
945	893025	843908625	30.7409	9.8132	995	990025	985074875	31.5436	9.9833
946	894916	846590536	30.7571	9.8167	996	992016	988047936	31.5595	9.9866
947	896809	849278123	30.7734	9.8201	997	994009	991026973	31.5753	9.9900
948	898704	851971392	30.7896	9.8236	998	996004	994011992	31.5911	9.9933
949	900601	854670349	30.8058	9.8270	999	998001	997002999	31.6070	9.9967
950	902500	857375000	30.8221	9.8305	1000	1000000	1000000000	31.6228	10.0000

AREAS AND CIRCUMFERENCES OF CIRCLES FROM 1 TO 100

Dia.	Area	Circum.	Dia.	Area	Circum.	Dia.	Area	Circum.
1/32	0.00077	0.098175	2	3.1416	6.28319	5	19.635	15.7080
3/64	0.00173	0.147262	2 1/16	3.3410	6.47953	5 1/16	20.129	15.9043
1/16	0.00307	0.196350	2 1/8	3.5466	6.67588	5 1/8	20.629	16.1007
3/32	0.00690	0.294524	2 3/16	3.7583	6.87223	5 3/16	21.135	16.2970
1/8	0.01227	0.392699	2 1/4	3.9761	7.06858	5 1/4	21.648	16.4934
5/32	0.01917	0.490874	2 5/16	4.2000	7.26493	5 5/16	22.166	16.6897
3/16	0.02761	0.589049	2 3/8	4.4301	7.46128	5 3/8	22.691	16.8861
7/32	0.03758	0.687223	2 7/16	4.6664	7.65763	5 7/16	23.221	17.0824
1/4	0.04909	0.785398	2 1/2	4.9087	7.85398	5 1/2	23.758	17.2788
9/32	0.06213	0.883573	2 9/16	5.1572	8.05033	5 9/16	24.301	17.4751
5/16	0.07670	0.981748	2 5/8	5.4119	8.24668	5 5/8	24.850	17.6715
11/32	0.09281	1.07992	2 11/16	5.6727	8.44303	5 11/16	25.406	17.8678
3/8	0.11045	1.17810	2 3/4	5.9396	8.63938	5 3/4	25.967	18.0642
13/32	0.12962	1.27627	2 13/16	6.2126	8.83573	5 13/16	26.535	18.2605
7/16	0.15033	1.37445	2 7/8	6.4918	9.03208	5 7/8	27.109	18.4569
15/32	0.17257	1.47262	2 15/16	6.7771	9.22843	5 15/16	27.688	18.6532
1/2	0.19635	1.57080	3	7.0686	9.42478	6	28.274	18.8496
17/32	0.22166	1.66897	3 1/16	7.3662	9.62113	6 1/8	29.465	19.2423
9/16	0.24850	1.76715	3 1/8	7.6699	9.81748	6 1/4	30.680	19.6350
19/32	0.27688	1.86532	3 3/16	7.9798	10.0138	6 3/8	31.919	20.0277
5/8	0.30680	1.96350	3 1/4	8.2958	10.2102	6 1/2	33.183	20.4204
21/32	0.33824	2.06167	3 5/16	8.6179	10.4065	6 5/8	34.472	20.8131
11/16	0.37122	2.15984	3 3/8	8.9462	10.6029	6 3/4	35.785	21.2058
23/32	0.40574	2.25802	3 7/16	9.2806	10.7992	6 7/8	37.122	21.5984
3/4	0.44179	2.35619	3 1/2	9.6211	10.9956	7	38.485	21.9911
25/32	0.47937	2.45437	3 9/16	9.9678	11.1919	7 1/8	39.871	22.3838
13/16	0.51849	2.55254	3 5/8	10.321	11.3883	7 1/4	41.282	22.7765
27/32	0.55914	2.65072	3 11/16	10.680	11.5846	7 3/8	42.718	23.1692
7/8	0.60132	2.74889	3 3/4	11.045	11.7810	7 1/2	44.179	23.5619
29/32	0.64504	2.84707	3 13/16	11.416	11.9773	7 5/8	45.664	23.9546
15/16	0.69029	2.94524	3 7/8	11.793	12.1737	7 3/4	47.173	24.3473
31/32	0.73708	3.04342	3 15/16	12.177	12.3700	7 7/8	48.707	24.7400
1	0.78540	3.14159	4	12.566	12.5664	8	50.265	25.1327
1 1/16	0.88664	3.33794	4 1/16	12.962	12.7627	8 1/8	51.849	25.5224
1 1/8	0.99402	3.53429	4 1/8	13.364	12.9591	8 1/4	53.456	25.9181
1 3/16	1.1075	3.73064	4 3/16	13.772	13.1554	8 3/8	55.088	26.3108
1 1/4	1.2272	3.92699	4 1/4	14.186	13.3518	8 1/2	56.745	26.7035
1 5/16	1.3530	4.12334	4 5/16	14.607	13.5481	8 5/8	58.426	27.0962
1 3/8	1.4849	4.31969	4 3/8	15.033	13.7445	8 3/4	60.132	27.4889
1 7/16	1.6230	4.51604	4 7/16	15.466	13.9408	8 7/8	61.862	27.8816
1 1/2	1.7671	4.71239	4 1/2	15.904	14.1372	9	63.617	28.2743
1 9/16	1.9175	4.90874	4 9/16	16.349	14.3335	9 1/8	65.397	28.6670
1 5/8	2.0739	5.10509	4 5/8	16.800	14.5299	9 1/4	67.201	29.0597
1 11/16	2.2365	5.30144	4 11/16	17.257	14.7262	9 3/8	69.029	29.4524
1 3/4	2.4053	5.49779	4 3/4	17.721	14.9226	9 1/2	70.882	29.8451
1 13/16	2.5802	5.69414	4 13/16	18.190	15.1189	9 5/8	72.760	30.2378
1 7/8	2.7612	5.89049	4 7/8	18.665	15.3153	9 3/4	74.662	30.6305
1 15/16	2.9483	6.08684	4 15/16	19.147	15.5116	9 7/8	76.589	31.0232

AREAS AND CIRCUMFERENCES OF CIRCLES FROM 1 TO 100

Dia.	Area	Circum.	Dia.	Area	Circum.	Dia.	Area	Circum.
10	78.540	31.4159	16	201.06	50.2655	22	380.13	69.1150
1/8	80.516	31.8086	1/8	204.22	50.6582	1/8	384.46	69.5077
1/4	82.516	32.2013	1/4	207.39	51.0509	1/4	388.82	69.9004
3/8	84.541	32.5940	3/8	210.60	51.4436	3/8	393.20	70.2931
1/2	86.590	32.9867	1/2	213.82	51.8363	1/2	397.61	70.6858
5/8	88.664	33.3794	5/8	217.08	52.2290	5/8	402.04	71.0785
3/4	90.763	33.7721	3/4	220.35	52.6217	3/4	406.49	71.4712
7/8	92.886	34.1648	7/8	223.65	53.0144	7/8	410.97	71.8639
11	95.033	34.5575	17	226.98	53.4071	23	415.48	72.2566
1/8	97.205	34.9502	1/8	230.33	53.7998	1/8	420.00	72.6493
1/4	99.402	35.3429	1/4	233.71	54.1925	1/4	424.56	73.0420
3/8	101.62	35.7356	3/8	237.10	54.5852	3/8	429.13	73.4347
1/2	103.87	36.1283	1/2	240.53	54.9779	1/2	433.74	73.8274
5/8	106.14	36.5210	5/8	243.98	55.3706	5/8	438.36	74.2201
3/4	108.43	36.9137	3/4	247.45	55.7633	3/4	443.01	74.6128
7/8	110.75	37.3064	7/8	250.95	56.1560	7/8	447.69	75.0055
12	113.10	37.6991	18	254.47	56.5487	24	452.39	75.3982
1/8	115.47	38.0918	1/8	258.02	56.9414	1/8	457.11	75.7909
1/4	117.86	38.4845	1/4	261.59	57.3341	1/4	461.86	76.1836
3/8	120.28	38.8772	3/8	265.18	57.7268	3/8	466.64	76.5765
1/2	122.72	39.2699	1/2	268.80	58.1195	1/2	471.44	76.9690
5/8	125.19	39.6626	5/8	272.45	58.5122	5/8	476.26	77.3617
3/4	127.68	40.0553	3/4	276.12	58.9049	3/4	481.11	77.7544
7/8	130.19	40.4480	7/8	279.81	59.2976	7/8	485.98	78.1471
13	132.73	40.8407	19	283.53	59.6903	25	490.87	78.5398
1/8	135.30	41.2334	1/8	287.27	60.0830	1/8	495.79	78.9325
1/4	137.89	41.6261	1/4	291.04	60.4757	1/4	500.74	79.3252
3/8	140.50	42.0188	3/8	294.83	60.8684	3/8	505.71	79.7179
1/2	143.14	42.4115	1/2	298.65	61.2611	1/2	510.71	80.1105
5/8	145.80	42.8042	5/8	302.49	61.6538	5/8	515.72	80.5033
3/4	148.49	43.1969	3/4	306.35	62.0465	3/4	520.77	80.8960
7/8	151.20	43.5896	7/8	310.24	62.4392	7/8	525.84	81.2887
14	153.94	43.9823	20	314.16	62.8319	26	530.93	81.6814
1/8	156.70	44.3750	1/8	318.10	63.2246	1/8	536.05	82.0741
1/4	159.48	44.7677	1/4	322.06	63.6173	1/4	541.19	82.4668
3/8	162.30	45.1604	3/8	326.05	64.0100	3/8	546.35	82.8595
1/2	165.13	45.5531	1/2	330.06	64.4026	1/2	551.55	83.2522
5/8	167.99	45.9458	5/8	334.10	64.7953	5/8	556.76	83.6449
3/4	170.87	46.3385	3/4	338.16	65.1880	3/4	562.00	84.0376
7/8	173.78	46.7312	7/8	342.25	65.5807	7/8	567.27	84.4303
15	176.71	47.1239	21	346.36	65.9734	27	572.56	84.8230
1/8	179.67	47.5166	1/8	350.50	66.3661	1/8	577.87	85.2157
1/4	182.65	47.9093	1/4	354.66	66.7588	1/4	583.21	85.6084
3/8	185.66	48.3020	3/8	358.84	67.1515	3/8	588.57	86.0011
1/2	188.69	48.6947	1/2	363.05	67.5442	1/2	593.96	86.3938
5/8	191.75	49.0874	5/8	367.28	67.9369	5/8	599.37	86.7865
3/4	194.83	49.4801	3/4	371.54	68.3296	3/4	604.81	87.1792
7/8	197.93	49.8728	7/8	375.83	68.7223	7/8	610.27	87.5719

AREAS AND CIRCUMFERENCES OF CIRCLES FROM 1 TO 100

Dia.	Area	Circum.	Dia.	Area	Circum.	Dia.	Area	Circum.
28	615.75	87.9646	34	907.92	106.814	40	1256.6	125.664
1/8	621.26	88.3573	1/8	914.61	107.207	1/8	1264.5	126.056
1/4	626.80	88.7500	1/4	921.32	107.600	1/4	1272.4	126.449
3/8	632.36	89.1427	3/8	928.06	107.992	3/8	1280.3	126.842
1/2	637.94	89.5354	1/2	934.82	108.385	1/2	1288.2	127.235
5/8	643.55	89.9281	5/8	941.61	108.788	5/8	1296.2	127.627
3/4	649.18	90.3208	3/4	948.42	109.170	3/4	1304.2	128.020
7/8	656.84	90.7135	7/8	955.25	109.563	7/8	1312.2	128.413
29	660.52	91.1062	35	962.11	109.956	41	1320.3	128.805
1/8	666.23	91.4989	1/8	969.00	110.348	1/8	1328.3	129.198
1/4	671.96	91.8916	1/4	975.91	110.741	1/4	1336.4	129.591
3/8	677.71	92.2843	3/8	982.84	111.134	3/8	1344.5	129.993
1/2	683.49	92.6770	1/2	989.80	111.527	1/2	1352.7	130.376
5/8	689.30	93.0697	5/8	996.78	111.919	5/8	1360.8	130.769
3/4	695.13	93.4624	3/4	1003.8	112.312	3/4	1369.0	131.161
7/8	700.98	93.8551	7/8	1010.8	112.705	7/8	1377.2	131.554
30	706.86	94.2478	36	1017.9	113.097	42	1385.4	131.947
1/8	712.76	94.6405	1/8	1025.0	113.490	1/8	1393.7	132.340
1/4	718.69	95.0332	1/4	1032.1	113.883	1/4	1402.0	132.732
3/8	724.64	95.4259	3/8	1039.2	114.275	3/8	1410.3	133.125
1/2	730.62	95.8186	1/2	1046.3	114.668	1/2	1418.6	133.518
5/8	736.62	96.2113	5/8	1053.5	115.061	5/8	1427.0	133.910
3/4	742.64	96.6040	3/4	1060.7	115.454	3/4	1435.4	134.303
7/8	748.69	96.9967	7/8	1068.0	115.846	7/8	1443.8	134.696
31	754.77	97.3894	37	1075.2	116.239	43	1452.2	135.088
1/8	760.87	97.7821	1/8	1082.5	116.632	1/8	1460.7	135.481
1/4	766.99	98.1748	1/4	1089.8	117.024	1/4	1469.1	135.874
3/8	773.14	98.5675	3/8	1097.1	117.417	3/8	1477.6	136.267
1/2	779.31	98.9602	1/2	1104.5	117.810	1/2	1486.2	136.659
5/8	785.51	99.3529	5/8	1111.8	118.202	5/8	1494.7	137.052
3/4	791.73	99.7456	3/4	1119.2	118.596	3/4	1503.3	137.445
7/8	797.98	100.138	7/8	1126.7	118.988	7/8	1511.9	137.837
32	804.25	100.531	38	1134.1	119.381	44	1520.5	138.230
1/8	810.54	100.924	1/8	1141.6	119.773	1/8	1529.2	138.623
1/4	816.86	101.316	1/4	1149.1	120.166	1/4	1537.9	139.015
3/8	823.21	101.709	3/8	1156.6	120.559	3/8	1546.6	139.408
1/2	829.58	102.102	1/2	1164.2	120.951	1/2	1555.3	139.801
5/8	835.97	102.494	5/8	1171.7	121.344	5/8	1564.0	140.194
3/4	842.39	102.887	3/4	1179.3	121.737	3/4	1572.8	140.586
7/8	848.83	103.280	7/8	1186.9	122.129	7/8	1581.6	140.979
33	855.30	103.673	39	1194.6	122.522	45	1590.4	141.372
1/8	861.79	104.065	1/8	1202.3	122.915	1/8	1599.3	141.764
1/4	868.31	104.458	1/4	1210.0	123.308	1/4	1608.2	142.157
3/8	874.85	104.851	3/8	1217.7	123.700	3/8	1617.0	142.550
1/2	881.41	105.243	1/2	1225.4	124.093	1/2	1626.0	142.942
5/8	888.00	105.636	5/8	1233.2	124.486	5/8	1634.9	143.335
3/4	894.62	106.029	3/4	1241.0	124.878	3/4	1643.9	143.728
7/8	901.26	106.421	7/8	1248.8	125.271	7/8	1652.9	144.121

AREAS AND CIRCUMFERENCES OF CIRCLES FROM 1 TO 100

Dia.	Area	Circum.	Dia.	Area	Circum.	Dia.	Area	Circum.
46	1661.9	144.513	52	2123.7	163.363	58	2642.1	182.212
1/8	1670.9	144.906	1/8	2133.9	163.756	1/8	2653.5	182.605
1/4	1680.0	145.299	1/4	2144.2	164.148	1/4	2664.9	182.998
3/8	1689.1	145.691	3/8	2154.5	164.541	3/8	2676.4	183.390
1/2	1698.2	146.084	1/2	2164.8	164.934	1/2	2687.8	183.783
5/8	1707.4	146.477	5/8	2175.1	165.326	5/8	2699.3	184.176
3/4	1716.5	146.869	3/4	2185.4	165.719	3/4	2710.9	184.569
7/8	1725.7	147.262	7/8	2195.8	166.112	7/8	2722.4	184.961
47	1734.9	147.655	53	2206.2	166.504	59	2734.0	185.354
1/8	1744.2	148.048	1/8	2216.6	166.897	1/8	2745.6	185.747
1/4	1753.5	148.440	1/4	2227.0	167.290	1/4	2757.2	186.139
3/8	1762.7	148.833	3/8	2237.5	167.683	3/8	2768.8	186.532
1/2	1772.1	149.226	1/2	2248.0	168.075	1/2	2780.5	186.925
5/8	1781.4	149.618	5/8	2258.5	168.468	5/8	2792.2	187.317
3/4	1790.8	150.011	3/4	2269.1	168.861	3/4	2803.9	187.710
7/8	1800.1	150.404	7/8	2279.6	169.253	7/8	2815.7	188.103
48	1809.6	150.796	54	2290.2	169.646	60	2827.4	188.496
1/8	1819.0	151.189	1/8	2300.8	170.039	1/8	2839.2	188.888
1/4	1828.5	151.582	1/4	2311.5	170.431	1/4	2851.0	189.281
3/8	1837 9	151.975	3/8	2322.1	170.824	3/8	2862.9	189.674
1/2	1847.5	152.367	1/2	2332.8	171.217	1/2	2874.8	190.066
5/8	1857.0	152.760	5/8	2343.5	171.609	5/8	2886.6	190.459
3/4	1866.5	153.153	3/4	2354.3	172.002	3/4	2898.6	190.852
7/8	1876.1	153.544	7/8	2365.0	172.395	7/8	2910.5	191.244
49	1885.7	153.938	55	2375.8	172.788	61	2922.5	191.637
1/8	1895.4	154.331	1/8	2386.6	173.180	1/8	2934.5	192.030
1/4	1905.0	154.723	1/4	2397.5	173.573	1/4	2946.5	192.423
3/8	1914.7	155.116	3/8	2408.3	173.966	3/8	2958.5	192.815
1/2	1924.2	155.509	1/2	2419.2	174.358	1/2	2970.6	193.208
5/8	1934.2	155.904	5/8	2430.1	174.751	5/8	2982.7	193.601
3/4	1943.9	156.294	3/4	2441.1	175.144	3/4	2994.8	193.993
7/8	1953.7	156.687	7/8	2452.0	175.536	7/8	3006.9	194.386
50	1963.5	157.080	56	2463.0	175.929	62	3019.1	194.779
1/8	1973.3	157.472	1/8	2474.0	176.322	1/8	3031.3	195.171
1/4	1983.2	157.865	1/4	2485.0	176.715	1/4	3043.5	195.564
3/8	1993.1	158.258	3/8	2496.1	177.107	3/8	3055.7	195.957
1/2	2003.0	158.650	1/2	2507.2	177.500	1/2	3068.0	196.350
5/8	2012.9	159.043	5/8	2518.3	177.893	5/8	3080.3	196.742
3/4	2022.8	159.436	3/4	2529.4	178.285	3/4	3092.6	197.135
7/8	2032.8	159.829	7/8	2540.6	178.678	7/8	3104.9	197.528
51	2042.8	160.221	57	2551.8	179.071	63	3117.2	197.920
1/8	2052.8	160.614	1/8	2563.0	179.463	1/8	3129.6	198.313
1/4	2062.9	161.007	1/4	2574.2	179.856	1/4	3142.0	198.706
3/8	2073.0	161.399	3/8	2585.4	180.249	3/8	3154.5	199.098
1/2	2083.1	161.792	1/2	2596.7	180.642	1/2	3166.9	199.491
5/8	2093.2	162.185	5/8	2608.0	181.034	5/8	3179.4	199.884
3/4	2103.3	162.577	3/4	2619.4	181.427	3/4	3191.9	200.277
7/8	2113.5	162.970	7/8	2630.7	181.820	7/8	3204.4	200.669

AREAS AND CIRCUMFERENCES OF CIRCLES FROM 1 TO 100

Dia.	Area	Circum.	Dia.	Area	Circum.	Dia.	Area	Circum.
64	3217.0	201.062	70	3848.5	219.911	76	4536.5	238.761
⅛	3229.6	201.455	⅛	3862.2	220.304	⅛	4551.4	239.154
¼	3242.2	201.847	¼	3876.0	220.697	¼	4566.4	239.546
⅜	3254.8	202.240	⅜	3889.8	221.090	⅜	4581.3	239.939
½	3267.5	202.633	½	3903.6	221.482	½	4596.3	240.332
⅝	3280.1	203.025	⅝	3917.5	221.875	⅝	4611.4	240.725
¾	3292.8	203.418	¾	3931.4	222.268	¾	4626.4	241.117
⅞	3305.6	203.811	⅞	3945.3	222.660	⅞	4641.5	241.510
65	3318.3	204.204	71	3959.2	223.053	77	4656.6	241.903
⅛	3331.1	204.596	⅛	3973.1	223.446	⅛	4671.8	242.295
¼	3343.9	204.989	¼	3987.1	223.838	¼	4686.9	242.688
⅜	3356.7	205.382	⅜	4001.1	224.231	⅜	4702.1	243.081
½	3369.6	205.774	½	4015.2	224.624	½	4717.3	243.473
⅝	3382.4	206.167	⅝	4029.2	225.017	⅝	4732.5	243.866
¾	3395.3	206.560	¾	4043.3	225.409	¾	4747.8	244.259
⅞	3408.2	206.952	⅞	4057.4	225.802	⅞	4763.1	244.652
66	3421.2	207.345	72	4071.5	226.195	78	4778.4	245.044
⅛	3434.3	207.738	⅛	4085.7	226.587	⅛	4793.7	245.437
¼	3447.2	208.131	¼	4099.8	226.930	¼	4809.0	245.830
⅜	3460.2	208.523	⅜	4114.0	227.373	⅜	4824.4	246.222
½	3473.2	208.916	½	4128.2	227.765	½	4839.8	246.615
⅝	3486.3	209.309	⅝	4142.5	228.158	⅝	4855.2	247.008
¾	3499.4	209.701	¾	4156.8	228.551	¾	4870.7	247.400
⅞	3512.5	210.094	⅞	4171.1	228.944	⅞	4886.2	247.793
67	3525.7	210.487	73	4185.4	229.336	79	4901.7	248.186
⅛	3538.8	210.879	⅛	4199.7	229.729	⅛	4917.2	248.579
¼	3552.0	211.272	¼	4214.1	230.122	¼	4932.7	248.971
⅜	3565.2	211.665	⅜	4228.5	230.514	⅜	4948.3	249.364
½	3578.5	212.058	½	4242.9	230.907	½	4963.9	249.757
⅝	3591.7	212.450	⅝	4257.4	231.300	⅝	4979.5	250.149
¾	3605.0	212.843	¾	4271.8	231.692	¾	4995.2	250.542
⅞	3618.3	213.236	⅞	4286.3	232.085	⅞	5010.9	250.935
68	3631.7	213.628	74	4300.8	232.478	80	5026.5	251.327
⅛	3645.0	214.021	⅛	4315.4	232.871	⅛	5042.3	251.720
¼	3658.4	214.414	¼	4329.9	233.263	¼	5058.0	252.113
⅜	3671.8	214.806	⅜	4344.5	233.656	⅜	5073.8	252.506
½	3685.3	215.199	½	4359.2	234.049	½	5089.6	252.898
⅝	3698.7	215.592	⅝	4373.8	234.441	⅝	5105.4	253.291
¾	3712.2	215.984	¾	4388.5	234.834	¾	5121.2	253.684
⅞	3725.7	216.337	⅞	4403.1	235.227	⅞	5137.1	254.076
69	3739.3	216.770	75	4417.9	235.619	81	5153.0	254.469
⅛	3752.8	217.163	⅛	4432.6	236.012	⅛	5168.9	254.862
¼	3766.4	217.555	¼	4447.4	236.405	¼	5184.9	255.254
⅜	3780.0	217.948	⅜	4462.2	236.798	⅜	5200.8	255.647
½	3793.7	218.341	½	4477.0	237.190	½	5216.8	256.040
⅝	3807.3	218.733	⅝	4491.8	237.583	⅝	5232.8	256.433
¾	3821.0	219.126	¾	4506.7	237.976	¾	5248.9	256.825
⅞	3834.7	219.519	⅞	4521.5	238.368	⅞	5264.9	257.218

AREAS AND CIRCUMFERENCES OF CIRCLES FROM 1 TO 100

Dia.	Area	Circum.	Dia.	Area	Circum.	Dia.	Area	Circum.
82	5281.0	257.611	88	6082.1	276.460	94	6939.8	295.310
1/8	5297.1	258.003	1/8	6099.4	276.853	1/8	6958.2	295.702
1/4	5313.3	258.396	1/4	6116.7	277.246	1/4	6976.7	296.095
3/8	5329.4	258.789	3/8	6134.1	277.638	3/8	6995.3	296.488
1/2	5345.6	259.181	1/2	6151.4	278.031	1/2	7013.8	296.881
5/8	5361.8	259.574	5/8	6168.8	278.424	5/8	7032.4	297.273
3/4	5378.1	259.967	3/4	6186.2	278.816	3/4	7051.0	297.666
7/8	5394.3	260.359	7/8	6203.7	279.209	7/8	7069.6	298.059
83	5410.6	260.752	89	6221.1	279.602	95	7088.2	298.451
1/8	5426.9	261.145	1/8	6238.6	279.994	1/8	7106.9	298.844
1/4	5443.3	261.538	1/4	6256.1	280.387	1/4	7125.6	299.237
3/8	5459.6	261.930	3/8	6273.7	280.780	3/8	7144.3	299.629
1/2	5476.0	262.323	1/2	6291.2	281.173	1/2	7163.0	300.022
5/8	5492.4	262.716	5/8	6308.8	281.565	5/8	7181.8	300.415
3/4	5508.8	263.103	3/4	6326.4	281.958	3/4	7200.6	300.807
7/8	5525.3	263.501	7/8	6344.1	282.351	7/8	7219.4	301.200
84	5541.8	263.894	90	6361.7	282.743	96	7238.2	301.593
1/8	5558.3	264.286	1/8	6379.4	283.136	1/8	7257.1	301.986
1/4	5574.8	264.679	1/4	6397.1	283.529	1/4	7276.0	302.378
3/8	5591.4	265.072	3/8	6414.9	283.921	3/8	7294.9	302.771
1/2	5607.9	265.465	1/2	6432.6	284.314	1/2	7313.8	303.164
5/8	5624.5	265.857	5/8	6450.4	284.707	5/8	7332.8	303.556
3/4	5641.2	266.250	3/4	6468.2	285.100	3/4	7351.8	303.949
7/8	5657.8	266.643	7/8	6486.0	285.492	7/8	7370.8	304.342
85	5674.5	267.035	91	6503.9	285.885	97	7389.8	304.734
1/8	5691.2	267.428	1/8	6521.8	286.278	1/8	7408.9	305.127
1/4	5707.9	267.821	1/4	6539.7	286.670	1/4	7428.0	305.520
3/8	5724.7	268.213	3/8	6557.6	287.063	3/8	7447.1	305.913
1/2	5741.5	268.606	1/2	6575.5	287.456	1/2	7466.2	306.305
5/8	5758.3	268.999	5/8	6593.5	287.848	5/8	7485.3	306.698
3/4	5775.1	269.392	3/4	6611.5	288.241	3/4	7504.5	307.091
7/8	5791.9	269.784	7/8	6629.6	288.634	7/8	7523.7	307.483
86	5808.8	270.177	92	6647.6	289.027	98	7543.0	307.876
1/8	5825.7	270.570	1/8	6665.7	289.419	1/8	7562.2	308.269
1/4	5842.6	270.962	1/4	6683.8	289.812	1/4	7581.5	308.661
3/8	5859.6	271.355	3/8	6701.9	290.205	3/8	7600.8	309.064
1/2	5876.5	271.748	1/2	6720.1	290.597	1/2	7620.1	309.447
5/8	5893.5	272.140	5/8	6738.2	290.990	5/8	7639.5	309.840
3/4	5910.6	272.533	3/4	6756.4	291.383	3/4	7658.9	310.232
7/8	5927.6	272.926	7/8	6774.7	291.775	7/8	7678.3	310.625
87	5944.7	273.319	93	6792.9	292.168	99	7697.7	311.018
1/8	5961.8	273.711	1/8	6811.2	292.561	1/8	7717.1	311.410
1/4	5978.9	274.104	1/4	6829.5	292.954	1/4	7736.6	311.803
3/8	5996.0	274.497	3/8	6847.8	293.346	3/8	7756.1	312.196
1/2	6013.2	274.889	1/2	6866.1	293.739	1/2	7775.6	312.588
5/8	6030.4	275.282	5/8	6884.5	294.132	5/8	7795.2	312.981
3/4	6047.6	275.675	3/4	6902.9	294.524	3/4	7814.8	313.374
7/8	6064.9	276.067	7/8	6921.3	294.917	7/8	7834.4	313.767

AREAS AND CIRCUMFERENCES OF CIRCLES FROM 100 TO 1000

Diam.	Area.	Circum.	Diam.	Area	Circum.	Diam.	Area	Circum.
100	7853.98	314.16	150	17671.46	471.24	200	31415.93	628.32
101	8011.85	317.30	151	17907.86	474.38	201	31730.87	631.46
102	8171.28	320.44	152	18145.84	477.52	202	32047.39	634.60
103	8332.29	323.58	153	18385.39	480.66	203	32365.47	637.74
104	8494.87	326.73	154	18626.50	483.81	204	32685.13	640.88
105	8659.01	329.87	155	18869.19	486.95	205	33006.36	644.03
106	8824.73	333.01	156	19113.45	490.09	206	33329.16	647.17
107	8992.02	336.15	157	19359.28	493.23	207	33653.53	650.31
108	9160.88	339.29	158	19606.68	496.37	208	33979.47	653.45
109	9331.32	342.43	159	19855.65	499.51	209	34306.98	656.59
110	9503.32	345.58	160	20106.19	502.65	210	34636.06	659.73
111	9676.89	348.72	161	20358.31	505.80	211	34966.71	662.88
112	9852.03	351.86	162	20611.99	508.94	212	35298.94	666.02
113	10028.75	355.00	163	20867.24	512.08	213	35632.73	669.16
114	10207.03	358.14	164	21124.07	515.22	214	35968.09	672.30
115	10386.89	361.28	165	21382.46	518.36	215	36305.03	675.44
116	10568.32	364.42	166	21642.43	521.50	216	36643.54	678.58
117	10751.32	367.57	167	21903.97	524.65	217	36983.61	681.73
118	10935.88	370.71	168	22167.08	527.79	218	37325.26	684.87
119	11122.02	373.85	169	22431.76	530.93	219	37668.48	688.01
120	11309.73	376.99	170	22698.01	534.07	220	38013.27	691.15
121	11499.01	380.13	171	22965.83	537.21	221	38359.63	694.29
122	11689.87	383.27	172	23235.22	540.35	222	38707.56	697.43
123	11882.29	386.42	173	23506.18	543.50	223	39057.07	700.58
124	12076.28	389.56	174	23778.71	546.64	224	39408.14	703.72
125	12271.85	392.70	175	24052.82	549.78	225	39760.78	706.86
126	12468.98	395.84	176	24328.49	552.92	226	40115.00	710.00
127	12667.69	398.98	177	24605.74	556.06	227	40470.78	713.14
128	12867.96	402.12	178	24884.56	559.20	228	40828.14	716.28
129	13069.81	405.27	179	25164.94	562.35	229	41187.07	719.42
130	13273.23	408.41	180	25446.90	565.49	230	41547.56	722.57
131	13478.22	411.55	181	25730.43	568.63	231	41909.63	725.71
132	13684.78	414.69	182	26015.53	571.77	232	42273.27	728.85
133	13892.91	417.83	183	26302.20	574.91	233	42638.48	731.99
134	14102.61	420.97	184	26590.44	578.05	234	43005.26	735.13
135	14313.88	424.12	185	26880.25	581.19	235	43373.61	738.27
136	14526.72	427.26	186	27171.63	584.34	236	43743.54	741.42
137	14741.14	430.40	187	27464.59	587.48	237	44115.03	744.56
138	14957.12	433.54	188	27759.11	590.62	238	44488.09	747.70
139	15174.68	436.68	189	28055.21	593.76	239	44862.73	750.84
140	15393.80	439.82	190	28352.87	596.90	240	45238.93	753.08
141	15614.50	442.96	191	28652.11	600.04	241	45616.71	757.12
142	15836.77	446.11	192	28952.92	603.19	242	45996.06	760.27
143	16060.61	449.25	193	29255.30	606.33	243	46376.98	763.41
144	16286.02	452.39	194	29559.25	609.47	244	46759.47	766.55
145	16513.00	455.53	195	29864.77	612.61	245	47143.52	769.69
146	16741.55	458.67	196	30171.86	615.75	246	47529.16	772.83
147	16971.67	461.81	197	30480.52	618.89	247	47916.36	775.97
148	17203.36	464.96	198	30790.75	622.04	248	48305.13	779.11
149	17436.62	468.10	199	31102.55	625.18	249	48695.47	782.26

AREAS AND CIRCUMFERENCES OF CIRCLES FROM 100 TO 1000

Diam.	Area	Circum.	Diam.	Area	Circum.	Diam.	Area	Circum.
250	49087.39	785.40	300	70685.83	942.48	350	96211.28	1099.56
251	49480.87	788.54	301	71157.86	945.62	351	96761.84	1102.70
252	49875.92	791.68	302	71631.45	948.76	352	97313.97	1105.84
253	50272.55	794.82	303	72106.62	951.90	353	97867.68	1108.98
254	50670.75	797.96	304	72583.36	955.04	354	98422.96	1112.12
255	51070.52	801.11	305	73061.66	958.19	355	98979.80	1115.27
256	51471.85	804.25	306	73541.54	961.33	356	99538.22	1118.41
257	51874.76	807.39	307	74022.09	964.47	357	100098.21	1121.55
258	52279.24	810.53	308	74506.01	967.61	358	100659.77	1124.69
259	52685.29	813.67	309	74990.60	970.75	359	101222.90	1127.83
260	53092.92	816.81	310	75476.76	973.89	360	101787.60	1130.97
261	53502.11	819.96	311	75964.50	977.04	361	102353.87	1134.11
262	53912.87	823.10	312	76453.80	980.18	362	102921.72	1137.26
263	54325.21	826.24	313	76944.67	983.32	363	103491.13	1140.40
264	54739.11	829.38	314	77437.12	986.46	364	104062.12	1143.54
265	55154.59	832.52	315	77931.13	989.60	365	104634.67	1146.68
266	55571.63	835.66	316	78426.72	992.74	366	105208.80	1149.82
267	55990.25	838.81	317	78923.88	995.88	367	105784.49	1152.96
268	56410.44	841.95	318	79422.60	999.03	368	106361.76	1156.11
269	56832.20	845.09	319	79922.90	1002.17	369	106940.60	1159.25
270	57255.53	848.23	320	80424.77	1005.31	370	107521.01	1162.39
271	57680.43	851.37	321	80928.21	1008.45	371	108102.99	1165.53
272	58106.90	854.51	322	81433.22	1011.59	372	108686.54	1168.67
273	58534.94	857.65	323	81939.80	1014.73	373	109271.66	1171.81
274	58964.55	860.80	324	82447.96	1017.88	374	109858.35	1174.96
275	59395.74	863.94	325	82957.68	1021.02	375	110446.62	1178.10
276	59828.49	867.08	326	83468.98	1024.16	376	111036.45	1181.24
277	60262.82	870.22	327	83981.84	1027.30	377	111627.86	1184.38
278	60698.71	873.36	328	84496.28	1030.44	378	112220.83	1187.52
279	61136.18	876.50	329	85012.28	1033.58	379	112815.38	1190.66
280	61575.22	879.65	330	85529.86	1036.73	380	113411.49	1193.81
281	62015.82	882.79	331	86049.01	1039.87	381	114009.18	1196.95
282	62458.00	885.93	332	86569.73	1043.01	382	114608.44	1200.09
283	62901.75	889.07	333	87092.02	1046.15	383	115209.27	1203.23
284	63347.07	892.21	334	87615.88	1049.29	384	115811.67	1206.37
285	63793.97	895.35	335	88141.31	1052.43	385	116415.64	1209.51
286	64242.43	898.50	336	88668.31	1055.58	386	117021.18	1212.65
287	64692.46	901.64	337	89196.88	1058.72	387	117628.30	1215.80
288	65144.07	904.78	338	89727.03	1061.86	388	118236.98	1218.94
289	65597.24	907.92	339	90258.74	1065.00	389	118847.24	1222.08
290	66051.99	911.06	340	90792.03	1068.14	390	119459.06	1225.22
291	66508.30	914.20	341	91326.88	1071.28	391	120072.46	1228.36
292	66966.10	917.35	342	91863.31	1074.42	392	120687.42	1231.50
293	67425.65	920.49	343	92401.31	1077.57	393	121303.96	1234.65
294	67886.68	923.63	344	92940.88	1080.71	394	121922.07	1237.79
295	68349.28	926.77	345	93482.02	1083.85	395	122541.75	1240.93
296	68813.45	929.91	346	94024.73	1086.99	396	123163.00	1244.07
297	69279.19	933.05	347	94569.01	1090.13	397	123785.82	1247.21
298	69746.50	936.19	348	95114.86	1093.27	398	124410.21	1250.35
299	70215.38	939.34	349	95662.28	1096.42	399	125036.17	1253.50

Areas and Circumferences of Circles from 100 to 1000

Diam.	Area	Circum.	Diam.	Area	Circum.	Diam.	Area	Circm.
400	125663.71	1256.64	450	159043.13	1413.72	500	196349.54	1570.80
401	126292.81	1259.78	451	159750.77	1416.86	501	197135.72	1573.94
402	126923.48	1262.92	452	160459.99	1420.00	502	197923.48	1577.08
403	127555.73	1266.06	453	161170.77	1423.14	503	198712.80	1580.22
404	128189.55	1269.20	454	161883.13	1426.28	504	199503.70	1583.36
405	128824.93	1272.35	455	162597.05	1429.42	505	200296.17	1586.50
406	129461.89	1275.49	456	163312.55	1432.57	506	201090.20	1589.65
407	130100.42	1278.63	457	164029.62	1435.71	507	201885.81	1592.79
408	130740.52	1281.77	458	164748.26	1438.85	508	202682.99	1595.93
409	131382.19	1284.91	459	165468.47	1441.99	509	203481.74	1599.07
410	132025.43	1288.05	460	166190.25	1445.13	510	204282.06	1602.21
411	132670.24	1291.19	461	166913.60	1448.27	511	205083.95	1605.35
412	133316.63	1294.34	462	167638.53	1451.42	512	205887.42	1608.50
413	133964.58	1297.48	463	168365.02	1454.56	513	206692.45	1611.64
414	134614.10	1300.62	464	169093.08	1457.70	514	207499.05	1614.78
415	135265.20	1303.76	465	169822.72	1460.84	515	208307.23	1617.92
416	135917.86	1306.90	466	170553.92	1463.98	516	209116.97	1621.06
417	136572.10	1310.04	467	171286.70	1467.12	517	209928.29	1624.20
418	137227.91	1313.19	468	172021.05	1470.27	518	210741.18	1627.34
419	137885.29	1316.33	469	172756.97	1473.41	519	211555.63	1630.49
420	138544.24	1319.47	470	173494.45	1476.55	520	212371.66	1633.63
421	139204.76	1322.61	471	174233.51	1479.69	521	213189.26	1636.77
422	139866.85	1325.75	472	174974.14	1482.83	522	214008.43	1639.91
423	140530.51	1328.89	473	175716.35	1485.97	523	214829.17	1643.05
424	141195.74	1332.04	474	176460.12	1489.11	524	215651.49	1646.19
425	141862.54	1335.18	475	177205.46	1492.26	525	216475.37	1649.34
426	142530.92	1338.32	476	177952.37	1495.40	526	217300.82	1652.48
427	143200.86	1341.46	477	178700.86	1498.54	527	218127.85	1655.62
428	143872.38	1344.60	478	179450.91	1501.68	528	218956.44	1658.76
429	144545.46	1347.74	479	180202.54	1504.82	529	219786.61	1661.90
430	145220.12	1350.88	480	180955.74	1507.96	530	220618.34	1665.04
431	145896.35	1354.03	481	181710.50	1511.11	531	221451.65	1668.19
432	146574.15	1357.17	482	182466.84	1514.25	532	222286.53	1671.33
433	147253.52	1360.31	483	183224.75	1517.39	533	223122.98	1674.47
434	147934.46	1363.45	484	183984.23	1520.53	534	223961.00	1677.61
435	148616.97	1366.59	485	184745.28	1523.67	535	224800.59	1680.75
436	149301.05	1369.73	486	185507.90	1526.81	536	225641.75	1883.89
437	149986.70	1372.88	487	186272.10	1529.96	537	226484.48	1687.04
438	150673.93	1376.02	488	187037.86	1533.10	538	227328.79	1690.18
439	151362.72	1379.16	489	187805.19	1536.24	539	228174.66	1693.32
440	152053.08	1382.30	490	188574.10	1539.38	540	229022.10	1696.46
441	152745.02	1385.44	491	189344.57	1542.52	541	229871.12	1699.60
442	153438.53	1388.58	492	190116.62	1545.66	542	230721.71	1702.74
443	154133.60	1391.73	493	190890.24	1548.81	543	231573.86	1705.88
444	154830.25	1394.87	494	191665.43	1551.95	544	232427.59	1709.03
445	155528.47	1398.01	495	192442.18	1555.09	545	233282.89	1712.17
446	156228.26	1401.15	496	193220.51	1558.23	546	234139.76	1715.31
447	156929.62	1404.29	497	194000.41	1561.37	547	234998.20	1718.45
448	157632.55	1407.43	498	194781.89	1564.51	548	235858.21	1721.59
449	158337.06	1410.58	499	195564.93	1567.65	549	236719.79	1724.73

AREAS AND CIRCUMFERENCES OF CIRCLES FROM 100 TO 1000

Diam.	Area	Circum.	Diam.	Area	Circum.	Diam.	Area	Circum.
550	237582.94	1727.88	600	282743.34	1884.96	650	331830.72	2042.04
551	238447.67	1731.02	601	283686.60	1888.10	651	332852.53	2045.18
552	239313.06	1734.16	602	284631.44	1891.24	652	333875.90	2048.32
553	240181.83	1737.30	603	285577.84	1894.38	653	334900.85	2051.46
554	241051.26	1740.44	604	286525.82	1897.52	654	335927.36	2054.60
555	241922.27	1743.58	605	287475.36	1900.66	655	336955.45	2057.74
556	242794.85	1746.73	606	288426.48	1903.81	656	337985.10	2060.88
557	243668.99	1749.87	607	289379.17	1906.95	657	339016.33	2064.03
558	244544.71	1753.01	608	290333.43	1910.09	658	340049.13	2067.17
559	245422.00	1756.15	609	291289.26	1913.23	659	341083.50	2070.31
560	246300.86	1759.29	610	292246.66	1916.37	660	342119.44	2073.45
561	247181.30	1762.43	611	293205.63	1919.51	661	343156.95	2076.59
562	248063.30	1765.58	612	294166.17	1922.65	662	344196.03	2079.73
563	248946.87	1768.72	613	295128.28	1925.80	663	345236.69	2082.88
564	249832.01	1771.86	614	296091.97	1928.94	664	346278.91	2086.02
565	250718.73	1775.00	615	297057.22	1932.08	665	347322.70	2089.16
566	251607.01	1778.14	616	298024.05	1935.22	666	348368.07	2092.30
567	252496.87	1781.28	617	298992.44	1938.36	667	349415.00	2095.44
568	253388.30	1784.42	618	299962.41	1941.50	668	350463.51	2098.58
569	254281.29	1787.57	619	300933.95	1944.65	669	351513.59	2101.73
570	255175.86	1790.71	620	301907.05	1947.79	670	352565.24	2104.87
571	256072.00	1793.85	621	302881.73	1950.93	671	353618.45	2108.01
572	256969.71	1796.99	622	303857.98	1954.07	672	354673.24	2111.15
573	257868.99	1800.13	623	304835.80	1957.21	673	355729.60	2114.29
574	258769.85	1803.27	624	305815.20	1960.35	674	356787.54	2117.43
575	259672.27	1806.42	625	306796.16	1963.50	675	357847.04	2120.58
576	260576.26	1809.56	626	307778.69	1966.64	676	358908.11	2123.72
577	261481.83	1812.70	627	308762.79	1969.78	677	359970.75	2126.86
578	262388.96	1815.84	628	309748.47	1972.92	678	361034.97	2130.00
579	263297.67	1818.98	629	310735.71	1976.06	679	362100.75	2133.14
580	264207.94	1822.12	630	311724.53	1979.20	680	363168.11	2136.28
581	265119.79	1825.27	631	312714.92	1982.35	681	364237.04	2139.42
582	266033.21	1828.41	632	313706.88	1985.49	682	365307.54	2142.57
583	266948.20	1831.55	633	314700.40	1988.63	683	366379.60	2145.71
584	267864.76	1834.69	634	315695.50	1991.77	684	367453.24	2148.85
585	268782.89	1837.83	635	316692.17	1994.91	685	368528.45	2151.99
586	269702.59	1840.97	636	317690.42	1998.05	686	369605.23	2155.13
587	270623.86	1844.11	637	318690.23	2001.19	687	370683.59	2158.27
588	271546.70	1847.26	638	319691.61	2004.34	688	371763.51	2161.42
589	272471.12	1850.40	639	320694.56	2007.48	689	372845.00	2164.56
590	273397.10	1853.54	640	321699.09	2010.62	690	373928.07	2167.70
591	274324.66	1856.68	641	322705.18	2013.76	691	375012.70	2170.84
592	275253.78	1859.82	642	323712.85	2016.90	692	376098.91	2173.98
593	276184.48	1862.96	643	324722.09	2020.04	693	377186.68	2177.12
594	277116.75	1866.11	644	325732.89	2023.19	694	378276.03	2180.27
595	278050.58	1869.25	645	326745.27	2026.33	695	379366.93	2183.41
596	278985.99	1872.39	646	327759.22	2029.47	696	380459.44	2186.55
597	279922.97	1875.53	647	328774.74	2032.61	697	381553.50	2189.69
598	280861.52	1878.67	648	329791.83	2035.75	698	382649.13	2192.83
599	281801.65	1881.81	649	330810.49	2038.89	699	383746.33	2195.97

Areas and Circumferences of Circles from 100 to 1000

Diam.	Area	Circum.	Diam.	Area	Circum.	Diam.	Area	Circum.
700	384845.10	2199.11	750	441786.47	2356.19	800	502654.82	2513.27
701	385945.44	2202.26	751	442965.35	2359.34	801	503912.25	2516.42
702	387047.36	2205.40	752	444145.80	2362.48	802	505171.24	2519.56
703	388150.84	2208.54	753	445327.83	2365.62	803	506431.80	2522.70
704	389255.90	2211.68	754	446511.42	2368.76	804	507693.94	2525.84
705	390362.52	2214.82	755	447696.59	2371.90	805	508957.64	2528.98
706	391470.72	2217.96	756	448883.32	2375.04	806	510222.92	2532.12
707	392580.49	2221.11	757	450071.63	2378.19	807	511489.77	2535.27
708	393691.82	2224.25	758	451261.51	2381.33	808	512758.19	2538.41
709	394804.73	2227.39	759	452452.96	2384.47	809	514028.18	2541.55
710	395919.21	2230.53	760	453645.98	2387.61	810	515299.74	2544.69
711	397035.26	2233.67	761	454840.57	2390.75	811	516572.87	2547.83
712	398152.89	2236.81	762	456036.73	2393.89	812	517847.57	2550.97
713	399272.08	2239.96	763	457234.46	2397.04	813	519123.84	2554.11
714	400392.84	2243.10	764	458433.77	2400.18	814	520401.68	2557.26
715	401515.18	2246.24	765	459634.64	2403.32	815	521681.10	2560.40
716	402639.08	2249.38	766	460837.08	2406.46	816	522962.08	2563.54
717	403764.56	2252.52	767	462041.10	2409.60	817	524244.63	2566.68
718	404891.60	2255.66	768	463246.69	2412.74	818	525528.76	2569.82
719	406020.22	2258.81	769	464453.84	2415.88	819	526814.46	2572.96
720	407150.41	2261.95	770	465662.57	2419.03	820	528101.73	2576.11
721	408282.17	2265.09	771	466872.87	2422.17	821	529390.56	2579.25
722	409415.50	2268.23	772	468084.74	2425.31	822	530680.97	2582.39
723	410550.40	2271.37	773	469298.18	2428.45	823	531972.95	2585.53
724	411686.87	2274.51	774	470513.19	2431.59	824	533266.50	2588.67
725	412824.91	2277.65	775	471729.77	2434.73	825	534561.62	2591.81
726	413964.52	2280.80	776	472947.92	2437.88	826	535858.32	2594.96
727	415105.71	2283.94	777	474167.65	2441.02	827	537156.58	2598.10
728	416248.46	2287.08	778	475388.94	2444.16	828	538456.41	2601.24
729	417392.79	2290.22	779	476611.81	2447.30	829	539757.82	2604.38
730	418538.68	2293.36	780	477836.24	2450.44	830	541060.79	2607.52
731	419686.15	2296.50	781	479062.25	2453.58	831	542365.34	2610.66
732	420835.19	2299.65	782	480289.83	2456.73	832	543671.46	2613.81
733	421985.79	2302.79	783	481518.97	2459.87	833	544979.15	2616.95
734	423137.97	2305.93	784	482749.69	2463.01	834	546288.40	2620.09
735	424291.72	2309.07	785	483981.98	2466.15	835	547599.23	2623.23
736	425447.04	2312.21	786	485215.84	2469.29	836	548911.63	2626.37
737	426603.94	2315.35	787	486451.28	2472.43	837	550225.61	2629.51
738	427762.40	2318.50	788	487688.28	2475.58	838	551541.15	2632.65
739	428922.43	2321.64	789	488926.85	2478.72	839	552858.26	2635.80
740	430084.03	2324.78	790	490166.99	2481.86	840	554176.94	2638.94
741	431247.21	2327.92	791	491408.71	2485.00	841	555497.20	2642.08
742	432411.95	2331.06	792	492651.99	2488.14	842	556819.02	2645.22
743	433578.27	2334.20	793	493896.85	2491.28	843	558142.42	2648.36
744	434746.16	2337.34	794	495143.28	2494.42	844	559467.39	2651.50
745	435915.62	2340.49	795	496391.27	2497.57	845	560793.92	2654.65
746	437086.64	2343.63	796	497640.84	2500.71	846	562122.03	2657.79
747	438259.24	2346.77	797	498891.98	2503.85	847	563451.71	2660.93
748	439433.41	2349.91	798	500144.69	2506.99	848	564782.96	2664.07
749	440609.16	2353.05	799	501398.97	2510.13	849	566115.78	2667.21

AREAS AND CIRCUMFERENCES OF CIRCLES FROM 100 TO 1000

Diam.	Area	Circum.	Diam.	Area	Circum.	Diam.	Area	Circum.
850	567450.17	2670.35	900	636172.51	2827.43	050	708821.84	2984.51
851	568786.14	2673.50	901	637587.01	2830.58	951	710314.88	2987.65
852	570123.67	2676.64	902	639003.09	2833.72	952	711809.50	2990.80
853	571462.77	2679.78	903	640420.73	2836.86	953	713305.68	2993.94
854	572803.45	2682.92	904	641839.95	2840.00	954	714803.43	2997.08
855	574145.69	2686.06	905	643260.73	2843.14	955	716302.76	3000.22
856	575489.51	2689.20	906	644683.09	2846.28	956	717803.66	3003.36
857	576834.90	2692.34	907	646107.01	2849.42	957	719306.12	3006.50
858	578181.85	2695.49	908	647532.51	2852.57	958	720810.16	3009.65
859	579530.38	2698.63	909	648959.58	2855.71	959	722315.77	3012.79
860	580880.48	2701.77	910	650388.22	2858.85	960	723822.95	3015.93
861	582232.15	2704.91	911	651818.43	2861.99	961	725331.70	3019.07
862	583585.39	2708.05	912	653250.21	2865.13	962	726842.02	3022.21
863	584940.20	2711.19	913	654683.56	2868.27	963	728353.91	3025.35
864	586296.59	2714.34	914	656118.48	2871.42	964	729867.37	3028.50
865	587654.54	2717.48	915	657554.98	2874.56	965	731382.40	3031.64
866	589014.07	2720.62	916	658993.04	2877.70	966	732899.01	3034.78
867	590375.16	2723.76	917	660432.68	2880.84	967	734417.18	3037.92
868	591737.83	2726.90	918	661873.88	2883.98	968	735936.93	3041.06
869	593102.06	2730.04	919	663316.66	2887.12	969	737458.24	3044.20
870	594467.87	2733.19	920	664761.01	2890.27	970	738981.13	3047.34
871	595835.25	2736.33	921	666206.92	2893.41	971	740505.59	3050.49
872	597204.20	2739.47	922	667654.41	2896.55	972	742031.62	3053.63
873	598574.72	2742.61	923	669103.47	2899.69	973	743559.22	3056.77
874	599946.81	2745.75	924	670554.10	2902.83	974	745088.39	3059.91
875	601320.47	2748.89	925	672006.30	2905.97	975	746619.13	3063.05
876	602695.70	2752.04	926	673460.08	2909.11	976	748151.44	3066.19
877	604072.50	2755.18	927	674915.42	2912.26	977	749685.32	3069.34
878	605450.88	2758.32	928	676372.33	2915.40	978	751220.78	3072.48
879	606830.82	2761.46	929	677830.82	2918.54	979	752757.80	3075.62
880	608212.34	2764.60	930	679290.87	2921.68	980	754296.40	3078.76
881	609595.42	2767.74	931	680752.50	2924.82	981	755836.59	3081.90
882	610980.08	2770.88	932	682215.69	2927.96	982	757378.30	3085.04
883	612366.31	2774.03	933	683680.46	2931.11	983	758921.61	3088.19
884	613754.11	2777.17	934	685146.80	2934.25	984	760466.48	3091.33
885	615143.48	2780.31	935	686614.71	2937.39	985	762012.93	3094.47
886	616534.42	2783.45	936	688084.19	2940.53	986	763560.95	3097.61
887	617926.93	2786.59	937	689555.24	2943.67	987	765110.54	3100.75
888	619321.01	2789.73	938	691027.86	2946.81	988	766661.70	3103.89
889	620716.66	2792.88	939	692502.05	2949.96	989	768214.44	3107.04
890	622113.89	2796.02	940	693977.82	2953.10	990	769768.74	3110.18
891	623512.68	2799.16	941	695455.15	2956.24	991	771324.61	3113.32
892	624913.04	2802.30	942	696934.06	2959.38	992	772882.06	3116.46
893	626314.98	2805.44	943	698414.53	2962.52	993	774441.07	3119.60
894	627718.49	2808.58	944	699896.58	2965.66	994	776001.66	3122.74
895	629123.56	2811.73	945	701380.19	2968.81	995	777563.82	3125.88
896	630530.21	2814.87	946	702865.38	2971.95	996	779127.54	3129.03
897	631938.43	2818.01	947	704352.14	2975.09	997	780692.84	3132.17
898	633348.22	2821.15	948	705840.47	2978.23	998	782259.71	3135.31
899	634759.58	2824.29	949	707330.37	2981.37	999	783828.15	3138.45
						1000	785398.16	3141.59

CIRCUMFERENCES AND DIAMETERS OF CIRCLES

Cir-cum.	Diameter	Cir-cum.	Diameter	Cir-cum.	Diameter	Cir-cum.	Diameter
1	.3183	51	16.2338	101	32.1493	151	48.0648
2	.6366	52	16.5521	102	32.4676	152	48.3831
3	.9549	53	16.8704	103	32.7859	153	48.7014
4	1.2732	54	17.1887	104	33.1042	154	49.0197
5	1.5915	55	17.5070	105	33.4225	155	49.3380
6	1.9099	56	17.8254	106	33.7408	156	49.6563
7	2.2282	57	18.1437	107	34.0592	157	49.9747
8	2.5465	58	18.4620	108	34.3775	158	50.2930
9	2.8648	59	18.7803	109	34.6958	159	50.6113
10	3.1831	60	19.0986	110	35.0141	160	50.9296
11	3.5014	61	19.4169	111	35.3324	161	51.2479
12	3.8197	62	19.7352	112	35.6507	162	51.5662
13	4.1380	63	20.0535	113	35.9690	163	51.8845
14	4.4563	64	20.3718	114	36.2873	164	52.2028
15	4.7746	65	20.6901	115	36.6056	165	52.5211
16	5.0930	66	21.0085	116	36.9239	166	52.8394
17	5.4113	67	21.3268	117	37.2423	167	53.1578
18	5.7296	68	21.6451	118	37.5606	168	53.4761
19	6.0479	69	21.9634	119	37.8789	169	53.7944
20	6.3662	70	22.2817	120	38.1972	170	54.1127
21	6.6845	71	22.6000	121	38.5155	171	54.4310
22	7.0028	72	22.9183	122	38.8338	172	54.7493
23	7.3211	73	23.2366	123	39.1521	173	55.0676
24	7.6394	74	23.5549	124	39.4704	174	55.3859
25	7.9577	75	23.8732	125	39.7887	175	55.7042
26	8.2761	76	24.1916	126	40.1070	176	56.0225
27	8.5944	77	24.5099	127	40.4254	177	56.3408
28	8.9127	78	24.8282	128	40.7437	178	56.6592
29	9.2310	79	25.1465	129	41.0620	179	56.9775
30	9.5493	80	25.4648	130	41.3803	180	57.2958
31	9.8676	81	25.7831	131	41.6986	181	57.6141
32	10.1859	82	26.1014	132	42.0169	182	57.9324
33	10.5042	83	26.4197	133	42.3352	183	58.2507
34	10.8225	84	26.7380	134	42.6535	184	58.5690
35	11.1408	85	27.0563	135	42.9718	185	58.8873
36	11.4592	86	27.3747	136	43.2901	186	59.2056
37	11.7775	87	27.6930	137	43.6085	187	59.5239
38	12.0958	88	28.0113	138	43.9268	188	59.8423
39	12.4141	89	28.3296	139	44.2451	189	60.1606
40	12.7324	90	28.6479	140	44.5634	190	60.4789
41	13.0507	91	28.9662	141	44.8817	191	60.7972
42	13.3690	92	29.2845	142	45.2000	192	61.1155
43	13.6873	93	29.6028	143	45.5183	193	61.4338
44	14.0056	94	29.9211	144	45.8366	194	61.7521
45	14.3239	95	30.2394	145	46.1549	195	62.0704
46	14.6423	96	30.5577	146	46.4732	196	62.3887
47	14.9606	97	30.8761	147	46.7916	197	62.7070
48	15.2789	98	31.1944	148	47.1099	198	63.0254
49	15.5972	99	31.5127	149	47.4282	199	63.3437
50	15.9155	100	31.8310	150	47.7465	200	63.6620

RECIPROCALS OF NUMBERS FROM 1 TO 1000

No.	Reciprocal	No.	Reciprocal	No.	Reciprocal	No.	Reciprocal
1	1.00000000	51	.01960784	101	.00990099	151	.00662252
2	.50000000	52	.01923077	102	.00980392	152	.00657895
3	.33333333	53	.01886792	103	.00970874	153	.00653595
4	.25000000	54	.01851852	104	.00961538	154	.00649351
5	.20000000	55	.01818182	105	.00952381	155	.00645161
6	.16666667	56	.01785714	106	.00943396	156	.00641026
7	.14285714	57	.01754386	107	.00934579	157	.00636943
8	.12500000	58	.01724138	108	.00925926	158	.00632911
9	.11111111	59	.01694915	109	.00917431	159	.00628931
10	.10000000	60	.01666667	110	.00909091	160	.00625000
11	.09090909	61	.01639344	111	.00900901	161	.00621118
12	.08333333	62	.01612903	112	.00892857	162	.00617284
13	.07692308	63	.01587302	113	.00884956	163	.00613497
14	.07142857	64	.01562500	114	.00877193	164	.00609756
15	.06666667	65	.01538461	115	.00869565	165	.00606061
16	.06250000	66	.01515151	116	.00862069	166	.00602410
17	.05882353	67	.01492537	117	.00854701	167	.00598802
18	.05555556	68	.01470588	118	.00847458	168	.00595238
19	.05263158	69	.01449275	119	.00840336	169	.00591716
20	.05000000	70	.01428571	120	.00833333	170	.00588235
21	.04761905	71	.01408451	121	.00826446	171	.00584795
22	.04545455	72	.01388889	122	.00819672	172	.00581395
23	.04347826	73	.01369863	123	.00813008	173	.00578035
24	.04166667	74	.01351351	124	.00806452	174	.00574713
25	.04000000	75	.01333333	125	.00800000	175	.00571429
26	.03846154	76	.01315789	126	.00793651	176	.00568182
27	.03703704	77	.01298701	127	.00787402	177	.00564972
28	.03571429	78	.01282051	128	.00781250	178	.00561798
29	.03448276	79	.01265823	129	.00775194	179	.00558659
30	.03333333	80	.01250000	130	.00769231	180	.00555556
31	.03225806	81	.01234568	131	.00763359	181	.00552486
32	.03125000	82	.01219512	132	.00757576	182	.00549451
33	.03030303	83	.01204819	133	.00751880	183	.00546448
34	.02941176	84	.01190476	134	.00746269	184	.00543478
35	.02857143	85	.01176471	135	.00740741	185	.00540540
36	.02777778	86	.01162791	136	.00735294	186	.00537634
37	.02702703	87	.01149425	137	.00729927	187	.00534759
38	.02631579	88	.01136364	138	.00724638	188	.00531914
39	.02564103	89	.01123595	139	.00719424	189	.00529100
40	.02500000	90	.01111111	140	.00714286	190	.00526316
41	.02439024	91	.01098901	141	.00709220	191	.00523560
42	.02380952	92	.01086956	142	.00704225	192	.00520833
43	.02325581	93	.01075269	143	.00699301	193	.00518135
44	.02272727	94	.01063830	144	.00694444	194	.00515464
45	.02222222	95	.01052632	145	.00689655	195	.00512820
46	.02173913	96	.01041667	146	.00684931	196	.00510204
47	.02127660	97	.01030928	147	.00680272	197	.00507614
48	.02083333	98	.01020408	148	.00675676	198	.00505051
49	.02040816	99	.01010101	149	.00671141	199	.00502513
50	.02000000	100	.01000000	150	.00666667	200	.00500000

RECIPROCALS OF NUMBERS FROM 1 TO 1000

No.	Reciprocal	No.	Reciprocal	No.	Reciprocal	No.	Reciprocal
201	.00497512	251	.00398406	301	.00332226	351	.00284900
202	.00495049	252	.00396825	302	.00331126	352	.00284091
203	.00492611	253	.00395257	303	.00330033	353	.00283286
204	.00490196	254	.00393701	304	.00328947	354	.00282486
205	.00487805	255	.00392157	305	.00327869	355	.00281690
206	.00485437	256	.00390625	306	.00326797	356	.00280899
207	.00483092	257	.00389105	307	.00325733	357	.00280112
208	.00480769	258	.00387597	308	.00324675	358	.00279330
209	.00478469	259	.00386100	309	.00323625	359	.00278551
210	.00476190	260	.00384615	310	.00322581	360	.00277778
211	.00473934	261	.00383142	311	.00321543	361	.00277008
212	.00471698	262	.03381679	312	.00320513	362	.00276243
213	.00469484	263	.00380228	313	.00319489	363	.00275482
214	.00467292	264	.00378788	314	.00318471	364	.00274725
215	.00465116	265	.00377358	315	.00317460	365	.00273073
216	.00462963	266	.00375940	316	.00316456	366	.00273224
217	.00460829	267	.00374532	317	.00315457	367	.00272480
218	.00458716	268	.00373134	318	.00314465	368	.00271739
219	.00456621	269	.00371747	319	.00313480	369	.00271003
220	.00454545	270	.00370370	320	.00312500	370	.00270270
221	.00452489	271	.00369004	321	.00311526	371	.00269542
222	.00450450	272	.00367647	322	.00310559	372	.00268817
223	.00448430	273	.00366300	323	.00309597	373	.00268096
224	.00446429	274	.00364963	324	.00308642	374	.00267380
225	.00444444	275	.00363636	325	.00307692	375	.00266667
226	.00442478	276	.00362319	326	.00306748	376	.00265957
227	.00440529	277	.00361011	327	.00305810	377	.00265252
228	.00438596	278	.00359712	328	.00304878	378	.00264550
229	.00436681	279	.00358423	329	.00303951	379	.00263852
230	.00434783	280	.00357143	330	.00303030	380	.00263158
231	.00432900	281	.00355872	331	.00302115	381	.00262467
232	.00431034	282	.00354610	332	.00301205	382	.00261780
233	.00429184	283	.00353357	333	.00300300	383	.00261097
234	.00427350	284	.00352113	334	.00299401	384	.00260417
235	.00425532	285	.00350877	335	.00298507	385	.00259740
236	.00423729	286	.00349650	336	.00297619	386	.00259067
237	.00421941	287	.00348432	337	.00296736	387	.00258398
238	.00420168	288	.00347222	338	.00295858	388	.00257732
239	.00418410	289	.00346021	339	.00294985	389	.00257069
240	.00416667	290	.00344828	340	.00294118	390	.00256410
241	.00414938	291	.00343643	341	.00293255	391	.00255754
242	.00413223	292	.00342466	342	.00292398	392	.00255102
243	.00411523	293	.00341297	343	.00291545	393	.00254453
244	.00409836	294	.00340136	344	.00290608	394	.00253807
245	.00408163	295	.00338983	345	.00289855	395	.00253165
246	.00406504	296	.00337838	346	.00289017	396	.00252525
247	.00404858	297	.00336700	347	.00288184	397	.00251889
248	.00403226	298	.00335570	348	.00287356	398	.00251256
249	.00401606	299	.00334448	349	.00286533	399	.00250627
250	.00400000	300	.00333333	350	.00285714	400	.00250000

RECIPROCALS OF NUMBERS FROM 100 TO 1000

No.	Reciprocal	No.	Reciprocal	No.	Reciprocal	No.	Reciprocal
401	.00249377	451	.00221729	501	.00199601	551	.00181488
402	.00248756	452	.00221239	502	.00199203	552	.00181159
403	.00248139	453	.00220751	503	.00198807	553	.00180832
404	.00247525	454	.00220264	504	.00198413	554	.00180505
405	.00246914	455	.00219780	505	.00198020	555	.00180180
406	.00246305	456	.00219298	506	.00197628	556	.00179856
407	.00245700	457	.00218818	507	.00197239	557	.00179533
408	.00245098	458	.00218341	508	.00196850	558	.00179211
409	.00244499	459	.00217865	509	.00196464	559	.00178891
410	.00243902	460	.00217391	510	.00196078	560	.00178571
411	.00243309	461	.00216920	511	.00195695	561	.00178253
412	.00242718	462	.00216450	512	.00195312	562	.00177936
413	.00242131	463	.00215983	513	.00194932	563	.00177620
414	.00241546	464	.00215517	514	.00194552	564	.00177305
415	.00240964	465	.00215054	515	.00194175	565	.00176991
416	.00240385	466	.00214592	516	.00193798	566	.00176678
417	.00239808	467	.00214133	517	.00193424	567	.00176367
418	.00239234	468	.00213675	518	.00193050	568	.00176056
419	.00238663	469	.00213220	519	.00192678	569	.00175747
420	.00238095	470	.00212766	520	.00192308	570	.00175439
421	.00237530	471	.00212314	521	.00191939	571	.00175131
422	.00236967	472	.00211864	522	.00191571	572	.00174825
423	.00236407	473	.00211416	523	.00191205	573	.00174520
424	.00235849	474	.00210970	524	.00190840	574	.00174216
425	.00235294	475	.00210526	525	.00190476	575	.00173913
426	.00234742	476	.00210084	526	.00190114	576	.00173611
427	.00234192	477	.00209644	527	.00189753	577	.00173310
428	.00233645	478	.00209205	528	.00189394	578	.00173010
429	.00233100	479	.00208768	529	.00189036	579	.00172712
430	.00232558	480	.00208333	530	.00188679	580	.00172414
431	.00232019	481	.00207900	531	.00188324	581	.00172117
432	.00231481	482	.00207469	532	.00187970	582	.00171821
433	.00230947	483	.00207039	533	.00187617	583	.00171527
434	.00230415	484	.00206612	534	.00187266	584	.00171233
435	.00229885	485	.00206186	535	.00186916	585	.00170940
436	.00229358	486	.00205761	536	.00186567	586	.00170648
437	.00228833	487	.00205339	537	.00186220	587	.00170358
438	.00228310	488	.00204918	538	.00185874	588	.00170068
439	.00227790	489	.00204499	538	.00185528	589	.00169779
440	.00227273	490	.00204082	540	.00185185	590	.00169491
441	.00226757	491	.00203666	541	.00184843	591	.00169205
442	.00226244	492	.00203252	542	.00184502	592	.00168919
443	.00225734	493	.00202840	543	.00184162	593	.00168634
444	.00225225	494	.00202429	544	.00183823	594	.00168350
445	.00224719	495	.00202020	545	.00183486	595	.00168067
446	.00224215	496	.00201613	546	.00183150	596	.00167785
447	.00223714	497	.00201207	547	.00182815	597	.00167504
448	.00223214	498	.00200803	548	.00182482	598	.00167224
449	.00222717	499	.00200401	549	.00182149	599	.00166945
450	.00222222	500	.00200000	550	.00181818	600	.00166667

RECIPROCALS OF NUMBERS FROM 1 TO 1000

No.	Reciprocal	No.	Reciprocal	No.	Reciprocal	No.	Reciprocal
601	.00166389	651	.00153610	701	.00142653	751	.00133156
602	.00166113	652	.00153374	702	.00142450	752	.00132979
603	.00165837	653	.00153140	703	.00142247	753	.00132802
604	.00165563	654	.00152905	704	.00142045	754	.00132626
605	.00165289	655	.00152672	705	.00141844	755	.00132450
606	.00165016	656	.00152439	706	.00141643	756	.00132275
607	.00164745	657	.00152207	707	.00141443	757	.00132100
608	.00164474	658	.00151975	708	.00141243	758	.00131926
609	.00164204	659	.00151745	709	.00141044	759	.00131752
610	.00163934	660	.00151515	710	.00140845	760	.00131579
611	.00163666	661	.00151286	711	.00140647	761	.00131406
612	.00163399	662	.00151057	712	.00140449	762	.00131234
613	.00163132	663	.00150830	713	.00140252	763	.00131062
614	.00162866	664	.00150602	714	.00140056	764	.00130890
615	.00162602	665	.00150376	715	.00139860	765	.00130719
616	.00162338	666	.00150150	716	.00139665	766	.00130548
617	.00162075	667	.00149925	717	.00139470	767	.00130378
618	.00161812	668	.00149701	718	.00139276	768	.00130208
619	.00161551	669	.00149477	719	.00139082	769	.00130039
620	.00161290	670	.00149254	720	.00138889	770	.00129870
621	.00161031	671	.00149031	721	.00138696	771	.00129702
622	.00160772	672	.00148809	722	.00138504	772	.00129534
623	.00160514	673	.00148588	723	.00138313	773	.00129366
624	.00160256	674	.00148368	724	.00138121	774	.00129199
625	.00160000	675	.00148148	725	.00137931	775	.00129032
626	.00159744	676	.00147929	726	.00137741	776	.00128866
627	.00159490	677	.00147710	727	.00137552	777	.00128700
628	.00159236	678	.00147493	728	.00137363	778	.00128535
629	.00158982	679	.00147275	729	.00137174	779	.00128370
630	.00158730	680	.00147059	730	.00136986	780	.00128205
631	.00158479	681	.00146843	731	.00136799	781	.00128041
632	.00158228	682	.00146628	732	.00136612	782	.00127877
633	.00157978	683	.00146413	733	.00136426	783	.00127714
634	.00157729	684	.00146199	734	.00136240	784	.00127551
635	.00157480	685	.00145985	735	.00136054	785	.00127388
636	.00157233	686	.00145773	736	.00135870	786	.00127226
637	.00156986	687	.00145560	737	.00135685	787	.00127065
638	.00156740	688	.00145349	738	.00135501	788	.00126904
639	.00156494	689	.00145137	739	.00135318	789	.00126743
640	.00156250	690	.00144927	740	.00135135	790	.00126582
641	.00156006	691	.00144718	741	.00134953	791	.00126422
642	.00155763	692	.00144509	742	.00134771	792	.00126263
643	.00155521	693	.00144300	743	.00134589	793	.00126103
644	.00155279	694	.00144092	744	.00134409	794	.00125945
645	.00155039	695	.00143885	745	.00134228	795	.00125786
646	.00154799	696	.00143678	746	.00134048	796	.00125628
647	.00154559	697	.00143472	747	.00133869	797	.00125470
648	.00154321	698	.00143266	748	.00133690	798	.00125313
649	.00154083	699	.00143061	749	.00133511	799	.00125156
650	.00153846	700	.00142857	750	.00133333	800	.00125000

RECIPROCALS OF NUMBERS FROM 1 TO 1000

No.	Reciprocal	No.	Reciprocal	No.	Reciprocal	No.	Reciprocal
801	.00124844	851	.00117509	901	.00110988	951	.00105152
802	.00124688	852	.00117371	902	.00110865	952	.00105042
803	.00124533	853	.00117233	903	.00110742	953	.00104932
804	.00124378	854	.00117096	904	.00110619	954	.00104822
805	.00124224	855	.00116959	905	.00110497	955	.00104712
806	.00124069	856	.00116822	906	.00110375	956	.00104602
807	.00123916	857	.00116686	907	.00110254	957	.00104493
808	.00123762	858	.00116550	908	.00110132	958	.00104384
809	.00123609	859	.00116414	909	.00110011	959	.00104275
810	.00123457	860	.00116279	910	.00109890	960	.00104167
811	.00123305	861	.00116144	911	.00109769	961	.00104058
812	.00123153	862	.00116009	912	.00109649	962	.00103950
813	.00123001	863	.00115875	913	.00109529	963	.00103842
814	.00122850	864	.00115741	914	.00109409	964	.00103734
815	.00122699	865	.00115607	915	.00109290	965	.00103627
816	.00122549	866	.00115473	916	.00109170	966	.00103520
817	.00122399	867	.00115340	917	.00109051	967	.00103413
818	.00122249	868	.00115207	918	.00108932	968	.00103306
819	.00122100	869	.00115075	919	.00108814	969	.00103199
820	.00121951	870	.00114942	920	.00108696	970	.00103093
821	.00121803	871	.00114811	921	.00108578	971	.00102987
822	.00121654	872	.00114679	922	.00108460	972	.00102881
823	.00121507	873	.00114547	923	.00108342	973	.00102775
824	.00121359	874	.00114416	924	.00108225	974	.00102669
825	.00121212	875	.00114286	925	.00108108	975	.00102564
826	.00121065	876	.00114155	926	.00107991	976	.00102459
827	.00120919	877	.00114025	927	.00107875	977	.00102354
828	.00120773	878	.00113895	928	.00107759	978	.00102250
829	.00120627	879	.00113766	929	.00107643	979	.00102145
830	.00120482	880	.00113636	930	.00107527	980	.00102041
831	.00120337	881	.00113507	931	.00107411	981	.00101937
832	.00120192	882	.00113379	932	.00107296	982	.00101833
833	.00120048	883	.00113250	933	.00107181	983	.00101729
834	.00119904	884	.00113122	934	.00107066	984	.00101626
835	.00119760	885	.00112994	935	.00106952	985	.00101523
836	.00119617	886	.00112867	936	.00106838	986	.00101420
837	.00119474	887	.00112740	937	.00106724	987	.00101317
838	.00119332	888	.00112613	938	.00106610	988	.00101215
839	.00119189	889	.00112486	939	.00106496	989	.00101112
840	.00119048	890	.00112360	940	.00106383	990	.00101010
841	.00118906	891	.00112233	941	.00106270	991	.00100908
842	.00118765	892	.00112108	942	.00106157	992	.00100806
843	.00118624	893	.00111982	943	.00106044	993	.00100705
844	.00118483	894	.00111857	944	.00105932	994	.00100604
845	.00118343	895	.00111732	945	.00105820	995	.00100502
846	.00118203	896	.00111607	946	.00105708	996	.00100402
847	.00118064	897	.00111483	947	.00105597	997	.00100301
848	.00117924	898	.00111359	948	.00105485	998	.00100200
849	.00117786	899	.00111235	949	.00105374	999	.00100100
850	.00117647	900	.00111111	950	.00105263	1000	.00100000

SHOP TRIGONOMETRY

THE laying out of angles is sometimes difficult by ordinary methods and a little knowledge of shop "trig" is very useful and much easier than as though we called it by its full name.

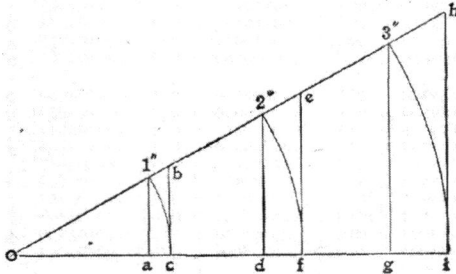

FIG. 1

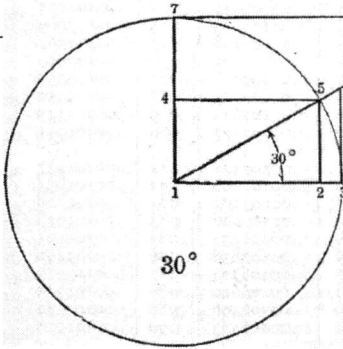

30°

FIG. 2

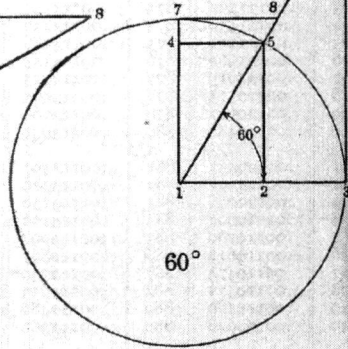

60°

FIG. 3

It is really a system of constants or multipliers based on the fact that there are always fixed proportions between the sides and angles of triangles and other figures. Fig. 1 shows a 30-degree angle with 1, 2 and 3-inch arcs, 1 c, 2 f, and 3 i. It will be found that every similar measurement is in exact proportion to the radius, thus 2 d is exactly twice the length of 1 a, and $h i$ is just three times $b c$. So, if we know the distance $a c$ for a 1-inch radius for any angle, a similar distance as $g i$ for the same angle, will be in exact proportion to the radius of the circle to one, which is the base. All these parts are named as shown in Figs. 2, 3, and 4.

The exact proportion of all·the various parts have been figured
for each part of a degree that is likely to be needed in ordinary work,
and these figures are given in the tables which follow; These numbers are simply multipliers or constants for a radius of one, and for
any other radius we multiply the numbers given by the radius we
are using. These tables form the most accurate means of calculating
many problems as will be shown. These constants can represent
one of anything, inches, feet, meters, or miles, and the answer will
be in the same unit. In tool work they are usually in inches, but
the relation is the same regardless of the unit.

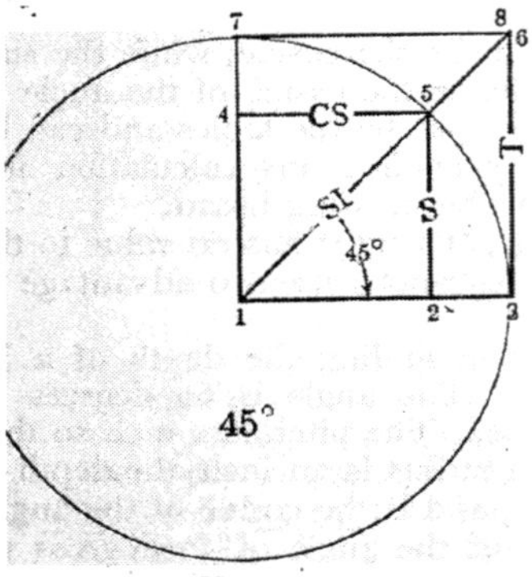

FIG. 4 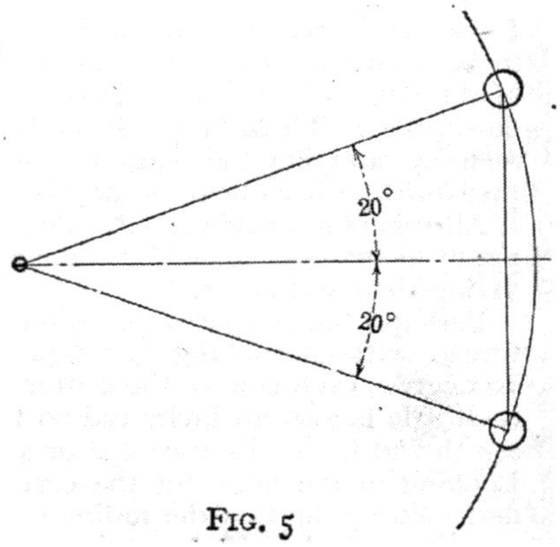   FIG. 5

ANGLE IS ALWAYS TAKEN EACH SIDE OF THE CENTER LINE AS
SHOWN

Lines 1–3 and 1–7 are called radius of the circle.
    1–2 is called cosine of the angle.
    4–5 is always the same as cosine of the angle.
    2–3 is called the versed sine of the angle.
    4–7 "   "   " co-versed sine of the angle.
    2–5 "   "   " sine   "   "   "
    3–6 "   "   " tangent   "   "   "
    7–8 "   "   " co-tangent   "   "   "
    1–6 "   "   " secant   "   "   "
    1–8 "   "   . " co-secant   "   "   "

The names always refer to the angle on one side of the center
line and not to the total or included angle. In dealing with a 60-
degree thread we divide this by a center line and call the angle 30
degrees in all our calculations. Everything is based on the radius
of a circle, and a 1 radius is used as this base. Perhaps the three
most important parts are the *sine*, the *tangent*, and the *secant*, these
being 2–5, 3–6, and 1–6 in all three of the figures. From this it
will be seen that the sine is half the chord or the distance from the
radius to the horizontal. The tangent 3–6 is the distance from

the horizontal radius to an extension of the radius at the angle given. The secant is the distance along the radius from the center to the tangent. From 2 to 3 is called the *versed sine*, and is the distance from the chord to the outer circle.

The angle considered in this work is always less than 90 degrees, and the angle between the angle used and 90 degrees, or the angle which is necessary to complete this to 90 degrees is called the complementary angle. In the first case the complementary angle is 60 degrees, in the second case 45 degrees, and in the third case 30 degrees. The *co-sine* is the distance 4–5, the *co-tangent* is 7–8, the *co-secant* is 1–8, and the *co-versed sine* is 4–7 in all three examples. In the 45-degree angle it will be seen that the various parts are alike in both angles, as the sine is the same as the cosine, while the sine of the angle of 30 degrees is the same as the cosine of the angle of 60 degrees. These facts will be borne out by the tables and can be seen by studying the diagrams or by making any calculation and then proving it as near as may be on the drawing board.

All this is interesting, but unless it is useful it has no value to the practical man, so we will see where it can be used to advantage in saving time and labor.

Perhaps the easiest application is in finding the depth of a V-thread without making any figures. The angle is 60 degrees or 30 degrees each side of the center line. The pitch is 1 inch so that each side is also an inch, and so the radius is an inch, the depth of the thread is the distance 1–2 or 4–5, and is the cosine of the angle. Looking in the table for the cosine of the angle of 30 degrees we find 0.86603, and as the radius is 1 this gives us the depth directly as 0.86603 inch. If the radius was 2 inches we would multiply by 2, or if it was ½ inch, divide by 2 and get the exact depth with almost no figuring. Suppose, on the other hand, that the thread was one inch deep and we want to find the length of one side, the angle remaining the same as before. In this case we have the depth which is the line 1–3, and we wish to find 1–6 which is the secant, so we look at the table again and find the secant of 30 degrees to be 1.1547 inches as the length of the side.

Suppose you have a square bar 2½ inches on each side, what is the distance across the corners? ·Looking at the second example we see that the side of the square bar is represented by line 1–3 and the corner distance by the secant 1–6 so we look for the secant of 45 degrees (because we know that half the 90 degree angle of a square bar must be 45 degrees) and find 1.4142 which would be the distance if the bar was one inch square, so we multiply 1.4142 by 2½ and get 3.5355 inches as the distance across the corners, and can know that this is closer than we can measure, and is not a guess by any means.

Reversing this we can find the side of a square that can be milled out of a round bar, such as the end of a reamer or tap. What square can we make on a 2-inch round reamer shank? The diameter of the bar is the radius as 1–5 and the angle 45 degrees as before, half the side of the square will be the sine 2–5, which the table shows to be 0.70711, and as this is half the chord which makes the flat across the bar, we multiply this by 2 and get 1.41422 inches as the distance across the flats for a reamer shank of this size.

Suppose we have a bar of $1\frac{1}{2} \times \frac{3}{4}$-inch steel and want to find the distance across the corners, and the angle it will make with the base. The $1\frac{1}{2}$-inch side is the radius, the diagonal is the secant, and the $\frac{3}{4}$-inch side is the tangent of the angle. Reducing these to a basis of one inch we have a bar 1 inch by $\frac{1}{2}$ inch and the $\frac{1}{2}$ inch is the tangent of the angle. Looking in the table we find this to be almost exactly the tangent of 26 degrees and 34 minutes. With this angle the secant or diagonal is 1.1180 for a radius of 1 inch and $1\frac{1}{2}$ times this gives 1.6770 as the distance across corners.

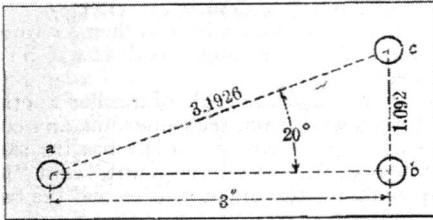

FIG. 6

A very practical use for this kind of calculation is in spacing bolt holes or otherwise dividing a circle into any number of equal parts. It is easy enough to get the length of each arc of the circumference by dividing 360 degrees by the number of divisions, but what we want is to find the chord or the distance from one point to the next in a straight line as a pair of dividers would step it off. First divide 360 by the number of divisions — say 9 — and get 40 degrees in each part. Fig. 5 shows this and we want the distance shown or the chord of the angle. This equals twice the sine of half the angle. Half the angle is 20 degrees and the sine for this is .342. Twice this or 0.684 is the chord of the 40-degree angle for every inch

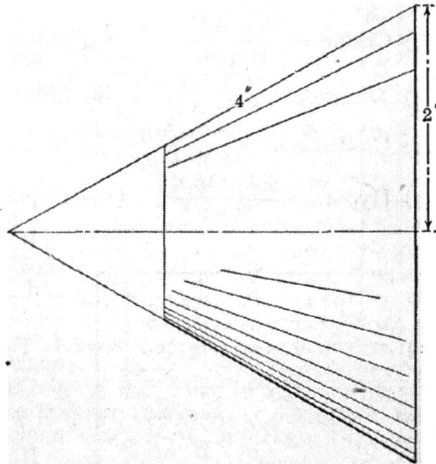

FIG. 7

of radius. If the circle is 14 inches in diameter the distance between the holes will be 7 times 0.684 or 4.788 inches. This is very quick and the most accurate method known.

Draftsmen often lay out jigs with the angles marked in degrees as in Fig. 6, overlooking the fact that the toolmaker has no convenient or accurate protractor for measuring the angle. Assume that a drawing shows three holes as a, b, and c, with b and c 20 degrees apart. The distance from a to b is 3 inches, what is the distance from b to c or from a to c?

As the known radius is from a to b, the distance $b\,c$ is the tangent of the angle and the tangent for a one-inch radius is .36397, so for a 3-inch radius it is $3 \times .36397 = 1.09191$ inches from b to c and at right angles to it.

But we need not depend on the accuracy of the square or of the way we use it, as we can find the distance from a to c just as easily and just as accurately as we did $b\,c$. This distance is the secant, and is 1.0642 for a one-inch radius. Multiplying this by $3 = 3.1926$ as the distance which can be accurately measured.

If the distance between a and c had been 3 inches, then $b\,c$ would have been the sine and $a\,b$ the cosine of the angle, both of which can be easily found from the tables.

It often happens that we want to find the angle of a roller or other piece of work as Fig. 7. Always work from the center line and continue the lines to complete the angle. Every triangle has the sides and they are called the "side opposite," "side adjacent," and "hypotenuse," the first being opposite the angle, the second the base line, and the third the slant line.

The following rules are very useful in this kind of work:

(1) Sine $= \dfrac{\text{Side Opp.}}{\text{Hypot.}}$

(2) Cosine $= \dfrac{\text{Side Adj.}}{\text{Hypot.}}$

(3) Tangent $= \dfrac{\text{Side Opp.}}{\text{Side Adj.}}$

(4) Co-Tangent $= \dfrac{\text{Side Adj.}}{\text{Side Opp.}}$

(5) Hypot. $= \dfrac{\text{Side Opp.}}{\text{Sine.}}$

(6) Side Opp. $=$ Hypot. $\times$ Sine.

(7) Side Adj. $=$ Hypot. $\times$ Cosine.

(8) Side Opp. $=$ Side Adj. $\times$ Tangent.

(9) Side Adj. $=$ Co-Tan. $\times$ Side Opp.

(10) Hypot. $= \dfrac{\text{Side Adj.}}{\text{Cosine.}}$

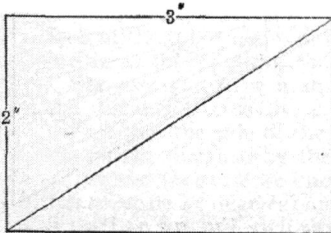

FIG. 8

If we have the dimensions shown in Fig. 7, the side opposite, and the hypotenuse, we use formula No. 1, and dividing 2 by 4 we get $\frac{1}{2}$ or .5 as the sine of the angle. The table shows this to be the sine of the angle of 30 degrees, consequently this is a 30-degree angle.

If we have the side opposite and the side adjacent we use formula No. 3, and find that $\frac{2}{4} = \frac{1}{2}$ or .5 = the tangent of the angle. The table shows this to be the tangent of 26 degrees and 34 minutes.

Should it happen that we only knew the hypotenuse and the angle we use formula No. 6 and multiply $4 \times .5 = 2$, the side opposite. In the same way we can find the side adjacent by using formula No. 7. The cosine of 30 degrees is .866 and $4 \times .866 = 3.464$ inches as the side adjacent.

Having a bar of steel 2 by 3 inches, Fig. 8, what is the distance across the corners? Either formulas 3 or 4 will answer for this.

Taking No. 4 we have 2 as the side opposite, 3 as the side adjacent. Dividing 3 by 2 gives 1.5. Looking under co-tangents for this we find 1.5003 after 33 degrees 41 minutes, which is nearly the correct angle. Then look for the secant of this and find 1.2017. Multiply this by 3 and get 3.6051 as the distance across the corners.

Complete tables of sines, tangents, secants, etc., will be on pages 529 to 563,

USING THE TABLE OF REGULAR POLYGONS

THE easiest way to lay out figures of this kind is to draw a circle and space it off, but it saves lots of time to know what spacing to use or how large a circle to draw to get a figure of the right size. Suppose we wish to lay out any regular figure, such as pentagon or five-sided figure, having sides 1½ inches long.

Number of Sides	Name of Figure	Diameter of Circle that will just enclose when side is 1	Diameter of circle that will just go inside when side is 1	Length of side where diameter of enclosure circle equals 1	Length of side where inside circle equals 1	Angle formed by lines drawn from center to corners	Angle formed by outer sides of figures	To find Area of Figure multiply side by itself and by number in this column
3	Triangle ..	1.1546	.5774	.866	1.732	120°	60°	.4330
4	Square	1.4142	1.	.7071	1.	90	90	1.
5	Pentagon ..	1.7012	1.3764	.5878	.7265	72	108	1.7204
6	Hexagon ..	2.	1.732	.5	.5774	60	120	2.5980
7	Heptagon .	2.3048	2.0766	.4338	.4815	51°-26′	128 4⁄7	3.6339
8	Octagon...	2.6132	2.4142	.3827	.4142	45	135	4.8284
9	Nonagon ..	2.9238	2.7474	.342	.3639	40	140	6.1818
10	Decagon ..	3.236	3.0776	.309	.3247	36	144	7.6942
11	Undecagon	3.5494	3.4056	.2817	.2936	32°-43	147 3⁄11	9.3656
12	Dodecagon	3.8638	3.732	.2588	.2679	30	150	11.1961

Table of Regular Polygons

Looking in the third column we find "Diameter of circle that will just enclose it," and opposite pentagon we find 1.7012 as the circle that will just enclose a pentagon having a side equal to 1. This may be 1 inch or 1 anything else, so as we are dealing in inches we call it inches. As the side of the pentagon is to be 1½ inches we multiply 1.7012 by 1½ and get 2.5518 as the diameter of circle to draw, and take half of this or the radius 1.2759 in the compass to draw the circle. Then with 1½ inches in the dividers we space round circle, and if the work has been carefully done it will just divide it into five equal parts. Connect these points by straight lines, and you have a pentagon with sides 1½ inches long.

If the pentagon is to go inside a circle of given diameter, say 2 inches, look under column 5 which gives "Length of side when diameter of enclosing circle equals 1," and find .5878. Multiply by 2 as this is for a 2-inch circle, and the side will be 2 × .5878 = 1.1756. Take this distance in the dividers and step around the 2-inch circle.

Assume that it is necessary to have a triangular end on a round shaft, how large must the shaft be to give a triangle 1.5 inches on a side?

Look in the table under column 3, and opposite triangle find 1.1546, meaning that where the side of a triangle is 1, the diameter of a circle that will just enclose it is 1.1546. As the side is 1.5, we have 1.5 × 1.1546 = 1.7318, the diameter of the shaft required. If the corners need not be sharp probably a shaft 1.625 would be ample.

Reversing this to find the size of a bearing that can be turned on a triangular bar of this size, look in column 4, which gives the largest circle that will go inside a triangle with a side equal to 1. This gives .5774. Multiply this by 1.5 = .8661.

A square taper reamer is to be used which must ream 1 inch at the small end and 1.5 at the back, what size must this be across the flats at both places?

Under column 5 find .7071 as the length of the side of a square when the diameter of the enclosing circle is 1, so this will be the side of the small end of the reamer and 1.5 × .7071 = 1.0606 is the side of the reamer at the large end.

FINDING THE RADIUS WITHOUT THE CENTER

It sometimes happens in measuring up a machine that we need to know the radius of curves when the center is not accessible. Three such cases are shown in Figs. 9, 10, and 11, the first two being a machine and the last a broken pulley. In Fig. 9 the rule is short enough to go in the curve while in Fig. 10 it has one end touching and the other across the sides. It makes no difference which is used so long as the distances are measured correctly, the short distance or *versed sine* being taken at the exact center of the chord and at right angles to it. It is easier figuring when the chord or the hight are even inches, so in measuring slip the rule until one or the other comes even; sometimes it is better to make the hight come 1 inch and let the chord go as it will, while at others the reverse may be true. The rule for finding the diameter is: Square half the chord, add to this the square of the hight, and divide the whole thing by the hight.

If the chord is 6 inches, as in Fig. 9, and the hight $1\frac{1}{2}$ inches we have

$$\frac{\frac{1}{2}\text{ chord}^2 + \text{hight}^2}{\text{hight}} = \frac{3^2 + 1\frac{1}{2}^2}{1\frac{1}{2}} = \frac{9 + 2\frac{1}{4}}{1\frac{1}{2}} = \frac{11\frac{1}{4}}{1\frac{1}{2}} = 7\frac{1}{2} \text{ inches.}$$

Or as shown in Fig. 10 the chord is 10 inches and the hight 1 inch, then the figures are

$$\frac{5^2 + 1^2}{1} = \frac{25 + 1}{1} = 26 \text{ inches.}$$

In Fig. 11 we have a piece of a broken pulley, and find the chord B to be 24 inches, and the hight A to be 2 inches. This becomes $\frac{12^2 + 2^2}{2} = \frac{144 + 4}{2} = \frac{148}{2} = 74$, so that the diameter of the pulley is 74 inches.

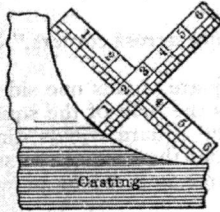

FIG. 9

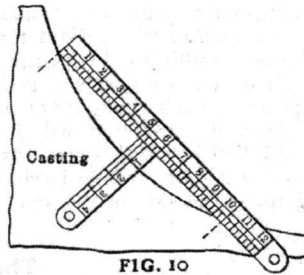

FIG. 10
Finding the Radius

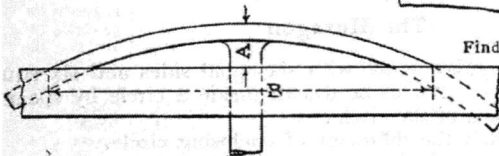

FIG. 11
Finding the Radius without Center

PROPERTIES OF REGULAR FIGURES

The Circle

A circle is a continuous curved line having every point at an equal distance from the center.

Its *perimeter* or circumference is always 3.14159265359 times the diameter, although 3.1416 is generally used and $3\frac{1}{7}$ is a very close approximation.

Area equals the diameter squared $\times$ .7854, or half the diameter squared $\times$ 3.1416, or half the diameter $\times$ half the circumference.

Diameter of a square having equal area = diameter of circle times .89 very nearly.

Triangle

Equilateral triangle is a regular figure having three equal sides and three equal angles of 60 degrees each.

The *side* equals .866 times the diameter of enclosing circle.

Distance from one side to opposite point equals the side times .866 or diameter of enclosing circle $\times$ .75 or inside circle $\times$ $1\frac{1}{2}$.

Diameter of enclosing circle equals the side times 1.1546 or $1\frac{1}{3}$ times distance from side to point or twice inside circle.

Diameter of inside circle equals side times .5774 or $\frac{1}{2}$ the enclosing circle.

The *area* equals one side multiplied by itself and by .433013.

Diameter of circle having equal area equals side of triangle times .73.

The Square

A square is a figure with four equal sides and four equal angles of 90 degrees.

Its *perimeter* or outside surface is four times the length of one side.

Area equals one side multiplied by the other which is the same as multiplying by itself or "squaring."

Diagonal or "long diameter," or "distance across corners," equals the side multiplied by 1.414.

Area of circle that will go inside the square equals one side multiplied by itself times .7854 or .7854 times the area of the square.

Area of circle that will just enclose the square equals diagonal multiplied by itself times .7854 or 1.27 times the area of the square.

Diameter of a circle having an equal area is 1.126 or practically 1⅛ times the side of the square.

The Hexagon

A hexagon is a regular figure with six equal sides and six equal angles of 120 degrees. It can be drawn inside a circle by spacing around with the radius of the circle.

The *side* equals half the diameter of enclosing circle.

The *long diameter* equals diameter of enclosing circle or twice the length of one side.

The *short diameter* equals the long diameter multiplied by .866 or 1.732 times one side.

The *area* equals one side multiplied by itself and by 2.5981.

The *area* of enclosing circle is one side multiplied by itself and by 3.1416.

The *area* of an inside circle is the short diameter multiplied by itself and by .7854.

Diameter of circle having equal area is practically .9 times long diameter.

The Octagon

An octagon is a regular figure with eight equal sides and eight equal angles of 135 degrees.

The *side* equals the long diameter multiplied by .382.

The *side* equals the short diameter multiplied by .415.

The *long diameter* equals diameter of enclosing circle or one side multiplied by 2.62.

The *short diameter* equals the long diameter multiplied by .93, or one side multiplied by 2.45.

The *area* equals one side multiplied by itself and by 4.8284.

The area of enclosing circle is 1.126 times area of octagon.

The area of inside circle is .972 times area of octagon.

The diameter of a circle having equal area is .953 times the long diameter of the octagon.

′	0° TAN.	0° CO-TAN.	1° TAN.	1° CO-TAN.	2° TAN.	2° CO-TAN.	3° TAN.	3° CO-TAN.	′
0	.00000	Infinite.	.01746	57.2900	.03492	28.6363	.05241	19.0811	60
1	.00029	3437.750	.01775	56.3506	.03521	28.3994	.05270	18.9755	59
2	.00058	1718.870	.01804	55.4415	.03550	28.1664	.05299	18.8711	58
3	.00087	1145.920	.01833	54.5613	.03579	27.9372	.05328	18.7678	57
4	.00116	859.436	.01862	53.7086	.03609	27.7117	.05357	18.6656	56
5	.00145	687.549	.01891	52.8821	.03638	27.4899	.05387	18.5645	55
6	.00175	572.957	.01920	52.0807	.03667	27.2715	.05416	18.4645	54
7	.00204	491.106	.01949	51.3032	.03696	27.0566	.05445	18.3655	53
8	.00233	429.718	.01978	50.5485	.03725	26.8450	.05474	18.2677	52
9	.00262	381.971	.02007	49.8157	.03754	26.6367	.05503	18.1708	51
10	.00291	343.774	.02036	49.1039	.03783	26.4316	.05533	18.0750	50
11	.00320	312.521	.02066	48.4121	.03812	26.2296	.05562	17.9802	49
12	.00349	286.478	.02095	47.7395	.03842	26.0307	.05591	17.8863	48
13	.00378	264.441	.02124	47.0853	.03871	25.8348	.05620	17.7934	47
14	.00407	245.552	.02153	46.4489	.03900	25.6418	.05649	17.7015	46
15	.00436	229.182	.02182	45.8294	.03929	25.4517	.05678	17.6106	45
16	.00465	214.858	.02211	45.2261	.03958	25.2644	.05708	17.5205	44
17	.00495	202.219	.02240	44.6386	.03987	25.0798	.05737	17.4314	43
18	.00524	190.984	.02269	44.0661	.04016	24.8978	.05766	17.3432	42
19	.00553	180.032	.02298	43.5081	.04046	24.7185	.05795	17.2558	41
20	.00582	171.885	.02328	42.9641	.04075	24.5418	.05824	17.1693	40
21	.00611	163.700	.02357	42.4335	.04104	24.3675	.05854	17.0837	39
22	.00640	156.259	.02386	41.9158	.04133	24.1957	.05883	16.9990	38
23	.00669	149.465	.02415	41.4106	.04162	24.0263	.05912	16.9150	37
24	.00698	143.237	.02444	40.9174	.04191	23.8593	.05941	16.8319	36
25	.00727	137.507	.02473	40.4358	.04220	23.6945	.05970	16.7496	35
26	.00756	132.219	.02502	39.9655	.04250	23.5321	.05999	16.6681	34
27	.00785	127.321	.02531	39.5059	.04279	23.3718	.06029	16.5874	33
28	.00814	122.774	.02560	39.0568	.04308	23.2137	.06058	16.5075	32
29	.00844	118.540	.02589	38.6177	.04337	23.0577	.06087	16.4283	31
30	.00873	114.589	.02619	38.1885	.04366	22.9038	.06116	16.3499	30
31	.00902	110.892	.02648	37.7686	.04395	22.7519	.06145	16.2722	29
32	.00931	107.426	.02677	37.3579	.04424	22.6020	.06175	16.1952	28
33	.00960	104.171	.02706	36.9560	.04454	22.4541	.06204	16.1190	27
34	.00989	101.107	.02735	36.5627	.04483	22.3081	.06233	16.0435	26
35	.01018	98.2179	.02764	36.1776	.04512	22.1640	.06262	15.9687	25
36	.01047	95.4895	.02793	35.8006	.04541	22.0217	.06291	15.8945	24
37	.01076	92.9085	.02822	35.4313	.04570	21.8813	.06321	15.8211	23
38	.01105	90.4633	.02851	35.0695	.04599	21.7426	.06350	15.7483	22
39	.01135	88.1436	.02881	34.7151	.04628	21.6056	.06379	15.6762	21
40	.01164	85.9398	.02910	34.3678	.04658	21.4704	.06408	15.6048	20
41	.01193	83.8435	.02939	34.0273	.04687	21.3369	.06437	15.5340	19
42	.01222	81.8470	.02968	33.6935	.04716	21.2049	.06467	15.4638	18
43	.01251	79.9434	.02997	33.3662	.04745	21.0747	.06496	15.3943	17
44	.01280	78.1263	.03026	33.0452	.04774	20.9460	.06525	15.3254	16
45	.01309	76.3900	.03055	32.7303	.04803	20.8188	.06554	15.2571	15
46	.01338	74.7292	.03084	32.4213	.04832	20.6932	.06584	15.1893	14
47	.01367	73.1390	.03114	32.1181	.04862	20.5691	.06613	15.1222	13
48	.01396	71.6151	.03143	31.8205	.04891	20.4465	.06642	15.0557	12
49	.01425	70.1533	.03172	31.5284	.04920	20.3253	.06671	14.9898	11
50	.01455	68.7501	.03201	31.2416	.04949	20.2056	.06700	14.9244	10
51	.01484	67.4019	.03230	30.9599	.04978	20.0872	.06730	14.8596	9
52	.01513	66.1055	.03259	30.6833	.05007	19.9702	.06759	14.7954	8
53	.01542	64.8580	.03288	30.4116	.05037	19.8546	.06788	14.7317	7
54	.01571	63.6567	.03317	30.1446	.05066	19.7403	.06817	14.6685	6
55	.01600	62.4992	.03346	29.8823	.05095	19.6273	.06847	14.6059	5
56	.01629	61.3829	.03376	29.6245	.05124	19.5156	.06876	14.5438	4
57	.01658	60.3058	.03405	29.3711	.05153	19.4051	.06905	14.4823	3
58	.01687	59.2659	.03434	29.1220	.05182	19.2959	.06934	14.4212	2
59	.01716	58.2612	.03463	28.8771	.05212	19.1879	.06963	14.3607	1
60	.01746	57.2900	.03492	28.6363	.05241	19.0811	.06993	14.3007	0
′	CO-TAN.	TAN.	CO-TAN.	TAN.	CO-TAN.	TAN.	CO-TAN.	TAN.	′
	89°		88°		87°		86°		

′	4° TAN.	CO-TAN.	5° TAN.	CO-TAN.	6° TAN.	CO-TAN.	7° TAN.	CO-TAN.	′
0	.06993	14.3007	.08749	11.4301	.10510	9.51436	.12278	8.14435	60
1	.07022	14.2411	.08778	11.3919	.10540	9.48781	.12308	8.12481	59
2	.07051	14.1821	.08807	11.3540	.10569	9.46141	.12338	8.10536	58
3	.07080	14.1235	.08837	11.3163	.10599	9.43515	.12367	8.08600	57
4	.07110	14.0655	.08866	11.2789	.10628	9.40904	.12397	8.06674	56
5	.07139	14.0079	.08895	11.2417	.10657	9.38307	.12426	8.04756	55
6	.07168	13.9507	.08925	11.2048	.10687	9.35724	.12456	8.02848	54
7	.07197	13.8940	.08954	11.1681	.10716	9.33154	.12485	8.00948	53
8	.07227	13.8378	.08983	11.1316	.10746	9.30599	.12515	7.99058	52
9	.07256	13.7821	.09013	11.0954	.10775	9.28058	.12544	7.97176	51
10	.07285	13.7267	.09042	11.0594	.10805	9.25530	.12574	7.95302	50
11	.07314	13.6719	.09071	11.0237	.10834	9.23016	.12603	7.93438	49
12	.07344	13.6174	.09101	10.9882	.10863	9.20516	.12633	7.91582	48
13	.07373	13.5634	.09130	10.9529	.10893	9.18028	.12662	7.89734	47
14	.07402	13.5098	.09159	10.9178	.10922	9.15554	.12692	7.87895	46
15	.07431	13.4566	.09189	10.8829	.10952	9.13093	.12722	7.86064	45
16	.07461	13.4039	.09218	10.8483	.10981	9.10646	.12751	7.84242	44
17	.07490	13.3515	.09247	10.8139	.11011	9.08211	.12781	7.82428	43
18	.07519	13.2996	.09277	10.7797	.11040	9.05789	.12810	7.80622	42
19	.07548	13.2480	.09306	10.7457	.11070	9.03379	.12840	7.78825	41
20	.07578	13.1969	.09335	10.7119	.11099	9.00983	.12869	7.77035	40
21	.07607	13.1461	.09365	10.6783	.11128	8.98598	.12899	7.75254	39
22	.07636	13.0958	.09394	10.6450	.11158	8.96227	.12929	7.73480	38
23	.07665	13.0458	.09423	10.6118	.11187	8.93867	.12958	7.71715	37
24	.07695	12.9962	.09453	10.5789	.11217	8.91520	.12988	7.69957	36
25	.07724	12.9469	.09482	10.5462	.11246	8.89185	.13017	7.68208	35
26	.07753	12.8981	.09511	10.5136	.11276	8.86862	.13047	7.66466	34
27	.07782	12.8496	.09541	10.4813	.11305	8.84551	.13076	7.64732	33
28	.07812	12.8014	.09570	10.4491	.11335	8.82252	.13106	7.63005	32
29	.07841	12.7536	.09600	10.4172	.11364	8.79964	.13136	7.61287	31
30	.07870	12.7062	.09629	10.3854	.11394	8.77689	.13165	7.59575	30
31	.07899	12.6591	.09658	10.3538	.11423	8.75425	.13195	7.57872	29
32	.07929	12.6124	.09688	10.3224	.11452	8.73172	.13224	7.56176	28
33	.07958	12.5660	.09717	10.2913	.11482	8.70931	.13254	7.54487	27
34	.07987	12.5199	.09746	10.2602	.11511	8.68701	.13284	7.52806	26
35	.08017	12.4742	.09776	10.2294	.11541	8.66482	.13313	7.51132	25
36	.08046	12.4288	.09805	10.1988	.11570	8.64275	.13343	7.49465	24
37	.08075	12.3838	.09834	10.1683	.11600	8.62078	.13372	7.47806	23
38	.08104	12.3390	.09864	10.1381	.11629	8.59893	.13402	7.46154	22
39	.08134	12.2946	.09893	10.1080	.11659	8.57718	.13432	7.44509	21
40	.08163	12.2505	.09923	10.0780	.11688	8.55555	.13461	7.42871	20
41	.08192	12.2067	.09952	10.0483	.11718	8.53402	.13491	7.41240	19
42	.08221	12.1632	.09981	10.0187	.11747	8.51259	.13521	7.39616	18
43	.08251	12.1201	.10011	9.98031	.11777	8.49128	.13550	7.37999	17
44	.08280	12.0772	.10040	9.96007	.11806	8.47007	.13580	7.36389	16
45	.08309	12.0346	.10069	9.93101	.11836	8.44896	.13609	7.34786	15
46	.08339	11.9923	.10099	9.90211	.11865	8.42795	.13639	7.33190	14
47	.08368	11.9504	.10128	9.87338	.11895	8.40705	.13669	7.31600	13
48	.08397	11.9087	.10158	9.84482	.11924	8.38625	.13698	7.30018	12
49	.08427	11.8673	.10187	9.81641	.11954	8.36555	.13728	7.28442	11
50	.08456	11.8262	.10216	9.78817	.11983	8.34496	.13758	7.26873	10
51	.08485	11.7853	.10246	9.76009	.12013	8.32446	.13787	7.25310	9
52	.08514	11.7448	.10275	9.73217	.12042	8.30406	.13817	7.23754	8
53	.08544	11.7045	.10305	9.70441	.12072	8.28376	.13846	7.22204	7
54	.08573	11.6645	.10334	9.67680	.12101	8.26355	.13876	7.20661	6
55	.08602	11.6248	.10363	9.64935	.12131	8.24345	.13906	7.19125	5
56	.08632	11.5853	.10393	9.62205	.12160	8.22344	.13935	7.17594	4
57	.08661	11.5461	.10422	9.59490	.12190	8.20352	.13965	7.16071	3
58	.08690	11.5072	.10452	9.56791	.12219	8.18370	.13995	7.14553	2
59	.08720	11.4685	.10481	9.54106	.12249	8.16398	.14024	7.13042	1
60	.08749	11.4301	.10510	9.51436	.12278	8.14435	.14054	7.11537	0
′	CO-TAN.	TAN.	CO-TAN.	TAN.	CO-TAN.	TAN.	CO-TAN.	TAN.	′
	85°		84°		83°		82°		

′	8° TAN.	8° CO-TAN.	9° TAN.	9° CO-TAN.	10° TAN.	10° CO-TAN.	11° TAN.	11° CO-TAN.	′
0	.14054	7.11537	.15838	6.31375	.17633	5.67128	.19438	5.14455	60
1	.14084	7.10038	.15868	6.30189	.17663	5.66165	.19468	5.13658	59
2	.14113	7.08546	.15898	6.29007	.17693	5.65205	.19498	5.12862	58
3	.14143	7.07059	.15928	6.27829	.17723	5.64248	.19529	5.12069	57
4	.14173	7.05579	.15958	6.26655	.17753	5.63295	.19559	5.11279	56
5	.14202	7.04105	.15988	6.25486	.17783	5.62344	.19589	5.10490	55
6	.14232	7.02637	.16017	6.24321	.17813	5.61397	.19619	5.09704	54
7	.14262	7.01174	.16047	6.23160	.17843	5.60452	.19649	5.08921	53
8	.14291	6.99718	.16077	6.22003	.17873	5.59511	.19680	5.08139	52
9	.14321	6.98268	.16107	6.20851	.17903	5.58573	.19710	5.07360	51
10	.14351	6.96823	.16137	6.19703	.17933	5.57638	.19740	5.06584	50
11	.14381	6.95385	.16167	6.18559	.17963	5.56706	.19770	5.05809	49
12	.14410	6.93952	.16196	6.17419	.17993	5.55777	.19801	5.05037	48
13	.14440	6.92525	.16226	6.16283	.18023	5.54851	.19831	5.04267	47
14	.14470	6.91104	.16256	6.15151	.18053	5.53927	.19861	5.03499	46
15	.14499	6.89688	.16286	6.14023	.18083	5.53007	.19891	5.02734	45
16	.14529	6.88278	.16316	6.12899	.18113	5.52090	.19921	5.01971	44
17	.14559	6.86874	.16346	6.11779	.18143	5.51176	.19952	5.01210	43
18	.14588	6.85475	.16376	6.10664	.18173	5.50264	.19982	5.00451	42
19	.14618	6.84082	.16405	6.09552	.18203	5.49356	.20012	4.99695	41
20	.14648	6.82694	.16435	6.08444	.18233	5.48451	.20042	4.98940	40
21	.14678	6.81312	.16465	6.07340	.18263	5.47548	.20073	4.98188	39
22	.14707	6.79936	.16495	6.06240	.18293	5.46648	.20103	4.97438	38
23	.14737	6.78564	.16525	6.05143	.18323	5.45751	.20133	4.96690	37
24	.14767	6.77199	.16555	6.04051	.18353	5.44857	.20164	4.95945	36
25	.14796	6.75838	.16585	6.02962	.18383	5.43966	.20194	4.95201	35
26	.14826	6.74483	.16615	6.01878	.18414	5.43077	.20224	4.94460	34
27	.14856	6.73133	.16645	6.00797	.18444	5.42192	.20254	4.93721	33
28	.14886	6.71789	.16674	5.99720	.18474	5.41309	.20285	4.92984	32
29	.14915	6.70450	.16704	5.98646	.18504	5.40429	.20315	4.92249	31
30	.14945	6.69116	.16734	5.97576	.18534	5.39552	.20345	4.91516	30
31	.14975	6.67787	.16764	5.96510	.18564	5.38677	.20376	4.90785	29
32	.15005	6.66463	.16794	5.95448	.18594	5.37805	.20406	4.90056	28
33	.15034	6.65144	.16824	5.94390	.18624	5.36936	.20436	4.89330	27
34	.15064	6.63831	.16854	5.93335	.18654	5.36070	.20466	4.88605	26
35	.15094	6.62523	.16884	5.92283	.18684	5.35206	.20497	4.87882	25
36	.15124	6.61219	.16914	5.91235	.18714	5.34345	.20527	4.87162	24
37	.15153	6.59921	.16944	5.90191	.18745	5.33487	.20557	4.86444	23
38	.15183	6.58627	.16974	5.89151	.18775	5.32631	.20588	4.85727	22
39	.15213	6.57339	.17004	5.88114	.18805	5.31778	.20618	4.85013	21
40	.15243	6.56055	.17033	5.87080	.18835	5.30928	.20648	4.84300	20
41	.15272	6.54777	.17063	5.86051	.18865	5.30080	.20679	4.83590	19
42	.15302	6.53503	.17093	5.85024	.18895	5.29235	.20709	4.82882	18
43	.15332	6.52234	.17123	5.84001	.18925	5.28393	.20739	4.82175	17
44	.15362	6.50970	.17153	5.82982	.18955	5.27553	.20770	4.81471	16
45	.15391	6.49710	.17183	5.81966	.18986	5.26715	.20800	4.80769	15
46	.15421	6.48456	.17213	5.80953	.19016	5.25880	.20830	4.80068	14
47	.15451	6.47206	.17243	5.79944	.19046	5.25048	.20861	4.79370	13
48	.15481	6.45961	.17273	5.78938	.19076	5.24218	.20891	4.78673	12
49	.15511	6.44720	.17303	5.77936	.19106	5.23391	.20921	4.77978	11
50	.15540	6.43484	.17333	5.76937	.19136	5.22566	.20952	4.77286	10
51	.15570	6.42253	.17363	5.75941	.19166	5.21744	.20982	4.76595	9
52	.15600	6.41026	.17393	5.74949	.19197	5.20925	.21013	4.75906	8
53	.15630	6.39804	.17423	5.73960	.19227	5.20107	.21043	4.75219	7
54	.15660	6.38587	.17453	5.72974	.19257	5.19293	.21073	4.74534	6
55	.15689	6.37374	.17483	5.71992	.19287	5.18480	.21104	4.73851	5
56	.15719	6.36165	.17513	5.71013	.19317	5.17671	.21134	4.73170	4
57	.15749	6.34961	.17543	5.70037	.19347	5.16863	.21164	4.72490	3
58	.15779	6.33761	.17573	5.69064	.19378	5.16058	.21195	4.71813	2
59	.15809	6.32566	.17603	5.68094	.19408	5.15256	.21225	4.71137	1
60	.15838	6.31375	.17633	5.67128	.19438	5.14455	.21256	4.70463	0
′	CO-TAN.	TAN.	CO-TAN.	TAN.	CO-TAN.	TAN.	CO-TAN.	TAN.	′
	81°		80°		79°		78°		

′	12° Tan.	Co-tan.	13° Tan.	Co-tan.	14° Tan.	Co-tan.	15° Tan.	Co-tan	′
0	.21256	4.70463	.23087	4.33148	.24933	4.01078	.26795	3.73205	60
1	.21286	4.69791	.23117	4.32573	.24964	4.00582	.26826	3.72771	59
2	.21316	4.69121	.23148	4.32001	.24995	4.00086	.26857	3.72338	58
3	.21347	4.68452	.23179	4.31430	.25026	3.99592	.26888	3.71907	57
4	.21377	4.67786	.23209	4.30860	.25056	3.99099	.26920	3.71476	56
5	.21408	4.67121	.23240	4.30291	.25087	3.98607	.26951	3.71046	55
6	.21438	4.66458	.23271	4.29724	.25118	3.98117	.26982	3.70616	54
7	.21469	4.65797	.23301	4.29159	.25149	3.97627	.27013	3.70188	53
8	.21499	4.65138	.23332	4.28595	.25180	3.97139	.27044	3.69761	52
9	.21529	4.64480	.23363	4.28032	.25211	3.96651	.27076	3.69335	51
10	.21500	4.63825	.23393	4.27471	.25242	3.96165	.27107	3.68909	50
11	.21590	4.63171	.23424	4.26911	.25273	3.95680	.27138	3.68485	49
12	.21621	4.62518	.23455	4.26352	.25304	3.95196	.27169	3.68061	48
13	.21651	4.61868	.23485	4.25795	.25335	3.94713	.27201	3.67638	47
14	.21682	4.61219	.23516	4.25239	.25366	3.94232	.27232	3.67217	46
15	.21712	4.60572	.23547	4.24685	.25397	3.93751	.27263	3.66796	45
16	.21743	4.59927	.23578	4.24132	.25428	3.93271	.27294	3.66376	44
17	.21773	4.59283	.23608	4.23580	.25459	3.92793	.27326	3.65957	43
18	.21804	4.58641	.23639	4.23030	.25490	3.92316	.27357	3.65538	42
19	.21834	4.58001	.23670	4.22481	.25521	3.91839	.27388	3.65121	41
20	.21864	4.57363	.23700	4.21933	.25552	3.91364	.27419	3.64705	40
21	.21895	4.56726	.23731	4.21387	.25583	3.90890	.27451	3.64289	39
22	.21925	4.56091	.23762	4.20842	.25614	3.90417	.27482	3.63874	38
23	.21956	4.55458	.23793	4.20298	.25645	3.89945	.27513	3.63461	37
24	.21986	4.54826	.23823	4.19756	.25676	3.89474	.27545	3.63048	36
25	.22017	4.54196	.23854	4.19215	.25707	3.89004	.27576	3.62636	35
26	.22047	4.53568	.23885	4.18675	.25738	3.88536	.27607	3.62224	34
27	.22078	4.52941	.23916	4.18137	.25769	3.88068	.27638	3.61814	33
28	.22108	4.52316	.23946	4.17600	.25800	3.87601	.27670	3.61405	32
29	.22139	4.51693	.23977	4.17064	.25831	3.87136	.27701	3.60996	31
30	.22169	4.51071	.24008	4.16530	.25862	3.86671	.27732	3.60588	30
31	.22200	4.50451	.24039	4.15997	.25893	3.86208	.27764	3.60181	29
32	.22231	4.49832	.24069	4.15465	.25924	3.85745	.27795	3.59775	28
33	.22261	4.49215	.24100	4.14934	.25955	3.85284	.27826	3.59370	27
34	.22292	4.48600	.24131	4.14405	.25986	3.84824	.27858	3.58966	26
35	.22322	4.47986	.24162	4.13877	.26017	3.84364	.27889	3.58562	25
36	.22353	4.47374	.24193	4.13350	.26048	3.83906	.27920	3.58160	24
37	.22383	4.46764	.24223	4.12825	.26079	3.83449	.27952	3.57758	23
38	.22414	4.46155	.24254	4.12301	.26110	3.82992	.27983	3.57357	22
39	.22444	4.45548	.24285	4.11778	.26141	3.82537	.28015	3.56957	21
40	.22475	4.44942	.24316	4.11256	.26172	3.82083	.28046	3.56557	20
41	.22505	4.44338	.24347	4.10736	.26203	3.81630	.28077	3.56159	19
42	.22536	4.43735	.24377	4.10216	.26235	3.81177	.28109	3.55761	18
43	.22567	4.43134	.24408	4.09699	.26266	3.80726	.28140	3.55364	17
44	.22597	4.42534	.24439	4.09182	.26297	3.80276	.28172	3.54968	16
45	.22628	4.41936	.24470	4.08666	.26328	3.79827	.28203	3.54573	15
46	.22658	4.41340	.24501	4.08152	.26359	3.79378	.28234	3.54179	14
47	.22689	4.40745	.24532	4.07639	.26390	3.78931	.28266	3.53785	13
48	.22719	4.40152	.24562	4.07127	.26421	3.78485	.28297	3.53393	12
49	.22750	4.39560	.24593	4.06616	.26452	3.78040	.28329	3.53001	11
50	.22781	4.38969	.24624	4.06107	.26483	3.77595	.28360	3.52609	10
51	.22811	4.38381	.24655	4.05590	.26515	3.77152	.28391	3.52219	9
52	.22842	4.37793	.24686	4.05092	.26546	3.76709	.28423	3.51829	8
53	.22872	4.37207	.24717	4.04586	.26577	3.76268	.28454	3.51441	7
54	.22903	4.36623	.24747	4.04081	.26608	3.75828	.28486	3.51053	6
55	.22934	4.36040	.24778	4.03578	.26639	3.75388	.28517	3.50666	5
56	.22964	4.35459	.24800	4.03075	.26670	3.74950	.28549	3.50279	4
57	.22995	4.34879	.24840	4.02574	.26701	3.74512	.28580	3.49894	3
58	.23026	4.34300	.24871	4.02074	.26733	3.74075	.28612	3.49509	2
59	.23056	4.33723	.24902	4.01576	.26764	3.73640	.28643	3.49125	1
60	.23087	4.33148	.24933	4.01078	.26795	3.73205	.28675	3.48741	0
′	Co-tan.	Tan.	Co-tan.	Tan.	Co-tan.	Tan.	Co-tan.	Tan.	′
	77°		76°		75°		74°		

′	16° Tan.	Co-tan.	17° Tan.	Co-tan.	18° Tan.	Co-tan.	19° Tan.	Co-tan.	′
0	.28675	3.48741	.30573	3.27085	.32492	3.07768	.34433	2.90421	60
1	.28706	3.48359	.30605	3.26745	.32524	3.07464	.34465	2.90147	59
2	.28738	3.47977	.30637	3.26406	.32556	3.07160	.34498	2.89873	58
3	.28769	3.47596	.30669	3.26067	.32588	3.06857	.34530	2.89600	57
4	.28800	3.47216	.30700	3.25729	.32621	3.06554	.34563	2.89327	56
5	.28832	3.46837	.30732	3.25392	.32653	3.06252	.34596	2.89055	55
6	.28864	3.46458	.30764	3.25055	.32685	3.05950	.34628	2.88783	54
7	.28895	3.46080	.30796	3.24719	.32717	3.05649	.34661	2.88511	53
8	.28927	3.45703	.30828	3.24383	.32749	3.05349	.34693	2.88240	52
9	.28958	3.45327	.30860	3.24049	.32782	3.05049	.34726	2.87970	51
10	.28990	3.44951	.30891	3.23714	.32814	3.04749	.34758	2.87700	50
11	.29021	3.44576	.30923	3.23381	.32846	3.04450	.34791	2.87430	49
12	.29053	3.44202	.30955	3.23048	.32878	3.04152	.34824	2.87161	48
13	.29084	3.43829	.30987	3.22715	.32911	3.03854	.34856	2.86892	47
14	.29116	3.43456	.31019	3.22384	.32943	3.03556	.34889	2.86624	46
15	.29147	3.43084	.31051	3.22053	.32975	3.03260	.34922	2.86356	45
16	.29179	3.42713	.31083	3.21722	.33007	3.02963	.34954	2.86089	44
17	.29210	3.42343	.31115	3.21392	.33040	3.02667	.34987	2.85822	43
18	.29242	3.41973	.31147	3.21063	.33072	3.02372	.35019	2.85555	42
19	.29274	3.41604	.31178	3.20734	.33104	3.02077	.35052	2.85289	41
20	.29305	3.41236	.31210	3.20406	.33136	3.01783	.35085	2.85023	40
21	.29337	3.40869	.31242	3.20079	.33169	3.01489	.35117	2.84758	39
22	.29368	3.40502	.31274	3.19752	.33201	3.01196	.35150	2.84494	38
23	.29400	3.40136	.31306	3.19426	.33233	3.00903	.35183	2.84229	37
24	.29432	3.39771	.31338	3.19100	.33266	3.00611	.35216	2.83965	36
25	.29463	3.39406	.31370	3.18775	.33298	3.00319	.35248	2.83702	35
26	.29495	3.39042	.31402	3.18451	.33330	3.00028	.35281	2.83439	34
27	.29526	3.38679	.31434	3.18127	.33363	2.99738	.35314	2.83176	33
28	.29558	3.38317	.31466	3.17804	.33395	2.99447	.35346	2.82914	32
29	.29590	3.37955	.31498	3.17481	.33427	2.99158	.35379	2.82653	31
30	.29621	3.37594	.31530	3.17159	.33460	2.98868	.35412	2.82391	30
31	.29653	3.37234	.31562	3.16838	.33492	2.98580	.35445	2.82130	29
32	.29685	3.36875	.31594	3.16517	.33524	2.98292	.35477	2.81870	28
33	.29716	3.36516	.31626	3.16197	.33557	2.98004	.35510	2.81610	27
34	.29748	3.36158	.31658	3.15877	.33589	2.97717	.35543	2.81350	26
35	.29780	3.35800	.31690	3.15558	.33621	2.97430	.35576	2.81091	25
36	.29811	3.35443	.31722	3.15240	.33654	2.97144	.35608	2.80833	24
37	.29843	3.35087	.31754	3.14922	.33686	2.96858	.35641	2.80574	23
38	.29875	3.34732	.31786	3.14605	.33718	2.96573	.35674	2.80316	22
39	.29906	3.34377	.31818	3.14288	.33751	2.96288	.35707	2.80059	21
40	.29938	3.34023	.31850	3.13972	.33783	2.96004	.35740	2.79802	20
41	.29970	3.33670	.31882	3.13656	.33816	2.95721	.35772	2.79545	19
42	.30001	3.33317	.31914	3.13341	.33848	2.95437	.35805	2.79289	18
43	.30033	3.32965	.31946	3.13027	.33881	2.95155	.35838	2.79033	17
44	.30065	3.32614	.31978	3.12713	.33913	2.94872	.35871	2.78778	16
45	.30097	3.32264	.32010	3.12400	.33945	2.94590	.35904	2.78523	15
46	.30128	3.31914	.32042	3.12087	.33978	2.94309	.35937	2.78269	14
47	.30160	3.31565	.32074	3.11775	.34010	2.94028	.35969	2.78014	13
48	.30192	3.31216	.32106	3.11464	.34043	2.93748	.36002	2.77761	12
49	.30224	3.30868	.32139	3.11153	.34075	2.93468	.36035	2.77507	11
50	.30255	3.30521	.32171	3.10842	.34108	2.93189	.36068	2.77254	10
51	.30287	3.30174	.32203	3.10532	.34140	2.92910	.36101	2.77002	9
52	.30319	3.29829	.32235	3.10223	.34173	2.92632	.36134	2.76750	8
53	.30351	3.29483	.32267	3.09914	.34205	2.92354	.36167	2.76498	7
54	.30382	3.29139	.32299	3.09606	.34238	2.92076	.36199	2.76247	6
55	.30414	3.28795	.32331	3.09298	.34270	2.91799	.36232	2.75996	5
56	.30446	3.28452	.32363	3.08991	.34303	2.91523	.36265	2.75746	4
57	.30478	3.28109	.32396	3.08685	.34335	2.91246	.36298	2.75496	3
58	.30509	3.27767	.32428	3.08379	.34368	2.90971	.36331	2.75246	2
59	.30541	3.27426	.32460	3.08073	.34400	2.90696	.36364	2.74997	1
60	.30573	3.27085	.32492	3.07768	.34433	2.90421	.36397	2.74748	0
′	Co-tan.	Tan.	Co-tan.	Tan.	Co-tan.	Tan.	Co-tan.	Tan.	′
		73°		72°		71°		70°	

′	20° TAN.	CO-TAN.	21° TAN.	CO-TAN.	22° TAN.	CO-TAN.	23° TAN.	CO-TAN.	′
0	.36397	2.74748	.38386	2.60509	.40403	2.47509	.42447	2.35585	60
1	.36430	2.74499	.38420	2.60283	.40436	2.47302	.42482	2.35395	59
2	.36463	2.74251	.38453	2.60057	.40470	2.47095	.42516	2.35205	58
3	.36496	2.74004	.38487	2.59831	.40504	2.46888	.42551	2.35015	57
4	.36529	2.73756	.38520	2.59606	.40538	2.46682	.42585	2.34825	56
5	.36562	2.73509	.38553	2.59381	.40572	2.46476	.42619	2.34636	55
6	.36595	2.73263	.38587	2.59156	.40606	2.46270	.42654	2.34447	54
7	.36628	2.73017	.38620	2.58932	.40640	2.46065	.42688	2.34258	53
8	.36661	2.72771	.38654	2.58708	.40674	2.45860	.42722	2.34069	52
9	.36694	2.72526	.38687	2.58484	.40707	2.45655	.42757	2.33881	51
10	.36727	2.72281	.38721	2.58261	.40741	2.45451	.42791	2.33693	50
11	.36760	2.72036	.38754	2.58038	.40775	2.45246	.42826	2.33505	49
12	.36793	2.71792	.38787	2.57815	.40809	2.45043	.42860	2.33317	48
13	.36826	2.71548	.38821	2.57593	.40843	2.44839	.42894	2.33130	47
14	.36859	2.71305	.38854	2.57371	.40877	2.44636	.42929	2.32943	46
15	.36892	2.71062	.38888	2.57150	.40911	2.44433	.42963	2.32756	45
16	.36925	2.70819	.38921	2.56928	.40945	2.44230	.42998	2.32570	44
17	.36958	2.70577	.38955	2.56707	.40979	2.44027	.43032	2.32383	43
18	.36991	2.70335	.38988	2.56487	.41013	2.43825	.43067	2.32197	42
19	.37024	2.70094	.39022	2.56266	.41047	2.43623	.43101	2.32012	41
20	.37057	2.69853	.39055	2.56046	.41081	2.43422	.43136	2.31826	40
21	.37090	2.69612	.39089	2.55827	.41115	2.43220	.43170	2.31641	39
22	.37124	2.69371	.39122	2.55608	.41149	2.43019	.43205	2.31456	38
23	.37157	2.69131	.39156	2.55389	.41183	2.42819	.43239	2.31271	37
24	.37190	2.68892	.39190	2.55170	.41217	2.42618	.43274	2.31086	36
25	.37223	2.68653	.39223	2.54952	.41251	2.42418	.43308	2.30902	35
26	.37256	2.68414	.39257	2.54734	.41285	2.42218	.43343	2.30718	34
27	.37289	2.68175	.39290	2.54516	.41319	2.42019	.43378	2.30534	33
28	.37322	2.67937	.39324	2.54299	.41353	2.41819	.43412	2.30351	32
29	.37355	2.67700	.39357	2.54082	.41387	2.41620	.43447	2.30167	31
30	.37388	2.67462	.39391	2.53865	.41421	2.41421	.43481	2.29984	30
31	.37422	2.67225	.39425	2.53648	.41455	2.41223	.43516	2.29801	29
32	.37455	2.66989	.39458	2.53432	.41490	2.41025	.43550	2.29619	28
33	.37488	2.66752	.39492	2.53217	.41524	2.40827	.43585	2.29437	27
34	.37521	2.66516	.39526	2.53001	.41558	2.40629	.43620	2.29254	26
35	.37554	2.66281	.39559	2.52786	.41592	2.40432	.43654	2.29073	25
36	.37588	2.66046	.39593	2.52571	.41626	2.40235	.43689	2.28891	24
37	.37621	2.65811	.39626	2.52357	.41660	2.40038	.43724	2.28710	23
38	.37654	2.65576	.39660	2.52142	.41694	2.39841	.43758	2.28528	22
39	.37687	2.65342	.39694	2.51929	.41728	2.39645	.43793	2.28348	21
40	.37720	2.65109	.39727	2.51715	.41763	2.39449	.43828	2.28167	20
41	.37754	2.64875	.39761	2.51502	.41797	2.39253	.43862	2.27987	19
42	.37787	2.64642	.39795	2.51289	.41831	2.39058	.43897	2.27806	18
43	.37820	2.64410	.39829	2.51076	.41865	2.38862	.43932	2.27626	17
44	.37853	2.64177	.39862	2.50864	.41899	2.38668	.43966	2.27447	16
45	.37887	2.63945	.39896	2.50652	.41933	2.38473	.44001	2.27267	15
46	.37920	2.63714	.39930	2.50440	.41968	2.38279	.44036	2.27088	14
47	.37953	2.63483	.39963	2.50229	.42002	2.38084	.44071	2.26909	13
48	.37986	2.63252	.39997	2.50018	.42036	2.37891	.44105	2.26730	12
49	.38020	2.63021	.40031	2.49807	.42070	2.37697	.44140	2.26552	11
50	.38053	2.62791	.40065	2.49597	.42105	2.37504	.44175	2.26374	10
51	.38086	2.62561	.40098	2.49386	.42139	2.37311	.44210	2.26196	9
52	.38120	2.62332	.40132	2.49177	.42173	2.37118	.44244	2.26018	8
53	.38153	2.62103	.40166	2.48967	.42207	2.36925	.44279	2.25840	7
54	.38186	2.61874	.40200	2.48758	.42242	2.36733	.44314	2.25663	6
55	.38220	2.61646	.40234	2.48549	.42276	2.36541	.44349	2.25486	5
56	.38253	2.61418	.40267	2.48340	.42310	2.36349	.44384	2.25309	4
57	.38286	2.61190	.40301	2.48132	.42345	2.36158	.44418	2.25132	3
58	.38320	2.60963	.40335	2.47924	.42379	2.35967	.44453	2.24956	2
59	.38353	2.60736	.40369	2.47716	.42413	2.35776	.44488	2.24780	1
60	.38386	2.60509	.40403	2.47509	.42447	2.35585	.44523	2.24604	0
′	CO-TAN.	TAN.	CO-TAN.	TAN.	CO-TAN.	TAN.	CO-TAN.	TAN.	′
	69°		68°		67°		66°		

′	24° Tan.	Co-tan.	25° Tan.	Co-tan.	26° Tan.	Co-tan.	27° Tan.	Co-tan.	
0	.44523	2.24604	.46631	2.14451	.48773	2.05030	.50953	1.96261	60
1	.44558	2.24428	.46666	2.14288	.48809	2.04879	.50989	1.96120	59
2	.44593	2.24252	.46702	2.14125	.48845	2.04728	.51026	1.95979	58
3	.44627	2.24077	.46737	2.13963	.48881	2.04577	.51063	1.95838	57
4	.44662	2.23902	.46772	2.13801	.48917	2.04426	.51099	1.95698	56
5	.44697	2.23727	.46808	2.13639	.48953	2.04276	.51136	1.95557	55
6	.44732	2.23553	.46843	2.13477	.48989	2.04125	.51173	1.95417	54
7	.44767	2.23378	.46879	2.13316	.49026	2.03975	.51209	1.95277	53
8	.44802	2.23204	.46914	2.13154	.49062	2.03825	.51246	1.95137	52
9	.44837	2.23030	.46950	2.12993	.49098	2.03675	.51283	1.94997	51
10	.44872	2.22857	.46985	2.12832	.49134	2.03526	.51319	1.94858	50
11	.44907	2.22683	.47021	2.12671	.49170	2.03376	.51356	1.94718	49
12	.44942	2.22510	.47056	2.12511	.49206	2.03227	.51393	1.94579	48
13	.44977	2.22337	.47092	2.12350	.49242	2.03078	.51430	1.94440	47
14	.45012	2.22164	.47128	2.12190	.49278	2.02929	.51467	1.94301	46
15	.45047	2.21992	.47163	2.12030	.49315	2.02780	.51503	1.94162	45
16	.45082	2.21819	.47199	2.11871	.49351	2.02631	.51540	1.94023	44
17	.45117	2.21647	.47234	2.11711	.49387	2.02483	.51577	1.93885	43
18	.45152	2.21475	.47270	2.11552	.49423	2.02335	.51614	1.93746	42
19	.45187	2.21304	.47305	2.11392	.49459	2.02187	.51651	1.93608	41
20	.45222	2.21132	.47341	2.11233	.49495	2.02039	.51688	1.93470	40
21	.45257	2.20961	.47377	2.11075	.49532	2.01891	.51724	1.93332	39
22	.45292	2.20790	.47412	2.10916	.49568	2.01743	.51761	1.93195	38
23	.45327	2.20619	.47448	2.10758	.49604	2.01596	.51798	1.93057	37
24	.45362	2.20449	.47483	2.10600	.49640	2.01449	.51835	1.92920	36
25	.45397	2.20278	.47519	2.10442	.49677	2.01302	.51872	1.92782	35
26	.45432	2.20108	.47555	2.10284	.49713	2.01155	.51909	1.92645	34
27	.45467	2.19938	.47590	2.10126	.49749	2.01008	.51946	1.92508	33
28	.45502	2.19769	.47626	2.09969	.49786	2.00862	.51983	1.92371	32
29	.45537	2.19599	.47662	2.09811	.49822	2.00715	.52020	1.92235	31
30	.45573	2.19430	.47698	2.09654	.49858	2.00569	.52057	1.92098	30
31	.45608	2.19261	.47733	2.09498	.49894	2.00423	.52094	1.91962	29
32	.45643	2.19092	.47769	2.09341	.49931	2.00277	.52131	1.91826	28
33	.45678	2.18923	.47805	2.09184	.49967	2.00131	.52168	1.91690	27
34	.45713	2.18755	.47840	2.09028	.50004	1.99986	.52205	1.91554	26
35	.45748	2.18587	.47876	2.08872	.50040	1.99841	.52242	1.91418	25
36	.45784	2.18419	.47912	2.08716	.50076	1.99695	.52279	1.91282	24
37	.45819	2.18251	.47948	2.08560	.50113	1.99550	.52316	1.91147	23
38	.45854	2.18084	.47984	2.08405	.50149	1.99406	.52353	1.91012	22
39	.45889	2.17916	.48019	2.08250	.50185	1.99261	.52390	1.90876	21
40	.45924	2.17749	.48055	2.08094	.50222	1.99116	.52427	1.90741	20
41	.45960	2.17582	.48091	2.07939	.50258	1.98972	.52464	1.90607	19
42	.45995	2.17416	.48127	2.07785	.50295	1.98828	.52501	1.90472	18
43	.46030	2.17249	.48163	2.07630	.50331	1.98684	.52538	1.90337	17
44	.46065	2.17083	.48198	2.07476	.50368	1.98540	.52575	1.90203	16
45	.46101	2.16917	.48234	2.07321	.50404	1.98396	.52613	1.90069	15
46	.46136	2.16751	.48270	2.07167	.50441	1.98253	.52650	1.89935	14
47	.46171	2.16585	.48306	2.07014	.50477	1.98110	.52687	1.89801	13
48	.46206	2.16420	.48342	2.06860	.50514	1.97966	.52724	1.89667	12
49	.46242	2.16255	.48378	2.06706	.50550	1.97823	.52761	1.89533	11
50	.46277	2.16090	.48414	2.06553	.50587	1.97680	.52798	1.89400	10
51	.46312	2.15925	.48450	2.06400	.50623	1.97538	.52836	1.89266	9
52	.46348	2.15760	.48486	2.06247	.50660	1.97395	.52873	1.89133	8
53	.46383	2.15596	.48521	2.06094	.50696	1.97253	.52910	1.89000	7
54	.46418	2.15432	.48557	2.05942	.50733	1.97111	.52947	1.88867	6
55	.46454	2.15268	.48593	2.05790	.50769	1.96969	.52984	1.88734	5
56	.46489	2.15104	.48629	2.05637	.50806	1.96827	.53022	1.88602	4
57	.46525	2.14940	.48665	2.05485	.50843	1.96685	.53059	1.88469	3
58	.46560	2.14777	.48701	2.05333	.50879	1.96544	.53096	1.88337	2
59	.46595	2.14614	.48737	2.05182	.50916	1.96402	.53134	1.88205	1
60	.46631	2.14451	.48773	2.05030	.50953	1.96261	.53171	1.88073	0
′	Co-tan.	Tan.	Co-tan.	Tan.	Co-tan.	Tan.	Co-tan.	Tan.	′
		65°		64°		63°		62°	

	28°		29°		30°		31°		
	Tan.	Co-tan.	Tan.	Co-tan.	Tan.	Co-tan.	Tan.	Co-tan.	
0	.53171	1.88073	.55431	1.80405	.57735	1.73205	.60086	1.66428	60
1	.53208	1.87941	.55469	1.80281	.57774	1.73089	.60126	1.66318	59
2	.53246	1.87809	.55507	1.80158	.57813	1.72973	.60165	1.66209	58
3	.53283	1.87677	.55545	1.80034	.57851	1.72857	.60205	1.66099	57
4	.53320	1.87546	.55583	1.79911	.57890	1.72741	.60245	1.65990	56
5	.53358	1.87415	.55621	1.79788	.57929	1.72625	.60284	1.65881	55
6	.53395	1.87283	.55659	1.79665	.57968	1.72509	.60324	1.65772	54
7	.53432	1.87152	.55697	1.79542	.58007	1.72393	.60364	1.65663	53
8	.53470	1.87021	.55736	1.79419	.58046	1.72278	.60403	1.65554	52
9	.53507	1.86891	.55774	1.79296	.58085	1.72163	.60443	1.65445	51
10	.53545	1.86760	.55812	1.79174	.58124	1.72047	.60483	1.65337	50
11	.53582	1.86630	.55850	1.79051	.58162	1.71932	.60522	1.65228	49
12	.53620	1.86499	.55888	1.78929	.58201	1.71817	.60562	1.65120	48
13	.53657	1.86369	.55926	1.78807	.58240	1.71702	.60602	1.65011	47
14	.53694	1.86239	.55964	1.78685	.58279	1.71588	.60642	1.64903	46
15	.53732	1.86109	.56003	1.78563	.58318	1.71473	.60681	1.64795	45
16	.53769	1.85979	.56041	1.78441	.58357	1.71358	.60721	1.64687	44
17	.53807	1.85850	.56079	1.78319	.58396	1.71244	.60761	1.64579	43
18	.53844	1.85720	.56117	1.78198	.58435	1.71129	.60801	1.64471	42
19	.53882	1.85591	.56156	1.78077	.58474	1.71015	.60841	1.64363	41
20	.53920	1.85462	.56194	1.77955	.58513	1.70901	.60881	1.64256	40
21	.53957	1.85333	.56232	1.77834	.58552	1.70787	.60921	1.64148	39
22	.53995	1.85204	.56270	1.77713	.58591	1.70673	.60960	1.64041	38
23	.54032	1.85075	.56309	1.77592	.58631	1.70560	.61000	1.63934	37
24	.54070	1.84946	.56347	1.77471	.58670	1.70446	.61040	1.63826	36
25	.54107	1.84818	.56385	1.77351	.58709	1.70332	.61080	1.63719	35
26	.54145	1.84689	.56424	1.77230	.58748	1.70219	.61120	1.63612	34
27	.54183	1.84561	.56462	1.77110	.58787	1.70106	.61160	1.63505	33
28	.54220	1.84433	.56500	1.76990	.58826	1.69992	.61200	1.63398	32
29	.54258	1.84305	.56539	1.76869	.58865	1.69879	.61240	1.63292	31
30	.54296	1.84177	.56577	1.76749	.58904	1.69766	.61280	1.63185	30
31	.54333	1.84049	.56616	1.76630	.58944	1.69653	.61320	1.63079	29
32	.54371	1.83922	.56654	1.76510	.58983	1.69541	.61360	1.62972	28
33	.54409	1.83794	.56693	1.76390	.59022	1.69428	.61400	1.62866	27
34	.54446	1.83667	.56731	1.76271	.59061	1.69316	.61440	1.62760	26
35	.54484	1.83540	.56769	1.76151	.59101	1.69203	.61480	1.62654	25
36	.54522	1.83413	.56808	1.76032	.59140	1.69091	.61520	1.62548	24
37	.54560	1.83286	.56846	1.75913	.59179	1.68979	.61561	1.62442	23
38	.54597	1.83159	.56885	1.75794	.59218	1.68866	.61601	1.62336	22
39	.54635	1.83033	.56923	1.75675	.59258	1.68754	.61641	1.62230	21
40	.54673	1.82906	.56962	1.75556	.59297	1.68643	.61681	1.62125	20
41	.54711	1.82780	.57000	1.75437	.59336	1.68531	.61721	1.62019	19
42	.54748	1.82654	.57039	1.75319	.59376	1.68419	.61761	1.61914	18
43	.54786	1.82528	.57078	1.75200	.59415	1.68308	.61801	1.61808	17
44	.54824	1.82402	.57116	1.75082	.59454	1.68196	.61842	1.61703	16
45	.54862	1.82276	.57155	1.74964	.59494	1.68085	.61882	1.61598	15
46	.54900	1.82150	.57193	1.74846	.59533	1.67974	.61922	1.61493	14
47	.54938	1.82025	.57232	1.74728	.59573	1.67863	.61962	1.61388	13
48	.54975	1.81899	.57271	1.74610	.59612	1.67752	.62003	1.61283	12
49	.55013	1.81774	.57309	1.74492	.59651	1.67641	.62043	1.61179	11
50	.55051	1.81649	.57348	1.74375	.59691	1.67530	.62083	1.61074	10
51	.55089	1.81524	.57386	1.74257	.59730	1.67419	.62124	1.60970	9
52	.55127	1.81399	.57425	1.74140	.59770	1.67309	.62164	1.60865	8
53	.55165	1.81274	.57464	1.74022	.59809	1.67198	.62204	1.60761	7
54	.55203	1.81150	.57503	1.73905	.59849	1.67088	.62245	1.60657	6
55	.55241	1.81025	.57541	1.73788	.59888	1.66978	.62285	1.60553	5
56	.55279	1.80901	.57580	1.73671	.59928	1.66867	.62325	1.60449	4
57	.55317	1.80777	.57619	1.73555	.59967	1.66757	.62366	1.60345	3
58	.55355	1.80653	.57657	1.73438	.60007	1.66647	.62406	1.60241	2
59	.55393	1.80529	.57696	1.73321	.60046	1.66538	.62446	1.60137	1
60	.55431	1.80405	.57735	1.73205	.60086	1.66428	62487	1.60033	0
	Co-tan.	Tan.	Co-tan.	Tan.	Co-tan.	Tan.	Co-tan.	Tan.	
	61°		60°		59°		58°		

,	32° TAN.	32° CO-TAN.	33° TAN.	33° CO-TAN.	34° TAN.	34° CO-TAN.	35° TAN.	35° CO-TAN.	,
0	.62487	1.60033	.64941	1.53986	.67451	1.48256	.70021	1.42815	60
1	.62527	1.59930	.64982	1.53888	.67493	1.48163	.70064	1.42726	59
2	.62568	1.59826	.65023	1.53791	.67536	1.48070	.70107	1.42638	58
3	.62608	1.59723	.65065	1.53693	.67578	1.47977	.70151	1.42550	57
4	.62649	1.59620	.65106	1.53595	.67620	1.47885	.70194	1.42462	56
5	.62689	1.59517	.65148	1.53497	.67663	1.47792	.70238	1.42374	55
6	.62730	1.59414	.65189	1.53400	.67705	1.47699	.70281	1.42286	54
7	.62770	1.59311	.65231	1.53302	.67748	1.47607	.70325	1.42198	53
8	.62811	1.59208	.65272	1.53205	.67790	1.47514	.70368	1.42110	52
9	.62852	1.59105	.65314	1.53107	.67832	1.47422	.70412	1.42022	51
10	.62892	1.59002	.65355	1.53010	.67875	1.47330	.70455	1.41934	50
11	.62933	1.58900	.65397	1.52913	.67917	1.47238	.70499	1.41847	49
12	.62973	1.58797	.65438	1.52816	.67960	1.47146	.70542	1.41759	48
13	.63014	1.58695	.65480	1.52719	.68002	1.47053	.70586	1.41672	47
14	.63055	1.58593	.65521	1.52622	.68045	1.46962	.70629	1.41584	46
15	.63095	1.58490	.65563	1.52525	.68088	1.46870	.70673	1.41497	45
16	.63136	1.58388	.65604	1.52429	.68130	1.46778	.70717	1.41409	44
17	.63177	1.58286	.65646	1.52332	.68173	1.46686	.70760	1.41322	43
18	.63217	1.58184	.65688	1.52235	.68215	1.46595	.70804	1.41235	42
19	.63258	1.58083	.65729	1.52139	.68258	1.46503	.70848	1.41148	41
20	.63299	1.57981	.65771	1.52043	.68301	1.46411	.70891	1.41061	40
21	.63340	1.57870	.65813	1.51946	.68343	1.46320	.70935	1.40974	39
22	.63380	1.57778	.65854	1.51850	.68386	1.46229	.70979	1.40887	38
23	.63421	1.57676	.65896	1.51754	.68429	1.46137	.71023	1.40800	37
24	.63462	1.57575	.65938	1.51658	.68471	1.46046	.71066	1.40714	36
25	.63503	1.57474	.65980	1.51562	.68514	1.45955	.71110	1.40627	35
26	.63544	1.57372	.66021	1.51466	.68557	1.45864	.71154	1.40540	34
27	.63584	1.57271	.66063	1.51370	.68600	1.45773	.71198	1.40454	33
28	.63625	1.57170	.66105	1.51275	.68642	1.45682	.71242	1.40367	32
29	.63666	1.57069	.66147	1.51179	.68685	1.45592	.71285	1.40281	31
30	.63707	1.56969	.66189	1.51084	.68728	1.45501	.71329	1.40195	30
31	.63748	1.56868	.66230	1.50988	.68771	1.45410	.71373	1.40109	29
32	.63789	1.56767	.66272	1.50893	.68814	1.45320	.71417	1.40022	28
33	.63830	1.56667	.66314	1.50797	.68857	1.45229	.71461	1.39936	27
34	.63871	1.56566	.66356	1.50702	.68900	1.45139	.71505	1.39850	26
35	.63912	1.56466	.66398	1.50607	.68942	1.45049	.71549	1.39764	25
36	.63953	1.56366	.66440	1.50512	.68985	1.44958	.71593	1.39679	24
37	.63994	1.56265	.66482	1.50417	.69028	1.44868	.71637	1.39593	23
38	.64035	1.56165	.66524	1.50322	.69071	1.44778	.71681	1.39507	22
39	.64076	1.56065	.66566	1.50228	.69114	1.44688	.71725	1.39421	21
40	.64117	1.55966	.66608	1.50133	.69157	1.44598	.71769	1.39336	20
41	.64158	1.55866	.66650	1.50038	.69200	1.44508	.71813	1.39250	19
42	.64199	1.55766	.66692	1.49944	.69243	1.44418	.71857	1.39165	18
43	.64240	1.55666	.66734	1.49849	.69286	1.44329	.71901	1.39079	17
44	.64281	1.55567	.66776	1.49755	.69329	1.44239	.71946	1.38994	16
45	.64322	1.55467	.66818	1.49661	.69372	1.44149	.71990	1.38909	15
46	.64363	1.55368	.66860	1.49566	.69416	1.44060	.72034	1.38824	14
47	.64404	1.55269	.66902	1.49472	.69459	1.43970	.72078	1.38738	13
48	.64446	1.55170	.66944	1.49378	.69502	1.43881	.72122	1.38653	12
49	.64487	1.55071	.66986	1.49284	.69545	1.43792	.72166	1.38568	11
50	.64528	1.54972	.67028	1.49190	.69588	1.43703	.72211	1.38484	10
51	.64569	1.54873	.67071	1.49097	.69631	1.43614	.72255	1.38399	9
52	.64610	1.54774	.67113	1.49003	.69675	1.43525	.72299	1.38314	8
53	.64652	1.54675	.67155	1.48909	.69718	1.43436	.72344	1.38229	7
54	.64693	1.54576	.67197	1.48816	.69761	1.43347	.72388	1.38145	6
55	.64734	1.54478	.67239	1.48722	.69804	1.43258	.72432	1.38060	5
56	.64775	1.54379	.67282	1.48629	.69847	1.43169	.72477	1.37976	4
57	.64817	1.54281	.67324	1.48536	.69891	1.43080	.72521	1.37891	3
58	.64858	1.54183	.67366	1.48442	.69934	1.42992	.72565	1.37807	2
59	.64899	1.54085	.67409	1.48349	.69977	1.42903	.72610	1.37722	1
60	.64941	1.53986	.67451	1.48256	.70021	1.42815	.72654	1.37638	0
,	CO-TAN.	TAN.	CO-TAN.	TAN.	CO-TAN.	TAN.	CO-TAN.	TAN.	,
	57°		56°		55°		54°		

′	36° TAN.	CO-TAN.	37° TAN.	CO-TAN.	38° TAN.	CO-TAN.	39° TAN.	CO-TAN.	′
0	.72654	1.37638	.75355	1.32704	.78129	1.27994	.80978	1.23490	60
1	.72699	1.37554	.75401	1.32624	.78175	1.27917	.81027	1.23416	59
2	.72743	1.37470	.75447	1.32544	.78222	1.27841	.81075	1.23343	58
3	.72788	1.37386	.75492	1.32464	.78269	1.27764	.81123	1.23270	57
4	.72832	1.37302	.75538	1.32384	.78316	1.27688	.81171	1.23196	56
5	.72877	1.37218	.75584	1.32304	.78363	1.27611	.81220	1.23123	55
6	.72921	1.37134	.75629	1.32224	.78410	1.27535	.81268	1.23050	54
7	.72966	1.37050	.75675	1.32144	.78457	1.27458	.81316	1.22977	53
8	.73010	1.36967	.75721	1.32064	.78504	1.27382	.81364	1.22904	52
9	.73055	1.36883	.75767	1.31984	.78551	1.27306	.81413	1.22831	51
10	.73100	1.36800	.75812	1.31904	.78598	1.27230	.81461	1.22758	50
11	.73144	1.36716	.75858	1.31825	.78645	1.27153	.81510	1.22685	49
12	.73189	1.36633	.75904	1.31745	.78692	1.27077	.81558	1.22612	48
13	.73234	1.36549	.75950	1.31666	.78739	1.27001	.81606	1.22539	47
14	.73278	1.36466	.75996	1.31586	.78786	1.26925	.81655	1.22467	46
15	.73323	1.36383	.76042	1.31507	.78834	1.26849	.81703	1.22394	45
16	.73368	1.36300	.76088	1.31427	.78881	1.26774	.81752	1.22321	44
17	.73413	1.36217	.76134	1.31348	.78928	1.26698	.81800	1.22249	43
18	.73457	1.36133	.76180	1.31269	.78975	1.26622	.81849	1.22176	42
19	.73502	1.36051	.76226	1.31190	.79022	1.26546	.81898	1.22104	41
20	.73547	1.35968	.76272	1.31110	.79070	1.26471	.81946	1.22031	40
21	.73592	1.35885	.76318	1.31031	.79117	1.26395	.81995	1.21959	39
22	.73637	1.35802	.76364	1.30952	.79164	1.26319	.82044	1.21886	38
23	.73681	1.35719	.76410	1.30873	.79212	1.26244	.82092	1.21814	37
24	.73726	1.35637	.76456	1.30795	.79259	1.26169	.82141	1.21742	36
25	.73771	1.35554	.76502	1.30716	.79306	1.26093	.82190	1.21670	35
26	.73816	1.35472	.76548	1.30637	.79354	1.26018	.82238	1.21598	34
27	.73861	1.35389	.76594	1.30558	.79401	1.25943	.82287	1.21526	33
28	.73906	1.35307	.76640	1.30480	.79449	1.25867	.82336	1.21454	32
29	.73951	1.35224	.76686	1.30401	.79496	1.25792	.82385	1.21382	31
30	.73996	1.35142	.76733	1.30323	.79544	1.25717	.82434	1.21310	30
31	.74041	1.35060	.76779	1.30244	.79591	1.25642	.82483	1.21238	29
32	.74086	1.34978	.76825	1.30166	.79639	1.25567	.82531	1.21166	28
33	.74131	1.34896	.76871	1.30087	.79686	1.25492	.82580	1.21094	27
34	.74176	1.34814	.76918	1.30009	.79734	1.25417	.82629	1.21023	26
35	.74221	1.34732	.76964	1.29931	.79781	1.25343	.82678	1.20951	25
36	.74267	1.34650	.77010	1.29853	.79829	1.25268	.82727	1.20879	24
37	.74312	1.34568	.77057	1.29775	.79877	1.25193	.82776	1.20808	23
38	.74357	1.34487	.77103	1.29696	.79924	1.25118	.82825	1.20736	22
39	.74402	1.34405	.77149	1.29618	.79972	1.25044	.82874	1.20665	21
40	.74447	1.34323	.77196	1.29541	.80020	1.24969	.82923	1.20593	20
41	.74492	1.34242	.77242	1.29463	.80067	1.24895	.82972	1.20522	19
42	.74538	1.34160	.77289	1.29385	.80115	1.24820	.83022	1.20451	18
43	.74583	1.34079	.77335	1.29307	.80163	1.24746	.83071	1.20379	17
44	.74628	1.33998	.77382	1.29229	.80211	1.24672	.83120	1.20308	16
45	.74674	1.33916	.77428	1.29152	.80258	1.24597	.83169	1.20237	15
46	.74710	1.33835	.77475	1.29074	.80306	1.24523	.83218	1.20166	14
47	.74764	1.33754	.77521	1.28997	.80354	1.24449	.83268	1.20095	13
48	.74810	1.33673	.77568	1.28919	.80402	1.24375	.83317	1.20024	12
49	.74855	1.33592	.77615	1.28842	.80450	1.24301	.83366	1.19953	11
50	.74900	1.33511	.77661	1.28764	.80498	1.24227	.83415	1.19882	10
51	.74946	1.33430	.77708	1.28687	.80546	1.24153	.83465	1.19811	9
52	.74991	1.33349	.77754	1.28610	.80594	1.24079	.83514	1.19740	8
53	.75037	1.33268	.77801	1.28533	.80642	1.24005	.83564	1.19669	7
54	.75082	1.33187	.77848	1.28456	.80690	1.23931	.83613	1.19599	6
55	.75128	1.33107	.77895	1.28379	.80738	1.23858	.83662	1.19528	5
56	.75173	1.33026	.77941	1.28302	.80786	1.23784	.83712	1.19457	4
57	.75219	1.32946	.77988	1.28225	.80834	1.23710	.83761	1.19387	3
58	.75264	1.32865	.78035	1.28148	.80882	1.23637	.83811	1.19316	2
59	.75310	1.32785	.78082	1.28071	.80930	1.23563	.83860	1.19246	1
60	.75355	1.32704	.78129	1.27994	.80978	1.23490	.83910	1.19175	0
′	CO-TAN.	TAN.	CO-TAN.	TAN.	CO-TAN.	TAN.	CO-TAN.	TAN	′
		53°		52°		51°		50°	

′	40° TAN.	40° CO-TAN.	41° TAN.	41° CO-TAN.	42° TAN.	42° CO-TAN.	43° TAN.	43° CO-TAN.	′
0	.83910	1.19175	.86929	1.15037	.90040	1.11061	.93252	1.07237	60
1	.83960	1.19105	.86980	1.14969	.90093	1.10996	.93306	1.07174	59
2	.84009	1.19035	.87031	1.14902	.90146	1.10931	.93360	1.07112	58
3	.84059	1.18964	.87082	1.14834	.90199	1.10867	.93415	1.07049	57
4	.84108	1.18894	.87133	1.14767	.90251	1.10802	.93469	1.06987	56
5	.84158	1.18824	.87184	1.14699	.90304	1.10737	.93524	1.06925	55
6	.84208	1.18754	.87236	1.14632	.90357	1.10672	.93578	1.06862	54
7	.84258	1.18684	.87287	1.14565	.90410	1.10607	.93633	1.06800	53
8	.84307	1.18614	.87338	1.14498	.90463	1.10543	.93688	1.06738	52
9	.84357	1.18544	.87389	1.14430	.90516	1.10478	.93742	1.06676	51
0	.84407	1.18474	.87441	1.14363	.90569	1.10414	.93797	1.06613	50
1	.84457	1.18404	.87492	1.14296	.90621	1.10349	.93852	1.06551	49
2	.84507	1.18334	.87543	1.14229	.90674	1.10285	.93906	1.06489	48
3	.84556	1.18264	.87595	1.14162	.90727	1.10220	.93961	1.06427	47
4	.84606	1.18194	.87646	1.14095	.90781	1.10156	.94016	1.06365	46
5	.84656	1.18125	.87698	1.14028	.90834	1.10091	.94071	1.06303	45
6	.84706	1.18055	.87749	1.13961	.90887	1.10027	.94125	1.06241	44
7	.84756	1.17986	.87801	1.13894	.90940	1.09963	.94180	1.06179	43
8	.84806	1.17916	.87852	1.13828	.90993	1.09899	.94235	1.06117	42
9	.84856	1.17846	.87904	1.13761	.91046	1.09834	.94290	1.06056	41
0	.84906	1.17777	.87955	1.13694	.91099	1.09770	.94345	1.05994	40
1	.84956	1.17708	.88007	1.13627	.91153	1.09706	.94400	1.05932	39
2	.85006	1.17638	.88059	1.13561	.91206	1.09642	.94455	1.05870	38
3	.85057	1.17569	.88110	1.13494	.91259	1.09578	.94510	1.05809	37
4	.85107	1.17500	.88162	1.13428	.91313	1.09514	.94565	1.05747	36
5	.85157	1.17430	.88214	1.13361	.91366	1.09450	.94620	1.05685	35
6	.85207	1.17361	.88265	1.13295	.91419	1.09386	.94676	1.05624	34
7	.85257	1.17292	.88317	1.13228	.91473	1.09322	.94731	1.05562	33
8	.85307	1.17223	.88369	1.13162	.91526	1.09258	.94786	1.05501	32
9	.85358	1.17154	.88421	1.13096	.91580	1.09195	.94841	1.05439	31
0	.85408	1.17085	.88473	1.13029	.91633	1.09131	.94896	1.05378	30
1	.85458	1.17016	.88524	1.12963	.91687	1.09067	.94952	1.05317	29
2	.85509	1.16947	.88576	1.12897	.91740	1.09003	.95007	1.05255	28
3	.85559	1.16878	.88628	1.12831	.91794	1.08940	.95062	1.05194	27
4	.85609	1.16809	.88680	1.12765	.91847	1.08876	.95118	1.05133	26
5	.85660	1.16741	.88732	1.12699	.91901	1.08813	.95173	1.05072	25
6	.85710	1.16672	.88784	1.12633	.91955	1.08749	.95229	1.05010	24
7	.85761	1.16603	.88836	1.12567	.92008	1.08686	.95284	1.04949	23
8	.85811	1.16535	.88888	1.12501	.92062	1.08622	.95340	1.04888	22
9	.85862	1.16466	.88940	1.12435	.92116	1.08559	.95395	1.04827	21
0	.85912	1.16398	.88992	1.12369	.92170	1.08496	.95451	1.04766	20
1	.85963	1.16329	.89045	1.12303	.92224	1.08432	.95506	1.04705	19
2	.86014	1.16261	.89097	1.12238	.92277	1.08369	.95562	1.04644	18
3	.86064	1.16192	.89149	1.12172	.92331	1.08306	.95618	1.04583	17
4	.86115	1.16124	.89201	1.12106	.92385	1.08243	.95673	1.04522	16
5	.86166	1.16056	.89253	1.12041	.92439	1.08179	.95729	1.04461	15
6	.86216	1.15987	.89306	1.11975	.92493	1.08116	.95785	1.04401	14
7	.86267	1.15919	.89358	1.11909	.92547	1.08053	.95841	1.04340	13
8	.86318	1.15851	.89410	1.11844	.92601	1.07990	.95897	1.04279	12
9	.86368	1.15783	.89463	1.11778	.92655	1.07927	.95952	1.04218	11
0	.86419	1.15715	.89515	1.11713	.92709	1.07864	.96008	1.04158	10
1	.86470	1.15647	.89567	1.11648	.92763	1.07801	.96064	1.04097	9
2	.86521	1.15579	.89620	1.11582	.92817	1.07738	.96120	1.04036	8
3	.86572	1.15511	.89672	1.11517	.92872	1.07676	.96176	1.03976	7
4	.86623	1.15443	.89725	1.11452	.92926	1.07613	.96232	1.03915	6
5	.86674	1.15375	.89777	1.11387	.92980	1.07550	.96288	1.03855	5
6	.86725	1.15308	.89830	1.11321	.93034	1.07487	.96344	1.03794	4
7	.86776	1.15240	.89883	1.11256	.93088	1.07425	.96400	1.03734	3
8	.86827	1.15172	.89935	1.11191	.93143	1.07362	.96457	1.03674	2
9	.86878	1.15104	.89988	1.11126	.93197	1.07299	.96513	1.03613	1
0	.86929	1.15037	.90040	1.11061	.93252	1.07237	.96569	1.03553	0
′	CO-TAN. 49°	TAN.	CO-TAN. 48°	TAN.	CO-TAN. 47°	TAN.	CO-TAN. 46°	TAN.	′

44°

'	Tan.	Co-tan.	'	'	Tan.	Co-tan.	'	'	Tan.	Co-tan.	'
0	.96569	1.03553	60	21	.97756	1.02295	39	41	.98901	1.01112	19
1	.96625	1.03493	59	22	.97813	1.02236	38	42	.98958	1.01053	18
2	.96681	1.03433	58	23	.97870	1.02176	37	43	.99016	1.00994	17
3	.96738	1.03372	57	24	.97927	1.02117	36	44	.99073	1.00935	16
4	.96794	1.03312	56	25	.97984	1.02057	35	45	.99131	1.00876	15
5	.96850	1.03252	55	26	.98041	1.01998	34	46	.99189	1.00818	14
6	.96907	1.03192	54	27	.98098	1.01939	33	47	.99247	1.00759	13
7	.96963	1.03132	53	28	.98155	1.01879	32	48	.99304	1.00701	12
8	.97020	1.03072	52	29	.98213	1.01820	31	49	.99362	1.00642	11
9	.97076	1.03012	51	30	.98270	1.01761	30	50	.99420	1.00583	10
10	.97133	1.02952	50	31	.98327	1.01702	29	51	.99478	1.00525	9
11	.97189	1.02892	49	32	.98384	1.01642	28	52	.99536	1.00467	8
12	.97246	1.02832	48	33	.98441	1.01583	27	53	.99594	1.00408	7
13	.97302	1.02772	47	34	.98499	1.01524	26	54	.99652	1.00350	6
14	.97359	1.02713	46	35	.98556	1.01465	25	55	.99710	1.00291	5
15	.97416	1.02653	45	36	.98613	1.01406	24	56	.99768	1.00233	4
16	.97472	1.02593	44	37	.98671	1.01347	23	57	.99826	1.00175	3
17	.97529	1.02533	43	38	.98728	1.01288	22	58	.99884	1.00116	2
18	.97586	1.02474	42	39	.98786	1.01229	21	59	.99942	1.00058	1
19	.97643	1.02414	41	40	.98843	1.01170	20	60	1	1	0
20	.97700	1.02355	40								
'	Co-tan.	Tan.	'	'	Co-tan.	Tan.	'	'	Co-tan.	Tan.	'

45°

NATURAL SINES AND COSINES

0°

'	Sine	Cosine	'	'	Sine	Cosine	'	'	Sine	Cosine	'
0	.00000	1	60	21	.00611	.99998	39	41	.01193	.99993	19
1	.00029	1	59	22	.00640	.99998	38	42	.01222	.99993	18
2	.00058	1	58	23	.00669	.99998	37	43	.01251	.99992	17
3	.00087	1	57	24	.00698	.99998	36	44	.01280	.99992	16
4	.00116	1	56	25	.00727	.99997	35	45	.01309	.99991	15
5	.00145	1	55	26	.00756	.99997	34	46	.01338	.99991	14
6	.00175	1	54	27	.00785	.99997	33	47	.01367	.99991	13
7	.00204	1	53	28	.00814	.99997	32	48	.01396	.99990	12
8	.00233	1	52	29	.00844	.99996	31	49	.01425	.99990	11
9	.00262	1	51	30	.00873	.99996	30	50	.01454	.99989	10
10	.00291	1	50	31	.00902	.99996	29	51	.01483	.99989	9
11	.00320	.99999	49	32	.00931	.99996	28	52	.01513	.99989	8
12	.00349	.99999	48	33	.00960	.99995	27	53	.01542	.99988	7
13	.00378	.99999	47	34	.00989	.99995	26	54	.01571	.99988	6
14	.00407	.99999	46	35	.01018	.99995	25	55	.01600	.99987	5
15	.00436	.99999	45	36	.01047	.99995	24	56	.01629	.99987	4
16	.00465	.99999	44	37	.01076	.99994	23	57	.01658	.99986	3
17	.00495	.99999	43	38	.01105	.99994	22	58	.01687	.99986	2
18	.00524	.99999	42	39	.01134	.99994	21	59	.01716	.99985	1
19	.00553	.99998	41	40	.01164	.99993	20	60	.01745	.99985	0
20	.00582	.99998	40								
'	Cosine	Sine	'	'	Cosine	Sine	'	'	Cosine	Sine	'

89°

| ' | 1° | | 2° | | 3° | | 4° | | ' |
	SINE	COSINE	SINE	COSINE	SINE	COSINE	SINE	COSINE	
0	.01745	.99985	.03490	.99939	.05234	.99863	.06076	.99756	60
1	.01774	.99984	.03519	.99938	.05263	.99861	.07005	.99754	59
2	.01803	.99984	.03548	.99937	.05292	.99860	.07034	.99752	58
3	.01832	.99983	.03577	.99936	.05321	.99858	.07063	.99750	57
4	.01862	.99983	.03606	.99935	.05350	.99857	.07092	.99748	56
5	.01891	.99982	.03635	.99934	.05379	.99855	.07121	.99746	55
6	.01920	.99982	.03664	.99933	.05408	.99854	.07150	.99744	54
7	.01949	.99981	.03693	.99932	.05437	.99852	.07179	.99742	53
8	.01978	.99980	.03723	.99931	.05466	.99851	.07208	.99740	52
9	.02007	.99980	.03752	.99930	.05495	.99849	.07237	.99738	51
10	.02036	.99979	.03781	.99929	.05524	.99847	.07266	.99736	50
11	.02065	.99979	.03810	.99927	.05553	.99846	.07295	.99734	49
12	.02094	.99978	.03830	.99926	.05582	.99844	.07324	.99731	48
13	.02123	.99977	.03868	.99925	.05611	.99842	.07353	.99729	47
14	.02152	.99977	.03897	.99924	.05640	.99841	.07382	.99727	46
15	.02181	.99976	.03926	.99923	.05669	.99839	.07411	.99725	45
16	.02211	.99976	.03955	.99922	.05698	.99838	.07440	.99723	44
17	.02240	.99975	.03984	.99921	.05727	.99836	.07469	.99721	43
18	.02269	.99974	.04013	.99919	.05756	.99834	.07498	.99719	42
19	.02298	.99974	.04042	.99918	.05785	.99833	.07527	.99716	41
20	.02327	.99973	.04071	.99917	.05814	.99831	.07556	.99714	40
21	.02356	.99972	.04100	.99916	.05844	.99829	.07585	.99712	39
22	.02385	.99972	.04129	.99915	.05873	.99827	.07614	.99710	38
23	.02414	.99971	.04159	.99913	.05902	.99826	.07643	.99708	37
24	.02443	.99970	.04188	.99912	.05931	.99824	.07672	.99705	36
25	.02472	.99969	.04217	.99911	.05960	.99822	.07701	.99703	35
26	.02501	.99969	.04246	.99910	.05989	.99821	.07730	.99701	34
27	.02530	.99968	.04275	.99909	.06018	.99819	.07759	.99699	33
28	.02560	.99967	.04304	.99907	.06047	.99817	.07788	.99696	32
29	.02589	.99966	.04333	.99906	.06076	.99815	.07817	.99694	31
30	.02618	.99966	.04362	.99905	.06105	.99813	.07846	.99692	30
31	.02647	.99965	.04391	.99904	.06134	.99812	.07875	.99689	29
32	.02676	.99964	.04420	.99902	.06163	.99810	.07904	.99687	28
33	.02705	.99963	.04449	.99901	.06192	.99808	.07933	.99685	27
34	.02734	.99963	.04478	.99900	.06221	.99806	.07962	.99683	26
35	.02763	.99962	.04507	.99898	.06250	.99804	.07991	.99680	25
36	.02792	.99961	.04536	.99897	.06279	.99803	.08020	.99678	24
37	.02821	.99960	.04565	.99896	.06308	.99801	.08049	.99676	23
38	.02850	.99959	.04594	.99894	.06337	.99799	.08078	.99673	22
39	.02879	.99959	.04623	.99893	.06366	.99797	.08107	.99671	21
40	.02908	.99958	.04653	.99892	.06395	.99795	.08136	.99668	20
41	.02938	.99957	.04682	.99890	.06424	.99793	.08165	.99666	19
42	.02967	.99956	.04711	.99889	.06453	.99792	.08194	.99664	18
43	.02996	.99955	.04740	.99888	.06482	.99790	.08223	.99661	17
44	.03025	.99954	.04769	.99886	.06511	.99788	.08252	.99659	16
45	.03054	.99953	.04798	.99885	.06540	.99786	.08281	.99657	15
46	.03083	.99952	.04827	.99883	.06569	.99784	.08310	.99654	14
47	.03112	.99952	.04856	.99882	.06598	.99782	.08339	.99652	13
48	.03141	.99951	.04885	.99881	.06627	.99780	.08368	.99649	12
49	.03170	.99950	.04914	.99879	.06656	.99778	.08397	.99647	11
50	.03199	.99949	.04943	.99878	.06685	.99776	.08426	.99644	10
51	.03228	.99948	.04972	.99876	.06714	.99774	.08455	.99642	9
52	.03257	.99947	.05001	.99875	.06743	.99772	.08484	.99639	8
53	.03286	.99946	.05030	.99873	.06773	.99770	.08513	.99637	7
54	.03316	.99945	.05059	.99872	.06802	.99768	.08542	.99635	6
55	.03345	.99944	.05088	.99870	.06831	.99766	.08571	.99632	5
56	.03374	.99943	.05117	.99869	.06860	.99764	.08600	.99630	4
57	.03403	.99942	.05146	.99867	.06889	.99762	.08629	.99627	3
58	.03432	.99941	.05175	.99866	.06918	.99760	.08658	.99625	2
59	.03461	.99940	.05205	.99864	.06947	.99758	.08687	.99622	1
60	.03490	.99939	.05234	.99863	.06976	.99756	.08716	.99619	0
'	COSINE	SINE	COSINE	SINE	COSINE	SINE	COSINE	SINE	'
	88°		87°		86°		85°		

′	5° SINE	5° COSINE	6° SINE	6° COSINE	7° SINE	7° COSINE	8° SINE	8° COSINE	′
0	.08716	.99619	.10453	.99452	.12187	.99255	.13917	.99027	60
1	.08745	.99617	.10482	.99449	.12216	.99251	.13946	.99023	59
2	.08774	.99614	.10511	.99446	.12245	.99248	.13975	.99019	58
3	.08803	.99612	.10540	.99443	.12274	.99244	.14004	.99015	57
4	.08831	.99609	.10569	.99440	.12302	.99240	.14033	.99011	56
5	.08860	.99607	.10597	.99437	.12331	.99237	.14061	.99006	55
6	.08889	.99604	.10626	.99434	.12360	.99233	.14090	.99002	54
7	.08918	.99602	.10655	.99431	.12389	.99230	.14119	.98998	53
8	.08947	.99599	.10684	.99428	.12418	.99226	.14148	.98994	52
9	.08976	.99596	.10713	.99424	.12447	.99222	.14177	.98990	51
10	.09005	.99594	.10742	.99421	.12476	.99219	.14205	.98986	50
11	.09034	.99591	.10771	.99418	.12504	.99215	.14234	.98982	49
12	.09063	.99588	.10800	.99415	.12533	.99211	.14263	.98978	48
13	.09092	.99586	.10829	.99412	.12562	.99208	.14292	.98973	47
14	.09121	.99583	.10858	.99409	.12591	.99204	.14320	.98969	46
15	.09150	.99580	.10887	.99406	.12620	.99200	.14349	.98965	45
16	.09179	.99578	.10916	.99402	.12640	.99197	.14378	.98961	44
17	.09208	.99575	.10945	.99399	.12678	.99193	.14407	.98957	43
18	.09237	.99572	.10973	.99396	.12706	.99189	.14436	.98953	42
19	.09266	.99570	.11002	.99393	.12735	.99186	.14464	.98948	41
20	.09295	.99567	.11031	.99390	.12764	.99182	.14493	.98944	40
21	.09324	.99564	.11060	.99386	.12793	.99178	.14522	.98940	39
22	.09353	.99562	.11089	.99383	.12822	.99175	.14551	.98936	38
23	.09382	.99559	.11118	.99380	.12851	.99171	.14580	.98931	37
24	.09411	.99556	.11147	.99377	.12880	.99167	.14608	.98927	36
25	.09440	.99553	.11176	.99374	.12908	.99163	.14637	.98923	35
26	.09469	.99551	.11205	.99370	.12937	.99160	.14666	.98919	34
27	.09498	.99548	.11234	.99367	.12966	.99156	.14695	.98914	33
28	.09527	.99545	.11263	.99364	.12995	.99152	.14723	.98910	32
29	.09556	.99542	.11291	.99360	.13024	.99148	.14752	.98906	31
30	.09585	.99540	.11320	.99357	.13053	.99144	.14781	.98902	30
31	.09614	.99537	.11349	.99354	.13081	.99141	.14810	.98897	29
32	.09642	.99534	.11378	.99351	.13110	.99137	.14838	.98893	28
33	.09671	.99531	.11407	.99347	.13139	.99133	.14867	.98889	27
34	.09700	.99528	.11436	.99344	.13168	.99129	.14896	.98884	26
35	.09729	.99526	.11465	.99341	.13197	.99125	.14925	.98880	25
36	.09758	.99523	.11494	.99337	.13226	.99122	.14954	.98876	24
37	.09787	.99520	.11523	.99334	.13254	.99118	.14982	.98871	23
38	.09816	.99517	.11552	.99331	.13283	.99114	.15011	.98867	22
39	.09845	.99514	.11580	.99327	.13312	.99110	.15040	.98863	21
40	.09874	.99511	.11609	.99324	.13341	.99106	.15069	.98858	20
41	.09903	.99508	.11638	.99320	.13370	.99102	.15097	.98854	19
42	.09932	.99506	.11667	.99317	.13399	.99098	.15126	.98849	18
43	.09961	.99503	.11696	.99314	.13427	.99094	.15155	.98845	17
44	.09990	.99500	.11725	.99310	.13456	.99091	.15184	.98841	16
45	.10019	.99497	.11754	.99307	.13485	.99087	.15212	.98836	15
46	.10048	.99494	.11783	.99303	.13514	.99083	.15241	.98832	14
47	.10077	.99491	.11812	.99300	.13543	.99079	.15270	.98827	13
48	.10106	.99488	.11840	.99297	.13572	.99075	.15299	.98823	12
49	.10135	.99485	.11869	.99293	.13600	.99071	.15327	.98818	11
50	.10164	.99482	.11898	.99290	.13629	.99067	.15356	.98814	10
51	.10192	.99470	.11927	.99286	.13658	.99063	.15385	.98800	9
52	.10221	.99476	.11956	.99283	.13687	.99059	.15414	.98805	8
53	.10250	.99473	.11985	.99279	.13716	.99055	.15442	.98800	7
54	.10279	.99470	.12014	.99276	.13744	.99051	.15471	.98796	6
55	.10308	.99467	.12043	.99272	.13773	.99047	.15500	.98791	5
56	.10337	.99464	.12071	.99269	.13802	.99043	.15529	.98787	4
57	.10366	.99461	.12100	.99265	.13831	.99039	.15557	.98782	3
58	.10395	.99458	.12129	.99262	.13860	.99035	.15586	.98778	2
59	.10424	.99455	.12158	.99258	.13889	.99031	.15615	.98773	1
60	.10453	.99452	.12187	.99255	.13917	.99027	.15643	.98769	0
′	COSINE	SINE	COSINE	SINE	COSINE	SINE	COSINE	SINE	′
	84°		83°		82°		81°		

'	9° SINE	COSINE	10° SINE	COSINE	11° SINE	COSINE	12° SINE	COSINE	'
0	.15643	.98769	.17365	.98481	.1908.	.98163	.20791	.97815	60
1	.15672	.98764	.17393	.98476	.19100	.98157	.20820	.97809	59
2	.15701	.98760	.17422	.98471	.1913.	.98152	.20848	.97803	58
3	.15730	.98755	.17451	.98466	.19167	.98146	.20877	.97797	57
4	.15758	.98751	.17479	.98461	.1919.	.98140	.20905	.97791	56
5	.15787	.98746	.17508	.98455	.19224	.98135	.20933	.97784	55
6	.15816	.98741	.17537	.98450	.19252	.98129	.20962	.97778	54
7	.15845	.98737	.17565	.98445	.19281	.98124	.20990	.97772	53
8	.15873	.98732	.17594	.98440	.19309	.98118	.21019	.97766	52
9	.15902	.98728	.17623	.98435	.19338	.98112	.21047	.97760	51
10	.15931	.98723	.17651	.98430	.19366	.98107	.21076	.97754	50
11	.15950	.98718	.17680	.98425	.19395	.98101	.21104	.97748	49
12	.15988	.98714	.17708	.98420	.19423	.98096	.21132	.97742	48
13	.16017	.98709	.17737	.98414	.19452	.98090	.21161	.97735	47
14	.16046	.98704	.17766	.98409	.19481	.98084	.21189	.97729	46
15	.16074	.98700	.17794	.98404	.19509	.98079	.21218	.97723	45
16	.16103	.98695	.17823	.98399	.19538	.98073	.21246	.97717	44
17	.16132	.98690	.17852	.98304	.19566	.98067	.21275	.97711	43
18	.16160	.98689	.17880	.98389	.19595	.98061	.21303	.97705	42
19	.16189	.98681	.17909	.98383	.19623	.98056	.21331	.97698	41
20	.16218	.98676	.17937	.98378	.19652	.98050	.21360	.97692	40
21	.16246	.98671	.17966	.98373	.19680	.98044	.21388	.97686	39
22	.16275	.98667	.17995	.98368	.19709	.98039	.21417	.97680	38
23	.16304	.98662	.18023	.98362	.19737	.98033	.21445	.97673	37
24	.16333	.98657	.18052	.98357	.19766	.98027	.21474	.97667	36
25	.16361	.98652	.18081	.98352	.19794	.98021	.21502	.97661	35
26	.16390	.98648	.18109	.98347	.19823	.98016	.21530	.97655	34
27	.16419	.98643	.18138	.98341	.19851	.98010	.21559	.97648	33
28	.16447	.98638	.18166	.98336	.19880	.98004	.21587	.97642	32
29	.16476	.98633	.18195	.98331	.19908	.97997	.21616	.97636	31
30	.16505	.98629	.18224	.98325	.19937	.97992	.21644	.97630	30
31	.16533	.98624	.18252	.98320	.19965	.97987	.21672	.97623	29
32	.16562	.98619	.18281	.98315	.19994	.97981	.21701	.97617	28
33	.16591	.98614	.18309	.98310	.20022	.97975	.21729	.97611	27
34	.16620	.98609	.18338	.98304	.20051	.97969	.21758	.97604	26
35	.16648	.98604	.18367	.98299	.20079	.97963	.21786	.97598	25
36	.16677	.98600	.18395	.98294	.20108	.97958	.21814	.97592	24
37	.16706	.98595	.18424	.98288	.20136	.97952	.21843	.97585	23
38	.16734	.98590	.18452	.98283	.20165	.97946	.21871	.97579	22
39	.16763	.98585	.18481	.98277	.20193	.97940	.21899	.97573	21
40	.16792	.98580	.18509	.98272	.20222	.97934	.21928	.97566	20
41	.16820	.98575	.18538	.98267	.20250	.97928	.21956	.97560	19
42	.16849	.98570	.18567	.98261	.20279	.97922	.21985	.97553	18
43	.16878	.98565	.18595	.98256	.20307	.97916	.22013	.97547	17
44	.16906	.98561	.18624	.98250	.20336	.97910	.22041	.97541	16
45	.16935	.98556	.18652	.98245	.20364	.97905	.22070	.97534	15
46	.16964	.98551	.18681	.98240	.20393	.97899	.22098	.97528	14
47	.16992	.98546	.18710	.98234	.20421	.97893	.22126	.97521	13
48	.17021	.98541	.18738	.98229	.20450	.97887	.22155	.97515	12
49	.17050	.98536	.18767	.98223	.20478	.97881	.22183	.97508	11
50	.17078	.98531	.18795	.98218	.20507	.97875	.22212	.97502	10
51	.17107	.98526	.18824	.98212	.20535	.97869	.22240	.97496	9
52	.17136	.98521	.18852	.98207	.20563	.97863	.22268	.97489	8
53	.17164	.98516	.18881	.98201	.20592	.97857	.22297	.97483	7
54	.17193	.98511	.18910	.98196	.20620	.97851	.22325	.97476	6
55	.17222	.98506	.18938	.98190	.20649	.97845	.22353	.97470	5
56	.17250	.98501	.18967	.98185	.20677	.97839	.22382	.97463	4
57	.17279	.98496	.18995	.98179	.20706	.97833	.22410	.97457	3
58	.17308	.98491	.19024	.98174	.20734	.97827	.22438	.97450	2
59	.17336	.98486	.19052	.98168	.20763	.97821	.22467	.97444	1
60	.17365	.98481	.19081	.98163	.20791	.97815	.22495	.97437	0

'	COSINE	SINE	COSINE	SINE	COSINE	SINE	COSINE	SINE	'
	80°		79°		78°		77°		

'	13°		14°		15°		16°		'
	SINE	COSINE	SINE	COSINE	SINE	COSINE	SINE	COSINE	
0	.22495	.97437	.24192	.97030	.25882	.96593	.27564	.96126	60
1	.22523	.97430	.24220	.97023	.25910	.96585	.27592	.96118	59
2	.22552	.97424	.24249	.97015	.25938	.96578	.27620	.96110	58
3	.22580	.97417	.24277	.97008	.25966	.96570	.27648	.96102	57
4	.22608	.97411	.24305	.97001	.25994	.96562	.27676	.96094	56
5	.22637	.97404	.24333	.96994	.26022	.96555	.27704	.96086	55
6	.22665	.97398	.24362	.96987	.26050	.96547	.27731	.96078	54
7	.22693	.97391	.24390	.96980	.26079	.96540	.27759	.96070	53
8	.22722	.97384	.24418	.96973	.26107	.96532	.27787	.96062	52
9	.22750	.97378	.24446	.96966	.26135	.96524	.27815	.96054	51
10	.22778	.97371	.24474	.96959	.26163	.96517	.27843	.96046	50
11	.22807	.97365	.24503	.96952	.26191	.96509	.27871	.96037	49
12	.22835	.97358	.24531	.96945	.26219	.96502	.27899	.96029	48
13	.22863	.97351	.24559	.96937	.26247	.96494	.27927	.96021	47
14	.22892	.97345	.24587	.96930	.26275	.96486	.27955	.96013	46
15	.22920	.97338	.24615	.96923	.26303	.96479	.27983	.96005	45
16	.22948	.97331	.24644	.96916	.26331	.96471	.28011	.95997	44
17	.22977	.97325	.24672	.96909	.26359	.96463	.28039	.95989	43
18	.23005	.97318	.24700	.96902	.26387	.96456	.28067	.95981	42
19	.23033	.97311	.24728	.96894	.26415	.96448	.28095	.95972	41
20	.23062	.97304	.24756	.96887	.26443	.96440	.28123	.95964	40
21	.23090	.97298	.24784	.96880	.26471	.96433	.28150	.95956	39
22	.23118	.97291	.24813	.96873	.26500	.96425	.28178	.95948	38
23	.23146	.97284	.24841	.96866	.26528	.96417	.28206	.95940	37
24	.23175	.97278	.24869	.96858	.26556	.96410	.28234	.95931	36
25	.23203	.97271	.24897	.96851	.26584	.96402	.28262	.95923	35
26	.23231	.97264	.24925	.96844	.26612	.96394	.28290	.95915	34
27	.23260	.97257	.24954	.96837	.26640	.96386	.28318	.95907	33
28	.23288	.97251	.24982	.96829	.26668	.96379	.28346	.95898	32
29	.23316	.97244	.25010	.96822	.26696	.96371	.28374	.95890	31
30	.23345	.97237	.25038	.96815	.26724	.96363	.28402	.95882	30
31	.23373	.97230	.25066	.96807	.26752	.96355	.28429	.95874	29
32	.23401	.97223	.25094	.96800	.26780	.96347	.28457	.95865	28
33	.23429	.97217	.25122	.96793	.26808	.96340	.28485	.95857	27
34	.23458	.97210	.25151	.96786	.26836	.96332	.28513	.95849	26
35	.23486	.97203	.25179	.96778	.26864	.96324	.28541	.95841	25
36	.23514	.97196	.25207	.96771	.26892	.96316	.28569	.95832	24
37	.23542	.97189	.25235	.96764	.26920	.96308	.28597	.95824	23
38	.23571	.97182	.25263	.96756	.26948	.96301	.28625	.95816	22
39	.23599	.97176	.25291	.96749	.26976	.96293	.28652	.95807	21
40	.23627	.97169	.25320	.96742	.27004	.96285	.28680	.95799	20
41	.23656	.97162	.25348	.96734	.27032	.96277	.28708	.95791	19
42	.23684	.97155	.25376	.96727	.27060	.96269	.28736	.95782	18
43	.23712	.97148	.25404	.96719	.27088	.96261	.28764	.95774	17
44	.23740	.97141	.25432	.96712	.27116	.96253	.28792	.95766	16
45	.23769	.97134	.25460	.96705	.27144	.96246	.28820	.95757	15
46	.23797	.97127	.25488	.96697	.27172	.96238	.28847	.95749	14
47	.23825	.97120	.25516	.96690	.27200	.96230	.28875	.95740	13
48	.23853	.97113	.25545	.96682	.27228	.96222	.28903	.95732	12
49	.23882	.97106	.25573	.96675	.27256	.96214	.28931	.95724	11
50	.23910	.97100	.25601	.96667	.27284	.96206	.28959	.95715	10
51	.23938	.97093	.25629	.96660	.27312	.96198	.28987	.95707	9
52	.23966	.97086	.25657	.96653	.27340	.96190	.29015	.95698	8
53	.23995	.97079	.25685	.96645	.27368	.96182	.29042	.95690	7
54	.24023	.97072	.25713	.96638	.27396	.96174	.29070	.95681	6
55	.24051	.97065	.25741	.96630	.27424	.96166	.29098	.95673	5
56	.24079	.97058	.25769	.96623	.27452	.96158	.29126	.95664	4
57	.24108	.97051	.25798	.96615	.27480	.96150	.29154	.95656	3
58	.24136	.97044	.25826	.96608	.27508	.96142	.29182	.95647	2
59	.24164	.97037	.25854	.96600	.27536	.96134	.29209	.95639	1
60	.24192	.97030	.25882	.96593	.27564	.96126	.29237	.95630	0
'	COSINE	SINE	COSINE	SINE	COSINE	SINE	COSINE	SINE	'
	76°		75°		74°		73°		

'	17° SINE	COSINE	18° SINE	COSINE	19° SINE	COSINE	20° SINE	COSINE	'
0	.29237	.95630	.30902	.95106	.32557	.94552	.34202	.93969	60
1	.29265	.95622	.30929	.95097	.32584	.94542	.34229	.93959	59
2	.29293	.95613	.30957	.95088	.32612	.94533	.34257	.93949	58
3	.29321	.95605	.30985	.95079	.32639	.94523	.34284	.93939	57
4	.29348	.95596	.31012	.95070	.32667	.94514	.34311	.93929	56
5	.29376	.95588	.31040	.95061	.32694	.94504	.34339	.93919	55
6	.29404	.95579	.31068	.95052	.32722	.94495	.34366	.93909	54
7	.29432	.95571	.31095	.95043	.32749	.94485	.34393	.93899	53
8	.29460	.95562	.31123	.95033	.32777	.94476	.34421	.93889	52
9	.29487	.95554	.31151	.95024	.32804	.94466	.34448	.93879	51
10	.29515	.95545	.31178	.95015	.32832	.94457	.34475	.93869	50
11	.29543	.95536	.31206	.95006	.32859	.94447	.34503	.93859	49
12	.29571	.95528	.31233	.94997	.32887	.94438	.34530	.93849	48
13	.29599	.95519	.31261	.94988	.32914	.94428	.34557	.93839	47
14	.29626	.95511	.31289	.94979	.32942	.94418	.34584	.93829	46
15	.29654	.95502	.31316	.94970	.32969	.94409	.34612	.93819	45
16	.29682	.95493	.31344	.94961	.32997	.94399	.34639	.93809	44
17	.29710	.95485	.31372	.94952	.33024	.94390	.34666	.93799	43
18	.29737	.95476	.31399	.94943	.33051	.94380	.34694	.93789	42
19	.29765	.95467	.31427	.94933	.33079	.94370	.34721	.93779	41
20	.29793	.95459	.31454	.94924	.33106	.94361	.34748	.93769	40
21	.29821	.95450	.31482	.94915	.33134	.94351	.34775	.93759	39
22	.29849	.95441	.31510	.94906	.33161	.94342	.34803	.93748	38
23	.29876	.95433	.31537	.94897	.33189	.94332	.34830	.93738	37
24	.29904	.95424	.31565	.94888	.33216	.94322	.34857	.93728	36
25	.29932	.95415	.31593	.94878	.33244	.94313	.34884	.93718	35
26	.29960	.95407	.31620	.94869	.33271	.94303	.34912	.93708	34
27	.29987	.95398	.31648	.94860	.33298	.94293	.34939	.93698	33
28	.30015	.95389	.31675	.94851	.33326	.94284	.34966	.93688	32
29	.30043	.95380	.31703	.94842	.33353	.94274	.34993	.93677	31
30	.30071	.95372	.31730	.94832	.33381	.94264	.35021	.93667	30
31	.30098	.95363	.31758	.94823	.33408	.94254	.35048	.93657	29
32	.30126	.95354	.31786	.94814	.33436	.94245	.35075	.93647	28
33	.30154	.95345	.31813	.94805	.33463	.94235	.35102	.93637	27
34	.30182	.95337	.31841	.94795	.33490	.94225	.35130	.93626	26
35	.30209	.95328	.31868	.94786	.33518	.94215	.35157	.93616	25
36	.30237	.95319	.31896	.94777	.33545	.94206	.35184	.93606	24
37	.30265	.95310	.31923	.94768	.33573	.94196	.35211	.93596	23
38	.30292	.95301	.31951	.94758	.33600	.94186	.35239	.93585	22
39	.30320	.95293	.31979	.94749	.33627	.94176	.35266	.93575	21
40	.30348	.95284	.32006	.94740	.33655	.94167	.35293	.93565	20
41	.30376	.95275	.32034	.94730	.33682	.94157	.35320	.93555	19
42	.30403	.95266	.32061	.94721	.33710	.94147	.35347	.93544	18
43	.30431	.95257	.32089	.94712	.33737	.94137	.35375	.93534	17
44	.30459	.95248	.32116	.94702	.33764	.94127	.35402	.93524	16
45	.30486	.95240	.32144	.94693	.33792	.94118	.35429	.93514	15
46	.30514	.95231	.32171	.94684	.33819	.94108	.35456	.93503	14
47	.30542	.95222	.32199	.94674	.33846	.94098	.35484	.93493	13
48	.30570	.95213	.32227	.94665	.33874	.94088	.35511	.93483	12
49	.30597	.95204	.32254	.94656	.33901	.94078	.35538	.93472	11
50	.30625	.95195	.32282	.94646	.33929	.94068	.35565	.93462	10
51	.30653	.95186	.32309	.94637	.33956	.94058	.35592	.93452	9
52	.30680	.95177	.32337	.94627	.33983	.94049	.35619	.93441	8
53	.30708	.95168	.32364	.94618	.34011	.94039	.35647	.93431	7
54	.30736	.95159	.32392	.94609	.34038	.94029	.35674	.93420	6
55	.30763	.95150	.32419	.94600	.34065	.94019	.35701	.93410	5
56	.30791	.95142	.32447	.94590	.34093	.94009	.35728	.93400	4
57	.30819	.95133	.32474	.94580	.34120	.93999	.35755	.93389	3
58	.30846	.95124	.32502	.94571	.34147	.93989	.35782	.93379	2
59	.30874	.95115	.32529	.94561	.34175	.93979	.35810	.93368	1
60	.30902	.95106	.32557	.94552	.34202	.93969	.35837	.93358	0
'	COSINE	SINE	COSINE	SINE	COSINE	SINE	COSINE	SINE	'
	72°		71°		70°		69°		

′	21° SINE	21° COSINE	22° SINE	22° COSINE	23° SINE	23° COSINE	24° SINE	24° COSINE	′
0	.35837	.93358	.37461	.92718	.39073	.92050	.40674	.91355	60
1	.35864	.93348	.37488	.92707	.39100	.92039	.40700	.91343	59
2	.35891	.93337	.37515	.92697	.39127	.92028	.40727	.91331	58
3	.35918	.93327	.37542	.92686	.39153	.92016	.40753	.91319	57
4	.35945	.93316	.37569	.92675	.39180	.92005	.40780	.91307	56
5	.35973	.93306	.37595	.92664	.39207	.91994	.40806	.91295	55
6	.36000	.93295	.37622	.92653	.39234	.91982	.40833	.91283	54
7	.36027	.93285	.37649	.92642	.39260	.91971	.40860	.91272	53
8	.36054	.93274	.37676	.92631	.39287	.91959	.40886	.91260	52
9	.36081	.93264	.37703	.92620	.39314	.91948	.40913	.91248	51
10	.36108	.93253	.37730	.92609	.39341	.91936	.40939	.91236	50
11	.36135	.93243	.37757	.92598	.39367	.91925	.40966	.91224	49
12	.36162	.93232	.37784	.92587	.39394	.91914	.40992	.91212	48
13	.36190	.93222	.37811	.92576	.39421	.91902	.41019	.91200	47
14	.36217	.93211	.37838	.92565	.39448	.91891	.41045	.91188	46
15	.36244	.93201	.37865	.92554	.39474	.91879	.41072	.91176	45
16	.36271	.93190	.37892	.92543	.39501	.91868	.41098	.91164	44
17	.36298	.93180	.37919	.92532	.39528	.91856	.41125	.91152	43
18	.36325	.93169	.37946	.92521	.39555	.91845	.41151	.91140	42
19	.36352	.93159	.37973	.92510	.39581	.91833	.41178	.91128	41
20	.36379	.93148	.37999	.92499	.39608	.91822	.41204	.91116	40
21	.36406	.93137	.38026	.92488	.39635	.91810	.41231	.91104	39
22	.36434	.93127	.38053	.92477	.39661	.91799	.41257	.91092	38
23	.36461	.93116	.38080	.92466	.39688	.91787	.41284	.91080	37
24	.36488	.93106	.38107	.92455	.39715	.91775	.41310	.91068	36
25	.36515	.93095	.38134	.92444	.39741	.91764	.41337	.91056	35
26	.36542	.93084	.38161	.92432	.39768	.91752	.41363	.91044	34
27	.36569	.93074	.38188	.92421	.39795	.91741	.41390	.91032	33
28	.36596	.93063	.38215	.92410	.39822	.91729	.41416	.91020	32
29	.36623	.93052	.38241	.92399	.39848	.91718	.41443	.91008	31
30	.36650	.93042	.38268	.92388	.39875	.91706	.41469	.90996	30
31	.36677	.93031	.38295	.92377	.39902	.91694	.41496	.90984	29
32	.36704	.93020	.38322	.92366	.39928	.91683	.41522	.90972	28
33	.36731	.93010	.38349	.92355	.39955	.91671	.41549	.90960	27
34	.36758	.92999	.38376	.92343	.39982	.91660	.41575	.90948	26
35	.36785	.92988	.38403	.92332	.40008	.91648	.41602	.90936	25
36	.36812	.92978	.38430	.92321	.40035	.91636	.41628	.90924	24
37	.36839	.92967	.38456	.92310	.40062	.91625	.41655	.90911	23
38	.36867	.92956	.38483	.92299	.40088	.91613	.41681	.90899	22
39	.36894	.92945	.38510	.92287	.40115	.91601	.41707	.90887	21
40	.36921	.92935	.38537	.92276	.40141	.91590	.41734	.90875	20
41	.36948	.92924	.38564	.92265	.40168	.91578	.41760	.90863	19
42	.36975	.92913	.38591	.92254	.40195	.91566	.41787	.90851	18
43	.37002	.92902	.38617	.92243	.40221	.91555	.41813	.90839	17
44	.37029	.92892	.38644	.92231	.40248	.91543	.41840	.90826	16
45	.37056	.92881	.38671	.92220	.40275	.91531	.41866	.90814	15
46	.37083	.92870	.38698	.92209	.40301	.91519	.41892	.90802	14
47	.37110	.92859	.38725	.92198	.40328	.91508	.41919	.90790	13
48	.37137	.92849	.38752	.92186	.40355	.91496	.41945	.90778	12
49	.37164	.92838	.38778	.92175	.40381	.91484	.41972	.90766	11
50	.37191	.92827	.38805	.92164	.40408	.91472	.41998	.90753	10
51	.37218	.92816	.38832	.92152	.40434	.91461	.42024	.90741	9
52	.37245	.92805	.38859	.92141	.40461	.91449	.42051	.90729	8
53	.37272	.92794	.38886	.92130	.40488	.91437	.42077	.90717	7
54	.37299	.92784	.38912	.92119	.40514	.91425	.42104	.90704	6
55	.37326	.92773	.38939	.92107	.40541	.91414	.42130	.90692	5
56	.37353	.92762	.38966	.92096	.40567	.91402	.42156	.90680	4
57	.37380	.92751	.38993	.92085	.40594	.91390	.42183	.90668	3
58	.37407	.92740	.39020	.92073	.40621	.91378	.42209	.90655	2
59	.37434	.92729	.39046	.92062	.40647	.91366	.42235	.90643	1
60	.37461	.92718	.39073	.92050	.40674	.91355	.42262	.90631	0
′	COSINE	SINE	COSINE	SINE	COSINE	SINE	COSINE	SINE	′
	68°		67°		66°		65°		

′	25° Sine	Cosine	26° Sine	Cosine	27° Sine	Cosine	28° Sine	Cosine	′
0	.42262	.90631	.43837	.89879	.45399	.89101	.46947	.88295	60
1	.42288	.90618	.43863	.89867	.45425	.89087	.46973	.88281	59
2	.42315	.90606	.43889	.89854	.45451	.89074	.46999	.88267	58
3	.42341	.90594	.43916	.89841	.45477	.89061	.47024	.88254	57
4	.42367	.90582	.43942	.89828	.45503	.89048	.47050	.88240	56
5	.42394	.90569	.43968	.89816	.45529	.89035	.47076	.88226	55
6	.42420	.90557	.43994	.89803	.45554	.89021	.47101	.88213	54
7	.42446	.90545	.44020	.89790	.45580	.89008	.47127	.88199	53
8	.42473	.90532	.44046	.89777	.45606	.88995	.47153	.88185	52
9	.42499	.90520	.44072	.89764	.45632	.88981	.47178	.88172	51
10	.42525	.90507	.44098	.89752	.45658	.88968	.47204	.88158	50
11	.42552	.90495	.44124	.89730	.45684	.88955	.47229	.88144	49
12	.42578	.90483	.44151	.89720	.45710	.88942	.47255	.88130	48
13	.42604	.90470	.44177	.89713	.45736	.88928	.47281	.88117	47
14	.42631	.90458	.44203	.89700	.45762	.88915	.47306	.88103	46
15	.42657	.90446	.44229	.89687	.45787	.88902	.47332	.88089	45
16	.42683	.90433	.44255	.89674	.45813	.88888	.47358	.88075	44
17	.42709	.90421	.44281	.89662	.45839	.88875	.47383	.88062	43
18	.42736	.90408	.44307	.89649	.45865	.88862	.47409	.88048	42
19	.42762	.90396	.44333	.89636	.45891	.88848	.47434	.88034	41
20	.42788	.90383	.44359	.89623	.45917	.88835	.47460	.88020	40
21	.42815	.90371	.44385	.89610	.45942	.88822	.47486	.88006	39
22	.42841	.90358	.44411	.89597	.45968	.88808	.47511	.87993	38
23	.42867	.90346	.44437	.89584	.45994	.88795	.47537	.87979	37
24	.42894	.90334	.44464	.89571	.46020	.88782	.47562	.87965	36
25	.42920	.90321	.44490	.89558	.46046	.88768	.47588	.87951	35
26	.42946	.90309	.44516	.89545	.46072	.88755	.47614	.87937	34
27	.42972	.90296	.44542	.89532	.46097	.88741	.47639	.87923	33
28	.42999	.90284	.44568	.89519	.46123	.88728	.47665	.87909	32
29	.43025	.90271	.44594	.89506	.46149	.88715	.47690	.87896	31
30	.43051	.90259	.44620	.89493	.46175	.88701	.47716	.87882	30
31	.43077	.90246	.44646	.89480	.46201	.88688	.47741	.87868	29
32	.43104	.90233	.44672	.89467	.46226	.88674	.47767	.87854	28
33	.43130	.90221	.44698	.89454	.46252	.88661	.47793	.87840	27
34	.43156	.90208	.44724	.89441	.46278	.88647	.47818	.87826	26
35	.43182	.90196	.44750	.89428	.46304	.88634	.47844	.87812	25
36	.43209	.90183	.44776	.89415	.46330	.88620	.47869	.87798	24
37	.43235	.90171	.44802	.89402	.46355	.88607	.47895	.87784	23
38	.43261	.90158	.44828	.89389	.46381	.88593	.47920	.87770	22
39	.43287	.90146	.44854	.89376	.46407	.88580	.47946	.87756	21
40	.43313	.90133	.44880	.89363	.46433	.88566	.47971	.87743	20
41	.43340	.90120	.44906	.89350	.46458	.88553	.47997	.87729	19
42	.43366	.90108	.44932	.89337	.46484	.88539	.48022	.87715	18
43	.43392	.90095	.44958	.89324	.46510	.88526	.48048	.87701	17
44	.43418	.90082	.44984	.89311	.46536	.88512	.48073	.87687	16
45	.43445	.90070	.45010	.89298	.46561	.88499	.48099	.87673	15
46	.43471	.90057	.45036	.89285	.46587	.88485	.48124	.87659	14
47	.43497	.90045	.45062	.89272	.46613	.88472	.48150	.87645	13
48	.43523	.90032	.45088	.89259	.46630	.88458	.48175	.87631	12
49	.43549	.90019	.45114	.89245	.46664	.88445	.48201	.87617	11
50	.43575	.90007	.45140	.89232	.46690	.88431	.48226	.87603	10
51	.43602	.89994	.45166	.89219	.46716	.88417	.48252	.87589	9
52	.43628	.89981	.45192	.89206	.46742	.88404	.48277	.87575	8
53	.43654	.89968	.45218	.89193	.46767	.88390	.48303	.87561	7
54	.43680	.89956	.45243	.89180	.46793	.88377	.48328	.87546	6
55	.43706	.89943	.45269	.89167	.46819	.88363	.48354	.87532	5
56	.43733	.89930	.45295	.89153	.46844	.88349	.48370	.87518	4
57	.43759	.89918	.45321	.89140	.46870	.88336	.48405	.87504	3
58	.43785	.89905	.45347	.89127	.46896	.88322	.48430	.87490	2
59	.43811	.89892	.45373	.89114	.46921	.88308	.48456	.87476	1
60	.43837	.89879	.45399	.89101	.46947	.88295	.48481	.87462	0
′	Cosine	Sine	Cosine	Sine	Cosine	Sine	Cosine	Sine	′
		64°		63°		62°		61°	

′	29° SINE	COSINE	30° SINE	COSINE	31° SINE	COSINE	32° SINE	COSINE	′
0	.48481	.87462	.50000	.86603	.51504	.85717	.52992	.84805	60
1	.48506	.87448	.50025	.86588	.51529	.85702	.53017	.84789	59
2	.48532	.87434	.50050	.86573	.51554	.85687	.53041	.84774	58
3	.48557	.87420	.50076	.86559	.51579	.85672	.53066	.84759	57
4	.48583	.87406	.50101	.86544	.51604	.85657	.53091	.84743	56
5	.48608	.87391	.50126	.86530	.51628	.85642	.53115	.84728	55
6	.48634	.87377	.50151	.86515	.51653	.85627	.53140	.84712	54
7	.48659	.87363	.50176	.86501	.51678	.85612	.53164	.84697	53
8	.48684	.87349	.50201	.86486	.51703	.85597	.53189	.84681	52
9	.48710	.87335	.50227	.86471	.51728	.85582	.53214	.84666	51
10	.48735	.87321	.50252	.86457	.51753	.85567	.53238	.84650	50
11	.48761	.87306	.50277	.86442	.51778	.85551	.53263	.84635	49
12	.48786	.87292	.50302	.86427	.51803	.85536	.53288	.84619	48
13	.48811	.87278	.50327	.86413	.51828	.85521	.53312	.84604	47
14	.48837	.87264	.50352	.86398	.51852	.85506	.53337	.84588	46
15	.48862	.87250	.50377	.86384	.51877	.85491	.53361	.84573	45
16	.48888	.87235	.50403	.86369	.51902	.85476	.53386	.84557	44
17	.48913	.87221	.50428	.86354	.51927	.85461	.53411	.84542	43
18	.48938	.87207	.50453	.86340	.51952	.85446	.53435	.84526	42
19	.48964	.87193	.50478	.86325	.51977	.85431	.53460	.84511	41
20	.48989	.87178	.50503	.86310	.52002	.85416	.53484	.84495	40
21	.49014	.87164	.50528	.86295	.52026	.85401	.53509	.84480	39
22	.49040	.87150	.50553	.86281	.52051	.85385	.53534	.84464	38
23	.49065	.87136	.50578	.86266	.52076	.85370	.53558	.84448	37
24	.49090	.87121	.50603	.86251	.52101	.85355	.53583	.84433	36
25	.49116	.87107	.50628	.86237	.52126	.85340	.53607	.84417	35
26	.49141	.87093	.50654	.86222	.52151	.85325	.53632	.84402	34
27	.49166	.87079	.50679	.86207	.52175	.85310	.53656	.84386	33
28	.49192	.87064	.50704	.86192	.52200	.85294	.53681	.84370	32
29	.49217	.87050	.50729	.86178	.52225	.85279	.53705	.84355	31
30	.49242	.87036	.50754	.86163	.52250	.85264	.53730	.84339	30
31	.49268	.87021	.50779	.86148	.52275	.85249	.53754	.84324	29
32	.49293	.87007	.50804	.86133	.52299	.85234	.53779	.84308	28
33	.49318	.86993	.50829	.86119	.52324	.85218	.53804	.84292	27
34	.49344	.86978	.50854	.86104	.52349	.85203	.53828	.84277	26
35	.49369	.86964	.50879	.86089	.52374	.85188	.53853	.84261	25
36	.49394	.86949	.50904	.86074	.52399	.85173	.53877	.84245	24
37	.49419	.86935	.50929	.86059	.52423	.85157	.53902	.84230	23
38	.49445	.86921	.50954	.86045	.52448	.85142	.53926	.84214	22
39	.49470	.86906	.50979	.86030	.52473	.85127	.53951	.84198	21
40	.49495	.86892	.51004	.86015	.52498	.85112	.53975	.84182	20
41	.49521	.86878	.51029	.86000	.52522	.85096	.54000	.84167	19
42	.49546	.86863	.51054	.85985	.52547	.85081	.54024	.84151	18
43	.49571	.86849	.51079	.85970	.52572	.85066	.54049	.84135	17
44	.49596	.86834	.51104	.85956	.52597	.85051	.54073	.84120	16
45	.49622	.86820	.51129	.85941	.52621	.85035	.54097	.84104	15
46	.49647	.86805	.51154	.85926	.52646	.85020	.54122	.84088	14
47	.49672	.86791	.51179	.85911	.52671	.85005	.54146	.84072	13
48	.49697	.86777	.51204	.85896	.52696	.84989	.54171	.84057	12
49	.49723	.86762	.51229	.85881	.52720	.84974	.54195	.84041	11
50	.49748	.86748	.51254	.85866	.52745	.84959	.54220	.84025	10
51	.49773	.86733	.51279	.85851	.52770	.84943	.54244	.84009	9
52	.49798	.86719	.51304	.85836	.52794	.84928	.54269	.83994	8
53	.49824	.86704	.51329	.85821	.52819	.84913	.54293	.83978	7
54	.49849	.86690	.51354	.85806	.52844	.84897	.54317	.83962	6
55	.49874	.86675	.51379	.85792	.52869	.84882	.54342	.83946	5
56	.49899	.86661	.51404	.85777	.52893	.84866	.54366	.83930	4
57	.49924	.86646	.51429	.85762	.52918	.84851	.54391	.83915	3
58	.49950	.86632	.51454	.85747	.52943	.84836	.54415	.83899	2
59	.49975	.86617	.51479	.85732	.52967	.84820	.54440	.83883	1
60	.50000	.86603	.51504	.85717	.52992	.84805	.54464	.83867	0
′	COSINE	SINE	COSINE	SINE	COSINE	SINE	COSINE	SINE	′
	60°		59°		58°		57°		

′	33° SINE	33° COSINE	34° SINE	34° COSINE	35° SINE	35° COSINE	36° SINE	36° COSINE	′
0	.54464	.83867	.55919	.82904	.57358	.81915	.58779	.80902	60
1	.54488	.83851	.55943	.82887	.57381	.81899	.58802	.80885	59
2	.54513	.83835	.55968	.82871	.57405	.81882	.58826	.80867	58
3	.54537	.83819	.55992	.82855	.57429	.81865	.58849	.80850	57
4	.54561	.83804	.56016	.82839	.57453	.81848	.58873	.80833	56
5	.54586	.83788	.56040	.82822	.57477	.81832	.58896	.80816	55
6	.54610	.83772	.56064	.82806	.57501	.81815	.58920	.80799	54
7	.54635	.83756	.56088	.82790	.57524	.81798	.58943	.80782	53
8	.54659	.83740	.56112	.82773	.57548	.81782	.58967	.80765	52
9	.54683	.83724	.56136	.82757	.57572	.81765	.58990	.80748	51
10	.54708	.83708	.56160	.82741	.57596	.81748	.59014	.80730	50
11	.54732	83692	.56184	.82724	.57619	.81731	.59037	.80713	49
12	.54756	.83676	.56208	.82708	.57643	.81714	.59061	.80696	48
13	.54781	.83660	.56232	.82692	.57667	.81698	.59084	.80679	47
14	.54805	.83645	.56256	.82675	.57691	.81681	.59108	.80662	46
15	.54829	.83629	.56280	.82659	.57715	.81664	.59131	.80644	45
16	.54854	.83613	.56305	.82643	.57738	.81647	.59154	.80627	44
17	.54878	.83597	.56329	.82626	.57762	.81631	.59178	.80610	43
18	.54902	.83581	.56353	.82610	.57786	.81614	.59201	.80593	42
19	.54927	.83565	.56377	.82593	.57810	.81597	.59225	.80576	41
20	.54951	.83549	.56401	.82577	.57833	.81580	.59248	.80558	40
21	.54975	.83533	.56425	.82561	.57857	.81563	.59272	.80541	39
22	.54999	.83517	.56449	.82544	.57881	.81546	.59295	.80524	38
23	.55024	.83501	.56473	.82528	.57904	.81530	.59318	.80507	37
24	.55048	.83485	.56497	.82511	.57928	.81513	.59342	.80489	36
25	.55072	.83469	.56521	.82495	.57952	.81496	.59365	.80472	35
26	.55097	.83453	.56545	.82478	.57976	.81479	.59389	.80455	34
27	.55121	.83437	.56569	.82462	.57999	.81462	.59412	.80438	33
28	.55145	.83421	.56593	.82446	.58023	.81445	.59436	.80420	32
29	.55169	.83405	.56617	.82429	.58047	.81428	.59459	.80403	31
30	.55194	.83389	.56641	.82413	.58070	.81412	.59482	.80386	30
31	.55218	.83373	.56665	.82396	.58094	.81395	.59506	.80368	29
32	.55242	.83356	.56689	.823 0	.58118	.81378	.59529	.80351	28
33	.55266	.83340	.56713	.82363	.58141	.81361	.59552	.80334	27
34	.55291	.83324	.56736	.82347	.58165	.81344	.59576	.80316	26
35	.55315	.83308	.56760	.82330	.58189	.81327	.59599	.80299	25
36	.55339	.83292	.56784	.82314	.58212	.81310	.59622	.80282	24
37	.55363	.83276	.56808	.82297	.58236	.81293	.59646	.80264	23
38	.55388	.83260	.56832	.82281	.58260	.81276	.59669	.80247	22
39	.55412	.83244	.56856	.82264	.58283	.81259	.59693	.80230	21
40	.55436	.83228	.56880	.82248	.58307	.81242	.59716	.80212	20
41	.55460	.83212	.56904	.82231	.58330	.81225	.59739	.80195	19
42	.55484	.83195	.56928	.82214	.58354	.81208	.59763	.80178	18
43	.55509	.83179	.56952	.82198	.58378	.81191	.59786	.80160	17
44	.55533	.83163	.56976	.82181	.58401	.81174	.59809	.80143	16
45	.55557	.83147	.57000	.82165	.58425	.81157	.59832	.80125	15
46	.55581	.83131	.57024	.82148	.58449	.81140	.59856	.80108	14
47	.55605	.83115	.57047	.82132	.58472	.81123	.59879	.80091	13
48	.55630	.83098	.57071	.82115	.58496	.81106	.59902	.80073	12
49	.55654	.83082	.57095	.82098	.58519	.81089	.59926	.80056	11
50	.55678	.83066	.57119	.82082	.58543	.81072	.59949	.80038	10
51	.55702	.83050	.57143	.82065	.58567	.81055	.59972	.80021	9
52	.55726	.83034	.57167	.82048	.58590	.81038	.59995	.80003	8
53	.55750	.83017	.57191	.82032	.58614	.81021	.60019	.79986	7
54	.55775	.83001	.57215	.82015	.58637	.81004	.60042	.79968	6
55	.55799	.82985	.57238	.81999	.58661	.80987	.60065	.79951	5
56	.55823	.82969	.57262	.81982	.58684	.80970	.60089	.79934	4
57	.55847	.82953	.57286	.81965	.58708	.80953	.60112	.79916	3
58	.55871	.82936	.57310	.81949	.58731	.80936	.60135	.79899	2
59	.55895	.82920	.57334	.81932	.58755	.80919	.60158	.79881	1
60	.55919	.82904	.57358	.81915	.58779	.80902	.60182	.79864	0
′	COSINE	SINE	COSINE	SINE	COSINE	SINE	COSINE	SINE	′
	56°		55°		54°		53°		

′	37° SINE	COSINE	38° SINE	COSINE	39° SINE	COSINE	40° SINE	COSINE	′
0	.60182	.79864	.61566	.78801	.62932	.77715	.64279	.76604	60
1	.60205	.79846	.61589	.78783	.62955	.77696	.64301	.76586	59
2	.60228	.79829	.61612	.78765	.62977	.77678	.64323	.76567	58
3	.60251	.79811	.61635	.78747	.63000	.77660	.64346	.76548	57
4	.60274	.79793	.61658	.78729	.63022	.77641	.64368	.76530	56
5	.60298	.79776	.61681	.78711	.63045	.77623	.64390	.76511	55
6	.60321	.79758	.61704	.78694	.63068	.77605	.64412	.76492	54
7	.60344	.79741	.61726	.78676	.63090	.77586	.64435	.76473	53
8	.60367	.79723	.61740	.78658	.63113	.77568	.64457	.76455	52
9	.60390	.79706	.61772	.78640	.63135	.77550	.64479	.76436	51
10	.60414	.79688	.61795	.78622	.63158	.77531	.64501	.76417	50
11	.60437	.79671	.61818	.78604	.63180	.77513	.64524	.76398	49
12	.60460	.79653	.61841	.78586	.63203	.77494	.64546	.76380	48
13	.60483	.79635	.61864	.78568	.63225	.77476	.64568	.76361	47
14	.60506	.79618	.61887	.78550	.63248	.77458	.64590	.76342	46
15	.60529	.79600	.61909	.78532	.63271	.77439	.64612	.76323	45
16	.60553	.79583	.61932	.78514	.63293	.77421	.64635	.76304	44
17	.60576	.79565	.61955	.78496	.63316	.77402	.64657	.76286	43
18	.60599	.79547	.61978	.78478	.63338	.77384	.64679	.76267	42
19	.60622	.79530	.62001	.78460	.63361	.77366	.64701	.76248	41
20	.60645	.79512	.62024	.78442	.63383	.77347	.64723	.76229	40
21	.60668	.79494	.62046	.78424	.63406	.77329	.64746	.76210	39
22	.60691	.79477	.62069	.78405	.63428	.77310	.64768	.76192	38
23	.60714	.79459	.62092	.78387	.63451	.77292	.64790	.76173	37
24	.60738	.79441	.62115	.78369	.63473	.77273	.64812	.76154	36
25	.60761	.79424	.62138	.78351	.63496	.77255	.64834	.76135	35
26	.60784	.79406	.62160	.78333	.63518	.77236	.64856	.76116	34
27	.60807	.79388	.62183	.78315	.63540	.77218	.64878	.76097	33
28	.60830	.79371	.62206	.78297	.63563	.77199	.64901	.76078	32
29	.60853	.79353	.62229	.78279	.63585	.77181	.64923	.76059	31
30	.60876	.79335	.62251	.78261	.63608	.77162	.64945	.76041	30
31	.60899	.79318	.62274	.78243	.63630	.77144	.64967	.76022	29
32	.60922	.79300	.62297	.78225	.63653	.77125	.64989	.76003	28
33	.60945	.79282	.62320	.78206	.63675	.77107	.65011	.75984	27
34	.60968	.79264	.62342	.78188	.63698	.77088	.65033	.75965	26
35	.60991	.79247	.62365	.78170	.63720	.77070	.65055	.75946	25
36	.61015	.79229	.62388	.78152	.63742	.77051	.65077	.75927	24
37	.61038	.79211	.62411	.78134	.63765	.77033	.65100	.75908	23
38	.61061	.79193	.62433	.78116	.63787	.77014	.65122	.75889	22
39	.61084	.79176	.62456	.78098	.63810	.76996	.65144	.75870	21
40	.61107	.79158	.62479	.78079	.63832	.76977	.65166	.75851	20
41	.61130	.79140	.62502	.78061	.63854	.76959	.65188	.75832	19
42	.61153	.79122	.62524	.78043	.63877	.76940	.65210	.75813	18
43	.61176	.79105	.62547	.78025	.63899	.76921	.65232	.75794	17
44	.61199	.79087	.62570	.78007	.63922	.76903	.65254	.75775	16
45	.61222	.79069	.62592	.77988	.63944	.76884	.65276	.75756	15
46	.61245	.79051	.62615	.77970	.63966	.76866	.65298	.75738	14
47	.61268	.79033	.62638	.77952	.63989	.76847	.65320	.75719	13
48	.61291	.79016	.62660	.77934	.64011	.76828	.65342	.75700	12
49	.61314	.78998	.62683	.77916	.64033	.76810	.65364	.75680	11
50	.61337	.78980	.62706	.77897	.64056	.76791	.65386	.75661	10
51	.61360	.78962	.62728	.77879	.64078	.76772	.65408	.75642	9
52	.61383	.78944	.62751	.77861	.64100	.76754	.65430	.75623	8
53	.61406	.78926	.62774	.77843	.64123	.76735	.65452	.75604	7
54	.61429	.78908	.62796	.77824	.64145	.76717	.65474	.75585	6
55	.61451	.78891	.62819	.77806	.64167	.76698	.65496	.75566	5
56	.61474	.78873	.62842	.77788	.64190	.76679	.65518	.75547	4
57	.61497	.78855	.62864	.77769	.64212	.76661	.65540	.75528	3
58	.61520	.78837	.62887	.77751	.64234	.76642	.65562	.75509	2
59	.61543	.78819	.62909	.77733	.64256	.76623	.65584	.75490	1
60	.61566	.78801	.62932	.77715	.64279	.76604	.65606	.75471	0
′	COSINE	SINE	COSINE	SINE	COSINE	SINE	COSINE	SINE	′
	52°		51°		50°		49°		

′	41° Sine	41° Cosine	42° Sine	42° Cosine	43° Sine	43° Cosine	44° Sine	44° Cosine	′
0	.65606	.75471	.66913	.74314	.68200	.73135	.69466	.71934	60
1	.65628	.75452	.66935	.74295	.68221	.73116	.69487	.71914	59
2	.65650	.75433	.66956	.74276	.68242	.73096	.69508	.71894	58
3	.65672	.75414	.66978	.74256	.68264	.73076	.69529	.71873	57
4	.65694	.75395	.66999	.74237	.68285	.73056	.69549	.71853	56
5	.65716	.75375	.67021	.74217	.68306	.73036	.69570	.71833	55
6	.65738	.75356	.67043	.74198	.68327	.73016	.69591	.71813	54
7	.65759	.75337	.67064	.74178	.68349	.72996	.69612	.71792	53
8	.65781	.75318	.67086	.74159	.68370	.72976	.69633	.71772	52
9	.65803	.75299	.67107	.74139	.68391	.72957	.69654	.71752	51
10	.65825	.75280	.67129	.74120	.68412	.72937	.69675	.71732	50
11	.65847	.75261	.67151	.74100	.68434	.72917	.69696	.71711	49
12	.65869	.75241	.67172	.74080	.68455	.72897	.69717	.71691	48
13	.65891	.75222	.67194	.74061	.68476	.72877	.69737	.71671	47
14	.65913	.75203	.67215	.74041	.68497	.72857	.69758	.71650	46
15	.65935	.75184	.67237	.74022	.68518	.72837	.69779	.71630	45
16	.65956	.75165	.67258	.74002	.68539	.72817	.69800	.71610	44
17	.65978	.75146	.67280	.73983	.68561	.72797	.69821	.71590	43
18	.66000	.75126	.67301	.73963	.68582	.72777	.69842	.71569	42
19	.66022	.75107	.67323	.73944	.68603	.72757	.69862	.71549	41
20	.66044	.75088	.67344	.73924	.68624	.72737	.69883	.71529	40
21	.66066	.75069	.67366	.73904	.68645	.72717	.69904	.71508	39
22	.66088	.75050	.67387	.73885	.68666	.72697	.69925	.71488	38
23	.66109	.75030	.67409	.73865	.68688	.72677	.69946	.71468	37
24	.66131	.75011	.67430	.73846	.68709	.72657	.69966	.71447	36
25	.66153	.74992	.67452	.73826	.68730	.72637	.69987	.71427	35
26	.66175	.74973	.67473	.73806	.68751	.72617	.70008	.71407	34
27	.66197	.74953	.67495	.73787	.68772	.72597	.70029	.71386	33
28	.66218	.74934	.67516	.73767	.68793	.72577	.70049	.71366	32
29	.66240	.74915	.67538	.73747	.68814	.72557	.70070	.71345	31
30	.66262	.74896	.67559	.73728	.68835	.72537	.70091	.71325	30
31	.66284	.74876	.67580	.73708	.68857	.72517	.70112	.71305	29
32	.66306	.74857	.67602	.73688	.68878	.72497	.70132	.71284	28
33	.66327	.74838	.67623	.73669	.68899	.72477	.70153	.71264	27
34	.66349	.74818	.67645	.73649	.68920	.72457	.70174	.71243	26
35	.66371	.74799	.67666	.73629	.68941	.72437	.70195	.71223	25
36	.66393	.74780	.67688	.73610	.68962	.72417	.70215	.71203	24
37	.66414	.74760	.67709	.73590	.68983	.72397	.70236	.71182	23
38	.66436	.74741	.67730	.73570	.69004	.72377	.70257	.71162	22
39	.66458	.74722	.67752	.73551	.69025	.72357	.70277	.71141	21
40	.66480	.74703	.67773	.73531	.69046	.72337	.70298	.71121	20
41	.66501	.74683	.67795	.73511	.69067	.72317	.70319	.71100	19
42	.66523	.74664	.67816	.73491	.69088	.72297	.70339	.71080	18
43	.66545	.74644	.67837	.73472	.69109	.72277	.70360	.71059	17
44	.66566	.74625	.67859	.73452	.69130	.72257	.70381	.71039	16
45	.66588	.74606	.67880	.73432	.69151	.72236	.70401	.71019	15
46	.66610	.74586	.67901	.73413	.69172	.72216	.70422	.70998	14
47	.66632	.74567	.67923	.73393	.69193	.72196	.70443	.70978	13
48	.66653	.74548	.67944	.73373	.69214	.72176	.70463	.70957	12
49	.66675	.74528	.67965	.73353	.69235	.72156	.70484	.70937	11
50	.66697	.74509	.67987	.73333	.69256	.72136	.70505	.70916	10
51	.66718	.74489	.68008	.73314	.69277	.72116	.70525	.70896	9
52	.66740	.74470	.68029	.73294	.69298	.72095	.70546	.70875	8
53	.66762	.74451	.68051	.73274	.69319	.72075	.70567	.70855	7
54	.66783	.74431	.68072	.73254	.69340	.72055	.70587	.70834	6
55	.66805	.74412	.68093	.73234	.69361	.72035	.70608	.70813	5
56	.66827	.74392	.68115	.73215	.69382	.72015	.70628	.70793	4
57	.66848	.74373	.68136	.73195	.69403	.71995	.70649	.70772	3
58	.66870	.74353	.68157	.73175	.69424	.71974	.70670	.70752	2
59	.66891	.74334	.68179	.73155	.69445	.71954	.70690	.70731	1
60	.66913	.74314	.68200	.73135	.69466	.71934	.70711	.70711	0
′	Cosine	Sine	Cosine	Sine	Cosine	Sine	Cosine	Sine	′
	48°		47°		46°		45°		

′	0° Sec.	Co-sec.	1° Sec.	Co-sec.	2° Sec.	Co-sec.	3° Sec.	Co-sec.	′
0	1	Infinite.	1.0001	57.299	1.0006	28.654	1.0014	19.107	60
1	1	3437.70	1.0001	56.359	1.0006	28.417	1.0014	19.002	59
2	1	1718.90	1.0002	55.450	1.0006	28.184	1.0014	18.897	58
3	1	1145.90	1.0002	54.570	1.0006	27.955	1.0014	18.794	57
4	1	859.44	1.0002	53.718	1.0006	27.730	1.0014	18.692	56
5	1	687.55	1.0002	52.891	1.0007	27.508	1.0014	18.591	55
6	1	572.96	1.0002	52.090	1.0007	27.290	1.0015	18.491	54
7	1	491.11	1.0002	51.313	1.0007	27.075	1.0015	18.393	53
8	1	429.72	1.0002	50.558	1.0007	26.864	1.0015	18.295	52
9	1	381.97	1.0002	49.826	1.0007	26.655	1.0015	18.198	51
10	1	343.77	1.0002	49.114	1.0007	26.450	1.0015	18.103	50
11	1	312.52	1.0002	48.422	1.0007	26.249	1.0015	18.008	49
12	1	286.48	1.0002	47.750	1.0007	26.050	1.0016	17.914	48
13	1	264.44	1.0002	47.096	1.0007	25.854	1.0016	17.821	47
14	1	245.55	1.0002	46.460	1.0008	25.661	1.0016	17.730	46
15	1	229.18	1.0002	45.840	1.0008	25.471	1.0016	17.639	45
16	1	214.86	1.0002	45.237	1.0008	25.284	1.0016	17.549	44
17	1	202.22	1.0002	44.650	1.0008	25.100	1.0016	17.460	43
18	1	190.99	1.0002	44.077	1.0008	24.918	1.0017	17.372	42
19	1	180.73	1.0003	43.520	1.0008	24.739	1.0017	17.285	41
20	1	171.89	1.0003	42.976	1.0008	24.562	1.0017	17.198	40
21	1	163.70	1.0003	42.445	1.0008	24.358	1.0017	17.113	39
22	1	156.26	1.0003	41.928	1.0008	24.216	1.0017	17.028	38
23	1	149.47	1.0003	41.423	1.0009	24.047	1.0017	16.944	37
24	1	143.24	1.0003	40.930	1.0009	23.880	1.0018	16.861	36
25	1	137.51	1.0003	40.448	1.0009	23.716	1.0018	16.779	35
26	1	132.22	1.0003	39.978	1.0009	23.553	1.0018	16.698	34
27	1	127.32	1.0003	39.518	1.0009	23.393	1.0018	16.617	33
28	1	122.78	1.0003	39.069	1.0009	23.235	1.0018	16.538	32
29	1	118.54	1.0003	38.631	1.0009	23.079	1.0018	16.459	31
30	1	114.59	1.0003	38.201	1.0009	22.925	1.0019	16.380	30
31	1	110.90	1.0003	37.782	1.0010	22.774	1.0019	16.303	29
32	1	107.43	1.0003	37.371	1.0010	22.624	1.0019	16.226	28
33	1	104.17	1.0004	36.969	1.0010	22.476	1.0019	16.150	27
34	1	101.11	1.0004	36.576	1.0010	22.330	1.0019	16.075	26
35	1	95.223	1.0004	36.191	1.0010	22.186	1.0019	16.000	25
36	1	95.405	1.0004	35.814	1.0010	22.044	1.0020	15.926	24
37	1	92.914	1.0004	35.445	1.0010	21.904	1.0020	15.853	23
38	1.0001	92.469	1.0004	35.084	1.0010	21.765	1.0020	15.780	22
39	1.0001	88.149	1.0004	34.729	1.0011	21.629	1.0020	15.708	21
40	1.0001	85.946	1.0004	34.382	1.0011	21.494	1.0020	15.637	20
41	1.0001	83.849	1.0004	34.042	1.0011	21.360	1.0021	15.566	19
42	1.0001	81.853	1.0004	33.708	1.0011	21.228	1.0021	15.496	18
43	1.0001	79.950	1.0004	33.381	1.0011	21.098	1.0021	15.427	17
44	1.0001	78.133	1.0004	33.060	1.0011	20.970	1.0021	15.358	16
45	1.0001	76.396	1.0005	32.745	1.0011	20.843	1.0021	15.290	15
46	1.0001	74.736	1.0005	32.437	1.0012	20.717	1.0022	15.222	14
47	1.0001	73.146	1.0005	32.134	1.0012	20.593	1.0022	15.155	13
48	1.0001	71.622	1.0005	31.836	1.0012	20.471	1.0022	15.089	12
49	1.0001	71.160	1.0005	31.544	1.0012	20.350	1.0022	15.023	11
50	1.0001	68.757	1.0005	31.257	1.0012	20.230	1.0022	14.958	10
51	1.0001	67.409	1.0005	30.976	1.0012	20.112	1.0023	14.893	9
52	1.0001	66.113	1.0005	30.699	1.0012	19.995	1.0023	14.829	8
53	1.0001	64.866	1.0005	30.428	1.0013	19.880	1.0023	14.765	7
54	1.0001	63.664	1.0005	30.161	1.0013	19.766	1.0023	14.702	6
55	1.0001	62.507	1.0005	29.899	1.0013	19.653	1.0023	14.640	5
56	1.0001	61.391	1.0006	29.641	1.0013	19.541	1.0024	14.578	4
57	1.0001	61.314	1.0006	29.388	1.0013	19.431	1.0024	14.517	3
58	1.0001	59.274	1.0006	29.139	1.0013	19.322	1.0024	14.456	2
59	1.0001	58.270	1.0006	28.894	1.0013	19.214	1.0024	14.395	1
60	1.0001	57.299	1.0006	28.654	1.0014	19.107	1.0024	14.335	0
′	Co-sec.	Sec.	Co-sec.	Sec.	Co-sec.	Sec.	Co-sec.	Sec.	
		89°		88°		87°		86°	

′	4° Sec.	Co-sec.	5° Sec.	Co-sec.	6° Sec.	Co-sec.	7° Sec.	Co-sec.	′
0	1.0024	14.335	1.0038	11.474	1.0055	9.5668	1.0075	8.2055	60
1	1.0025	14.276	1.0038	11.436	1.0055	9.5404	1.0075	8.1861	59
2	1.0025	14.217	1.0039	11.398	1.0056	9.5141	1.0076	8.1668	58
3	1.0025	14.159	1.0039	11.360	1.0056	9.4880	1.0076	8.1476	57
4	1.0025	14.101	1.0039	11.323	1.0056	9.4620	1.0076	8.1285	56
5	1.0025	14.043	1.0039	11.286	1.0057	9.4362	1.0077	8.1094	55
6	1.0026	13.986	1.0040	11.249	1.0057	9.4105	1.0077	8.0905	54
7	1.0026	13.930	1.0040	11.213	1.0057	9.3850	1.0078	8.0717	53
8	1.0026	13.874	1.0040	11.176	1.0057	9.3596	1.0078	8.0529	52
9	1.0026	13.818	1.0040	11.140	1.0058	9.3343	1.0078	8.0342	51
10	1.0026	13.763	1.0041	11.104	1.0058	9.3092	1.0079	8.0156	50
11	1.0027	13.708	1.0041	11.069	1.0058	9.2842	1.0079	7.9971	49
12	1.0027	13.654	1.0041	11.033	1.0059	9.2593	1.0079	7.9787	48
13	1.0027	13.600	1.0041	10.988	1.0059	9.2346	1.0080	7.9604	47
14	1.0027	13.547	1.0042	10.963	1.0059	9.2100	1.0080	7.9421	46
15	1.0027	13.494	1.0042	10.929	1.0060	9.1855	1.0080	7.9240	45
16	1.0028	13.441	1.0042	10.894	1.0060	9.1612	1.0081	7.9059	44
17	1.0028	13.389	1.0043	10.860	1.0060	9.1370	1.0081	7.8879	43
18	1.0028	13.337	1.0043	10.826	1.0061	9.1129	1.0082	7.8700	42
19	1.0028	13.286	1.0043	10.792	1.0061	9.0890	1.0082	7.8522	41
20	1.0029	13.235	1.0043	10.758	1.0061	9.0651	1.0082	7.8344	40
21	1.0029	13.184	1.0044	10.725	1.0062	9.0414	1.0083	7.8168	39
22	1.0029	13.134	1.0044	10.692	1.0062	9.0179	1.0083	7.7992	38
23	1.0029	13.084	1.0044	10.659	1.0062	8.9944	1.0084	7.7817	37
24	1.0029	13.034	1.0044	10.626	1.0063	8.9711	1.0084	7.7642	36
25	1.0030	12.985	1.0045	10.593	1.0063	8.9479	1.0084	7.7469	35
26	1.0030	12.937	1.0045	10.561	1.0063	8.9248	1.0085	7.7296	34
27	1.0030	12.888	1.0045	10.529	1.0064	8.9018	1.0085	7.7124	33
28	1.0030	12.840	1.0046	10.497	1.0064	8.8790	1.0085	7.6953	32
29	1.0031	12.793	1.0046	10.465	1.0064	8.8563	1.0086	7.6783	31
30	1.0031	12.745	1.0046	10.433	1.0065	8.8337	1.0086	7.6613	30
31	1.0031	12.698	1.0046	10.402	1.0065	8.8112	1.0087	7.6444	29
32	1.0031	12.652	1.0047	10.371	1.0065	8.7888	1.0087	7.6276	28
33	1.0032	12.606	1.0047	10.340	1.0066	8.7665	1.0087	7.6108	27
34	1.0032	12.560	1.0047	10.309	1.0066	8.7444	1.0088	7.5942	26
35	1.0032	12.514	1.0048	10.278	1.0066	8.7223	1.0088	7.5776	25
36	1.0032	12.469	1.0048	10.248	1.0067	8.7004	1.0089	7.5611	24
37	1.0032	12.424	1.0048	10.217	1.0067	8.6786	1.0089	7.5446	23
38	1.0033	12.379	1.0048	10.187	1.0067	8.6569	1.0089	7.5282	22
39	1.0033	12.335	1.0049	10.157	1.0068	8.6353	1.0090	7.5119	21
40	1.0033	12.291	1.0049	10.127	1.0068	8.6138	1.0090	7.4957	20
41	1.0033	12.248	1.0049	10.098	1.0068	8.5924	1.0090	7.4795	19
42	1.0034	12.204	1.0050	10.068	1.0069	8.5711	1.0091	7.4634	18
43	1.0034	12.161	1.0050	10.039	1.0069	8.5499	1.0091	7.4474	17
44	1.0034	12.118	1.0050	10.010	1.0069	8.5289	1.0092	7.4315	16
45	1.0034	12.076	1.0050	9.9812	1.0070	8.5079	1.0092	7.4156	15
46	1.0035	12.034	1.0051	9.9525	1.0070	8.4871	1.0092	7.3998	14
47	1.0035	11.992	1.0051	9.9239	1.0070	8.4663	1.0093	7.3840	13
48	1.0035	11.950	1.0051	9.8955	1.0071	8.4457	1.0093	7.3683	12
49	1.0035	11.909	1.0052	9.8672	1.0071	8.4251	1.0094	7.3527	11
50	1.0036	11.868	1.0052	9.8391	1.0071	8.4046	1.0094	7.3372	10
51	1.0036	11.828	1.0052	9.8112	1.0072	8.3843	1.0094	7.3217	9
52	1.0036	11.787	1.0053	9.7834	1.0072	8.3640	1.0095	7.3063	8
53	1.0036	11.747	1.0053	9.7558	1.0073	8.3439	1.0095	7.2909	7
54	1.0037	11.707	1.0053	9.7283	1.0073	8.3238	1.0096	7.2757	6
55	1.0037	11.668	1.0053	9.7010	1.0073	8.3039	1.0096	7.2604	5
56	1.0037	11.628	1.0054	9.6730	1.0074	8.2840	1.0097	7.2453	4
57	1.0037	11.589	1.0054	9.6469	1.0074	8.2642	1.0097	7.2302	3
58	1.0038	11.550	1.0054	9.6200	1.0074	8.2446	1.0097	7.2152	2
59	1.0038	11.512	1.0055	9.5933	1.0075	8.2250	1.0098	7.2002	1
60	1.0038	11.474	1.0055	9.5668	1.0075	8.2055	1.0098	7.1853	0
′	Co-sec.	Sec.	Co-sec.	Sec.	Co-sec.	Sec.	Co-sec.	Sec.	′
	85°		84°		83°		82°		

′	8° SEC.	CO-SEC.	9° SEC.	CO-SEC.	10° SEC.	CO-SEC.	11° SEC.	CO-SEC.	′
0	1.0098	7.1853	1.0125	6.3924	1.0154	5.7588	1.0187	5.2408	60
1	1.0099	7.1704	1.0125	6.3807	1.0155	5.7493	1.0188	5.2330	59
2	1.0099	7.1557	1.0125	6.3690	1.0155	5.7398	1.0188	5.2252	58
3	1.0099	7.1409	1.0126	6.3574	1.0156	5.7304	1.0189	5.2174	57
4	1.0100	7.1263	1.0126	6.3458	1.0156	5.7210	1.0189	5.2097	56
5	1.0100	7.1117	1.0127	6.3343	1.0157	5.7117	1.0190	5.2019	55
6	1.0101	7.0972	1.0127	6.3228	1.0157	5.7023	1.0191	5.1942	54
7	1.0101	7.0827	1.0128	6.3113	1.0158	5.6930	1.0191	5.1865	53
8	1.0102	7.0683	1.0128	6.2999	1.0158	5.6838	1.0192	5.1788	52
9	1.0102	7.0539	1.0129	6.2885	1.0159	5.6745	1.0192	5.1712	51
10	1.0102	7.0396	1.0129	6.2772	1.0159	5.6653	1.0193	5.1636	50
11	1.0103	7.0254	1.0130	6.2659	1.0160	5.6561	1.0193	5.1560	49
12	1.0103	7.0112	1.0130	6.2546	1.0160	5.6470	1.0194	5.1484	48
13	1.0104	6.9971	1.0131	6.2434	1.0161	5.6379	1.0195	5.1409	47
14	1.0104	6.9830	1.0131	6.2322	1.0162	5.6288	1.0195	5.1333	46
15	1.0104	6.9690	1.0132	6.2211	1.0162	5.6197	1.0196	5.1258	45
16	1.0105	6.9550	1.0132	6.2100	1.0163	5.6107	1.0196	5.1183	44
17	1.0105	6.9411	1.0133	6.1990	1.0163	5.6017	1.0197	5.1109	43
18	1.0106	6.9273	1.0133	6.1880	1.0164	5.5928	1.0198	5.1034	42
19	1.0106	6.9135	1.0134	6.1770	1.0164	5.5838	1.0198	5.0960	41
20	1.0107	6.8998	1.0134	6.1661	1.0165	5.5749	1.0199	5.0886	40
21	1.0107	6.8861	1.0135	6.1552	1.0165	5.5660	1.0199	5.0812	39
22	1.0107	6.8725	1.0135	6.1443	1.0166	5.5572	1.0200	5.0739	38
23	1.0108	6.8589	1.0136	6.1335	1.0166	5.5484	1.0201	5.0666	37
24	1.0108	6.8454	1.0136	6.1227	1.0167	5.5336	1.0201	5.0593	36
25	1.0109	6.8320	1.0136	6.1120	1.0167	5.5308	1.0202	5.0520	35
26	1.0109	6.8185	1.0137	6.1013	1.0168	5.5221	1.0202	5.0447	34
27	1.0110	6.8052	1.0137	6.0906	1.0169	5.5134	1.0203	5.0375	33
28	1.0110	6.7919	1.0138	6.0800	1.0169	5.5047	1.0204	5.0302	32
29	1.0111	6.7787	1.0138	6.0694	1.0170	5.4960	1.0204	5.0230	31
30	1.0111	6.7655	1.0139	6.0588	1.0170	5.4874	1.0205	5.0158	30
31	1.0111	6.7523	1.0139	6.0483	1.0171	5.4788	1.0205	5.0087	29
32	1.0112	6.7392	1.0140	6.0379	1.0171	5.4702	1.0206	5.0015	28
33	1.0112	6.7262	1.0140	6.0274	1.0172	5.4617	1.0207	4.9944	27
34	1.0113	6.7132	1.0141	6.0170	1.0172	5.4532	1.0207	4.9873	26
35	1.0113	6.7003	1.0141	6.0066	1.0173	5.4447	1.0208	4.9802	25
36	1.0114	6.6874	1.0142	5.9963	1.0174	5.4362	1.0208	4.9732	24
37	1.0114	6.6745	1.0142	5.9860	1.0174	5.4278	1.0209	4.9661	23
38	1.0115	6.6617	1.0143	5.9758	1.0175	5.4194	1.0210	4.9591	22
39	1.0115	6.6490	1.0143	5.9655	1.0175	5.4110	1.0210	4.9521	21
40	1.0115	6.6363	1.0144	5.9554	1.0176	5.4026	1.0211	4.9452	20
41	1.0116	6.6237	1.0144	5.9452	1.0176	5.3943	1.0211	4.9382	19
42	1.0116	6.6111	1.0145	5.9351	1.0177	5.3860	1.0212	4.9313	18
43	1.0117	6.5985	1.0145	5.9250	1.0177	5.3777	1.0213	4.9243	17
44	1.0117	6.5860	1.0146	5.9150	1.0178	5.3695	1.0213	4.9175	16
45	1.0118	6.5736	1.0146	5.9049	1.0179	5.3612	1.0214	4.9106	15
46	1.0118	6.5612	1.0147	5.8950	1.0179	5.3530	1.0215	4.9037	14
47	1.0119	6.5488	1.0147	5.8850	1.0180	5.3449	1.0215	4.8969	13
48	1.0119	6.5365	1.0148	5.8751	1.0180	5.3367	1.0216	4.8901	12
49	1.0119	6.5243	1.0148	5.8652	1.0181	5.3286	1.0216	4.8833	11
50	1.0120	6.5121	1.0149	5.8554	1.0181	5.3205	1.0217	4.8765	10
51	1.0120	6.4999	1.0150	5.8456	1.0182	5.3124	1.0218	4.8697	9
52	1.0121	6.4878	1.0150	5.8358	1.0182	5.3044	1.0218	4.8630	8
53	1.0121	6.4757	1.0151	5.8261	1.0183	5.2963	1.0219	4.8563	7
54	1.0122	6.4637	1.0151	5.8163	1.0184	5.2883	1.0220	4.8496	6
55	1.0122	6.4517	1.0152	5.8067	1.0184	5.2803	1.0220	4.8429	5
56	1.0123	6.4398	1.0152	5.7970	1.0185	5.2724	1.0221	4.8362	4
57	1.0123	6.4270	1.0153	5.7874	1.0185	5.2645	1.0221	4.8296	3
58	1.0124	6.4160	1.0153	5.7778	1.0186	5.2566	1.0222	4.8229	2
59	1.0124	6.4042	1.0154	5.7683	1.0186	5.2487	1.0223	4.8163	1
60	1.0125	6.3924	1.0154	5.7588	1.0187	5.2408	1.0223	4.8097	0
′	CO-SEC.	SEC.	CO-SEC.	SEC.	CO-SEC.	SEC.	CO-SEC.	SEC.	′
	81°		80°		79°		78°		

'	12° SEC.	CO-SEC.	13° SEC.	CO-SEC.	14° SEC.	CO-SEC.	15° SEC.	CO-SEC.	'
0	1.0223	4.8097	1.0263	4.4454	1.0306	4.1336	1.0353	3.8637	60
1	1.0224	4.8032	1.0264	4.4398	1.0307	4.1287	1.0353	3.8595	59
2	1.0225	4.7966	1.0264	4.4342	1.0308	4.1239	1.0354	3.8553	58
3	1.0225	4.7901	1.0265	4.4287	1.0308	4.1191	1.0355	3.8512	57
4	1.0226	4.7835	1.0266	4.4231	1.0309	4.1144	1.0356	3.8470	56
5	1.0226	4.7770	1.0266	4.4176	1.0310	4.1096	1.0357	3.8428	55
6	1.0227	4.7706	1.0267	4.4121	1.0311	4.1048	1.0358	3.8387	54
7	1.0228	4.7641	1.0268	4.4065	1.0311	4.1001	1.0358	3.8346	53
8	1.0228	4.7576	1.0268	4.4011	1.0312	4.0953	1.0359	3.8304	52
9	1.0229	4.7512	1.0269	4.3956	1.0313	4.0906	1.0360	3.8263	51
10	1.0230	4.7448	1.0270	4.3910	1.0314	4.0859	1.0361	3.8222	50
11	1.0230	4.7384	1.0271	4.3847	1.0314	4.0812	1.0362	3.8181	49
12	1.0231	4.7320	1.0271	4.3792	1.0315	4.0765	1.0362	3.8140	48
13	1.0232	4.7257	1.0272	4.3738	1.0316	4.0718	1.0363	3.8100	47
14	1.0232	4.7193	1.0273	4.3684	1.0317	4.0672	1.0364	3.8059	46
15	1.0233	4.7130	1.0273	4.3630	1.0317	4.0625	1.0365	3.8018	45
16	1.0234	4.7067	1.0274	4.3576	1.0318	4.0579	1.0366	3.7978	44
17	1.0234	4.7004	1.0275	4.3522	1.0319	4.0532	1.0367	3.7937	43
18	1.0235	4.6942	1.0276	4.3469	1.0320	4.0486	1.0367	3.7897	42
19	1.0235	4.6879	1.0276	4.3415	1.0320	4.0440	1.0368	3.7857	41
20	1.0236	4.6817	1.0277	4.3362	1.0321	4.0394	1.0369	3.7816	40
21	1.0237	4.6754	1.0278	4.3309	1.0322	4.0348	1.0370	3.7776	39
22	1.0237	4.6692	1.0278	4.3256	1.0323	4.0302	1.0371	3.7736	38
23	1.0238	4.6631	1.0279	4.3203	1.0323	4.0256	1.0371	3.7697	37
24	1.0239	4.6569	1.0280	4.3150	1.0324	4.0211	1.0372	3.7657	36
25	1.0239	4.6507	1.0280	4.3098	1.0325	4.0165	1.0373	3.7617	35
26	1.0240	4.6446	1.0281	4.3045	1.0326	4.0120	1.0374	3.7577	34
27	1.0241	4.6385	1.0282	4.2993	1.0327	4.0074	1.0375	3.7538	33
28	1.0241	4.6324	1.0283	4.2941	1.0327	4.0029	1.0376	3.7498	32
29	1.0242	4.6263	1.0283	4.2888	1.0328	3.9984	1.0376	3.7459	31
30	1.0243	4.6202	1.0284	4.2836	1.0329	3.9939	1.0377	3.7420	30
31	1.0243	4.6142	1.0285	4.2785	1.0330	3.9894	1.0378	3.7380	29
32	1.0244	4.6081	1.0285	4.2733	1.0330	3.9850	1.0379	3.7341	28
33	1.0245	4.6021	1.0286	4.2681	1.0331	3.9805	1.0380	3.7302	27
34	1.0245	4.5961	1.0287	4.2630	1.0332	3.9760	1.0381	3.7263	26
35	1.0246	4.5901	1.0288	4.2579	1.0333	3.9716	1.0382	3.7224	25
36	1.0247	4.5841	1.0288	4.2527	1.0334	3.9672	1.0382	3.7186	24
37	1.0247	4.5782	1.0289	4.2476	1.0334	3.9627	1.0383	3.7147	23
38	1.0248	4.5722	1.0290	4.2425	1.0335	3.9583	1.0384	3.7108	22
39	1.0249	4.5663	1.0291	4.2375	1.0336	3.9539	1.0385	3.7070	21
40	1.0249	4.5604	1.0291	4.2324	1.0337	3.9495	1.0386	3.7031	20
41	1.0250	4.5545	1.0292	4.2273	1.0338	3.9451	1.0387	3.6993	19
42	1.0251	4.5486	1.0293	4.2223	1.0338	3.9408	1.0387	3.6955	18
43	1.0251	4.5428	1.0293	4.2173	1.0339	3.9364	1.0388	3.6917	17
44	1.0252	4.5369	1.0294	4.2122	1.0340	3.9320	1.0389	3.6878	16
45	1.0253	4.5311	1.0295	4.2072	1.0341	3.9277	1.0390	3.6840	15
46	1.0253	4.5253	1.0296	4.2022	1.0341	3.9234	1.0391	3.6802	14
47	1.0254	4.5195	1.0296	4.1972	1.0342	3.9190	1.0392	3.6765	13
48	1.0255	4.5137	1.0297	4.1923	1.0343	3.9147	1.0393	3.6727	12
49	1.0255	4.5079	1.0298	4.1873	1.0344	3.9104	1.0393	3.6689	11
50	1.0256	4.5021	1.0299	4.1824	1.0345	3.9061	1.0394	3.6651	10
51	1.0257	4.4964	1.0299	4.1774	1.0345	3.9018	1.0395	3.6614	9
52	1.0257	4.4907	1.0300	4.1725	1.0346	3.8976	1.0396	3.6576	8
53	1.0258	4.4850	1.0301	4.1676	1.0347	3.8933	1.0397	3.6539	7
54	1.0259	4.4793	1.0302	4.1627	1.0348	3.8990	1.0398	3.6502	6
55	1.0260	4.4736	1.0302	4.1578	1.0340	3.8848	1.0399	3.6464	5
56	1.0260	4.4679	1.0303	4.1529	1.0340	3.8805	1.0399	3.6427	4
57	1.0261	4.4623	1.0304	4.1481	1.0350	3.8763	1.0400	3.6390	3
58	1.0262	4.4566	1.0305	4.1432	1.0351	3.8721	1.0401	3.6353	2
59	1.0262	4.4510	1.0305	4.1384	1.0352	3.8679	1.0402	3.6316	1
60	1.0263	4.4454	1.0306	4.1336	1.0353	3.8637	1.0403	3.6279	0
'	CO-SEC.	SEC.	CO-SEC.	SEC.	CO-SEC.	SEC.	CO-SEC.	SEC.	'
	77°		76°		75°		74°		

'	16° SEC.	CO-SEC.	17° SEC.	CO-SEC.	18° SEC.	CO-SEC.	19° SEC.	CO-SEC.	'
0	1.0403	3.6279	1.0457	3.4203	1.0515	3.2361	1.0576	3.0715	60
1	1.0404	3.6243	1.0458	3.4170	1.0516	3.2332	1.0577	3.0690	59
2	1.0405	3.6206	1.0459	3.4138	1.0517	3.2303	1.0578	3.0664	58
3	1.0406	3.6169	1.0460	3.4106	1.0518	3.2274	1.0579	3.0638	57
4	1.0406	3.6133	1.0461	3.4073	1.0519	3.2245	1.0580	3.0612	56
5	1.0407	3.6096	1.0461	3.4041	1.0520	3.2216	1.0581	3.0586	55
6	1.0408	3.6060	1.0462	3.4009	1.0521	3.2188	1.0582	3.0561	54
7	1.0409	3.6024	1.0463	3.3977	1.0522	3.2159	1.0584	3.0535	53
8	1.0410	3.5987	1.0464	3.3945	1.0523	3.2131	1.0585	3.0509	52
9	1.0411	3.5951	1.0465	3.3913	1.0524	3.2102	1.0586	3.0484	51
10	1.0412	3.5915	1.0466	3.3881	1.0525	3.2074	1.0587	3.0458	50
11	1.0413	3.5879	1.0467	3.3849	1.0526	3.2045	1.0588	3.0433	49
12	1.0413	3.5843	1.0468	3.3817	1.0527	3.2017	1.0589	3.0407	48
13	1.0414	3.5807	1.0469	3.3785	1.0528	3.1989	1.0590	3.0382	47
14	1.0415	3.5772	1.0470	3.3754	1.0529	3.1960	1.0591	3.0357	46
15	1.0416	3.5736	1.0471	3.3722	1.0530	3.1932	1.0592	3.0331	45
16	1.0417	3.5700	1.0472	3.3690	1.0531	3.1904	1.0593	3.0306	44
17	1.0418	3.5665	1.0473	3.3659	1.0532	3.1876	1.0594	3.0281	43
18	1.0419	3.5629	1.0474	3.3627	1.0533	3.1848	1.0595	3.0256	42
19	1.0420	3.5594	1.0475	3.3596	1.0534	3.1820	1.0596	3.0231	41
20	1.0420	3.5559	1.0476	3.3565	1.0535	3.1792	1.0598	3.0206	40
21	1.0421	3.5523	1.0477	3.3534	1.0536	3.1764	1.0599	3.0181	39
22	1.0422	3.5488	1.0478	3.3502	1.0537	3.1736	1.0600	3.0156	38
23	1.0423	3.5453	1.0478	3.3471	1.0538	3.1708	1.0601	3.0131	37
24	1.0424	3.5418	1.0479	3.3440	1.0539	3.1681	1.0602	3.0106	36
25	1.0425	3.5383	1.0480	3.3409	1.0540	3.1653	1.0603	3.0081	35
26	1.0426	3.5348	1.0481	3.3378	1.0541	3.1625	1.0604	3.0056	34
27	1.0427	3.5313	1.0482	3.3347	1.0542	3.1598	1.0605	3.0031	33
28	1.0428	3.5279	1.0483	3.3316	1.0543	3.1570	1.0606	3.0007	32
29	1.0428	3.5244	1.0484	3.3286	1.0544	3.1543	1.0607	2.9982	31
30	1.0429	3.5209	1.0485	3.3255	1.0545	3.1515	1.0608	2.9957	30
31	1.0430	3.5175	1.0486	3.3224	1.0546	3.1488	1.0609	2.9933	29
32	1.0431	3.5140	1.0487	3.3194	1.0547	3.1461	1.0611	2.9908	28
33	1.0432	3.5106	1.0488	3.3163	1.0548	3.1433	1.0612	2.9884	27
34	1.0433	3.5072	1.0489	3.3133	1.0549	3.1406	1.0613	2.9859	26
35	1.0434	3.5037	1.0490	3.3102	1.0550	3.1379	1.0614	2.9835	25
36	1.0435	3.5003	1.0491	3.3072	1.0551	3.1352	1.0615	2.9810	24
37	1.0436	3.4969	1.0492	3.3042	1.0552	3.1325	1.0616	2.9786	23
38	1.0437	3.4935	1.0493	3.3011	1.0553	3.1298	1.0617	2.9762	22
39	1.0438	3.4901	1.0494	3.2981	1.0554	3.1271	1.0618	2.9738	21
40	1.0438	3.4867	1.0495	3.2951	1.0555	3.1244	1.0619	2.9713	20
41	1.0439	3.4833	1.0496	3.2921	1.0556	3.1217	1.0620	2.9689	19
42	1.0440	3.4799	1.0497	3.2891	1.0557	3.1190	1.0622	2.9665	18
43	1.0441	3.4766	1.0498	3.2861	1.0558	3.1163	1.0623	2.9641	17
44	1.0442	3.4732	1.0499	3.2831	1.0559	3.1137	1.0624	2.9617	16
45	1.0443	3.4698	1.0500	3.2801	1.0560	3.1110	1.0625	2.9593	15
46	1.0444	3.4665	1.0501	3.2772	1.0561	3.1083	1.0626	2.9569	14
47	1.0445	3.4632	1.0502	3.2742	1.0562	3.1057	1.0627	2.9545	13
48	1.0446	3.4598	1.0503	3.2712	1.0563	3.1030	1.0628	2.9521	12
49	1.0447	3.4565	1.0504	3.2683	1.0564	3.1004	1.0629	2.9497	11
50	1.0448	3.4532	1.0505	3.2653	1.0566	3.0977	1.0630	2.9474	10
51	1.0448	3.4498	1.0506	3.2624	1.0567	3.0951	1.0632	2.9450	9
52	1.0449	3.4465	1.0507	3.2594	1.0568	3.0925	1.0633	2.9426	8
53	1.0450	3.4432	1.0508	3.2565	1.0569	3.0898	1.0634	2.9402	7
54	1.0451	3.4399	1.0509	3.2535	1.0570	3.0872	1.0635	2.9379	6
55	1.0452	3.4366	1.0510	3.2506	1.0571	3.0846	1.0636	2.9355	5
56	1.0453	3.4334	1.0511	3.2477	1.0572	3.0820	1.0637	2.9332	4
57	1.0454	3.4301	1.0512	3.2448	1.0573	3.0793	1.0638	2.9308	3
58	1.0455	3.4268	1.0513	3.2419	1.0574	3.0767	1.0639	2.9285	2
59	1.0456	3.4236	1.0514	3.2390	1.0575	3.0741	1.0641	2.9261	1
60	1.0457	3.4203	1.0515	3.2361	1.0576	3.0715	1.0642	2.9238	0
'	CO-SEC.	SEC.	CO-SEC.	SEC.	CO-SEC.	SEC.	CO-SEC.	SEC.	'
	73°		72°		71°		70°		

′	20° Sec.	20° Co-sec.	21° Sec.	21° Co-sec.	22° Sec.	22° Co-sec.	23° Sec.	23° Co-sec.	′
0	1.0642	2.9238	1.0711	2.7904	1.0785	2.6695	1.0864	2.5593	60
1	1.0643	2.9215	1.0713	2.7883	1.0787	2.6675	1.0865	2.5575	59
2	1.0644	2.9191	1.0714	2.7862	1.0788	2.6656	1.0866	2.5558	58
3	1.0645	2.9168	1.0715	2.7841	1.0789	2.6637	1.0868	2.5540	57
4	1.0646	2.9145	1.0716	2.7820	1.0790	2.6618	1.0869	2.5523	56
5	1.0647	2.9122	1.0717	2.7799	1.0792	2.6599	1.0870	2.5506	55
6	1.0648	2.9098	1.0719	2.7778	1.0793	2.6580	1.0872	2.5488	54
7	1.0650	2.9075	1.0720	2.7757	1.0794	2.6561	1.0873	2.5471	53
8	1.0651	2.9052	1.0721	2.7736	1.0795	2.6542	1.0874	2.5453	52
9	1.0652	2.9029	1.0722	2.7715	1.0797	2.6523	1.0876	2.5436	51
10	1.0653	2.9006	1.0723	2.7694	1.0798	2.6504	1.0877	2.5419	50
11	1.0654	2.8983	1.0725	2.7674	1.0799	2.6485	1.0878	2.5402	49
12	1.0655	2.8960	1.0726	2.7653	1.0801	2.6466	1.0880	2.5384	48
13	1.0656	2.8937	1.0727	2.7632	1.0802	2.6447	1.0881	2.5367	47
14	1.0658	2.8915	1.0728	2.7611	1.0803	2.6428	1.0882	2.5350	46
15	1.0659	2.8892	1.0729	2.7591	1.0804	2.6410	1.0884	2.5333	45
16	1.0660	2.8869	1.0731	2.7570	1.0806	2.6391	1.0885	2.5316	44
17	1.0661	2.8846	1.0732	2.7550	1.0807	2.6372	1.0886	2.5299	43
18	1.0662	2.8824	1.0733	2.7529	1.0808	2.6353	1.0888	2.5281	42
19	1.0663	2.8801	1.0734	2.7509	1.0810	2.6335	1.0889	2.5264	41
20	1.0664	2.8778	1.0736	2.7488	1.0811	2.6316	1.0891	2.5247	40
21	1.0666	2.8756	1.0737	2.7468	1.0812	2.6297	1.0892	2.5230	39
22	1.0667	2.8733	1.0738	2.7447	1.0813	2.6279	1.0893	2.5213	38
23	1.0668	2.8711	1.0739	2.7427	1.0815	2.6260	1.0895	2.5196	37
24	1.0669	2.8688	1.0740	2.7406	1.0816	2.6242	1.0896	2.5179	36
25	1.0670	2.8666	1.0742	2.7386	1.0817	2.6223	1.0897	2.5163	35
26	1.0671	2.8644	1.0743	2.7366	1.0819	2.6205	1.0899	2.5146	34
27	1.0673	2.8621	1.0744	2.7346	1.0820	2.6186	1.0900	2.5129	33
28	1.0674	2.8599	1.0745	2.7325	1.0821	2.6168	1.0902	2.5112	32
29	1.0675	2.8577	1.0747	2.7305	1.0823	2.6150	1.0903	2.5095	31
30	1.0676	2.8554	1.0748	2.7285	1.0824	2.6131	1.0904	2.5078	30
31	1.0677	2.8532	1.0749	2.7265	1.0825	2.6113	1.0906	2.5062	29
32	1.0678	2.8510	1.0750	2.7245	1.0826	2.6095	1.0907	2.5045	28
33	1.0679	2.8488	1.0751	2.7225	1.0828	2.6076	1.0908	2.5028	27
34	1.0681	2.8466	1.0753	2.7205	1.0829	2.6058	1.0910	2.5011	26
35	1.0682	2.8444	1.0754	2.7185	1.0830	2.6040	1.0911	2.4995	25
36	1.0683	2.8422	1.0755	2.7165	1.0832	2.6022	1.0913	2.4978	24
37	1.0684	2.8400	1.0756	2.7145	1.0833	2.6003	1.0914	2.4961	23
38	1.0685	2.8378	1.0758	2.7125	1.0834	2.5985	1.0915	2.4945	22
39	1.0686	2.8356	1.0759	2.7105	1.0836	2.5967	1.0917	2.4928	21
40	1.0688	2.8334	1.0760	2.7085	1.0837	2.5949	1.0918	2.4912	20
41	1.0689	2.8312	1.0761	2.7065	1.0838	2.5931	1.0920	2.4895	19
42	1.0690	2.8290	1.0763	2.7045	1.0840	2.5913	1.0921	2.4879	18
43	1.0691	2.8269	1.0764	2.7026	1.0841	2.5895	1.0922	2.4862	17
44	1.0692	2.8247	1.0765	2.7006	1.0842	2.5877	1.0924	2.4846	16
45	1.0694	2.8225	1.0766	2.6986	1.0844	2.5859	1.0925	2.4829	15
46	1.0695	2.8204	1.0768	2.6967	1.0845	2.5841	1.0927	2.4813	14
47	1.0696	2.8182	1.0769	2.6947	1.0846	2.5823	1.0928	2.4797	13
48	1.0697	2.8160	1.0770	2.6927	1.0847	2.5805	1.0929	2.4780	12
49	1.0698	2.8139	1.0771	2.6908	1.0849	2.5787	1.0931	2.4764	11
50	1.0699	2.8117	1.0773	2.6888	1.0850	2.5770	1.0932	2.4748	10
51	1.0701	2.8096	1.0774	2.6869	1.0851	2.5752	1.0934	2.4731	9
52	1.0702	2.8074	1.0775	2.6849	1.0853	2.5734	1.0935	2.4715	8
53	1.0703	2.8053	1.0776	2.6830	1.0854	2.5716	1.0936	2.4699	7
54	1.0704	2.8032	1.0778	2.6810	1.0855	2.5699	1.0938	2.4683	6
55	1.0705	2.8010	1.0779	2.6791	1.0857	2.5681	1.0939	2.4666	5
56	1.0707	2.7989	1.0780	2.6772	1.0858	2.5663	1.0941	2.4650	4
57	1.0708	2.7968	1.0781	2.6752	1.0859	2.5646	1.0942	2.4634	3
58	1.0709	2.7947	1.0783	2.6733	1.0861	2.5628	1.0943	2.4618	2
59	1.0710	2.7925	1.0784	2.6714	1.0862	2.5610	1.0945	2.4602	1
60	1.0711	2.7904	1.0785	2.6695	1.0864	2.5593	1.0946	2.4586	0
′	Co-sec.	Sec.	Co-sec.	Sec.	Co-sec.	Sec.	Co-sec.	Sec.	′
	69°		68°		67°		66°		

′	24° SEC.	CO-SEC.	25° SEC.	CO-SEC.	26° SEC.	CO-SEC.	27° SEC.	CO-SEC.	′
0	1.0946	2.4586	1.1034	2.3662	1.1126	2.2812	1.1223	2.2027	60
1	1.0948	2.4570	1.1035	2.3647	1.1127	2.2798	1.1225	2.2014	59
2	1.0949	2.4554	1.1037	2.3632	1.1129	2.2784	1.1226	2.2002	58
3	1.0951	2.4538	1.1038	2.3618	1.1131	2.2771	1.1228	2.1989	57
4	1.0952	2.4522	1.1040	2.3603	1.1132	2.2757	1.1230	2.1977	56
5	1.0953	2.4506	1.1041	2.3588	1.1134	2.2744	1.1231	2.1964	55
6	1.0955	2.4490	1.1043	2.3574	1.1135	2.2730	1.1233	2.1952	54
7	1.0956	2.4474	1.1044	2.3559	1.1137	2.2717	1.1235	2.1939	53
8	1.0958	2.4458	1.1046	2.3544	1.1139	2.2703	1.1237	2.1927	52
9	1.0959	2.4442	1.1047	2.3530	1.1140	2.2690	1.1238	2.1914	51
10	1.0961	2.4426	1.1049	2.3515	1.1142	2.2676	1.1240	2.1902	50
11	1.0962	2.4411	1.1050	2.3501	1.1143	2.2663	1.1242	2.1889	49
12	1.0963	2.4395	1.1052	2.3486	1.1145	2.2650	1.1243	2.1877	48
13	1.0965	2.4379	1.1053	2.3472	1.1147	2.2636	1.1245	2.1865	47
14	1.0966	2.4363	1.1055	2.3457	1.1148	2.2623	1.1247	2.1852	46
15	1.0968	2.4347	1.1056	2.3443	1.1150	2.2610	1.1248	2.1840	45
16	1.0969	2.4332	1.1058	2.3428	1.1151	2.2596	1.1250	2.1828	44
17	1.0971	2.4316	1.1059	2.3414	1.1153	2.2583	1.1252	2.1815	43
18	1.0972	2.4300	1.1061	2.3399	1.1155	2.2570	1.1253	2.1803	42
19	1.0973	2.4285	1.1062	2.3385	1.1156	2.2556	1.1255	2.1791	41
20	1.0975	2.4269	1.1064	2.3371	1.1158	2.2543	1.1257	2.1778	40
21	1.0976	2.4254	1.1065	2.3356	1.1159	2.2530	1.1258	2.1766	39
22	1.0978	2.4238	1.1067	2.3342	1.1161	2.2517	1.1260	2.1754	38
23	1.0979	2.4222	1.1068	2.3328	1.1163	2.2503	1.1262	2.1742	37
24	1.0981	2.4207	1.1070	2.3313	1.1164	2.2490	1.1264	2.1730	36
25	1.0982	2.4191	1.1072	2.3299	1.1166	2.2477	1.1265	2.1717	35
26	1.0984	2.4176	1.1073	2.3285	1.1167	2.2464	1.1267	2.1705	34
27	1.0985	2.4160	1.1075	2.3271	1.1169	2.2451	1.1269	2.1693	33
28	1.0986	2.4145	1.1076	2.3256	1.1171	2.2438	1.1270	2.1681	32
29	1.0988	2.4130	1.1078	2.3242	1.1172	2.2425	1.1272	2.1669	31
30	1.0989	2.4114	1.1079	2.3228	1.1174	2.2411	1.1274	2.1657	30
31	1.0991	2.4099	1.1081	2.3214	1.1176	2.2398	1.1275	2.1645	29
32	1.0992	2.4083	1.1082	2.3200	1.1177	2.2385	1.1277	2.1633	28
33	1.0994	2.4068	1.1084	2.3186	1.1179	2.2372	1.1279	2.1620	27
34	1.0995	2.4053	1.1085	2.3172	1.1180	2.2359	1.1281	2.1608	26
35	1.0997	2.4037	1.1087	2.3158	1.1182	2.2346	1.1282	2.1596	25
36	1.0998	2.4022	1.1088	2.3143	1.1184	2.2333	1.1284	2.1584	24
37	1.1000	2.4007	1.1090	2.3129	1.1185	2.2320	1.1286	2.1572	23
38	1.1001	2.3992	1.1092	2.3115	1.1187	2.2307	1.1287	2.1560	22
39	1.1003	2.3976	1.1093	2.3101	1.1189	2.2294	1.1289	2.1548	21
40	1.1004	2.3961	1.1095	2.3087	1.1190	2.2282	1.1291	2.1536	20
41	1.1005	2.3946	1.1096	2.3073	1.1192	2.2269	1.1293	2.1525	19
42	1.1007	2.3931	1.1098	2.3059	1.1193	2.2256	1.1294	2.1513	18
43	1.1008	2.3916	1.1099	2.3046	1.1195	2.2243	1.1296	2.1501	17
44	1.1010	2.3901	1.1101	2.3032	1.1197	2.2230	1.1298	2.1489	16
45	1.1011	2.3886	1.1102	2.3018	1.1198	2.2217	1.1299	2.1477	15
46	1.1013	2.3871	1.1104	2.3004	1.1200	2.2204	1.1301	2.1465	14
47	1.1014	2.3856	1.1106	2.2990	1.1202	2.2192	1.1303	2.1453	13
48	1.1016	2.3841	1.1107	2.2976	1.1203	2.2179	1.1305	2.1441	12
49	1.1017	2.3826	1.1109	2.2962	1.1205	2.2166	1.1306	2.1430	11
50	1.1019	2.3811	1.1110	2.2949	1.1207	2.2153	1.1308	2.1418	10
51	1.1020	2.3796	1.1112	2.2935	1.1208	2.2141	1.1310	2.1406	9
52	1.1022	2.3781	1.1113	2.2921	1.1210	2.2128	1.1312	2.1394	8
53	1.1023	2.3766	1.1115	2.2907	1.1212	2.2115	1.1313	2.1382	7
54	1.1025	2.3751	1.1116	2.2894	1.1213	2.2103	1.1315	2.1371	6
55	1.1026	2.3736	1.1118	2.2880	1.1215	2.2090	1.1317	2.1359	5
56	1.1028	2.3721	1.1120	2.2866	1.1217	2.2077	1.1319	2.1347	4
57	1.1029	2.3706	1.1121	2.2853	1.1218	2.2065	1.1320	2.1335	3
58	1.1031	2.3691	1.1123	2.2839	1.1220	2.2052	1.1322	2.1324	2
59	1.1032	2.3677	1.1124	2.2825	1.1222	2.2039	1.1324	2.1312	1
60	1.1034	2.3662	1.1126	2.2812	1.1223	2.2027	1.1326	2.1300	0
′	CO-SEC.	SEC.	CO-SEC.	SEC.	CO-SEC	SEC.	CO-SEC.	SEC.	′
	65°		64°		63°		62°		

′	28° SEC	CO-SEC	29° SEC	CO-SEC	30° SEC	CO-SEC	31° SEC	CO-SEC	′
0	1.1326	2.1300	1.1433	2.0627	1.1547	2.0000	1.1666	1.9416	60
1	1.1327	2.1289	1.1435	2.0616	1.1549	1.9990	1.1668	1.9407	59
2	1.1329	2.1277	1.1437	2.0605	1.1551	1.9980	1.1670	1.9397	58
3	1.1331	2.1266	1.1439	2.0594	1.1553	1.9970	1.1672	1.9388	57
4	1.1333	2.1254	1.1441	2.0583	1.1555	1.9960	1.1674	1.9378	56
5	1.1334	2.1242	1.1443	2.0573	1.1557	1.9950	1.1676	1.9369	55
6	1.1336	2.1231	1.1445	2.0562	1.1559	1.9940	1.1678	1.9360	54
7	1.1338	2.1219	1.1446	2.0551	1.1561	1.9930	1.1681	1.9350	53
8	1.1340	2.1208	1.1448	2.0540	1.1562	1.9920	1.1683	1.9341	52
9	1.1341	2.1196	1.1450	2.0530	1.1564	1.9910	1.1685	1.9332	51
10	1.1343	2.1185	1.1452	2.0519	1.1566	1.9900	1.1687	1.9322	50
11	1.1345	2.1173	1.1454	2.0508	1.1568	1.9890	1.1689	1.9313	49
12	1.1347	2.1162	1.1456	2.0498	1.1570	1.9880	1.1691	1.9304	48
13	1.1349	2.1150	1.1458	2.0487	1.1572	1.9870	1.1693	1.9295	47
14	1.1350	2.1139	1.1459	2.0476	1.1574	1.9860	1.1695	1.9285	46
15	1.1352	2.1127	1.1461	2.0466	1.1576	1.9850	1.1697	1.9276	45
16	1.1354	2.1116	1.1463	2.0455	1.1578	1.9840	1.1699	1.9267	44
17	1.1356	2.1104	1.1465	2.0444	1.1580	1.9830	1.1701	1.9258	43
18	1.1357	2.1093	1.1467	2.0434	1.1582	1.9820	1.1703	1.9248	42
19	1.1359	2.1082	1.1469	2.0423	1.1584	1.9811	1.1705	1.9239	41
20	1.1361	2.1070	1.1471	2.0413	1.1586	1.9801	1.1707	1.9230	40
21	1.1363	2.1059	1.1473	2.0402	1.1588	1.9791	1.1709	1.9221	39
22	1.1365	2.1048	1.1474	2.0392	1.1590	1.9781	1.1712	1.9212	38
23	1.1366	2.1036	1.1476	2.0381	1.1592	1.9771	1.1714	1.9203	37
24	1.1368	2.1025	1.1478	2.0370	1.1594	1.9761	1.1716	1.9193	36
25	1.1370	2.1014	1.1480	2.0360	1.1596	1.9752	1.1718	1.9184	35
26	1.1372	2.1002	1.1482	2.0349	1.1598	1.9742	1.1720	1.9175	34
27	1.1373	2.0991	1.1484	2.0339	1.1600	1.9732	1.1722	1.9166	33
28	1.1375	2.0980	1.1486	2.0329	1.1602	1.9722	1.1724	1.9157	32
29	1.1377	2.0969	1.1488	2.0318	1.1604	1.9713	1.1726	1.9148	31
30	1.1379	2.0957	1.1489	2.0308	1.1606	1.9703	1.1728	1.9139	30
31	1.1381	2.0946	1.1491	2.0297	1.1608	1.9693	1.1730	1.9130	29
32	1.1382	2.0935	1.1493	2.0287	1.1610	1.9683	1.1732	1.9121	28
33	1.1384	2.0924	1.1495	2.0276	1.1612	1.9674	1.1734	1.9112	27
34	1.1386	2.0912	1.1497	2.0266	1.1614	1.9664	1.1737	1.9102	26
35	1.1388	2.0901	1.1499	2.0256	1.1616	1.9654	1.1739	1.9093	25
36	1.1390	2.0890	1.1501	2.0245	1.1618	1.9645	1.1741	1.9084	24
37	1.1391	2.0879	1.1503	2.0235	1.1620	1.9635	1.1743	1.9075	23
38	1.1393	2.0868	1.1505	2.0224	1.1622	1.9625	1.1745	1.9066	22
39	1.1395	2.0857	1.1507	2.0214	1.1624	1.9616	1.1747	1.9057	21
40	1.1397	2.0846	1.1508	2.0204	1.1626	1.9606	1.1749	1.9048	20
41	1.1399	2.0835	1.1510	2.0194	1.1628	1.9596	1.1751	1.9039	19
42	1.1401	2.0824	1.1512	2.0183	1.1630	1.9587	1.1753	1.9030	18
43	1.1402	2.0812	1.1514	2.0173	1.1632	1.9577	1.1756	1.9021	17
44	1.1404	2.0801	1.1516	2.0163	1.1634	1.9568	1.1758	1.9013	16
45	1.1406	2.0790	1.1518	2.0152	1.1636	1.9558	1.1760	1.9004	15
46	1.1408	2.0779	1.1520	2.0142	1.1638	1.9549	1.1762	1.8995	14
47	1.1410	2.0768	1.1522	2.0132	1.1640	1.9539	1.1764	1.8986	13
48	1.1411	2.0757	1.1524	2.0122	1.1642	1.9530	1.1766	1.8977	12
49	1.1413	2.0746	1.1526	2.0111	1.1644	1.9520	1.1768	1.8968	11
50	1.1415	2.0735	1.1528	2.0101	1.1646	1.9510	1.1770	1.8959	10
51	1.1417	2.0725	1.1530	2.0091	1.1648	1.9501	1.1772	1.8950	9
52	1.1419	2.0714	1.1531	2.0081	1.1650	1.9491	1.1775	1.8941	8
53	1.1421	2.0703	1.1533	2.0071	1.1652	1.9482	1.1777	1.8932	7
54	1.1422	2.0692	1.1535	2.0061	1.1654	1.9473	1.1779	1.8924	6
55	1.1424	2.0681	1.1537	2.0050	1.1656	1.9463	1.1781	1.8915	5
56	1.1426	2.0670	1.1539	2.0040	1.1658	1.9454	1.1783	1.8906	4
57	1.1428	2.0659	1.1541	2.0030	1.1660	1.9444	1.1785	1.8897	3
58	1.1430	2.0648	1.1543	2.0020	1.1662	1.9435	1.1787	1.8888	2
59	1.1432	2.0637	1.1545	2.0010	1.1664	1.9425	1.1790	1.8879	1
60	1.1433	2.0627	1.1547	2.0000	1.1666	1.9416	1.1792	1.8871	0
′	CO-SEC	SEC	CO-SEC	SEC	CO-SEC	SEC	CO-SEC	SEC	′
	61°		60°		59°		58°		

′	32° SEC.	32° CO-SEC.	33° SEC.	33° CO-SEC.	34° SEC.	34° CO-SEC.	35° SEC.	35° CO-SEC.	′
0	1.1792	1.8871	1.1024	1.8361	1.2062	1.7883	1.2208	1.7434	60
1	1.1794	1.8862	1.1026	1.8352	1.2064	1.7875	1.2210	1.7427	59
2	1.1796	1.8853	1.1928	1.8344	1.2067	1.7867	1.2213	1.7420	58
3	1.1798	1.8844	1.1930	1.8336	1.2069	1.7860	1.2215	1.7413	57
4	1.1800	1.8836	1.1933	1.8328	1.2072	1.7852	1.2218	1.7405	56
5	1.1802	1.8827	1.1935	1.8320	1.2074	1.7844	1.2220	1.7398	55
6	1.1805	1.8818	1.1937	1.8311	1.2076	1.7837	1.2223	1.7391	54
7	1.1807	1.8809	1.1939	1.8303	1.2079	1.7829	1.2225	1.7384	53
8	1.1809	1.8801	1.1942	1.8295	1.2081	1.7821	1.2228	1.7377	52
9	1.1811	1.8792	1.1944	1.8287	1.2083	1.7814	1.2230	1.7369	51
10	1.1813	1.8783	1.1946	1.8279	1.2086	1.7806	1.2233	1.7362	50
11	1.1815	1.8785	1.1948	1.8271	1.2088	1.7798	1.2235	1.7355	49
12	1.1818	1.8766	1.1951	1.8263	1.2091	1.7791	1.2238	1.7348	48
13	1.1820	1.8757	1.1953	1.8255	1.2093	1.7783	1.2240	1.7341	47
14	1.1822	1.8749	1.1955	1.8246	1.2095	1.7776	1.2243	1.7334	46
15	1.1824	1.8740	1.1958	1.8238	1.2098	1.7768	1.2245	1.7327	45
16	1.1826	1.8731	1.1960	1.8230	1.2100	1.7760	1.2248	1.7319	44
17	1.1828	1.8723	1.1962	1.8222	1.2103	1.7753	1.2250	1.7312	43
18	1.1831	1.8714	1.1964	1.8214	1.2105	1.7745	1.2253	1.7305	42
19	1.1833	1.8706	1.1967	1.8206	1.2107	1.7738	1.2255	1.7298	41
20	1.1835	1.8697	1.1969	1.8198	1.2110	1.7730	1.2258	1.7291	40
21	1.1837	1.8688	1.1971	1.8190	1.2112	1.7723	1.2260	1.7284	39
22	1.1839	1.8680	1.1974	1.8182	1.2115	1.7715	1.2263	1.7277	38
23	1.1841	1.8671	1.1976	1.8174	1.2117	1.7708	1.2265	1.7270	37
24	1.1844	1.8663	1.1978	1.8166	1.2119	1.7700	1.2268	1.7263	36
25	1.1846	1.8654	1.1980	1.8158	1.2122	1.7693	1.2270	1.7256	35
26	1.1848	1.8646	1.1983	1.8150	1.2124	1.7685	1.2273	1.7249	34
27	1.1850	1.8637	1.1985	1.8142	1.2127	1.7678	1.2276	1.7242	33
28	1.1852	1.8629	1.1987	1.8134	1.2129	1.7670	1.2278	1.7234	32
29	1.1855	1.8620	1.1990	1.8126	1.2132	1.7663	1.2281	1.7227	31
30	1.1857	1.8611	1.1992	1.8118	1.2134	1.7655	1.2283	1.7220	30
31	1.1859	1.8603	1.1994	1.8110	1.2136	1.7648	1.2286	1.7213	29
32	1.1861	1.8595	1.1997	1.8102	1.2139	1.7640	1.2288	1.7206	28
33	1.1863	1.8586	1.1999	1.8094	1.2141	1.7633	1.2291	1.7199	27
34	1.1866	1.8578	1.2001	1.8086	1.2144	1.7625	1.2293	1.7192	26
35	1.1868	1.8569	1.2004	1.8078	1.2146	1.7618	1.2296	1.7185	25
36	1.1870	1.8561	1.2006	1.8070	1.2149	1.7610	1.2298	1.7178	24
37	1.1872	1.8552	1.2008	1.8062	1.2151	1.7603	1.2301	1.7171	23
38	1.1874	1.8544	1.2010	1.8054	1.2153	1.7596	1.2304	1.7164	22
39	1.1877	1.8535	1.2013	1.8047	1.2156	1.7588	1.2306	1.7157	21
40	1.1879	1.8527	1.2015	1.8039	1.2158	1.7581	1.2309	1.7151	20
41	1.1881	1.8519	1.2017	1.8031	1.2161	1.7573	1.2311	1.7144	19
42	1.1883	1.8510	1.2020	1.8023	1.2163	1.7566	1.2314	1.7137	18
43	1.1886	1.8502	1.2022	1.8015	1.2166	1.7559	1.2316	1.7130	17
44	1.1888	1.8493	1.2024	1.8007	1.2168	1.7551	1.2319	1.7123	16
45	1.1890	1.8485	1.2027	1.7099	1.2171	1.7544	1.2322	1.7116	15
46	1.1892	1.8477	1.2029	1.7992	1.2173	1.7537	1.2324	1.7109	14
47	1.1894	1.8468	1.2031	1.7084	1.2175	1.7529	1.2327	1.7102	13
48	1.1897	1.8460	1.2034	1.7976	1.2178	1.7522	1.2329	1.7095	12
49	1.1899	1.8452	1.2036	1.7968	1.2180	1.7514	1.2332	1.7088	11
50	1.1901	1.8443	1.2039	1.7960	1.2183	1.7507	1.2335	1.7081	10
51	1.1903	1.8435	1.2041	1.7953	1.2185	1.7500	1.2337	1.7075	9
52	1.1906	1.8427	1.2043	1.7945	1.2188	1.7493	1.2340	1.7068	8
53	1.1908	1.8418	1.2046	1.7937	1.2190	1.7485	1.2342	1.7061	7
54	1.1910	1.8410	1.2048	1.7929	1.2193	1.7478	1.2345	1.7054	6
55	1.1912	1.8402	1.2050	1.7921	1.2195	1.7471	1.2348	1.7047	5
56	1.1915	1.8394	1.2053	1.7914	1.2198	1.7463	1.2350	1.7040	4
57	1.1917	1.8385	1.2055	1.7906	1.2200	1.7456	1.2353	1.7033	3
58	1.1919	1.8377	1.2057	1.7898	1.2203	1.7449	1.2355	1.7027	2
59	1.1921	1.8369	1.2060	1.7891	1.2205	1.7442	1.2358	1.7020	1
60	1.1922	1.8361	1.2062	1.7883	1.2208	1.7434	1.2361	1.7013	0
′	CO-SEC.	SEC.	CO-SEC.	SEC.	CO-SEC.	SEC.	CO-SEC.	SEC.	′
	57°		56°		55°		54°		

′	36° SEC.	36° CO-SEC.	37° SEC.	37° CO-SEC.	38° SEC.	38° CO-SEC.	39° SEC.	39° CO-SEC.	′
0	1.2361	1.7013	1.2521	1.6616	1.2690	1.6243	1.2867	1.5890	60
1	1.2363	1.7006	1.2524	1.6610	1.2693	1.6237	1.2871	1.5884	59
2	1.2366	1.6999	1.2527	1.6603	1.2696	1.6231	1.2874	1.5879	58
3	1.2368	1.6993	1.2530	1.6597	1.2699	1.6224	1.2877	1.5873	57
4	1.2371	1.6986	1.2532	1.6591	1.2702	1.6218	1.2880	1.5867	56
5	1.2374	1.6979	1.2535	1.6584	1.2705	1.6212	1.2883	1.5862	55
6	1.2376	1.6972	1.2538	1.6578	1.2707	1.6206	1.2886	1.5856	54
7	1.2379	1.6965	1.2541	1.6572	1.2710	1.6200	1.2889	1.5850	53
8	1.2382	1.6959	1.2543	1.6565	1.2713	1.6194	1.2892	1.5845	52
9	1.2384	1.6952	1.2546	1.6559	1.2716	1.6188	1.2895	1.5839	51
10	1.2387	1.6945	1.2549	1.6552	1.2719	1.6182	1.2898	1.5833	50
11	1.2389	1.6938	1.2552	1.6546	1.2722	1.6176	1.2901	1.5828	49
12	1.2392	1.6932	1.2554	1.6540	1.2725	1.6170	1.2904	1.5822	48
13	1.2395	1.6925	1.2557	1.6533	1.2728	1.6164	1.2907	1.5816	47
14	1.2397	1.6918	1.2560	1.6527	1.2731	1.6159	1.2910	1.5811	46
15	1.2400	1.6912	1.2563	1.6521	1.2734	1.6153	1.2913	1.5805	45
16	1.2403	1.6905	1.2565	1.6514	1.2737	1.6147	1.2916	1.5799	44
17	1.2405	1.6898	1.2568	1.6508	1.2739	1.6141	1.2919	1.5794	43
18	1.2408	1.6891	1.2571	1.6502	1.2742	1.6135	1.2922	1.5788	42
19	1.2411	1.6885	1.2574	1.6496	1.2745	1.6129	1.2926	1.5783	41
20	1.2413	1.6878	1.2577	1.6489	1.2748	1.6123	1.2929	1.5777	40
21	1.2416	1.6871	1.2579	1.6483	1.2751	1.6117	1.2932	1.5771	39
22	1.2419	1.6865	1.2582	1.6477	1.2754	1.6111	1.2935	1.5766	38
23	1.2421	1.6858	1.2585	1.6470	1.2757	1.6105	1.2938	1.5760	37
24	1.2424	1.6851	1.2588	1.6464	1.2760	1.6099	1.2941	1.5755	36
25	1.2427	1.6845	1.2591	1.6458	1.2763	1.6093	1.2944	1.5749	35
26	1.2429	1.6838	1.2593	1.6452	1.2766	1.6087	1.2947	1.5743	34
27	1.2432	1.6831	1.2596	1.6445	1.2769	1.6081	1.2950	1.5738	33
28	1.2435	1.6825	1.2599	1.6439	1.2772	1.6077	1.2953	1.5732	32
29	1.2437	1.6818	1.2602	1.6433	1.2775	1.6070	1.2956	1.5727	31
30	1.2440	1.6812	1.2605	1.6427	1.2778	1.6064	1.2960	1.5721	30
31	1.2443	1.6805	1.2607	1.6420	1.2781	1.6058	1.2963	1.5716	29
32	1.2445	1.6798	1.2610	1.6414	1.2784	1.6052	1.2966	1.5710	28
33	1.2448	1.6792	1.2613	1.6408	1.2787	1.6046	1.2969	1.5705	27
34	1.2451	1.6785	1.2616	1.6402	1.2790	1.6040	1.2972	1.5699	26
35	1.2453	1.6779	1.2619	1.6396	1.2793	1.6034	1.2975	1.5694	25
36	1.2456	1.6772	1.2622	1.6389	1.2795	1.6029	1.2978	1.5688	24
37	1.2459	1.6766	1.2624	1.6383	1.2798	1.6023	1.2981	1.5683	23
38	1.2461	1.6759	1.2627	1.6377	1.2801	1.6017	1.2985	1.5677	22
39	1.2464	1.6752	1.2630	1.6371	1.2804	1.6011	1.2988	1.5672	21
40	1.2467	1.6746	1.2633	1.6365	1.2807	1.6005	1.2991	1.5666	20
41	1.2470	1.6739	1.2636	1.6359	1.2810	1.6000	1.2994	1.5661	19
42	1.2472	1.6733	1.2639	1.6352	1.2813	1.5994	1.2997	1.5655	18
43	1.2475	1.6726	1.2641	1.6346	1.2816	1.5988	1.3000	1.5650	17
44	1.2478	1.6720	1.2644	1.6340	1.2819	1.5982	1.3003	1.5644	16
45	1.2480	1.6713	1.2647	1.6334	1.2822	1.5976	1.3006	1.5639	15
46	1.2483	1.6707	1.2650	1.6328	1.2825	1.5971	1.3010	1.5633	14
47	1.2486	1.6700	1.2653	1.6322	1.2828	1.5965	1.3013	1.5628	13
48	1.2488	1.6694	1.2656	1.6316	1.2831	1.5959	1.3016	1.5622	12
49	1.2490	1.6687	1.2659	1.6309	1.2834	1.5953	1.3019	1.5617	11
50	1.2494	1.6681	1.2661	1.6303	1.2837	1.5947	1.3022	1.5611	10
51	1.2497	1.6674	1.2664	1.6297	1.2840	1.5942	1.3025	1.5606	9
52	1.2499	1.6668	1.2667	1.6291	1.2843	1.5936	1.3029	1.5600	8
53	1.2502	1.6661	1.2670	1.6285	1.2846	1.5930	1.3032	1.5595	7
54	1.2505	1.6655	1.2673	1.6279	1.2849	1.5924	1.3035	1.5590	6
55	1.2508	1.6648	1.2676	1.6273	1.2852	1.5919	1.3038	1.5584	5
56	1.2510	1.6642	1.2679	1.6267	1.2855	1.5913	1.3041	1.5579	4
57	1.2513	1.6636	1.2681	1.6261	1.2858	1.5907	1.3044	1.5573	3
58	1.2516	1.6629	1.2684	1.6255	1.2861	1.5901	1.3048	1.5568	2
59	1.2519	1.6623	1.2687	1.6249	1.2864	1.5896	1.3051	1.5563	1
60	1.2521	1.6616	1.2690	1.6243	1.2867	1.5890	1.3054	1.5557	0
′	CO-SEC. 53°	SEC.	CO-SEC. 52°	SEC.	CO-SEC. 51°	SEC.	CO-SEC. 50°	SEC.	′

′	40° SEC.	CO-SEC.	41° SEC.	CO-SEC.	42° SEC.	CO-SEC.	43° SEC.	CO-SEC.	′
0	1.3054	1.5557	1.3250	1.5242	1.3456	1.4945	1.3673	1.4663	60
1	1.3057	1.5552	1.3253	1.5237	1.3460	1.4940	1.3677	1.4658	59
2	1.3060	1.5546	1.3257	1.5232	1.3463	1.4935	1.3681	1.4654	58
3	1.3064	1.5541	1.3260	1.5227	1.3467	1.4930	1.3684	1.4649	57
4	1.3067	1.5536	1.3263	1.5222	1.3470	1.4925	1.3688	1.4644	56
5	1.3070	1.5530	1.3267	1.5217	1.3474	1.4921	1.3692	1.4640	55
6	1.3073	1.5525	1.3270	1.5212	1.3477	1.4916	1.3695	1.4635	54
7	1.3076	1.5520	1.3274	1.5207	1.3481	1.4911	1.3699	1.4631	53
8	1.3080	1.5514	1.3277	1.5202	1.3485	1.4906	1.3703	1.4626	52
9	1.3083	1.5509	1.3280	1.5197	1.3488	1.4901	1.3707	1.4622	51
10	1.3086	1.5503	1.3284	1.5192	1.3492	1.4897	1.3710	1.4617	50
11	1.3089	1.5498	1.3287	1.5187	1.3495	1.4892	1.3714	1.4613	49
12	1.3092	1.5493	1.3290	1.5182	1.3499	1.4887	1.3718	1.4608	48
13	1.3096	1.5487	1.3294	1.5177	1.3502	1.4882	1.3722	1.4604	47
14	1.3099	1.5482	1.3297	1.5171	1.3506	1.4877	1.3725	1.4599	46
15	1.3102	1.5477	1.3301	1.5166	1.3509	1.4873	1.3729	1.4595	45
16	1.3105	1.5471	1.3304	1.5161	1.3513	1.4868	1.3733	1.4590	44
17	1.3109	1.5466	1.3307	1.5156	1.3517	1.4863	1.3737	1.4586	43
18	1.3112	1.5461	1.3311	1.5151	1.3520	1.4858	1.3740	1.4581	42
19	1.3115	1.5456	1.3314	1.5146	1.3524	1.4854	1.3744	1.4577	41
20	1.3118	1.5450	1.3318	1.5141	1.3527	1.4849	1.3748	1.4572	40
21	1.3121	1.5445	1.3321	1.5136	1.3531	1.4844	1.3752	1.4568	39
22	1.3125	1.5440	1.3324	1.5131	1.3534	1.4839	1.3756	1.4563	38
23	1.3128	1.5434	1.3328	1.5126	1.3538	1.4835	1.3759	1.4559	37
24	1.3131	1.5429	1.3331	1.5121	1.3542	1.4830	1.3763	1.4554	36
25	1.3134	1.5424	1.3335	1.5116	1.3545	1.4825	1.3767	1.4550	35
26	1.3138	1.5419	1.3338	1.5111	1.3549	1.4821	1.3771	1.4545	34
27	1.3141	1.5413	1.3342	1.5106	1.3552	1.4816	1.3774	1.4541	33
28	1.3144	1.5408	1.3345	1.5101	1.3556	1.4811	1.3778	1.4536	32
29	1.3148	1.5403	1.3348	1.5096	1.3560	1.4806	1.3782	1.4532	31
30	1.3151	1.5398	1.3352	1.5092	1.3563	1.4802	1.3786	1.4527	30
31	1.3154	1.5392	1.3355	1.5087	1.3567	1.4707	1.3790	1.4523	29
32	1.3157	1.5387	1.3359	1.5082	1.3571	1.4702	1.3794	1.4518	28
33	1.3161	1.5382	1.3362	1.5077	1.3574	1.4788	1.3797	1.4514	27
34	1.3164	1.5377	1.3366	1.5072	1.3578	1.4783	1.3801	1.4510	26
35	1.3167	1.5371	1.3369	1.5067	1.3581	1.4778	1.3805	1.4505	25
36	1.3170	1.5366	1.3372	1.5062	1.3585	1.4774	1.3809	1.4501	24
37	1.3174	1.5361	1.3376	1.5057	1.3589	1.4769	1.3813	1.4496	23
38	1.3177	1.5356	1.3379	1.5052	1.3592	1.4764	1.3816	1.4492	22
39	1.3180	1.5351	1.3383	1.5047	1.3596	1.4760	1.3820	1.4487	21
40	1.3184	1.5345	1.3386	1.5042	1.3600	1.4755	1.3824	1.4483	20
41	1.3187	1.5340	1.3390	1.5037	1.3603	1.4750	1.3828	1.4479	19
42	1.3190	1.5335	1.3393	1.5032	1.3607	1.4746	1.3832	1.4474	18
43	1.3193	1.5330	1.3397	1.5027	1.3611	1.4741	1.3836	1.4470	17
44	1.3197	1.5325	1.3400	1.5022	1.3614	1.4736	1.3839	1.4465	16
45	1.3200	1.5319	1.3404	1.5018	1.3618	1.4732	1.3843	1.4461	15
46	1.3203	1.5314	1.3407	1.5013	1.3622	1.4727	1.3847	1.4457	14
47	1.3207	1.5309	1.3411	1.5008	1.3625	1.4723	1.3851	1.4452	13
48	1.3210	1.5304	1.3414	1.5003	1.3629	1.4718	1.3855	1.4448	12
49	1.3213	1.5299	1.3418	1.4998	1.3633	1.4713	1.3859	1.4443	11
50	1.3217	1.5294	1.3421	1.4993	1.3636	1.4709	1.3863	1.4439	10
51	1.3220	1.5289	1.3425	1.4988	1.3640	1.4704	1.3867	1.4435	9
52	1.3223	1.5283	1.3428	1.4983	1.3644	1.4699	1.3870	1.4430	8
53	1.3227	1.5278	1.3432	1.4979	1.3647	1.4695	1.3874	1.4426	7
54	1.3230	1.5273	1.3435	1.4974	1.3651	1.4690	1.3878	1.4422	6
55	1.3233	1.5268	1.3439	1.4969	1.3655	1.4686	1.3882	1.4417	5
56	1.3237	1.5263	1.3442	1.4964	1.3658	1.4681	1.3886	1.4413	4
57	1.3240	1.5258	1.3446	1.4959	1.3662	1.4676	1.3890	1.4408	3
58	1.3243	1.5253	1.3449	1.4954	1.3666	1.4672	1.3894	1.4404	2
59	1.3247	1.5248	1.3453	1.4949	1.3669	1.4667	1.3898	1.4400	1
60	1.3250	1.5242	1.3456	1.4945	1.3673	1.4663	1.3902	1.4395	0
′	CO-SEC.	SEC.	CO-SEC.	SEC.	CO-SEC.	SEC.	CO-SEC.	SEC.	′
	49°		48°		47°		46°		

′	44° SEC.	44° CO-SEC.	′	′	44° SEC.	44° CO-SEC.	′	′	44° SEC	44° CO-SEC.	′
0	1.3902	1.4395	60	21	1.3984	1.4305	39	41	1.4065	1.4221	19
1	1.3905	1.4391	59	22	1.3988	1.4301	38	42	1.4069	1.4217	18
2	1.3909	1.4387	58	23	1.3992	1.4297	37	43	1.4073	1.4212	17
3	1.3913	1.4382	57	24	1.3996	1.4292	36	44	1.4077	1.4208	16
4	1.3917	1.4378	56	25	1.4000	1.4288	35	45	1.4081	1.4204	15
5	1.3921	1.4374	55	26	1.4004	1.4284	34	46	1.4085	1.4200	14
6	1.3925	1.4370	54	27	1.4008	1.4280	33	47	1.4089	1.4196	13
7	1.3929	1.4365	53	28	1.4012	1.4276	32	48	1.4093	1.4192	12
8	1.3933	1.4361	52	29	1.4016	1.4271	31	49	1.4097	1.4188	11
9	1.3937	1.4357	51	30	1.4020	1.4267	30	50	1.4101	1.4183	10
10	1.3941	1.4352	50	31	1.4024	1.4263	29	51	1.4105	1.4179	9
11	1.3945	1.4348	49	32	1.4028	1.4259	28	52	1.4109	1.4175	8
12	1.3949	1.4344	48	33	1.4032	1.4254	27	53	1.4113	1.4171	7
13	1.3953	1.4339	47	34	1.4036	1.4250	26	54	1.4117	1.4167	6
14	1.3957	1.4335	46	35	1.4040	1.4246	25	55	1.4122	1.4163	5
15	1.3960	1.4331	45	36	1.4044	1.4242	24	56	1.4126	1.4159	4
16	1.3964	1.4327	44	37	1.4048	1.4238	23	57	1.4130	1.4154	3
17	1.3968	1.4322	43	38	1.4052	1.4233	22	58	1.4134	1.4150	2
18	1.3972	1.4318	42	39	1.4056	1.4229	21	59	1.4138	1.4146	1
19	1.3976	1.4314	41	40	1.4060	1.4225	20	60	1.4142	1.4142	0
20	1.3980	1.4310	40								

′	CO-SEC.	SEC.	′	′	CO-SEC.	SEC.	′	′	CO-SEC.	SEC.	′
	45°				45°				45°		

DICTIONARY OF MACHINE·SHOP TERMS

THIS has been compiled to assist in a definite understanding of the names of tools, appliances and shop terms which are used in various parts of the country, and will, we trust, prove of value in this way. Cross references have been used in many cases, and we believe that no trouble will be experienced in finding the definition desired even where it may not be under the letter expected. Cutters of all kinds are under "cutters," twist drills under "drills," and by bearing this in mind no delay will be experienced. Practical suggestions as to additions to this section will be appreciated.

DICTIONARY OF SHOP TERMS

A

Ampere — The unit of electric current. The amount of current which one volt can force through a resistance of one ohm.

Ampere Hour. — One ampere flowing for one hour.

Ampere Turns. — Used in magnet work to represent the number of turns times the number of amperes.

Angle Irons — Pieces, usually castings, for holding work at an angle with the face-plate of a lathe, the platen of a planer or other similar work. Usually at right angles but can be anything desired.

Angle Plate — A cast-iron plate with two surfaces at right angles to each other; one side is bolted to a machine table, the other carries the work.

Annealing — Softening steel, rolled brass or copper by heating to a low heat and allowing to cool gradually.

Annealing Boxes — Boxes, usually of cast iron, in which steel is packed with lime or sand to retard the cooling as much as possible.

Anode — The positive terminal of any source of electricity as a battery, or where the current goes into a plating bath.

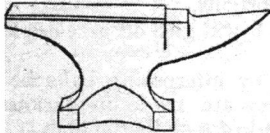

Anvils — Blocks of iron or steel on which metals are hammered or forged. Usually have a steel face. A square hole is usually provided for holding hardies, fuller blocks, etc.

Apron — A protecting or covering piece which encloses or covers any mechanism, as the apron of a lathe.

Arbor — Shaft or bar to hold work while it is being turned or otherwise worked on. Usually made with a slight taper (about .010 inch per foot) to drive into work and hold by friction. Also applied to shaft for holding circular saws, milling cutters, etc. Often called mandrel.

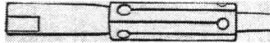

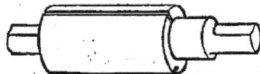

Arbor, Expansion — Arbor which can be varied in diameter to hold different sized work. These vary greatly in design, as shown. The first and last are spring sleeves of different types, the second has blades which can be adjusted to size.

Arc — The passage of current across the space between two separated points.

Armature. — Usually the revolving part of a dynamo or motor or the movable part of any magnetic device.

565

B

Babbitt Metal — A good mixture for bearings where the load is not too heavy. Consists of varying proportions of tin, antimony, and copper, and sometimes lead. Tin is the base.

Back-lash — Usually applied to lost motion in gears, sometimes to screw in a nut.

Backing-off — Removing metal behind the cutting edge to relieve friction in taps, reamers, drills, etc. Also called "relieving."

Back Rest — A rest attached to the lathe ways for supporting long, slender shafts or other work being turned.

Balance, Running — High-speed pulleys require balancing by running at speed and seeing that they run without tremor or vibration. This is called running balance.

Balance, Standing — When a pulley has been balanced on the balancing ways it is called a standing balance. See Balance-running.

Balancing Ways — Level strips on which the shaft carrying the pulley or other revolving body is placed. If the pulley is unbalanced the heavy side will roll to bottom.

Ball Reamer — See Reamer, Ball.

Bastard — Not regular. The term is usually applied to a file, meaning a cut between the rough and second cut, or to a thread, meaning one that is not of the standard proportions.

Battery. — A combination of chemicals which will give off an electric current.

Bearings, Ball — Made to reduce friction by interposing balls between the shaft and the bearing. They are made in various ways but all aim to have a rolling instead of a sliding action.

Bearings, Roller — Similar to ball bearings except rollers are used instead of balls. In some cases the rollers are practically hollow round springs from square stock. These are known as flexible roller bearings (Hyatt).

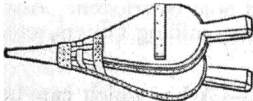

Bellows — Devices of wood and leather for producing a current of air for fanning fires or blowing dust.

Bearing, Base Plate — For supporting pillow blocks or journal boxes.

Belt Carriers — Pulleys for supporting a long belt between driving and driven pulleys. May or may not have flanges.

Belt Dressing — Preparation for preserving or cleaning a belt or making it cling to pulleys.

Belt Fastener — Hooks or other device for joining the ends of belt.

Belt Lacing — Methods of fastening ends of belt with a more or less flexible joint by means of leather or wire lacing.

Belt, Muley — A belt running around a corner guided by idler pulleys on a muley shaft.

Belt Polisher or Strap — A belt covered with glue and emery or other abrasive is driven over pulleys and work held against it.

Belt Shifter — Device for shifting belt or belts on countershaft or elsewhere, from loose to tight pulleys and vice-versa. These are made in many varieties. Not used where clutches are employed.

Belt Tightener — Loose pulleys arranged for taking up slack of belts; often called idlers.

Bench — Usual hight is 34 to 35 inches from floor to top of bench, width about 29 inches. Should be 3 inches from wall to allow circulation of air, in order to give sprinklers a chance at a fire underneath.

Bench, Leveling — Bench with a level surface so that work can be laid on it to test. Made of iron.

Bending Machine — For bending rods, beams, rails, plate, etc. Run by hydraulic or other power.

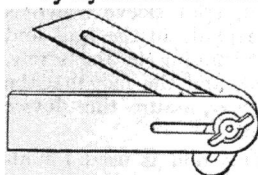

Bevel — A tool for measuring or laying off bevels as shown. Also a surface not at right angles to the main surface; may be any angle. When at 45 degrees sometimes called a miter.

Blocks, Differential — Hoisting apparatus consisting of differential gears for lifting heavy loads.

Blocks, Tackle — Sheaves or pulleys mounted in a shell or case, used with hoisting ropes or chains to raise heavy weights.

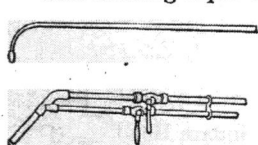

Blow Pipe — A pipe for blowing a jet of air into a flame for heating work locally, such as soldering. The upper picture is a plain one for use with an alcohol lamp, the other has a gas and an air tube. Each is regulated by the small valve so as to make the hottest flame.

BOLTS

Agricultural Bolt. Agricultural bolts, as indicated by the name, are used in farm machines and appliances. The body of the bolt has a series of helical lands and grooves which are formed by a rolling process.

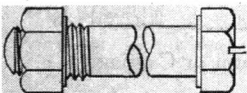

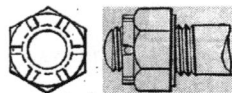

A. L. A. M. Bolt — This bolt is adopted by the Association of Licensed Automobile Manufacturers. It has a slotted head and castellated nut.

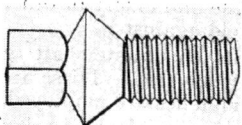

Boiler Patch Bolt — A bolt used in fastening patches on boilers. The patch is countersunk for the cone head, and boiler shell tapped for bolt thread. The square head is knocked off after bolt is screwed in place.

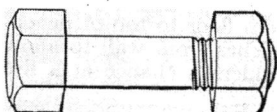

Coupling Bolt — Bolts for shaft couplings are finished all over and must be a close fit in the hole reamed in the two flanges of the coupling, so that the sections shall be rigidly secured together.

Expansion Bolt — In attaching parts to brick, stone or concrete walls and floors, expansion bolts are frequently employed. The

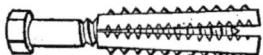

"Star" bolt in the illustration has an internally threaded, split sleeve which is slipped into a hole made in the wall and then expanded by running in the screw. The projections on the surface of the shell, and the fact that the hole receiving it is made larger at the rear, assure the device holding fast when the expander is in place.

Hanger Bolt — This bolt is used for attaching hangers to woodwork and consists of a lag screw at one end with a machine bolt thread and nut at the other.

Machine Bolts

Hexagon Head

Square Head

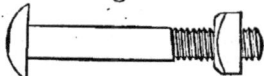

Round Head

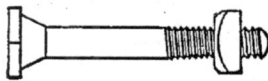

Square Countersunk Head

Miscellaneous Bolts

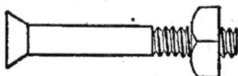

Tire

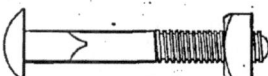

Loom or Carriage

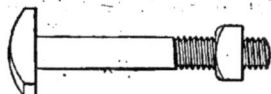

Oval T-Head

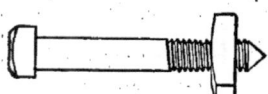

Joint

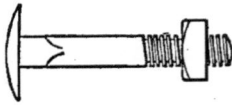

Step

Eye

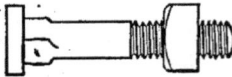

Deck

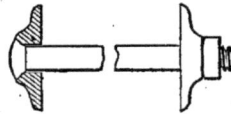

Bridge or Roof

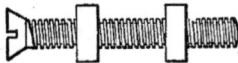

Sink

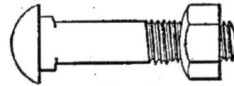

Track

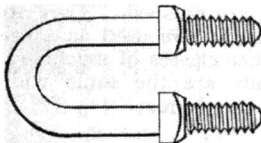

U

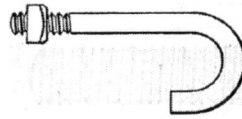

Hook

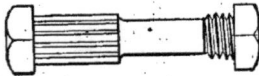

"North" Bolt — The "North" bolt is used in agricultural machinery and appliances and has a series of longitudinal lands rolled on the body to the same diameter as the bolt.

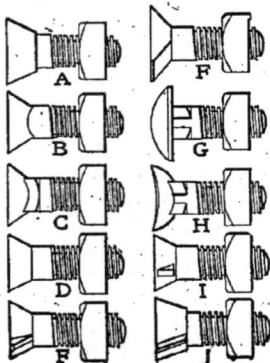

Plow Bolt — Several types of plow and cultivator bolts are shown in the accompanying engravings, the forms illustrated being typical of a variety of bolts manufactured for agricultural apparatus.

A — Large Round Head
B — Square Head
C — Round Head, Square Shank
D — Round Head
E — Key Head
F — Tee Head
G — Button Head
H — Concave Head
I — Reverse Key Head
J — Large Key Head.

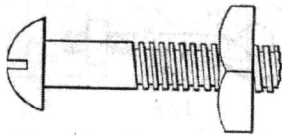

Round or Button Head

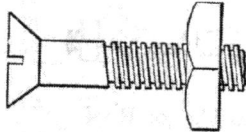

Flat or Countersunk
Head

Stove Bolt — Stove bolts are made in sizes ranging from $\frac{1}{8}$ to $\frac{3}{8}$ inch. There is no standard form of thread for these bolts to which all makers adhere, and even the same makers in some cases have a different shape of thread for different sizes of bolts. The heads commonly formed are the round, or button head, and the flat or countersunk head.

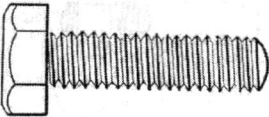

Hexagon Head

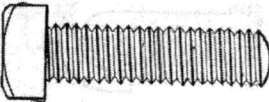

Square Head

Tap Bolt — Tap bolts are usually threaded the full length of the body, which is not machined prior to running on the die. Only the point and the under side of the head are finished. They are not hardened and are used as a rule for the rougher classes of machine work. The heads are the same width as machine bolt heads.

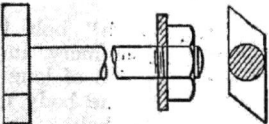

T-Head Planer Bolt

T-Head Planer Bolt — A bolt with a T-head having oblique ends which may be dropped into the T-slot of a planer and locked by giving it a quarter turn, until the sloping ends strike against the sides of the slot. Commonly employed for holding work on the planer table.

Bolt Cutter — Machine for threading bolts, cutting threads on them.

Bolt Header — Machine for upsetting the bolt body to form the head.

Bolster — A block sometimes called the die block, in which a punch press die is held. It is attached to the bed by bolts at either end.

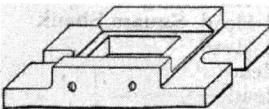

Bolster

Boring and Turning Mill — Machine having a rotating horizontal table for the work with one or more stationary vertical tools for boring, turning or facing; a turret is often provided for holding a number of tools in one of the heads. Often called "vertical mill." Horizontal boring machines are not called "mills."

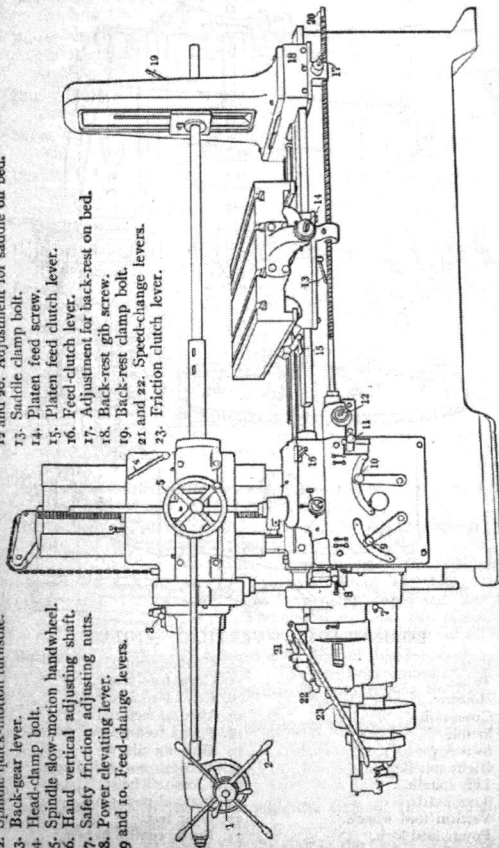

BORING MACHINE — HORIZONTAL — LUCAS

2. Spindle quick-motion turnstile.
3. Back-gear lever.
4. Head-clamp bolt.
5. Spindle slow-motion handwheel.
6. Hand vertical adjusting shaft.
7. Safety friction adjusting nuts.
8. Power elevating lever.
9 and 10. Feed-change levers.

11. Feed-screw lever.
12 and 20. Adjustment for saddle on bed.
13. Saddle clamp bolt.
14. Platen feed screw.
15. Platen feed clutch lever.
16. Feed-clutch lever.
17. Adjustment for back-rest on bed.
18. Back-rest gib screw.
19. Back-rest clamp bolt.
21 and 22. Speed-change levers.
23. Friction clutch lever.

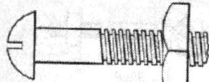

Round or Button Head

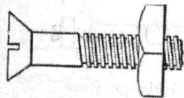

Flat or Countersunk Head

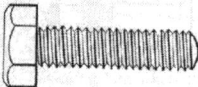

Hexagon Head

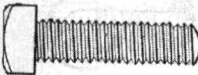

Square Head

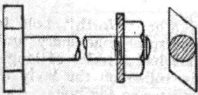

T-Head Planer Bolt

Stove Bolt — Stove bolts are made in sizes ranging from ⅛ to ⅜ inch. There is no standard form of thread for these bolts to which all makers adhere, and even the same makers in some cases have a different shape of thread for different sizes of bolts. The heads commonly formed are the round, or button head, and the flat or countersunk head.

Tap Bolt — Tap bolts are usually threaded the full length of the body, which is not machined prior to running on the die. Only the point and the under side of the head are finished. They are not hardened and are used as a rule for the rougher classes of machine work. The heads are the same width as machine bolt heads.

T-Head Planer Bolt — A bolt with T-head having oblique ends which may be dropped into the T-slot of planer and locked by giving it a quarter turn, until the sloping ends strike against the sides of the slot. Commonly employed for holding work on the planer table.

Bolt Cutter — Machine for threading bolts, cutting threads on them.

Bolt Header — Machine for upsetting the bolt body to form the head.

Bolster — A block sometimes called the die block, in which a punch press die is held. It is attached to the bed by bolts at either end.

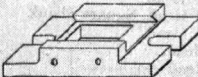

Bolster

Boring and Turning Mill — Machine having a rotating horizontal table for the work with one or more stationary vertical tools for boring turning or facing; a turret is often provided for holding a number of tools in one of the heads. Often called "vertical mill." Horizontal boring machines are not called "mills."

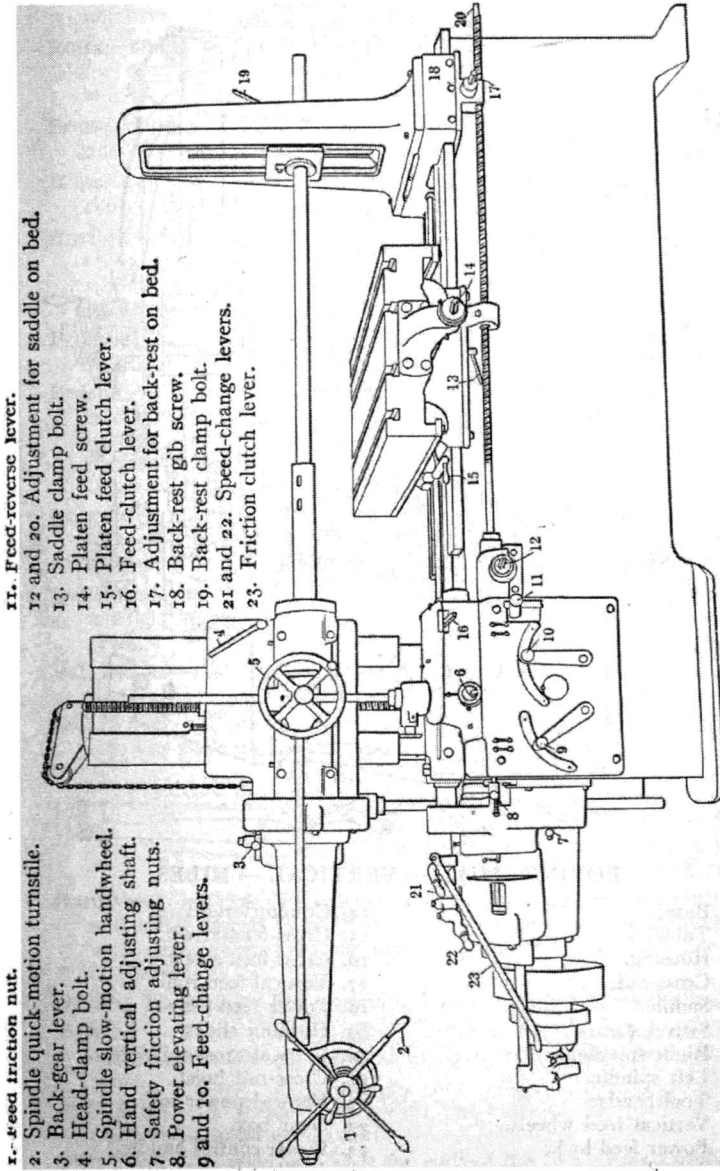

BORING MACHINE—HORIZONTAL—LUCAS

1. Feed friction nut.
2. Spindle quick-motion turnstile.
3. Back-gear lever.
4. Head-clamp bolt.
5. Spindle slow-motion handwheel.
6. Hand vertical adjusting shaft.
7. Safety friction adjusting nuts.
8. Power elevating lever.
9 and 10. Feed-change levers.
11. Feed-reverse lever.
12 and 20. Adjustment for saddle on bed.
13. Saddle clamp bolt.
14. Platen feed screw.
15. Platen feed clutch lever.
16. Feed-clutch lever.
17. Adjustment for back-rest on bed.
18. Back-rest gib screw.
19. Back-rest clamp bolt.
21 and 22. Speed-change levers.
23. Friction clutch lever.

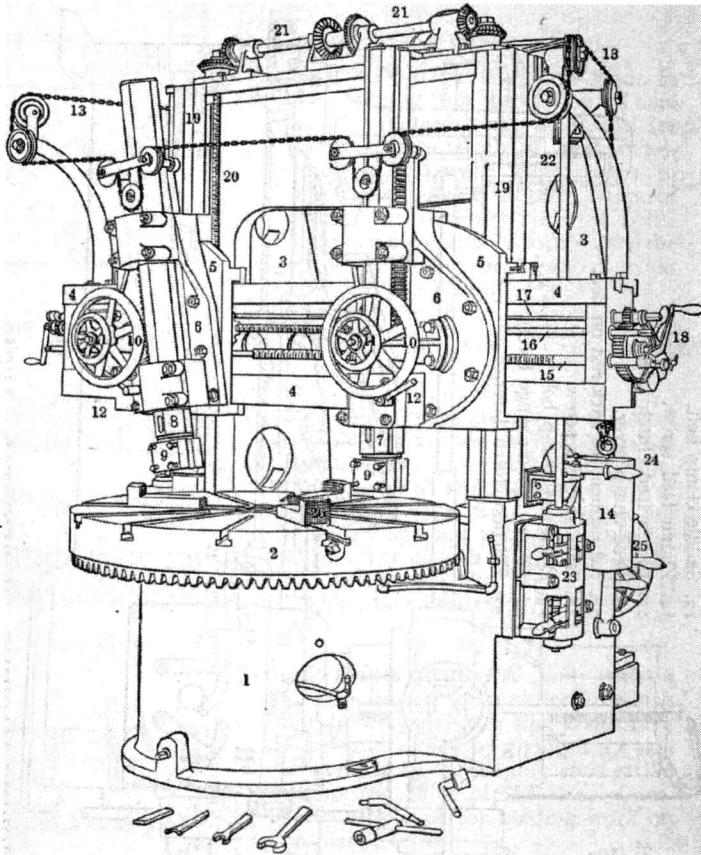

BORING MILL — VERTICAL — NILES

1. Base.
2. Table.
3. Housing.
4. Cross-rail.
5. Saddle.
6. Swivel.
7. Right spindle.
8. Left spindle.
9. Tool heads.
10. Vertical feed wheels.
11. Power feed lock.
12. Spindle bearings.
13. Counterweight chain.

14. Counterweight.
15. Cross-feed screw.
16. Cross-feed screw.
17. Vertical feed rod.
18. Power feed gears.
19. Housing slides.
20. Vertical cross-rail screw.
21. Cross-rail hoist.
22. Vertical power rod.
23. Gear box.
24. Power control handle.
25. Driving pulleys.
26. Chuck jaws.

Box Chuck — A two-jawed chuck of rectangular form used by brass finishers.

Brass — Alloy of copper and zinc although a little tin is often added for strength and density. Common proportion is copper 66, zinc 34. See bronzes, also low and high brass.

Brass, High — Only applied to rolled material. Two parts copper, one of zinc. Color is light yellow.

Brass, Low — Only applied to rolled material. Ranges from 75 per cent. copper to 25 of zinc to 88 per cent. copper and 12 of zinc.

Brazing — The joining of metals by the use of copper filings or chips and borax or some other flux. This is usually called spelter or hard solder and can be applied to almost any of the harder metals.

Brazing Clamps — Clamps to hold the ends of band saw or other work for brazing.

Broach — A tool which is practically a series of chisels or cutting edges for enlarging holes or changing their shape. Generally used for odd shaped holes but occasionally for rounds. The teeth should be on an angle to give a shearing cut. Name is sometimes given to a small reamer used by jewelers.

Bronzes — Alloy of Copper and Tin. Used in coinage, in bells, statuary, musical instruments and mirrors. Bell metal is 80 copper, 20 tin to 84 copper, 16 tin.

Bulldozer — Heavy forming machine for bending iron or steel and in which the dies move horizontally. Very similar to a forging press.

Bull Blocks — Blocks through which wire or rods are drawn to reduce size.

Bull Wheel — Usually applied to the gear of a planer which meshes into the rack under the table and drives it.

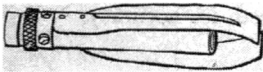

Bunsen Burner — A device for securing a very hot flame by mixing air and gas in a chamber behind the flame. The one shown has two pieces which make the flame flat instead of round.

Burnishers — Tools of hardened and polished steel for finishing brass and softer metals by friction. They are held against the revolving work and give a smooth surface by compressing the outer layer of the metal.

Burring Machine — For removing burrs from hot pressed nuts.

Bushing — Tube or shell which reduces the diameter of a hole. Hardened bushings are used in jig work to guide drills or other tools.

Butt Joint — A riveted joint with the ends of the plates abutting squarely against each other.

Butt Weld — A weld in which the ends of the two pieces simply abut against each other for welding together.

Button — A steel bushing, hardened and ground, used for locating a jig plate or some similar piece in which holes have to be bored in exact position. The button is attached to the work by a small screw and is then adjusted by a micrometer or otherwise until it is central at the exact point where it is desired to bore the hole. The work is then placed on the face plate of the lathe, and with a test indicator resting on the outside of the button, the piece is readily set central. It is then clamped fast to the face plate, the button is removed and the hole bored. Frequently, several buttons are used on the same piece of work, their relative positions being adjusted to conform to the center distances required between holes. The work is then indicated true by each button in succession, and one hole after another bored.

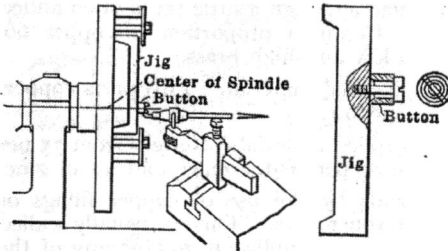

C

CALIPERS

Firm Joint Calipers — Having a large, firm joint in place of old style plain riveted joint. This is an inside caliper.

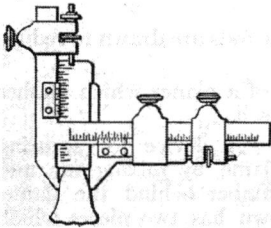

Gear Tooth Caliper — A caliper with two beams at right angles. The vertical beam gives tooth depth to pitch line and the other the thickness at pitch line. Both have verniers. Used in measuring teeth for accuracy.

Hermaphrodite Caliper — A combination of one leg of a divider and one leg of a caliper. Used in testing centered work and in laying off distances from the edge of a piece.

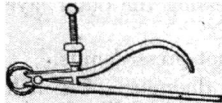

Keyhole Caliper — Has one straight leg and the other curved.

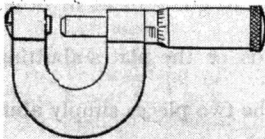

Micrometer Caliper — A measuring instrument consisting of a screw and having its barrel divided into small parts so as to measure slight degrees of rotation. Usually measure to thousandths, sometimes to ten-thousandths

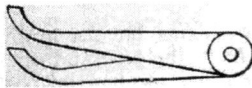

Odd Leg Caliper — Calipers having both legs pointing in the same direction. Used in measuring shoulder distances on flat work, boring half round, boxes etc.

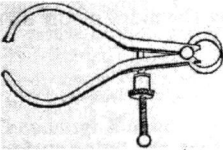

Outside, Spring Caliper — Tool for measuring the outside diameter of work. Controlled by spring and threaded nut. Nuts are sometimes split or otherwise designed to allow rapid movement when desired, final adjustment being made by screw.

Slide Caliper — A beam caliper made with a graduated slide. Generally made small for carrying in the pocket.

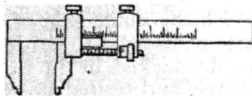

Square-micrometer Caliper — A beam caliper having jaws square with the blade, and having a micrometer adjustment to read to thousandths of an inch.

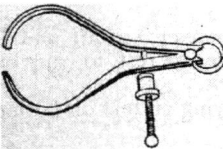

Thread Caliper — Similar to outside calipers except it has broad points to go over the tops of several threads.

Transfer Caliper. — Caliper which can be set to a given size, the auxiliary arm set, and the calipers opened at will, as they can be reset to the auxiliary arm at any time. Used to caliper recesses and places where they must be moved to get them out.

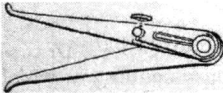

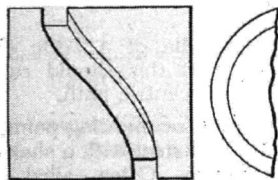

Cam, Drum or Barrel — The drum cam has a path for the roll cut around the periphery, and imparts a to-and-for motion to a slide or lever in a plane parallel to the axis of the cam. Sometimes these cams are built up of a plain drum with cam plates attached.

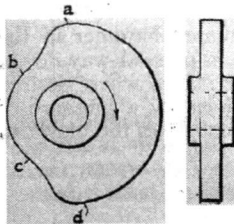

Cam, Edge — Edge or peripheral cams (also called disk cams) operate a mechanism in one direction only, gravity, or a spring, being relied upon to hold the cam roll in contact with the edge of the cam. On the cam shown, a to b is the drop; b to c the dwell; c to d, rise; d to a, dwell.

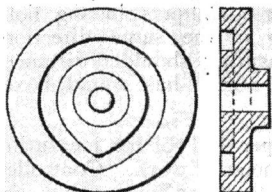

Cam, Face — Face cams have a groove or roll path cut in the face and operate a lever or other mechanism positively in both directions, as the roll is always guided by the sides of the slot.

"C" Clamp — See Clamp "C."

"C" Washer. — See Washer, Open.

Carbonizing — The heat treatment of steel so that the outer surface will be hard. The surface absorbs carbon from the material used.

Card Patterns — Patterns made on a gate so as to be all molded at once and to provide gates for the metal to flow.

Case-hardening — A surface hardening by which the outer skin of a piece of iron or steel absorbs carbon or carbonizes so as to harden when cooled in water. The piece is usually packed in an iron box with bone, leather or charcoal, or all three, and heated slowly several hours, then quenched.

Cat Head — A collar or sleeve which fits loosely over a shaft and is clamped to it by set screws. Used for steady rest to run on where it is not desired to run it on the work.

Same name is also given to the head carrying cutters on boring bars.

Cat Head Chuck — A chuck in which the end of a shaft or other piece is driven by a number of set screws tapped through the wall of the chuck.

Cathode — The negative terminal of an electric bath or battery.

Center, Dead — The back center or the stationary center on which the work revolves. On many grinding machines both centers are dead.

Center, Live — The center in the revolving spindle of a lathe or similar machine. It is highly important that this should run true or it will cause the work to move in an eccentric path.

Center Punch — Punch for marking points on metal. Made of steel with a sharp point and hardened. Often called a prick punch.

Center Punch, Automatic — Has a spring actuated hammer in the handle, which is released when the handle is pressed way down. The point can be placed where desired and the blow given by a pressure of the hand. In some cases the blow can be varied.

Center Punch, Bell or Self-centering — A center punch sliding in a bell or cone mouthed casing so when placed square over the end of any bar it will locate the center with sufficient accuracy for most purposes.

Center Punch, Locating — Having an extra leg which has a spring point and is adjustable. The spring point is placed in the first punch mark and so locates the next punch mark at the right distance from the first.

Centering Machines — For drilling and reaming center of work for the lathe or grinder.

Chamber — A long recess. See Recess.

Chasers — Tools used for cutting threads by chasing. Usually have several teeth of right pitch, but name is sometimes applied to a single point tool used in brass work on a Fox lathe. Chasers are made circular or flat and in the old days many were used by hand.

Chasing Threads — Cutting threads by moving a tool along the work at the right speed to give the proper pitch. Distinguishes between threads cut with a die and those cut with a threading tool.

Chattering — A slight jumping of the tool away from the work or vice-versa, and which leaves little ridges in same direction as the teeth. Occurs at times in any class of work and with any kind of tool. Due to springing of some parts of the machine.

Cherry — See Cutters, Milling.

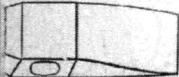

Chisel, Blacksmith's Hot — A chisel for cutting hot metal. Has a handle so that it can be used without getting the hand too near the heated metal.

Chipping — The cutting of metal with cold chisel and hammer. Also used when a piece "chips" or breaks out of a piece or punch.

Chisel, Cape — Chisel with a narrow blade for cutting keyways and similar work.

Flat Cold Chisel

Diamond

Cape

Round

Chisel, Cold — The usual machinists' chisel for cutting or "chipping" metal with a plain cutting edge as in illustration.

Chisel, Diamond or Lozenge — Similar to a cape chisel but with square end and cutting edge at one corner. Used for cutting a sharp-bottomed groove.

Chisel, Round — A round end chisel with the cutting edge ground back at an angle. Used for cutting oil grooves and similar work.

Chuck, Draw — Operated by moving longitudinally in a taper bearing. Used on precision work.

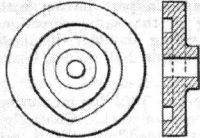

Cam, Face — Face cams have a groove or roll path cut in the face and operate a lever or other mechanism positively in both directions, as the roll is always guided by the sides of the slot.

"C" Clamp — See Clamp "C."

"C" Washer. — See Washer, Open.

Carbonizing — The heat treatment of steel so that the outer surface will be hard. The surface absorbs carbon from the material used.

Card Patterns — Patterns made on a gate so as to be all molded at once and to provide gates for the metal to flow.

Case-hardening — A surface hardening by which the outer skin of a piece of iron or steel absorbs carbon or carbonizes so as to harden when cooled in water. The piece is usually packed in an iron box with bone, leather or charcoal, or all three, and heated slowly several hours, then quenched.

Cat Head — A collar or sleeve which fits loosely over a shaft and is clamped to it by set screws. Used for steady rest to run on where it is not desired to run it on the work.

Same name is also given to the head carrying cutters on boring bars.

Cat Head Chuck — A chuck in which the end of a shaft or other piece is driven by a number of set screws tapped through the wall of the chuck.

Cathode — The negative terminal of an electric bath or battery.

Center, Dead — The back center or the stationary center on which the work revolves. On many grinding machines both centers are dead.

Center, Live — The center in the revolving spindle of a lathe or similar machine. It is highly important that this should run true or it will cause the work to move in an eccentric path.

Center Punch — Punch for marking points on metal. Made of steel with a sharp point and hardened. Often called a prick punch.

Center Punch, Automatic — Has a spring actuated hammer in the handle, which is released when the handle is pressed way down. The point can be placed where desired and the blow given by a pressure of the hand. In some cases the blow can be varied.

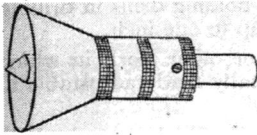

Center Punch, Bell or Self-centering — A center punch sliding in a bell or cone mouthed casing so when placed square over the end of any bar it will locate the center with sufficient accuracy for most purposes.

Center Punch, Locating — Having an extra leg which has a spring point and is adjustable. The spring point is placed in the first punch mark and so locates the next punch mark at the right distance from the first.

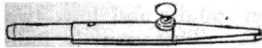

Centering Machines — For drilling and reaming center of work for the lathe or grinder.

Chamber — A long recess. See Recess.

Chasers — Tools used for cutting threads by chasing. Usually have several teeth of right pitch, but name is sometimes applied to a single point tool used in brass work on a Fox lathe. Chasers are made circular or flat and in the old days many were used by hand.

Chasing Threads — Cutting threads by moving a tool along the work at the right speed to give the proper pitch. Distinguishes between threads cut with a die and those cut with a threading tool.

Chattering — A slight jumping of the tool away from the work or vice-versa, and which leaves little ridges in same direction as the teeth. Occurs at times in any class of work and with any kind of tool. Due to springing of some parts of the machine.

Cherry — See Cutters, Milling.

Chisel, Blacksmith's Hot — A chisel for cutting hot metal. Has a handle so that it can be used without getting the hand too near the heated metal.

Chipping — The cutting of metal with cold chisel and hammer. Also used when a piece "chips" or breaks out of a piece or punch.

Chisel, Cape — Chisel with a narrow blade for cutting keyways and similar work.

Flat Cold Chisel

Diamond

Cape

Round

Chisel, Cold — The usual machinists' chisel for cutting or "chipping" metal with a plain cutting edge as in illustration.

Chisel, Diamond or Lozenge — Similar to a cape chisel but with square end and cutting edge at one corner. Used for cutting a sharp-bottomed groove.

Chisel, Round — A round end chisel with the cutting edge ground back at an angle. Used for cutting oil grooves and similar work.

Chuck, Draw — Operated by moving longitudinally in a taper bearing. Used on precision work.

Chuck, Drill — A chuck made especially for holding drills in drilling machines. Sizes run from the smallest up to one inch.

Chuck, Eccentric — For turning eccentrics or other work in which hole is not concentric with outside. Usually made adjustable to suit varying degrees of eccentricity.

Chuck, Expanding — For turning hollow work which must be held on inside. Jaws go inside of work.

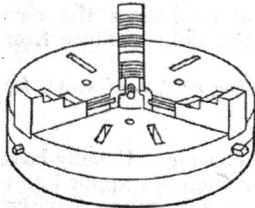

Chucks, Lathe — Devices for holding work. Usually screw on spindle and have two, three or four jaws. These may be independent or move together by screws only (in case of two jawed) or screws and gears in case of more than two. There is also a spiral or scroll chuck without gears or screws of the ordinary kind.

Chuck, Magnetic — Has no jaws but holds iron and steel by magnetism.

Chuck, Master — The main body of a screw chuck which screws on the nose of the lathe spindle and which carries the sub- or screw-chuck for holding the work. Mostly used in brass work.

Chuck, Nipple — For holding short piece of pipe to be threaded.

Chuck, Oval — Chuck designed to move the work to and from the tool so as to produce an oval instead of a round. Sometimes called an elliptic chuck.

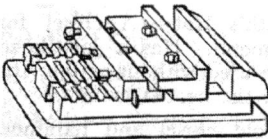

Plain Base

Chuck, Planer — For holding work on bed or platen of planer, shaper or milling machine. Sometimes called a vise. They are made with both plain and swivel bases as shown, and usually have locking strips which hold the piece carrying the set screws.

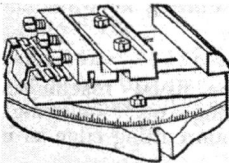

Swivel Base

Chuck, Screw — Chucks made with internal or external thread to hold work which has been already threaded. These very often screw into a master chuck. Mostly used in brass work.

Chuck, Spring — See Screw Machine Tools.

Chucking Machines — Usually have a turret for tools, a revolving chuck or table for work, and generally used for boring and reaming. May be either vertical or horizontal.

Circuit — The path in which an electric current flows.

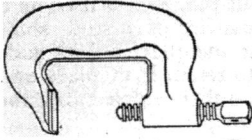

Clamp, "C" — Clamp shaped like a letter "C" for holding work in various ways. Are sometimes cast but more often drop forged for heavier work.

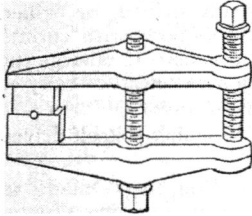

Clamps, Machinist — Clamps for holding work together, holding jigs or templets on work, etc.

Clash Gears — Gears which are thrown into mesh by moving the centers together and sometimes by sliding the gears on parallel shafts till the teeth get a full bearing. The latter are sometimes called sliding gears.

Clutch — Any device which permits one shaft to engage and drive another, may be either friction or positive, usually the former. Made of all sorts of combinations of cams, levers and toggles.

Clutch, Friction — A device whereby motion of loose pulley is transmitted to shaft to be driven. Various methods are employed but all depend on forcing some kind of friction surfaces together so that one drives the other.

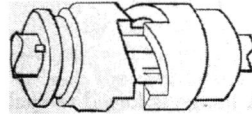

Ratchet Tooth Clutch

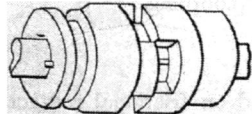

Clutches, Positive — Devices for connecting machines to a constantly running shaft or one part to another, at will. There are many kinds, both positive and friction. The illustrations show two of the most common of the positive clutches.

Square Jaw Clutch

Collar — A ring used for holding shafting, loose pulleys, in proper position or for fastening to boring tools to prevent them going in too deep.

Collar, Safety — Having a clamping device instead of set screw or having set screw below surface or so covered as not to catch anything brought in contact with it.

Commutator — The part of a dynamo or motor which takes off or leads current into the machine.

Compound Rest — An auxiliary tool slide on lathe carriage arranged to swivel so as to turn at any desired angle with the lathe centers or with cross slide. Usually graduated into degrees.

Cotter, Spring — Also called split cotter, split pin, etc., is used in a hole drilled crosswise of a stud, shaft or some similar member, and its ends spread apart to retain it in place and keep some member carried by the shaft from slipping off.

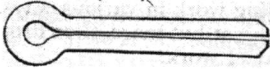

Counterbore — Has a pilot to fit a hole already drilled, or drilled and reamed, and its body with cutting edges on the end is used to enlarge the hole to receive a screw head or body or for some similar purpose.

Countershaft — The shaft for driving a machine which is itself driven by the main or line shaft.

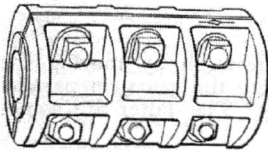

Coupling, Clamp — Couplings made in two or more parts, clamping around the shafts by transverse bolts. Hold either by friction or have dowels in shaft. Sometimes called compression although this is confusing.

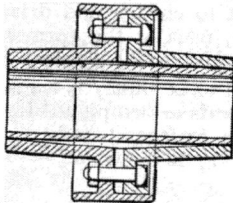

Coupling, Compression — Grips shafting by drawing together tapered parts. This forces them against shaft and holds it firmly. Bolts parallel with shaft draw parts together.

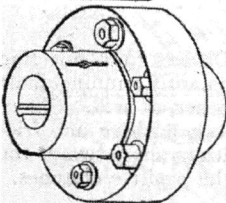

Coupling, Flanged — A flange is keyed to each shaft and these flanges are bolted together. Also called "plate" coupling.

Coupling, Friction — Couplings which depend on frictional contact.

Coupling, Jaw or Clutch — Positively engaged by jaws or projections on the face of opposing parts.

Coupling, Shaft — Devices for fastening ends of shafting together so that both may be driven as one shaft. These are made in a great variety of ways, from plain set screw coupling to elaborate compression devices.

Coupling, Wedge — Coupling that clamps the shaft with a wedging action. Practically like a compression coupling. Generally enclosed in a sleeve. Also called vise coupling.

Cope — The upper part of a flask.

Coping Machine — For cutting away the flanges and corners of beams and bending the ends.

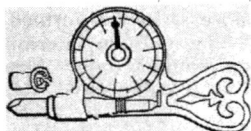

Counter, Revolution — Device for counting the revolutions of a shaft. Generally made with a worm and a gear having 100 teeth so that one turn of dial equals 100 revolutions.

Countershaft — Shaft carrying tight and loose pulleys (or friction clutch pulleys) for starting and stopping machines or reversing their motion.

Crane, Gantry — Traveling crane mounted on posts or legs for yard use.

Crane, Jib — Crane with a swinging boom or arm.

Crane, Locomotive — Crane mounted on a car with an engine so as to be self-propelling on a track.

Crane, Pillar — Having the boom or moving arm fastened to pillar or post.

Crane, Portable — Hoisting frame on wheels which can be run around to the work and used to handle work in and out of lathes and other machines.

Crane, Post — See Crane, Pillar.

Crane, Swing — Same as Jib Crane.

Crane, Traveling — Crane with a bridge or cross beam having wheels at each end so it can be run on overhead tracks to any point in the shop.

Crimping — Fluting, corrugating or compressing metal ring to reduce its diameter.

Cross-rail — The part of a planer, boring mill or similar machine on which the tool heads or slides move and are supported.

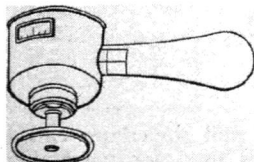

Cut Meter — Instrument for measuring the surface speed of work either in lathe or planer. A wheel is pressed against the moving surface and the speed is shown in feet per minute.

Cutters, Flue Sheet — Special cutters for making holes as for flues, in flue sheets or in other sheet metal or structural work.

CUTTERS, MILLING

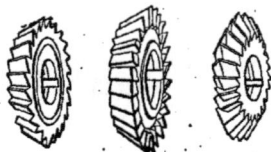

Angular Cutters — Such cutters are used for milling straight and spiral mills, ratchet teeth, etc. Cutters for spiral mill grooving are commonly made with an angle of 12 degrees on one side and 40, 48 or 53 degree angle on the other.

Cherry—A form of milling cutter which is more strictly a formed reamer, for finishing out the interior of a die or some similar tool. The cherry shown is for a bullet mold.

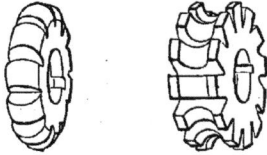

Convex and Concave Cutters — Convex and concave cutters are used for milling half circles. The convex cutter is often used for fluting taps and other tools. Like all other formed cutters the shape is not affected by the process of sharpening.

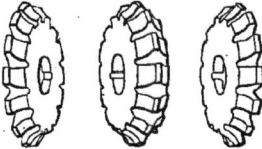

Corner Rounding Cutters — Left hand double and right hand cutters of this type are used for finishing rounded corners and edges of work. The shape of the cutter is not altered by grinding on the face of the teeth.

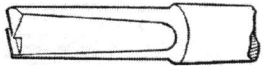

Cotter Mill — This type of mill is used for cutting keyseats and other slots and grooves.

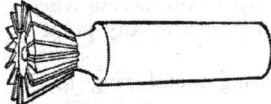

Dovetail Cutters — Male and female dovetails are milled with these tools, and edges of work conveniently beveled.

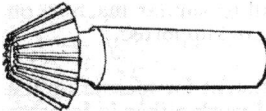

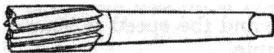

End Mill — This mill sometimes called a butt mill, is used for machining slots, milling edges of work, cutting cams, etc.

Left Hand   Right Hand

End Mill (with center cut). This end mill has clearance on the inner side of the end teeth and is adapted to cut into the work to a depth equal to the length of the end teeth and then feed along, dispensing with the necessity of first drilling a hole, which has to be done when the inner sides of the teeth are not relieved.

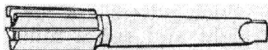

Left Hand Mill

Left Hand   Right Hand

The mills are often used for heavy cuts particularly in cast iron.

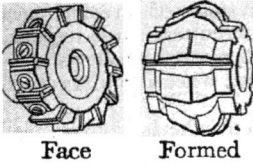

Face and Formed Cutters — The face cutter to the left, of Brown & Sharpe inserted tooth type is made in large sizes and cuts on the periphery and ends of teeth.

The formed cutter to the right may be sharpened by grinding on the face without changing the shape. For milling wide forms several cutters are often placed side by side in a gang.

Fish Tail Cutter — A simple cutter for milling a seat or groove in a shaft or other piece. Usually operated at rapid speed and light cut and feed.

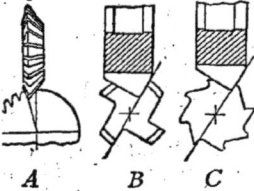

Fluting Cutters — Cutter *A* is an angular mill for cutting the teeth in spiral mills, cutter *B* is for tap fluting and *C* for milling reamer flutes. In each case the cutter is shown with one face set radial to the center of the work.

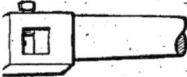

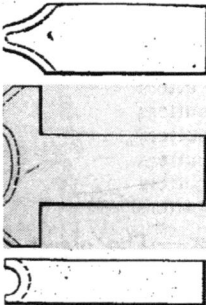

Fly Cutters — Fly cutters are simple formed cutters which may be held in an arbor like that shown at the top of the group. The arbor is placed in the miller spindle and the tool or other work to be formed is given a slow feed past the revolving cutter. After roughing out, the cutter can be held stationary and used like a planer tool for finishing the work which is fed past it and so given a scraping cut.

Gang Cutters — Cutters are used in a gang on an arbor for milling a broad surface of any desired form. The cutters shown have interlocking and overlapping teeth so that proper spacing may be maintained. In extensive manufacturing operation the gangs of cutters are usually kept set up on their arbor and never removed except for grinding.

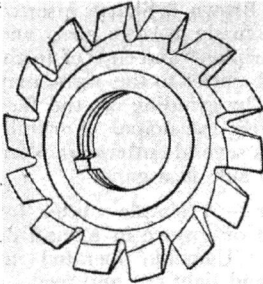

Gear Cutter (Involute). In the Brown & Sharpe system of involute gear cutters, eight cutters are regularly made for each pitch, as follows:

No. 1 will cut wheels from 135 teeth to a rack.

No. 2 will cut wheels from 55 teeth to 134 teeth.

No. 3 will cut wheels from 35 teeth to 54 teeth.

No. 4 will cut wheels from 26 teeth to 34 teeth.

No. 5 will cut wheels from 21 teeth to 25 teeth.

No. 6 will cut wheels from 17 teeth to 20 teeth.

No. 7 will cut wheels from 14 teeth to 16 teeth.

No. 8 will cut wheels from 12 teeth to 13 teeth.

Such cutters are always accurately formed and can be sharpened without affecting the shape of the teeth.

Gear Cutters, Duplex — The Gould & Eberhart duplex cutters are used in gangs of two or more; the number of cutters in the gang depending on the number of teeth in the gear to be cut. The following table gives the number of cutters which may be used in cutting different numbers of teeth.

Under	30 teeth	1 cutter
Over	30 teeth	2 cutters
Over	50 teeth	3 cutters
Over	70 teeth	4 cutters
Over	95 teeth	5 cutters
Over	120 teeth	6 cutters
Over	150 teeth	7 cutters
Over	180 teeth	8 cutters
Over	230 teeth	10 cutters
Over	260 teeth	12 cutters.

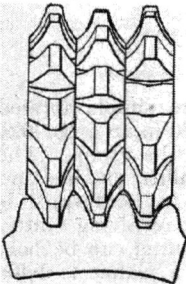

Gear Stocking Cutter — The object of stocking cutters is to rough out the teeth in gears, leaving a smaller amount of metal to be removed by the finishing cutter. They increase the accuracy with which gears may be cut, and save the finishing cutter as well.

In all cases where accuracy and smooth running are necessary the gears should first be roughed out. One stocking cutter answers for all gears of the same pitch.

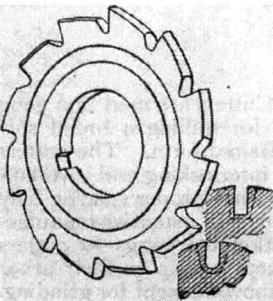

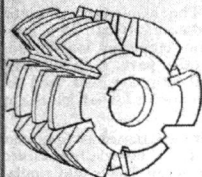

Hob — A form of milling cutter with teeth spirally arranged like a thread on a screw and with flutes to give cutting edges as indicated. Used for cutting the teeth of worm gears to suit the worm which is to operate the gear. Hobs are formed and backed off so that the faces of the teeth may be ground without changing the shape.

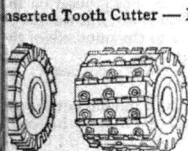

Inserted Tooth Cutter — Brown & Sharpe inserted tooth cutters have taper bushings and screws for holding the blades in position in the bodies. Inserted tooth construction is generally recommended for cutters 6 inches or larger in diameter. There are many types of inserted tooth cutters and in most cases the blades are readily removed and replaced when broken or worn out.

Inserted Tooth Cutter (Pratt & Whitney). In this type of cutter the teeth or blades are secured in position by taper pins driven into holes between every other pair of blades; the cutter head being slotted as shown to allow the metal at each side of the taper pin to be pressed firmly against the inserted blades.

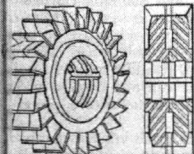

Interlocking Side Cutters — These cutters have overlapping teeth and may be adjusted apart to maintain a definite width for milling slots, etc., by using packing between the inner faces.

Plain Cutters — These cutters are for milling flat surfaces. When over ¾ inch wide the teeth are usually cut spirally at an angle of from 10 to 15 degrees, to give an easy shearing cut. When of considerable length relative to diameter they are called slabbing mills.

Gear Cutter (Involute). In the Bro[
& Sharpe system of involute g[
cutters, eight cutters are regula[
made for each pitch, as follows:

No. 1 will cut wheels from 135 te[
to a rack.

No. 2 will cut wheels from 55 te[
to 134 teeth.

No. 3 will cut wheels from 35 te[
to 54 teeth.

No. 4 will cut wheels from 26 te[
to 34 teeth.

No. 5 will cut wheels from 21 te[
to 25 teeth.

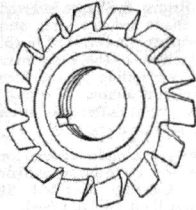

No. 6 will cut wheels from 17 teeth to 20 teeth.
No. 7 will cut wheels from 14 teeth to 16 teeth.
No. 8 will cut wheels from 12 teeth to 13 teeth.

Such cutters are always accurately formed and can be sha[
ened without affecting the shape of the teeth.

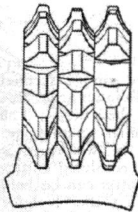

Gear Cutters, Duplex — The Gould & Eberh[
duplex cutters are used in gangs of two [
more; the number of cutters in the ga[
depending on the number of teeth in [
gear to be cut. The following table gi[
the number of cutters which may be used [
cutting different numbers of teeth.

Under	30 teeth	1 cutter
Over	30 teeth	2 cutters
Over	50 teeth	3 cutters
Over	70 teeth	4 cutters
Over	95 teeth	5 cutters
Over	120 teeth	6 cutters
Over	150 teeth	7 cutters
Over	180 teeth	8 cutters
Over	230 teeth	10 cutters
Over	260 teeth	12 cutters.

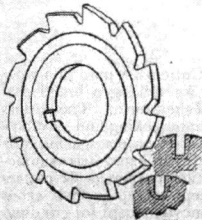

Gear Stocking Cutter — The object [
stocking cutters is to rough out [
teeth in gears, leaving a smal[
amount of metal to be removed [
the finishing cutter. They incre[
the accuracy with which gears may [
cut, and save the finishing cutter [
well.

In all cases where accuracy and smo[
running are necessary the gears shou[
first be roughed out. One stocki[
cutter answers for all gears of [
same pitch.

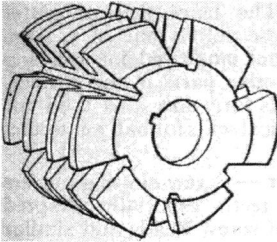

Hob — A form of milling cutter with teeth spirally arranged like a thread on a screw and with flutes to give cutting edges as indicated. Used for cutting the teeth of worm gears to suit the worm which is to operate the gear. Hobs are formed and backed off so that the faces of the teeth may be ground without changing the shape.

Inserted Tooth Cutter — Brown & Sharpe inserted tooth cutters have taper bushings and screws for holding the blades in position in the bodies. Inserted tooth construction is generally recommended for cutters 6 inches or larger in diameter. There are many types of inserted tooth cutters and in most cases the blades are readily removed and replaced when broken or worn out.

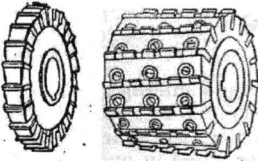

Inserted Tooth Cutter (Pratt & Whitney). In this type of cutter the teeth or blades are secured in position by taper pins driven into holes between every other pair of blades; the cutter head being slotted as shown to allow the metal at each side of the taper pin to be pressed firmly against the inserted blades.

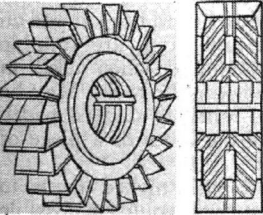

Interlocking Side Cutters — These cutters have overlapping teeth and may be adjusted apart to maintain a definite width for milling slots, etc., by using packing between the inner faces.

Plain Cutters — These cutters are for milling flat surfaces. When over ¾ inch wide the teeth are usually cut spirally at an angle of from 10 to 15 degrees, to give an easy shearing cut. When of considerable length relative to diameter they are called slabbing mills.

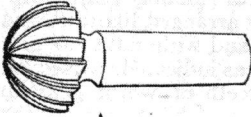

Rose Cutter — The hemispherical cutter known as a rose mill is one of a large variety of forms employed for working out dies and other parts in the profiler. Cutters of this form are also used for making spherical seats for ball joints, etc.

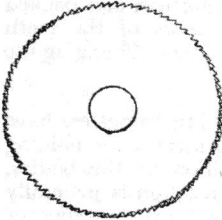

Screw Slotting Cutter — Screw slotting cutters have fine pitch teeth especially adapted for the slotting of screw heads and similar work. The cutters are not ground on the sides. They are made of various thicknesses corresponding to the numbers of the American Wire Gage.

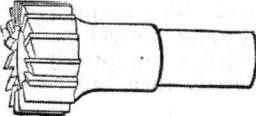

Shank Cutter — Shank milling cutters are made in all sorts of forms with shanks which can be conveniently held true in miller or profiler while in operation.

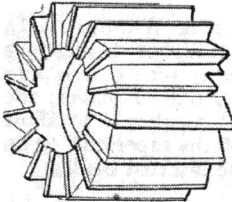

Shell End Cutter — Shell end mills are designed to do heavier work than that for which the regular type of end mills are suited. They are made to be used on an arbor and are secured by a screw in the end of the arbor. The end of the cutter is counterbored to receive the head of the screw and the back end is slotted for driving as indicated.

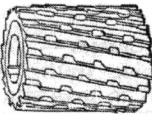

Side   Slabbing

Side or Straddle, and Slabbing Cutters — Side cutters like that to the left cut on the periphery and sides, are suitable for milling slots and when used in pairs are called straddle mills. May be packed out to mill any desired width of slot or opposite faces of a piece of any thickness.

Slabbing cutters are frequently made with nicked teeth to break up the chip and so give an easier cut than would be possible with a plain tooth.

Slitting Saw, Metal — Metal slitting saws are thin milling cutters. The sides are finished true by grinding, and a little thicker at the outside edge than near the center, for proper clearance. Coarse teeth are best adapted for brass work and deep slots and fine teeth for cutting thin metal.

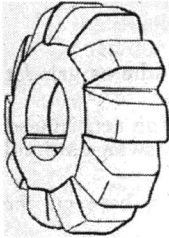

Sprocket Wheel Cutter — Cutters for milling the teeth on sprocket wheels for chains are formed to the necessary outline and admit of grinding on the face like regular gear cutters, without changing the form of the tooth.

Straight Shank Cutter — Straight shank cutters of small size are extensively used in profilers and vertical millers for die sinking, profiling, routing, etc. They are held in spring chucks or collets.

Left Hand

Left Hand Cutter

Right Hand Cutter

T-Slot Cutter — Slots for bolts in miller and other tables are milled with T-slot cutters. They are made to standard dimensions to suit bolts of various sizes. The narrow part of the slot is first milled in the casting, then the bottom portion is widened out with the T-slot cutter.

Woodruff Key Cutter — The Whitney Mfg. Co's keys are semi-circular in form and for cutting the seats in the shaft to receive them a cutter of the type shown is used. These cutters are made of right diameter and thickness to suit all the different sizes of keys in the Woodruff system.

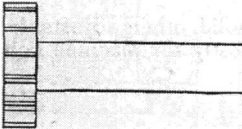

Cutting-off Machine — For cutting desired lengths from commercial bars of iron, steel or other material, usually has stationary tools and revolves the work. The latter is gripped by the rotating chuck; and as the tools are fed toward the center, the spindle in some types of machines is driven at an accelerated speed so that as the diameter of the cut is reduced, the speed of rotation is increased to maintain a practically uniform surface speed of work. In cold-saw cutting-off machines, the work is held in a vise and a rotating circular cutter is fed against it. Such machines are used not only for severing round stock but also for cutting off square and rectangular bars, rails, I-beams, channels and other structural steel shapes.

Cutting-off Tool Post — The tool block used on the cross slide of a turret lathe or other machine for carrying the tool for cutting off the completed piece of work from the bar of material held in the chuck. The tool post may be made to receive a straight tool or a circular cutter.

D

Daniels Planer — See Planer.

Dead Center — The center in the tail spindle of a lathe or grinder which does not revolve.

Derrick — Structure consisting of a fixed upright and an arm hinged at bottom, which is raised and lowered and usually swings around to handle heavy loads.

Dial Feed — A revolving disk which carries blanks between the punch and die.

Diamond Hand Tool — Used for dressing grinding wheels after they have been roughed out with the cheaper forms of cutters. Fixed diamonds are usually considered better than those held by hand.

Die Chasers — Threaded sections inserted in a die head for cutting bolts and screws.

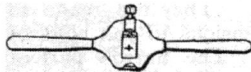

Die, Screw Plate or Stock — A frame or handle for holding a threading die. Sometimes die and handles are of one piece.

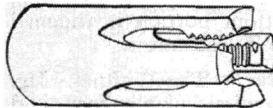

Die, Spring or Prong — Die with cutting portions in the end of prongs; can be adjusted somewhat by springing prongs together with a collar on outside.

Dies, Bolt — Dies for cutting bolts. Some are solid, others adjustable. Some for hand die stocks or plates but mostly for machine bolt cutters.

DIES, PUNCH PRESS

Bending Dies, Compound — In compound bending dies of the type shown the work is carried down into the die by punch *A*, and held there while the beveled fingers *B* act upon the slides *C* and cause them to move forward in the top of die *D* and bend the material to the outline of the punch. Upon the up-stroke of the punch the slides *C* are pressed outwardly by their springs and the bent piece of work is removed by the punch from the die. It will be seen that the holder for punch *A*, upon which depends the interior form of the piece being bent, is not positively secured in its holder, but is instead adapted to slide up and down in its seat,

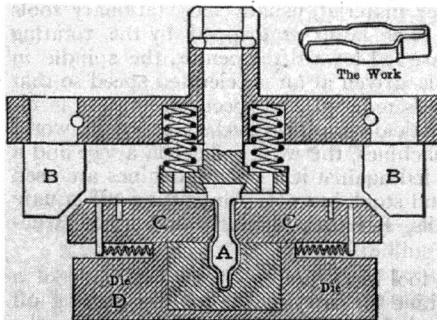

although prevented from turning by a small pin at the upper end of the shank which is engaged by a slot in the punch carrier. The springs shown above the punch proper tend to hold the punch in its lower position and at the same time after the punch has passed down into the die allow the punch carrier to descend still further to press fingers *B* into operation against slides *C* which bend the work to the outline of the punch.

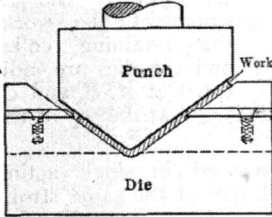

Bending Dies, Plain — Simple bending dies are made with the upper face of the die and the bottom of the punch shaped to conform to the bend it is desired to give the blank. A common type is shown in the engraving.

In simple bending dies the upper face of the die is cut out to the desired form and the piece of work formed to required shape by being pressed directly down into the die by the punch.

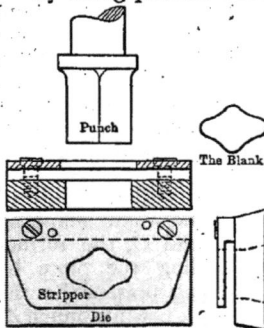

Blanking Dies — Blanking dies are about the most commonly used of all the varieties of press tools. A simple form of die is seen in the illustration. The strip of sheet metal is fed under the stripper and is prevented by that member from lifting with the punch upon the up-stroke, following the punching out of the blank. Where several punches are combined in one hole for blanking as many pieces simultaneously, they are known as multiple blanking tools.

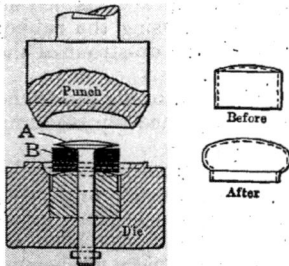

Bulging Dies — The "before and after" sketches show the character of the work handled in bulging dies. The shell after being drawn up straight is placed over mushroom plunger *A* in the bulging die, and when the punch descends the rubber disk *B* is forced out, expanding the shell into the curved chamber formed by the punch and die. Upon the punch ascending, the rubber returns to its original form and the expanded work is then removed.

Burnishing Dies — Burnishing dies are made a little smaller at the bottom than at the top and when the work is forced down through the die, the edge of the piece is given a very high finish making polishing and hand finishing operations unnecessary. The burnishing process forms a very accurate sizing method also.

Coining Dies — Coining dies are operated in very powerful presses of the embossing type similar to those used for forming designs on silverware, medals, jewelry, etc. The position of the work, the retaining collar and the dies are indicated at *A, B,* and *C.*

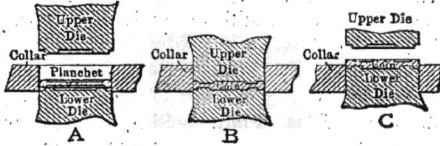

In the latter section the coin is shown delivered at the top of the die.

Combination Dies — Combination dies are used in single acting presses for such work as cutting a blank and at the same stroke turning down the edge and drawing the piece into the required shape. In most cases the work is pushed out of the dies by the action of a spring. Such a set of dies is shown in the engraving, for making a box cover and body. The work is blanked by cutting-punch *A,* and formed to the right shape by *B* and *C,* the former holding the piece by spring pressure to the block *C* while punch *A,* continuing to descend, draws the box to the required shape. Ring *D* acts as an ejector or shedder and is pressed down, compressing the rubber at *E* during the drawing operation, and upon the up-stroke of the punch, ascends and ejects the work from the dies.

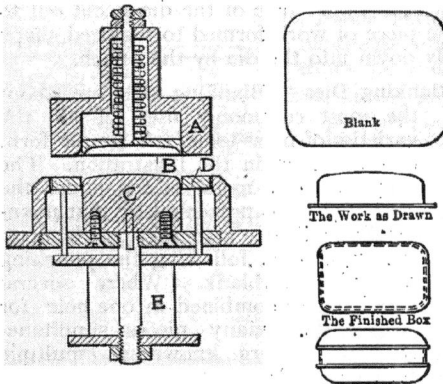

Dies of this type, with a spring actuated punch or die inside the regular blanking tool, are often used for simultaneously blanking and piercing, blanking and bending, etc.

It will be noticed that the lower view in the group showing the work at the right-hand side of the sectional illustration of the die, represents the box cover and body as they appear when assembled after the superfluous metal in the flange or "fin" has been removed in a trimming die. This fin as left on the piece when coming from the combination die is shown in the view immediately under the blank. A trimming die for finishing such work evenly is shown on page 597.

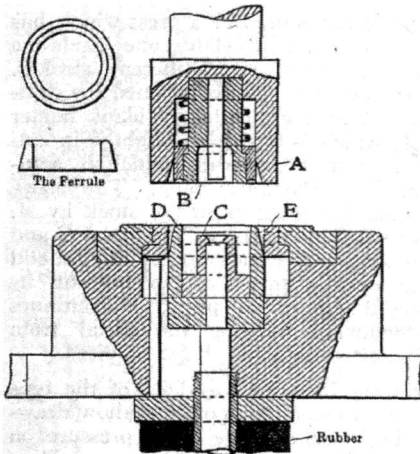

Compound Dies — Compound dies have a die in the upper punch and a punch in the lower die. The ferrule-making tools shown have a blanking and outer drawing punch *A*, with a central die *B*, to receive lower punch *C* which cuts out the center of the ferrule blank and allows the metal to be drawn down inside as well as outside of the bevel edged member *D*. As the work is drawn down ring *E* descends compressing rubber cushion *F* below and upon the return movement the ferrule is ejected from the die.

Cupping Dies — Used for drawing up a cup from a disk or planchet. Same as drawing dies.

Curling Dies — Curling dies are used for producing a curled edge around the top of a piece drawn up from sheet metal. When the top is to be stiffened by a wire ring around which the metal is curled, a wiring die is used, the construction of which is practically the same as the curling die. The illustration shows a curling die and the appearance of a shell at various stages during the operation of curling over the edge. The diagrams *A*, *B*, *C*, *D*, show the progress in the curling process as the punch descends, pressing down on the edge of the straight drawn shell.

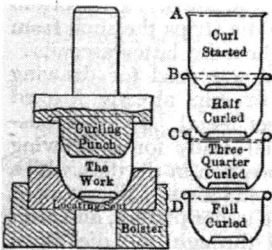

Dinking Dies — Dinking dies, or hollow cutters, although not usually classed with regular dies are used so commonly as to entitle them to be listed in that class. They are adapted to punching out all sorts of shapes from leather, cloth, or paper. The edges of the dies (a few specimens of which are shown in the engraving) are usually beveled about 20 degrees outside. Where made for press use the handle is omitted. As a surface for

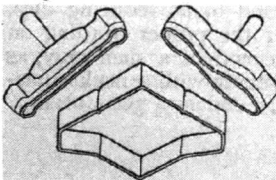

the cutting edge of the die to strike on, a block is built up of seasoned rock maple, set endwise of the grain.

Double Action Dies — This type of die is used in a press which has a double acting ram; that is, there are two slides, one inside the other, which have different strokes. To the outer slide is fastened the combined cutting punch and blank holder *A*, which is operated slightly in advance of the drawing punch *B* actuated by the inner slide. The blank upon being cut from the stock by *A*, drops into the top of the die at *C* and is kept under pressure by the flat end of cutting punch *A* to prevent its wrinkling, while punch *B* continues downward drawing the metal from between the pressure surfaces and into the shape required.

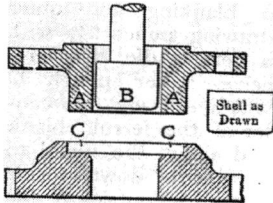

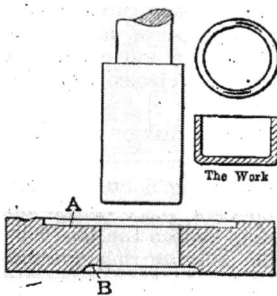

Drawing Dies, Plain — Dies of the type shown can be used for shallow drawing only, as there is no pressure on the blank to prevent its wrinkling when forced down into the die by the punch. The blank fits the recess *A* in the upper face of the die and the die itself which is slightly tapering is made the diameter of the punch plus twice the thickness of the wall required for the shell. The bottom edge *B* of the die strips the shell from the punch when the latter ascends.

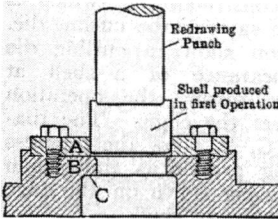

Re-drawing dies are used for drawing out a shell or cup already formed from the sheet metal. In the illustration, a shell ready for re-drawing is shown in position in the dies, which need little explanation. The work is located in the upper plate *A*, and after being forced through the die *B*, is stripped from the punch by edge *C*. Ordinarily, a shell which is to be given considerable elongation, is passed through a number of re-drawing dies.

Re-drawing dies are sometimes referred to as reducing dies, although the latter, as explained under the proper heading on page 594, are used for drawing down the end of a shell only, as in the case of a cartridge shell, which is made with a neck somewhat smaller in diameter than the body.

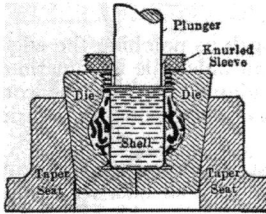

Fluid Dies — Water or fluid dies are used for forming artistic hollow ware of silver, and other soft metals, in exact reproduction of chased work. The die as shown is a hinged mold cast from carved models and finished with all details clean and sharp. The shell to be worked is filled with liquid and enclosed in the die and a plunger in the press ram then descends and causes the fluid to force the metal out into the design in the die.

Follow Dies — Follow tools consist of two or more punches and dies in one punch holder and die body, these being arranged in tandem fashion so that after the first operation the stock is fed to the next point and a second operation performed; and so on. In the die shown, which is for making piece *A*, the strip of metal is first entered beneath stripper. *B* far enough to allow the first shell to be drawn at the first stroke by punch *C* and die *D*. The metal is then moved along one space and the shell drawn at the first stroke is centered and located within the locating portion of piercing die. *E*. At the next stroke the hole in the center is pierced with punch *F*, and a second shell drawn in the stock by punch and die *C* and *D*. The stock is then fed forward another space and the blanking punch *G* cuts out the piece from the metal. At the same stroke a third piece is being formed on the end of the stock and a second hole pierced. Thus three operations are carried on simultaneously.

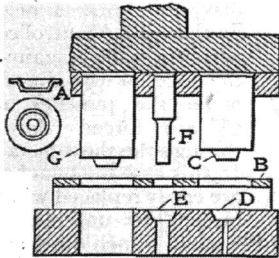

Gang Dies — Gang tools have two or more punches and dies in one holder for making as many openings in a blank at one stroke of the press. Sometimes dies which perform a number of operations on a piece which is fed along successively under one punch after another are called "gang" dies; strictly speaking, however, such tools are "follow" dies. Where a large number of punches are combined they are called a multiple punch, or if they are of quite small diameter for piercing are sometimes known as perforating punches.

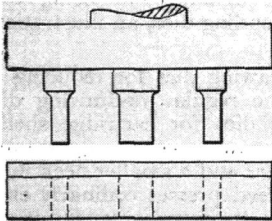

Heading Dies — Heading dies strike up the heads on cartridges and other shells, and are generally operated in a horizontal heading machine.

Index Dies — For certain classes of work such as notching the edges of large disks or armature punchings, an index die is sometimes used consisting of a rotary index plate adapted to carry the work step by step past the punches which cut out one notch or a series of notches at each stroke of the press.

Perforating Dies — Perforating tools consist of a number of piercing tools in one set of dies and may be called also multiple piercing tools. In the example shown, which punches a large number of holes in a disk, the work is held by the spring-controlled pressure-pad A against the face of the die B while the punches at C are forced down through the sheet metal. In this case the punches are easily replaced when broken, by unscrewing the holder from the shank and slipping the small punch out from the back.

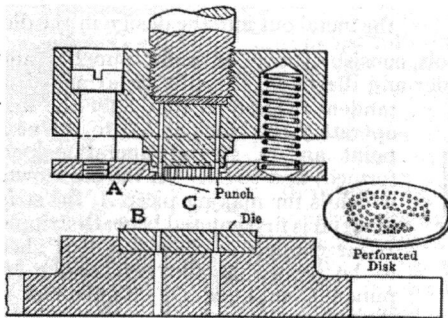

Piercing Dies — Piercing tools are used for punching small holes through sheet metal. Where arranged for punching a large number of holes simultaneously they are often called perforating dies.

Piercing Dies, Compound — Compound piercing tools have, in addition to the regular punches carried by the holder in the ram, a set of horizontal punches for making holes through the sides of the work. These side punches are operated by slides moved inward by wedge-shaped fingers, the arrangement being the same as in the case of the compound bending dies, an illustration of which is given under that head.

Reducing Dies — Reducing dies are re-drawing dies for reducing a portion of the shell only, whereas the regular re-drawing die reduces the whole length. Reducing dies for cartridge shells form the familiar "bottle neck" shell now so commonly manufactured, with a larg body for the powder and a smaller neck into which the bullet is secured. In dial feed presses ordinarily employed for cartridge making operations, two or more reducing dies are often used for shaping the neck of the shell to the required dimensions, each die operating in turn upon the shell as it is carried around step by step under the press tools by the intermittent rotary movement of the feeding dial.

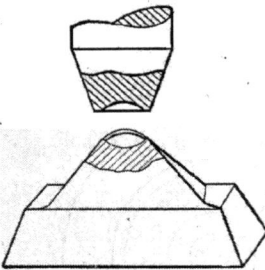

Riveting Dies — Riveting dies for the punch press are provided with cavities in the working faces to suit the shape of the head it is desired to produce on the ends of the rivets.

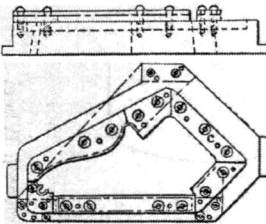

Sectional Dies — Frequently dies of complicated outline are built up in sections to enable them to be more easily constructed and kept in order. This form is resorted to often in the case of large dies where a break at one point would mean considerable expense for a new die. Also the difficulties of hardening are reduced with the sectional construction. As shown, the various parts are secured to a common base or holder.

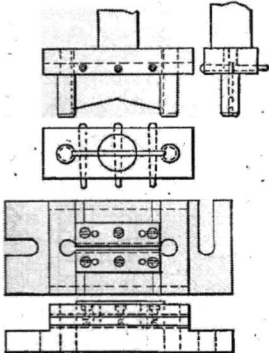

Shearing Dies — Shearing dies are used for cutting-off operations, and are frequently combined with other press tools so that after certain operations on a piece it can be severed from the end of the stock. The shearing tools in the engraving are arranged for simply cutting up stock into pieces of the required length and the punch itself is of the inserted type secured by pins in its holder.

Split Dies — Split dies form one type of sectional die — the simplest; they are made in halves to facilitate working out to shape, hardening, and economical maintainance.

Sub-press Dies — A sub-press and its tools are represented on the following page. Such tools are used for small parts which have to be made accurately and are very common in watch and typewriter shops and similar places. The tools are held positively in line in this press and as a result their efficiency is maintained indefinitely. The press is slipped bodily into the regular power press with the base clamped to the press bed and the neck of the sub-press plunger connected with the ram of the press.

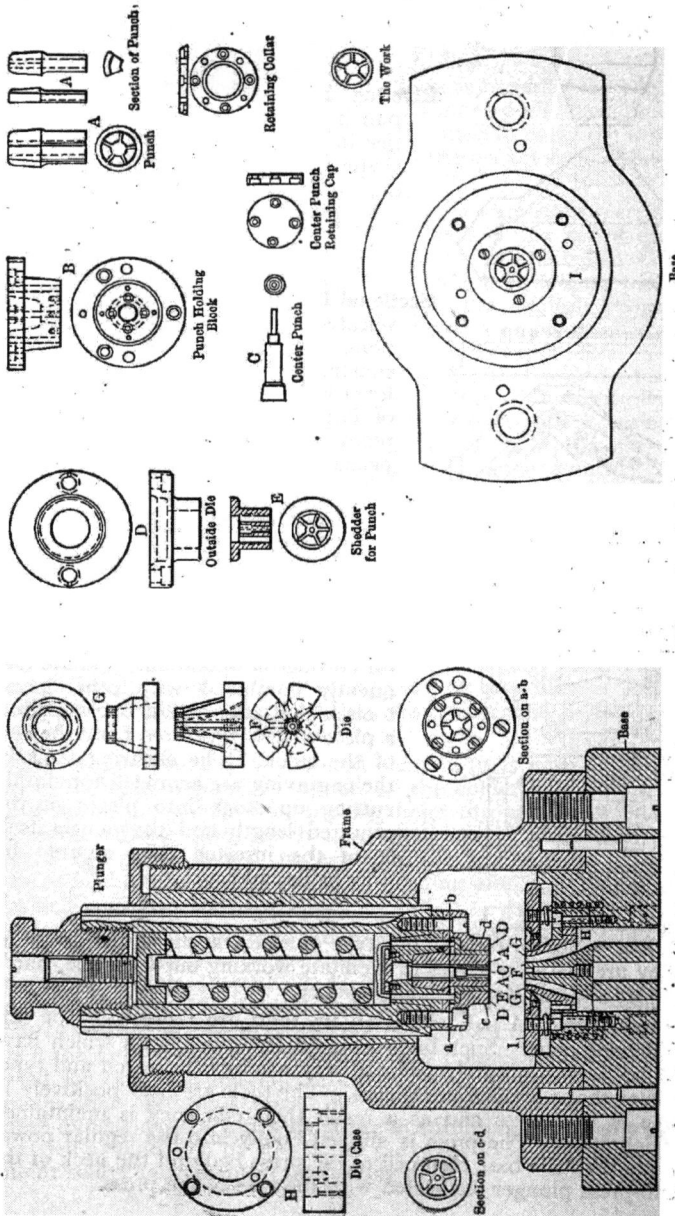

Sub-Press with Tools for a Watch Wheel

Swaging Dies — Swaging operations are resorted to where it is desired to shape up or round over the edges of work already blanked out. Thus in watch wheel work the arms and inside edges of the rims are sometimes swaged to a nicely rounded form subsequently to the blanking out of the wheel in the sub-press. Swaging dies for such work are of course made with shallow impressions which correspond to a split mold between the two halves of which the blank is properly shaped.

Bullet swaging dies receive the slug as it comes from the bullet mold and shape the end to the required cone point.

Trimming Dies — Trimming dies remove the superfluous metal left around the edges or ends of various classes of drawn and formed work. In the case shown, the box body A has been drawn up and a fin left all the way round; this is dropped into the trimming die B and the punch C in carrying it through the die trims the edge off evenly, as indicated. Work of the nature shown in this illustration is blanked, drawn up and formed ready for trimming, by means of combination tools, a typical example of which will be found under the combination die heading on page 590. The box body illustrated here as it appears before and after trimming is shown in connection with the combination dies as it appears in the blank, after it is formed, and after assembling with its cover.

Triple-action Dies — These dies are used in triple-acting presses, where in addition to the double-action slides which take the place of the regular single-acting ram, there is also a third slide or plunger which operates under the table or die bed. Thus a piece like that shown which has to be blanked, drawn and embossed, is operated upon from above by the cutting and drawing punches A and B, and upon the latter carrying the drawn work down to the face of the embossing die C, that die is forced upward by the plunger D beneath and gives the piece the desired impression. On the up-stroke of the punch the work is stripped from it by edge E and falls out of the press.

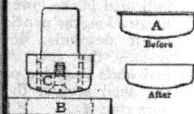

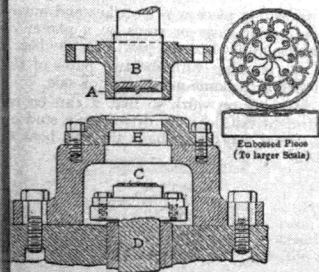

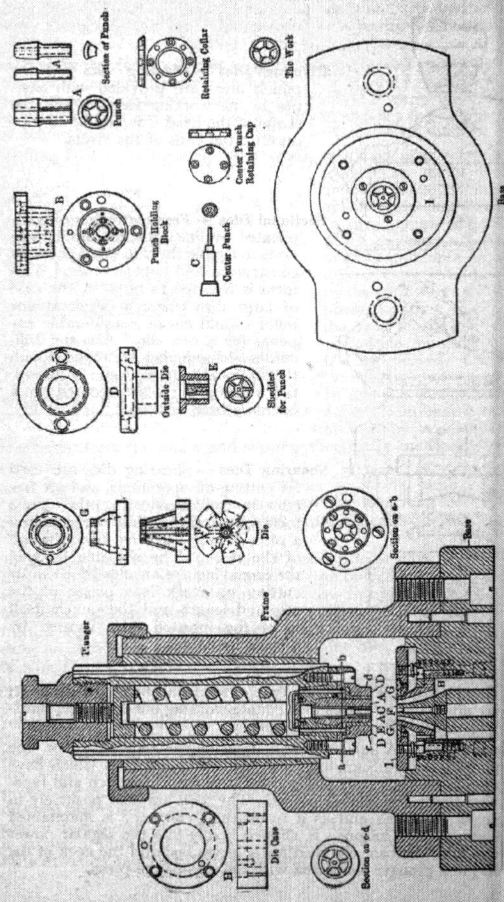

Section of Punch

Punch

Retaining Collar

Die Nest

A

Center Punch Retaining Cap

Punch Holding Block

B

C

Center Punch

Outside Die

D

E

Shoulder for Punch

Die

G

Section on a-b

Base

Plunger

Frame

DEAD

Die Case

H

Section on c-d

Base

Sub-Press with Tools for a Watch Wheel

Swaging Dies — Swaging operations are resorted to where it is desired to shape up or round over the edges of work already blanked out. Thus in watch wheel work the arms and inside edges of the rims are sometimes swaged to a nicely rounded form subsequently to the blanking out of the wheel in the sub-press. Swaging dies for such work are of course made with shallow impressions which correspond to a split mold between the two halves of which the blank is properly shaped.

Bullet swaging dies receive the slug as it comes from the bullet mold and shape the end to the required cone point.

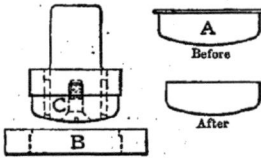

Trimming Dies — Trimming dies remove the superfluous metal left around the edges or ends of various classes of drawn and formed work. In the case shown, the box body *A* has been drawn up and a fin left all the way round; this is dropped into the trimming die *B* and the punch *C* in carrying it through the die trims the edge off evenly, as indicated. Work of the nature shown in this illustration is blanked, drawn up and formed ready for trimming, by means of combination tools, a typical example of which will be found under the combination die heading on page 590. The box body illustrated here as it appears before and after trimming is shown in connection with the combination dies as it appears in the blank, after it is formed, and after assembling with its cover.

Triple-action Dies — These dies are used in triple-acting presses, where in addition to the double-action slides which take the place of the regular single-acting ram, there is also a third slide or plunger which operates under the table or die bed. Thus a piece like that shown which has to be blanked, drawn and embossed, is operated upon from above by the cutting and drawing punches *A* and *B*, and upon the latter carrying the drawn work down to the face of the embossing die *C*, that die is forced upward by the plunger *D* beneath and gives the piece the desired impression. On the up-stroke of the punch the work is stripped from it by edge *E* and falls out of the press.

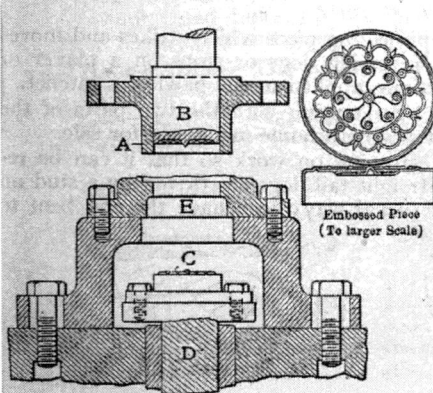

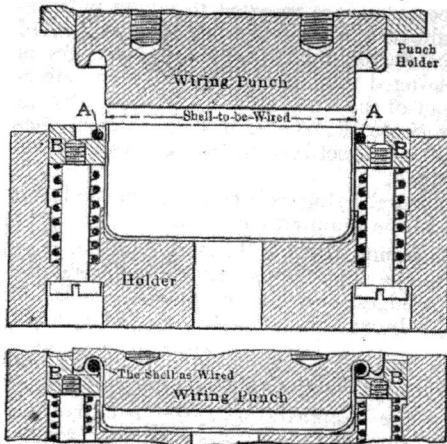

Wiring Dies — Wiring dies are much the same in construction as plain curling dies. In the engraving, the wire ring is shown at *A* around the top of the shell to be wired and in a channel at the top of the spring-supported ring *B*. As indicated in the lower illustration, the punch as it descends, depresses the ring *B* and curls the edge of the shell around the wire ring *A*.

Disks, Reference — Accurate disks of standard dimensions for setting calipers and measuring with. Usually of hardened steel.

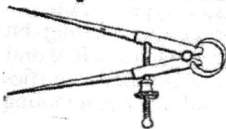

Divider, Spring — The spring tends to force the points apart and adjustments are made by the nurled nut on the screw.

Doctor — Local term for adjuster or adapter so that chucks from one lathe can be used on another. Sometimes used same as "dutchman."

Dog — Name given to any projecting piece which strikes and moves some other part, as the reversing dogs or stops on a planer or milling machine. Sometimes applied to the pawl of a ratchet.

Dog, Clamp — Grips work by clamping with the two parts of the dog. There are many types both home-made and for sale.

Dog, Lathe — Devices for clamping on work so that it can be revolved by face-plate. Straight tail dogs are driven by a stud on face-plate. Curved tail (usual way) dogs have the end bent to go into a slot in face-plate.

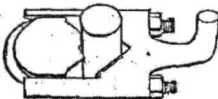

Clamp Dog

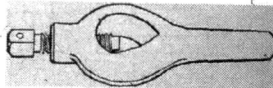

Straight Tail

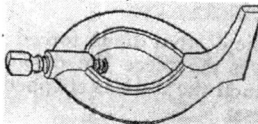

Bent Tail

Drag — The bottom part of a flask, sometimes called the nowell.

Draw Bench — Place where wire is drawn from rods, being drawn through plates or bull blocks with successively smaller openings.

Drift — A tool for cutting out the sides of an opening while driven through with a hammer.

DRILLS

Center Drill — The short drills used for centering shafts before facing and turning are called center drills. The drill and reamer or countersink for the 60 degree center hole when combined as shown allow the centering to be done more readily than when separate tools are used.

Drill

Combination

Core Drill — The core drill is a hollow tool which cuts out a core instead of removing the metal in the form of chips. Such drills are generally used to procure a core from the center of castings or forgings for the determination of the tensile strength or other physical properties of the metal.

Gun Barrel Drill — Gun barrel drills are run at high speed and under very light feed, oil being forced through a hole in the drill to clear the chips and cool the cutting point and work. The drill itself is short and fastened to a shank of suitable length.

Hog Nose Drill — More like a boring tool. Mostly used for boring out cored holes. Must be very stiff to be effective but when made right and used to advantage, does lots of hard work.

Hollow Drill — The hollow drill is for deep-hole drilling. It has an opening through the body and is attached to a shank of the necessary length for the depth of hole to be drilled.

Oil-drill (Morse) — These drills convey lubricant to the point, through holes formed in the solid metal. Where the drills are larger than $2\frac{1}{4}$ inches an inserted copper tube is employed to carry the oil to the drill point and wash out the chips and keep the drill cool. The oil enters through the hollow shank or through a connection at the side as shown.

Twist

Ratchet Drill — The square taper shanks of these drills are made to fit a ratchet for drilling holes by hand.

Flat

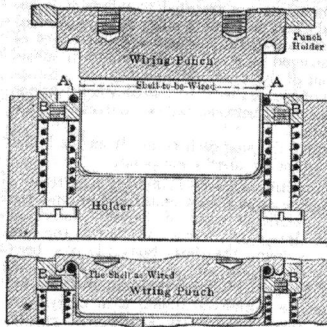

Wiring Dies — Wiring dies are much the same in construction as plain curling dies. In the engraving, the wire ring is shown a A around the top o the shell to be wire and in a channel a the top of the spring supported ring B. A indicated in the lowe illustration, the punc as it descends, de presses the ring A and curls the edge o the shell around th wire ring A.

Disks, Reference — Accurate disks of standard dimensions for settin calipers and measuring with. Usually of hardened steel.

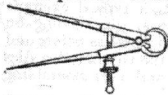

Divider, Spring — The spring tends to forc the points apart and adjustments are mad by the nurled nut on the screw.

Doctor — Local term for adjuster or adapter so that chucks fro one lathe can be used on another. Sometimes used same a "dutchman."

Dog — Name given to any projecting piece which strikes and move some other part, as the reversing dogs or stops on a planer o milling machine. Sometimes applied to the pawl of a ratchet.

Dog, Clamp — Grips work by clamping with the two parts of th dog. There are many types both home-made and for sale.

Dog, Lathe — Devices for clamping on work so that it can be re volved by face-plate. Straight tail dogs are driven by a stud o face-plate. Curved tail (usual way) dogs have the end bent t go into a slot in face-plate.

Clamp Dog   Straight Tail

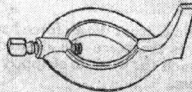

Bent Tail

Drag — The bottom part of a flask, sometimes called the nowell.

Draw Bench — Place where wire is drawn from rods, being drawn through plates or bull blocks with successively smaller openings.

Drift — A tool for cutting out the sides of an opening while driven through with a hammer.

DRILLS

Center Drill — The short drills used for centering shafts before facing and turning are called center drills. The drill and reamer or countersink for the 60 degree center hole when combined as shown allow the centering to be done more readily than when separate tools are used.

Drill

Combination

Core Drill — The core drill is a hollow tool which cuts out a core instead of removing the metal in the form of chips. Such drills are generally used to procure a core from the center of castings or forgings for the determination of the tensile strength or other physical properties of the metal.

Gun Barrel Drill — Gun barrel drills are run at high speed and under very light feed, oil being forced through a hole in the drill to clear the chips and cool the cutting point and work. The drill itself is short and fastened to a shank of suitable length.

Hog Nose Drill — More like a boring tool. Mostly used for boring out cored holes. Must be very stiff to be effective but when made right and used to advantage, does lots of hard work.

Hollow Drill — The hollow drill is for deep-hole drilling. It has an opening through the body and is attached to a shank of the necessary length for the depth of hole to be drilled.

Oil-drill (Morse) — These drills convey lubricant to the point, through holes formed in the solid metal. Where the drills are larger than 2½ inches an inserted copper tube is employed to carry the oil to the drill point and wash out the chips and keep the drill cool. The oil enters through the hollow shank or through a connection at the side as shown.

Twist

Ratchet Drill — The square taper shanks of these drills are made to fit a ratchet for drilling holes by hand.

Flat

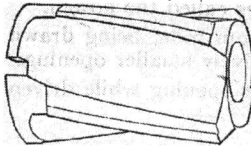

Shell Drill — Shell drills are fitted to a taper shank and used for chucking out cored holes and enlarging holes drilled with a two-flute twist drill. The angle of the spiral lips is about 15 degrees.

Straight Flute Drill — The straight flute, or "Farmer" drill as it is frequently called after its inventor, does not clear itself as well as the twist drill does, but is stiffer, and does not "run" or follow blow-holes or soft spots as readily as the twist drill. It is also better for drilling brass and other soft metals.

Three Groove

Four Groove

Three and Four-groove Drills — Where large holes are to be made in solid stock, it is advisable to use a three or four groove drill after running the required two-flute drill through the piece. These drills will enlarge the hole to the size required and are also useful in boring out cored holes in castings.

Twist Drill — Usually made with two flutes or grooves, running around the body. This furnishes cutting edges and the chips follow the flutes out of the hole being drilled.

Pod

Bit Point

Single Flute

Wood Drill (Bit) — Bits for wood drilling are made in various forms. The pod drill is cut out hollow at the working end; the double flute spiral drill has a regular bit point; the single flute drill is full diameter for a short distance only and is cleared the rest of the length as indicated.

Drill, Chain — Device to be used in connection with a brace or breast drill in many places where it is not convenient to bring a ratchet drill into use.

Drill Speeder — Device which goes on drill spindle and gears up the speed of drills so that small drills can be used economically on large drill presses.

Drill Vise — See Vise, Drill.

Drill, Radial — Parts of

1. Vertical driving-shaft gear.
2. Center driving-shaft gear.
3. Elevating tumble-plate segment.
4. Elevating-screw gear.
5. Column cap.
6. Vertical driving shaft.
7. Column sleeve.
8. Elevating-lever shaft.
9. Elevating screw.
10. Arm girdle.
11. Arm-binder handle.

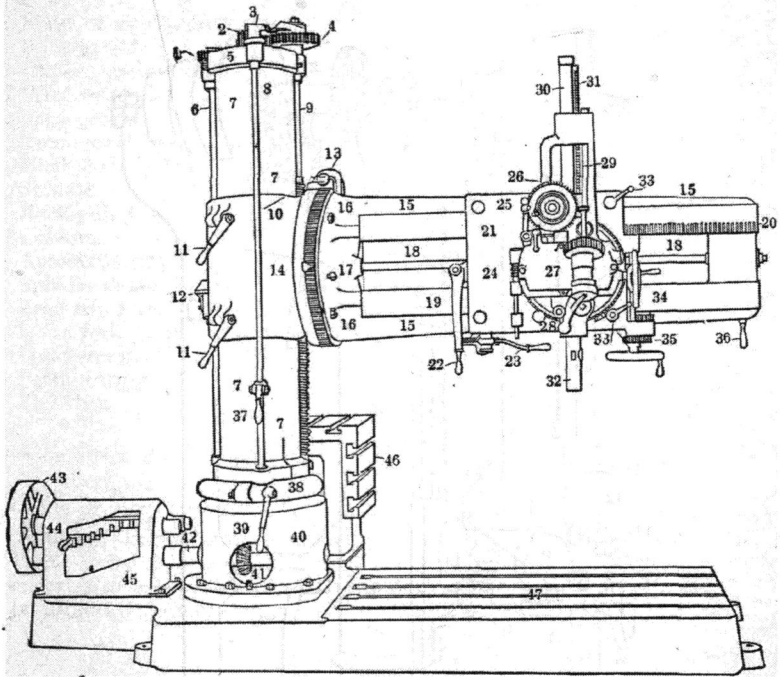

RADIAL DRILL—FULL UNIVERSAL—BICKFORD

12. Arm-miter gear guard.
13. Arm-worm box.
14. Arm pointer.
15. Full universal arm.
16. Arm-clamping nuts.
17. Arm-dowel pin.
18. Arm shaft.
19. Arm ways.
20. Arm rack.
21. Saddle.
22. Reversing lever.
23. Back-gear lever.
24. Head-swiveling worm.
25. Feed-trip lever.
26. Index gear.
27. Universal head.
28. Quick-return lever.
29. Feed-rack worm shaft.
30. Spindle sleeve.
31. Feed rack.
32. Spindle.
33. Saddle-binding lever.
34. Feed hand wheel.
35. Head-moving gear.
36. Arm-swinging handle.
37. Elevating lever.
38. Clamping ring.
39. Clamping-ring handle.
40. Column.
41. Column driving-miters.
42. Driving-shaft coupling.
43. Driving pulley.
44. Speed-change lever.
45. Speed-box case.
46. Box table.
47. Base.

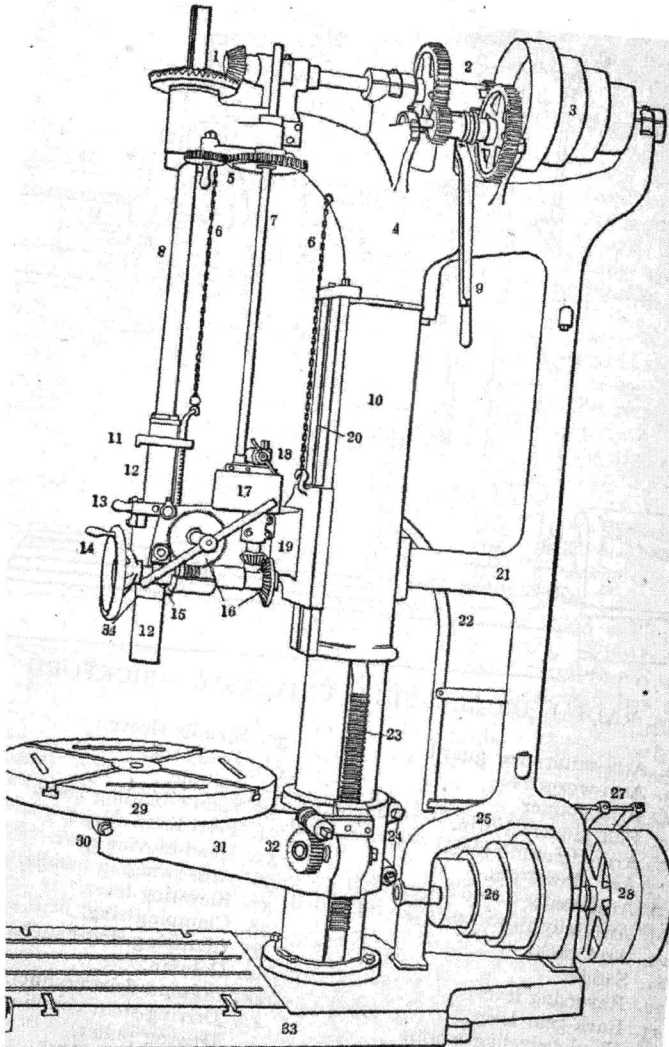

DRILL PRESS — CINCINNATI MACHINE
TOOL COMPANY

Drill Press — Parts of

1. Main driving gears, bevel.
2. Back gears.
3. Upper cone pulley.
4. Yoke to frame.
5. Feed gears.
6. Counterweight chains.
7. Feed shaft.
8. Spindle.
9. Back-gear lever
10. Column.
11. Automatic stop.
12. Spindle sleeve.
13. Feed-trip lever.
14. Hand-feed wheel.
15. Quick-return lever.
16. Feed gearing.
17. Feed box.
18. Feed-change handle.
19. Sliding head.
20. Face of column.
21. Back brace.
22. Belt shifter.
23. Rack for elevating table.
24. Table-arm clamping screws.
25. Pulley stand.
26. Lower cone pulley.
27. Belt-shifting fingers.
28. Tight and loose pulleys
29. Table.
30. Table-clamp screw.
31. Table arm.
32. Table-adjusting gear.
33. Base.
34. Ball-thrust bearing.

Drive or Force Fit — See Fit.

Dry Sand Molds — Molds made of green sand and baked dry in ovens or otherwise dried out before pouring.

Dutchman — Local term for a wedge or liner to make a piece fit. Used to make a poor job useable. A round key or pin fitting endwise in a hole drilled half in a shaft and half in the piece to be attached thereto.

E

Ejector — An ejector on punch press work is a ring, collar or disk actuated by spring pressure or by pressure of a rubber disk, to remove blanks from the interior of compound and other dies. It is often called a shedder.

Elliptic Chuck — See Chuck, Oval.

Emery Jointer — Grinder for making a close joint between the share and mold board of steel plows.

Emery Wheel Dressers — See Grinding Wheels and Diamonds.

End Measuring Rod — Arranged for internal measurements similar to the internal cylindrical gages.

Expanding Arbor or Mandrel — See Arbor.

Extractor, Oil — Machine for extracting oil from iron and metal chips. Revolves rapidly and throws out the oil by centrifugal force.

F

Face Cam — See Cam, Face.

Face Plate — The plate or disk which screws on the nose of a lathe spindle and drives or carries work to be turned or bored. Sometimes applied to table of vertical boring mill.

Face Reamer — See Reamer, Face.

Feather — Might be called a sliding key — sometimes called a spline. Used to prevent a pulley, gear or other part, from turning on the shaft but allows it to move lengthwise as in the feed shaft used on most lathes and other tools. Feather is nearly always fastened to the sliding piece.

Field — Usually the stationary part of a dynamo or motor.

Files — Tools of hardened steel having sharp cutting points or teeth across their surface. These are forced up by a chisel and hammer.

Filing Machine — Runs a file by power, usually vertically. Useful in many kinds of small work.

Fin — The thin edge or mark left by the parting of a mold or die. In drop forge work this is called the "flash."

Fit, Drive or Force or Press — Fitting a shaft to a hole by making the hole so the shaft can be driven or forced in with a sledge or some power press, often requiring many tons pressure.

Fit, Running or Sliding — Enough allowance between shaft and hole to allow it to run or slide without sticking or heating.

Fit, Shrink — Fitting a shaft to a hole by making the hole slightly smaller than the shaft, then heating the piece with the hole till it expands enough to allow shaft to enter. When cool the shaft is very tightly seized if the allowance is right.

Fit, Wringing — A smaller allowance than for running but so that the shaft can be twisted into the hole by hand. Usually applied to some such work as a boring bar in a horizontal boring machine. Sometimes used in connection with twisting two flat surfaces together to exclude the air.

Flask — The frame which holds the sand mold for the casting. Includes both the cope and drag.

Flat Reamer — See Reamer, Flat.

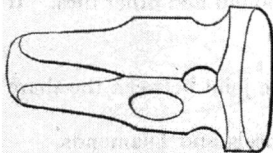

Flatter — Round face. A blacksmith's tool which is held on the work and struck by a sledge. Used to take out hammer marks and smooth up a forging.

Flute — Shop name for a groove. Applied to taps, reamers, drills and other tools.

Fly-wheel — Heavy wheel for steadying motion of machinery. On an engine it carries the crank past the center and produces a uniform rotation.

Follower Rest — A back rest for supporting long lathe work; attached to the carriage and following immediately behind the turning tool.

Foot Stock — The tail stock or tail block of a lathe, grinder, etc.

Force — A master punch which is used under a powerful press to form an impression in a die. Forces are commonly employed in the making of coining and other embossing dies. A similar tool used by jewelers is called a "hub." It is sometimes referred to incorrectly as a "hob."

Forge — Open fireplace for heating metals for welding, forging, etc. Has forced draft by fan or bellows.

Forging Press — Heavy machine for shaping metal by forcing into dies by a steady pressure instead of a sudden blow as in drop forging. Similar to a bulldozer.

Fox Center — A center for driving woodwork in the lathe. Also used in hand or fox lathes for driving special work.

Fox Lathe — Lathe for brass workers having a "chasing bar" for cutting threads and often has a turret on the tail stock.

Franklin Metal — An alloy having zinc as a base, used for casting in metal molds.

Fuller — Blacksmith's tool something like a hammer, having a round nose for spreading or fulling the iron under hammer blowers.

   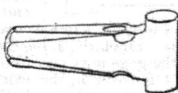

Anvil Fuller   Hand Fuller

 **Furnace, Muffle** — Furnace for heating steel to harden, in which the flame does not come in contact with the metals.

Furniture — In machine shops applies to tool racks, lathe pans, tote boxes, etc.

Fuse — A piece of metal which melts when too much current passes and acts as a safety valve.

GAGES

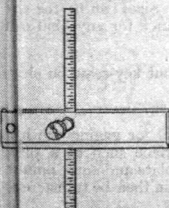 **Depth Gage** — A tool for measuring the depth of holes or recesses. The body is placed across the hole while the rule is slipped down into the hole to be measured. In many cases the rod is simply a wire and not graduated.

Drill Gage — Flat steel plate drilled with different size drills and each hole marked with correct size or number.

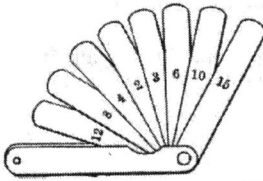

Feeler or Thickness Gage — Has blades of different thicknesses, in thousandths of an inch, so that slight variations can be felt or measured.

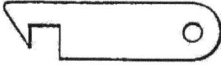

Gear Tooth Depth Gage — A gage for measuring the depth of gear teeth. Requires a different gage for each pitch.

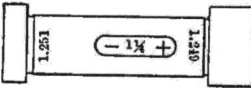

Limit Gage — A plug or other gage having one end larger and the other smaller than the nominal size. If the small end of the plug goes in but the large end does not, the size is between the two and within the limits of the gage. Similarly, in the case of a female limit gage, if the large end of the gage goes over the piece of work and the small end does not go over it, the work is within the established limits. Ordinarily, one end of a limit gage is marked "Go," and the other end "Not Go," or else they are stamped + and —.

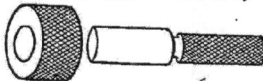

Plug and Ring Gage — Gages for use in measuring inside and outside work or for use in setting calipers.

Radius or Curve Gage — Made like a feeler or thread gage but has each blade with a given outside radius on one end and inside radius on the other for gaging small fillets or round edges.

Scratch Gage — For scratching a line at a given distance from one side of a piece. Adjustable for different lengths.

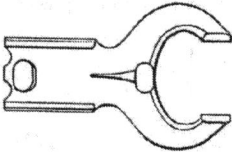

Snap Gage — A solid caliper used for either inside or outside measurement. This shows a combined gage for outside and inside work. Sizes can be the same or give the allowance for any kind of fit desired.

Splining or Key-seat Gage — Gage for laying out key-seats on shafts.

Surface Gage — A tool for gaging the hight between a flat surface such as a planer table or a surface plate and some point on the work. This can then be transfered to any other point.

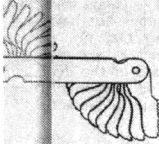

Thread Gage — Tool with a number of blades, each having the same number of notches per inch as the thread it represents. Made for different kinds of threads and in various forms.

Wire Gage — Gage for measuring sizes of wire. The wire fits between the sides of the opening, not in the holes. Sometimes made in the form of a circular disk.

rm Thread Tool Gage — For grinding thread tool for worm threads — 29 gree angle.

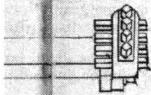

Gang Tool — A holder with a number of tools, generally used in the planer but sometimes in the lathe. Each tool cuts a little deeper than the one ahead of it.

GEARS

ular Gars — Sometimes applied to bevel gears and also to spur gears ith helical or skew teeth. See those terms for definition.

ular ar — Toothed ring for use in universal chucks and similar pla s. Teeth can be on any of the four faces although when inside is usually called an internal gear.

Bevel Gears — Gears cut on conical surfaces to transmit power with shafts at an angle to each other. When made for shafts at right angles and with both gears of the same size are often called "miter" gears. Teeth may be either straight, skew or herring bone.

wn Ge — A gear with teeth on the side of rim. Used before faciliti for cutting bevel gears existed. Seldom found now.

Elliptical or Eccentric Gears — Gears in which the shaft is not in the center. May be of almost any shape, oval, heart-shape, etc. Printing presses usually have good examples of this.

ical Gers — Gears having teeth at an angle across the face to give a ore constant pull. Also give side thrust. More often called kew" teeth.

Herring-bone Gears — Gears having teeth cut at a double angle. Made by putting two helical or "skew" tooth gears together. Does away with side or end thrust.

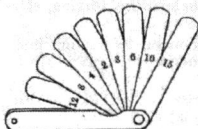

Feeler or Thickness Gage — Has bl[a]es of different thicknesses, in thousan[t]hs of an inch, so that slight variatio[n] can be felt or measured.

Gear Tooth Depth Gage — A gage fo[r] [m]eas-uring the depth of gear teeth. R[eq]uires a different gage for each pitch.

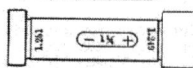

Limit Gage — A plug or other gage [ha]ving one end larger and the other [sm]aller than the nominal size. If th[e s]mall end of the plug goes in but th[e l]arge end does not, the size is between the two and within the li[mi]ts of the gage. Similarly, in the case of a female limit gage, if th[e l]arge end of the gage goes over the piece of work and the sm[all] end does not go over it, the work is within the established [li]mits. Ordinarily, one end of a limit gage is marked "Go," a[nd] the other end "Not Go," or else they are stamped + and − [.]

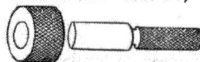

Plug and Ring Gage — Gages fo[r u]se in measuring inside and outside [wo]rk or for use in setting calipers.

Radius or Curve Gage — Made like a feeler or thread gage [. I]t has each blade with a given outside radius on one end an[d] [i]nside radius on the other for gaging small fillets or round edge[s.]

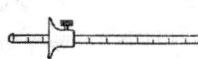

Scratch Gage — For scratching a [li]ne at a given distance from one [si]de of a piece. Adjustable for [diff]erent lengths.

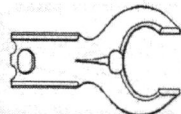

Snap Gage — A solid caliper used f[or] [e]ither inside or outside measuremen[t.] This shows a combined gage for [ou]tside and inside work. Sizes can be t[he] [s]ame or give the allowance for any ki[nd] [of] fit desired.

Splining or Key-seat Gage — Gage for laying out key-seats o[n s]hafts.

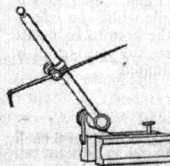

Surface Gage — A tool for gaging t[he] [h]ight between a flat surface such as a [p]laner table or a surface plate and some [po]int on the work. This can then be tran[sfer]red to any other point.

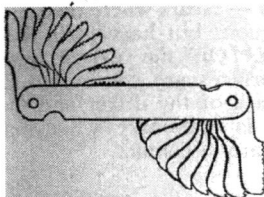

Thread Gage — Tool with a number of blades, each having the same number of notches per inch as the thread it represents. Made for different kinds of threads and in various forms.

Wire Gage — Gage for measuring sizes of wire. The wire fits between the sides of the opening, not in the holes. Sometimes made in the form of a circular disk.

Worm Thread Tool Gage — For grinding thread tool for worm threads — 29 degree angle.

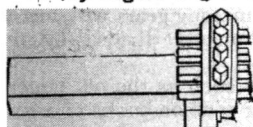

Gang Tool — A holder with a number of tools, generally used in the planer but sometimes in the lathe. Each tool cuts a little deeper than the one ahead of it.

GEARS

Angular Gears — Sometimes applied to bevel gears and also to spur gears with helical or skew teeth. See those terms for definition.

Annular Gear — Toothed ring for use in universal chucks and similar places. Teeth can be on any of the four faces although when inside it is usually called an internal gear.

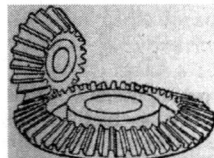

Bevel Gears — Gears cut on conical surfaces to transmit power with shafts at an angle to each other. When made for shafts at right angles and with both gears of the same size are often called "miter" gears. Teeth may be either straight, skew or herring bone.

Crown Gear — A gear with teeth on the side of rim. Used before facilities for cutting bevel gears existed. Seldom found now.

Elliptical or Eccentric Gears — Gears in which the shaft is not in the center. May be of almost any shape, oval, heart-shape, etc. Printing presses usually have good examples of this.

Helical Gears — Gears having teeth at an angle across the face to give a more constant pull. Also give side thrust. More often called "skew" teeth.

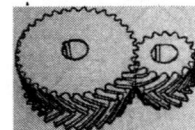

Herring-bone Gears — Gears having teeth cut at a double angle. Made by putting two helical or "skew" tooth gears together. Does away with side or end thrust.

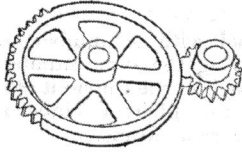

Intermittent Gears — Gears where the teeth are not continuous but have plain surfaces between. On the driven gear these plain surfaces are concave to fit the plain surface of the driver and the driven wheel is stationary while the plain surfaces are in contact.

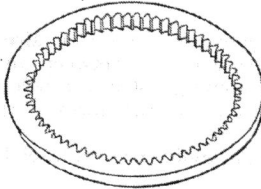

Internal Gears — Gears having teeth on the inside of a ring or shell.

Module or Metric Gears — French system of making gears with metric measurement. Pitch diameter in millimeters divided by the number of teeth in the gear.

Pin Gear — Gear with teeth formed by pins such as the old lantern pinion. Also formed by short projecting pins or knobs and only used now in some feeding devices.

Quill Gears — Gears or pinions cut on a quill or sleeve.

Skew Gears — See Helical.

Spiral Gears — Spur gears with spiral teeth which run together at an angle and do the work of bevel gears.

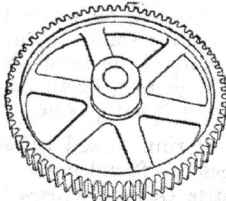

Spur Gears — Wheels or cylinders whose shafts are parallel, having teeth across face. Teeth can be straight, helical or skew or herring bone.

Staggered Tooth Gears — Made up of two or more straight tooth spur gears, teeth set so that teeth and spaces break joints instead of presenting a continuous pull.

Worm Gears — Spur gears with teeth cut on angle to be driven by a worm. Teeth are usually cut out with a hob to fit the worm.

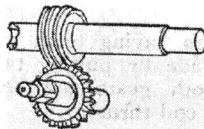

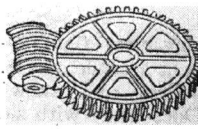

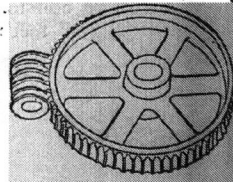

Sprocket Gears — Toothed wheels for chain driving. A is the regular and B is a hook tooth for running one way only.

B

Gear Teeth — The projections which, meshing together, transmit a positive motion. The involute curve tooth is now almost universal. The older form has a $14\frac{1}{2}$ degree pressure angle but some are using a shorter tooth, known as a "stub" tooth, with 20 degrees pressure angle. An involute tooth rack has straight sides to the teeth.

Gear, Pitch of — *Chordal,* distance from center of one tooth to center of next in a direct line.

Circular, distance from center of one tooth to center of next along the pitch line.

Diametral, number of teeth per inch of diameter.

Geneva Motion — A device which gives a positive but intermittent motion to the driven wheel but prevents its moving in either direction without the driver. The driver may have one tooth as shown or a number if desired. Also made so as to prevent a complete revolution of the driven wheel.

German Silver — An alloy of copper 60 parts, zinc 20 parts, nickel 20 parts.

Gib — A piece located alongside a sliding member to take up wear.

Gland — A cylindrical piece enveloping a stem and used in a stuffing-box to make a tight joint.

Green Sand Molds — Molds made of sand that is moistened for molding and not dried out or baked before pouring.

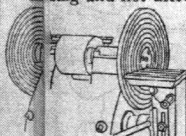

Grinder, Disk — A grinding machine having steel disks which are covered with emery cloth. Some disks have spiral grooves to give cushions under the emery cloth.

Grinding Wheel Dresser — A tool consisting of pointed or corrugated disks of hard metal which really break or pry off small particles of the grinding wheel when held against its rapidly revolving surface.

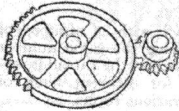

Intermittent Gears — Gears where the teeth are not continuous but have plain surfaces between. On the driven gear these plain surfaces are concave to fit the plain surface of the driver and the driven wheel is stationary while the plain surfaces are in contact.

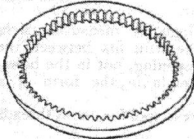

Internal Gears — Gears having teeth on the inside of a ring or shell.

Module or Metric Gears — French system of making gears with metric measurement. Pitch diameter in millimeters divided by the number of teeth in the gear.

Pin Gear — Gear with teeth formed by pins such as the old lantern pinion. Also formed by short projecting pins or knobs and only used now in some feeding devices.

Quill Gears — Gears or pinions cut on a quill or sleeve.

Skew Gears — See Helical.

Spiral Gears — Spur gears with spiral teeth which run together at an angle and do the work of bevel gears.

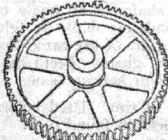

Spur Gears — Wheels or cylinders whose shafts are parallel, having teeth across face. Teeth can be straight, helical or skew or herring bone.

Staggered Tooth Gears — Made up of two or more straight tooth spur gears, teeth set so that teeth and spaces break joints instead of presenting a continuous pull.

Worm Gears — Spur gears with teeth cut on angle to be driven by a worm. Teeth are usually cut out with a hob to fit the worm.

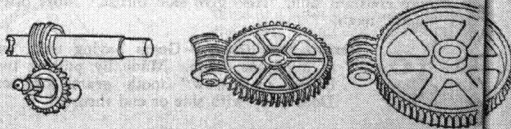

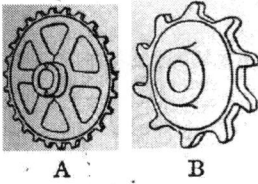

Sprocket Gears — Toothed wheels for chain driving. A is the regular and B is a hook tooth for running one way only.

A   B

Gear Teeth — The projections which, meshing together, transmit a positive motion. The involute curve tooth is now almost universal. The older form has a $14\frac{1}{2}$ degree pressure angle but some are using a shorter tooth, known as a "stub" tooth, with 20 degrees pressure angle. An involute tooth rack has straight sides to the teeth.

Gears, Pitch of — *Chordal*, distance from center of one tooth to center of next in a direct line.

Circular, distance from center of one tooth to center of next along the pitch line.

Diametral, number of teeth per inch of diameter.

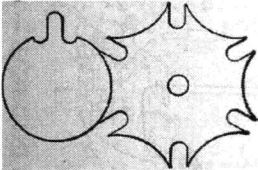

Geneva Motion — A device which gives a positive but intermittent motion to the driven wheel but prevents its moving in either direction without the driver. The driver may have one tooth as shown or a number if desired. Also made so as to prevent a complete revolution of the driven wheel.

German Silver — An alloy of copper 60 parts, zinc 20 parts, nickel 20 parts.

Jib — A piece located alongside a sliding member to take up wear.

Gland — A cylindrical piece enveloping a stem and used in a stuffing-box to make a tight joint.

Green Sand Molds — Molds made of sand that is moistened for molding and not dried out or baked before pouring.

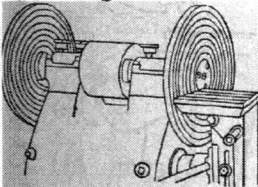

Grinder, Disk — A grinding machine having steel disks which are covered with emery cloth. Some disks have spiral grooves to give cushions under the emery cloth.

Grinder Wheel Dresser — A tool consisting of pointed or corrugated disks of hard metal which really break or pry off small particles of the grinding wheel when held against its rapidly revolving surface.

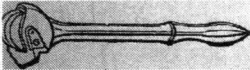

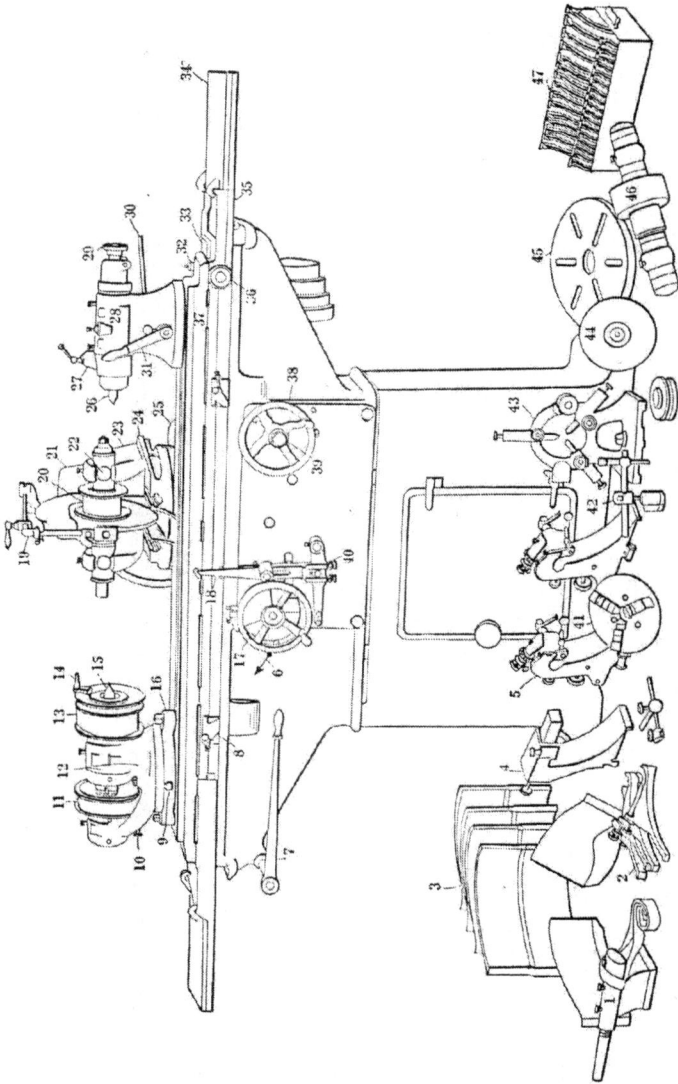

GRINDING MACHINE — CYLINDRICAL — BROWN & SHARPE

Grinding Machine — Parts of

1. Internal grinding fixture.	25. Wheel-stand slide.
2. Water guard supports.	26. Footstock center.
3. Water guards.	27. Diamond tool-holder.
4. Plain back rests.	28. Footstock.
5. Universal back rest.	29. Tension adjusting knob.
6. Automatic cross-feed pawl.	30. Quick-adjusting lever.
7. Starting and stopping lever.	31. Clamping lever
8. Table-reversing dogs.	32. Clamping bolt.
9. Headstock index finger.	33. Table scale.
10. Live spindle-locking pin.	34. Bed water guard.
11. Live spindle-driving pulley.	35. Sliding table.
12. Headstock.	36. Swivel table knob.
13. Dead center pulley.	37. Swivel table.
14. Work driving arm and pin.	38. Hand wheel.
15. Headstock center.	39. Table travel control.
16. Headstock base.	40. Automatic cross-feed.
17. Cross-feed hand wheel.	41. Universal chuck.
18. Reversing lever.	42. Tooth rest.
19. Water piping.	43. Center rest.
20. Wheel-driving pulley.	44. Face-grinding chuck.
21. Wheel guards.	45. Face plate.
22. Spindle box.	46. Internal grinding counter.
23. Wheel stand.	47. Work-driving dogs.
24. Wheel-stand platen.	

Grinding Wheels — Common types of grinding wheels made of emery, corundum, carborundum and alundum, are the disk, ring, saucer, cup and cylinder. Disk and ring wheels are used on the periphery; saucer wheels on the thin edge; cup and cylinder wheels on the end. The latter are commonly used for surface grinding. See pages 224 and 225 for other shapes.

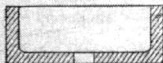

Cup

Disk

Cylinder

Ring

Saucer or Dish

Gripe — Local name for machine clamp.

Ground joint — A joint finished by grinding the two parts together with emery and oil or by other abrasives.

Ground — A connection between the electric circuit and the earth.

Gudgeon — Local name for a trunnion or bearing which projects from a piece as a cannon.

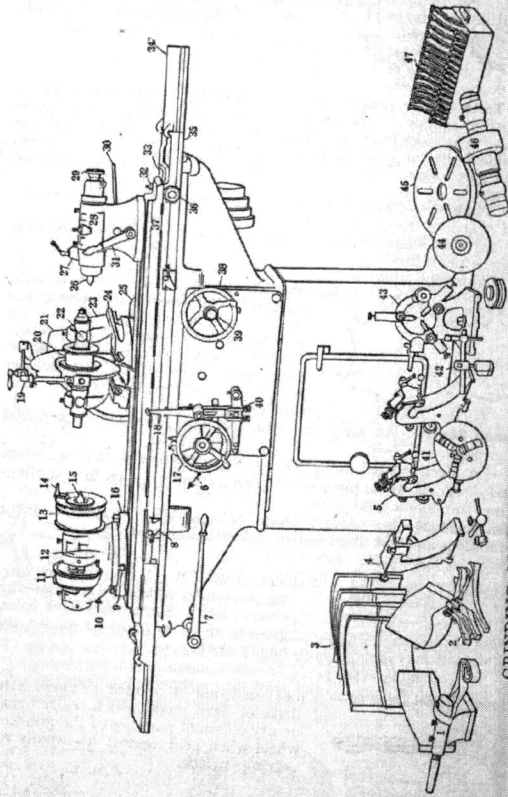

GRINDING MACHINE, CYLINDRICAL, BROWN & SHARPE

Grinding Machine — Parts of

1. Internal grinding fixture.	25. Wheel-stand slide.
2. Water guard supports.	26. Footstock center.
3. Water guards.	27. Diamond tool-holder.
4. Plain back rests.	28. Footstock.
5. Universal back rest.	29. Tension adjusting knob.
6. Automatic cross-feed pawl.	30. Quick-adjusting lever.
7. Starting and stopping lever.	31. Clamping lever.
8. Table-reversing dogs.	32. Clamping bolt.
9. Headstock index finger.	33. Table scale.
10. Live spindle-locking pin.	34. Bed water guard.
11. Live spindle-driving pulley.	35. Sliding table.
12. Headstock.	36. Swivel table knob.
13. Dead center pulley.	37. Swivel table.
14. Work driving arm and pin.	38. Hand wheel.
15. Headstock center.	39. Table travel control.
16. Headstock base.	40. Automatic cross-feed.
17. Cross-feed hand wheel.	41. Universal chuck.
18. Reversing lever.	42. Tooth rest.
19. Water piping.	43. Center rest.
20. Wheel-driving pulley.	44. Face-grinding chuck.
21. Wheel guards.	45. Face plate.
22. Spindle box.	46. Internal grinding counter.
23. Wheel stand.	47. Work-driving dogs.
24. Wheel-stand platen.	

Grinding Wheels — Common types of grinding wheels made of emery, corundum, carborundum and alundum, are the disk, ring, saucer, cup and cylinder. Disk and ring wheels are used on the periphery; saucer wheels on the thin edge; cup and cylinder wheels on the end. The latter are commonly used for surface grinding. See pages 224 and 225 for other shapes.

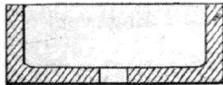

Cup

Disk

Ring

Cylinder

Saucer or Dish

Gripe — Local name for machine clamp.

Ground joint — A joint finished by grinding the two parts together with emery and oil or by other abrasives.

Ground — A connection between the electric circuit and the earth.

Gudgeon — Local name for a trunnion or bearing which projects from a piece as a cannon.

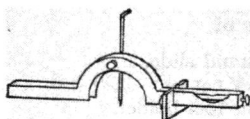

Guide Liner — A tool for use in locomotive work for lining up guides and cross heads.

H

Half Nut — A nut which is split lengthwise. Sometimes half is used and rides on screw, in others both halves clamp around screw as in the half nut of a lathe carriage.

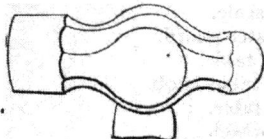

Ball Peen

Hammer — The common types of machinists' hammers are the ball peen, straight peen and cross peen, as shown. The so-called engineer's and the riveting hammers have cross peens.

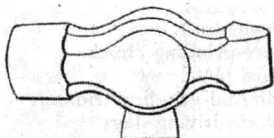

Straight Peen

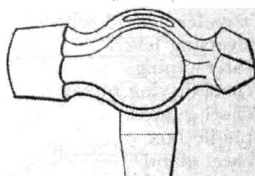

Cross Peen

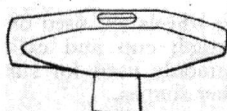

Riveting

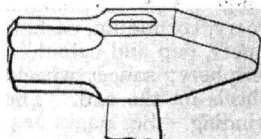

Engineers

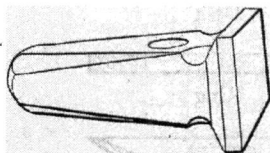

Hammer, Blacksmith's Flatter — A flat-faced hammer used to smooth the surfaces of forgings. Is held on the work and struck by a helper with a sledge.

Hammer, Bumping or Horning — For closing seams on large cans, buckets, etc.

Hammer, Drop — Hammer head or "monkey" or "drop" is raised by hand or power and falls by gravity. Sometimes raised by a board attached to top of hammer head and running between pulleys. Others use a belt.

Hammer, Helve — Power hammer in which there is an arm pivoted in the center and power applied at the back end while the hammer is at the other and strikes the work on an anvil.

Hammer, Lever Trip — Trips the hammer by a cam or lever and allows it to fall.

Hammer, Spring — Comparatively small hammer giving a great variety in the force of blow. This is controlled by pressure of foot on lever.

Hand Wheels, Clutched — Hand wheels connected to shaft by a clutch which can be thrown out by a knob or otherwise so that accidental movement of wheel will not disturb setting. Used on milling machines and similar places.

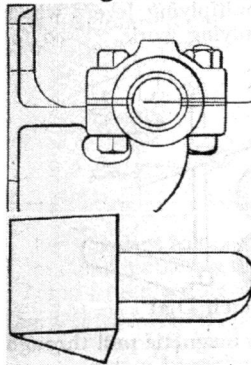

Hanger, Drop — Shaft hanger to be fastened to ceiling with bearing held in lower end.

Hanger, Post — Shafting hanger for fastening to posts or other vertical structures.

Hardie — Blacksmith's cutting chisel which fits a hole in the anvil and forms the lower tool in cutting off work.

Harveyizing — The surface hardening of steel armor plates by using a bed of charcoal over the work and then gas turned on so it will soak in from the top. Not adapted to small work.

Hindley Worm — See Worm.

Hoist, Chain — Hoist with chain passing through pulley block used for hoisting.

Holder, Drill — Device for holding drill stationary while work is revolved by lathe chuck, or face place. Not a drill chuck.

Hooks, Twin or Sister — Double crane hook which resembles an anchor and allows load to be carried on either side.

Hub — A master punch used in making jewelry dies for fancy embossing, and various forms to which articles of gold and silver are to be struck.

Hunting Tooth — An extra tooth in a wheel to give it one more tooth than its mate in order to prevent the same teeth from meshing together all the time.

I

Idler or Idler Pulley — See Pulley, Idler.

Incandescent — A substance heated to white heat as in the bulb of a lamp.

Indexing, Compound — Indexing by combination of two settings of index, either by adding or subtracting.

Indexing, Differential — Indexing with the index plate geared to the spindle, thus giving a differential motion that allows the indexing to be done with one circle of holes and with the index crank turned in the same direction, as in plain indexing.

Indexing, Direct — Indexing work by direct use of dividing head of milling machine.

Indicator, Lathe Test — Instrument with multiplying levers which shows slight variations in the truth of revolving work. Used for setting work in lathe or on face-plate.

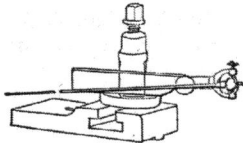

Plain Indicator

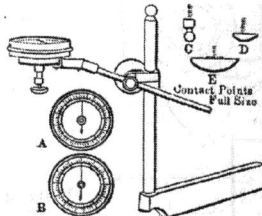

Watch Dial

Induction Motor — A motor which runs by the magnetic pull through the air without contact. Usually a constant-speed motor.

J

Jack, Hydraulic — Device for raising weight or exerting pressure by pumping oil or other liquid under a piston or ram.

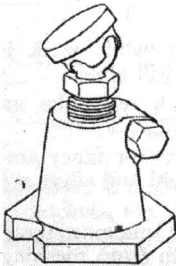

Jack, Leveling — Small jacks (usually screw jacks) for leveling and holding work on planer beds and similar places. Practically adjustable blocking.

Jack, Screw — Device for elevating weights by means of a screw.

Jack Shaft — See Shaft, Jack.

Jam Plates — Old name for screw plates and in many cases a true one as the thread was jammed instead of cut.

Jig, Drill — A device for holding work while drilling, having bushings through which the drill is guided so that the holes are correctly located in the piece. Milling and planing jigs (commonly called fixtures) hold work while it is machined in the milling machine and planer. Parts produced in jigs and fixtures are interchangeable.

Joint, Universal — Shaft connection which allows freedom in any direction and still conveys a positive motion. Most of them can transmit power through any angle up to 45 degrees.

Journal Box — The part of a bearing in which the shaft revolves.

K

Kerf — The slot or passageway cut by a saw.

Key — The piece used to fasten any hollow object to a shaft or rod. Usually applied to fastening pulleys and fly-wheels to shafts; or locomotive driving wheels to their axles. Keys may be square, rectangular, round or other shape and fasten in any way. Are usually rectangular and run lengthwise of shaft.

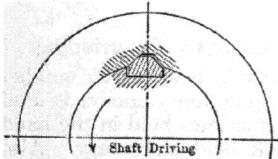

Key, Barth — This key was invented several years ago by Carl G. Barth. It is simply a rectangular key with one-half of both sides beveled off at 45 degrees. The key need not fit tightly, as the pressure tends to drive it better into its seat. As a feather key this key has been used in a great many cases to replace rectangular feather keys which have given trouble. It has also been used to replace keys which were sheared off under heavy load.

Key, Center — A flat piece of steel, with tapered sides, for removing taper shank drills from drill spindle or similar work.

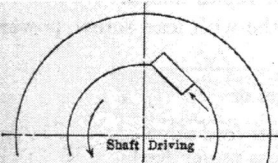

Key, Lewis — A key invented by Wilfred Lewis about 20 years ago. Its position is such that it is subjected to compression only.

Key, Round End — Is fitted into a shaft by end milling a seat into which the key is secured. Where a key of some length is fixed in the shaft and a member arranged to slide thereon it is called a feather or feather key.

Key Seater — Machine for cutting keyways in shafts or hubs of pulleys or gears.

Key, Taper — The taper key is made with and without head. The taper is commonly $\frac{1}{8}$ or $\frac{3}{16}$ inch per foot.

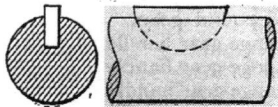

Key, Woodruff — A semi-circular key used in various kinds of shafts, studs, etc. It is fitted in place by merely sinking a seat with a shank mill such as the Whitney cutter.

Keyway — A groove, usually square or rectangular, in which the key is driven or in which a "feather" slides. The groove in both the shaft and piece which is to be fastened to it, or guided on it, is called a keyway.

Knurling — See Nurling.

L

Land — Space between flutes or grooves in drills, taps, reamers or other tools.

Lap — Applied to seams which lap each other. To the distance a valve must move before opening its port when valve is central on seat. To a tool usually consisting of lead, iron or copper charged with abrasive for fine grinding. See Lap, Lead.

Lap Cutter — For preparing the ends of band-saws with bands for brazing. Uses milling cutters.

Lap Grinder — This prepares the laps of band-saws by grinding.

Lap, Lead — Usually a bar of lead or covered with lead, a trifle smaller than the hole to be ground. Emery or some fine abrasive is used which gives a fine surface. Laps are sometimes held in the hand or are run in a machine and the work held stationary. Also consists at times of a lead-covered disk, revolving horizontally, which is used for grinding flat surfaces. Very similar in action to a potter's wheel.

Lathe, Double Spindle — Has two working spindles, so located that one gives a much larger swing than the other, and both can be used to advantage. Especially good for repair shops.

Lathe, Engine — The ordinary form of lathe with lead screw, power feed, etc.

Lathe, Engine — Parts of

1. Rear bearing.	20. Cross-feed screw.
2. Back-gear case.	21. Cross-power feed.
3. Cone pulley.	22. Half-nut handle.
4. Face-gear guard.	23. Regular power feed.
5. Front bearing.	24. Feed reverse.
6. Face plate.	25. Gear stud.
7. Live center.	26. Hand feed.
8. Dead center.	27. Front apron.
9. Tail spindle.	28. Rear apron.
10. Tail-spindle lock.	29. Lead screw.
11. Tailstock slide.	30. Feed rod.
12. Locking bolts.	31. Feed gears.
13. Tailstock base.	32. Feed box.
14. Tailstock pinion.	33. Change gear handle.
15. Tailstock hand wheel.	34. Compound gears.
16. Steady rest.	35. Change-gear handle.
17. Tool post.	36. Change-gear handle.
18. Compound rest.	37. Change-gear handle.
19. Cross-slide.	38. Bed.

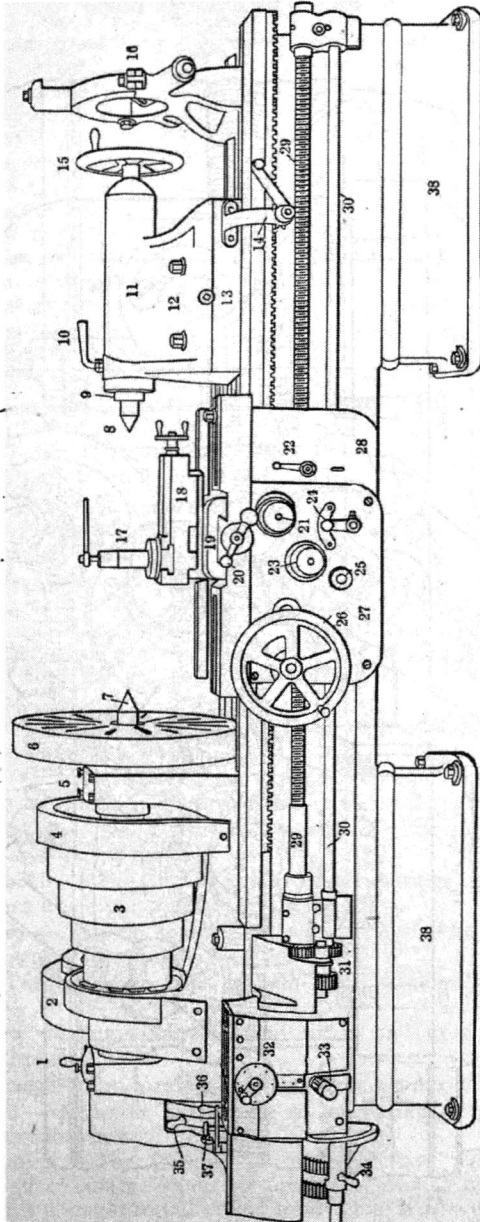

LATHE—ENGINE—SCHUMACHER & BOYE

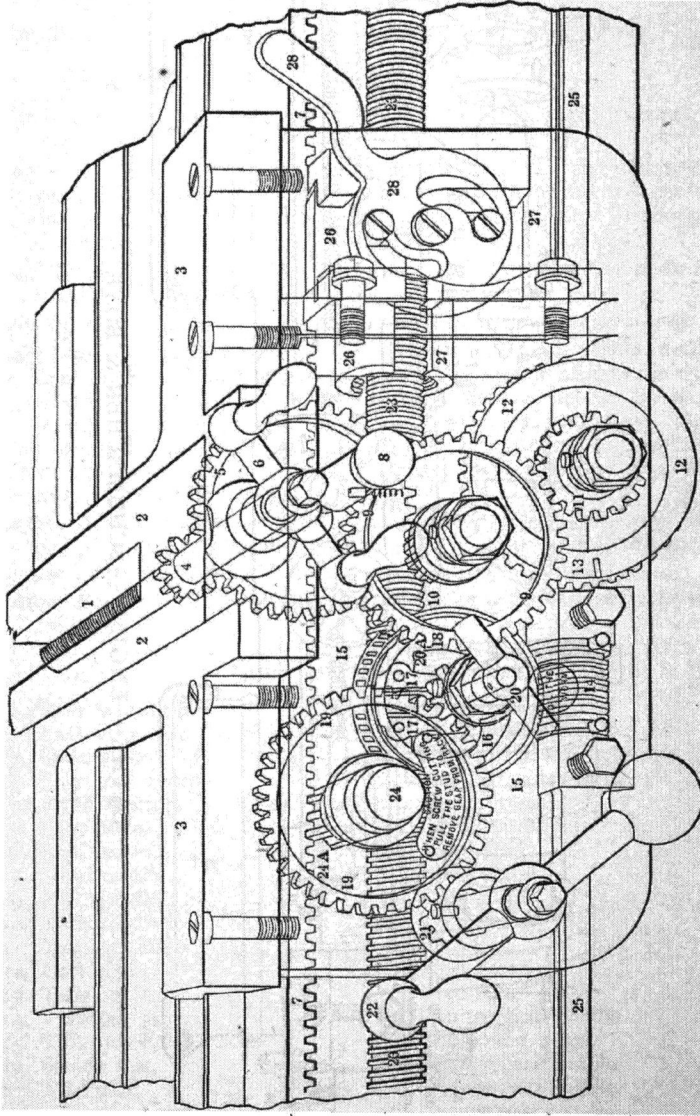

Lathe Apron, Reed — Parts of

1. Cross-feed screw.	16. Clutch ring.
2. Cross-slides.	17. Clutch levers.
3. Wing of saddle.	18. Pinion.
4. Cross-feed pinion.	19. Gear in train.
5. Cross-feed gear.	20. Feed-clutch handle.
6. Cross-feed handle.	20A. Clutch spreader.
7. Rack.	21. Hand pinion.
8. Power cross-feed and control.	22. Carriage handle.
9. Gear in train.	23. Lead screw.
10. Pinion for cross-feed.	24. Rack pinion knob.
11. Main driving pinion.	24A Rack pinion.
12. Bevel gear.	25. Feed rod.
13. Bevel pinion.	26. Upper-half nut.
14. Feed-worm.	27. Lower-half nut.
15. Feed-worm wheel.	28. Half-nut cam.

NOTE:—Cross-feed is from bevel pinion 13, through gears 12, 11, 9, 10, and 4. Regular feed is through worm 14, worm wheel 15, clutch 16, pinion 18, gears 19 and 24A. Hand movement is through handle 22, pinion 21, 19 and 24A.

Lathe, Extension — So made that bed can be lengthened or shortened. When bed is made longer, there is a gap near head, increasing the swing for face-plate work.

Lathe, Fox — Brass workers' lathe having a "fox" or chasing bar for cutting threads. The bar has a "leader" which acts as a nut on a short lead screw or "hob" of the desired pitch (or half the pitch if the hob is geared down 2 to 1) and carries a tool along at the right feed for the thread. Sometimes has a turret on the back head.

Lathe, Gap — Has V-shaped gap in front of head stock to increase swing for face-plate work.

Lathe, Gun — For boring and turning cannons and rapid-fire guns.

Lathe, Ingot — For boring, turning and cutting off steel ingots.

Lathe, Precision — Bench lathe made especially for small and very accurate die, jig or model work.

Lathe, Projectile.— Simply a heavy lathe for turning up projectiles. Sometimes has attachment for pointing them.

Lathe, Pulley — Especially designed for turning pulleys, can turn them crowning or straight.

Lathe, Roll Turning — For turning rolling mill, steel mill and calendar rolls.

Lathe, Screw Cutting — Having lead screw and change gears for cutting threads.

Lathe, Shafting — For turning long shafts or similar work.

Lathe, Speed — A simple lathe with no mechanically actuated carriage or attachments.

Lathe, Spinning — For forming sheet metal into various hollow shapes, all circular. Done by forcing against a form of some kind (with a single round ended tool) while it is revolving.

Lathe, Stone Turning — Specially designed for turning stone columns or similar shapes.

Lathe, Turret — Having a multiple tool holder which revolves. This is the turret. Usually takes place of tail or foot stock but not always. Usually has automatic devices for turning turret and sometimes for feeding tools against work.

Lathe, Vertical — Name given one type of Bullard boring mill on account of a side head which acts very much like a lathe carriage and does a large variety of work that would ordinarily be done on the face-plate of a lathe.

Lathe, Watchmaker's — A very small precision lathe.

Lead — The advance made by one turn of a screw. Often confused with pitch of thread but not the same unless in the case of a single thread. With a double thread the lead is twice as much as the pitch.

Level — Instrument with a glass tube or vial containing a liquid which does not quite fill it. The tube is usually ground on an arc so that bubble can easily get to the center. Alcohol is generally used as it does not freeze at ordinary temperatures.

Level, Engineers' — Level mounted on tripod and having telescope for leveling distant objects.

Level, Pocket — Small level to be carried in pocket.

Level, Quartering — A tool for testing driving wheels to see if crank-pins are set 90 degrees apart. The level has a forked end and with the angles shown. Placing this on the crank-pin and lining the edge with the center of axle should bring the bubble of level in the center. If the same result is obtained on the other wheel the crank-pins are 90 degrees apart.

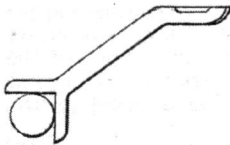

1st Class

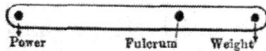

Power   Fulcrum   Weight

2nd Class

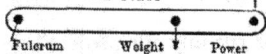

Fulcrum   Weight   Power

3rd Class

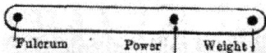

Fulcrum   Power   Weight

Levers — Arms pivoted or bearing on points called fulcrums. Divided into three classes as shown. First has fulcrum or bearing point between power and weight, second has weight between power and fulcrum and third has power between weight and fulcrum.

Line Shaft — See Shaft, Line.

Liner — A piece for separating pieces a desired distance; also called shim.

Live Center — See Center, Live.

Loam Mold — Made with a mixture of coarse sand and loam into a sort of plaster which is spread over brick or other framework to make the mold. Used on large castings to produce a smoother finish than is to be had with green sand.

M

Machinists' Clamp — See Clamp.

Magnet Electro — Usually a bar of iron having coils of insulated wire around it which carry current. Permanent magnets are of hardened steel with no wire or current around them.

Mandrel — See Arbor.

Marking Machine — For stamping trade-marks, patent dates, etc., on cutlery, gun barrels, etc. Stamps are usually on rolls and rolled into work.

Master Die — A die made standard and used only for reference purposes or for threading taps.

Master Plate — See Plate, Master.

Master Tap — A tap cut to standard dimensions and used only for reference purposes or for tapping master dies.

Match Board — The board used to hold patterns, half on each side, while being molded on some types of molding machines.

Measuring Machine — Practically a large bench caliper of any desired form to measure work such as taps, reamers, gages, etc.

Measuring Rods — See End Measuring Rods.

Milling Cutters — See Cutters, Milling.

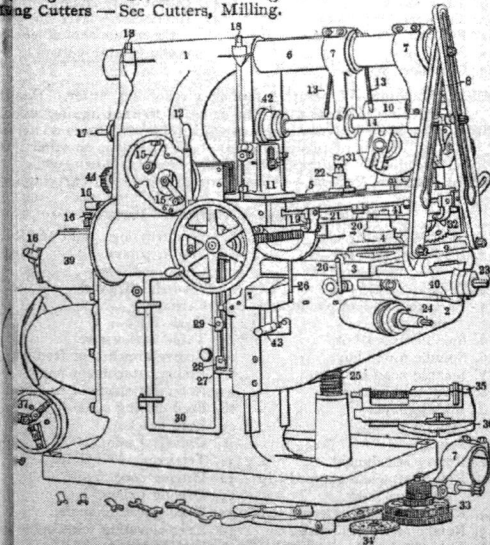

MILLING MACHINE — UNIVERSAL — MILWAUKEE

Lathe, Stone Turning — Specially designed for turning stone colum
or similar shapes.

Lathe, Turret — Having a multiple tool holder which revolv
This is the turret. Usually takes place of tail or foot stock b
not always. Usually has automatic devices for turning tur
and sometimes for feeding tools against work.

Lathe, Vertical — Name given one type of Bullard boring mill
account of a side head which acts very much like a lathe carria
and does a large variety of work that would ordinarily be done
the face-plate of a lathe.

Lathe, Watchmaker's — A very small precision lathe.

Lead — The advance made by one turn of a screw. Often confus
with pitch of thread but not the same unless in the case of
single thread. With a double thread the lead is twice as mu
as the pitch.

Level — Instrument with a glass tube or vial containing a liqu
which does not quite fill it. The tube is usually ground on
arc so that bubble can easily get to the center. Alcohol is ge
erally used as it does not freeze at ordinary temperatures.

Level, Engineers' — Level mounted on tripod and having telesco
for leveling distant objects.

Level, Pocket — Small level to be carried in pocket.

Level, Quartering — A tool for testing driving wheels to see if cran
pins are set 90 degrees apart. The le
has a forked end and with the angles show
Placing this on the crank-pin and lining t
edge with the center of axle should bri
the bubble of level in the center. If t
same result is obtained on the other wh
the crank-pins are 90 degrees apart.

1st Class

Power   Fulcrum   Weight

2nd Class

Fulcrum   Weight   Power

3rd Class

Fulcrum   Power   Weight

Levers — Arms pivoted or bearing
points called fulcrums. Divided in
three classes as shown. First has f
crum or bearing point between pow
and weight, second has weight b
tween power and fulcrum and thi
has power between weight and fu
crum.

Line Shaft — See Shaft, Line.

Liner — A piece for separating pieces a desired distance; also call
shim.

Live Center — See Center, Live.

Loam Mold — Made with a mixture of coarse sand and loam into
sort of plaster which is spread over brick or other framework
make the mold. Used on large castings to produce a smooth
finish than is to be had with green sand.

M

Machinists' Clamp — See Clamp.

Magnet Electro — Usually a bar of iron having coils of insulated wire around it which carry current. Permanent magnets are of hardened steel with no wire or current around them.

Mandrel — See Arbor.

Marking Machine — For stamping trade-marks, patent dates, etc., on cutlery, gun barrels, etc. Stamps are usually on rolls and rolled into work.

Master Die — A die made standard and used only for reference purposes or for threading taps.

Master Plate — See Plate, Master.

Master Tap — A tap cut to standard dimensions and used only for reference purposes or for tapping master dies.

Match Board — The board used to hold patterns, half on each side, while being molded on some types of molding machines.

Measuring Machine — Practically a large bench caliper of any desired form to measure work such as taps, reamers, gages, etc.

Measuring Rods — See End Measuring Rods.

Milling Cutters — See Cutters, Milling.

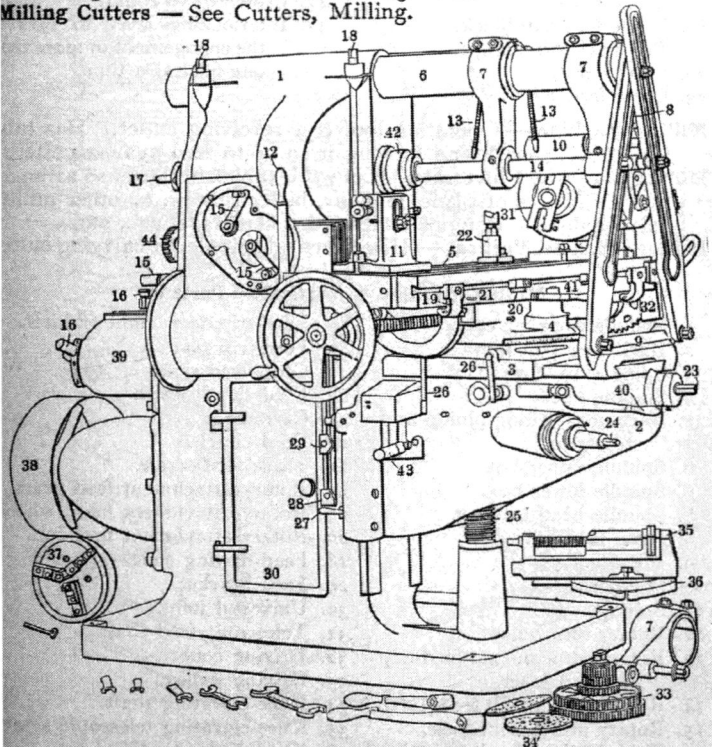

MILLING MACHINE — UNIVERSAL — MILWAUKEE

Milling Machine — Universal — Parts of

1. Column.
2. Knee.
3. Saddle.
4. Swivel carriage.
5. Work table.
6. Over arm.
7. Arm brackets (arbor supports.)
8. Arm braces (harness).
9. Knee clamp (for arm braces).
10. Spiral dividing head.
11. Tailstock.
12. Starting lever.
13. Oil tubes.
14. Cutter arbor.
15. Speed-changing lever.
16. Feed-changing lever.
17. Draw-in rod for arbor.
18. Arm-clamp screws.
19. Table stops.
20. Table-feed trip block.
21. Fixed table-feed trips.
22. Steady rest.
23. Cross-feed screw.

24. Elevating shaft.
25. Elevating screw (telescopic).
26. Saddle-clamp levers.
27. Knee-clamp levers.
28. Fixed vertical feed trip.
29. Vertical feed-trip blocks.
30. Door.
31. Dog driver.
32. Change-gear bracket.
33. Change gears.
34. Index plates.
35. Vise.
36. Swivel base.
37. Universal chuck.
38. Driving pulley.
39. Feed box.
40. Cross and vertical feed handle.
41. Table-feed handle.
42. Clutch-drive collar.
43. Interlocking lever to prevent the engagement of more than one feed at a time.

Milling Machine — Operating tool is a revolving cutter. Has table for carrying work and moving it so as to feed against cutter.
Milling Machine, Universal — Has work table and feeds so arranged that all classes of plane, circular, helical, index, or other milling may be done. Equipped with index centers, chuck, etc.
Milling Machine, Vertical — Has a vertical spindle for carrying cutter.

Milling Machine — Vertical — Parts of

1. Spindle drawbar cap.
2. Back-gear pull pin.
3. Spindle-driving pulley.
4. Spindle head.
5. Back-gear sliding pinion and stem gear.
6. Spindle upper box.
6. Spindle lower box.
7. Spindle head bearing.
8. Head-feed gear.
9. Idler pulleys.
10. Standard.
11. Spindle.
12. Rotary attachment.
13. Rotary attachment feed-trip dog and lever.
14. Rotary attachment feed clutch.
15. Rotary attachment base.
16. Table and table oil pans.
17. Rotary attachment binder.

18. Feed-trip dogs, right and left.
19. Feed-trip plate.
20. Cross-feed screw.
21. Feed-clutch lever.
22. Carriage.
23. Feed clutch.
24. Table-feed screw.
25. Rotary attachment feed gears.
26. Rotary attachment hand wheel.
27. Rotary attachment feed rod.
28. Feed-driving cone.
29. Feed bracket.
30. Universal joint.
31. Telescopic feed shaft.
32. Driving cone.
33. Driving pulley.
34. Knee-elevating shaft.
35. Knee-elevating telescopic screw.
36. Face of standard.
37. Base.

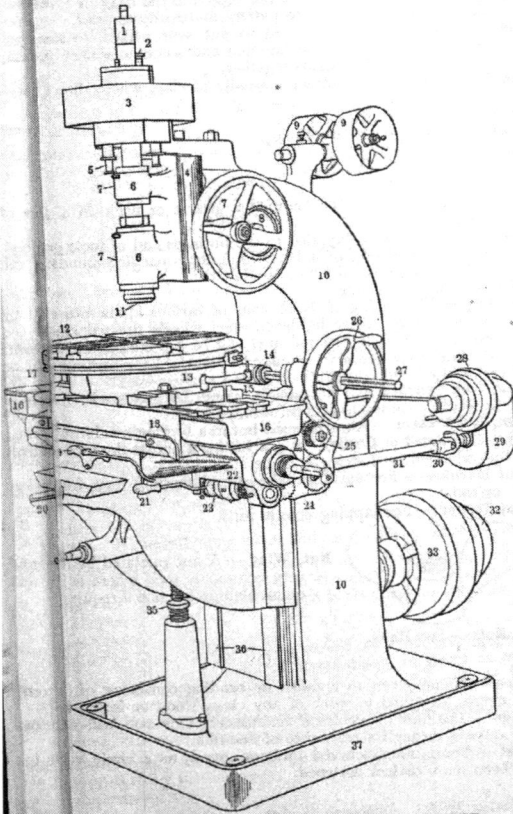

MILLING MACHINE — VERTICAL — BECKER

Milling Machine — Universal — Parts of

1. Column.
2. Knee.
3. Saddle.
4. Swivel carriage.
5. Work table.
6. Over arm.
7. Arm brackets (arbor supports.)
8. Arm braces (harness).
9. Knee clamp (for arm braces).
10. Spiral dividing head.
11. Tailstock.
12. Starting lever.
13. Oil tubes.
14. Cutter arbor.
15. Speed-changing lever.
16. Feed-changing lever.
17. Draw-in rod for arbor.
18. Arm-clamp screws.
19. Table stops.
20. Table-feed trip block.
21. Fixed table-feed trips.
22. Steady rest.
23. Cross-feed screw.
24. Elevating shaft.
25. Elevating screw (telescope).
26. Saddle-clamp levers.
27. Knee-clamp levers.
28. Fixed vertical feed trip.
29. Vertical feed-trip blocks.
30. Door.
31. Dog driver.
32. Change-gear bracket.
33. Change gears.
34. Index plates.
35. Vise.
36. Swivel base.
37. Universal chuck.
38. Driving pulley.
39. Feed box.
40. Cross and vertical feed handle.
41. Table-feed handle.
42. Clutch-drive collar.
43. Interlocking lever to prevent the engagement of more than one feed at a time.

Milling Machine — Operating tool is a revolving cutter. Has table for carrying work and moving it so as to feed against cutter.

Milling Machine, Universal — Has work table and feeds so arranged that all classes of plane, circular, helical, index, or other milling may be done. Equipped with index centers, chuck, etc.

Milling Machine, Vertical — Has a vertical spindle for carrying cutter.

Milling Machine — Vertical — Parts of

1. Spindle drawbar cap.
2. Back-gear pull pin.
3. Spindle-driving pulley.
4. Spindle head.
5. Back-gear sliding pinion and stem gear.
6. Spindle upper box.
6. Spindle lower box.
7. Spindle head bearing.
8. Head feed gear.
9. Idler pulleys.
10. Standard.
11. Spindle.
12. Rotary attachment.
13. Rotary attachment feed-trip dog and lever.
14. Rotary attachment feed clutch.
15. Rotary attachment base.
16. Table and table oil pans.
17. Rotary attachment binder.
18. Feed-trip dogs, right and left.
19. Feed-trip plate.
20. Cross-feed screw.
21. Feed-clutch lever.
22. Carriage.
23. Feed clutch.
24. Table-feed screw.
25. Rotary attachment feed gear.
26. Rotary attachment hand wheel.
27. Rotary attachment feed roll.
28. Feed-driving cone.
29. Feed bracket.
30. Universal joint.
31. Telescopic feed shaft.
32. Driving cone.
33. Driving pulley.
34. Knee-elevating shaft.
35. Knee-elevating telescopic screw.
36. Face of standard.
37. Base.

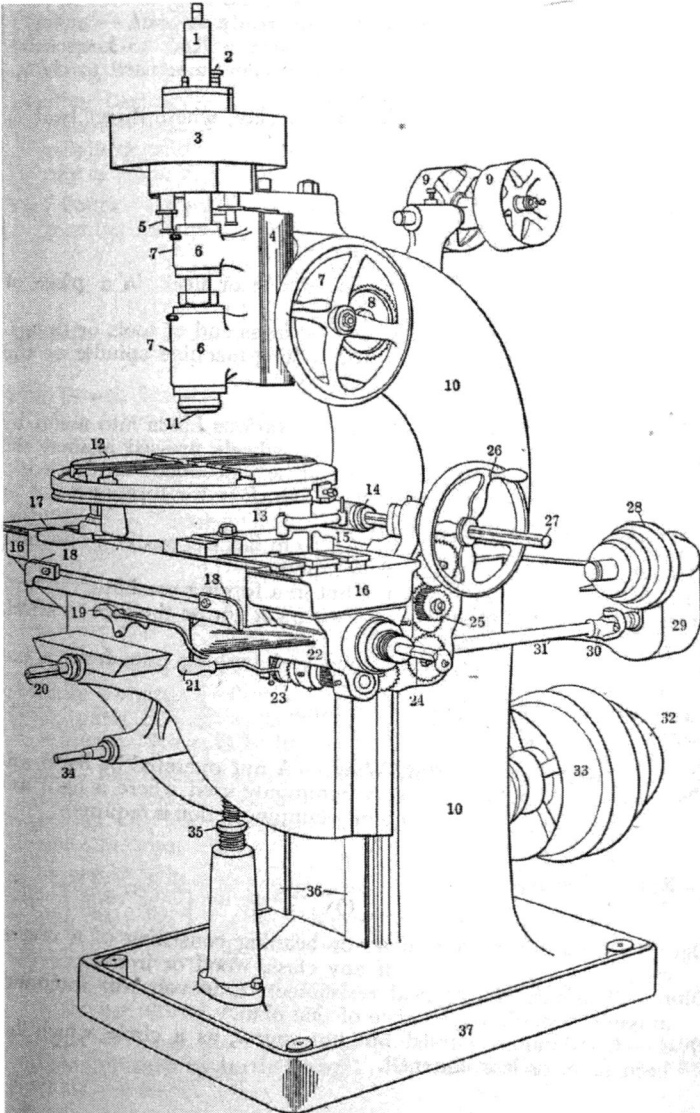

MILLING   MACHINE — VERTICAL — BECKER

Miter — A bevel of 45 degrees.

Mold — The mold consists of the cope and the drag or nowel, with the sand inside molded to pattern and ready to pour.

Mold Board — The board used to put over a flask to keep sand from falling when being handled and sometimes used to clamp on when fastening molds together.

Mufflers — Ovens or furnaces, usually of clay, where direct heat is not required.

Muley Belt — See Belt, Muley.

Muley Shaft — See Shaft, Muley.

N

Necking Tool — Tool for turning a groove or neck in a piece of work.

Nose — In shop work applied to the business end of tools or things. The threaded end of a lathe or milling-machine spindle or the end of "hog nose drill" or similar tool.

Nowel — Same as Drag.

Nurling — The rolling of depressions of various kinds into metal by the use of revolving hardened steel wheels pressed against the work. The design on the nurl will be reproduced on the work. Generally used to give a roughened surface for turning a nut or screw by hand.

Nut, Cold Punched — A nut punched from flat bar stock. The hole is usually reamed to size before tapping.

Nut, Hot Pressed — A nut formed hot in a forging machine.

Nut, Castellated or Castle — A nut with slot across the face to admit a cotter pin for locking in place.

Nut Machine — For cutting, drilling and tapping nuts from a bar or rod.

Nut Tapper — For tapping hole in nuts.

Nut, Wing — A nut operated by hand and very commonly used where a light and quick clamping action is required.

Nuts — See Bolts.

O

Ogee — Name given to a finish or beading consisting of a reverse curve. Applied to work of any class, wood or iron.

Ohm — The unit of electrical resistance. One volt will force one ampere through a resistance of one ohm.

Oval — Continuously curved but not round, as a circle which has been more or less flattened.

P

Pawl — A hinged piece which engages teeth in a gear, rack or ratchet for moving it or for arresting its motion. Sometimes used to designate a piece such as a reversing dog on a planer or milling machine.

Peening — The stretching of metal by hammering or rolling the surface. Used to stretch babbitt to fit tightly in a bearing, to straighten bars by stretching the short or concave side, etc.

Pickling; Castings — Dipping into acid solution to soften scale and remove sand. Solution of three or four parts of water to one of sulphuric acid is used for iron. For brass use five parts water to one of nitric acid.

Pin, Collar — A collar pin is driven tight into a machine frame or member and adapted to carry a roll, gear, or other part at the outer end. It differs from the collar stud in not having a thread at the inner end. When drilled through the end for a cotter pin it is known as a fulcrum pin, as it is then especially suited for carrying rocker arms, etc.

Pin, Dowel, Screw — Dowel pins are customarily made straight, or plain taper and fitted into reamed holes. When applied in such a position in a mechanism that it is impossible to remove them by driving out, they are sometimes threaded and screwed into place.

Pin, Taper — Taper pins for dowels and other purposes are regularly manufactured with a taper of $\frac{1}{4}$ inch to the foot and from $\frac{3}{4}$ to 6 inches long, the diameters at the large end of the sizes in the series ranging from about $\frac{5}{32}$ to $\frac{13}{16}$ inch. The reamers for these pins are so proportioned that each size overlaps" the next smaller size by about $\frac{1}{2}$ inch.

Pickling Forgings — Putting in bath of 1 part sulphuric acid to 25 parts boiling water to remove scale. Can be done in 10 minutes. Rinse in boiling water and they will dry before rusting.

Pitch — The distance from the center of one screw thread, or gear tooth or serration of any kind to the center of the next. In screws with a single thread the pitch is the same as the lead but not otherwise.

Pillow Blocks — Low shaft bearings, resting on foundations, or floors or other supports.

Pitman — A connecting rod; term used more commonly in connection with agricultural implements.

Planchet — Blank piece of metal punched out of a sheet before being finished by further work. Such as the blanks from which coins are made.

Planer — For producing plane surfaces on metals. Work is held on table or platen which runs back and forth under the tool which is stationary.

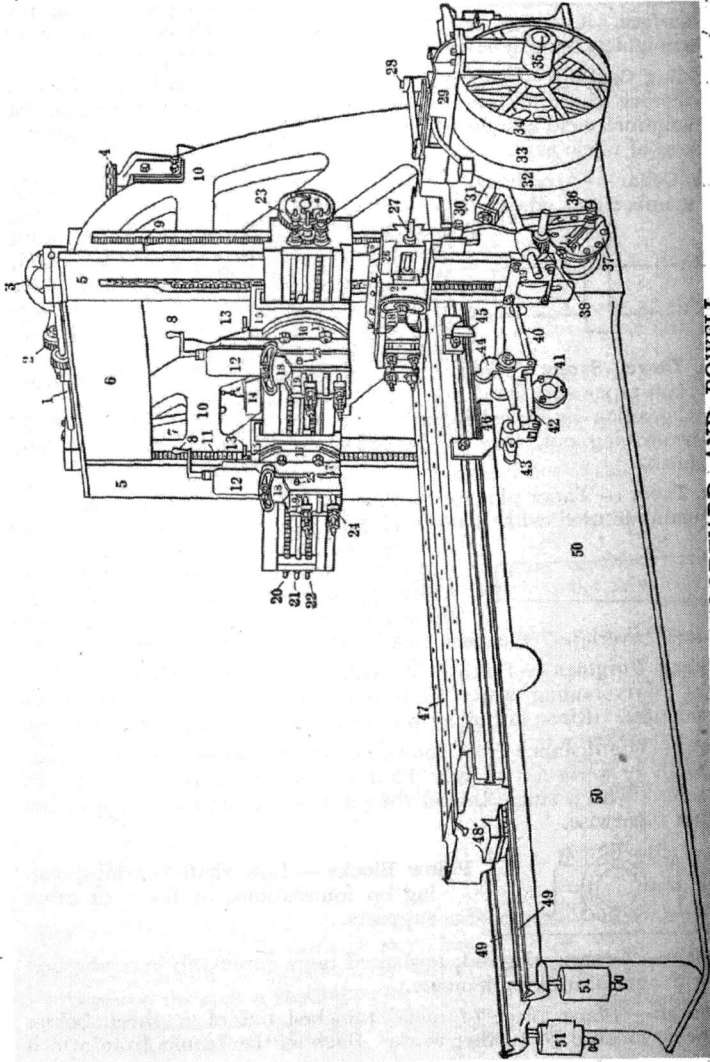

PLANER — WOODWARD AND POWELL

Planer — Parts of

1. Shaft for raising cross-rail.
2. Gears for raising cross-rail.
3. Pulley drive for raising cross-rail.
4. Chain for counterweighting the cross-rail.
5. Face of uprights.
6. Tie piece between uprights.
7. Handle controlling.
8. Crank handle for raising tool block.
9. Rack for moving feed screw in cross-rail.
10. Upright or housing.
11. Screw for elevating cross-rail.
12. Tool slide.
13. Screw to clamp saddle to cross-rail.
14. Counterweight for left side of cross-rail.
15. Saddle.
16. Swivel.
17. Clamping bolt.
18. Clapper box.
19. Clapper block.
20. Feed screw for left-hand head.
21. Vertical feed rod.
22. Feed screw for right-hand head.
23. Feed mechanism on end of cross-rail.
24. Tool-holding straps.
25. Clapper block pin.
26. Side head.
27. Side head for feed screw.
28. Belt shifter.
29. Drive-pulley support.
30. Connection to feed rack.
31. Regulator for vertical feed.
32. Forward driving pulley.
33. Loose pulley.
34. Return Iriving pulley
35. Driving shaft.
36. Regulator cross-feed.
37. Cross-feed drive.
38. Vertical feed pinion.
39. Vertical feed rod.
40. Rod to belt shifter for reversing
41. Bull or driving-wheel shaft.
42. Connections to safety lock.
43. Lock to prevent table being moved.
44. Reversing latch or trip.
45. Forward stop dog.
46. Backward stop dog.
47. Platen or table.
48. Rack under platen.
49. Ways or V's
50. Bed.
51. Oil reservoirs.

Planer Centers — A pair of index centers to hold work for planing. Similar to plain milling machine centers.

Planer, Daniels — Wood planer with a table for carrying work under a two-armed knife swung horizontally from a vertical spindle. Very similar to a vertical spindle-milling machine of the planer type. Excellent for taking warp or wind out of lumber.

Planer, Open Side — A planer with only one upright or housing, supporting an overhanging arm which takes the place of the usual cross rail. Useful in planing work too wide to go in the ordinary planer.

Planer, Radius — For planing parts of circles such as links for locomotive or stationary engine valve motion.

Planer, Rotary — Really a large milling machine in which the work is carried past a rotary cutter by the platen.

Planer Tools — See Tools, Planer.

Planer, Traveling Head — Planer in which work is stationary and tool moves over it.

Planishing — The finishing of sheet metal by hammering with smooth faced hammers or their equivalents.

Plate, Master — A steel plate serving as a model by which holes in jigs, fixtures and other tools are accurately located for boring. In the illustration the piece to be bored is shown dowelled to the master plate which is mounted on the face plate of the lathe. In the master plate there are as many holes as are to be bored in the work, and the center distances are correct. The plate is located on a center plug fitting the lathe spindle, and after a given hole is bored in the work, the master plate and work are shifted and relocated with the center plug in the next hole in the plate and the corresponding hole in the work is then bored out. This is one of the most accurate methods employed by the toolmaker on precision work.

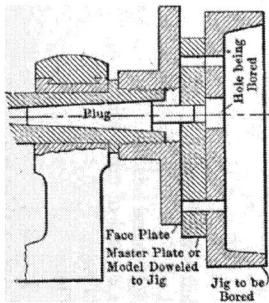

Platen — A work holding table on miller, planer or drill.

Plumb Bob, Mercury — Plumb bob filled with mercury to secure weight in a small space.

Potter's Wheel — Probably the oldest machine known. Consists of a vertical shaft with a disk mounted horizontally at the top. The potter puts a lump of clay in the center, revolves the wheel with his foot or by power, and shapes the revolving clay as desired. See Lap; Lead for modern application of this in machine work.

Press, Blanking — For heavy punching or swaging.

Press, Broaching — A press for forcing broaches through holes in metal work. Usually cleans out or forms holes that are not round.

Press, Cabbaging — For compressing loose sheet metal scrap into convenient form for handling and remelting.

Press, Coining — For making metal planchets from which coins are stamped.

Press, Double Action — Has a telescoping ram or one ram inside the other, each driven by an independent cam so that one motion follows the other and performs two operations for each revolution of the press.

Press Fit — See Fit.

Press, Forcing — For forcing one piece into another, such as a rod brass into a rod.

Press, Forging — For forging metal by subjecting it to heavy pressure between formers or dies.

Press, Horning — For closing side seams on pieced tinware.

Press, Inclinable — One that can be used in vertical or inclined position.

Press, Screw — Pressure is applied by screw. Heavier work is done in this way than by foot or hand press.

Press, Straight-sided — Made with perfectly straight sides so as to give great strength and rigidity for heavy work.

Press, Pendulum — Foot press having a pendulum like lever for applying power to the ram.

Profiling Machine — Has rotary cutter that can be made to follow outline or pattern in shaping small parts of machines. Practically a vertical milling machine.

Protractor, Bevel — Graduated semicircular protractor having a pivoted arm for measuring off angles.

Pull-pin — A means of locking or unlocking two parts of machinery. Sometimes slides gears in or out of mesh and at others operates a sliding key which engages any desired gear of a number on stud.

Pulley, Gallow or Guide — Loose pulley mounted in movable frames to guide and tighten belts.

Pulley, Idler — A pulley running loose on a shaft and driving no machinery, merely guiding the belt. Practically same as a "loose pulley."

Pulley, Loose — Pulley running loosely on shaft doing no work. Carries belt when not driving tight (or fast, or working) pulley. Used on countershafts, planers, grinders, etc., where machine is idle part of time. Belt is then on the loose pulley but when shifted to tight pulley the machine starts up. See Belt Shifter, Friction Clutch.

Punching — A piece cut out of sheet stock by punch and die; the same as blank.

Punch, Belt — Hollow, round or elliptical punch for cutting holes for belt lacing.

Q

Quadrant — A piece forming a quarter circle. A segment of a circle. The swinging plate carrying the change gears in the feed train at the end of the lathe.

Quick Return — A mechanism employed in various machine tools to give a table, ram or other member a rapid movement during the return or non-cutting stroke.

Quill — A hollow shaft which revolves on a solid shaft, carrying pulleys or clutches. When clutches are closed the quill and shaft revolve together.

R

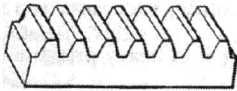

Rack — A strip cut with teeth so that a gear can mesh with it to convert rotary into reciprocating motion or vice versa.

Rack Cutter — Cuts regularly spaced teeth in a straight line. Cutting tool is either a milling cutter or a single point tool.

Ratchet — A gear with triangular shaped teeth adapted to be engaged by a pawl which either imparts intermittent motion to the ratchet or else locks it against backward movement when operated otherwise.

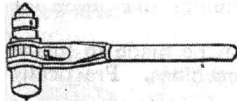

Ratchet Drill — Device for turning a drill when the handle cannot make a complete revolution. A pawl on the handle drops into a ratchet wheel on the barrel so that it can be turned one or more teeth.

Recess — A groove below the normal surface of work. On flat work a groove to allow tool to run into as a planer, or a slide to run over as a cross-head on a guide. In boring a groove inside a hole. If long it is often called a chamber.

Relief or Relieving — The removing of, or the amount removed to reduce friction back of cutting edge of a drill, reamer, tap, etc. Also applied to other than cutting tools. See "backing off."

REAMERS

Reamer — A tool to enlarge a hole already existing, whether a cast or cored hole or one made by a drill or boring bar. Reamers are of many kinds and shape as indicated below. Usually a reamer gives the finishing touch to a hole.

Ball Reamer — Usually a fluted or rose reamer for making the female portion of a ball joint. It is considered advisable to space the teeth irregularly as this tends to prevent chattering.

Bridge Reamer — A reamer used by boiler-makers, bridge builders, ship-builders, etc., has a straight body from A to B and tapered end from B to C. This reamer has a taper shank and can be used in an air drill.

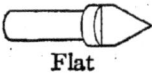

Flat

Fluted

Center Reamer — Center reamers, or countersinks for centering the ends of shafts, etc., are usually made 60 degrees included angle.

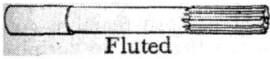

Fluted

Rose

Chucking Reamer — Chucking reamers are used in turret machines. The plain, fluted type has teeth relieved the whole length; while the rose reamer cuts only on the end as there is no peripheral clearance. Where possible reamers used in the turret should be mounted in floating holders which allow the reamer to play sidewise sufficiently to line up with the hole in the work which may be so drilled or bored as not to run perfectly true prior to the reaming operation.

Chucking Reamer (Three-groove) — Spiral fluted chucking reamers with three and four grooves are employed for enlarging cored holes, etc. They are also made with

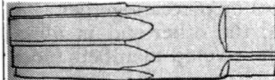

oil passages through them and in this form are adapted to operating in steel.

Flat Reamer — A reamer made of a flat piece of steel. Not much used except on brass work and then usually packed with wooden strips to fit the hole tightly. Flat reamers are not much used except for taper work.

Half-round Reamer — Used considerably in some classes of work, particularly in small sizes and taper work when taper is slight. Not much used in large sizes. Somewhat resembles the "hog-nose drill" in general appearance except that this is always quite short on cutting edge.

Straight

Threaded End

Spiral

Hand Reamer — Reamers enlarge and finish a hole produced by drilling, boring, etc. The cut should be light for hand reamers and the reamer held straight to avoid ruining the hole. The threaded end reamer has a fine thread to assist in drawing the reamer into the work. The spiral reamer is cut left-hand to prevent its drawing into the hole too rapidly. Reamers are slightly tapered at the point to enable them to enter.

Pipe Reamer (Briggs) — Pipe reamers to the Briggs standard taper of ¾-inch per foot are used for reaming out work prior to tapping with the pipe tap.

Shell Reamer — Shell reamers have taper holes to fit the end of an arbor on which they are held in the chucking machine. They are made with both straight and spiral flutes.

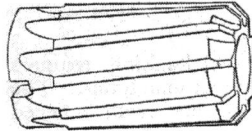

Shell Reamer (Rose) — Rose reamers cut on the end only as there is no peripheral clearance. They are very accurate tools for finishing holes. The shell reamers are made with taper holes to fit an arbor for holding them in the turret machine.

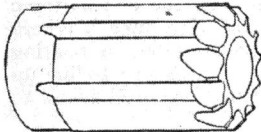

Taper Reamer — For finishing taper holes two or more reamers are sometimes used. The roughing reamer is often provided with nicked or stepped teeth to break up the chip. Taper reamers are also made with spiral teeth. Where the taper is slight the spiral should be left-hand to prevent the reamer from drawing in too fast; where the taper is abrupt the teeth, if cut with right-hand spiral, will help hold the reamer to the cut and make the operation more satisfactory.

Roughing

Finishing

Taper Pin Reamer — Standard taper pin reamers are made $\frac{1}{4}$-inch taper per foot and each size in the series will overlap the next size smaller by about one-half inch.

Taper Reamer (Locomotive) — Reamers for locomotive taper pins have a taper of $\frac{1}{16}$ inch per foot.

Rests, Slide — Detachable rests capable of being clamped to brass lathe bed at any desired point and usually arranged to give motion to tool in two ways; across the bed to reduce diameter or cut-off, and with the bed for turning. Invented by Henry Maudsley.

Rheostat — An adjustable resistance box so that part of the current can be cut out of the motor.

Riddle — Name given to a sieve used in foundries for siftings and for the molds.

Riffle — Name given a small file used by die sinkers and on similar work.

Rivet — A pin for holding two or more plates or pieces together. A head is formed on one end when made; the other end is upset after the rivet is put in place and draws the riveted members close together.

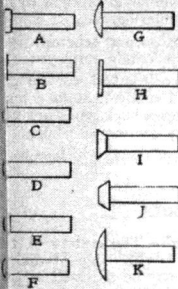

Rivets

A — Machine Head
B — Cone Head
C — Wheel Head
D — Oval Countersunk Head
E — Globe Head
F — Round Head
G — Truss Head
H — Flat Head
I — Countersunk Head
J — Bevel Head
K — Wagon-Box Head.

Rivet Machine — For making rivets from metal rods.

Roller Bearing — See Bearing.

Rule, Hook — Rule with a hook on the end for measuring through pulley holes and in similar places.

Rule, Key-seat — For laying out key-seats on shaft or in hubs.

Rule, Shrink — Graduated to allow for shrinkage in casting. Used by pattern-makers and varies with metal to be cast.

Run — Applied to drilling or reaming when the tool shows a tendency to leave the straight or direct path. Caused by one lip or cutting edge being less sharp than the other, being ground so one lip leads the other, or from uneven hardness of material being drilled.

Running or Sliding Fit — See Fits.

Rust Joint — A joint made by application of cast-iron turnings mixed with sal-ammoniac and sulphur to cause the turnings to rust and become a solid body.

S

Salamander — The mass of iron left in the hearth when a furnace is blown out for repairs.

Sand Blast — Sand is blown by compressed air through a hose as desired. Used to clean castings, stonework, etc.

Sanding Machine — A machine in which woodwork is finished by means of rolls or wheels covered with sandpaper.

Sanding Belt — Endless belt of some strong fabric, charged with glue and sand. For sandpapering wood held in hand or by clamps.

Saw, Band — Continuous metal band, toothed on one edge and guided between rolls. Mostly used on woodwork, but occasionally on metal work, especially in European shops.

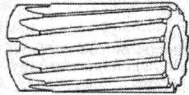

Shell Reamer — Shell reamers have tap
holes to fit the end of an arbor on whic
they are held in the chucking machin
They are made with both straight an
spiral flutes.

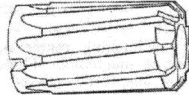

Shell Reamer (Rose) — Rose reamers c
on the end only as there is no perip
eral clearance. They are very a
curate tools for finishing holes. T
shell reamers are made with tap
holes to fit an arbor for holding the
in the turret machine.

Taper Reamer — For finishing taper holes two or more reamers a
sometimes used. The roughing reamer is often provided wi
nicked or stepped teeth to break up t
chip. Taper reamers are also ma
with spiral teeth. Where the taper
slight the spiral should be left-hand
prevent the reamer from drawing in t
fast; where the taper is abrupt the tee
if cut with right-hand spiral, will h
hold the reamer to the cut and make t
operation more satisfactory.

Roughing

Finishing

Taper Pin Reamer — Standard taper pin reamers are made $\frac{1}{4}$-in
taper per foot and each size in
series will overlap the next size smal
by about one-half inch.

Taper Reamer (Locomotive) — Ream
for locomotive taper pins have a tap
of $\frac{1}{16}$ inch per foot.

Rests, Slide — Detachable rests capable of being clamped to brass la
bed at any desired point and usually arranged to give motion
tool in two ways; across the bed to reduce diameter or cut-
and with the bed for turning. Invented by Henry Maudsley.

Rheostat — An adjustable resistance box so that part of the curr
can be cut out of the motor.

Riddle — Name given to a sieve used in foundries for siftings a
for the molds.

Riffle — Name given a small file used by die sinkers and on simi
work.

Rivet — A pin for holding two or more plates or pieces together.
head is formed on one end when made; the other end is up
after the rivet is put in place and draws the riveted members cl
together.

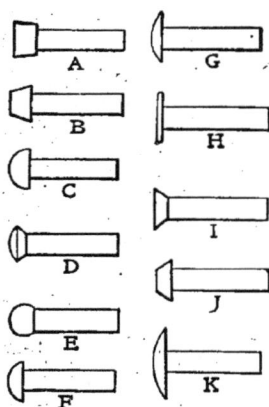

Rivets

A — Machine Head
B — Cone Head
C — Wheel Head
D — Oval Countersunk Head
E — Globe Head
F — Round Head
G — Truss Head
H — Flat Head
I — Countersunk Head
J — Bevel Head
K — Wagon-Box Head.

Rivet Machine — For making rivets from metal rods.

Roller Bearing — See Bearing.

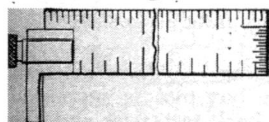

Rule, Hook — Rule with a hook on the end for measuring through pulley holes and in similar places.

Rule, Key-seat — For laying out key-seats on shaft or in hubs.

Rule, Shrink — Graduated to allow for shrinkage in casting. Used by pattern-makers and varies with metal to be cast.

Run — Applied to drilling or reaming when the tool shows a tendency to leave the straight or direct path. Caused by one lip or cutting edge being less sharp than the other, being ground so one lip leads the other, or from uneven hardness of material being drilled.

Running or Sliding Fit — See Fits.

Rust Joint — A joint made by application of cast-iron turnings mixed with sal-ammoniac and sulphur to cause the turnings to rust and become a solid body.

S

Salamander — The mass of iron left in the hearth when a furnace is blown out for repairs.

Sand Blast — Sand is blown by compressed air through a hose as desired. Used to clean castings, stonework, etc.

Sanding Machine — A machine in which woodwork is finished by means of rolls or wheels covered with sandpaper.

Sanding Belt — Endless belt of some strong fabric, charged with glue and sand. For sandpapering wood held in hand or by clamps.

Saw, Band — Continuous metal band, toothed on one edge and guided between rolls. Mostly used on woodwork, but occasionally on metal work, especially in European shops.

Saw Bench, Universal — Bench on which lumber is brought to the saw for ripping, cross-cutting, dadoing, mitering, etc.

Saw, Cold — For sawing metal. Circular saws are generally used though not always, band saws being occasionally employed.

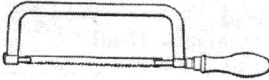

Saw, Hack — Close-toothed saw for cutting metal. Usually held in a hand frame but power hack saws are now becoming very common in shops.

Scarf — The bevel edge formed on a piece of metal which is to be lap-welded.

SCREW MACHINE TOOLS

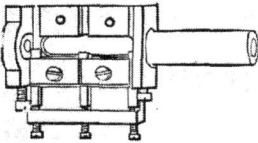

Box Tool, Bushing — The cutters in this tool are placed with edges radial to the stock and may be adjusted to turn the required diameter by the screws in the rear. The stock is supported in a bushing and must therefore be very true and accurate as to size.

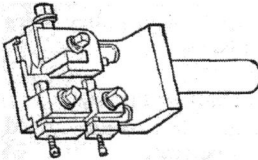

Box Tool, Finishing — The material turned in this box tool is supported by adjustable back rest jaws and the cutters are also adjustable in and out as well as lengthwise of the tool body.

Box Tool, Roughing — This tool has one or more cutters inverted over the work and with cutting edges tangent to the material.

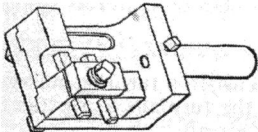

The back rest is bored out the size the screw or other piece is to be turned and the cutter turns the end of the piece to size before it enters the back rest. Sometimes a pointing tool is inserted in the shank for finishing the end of the work.

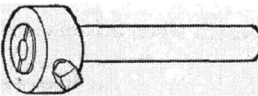

Drill Holder — The end of the drill holder is split and provided with a clamp collar by which the holder is closed on the drill.

Feed Tube — The screw-machine feed tube or feed finger is closed prior to hardening and maintains at all times a grip on the stock.

The rear end is threaded and screwed into the tube by which it is operated. It is drawn back over the stock and when the chuck opens is moved forward feeding the stock the right distance for the next piece.

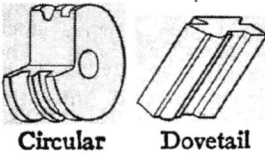

Forming Tools — Circular forming cutters are generally cut below center to give proper clearance and the tool post is bored a corresponding amount above center to bring the tool on the center line. Dovetail cutters are made at an angle of about 10 degrees for clearance.

Circular   Dovetail

Hollow Mill — Usually made with 3 prongs or cutting edges and with a slight taper inside toward the rear. A clamp collar is used on mill like a spring die collar and a reasonable amount of adjustment may be obtained by this collar. Hollow mills are frequently used in place of box tools for turning work in the screw machine.

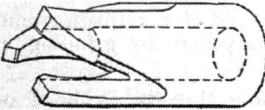

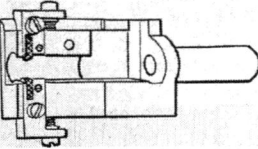

Nurling Tool — The two nurls in this box are adjustable to suit different diameters of work.

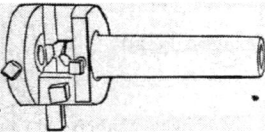

Pointing Tool — The bushing in this tool receives and supports the end of the round stock and the cutters carried in the frame form and point the end.

Revolving Die Holder — The common type of revolving die holder which is generally used with spring dies, has a pair of driving pins behind the head and in the flange of the sleeve which fits into the turret hole. At the rear end of the sleeve is a cam surface which engages a pin in the shank of the head when the die is reversed. The die is run on to the work with the driving pins engaged. When the work is reversed, the cam at the rear engages the pin in the shank and holds the die from turning so that it must draw off the work.

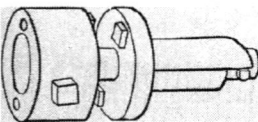

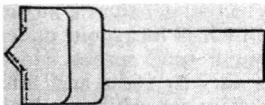

Spotting Tool — This tool spots a center in the end of the bar of stock to allow the drill to start properly, and also faces the end of the piece true. Sometimes called "centering and facing" tool. It is desirable to have the included angle of the cutting point less than that of the drill which follows it in order that the latter may start true by cutting at the corners first.

Spring Collet — Spring collets or chucks are made to receive round,
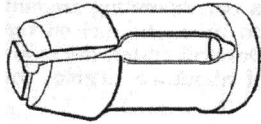 square, hexagonal or other stock worked in the screw machine. The collet is hardened and is closed in operation by being pressed into the conical cap into which it fits. When released it springs open sufficiently to free the stock and allow it to be fed through the collet.

Spring Die and Extension — Spring dies
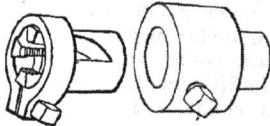 or prong dies are provided with a collar at the end for adjusting and are easily sharpened by grinding in the flutes.

Screw Plates — Holders for dies for cutting threads on bolts or screws. Dies are usually separate but sometimes cut in the piece which forms the holder.

SCREWS

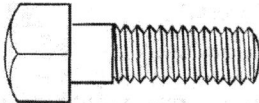

Square Head

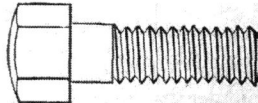

Hexagon Head

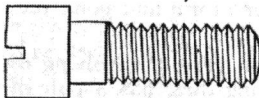

Flat Fillister Head

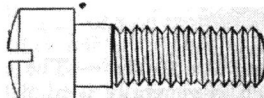

Oval Fillister Head

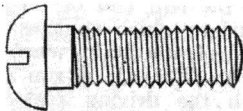

Button Head

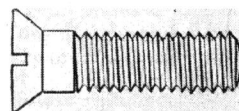

Countersunk Head

Cap Screws — Cap screws are machined straight from point to head, have finished heads and up to 4 inches in length are usually threaded three-fourths of the length. When longer than 4 inches they are threaded one half the length, which is measured under the head, except in the case of countersunk head screws which are measured over all. Cap-screw sizes vary by 16ths and 8ths and are regularly made up to 1 or 1¼ inch diameter, while machine screws with which they are frequently confused are made to the machine-screw gage sizes.

Flat fillister heads on cap screws are often called "round" heads; oval fillister heads are frequently designated as "fillister" heads, and countersunk heads as "flat" heads. When a countersunk or flat head has an oval top it is called a "French" head.

Fillister heads are also made with rounded corners as well as with the oval head shown above. Fillister head screws are known in England as cheese-head screws. The included angle of the countersunk or flat head is 70 degrees.

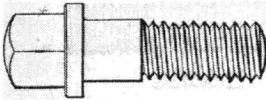

Collar Screw — Collar or collar head screws are used for much the same purposes as regular cap screws, and, in fact, are sometimes designated as "collar" cap or "collar head" cap screws.

Lag Screw — Lag screws, or coach screws, as they are often called, have a thread like a wood screw and a square or a hexagonal

head. They are used for attaching countershaft hangers to over-head joists for fastening machines to wood floors and for many other purposes where a heavy wood screw is required.

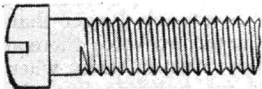

Machine Screws — Machine screws are made to the sizes of the machine-screw gage instead of running like cap screws in even fractions of an inch.

Fillister Head

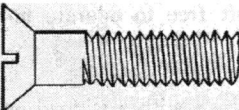

Counter Sunk or Flat Head

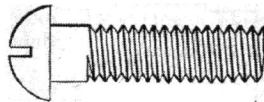

Button or Round

Set Screws — Set screws are threaded the full length of body and may or may not be necked under the head. They are usually case-hardened. Ordinarily the width of head across flats and the length of head are equal to the diameter of the screw. The headless set screw is known in England as a "grub" screw.

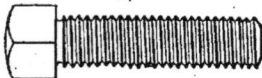

Flat Point

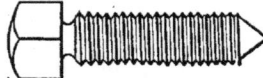

Cone Point

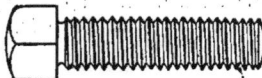

Round Point

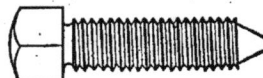

Hanger Point

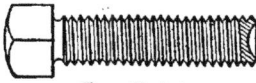

Cup Point

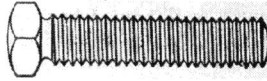

Low Head

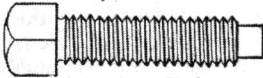

Flat Pivot Point

Headless

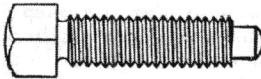

Round Pivot Point

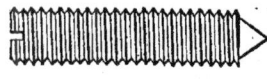

Cone Point Headless

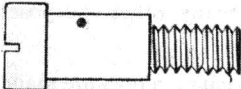

Single Shoulder

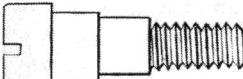

Double Shoulder

Shoulder Screw — Shoulder screws are commonly used for carrying levers and other machine parts that have to operate freely. The screw body is enough longer than the thickness of the piece pivoted thereon to allow the latter to work easily when the screw is set up tight against the bottom of the shoulder. With double shoulders two members may be mounted side by side and left free to operate independently of each other.

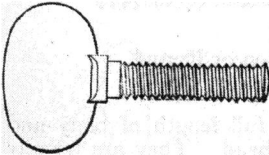

Thumb Screw — A screw with a winged or knurled head which may be operated by hand when a quick and light clamping effect is desired.

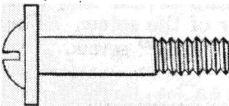

Washer-head Screw — The washer formed on this screw enables it to be used for holding pieces with large holes without applying a loose washer.

Wood Screws — Wood screws are made in an endless variety of forms, a number of which are shown on the following page. They range in size from No. o to No. 30 by the American Screw Company's gage and are regularly made in lengths from ¼ inch to 6 inches. Generally the thread is cut about seven tenths of the total length of the screw. The flat-head wood screw has an included angle of head of 82 degrees.

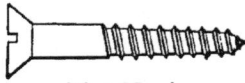
Flat Head

Oval Head

Round Head

Piano Head

Oval Fillister Head

Countersunk Fillister Head

Felloe

Clove Head

Hexagon Head

Headless

Grooved

Square Bung Head

Pinched Head

Round Bung Head

Dowel

Winged

Drive

Winged

Winged Head

Screw Thread, Acme 29 degree Standard —

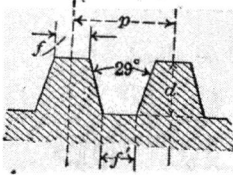

$$p = \text{pitch} = \frac{1}{\text{no. threads per inch}}$$

d = depth = $\frac{1}{2}$ p + .010.
f = flat on top of thread = p x .3707
The Acme screw thread is practically the same depth as the square thread and much stronger. It is used extensively for lead screws, feed screws, etc.

Screw Thread, British Association Standard—
p=pitch
d=depth=p x .6

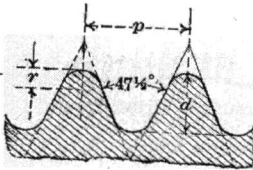

$$r = \text{radius} = \frac{2 \times p}{11}$$

This thread has been adopted in England for small screws used by opticians and in telegraph work, upon recommendations made by the Committee of the British Association. The diameter and pitches in this system are in millimeters.

Screw Thread, Buttress —

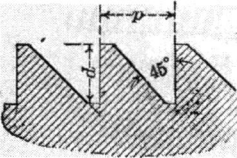

$$p = \text{pitch} = \frac{1}{\text{no. threads per inch}}$$

d=depth=$\frac{3}{4}$ p

The buttress thread takes a bearing on one side only and is very strong in that direction. The ratchet thread is of practically the same form but sharper.

Screw Thread, International (Metric) Standard—
p=pitch
d=depth=p x .6495

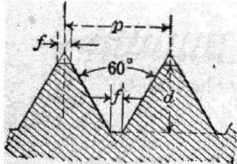

$$f = \text{flat} = \frac{p}{8}$$

The International thread is of the same form as the Sellers or U. S. Standard. This system was recommended by a Congress held at Zurich in 1898, and is much the same as the metric system of threads generally used in France. The sizes and pitches in the system are in millimeters.

Screw Thread, Square —

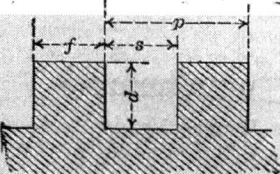

$$p = \text{pitch} = \frac{1}{\text{no. threads per inch}}$$

d=depth=$\frac{1}{2}$ p
f =width of flat =$\frac{1}{2}$ p
s=width of space=$\frac{1}{2}$ p.

While theoretically depth, width of space and thread are each one half the pitch, in practice the groove is cut slightly wider and deeper.

Screw Thread, United States Standard —

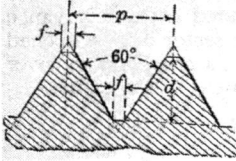

$$p = pitch = \frac{1}{\text{no. threads per inch}}$$

$$d = depth = p \times .6495$$

$$f = flat = \frac{p}{8}$$

This thread was devised by Wm. Sellers, and recommended by the Franklin Institute in 1869. It is called the U. S. Standard, the Franklin Institute, and the Sellers thread. The advantages of this thread are, that it is not easily injured, tap and dies will retain their size longer, and bolts and screws with this thread are stronger and better appearing. The system has been adopted by the United States Government, Master Mechanics and Master Car Builders' Associations, Machine Bolt Makers, and by many manufacturing establishments.

Screw Thread, V, 60 degree Sharp —

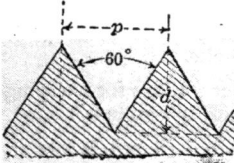

$$p = pitch = \frac{1}{\text{no. threads per inch}}$$

$$d = depth = p \times .8660$$

While the sharp V form gives a deeper thread than the U. S. Standard, the objections urged against the thread are, that the sharp top is injured by the slightest accident, and, in the case of taps and dies, the fine edge is quickly lost, causing constant variation in fitting.

Screw Thread, Whitworth Standard —

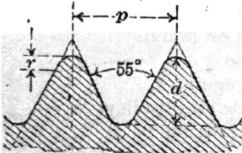

$$p = pitch = \frac{1}{\text{no. threads per inch}}$$

$$d = depth = p \times .64033$$

$$r = radius = p \times .1373$$

The Whitworth thread is the standard in use in England. It was devised by Sir Joseph Whitworth in 1841, the system then proposed by him being slightly modified in 1857 and 1861.

Worm Thread, Brown & Sharpe 29 degree —

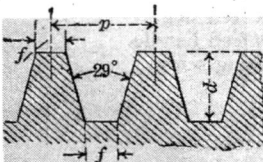

$$p = pitch = \frac{1}{\text{no. threads per inch}}$$

$$d = depth = p \times .6866$$

f = flat on top of thread = $p \times .335$
This thread is commonly used in America for worms. It is considerably deeper than the Acme screw thread of the same angle, namely 29 degrees.

Sector — A device used on an index plate of a dividing head for indicating the number of holes to be included at each advance of the index crank in dividing circles. The sector can be opened or closed to form as large or small an arc as necessary to cover the desired number of holes for each movement of the crank.

Set — The bend to one side of the teeth of a saw.

Set Screw — See Screws.

Shaft-bearing Stand — Shaft bearing which is fastened to floor.

Shaft Coupling — See Coupling.

Shaft, Flexible — Shaft made of a helical spring or of jointed parts, usually confined in a leather or fabric casing, to transmit power in varying directions.

Shaft, Jack — A secondary or auxiliary shaft, driven by the engine and in turn driving the dynamos or other machinery. Jack shafts are often introduced between a regular machine countershaft and the line shaft.

Shaft, Line — The shafting driving the machinery of a shop or section of a shop by means of pulleys and belts.

Shaft, Muley — A vertical shaft carrying two idler pulleys for carrying a belt around a corner. To be avoided where possible.

Shaper — Work is held on table or knee and tool moves across it, held by a tool post on the moving ram. Table adjustable for depth of cut, etc.

Shaper — Parts of

1. Tool post.
2. Clapper block.
3. Clapper box.
4. Clamping bolts.
5. Down-feed screw.
6. Tool slide.
7. Tool head.
8. Binder for head.
9. Stop for down feed.
10. Down-feed adjustment.
11. Ram adjuster.
12. Ram.
13. Position lever.
14. Clamp for down feed.
15 Ram slide.
16. Face of column.
17. Ram guide.
18. Frame or body.
19. Feed box.
20. Feed regulator.
21. Cone-driving pulley.
22. Lever bearing.
23. Power elevation of table.
24. Vise.
25. Swiveling base.
26. Table.
27. Saddle.
28. Cross-feed screw.
29. Cross-feed dog.
30. Cross-feed handle.
31. Elevating screw.

Shaper, Crank — Ram is driven by a crank motion.

Shaper, Draw Cut — Cutting stroke takes place when tool is moving toward frame of machine. This tends to draw the parts together.

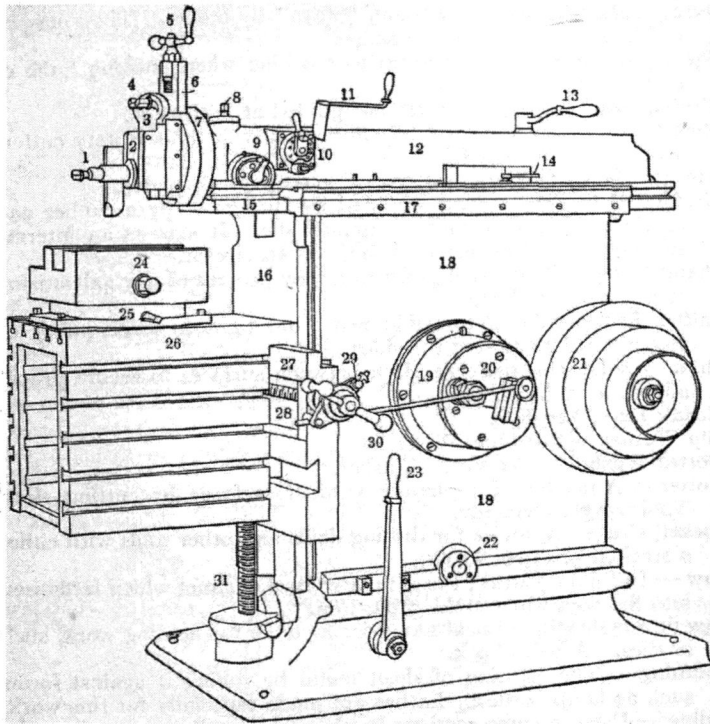

SHAPER — POTTER AND JOHNSTON

Shaper, Friction — Ram is driven by rack and pinion through friction clutches. Ram is reversed by simultaneous release and engagement of these clutches. These are driven by open and crossed belts in opposite directions.

Shaper, Gear — Planes gear teeth by using a hardened cutter, shaped like a pinion gear, and moving across the face of the gear with a planing or shaping cut.

Shaper, Geared — Ram is driven by rack and pinion with a slow cutting stroke and a quick return by shifting open and crossed belts the same as on a planer.

Shapers, Traverse or Traveling Head — Ram feeds across work, which is stationary.

Shear — Tool for cutting metals between two blades. The name given to the way or V of a lathe or planer. A hoisting apparatus used on wharves or docks, consisting of two heavy struts like a long inverted V.

Shears — The ways on which the lathe carriage and tail stock move are called "shears" by some, "ways" by others. They may be either V, flat or any other shape.

Shears, Alligator — Name given to machine where moving knife or cutter works on a pivot.

Shears, Squaring — Has cutter bar guided at both ends.

Shears, Slitting — Arranged for slitting sheet metal. Rotary cutters are usually employed.

Shearing Machine — For cutting off rods, bars or plates.

Shedder — A plate or ring operated by springs or by a rubber pad to eject a blank from a compound die. It acts as an internal stripper, and is sometimes known as an ejector.

Sherardizing — The name given to a new process of dry galvanizing of any iron product.

Shifter Forks — Arms to guide belt from tight to loose pulley or vice versa, by pressing the sides.

Shim — A liner or piece to place between surfaces to secure proper adjustment.

Shrink Fit — See Fits.

Slip Washer — See Open Washer.

Slotted Washer — See Open Washer.

Slotter — A machine for planing vertical surfaces or cutting slots. Tool travels vertically.

Socket, Grip — A device for driving drills and other tools with either a straight or taper shank.

Sow — In foundry work, the gate or central channel which feeds iron into the pigs when making pig iron.

Sow or Sow-block — Local name for a chuck for holding work, such as dies. A ball chuck.

Spinning — The forming of sheet metal by rolling it against forms such as lamp bodies. Lathes are made especially for this work.

Spline — Used in some sections in place of "key" and in others the same as "feather." See Key and Feather.

Split Nut — Nut split lengthwise so as to open for quick adjustment.

Spot or Spotting — Spotting is making a spot or flat surface for a set-screw point or to lay out from.

Spring, Compression — A helical spring which tends to shorten in action.

Spring, Helical — A spring coiled lengthwise of its axis like a screw thread. Often incorrectly called a spiral spring.

Spring, Leaf — A built up spring made of flat stock like a carriage spring or locomotive driving spring.

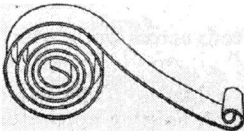

Spring, Spiral — A spring wound with one coil over the other as in a clock spring. Usually of flat stock, but not always.

Spring, Tension — A helical spring which tends to lengthen in action.

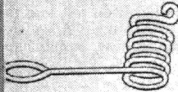

Spring, Torsion — A helical spring which operates with a coiling or uncoiling action as a door spring.

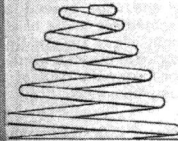

Spring, Valve — A helical spring used on valve stems and similar places; each coil being smaller than the one below, in order that the spring may close up into a very small space and then have a considerable range of action.

Spring Cotter — See Cotter.

Sprue Cutter — A cutting punch for trimming sprues from soft metal castings.

Square, Caliper — A square with a caliper adjustment for laying out work.

Square, Combination — A tool combining square, level and protractor in one tool.

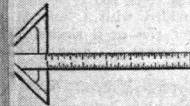

Square, Center — For finding the center of a round bar by placing across the end and scribing lines in two different positions. Also used as a T-square. Not so much used as formerly.

Square — A straight edge with a head at one end commonly used on the drawing board for drawing straight lines. It forms a guide also, along which triangles are slid. Generally made of wood, although sometimes of metal and often provided with a swiveling head which serves as a protractor when graduated in degrees.

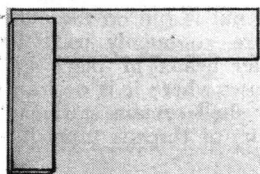

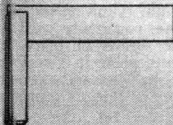

Square, Try — Small square for testing work as to its being at right angles.

Stand, Vise — Stand, usually of metal, for holding a vise firmly in any desired part of the shop, making it a portable vise.

Steady Rest — A rest attached to the lathe ways for supporting long, slender work.

Steel, High Speed — A name given to steels which do not lose their hardness by being heated under high speed cuts. Alloy steels which depend on tungsten, chromium, manganese, molybdenum, etc., for their hardness.

Stocks, Ratchet — Die stocks with ratchet handles.

Straight Edge — A piece of metal having one edge ground and scraped flat and true. Small ones are sometimes made of steel but large, straight edges are usually of cast iron, proportioned to resist bending, and are used for testing the truth of flat surfaces such as plane ways.

Strap — See Belt Polisher.

Strapping — A method of buffing by the use of a flexible strap or belt, usually made of cloth and covered with abrasive held in place by glue. Runs over two pulleys or one pulley and a rod or plate at high speed.

String Jig — Fixture for holding a row of pieces to be milled or planed.

Stripper — A thin plate placed over the die, in a punch press, with a gap beneath to admit the sheet stock and an opening to allow the punch to pass freely; upon the up-stroke of the punch it prevents the strip of metal from lifting with the punch.

Stripping-plate — A plate containing holes of the same outline as the pattern and used to prevent sand following the patterns when drawn out on some molding machines.

Stud, Collar — The collar stud forms a satisfactory device for carrying gears, cam rolls, rocker levers, etc. It is often provided with a hole at the end for a cutter pin or is slotted for a split washer, to retain the gear, or other part in place.

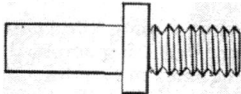

Stud, Shoulder — A stud of this form is used for mounting levers and other parts which could be operated on a plain, unthreaded stud, which stud, however, cannot be conveniently set or removed when necessary. It is also a form of post or guide sometimes employed in machine construction for carrying one or more sliding parts.

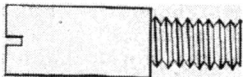

Stud, Threaded — Studs are threaded on both ends to lengths required and screwed tight into place. A nut is run on the outer end. They are commonly used for holding cylinder heads in place and for other purposes where it is desirable that the screw shall remain stationary to prevent injury of threads tapped in the main piece.

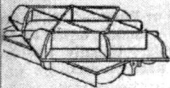

Surface Plates — Cast-iron plates have surfaces scraped flat for use in testing work. Should be made in sets of three and so scraped that each one has a perfect bearing with the other two.

Swaging — Changing the sectional shape of a piece of metal by hammering, rolling or otherwise forcing the particles to change shape without cutting.

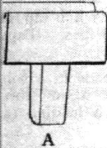

Swaging Blocks — Blocks of cast or wrought iron to assist blacksmith in swaging and bending iron to various shapes. *A* is for use in the hardy hole in the anvil, *B* can be used anywhere but is usually on or beside the anvil.

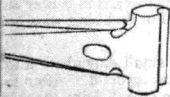

A   B

Swaging Hammer — A connection with the swaging block to swage metal to the desired size and shape.

Swaging Machine — For reducing tapering or pointing wire or tubing either between rolling dies or by hammering with rapid blows between dies of suitable shape.

Sweating — Another name for soldering.

Swing of a Lathe — In the United States the swing of a lathe means the largest diameter of the work that can be swung over the ways or shears. In England it means the distance from lathe center to the ways or one half the U. S. measurements.

T

Take-up — Name given to device for taking up slack in belt or rope drives.

Tap — Hardened and tempered steel tool for cutting internal threads. Has a thread cut on it and flutes to give cutting edges.

Tap, Bit-brace — Tap of any kind, usually on all bolt taps, with shank made square to be driven by bit-brace.

Tap, Echols Thread — This form of tap has every other thread cut away on each land, but these are staggered so that a space on one land has a tooth behind it on the next land. This is done for chip clearance.

Tap, Hand, First or Taper — Bolt tap usually for hand use. The first or taper tap has the front end tapered to enter easily.

Tap, Hand, Second or Plug — The second tap with only a small taper to the first two threads. Usually this tap is the last that need be used.

Tap, Hand, Third or Bottoming — Tap with full thread clear to the end. For cutting a thread clear to the bottom of a hole.

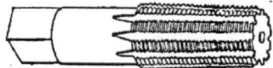

Tap, Hob for Pipe Dies — A hob tap for cutting threads in pipe dies. Taper ¾ inch per foot.

Tap, Hob for Solid Dies — Used for cutting the threads in a solid die. It is best to remove about three fourths of the stock with a leading tap but is not necessary.

Tap, Hob, Sellers — Has threads in center and numerous flutes. For hobbing dies and chasers.

Tap, Machine or Nut — Tap with long shank small enough to allow tapped nuts to pass over it. After tap is full the tap is removed from machine and nuts slid off the shank.

Tap, Machine Screw — Taps made with sizes and threads of machine screws. Made with shank the size of screw and pointed ends on small sizes.

Tap, Master — Tap for cutting solid and open dies.

Tap, Patch-bolt — Tap for boiler-makers use in patching boilers. Sizes vary by sixteenths from ½ inch to 1¼ inches. All threads are 12 to inch and taper is ¾ inch per foot.

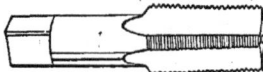

Tap, Pipe — Taper tap, ¾ inch taper per foot for pipe fitting.

Tap, Pulley — Tap with a long shank to reach the hub of pulley for tapping set-screw holes.

Tap Remover — Device for removing broken taps. Usually have prongs which go down in the flutes and around the central portion.

Tap, Staybolt — Tap for threading boiler sheets for staybolts. *A* reams the hole, *B* is a taper thread, *C* is straight thread of right size. *D* square for driving tap. All standard staybolt taps have 12 threads per inch.

D   C   B   A

Tap, Step — Tap made with "steps" or varying diameters. Front end cuts part of thread, next step takes out more and so on to the end. Only used for heavy threads, usually square or Acme.

Tap, Stove-bolt — Made same way as machine-screw taps but in only six standard sizes.

Tap, Tapper — Similar to a machine tap except that it has no square on the end.

Taper Reamer — See Reamer, Taper.

Tapped Face-plate — Having a number of tapped holes instead of slots. Studs screw in at any desired point.

Tapping Machine — For cutting threads with taps (tapping) in nuts or other holes.

Threads, Screw — See Screw Threads.

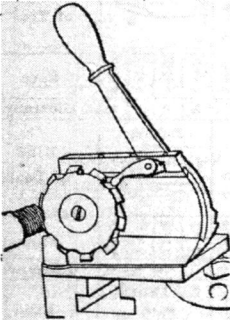

Threading Tool, Rivet-Dock — The tool is a rotary cutter with cutting teeth of different depths. The first tooth starts the cut, then instead of feeding the carriage into the work, the cutter is turned and the next tooth takes the next cut.

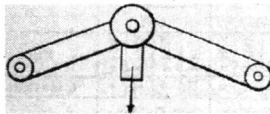

Toggle — Arrangement of levers to multiply pressure obtained by making movement given to work very much less than movement of applied power.

Tongs — Tools for holding hot or cold metals.

Tool, Boring — For operating on internal surface of holes.

Tool, Cutting-off — For cutting work apart on lathe or cutting-off machine.

Tool, Diamond — Black diamond set in metal for tracing emery or other abrasive wheels. Also used to some extent for truing up hardened steel or iron.

Tool Holder, Lathe or Planer — A body or shank, adopted to hold small pieces of tool steel for cutting tools. These can be removed for sharpening or renewal without moving the holder and saves resetting the tool to the work.

Tools, Inserted Cutter — Holders in which are held small steel cutting tools. These are usually removed for grinding or replacing when broken or worn out. Usually made of self-hardening steel.

Tool, Nurling — For roughing or checking the outside of turned work so it can be readily grasped by hand. The tool is a wheel with the desired markings cut in the edge and hardened. It is forced against the work and actually forces the metal up into the depressions in the wheel. Most nurls are held in the end of a hand tool but for heavy nurling they are made to go in the tool post as shown.

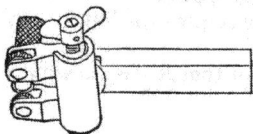

TOOLS, LATHE — WM. SELLERS & CO.

Lathe

Square Thread	60° V Thread	Bent Side	Side	Bent Roughing	Roughing	
Right	Right	Right	Right	Top Rake 8° / 30°	Top Rake 8°	Kind of Tool
Top d 0° / End c 0° / Side b 10° / Side a 10°	Top d 0° / End c 15° / Side b 7° / Side a 12°	Top d 12° / End c 0° / Side a 6°	Top d 12° / End c 0° / Side a 6°	Top d 22° / Side a 6°	Top d 22° / Side a 5°	Face / Clearance
Square Thread	**60° V Thread**	**Bent Side**	**Side**	**Nicking**	**Finishing**	
Left	Left	Left	Left			Kind of Tool
Top d 0° / End c 0° / Side b 10° / Side a 10°	Top d 0° / End c 15° / Side b 7° / Side a 12°	Top d 12° / End c 0° / Side a 6°	Top d 12° / End c 0° / Side a 6°	Top d 1° / End c 0° / Side b 3° / Side a 3°	Top d 15° / End c 0° / Side b 4° / Side a 4°	Face / Clearance
Square Thread Bent	**60° V Thread Bent**	**Inside Bent**	**Bent Brass**	**Bent Nicking**	**Bent Finishing**	
Right	Right	Left	Right	Left	Left	Kind of Tool
Top d 0° / End c 0° / Side b 0° / Side a 10°	Top d 0° / End c 15° / Side b 7° / Side a 12°	Top d 12° / End c 0° / Side a 6°	Top d 0° / End c 10° / Side b 0° / Side a 10°	Top d 1° / End c 0° / Side b 3° / Side a 3°	Top d 15° / End c 0° / Side b 4° / Side a 4°	Face / Clearance
Square Thread Bent	**60° V Thread Bent**	**Inside Bent**	**Brass**	**Bent Nicking**	**Bent Finishing**	
Left	Left	Right	Right	Right	Right	Kind of Tool
Top d 0° / End c 0° / Side b 0° / Side a 10°	Top d 0° / End c 15° / Side b 7° / Side a 12°	Top d 12° / End c 0° / Side a 6°	Top d 0° / End c 10° / Side b 0° / Side a 10°	Top d 1° / End c 0° / Side b 3° / Side a 3°	Top d 15° / End c 0° / Side b 4° / Side a 4°	Face / Clearance

TOOLS, LATHE

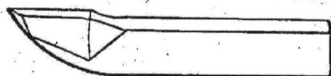

Left-hand Side Tool

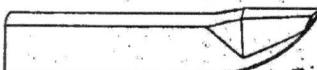

Right-hand Side Tool

Left-hand Bent Side Tool

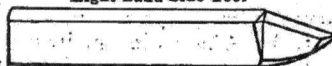

Right-hand Bent Side Tool

Left-hand Diamond Point

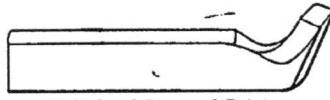

Right-hand Diamond Point

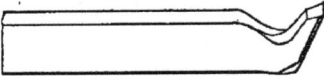

Bent Right hand Diamond Point

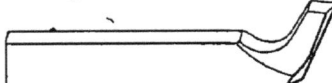

Half Diamond Point, R.H.

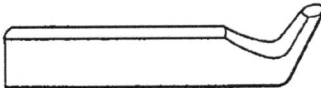

Round Nose.

Water Polishing Tool.

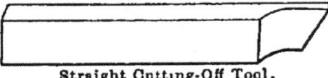

Straight Cutting-Off Tool.

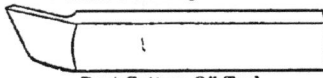

Bent Cutting-Off Tool.

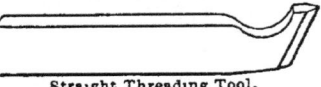

Straight Threading Tool.

Bent Threading Tool.

Inside Boring Tool.

Inside Threading Tool.

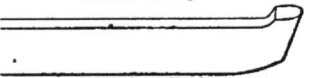

Bull Nose Tool.

Finishing or Necking Tool.

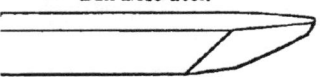

Scaling Tool.

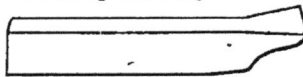

For Trueing Up Centers, &c.

TOOLS, PLANER

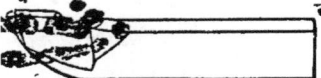

Left-hand Side Tool

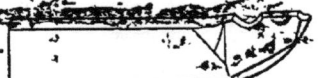

Right-hand Side Tool

Left-hand Diamond Point Tool

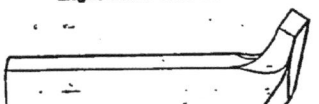

Right-hand Diamond Point Tool

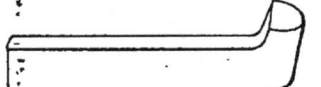

Bull Nose, for Heavy Cuts.

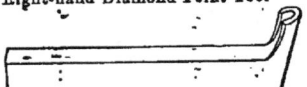

Gouge Nose Tool.

Broad Nose or Stocking Tool.

Scaling Tool.

Right-hand Siding Tool.

Left-hand Siding Tool.

For Finishing in Corners.

Cutting-Off Tool

Left-hand Bevel Tool.

Right-hand Bevel Tool.

For Smoothing Wrought Iron or Steel.

Smoothing Tool for Cast Iron

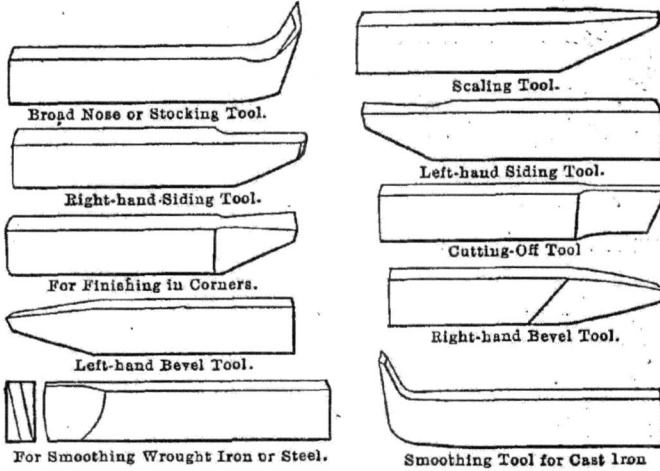

TOOLS, PLANER AND SLOTTER

Slotter	Planer						Kind of Tool
Corner	**Chamfering** Right	**Bent Finishing** Right	**30° Angle** Right	**Side Finishing** Right	**Finishing**		**Kind of Tool**
End c / Side b / Side a	Top d / Side b / Side a	Top d / End c / Side a	Top d / End c / Side b / Side a	Top d / End c / Side b / Side a	Top d / End c / Side b / Side a		**Face**
							Clearance
Square Right & Left	**45° Angle Slot**	**Bent Finishing** Left	**30° Angle** Left	**Side Finishing** Left	**Splining**		**Kind of Tool**
End c / Side d / Side b / Side a	Top d / End c / Side b / Side a / Side f	Top d / End c / Side a	Top d / End c / Side b / Side a	Top d / End c / Side b / Side a	Top d / End c / Side b / Side a		**Face**
							Clearance
Splining Left	**30° Angle Slot** Left	**45° Angle** Left	**40° Angle** Left	**Bent Side Finishing** Left	**Cutting Down** Left		**Kind of Tool**
Top d / End c / Side b / Side a	Top d / End c / Side b / Side a	Top d / End c / Side b / Side a	Top d / End c / Side b / Side a	Top d / End c / Side b / Side a	Top d / End c / Side a		**Face**
							Clearance
Hexagon For Wrenches	**30° Angle Slot** Right	**45° Angle** Right	**40° Angle** Right	**Bent Side Finishing** Right	**Cutting Down** Right		**Kind of Tool**
Top d / Side c / Side b / Side a	Top d / End c / Side b / Side a	Top d / End c / Side b / Side a	Top d / End c / Side b / Side a	Top d / End c / Side b / Side a	Top d / End c / Side a		**Face**
							Clearance

Tote Boxes — See Tote Pans.

Tote Pans — Pans or trays of steel for carrying small parts from one part of shop to another.

Train — A series of gears, as the feed train of a lathe connecting spindle with lead screw.

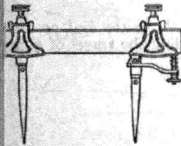

Trammels — For drawing large circles. Fit on a beam and their capacity depends on the length of the beam.

Trepanning Tool — Tool for cutting an annular groove outside or around a bored hole.

Tripper — Device that trips any piece of mechanism at the desired time. An example is found in conveyers where the tripper dumps the material at the desired point.

Tumbler Gear — An intermediate gear which meshes in between other gears to reverse the direction of the driven gear of the train.

Stub End

Turn Buckle — Turn buckles are for connecting and tightening truss rods, tie rods, etc., used in construction work.

Hook and Eye

Tuyere — The pipe or opening into forge through which air is forced.

V

Veeder Metal — An alloy with tin as a base, used for casting in metal molds.

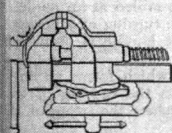

Vise, Chipping or Filing — Heavy bench vise used for holding work to chip. Vises for filing only are similar but lighter.

Vise, Drill — Vise for use on drill press to hold work being drilled.

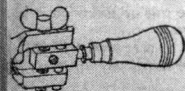

Vise, Hand — A small vise to be held in the hand. For small work that requires turning frequently to get at different sides.

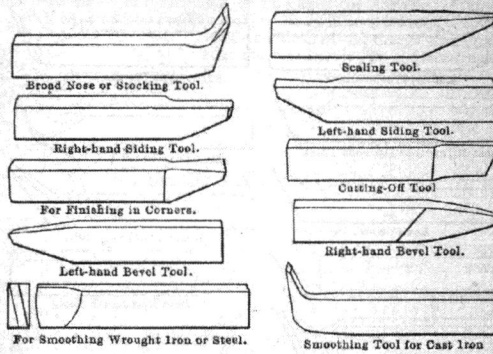

Broad Nose or Stocking Tool.

Scaling Tool.

Right-hand Siding Tool.

Left-hand Siding Tool.

For Finishing in Corners.

Cutting-Off Tool.

Left-hand Bevel Tool.

Right-hand Bevel Tool.

For Smoothing Wrought Iron or Steel.

Smoothing Tool for Cast Iron.

TOOLS, PLANER AND SLOTTER

Slotter	Planer					
Corner	Chamfering	Bent Finishing	80° Angle	Side Finishing	Finishing	Kind of Tool
		Right	Right	Right		
						Face
						Clearance
Square	45° Angle Slot	Bent Finishing	80° Angle	Side Finishing	Splining	Kind of Tool
	Right & Left	Left	Left	Left		
						Face
						Clearance
Splining	30° Angle Slot	45° Angle	40° Angle	Bent Side Finishing	Cutting Down	Kind of Tool
	Left	Left	Left	Left	Left	
						Face
						Clearance
Hexagon	30° Angle Slot	45° Angle	40° Angle	Bent Side Finishing	Cutting Down	Kind of Tool
For Wrenches	Right	Right	Right	Right	Right	
						Face
						Clearance

Tote Boxes — See Tote Pans.

Tote Pans — Pans or trays of steel for carrying small parts from one part of shop to another.

Train — A series of gears, as the feed train of a lathe connecting spindle with lead screw.

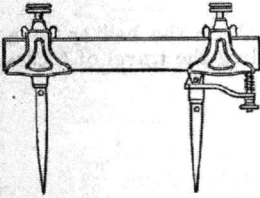

Trammels — For drawing large circles. Fit on a beam and their capacity depends on the length of the beam.

Trepanning Tool — Tool for cutting an annular groove outside or around a bored hole.

Tripper — Device that trips any piece of mechanism at the desired time. An example is found in conveyers where the tripper dumps the material at the desired point.

Tumbler Gear — An intermediate gear which meshes in between other gears to reverse the direction of the driven gear of the train.

Stub End

Turn Buckle — Turn buckles are for connecting and tightening truss rods, tie rods, etc., used in construction work.

Hook and Eye

Tuyere — The pipe or opening into forge through which air is forced.

V

Veeder Metal — An alloy with tin as a base, used for casting in metal molds.

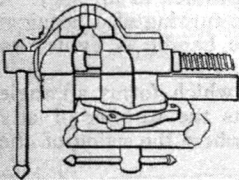

Vise, Chipping or Filing — Heavy bench vise used for holding work to chip. Vises for filing only are similar but lighter.

Vise, Drill — Vise for use on drill press to hold work being drilled.

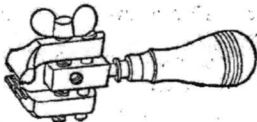

Vise, Hand—A small vise to be held in the hand. For small work that requires turning frequently to get at different sides.

Vise, Jig — A drill vise with arms which carry bushings so that pieces can be drilled in duplicate without special jigs for them.

Vise, Pin — Small hand vise for holding small wire rods.

Vise Stands — See Stands, Vise.

V's — Ways shaped like a V, either raised above the bed as on a lathe or cut below as in a planer, for guiding the travel of a carriage or table.

Volt — The unit of electrical pressure.

W

Washer, Open — Washers with one side open so as to be removed or slipped under the nut to avoid necessity of taking the nut entirely off. Also called a "C" washer.

Watt — The unit of electrical power and equals volts multiplied by amperes. 746 watts are equal to one horse-power.

Ways — The guiding or bearing surfaces on which moving parts slide, as in a lathe plane or milling machine. The ways may be of any form, flat, V or any other shape.

Welding — The joining of metals by heating the parts to be joined to the fusing point and making a union by hammering or forcing them together. Welding in an open fire is usually confined to iron and steel but nearly all metals can be joined in this way by electric heating.

Wind — Pronounced with a long *i* as in "mind" and refers to a twist or warping away from straightness and parallelism.

Wrench, Bridge Builders' — Large heavy wrench with a hole in end for a tackle to apply power.

WRENCHES, MACHINE

15 degree angle wrenches have an opening milled at an angle of 15 degrees with the handle, which permits the turning of a hexagon nut completely around where the swing of the handle is limited to 30 degrees.

$22\frac{1}{2}$ degree angle wrenches have an opening which forms an angle of $22\frac{1}{2}$ degrees with the handle, which permits the turning of any square head bolt or screw completely around where the swing of the handle is limited to 45 degrees.

Unfinished drop-forged wrenches are plain forgings, with openings milled to fit the nut or screw on which they are to be used.

Semi-finished wrenches are milled to fit the nut or screw on which they are to be used and case-hardened all over.

Finished wrenches are milled to fit the nut or screw on which they are to be used and are ground, polished, case-hardened all over, lacquered, with heads bright.

Single End, Hex.

Double End, Hex.

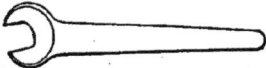

15° Angle, Single End

15° Angle, Double End

22½° Angle, Double End

S — 22½° Angle

Single End, Set Screw and Machine

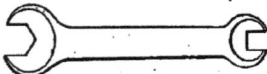

Double End, Set Screw and Machine

"Box"-Tool Post

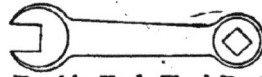

Double End, Tool Post

Hex. Box, 15° Angle

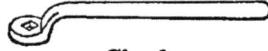

Chuck

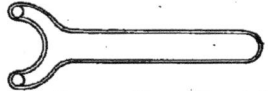

Pin-face, For Round Nuts Having Holes in their Face to Receive the two Wrench Pins

Hook Spanner, Milled out to suit Round Nuts Having Notches in the Periphery to Receive the Hook at the End of Spanner

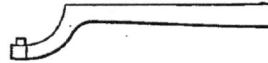

Pin Spanner Used on Round Nuts which have Holes in the Periphery to receive the Spanner Pin

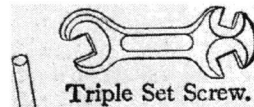

Triple Set Screw.

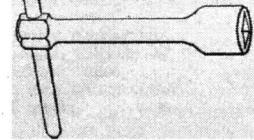

Socket

WRENCHES, MISCELLANEOUS

Monkey or Screw

Stillson Pipe

Pocket Adjustable

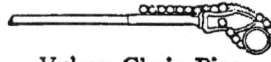

Vulcan Chain Pipe

General Utility

Pipe Tong

Construction

Track

Wrench, Tap — Wrench for holding and turning taps. Usually made adjustable for different sizes.

Wringing Fits — See Fits.

INDEX

LIST OF AUTHORITIES

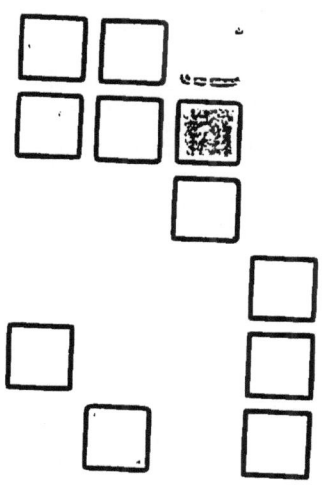

9 781360 229874